Texts in Theoretical Computer Science
An EATCS Series

Springer
Berlin
Heidelberg
New York
Hong Kong
London
Milan
Paris
Tokyo

Klaus Schneider

Verification of Reactive Systems

Formal Methods and Algorithms

With 149 Figures

Springer

Author

Prof. Dr. Klaus Schneider

FB Informatik
AG Reaktive Systeme
Universität Kaiserslautern
67653 Kaiserslautern
Germany

klaus.schneider@informatik.uni-kl.de

Series Editors

Prof. Dr. Wilfried Brauer
Institut für Informatik
Technische Universität München
Arcisstrasse 21, 80333 München, Germany
brauer@informatik.tu-muenchen.de

Prof. Dr. Grzegorz Rozenberg
Leiden Institute of Advanced Computer Science
University of Leiden
Niels Bohrweg 1, 2333 CA Leiden, The Netherlands
rozenber@liacs.nl

Prof. Dr. Arto Salomaa
Data City
Turku Centre for Computer Science
20 500 Turku, Finland
asalomaa@utu.fi

Library of Congress Cataloging-in-Publication Data applied for

Bibliographic information published by Die Deutsche Bibliothek
Die Deutsche Bibliothek lists this publication in the Deutsche Nationalbibliographie; detailed bibliographic data is available in the Internet at <http://dnd.dd.de>

ACM Computing Classification (1998): F.3.1, D.2.4, F.4.1

ISBN 978-3-642-05555-3

Springer-Verlag is a part of Springer Science+Business Media
springeronline.com

Softcover reprint of the hardcover 1st edition 2004

Cover Design: KünkelLopka, Heidelberg

45/3142 – 5 4 3 2 1 0 – Printed on acid-free paper

To Tim, Katja and Kai

Foreword

Computer systems are becoming ubiquitous. Many of the most important and prevalent ones are reactive systems. Reactive systems include microprocessors, computer operating systems, air traffic control systems, as well as on-board avionics and other embedded systems. These systems are characterized technically by their ongoing, ideally infinite behavior; termination is impossible or aberrant behavior, in contrast to classical theories of computation. Reactive systems tend to be characterized in practice by having failure modes that can severely compromise safety, even leading to loss of life. Alternatively, errors can have serious financial repercussions such as expensive recalls. Reactive systems need to be correct before being deployed.

To determine whether such reactive systems do behave correctly, a rich mathematical theory of verification of reactive systems has been developed over the last two decades or so. In contrast to earlier work emphasizing the role of proofs in deductive systems to establish correctness, the alternative suggestion is to take a model-theoretic view. It turns out that this permits the process of reasoning about program correctness to be fully automated in principle and partially automated to a high degree in practice.

It is my pleasure to introduce Klaus Schneider's excellent book *Verification of Reactive Systems: Formal Methods and Algorithms*. This book is the story of reactive systems verification, reflecting Klaus's broad expertise on the subject. It addresses both applications and theory, providing especially strong coverage of basic as well as advanced theory not otherwise available in book form. Key topics include Kripke and related transition structures, temporal logics, automata on infinite strings including Safra's determinization construction, expressiveness and Borel hierarchies of ω-languages, as well as monadic predicate logics. An underlying theme is the use of the vectored μ-calculus to provide an elegant "Theory of Everything". *Verification of Reactive Systems* belongs on the bookshelf of every serious researcher into the topic. It should also serve as a valuable text for graduate students and advanced undergraduates.

April 2003

E. Allen Emerson,
Endowed Professor of Computer Sciences
University of Texas at Austin

Preface

The design of modern information processing systems like digital circuits or protocols is becoming more and more difficult. A large part of the design costs and time (about 70%) is currently spent on methods that try to guarantee the absence of design errors. For this reason, designing systems is now more and more a synonym for verifying systems.

The research into the verification of reactive systems, in particular, into model checking, is one of the most impressive successes of theoretical computer science. Two decades after the publication of the basic papers on the formal foundation, the methods became mature enough for industrial usage. Nowadays, the hardware industry employs hundreds of highly specialized researchers working with formal methods to detect design bugs.

When I entered this field, it was an enormous effort to read hundreds of papers to understand the relationships between the different formal methods that are currently in use. It was surprising to me that there was no book covering all these methods, even the basic ones, although there is such a huge interest in them. For this reason, I decided to write this book to provide newcomers and researchers with a textbook that covers most of the relevant logics, with a particular emphasis on (verification and translation) algorithms.

The book is intended for graduate students as well as for researchers already working in this area. It is self-contained and gives proofs and algorithms for all important constructions. For a less detailed and formal introduction, I want to recommend the book of Clarke, Grumberg, and Peled [111]. Supplemental material on actual tools is found in [38], and further topics on the μ-calculus and infinite games are found in [221].

There are many persons I have to thank for helping me to write this book. In particular, I want to thank Detlef Schmid and the hardware verification group at the University of Karlsruhe, in particular Jorgos Logothetis, Tobias Schüle, and Roberto Ziller. Many discussions with Moshe Vardi moved me to improve the book. Allen Emerson was soon interested in the project and also gave fruitful comments. Moreover, I want to thank Amir Pnueli, Wolfgang Thomas, and Peter Schmitt for comments on early versions of the manuscript. Last, but not least, it should be mentioned that the editors of the EATCS series, in particular, Prof. Brauer, and the team at Springer-Verlag helped me to publish this book.

Kaiserslautern, September 2003 *Klaus Schneider*

Contents

1

Introduction

Quo facto, quando orientur controversiae, non magis disputatione
opus erit inter duos philosophos, quam inter duos computistas.
Sufficiet enim calamos in manus sumere sedereque ad abacos,
et sibi mutuo (accito si placet amico) dicere: calculemus[1].
— *Gottfried Wilhelm Leibniz (1646-1716)*

1.1 Formal Methods in System Design

1.1.1 General Remarks and Taxonomy

The development of information processing systems, especially if these consist of concurrent processes, is a very complicated task. In fact, modern computer systems are the most complicated structures mankind has ever built in its history: Modern microprocessors are implemented by millions of transistors; operating systems and software applications consist of millions of lines of code. Therefore, it is no wonder that these systems often have errors that lead to serious malfunctions, even if the systems have been extensively tested to validate their correctness.

While the construction of erroneous systems has never been tolerated, the need to avoid errors in design is becoming more and more important. One reason for this is that system sizes are rapidly growing. If we assume that the number of errors in these systems grows with their size, it becomes clear that the larger the systems are, the more troublesome they will be, and the probability that they will actually work is reduced. Very large systems

[1] The translation is roughly as follows: whenever there are different opinions about certain facts, one should not discuss them like philosophers usually do; instead one should 'calculate' the truth. Leibniz and Newton were the first who tried to replace at least some parts of the creativity used by mathematicians by rules of a calculus that could be implemented by machines.

could contain so many errors that they will never successfully run. A couple of large software projects have demonstrated this already.

But even if the system's development can be successfully completed, the time spent for debugging and testing grows rapidly with the system's size. It is not unusual that more than 70% of the design time is spent on simulation. Errors found late in the design may lead to expensive redesigns that in turn lead to delays in the time-to-market. Even if this delay is only about two or three months, the overall economic success of the product may be endangered.

Another reason for the increased pressure to avoid design errors is that computer systems are used more and more in applications where their malfunctioning can cause extensive damage or could even endanger human lives. Nuclear plants, aircrafts, and automobiles are more and more controlled by so-called *embedded systems*. These embedded systems are in principle complete computer systems, since they usually consist of a microprocessor that runs special software. Often more than one task has to be performed by the system, and for this reason, it is often divided into several processes or threads that implement the desired tasks. For reasons of efficiency, specialized hardware is often used to increase the throughput. For example, image processing systems often have special processing units like JPEG and MPEG decoders for compressing and decompressing image data to increase the throughput.

While the complexity of systems steadily increases, the design methods to guarantee correct systems have not emerged at the same speed. In software design, the introduction of object-oriented analysis and design has helped to structure the designs to obtain reusable designs. In hardware design, special design flows and design tools are used to translate a high-level algorithmic description given in hardware description languages like VHDL or Verilog to a circuit netlist. This way, it is possible to design quite large systems, much larger and faster than one expected some years ago.

However, the design of embedded systems does not only involve the design of hardware or software. Instead, the combination of both is a critical problem since the tasks that are implemented in hardware or software must be carefully selected. For this reason, hardware-software codesign methods are in use that start with a realization-independent description of the system, which may however already be partitioned into several tasks. In an analysis phase, modules are detected whose functions influence the speed of the system. Moreover, estimates for implementation costs also need to be considered. Dependent on these facts, a partition into hardware and software is made and the design of the hardware and software parts is done in a conventional manner.

So, there are already design flows that allow hardware and software development and also hardware/software codesigns. However, these design flows are very complex. If an error is detected late in the design, its correction may influence even the hardware-software partitioning so that a complete redesign has to be made. It is therefore mandatory that design errors are detected as soon as possible, i.e., at the level of the realization-independent description.

One way to detect design errors is clearly to test the design by means of implementing prototypes. This is a standard task in software design, but is not so simple for the design of hardware. Here, one is usually forced to simulate the circuits as it is too expensive to fabricate prototype circuits. However, in the last few years, programmable hardware such as field-programmable gate arrays (FPGAs) [70, 122] have been developed that allow the implementation of hardware prototypes. However, the speed of these prototypes is slower than the speed that will be obtained by a later implementation as an application-specific integrated circuit (ASIC). Therefore, simulation of the hardware-software system is often still necessary to check the correct interaction between the software and hardware parts. However, the problem with simulation is that it is quite slow when large designs are to be simulated, and what is even more intrinsic to the approach is that only errors can be found, while the *absence of errors* can never be shown.

For this reason, the application of formal methods in the design of software, hardware, and hardware-software codesign is more and more frequently discussed. There are some approaches that are independent of the kind of system to be verified. However, in most cases, the kind of system determines the kinds of properties to be verified, and this in turn makes one or another verification formalism more or less suited. For example, when a hardware controller is to be verified, we will usually not have to consider abstract data types. Instead, we are confronted with some sort of finite state machine that has to emit the desired control signals at the right point of time. For this reason, the kind of system is important for the choice of a suitable verification formalism.

Therefore, it is no wonder that a plethora of formal methods has been developed over time. Some of them consider the same problem and try to solve it in different ways, but there are also very different approaches that have almost nothing in common. In fact, only a few of the formal methods that are considered nowadays are discussed in this book, as it has a special focus on so-called *reactive systems* and *finite-state based verification procedures*.

For this reason, we will first consider in the next section different ways to apply formal methods to the design of complex systems. In particular, we distinguish between three main approaches: formal specification, verification, and formal synthesis or program derivation. While these approaches only explain where and how formal methods are applied in the design flow, no formal method has yet been determined. The particular choice of a formal method crucially depends, as already mentioned, on the kind of system, and also on the kind of specification, that is considered. Therefore, in Section 1.1.3, we give a classification of systems with their related properties. Having then seen the important classifications of formal methods, systems and properties, we then consider in Section 1.2 the history of some formal methods.

The content of Section 1.2 is however rather limited to the focus of this book and does not consider the genealogy of other formalisms. Nevertheless, it is very fruitful to see the relationship between the considered approaches.

1.1.2 Classification of Formal Methods

So far, we have discussed the usefulness of formal methods in the design of software, hardware or hardware-software codesigns. There are, however, very different formal methods and, furthermore, very different ways that these formal methods can be used in the design.

In this section, we discuss the main applications of formal methods in system design and can therefore give a first classification of formal methods. We can also explain what can be achieved by formal methods in system design and what they can not do. There are at least the following ways to use formal methods in system design:

- writing formal specifications
- proving properties about the specification
- deriving implementations from a given specification
- verifying specifications w.r.t. a given implementation

We will discuss these different approaches and, moreover, discuss the limitations of formal methods in the design process.

Writing a formal specification. Formal methods are used to reason about mathematical objects. However, hardware circuits are, e.g., not mathematical objects, but physical objects of the real world. Therefore, it is necessary to develop a mathematical model of the system and also to describe the properties that the system should have by means of some mathematical language. This should be clear, but it must be stressed for two reasons: First, the properties are normally given in an informal manner, i.e., by means of natural language. It is frequently the case that these requirements are inconsistent, and therefore, they can not be satisfied at all. Secondly, no matter what formal method is used, it can only argue about the formally given system description and the formally given properties. If these are not what is actually intended, the application of the formal methods will prove things that nobody is really interested in.

For the system's model, this problem is often overestimated. Any programming language with a formal semantics is a mathematical model that can in principle be used for the application of formal methods. At least, it can be converted into another mathematical model. Hence, any programmer and any hardware designer already deals with formal models even if 'formal methods' are not believed to be applied in the design flow.

Additionally, the environment of the system has often to be modeled to show that the system meets its specification. The environment often restricts the inputs that can occur by physical restrictions. For example, a robot's arm can not reach every place and therefore, it is not necessary to consider all locations of it. But even if the environment model has to be taken into account, the problem is overestimated. In any engineering discipline mathematical models are used; and nobody who finds a problem in the construction of a crane would suggest that crane builders should abandon mathematics.

Proving properties of the specification. We have already pointed out that specifications are often given in an informal language and must therefore be first rephrased in a formal specification language. This is an error-prone task, and therefore, it is often desirable to prove some properties of a given specification to see that it actually means what one has in mind. In particular, it is important to show its satisfiability to assure that at least one solution exists. For example, the specification $a^{(0)} \wedge a^{(1)} \wedge \forall t.a^{(t+1)} = \neg a^{(t)}$, that should express that a is true for the first two points of time and then oscillates, is not satisfiable (a correct specification would be $a^{(0)} \wedge a^{(1)} \wedge \neg a^{(2)} \wedge \forall t.a^{(t+3)} = \neg a^{(t+2)}$).

It is often fruitful to prove the equivalence of different specifications to get a deeper understanding of the task that is to be implemented. Even if the specifications are not verified against a later implementation these steps often lead to a deeper understanding and a better structuring of the problem. Therefore, formal methods allow us to find errors in the specification phase. Hall writes in his article [231] about his experience with formal methods in software design in his company:

> *In an informal specification, it is hard to tell what is an error because it is not clear what is being said. When challenged, people try to defend their informal specification by reinterpreting it to meet the criticism. With a formal specification, we have found that errors are much more easily found – and, once they are found, everyone is more ready to agree that they are errors.*

Deriving implementations from a specification. Once a specification has been set up and one has figured out that it is indeed what is desired, it would be helpful to have a design method that could automatically derive a system's implementation that fulfills the given requirements. This has actually been the idea of the fifth generation programming languages like PROLOG, where the specification and implementation phases become closely related to each other.

However, specifications are often given in a declarative manner and not in a constructive manner. This means that these specifications only describe *what* the system should do, but not *how* this function can be achieved. It is certainly not possible to derive correct programs from declarative specifications since these problems are intrinsically undecidable so that machines can never solve them. Therefore, the construction of appropriate implementations will always remain a creative task for human beings.

Nevertheless, the algorithm can be given in an abstract manner where many implementation details are ignored. It is then possible to use appropriate design tools to construct a more detailed system's implementation out of such an abstract system description. For example, the algorithm can be written in a high-level programming language and a compiler can then be used to translate the algorithm to some machine language so that it can be executed on a microprocessor. In hardware design, a high-level hardware description can be translated by so-called synthesis tools to a low level description that can be physically implemented. Similarly, software and hardware descriptions can be generated from abstract and realization independent descriptions for example those given in SDL [139, 524] or synchronous languages [42, 230]. Therefore, *formal software* [93] and *hardware synthesis* [57, 58, 297] have their applications here.

Verifying specifications w.r.t. a given implementation. As it may be possible to automatically derive detailed system descriptions by less detailed ones, or at least to use tools that assure the correctness of the manually applied design steps, there is no need to reprove properties at different levels of abstraction. The design steps that are used to refine the system's description must not affect the validity of the specification. However, it still remains to check whether the abstract implementation satisfies the originally given specifications. This process is normally called formal verification of the system and this is also the main topic of this book.

There are two main ways formal verification can be applied. On the one hand, one can describe both the system's model Φ_{imp} and the specification Φ_{spec} in a formal language and consider the resultant formulas with a special calculus that is suited for the chosen formal language. As both the specification and the system are given as formulas of the same logic, the remaining task is to prove properties of the language such as $\Phi_{\mathsf{imp}} \rightarrow \Phi_{\mathsf{spec}}$ or $\Phi_{\mathsf{imp}} \leftrightarrow \Phi_{\mathsf{spec}}$. Therefore, these methods are based on *automated theorem proving* for certain formal languages (logics). Usually, one wants to confirm that the formula $\Phi_{\mathsf{imp}} \rightarrow \Phi_{\mathsf{spec}}$ holds, i.e., to check that the specification holds for the implementation. The specification can therefore, and in general will, only describe a partial behavior of the system.

While the above mentioned approach is reduced to the theorem proving problem $\Phi_{\mathsf{imp}} \rightarrow \Phi_{\mathsf{spec}}$ of a certain logic, another approach has been developed since the 1980s which is called *model checking*. In model checking, the system's description is not given in the logic. Instead, it is given as an interpretation $\mathcal{M}_{\mathsf{imp}}$ of the considered logic. A model checking procedure has the task of evaluating the specification Φ_{spec} in the interpretation $\mathcal{M}_{\mathsf{imp}}$.

It is often the case that the model checking problem of a logic is simpler than the related theorem proving or *satisfiability problem*, but both may also share the same complexity. It can however be easily seen that model

checking is somehow simpler than satisfiability checking on nondeterministic algorithms: Model checking must evaluate a given formula in a *given model* while satisfiability checking must check *whether an interpretation exists* such that the formula can be evaluated to true. In particular, nondeterministic machines can guess a suitable interpretation, if one exists, and can then use the corresponding model checking procedure to evaluate the formula in the model. Therefore, model checking is often less complex than the related theorem proving problem, at least when nondeterministic computation models are considered.
The difference is best seen by a simple example: Consider as specification logic the simple propositional logic. Interpretations of this logic are simply truth assignments to the variables that occur in the formulas, and model checking is simply performed by evaluating a propositional formula with such an assignment. It is clear that the latter can be done in linear time with respect to the length of the formula. Theorem proving for propositional logic is however equivalent to the satisfiability problem and therefore known to be NP-complete [124, 204].

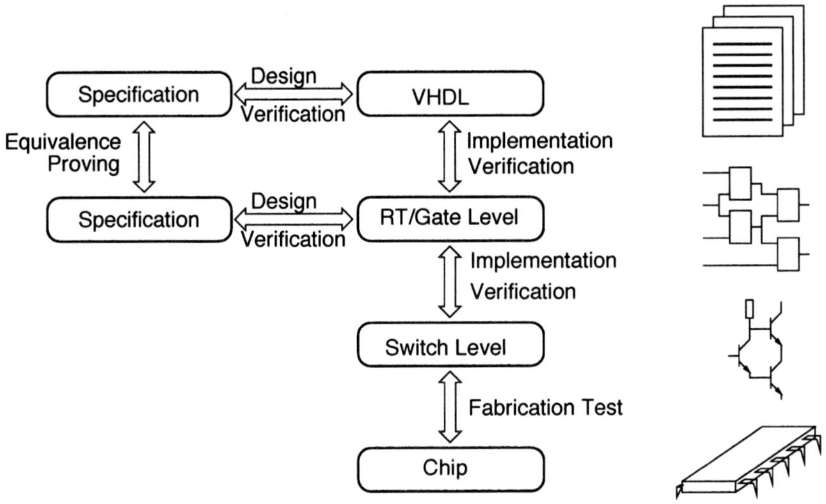

Fig. 1.1. Different ways to apply formal methods in the design

Different ways to apply formal methods for the hardware design are pictorially given in Fig. 1.1, but the restriction to hardware design is not important to the discussion at the moment. Specifications can be compared with each other, where equivalence between specifications can be checked and where one specification implies another one. *Implementation verification*, or *equivalence checking* compares different implementation descriptions with each other. This approach is often called 'vertical verification' which is shown in Fig. 1.1. If one implementation is obtained by derivation with a formal method from another one, one speaks about *formal synthesis or program derivation*. Finally, formal specifications can be checked for a given implementation description, which is often called *property checking* or simply *(formal) verification*. In general, we may define verification to be the process of constructing a mathematical proof that shows that an implementation fulfills a given specification.

While all the mentioned ways of using formal methods in the design of complex systems are important in assuring the correctness of the system that is to be developed, we mainly consider the verification of properties in this book. Moreover, for some formalisms in this book, the verification problem, which is normally interpreted as a model checking problem can be solved by the same methods as the satisfiability problem. Therefore, we will also consider satisfiability problems for some formalisms.

One point to be discussed here is that it is often argued that the verification of a system guarantees that the system will be free of errors. This is normally not the case. What is shown in a formal verification is that the formal model of the system satisfies a formal specification. Therefore, we need to additionally assure that the specification actually describes the properties that are to be fulfilled and that the system's model is actually what is implemented later on. We already addressed the problem in the paragraph on 'writing a formal specification': Programming languages, hardware description languages and other system level description languages are already formal models that can be used for the verification as well as for the refinement of the implementation. Hence, the problem of the system's formal model being different from the later implementation is not a severe one. This not so simple with the specification: As it is impossible to guess what a specification engineer had in mind, when he or she wrote a specification, the only way to check if the specification is what is wanted is to prove the properties of the specification. A major point here is that the specification language should be as readable as possible so that it can be easily understood. Many complaints about formal methods are prejudiced by the fact that many are hard to understand. Nevertheless, even if a readable formalism is chosen, engineering practice has shown [231] that any formally given specification should additionally be explained in natural language to be better understood. This is also for reasons of redundancy.

However, even if the specification and the system are correctly given and successfully verified, there are some problems that can nevertheless lead to a malfunctioning system. For example, it may be the case that the underlying physical components that finally execute the systems computations are damaged. This is a particular problem for the fabrication of hardware circuits: Layout defects that may occur during the fabrication process may also lead to malfunctioning chips. These defects can not be checked by formal verification, and are normally avoided by *testing*. This means that a chip is tested under a given set of test pattern sequences that distinguish a correct from a faulty circuit. The test patterns are usually automatically generated. As for large circuits the number of test patterns may become prohibitively large, additional test circuitry like scan-paths and self-tests, may become necessary. Modern test procedures establish a high quality, so that normally less than five bad chips out of one million are delivered [282].

Moreover, correct systems can be used in a wrong manner which results in *errors by wrong usage*. This is a general problem as systems are usually designed in a modular manner and are therefore implemented with assumptions on their environment. Such a problem has occurred with the Ariane 5, since a software module had been reused from the Ariane 3 that assumed certain values on the acceleration that did not hold for the Ariane 5.

Wrong usage is, in particularly, a problem for embedded systems as these systems are by definition integrated into an environment which corresponds with certain assumptions in the design phase. Hence, there will always be some assumptions on the interaction between the system and its environment which may be functional, or of other kinds. For example, temperature, voltages, physical size, and many more requirements may have to be considered. Hence, the correct usage of the systems must also be specified.

Furthermore, it may be the case that the system is correct and is used in a correct manner, but *aging of the system* may lead after some years to defects. These kinds of errors can not be avoided by verification approaches. The solution here is to use fault tolerance methods, e.g., to implement redundant systems that are able to run even if one or two system's components fail.

Therefore, to guarantee 'trustworthy' systems, formal verification, test, and fault tolerance methods must all be used. There are many examples, ranging from the verification of train stations, the Pentium bug, the Ariane 5, and many others, that show the necessity of formal methods in system design. Formal methods have already led to the discovery of several errors in systems that are already in use and in standards that have been signed-off as correct.

Having outlined the limitations of formal methods, it is important to say that their usage is still essential for avoiding design errors. Modern system design flows will benefit from formal methods in that design errors can be avoided or found quicker than by traditional test and simulation methods. According to a recent investigation [449], in 82% of the cases, design errors were responsible for the malfunctioning of systems. Moreover, it has been reported [231] that the usage of formal methods has led to a better structure of a system since the different tasks that the system should perform are better understood from the beginning of its design. It might be surprising, but it is often the case that designers have captured the problem that they should have solved only after they have made the implementation. An indication for this phenomenon is that re-implementations are often much better than the first ones.

So, we have outlined different ways on how formal methods can be applied in modern system design. We have already distinguished between verification, formal synthesis, and the theorem proving of properties to check the specifications. For a further discussion, we will now try to classify different kinds of systems and their related properties in the next section. We will then finally be able to describe the kind of systems and kind of formalisms that will be considered in this book.

1.1.3 Classification of Systems

In the previous section, we outlined several ways of applying formal methods in the design of complex systems. We now refine this view in considering different kinds of systems, their different properties, and thereby, a certain preselection of verification formalisms. Depending on their architecture, systems can be classified in several ways, for example:

- asynchronous / synchronous hardware
- analog / digital hardware
- mono- or multi-processor systems
- imperative / functional / logic-based / object-oriented software
- multi-threaded or sequential software
- conventional vs. real-time operating systems
- embedded systems vs. local systems vs. distributed systems

As specific architectures such as the ones given above are dedicated to specific tasks, it is clear that one formal method will be more or less suited than the other. For example, the behavior of analog hardware is essentially based on differential equations so that their formal verification is closely related with solving these equations. In contrast to this, digital hardware only considers Boolean valued data types that may be collected in so-called bitvectors to encode finite data types like 16-bit integers. Clearly, infinite data types and complex abstract data types play no particular role in hardware systems (at least at the register-transfer level), and are therefore solely considered in software design (or in high-level design phases of hardware designs). The problems that occur for the verification of digital hardware circuits are intrinsically based on finite-state machines and are therefore, in principle, solvable by computers. However, the number of states may become prohibitively large, so that the verification approaches must fight the state-explosion problem.

Digital hardware design becomes more and more 'soft', which means that the hardware design starts at the level of algorithmic descriptions. For example, special applications such as image processing algorithms like the JPEG and the MPEG algorithms are often implemented in special hardware circuits that are found in modern digital cameras. On the other hand, the performance of modern microprocessors is so good that often elaborate hardware designs are not much faster than the highly optimized microprocessor structures where many person-years of development have been invested. Therefore, hardware implementations are only recommended when efficiency is crucial for the functioning of the system or if large numbers of circuits are expected to be sold. The reason for the latter issue is that the development of a hardware circuit is much more expensive than that for an equivalent software component, and these development costs need to be recovered by the sale of a large number of circuits.

However, as more and more complex algorithms are implemented in hardware, the requirements for hardware verification also changes. The need to consider complex multi-threaded systems whose threads heavily interact with each other becomes more and more challenging. Even if no complex data types need to be considered, the tasks that are performed by modern hardware systems are more and more complex, and the number of states in these systems has reached very large numbers. The implementation of complex control tasks will moreover require the consideration of high-level description languages that can deal with many interacting threads.

Hence, the difference between this high-level hardware design and the design of multi-threaded software diminishes, so that we need, in principle, not to distinguish between hardware-oriented multi-threaded software with low-level data types and high-level hardware descriptions. A more distinguishing criterion is the paradigm of the underlying programming language, i.e., whether it is imperative, functional, logic-based or object-oriented. Logic-based languages such as PROLOG, and functional languages such as ML, Haskell, and many more are well-suited w.r.t. verification. However these languages are rarely extended by multiple threads which limits their usefulness in system design. Moreover, these languages require, in general, more memory than imperative languages, at least when the user is responsible for storage management.

Hence, for the implementation of *embedded systems*, these languages have not really been considered, since memory requirements are often of an essential importance for these systems. This domain is completely determined by imperative languages like C. With the increasing complexity and therefore the increasing need to reuse components, it is probable that object-oriented languages as C++ and maybe Java will be used in future. Therefore, software and hardware designs will come closer in the future.

Another issue is added by embedded and distributed systems. As the components of these systems have to interact with each other or with the environment, it is important to guarantee that this interaction is done in a correct and efficient manner. For example, it must be guaranteed that messages are never lost and arrive within some time constraints. The interaction of different system components with each other gives us another major distinction. From the viewpoint of a component all other components belong to the environment, we simply consider a component together with its environment in the following. Depending on the type of interaction, we distinguish the following important classes of system:

Transformational Systems: After being started by the environment, these systems read, at the beginning of their computations, some input data and produce the desired output data. It is assumed that these systems should always terminate, because the outputs are only available after the termination. An example of a transformational system is a compiler that translates a program of a high-level programming language (which is the input data) to a machine language (which is the output data).

Interactive Systems differ from transformational systems in that it is not desired that they terminate unless the user explicitly instructs them to do so. Instead, they continuously run and interact with the environment (the user). These interactions are split into the *action* that is given by the environment and the *reaction* which is the answer of the system to the given action. It is important for the distinguishing from the next category that the environment of an interactive system has to wait until the system is ready for new inputs. This means that the frequency of interactions is completely determined by the performance of the system.

Reactive Systems differ from interactive systems in that the environment can freely determine the points in time when an interaction is desired. This means that a reactive system must be at least fast enough to react on a given environment action before the next action of the environment occurs. For this reason, reactive systems must satisfy some real-time constraints and therefore fall into the category of *real-time systems*. Two different kinds of real-time constraints are distinguished: these are hard and soft real-time constraints. The former are necessary for a correct functioning of the system, while the latter ones are wanted to increase the comfort. Because of their nature, reactive systems must often satisfy hard real-time constraints and are therefore usually implemented as concurrent systems. This means that these systems consist of a couple of concurrent threads that may be dynamically generated and aborted.

The implementation of reactive systems is not an easy task. The environment often gives clear real-time constraints by the physical construction of the system. For example, a valve can be closed within a certain amount of time, a car can be stopped within a certain amount of time, or an airbag can be opened within a certain interval of time.

As it is quite clear what real-time constraints are to be met, it is not so clear, how a reactive system should be implemented to meet these constraints. In general, to be as fast as possible, one might suggest a complete hardware solution. However, this is in most cases not necessary and would be far more expensive than it should be. Therefore, the systems are normally implemented partly in hardware and in software, so that a compromise between the costs and the efficiency has to be made.

Reconsidering the system classes that we have previously considered by examining the architecture, we first note that nearly all hardware circuits are reactive systems in the following sense: In the design of asynchronous hardware, it is required that all signals become stable within a certain amount of time so that oscillating signals are avoided. In the design of synchronous hardware circuits, the points of time where the interactions will occur are fixed by the system's clock which synchronizes all parts of the circuit. The 'real-time' constraint of any submodule of such a circuit is therefore that any signal must be propagated through the circuit and all signals have stabilized before the next clock cycle occurs. CAD tools for designing hardware circuits determine the critical path of a hardware circuit and can minimize its length so that the clock speed can be increased. Hence, hardware designs do always have to consider real-time constraints.

In contrast to that, the software design does not usually aim to construct reactive systems. However, there are new applications that make software obey given real-time constraints. For example, a distributed data base to manage flight reservations must be updated fast enough for all requests to be considered w.r.t. the actual state of the data base. Moreover, computers are used to control complex systems such as aircrafts or even nuclear plants, and must therefore be able to react on unforeseen situations before serious damages occur. For this reason it is usually important to use real-time operating systems that guarantee fixed time bounds for interrupting processes and executing interrupt routines. It is very important for the implementation of reactive systems that process management is done within guaranteed real-time constraints: Everybody who has ever erroneously deleted a directory on a Unix system that contains many files, and tried to abort the deletion process without success, will agree that Unix is certainly not a real-time operating system.

Special programming languages for the development of reactive systems have been suggested in the past decade, in particular the *synchronous languages* [230]. The main paradigm of these languages is the *perfect synchrony paradigm* that is most easily explained with the synchronous language Esterel [42, 43]. The perfect synchrony paradigm is achieved in Esterel as follows: By the Esterel semantics, almost all program statements do not require time for their execution. There is only one basic statement, namely the **pause** statement that does consume time, and this is actually all it does. Each time a **pause** statement is executed, one logical unit of time is consumed, which means that the control flow rests for one unit of time on that **pause** statement. Therefore, threads run synchronously to each other since they will always execute all statements between two **pause** statements in zero time and will then synchronize (by the semantics of Esterel) at the next **pause** statement.

Clearly, it is only an idealized view that the other Esterel statement can be executed without consuming time. However, the same idealization has been used for designing complex hardware circuits. There, the designer assumes that the signals propagate through a combinational circuit without delays, although this is physically not possible. However, if the clock cycle is not too fast, this idealization is legal and liberates the designer from the burden to consider the circuits in a more detailed manner than necessary. The complexity of actual hardware designs proves that this idealization is reasonable. Berry, the main developer of the Esterel language, compares this idealization with the models that are used in mechanics [41]: Although we know that Newtonian mechanics is not precisely true and that it is only an approximation of the relativistic mechanics due to Einstein, most applications nowadays still use Newtonian models, simply because these are much more efficiently computed, and for most applications the results are precise enough.

After a (synchronous) program has been written, it can be translated to a finite state machine that controls the manipulation of the data variables. The states of this finite state machine correspond with the possible locations of the control flow in the program text. As the program text is finite, it follows that the control flow can always be modeled with finitely many states. However, if the values of the data variables are considered, the state set may become infinite when infinite data types come into play. In practice, however, there is no system that is able to really handle infinite data types, so that we usually have finite data types: Integers in most programming languages like C have a certain bitwidth and are therefore finite data types. For this reason, we can compile most programs to finite state machines, even if these have an astronomical number of states.

Synchronous languages have a nice property in that the concurrency of the programs can be handled at compile-time: due to the semantics all programs are deterministic, and therefore the interactions of the threads are known at compile-time. The languages moreover provide convenient statements for controlling the complex interactions of threads like different variants of abortion and suspension. Even if these programs are quite readable, the important properties that one is interested in the verification of reactive systems are nevertheless concerned with the correct temporal behavior. Particular problems are to prove the absence of deadlocks, absence of live-locks, mutual exclusion, and write clashes, and in general, that signals occur at the right time so that, for example, protocols are correctly implemented.

An important taxonomy of properties, as given below, is found in many books and papers, in particular in [351, 352]. It is based on both practical and theoretical observations. On the one hand, the properties below can often be found more or less directly in many specifications. On the other hand, many formalisms can be classified when they are either able to express these properties or not.

Safety properties state that for all computations of the system, and for all instances of time, some property will invariantly hold. For example, a safety property of a traffic light controller would be that at no point of time, the traffic lights of crossing streets will have a green light.

Liveness properties state that some desired state of the system can eventually be reached. There is no fixed bound of time given in which the state must be reached. For example, a liveness property could be that the initialization phase will definitely terminate and that the system will therefore become ready for computations.

Persistence properties are related to the stabilization of certain properties. In general, a persistence property describes that for all possible computations, there is a point of time when a certain property will always hold afterwards.

Fairness properties state that some property will infinitely often hold. The notions of fairness and liveness are often mixed up since, for example liveness properties in the theory of Petri nets means that the net is always alive, i.e., that there is always some progress. In our classification, this is however a fairness property. Manna and Pnueli call these properties *recurrence* properties [351, 352].

The notion of 'fairness' is derived from specifications, where these properties are used to state that no process is ignored infinitely often by an operating system that should schedule the processes on a processor. Several notions of fairness have been introduced such as strong fairness, unconditional fairness, and many others (see [175, 197] for a more detailed discussion of these fairness properties).

From a viewpoint of expressiveness, we will see in Section 4.6, that liveness, safety, and persistence properties can be reduced to equivalent fairness properties when appropriate observers are added. The above properties are used to define a hierarchy for ω-automata given in Section 4.6, which is then adapted to temporal logic in Section 5.4.3. We will moreover see that the first three classes can be translated to very simple fixpoint expressions, while the latter class requires a higher effort, since it requires mutually dependent nested fixpoints for its description. Hence, these properties can be used to structure many formalisms in a hierarchy. We will elaborate this issue in detail throughout this book.

Safety and liveness properties are of particular interest, even they can both be reduced to persistence and fairness properties when appropriate observers are used. One reason is simply that most specifications are safety properties, and another reason is that the verification of safety properties can be done by specialized verification procedures. For example, these properties can be verified by induction, so that no traversal of the state spaces is necessary. Therefore, safety properties can also be proved for infinite state spaces. For example, induction-less induction methods that are based on term rewriting can verify safety properties.

To summarize, we have now seen where and how formal methods can be applied in modern system design. Our main interest is the formal verification of already implemented systems. We have furthermore classified the systems in many ways, and the most relevant systems for this book are reactive systems that can often be reduced to finite-state machines. Hence, we are interested in the formal verification of finite state systems. Moreover, we have already mentioned important classes of properties, without taking a specific formalism into account.

The kind of system clearly influences the properties to be specified, and therefore the choice of a suitable verification formalism. A plethora of formalisms has been developed, and still new formalisms are invented for different purposes. Therefore, we will consider in the next section some of the most popular ones and will, in particular, list how these formalisms have evolved over the time.

1.2 Genealogy of Formal Verification

In the previous section, we defined what classes of formal methods exist, and have seen the application of formal methods in specification, formal synthesis, and formal verification. Moreover, we have found reactive systems to be of particular interest for formal verification, since their design is an error-prone task due to the intensive use of multi-threading and the heterogeneous design which is often split into hardware and software. Moreover, reactive systems are well-suited to formal verification, since they can often be reduced to finite state systems so that the verification problem becomes decidable.

In this section, we consider approaches that are used for the formal verification of properties in a more detailed manner. In particular, we give some historical notes on the formalisms that are considered in detail throughout this book. Parts of the next section are based on [50], who themselves borrowed material from [140]. The other sections are a summary of other research papers of the corresponding formalisms.

1.2.1 Early Beginnings of Mathematical Logic

The idea that formal reasoning could be mechanized such that machines can generate mathematical proofs is an old dream that has its origins in the seventeenth century. *Déscartes (1596-1650)* developed an algebraic foundation of the ancient Euclidian geometry known from the Greek philosophers. Based on the introduction of coordinate systems, he was able to express all geometric problems by means of algebraic equations that are then solvable by purely algebraic means. Déscartes was aware of the fact that his 'decision procedure' could be mechanized in a similar way to the arithmetic computations have been mechanized by the calculators of Schickard (1592-1653) and Pascal (1623-1662). In his work, he wrote:

> *...it is possible to construct all the problems of ordinary geometry by doing no more than the little covered in the four figures that I have explained. This*

> *is one thing which I believe the ancients did not notice, for otherwise they would not have put so much labor into writing so many books in which the very sequence of the propositions showed that they did not have a sure method of finding all ...*

Leibniz (1646-1716) had an even more general vision: His aim was to do the same for all fields of mathematics and even more for any kind of human thinking. In a research project that he planned for the next three centuries (!), his aims were to develop a formal language called the *'lingua characteristica'*, and to develop a corresponding calculus, called the *'calculus ratiocinator'*. The lingua characteristica would be powerful enough to express all kind of properties, and the calculus ratiocinator would provide laws that could be implemented – in modern words – in some sort of decision procedure, so that one could build a machine that would be able to derive any kind of truth.

However, the contribution of Leibniz to this project was not very promising, although his research in the differential calculus went in that direction. A first calculus in the sense of Leibniz was then developed by *A. de Morgan* and *G. Boole (1815-1864)* for propositional logic. Originally, Boolean algebra had been developed for the formalization of set theory. Boole himself viewed his work as a contribution to Leibniz's research programme. It is remarkable to mention that in 1869 S. Javins built a machine that was able to check Boolean expressions so that Leibniz's research programme had already been successful for propositional logic at that time.

The next step was then taken by *Gottlob Frege (1848-1925)*. In his book [198] entitled 'Begriffsschrift', he actually developed what we now call first order predicate logic. This logic is a convenient formalism that can express many interesting properties. In particular, it extends propositional logic by quantified formulas of the form $\exists x.\Phi$ and $\forall x.\Phi$ which express that the property Φ must hold for at least one or for all elements x. Atomic formulas are not only propositional constants, but may also depend on arguments, i.e., they may be of the form $p(\tau_1, \ldots, \tau_n)$, where the τ_i's are terms of the logic. These terms are recursively constructed of variables, constants and function applications which look like $f(\tau_1, \ldots, \tau_n)$. Note however that $f(\tau_1, \ldots, \tau_n)$ is interpreted as an element of the considered domain, while atomic formulas are interpreted to be either true or false. Additionally, equality $\doteq$ is often added in that for two terms τ_1 and τ_2, the expression $\tau_1 \doteq \tau_2$ is an atomic formula that expresses that the elements τ_1 and τ_2 are the same. The domain $\mathcal{D}$ that is used for interpretation of the terms and formulas is thereby given by an interpretation of the logic. An interpretation must moreover provide a function $\mathcal{J}$ that maps predicates p of arity n to a relation $\mathcal{J}(p) \subseteq \mathcal{D}^n$, and function symbols f of arity n to functions of type $\mathcal{D}^n \to \mathcal{D}$. In contrast to propositional logic, first order logic therefore allows reasoning about infinite domains.

Although Frege's work has not become very famous, his contribution is important when one considers the argumentations that were used at that time. In particular, it was not clear at that time what the basic constructs and axioms of mathematics were. Therefore, many proofs were not sound since they are based on other things that were, in turn, based on the theorem that was to be proved. Frege's work mainly contributed to the formal language, i.e., lingua characteristica, although he made proofs by the 'modus ponens' which was his 'calculus ratiocinator'. Frege's work was moreover important because he was the first who distinguished between *syntax and semantics* of a formal language and therefore, his work is an early forerunner of the principles that are used nowadays in computer science.

G. Peano applied Frege's mathematical logic to other fields of science. He wrote:

> ...*'I think that the propositions of any science can be expressed by these signs alone, provided we add signs representing the objects of that science.'*

Therefore, Peano's aim was to eliminate natural language for the precise formulation of properties in a precise formal manner. However, his reasoning about these properties was then done in natural language so that he ignored the initial work of Frege in terms of the 'calculus ratiocinator'.

Automated reasoning has however been controversially discussed from its beginning: For example, the famous mathematician *H. Poincaré* wrote:

> *Thus it will be readily understood that in order to present a theorem, it is no longer necessary or even useful to know what it means. We might replace geometry by the reasoning piano imagined by Stanley Javins; or if we prefer, we might imagine a machine where we could put in axioms at one end and take out theorems at the other, like that legendary machine in Chicago where pigs go in alive and come out transformed into hams and sausages. It is no more necessary for the mathematician than it is for these machines to know what he is doing.'*

Nevertheless, it became clear that mathematics had to be put on a sound basis with a clearly defined set of axioms and inference rules. *Whitehead* and *Russel* have proved in their famous work, the 'Principia Mathematica', that such a formal foundation was possible for all known mathematics. At this time, the formalization of *higher order predicate logics*, or as it is sometimes called the *type theory*, started in order to circumvent antinomies like Russel's paradox (to construct the set of all sets which could not be correctly typed).

The classical mathematical logic was then quickly developed: *Th. Skolem* developed in [461] and [462] a systematic way to check the satisfiability of logical formulas. In [461] he developed his quantifier elimination method that became known as 'skolemization'. The essential idea is thereby that formulas of the form $\forall x.\exists y.\Phi(x,y)$ denote some dependency between y and x so that there must be a function f that maps any element x to an element y so that the relation $\Phi(x,y)$ holds. Hence, the formula $\forall x.\exists y.\Phi(x,y)$ is satisfiable if and only if the formula $\forall x.\Phi(x,f(x))$ is satisfiable (where f should not already occur in Φ). The skolemization therefore eliminates positive occurrences of $\exists$ quantifiers for the consideration of satisfiability. As a result, only universally quantified formulas need to be considered, which can be moreover brought into prenex normal form, so that only formulas of the form $\forall x_1 \ldots . \forall x_n . \Phi$ have to be considered, where Φ does not contain quantifiers at all.

In [462], Skolem constructed a 'standard model' for the universal fragment of first order predicate logic, namely the Herbrand universe, whose name is therefore not attributed to its inventor. The essential idea is that for any considerations of satisfiability, one can use the set of (variable-free) terms as domain $\mathcal{D}$, hence, interpreting terms by themselves, and predicates as relations between terms. Hence, Skolem proved that any satisfiable first order logic formula does also has a *countable* model, which means that uncountable domains such as the real numbers can not be characterized by first order logic.

In the same year, *Hilbert* and *Ackermann* [246] presented in their book 'Grundzüge der theoretischen Logik' an axiomatization of the first order predicate calculus and imposed two important questions: firstly, the completeness of this axiomatization, i.e., whether it is possible to derive any valid property with it, and secondly, its decidability, i.e., whether one can build a machine to deduce truth.

Both problems have been solved by *Gödel*: In 1930, he showed [211] that the calculus given by Hilbert and Ackermann was in fact complete, which was then a promising approach to automated reasoning. However, one year later, Gödel showed [212] that any formal system that is strong enough to express arithmetic can either be not complete, or it is not decidable whether a formula is an axiom of the system. In particular, he presented a construction of a formula in any such formal system that can neither be proved nor disproved. To this end, he encoded the notions of derivation in a calculus as first-order formulas and considered the formula that says 'I am not derivable'. If this formula was valid, it could be used as a witness for a valid formula that can not be derived. If it was false, it must be derivable, but then the calculus is not correct since it derives the wrong formulas. Therefore any formalism that is powerful enough to formalize arithmetic with natural numbers is incomplete and therefore has 'leaks' (i.e., formulas that are neither true nor false). Some of the yet unsolved propositions of number theory such as Goldbach's conjecture are supposed to be examples of such leaks (however the same had been thought about Fermat's theorem until a proof was recently found).

The decidability problem for first order logic as raised by Hilbert and Ackermann was then independently solved by *A. Turing* and *A. Church* [99] in 1936 in that they showed the undecidability of the problem. While Turing reduced the problem to the termination problem of his Turing machines, Church found a similar reduction in the evaluation of λ-calculus expressions.

These negative results evidently destroyed the dream of implementing a 'calculus ratiocinator' as implied by Leibniz.

However, *Herbrand* already pointed out in his dissertation of 1930 that any valid sentence can be proved in finite time, i.e., we can define algorithms that are able to prove any valid formula of first-order predicate calculus. The essential property of first order logic that enables us to do this is the compactness property which states that a (possibly infinite) set of formulas is satisfiable iff each finite subset of it is satisfiable. In other words, a possibly infinite set of formulas is unsatisfiable iff there is a *finite subset* of it that is unsatisfiable. The objective of Herbrand's proof procedure is therefore to replace quantified formulas $\forall x.\Phi$ by the set $\{[\Phi]_x^\tau \mid \mathcal{T}\}$ where $\mathcal{T}$ is the set of all terms and $[\Phi]_x^\tau$ is obtained from Φ by replacing x by τ.

However, if the formula is satisfiable, the procedure may run into an infinite loop that encounters an infinite model and will therefore never terminate. The problem is that as long as the algorithm does not terminate, we know nothing about the truth value of the formula. As we have no upper bound on how long the algorithm will run, there will be no result found unless the algorithm successfully terminates.

1.2.2 Automated Theorem Proving

The rapid development of the first computers started a new kind of research, namely *automated theorem proving*. It now became possible to build, in a much simpler way than ever before, a 'calculus ratiocinator', simply by programming a computer. The first program in that direction, a decision procedure due to Presburger for his arithmetic [415], was implemented in 1954 by *M. Davis* on a Johniac, a 'Röhrencomputer'. A big success was achieved by the proof of the fact that the sum of two even numbers is again an even number. This was the first proof made by a machine.

Based on more powerful computers, better implementations followed: *H. Wang* developed in 1958 at IBM, and afterwards from 1959-1964 at Bell-Labs, an automated theorem prover that was able to prove 350 theorems of the 'Principia Mathematica' (quite simple laws of predicate calculus with equality). In 1960-1962, *Martin Davis* and *Hillary Putnam* presented a new proof procedure which was split into two parts [141]: firstly, a part that instantiates the quantified formulas in a systematic way (by terms of the Herbrand universe), and a second part for efficient evaluation of propositional logic. The latter part is still in use, but the former part was more important in the 1960s.

In 1960, *Prawitz* [414] recognized that the enumeration of all terms of the Herbrand universe was not reasonable, and therefore developed an algorithm for computing only the relevant instantiations by a process that we call *unification*. His idea was implemented by Davis, McIllroy and others. In 1965, *Robinson* [425] integrated Prawitz's unification algorithm in a single deduction rule, namely the resolution principle. In the meantime, a lot of refinements of resolution calculus such as hyper-resolution or theory-resolution [470] have been developed and implemented in efficient theorem provers like Otter, Setheo, or SPASS. Moreover, other representations like clausal graphs, the connection graphs of Kowalski [287], the matings of *P. Andrews* [16], or the connection method [48] of *Bibel* have been developed for the implementation of more efficient theorem provers.

The field of automated theorem proving is still a major topic of research. Many refinements have been added and many new calculi and specialized logics have been invented. For example, tableau calculi [195, 464] are a promising way to construct automated theorem provers for special kinds of logics, such a modal logics [98, 255, 292]. The relationship between tableau and the more frequently used resolution calculi is outlined in detail by *Fitting* in [195]. Eder considers in [150] the complexity of different calculi, and d'Agostino [134] points out some improvements for tableau calculi so that theorem provers based on them may reach the same efficiency as the resolution-based ones.

Nearly all automated theorem provers are designed for first order predicate logic. We have already mentioned that the compactness property of first order logic leads directly to a semi-decision procedure for the logic. However, as there are sound and complete calculi for first order logic, it follows by Gödel's result that first order logic can not express Peano's arithmetic. As any abstract data type such as lists, can be used to encode numbers, it moreover follows that first-order logic can not characterize such abstract data types (up to isomorphisms between the interpretations).

For this reason, extensions of the first-order logic have been investigated that extend the logic by means of induction principles. The most popular provers for first order logic (with induction) are ACL2 [277], Eves [132], LP [205], Nqthm [60], Reve [322], and RRL [276]. In general, these fall into the two classes of *explicit* and *implicit* induction provers. Explicit induction provers like [25, 60, 61, 92, 206] use induction rules as explicitly given proof rules, e.g., for tableau construction. These induction rules are based on a well-founded ordering of the terms and require that the induction step transfers results from smaller terms to larger ones.

Implicit induction calculi, also known as inductionless induction, are based on term rewriting and have been developed since the eighties [59, 199, 254, 267, 268, 385]. These calculi are based on the consideration that an equation γ is a consequence of a set of equations Γ if and only if the same set of (variable-free) formulas can be derived from both Γ and $\Gamma \cup \{\gamma\}$. The restriction to equation systems is not as severe, as it might look at a first glance: any proposition can be written as an equation of the form $\Phi = \mathsf{true}$. Moreover, there are extensions [144, 275, 286] that consider conditional equation systems. The advantage of the inductionless induction methods is that they are able to automatically deduce all lemmas that are required for the proof, while in explicit induction provers, the user has to manually set up the appropriate lemmas. Note that the induction often fails for valid formulas and must then be applied to a stronger property.

Another, and even more powerful extension of first order logic is obtained by *higher order logics*. While first order logics only quantify over elements of the considered domain $\mathcal{D}$, higher order logics additionally quantify over sets of such elements, and functions of such elements. These additional extensions enhance the expressiveness of the logics so that all facts of mathematics can be expressed. For example, Peano's axioms for the natural numbers can be easily expressed in higher order logic, and hence, the natural numbers can be formalized with this formalism.

Clearly, this means by Gödel's result that there is no complete calculus for this logic. Therefore, it is hardly possible that automated proof procedures can be implemented for it (Andrews et. al. [18] have implemented an automated theorem prover for higher order logic, and Kerber showed in [279, 280] how simple properties of higher order logics can be proved by means of a first order theorem prover). Hence, theorem provers for higher order logic are usually proof assistants, where the user has to manually invoke proof steps that are then checked by the system. The system has therefore only the task of book-keeping subgoals, checking the applicability of the rules, and clearly to generate the subgoals by applying the rules.

In particular, theorem provers for higher order logic are interesting for the formal verification of systems. In fact, one of the main applications of these theorem provers is verification. The most popular higher order logic theorem provers that are used for this purpose are HOL [216], PVS [396], Coq [125], Veritas [233], Nuprl [123], and Isabelle [398]. These provers differ in the kind of higher order logic they use, e.g., PVS uses dependent types[2], while HOL is based on simple types. Nuprl is based on intuitionistic logic, while the others are based on classic logic. Moreover, the theorem provers differ in the comfort they provide. In particular, PVS and HOL provide a rich set of efficient decision procedures including Presburger arithmetic, propositional logic, and also proof procedures for first order logic.

Both induction provers, and theorem provers for higher order logics, in particular HOL and PVS, have been used to verify different kinds of systems. For example, in 1986 Camilleri, Gordon and Melham verified a n-bit broad CMOS adder and a sequential switch level circuit for the computation of $n!$ [94]. Herbert formalized delay times in combinational hardware circuits [245] in 1988, as well as a network chip in ECL logic. Gordon verified a n-bit sequential multiplier and many other circuits [215] around the mid-eighties. Kumar, Schneider, and Kropf presented, in 1991, a structured approach for the verification of register-transfer circuits in HOL [298, 440, 441]. HOL has also been used to show the correctness of microprocessors like TAMARACK-

[2] In simple type theory, the types are defined independently of the terms. In dependent type theory, the set of types and terms are mutually recursive. Therefore, it is in general not decidable whether a term is correctly typed.

1 [269], Viper [121, 133, 517], and DLX [480]. PVS has also been used for the same purpose, e.g., the processor AAMP5 has been verified by Miller and Srivas [368]. Nqthm has been used by Hunt [256] to verify the 16-bit microprocessor FM8501 whose complexity is comparable with a PDP-11. The work has been extended to the verification of the 32-bit processor FM8502 that has also a more powerful instruction set [257]. The verification of the FM8502 was part of a larger verification project where also a code generator, an assembler, and even a kernel of an operating system were verified [45].

1.2.3 Beginnings of Program Verification

In the so-far mentioned work, we mainly considered pure theorem proving for first and higher order predicate calculus that had been successfully applied to the verification of some systems, but that is still not specialized, neither in terms of the formal language nor in terms of the proof methods. As there was however an early interest in the verification of computer systems by mathematical proofs, specialized logics and proof procedures were invented in the late 1960s. Thus, a new field for automated reasoning, namely the *verification of computer programs and systems* was born.

The earliest work in this area probably stems from *Floyd* [196] and *Hoare* [248]. They proposed guarantee commitment style proof rules for computer programs: Given that Φ and Ψ were formulas of some predicate logic, and P is a program statement, then the 'Hoare triple' $\{\Phi\}P\{\Psi\}$ means that: if Φ holds when the program P is started, and P terminates, then the property Ψ holds. In this 'Hoare triple' the condition Φ is called the precondition and Ψ is called the postcondition. The most interesting rule of Hoare's calculus is the one for the verification of loops. The rule is based on so-called invariants Φ_I and is as follows:

$$\frac{\Phi \rightarrow \Phi_I \quad \{\Phi_I \wedge B\}P\{\Phi_I\} \quad \Phi_I \wedge \neg B \rightarrow \Psi}{\{\Phi\}\mathbf{while}\ B\ \mathbf{do}\ P\ \mathbf{end}\{\Psi\}}$$

If a specification Ψ is to be shown for the loop **while** B **do** P **end**, where we can assume the precondition Φ, we must first search a suitable invariant Φ_I so that we can apply the above rule. The remaining problem is then to prove the propositions that are given above the line. In particular, the condition $\{\Phi_I \wedge B\}P\{\Phi_I\}$ amounts to saying that Φ_I is an invariant of P: if it holds before the execution of P, it will also remain true after the termination of P (it may however be false during the execution of P). The problem is that invariants are not always detected easily so that the conditions above the line hold.

For this reason, some investigations started to compute or approximate invariants. In particular, *Dijkstra* [145] suggested to compute weakest preconditions for a specification Ψ and a given program P. Informally, the weakest precondition $wp(P, \Psi)$ satisfies the Hoare triple $\{wp(P, \Psi)\}P\{\Psi\}$, and for any other precondition Φ that satisfies $\{\Phi\}P\{\Psi\}$, we have $\Phi \to wp(P, \Psi)$. Weakest preconditions can be used to give a fixpoint characterization of invariants. We will consider these relationships in the next paragraph, and in more detail in Section 3.8.3. Moreover, we note that Owicki and Gries extended these proof methods for safety properties to deal with concurrency in [394, 395].

1.2.4 Dynamic Logics and Fixpoint Calculi

Dynamic logics, also called program logics, due to *Pratt* and *Harel* [235, 411] can be used as a formal foundation of both Hoare's calculus and Dijkstra's weakest preconditions. Both can be defined in dynamic logic, and the rules revealed by Hoare and Dijkstra can then be proved.

Dynamic logics are special cases of modal logics [98, 255, 292] which have been developed in philosophy. In modal logics, the truth values of the atomic propositions of the logic are no longer fixed by a particular interpretation as in the previously mentioned predicate logics. Instead, it depends on a current state, which is often called the 'current world'. Moreover, an interpretation of modal logic determines what the next state of a state could be. Models of modal logics are therefore Kripke structures $\mathcal{K} = (\mathcal{S}, \mathcal{I}, \mathcal{R}, \xi)$ where $\mathcal{S}$ is the set of possible states, $\mathcal{I} \subseteq \mathcal{S}$ is the set of initial states, $\mathcal{R} \subseteq \mathcal{S} \times \mathcal{S}$ determines the transition relation, and ξ is finally a function that maps any state $s \in \mathcal{S}$ to an interpretation of the atomic formulas. $(s, s') \in \mathcal{R}$ means that the state s' can be reached from the set s, i.e., it is a possible successor state of s. There may be more than one successor state, and sometimes a condition α may be given to select a particular next state. This roughly explains the semantic models for modal logics. Several modal logics are distinguishable in that one often gives additional requirements on the transition relation, for example, that it must be symmetric or transitive.

For the syntax of dynamic logics, there are two important additional operators for modal logics: $\langle\alpha\rangle\Psi$ holds in a state s if this state has a successor state s' that can be reached from s with the condition α such that the formula Ψ holds in s'. The dual operator $[\alpha]\Psi$, defined as $[\alpha]\Psi :\equiv \neg\langle\alpha\rangle\neg\Psi$, states that all successor states s' that can be reached under the condition α must satisfy Ψ.

It is quite clear, how modal logics and program logics are related to each other: States of a Kripke structure $\mathcal{K}_P$ can be used to model different stages of the computation of a program P. The transition relation $\mathcal{R}_P$ can be derived with the semantics of the programming language used to implement the program P. Hence, by means of the programming language's semantics, we can transform every program into a corresponding Kripke structure (e.g. see [435, 436, 438] to derive a Kripke structure from Esterel programs). Therefore, modal logics are particularly well-suited for reasoning about the before-after behavior of programs, when we consider all the situations that could occur during the execution of a program.

In dynamic logics, the modal operators $\langle\alpha\rangle\Psi$ and $[\alpha]\Psi$ are extended in that the conditions α need not necessarily be atomic program statements (this distinguishes them from *Hennessy-Milner* logic [239]). Instead, they may be entire program statements P, and in this case, the formula $\langle P\rangle\Psi$ intuitively holds in a particular state s if the program statement P can be executed from this state so that after termination of P a state s' is reached where Ψ holds. Note that several transitions can be taken during the execution of P. In a similar way, the formula $[P]\Psi$ holds iff for all executions of the program P the property Ψ must hold after termination (P may be nondeterministic or its execution may depend on the inputs). If no terminating execution of P can be started in this state, the formula does trivially hold. Usually, dynamic logics consider some set of program constructs for determining the statements that are allowed in the formulas. A detailed definition is given in Section 3.8.3.

Using dynamic logics, Hoare triples $\{\Phi\}P\{\Psi\}$ can be defined as an abbreviation of the formula $\Phi \rightarrow [P]\Psi$. Therefore, Hoare's rules can also be given as formulas in dynamic logic and therefore the correctness of the rules can be proved. For example, the above mentioned rule for loops is translated to the following valid dynamic logic formula:

$$\left(\begin{array}{l}\Phi\wedge \\ (\Phi \rightarrow \Phi_I)\wedge \\ (\Phi_I \wedge B \rightarrow [P]\Phi_I)\wedge \\ (\Phi_I \wedge \neg B \rightarrow \Psi)\end{array}\right) \rightarrow [\textbf{while } B \textbf{ do } P \textbf{ end}]\Psi$$

Also the correctness of the rules for the computation of weakest preconditions can be proved. In particular, it turns out that the weakest preconditions of loops can be defined as greatest fixpoints:

$$wp(\textbf{while } B \textbf{ do } S \textbf{ end}, \Psi) := \nu x.(\neg B \wedge \Psi) \vee (B \wedge wp(S, x))$$

Thus, the expression $\nu x.\Phi$ denotes the greatest fixpoint of Φ. To explain what this means in our setting, recall that the models are Kripke structures and that the formulas are interpreted on states of the Kripke structure. Therefore, we can compute for any formula Φ and any Kripke structure $\mathcal{K}$ the set of states $[\![\Phi]\!]_{\mathcal{K}}$ of $\mathcal{K}$ where Φ holds. If we change the structure $\mathcal{K}$ to $\mathcal{K}_x^S$ such that the variable x holds in the states $S \subseteq \mathcal{S}$, we obtain a so-called *state transformer* by defining $f(S) := [\![\Phi]\!]_{\mathcal{K}_x^S}$. Note that f is a function of type $f : 2^{\mathcal{S}} \rightarrow 2^{\mathcal{S}}$. $S \subseteq \mathcal{S}$ a fixpoint of this state transformer iff the condition $S = f(S)$ holds. As the set of all subsets $2^{\mathcal{S}}$ is ordered by the set inclusion, we can furthermore talk about least and greatest fixpoints, and denote these as $\mu x.\Phi$ and $\nu x.\Phi$, respectively.

These observations showed the usefulness of fixpoint expressions and stimulated the construction of fixpoint logics. In 1975, *Kfoury and Park* proved that properties like termination and totality of programs can not be expressed in first order logics [283] (see Section 6.2.2). For this reason, *Park* [397], *Hitchcock* and *Park* [247], and *de Bakker* and *de Roever* [142] introduced a least fixpoint operator to remedy these deficiencies. *Emerson* and *Clarke* showed in

1980 [160] how fixpoints can be used to formulate correctness properties of parallel programs. The resulting formal systems were powerful enough to express properties like termination, liveness, and freedom from deadlocks or starvation. Based on these forerunners, *Pratt* [413] and *Kozen* [288, 289] have developed the propositional μ-calculus. This formalism is discussed in detail in Chapter 3 of this book and we will see that it is a very powerful basis for all other formalisms in this book. In particular, we will see in Section 3.8.3 that dynamic logics can be easily defined in terms of the μ-calculus.

In the early 1980s, it was not immediately clear, whether the propositional μ-calculus was decidable. It should be noted that the compactness property that is the reason for the semi-decidability of first order logic does neither hold for propositional dynamic logic nor for the propositional μ-calculus. In 1983-1984, Kozen [288, 289], Vardi and Wolper [499] developed exponential time decision procedures for fragments of Kozen's μ-calculus. In 1983, Kozen and Parikh [290] and independently, Niwiński showed that the satisfiability problem of μ-calculus formulas can be reduced to the second order theory of n successors (SnS). By Rabin's results [418] (Rabin has proved the decidability of SnS), a first decision procedure was obtained for the propositional μ-calculus. However, like Streett and Emerson's decision procedure of 1984 [477], its runtime complexity was nonelementary, which means that the runtime can not be bound by a finite number of exponential nestings. Better decision procedures were found afterwards: Streett and Emerson found, in 1989 [478], a triple exponential time decision procedure for the propositional μ-calculus. Based on further improvements for (1) determinizing ω-automata in exponential time by Safra's construction (cf. Definition 4.29), and (2) checking the emptiness of ω-automata on trees in exponential time [165, 168, 304, 409] this was reduced to a single exponential time decision procedure (cf. Appendix B.3). The decidability and complexity of the extension to past time modalities was finally shown by Vardi [430, 496] in 1998.

Beneath the test for satisfiability, the evaluation of a given μ-calculus formula in a given Kripke structure is of interest, i.e., the *model checking problem of the μ-calculus*. In particular, the verification problem can be reduced to such model checking problems. In general, one distinguishes between local and global approaches. Global approaches aim at computing the set of states where the formula holds, while local approaches only try to check whether the formula holds in a particular state or not. In general, local model checking approaches may be more efficient than global ones, since the validity in a given state can possibly be answered by considering only a part of the entire state set. In the worst case however, the same complexity is reached as in global approaches. Global approaches, on the other hand, have the advantage that they can make use of a breadth-first search which can be very efficiently implemented by means of symbolic traversals with binary decision diagrams [44, 88]. Therefore, global approaches can cope with very large structures, i.e., structures with up to 10^{100} states.

A first model checking procedure, given by Emerson and Lei in 1986 [174], runs in time $O\left(|\mathcal{K}|\,(|\mathcal{S}|\,|\Phi|)^{\mathsf{ad}(\Phi)+1}\right)$, where $|\mathcal{S}|$ is the number of states, $|\mathcal{K}|$ is the size of the Kripke structure (maximum of transitions and states), and $\mathsf{ad}(\Phi)$ is the number of alternating nestings of fixpoint operators (see page 116). In 1991, Cleaveland and Steffen [118, 119] presented a sophisticated model checking procedure for the alternation free μ-calculus (this is the set of μ-calculus formulas with $\mathsf{ad}(\Phi) \leq 1$) that runs in time $O(|\mathcal{K}|\,|\Phi|)$ and therefore improved the previous result. Therefore, the alternation-free μ-calculus is a promising language for the automated verification since it has very efficient model checking procedures. Cleaveland, Klein, and Steffen extended their model checking procedure afterwards to formulas of arbitrary alternation depth and obtained a runtime of order $O\left(\left(\frac{1}{d}\,|\mathcal{S}|\,|\Phi|\right)^{d-1}|\mathcal{K}|\,|\Phi|\right)$ [116] with $d := \mathsf{ad}(\Phi)$.

In 1993, Emerson, Jutla and Sistla [169] presented some more fragments of the μ-calculus that can be checked in time $O\left(|\mathcal{K}|\,|\Phi|^2\right)$, i.e, linear in terms of the system's size and quadratic in terms of the length of the formula. As the system's size is usually the limiting factor, this is still an acceptable result. In 1994, Long, Browne, Clarke, Jha, and Marrero showed that the previous results on μ-calculus model checking can be improved to $O\left((|\mathcal{S}|\,|\Phi|)^{\frac{d}{2}}\,|\mathcal{K}|\,|\Phi|\right)$ [333]. We will give proofs for these results in Chapter 3.

Local model checking procedures (see Appendix B) for the μ-calculus have been given by Stirling and Walker [471, 472] (1989-1991), Cleaveland [115] (1989), and Bradfield and Stirling [67] (1992). Bradfield [63] also discusses model checking procedures for infinite state spaces.

The μ-calculus is of particular interest for the complexity theory, since the model checking problem of the μ-calculus is known to be in NP and also in the complement coNP [168–170], as shown by Emerson, Jutla and Sistla in 1993. This means that there is a nondeterministic procedure that can check μ-calculus formulas in polynomial time. There are very few problems that belong to NP ∩ coNP for which no polynomial deterministic procedure is known. The model checking problem for the μ-calculus is one of them. The result was even refined to membership in UP ∩ coUP by Jurdziński in 1998 [270].

Another question related to the alternation depth was independently solved by Bradfield [64, 65] and Lenzi [321] in 1996. They proved that the alternation hierarchy of the μ-calculus is strict, i.e., for every number n, there are μ-calculus formulas of alternation depth n which can not be expressed by μ-calculus formulas of lower alternation depth. All currently known model checking procedures are, however, exponential in the alternation depth.

The research on efficient decision procedures for the μ-calculus is still not complete. In particular, it is not clear whether a polynomial model checking procedure exists or not, although the existence of a polynomial algorithm is unlikely. Moreover, efficient decision procedures for the μ-calculus are important, since we will see throughout the book that most formalisms can be translated to the μ-calculus.

1.2.5 Temporal Logics

μ-calculus formulas are quite hard to understand, in particular when interdependent fixpoints are nested. For this reason, there is a need for more readable specification languages. Special modal logics have been developed with the view that the change from one state to another requires one unit of time by Prior in 1957 [416, 417]. Therefore, the resulting logics are called *temporal logics*. Beneath the simple next-time operator, which we discussed in the previous section, temporal logics provide further temporal operators for describing complex temporal properties. The most important temporal operator is the $\underline{\mathsf{U}}$ operator that has the following meaning: $[\varphi\ \underline{\mathsf{U}}\ \psi]$ holds if there is a point of time in the future where ψ holds and up to this point the condition φ holds. Other temporal operators are G and F with the following meaning: $\mathsf{G}\varphi$ states that φ must always hold, and $\mathsf{F}\varphi$ states that φ must hold at least once. The next time operator is usually written as X, so that $\mathsf{X}\varphi$ means that φ holds at the next point of time. Note here that all mentioned temporal operators do refer to a particular computation of a system, i.e., to a *path through the Kripke structure*.

From the viewpoint of temporal operators, Kamp [274] used, in 1968, a combined form of the $\underline{\mathsf{U}}$ and the X operator, which we denote as $\underline{\mathsf{XU}}$. The operator is defined as $[\varphi\ \underline{\mathsf{XU}}\ \psi] := \mathsf{X}\,[\varphi\ \underline{\mathsf{U}}\ \psi]$, i.e., it behaves like $\underline{\mathsf{U}}$ except that the present point of time is ignored. Moreover, Kamp considered the corresponding past-time operator: $[\varphi\ \overleftarrow{\underline{\mathsf{XU}}}\ \psi]$ holds iff there was a point of time in the past, where ψ held and since then φ holds up to this point. Kamp proved that $\underline{\mathsf{XU}}$ is able to express all previously mentioned future temporal operators and is strictly more expressive than the temporal operators G and F (see page 289). Kamp also proved that his temporal logic is as expressive as the first order theory of linear order (see Section 6.4). The same was proved [203] in 1980 for the future time fragment of the logic by Gabbay, Pnueli, Shelah and Stavi so that past time operators have been viewed as unnecessary since then. However, in 1985, Lichtenstein, Pnueli, and Zuck [326] reintroduced past operators for reasons of clear and uniform specifications. Laroussinie and Schnoebelen, also favored past operators for sake of simple and succinct specifications [315, 316, 355, 443] (for example: 'when an accident happens, then a mistake is made before hand'). Further operators, such as the X operator, the precede operator, and the weak U operator were introduced by Manna and Pnueli in 1979 and 1982 [343, 345, 346]. We will discuss these operators in Chapter 5.

We have already remarked that temporal operators consider a particular computation of a system, i.e., a path through a Kripke structure. In 1980, Emerson and Clarke [160], and in 1981, *Ben-Ari, Manna and Pnueli* [36] explicitly used, for the first time, the path quantifiers E and A to quantify over computation paths of a particular state. Hence, $\mathsf{E}\Phi$ holds in a state of a Kripke structure iff at least one infinite computation path starts in that state that satisfies Φ. Analogously $\mathsf{A}\Phi$ holds in a state iff all infinite computation paths that start in that state satisfy Φ. If a temporal logic provides these path quantifiers, one usually says that the temporal logic is a branching time temporal logic, otherwise it is called a linear time temporal logic. This is motivated by the fact that the use of a path quantifier allows branching to another path when the formula is evaluated along a certain path. Hence, these formulas can state properties about the 'branching behavior' of a system, which is not possible for linear time temporal logics. The linear time temporal logic with the temporal operators X and $\underline{\mathsf{U}}$ is usually denoted as LTL (we will call it LTL_p). By Kamp's result, the temporal operators G and F, and many more can be defined, since this set of operators is already expressively complete w.r.t. the monadic first order theory of linear orders $\mathsf{MFO}_<$. We prove this in Section 6.4.

The branching time temporal logic given by Ben-Ari, Manna and Pnueli in 1981 was called UB and is discussed in Chapter 5. In the same year, Emerson and Clarke [160, 161] pointed out that some forms of temporal logic formulas can be directly interpreted as fixpoint formulas of μ-calculus and therefore introduced the temporal logic CTL as a macro language of a fragment of the alternation-free μ-calculus. CTL consists of macro operators that are formed by coupling path quantifiers and temporal operators in pairs. This however makes it hard to express complex temporal properties for one computation path since each temporal operator must be preceded by a path quantifier that has the freedom to choose a new path for its evaluation.

The following decade saw an extensive debate [163, 172, 310, 324, 497] on whether the branching time logic CTL or the linear time temporal logic LTL is more suited for the specification and verification of finite state systems. In general, LTL specifications tend to be more readable than CTL specifications, since LTL directly allows the formalization of properties with more than one event, as temporal operators may be nested arbitrarily. For example, the property 'a has to hold until b holds the second time' can be expressed in LTL as $[a\ \underline{\mathsf{U}}\ (a \wedge b \wedge \mathsf{X}\,[a\ \underline{\mathsf{U}}\ b])]$. In 1985, Lichtenstein and Pnueli presented [324] a model checking procedure for temporal logic that runs in time $O(|\mathcal{K}|\, 2^{c|\Phi|})$ for some constant $c > 0$. They argued that specifications Φ are rather short in comparison to the size of the model and that therefore their decision procedure is of practical use. In 1986, Clarke, Emerson, and Sistla gave a model checking procedure for CTL that runs in time $O(|\mathcal{K}|\,|\Phi|)$ [103] which was a strong argument for the use of CTL.

However, this good theoretical result need not necessarily have led to verification tools that were able to verify large systems. In fact, first implementations were only able to handle systems with a thousand states. The breakthrough of the CTL model checking procedures was achieved with the development of efficient data structures for symbolically traversing the structure. These *symbolic model checking procedures* are based on manipulating Boolean functions that are stored as binary decision diagrams (BDDs) [74] (cf. Appendix A). The application of these data structures in the model checking procedures is as follows: The states of the Kripke structures are encoded by a couple of state variables $q_1, \ldots, q_n$, and hence, the transition relation can be described as a Boolean formula in $q_1, \ldots, q_n$ and corresponding variables $q'_1, \ldots, q'_n$ for the next state. This description of the structure can then be efficiently stored as a BDD, as can the sets of states of the structure. As the evaluation of the temporal logic formula simply consists of some fixpoint iterations over such sets of states, the entire model checking procedure can be implemented with BDDs. Note that a structure with n state variables may have 2^n reachable states. Hence, small propositional formulas can encode large structures. In particular, note that if all the 2^n states were connected with each other, the transition relation would be simply represented by the formula 1 (denoting truth). The same holds for sets of states.

Symbolic model checking was introduced by Burch, Clarke, McMillan, Dill, Hwang in 1990 [87–89], and independently in the same year by Berthet, Coudert, and Madre [44]. The use of symbolic model checking had finally led to the breakthrough in the verification of finite state systems and allowed the checking of systems with more than 10^{20} states. For this reason, symbolic CTL model checking still plays a dominant role, and verification tools such as SMV [360] and VIS [69] have successfully verified lots of systems, including the alternating bit protocol [103], traffic light controllers [71], DMA controllers [360], the Gigamax cache coherence protocol [360], and the Futurebus cache coherence protocol [106].

A major drawback of CTL is however its limited expressiveness: In particular, CTL can not express *fairness*. Therefore, extensions of CTL have been defined which augment the temporal operators of CTL by additional fairness constraints. In [103], it was shown that model checking procedures of polynomial runtime can be obtained for the extension of fairness constraints, and the procedures would still require polynomial runtime in terms of the size of the structure.

Nevertheless, the expressiveness, and even worse, the readability of CTL is not satisfactory. Therefore, the search continued for more powerful temporal logics that could be efficiently checked by symbolic model checking. Emerson and Halpern therefore introduced the temporal logic CTL* in [163] as a superset of CTL and LTL, in that path quantifiers *may* be applied to every subformula. Emerson and Lei [172, 176] then showed that any model checking procedure for LTL can be transformed to a model checking procedure for CTL* with roughly the same complexity. Therefore, there is no additional cost when path quantifiers are added to LTL. Expressivenesses and complexities of several temporal logics were investigated by Emerson and Halpern [162] in 1985, and, in particular for CTL* by Emerson and Jutla in [165]. It turned out that both LTL and CTL* model checking problems are PSPACE-complete. Moreover, neither LTL nor CTL* can be directly checked by symbolic model checking (however, as we will discuss below, both can be translated to the μ-calculus which can be checked by symbolic model checking).

Recently, some new results have been added to the discussion. In 1994, Bernholtz and Grumberg presented a temporal logic CTL^2 that allows two nested temporal operators after a path quantifier. They showed that CTL^2 can still be checked in polynomial time. In 1997, Schneider presented the temporal logic $\mathsf{LeftCTL}^*$ that allows arbitrary deep nesting of temporal operators on one argument of the binary temporal operators without necessarily using path quantifiers. $\mathsf{LeftCTL}^*$ can be translated to the alternation-free μ-calculus, and in particular, to CTL. The size of the obtained CTL formula for a given $\mathsf{LeftCTL}^*$ formula Φ is thereby bound by $O(|\Phi|\, 2^{2|\Phi|})$, so that a $\mathsf{LeftCTL}^*$ model checking procedure with runtime $O(|\mathcal{K}|\, |\Phi|\, 2^{2|\Phi|})$ is obtained. Note that the blow-up shows that there are $\mathsf{LeftCTL}^*$ formulas that are exponentially more succinct than corresponding CTL formulas, and are therefore more readable.

In fact, from a result of Wilke [513], it follows that at least an exponential lower bound is required for this translation. Adler and Immerman [4] improved this result in 2001 to a lower bound $|\varphi|!$. In fact, the translation of $\mathsf{LeftCTL}^*$ to exponentially sized 'CTL' formulas given in Section 5.3.5 translates the formulas to CTL formulas where common subterms are shared. For this reason only a blow-up $O(|\Phi|\, 2^{2|\Phi|})$ is sufficient. Recently, Johannsen and Lange [266] proved that satisfiability checking of CTL^+ is 2EXPTIME-complete. As satisfiability checking of CTL is only EXPTIME-complete (as well as the sat-problem of the μ-calculus), it follows that every translation from CTL^+ to CTL (or to the μ-calculus) must necessarily have an exponential blow-up.

$\mathsf{LeftCTL}^*$ specifications tend to be as readable as LTL specifications (for the same reasons), but can be automatically translated to CTL, so that one benefits from the already existing efficient model checking tools for CTL. As an example, consider the $\mathsf{LeftCTL}^*$ formula $\mathsf{E}[\mathsf{F}a \wedge \mathsf{FG}b]$ that states that there is a path where a holds at least once and after some time b always holds. This formula is translated to the following equivalent, but less readable CTL formula:

$$\mathsf{EF}[a \wedge \mathsf{EFEG}b] \vee \mathsf{EF}\,[b\ \underline{\mathsf{U}}\ (a \wedge \mathsf{EG}b)]$$

We will consider the translation from $\mathsf{LeftCTL}^*$ to CTL in detail in Section 5.3.3 and 5.3.5. The expressiveness of $\mathsf{LeftCTL}^*$ is the same as the expressiveness of the well-known logic CTL, which suffices for most applications. Nevertheless, we will also consider some extensions of $\mathsf{LeftCTL}^*$. In particular, we will define a logic AFCTL^* in Section 5.4.5. AFCTL^* is strictly stronger than $\mathsf{LeftCTL}^*$ and CTL, but can still be translated to the alternation-free μ-calculus.

The translations of AFCTL^* and $\mathsf{LeftCTL}^*$ to the μ-calculus are very different. While we will translate $\mathsf{LeftCTL}^*$ directly to the alternation-free μ-calculus (Section 5.3.5), our translation of AFCTL^* is indirect via a translation to ω-automata (see Chapter 4 and Section 5.4). For this reason, the logic LeftCTL* is still interesting on its own. The construction of the logic AFCTL* is related to a result of Kupferman and Vardi [303] who characterized the intersection between the alternation-free μ-calculus and LTL. We will outline the relationship in Section 5.4.5. Therefore, the definition of the temporal logics LeftCTL* and AFCTL* is motivated by the well-known hierarchies of ω-automata and μ-calculus. It is thus of crucial importance that a good compromise between the expressiveness and the efficiency of the logics is found. In general, the stronger the expressiveness of a logic, the higher the complexity of its verification procedures.

In general, the expressiveness of temporal logics is well understood (cf. Theorem 5.76 on page 382). Kamp has already proved in 1968 that temporal logic is expressively complete w.r.t. the monadic first order theories of linear order $\mathsf{MFO}_<$. In 1971, McNaughton and Papert [364] characterized the corresponding subset of ω-automata whose expressiveness matches that of temporal logics and also introduced star-free regular expressions for the characterization of this class. As temporal logics are less expressive than ω-automata, there are properties that can not be expressed by temporal logics, but with ω-automata. As an example, Wolper [519] mentioned the property that a variable a should hold for *at least* all even points of time. As these properties can, however, be expressed as μ-calculus formulas and also as ω-automata, Wolper suggested to extend temporal logic by operators based on regular languages [523]. Wolper also proposed a deductive proof system for his logic, which was shown to be complete, after some corrections, by Banieqbal and Barringer in 1986 [28]. The branching time analog was considered by Vardi and Wolper [500] in 1984. Wolper's extension had also some relationship to quantified temporal logic which was considered in [460, 519], and its complexity has been analyzed by Sistla, Vardi and Wolper in 1987 [459].

We conclude this section with some further historical remarks and a listing of temporal logics that are not considered in this book. First applications of temporal logics for the specification of computer systems were given in 1977 by *Kröger* [294] and *Pnueli* [407], who used temporal logics for the specification of sequential and concurrent program properties, respectively. Other authors that used temporal logics around the early 1980s as specification language were Hailpern [228], Owicki [229], and Lamport [311], and Manna and Pnueli [344, 346, 347]. Bochmann [53] was probably the first who specified the behavior of hardware circuits by temporal logics. Using temporal logic, Malachi and Owicki specified 'self-timed systems' [340] in 1981, and Manna and Wolper described the synchronization of communication processes by temporal logics in 1984 [353]. There are many more of these early applications that are not listed.

New directions of research mainly consider the state-explosion problem, which roughly means that the number of states that must be considered for verification grows exponentially with the size of the system. Promising results has been obtained by (data) abstraction (see Appendix C.4) by Clarke,

Grumberg, and Long [108, 109, 332] and also by Graf, Loiseaux, Sifakis, Bouajjani, and Bensalem [222, 331]. Other methods of solving the state explosion problem have been considered in the previous decade. Among them are reduction by exploiting symmetry of the structures [113, 178, 180, 181, 260] (see Appendix C.5), partial order reductions [400] that abstract away from different interleavings of asynchronous threads, on-the-fly methods [208], as well as combinations of these approaches [164].

So far, we have only discussed temporal logics whose semantics are based on discrete Kripke structures. However, there are also temporal logics that have different semantics. We will not consider these logics in this book, but list at least some of them to conclude this section. For example, there are real-time temporal logics which are either based on a continuous time model [9, 30, 90, 91] or on a discrete time model where transitions may require more than one unit of time [10, 11, 95, 238, 243, 316, 329, 330, 392, 427]. Furthermore, there are other variants such as first order temporal logics [1, 345], partial order temporal logics [406], and interval temporal logics [377, 450].

The semantics of the temporal interval logic ITL [232] maps sequences of states to variables, so that the truth value of a variable does not simply depend on a state of the Kripke structure, but on a sequence of states. The important operator of ITL is the chop operator ';' that has the following meaning: $\varphi;\psi$ holds on a sequence of states $s_0, \ldots, s_n$ iff this sequence can be split into two parts $s_0, \ldots, s_i$ and $s_i, \ldots, s_n$ such that φ holds on $s_0, \ldots, s_i$ and ψ holds on $s_i, \ldots, s_n$. Using this chop operator, many other interval based temporal operators can be described. However, the major drawback of ITL is that the satisfiability is no longer decidable [232]. Moszkowski [378, 379] used ITL to establish executable specifications and in this way verified entire arithmetic-logic units of microprocessors at the transistor level. Leeser [319] extended Moszkowski's model by setup and hold times and used temporal PROLOG to also verify an arithmetic-logic unit at transistor level.

1.2.6 Decidable Theories and ω-Automata

A lot of decision procedures for special logics have been developed independently of the research in the verification of computer systems and the development of automated theorem proving procedures for first and higher order predicate logics. Based on the disappointing result of Gödel's incompleteness theorem in 1931 and the undecidability theorem of first order logic of Church and Turing in 1936/1937 [99, 492], a considerable amount of work has been put on the investigation of decidable mathematical theories.

The first investigations to find decidable fragments were to study quantifier prefix classes (see Section 6.2.3). This means that first order formulas of the form $\Theta_1 x_1. \ldots \Theta_n x_n.\varphi$ with $\Theta_i \in \{\forall, \exists\}$ and quantifier-free φ are considered with restricted patterns of quantifiers Θ_i. For example, Bernays and Schönfinkel [39], and Ramsey [422] showed that the sat-problem of the formulas where only one change from $\exists$ to $\forall$ quantifiers is allowed, i.e., the fragment $\mathsf{FO}(\exists^*\forall^*)$, is decidable. Other fragments with decidable sat-problem have been found by Ackermann [3] ($\mathsf{FO}(\exists^*\forall\exists^*)$) and Gödel, Kalmár, and Schütte [213, 273, 448] ($\mathsf{FO}(\exists^*\forall^2\exists^*)$). These are the maximal decidable classes, since there are formulas with quantifier prefixes $\forall^3\exists$ (Surányi [479], 1959) and $\forall\exists\forall$ (Kahr, Wang, and Moore [272], 1962) that can describe undecidable problems. Hence, the prefix classes $\mathsf{FO}(\alpha)$ were completely classified in 1962 for first order logic without equality. Only the result for $\mathsf{FO}(\exists^*\forall^2\exists^*)$ with equality was missing, that has been answered by Goldfarb [214] in 1984 to the negative. Besides the quantifier prefix classes, also restrictions to a finite number of variables have been considered. It is remarkable that first order logic with only two variables, but arbitrary quantification, is decidable [218, 219, 375], which has been essentially shown by Mortimer in 1975. As modal logic can be embedded in predicate logic with only two variables, Vardi posed the question [495] whether this could be a reason for the robust decidability of modal logic. Section 6.2.3 gives more details on these classes, and for further reading, we refer to the original literature, and excellent books on this topic like [56, 146, 323].

Many other decidable theories have been considered, in particular fragments of arithmetic such as Presburger arithmetic [415] or Skolem arithmetic, and interesting decision procedures have been found for them [83, 84, 336, 446, 447, 521, 522]. Furthermore, the monadic second order theory of one successor S1S [80, 455, 486], which is equivalent to the monadic second order theory of linear orders $\mathsf{MSO}_<$ is another decidable theory that subsumes Presburger arithmetic (see page 433).

We have to explain, what a 'theory' in this sense is. We have already explained that the domain $\mathcal{D}$ that is used for interpreting the variables of predicate logic is chosen arbitrarily for the interpretation. For special theories, one accepts certain axioms which are formulas that are assumed to be valid. Hence, the set of domains is thereby restricted to those domains that satisfy these axioms. The theory that is induced by these axioms is then the set of formulas that can be derived from this set[3].

For example, to only consider domains with more than n elements, we could establish the axiom $\exists x_1. \ldots \exists x_n. \bigwedge_{i=1}^{n} \bigwedge_{j=1,j\neq i}^{n} .x_i \neq x_j$. As another example, one could set up the following axioms to specify that $\leq$ is a total order:

$$\begin{aligned} \text{Reflexivity: } & \forall x.\ x \leq x \\ \text{Antisymmetry: } & \forall x.\forall y.\ x \leq y \wedge y \leq x \rightarrow x \doteq y \\ \text{Transitivity: } & \forall x.\forall y.\forall z.\ x \leq y \wedge y \leq z \rightarrow x \leq z \\ \text{Totality: } & \forall x.\forall y.\ x \leq y \vee y \leq x \end{aligned}$$

[3] As first order logic has complete proof procedures, this is the same as the set of formulas that are logical consequences of the axioms. For higher order logic, which is not complete, we must distinguish between theories that are *derived* by a special calculus and others that are obtained by *logical consequence*.

All first order formulas that can be derived from the above set of axioms form the first order theory of total orders. However, for the monadic first and second order theories of *linear order* $\mathsf{MFO}_<$ and $\mathsf{MSO}_<$, the domain is further restricted such that the elements are lined up in a chain. Hence, the domain is either a finite string, or isomorphic to the natural or the integer numbers. To axiomatize this, one has to add the Peano axioms (see page 405), which requires second order logic.

These theories are important for the formalisms we will consider in this book. However, at the beginning of the research, $\mathsf{MSO}_<$ has not been discussed. Instead, an equivalent variant of the logic has been considered, which is called the 'monadic second order logic of one successor' S1S. Note, however, that although the second order logics $\mathsf{MSO}_<$ and S1S are equally expressive, this is not the case for their first order fragments. Indeed, $\mathsf{MFO}_<$ is strictly more expressive than the first order fragment of S1S.

In 1960, J.R. Büchi succeeded in proving the decidability of S1S by reducing S1S to ω-automata. These ω-automata differ from classical finite state automata as introduced by Kleene[4] in 1956 [285] as follows: Kleene's finite state automata are used to decide whether a finite word belongs to a regular language or not. This is done by an automaton by reading the word letter by letter, and possibly changing the internal state each time a letter of the word is read. A word is accepted, iff the automaton is in one of its designated final states after reading the entire word.

In contrast to that, ω-automata accept or reject *infinite* words, and therefore their acceptance condition must be defined differently. A natural condition imposed by Büchi was that a word should be accepted if there is a run over this word that reaches at least one of the designated states infinitely often. As this acceptance condition has been introduced by Büchi, these automata are nowadays called Büchi automata. A lot of other variants of ω-automata were defined after Büchi's pioneering work including Muller automata [363, 380] (1963), Rabin automata [363, 418] (1969), Streett automata [476] (1982), and Parity automata [376] (1984). The other kinds of ω-automata have been introduced mainly for one reason: while for finite automata on finite words, it is possible to construct for any nondeterministic automaton an equivalent deterministic one, this does not hold for Büchi automata. However, for Muller, Rabin, Streett, and Parity automata this can be achieved. The complexity for determinizing these ω-automata automata is higher than for automata on finite words, although still exponential: While for the latter 2^n states are sufficient, the optimal construction of a deterministic Rabin automaton from a Büchi automaton requires $2^{O(n\log(n))}$ states (where n is the number of states of the given automaton). We will see that the automaton classes form a strict hierarchy that has moreover a strong relationship to

[4] Kleene's paper was actually a mathematical reworking of the ideas of W. McCulloch and W. Pitts [359], who, in 1943, had presented a logical model for the behavior of nerve systems that is in principle a finite automaton.

the Borel hierarchy known in topology. Details on the different kinds of ω-automata, the automaton hierarchy, and various translation procedures between ω-automata are given in detail in Chapter 4. We will also outline the relationship between algebraic structures and automata, and will characterize the important class of noncounting automata by algebraic properties.

The translation of S1S or $\mathsf{MSO}_<$ formulas of length n to equivalent Büchi automata is nonelementary. This means that the procedure runs in a time that can not be bound by a finite nesting of exponentials and has therefore been considered to be useless for a long time. However, recently the procedure has been implemented and been successfully applied to the verification of generic hardware circuits [31, 240, 265, 278, 442]. A possible future direction of research is therefore to develop decision procedures for timing diagrams which can be understood as graphical representations of S1S or $\mathsf{MSO}_<$ formulas. We consider translations between S1S and $\mathsf{MSO}_<$, and also to equivalent ω-automata in Chapter 6.

ω-automata are strongly related to temporal logic, in that they also establish a temporal relationship on the input sequences they accept. Therefore, translations from temporal logics to ω-automata have been considered, mainly for the construction of efficient decision procedures for temporal logics. We have already mentioned that Wolper [523] suggested the use of ω-automata as special temporal operators to extend the expressiveness of temporal logics. We will consider such a branching time temporal logic $\mathcal{L}_\omega$ in detail in Chapter 4. A basic translation from linear time temporal logic to $\mathcal{L}_\omega$ is then considered in Section 5.4. It is remarkable that the translation can be performed in linear time w.r.t. to the length of the given temporal logic formula, when a symbolic description of the automaton is derived (that can be directly used for symbolic model checking). We will study this translation procedure in detail, and will show some novel improvements. These improvements will then lead to the definition of temporal logic classes TL_κ in correspondence with the automaton hierarchy: We define for any automaton class κ, a logic TL_κ that can be translated to the automata in the class κ. We will also prove the completeness of the logics TL_κ, which follows from related results of Manna and Pnueli [350–352].

Moreover, we will see in Chapter 6 that both S1S and $\mathsf{MSO}_<$ can be easily translated to quantified temporal logic which can in turn be converted to ω-automata with a nonelementary translation procedure. Finally, we will prove in Chapter 6 Kamp's result that temporal logic is equal expressive as $\mathsf{MFO}_<$, the first order fragment of of $\mathsf{MSO}_<$. In Section 5.5.1, we will show how noncounting automata can be translated to temporal logic, the converse is simple. Hence, robust characterizations of all of these logics exists.

Therefore, ω-automata have served as a basic formalism whose decidability and the corresponding complexity is well-known. In order to prove the decidability of a theory such as $\mathsf{MSO}_<$, one simply has to give a translation to equivalent ω-automata. To determine the complexity, one simply has to add the complexity of the translation procedure to the complexity of the remaining decision procedure for the obtained ω-automaton.

We have also seen that the μ-calculus is a 'basic machinery' that can be used as a foundation for other formalisms. It is therefore natural to ask how ω-automata and μ-calculus are related to each other. However, this relationship has been considered relatively late. Thomas showed in 1988 [485] that the temporal logic that is obtained by using ω-automata as temporal operators is strictly less expressive than the second order theory of two successors (S2S). In contrast to S1S, where only one successor is available, the monadic second order logic of two successors, S2S has two successors. For this reason, its domains are not lined up, but form trees that may be finite or infinite. In particular, domains for S2S are binary trees, and for SnS trees of branching degree n. As Niwiński [389] has shown that S2S has the same expressiveness as the propositional μ-calculus, it follows that the μ-calculus is strictly more expressive than this temporal logic.

The same result follows by translating $\mathcal{L}_\omega$ to the μ-calculus (see Section 4.8). Such a translation procedure has been given by Dam in 1994 [135] where a given Büchi automaton with n states is translated to an equivalent μ-calculus formula of size $2^{O(n)}$ and an alternation depth ≤ 2. By Bradfield's and Lenzi's recent result (that the alternation hierarchy is strict), it thus follows that the μ-calculus is strictly more expressive than $\mathcal{L}_\omega$. We will present in Section 4.8 a translation procedure that constructs for given ω-automata equivalent vectorized μ-calculus formulas of size $O(n)$ with an alternation depth ≤ 2. Using this translation, the decision procedures obtained from the μ-calculus match the lower bounds of other decision procedures that directly work on ω-automata. Hence, the μ-calculus is indeed a very expressive language that can serve as a basic machinery for various problems.

If one restricts the consideration to single paths or linear time structures, where each state has a unique successor state, it is interesting to note that $\mathcal{L}_\omega$ and the μ-calculus become equal expressive. This shows that the additional expressiveness of the μ-calculus is due to statements on the branching behavior of the structures: while any formula of $\mathcal{L}_\omega$ can only have a finite number of nested E and A quantifiers, there are only finitely many choices of taking a new path along a considered path. In contrast to that, the fixpoint iterations for μ-calculus formulas can look arbitrarily deep in the branching of the structure. We will explain this in more detail in Section 4.8.

The situation changes when ω-automata on infinite trees are considered. Pioneering work of Rabin in 1969 [418] proved that the second order theory of two successors (S2S) is decidable by reducing it to equivalent ω-automata on infinite trees. Hence, this is a branching time analogon to Büchi's result of the equivalence of S1S and ω-automata on words. However, not all results that hold for ω-automata on infinite words have corresponding results for the tree automata. In particular, it can be shown that Rabin tree automata are equal expressive as the μ-calculus (see Appendix B.3), but strictly more expressive than Büchi tree automata.

Due to lack of space, we will not consider ω-automata on infinite trees in this book (apart from Appendix B.3), although their theory gives further insights into the formalisms considered here. The interested reader is referred to Thomas' survey [486, 489] that contains many more references and the new book of Grädel, Thomas, and Wilke [221]. Also, we will not consider *alternating ω-automata* [82, 96, 374] which are a generalization of nondeterministic automata. However, the symbolic descriptions that we use to embed automata in temporal logic are somehow related to alternating automata.

1.2.7 Summary

As can be seen, a plethora of formalisms for the verification of programs, and, in particular, for the verification of concurrent programs has been proposed. Up to now, their relationship is almost clear and for many different formalisms we already know if translations between them exist and how to translate them efficiently. In this book, the most important classical formalisms, namely μ-calculus, ω-automata, temporal logics, and predicate logic are considered and their relationship is outlined in detail. A special emphasis is thereby the existence of algorithms either for translation between these formalisms or for the implementation of decision procedures for the formalisms.

In particular, two basic machineries can be selected for the verification of most properties: we can reduce the property to an ω-automaton problem, or we could use the μ-calculus as a basic formalism. We have already discussed that $\mathcal{L}_\omega$ can be translated to the μ-calculus, so the decision procedure for the μ-calculus can be used to solve these problems with essentially the same complexity.

However, this complexity is determined in a theoretical manner. If the procedures are implemented, they behave rather differently. Therefore, we consider both solutions in the following: Given the ω-automaton $\mathfrak{A}$, a Kripke structure $\mathcal{K}$ and a state s of the Kripke structure, suppose we have to decide whether $\mathsf{E}\mathfrak{A}$ holds in s or not, i.e., we have to solve the model checking problem $(\mathcal{K}, s) \models \mathsf{E}\mathfrak{A}$. Then, as a first solution, we translate $\mathsf{E}\mathfrak{A}$ to an equivalent μ-calculus formula $\Phi_{\mathsf{E}\mathfrak{A}}$, and check the equivalent problem $(\mathcal{K}, s) \models \Phi_{\mathsf{E}\mathfrak{A}}$ by means of the model checking procedures for the μ-calculus. The second solution is to interpret the transition system of $\mathfrak{A}$ as a Kripke structure $\mathsf{Struct}(\mathfrak{A})$. Hence, the problem can be reduced to check whether the product structure $\mathcal{K} \times \mathsf{Struct}(\mathfrak{A})$ contains a path that satisfies the acceptance condition of $\mathfrak{A}$[5].

Both solutions have advantages and disadvantages: while the structure $\mathsf{Struct}(\mathfrak{A})$ can be symbolically represented, this is not the case for the formula $\Phi_{\mathsf{E}\mathfrak{A}}$, whose representation may therefore be exponentially larger than that of $\mathsf{Struct}(\mathfrak{A})$. On the other hand, the product structure $\mathcal{K} \times \mathsf{Struct}(\mathfrak{A})$

[5] This is not quite correct, but we omit details here. Consider the discussion in Section 4.8

that must be considered in the ω-automaton based approach may suffer from a state explosion, so that it may not be representable. However, this need not necessarily be the case. In fact, many combinations of states of $\mathcal{K}$ and $\mathsf{Struct}(\mathfrak{A})$ are inconsistent and therefore do not occur in the product structure $\mathcal{K} \times \mathsf{Struct}(\mathfrak{A})$. Hence, this structure may even be smaller than $\mathcal{K}$. This effect is best seen, when the automaton $\mathfrak{A}$ is deterministic and does only accept a single input sequence. In this case, the structure $\mathcal{K} \times \mathsf{Struct}(\mathfrak{A})$ will also consist of only one path.

This effect is exploited in on-the-fly approaches that aim at constructing the product structure $\mathcal{K} \times \mathsf{Struct}(\mathfrak{A})$ in such a way that inconsistencies between $\mathcal{K}$ and $\mathsf{Struct}(\mathfrak{A})$ are detected as soon as possible. Hence, the ω-automaton based approach may be much more efficient than the one obtained by a translation to the μ-calculus. However, in some cases, there may be not many inconsistencies, and therefore the structure $\mathcal{K} \times \mathsf{Struct}(\mathfrak{A})$ may really suffer from the state explosion. In these cases, the solution via the translation to the μ-calculus will probably be more efficient. However, this crucially depends on $\mathfrak{A}$ and $\mathcal{K}$, and can hardly be estimated before the computations are actually performed.

Apart from the choice of a basic machinery, it is important to have different ways to specify a particular property. Some properties can be better expressed by ω-automata, others better by temporal logics, and others even directly in $\mathsf{MSO}_<$. For reasons of redundancy, it is also desirable that a property is given in different formalisms, and additionally in natural language to explain the essential idea of the specification (preciseness is not necessary, and not even desired for the natural language description for that purpose).

The *readability of specifications* is a major issue. Considering the formalisms in this light, the μ-calculus may only be seen as a basic machinery since its formulas really tend to be unreadable. Therefore, specifications are rarely given directly in the μ-calculus. Another issue that is related with the complexity of the decision procedures and the expressiveness of a logic is how *succinct* the formalisms are. For example, it has already been noted that the translation from $\mathsf{MSO}_<$ to $\mathcal{L}_\omega$ suffers from a nonelementary blow-up. This means that there are formulas in $\mathsf{MSO}_<$ that can express something that can also be expressed in $\mathcal{L}_\omega$, but with an enormous blow-up of the formula's size.

This observation holds for many formalisms. For example, the temporal logic $\mathsf{LeftCTL}^*$ is equally expressive as the temporal logic CTL. However, the translation from $\mathsf{LeftCTL}^*$ to CTL involves an exponential blow-up, so that the model checking procedure for $\mathsf{LeftCTL}^*$ runs in time $O(|\mathcal{K}|\,|\Phi|\,2^{2|\Phi|})$, while the one for CTL runs in time $O(|\mathcal{K}|\,|\Phi|)$. But is this an advantage or a disadvantage of CTL? It can be shown that there are formulas in $\mathsf{LeftCTL}^*$ that can only be expressed by CTL formulas whose size can not be bound by a polynomial [4, 266, 513]. To illustrate this, simply take a NP-complete problem and describe it with a polynomially sized $\mathsf{LeftCTL}^*$ formula (see Section 5.2.2). As the model checking procedure for CTL runs in polynomial time, the existence of polynomially sized CTL formulas for that $\mathsf{LeftCTL}^*$ formula would imply $\mathsf{P} = \mathsf{NP}$, which probably does not hold (this is to date an unsolved problem). The necessity of the exponential blow-up for the translation from $\mathsf{LeftCTL}^*$ to CTL follows from results given in [4, 266, 513].

Hence, the complexity of the decision procedures for the formalisms should be taken with some care as an argument for or against a formalism. In fact, the complexity of a given verification problem is more inherent to the problem itself than to the formalism in which we describe it. Therefore, the readability should be of more interest. However, readability is a subjective issue and can not be quantified in a reasonable manner, unless by the length of the formulas. *Therefore, there are good reasons to consider all the mentioned formalisms, and to use whichever one best suits the problem.* Succinctness can also be viewed as the reciprocal of the complexity of the decision procedure. Hence, we may say that $\mathsf{LeftCTL}^*$ is exponentially more succinct than CTL, or that $\mathsf{MSO}_<$ is nonelementarily more succinct than ω-automata or temporal logic.

1.3 Outline of the Book

There is still no complete survey of all formal methods and their relationships, so we have to refer instead to a couple of surveys and books such as [158, 223, 486]. Clarke and Wing give an interesting survey on some formal methods and examples in [114]. Verification tools that are particularly well-suited for hardware verification are presented Kropf in [295] and also in the new book [38]. Furthermore, a good introductory textbook to model checking is given by Clarke, Grumberg, and Peled in [112].

The contents of this book is a self-contained and detailed treatment of the basic 'finite-state' formalisms, namely the μ-calculus, ω-automata, temporal logics, and (monadic) predicate logics. We describe translation procedures for any of these formalisms whenever they exist, and compare the expressivenesses and complexities of these logics. We will see that the μ-calculus is the most expressive logic of the ones mentioned, and that ω-automata and the second order theory of linear order $\mathsf{MSO}_<$ are equally expressive. Moreover, temporal logics are strictly less expressive than ω-automata, and equally expressive than the monadic first order theory of linear order $\mathsf{MFO}_<$. It is also well-known which subset of the ω-automata corresponds with the temporal logic formulas, namely the noncounting ω-automata, which furthermore correspond with star-free ω-regular expressions (cf. page 382). We will refine these relationships by considering many sublogics, such as μ-calculus formulas of a certain alternation depth, ω-automata with special acceptance conditions, and many temporal logics. We will consider in detail how these fragments are related to each other. In particular, we will consider the already mentioned temporal logics $\mathsf{LeftCTL}^*$ and AFCTL^* that can be translated to the alternation-free μ-calculus. Moreover, we consider a hierarchy of temporal logics TL_κ that corresponds with the automaton hierarchy (i.e., the Borel hierarchy).

For a comparison of these formalisms, we will combine them to obtain a unified specification language $\mathcal{L}_{\mathsf{spec}}$ that is essentially the union of μ-calculus, ω-automata, and temporal logics (formulas of different formalisms may however be nested). The semantics of $\mathcal{L}_{\mathsf{spec}}$ is defined over finite Kripke structures that are general models for reactive finite state systems.

Beyond the translation of the various formalisms into each other, and proving the expressiveness results of these formalisms, we will also consider verification procedures for these logics. For this reason, we will use both the μ-calculus and ω-automata as basic mechanisms. In particular, we also show how to translate ω-automata to μ-calculus so that μ-calculus can be used as our single basic decision procedure. However, as we have already discussed, the decision procedures for ω-automata have some advantages for practical usage. Therefore, both decision procedures, i.e., those for μ-calculus and those for ω-automata, have their own merits.

It has to be emphasized that the book is almost self-contained. Most of the theorems are given with detailed proofs so that the reader will find explanations in any detail that he or she wants. However, those who are only interested in the facts and do not want to find out (at least in a first reading) *why* these facts hold, may skip the proofs.

The outline of the book is as follows: in the next chapter, we define the unified specification logic $\mathcal{L}_{\mathsf{spec}}$, its models, and its semantics. We will also discuss some normal forms that will be used throughout the book. We will also present the syntax and semantics of the vectorized μ-calculus. This chapter is not meant for understanding the formalisms that are presented there in terms of their syntax and semantics. It simply lists the basic definitions of syntax and semantics of the different formalisms that are considered in more detail in the following chapters of the book. However, it presents the theory of Kripke structures, simulation and bisimulation relations, as well as products and quotients of Kripke structures that are fundamental constructions used in verification.

Chapter 3 will then define the μ-calculus both in its basic form as well as in its vectorized form. The vectorized form can be exponentially more succinct since it allows us to share common subformulas in equation systems without representing them several times. Starting from the theory of lattices and the fundamental theorem of Tarski and Knaster, we will develop efficient model checking procedures for the μ-calculus that are to date the best known algorithms to solve this problem. We will give detailed proofs and will determine the runtime complexity of the discussed model checking procedures. Appendix B discusses moreover local model checking procedures and decision procedures for the satisfiability of μ-calculus formulas. To this end, we need ω-tree automata, which is a formalism that is not used elsewhere in the book. At the end of Chapter 3, we consider reductions by (bi)simulation relations and the relationship to dynamic logic and infinite games.

Chapter 4 considers ω-automata on words. In order to incorporate ω-automata in our logic $\mathcal{L}_{\mathsf{spec}}$, we use symbolic descriptions of ω-automata.

In these descriptions, the states are encoded by a finite number of Boolean state variables. The initial states and the transition relation can then be given by an almost propositional formula. In particular, we will define different kinds of ω-automata, compute Boolean combinations of them and convert different acceptance conditions into each other. Moreover, we consider their expressiveness and therefore reveal the Borel hierarchy. It is straightforward to define, in Section 4.8, a branching time temporal logic $\mathcal{L}_\omega$ whose temporal operators are ω-automata. We will present transformations between different kinds of ω-automata and also procedures to check if such a reduction is possible. In Section 4.7, we explain the relationship between finite state automata and monoids. In particular, we consider aperiodic monoids and noncounting automata. Furthermore, we consider the determinization of ω-automata which will allow us to flatten nested expressions in $\mathcal{L}_\omega$ (however with a nonelementary blow-up). Finally, we will discuss model checking procedures for our automaton based logic $\mathcal{L}_\omega$ in Section 4.8, and translations to the μ-calculus.

Temporal logics are considered in Chapter 5. We will first consider well-known temporal logics, including CTL, LTL, CTL*, and some other variants like CTL^2 and the logic LeftCTL*. We will show basic translation principles in Section 5.3.3 and Section 5.3.4 that allow us to translate LeftCTL* to CTL. We note that these principles are not restricted to LeftCTL*, and can be applied to general CTL* formulas to reason about their equivalence, or to translate temporal logic to the μ-calculus. Translations of CTL and LeftCTL* to the μ-calculus are given in Section 5.3, and an optimized version is given in Section 5.3.5 by directly translating to the vectorized μ-calculus. In Section 5.4, we will consider the translation of temporal logics to ω-automata. We start with a simple translation procedure and consider improvements of it, which then lead to the definition of the temporal logic hierarchy (Section 5.4.3). This hierarchy was investigated by Manna and Pnueli in [350–352]. However, they only considered a restricted normal form of the logics that we will discuss in Section 5.4.3. A novel contribution is the definition of the logics TL_κ [437] and the observation that the future time fragments of these logics are expressively complete w.r.t. to the corresponding full logic TL_κ. This enables us to define, in Section 5.4.5, on page 373, the branching time logic AFCTL* that corresponds with the set of CTL* formulas that can be translated to the alternation-free μ-calculus. We will moreover present a translation from AFCTL* to $\mathcal{L}_\omega$ that runs in linear time (note however the symbolic representation of $\mathcal{L}_\omega$). Section 5.5.1 considers then the relationship between noncounting automata and temporal logic, and Section 5.5.2 shows the completeness of the TL_κ logics, because they have the separation property (Section 5.5.3). In Section 5.6, we briefly consider the complexity of some temporal logics.

Chapter 6 presents the relationship between ω-automata, temporal logics, and (monadic) predicate logics. After listing basic results on first and second order predicate logic, we list known results about decidable fragments of first order logic. In Section 6.3, we prove Büchi's result, i.e., the equal expressiveness of S1S, $\mathsf{MSO}_<$ and ω-automata, and in Section 6.4, we prove Kamp's result, i.e., the equal expressiveness of $\mathsf{MFO}_<$ and temporal logic. The equal expressiveness between noncounting ω-automata and temporal logic is presented in Section 5.5.1. Hence, the book covers all relevant translation procedures between different formalism used for the specification and verification of reactive systems. Finally, we will give some conclusions in Chapter 7.

2

A Unified Specification Language

In this chapter, we define the specification language $\mathcal{L}_{\mathsf{spec}}$ as a union different independent formalisms. In particular, we combine ω-automata, temporal logics, the propositional μ-calculus, and – to some extent – monadic predicate logics. We do not propose this logic as a new specification formalism, instead the purpose of this chapter is to define the models and semantics of these formalisms. The following chapters will then outline all details of the particular formalisms and will reveal their relationships.

2.1 Kripke Structures as Formal Models of Reactive Systems

We have already outlined in the introduction that the starting point for the verification is an appropriate model of the system that is to be verified. In this book, we only consider *formal models* of reactive finite state systems that can be obtained by compilation of programs or hardware descriptions. However, we do not consider how these models are obtained of such descriptions, the interested reader is referred to [435, 436, 438] to see how this can be done for synchronous languages. Instead, we only consider the end-product of the compilation in a very simple model that captures the computations of the reactive finite state system. The models we will consider throughout this book are the following:

Definition 2.1 (Kripke Structures). *A Kripke structure* $\mathcal{K} = (\mathcal{I}, \mathcal{S}, \mathcal{R}, \mathcal{L})$ *for a finite set of variables* V_Σ *is given by a finite set of states* $\mathcal{S}$*, a set of initial states* $\mathcal{I} \subseteq \mathcal{S}$*, a transition relation* $\mathcal{R} \subseteq \mathcal{S} \times \mathcal{S}$*, and a label function* $\mathcal{L} : \mathcal{S} \to 2^{V_\Sigma}$ *that maps each state to a set of variables. The size of* $\mathcal{K}$ *is* $|\mathcal{K}| := \max\{|\mathcal{S}|, |\mathcal{R}|\}$.

Kripke structures are closely related to finite state automata, and in fact, Kripke structures may be viewed as Moore machines that read letters from a singleton alphabet [332] (the label function is then the output function). Note that a Kripke structure only defines the states and computations of a system, but it does not provide any form of *causality*. This means that Kripke structures do not explain why the system is in a specific state, or *why it moves to another state*. In particular, Kripke structures do not distinguish between inputs, outputs, program locations and local variables. Instead, they collect the possible values of the different variables that can occur in the computations of a system.

In many research papers, Kripke structures have to satisfy the restriction that their transition relations $\mathcal{R}$ must be total, i.e., that $\forall s.\exists s'.(s,s') \in \mathcal{R}$ must hold. This means that there are no deadend states, i.e., states without successor states. As we want to describe reactive systems that have an infinite behavior, we are also not interested in finite paths of a Kripke structure, and therefore do not want to consider deadend states. However, it is sometimes inconvenient to assure that $\mathcal{R}$ is total, since certain operations on Kripke structures like the computation of product structures (Definition 2.31) may destroy this property. Moreover, symbolic representations of Kripke structures necessarily encode state sets whose cardinalities are powers of two, and therefore normally many unreachable states. These unreachable states may have deadends. Hence, our definition of Kripke structures should consider unreachable states as well as deadend states. Of course, it is not too difficult to eliminate the finite paths by removing transitions, but we may alternatively define the semantics of our logics such that it will only consider infinite paths. Therefore, we do not require that $\mathcal{R}$ must be total, and instead, put that restriction on the semantics of our logics.

To this end, we have to consider the (infinite) paths of a Kripke structure. A path is thereby an infinite sequence $s_0, s_1, \ldots$ of states of the Kripke structure such that $(s_i, s_{i+1}) \in \mathcal{R}$ holds for all $i \in \mathbb{N}$. It is convenient to describe sequences of states as functions $\pi : \mathbb{N} \to \mathcal{S}$, so that $\pi^{(0)}$ is the first state of the path π, $\pi^{(1)}$ is the second one, and so on. We moreover define the following sets of infinite paths:

Definition 2.2 (Paths and Language of a Structure). *Given a Kripke structure $\mathcal{K} = (\mathcal{I}, \mathcal{S}, \mathcal{R}, \mathcal{L})$ for a set of variables V_Σ. For each $s \in \mathcal{S}$, we define the following sets:*

- $\mathsf{Paths}_\mathcal{K}(s) := \{\pi : \mathbb{N} \to \mathcal{S} \mid (\pi^{(0)} = s) \wedge \forall t \in \mathbb{N}.\ (\pi^{(t)}, \pi^{(t+1)}) \in \mathcal{R}\}$
- $\mathsf{RatPaths}_\mathcal{K}(s) := \{\pi \in \mathsf{Paths}_\mathcal{K}(s) \mid \exists n, \ell \in \mathbb{N}.\forall t.\ \pi^{(t+n)} = \pi^{((t \bmod \ell)+n)}\}$
- $\mathcal{S}_{\mathsf{inf}} := \{s \in \mathcal{S} \mid \mathsf{Paths}_\mathcal{K}(s) \neq \{\}\}$

Moreover, we define for sets $S \subseteq \mathcal{S}$ the sets $\mathsf{Paths}_\mathcal{K}(S) := \bigcup_{s\in S} \mathsf{Paths}_\mathcal{K}(s)$ *and* $\mathsf{RatPaths}_\mathcal{K}(S) := \bigcup_{s\in S} \mathsf{RatPaths}_\mathcal{K}(s)$.

For every path π, the sequence $\lambda t.\mathcal{L}(\pi^{(t)})$ is called its trace. The language $\mathsf{Lang}(s)$ *of a state $s \in \mathcal{S}$ of the structure is defined as the set* $\mathsf{Lang}(s) := \{\lambda t.\mathcal{L}(\pi^{(t)}) \mid \pi \in \mathsf{Paths}_\mathcal{K}(s)\}$ *of infinite words over the alphabet 2^{V_Σ}. The language* $\mathsf{Lang}(\mathcal{K})$ *of $\mathcal{K}$ is then defined as* $\mathsf{Lang}(\mathcal{K}) := \bigcup_{s\in\mathcal{I}} \mathsf{Lang}(s)$.

$\mathsf{Paths}_{\mathcal{K}}(s)$ is the set of paths that are starting in state s of the Kripke structure $\mathcal{K}$. $\mathsf{RatPaths}_{\mathcal{K}}(s)$ is a subset of $\mathsf{Paths}_{\mathcal{K}}(s)$ such that all paths in $\mathsf{RatPaths}_{\mathcal{K}}(s)$ end in a cycle. Paths with that property are called rational[1] in the following.

Sometimes, Kripke structures are additionally endowed with fairness constraints. For example, these fairness constraints may be given as a set $\mathcal{F} = \{F_1, \ldots, F_f\}$ with sets of states $F_i \subseteq \mathcal{S}$. The set of paths $\mathsf{Paths}_{\mathcal{K}}(s)$ is then restricted to those paths that visit at least one state of every fairness constraint F_i infinitely often.

Definition 2.3 (Fairness Constraints and Fair Paths). *Given a Kripke structure $\mathcal{K} = (\mathcal{I}, \mathcal{S}, \mathcal{R}, \mathcal{L})$ for a set of variables V_Σ, and a set of fairness constraints $\mathcal{F} = \{F_1, \ldots, F_f\}$ with sets of states $F_i \subseteq \mathcal{S}$. Then, we define:*

- $\mathsf{FairPaths}_{\mathcal{K},\mathcal{F}}(s) := \{\pi \in \mathsf{Paths}_{\mathcal{K}}(s) \mid \forall F \in \mathcal{F}.\forall t \in \mathbb{N}.\exists t' \in \mathbb{N}.\ \pi^{(t+t')} \in F\}$
- $\mathsf{RatFairPaths}_{\mathcal{K},\mathcal{F}}(s) := \mathsf{RatPaths}_{\mathcal{K}}(s) \cap \mathsf{FairPaths}_{\mathcal{K},\mathcal{F}}(s)$
- $\mathcal{S}_{\mathsf{fair}} := \{s \in \mathcal{S} \mid \mathsf{FairPaths}_{\mathcal{K},\mathcal{F}}(s) \neq \{\}\}$

The consideration of fairness constraints is often necessary after abstractions (see [328] for such an example). Note that it is not always possible to handle fairness by removing states to fulfill the equation $\mathsf{Paths}_{\mathcal{K}}(s) = \mathsf{FairPaths}_{\mathcal{K},\mathcal{F}}(s)$: There are cases where every state has a fair path, and therefore no state can be eliminated, but nevertheless there are unfair paths (see Figure 3.21 on page 165 as an example). Hence, eliminating states is no solution for dealing with fairness constraints. It is a matter of taste, whether fairness constraints are seen as part of the model, or as part of the specifications (which is more flexible). We prefer the latter. Moreover, the following fact is essential to restrict several considerations, like generating counterexamples, to rational fair paths:

Lemma 2.4 (Reduction to Rational Fair Paths). *Given a Kripke structure $\mathcal{K} = (\mathcal{I}, \mathcal{S}, \mathcal{R}, \mathcal{L})$ for a set of variables V_Σ and a set of fairness constraints $\mathcal{F}$, then the following holds for every state $s \in \mathcal{S}$:*

$$\exists \pi \in \mathsf{FairPaths}_{\mathcal{K},\mathcal{F}}(s) \quad \textit{iff} \quad \exists \pi_r \in \mathsf{RatFairPaths}_{\mathcal{K},\mathcal{F}}(s)$$

Proof. As $\mathsf{RatFairPaths}_{\mathcal{K},\mathcal{F}}(s) \subseteq \mathsf{FairPaths}_{\mathcal{K},\mathcal{F}}(s)$ holds by definition, the direction from right to left is trivial. For the proof of the other direction, consider a path $\pi \in \mathsf{FairPaths}_{\mathcal{K},\mathcal{F}}(s)$. As the number of states $\mathcal{S}$ of $\mathcal{K}$ is finite, the number of states occurring on π, i.e., the set $S_\pi := \{\pi^{(t)} \mid t \in \mathbb{N}\}$ must also be finite. Hence, at least one state $s_0 \in \mathcal{S}$ must occur infinitely often on π. Let n be any occurrence of s_0 on π, i.e., we have $\pi^{(n)} = s_0$.

Let $\mathcal{F} = \{F_1, \ldots, F_f\}$. As $\pi \in \mathsf{FairPaths}_{\mathcal{K},\mathcal{F}}(s)$ holds, there must be for each F_i a state $s_i \in F_i$ that occurs infinitely often on π. Choose for each of

[1] Some authors talk about ultimately periodic paths instead of rational fair paths. I feel that the notion of rational paths is quite well-motivated, since rational numbers are those real numbers whose radix representation is periodic after some finite index.

these states $s_1, \ldots, s_f$ an occurrence on π after the point n, i.e., choose $\delta_i \in \mathbb{N}$ such that $\pi^{(\delta_i+n)} = s_i$ holds. As there are infinitely many occurrences of s_0 on π, there must be a position $\ell+n$ such that $\ell+n \geq \max\{\delta_1+n, \ldots, \delta_f+n\}$. Using this position, we can now define the following rational path π_r:

$$\pi_r^{(t)} := \begin{cases} \pi^{(t)} & : \text{ for } t < \ell+n \\ \pi^{(((t-n) \bmod \ell)+n)} & : \text{ for } t \geq \ell+n \end{cases}$$

Clearly, π_r is a rational path that visits the state $s_i \in F_i$ infinitely often. □

The above lemma is an important result of the theory of ω-regular languages. Some people get confused by the result of the above lemma and wonder whether there are any irrational paths at all. To see that irrational paths do naturally exist, even with our restriction that Kripke structures are finite, consider the structure given in Figure 2.1. There is only one initial state s_i. Now take any irrational number, e.g. $\sqrt{2} = 1.4142136\ldots$ and construct a path as follows: $\pi^{(2t)} := s_i$ and $\pi^{(2t+1)}$ is 'the t-th digit in the decimal representation of $\sqrt{2}$. Clearly, this path is irrational, as $\sqrt{2}$ is irrational.

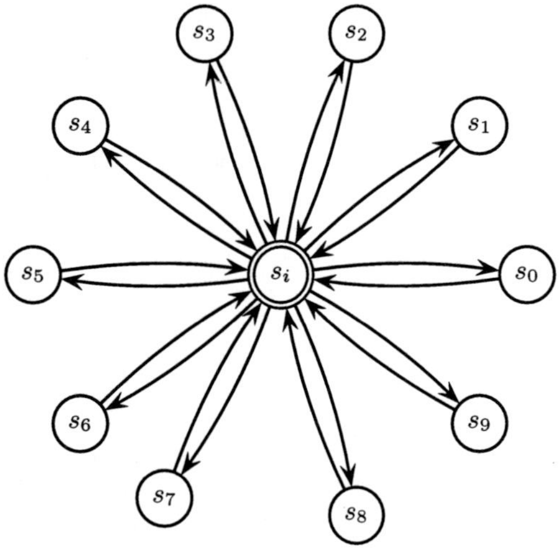

Fig. 2.1. Kripke structure with irrational paths

One might wonder about the form of the fairness constraints. The above definition of fairness constraints is used due to convenience and the efficiency of related algorithms. The fairness constraints we use require that fair paths must run infinitely often through at least one state $s \in F_i$ of each

$F_i \in \mathcal{F}$. There are also other kinds of fairness constraints that we will consider in Chapter 4 in the context of ω-automata. We will thus see that the types of fairness constraints we have chosen are very powerful ones.

Throughout this book, we will often illustrate Kripke structures as graphs as in Figure 2.1. States are drawn as vertices of a directed graph, where the edges of the graph correspond with transitions of the Kripke structure. Initial states are drawn with double lines and sets belonging to a fairness constraint are often colored (fortunately, we seldom have examples with more than one constraint).

We are however sloppy with the marking of the states: Sometimes, we write the name of the state inside the vertex, sometimes beside it. The reason for the latter case is that we then write the label $\mathcal{L}(s)$ of the state in the vertex. Again, we are often sloppy with that marking: Formally, $\mathcal{L}(s) \subseteq V_\Sigma$ is a set, so we should write sets of variables in the vertices as shown in Figure 2.4. However, for large sets, this is inconvenient, and therefore we sometimes prefer to use a shorthand description as shown in Figure 2.5: if $a \in \mathcal{L}(s)$, then the node will be labeled with a, and if $a \notin \mathcal{L}(s)$, then we label the node with $\overline{a}$. Such an example is given in Figure 2.5. However, this different notation should not lead to confusion.

For the semantics of our logics, we must reason about successor and predecessor states of a particular state or even, about successor and predecessor states of sets of states. These are formally defined as given below.

Definition 2.5 (Successor and Predecessor Sets). *Given a binary relation $\mathcal{R} \subseteq \mathcal{S}_1 \times \mathcal{S}_2$, we define for all sets $Q_1 \subseteq \mathcal{S}_1$ and $Q_2 \subseteq \mathcal{S}_2$ the following sets:*

- $\mathsf{pre}_\exists^{\mathcal{R}}(Q_2) := \{s_1 \in \mathcal{S}_1 \mid \exists s_2.(s_1, s_2) \in \mathcal{R} \wedge s_2 \in Q_2\}$
- $\mathsf{pre}_\forall^{\mathcal{R}}(Q_2) := \{s_1 \in \mathcal{S}_1 \mid \forall s_2.(s_1, s_2) \in \mathcal{R} \rightarrow s_2 \in Q_2\}$
- $\mathsf{suc}_\exists^{\mathcal{R}}(Q_1) := \{s_2 \in \mathcal{S}_2 \mid \exists s_1.(s_1, s_2) \in \mathcal{R} \wedge s_1 \in Q_1\}$
- $\mathsf{suc}_\forall^{\mathcal{R}}(Q_1) := \{s_2 \in \mathcal{S}_2 \mid \forall s_1.(s_1, s_2) \in \mathcal{R} \rightarrow s_1 \in Q_1\}$

We mainly use these definitions for the transition relations of Kripke structures to determine successor and predecessor states. In this case, $\mathsf{suc}_\exists^{\mathcal{R}}(Q_1)$ is the set of states where at least one predecessor belongs to Q_1 and $\mathsf{suc}_\forall^{\mathcal{R}}(Q_1)$ is the set of states where all predecessors are in Q_1. Analogously, $\mathsf{pre}_\exists^{\mathcal{R}}(Q_1)$ is the set of states that have at least one successor in Q_2, and for each state in $\mathsf{pre}_\forall^{\mathcal{R}}(Q_1)$ all successors are in Q_2. The functions $\mathsf{pre}_\exists^{\mathcal{R}}(Q_2)$, $\mathsf{pre}_\forall^{\mathcal{R}}(Q_2)$, $\mathsf{suc}_\exists^{\mathcal{R}}(Q_1)$, and $\mathsf{suc}_\forall^{\mathcal{R}}(Q_1)$ have the following properties that we will frequently use in the following.

Lemma 2.6 (Properties of Successor and Predecessor Sets). *The following properties hold for every binary relation $\mathcal{R} \subseteq \mathcal{S}_1 \times \mathcal{S}_2$:*

Duality:

- $\mathsf{pre}_\exists^{\mathcal{R}}(Q_2) = \mathcal{S}_1 \setminus \mathsf{pre}_\forall^{\mathcal{R}}(\mathcal{S}_2 \setminus Q_2)$
- $\mathsf{pre}_\forall^{\mathcal{R}}(Q_2) = \mathcal{S}_1 \setminus \mathsf{pre}_\exists^{\mathcal{R}}(\mathcal{S}_2 \setminus Q_2)$
- $\mathsf{suc}_\exists^{\mathcal{R}}(Q_1) = \mathcal{S}_2 \setminus \mathsf{suc}_\forall^{\mathcal{R}}(\mathcal{S}_1 \setminus Q_1)$
- $\mathsf{suc}_\forall^{\mathcal{R}}(Q_1) = \mathcal{S}_2 \setminus \mathsf{suc}_\exists^{\mathcal{R}}(\mathcal{S}_1 \setminus Q_1)$

Monotonicity:

- $Q_2 \subseteq Q_2'$ *implies* $\mathsf{pre}_\exists^{\mathcal{R}}(Q_2) \subseteq \mathsf{pre}_\exists^{\mathcal{R}}(Q_2')$
- $Q_1 \subseteq Q_1'$ *implies* $\mathsf{suc}_\exists^{\mathcal{R}}(Q_1) \subseteq \mathsf{suc}_\exists^{\mathcal{R}}(Q_1')$
- $Q_2 \subseteq Q_2'$ *implies* $\mathsf{pre}_\forall^{\mathcal{R}}(Q_2) \subseteq \mathsf{pre}_\forall^{\mathcal{R}}(Q_2')$
- $Q_1 \subseteq Q_1'$ *implies* $\mathsf{suc}_\forall^{\mathcal{R}}(Q_1) \subseteq \mathsf{suc}_\forall^{\mathcal{R}}(Q_1')$

Distributivity with $\cup$ *and* $\cap$*:*

- $\mathsf{pre}_\exists^{\mathcal{R}}(\bigcup_{i\in I} Q_i) = \bigcup_{i\in I} \mathsf{pre}_\exists^{\mathcal{R}}(Q_i)$
- $\mathsf{pre}_\exists^{\mathcal{R}}(\bigcap_{i\in I} Q_i) \subseteq \bigcap_{i\in I} \mathsf{pre}_\exists^{\mathcal{R}}(Q_i)$
- $\mathsf{pre}_\forall^{\mathcal{R}}(\bigcap_{i\in I} Q_i) = \bigcap_{i\in I} \mathsf{pre}_\forall^{\mathcal{R}}(Q_i)$
- $\bigcup_{i\in I} \mathsf{pre}_\forall^{\mathcal{R}}(Q_i) \subseteq \mathsf{pre}_\forall^{\mathcal{R}}(\bigcup_{i\in I} Q_i)$
- $\mathsf{suc}_\exists^{\mathcal{R}}(\bigcup_{i\in I} Q_i) = \bigcup_{i\in I} \mathsf{suc}_\exists^{\mathcal{R}}(Q_i)$
- $\mathsf{suc}_\exists^{\mathcal{R}}(\bigcap_{i\in I} Q_i) \subseteq \bigcap_{i\in I} \mathsf{suc}_\exists^{\mathcal{R}}(Q_i)$
- $\mathsf{suc}_\forall^{\mathcal{R}}(\bigcap_{i\in I} Q_i) = \bigcap_{i\in I} \mathsf{suc}_\forall^{\mathcal{R}}(Q_i)$
- $\bigcup_{i\in I} \mathsf{suc}_\forall^{\mathcal{R}}(Q_i) \subseteq \mathsf{suc}_\forall^{\mathcal{R}}(\bigcup_{i\in I} Q_i)$

The above lemma lists the essential properties of the predecessor and successor functions. Of particular importance is the monotonicity of these functions. There are certain restrictions on $\mathcal{R}$ that allow us to derive further laws, as shown in the next lemma:

Lemma 2.7 (Properties of Successor and Predecessor Sets). *The following properties hold for every binary relation* $\mathcal{R} \subseteq \mathcal{S}_1 \times \mathcal{S}_2$*:*

- $\forall Q_1 \subseteq \mathcal{S}_1.\ Q_1 \subseteq \mathsf{pre}_\forall^{\mathcal{R}}(\mathsf{suc}_\exists^{\mathcal{R}}(Q_1))$
- $\forall Q_2 \subseteq \mathcal{S}_2.\ \mathsf{suc}_\exists^{\mathcal{R}}(\mathsf{pre}_\forall^{\mathcal{R}}(Q_2)) \subseteq Q_2$
- $\mathcal{R}$ *is total on* $\mathcal{S}_1$ *(i.e.,* $\forall s_1 \in \mathcal{S}_1.\exists s_2 \in \mathcal{S}_2.\ (s_1, s_2) \in \mathcal{R}$*), holds if and only if* $\forall Q_2 \subseteq \mathcal{S}_2.\ \mathsf{pre}_\forall^{\mathcal{R}}(Q_2) \subseteq \mathsf{pre}_\exists^{\mathcal{R}}(Q_2)$
- $\mathcal{R}$ *is a total function (i.e.,* $\forall s_1 \in \mathcal{S}_1.\exists_1 s_2 \in \mathcal{S}_2.\ (s_1, s_2) \in \mathcal{R}$*) holds if and only if* $\forall Q_2 \subseteq \mathcal{S}_2.\ \mathsf{pre}_\forall^{\mathcal{R}}(Q_2) = \mathsf{pre}_\exists^{\mathcal{R}}(Q_2)$
- *If* $\mathcal{R}$ *is surjective, i.e., total on* $\mathcal{S}_2$ *(*$\forall s_2 \in \mathcal{S}_2.\exists s_1 \in \mathcal{S}_1.\ (s_1, s_2) \in \mathcal{R}$*), then* $\forall Q_1 \subseteq \mathcal{S}_1.\mathsf{suc}_\forall^{\mathcal{R}}(Q_1) \subseteq \mathsf{suc}_\exists^{\mathcal{R}}(Q_1)$
- *If* $\mathcal{R}^{-1}$ *is a total function, i.e.,* $\forall s_2 \in \mathcal{S}_2.\exists_1 s_1 \in \mathcal{S}_1.\ (s_1, s_2) \in \mathcal{R}$ *holds, then* $\forall Q_1 \subseteq \mathcal{S}_1.\ \mathsf{suc}_\forall^{\mathcal{R}}(Q_1) = \mathsf{suc}_\exists^{\mathcal{R}}(Q_1)$
- $\mathcal{R}$ *is total on* $\mathcal{S}_1$ *iff* $S_1 = \mathsf{pre}_\exists^{\mathcal{R}}(\mathcal{S}_2)$ *and iff* $\{\} = \mathsf{pre}_\forall^{\mathcal{R}}(\{\})$

Before going on with operations on Kripke structures like minimization by quotient construction or products, we will discuss some implementation issues. As a main part of a Kripke structure is its transition relation, we consider now how this relation can be represented. Clearly, relations are subsets of a cartesian product, and in particular, our transition relations are subsets of $\mathcal{S} \times \mathcal{S}$. For this reason, we could directly implement this relation as a set that contains the corresponding pairs. Another possibility that can be used for every binary relation is to represent it as the following Boolean square matrix:

$$\mathcal{M}_{\mathcal{R}} := \begin{pmatrix} (s_1, s_1) \in \mathcal{R} & \cdots & (s_1, s_n) \in \mathcal{R} \\ \vdots & & \vdots \\ (s_n, s_1) \in \mathcal{R} & \cdots & (s_n, s_n) \in \mathcal{R} \end{pmatrix}$$

In this case, it is interesting to see that a set of states corresponds with a Boolean vector, and that the (existential) predecessor and successor functions can be simply implemented by matrix multiplication as shown in Section 4.7.1.

All representations so-far discussed are explicit, and therefore their memory requirement directly depends on the number of states $|\mathcal{S}|$ or the number of transitions $|\mathcal{R}|$, which is limited by $|\mathcal{S}|^2$. This dependency is broken up by *implicit* set representations that have become very popular under the name *symbolic* set representations.

The basic idea of such a symbolic set representation is that we do not list the set elements in an explicit manner. Instead, the elements of the underlying set are encoded by Boolean variables. Sets are then simply encoded by propositional formulas, and for this reason, we first give the following definition[2]:

Definition 2.8 (Syntax of Propositional Logic $\mathcal{L}_{\mathsf{XProp}}$). *The set of propositional formulas $\mathcal{L}_{\mathsf{XProp}}$ over a finite set of variables V_Σ is the smallest set with the following properties:*

- $p \in \mathcal{L}_{\mathsf{XProp}}$ *for* $p \in V_\Sigma$
- $\mathsf{X}\varphi \in \mathcal{L}_{\mathsf{XProp}}$ *for* $\varphi \in \mathcal{L}_{\mathsf{XProp}}$
- $\neg\varphi, \varphi \wedge \psi, \varphi \vee \psi \in \mathcal{L}_{\mathsf{XProp}}$ *if* $\varphi, \psi \in \mathcal{L}_{\mathsf{XProp}}$

As well as the usual Boolean operators like negation $\neg$, conjunction $\wedge$, and disjunction $\vee$, we have additionally used the operator X to refer to the next point of time. However, this is not important at the moment; we could instead shift this operator inwards by the laws (we will see below that these are valid equations) $\mathsf{X}\neg\varphi = \neg\mathsf{X}\varphi$, $\mathsf{X}(\varphi \wedge \psi) = \mathsf{X}\varphi \wedge \mathsf{X}\psi$, and $\mathsf{X}(\varphi \vee \psi) = \mathsf{X}\varphi \vee \mathsf{X}\psi$. For this reason, we could restrict the application of X to variables, and then we could view $\mathsf{X}p$ just as another variable for $p \in V_\Sigma$. The semantics of our propositional formulas is therefore defined as follows:

Definition 2.9 (Propositional Evaluation). *Given a formula $\Phi \in \mathcal{L}_{\mathsf{XProp}}$ over the variables V_Σ, and two sets of variables $\vartheta_1, \vartheta_2 \subseteq V_\Sigma$, then, we define the evaluation $[\![\Phi]\!]_{\vartheta_1,\vartheta_2} \in \{\mathsf{true}, \mathsf{false}\}$ of Φ under ϑ_1 and ϑ_2 as follows for all $p \in V_\Sigma$ and $\varphi, \psi \in \mathcal{L}_{\mathsf{XProp}}$:*

$$
\begin{array}{ll}
[\![p]\!]_{\vartheta_1,\vartheta_2} := p \in \vartheta_1 & [\![\mathsf{X}p]\!]_{\vartheta_1,\vartheta_2} := p \in \vartheta_2 \\
[\![\neg\varphi]\!]_{\vartheta_1,\vartheta_2} := \neg\, [\![\varphi]\!]_{\vartheta_1,\vartheta_2} & [\![\mathsf{X}\neg\varphi]\!]_{\vartheta_1,\vartheta_2} := \neg\, [\![\mathsf{X}\varphi]\!]_{\vartheta_1,\vartheta_2} \\
[\![\varphi \wedge \psi]\!]_{\vartheta_1,\vartheta_2} := [\![\varphi]\!]_{\vartheta_1,\vartheta_2} \wedge [\![\psi]\!]_{\vartheta_1,\vartheta_2} & [\![\mathsf{X}(\varphi \wedge \psi)]\!]_{\vartheta_1,\vartheta_2} := [\![\mathsf{X}\varphi]\!]_{\vartheta_1,\vartheta_2} \wedge [\![\mathsf{X}\psi]\!]_{\vartheta_1,\vartheta_2} \\
[\![\varphi \vee \psi]\!]_{\vartheta_1,\vartheta_2} := [\![\varphi]\!]_{\vartheta_1,\vartheta_2} \vee [\![\psi]\!]_{\vartheta_1,\vartheta_2} & [\![\mathsf{X}(\varphi \vee \psi)]\!]_{\vartheta_1,\vartheta_2} := [\![\mathsf{X}\varphi]\!]_{\vartheta_1,\vartheta_2} \vee [\![\mathsf{X}\psi]\!]_{\vartheta_1,\vartheta_2}
\end{array}
$$

The above definition does more than evaluate propositional formulas as it can already deal with the X operator. Note that the meaning of ϑ_1 and ϑ_2 is that these sets contain the variables that are assumed to hold at the current

[2] We give the unary operators $\neg$ and X a higher priority, hence, $\neg\varphi \wedge \psi$ and $\mathsf{X}\varphi \wedge \psi$ should be read as $(\neg\varphi) \wedge \psi$ and $(\mathsf{X}\varphi) \wedge \psi$, respectively.

and next point of time, respectively. Note also that we have used the propositional operators at the 'meta level': while we have defined $\neg$, $\wedge$, $\vee$ to be operators of our logic $\mathcal{L}_{\mathsf{XProp}}$, we also use these symbols for operators on the set of Boolean values $\{\mathsf{true}, \mathsf{false}\}$. In principle, we should use different symbols for the two levels, but this would make the following more complicated than necessary. So, we shall use the same symbols for both levels.

We now turn back to the symbolic representation of sets, in particular the symbolic representation of transition relations and sets of states. To this end, we have to encode the states of the Kripke structure by a couple of Boolean variables. For example, we could directly use sets of these variables as states of the Kripke structure: if we use the state variables $p_1, \ldots, p_n$, then our states are subsets of $\{p_1, \ldots, p_n\}$. A set of states can then be associated with a propositional formula over the state variables, where no X operator occurs. Sets of transitions are encoded by a propositional formula with X operators.

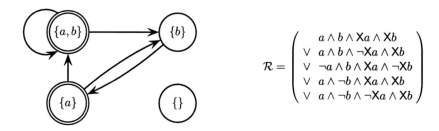

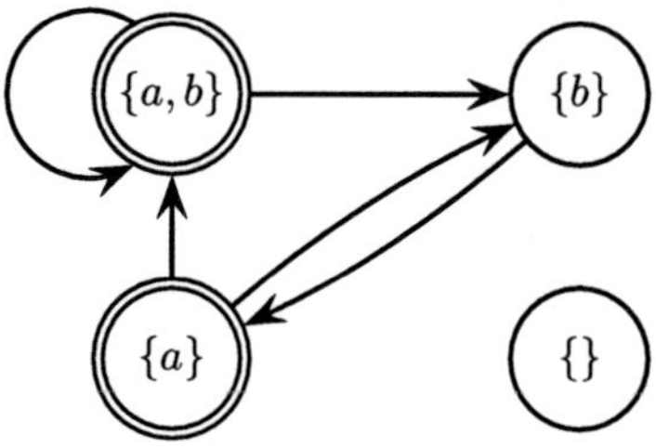

$$\mathcal{R} = \left(\begin{array}{ll} & a \wedge b \wedge \mathsf{X}a \wedge \mathsf{X}b \\ \vee & a \wedge b \wedge \neg\mathsf{X}a \wedge \mathsf{X}b \\ \vee & \neg a \wedge b \wedge \mathsf{X}a \wedge \neg\mathsf{X}b \\ \vee & a \wedge \neg b \wedge \mathsf{X}a \wedge \mathsf{X}b \\ \vee & a \wedge \neg b \wedge \neg\mathsf{X}a \wedge \mathsf{X}b \end{array}\right)$$

Fig. 2.2. Symbolic representation of Kripke structures

We consider an example to illustrate the idea: We encode the states of the Kripke structure in Figure 2.2 with the variables $\{a, b\}$, so that we obtain the four states shown. We are only interested in the three states $\{a, b\}$, $\{a\}$, $\{b\}$, but due to our encoding, we can only have powers of 2 as cardinalities of state sets. Thus, we normally have to do with unwanted states (and therefore, there can be unreachable deadend states even if our system does not suffer from deadlocks or other problems).

A possible propositional formula to encode the transition relation is given on the right hand side of Figure 2.2. The benefit of symbolic representations is however not visible here, since we have listed for every transition one disjunct. The power of symbolic representation comes from the fact that propositional formulas can have an exponential number of satisfying assignments, and therefore these formulas can encode an exponential number of states or transitions. In the above example, we could instead use the formula $a \wedge \mathsf{X}b \vee \neg a \wedge b \wedge \mathsf{X}a \wedge \neg\mathsf{X}b$ for the same purpose.

The development of efficient data structures like BDDs [74, 465, 466] for the manipulation of propositional formulas has lead to an enormous increase of efficiency in model checking procedures for almost all finite state problems [44, 88, 466]. The interested reader will find a short description of BDDs in Appendix A. We do not consider further details of these implementations, and stay at the more abstract level, where we consider sets explicitly. Nevertheless, most algorithms presented in this book can be implemented in a symbolic manner: in fact the automaton formulas of our specification logic $\mathcal{L}_{\mathsf{spec}}$, as well as the translations in Section 5.4 are tailored for that purpose.

There is another point that we have to discuss at this point: In the above encoding, we used state variables different from V_Σ to encode the states. One might argue that this is not necessary, since we could directly use the variables V_Σ for that purpose. In principle, this can be done (and is done by actual implementations), but there is the problem that we could have two different states s_1 and s_2 with the same label $\mathcal{L}(s_1) = \mathcal{L}(s_2)$. In this case, we have to introduce further variables, so that every state has a unique label.

2.1.1 Simulation and Bisimulation of Kripke Structures

We will see in the following chapters that the size of Kripke structures is a crucial factor in assessing the complexity of the verification procedures. If the Kripke structures are obtained from programs, then it can often be observed that the size of the structure grows exponentially with the size of the program. This relationship is sometimes called the *state explosion problem* and it is certainly the main problem for formal verification using finite state methods.

For this reason, several approaches to combat the state explosion problem have been proposed, one of these, namely the use of symbolic representations was discussed in the previous section. Another approach is to reduce the structure of a given program such that the validity of the specification is preserved. Clearly, it is desirable to directly compute the reduced structure from the program, and this is often possible.

In this section, we give the basic definitions and constructions for such reductions. We start by defining a preorder on the structures that will then lead to the definition of equivalent structures and finally to quotient structures, which are our minimized structures.

Definition 2.10 (Simulation Relations). *Given the structures $\mathcal{K}_1 = (\mathcal{I}_1, \mathcal{S}_1, \mathcal{R}_1, \mathcal{L}_1)$, $\mathcal{K}_2 = (\mathcal{I}_2, \mathcal{S}_2, \mathcal{R}_2, \mathcal{L}_2)$ over variables V_{Σ_1} and V_{Σ_2} respectively, with $V_{\Sigma_1} \subseteq V_{\Sigma_2}$. A relation $\zeta \subseteq \mathcal{S}_1 \times \mathcal{S}_2$ is called a simulation relation between $\mathcal{K}_1$ and $\mathcal{K}_2$ if the following holds:*

- **SIM1:** $(s_1, s_2) \in \zeta$ *implies* $\mathcal{L}_1(s_1) = \mathcal{L}_2(s_2) \cap V_{\Sigma_1}$
- **SIM2:** *for states $s_1, s_1' \in \mathcal{S}_1$ and $s_2 \in \mathcal{S}_2$ with $(s_1, s_2) \in \zeta$ and $(s_1, s_1') \in \mathcal{R}_1$, there is a state $s_2' \in \mathcal{S}_2$ such that $(s_1', s_2') \in \zeta$ and $(s_2, s_2') \in \mathcal{R}_2$*
- **SIM3:** *for any $s_1 \in \mathcal{I}_1$, there is a $s_2 \in \mathcal{I}_2$ with $(s_1, s_2) \in \zeta$.*

We write $\mathcal{K}_1 \preccurlyeq_\zeta \mathcal{K}_2$ for structures, if ζ is a simulation relation between $\mathcal{K}_1$ and $\mathcal{K}_2$.

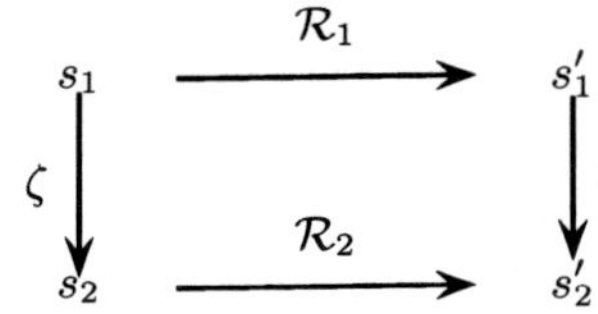

Fig. 2.3. Simulation relations between structures

The notion *simulation* relation is due to the fact that whenever we have two structures $\mathcal{K}_1$ and $\mathcal{K}_2$ with $\mathcal{K}_1 \preccurlyeq_\zeta \mathcal{K}_2$, then $\mathcal{K}_2$ is able to simulate each computation of $\mathcal{K}_1$ because for every path in $\mathcal{K}_1$ there is a corresponding one in $\mathcal{K}_2$ that carries the same labels (w.r.t. V_{Σ_1}) (cf. Figure 2.3).

We have neither taken care about deadend states nor about fairness constraints in the above definition. Deadend states are clearly considered in the definition, since **SIM2** only considers states that have transitions. However, fairness constraints are not considered. In particular, it is not sufficient to restrict the consideration to the fair states (page 164). Path based definitions of fair simulation relations as given in [26, 110, 332] are therefore not captured by this approach. In fact, these path based definitions yield a stricter notion of simulation, unless the fairness constraints $F \in \mathcal{F}$ are observable (i.e. represented by some formula).

The second property **SIM2**, that we will often call the 'simulation property', can be described in various ways:

Lemma 2.11 (Simulation Relations). *For every relation $\zeta \subseteq \mathcal{S}_1 \times \mathcal{S}_2$ between the states of two structures $\mathcal{K}_1 = (\mathcal{I}_1, \mathcal{S}_1, \mathcal{R}_1, \mathcal{L}_1)$ and $\mathcal{K}_2 = (\mathcal{I}_2, \mathcal{S}_2, \mathcal{R}_2, \mathcal{L}_2)$, the property* **SIM2** *is equivalent to each of the following properties:*

- $\mathcal{R}_1 \circ \zeta^{-1} \subseteq \zeta^{-1} \circ \mathcal{R}_2$
- $\mathsf{suc}_\exists^{\mathcal{R}_1}(\mathsf{pre}_\exists^{\zeta}(S)) \subseteq \mathsf{pre}_\exists^{\zeta}(\mathsf{suc}_\exists^{\mathcal{R}_2}(S))$ *for every* $S \subseteq \mathcal{S}_2$
- $\mathsf{suc}_\exists^{\zeta}(\mathsf{pre}_\exists^{\mathcal{R}_1}(S)) \subseteq \mathsf{pre}_\exists^{\mathcal{R}_2}(\mathsf{suc}_\exists^{\zeta}(S))$ *for every* $S \subseteq \mathcal{S}_1$
- $\mathsf{suc}_\exists^{\zeta}(\mathsf{pre}_\exists^{\mathcal{R}_1}(\{s\})) \subseteq \mathsf{pre}_\exists^{\mathcal{R}_2}(\mathsf{suc}_\exists^{\zeta}(\{s\}))$ *for every* $s \in \mathcal{S}_1$

Proof. Simply note that

$$\begin{aligned}
\mathcal{R}_2 \circ \mathcal{R}_1 &= \{(a,c) \mid \exists b.(a,b) \in \mathcal{R}_1 \wedge (b,c) \in \mathcal{R}_2\} \\
&= \{(a,c) \mid c \in \mathsf{suc}_\exists^{\mathcal{R}_2}(\mathsf{suc}_\exists^{\mathcal{R}_1}(\{a\}))\} \\
&= \{(a,c) \mid a \in \mathsf{pre}_\exists^{\mathcal{R}_1}(\mathsf{pre}_\exists^{\mathcal{R}_2}(\{c\}))\}
\end{aligned}$$

holds, and that the equation $\mathsf{pre}_\exists^{\mathcal{R}}(\bigcup_{i=1}^n S_i) = \bigcup_{i=1}^n \mathsf{pre}_\exists^{\mathcal{R}}(S_i)$ as well as the equation $\mathsf{suc}_\exists^{\mathcal{R}}(\bigcup_{i=1}^n S_i) = \bigcup_{i=1}^n \mathsf{suc}_\exists^{\mathcal{R}}(S_i)$ holds. Finally, we have $\mathsf{pre}_\exists^{\mathcal{R}}(S) = \mathsf{suc}_\exists^{\mathcal{R}^{-1}}(S)$ and $\mathsf{suc}_\exists^{\mathcal{R}}(S) = \mathsf{pre}_\exists^{\mathcal{R}^{-1}}(S)$. □

The above versions of the simulation property are sometimes more convenient than the one given in Definition 2.10. For example, we can argue as follows:

$$
\begin{aligned}
\mathsf{suc}_{\exists}^{\zeta}(\mathsf{pre}_{\exists}^{\mathcal{R}_1^{n+1}}(S)) &= \mathsf{suc}_{\exists}^{\zeta}(\mathsf{pre}_{\exists}^{\mathcal{R}_1}(\mathsf{pre}_{\exists}^{\mathcal{R}_1^n}(S))) \\
&\subseteq \mathsf{pre}_{\exists}^{\mathcal{R}_2}(\mathsf{suc}_{\exists}^{\zeta}(\mathsf{pre}_{\exists}^{\mathcal{R}_1^n}(S))) \\
&\subseteq \mathsf{pre}_{\exists}^{\mathcal{R}_2}(\mathsf{pre}_{\exists}^{\mathcal{R}_2}(\mathsf{suc}_{\exists}^{\zeta}(\mathsf{pre}_{\exists}^{\mathcal{R}_1^{n-1}}(S)))) \\
&\vdots \\
&\subseteq \mathsf{pre}_{\exists}^{\mathcal{R}_2^{n+1}}(\mathsf{suc}_{\exists}^{\zeta}(S))
\end{aligned}
$$

In a similar way, we obtain $\mathsf{suc}_{\exists}^{\mathcal{R}_1^n}(\mathsf{pre}_{\exists}^{\zeta}(S)) \subseteq \mathsf{pre}_{\exists}^{\zeta}(\mathsf{suc}_{\exists}^{\mathcal{R}_2^n}(S))$. Hence, we see that the simulation property does hold even for arbitrary $n \in \mathbb{N}$. Note further that we have $S \subseteq \mathsf{suc}_{\exists}^{\mathcal{R}}(\mathsf{pre}_{\exists}^{\mathcal{R}}(S))$ if $\mathcal{R}$ is right total, and that $S \subseteq \mathsf{pre}_{\exists}^{\mathcal{R}}(\mathsf{suc}_{\exists}^{\mathcal{R}}(S))$ if $\mathcal{R}$ is left total. These inclusions become equations if $\mathcal{R}$ is right and left unique, respectively. Furthermore, we have for any relation $\mathcal{R}$

$$
\begin{aligned}
\mathcal{R}^{-1} \circ \mathcal{R} &= \{(a, a') \mid \exists b.(a, b) \in \mathcal{R} \wedge (b, a') \in \mathcal{R}^{-1}\} \\
&= \{(a, a') \mid a' \in \mathsf{pre}_{\exists}^{\mathcal{R}}(\mathsf{suc}_{\exists}^{\mathcal{R}}(\{a\}))\} \\
&= \{(a, a') \mid a \in \mathsf{pre}_{\exists}^{\mathcal{R}}(\mathsf{suc}_{\exists}^{\mathcal{R}}(\{a'\}))\}
\end{aligned}
$$

and hence, if $\mathcal{R}$ is left and right total, then we have $(a, a) \in \mathsf{pre}_{\exists}^{\mathcal{R}}(\mathsf{suc}_{\exists}^{\mathcal{R}}(\{a\}))$ and also $(a, a) \in \mathsf{suc}_{\exists}^{\mathcal{R}}(\mathsf{pre}_{\exists}^{\mathcal{R}}(\{a\}))$. As any simulation relation $\zeta \subseteq \mathcal{S}_1 \times \mathcal{S}_2$ is left total, it follows that $id_{\mathcal{S}_1} \subseteq \zeta \circ \zeta^{-1}$. Moreover, if the simulation relation ζ is a function, i.e., ζ is right unique, then, we additionally have $id_{\mathcal{S}_2} = \zeta^{-1} \circ \zeta$.

Simulation relations are related in some way to language containment. To state a precise relationship between the two notions, we first make the following definition.

Definition 2.12 (Restricted Structure). *Given a structure $\mathcal{K} = (\mathcal{I}, \mathcal{S}, \mathcal{R}, \mathcal{L})$ over a set of variables V_Σ and a set of variables $\mathcal{V} \subseteq V_\Sigma$. The structure $\mathcal{K}_{\downarrow \mathcal{V}}$ is obtained by restricting $\mathcal{L}$ to the variables of $\mathcal{V}$, i.e., $\mathcal{K}_{\downarrow \mathcal{V}} := (\mathcal{I}, \mathcal{S}, \mathcal{R}, \mathcal{L}')$ with $\mathcal{L}'(s) := \mathcal{L}(s) \cap \mathcal{V}$.*

Now, we can prove the following relationship between language containment and the existence of a simulation relation.

Lemma 2.13 (Language Containment and Simulation Relations). *Given two structures $\mathcal{K}_1 = (\mathcal{I}_1, \mathcal{S}_1, \mathcal{R}_1, \mathcal{L}_1)$, $\mathcal{K}_2 = (\mathcal{I}_2, \mathcal{S}_2, \mathcal{R}_2, \mathcal{L}_2)$ over sets of variables V_{Σ_1} and V_{Σ_2}, respectively, with $V_{\Sigma_1} \subseteq V_{\Sigma_2}$. If there exists a simulation relation between $\mathcal{K}_1$ and $\mathcal{K}_2$, then $\mathsf{Lang}(\mathcal{K}_1) \subseteq \mathsf{Lang}(\mathcal{K}_{2\downarrow V_{\Sigma_1}})$ holds. In general, the converse does not hold.*

The proof follows almost directly from Definition 2.10. Hence, the existence of a simulation relation is a stronger requirement than language containment, i.e., there are structures $\mathcal{K}_1$ and $\mathcal{K}_2$ such that $\mathsf{Lang}(\mathcal{K}_1) \subseteq \mathsf{Lang}(\mathcal{K}_{2\downarrow V_{\Sigma_1}})$ holds, but there is no simulation relation between $\mathcal{K}_1$ and $\mathcal{K}_2$. As an example of such structures consider the structures given in Figure 2.4 (a proof is given after Lemma 2.15).

Language containment imposes a partial order on the languages of structures. The following lemma shows that also the existence of simulation relations leads to an ordering of the structures.

Lemma 2.14 (Simulation Preorder). *If we write $\mathcal{K}_1 \preccurlyeq \mathcal{K}_2$ to indicate that there exists a simulation relation between two structures $\mathcal{K}_1$ and $\mathcal{K}_2$, then $\preccurlyeq$ is a preorder on structures, i.e., the following holds:*

- *(Reflexivity) for any structure $\mathcal{K}$, $\mathcal{K} \preccurlyeq \mathcal{K}$*
- *(Transitivity) for any structures $\mathcal{K}_1, \mathcal{K}_2, \mathcal{K}_3$ over variables $V_{\Sigma_1}, V_{\Sigma_2}, V_{\Sigma_3}$ with $\mathcal{K}_1 \preccurlyeq \mathcal{K}_2$ and $\mathcal{K}_2 \preccurlyeq \mathcal{K}_3$, we have $\mathcal{K}_1 \preccurlyeq \mathcal{K}_3$.*

Proof. Reflexivity clearly holds, as we can use the relation $\{(s,s) \mid s \in \mathcal{S}\}$ as a simulation relation between $\mathcal{K}$ and $\mathcal{K}$. To prove the transitivity, assume there are structures $\mathcal{K}_1$, $\mathcal{K}_2$ and $\mathcal{K}_3$ with $\mathcal{K}_1 \preccurlyeq_{\zeta_{1,2}} \mathcal{K}_2$ and $\mathcal{K}_2 \preccurlyeq_{\zeta_{2,3}} \mathcal{K}_3$. Then, we define $\zeta_{1,3} := \zeta_{1,2} \circ \zeta_{2,3}$ as a simulation relation between $\mathcal{K}_1$ and $\mathcal{K}_3$. □

Definition 2.10 can not be easily used for constructing a decision procedure to check whether one of two given structures simulates the other one or not. The next lemma gives such a decision procedure. Moreover, it gives another interesting theoretical result: whenever there exists a simulation between two structures $\mathcal{K}_1$ and $\mathcal{K}_2$, then there is also a largest simulation relation that includes all other simulation relations between $\mathcal{K}_1$ and $\mathcal{K}_2$.

Lemma 2.15 (Checking Simulation Preorder). *Given two structures $\mathcal{K}_1 = (\mathcal{I}_1, \mathcal{S}_1, \mathcal{R}_1, \mathcal{L}_1)$, $\mathcal{K}_2 = (\mathcal{I}_2, \mathcal{S}_2, \mathcal{R}_2, \mathcal{L}_2)$ over sets of variables V_{Σ_1} and V_{Σ_2}, respectively, with $V_{\Sigma_1} \subseteq V_{\Sigma_2}$. We define the following sequence of relations over $\mathcal{S}_1 \times \mathcal{S}_2$:*

- $(s_1, s_2) \in \mathcal{H}_0 :\Leftrightarrow \mathcal{L}_1(s_1) = \mathcal{L}_2(s_2) \cap V_{\Sigma_1}$
- $(s_1, s_2) \in \mathcal{H}_{i+1} :\Leftrightarrow \left(\begin{array}{l} (s_1, s_2) \in \mathcal{H}_i \wedge \\ \forall s_1' \in \mathcal{S}_1. \exists s_2' \in \mathcal{S}_2. \\ \qquad (s_1, s_1') \in \mathcal{R}_1 \rightarrow (s_1', s_2') \in \mathcal{H}_i \wedge (s_2, s_2') \in \mathcal{R}_2 \end{array}\right)$

The sequence converges to a relation $\mathcal{H}_*$, i.e., from an index n_0 on, we have $\mathcal{H}_i = \mathcal{H}_*$ for all $i > n_0$. In any case, $\mathcal{H}_*$ is the largest relation on $\mathcal{S}_1 \times \mathcal{S}_2$ such that the conditions SIM1 and SIM2 given in Definition 2.10 hold. Moreover, if $\mathcal{I}_1 \subseteq \mathsf{pre}_\exists^{\mathcal{H}_*}(\mathcal{I}_2)$ holds then $\mathcal{H}_*$ is the largest simulation relation between $\mathcal{K}_1$ and $\mathcal{K}_2$; otherwise there is no simulation relation between $\mathcal{K}_1$ and $\mathcal{K}_2$.

Proof. Note first, that we always have $\mathcal{H}_{i+1} \subseteq \mathcal{H}_i$ by construction of the sequence. Therefore and by definition of $\mathcal{H}_0$, each $\mathcal{H}_i$ satisfies condition SIM1. The convergence of the sequence is easily seen as there is only a finite number of state pairs in $\mathcal{S}_1 \times \mathcal{S}_2$ and hence there is no infinitely strictly decreasing sequence of such relations. As $\mathcal{H}_*$ is the fixpoint of the sequence, it follows that it satisfies SIM2.

Now, let ζ be any simulation relation between $\mathcal{K}_1$ and $\mathcal{K}_2$. It is easily seen that ζ must be a subset of each $\mathcal{H}_i$ and hence also of $\mathcal{H}_*$, since ζ must satisfy SIM1 and SIM2. Hence, $\mathcal{H}_*$ is the largest relation that satisfies SIM1 and SIM2.

As any simulation relation ζ between $\mathcal{K}_1$ and $\mathcal{K}_2$ is hence a subset of $\mathcal{H}_*$, $\mathcal{I}_1 \not\subseteq \mathsf{pre}_\exists^{\mathcal{H}_*}(\mathcal{I}_2)$ implies that $\exists s_1 \in \mathcal{I}_1. \forall s_2 \in \mathcal{I}_2. (s_1, s_2) \notin \zeta$, which would contradicts SIM3. Hence, $\mathcal{I}_1 \not\subseteq \mathsf{pre}_\exists^{\mathcal{H}_*}(\mathcal{I}_2)$ implies that there is no simulation relation between $\mathcal{K}_1$ and $\mathcal{K}_2$. If, on the other hand $\mathcal{I}_1 \subseteq \mathsf{pre}_{\exists}^{\mathcal{H}_*}(\mathcal{I}_2)$ holds, then $\mathcal{H}_*$ is a simulation relation and hence, the largest one. □

The above lemma gives a construction of the largest simulation relation between two given structures. In addition, it also shows that if one of two structures simulates the other one, then *there is always a largest simulation relation*.

Fig. 2.4. Counterexample for the converse of lemma 2.13

Lemma 2.15 allows us to present a counterexample for the converse of Lemma 2.13. Consider the Kripke structures $\mathcal{K}_1$ and $\mathcal{K}_2$ over the variables $V_\Sigma = \{a, b, c, d\}$ given in Figure 2.4. It is easily seen that both structures $\mathcal{K}_1$ and $\mathcal{K}_2$ given in Figure 2.4 define the same language. However, there is no simulation relation ζ between $\mathcal{K}_1$ and $\mathcal{K}_2$. This is seen by the construction given in Lemma 2.15. We denote the states of $\mathcal{K}_1$ that are labeled with $\{a\}$, $\{b\}$, $\{c\}$, and $\{d\}$ as p_0, p_1, p_2, and p_3, respectively, and the states of $\mathcal{K}_2$ labeled with $\{a\}$, $\{b\}$ (left hand side), $\{b\}$ (right hand side), $\{c\}$, and $\{d\}$ as q_0, q_{1l}, q_{1r}, q_2, and q_3, respectively. Then the construction according to Lemma 2.15 is as follows:

$$\begin{aligned}\mathcal{H}_0 &:= \{(p_0, q_0), (p_1, q_{1l}), (p_1, q_{1r}), (p_2, q_2), (p_3, q_3)\}\\ \mathcal{H}_1 &:= \{(p_0, q_0), (p_2, q_2), (p_3, q_3)\}\\ \mathcal{H}_2 &:= \{(p_3, q_3)\} =: \mathcal{H}_*\end{aligned}$$

As $\mathcal{I}_1 \not\subseteq \mathsf{pre}_{\exists}^{\mathcal{H}_*}(\mathcal{I}_2) = \{\}$ holds, it follows that $\mathcal{K}_2$ does not simulate $\mathcal{K}_1$. However, the converse does hold: $\mathcal{K}_1$ simulates $\mathcal{K}_2$. The construction of the largest simulation relation between the structures is as follows:

$$\begin{aligned}\mathcal{H}_0 &:= \{(q_0, p_0), (q_{1l}, p_1), (q_{1r}, p_1), (q_2, p_2), (q_3, p_3)\}\\ \mathcal{H}_1 &:= \mathcal{H}_0 =: \mathcal{H}_*\end{aligned}$$

As $\mathcal{I}_2 = \{q_0\} \subseteq \mathsf{pre}_{\exists}^{\mathcal{H}_*}(\mathcal{I}_1) = \{q_0\}$ holds, it follows that $\mathcal{H}_*$ is the largest simulation relation between $\mathcal{K}_2$ and $\mathcal{K}_1$.

The question is now, how simulation preorders can be used to verify certain properties more efficiently. For this reason, assume the specification to be verified does depend on only a subset of the variables of the structure. Then, it is clear that the validity of the specification is independent of the labels of the variables not appearing in the specification. Hence, we can abstract away from those labels and identify all states that have the same label w.r.t. the variables occurring in the specification. The definition of this so-called collapsed structure is given formally in the next definition.

Definition 2.16 (Collapsed Structure). *Given a structure $\mathcal{K} = (\mathcal{I}, \mathcal{S}, \mathcal{R}, \mathcal{L})$ over a signature V_Σ. The collapsed structure* $\mathsf{collapse}(\mathcal{K}) := (\mathcal{I}_c, \mathcal{S}_c, \mathcal{R}_c, \mathcal{L}_c)$ *is also a structure over V_Σ and is defined as follows:*

- $\mathcal{S}_c := \{\mathcal{L}(s) \mid s \in \mathcal{S}\}$
- $\mathcal{I}_c := \{\mathcal{L}(s) \mid s \in \mathcal{I}\}$
- $\mathcal{R}_c := \{(\mathcal{L}(s_1), \mathcal{L}(s_2)) \mid (s_1, s_2) \in \mathcal{R}\}$
- $\mathcal{L}_c(s) := s$ *for each* $s \in \mathcal{S}_c$

Note also, that in general, there might be different states in a Kripke structure that have the same label. Hence, the structure $\mathsf{collapse}(\mathcal{K})$ can have less states than $\mathcal{K}$. This holds in particular for collapsed restrictions $\mathsf{collapse}(\mathcal{K}_{\downarrow\mathcal{V}})$. The next lemma shows that there is a simulation relation between $\mathcal{K}$ and $\mathsf{collapse}(\mathcal{K})$.

Lemma 2.17 (Simulation Preorder of Collapsed Structures). *Given a structure $\mathcal{K} = (\mathcal{I}, \mathcal{S}, \mathcal{R}, \mathcal{L})$ over a signature V_Σ and a set of variables $\mathcal{V} \subseteq V_\Sigma$. The relation $\zeta := \{(s, \mathcal{L}(s)) \mid s \in \mathcal{S}\}$ is a simulation relation between $\mathcal{K}$ and* $\mathsf{collapse}(\mathcal{K})$.

The proof is immediately seen by checking the requirements of a simulation relation. More interesting is the following fact:

Lemma 2.18 (Collapsing is Monotonic). *Given structures $\mathcal{K}_1$ and $\mathcal{K}_2$ over the sets of variables V_{Σ_1} and V_{Σ_2}, respectively. Then, for any simulation relation ζ between $\mathcal{K}_1$ and $\mathcal{K}_2$, there is a simulation relation ζ_c between* $\mathsf{collapse}(\mathcal{K}_1)$ *and* $\mathsf{collapse}(\mathcal{K}_2)$. *Hence, we have the following:*

$$\mathcal{K}_1 \preccurlyeq \mathcal{K}_2 \textit{ implies } \mathsf{collapse}(\mathcal{K}_1) \preccurlyeq \mathsf{collapse}(\mathcal{K}_2)$$

Proof. We assume, without loss of generality, that any state of $\mathcal{S}_1$ and any state of $\mathcal{S}_2$ is reachable from some initial state. Note that, since $\mathcal{K}_1 \preccurlyeq_\zeta \mathcal{K}_2$, it follows that $V_{\Sigma_1} \subseteq V_{\Sigma_2}$ and hence, the set of states of $\mathsf{collapse}(\mathcal{K}_1)$ is a subset of the set of states of $\mathsf{collapse}(\mathcal{K}_2)$. Hence, we define for any $\vartheta_1 \subseteq V_{\Sigma_1}$ and any $\vartheta_2 \subseteq V_{\Sigma_2}$ the following relation $(\vartheta_1, \vartheta_2) \in \zeta_c :\Leftrightarrow \vartheta_1 = \vartheta_2 \cap V_{\Sigma_1}$. It is then easily seen that ζ_c is a simulation relation. □

Note that $\mathsf{collapse}(\mathcal{K})$ is always a structure whose states can be identified with its labels. Hence, we need no additional state variables for a symbolic representation of these structures. Using a set of variables $\mathcal{V}$ that is smaller than V_Σ, we obtain much smaller structures by collapsing the restriction to $\mathcal{V}$.

Clarke, Grumberg, and Long [108, 109, 332] and Graf, Loiseaux, Sifakis, Bouajjani, and Bensalem [222, 331] considered reductions of given model checking problems by means of simulation relations. Of course, this requires that the properties that have to be verified must satisfy certain criteria (cf. page 173).

It is a common mathematical technique to define an equivalence relation $\approx$ for a given preorder $\preccurlyeq$ as follows $b \approx a :\Leftrightarrow a \preccurlyeq b \wedge b \preccurlyeq a$. Reflexivity and transitivity of $\preccurlyeq$ carry over to $\approx$ and the definition of $\approx$ certainly makes $\approx$ reflexive. Using $\preccurlyeq$ as the preorder on structures defined in Lemma 2.14, we could define an equivalence relation $\approx$ on structures in this manner. However, we do not follow this definition of $\approx$. Instead, we define symmetric simulation relations called bisimulation relations that naturally lead to such an equivalence relation.

Definition 2.19 (Bisimulation Relations). *Given two structures $\mathcal{K}_1 = (\mathcal{I}_1, \mathcal{S}_1, \mathcal{R}_1, \mathcal{L}_1)$ and $\mathcal{K}_2 = (\mathcal{I}_2, \mathcal{S}_2, \mathcal{R}_2, \mathcal{L}_2)$ over a signature V_Σ. A relation ζ over $\mathcal{S}_1 \times \mathcal{S}_2$ is called a bisimulation relation if ζ is both a simulation between $\mathcal{K}_1$ and $\mathcal{K}_2$ and also a simulation between $\mathcal{K}_2$ and $\mathcal{K}_1$. Hence, the following must hold:*

- **BISIM1:** $(s_1, s_2) \in \zeta$ *implies* $\mathcal{L}_1(s_1) = \mathcal{L}_2(s_2)$
- **BISIM2a:** *for states $s_1, s_1' \in \mathcal{S}_1$ and $s_2 \in \mathcal{S}_2$ with $(s_1, s_2) \in \zeta$ and $(s_1, s_1') \in \mathcal{R}_1$, there is a state $s_2' \in \mathcal{S}_2$ such that $(s_1', s_2') \in \zeta$ and $(s_2, s_2') \in \mathcal{R}_2$*
- **BISIM2b:** *for states $s_2, s_2' \in \mathcal{S}_2$ and $s_1 \in \mathcal{S}_1$ with $(s_1, s_2) \in \zeta$ and $(s_2, s_2') \in \mathcal{R}_2$, there is a state $s_1' \in \mathcal{S}_1$ such that $(s_1', s_2') \in \zeta$ and $(s_1, s_1') \in \mathcal{R}_1$*
- **BISIM3a:** *for every $s_1 \in \mathcal{I}_1$, there is a $s_2 \in \mathcal{I}_2$ with $(s_1, s_2) \in \zeta$*
- **BISIM3b:** *for every $s_2 \in \mathcal{I}_2$, there is a $s_1 \in \mathcal{I}_1$ with $(s_1, s_2) \in \zeta$*

Two paths π_1 and π_2 through $\mathcal{K}_1$ and $\mathcal{K}_2$, respectively, are called bisimulation equivalent if $\forall t \in \mathbb{N}.(\pi_1^{(t)}, \pi_2^{(t)}) \in \zeta$ holds. Moreover, we write $\mathcal{K}_1 \approx_\zeta \mathcal{K}_2$ for structures, if ζ is a bisimulation relation between $\mathcal{K}_1$ and $\mathcal{K}_2$.

The notional *bisimulation* relation stems from the fact that each bisimulation between two structures $\mathcal{K}_1$ and $\mathcal{K}_2$ is both a simulation relation between $\mathcal{K}_1$ and $\mathcal{K}_2$ and also between $\mathcal{K}_2$ and $\mathcal{K}_1$. The relationship between language containment and bisimulation relations is almost clear and stated in the next lemma.

Lemma 2.20 (Language Containment and Bisimulation Relation). *Given the structures $\mathcal{K}_1 = (\mathcal{I}_1, \mathcal{S}_1, \mathcal{R}_1, \mathcal{L}_1)$ and $\mathcal{K}_2 = (\mathcal{I}_2, \mathcal{S}_2, \mathcal{R}_2, \mathcal{L}_2)$ over a signature V_Σ. If there exists a bisimulation relation ζ between $\mathcal{K}_1$ and $\mathcal{K}_2$, then we have* $\mathsf{Lang}(\mathcal{K}_1) = \mathsf{Lang}(\mathcal{K}_2)$.

The proof is straightforward and follows almost directly from the definition of bisimulation relations. One might think that the converse would also hold, but the example given in Figure 2.4 already showed that this is not true. To see this, note that any bisimulation relation between $\mathcal{K}_1$ and $\mathcal{K}_2$ is also a simulation relation between $\mathcal{K}_1$ and $\mathcal{K}_2$.

We may now define an equivalence relation $\approx$ on structures, such that $\mathcal{K}_1 \approx \mathcal{K}_2$ holds iff a bisimulation between $\mathcal{K}_1$ and $\mathcal{K}_2$ exists. Then, $\approx$ partitions the set of structures into equivalence classes:

Lemma 2.21 (Bisimulation Equivalence). *If we write $\mathcal{K}_1 \approx \mathcal{K}_2$ to indicate that a bisimulation between $\mathcal{K}_1$ and $\mathcal{K}_2$ exists, then $\approx$ is an equivalence relation, i.e., the following holds:*

- *(Reflexivity) for any structure $\mathcal{K}$, $\mathcal{K} \approx \mathcal{K}$*
- *(Symmetry) for any structures $\mathcal{K}_1, \mathcal{K}_2$ with $\mathcal{K}_1 \approx \mathcal{K}_2$ we also have $\mathcal{K}_2 \approx \mathcal{K}_1$*
- *(Transitivity) for any structures $\mathcal{K}_1, \mathcal{K}_2, \mathcal{K}_3$ with $\mathcal{K}_1 \approx \mathcal{K}_2$ and $\mathcal{K}_2 \approx \mathcal{K}_3$, we also have $\mathcal{K}_1 \approx \mathcal{K}_3$.*

Proof. For each structure $\mathcal{K}$, we have $\mathcal{K} \approx \mathcal{K}$, since $\mathcal{S} \times \mathcal{S}$ is a bisimulation on $\mathcal{K}$, which proves the reflexivity of $\approx$. Given that ζ is a bisimulation relation between $\mathcal{K}_1$ and $\mathcal{K}_2$, then $\{(s_2, s_1) \in \mathcal{S}_2 \times \mathcal{S}_1 \mid (s_1, s_2) \in \zeta\}$ is a bisimulation relation between $\mathcal{K}_2$ and $\mathcal{K}_1$. This proves the symmetry of $\approx$. Transitivity of $\approx$ is shown by constructing a bisimulation relation $\zeta_{1,3}$ between $\mathcal{K}_1$ and $\mathcal{K}_3$ from bisimulation relations $\zeta_{1,2}$ between $\mathcal{K}_1$ and $\mathcal{K}_2$, and $\zeta_{2,3}$ between $\mathcal{K}_2$ and $\mathcal{K}_3$ as follows: $\zeta_{1,3} := \{(s_1, s_3) \in \mathcal{S}_1 \times \mathcal{S}_3 \mid \exists s_2 \in \mathcal{S}_2.(s_1, s_2) \in \zeta_{1,2} \wedge (s_2, s_3) \in \zeta_{2,3}\}$. □

Bisimulation equivalence is decidable as well as checking the simulation preorder. The decision procedure for checking it is a symmetric version of the one presented in Lemma 2.15 for checking the simulation preorder.

Lemma 2.22 (Checking Bisimulation Equivalence). *Given the structures $\mathcal{K}_1 = (\mathcal{I}_1, \mathcal{S}_1, \mathcal{R}_1, \mathcal{L}_1)$ and $\mathcal{K}_2 = (\mathcal{I}_2, \mathcal{S}_2, \mathcal{R}_2, \mathcal{L}_2)$ over a signature V_Σ. We define the following sequence of relations over $\mathcal{S}_1 \times \mathcal{S}_2$:*

- $(s_1, s_2) \in \mathcal{B}_0 :\Leftrightarrow \mathcal{L}_1(s_1) = \mathcal{L}_2(s_2)$
- $(s_1, s_2) \in \mathcal{B}_{i+1} :\Leftrightarrow \left(\begin{array}{l} (s_1, s_2) \in \mathcal{B}_i \wedge \\ \forall s_1' \in \mathcal{S}_1.\exists s_2' \in \mathcal{S}_2. \\ \qquad (s_1, s_1') \in \mathcal{R}_1 \to (s_1', s_2') \in \mathcal{B}_i \wedge (s_2, s_2') \in \mathcal{R}_2 \wedge \\ \forall s_2' \in \mathcal{S}_2.\exists s_1' \in \mathcal{S}_1. \\ \qquad (s_2, s_2') \in \mathcal{R}_2 \to (s_1', s_2') \in \mathcal{B}_i \wedge (s_1, s_1') \in \mathcal{R}_1 \end{array}\right)$

The sequence converges to a relation $\mathcal{B}_*$, i.e., from an index n_0 on, we have $\mathcal{B}_i = \mathcal{B}_*$ for all $i > n_0$. In any case, $\mathcal{B}_*$ is the largest relation on $\mathcal{S}_1 \times \mathcal{S}_2$ such that the conditions BISIM1, BISIM2a, and BISIM2b of Definition 2.19, hold. Moreover, if $\mathcal{I}_1 \subseteq \mathsf{pre}_\exists^{\mathcal{B}_*}(\mathcal{I}_2)$ and $\mathcal{I}_2 \subseteq \mathsf{suc}_\exists^{\mathcal{B}_*}(\mathcal{I}_1)$ hold then $\mathcal{B}_*$ is the largest bisimulation relation between $\mathcal{K}_1$ and $\mathcal{K}_2$; otherwise there is no bisimulation relation between $\mathcal{K}_1$ and $\mathcal{K}_2$.

The proof is done analogously to the proof of Lemma 2.15. If we consider bisimulations on a structure, i.e., between the structure and itself, it is disturbing that Definition 2.19 does not require that a bisimulation relation must be an equivalence relation. The following result, shows that we can restrict ourselves to bisimulations that are equivalence relations:

Lemma 2.23 (Bisimulations and Equivalence Relations). *Given two structures* $\mathcal{K}_1 = (\mathcal{I}_1, \mathcal{S}_1, \mathcal{R}_1, \mathcal{L}_1)$, $\mathcal{K}_2 = (\mathcal{I}_2, \mathcal{S}_2, \mathcal{R}_2, \mathcal{L}_2)$ *over a signature* V_Σ. *Then, the following holds:*

- *If* ζ_1 *and* ζ_2 *are bisimulation relations between* $\mathcal{K}_1$ *and* $\mathcal{K}_2$, *then* $\zeta_1 \cup \zeta_2$ *is also a bisimulation between* $\mathcal{K}_1$ *and* $\mathcal{K}_2$.
- *Each bisimulation relation on* $\mathcal{K}_1$ *is symmetric and transitive.*
- $\{(s, s) \mid s \in \mathcal{S}_1\}$ *is a bisimulation relation on* $\mathcal{K}_1$ *(and also an equivalence relation).*
- *If* ζ *is a bisimulation relation on* $\mathcal{K}_1$, *then* $\{(s_1, s_2) \in \mathcal{S}_1 \times \mathcal{S}_2) \mid (s_1, s_2) \in \zeta \vee s_1 = s_2\}$ *is the smallest bisimulation relation that is an equivalence relation and includes* ζ.

Hence, *the largest bisimulation relation on* $\mathcal{K}$ *must be an equivalence relation*. The proof of the above items is straightforward but tedious, and hence not outlined here. Note that an equivalence relation ζ is also a bisimulation relation iff BISIM1 and BISIM2a hold. The other properties hold due to the symmetry and reflexivity of ζ.

2.1.2 Quotient Structures

The next point is to show how we can construct for a given structure $\mathcal{K}$ another structure $\mathcal{K}'$ such that these structures are bisimilar. In particular, we are interested in the smallest such structure.

Definition 2.24 (Quotient Structures). *Let* $\mathcal{K} = (\mathcal{I}, \mathcal{S}, \mathcal{R}, \mathcal{L})$ *be a Kripke structure over a set of variables* V_Σ *and let* ζ *be an equivalence relation on* $\mathcal{S}$. *We denote the equivalence class of* $s \in \mathcal{S}$ *with* $\widetilde{s}$, *i.e.* $\widetilde{s} := \{s' \in \mathcal{S} \mid (s, s') \in \zeta\}$. *The quotient structure* $\mathcal{K}_{/\zeta} = (\widetilde{\mathcal{I}}, \widetilde{\mathcal{S}}, \widetilde{\mathcal{R}}, \widetilde{\mathcal{L}})$ *of* $\mathcal{K}$ *by* ζ *is then defined as follows:*

- $\widetilde{\mathcal{I}} := \{\widetilde{s} \mid s \in \mathcal{I}\}$
- $\widetilde{\mathcal{S}} := \{\widetilde{s} \mid s \in \mathcal{S}\}$
- $(\widetilde{s_1}, \widetilde{s_2}) \in \widetilde{\mathcal{R}}$ *iff* $\exists s_1 \in \widetilde{s_1}. \exists s_2' \in \widetilde{s_2}.(s_1', s_2') \in \mathcal{R}$
- $\widetilde{\mathcal{L}}(\widetilde{s}) := \{\mathcal{L}(s') \mid (s', s) \in \zeta\}$

If ζ *preserves labels, i.e. for each* $s_1, s_2 \in \mathcal{S}$ *with* $(s_1, s_2) \in \zeta$, *it follows that* $\mathcal{L}(s_1) = \mathcal{L}(s_2)$, *and we then define* $\widetilde{\mathcal{L}}(\widetilde{s}) := \mathcal{L}(s)$ *instead of* $\widetilde{\mathcal{L}}(\widetilde{s}) := \{\mathcal{L}(s)\}$.

If ζ preserves labels (in particular, if ζ is a bisimulation relation) then $\mathcal{K}_{/\zeta}$ is a structure over V_Σ and we will show in the next lemma that the structures $\mathcal{K}$ and $\mathcal{K}_{/\zeta}$ are bisimilar to each other. Hence, both structures describe the same system and the quotient structure can be used instead of the original one (note that the quotient structure has at most as many states as the original structure).

However, if ζ does not preserve labels, i.e., when there are states $s_1, s_2 \in \mathcal{S}$ with $(s_1, s_2) \in \zeta$, but $\mathcal{L}(s_1) \neq \mathcal{L}(s_2)$, the label $\widetilde{\mathcal{L}}(\widetilde{s_1})$ of $\widetilde{s_1}$ is a set of sets of variables. In this case, it is not clear which variables hold in a state and hence, it is in general not possible to argue whether a specification holds for this structure or not. In this case, the quotient construction only makes sense for the verification, when the truth value of the specification is independent of the choice of a specific label $\vartheta \in \widetilde{\mathcal{L}}(\widetilde{s_1})$. Such an application is given by the symmetry reduction of structures [113, 178, 180, 181, 260].

Lemma 2.25 (Bisimilarity of Quotient). *Given a structure $\mathcal{K} = (\mathcal{I}, \mathcal{S}, \mathcal{R}, \mathcal{L})$ over a signature V_Σ and an equivalence relation ζ on $\mathcal{S}$ that is also a bisimulation relation (hence, it preserves labels). Then $\mathcal{K}$ and $\mathcal{K}_{/\zeta}$ are bisimilar.*

Proof. We define the following relation $\approx$ on $\mathcal{S} \times \widetilde{\mathcal{S}}$: $s_1 \approx \widetilde{s_2} :\Leftrightarrow (s_1, s_2) \in \zeta$. $\approx$ is well-defined as $(s_1, s_2) \in \zeta$ implies that $(s_1, s_2') \in \zeta$ holds for each s_2' with $(s_2, s_2') \in \zeta$. It is easily seen that $\approx$ is a bisimulation relation. □

We have already pointed out that the construction of a quotient model with an equivalence relation that does not preserve labels only makes sense when specifications are checked that are robust w.r.t. to a particular choice of a label $\vartheta \in \widetilde{\mathcal{L}}(\widetilde{s})$. In this case, we assume that there is an equivalence relation $\approx$ on 2^{V_Σ} that is consistent with ζ, i.e., for all states $s_1, s_2 \in \mathcal{S}$ with $(s_1, s_2) \in \zeta$, we also have $\mathcal{L}(s_1) \approx \mathcal{L}(s_2)$. Then, the set $\widetilde{\mathcal{L}}(\widetilde{s})$ is a subset of an equivalence class w.r.t. $\approx$ and we can choose any of its member as a representative for checking specifications. Clearly, the definition of $\approx$ must be made in a way that respects the specification, i.e., the truth value of the specification must be independent of the particular choice of the chosen representative $\vartheta \in \widetilde{\mathcal{L}}(\widetilde{s})$.

The fact that a state of the quotient structure is defined as a set of states of the original structure, makes the use of the quotient $\mathcal{K}_{/\zeta}$ as given above often difficult. Instead, one can also choose a particular state of a class $\widetilde{s}$, as we have chosen labels of $\widetilde{\mathcal{L}}(\widetilde{s})$.

In this manner, a representative for $\mathcal{K}_{/\zeta}$ can be defined by using a selection function $\hbar : \mathcal{S} \to \mathcal{S}$ to choose one and only one representative state $\hbar(s)$ of each class $\widetilde{s}$. Using the representative for $\mathcal{K}_{/\zeta}$, we obtain a structure that is isomorphic to $\mathcal{K}_{/\zeta}$, but whose states are a subset of the original states $\mathcal{S}$. These structures are called canonical quotient structures and are defined as follows:

Definition 2.26 (Canonical Quotient Structures). *Given a structure $\mathcal{K} = (\mathcal{I}, \mathcal{S}, \mathcal{R}, \mathcal{L})$ over the variables V_Σ and a relation ζ on $\mathcal{S} \times \mathcal{S}$ that is a bisimulation relation or an equivalence relation. Each function $\hbar : \mathcal{S} \to \mathcal{S}$ is called a canonical selection function for ζ iff the following conditions hold:*

- $\forall s \in \mathcal{S}.(s, \hbar(s)) \in \zeta$
- $\forall s_1, s_2 \in \mathcal{S}.(s_1, s_2) \in \zeta \to (\hbar(s_1) = \hbar(s_2))$

For a canonical selection function $\hbar : \mathcal{S} \to \mathcal{S}$ for ζ, we define the canonical quotient structure of $\mathcal{K}_\hbar = (\mathcal{I}_\hbar, \mathcal{S}_\hbar, \mathcal{R}_\hbar, \mathcal{L}_\hbar)$ of $\mathcal{K}$ w.r.t. $\hbar$ as follows:

- $\mathcal{S}_\hbar := \{\hbar(s) \mid s \in \mathcal{S}\}$
- $\mathcal{I}_\hbar := \{\hbar(s) \mid s \in \mathcal{I}\}$
- $\mathcal{R}_\hbar := \{(\hbar(s_1), \hbar(s_2)) \mid (s_1, s_2) \in \mathcal{R}\}$
- $\mathcal{L}_\hbar(s) := \mathcal{L}(s)$ *for each* $s \in \mathcal{S}_\hbar$

Moreover, we define for each canonical selection function $\hbar : \mathcal{S} \to \mathcal{S}$ *its induced equivalence relation* $\zeta_\hbar$ *as* $(s_1, s_2) \in \zeta_\hbar :\Leftrightarrow \hbar(s_1) = \hbar(s_2)$.

Using canonical quotient structures as representatives enables us again to interpret[3] any specification on the (canonical) quotient. Also, the use of canonical quotient structures has some advantages for representations of the structures in practical implementations. In particular, it enables us to use the same data structures, and symbolic representations by propositional formulas that are used for the original structure.

The name 'canonical selection function' for $\hbar$ is motivated by the fact that $\hbar$ maps all equivalent states $(s_1, s_2) \in \zeta$ to a unique member $\hbar(s_1) = \hbar(s_2)$ of the equivalence class. As a consequence, the number of states of $\mathcal{K}_\hbar$ is the same as the number of equivalence classes of $\zeta_\hbar$. As another consequence, it follows that $\hbar(s)$ must be a fixpoint of $\hbar$. This is indeed the case, as stated in the next lemma:

Lemma 2.27 (Invariance of $\mathcal{S}_\hbar$ under $\hbar$). *Given a structure* $\mathcal{K} = (\mathcal{I}, \mathcal{S}, \mathcal{R}, \mathcal{L})$ *with a relation* ζ *that is either a or bisimulation relation or an equivalence relation on* $\mathcal{K}$ *that preserves labels, and a canonical selection function* $\hbar : \mathcal{S} \to \mathcal{S}$ *for* ζ. *Then, for each* $s \in \mathcal{S}_\hbar$, *we have* $\hbar(s) = s$, *and hence, for each* $s \in \mathcal{S}$, *we have* $\hbar(\hbar(s)) = \hbar(s)$.

Proof. Let $s \in \mathcal{S}_\hbar$ be given. Hence, there must be a $s' \in \mathcal{S}$ such that $s = \hbar(s')$. By condition (1) of Definition 2.26 we have $(s', \hbar(s')) \in \zeta$ for each $s' \in \mathcal{S}$, an by condition (2), it then follows that $\hbar(s') = \hbar(\hbar(s'))$. Hence, we have $s = \hbar(s)$ for each $s \in \mathcal{S}_\hbar$. □

So, each canonical selection function maps $\mathcal{S}$ surjectively on $\mathcal{S}_\hbar$ where each state of $\mathcal{S}_\hbar$ is a fixpoint under $\hbar$. As its name presupposes, the induced equivalence relation $\zeta_\hbar$ of a canonical selection function $\hbar$ is clearly an equivalence relation. The next lemma gives a precise relationship between ζ and $\zeta_\hbar$.

Lemma 2.28. *Given a structure* $\mathcal{K} = (\mathcal{I}, \mathcal{S}, \mathcal{R}, \mathcal{L})$ *with a bisimulation or equivalence relation* ζ *on* $\mathcal{K}$ *and a canonical selection function* $\hbar : \mathcal{S} \to \mathcal{S}$ *for* ζ. *Then, it follows for the induced equivalence relation* $\zeta_\hbar$, *that* $(s_1, s_2) \in \zeta_\hbar \Leftrightarrow s_1 = s_2 \vee (s_1, s_2) \in \zeta$ *holds for all states* $s_1, s_2 \in \mathcal{S}$.

If ζ *is an equivalence relation, this means that* $\zeta_\hbar$ *and* ζ *are the same, and if* ζ *is a bisimulation relation, then* $\zeta_\hbar$ *is the smallest bisimulative equivalence relation that includes* ζ.

[3] Clearly, some restrictions must hold for $\hbar$ and the specification that assures the truth of the specification is not affected.

Proof. The proposition $(s_1, s_2) \in \zeta_\hbar \Leftrightarrow s_1 = s_2 \vee (s_1, s_2) \in \zeta$ is proved by a case distinction:

ζ is an equivalence relation: In this case, our proposition is equivalent to $\zeta_\hbar = \zeta$, i.e. we have to show that for all states $s_1, s_2 \in \mathcal{S}$, we have $(s_1, s_2) \in \zeta \Leftrightarrow \hbar(s_1) = \hbar(s_2)$. The direction from left to right is already given by condition (2) of Definition 2.26, hence we only need to show the direction from right to left. Let $s_1, s_2 \in \mathcal{S}$ with $\hbar(s_1) = \hbar(s_2)$. As ζ is an equivalence relation, it follows by reflexivity of ζ that $(\hbar(s_1), \hbar(s_2)) \in \zeta$. By condition (1), we have $(s_1, \hbar(s_1)) \in \zeta$ and hence by transitivity of ζ that $(s_1, \hbar(s_2)) \in \zeta$ holds. Again, by condition (1), we have $(s_2, \hbar(s_2)) \in \zeta$ and by symmetry of ζ also $(\hbar(s_2), s_2) \in \zeta$. By transitivity of ζ, it finally follows that $(s_1, s_2) \in \zeta$.

ζ is a bisimulation relation: (not necessarily an equivalence relation). We define the smallest bisimulative equivalence relation $\approx$ that includes ζ according to Lemma 2.23 as $s_1 \approx s_2 :\Leftrightarrow s_1 = s_2 \vee (s_1, s_2) \in \zeta$. It is easily seen that $\hbar$ does also fulfill conditions (1) and (2) in Definition 2.26 for $\approx$ so that $\hbar$ is also a canonical selection function for $\approx$. Hence, it follows by the above case that $\approx = \zeta_\hbar$, which means by Lemma 2.23 that $\zeta_\hbar$ is the smallest bisimulative equivalence relation that includes ζ.

□

As $\zeta_\hbar$ is an equivalence relation, we can compute the quotient $\mathcal{K}_{/\zeta_\hbar}$ of $\mathcal{K}$ by $\zeta_\hbar$. The next lemma states that for each canonical selection function $\hbar$, the structures $\mathcal{K}_{/\zeta_\hbar}$ and $\mathcal{K}_\hbar$ are isomorphic, hence, they represent the same structure, up to renaming of states. An important consequence of the lemma is that the particular choice of a canonical selection function does not matter, since all structures $\mathcal{K}_\hbar$ are isomorphic to $\mathcal{K}_{/\zeta_\hbar}$ and hence, isomorphic to each other.

Lemma 2.29 (Isomorphism of Canonical Quotient Structures). *Given a structure $\mathcal{K} = (\mathcal{I}, \mathcal{S}, \mathcal{R}, \mathcal{L})$ with a bisimulation or equivalence relation ζ on $\mathcal{K}$ that preserves labels, and a canonical selection function $\hbar : \mathcal{S} \to \mathcal{S}$ for ζ with its induced equivalence relation $\zeta_\hbar$. Then, the canonical quotient structure $\mathcal{K}_\hbar$ is isomorphic to the quotient $\mathcal{K}_{/\zeta}$.*

Proof. First, note that the quotient with a bisimulation relation ζ is defined as the quotient with the smallest bisimulative equivalence relation that includes ζ. The last lemma proved that this is $\zeta_\hbar$ such that $\mathcal{K}_{/\zeta}$ is actually $\mathcal{K}_{/\zeta_\hbar}$. Hence, we have to show that $\mathcal{K}_{/\zeta_\hbar}$ and $\mathcal{K}_\hbar$ are isomorphic. For this reason, define the function $\Theta : \mathcal{S}_{/\zeta_\hbar} \to \mathcal{S}_\hbar$ as $\Theta(\widetilde{s}) := \hbar(s)$. It is easy to see that Θ is an isomorphism between $\mathcal{K}_\hbar$ and $\mathcal{K}_{/\zeta_\hbar}$. □

In the literature, e.g. in [164], often the consideration of the quotient structure $\mathcal{K}_{/\zeta}$ is replaced by the consideration of a canonical quotient structure $\mathcal{K}_{/\zeta_\hbar}$. The above lemma shows that under the given assumptions, $\mathcal{K}_{/\zeta}$ and $\mathcal{K}_{/\zeta_\hbar}$ are isomorphic for each canonical selection function $\hbar$ and hence it does not matter which one of the structures are used. In particular, it does not matter which canonical selection function is chosen. It is therefore only a matter of taste, whether to work with equivalence classes or representatives thereof. However, for practical implementations the use of abstract structures is recommended since it avoids implementing new data structures for transition relations between sets of states.

A bisimulation relation whose equivalence classes contain as many states as possible leads to quotient structures that are as small as possible. Lemma 2.22 shows how the largest bisimulation can be computed to lead to the smallest quotient structure.

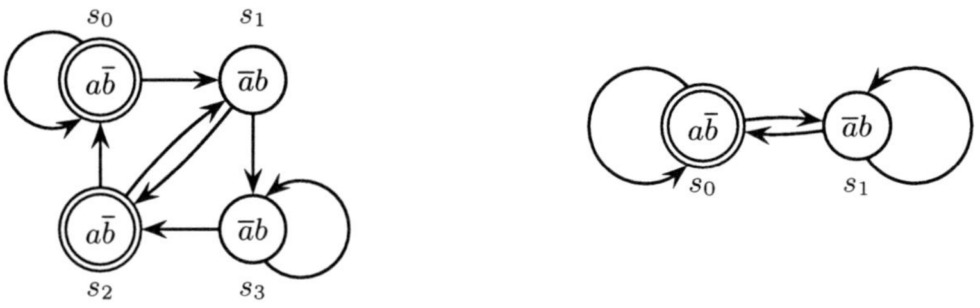

Fig. 2.5. Example of a bisimulation reduction

As an example, consider the structure given on the left hand side of Figure 2.5. The computation of the largest bisimulation on $\mathcal{K}$ results in the following relation: $\mathcal{B}_* := \{(s,s) \mid s \in \mathcal{S}\} \cup \{(s_0,s_2),(s_2,s_0),(s_1,s_3),(s_3,s_1)\}$. Hence, we have the following equivalence classes: $\{(s_0,s_2),\}$ and $\{(s_1,s_3)\}$. Using the canonical selection function $\hbar$ with $\hbar(s_0) = \hbar(s_2) = s_0$ and $\hbar(s_1) = \hbar(s_2) = s_1$ leads then to the canonical quotient structure given on the right hand side of Figure 2.5.

We will see in Section 3.8.1 that most of our logics can not distinguish between bisimilar states. For this reason, we can reduce the complexity of the model checking problem by computing quotient structures in advance. For this reason, the quotient construction can be used for all logics considered in this book to reduce the complexity of the model checking problems.

Having defined quotients, we can now characterize the collapsing procedure of Definition 2.16 in a different manner and see that quotients obtained from label preserving equivalence relations simulate given structures.

Lemma 2.30 (Simulation Preorder of Label Preserving Quotients). *Given a structure $\mathcal{K} = (\mathcal{I}, \mathcal{S}, \mathcal{R}, \mathcal{L})$ over a signature V_Σ and an equivalence relation ζ on $\mathcal{S}$ that preserves labels, i.e. $(s_1, s_2) \in \zeta$ implies that $\mathcal{L}(s_1) = \mathcal{L}(s_2)$. Then, it follows that $\mathcal{K} \preccurlyeq \mathcal{K}_{/\zeta}$ holds, i.e., there is a simulation relation between $\mathcal{K}$ and $\mathcal{K}_{/\zeta}$. Moreover, for $(s_1, s_2) \in \zeta :\Leftrightarrow \mathcal{L}(s_1) = \mathcal{L}(s_2)$, it follows that* $\mathsf{collapse}(\mathcal{K})$ *and $\mathcal{K}_{/\zeta}$ are isomorphic.*

Proof. Given that ζ is an equivalence relation that preserves labels. Then, we define $\widetilde{\zeta} := \{(s, \widetilde{s}) \mid s \in \mathcal{S}\}$ and prove that $\widetilde{\zeta}$ is a simulation relation. To prove the second statement, we define $\Theta(\widetilde{s}) := \mathcal{L}(s)$ and prove that Θ is an isomorphism between $\widetilde{\mathcal{S}}$ and collapse($\mathcal{K}$). Clearly, Θ is well-defined since equivalent states have the same label. Also, it is easy to see that Θ is injective, surjective, preserves transitions, and respects initial and fair states. □

Hence, we see that collapse($\mathcal{K}$) is a special quotient structure, namely the one under the equivalence relation $(s_1, s_2) \in \zeta :\Leftrightarrow \mathcal{L}(s_1) = \mathcal{L}(s_2)$ which is the largest equivalence relation that preserves labels.

2.1.3 Products of Kripke Structures

Usually, systems are given in a hierarchical manner, since they are decomposed into subsystems. For this reason, it is desirable to obtain the entire behavior of a system in terms of the behaviors of its subsystems. The final Kripke structure will then be obtained as a product of the subsequent Kripke structures. Hence, the product of Kripke structures means to compute a system that is obtained by executing the subsystems synchronously in parallel. Products of Kripke structures must be handled with some care, since there are some situations where products can not be defined.

Definition 2.31 (Product Structures). *Given two Kripke structures $\mathcal{K}_1 = (\mathcal{I}_1, \mathcal{S}_1, \mathcal{R}_1, \mathcal{L}_1)$ and $\mathcal{K}_2 = (\mathcal{I}_2, \mathcal{S}_2, \mathcal{R}_2, \mathcal{L}_2)$ over the sets of variables V_{Σ_1} and V_{Σ_2} respectively. The product $\mathcal{K}_1 \times \mathcal{K}_2 = (\mathcal{I}_\times, \mathcal{S}_\times, \mathcal{R}_\times, \mathcal{L}_\times)$ is defined as follows:*

- $\mathcal{S}_\times := \{(s_1, s_2) \in \mathcal{S}_1 \times \mathcal{S}_2 \mid \mathcal{L}_1(s_1) \cap V_{\Sigma_2} = \mathcal{L}_2(s_2) \cap V_{\Sigma_1}\}$
- $\mathcal{I}_\times := \mathcal{S}_\times \cap (\mathcal{I}_1 \times \mathcal{I}_2)$
- $\mathcal{R}_\times := \{((s_1, s_2), (s_1', s_2')) \in \mathcal{S}_\times \times \mathcal{S}_\times \mid (s_1, s_1') \in \mathcal{R}_1 \wedge (s_2, s_2') \in \mathcal{R}_2\}$
- $\mathcal{L}_\times((s_1, s_2)) := \mathcal{L}_1(s_1) \cup \mathcal{L}_2(s_2)$

Note that $\mathcal{K}_1 \times \mathcal{K}_2$ is a structure on $V_{\Sigma_1} \cup V_{\Sigma_2}$.

Note that $(s_1, s_2) \in \mathcal{S}_1 \times \mathcal{S}_2$ belongs to $\mathcal{S}_\times$ iff the label functions $\mathcal{L}_1(s_1)$ and $\mathcal{L}_2(s_2)$ do not differ at the common variables $V_{\Sigma_1} \cap V_{\Sigma_2}$. In the case $V_{\Sigma_1} = V_{\Sigma_2}$, this means that both label functions have to be the same. Therefore, there are cases, where the product of two structures can not be defined, because $\mathcal{S}_\times$ is empty since all states have inconsistent labels. As a simple example, consider two arbitrary structures over $V_\Sigma = \{a, b\}$ such that all states of the first structure are labeled with a and all states of the other structure are labeled with b.

The problem is that variables of $V_{\Sigma_1} \cap V_{\Sigma_2}$ are shared variables. Interpreting the structures $\mathcal{K}_1$ and $\mathcal{K}_2$ as processes that run synchronously in parallel, then the variables of $V_{\Sigma_1} \cap V_{\Sigma_2}$ are shared between these processes. Therefore their values must be well-defined for each point of time for the parallel execution. In the example mentioned above, the product yields in a Kripke structure with an empty state set. This means that this structure models a system where the processes ran into an inconsistent configuration.

Note also that even when $\mathcal{R}_1$ and $\mathcal{R}_2$ are total, $\mathcal{R}_\times$ can lead to deadend states, because all successor states generated by $\mathcal{R}_1$ and $\mathcal{R}_2$ from a state $(s_1, s_2) \in \mathcal{S}_\times$ could be inconsistent. However, we already mentioned that deadend states are harmless since they are ignored by our semantics, because the set of paths we consider are always infinite paths (see Definition 2.2).

Hence, the product structure will in general contain less computations than the union of the computations of the factor structures. The next lemma shows that $\mathcal{K}_1 \times \mathcal{K}_2$ will not generate new computations, i.e., both $\mathcal{K}_1$ and $\mathcal{K}_2$ simulate $\mathcal{K}_1 \times \mathcal{K}_2$ when $V_{\Sigma_1} = V_{\Sigma_2}$ holds.

Lemma 2.32 (Simulation of Products by Factors). *Given two structures $\mathcal{K}_1$ and $\mathcal{K}_2$ over the sets of variables V_{Σ_1} and V_{Σ_2} respectively. Then, $\mathcal{K}_1$ simulates $\mathcal{K}_1 \times \mathcal{K}_2$ restricted to V_{Σ_1} and $\mathcal{K}_2$ simulates $\mathcal{K}_1 \times \mathcal{K}_2$ restricted to V_{Σ_2} (formally $(\mathcal{K}_1 \times \mathcal{K}_2)_{\downarrow V_{\Sigma_1}} \preccurlyeq \mathcal{K}_1$ and $(\mathcal{K}_1 \times \mathcal{K}_2)_{\downarrow V_{\Sigma_2}} \preccurlyeq \mathcal{K}_2$).*

Proof. We only prove that $\mathcal{K}_1$ simulates $\mathcal{K}_1 \times \mathcal{K}_2$ restricted to V_{Σ_1}, since it can be easily seen that $\mathcal{K}_1 \times \mathcal{K}_2$ and $\mathcal{K}_2 \times \mathcal{K}_1$ are isomorphic, and hence bisimilar. Assume that $\mathcal{K}_1 = (\mathcal{I}_1, \mathcal{S}_1, \mathcal{R}_1, \mathcal{L}_1)$, $\mathcal{K}_2 = (\mathcal{I}_2, \mathcal{S}_2, \mathcal{R}_2, \mathcal{L}_2)$, and $\mathcal{K}_1 \times \mathcal{K}_2 = (\mathcal{I}_\times, \mathcal{S}_\times, \mathcal{R}_\times, \mathcal{L}_\times)$. We define the following relation $\zeta \subseteq \mathcal{S}_\times \times \mathcal{S}_1$: $((s_1, s_2), s_1') \in \zeta :\Leftrightarrow s_1 = s_1'$. It is easily seen that ζ is a simulation relation. □

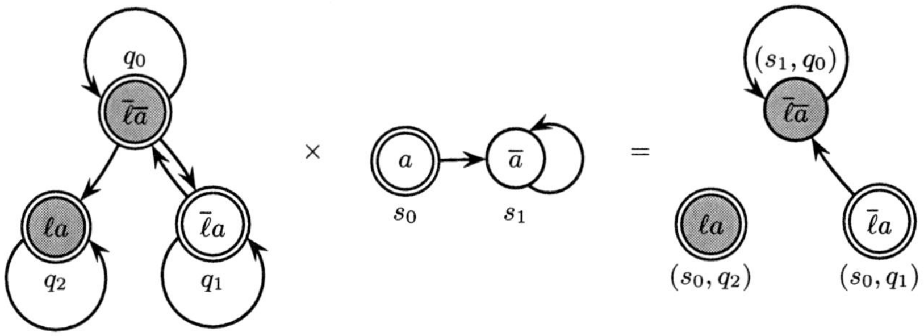

Fig. 2.6. Example for a product structure yielding in a deadend state

The converse of the above lemma does not hold in general, i.e., the structure $\mathcal{K}_1 \times \mathcal{K}_2$ restricted to V_{Σ_1} does not always simulate $\mathcal{K}_1$. This is because some computations of $\mathcal{K}_1$ are lost, because they do not match with any computation of $\mathcal{K}_2$. Clearly, this is the case, when a state $s_1 \in \mathcal{S}_1$ has no consistent state in $\mathcal{S}_2$ such that there is no product state $(s_1, s_2) \in \mathcal{S}_\times$. However, this is not the only reason for loosing a computation: Even when each state $s_1 \in \mathcal{S}_1$

has a consistent state $s_2 \in \mathcal{S}_2$ such that $(s_1, s_2) \in \mathcal{S}_\times$ follows, a computation may be lost, since a transition of $\mathcal{R}_1$ does not appear in the product. To see this, consider the product computation given in Figure 2.6. Each state q_0, q_1, q_2 of the first factor structure appears in a product state and also all states s_0 and s_1 of the other factor structure appears in a product state. Nevertheless, some transitions of the first structure do not appear in the product. For example, the transition from q_0 to q_2 does not appear in the product, and also the self-loops in q_1 and q_2 are lost.

We conclude this section by listing some further simple properties of product structures. For any set of variables V_Σ, there is moreover a structure $\mathcal{K}_{id}$ such that for any other structure $\mathcal{K}$ over V_Σ, the product $\mathcal{K} \times \mathcal{K}_{id}$ is isomorphic to $\mathcal{K}$. Moreover, the product computation is commutative and associative. Hence, the set of all models with the product operations fulfills all laws of an algebraic structure called a monoid.

Lemma 2.33 (Properties of Product Structures). *Given structures $\mathcal{K}_1$, $\mathcal{K}_2$, and $\mathcal{K}_3$ over the sets of variables V_{Σ_1}, V_{Σ_2} and V_{Σ_3}, respectively. Then, the following holds:*

- $\mathcal{K}_1 \times \mathcal{K}_2$ *and* $\mathcal{K}_2 \times \mathcal{K}_1$ *are isomorphic.*
- $(\mathcal{K}_1 \times \mathcal{K}_2) \times \mathcal{K}_3$ *and* $\mathcal{K}_1 \times (\mathcal{K}_2 \times \mathcal{K}_3)$ *are isomorphic.*
- $\mathcal{K}_1 \times \mathcal{K}_{id}$ *and* $\mathcal{K}_1$ *are isomorphic, where* $\mathcal{K}_{id} := (2^{V_\Sigma}, 2^{V_\Sigma}, \mathcal{R}_{id}, \lambda s.s)$ *with* $\mathcal{R}_{id} := \{(s, s) \mid s \subseteq V_\Sigma\}$ *is isomorphic to* $\mathcal{K}$.
- $\mathcal{K}_1 \preccurlyeq \mathcal{K}_2$ *implies* $\mathcal{K}_1 \times \mathcal{K}_3 \preccurlyeq \mathcal{K}_2 \times \mathcal{K}_3$

The proofs of the above statements are straightforward but tedious, and hence neglected here. For the computation of $\mathsf{collapse}(\mathcal{K})$, it is important that we can compute $\mathsf{collapse}(\mathcal{K})$ hierarchically, in case that $\mathcal{K}$ is given as a product of structures. This is stated in the next lemma (a proof can be found in [332], pp. 151).

Lemma 2.34 (Collapsing Commutes with Product). *Given structures $\mathcal{K}_1$ and $\mathcal{K}_2$ over the sets of variables V_{Σ_1} and V_{Σ_2}, respectively. Then, the following holds:*

$$\mathsf{collapse}(\mathcal{K}_1 \times \mathcal{K}_2) = \mathsf{collapse}(\mathcal{K}_1) \times \mathsf{collapse}(\mathcal{K}_2)$$

2.2 Syntax of the Specification Logic $\mathcal{L}_{\mathsf{spec}}$

In this section, we introduce a unified specification language $\mathcal{L}_{\mathsf{spec}}$ that is roughly speaking a union of the formalisms considered in this book. In particular, $\mathcal{L}_{\mathsf{spec}}$ contains the μ-calculus, ω-automata, and temporal logics. The introduction of $\mathcal{L}_{\mathsf{spec}}$ allows us to easily compare the different formalisms that we consider later on and to develop translation procedures between them.

In general, we have to distinguish by formulas that describe properties of computation paths, and other formulas that describe properties of computation states. We call these different formulas path formulas and state formulas, respectively. For the definition of automaton formulas, we directly make use of their symbolic representation that we outlined in the previous section.

Definition 2.35 (Syntax of $\mathcal{L}_{\mathsf{spec}}$). *The following mutually recursive definitions introduce the set of path formulas PF_Σ and the set of state formulas SF_Σ over a given finite set of variables V_Σ:*

- *The set of path formulas PF_Σ over the variables V_Σ is the smallest set which satisfies the following properties:*
  State Formulas: *each state formula is a path formula, i.e.,* $\mathsf{SF}_\Sigma \subseteq \mathsf{PF}_\Sigma$
  Boolean Operators: $\neg\varphi$, $\varphi \wedge \psi$, $\varphi \vee \psi \in \mathsf{PF}_\Sigma$ *if* $\varphi, \psi \in \mathsf{PF}_\Sigma$
  Future Temporal Operators: $\mathsf{X}\varphi$, $[\varphi\ \underline{\mathsf{U}}\ \psi]$, $[\varphi\ \mathsf{B}\ \psi] \in \mathsf{PF}_\Sigma$, *if* $\varphi, \psi \in \mathsf{PF}_\Sigma$
  Past Temp. Operators: $\overleftarrow{\underline{\mathsf{X}}}\varphi$, $\overleftarrow{\mathsf{X}}\varphi$, $[\varphi\ \overleftarrow{\underline{\mathsf{U}}}\ \psi]$, $[\varphi\ \overleftarrow{\mathsf{B}}\ \psi] \in \mathsf{PF}_\Sigma$, *if* $\varphi, \psi \in \mathsf{PF}_\Sigma$
  Automaton Operators: *Given a finite set of variables Q distinct from V_Σ, and 'propositional' formulas $\Phi_\mathcal{I}, \Phi_\mathcal{R} \in \mathcal{L}_{\mathsf{XProp}}$ over $V_\Sigma \cup Q$ where $\Phi_\mathcal{I}$ contains no* X *operator, then all formulas $\mathcal{A}_\exists(Q, \Phi_\mathcal{I}, \Phi_\mathcal{R}, \Phi_\mathcal{F})$, $\mathcal{A}_\forall(Q, \Phi_\mathcal{I}, \Phi_\mathcal{R}, \Phi_\mathcal{F}) \in \mathsf{PF}_\Sigma$, provided that $\Phi_\mathcal{F}$ is a a path formula over $V_\Sigma \cup Q$.*
- *The set of state formulas SF_Σ over the variables V_Σ is the smallest set which satisfies the following properties:*
  Variables: *each variable is a state formula, i.e.,* $V_\Sigma \subseteq \mathsf{SF}_\Sigma$
  Boolean Operators: $\neg\varphi$, $\varphi \wedge \psi$, $\varphi \vee \psi \in \mathsf{SF}_\Sigma$ *if* $\varphi, \psi \in \mathsf{SF}_\Sigma$
  Path Quantifiers: $\mathsf{E}\varphi$, $\mathsf{A}\varphi \in \mathsf{SF}_\Sigma$ *if* $\varphi \in \mathsf{PF}_\Sigma$
  Set Quantifiers: $\exists x.\varphi$, $\forall x.\varphi \in \mathsf{SF}_\Sigma$ *if* $\varphi \in \mathsf{SF}_\Sigma$
  Future Modalities: $\Diamond\varphi, \Box\varphi \in \mathsf{SF}_\Sigma$ *if* $\varphi \in \mathsf{SF}_\Sigma$
  Past Modalities: $\overleftarrow{\Diamond}\varphi, \overleftarrow{\Box}\varphi \in \mathsf{SF}_\Sigma$ *if* $\varphi \in \mathsf{SF}_\Sigma$
  Fixpoint Operators: $\mu x.\varphi$, $\nu x.\varphi \in \mathsf{SF}_\Sigma$ *if* $\varphi \in \mathsf{SF}_\Sigma$ *and each occurrence of x in φ is positive.*
  Vectorized Fixpoint Operators: *Given* $E = [x_1 \stackrel{\sigma_1}{=} \varphi_1, \ldots, x_n \stackrel{\sigma_n}{=} \varphi_n]$ *with* $x_i \in V_\Sigma$, $\sigma_i \in \{\mu, \nu\}$, $\varphi_i \in \mathsf{SF}_\Sigma$ *for* $i \in \{1, \ldots, n\}$, *and* $\varphi \in \mathsf{SF}_\Sigma$. *We define* $\mathsf{defvars}(E) := \{x_1, \ldots, x_n\}$. *Then,* $\mathsf{fix}\ E\ \mathsf{in}\ \varphi\ \mathsf{end} \in \mathsf{SF}_\Sigma$ *holds, provided that the following holds:*
  - *any occurrence of a variable in $\{x_1, \ldots, x_n\}$ in a right hand side formula φ_i is positive, i.e., under an even number of negations*
  - *no right hand side formula φ_i contains a variable that is bound in φ*

The set of $\mathcal{L}_{\mathsf{spec}}$ formulas is the set of state formulas SF_Σ.

As already mentioned, we have to distinguish between two kinds of formulas: Path formulas are interpreted on paths of a Kripke structure, while state formulas are interpreted on states of the structure. It should be noted that we can also interpret every state formula as a path formula: Given a path π and a state formula φ, we simply interpret φ on the first state of π and ignore all other states of π. Hence, all state formulas are also path formulas.

In general, the formulas of a logic depend on the set of atomic formulas, i.e., available variables and constants, and on the set of available operators. Our logic $\mathcal{L}_{\mathsf{spec}}$ provides different kinds of operators, that can be classified into different categories, namely Boolean operators, temporal operators, path quantifiers, fixpoint operators, and set quantifiers. We will discuss them briefly in the following before giving a formal definition.

Boolean operators like $\neg$, $\vee$, $\wedge$, $\rightarrow$, $\leftrightarrow$, $\overline{\wedge}$, $\overline{\vee}$ or $\oplus$ *map given Boolean values to Boolean values*. The mapping, i.e., the semantics of these Boolean operators, can be given by well-known truth tables, as for example, in Table 2.1. However, Table 2.1 may be misleading, since we define the semantics of our formulas with respect to a given Kripke structure. We will briefly explain the relationship: Boolean operators can be applied both to state and path formulas. Consequently, we can interpret them on states as well as on paths of a Kripke structure: Given, for example, the formula $\varphi \wedge \psi$ and a state s of a structure, then Table 2.1 means that $\varphi \wedge \psi$ holds on s, iff both φ and ψ hold on s. Given that $\varphi \wedge \psi$ is a path formula that is to be interpreted on the path π, then $\varphi \wedge \psi$ holds on π if both φ holds on π and ψ holds on π.

Clearly, there are $2^4 = 16$ different Boolean binary operators, but it is well-known that all Boolean operators can be expressed by one of the singleton bases $\{\overline{\wedge}\}$ or $\{\overline{\vee}\}$. It can be shown, that $\overline{\wedge}$ and $\overline{\vee}$ are the only operators which have this property. Other complete Boolean operator bases are $\{\neg, \wedge\}$, $\{\neg, \vee\}$, $\{\neg, \wedge, \vee\}$, and for Reed-Muller normal forms $\{\wedge, \oplus\}$.

φ ψ	$\neg\varphi$	$\varphi \vee \psi$	$\varphi \wedge \psi$	$\varphi \rightarrow \psi$	$\varphi \leftrightarrow \psi$	$\varphi \oplus \psi$	$\varphi \overline{\wedge} \psi$	$\varphi \overline{\vee} \psi$
0 0	1	0	0	1	1	0	1	1
0 1	1	1	0	1	0	1	1	0
1 0	0	1	0	0	0	1	1	0
1 1	0	1	1	1	1	0	0	0

Table 2.1. Semantics of several Boolean operators

Temporal operators generate path formulas. For example, $\mathsf{X}a$ holds on a path at a position t iff a holds on that path at position $t+1$. $[a\ \underline{\mathsf{U}}\ b]$ holds on a path at position t iff there is a point of time δ with $t \leq \delta$ such that b holds on that path at position δ, and a holds for all positions x with $t \leq x < \delta$. A lot of other temporal operators can be defined in terms of $\underline{\mathsf{U}}$ and X. In particular, we define the before operator as $[a\ \mathsf{B}\ b] :\equiv \neg [(\neg a)\ \underline{\mathsf{U}}\ b]$. $[a\ \mathsf{B}\ b]$ holds on a path at position t if either a holds before b on the remaining suffix from t on, or if for all states on this suffix, we have $\neg a \wedge \neg b$. Further operators can be defined with the until operator, e.g.:

$$
\begin{array}{ll}
\mathsf{G}a = [0\ \mathsf{B}\ (\neg a)] & \mathsf{F}a = [1\ \underline{\mathsf{U}}\ a] \\
[a\ \mathsf{U}\ b] = [b\ \mathsf{B}\ (\neg a \wedge \neg b)] & [a\ \underline{\mathsf{B}}\ b] = [(\neg b)\ \underline{\mathsf{U}}\ (a \wedge \neg b)] \\
[a\ \mathsf{W}\ b] = [(a \wedge b)\ \mathsf{B}\ (\neg a \wedge b)] & [a\ \underline{\mathsf{W}}\ b] = [(\neg b)\ \underline{\mathsf{U}}\ (a \wedge b)]
\end{array}
$$

$\mathsf{G}a$ holds on a path at position t, iff a holds for all positions x with $x \geq t$; and $\mathsf{F}a$ holds on a path at position t iff a holds for at least one position x with $x \geq t$. U is the weak 'until'-operator that can also be defined as $[a\ \mathsf{U}\ b] = [a\ \underline{\mathsf{U}}\ b] \vee \mathsf{G}a$ or equivalently as $[a\ \mathsf{U}\ b] = [a\ \underline{\mathsf{U}}\ b] \vee \mathsf{G}(a \wedge \neg b)$. In a similar way, $\underline{\mathsf{B}}$ is the strong before operator that can alternatively be defined as $[a\ \underline{\mathsf{B}}\ b] = [a\ \mathsf{B}\ b] \wedge \mathsf{F}a$. $[a\ \underline{\mathsf{W}}\ b]$ holds on a path at position t, iff there is a position δ where $a \wedge b$ holds, and for all positions x with $t \leq x < \delta$, b does not hold. Hence, $[a\ \underline{\mathsf{W}}\ b]$ holds at position t iff a holds when b holds for the first time after (or including) t. There is also a weak variant W of $\underline{\mathsf{W}}$ that can alternatively be defined as $[a\ \mathsf{W}\ b] = [a\ \underline{\mathsf{W}}\ b] \vee \mathsf{G}\neg b$.

Hence, one of the arguments of the binary temporal operators U, B, W, and their strong variants, is an *event that is awaited for* (this is the right hand argument of U, $\underline{\mathsf{U}}$, W, $\underline{\mathsf{W}}$, and the left hand argument of B and $\underline{\mathsf{B}}$). The first presence of this event determines a prefix of the considered path. The semantics of the temporal operator requires for the other argument some restrictions related with that prefix.

Strong variants of temporal operators are underlined throughout this book to distinguish them from their weak variants. The 'before' operator has three variants, since we could define an even stronger one by $[a\ \underline{\underline{\mathsf{B}}}\ b]$ which means that both a and b must occur and a must occur strictly before b. Note that $[a\ \underline{\mathsf{B}}\ b]$ holds also in this case, and additionally holds if b is never true. $[a\ \mathsf{B}\ b]$ is even weaker, i.e., it holds even if neither a nor b occurs, but if b occurs, then there must be some occurrence of a before that point of time.

Other variants of the operators are obtained by excluding the current point of time. While, for example, $[a\ \mathsf{U}\ b]$ also makes a proposition on the current instance of time, we could exclude this and use the following abbreviation $[a\ \mathsf{XU}\ b] := \mathsf{X}\,[a\ \mathsf{U}\ b]$, and similarly for the other operators to introduce the operators XW, XU, XB, $\underline{\mathsf{XW}}$, $\underline{\mathsf{XU}}$, $\underline{\mathsf{XB}}$.

Operator bases for Boolean operators can be proved as complete in the sense that the given set of operators is sufficient to express any Boolean function. The same can be done for temporal operators. For example, the sets $\{\mathsf{XW}\}$, $\{\underline{\mathsf{XW}}\}$, $\{\mathsf{W},\mathsf{X}\}$, $\{\underline{\mathsf{W}},\mathsf{X}\}$, $\{\mathsf{U},\mathsf{X}\}$, $\{\underline{\mathsf{U}},\mathsf{X}\}$, $\{\mathsf{B},\mathsf{X}\}$, and $\{\underline{\mathsf{B}},\mathsf{X}\}$ are all sufficient to express all the remaining temporal operators.

In addition to the future time temporal operators, we also consider the corresponding past time temporal operators. These are defined analogously, with the only difference being that the direction of the flow of time is reversed. For example, $[a\ \overleftarrow{\underline{\mathsf{U}}}\ b]$ holds on a path at position t iff there is a point of time δ with $\delta \leq t$ such that b holds on that path at position δ, and a holds for all positions x with $\delta < x \leq t$. The past time analogon of the next time operator, is called the previous operator. $\overleftarrow{\underline{\mathsf{X}}}b$ holds on a path at position t iff $t > 0$ and b holds at position $t-1$. Hence, there are two variants of previous operators, namely a strong and a weak variant. For the weak variant, we have that $\overleftarrow{\mathsf{X}}b$ holds on a path at position t iff $t = 0$ holds or b holds at position

$t-1$. Clearly, we can define the strong and weak variants in terms of each other: $\overleftarrow{\underline{\mathsf{X}}}a = \neg\overleftarrow{\mathsf{X}}\neg a$ and $\overleftarrow{\mathsf{X}}a = \neg\overleftarrow{\underline{\mathsf{X}}}\neg a$.

It is furthermore remarkable that the previous operator allows us to check whether we are in the initial position of a path: Note that $\overleftarrow{\mathsf{X}}0$ holds iff we are in the initial position. This is something that can not be expressed with future time operators, since these only consider the suffix of the path from the currently considered position. A further advantage of considering past time temporal operators is that it has been recently shown that their usage makes temporal logic exponentially more succinct [316, 355]. Again, we can define further past operators with analogous definitions as given above. We will give a formal definition of these operators in Definition 2.36 below.

As special temporal operators, we use *ω-automaton expressions*. These come in two forms, namely existential automata $\mathcal{A}_{\exists}(Q, \Phi_{\mathcal{I}}, \Phi_{\mathcal{R}}, \Phi_{\mathcal{F}})$ and universal automata $\mathcal{A}_{\forall}(Q, \Phi_{\mathcal{I}}, \Phi_{\mathcal{R}}, \Phi_{\mathcal{F}})$. The intuition behind the semantics of these operators is that we interpret them as finite state machines where the set of states is given as the set of subsets of the state variables Q. The initial states are those that satisfy the formula $\Phi_{\mathcal{I}}$. Note that a state $\sigma \subseteq Q$ can be viewed as as variable assignment in that we interpret the variables in σ to be true and those in $Q \setminus \sigma$ to be false. In a similar way, $\Phi_{\mathcal{R}}$ encodes the transitions of the automaton. An existential automaton formula $\mathcal{A}_{\exists}(Q, \Phi_{\mathcal{I}}, \Phi_{\mathcal{R}}, \Phi_{\mathcal{F}})$ holds on a path π at position t iff the trace $\lambda x.\mathcal{L}(\pi^{(x+t)})$ belongs to the language of the automaton, i.e., if there is a run for this word through the state transition diagram of the automaton such that the acceptance condition $\Phi_{\mathcal{F}}$ is satisfied. A universal automaton holds iff all runs of this word through the state transition diagram of the automaton satisfy the acceptance condition $\Phi_{\mathcal{F}}$.

Path quantifiers A and E are used to express that a path formula has to hold for all computation paths starting in a particular state or for at least one of them. Actually, only one of the path quantifiers E and A is necessary, as the equations $\mathsf{E}\varphi = \neg\mathsf{A}\neg\varphi$ and $\mathsf{A}\varphi = \neg\mathsf{E}\neg\varphi$ hold. Nevertheless, we use both quantifiers in order to have a comfortable language. Path quantifiers are used to transform path properties to state properties, while temporal operators transform state properties into path properties.

The *modal operators* $\Diamond\varphi$, $\Box\varphi$, $\overleftarrow{\Diamond}\varphi$ and $\overleftarrow{\Box}\varphi$ correspond with the universal/existential predecessor/successor states: $\Diamond\varphi$ holds in a state, if there is a successor state where φ holds. $\Box\varphi$ holds in a state if φ holds in all of its successor states. Similarly, $\overleftarrow{\Diamond}\varphi$ holds in a state, if there is a predecessor state where φ holds, and $\overleftarrow{\Box}\varphi$ holds in a state, if φ holds in all predecessor states of that state. We will see later that the modal operators can not be expressed by path quantifiers E, A and temporal operators like X, $\overleftarrow{\mathsf{X}}$, and $\overleftarrow{\underline{\mathsf{X}}}$.

Another category of operators are binders that take as arguments a variable x and a state formula φ. Given a binder σ, we will usually write $\sigma x.\varphi$ for the application of σ to x and φ. We call the variable x in these formulas a *bound variable*, while variables that are not arguments of a binder are called *free variables*. To be precise, we should preferably talk about free and bound occurrences of a variable since one and the same variable may have both free and bound occurrences. The semantics of atomic propositions is normally determined by the label function $\mathcal{L}$ of the Kripke structure. For a bound variable, however, we can freely choose labels such that the semantics of the binder holds. To this end, we define for a structure $\mathcal{K}$ its modified structure $\mathcal{K}_x^Q$ in that we change the labels of the variable x such that only the states in Q are labeled with x.

Important binders are the *quantifiers* $\forall$ and $\exists$, so that the formulas $\forall x.\varphi$ and $\exists x.\varphi$. $\exists x.\varphi$ hold in a state s of a structure $\mathcal{K}$ iff there is a set of states Q such that φ holds in state s of the modified structure $\mathcal{K}_x^Q$. Similarly, $\forall x.\varphi$ holds in s iff for any set of states Q, the formula φ holds in state s of the modified structure $\mathcal{K}_x^Q$. Therefore, the quantification is essentially made on sets of states of the considered Kripke structure.

fixpoint operator

Another category of binders are *fixpoint operators*. Given a state formula φ with a variable x, we use the formulas $\mu x.\varphi$ and $\nu x.\varphi$ to denote the least and greatest fixpoint of φ. A fixpoint of φ is thereby a set of states Q such that $Q = [\![\varphi]\!]_{\mathcal{K}_x^Q}$ holds, where $[\![\varphi]\!]_{\mathcal{K}}$ denotes the set of states of $\mathcal{K}$ where φ holds. Hence, $[\![\mu x.\varphi]\!]_{\mathcal{K}}$ denotes the least set Q such that $Q = [\![\varphi]\!]_{\mathcal{K}_x^Q}$ holds, and $[\![\nu x.\varphi]\!]_{\mathcal{K}}$ denotes the greatest set Q such that $Q = [\![\varphi]\!]_{\mathcal{K}_x^Q}$ holds.

We should also consider mutual recursive fixpoint equations $E = [x_1 \stackrel{\sigma_1}{=} \varphi_1, \ldots, x_n \stackrel{\sigma_n}{=} \varphi_n]$ with bound variables $x_i \in V_\Sigma$, binders $\sigma_i \in \{\mu, \nu\}$, and state formulas $\varphi \in \mathsf{SF}_\Sigma$. Using such a list of equations, we construct state formulas $\mathsf{fix}\ E\ \mathsf{in}\ \varphi\ \mathsf{end}$ where φ is a state formula. These formulas are called 'vectorized fixpoint formulas' since they compute several mutually interdependent fixpoints simultaneously: We have to find sets of states Q_i for which $Q_i = [\![\varphi_i]\!]_{\mathcal{K}_{x_1,\ldots,x_n}^{Q_1,\ldots,Q_n}}$ holds, and evaluate φ in $\mathcal{K}_{x_1,\ldots,x_n}^{Q_1,\ldots,Q_n}$. Intuitively, the set Q_i should be chosen as the least and greatest one when $\sigma_i \equiv \mu$ and $\sigma_i \equiv \nu$ holds, respectively. We will also write $\mathsf{min}\ E\ \mathsf{in}\ \varphi\ \mathsf{end}$ and $\mathsf{max}\ E\ \mathsf{in}\ \varphi\ \mathsf{end}$ for $\mathsf{fix}\ E\ \mathsf{in}\ \varphi\ \mathsf{end}$ when all σ_i are either μ or ν.

It is easily seen that $\mu x.\varphi$ and $\nu x.\varphi$ are equivalent to $\mathsf{min}\ \{x = \varphi\}\ \mathsf{in}\ x\ \mathsf{end}$ and $\mathsf{max}\ \{x = \varphi\}\ \mathsf{in}\ x\ \mathsf{end}$, respectively. Conversely, we can express vectorized fixpoint formulas in terms of simple ones. However, vectorized fixpoint formulas have the advantage that computed fixpoints can be shared and can therefore be exponentially more succinct. In general, we will see that fixpoint operators are very expressive and can be used to capture all properties that can be expressed by any other considered formalism in this book.

We have already discussed other operators that can be defined as abbreviations of the operators we have chosen to define $\mathcal{L}_{\mathsf{spec}}$. As we already outlined, it is often a matter of taste, which kind of operators are chosen. For example, we could also use $\overline{\wedge}$ as the only Boolean operator, or $[\cdot\ \mathsf{XU}\ \cdot]$ as the only temporal operator. In the remainder of this book, we will use the following abbreviations, and can reduce case distinctions in proofs to the base constructs of Definition 2.35.

Definition 2.36 (Abbreviations for the Syntax of $\mathcal{L}_{\mathsf{spec}}$). *We use the following macro operators to extend the specification logic $\mathcal{L}_{\mathsf{spec}}$:*

Boolean Operators / Constants:

- $0 := a \wedge \neg a$ *for some variable* $a \in V_\Sigma$
- $1 := a \vee \neg a$ *for some variable* $a \in V_\Sigma$
- $\varphi \rightarrow \psi := \neg\varphi \vee \psi$
- $\varphi \leftrightarrow \psi := (\varphi \rightarrow \psi) \wedge (\neg\varphi \rightarrow \neg\psi)$
- $(\varphi \Rightarrow \psi | \eta) := (\varphi \rightarrow \psi) \wedge (\neg\varphi \rightarrow \eta)$

Further Temporal Operators:

- $\mathsf{G}\varphi := [0\ \mathsf{B}\ (\neg\varphi)]$ *and* $\overleftarrow{\mathsf{G}}\varphi := [0\ \overleftarrow{\mathsf{B}}\ (\neg\varphi)]$
- $\mathsf{F}\varphi := [1\ \underline{\mathsf{U}}\ \varphi]$ *and* $\overleftarrow{\mathsf{F}}\varphi := [1\ \overleftarrow{\underline{\mathsf{U}}}\ \varphi]$
- $[\varphi\ \mathsf{W}\ \psi] := [(\varphi \wedge \psi)\ \mathsf{B}\ (\neg\varphi \wedge \psi)]$ *and* $[\varphi\ \overleftarrow{\mathsf{W}}\ \psi] := [(\varphi \wedge \psi)\ \overleftarrow{\mathsf{B}}\ (\neg\varphi \wedge \psi)]$
- $[\varphi\ \underline{\mathsf{W}}\ \psi] := [(\neg\psi)\ \underline{\mathsf{U}}\ (\varphi \wedge \psi)]$ *and* $[\varphi\ \overleftarrow{\underline{\mathsf{W}}}\ \psi] := [(\neg\psi)\ \overleftarrow{\underline{\mathsf{U}}}\ (\varphi \wedge \psi)]$
- $[\varphi\ \mathsf{U}\ \psi] := [\psi\ \mathsf{B}\ (\neg\varphi \wedge \neg\psi)]$ *and* $[\varphi\ \overleftarrow{\mathsf{U}}\ \psi] := [\psi\ \overleftarrow{\mathsf{B}}\ (\neg\varphi \wedge \neg\psi)]$
- $[\varphi\ \underline{\mathsf{B}}\ \psi] := [(\neg\psi)\ \underline{\mathsf{U}}\ (\varphi \wedge \neg\psi)]$ *and* $[\varphi\ \overleftarrow{\underline{\mathsf{B}}}\ \psi] := [(\neg\psi)\ \overleftarrow{\underline{\mathsf{U}}}\ (\varphi \wedge \neg\psi)]$

Further Fixpoint Operators:

- $\mathsf{min}\ [x_1 = \varphi_1, \ldots, x_n = \varphi_n]\ \mathsf{in}\ \varphi\ \mathsf{end}$
  $:= \mathsf{fix}\ [x_1 \stackrel{\mu}{=} \varphi_1, \ldots, x_n \stackrel{\mu}{=} \varphi_n]\ \mathsf{in}\ \varphi\ \mathsf{end}$
- $\mathsf{max}\ [x_1 = \varphi_1, \ldots, x_n = \varphi_n]\ \mathsf{in}\ \varphi\ \mathsf{end}$
  $:= \mathsf{fix}\ [x_1 \stackrel{\nu}{=} \varphi_1, \ldots, x_n \stackrel{\nu}{=} \varphi_n]\ \mathsf{in}\ \varphi\ \mathsf{end}$

Note that the equations in vectorized fixpoint expressions are sorted, i.e., we have *lists* of equations and not sets of equations. Note also, that the requirement that no right hand side formula contains bound variables forbids to construct formulas of the following form:

$$\mathsf{min} \begin{bmatrix} x_1 = z \wedge \varphi_1 \vee \mathsf{EX}x_1 \\ \vdots \\ x_n = z \wedge \varphi_n \vee \mathsf{EX}x_n \end{bmatrix} \mathsf{in}\ \mathsf{max} \left[z = \varphi \wedge \bigwedge_{i=1}^{n} \mathsf{EX}x_i \right] \mathsf{in}\ z\ \mathsf{end}\ \mathsf{end}$$

However, the following formula obeys the given syntactic requirements:

$$\mathsf{fix} \begin{bmatrix} x_1 \stackrel{\mu}{=} z \wedge \varphi_1 \vee \mathsf{EX}x_1 \\ \vdots \\ x_n \stackrel{\mu}{=} z \wedge \varphi_n \vee \mathsf{EX}x_n \\ z \stackrel{\nu}{=} \varphi \wedge \bigwedge_{i=1}^{n} \mathsf{EX}x_i \end{bmatrix} \mathsf{in}\ z\ \mathsf{end}$$

Before defining the semantics of $\mathcal{L}_{\mathsf{spec}}$, we need to give some further definitions. An important operation that is carried out on the syntax of formulas is the substitution of variables by formulas. These substitutions and their corresponding functions are defined formally below.

```
function [Φ]_Δ
  {(x_1, η_1), ..., (x_n, η_n)} ≡ Δ;
  V := {x_1, ..., x_n} ∪ ⋃_{i=1}^{n} FV(η_i);
  case Φ of
    is_var(Φ): for i := 1 to n do
                  if Φ = x_i then return η_i end;
               end;
               return Φ;
    ¬φ        : return ¬ [φ]_Δ;
    φ ∧ ψ     : return [φ]_Δ ∧ [ψ]_Δ;
    φ ∨ ψ     : return [φ]_Δ ∨ [ψ]_Δ;
    Xφ        : return X [φ]_Δ;
    [φ U̲ ψ]   : return [[φ]_Δ U̲ [ψ]_Δ];
    [φ B ψ]   : return [[φ]_Δ B [ψ]_Δ];
    X⃖ φ       : return X⃖ [φ]_Δ;
    X̲⃖ φ       : return X̲⃖ [φ]_Δ;
    [φ U̲⃖ ψ]   : return [[φ]_Δ U̲⃖ [ψ]_Δ];
    [φ B⃖ ψ]   : return [[φ]_Δ B⃖ [ψ]_Δ];
    A_σ (Q, Φ_I, Φ_R, Φ_F) :
               if V ∩ Q ≠ {} then fail
               else return A_σ (Q, [Φ_I]_Δ, [Φ_R]_Δ, [Φ_F]_Δ) end
    Eφ        : return E[φ]_Δ;
    Aφ        : return A[φ]_Δ;
    ◇φ        : return ◇ [φ]_Δ;
    □φ        : return □ [φ]_Δ;
    ◇⃖ φ       : return ◇⃖ [φ]_Δ;
    □⃖ φ       : return □⃖ [φ]_Δ;
    σy.φ      : if y ∈ V then fail else return σy. [φ]_Δ;
    fix [y_1 =^{σ_1} φ_1, ..., y_m =^{σ_m} φ_m] in φ end :
               if V ∩ {y_1, ..., y_m} ≠ {} then fail
               else
                  for i := 1 to m do ψ_i := [φ_1]_Δ end
                  return fix {y_1 =^{σ_1} ψ_1, ..., y_m =^{σ_m} ψ_m} in [φ]_Δ end end
               end;
  end
end
```

Fig. 2.7. Substitution of formulas

Definition 2.37 (Substitution of Formulas). *Given variables $x_1, \ldots, x_n \in V_\Sigma$ and formulas $\varphi_1, \ldots, \varphi_n \in \mathsf{PF}_\Sigma$. Then, the set $\{(x_i, \varphi_i) \mid i \in \{1, \ldots, n\}\}$ is called a substitution. The application of a substitution Δ to a formula $\Phi \in \mathsf{PF}_\Sigma$ results in another formula $[\Phi]_\Delta$ that is formally defined in Figure 2.7. For convenience, we often write $[\Phi]_x^\eta$ instead of $[\Phi]_{\{(x,\eta)\}}$ and additionally use* let $x = \eta$ in Φ end *as a formula with the same semantics as $[\Phi]_{\{(x,\eta)\}}$.*

function $|\Phi|$
  case Φ **of**
    is_var(Φ): **return** 1;
    $\neg\varphi$: **return** $|\varphi| + 1$;
    $\varphi \wedge \psi$: **return** $|\varphi| + |\psi| + 1$;
    $\varphi \vee \psi$: **return** $|\varphi| + |\psi| + 1$;
    $\mathsf{X}\varphi$: **return** $|\varphi| + 1$;
    $[\varphi\ \underline{\mathsf{U}}\ \psi]$: **return** $|\varphi| + |\psi| + 1$;
    $[\varphi\ \mathsf{B}\ \psi]$: **return** $|\varphi| + |\psi| + 1$;
    $\overleftarrow{\mathsf{X}}\varphi$: **return** $|\varphi| + 1$;
    $\overleftarrow{\underline{\mathsf{X}}}\varphi$: **return** $|\varphi| + 1$;
    $[\varphi\ \overleftarrow{\underline{\mathsf{U}}}\ \psi]$: **return** $|\varphi| + |\psi| + 1$;
    $[\varphi\ \overleftarrow{\mathsf{B}}\ \psi]$: **return** $|\varphi| + |\psi| + 1$;
    $\mathcal{A}_\sigma\,(Q, \Phi_\mathcal{I}, \Phi_\mathcal{R}, \Phi_\mathcal{F})$:
        return $|Q| + |\Phi_\mathcal{I}| + |\Phi_\mathcal{R}| + |\Phi_\mathcal{F}| + 1$
    $\mathsf{E}\varphi$: **return** $|\varphi| + 1$;
    $\mathsf{A}\varphi$: **return** $|\varphi| + 1$;
    $\Diamond\varphi$: **return** $|\varphi| + 1$;
    $\Box\varphi$: **return** $|\varphi| + 1$;
    $\overleftarrow{\Diamond}\varphi$: **return** $|\varphi| + 1$;
    $\overleftarrow{\Box}\varphi$: **return** $|\varphi| + 1$;
    $\sigma y.\varphi$: **return** $|\varphi| + 1$;
    fix $[y_1 \stackrel{\sigma_1}{=} \varphi_1, \ldots, y_m \stackrel{\sigma_m}{=} \varphi_m]$ in φ end :
        return $|\varphi| + 1 + \sum_{i=1}^{n} |\varphi_i|$
  end
end;

Fig. 2.8. Size of formulas

To be precise, the above definition of substitution is a simultaneous one. Simultaneous substitution means that the result of $[x \vee y]_{\{(x,y),(y,x)\}}$ is $y \vee x$. Note further that substitutions are not defined when there is an attempt to substitute a bound variable. In these cases, we assume suitable renaming of the bound variables to avoid conflicts. For example, $[\mu x.x \vee \Diamond y]_y^x$ will then be $[\mu z.z \vee \Diamond y]_y^x$, i.e., $\mu z.z \vee \Diamond x$, which is not equivalent to $\mu x.x \vee \Diamond x$.

We also sometimes use expressions like let $x = \eta$ in Φ end that we call let-expressions. These formulas can be much more succinct than the corresponding flattened one that is obtained by carrying out the substitution as given in Figure 2.7 where x is replaced with η. Many programming languages like C allow the representation of data structures by pointers. We may interpret let-expressions directly as such a data structure.

The complexity of many algorithms that receive a formula as an input is determined in terms of the length of the given input formula. Because of its importance, we should formally define this length of a formula, although this is straightforward.

Definition 2.38 (Length of Formulas). *For any formula $\Phi \in \mathcal{L}_{\mathsf{spec}}$, the algorithm given in Figure 2.8 computes the size $|\Phi| \in \mathbb{N}$ of Φ.*

2.3 Semantics of the Specification Logic $\mathcal{L}_{\mathsf{spec}}$

We have already given an intuitive, i.e., informal semantics for our language, that must now be formalized in a precise manner. In the last section, Kripke structures were introduced as models for describing reactive systems. We will now define how formulas of the logic $\mathcal{L}_{\mathsf{spec}}$ are interpreted over Kripke structures. For this reason, we need some additional definitions for the semantics of automaton formulas and for the semantics of vectorized fixpoint expressions.

Definition 2.39 (Associated Kripke Structure of an Automaton Formula). *Given an automaton formula $\mathfrak{A} = \mathcal{A}_\Theta(Q, \Phi_\mathcal{I}, \Phi_\mathcal{R}, \Phi_\mathcal{F})$ with $\Theta \in \{\exists, \forall\}$, we define its associated Kripke structure* $\mathsf{Struct}(\mathfrak{A}) = (\mathcal{I}_\mathfrak{A}, \mathcal{S}_\mathfrak{A}, \mathcal{R}_\mathfrak{A}, \mathcal{L}_\mathfrak{A})$ *of $\mathfrak{A}$ as follows:*

- $\mathcal{S}_\mathfrak{A} := 2^{Q \cup V_\Sigma}$
- $\mathcal{I}_\mathfrak{A} := \{\vartheta \subseteq Q \cup V_\Sigma \mid [\![\Phi_\mathcal{I}]\!]_{\vartheta,\{\}} = \mathsf{true}\}$
- $\mathcal{R}_\mathfrak{A} := \{(\vartheta_1, \vartheta_2) \mid [\![\Phi_\mathcal{R}]\!]_{\vartheta_1,\vartheta_2} = \mathsf{true}\}$
- $\mathcal{L}_\mathfrak{A}(\vartheta) := \vartheta$

Clearly, there is a strong relationship between the associated Kripke structure $\mathcal{K}_\mathfrak{A}$ and the given automaton formula $\mathfrak{A}$. In particular, $\Phi_\mathcal{I}$ is satisfied on every initial state of $\mathsf{Struct}(\mathfrak{A})$ and the transition relation $\Phi_\mathcal{R}$ of $\mathfrak{A}$ is respected on every transition of $\mathcal{K}_\mathfrak{A}$. We will state and prove this after we have established the semantics of $\mathcal{L}_{\mathsf{spec}}$.

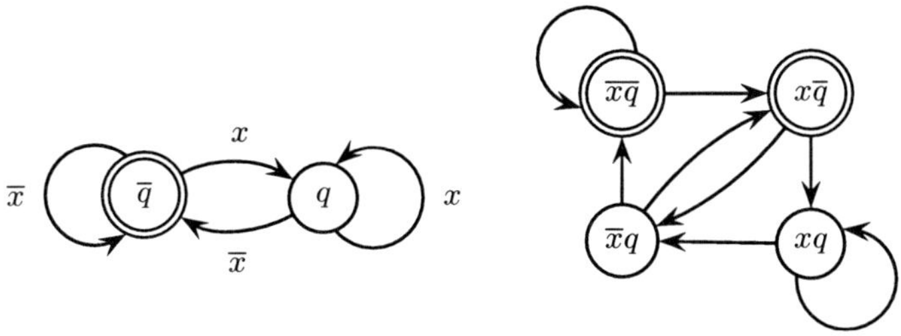

Fig. 2.9. Example for an associated Kripke structure of an automaton formula

We will often draw the transition diagrams of automaton formulas similar to those of Kripke structures. For example, consider the automaton formula $\mathfrak{A} = \mathcal{A}_\exists(\{q\}, \neg q, \mathsf{X}q \leftrightarrow x, \Phi_\mathcal{F})$ over the variables $\{x\}$. The left hand side of Figure 2.9 shows the transition diagram of $\mathfrak{A}$, and the right hand side shows the transition diagram of the associated Kripke structure $\mathsf{Struct}(\mathfrak{A})$. As can be seen, transitions of $\mathfrak{A}$ correspond with states in $\mathsf{Struct}(\mathfrak{A})$.

Given a Kripke structure $\mathcal{K} = (\mathcal{S}, \mathcal{I}, \mathcal{R}, \mathcal{L})$ over V_Σ, we can already compute the product structure $\mathcal{K} \times \mathsf{Struct}(\mathfrak{A}) = (\mathcal{S}_\times, \mathcal{I}_\times, \mathcal{R}_\times, \mathcal{L}_\times)$. According to the definition of product structures, it is easily seen that the result is as follows:

- $\mathcal{S}_\times := \{(s,\sigma) \mid s \in \mathcal{S} \wedge \sigma \subseteq Q \cup V_\Sigma \wedge \mathcal{L}(s) = \sigma \cap V_\Sigma\}$
- $\mathcal{I}_\times := \{(s,\sigma) \in \mathcal{S}_\times \mid s \in \mathcal{I} \wedge [\![\Phi_\mathcal{I}]\!]_\sigma = \mathsf{true}\}$
- $\mathcal{R}_\times := \{((s,\sigma),(s',\sigma')) \in \mathcal{S}_\times \times \mathcal{S}_\times \mid (s,s') \in \mathcal{R} \wedge [\![\Phi_\mathcal{R}]\!]_{\sigma,\sigma'} = \mathsf{true}\}$
- $\mathcal{L}_\times((s,\sigma)) := \mathcal{L}(s) \cup \sigma$

Note that states of the automaton are sets of state variables Q and inputs are sets of input variables V_Σ. The first component s of a state (s,σ) stems from the structure $\mathcal{K}$ and the second one from the structure $\mathsf{Struct}(\mathfrak{A})$. Note that the states of $\mathsf{Struct}(\mathfrak{A})$ are sets of state variables $\sigma \subseteq Q$ and those sets of input variables that belong to a transition leaving this state. Using these products, we can define the semantics of automaton formulas below.

The definition of the semantics of vectorized fixpoint expressions also requires some definitions in advance. Recall that let expressions that are defined as $\mathsf{let}\ x = \varphi\ \mathsf{in}\ \Phi\ \mathsf{end} := [\Phi]_x^\varphi$. In principle, we will try to define the semantics of vectorized fixpoint expressions in the same manner, i.e., by syntactic substitution, but this is not so simple, since in the equations $x_i \overset{\sigma_i}{=} \varphi_i$, the right hand side φ_i may also contain the variable x_i. As our substitutions are simultaneous, we have to eliminate the dependencies between the bound variables in an equation system. Therefore, we must construct an associated substitution $\mathsf{EqSubs}(E)$ for such an equation system E and this is formally defined below.

Definition 2.40 (Associated Substitution of Equation Systems). *Given an equation system E of a fixpoint formula* $\mathsf{fix}\ E\ \mathsf{in}\ \Phi\ \mathsf{end}$, *we define the application of the equation system E to a formula Φ recursively as follows:*

- $[\,]\langle\Phi\rangle := \Phi$
- $(E\&[x \overset{\sigma}{=} \varphi])\langle\Phi\rangle := [E\langle\Phi\rangle]_x^{\sigma x.E\langle\varphi\rangle}$

The application $E\langle E'\rangle$ of E to another equation system $E' = [y_1 \overset{\rho_1}{=} \psi_1, \ldots, y_m \overset{\rho_m}{=} \psi_m]$ is defined as $E\langle E'\rangle := [y_1 \overset{\rho_1}{=} E\langle\psi_1\rangle, \ldots, y_m \overset{\rho_m}{=} E\langle\psi_m\rangle]$. Furthermore, we define for $E = [x_1 \overset{\sigma_1}{=} \varphi_1, \ldots, x_n \overset{\sigma_n}{=} \varphi_n]$ the associated substitution $\mathsf{EqSubs}(E) :=$ $\{(x_1, E\langle x_1\rangle), \ldots, (x_n, E\langle x_n\rangle)\}$.

The associated substitution $\mathsf{EqSubs}(E)$ of E can alternatively be defined as follows:

- $\mathsf{EqSubs}([\,]) := \{\}$
- $\mathsf{EqSubs}\left(E\&[x \overset{\sigma}{=} \varphi]\right) = \{(x, \sigma x.E\langle\varphi\rangle)\} \circ \mathsf{EqSubs}(E)$

As an example, consider $E = [x \stackrel{\mu}{=} \Box x \vee \overleftarrow{\Diamond} y, y \stackrel{\mu}{=} a \wedge \Diamond x \wedge \overleftarrow{\Diamond} y]$. We first obtain $\mathsf{EqSubs}\left([x \stackrel{\mu}{=} \Box x \vee \overleftarrow{\Diamond} y]\right) = \{(x, \mu x.\Box x \vee \overleftarrow{\Diamond} y)\}$ and therefore

$$\begin{aligned}\mathsf{EqSubs}(E) &= \{(y, \nu y.a \wedge \Diamond(\mu x.\Box x \vee \overleftarrow{\Diamond} y) \wedge \overleftarrow{\Diamond} y\} \circ \{(x, \mu x.\Box x \vee \overleftarrow{\Diamond} y)\} \\ &= \{\ (y, \nu y.a \wedge \Diamond(\mu x.\Box x \vee \overleftarrow{\Diamond} y) \wedge \overleftarrow{\Diamond} y, \\ &\qquad (x, \mu x.\Box x \vee \overleftarrow{\Diamond} (\nu y.a \wedge \Diamond(\mu x.\Box x \vee \overleftarrow{\Diamond} y) \wedge \overleftarrow{\Diamond} y))\ \}\end{aligned}$$

The reason why we can not simply use $\{(x_1, \varphi_1), \ldots, (x_n, \varphi_n)\}$ as associated substitution for the equation system $[x_1 \stackrel{\sigma_1}{=} \varphi_1, \ldots, x_n \stackrel{\sigma_n}{=} \varphi_n]$ is that one of the right hand side formulas φ_i may contain one of the defined variables x_j. We prove now that this does not hold for $\mathsf{EqSubs}(E)$.

Lemma 2.41 (Associated Substitution of Equation Systems). *Given an equation system E of a fixpoint formula* fix E in Φ end *together with its associated substitution* $\mathsf{EqSubs}(E) = \{(x_1, \eta_1), \ldots, (x_n, \eta_n)\}$, *then, no variable of* $\{x_1, \ldots, x_n\}$ *occurs free in any* η_i.

Proof. For $n = 1$, we have $\mathsf{EqSubs}\left([x_1 \stackrel{\sigma_1}{=} \varphi_1]\right) = [(x_1, \sigma_1 x_1.\eta_1)]$, hence the lemma holds in this case. For the induction step, consider Definition 2.40. The induction hypothesis, we consider $E'\&[x_n \stackrel{\sigma_n}{=} \varphi_n]$ where E' contains equations $x_i \stackrel{\sigma_i}{=} \varphi_i$ for $i = 1, \ldots, n-1$. Let $\mathsf{EqSubs}(E') = \{(x_1, \eta_1), \ldots, (x_{n-1}, \eta_{n-1})\}$, then by the induction hypothesis, none of the variables $\{x_1, \ldots, x_{n-1}\}$ occurs free in any η_i for $i < n$. Therefore, these variables do also not occur free in $E'\langle\varphi_n\rangle$, and hence, none of $\{x_1, \ldots, x_n\}$ occurs free in $\sigma_n x_n.E'\langle\varphi_n\rangle$. The final substitutions $[\eta_i]_{x_n}^{\sigma_n x_n.E'\langle\varphi_n\rangle}$, which is by composition of $\{(x_n, \sigma_n x_n.E'\langle\varphi_n\rangle)\}$, therefore eliminates all free occurrences of x_n in η_i and do not introduce new free occurrences of the variables $\{x_1, \ldots, x_n\}$. □

We will discuss further properties of the associated substitutions of equation systems in the chapter on the μ-calculus and do not give further comments on that here. This completes all definitions that we need to define the semantics of $\mathcal{L}_{\mathsf{spec}}$. The definition is therefore given as follows.

Definition 2.42 (Semantics of $\mathcal{L}_{\mathsf{spec}}$). *Given a path π of a Kripke structure $\mathcal{K} = (\mathcal{I}, \mathcal{S}, \mathcal{R}, \mathcal{L})$, and a number $t \in \mathbb{N}$, the following rules define the semantics of $\mathcal{L}_{\mathsf{spec}}$ path formulas:*

- $(\mathcal{K}, \pi, t) \models \varphi$ *iff* $(\mathcal{K}, \pi^{(t)}) \models \varphi$ *for each state formula* φ
- $(\mathcal{K}, \pi, t) \models \neg\varphi$ *iff not* $(\mathcal{K}, \pi, t) \models \varphi$
- $(\mathcal{K}, \pi, t) \models \varphi \wedge \psi$ *iff* $(\mathcal{K}, \pi, t) \models \varphi$ *and* $(\mathcal{K}, \pi, t) \models \psi$
- $(\mathcal{K}, \pi, t) \models \varphi \vee \psi$ *iff* $(\mathcal{K}, \pi, t) \models \varphi$ *or* $(\mathcal{K}, \pi, t) \models \psi$
- $(\mathcal{K}, \pi, t) \models \mathsf{X}\varphi$ *iff* $(\mathcal{K}, \pi, t+1) \models \varphi$
- $(\mathcal{K}, \pi, t) \models [\varphi\ \underline{\mathsf{U}}\ \psi]$ *iff there is a* $\delta \geq t$ *such that* $(\mathcal{K}, \pi, \delta) \models \psi$ *holds and for all* x *with* $t \leq x < \delta$, *we have* $(\mathcal{K}, \pi, x) \models \varphi$
- $(\mathcal{K}, \pi, t) \models [\varphi\ \mathsf{B}\ \psi]$ *iff* $(\mathcal{K}, \pi, t) \models \neg[(\neg\varphi)\ \underline{\mathsf{U}}\ \psi]$

- $(\mathcal{K}, \pi, t) \models \overleftarrow{\mathsf{X}}\varphi$ *iff* $t = 0$ *or* $(\mathcal{K}, \pi, t-1) \models \varphi$
- $(\mathcal{K}, \pi, t) \models \overleftarrow{\underline{\mathsf{X}}}\varphi$ *iff* $t > 0$ *and* $(\mathcal{K}, \pi, t-1) \models \varphi$
- $(\mathcal{K}, \pi, t) \models [\varphi\ \overleftarrow{\underline{\mathsf{U}}}\ \psi]$ *iff there is a* $\delta \leq t$ *such that* $(\mathcal{K}, \pi, \delta) \models \psi$ *holds and for all* x *with* $\delta < x \leq t$, *we have* $(\mathcal{K}, \pi, x) \models \varphi$
- $(\mathcal{K}, \pi, t) \models [\varphi\ \overleftarrow{\mathsf{B}}\ \psi]$ *iff* $(\mathcal{K}, \pi, t) \models \neg[(\neg\varphi)\ \overleftarrow{\underline{\mathsf{U}}}\ \psi]$
- *Given an automaton formula* $\mathfrak{A} = \mathcal{A}_\exists(Q, \Phi_\mathcal{I}, \Phi_\mathcal{R}, \Phi_\mathcal{F})$ *with its associated structure* $\mathcal{K}_\mathfrak{A} = (\mathcal{I}_\mathfrak{A}, \mathcal{S}_\mathfrak{A}, \mathcal{R}_\mathfrak{A}, \mathcal{L}_\mathfrak{A})$, *we define:* $(\mathcal{K}, \pi, t) \models \mathfrak{A}$ *iff there is path* ξ *through* $\mathcal{K} \times \mathcal{K}_\mathfrak{A}$ *with* $\forall x.\mathsf{fst}(\xi^{(x)}) = \pi^{(x+t)}$ *such that* $(\mathcal{K} \times \mathcal{K}_\mathfrak{A}, \xi, 0) \models \Phi_\mathcal{I} \wedge \Phi_\mathcal{F}$ *holds.*
- $(\mathcal{K}, \pi, t) \models \mathcal{A}_\forall(Q, \Phi_\mathcal{I}, \Phi_\mathcal{R}, \Phi_\mathcal{F})$ *iff* $(\mathcal{K}, \pi, t) \models \neg\mathcal{A}_\exists(Q, \Phi_\mathcal{I}, \Phi_\mathcal{R}, \neg\Phi_\mathcal{F})$

For a given state s *of a structure* $\mathcal{K} = (\mathcal{I}, \mathcal{S}, \mathcal{R}, \mathcal{L})$, *the semantics of a state formula is given by the following definitions:*

- $(\mathcal{K}, s) \models x$ *iff* $x \in \mathcal{L}(s)$ *for all variables* $x \in V_\Sigma$
- $(\mathcal{K}, s) \models \neg\varphi$ *iff not* $(\mathcal{K}, s) \models \varphi$
- $(\mathcal{K}, s) \models \varphi \wedge \psi$ *iff* $(\mathcal{K}, s) \models \varphi$ *and* $(\mathcal{K}, s) \models \psi$
- $(\mathcal{K}, s) \models \varphi \vee \psi$ *iff* $(\mathcal{K}, s) \models \varphi$ *or* $(\mathcal{K}, s) \models \psi$
- $(\mathcal{K}, s) \models \mathsf{E}\varphi$ *iff there is a path* $\pi \in \mathsf{Paths}_\mathcal{K}(s)$ *such that* $(\mathcal{K}, \pi, 0) \models \varphi$
- $(\mathcal{K}, s) \models \mathsf{A}\varphi$ *iff for all paths* $\pi \in \mathsf{Paths}_\mathcal{K}(s)$ $(\mathcal{K}, \pi, 0) \models \varphi$ *holds.*
- $(\mathcal{K}, s) \models \Diamond\varphi$ *iff there is a* $s' \in \mathcal{S}$ *with* $(s, s') \in \mathcal{R}$ *and* $(\mathcal{K}, s') \models \varphi$
- $(\mathcal{K}, s) \models \Box\varphi$ *iff* $(\mathcal{K}, s) \models \neg\Diamond\neg\varphi$
- $(\mathcal{K}, s) \models \overleftarrow{\Diamond}\varphi$ *iff there is a* $s' \in \mathcal{S}$ *with* $(s', s) \in \mathcal{R}$ *and* $(\mathcal{K}, s') \models \varphi$
- $(\mathcal{K}, s) \models \overleftarrow{\Box}\varphi$ *iff* $(\mathcal{K}, s) \models \neg\overleftarrow{\Diamond}\neg\varphi$
- $(\mathcal{K}, s) \models \exists x.\varphi$ *iff there is a* $Q \subseteq \mathcal{S}$ *such that* $(\mathcal{K}_x^Q, s) \models \varphi$
- $(\mathcal{K}, s) \models \forall x.\varphi$ *iff for all* $Q \subseteq \mathcal{S}$ *we have* $(\mathcal{K}_x^Q, s) \models \varphi$
- $(\mathcal{K}, s) \models \mathsf{fix}\ E\ \mathsf{in}\ \varphi\ \mathsf{end}$ *iff* $(\mathcal{K}, s) \models E\langle\varphi\rangle$
- $(\mathcal{K}, s) \models \mu x.\varphi$ *iff* $s \in \check{Q}$, *where* $\check{Q}$ *is the least set of states* $Q \subseteq \mathcal{S}$ *that satisfies the equation* $Q = \{s' \in \mathcal{S} \mid (\mathcal{K}_x^Q, s') \models \varphi\}$
- $(\mathcal{K}, s) \models \nu x.\varphi$ *iff* $s \in \hat{Q}$, *where* $\hat{Q}$ *is the greatest set of states* $Q \subseteq \mathcal{S}$ *that satisfies the equation* $Q = \{s' \in \mathcal{S} \mid (\mathcal{K}_x^Q, s') \models \varphi\}$

The above definition formalizes the informal description of the operators that has already been given. The semantics of least and greatest fixpoint operators $\mu x.\varphi$ and $\nu x.\varphi$ is best explained if we define the corresponding state transformer $f_\varphi : \mathcal{S} \to \mathcal{S}$ as $f_\varphi(Q) := \{s \in \mathcal{S} \mid (\mathcal{K}_x^Q, s) \models \varphi\}$. Then, our requirements (each occurrence of the bound variable x must be positive in φ) assures that f is a monotonic function. An element $d \in \mathcal{D}$ is a fixpoint of a function $f : \mathcal{D} \to \mathcal{D}$ iff $f(d) = d$ holds. Without further restrictions, fixpoints need not exist, and if one exists, there might be more than one. If the set $\mathcal{D}$ is however a lattice (see Section 3.1) and f is monotonic, then f has fixpoints. Moreover, even a least and a greatest fixpoint exists. It is easily seen, that $(2^\mathcal{S}, \subseteq)$ is a lattice. Therefore, least and greatest fixpoints of our function f_φ exist and can be used to define the semantics of $\mu x.\varphi$ and $\nu x.\varphi$, such that $\mu x.\varphi$

holds in exactly those states that belong to the least fixpoint of f_φ, and analogously, $\nu x.\varphi$ holds in exactly those states that belong to the greatest fixpoint of f_φ. These explanations show that the above definition of the semantics of $\mathcal{L}_{\mathsf{spec}}$ is well-defined, i.e., the required least and greatest fixpoints exist.

Definition 2.42 explains when a formula holds in a certain state or along a certain path of a structure. For state formulas Φ, it is often desired to have the set of states $[\![\Phi]\!]_\mathcal{K}$ of a structure $\mathcal{K}$ where Φ holds, i.e., the set $[\![\Phi]\!]_\mathcal{K} := \{s \in \mathcal{S} \mid (\mathcal{K}, s) \models \Phi\}$. The following lemma gives some rules to directly compute $[\![\Phi]\!]_\mathcal{K}$ for some state formulas.

Lemma 2.43 (Satisfying States). *Given a Kripke structure $\mathcal{K} = (\mathcal{I}, \mathcal{S}, \mathcal{R}, \mathcal{L})$, we define the set of satisfying states of a state formula Φ as $[\![\Phi]\!]_\mathcal{K} := \{s \in \mathcal{S} \mid (\mathcal{K}, s) \models \Phi\}$. Given that $\mathcal{S}_{\mathsf{inf}} := \{s \in \mathcal{S} \mid \mathsf{Paths}_\mathcal{K}(s) \neq \{\}\}$, then the following rules hold for any state formulas φ and ψ:*

- $\mathcal{S}_{\mathsf{inf}} = [\![\nu x.\Diamond x]\!]_\mathcal{K}$
- $[\![x]\!]_\mathcal{K} = \{s \in \mathcal{S} \mid x \in \mathcal{L}(s)\}$ *for all variables* $x \in V_\Sigma$
- $[\![\neg\varphi]\!]_\mathcal{K} = \mathcal{S} \setminus [\![\mathcal{K}]\!]_\varphi$
- $[\![\varphi \wedge \psi]\!]_\mathcal{K} = [\![\varphi]\!]_\mathcal{K} \cap [\![\psi]\!]_\mathcal{K}$
- $[\![\varphi \vee \psi]\!]_\mathcal{K} = [\![\varphi]\!]_\mathcal{K} \cup [\![\psi]\!]_\mathcal{K}$
- $[\![\Diamond\varphi]\!]_\mathcal{K} = \mathsf{pre}_\exists^\mathcal{R}([\![\varphi]\!]_\mathcal{K})$
- $[\![\Box\varphi]\!]_\mathcal{K} = \mathsf{pre}_\forall^\mathcal{R}([\![\varphi]\!]_\mathcal{K})$
- $\left[\!\!\left[\overleftarrow{\Diamond}\varphi\right]\!\!\right]_\mathcal{K} = \mathsf{suc}_\exists^\mathcal{R}([\![\varphi]\!]_\mathcal{K})$
- $\left[\!\!\left[\overleftarrow{\Box}\varphi\right]\!\!\right]_\mathcal{K} = \mathsf{suc}_\forall^\mathcal{R}([\![\varphi]\!]_\mathcal{K})$
- $[\![\mathsf{EX}\varphi]\!]_\mathcal{K} = \mathsf{pre}_\exists^\mathcal{R}(\mathcal{S}_{\mathsf{inf}} \cap [\![\varphi]\!]_\mathcal{K})$
- $[\![\mathsf{AX}\varphi]\!]_\mathcal{K} = \mathsf{pre}_\forall^\mathcal{R}((\mathcal{S} \setminus \mathcal{S}_{\mathsf{inf}}) \cup [\![\varphi]\!]_\mathcal{K})$
- $[\![\mu x.\varphi]\!]_\mathcal{K}$ *is the least set of states* $Q \subseteq \mathcal{S}$ *such that* $Q = [\![\varphi]\!]_{\mathcal{K}_x^Q}$ *holds and analogously,* $[\![\nu x.\varphi]\!]_\mathcal{K}$ *is the greatest set of states* $Q \subseteq \mathcal{S}$ *such that* $Q = [\![\varphi]\!]_{\mathcal{K}_x^Q}$ *holds. Moreover,*
  - $[\![\mu x.\varphi]\!]_\mathcal{K} = \bigcap\{Q \subseteq \mathcal{S} \mid [\![\varphi]\!]_{\mathcal{K}_x^Q} \subseteq Q\}$
  - $[\![\nu x.\varphi]\!]_\mathcal{K} = \bigcup\{Q \subseteq \mathcal{S} \mid Q \subseteq [\![\varphi]\!]_{\mathcal{K}_x^Q}\}$
- $[\![\mathsf{fix}\ E\ \mathsf{in}\ \varphi\ \mathsf{end}]\!]_\mathcal{K} = [\![E\langle\varphi\rangle]\!]_\mathcal{K}$

For the latter equations, consider again the corresponding state transformer $f_\varphi : \mathcal{S} \to \mathcal{S}$, which is defined as $f_\varphi(Q) := \{s \in \mathcal{S} \mid (\mathcal{K}_x^Q, s) \models \varphi\}$. We have already remarked that $(2^\mathcal{S}, \subseteq)$ is a complete partial order and that f_φ is monotonic with respect to that order. Therefore, f_φ has fixpoints. In Section 3.1, we will see that the set of fixpoints of f_φ is closed with respect to $\cap$ and $\cup$. Therefore, if Q_1 and Q_2 are fixpoints, so are $Q_1 \cap Q_2$ and $Q_1 \cup Q_2$. Hence, the intersection of all fixpoints is the least and the union of all fixpoints is the greatest fixpoint of f_φ. In Section 3.1, we will see that this can be generalized to the above cases, i.e., to the intersection of prefixed points and the union of postfixed points. The proofs of the other facts are all straightforward, e.g., consider the following:

$$
\begin{aligned}
[\![\mathsf{EX}\varphi]\!]_{\mathcal{K}} &= \{s \in \mathcal{S} \mid (\mathcal{K}, s) \models \mathsf{EX}\varphi\} \\
&= \{s \in \mathcal{S} \mid \exists \pi \in \mathsf{Paths}_{\mathcal{K}}(s).(\mathcal{K}, \pi, 0) \models \mathsf{X}\varphi\} \\
&= \{s \in \mathcal{S} \mid \exists \pi \in \mathsf{Paths}_{\mathcal{K}}(s).(\mathcal{K}, \pi, 1) \models \varphi\} \\
&= \{s \in \mathcal{S} \mid \exists s' \in \mathcal{S}.(s, s') \in \mathcal{R} \wedge \exists \pi' \in \mathsf{Paths}_{\mathcal{K}}(s').(\mathcal{K}, \pi', 0) \models \varphi\} \\
&= \{s \in \mathcal{S} \mid \exists s' \in \mathcal{S}.(s, s') \in \mathcal{R} \wedge \exists \pi' \in \mathsf{Paths}_{\mathcal{K}}(s').(\mathcal{K}, s') \models \varphi\} \\
&= \{s \in \mathcal{S} \mid \exists s' \in \mathcal{S}.(s, s') \in \mathcal{R} \wedge \exists \pi' \in \mathsf{Paths}_{\mathcal{K}}(s').s' \in [\![\varphi]\!]_{\mathcal{K}}\} \\
&= \{s \in \mathcal{S} \mid \exists s' \in \mathcal{S}.(s, s') \in \mathcal{R} \wedge s' \in \mathcal{S}_{\mathsf{inf}} \wedge s' \in [\![\varphi]\!]_{\mathcal{K}}\} \\
&= \{s \in \mathcal{S} \mid \exists s' \in \mathcal{S}.(s, s') \in \mathcal{R} \wedge s' \in \mathcal{S}_{\mathsf{inf}} \cap [\![\varphi]\!]_{\mathcal{K}}\} \\
&= \{s \in \mathcal{S} \mid s \in \mathsf{pre}_{\exists}^{\mathcal{R}}(\mathcal{S}_{\mathsf{inf}} \cap [\![\varphi]\!]_{\mathcal{K}})\} \\
&= \mathsf{pre}_{\exists}^{\mathcal{R}}(\mathcal{S}_{\mathsf{inf}} \cap [\![\varphi]\!]_{\mathcal{K}})
\end{aligned}
$$

The above lemma can be used in proofs to make these more concise. In a similar way, we can sometimes omit the positions of paths when path formulas are to be evaluated. This is shown in the next lemma.

Lemma 2.44. *Given a Kripke structure $\mathcal{K} = (\mathcal{I}, \mathcal{S}, \mathcal{R}, \mathcal{L})$, a path π through $\mathcal{K}$ and a position $t \in \mathbb{N}$. Let φ be any path formula of $\mathcal{L}_{\mathsf{spec}}$ where no past temporal operator occurs. Then, we have $(\mathcal{K}, \pi, t) \models \varphi$ iff $(\mathcal{K}, \lambda x.\pi^{(x+t)}, 0) \models \varphi$.*

Essentially, the lemma states that only the past operators are able to look at the positions of the path that occur before t. If past operators do not occur then, we can simply consider the suffix of the path $\lambda x.\pi^{(x+t)}$ with the position 0. As we then always consider the position 0, this position is then omitted. This semantics is often given directly for logics that do not have past operators.

We have already introduced substitution as a basic operation on the syntax of formulas. The following lemma gives in some way the semantics of the substitution operation. Moreover, it shows how we can derive a single substitution from the composition of two given substitutions.

Lemma 2.45 (Substitution Lemma). *Given substitutions $\Delta = \{(x_i, \varphi_i) \mid i \in \{1, \ldots, n\}\}$ and Δ', a Kripke structure $\mathcal{K} = (\mathcal{I}, \mathcal{S}, \mathcal{R}, \mathcal{L})$, and a formula $\Phi \in \mathcal{L}_{\mathsf{spec}}$. Then, we have*

1. $\left[\!\!\left[[\Phi]_{\{(x_1,\varphi_1),\ldots,(x_n,\varphi_n)\}} \right]\!\!\right]_{\mathcal{K}} = [\![\Phi]\!]_{\mathcal{K}^{Q_1,\ldots,Q_n}_{x_1,\ldots,x_n}}$ *where* $Q_i = [\![\varphi_i]\!]_{\mathcal{K}}$
2. $\left[[\Phi]^{\varphi_1,\ldots,\varphi_n}_{x_1,\ldots,x_n} \right]_{\Delta'} = [\Phi]_{\Delta'' \cup \{(x_1,\varphi_1'),\ldots,(x_n,\varphi_n')\}}$ *where we abbreviated* $\varphi_i' := [\varphi_i]_{\Delta'}$ *and* $\Delta'' := \{(y, \eta) \in \Delta' \mid y \notin \{x_1, \ldots, x_n\}\}$

So far, the semantics did not consider initial states, except for semantics of automaton formulas. Initial states are however necessary to define what it means when a state formula Φ holds in a structure: There must be an initial state that satisfies Φ. In a similar manner, we define the validity of a formula.

Definition 2.46 (Satisfiability and Validity). *Let $\varphi \in \mathcal{L}_{\mathsf{spec}}$ and $\mathcal{K} = (\mathcal{I}, \mathcal{S}, \mathcal{R}, \mathcal{L})$ be a structure over V_Σ. Then, we define $\mathcal{K} \models \varphi$ iff $\mathcal{I} \subseteq [\![\varphi]\!]_{\mathcal{K}}$ holds. A formula $\varphi \in \mathcal{L}_{\mathsf{spec}}$ is said to be satisfiable, iff there exists a structure $\mathcal{K}$ such that $\mathcal{K} \models \varphi$ holds. Moreover, a formula is said to be valid iff for all structures $\mathcal{K}$, we have $\mathcal{K} \models \varphi$.*

Due to the above definition, it is possible that neither $\mathcal{K} \models \varphi$ nor $\mathcal{K} \models \neg\varphi$ holds, since both $\mathcal{I} \cap [\![\varphi]\!]_{\mathcal{K}}$ and $\mathcal{I} \cap [\![\neg\varphi]\!]_{\mathcal{K}}$ can be nonempty, and therefore we neither have $\mathcal{I} \subseteq [\![\varphi]\!]_{\mathcal{K}}$ nor $\mathcal{I} \subseteq [\![\neg\varphi]\!]_{\mathcal{K}}$.

For the interpretation of automaton formulas $\mathfrak{A}$, we use the product of $\mathcal{K}$ with the associated structures $\mathcal{K}_{\mathfrak{A}}$. One might think that is is more complicated than necessary. However, the product computation is necessary to generate appropriate copies of states as we will show with a small example: Consider the automaton formula $\mathfrak{A} := \mathcal{A}_{\exists}\left(\{q\}, q, \mathsf{X}q \leftrightarrow \neg q, \mathsf{G}[q \rightarrow a]\right)$. It is easily seen that $\mathfrak{A}$ has the two states $\{\}$ and $\{q\}$, and that the latter is the only initial state. There are only two transitions, namely one from state $\{\}$ to $\{q\}$, and another one from $\{q\}$ to $\{\}$. The acceptance condition requires that a must hold at least at the points of time where we are in state $\{q\}$, i.e., a must hold at least at all even points of time. Consider now the structure $\mathcal{K}$ given on the left of Figure 2.10. The structure given in the middle of Figure 2.10 shows the structure $\mathsf{Struct}(\mathfrak{A})$ that is associated with $\mathfrak{A}$, and the structure given on the right hand side is the product $\mathcal{K} \times \mathsf{Struct}(\mathfrak{A})$. According to the semantics of automaton formulas, we have $(\mathcal{K}, s_0) \models \mathsf{E}\mathfrak{A}$ iff $(\mathcal{K} \times \mathsf{Struct}(\mathfrak{A}), (p_0, s_0)) \models \mathsf{EG}[q \rightarrow a]$ holds. It is easily seen that such a path exists in $\mathcal{K} \times \mathsf{Struct}(\mathfrak{A})$, namely the path that toggles between (p_0, s_0) and (p_2, s_0). Hence, it follows that $(\mathcal{K}, s_0) \models \mathsf{E}\mathfrak{A}$ holds.

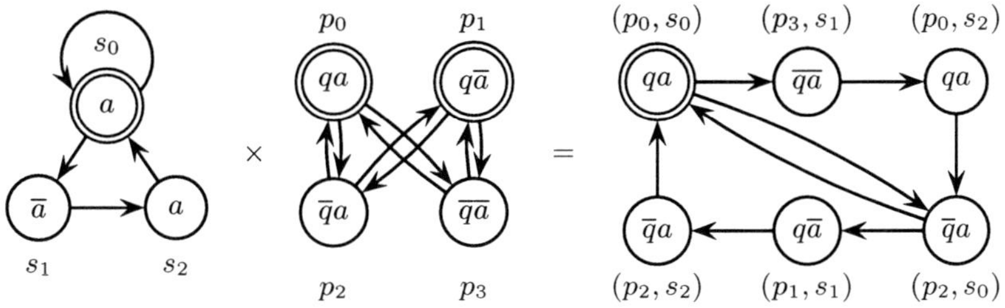

Fig. 2.10. Structure for discussing second order quantification

We can not express the same fact with a quantified formula of the form $\exists q.\varphi$ or $\forall q.\varphi$. Both kinds of formulas, automaton formulas $\mathcal{A}_{\exists}(Q, \Phi_{\mathcal{I}}, \Phi_{\mathcal{R}}, \Phi_{\mathcal{F}})$ and formulas $\exists q.\varphi$, provide some means for quantification. The difference between both is that automaton formulas are able to *quantify over occurrences of states on a path*, hence, the quantification over a state variable q of the automaton associates with q a set of natural numbers, while in formulas of type $\exists q.\varphi$ the bound variable q is associated with a subset of $\mathcal{S}$. Note that in $\exists q.\varphi$, we *quantify over sets of states*. Having seen that we need products with the associated structure $\mathcal{K}_{\mathfrak{A}}$, we can now state precisely the relationship between $\mathfrak{A}$ and $\mathcal{K}_{\mathfrak{A}}$:

Lemma 2.47 (Associated Kripke Structure). *Given an automaton formula* $\mathfrak{A} = \mathcal{A}_{\Theta}(Q, \Phi_{\mathcal{I}}, \Phi_{\mathcal{R}}, \Phi_{\mathcal{F}})$ *with* $\Theta \in \{\forall, \exists\}$*, and its associated Kripke structure* $\mathcal{K}_{\mathfrak{A}} = (\mathcal{I}_{\mathfrak{A}}, \mathcal{S}_{\mathfrak{A}}, \mathcal{R}_{\mathfrak{A}}, \mathcal{L}_{\mathfrak{A}})$ *of* $\mathfrak{A}$*, the following holds:*

- *for any* $s \in \mathcal{S}_{\mathfrak{A}}$*, we have* $s \in \mathcal{I}_{\mathfrak{A}}$ *iff* $(\mathcal{K}_{\mathfrak{A}}, s) \models \Phi_{\mathcal{I}}$
- *for any* $s \in \mathcal{S}_{\mathfrak{A}}$*, we have* $(\mathcal{K}_{\mathfrak{A}}, s) \models \mathsf{AG}\Phi_{\mathcal{R}}$

2.4 Normal Forms

Formulas of $\mathcal{L}_{\mathsf{spec}}$ can be brought into several normal forms. We will consider further normal forms related to sublogics in the corresponding chapters. Normal forms that can be applied to the general language $\mathcal{L}_{\mathsf{spec}}$ are considered here. The first one is given by shifting negation symbols inside such that these only occur in front of variables. This is done by rewriting with the equations of the following lemma.

Lemma 2.48 (Negation Normal Form (NNF)). *For every* $\mathcal{L}_{\mathsf{spec}}$ *formula* Φ*, there is an equivalent* $\mathcal{L}_{\mathsf{spec}}$ *formula* Ψ *of length* $O(|\Phi|)$ *where negation symbols only occur in front of variables. These formulas are said to be in negation normal form. These negation normal forms can be computed by rewriting with the following equations:*

$$
\begin{array}{ll}
\neg(\varphi \wedge \psi) = \neg\varphi \vee \neg\psi & \neg(\varphi \vee \psi) = \neg\varphi \wedge \neg\psi \\
\neg\neg\varphi = \varphi & \neg\mathsf{X}\varphi = \mathsf{X}\neg\varphi \\
\neg\mathsf{G}\varphi = \mathsf{F}\neg\varphi & \neg\mathsf{F}\varphi = \mathsf{G}\neg\varphi \\
\neg[\varphi\ \mathsf{W}\ \psi] = [(\neg\varphi)\ \underline{\mathsf{W}}\ \psi] & \neg[\varphi\ \underline{\mathsf{W}}\ \psi] = [(\neg\varphi)\ \mathsf{W}\ \psi] \\
\neg[\varphi\ \mathsf{U}\ \psi] = [(\neg\varphi)\ \underline{\mathsf{B}}\ \psi] & \neg[\varphi\ \underline{\mathsf{U}}\ \psi] = [(\neg\varphi)\ \mathsf{B}\ \psi] \\
\neg[\varphi\ \mathsf{B}\ \psi] = [(\neg\varphi)\ \underline{\mathsf{U}}\ \psi] & \neg[\varphi\ \underline{\mathsf{B}}\ \psi] = [(\neg\varphi)\ \mathsf{U}\ \psi] \\
\neg\overleftarrow{\mathsf{X}}\varphi = \overleftarrow{\underline{\mathsf{X}}}\neg\varphi & \neg\overleftarrow{\underline{\mathsf{X}}}\varphi = \overleftarrow{\mathsf{X}}\neg\varphi \\
\neg\overleftarrow{\mathsf{G}}\varphi = \overleftarrow{\mathsf{F}}\neg\varphi & \neg\overleftarrow{\mathsf{F}}\varphi = \overleftarrow{\mathsf{G}}\neg\varphi \\
\neg[\varphi\ \overleftarrow{\mathsf{W}}\ \psi] = [(\neg\varphi)\ \overleftarrow{\underline{\mathsf{W}}}\ \psi] & \neg[\varphi\ \overleftarrow{\underline{\mathsf{W}}}\ \psi] = [(\neg\varphi)\ \overleftarrow{\mathsf{W}}\ \psi] \\
\neg[\varphi\ \overleftarrow{\mathsf{U}}\ \psi] = [(\neg\varphi)\ \overleftarrow{\underline{\mathsf{B}}}\ \psi] & \neg[\varphi\ \overleftarrow{\underline{\mathsf{U}}}\ \psi] = [(\neg\varphi)\ \overleftarrow{\mathsf{B}}\ \psi] \\
\neg[\varphi\ \overleftarrow{\mathsf{B}}\ \psi] = [(\neg\varphi)\ \overleftarrow{\underline{\mathsf{U}}}\ \psi] & \neg[\varphi\ \overleftarrow{\underline{\mathsf{B}}}\ \psi] = [(\neg\varphi)\ \overleftarrow{\mathsf{U}}\ \psi] \\
\neg\mathsf{A}\varphi = \mathsf{E}\neg\varphi & \neg\mathsf{E}\varphi = \mathsf{A}\neg\varphi \\
\neg\Box\varphi = \Diamond\neg\varphi & \neg\Diamond\varphi = \Box\neg\varphi \\
\neg\overleftarrow{\Box}\varphi = \overleftarrow{\Diamond}\neg\varphi & \neg\overleftarrow{\Diamond}\varphi = \overleftarrow{\Box}\neg\varphi \\
\multicolumn{2}{l}{\neg\mathcal{A}_{\exists}(Q, \Phi_{\mathcal{I}}, \Phi_{\mathcal{R}}, \Phi_{\mathcal{F}}) = \mathcal{A}_{\forall}(Q, \Phi_{\mathcal{I}}, \Phi_{\mathcal{R}}, \neg\Phi_{\mathcal{F}})} \\
\multicolumn{2}{l}{\neg\mathcal{A}_{\forall}(Q, \Phi_{\mathcal{I}}, \Phi_{\mathcal{R}}, \Phi_{\mathcal{F}}) = \mathcal{A}_{\exists}(Q, \Phi_{\mathcal{I}}, \Phi_{\mathcal{R}}, \neg\Phi_{\mathcal{F}})} \\
\neg\mu x.\varphi = \nu x.\neg[\varphi]_x^{\neg x} & \neg\nu x.\varphi = \mu x.\neg[\varphi]_x^{\neg x} \\
\neg\forall x.\varphi = \exists x.\neg\varphi & \neg\exists x.\varphi = \forall x.\neg\varphi \\
\neg\mathsf{fix}\ E\ \mathsf{in}\ \varphi\ \mathsf{end} = \mathsf{fix}\ E\ \mathsf{in}\ \neg\varphi\ \mathsf{end} &
\end{array}
$$

The length of $\mathsf{NNF}(\Phi)$ is linear in terms of the length of Φ since in each case only a constant is added to the length. The above lemma allows us to consider formulas only where negation symbols are allowed before a variable.

Also note that not all operators are required for generating negation normal forms, and that each of the binary temporal operators can express the other binary operators. However, this does not help when negation normal forms are to be generated, since then we also need to have the negation of that operator, i.e., the dual operator. Note that we have defined the core language of $\mathcal{L}_{\mathsf{spec}}$ such that it allows the computation of negation normal forms.

The next normal form allows us to separate the state and path subformulas of a formula. We will establish this normal form in two steps. In the first step, we assume that the formula contains neither $\forall$, $\exists$ nor vectorized fixpoint expressions. Then, we have the following:

Theorem 2.49 (Path Quantifier Normal Form (PQNF)). *For every formula $\Phi \in \mathcal{L}_{\mathsf{spec}}$ without vectorized fixpoint expressions* $\mathsf{fix}\ E\ \mathsf{in}\ \varphi\ \mathsf{end}$ *and quantified subformulas of the form $\forall x.\varphi$ or $\exists x.\varphi$, the algorithm given in Figure 2.11 computes a pair $\mathsf{PQNF}(\Phi) = (E, \Psi)$ such that $\Phi = \mathsf{fix}\ E\ \mathsf{in}\ \Psi\ \mathsf{end}$ holds. Ψ is a formula without path quantifiers and without fixpoint formulas. The right hand sides of the equations $x_i \stackrel{\sigma}{=} \varphi_i$ in E are moreover of one the following forms:*

- $\varphi_i \equiv \mathsf{E}\varphi'$, *where φ' neither contains fixpoint operators nor path quantifiers*
- $\varphi_i \equiv \Diamond\varphi'$, *where φ' neither contains fixpoint operators nor path quantifiers*
- $\varphi_i \equiv \overleftarrow{\Diamond}\varphi'$, *where φ' neither contains fixpoint operators nor path quantifiers*
- φ_i *neither contains fixpoint operators nor path quantifiers*

Moreover, the size of $\mathsf{fix}\ E\ \mathsf{in}\ \Psi\ \mathsf{end}$ *is of order $O(|\Phi|)$.*

The task of the normal form $\mathsf{PQNF}(\Phi)$ is to separate between state and path formulas. We will use this separation when we convert model checking procedures for path formulas to a corresponding one for state formulas. In particular, we will use this normal form in Section 4.8.1, Section 5.3, and moreover in Section 5.4.5. It is furthermore possible to apply the following laws to shift binders outwards:

- $\mathsf{fix}\ E_1\ \mathsf{in}\ \mathsf{fix}\ E_2\ \mathsf{in}\ \Phi\ \mathsf{end}\ \mathsf{end} = \mathsf{fix}\ E_2\&E_1\ \mathsf{in}\ \Phi\ \mathsf{end}$
- $\varphi \wedge \mathsf{fix}\ E\ \mathsf{in}\ \psi\ \mathsf{end} = \mathsf{fix}\ E\ \mathsf{in}\ \varphi \wedge \psi\ \mathsf{end}$, provided that φ contains none of the defined variables of E
- $\varphi \vee \mathsf{fix}\ E\ \mathsf{in}\ \psi\ \mathsf{end} = \mathsf{fix}\ E\ \mathsf{in}\ \varphi \vee \psi\ \mathsf{end}$, provided that φ contains none of the defined variables of E
- $\varphi \wedge \forall x.\psi = \forall x.\varphi \wedge \psi$, provided that x not occur in φ
- $\varphi \wedge \exists x.\psi = \exists x.\varphi \wedge \psi$, provided that x not occur in φ
- $\varphi \vee \forall x.\psi = \forall x.\varphi \vee \psi$, provided that x not occur in φ
- $\varphi \vee \exists x.\psi = \exists x.\varphi \vee \psi$, provided that x not occur in φ

Further normal forms that we will sometimes use are related with normal forms of propositional logic, i.e., formulas that are only built up with Boolean operators from variables. The most important normal forms for these formulas are without doubt the disjunctive and conjunctive normal forms. In principle, the canonical disjunctive normal form is a complete listing of those

function $\mathsf{PQNF}(\Phi)$
(∗ Ψ *is in negation normal form* ∗)
case Ψ **of**

$\mathsf{is\_var}(\Psi)$	: **return** $([\,],\Psi)$;
$\neg\varphi$	: $(E_\varphi,\varphi') \equiv \mathsf{PQNF}(\varphi)$; **return** $(E_\varphi,\neg\varphi')$;
$\varphi \wedge \psi$	: $(E_\varphi,\varphi') \equiv \mathsf{PQNF}(\varphi)$; $(E_\psi,\psi') \equiv \mathsf{PQNF}(\psi)$; **return** $(E_\varphi \& E_\psi, \varphi' \wedge \psi')$;
$\varphi \vee \psi$	: $(E_\varphi,\varphi') \equiv \mathsf{PQNF}(\varphi)$; $(E_\psi,\psi') \equiv \mathsf{PQNF}(\psi)$; **return** $(E_\varphi \& E_\psi, \varphi' \vee \psi')$;
$\mathsf{X}\varphi$	: $(E_\varphi,\varphi') \equiv \mathsf{PQNF}(\varphi)$; **return** $(E_\varphi,\mathsf{X}\varphi')$;
$[\varphi\ \underline{\mathsf{U}}\ \psi]$	: $(E_\varphi,\varphi') \equiv \mathsf{PQNF}(\varphi)$; $(E_\psi,\psi') \equiv \mathsf{PQNF}(\psi)$; **return** $(E_\varphi \& E_\psi, [\varphi'\ \underline{\mathsf{U}}\ \psi'])$;
$[\varphi\ \mathsf{B}\ \psi]$	: $(E_\varphi,\varphi') \equiv \mathsf{PQNF}(\varphi)$; $(E_\psi,\psi') \equiv \mathsf{PQNF}(\psi)$; **return** $(E_\varphi \& E_\psi, [\varphi'\ \mathsf{B}\ \psi'])$;
$\overleftarrow{\mathsf{X}}\varphi$	: $(E_\varphi,\varphi') \equiv \mathsf{PQNF}(\varphi)$; **return** $(E_\varphi,\overleftarrow{\mathsf{X}}\varphi')$;
$\overleftarrow{\underline{\mathsf{X}}}\varphi$	: $(E_\varphi,\varphi') \equiv \mathsf{PQNF}(\varphi)$; **return** $(E_\varphi,\overleftarrow{\underline{\mathsf{X}}}\varphi')$;
$[\varphi\ \overleftarrow{\underline{\mathsf{U}}}\ \psi]$	: $(E_\varphi,\varphi') \equiv \mathsf{PQNF}(\varphi)$; $(E_\psi,\psi') \equiv \mathsf{PQNF}(\psi)$; **return** $(E_\varphi \& E_\psi, [\varphi'\ \overleftarrow{\underline{\mathsf{U}}}\ \psi'])$;
$[\varphi\ \overleftarrow{\mathsf{B}}\ \psi]$	: $(E_\varphi,\varphi') \equiv \mathsf{PQNF}(\varphi)$; $(E_\psi,\psi') \equiv \mathsf{PQNF}(\psi)$; **return** $(E_\varphi \& E_\psi, [\varphi'\ \overleftarrow{\mathsf{B}}\ \psi'])$;
$\mathcal{A}_\sigma(Q,\Phi_\mathcal{I},\Phi_\mathcal{R},\Phi_\mathcal{F})$	: $(E,\Phi'_\mathcal{F}) \equiv \mathsf{PQNF}(\Phi_\mathcal{F})$; **return** $(E,\mathcal{A}_\sigma(Q,\Phi_\mathcal{I},\Phi_\mathcal{R},\Phi'_\mathcal{F}))$;
$\mathsf{E}\varphi$	: $(E_\varphi,\varphi') \equiv \mathsf{PQNF}(\varphi)$; $\vartheta = \mathsf{newvar}$; **return** $(E_\varphi \& [\vartheta = \mathsf{E}\varphi'],\vartheta)$;
$\mathsf{A}\varphi$	: $(E_\varphi,\varphi') \equiv \mathsf{PQNF}(\neg\varphi)$; $\vartheta = \mathsf{newvar}$; **return** $(E_\varphi \& [\vartheta = \mathsf{E}\neg\varphi],\neg\vartheta)$;
$\Diamond\varphi$	: $(E_\varphi,\varphi') \equiv \mathsf{PQNF}(\varphi)$; $\vartheta = \mathsf{newvar}$; **return** $(E_\varphi \& [\vartheta = \Diamond\varphi'],\vartheta)$;
$\Box\varphi$	: $(E_\varphi,\varphi') \equiv \mathsf{PQNF}(\neg\varphi)$; $\vartheta = \mathsf{newvar}$; **return** $(E_\varphi \& [\vartheta = \Diamond\neg\varphi],\neg\vartheta)$;
$\overleftarrow{\Diamond}\varphi$	: $(E_\varphi,\varphi') \equiv \mathsf{PQNF}(\varphi)$; $\vartheta = \mathsf{newvar}$; **return** $(E_\varphi \& [\vartheta = \overleftarrow{\Diamond}\varphi'],\vartheta)$;
$\overleftarrow{\Box}\varphi$	: $(E_\varphi,\varphi') \equiv \mathsf{PQNF}(\neg\varphi)$; $\vartheta = \mathsf{newvar}$; **return** $(E_\varphi \& [\vartheta = \overleftarrow{\Diamond}\neg\varphi],\neg\vartheta)$;
$\sigma x.\varphi$	: $(E_\varphi,\varphi') \equiv \mathsf{PQNF}(\varphi)$; **return** $(E \& [x \stackrel{\sigma}{=} \varphi'],x)$;

end
end

Fig. 2.11. Transformation into path quantifier normal form

variable assignments that satisfy the formula. We have already identified variable assignment with subsets of variables (cf. page 51), and therefore compute these 'variable assignments' as follows:

Definition 2.50 (Models of Propositional Formulas). *For any propositional formula in negation normal form over the variables V_Σ, we define its models as follows:*

- $\mathsf{models}_{V_\Sigma}(x) := \{\vartheta \subseteq V_\Sigma \mid x \in \vartheta\}$
- $\mathsf{models}_{V_\Sigma}(\neg x) := \{\vartheta \subseteq V_\Sigma \mid x \notin \vartheta\}$
- $\mathsf{models}_{V_\Sigma}(\varphi \wedge \psi) := \mathsf{models}_{V_\Sigma}(\varphi) \cap \mathsf{models}_{V_\Sigma}(\psi)$
- $\mathsf{models}_{V_\Sigma}(\varphi \vee \psi) := \mathsf{models}_{V_\Sigma}(\varphi) \cup \mathsf{models}_{V_\Sigma}(\psi)$

Moreover, for any subset $\vartheta \subseteq V_\Sigma$, we define $\mathsf{minterm}_{V_\Sigma}(\vartheta) := \bigwedge_{x\in\vartheta} x \wedge \bigwedge_{x\in V_\Sigma\setminus\vartheta} \neg x.$

Intuitively, each member of $\mathsf{models}_{V_\Sigma}(\Phi)$ corresponds with exactly one variable assignment of the variables of V_Σ, such that $\mathsf{models}_{V_\Sigma}(\varphi)$ is the set of all assignments that satisfy φ. Hence, $\mathsf{models}_{V_\Sigma}(\Phi)$ can be viewed as a complete disjunctive normal form of Φ. Similarly, $\mathsf{minterm}_{V_\Sigma}(\vartheta)$ corresponds to a maximal minterm and the disjunction of all the minterms of the models is equivalent to the formula itself.

Note that in contrast to Definition 2.8 and 2.9, we do not consider X operators in the above definition. Hence, the semantics according to Definition 2.9 can be simplified to only use one set of variables. We then have:

Lemma 2.51 (Disjunctive Normal Form). *Given propositional formulas Φ and Ψ over the variables V_Σ. The following holds for the functions* $\mathsf{models}_{V_\Sigma}(\Phi)$ *and* $\mathsf{minterm}_{V_\Sigma}(\Phi)$ *for any $\vartheta \subseteq V_\Sigma$:*

- $[\![\Phi]\!]_\vartheta = \mathsf{true} \Leftrightarrow \vartheta \in \mathsf{models}_{V_\Sigma}(\Phi)$
- $\mathsf{models}_{V_\Sigma}(\mathsf{minterm}_{V_\Sigma}(\vartheta)) = \{\vartheta\}$
- $\vartheta \in \mathsf{models}_{V_\Sigma}(\Phi)$ *implies that* $\mathsf{minterm}_{V_\Sigma}(\vartheta) \rightarrow \Phi$ *holds*
- $\mathsf{models}_{V_\Sigma}(\Phi)$ *is a unique normal form for all equivalent propositional formulas, i.e.*
$$\Phi = \bigvee_{\vartheta\in\mathsf{models}_{V_\Sigma}(\Phi)} \mathsf{minterm}_{V_\Sigma}(\vartheta)$$

The above lemma proves that any formula of propositional logic can be transformed into disjunctive normal form. The next lemma shows that this can be extended to formulas that contain temporal operators and path quantifiers, in that subformulas that are starting with such operators are treated as propositional atoms.

Lemma 2.52 (TDNF). *For each $\mathcal{L}_{\mathsf{spec}}$ formula Φ, there is an equivalent $\mathcal{L}_{\mathsf{spec}}$ formula Ψ of the form $\bigvee_{i\in I} \bigwedge_{j\in J_i} \varphi_{i,j}$ for some finite index sets $I, J_i \subseteq \mathbb{N}$, where each $\varphi_{i,j}$ neither starts with $\wedge$ nor with $\vee$. The length of Ψ is of order $O(|\Phi|\, 2^{|\Phi|})$, and in particular, $|I| \in O(2^{|\Phi|})$ holds and $\left|\bigwedge_{j\in J_i} \varphi_{i,j}\right| \in O(|\Phi|)$ holds for each J_i.*

The proof is done by induction on Φ using the algorithm given in Figure 2.12, where the correctness is clear. To prove the upper bound, consider the case

```
function TDNF(Φ)
  (* Ψ is in negation normal form *)
  case Ψ of
    is_var(Φ): return Ψ;
    ¬φ       : return ¬φ; (* φ is a variable *)
    φ ∧ ψ    : ⋁_{i∈I} φ_i ≡ TDNF(φ) and ⋁_{i∈J} ψ_j ≡ TDNF(ψ);
             : return ⋁_{i∈I} ⋁_{i∈J} φ_i ∧ ψ_j;
    φ ∨ ψ    : return TDNF(φ) ∨ TDNF(ψ);
    else     : return Ψ;
  end
end
```

Fig. 2.12. Transformation into disjunctive normal form

$\varphi \wedge \psi$: due to the induction hypothesis, we have $|I| \in O(2^{|\varphi|})$, $|J| \in O(2^{|\psi|})$, $|\varphi_i| \in O(|\varphi|$, and $|\psi_j| \in O(|\psi|$. Hence, $|\bigvee_{i\in I}\bigvee_{i\in J}\varphi_i \wedge \psi_j| \in O(2^{|\varphi|}2^{|\psi|}(|\varphi| + |\psi|)) = O(2^{|\varphi|+|\psi|}(|\varphi|+|\psi|)) = O(2^{|\Phi|}\,|\Phi|)$. In the case $\varphi\vee\psi$, we have $|\varphi|\,2^{|\varphi|} + |\psi|\,2^{|\psi|} \leq |\varphi|\,2^{|\varphi|+|\psi|} + |\psi|\,2^{|\varphi|+|\psi|} = (|\varphi| + |\psi|)2^{|\varphi|+|\psi|}$.

3

Fixpoint Calculi

The propositional μ-calculus is a very expressive language: All languages discussed in this book can be translated to equivalent μ-calculus formulas, but none of them reaches the expressiveness of the μ-calculus. The development of the μ-calculus started in 1975, when Kfoury and Park proved that properties like termination and totality of programs can not be expressed in first order logics [283] (see also Section 6.2.2). For this reason, Park [397], Hitchcock and Park [247], and de Bakker and de Roever [142] introduced a least fixpoint operator to remedy such deficiencies. The resulting formal systems were powerful enough to express important properties like termination, liveness, and deadlocks or starvation.

Dynamic logic [235, 411] is closely related to the μ-calculus. It also makes use of modal operators to reason about the 'before-after behavior' of programs. For example, the dynamic logic constructs $\langle P\rangle\Psi$ and $[P]\,\Psi$ assert that after executing P the property Ψ can/must hold. In particular, the Hoare triples $\Phi\langle P\rangle\Psi$ and $\Phi\,[P]\,\Psi$ correspond to the special dynamic logic formulas $\Phi \to \langle P\rangle\Psi$ and $\Phi \to [P]\,\Psi$, respectively. Hence, $\Phi\langle P\rangle\Psi$ means that if Φ holds before program P is executed, then Ψ holds after termination of P. $\Phi\,[P]\,\Psi$ additionally adds the situation when P does not terminate (partial correctness). Beneath dynamic logic, Hennessy-Milner logic [239] (also closely related to propositional dynamic logic) is a forerunner of the propositional μ-calculus.

Propositional versions of the μ-calculus have been independently proposed by Pratt [413] and Kozen [288, 289] based on forerunners like those mentioned above or Emerson's and Clarke's work [160]. The propositional μ-calculus increases the expressive power of the propositional dynamic logic (PDL) of Fischer and Ladner [192] by means of fixpoint operators and resembles the version of PDL called PDL-Δ given by Streett [476]. Kozen and Parikh [290] showed that the satisfiability problem of μ-calculus formulas can be reduced to the second order theory of n successors (SnS) and Niwiński showed that S2S is expressively equivalent to the μ-calculus.

By Rabin's results [418], a decision procedure was obtained for the propositional μ-calculus, however, its runtime complexity was nonelementary like the decision procedure of Streett and Emerson [477] of 1984. While this runtime complexity can not be improved for SnS, better decision procedures were later found for the propositional μ-calculus: Streett and Emerson developed an automata theoretic decision procedure for the propositional μ-calculus that runs in triple exponential time [478]. Based on further improvements for (1) determinizing ω-automata in exponential time by Safra's construction (cf. Definition 4.29), and (2) checking the emptiness of ω-automata on trees in exponential time [165, 168, 304, 409] finally reduced the complexity to a single exponential time decision procedure (cf. Appendix B.3) so that the known lower bound has been reached: *satisfiability of the μ-calculus is* EXPTIME*-complete [165, 168], while the precise complexity for model checking is still an open problem*. The decidability of the extension to past time modalities in exponential time was finally shown by Vardi [430, 496] in 1998. On the 'deductive side', Stirling and Walker [471, 472], Bradfield and Stirling [67], and Cleaveland [115] developed tableau rules as proof systems for the μ-calculus. These rules can also be used for local model checking (Appendix B), i.e., to decide whether a formula holds in a particular state. Walukiewicz proved in [507] the completeness of Kozen's deductive system for the μ-calculus.

In this chapter, we first consider some basic background on partial orders and fixpoints, in particular the Tarski-Knaster theorem for the computation of fixpoints. Then, we introduce the syntax of the propositional μ-calculus, and prove the transformations to certain normal forms. In Section 3.4 and Section 3.5, we consider model checking procedures for the basic μ-calculus and the vectorized μ-calculus, respectively. In Section 3.6, we show how the runtime of the model checking procedures can be further reduced, which is currently the best known result. As an important application, we consider in Section 3.7 the computation of fair states of a Kripke structure. Section 3.8.1 shows then the relationship between (bi)simulation relations and the μ-calculus, and Section 3.8.3 sketches the relationship to dynamic logic. Appendix B discusses local model checking procedures, and also the satisfiability problem of the μ-calculus (Appendix B.3).

3.1 Partial Orders, Lattices and Fixpoints

In this section, we recall basic definitions and facts about partial orders, lattices and fixpoints. We first start with the definition of partial orders.

Definition 3.1 (Partial Orders, Least Upper and Greatest Lower Bounds). *For every set $\mathcal{D}$ with a relation $\sqsubseteq$ on $\mathcal{D} \times \mathcal{D}$, the pair $(\mathcal{D}, \sqsubseteq)$ is a partial order if the following laws hold:*

Reflexivity: $\forall x \in \mathcal{D}. x \sqsubseteq x$
Antisymmetry: $\forall x, y \in \mathcal{D}. x \sqsubseteq y \wedge y \sqsubseteq x \rightarrow x = y$
Transitivity: $\forall x, y, z \in \mathcal{D}. x \sqsubseteq y \wedge y \sqsubseteq z \rightarrow x \sqsubseteq z$

$(\mathcal{D}, \sqsubseteq)$ is a total order if all elements can be compared, i.e. if additionally $\forall x, y \in \mathcal{D}. x \sqsubseteq y \vee y \sqsubseteq x$ holds. For any set $M \subseteq \mathcal{D}$, an element m_u is an upper bound, if $\forall x \in M. x \sqsubseteq m_u$ holds. Moreover, m_u is the least upper bound of M if the following holds:

$$(\forall x \in M. x \sqsubseteq m_u) \wedge (\forall y \in \mathcal{D}.(\forall x \in M. x \sqsubseteq y) \rightarrow m_u \sqsubseteq y)$$

Similarly, m_l is a lower bound of M, if $\forall x \in M. m_l \sqsubseteq x$ holds, and it is the greatest lower bound of M if the following holds:

$$(\forall x \in M. m_l \sqsubseteq x) \wedge (\forall y \in \mathcal{D}.(\forall x \in M. y \sqsubseteq x) \rightarrow y \sqsubseteq m_l)$$

We denote the least upper and the greatest lower bound of M as $\mathsf{sup}(M)$ and $\mathsf{inf}(M)$, respectively, and often use the alternative names 'supremum' and 'infimum'. $\mathsf{sup}(M)$ is moreover the minimal element of M if $\mathsf{sup}(M) \in M$ holds. Analogously, $\mathsf{inf}(M)$ is the maximal element of M if $\mathsf{inf}(M) \in M$ holds.

Of course, a subset $M \subseteq \mathcal{D}$ need neither have lower upper nor greatest lower bounds at all. And even if such bounds exist, there is no need for the existence of the supremum or the infimum. For example, the sets of rational and real numbers are totally ordered with the usual ordering relation. The set $M := \{x \in \mathbb{Q} \mid \sqrt{2} \leq x < \sqrt{3}\}$ has upper and lower bounds, but neither a supremum nor an infimum in $\mathbb{Q}$. However, if either $\mathsf{sup}(M)$ or $\mathsf{inf}(M)$ does exist, then it is uniquely determined (by the reflexivity of $\sqsubseteq$).

Lemma 3.2. *For every partially ordered set $(\mathcal{D}, \sqsubseteq)$ and subsets $A, B \subseteq \mathcal{D}$, we have:*

- $\mathsf{sup}(A) = \mathsf{sup}(B)$ *iff*
  $\mathsf{sup}(A)$ *is an upper bound of B and* $\mathsf{sup}(B)$ *is an upper bound of A*
- $\mathsf{inf}(A) = \mathsf{inf}(B)$ *iff*
  $\mathsf{inf}(A)$ *is a lower bound of B and* $\mathsf{inf}(B)$ *is a lower bound of A*
- $\mathsf{sup}\left(\bigcup_{i \in I} A_i\right) = \mathsf{sup}\left(\bigcup_{i \in I} \mathsf{sup}(A_i)\right)$
- $\mathsf{inf}\left(\bigcap_{i \in I} A_i\right) = \mathsf{inf}\left(\bigcap_{i \in I} \mathsf{inf}(A_i)\right)$
- $A \subseteq B$ *implies* $\mathsf{sup}(A) \sqsubseteq \mathsf{sup}(B)$
- $A \subseteq B$ *implies* $\mathsf{inf}(B) \sqsubseteq \mathsf{inf}(A)$

Proof. Consider the first point: The direction from the left to the right is trivial. The other direction is seen as follows: If $\mathsf{sup}(A)$ is an upper bound of B, it immediately follows that $\mathsf{sup}(B) \sqsubseteq \mathsf{sup}(A)$ holds, since $\mathsf{sup}(B)$ is the *least* upper bound of B. Analogously, we conclude that $\mathsf{sup}(A) \sqsubseteq \mathsf{sup}(B)$ holds, if $\mathsf{sup}(B)$ is an upper bound of A. By antisymmetry of $\sqsubseteq$, it therefore follows that $\mathsf{sup}(A) = \mathsf{sup}(B)$. The second point is proved analogously, and the other points are proved by the help of the first two. □

In general, we do not have a reasonable relationship between least upper and greatest lower bounds. In particular, the equation $\mathsf{sup}(M) = \mathsf{inf}(\mathcal{D} \setminus M)$ does not hold: For example, in the totally ordered set $(\mathbb{R}, \leq)$, the set $M := \{x \in \mathbb{Q} \mid \sqrt{2} \leq x < \sqrt{3}\}$ has $\mathsf{sup}(M) = \sqrt{2}$ and $\mathsf{inf}(M) = \sqrt{3}$, but the complement set $\mathbb{R} \setminus M$ neither has a lower nor an upper bound.

In the following, we consider special partial orders that guarantee the existence of $\mathsf{sup}(M)$ and $\mathsf{inf}(M)$ for certain sets $M \subseteq \mathcal{D}$. These are called complete lattices and are defined as follows:

Definition 3.3 (Lattices and Complete Lattices). *A partially ordered set $(\mathcal{D}, \sqsubseteq)$ is a lattice, if for all elements $x, y \in \mathcal{D}$ both $\mathsf{sup}(\{x, y\})$ and $\mathsf{inf}(\{x, y\})$ exist. Moreover, $(\mathcal{D}, \sqsubseteq)$ is a complete lattice, if for every nonempty set $M \subseteq \mathcal{D}$, both $\mathsf{sup}(M)$ and $\mathsf{inf}(M)$ exist. In particular, we denote $\bot := \mathsf{inf}(\mathcal{D})$ and $\top := \mathsf{sup}(\mathcal{D})$.*

Of course, every total order is a lattice, and therefore $(\mathbb{N}, \leq)$ is also a lattice. However, $(\mathbb{N}, \leq)$ is not a complete lattice, since the set $\mathbb{N}$ itself has no supremum. However, if we extend this order to $\mathbb{N} \cup \{\top\}$ in that we define $n \sqsubseteq m :\Leftrightarrow n \leq m$ for $n, m \in \mathbb{N}$, and $n \sqsubseteq \top$ for every $n \in \mathbb{N}$, then $(\mathbb{N} \cup \{\top\}, \sqsubseteq)$ is a complete lattice.

It is interesting to note that in every lattice, we can define two operations as follows:

- $x \sqcup y := \mathsf{sup}(\{x, y\})$
- $x \sqcap y := \mathsf{inf}(\{x, y\})$

With this definitions, it is not too difficult to prove the following laws:

$$\begin{aligned}
\text{Commutative Laws: } & x \sqcap y = y \sqcap x \\
& x \sqcup y = y \sqcup x \\
\text{Associative Laws: } & x \sqcap (y \sqcap z) = (x \sqcap y) \sqcap z \\
& x \sqcup (y \sqcup z) = (x \sqcup y) \sqcup z \\
\text{Absorption: } & x \sqcap (x \sqcup y) = x \\
& x \sqcup (x \sqcap y) = x \\
\text{Distributive Laws: } & x \sqcap (y \sqcup z) = (x \sqcap y) \sqcup (x \sqcap z) \\
& x \sqcup (y \sqcap z) = (x \sqcup y) \sqcap (x \sqcup z) \\
\text{Neutral Elements: } & x \sqcap \top = x \\
& x \sqcup \bot = x
\end{aligned}$$

Moreover, if a set $\mathcal{D}$ with two operations $\sqcap$ and $\sqcup$ that satisfy the above laws is given, then we can define a relation $\sqsubseteq$ on $\mathcal{D} \times \mathcal{D}$ as follows: $x \sqsubseteq y :\Leftrightarrow x = x \sqcap y$. This relation then turns out to be a partial order. So, we see that there are interesting relationships between algebraic structures and partial orders.

Lemma 3.4 (Properties of Lattices). *In every lattice $(\mathcal{D}, \sqsubseteq)$, we have the following laws:*

- $\mathsf{inf}(\{e_1, \ldots, e_{n+1}\}) = \mathsf{inf}(\{e_{n+1}\} \cup \mathsf{inf}(\{e_1, \ldots, e_n\}))$
- $\mathsf{sup}(\{e_1, \ldots, e_{n+1}\}) = \mathsf{sup}(\{e_{n+1}\} \cup \mathsf{sup}(\{e_1, \ldots, e_n\}))$,

and therefore the following holds:

- $\mathsf{inf}(M)$ *and* $\mathsf{sup}(M)$ *exist for every finite subset* $M \subseteq \mathcal{D}$
- *every finite lattice is complete*

We now consider functions between partial orders. In particular, functions are of interest that maintain the order of the corresponding elements.

Definition 3.5 (Monotonic and Continuous Functions). *Given partially ordered sets $(\mathcal{D}, \sqsubseteq_{\mathcal{D}})$ and $(\mathcal{E}, \sqsubseteq_{\mathcal{E}})$. A function $f : \mathcal{D} \to \mathcal{E}$. f is monotonic, if the following holds:*

$$\forall x, y \in \mathcal{D}.\ x \sqsubseteq_{\mathcal{D}} y \to f(x) \sqsubseteq_{\mathcal{E}} f(y)$$

f is continuous if f is monotonic and for any directed set $M \subseteq \mathcal{D}$, it follows that $f(\mathsf{sup}\,(M)) = \mathsf{sup}\,(\{f(x) \mid x \in M\})$ and $f(\mathsf{inf}\,(M)) = \mathsf{inf}\,(\{f(x) \mid x \in M\})$ holds.

An element $d \in \mathcal{D}$ is a fixpoint of $f : \mathcal{D} \to \mathcal{D}$ if $f(d) = d$ holds, and $d \in \mathcal{D}$ is a prefixed point of $f : \mathcal{D} \to \mathcal{D}$ if $d \sqsubseteq f(d)$ holds. Clearly, not every function f has fixpoints. The following theorem due to Tarski and Knaster, states however, that any continuous function $f : \mathcal{D} \to \mathcal{D}$ over a complete lattice $(\mathcal{D}, \sqsubseteq)$ has fixpoints. Moreover, the theorem provides an iteration for computing the least and greatest fixpoint of any such function.

Theorem 3.6 (Tarski/Knaster Fixpoint Theorem [317, 482]). *Let $(\mathcal{D}, \sqsubseteq)$ be a complete lattice and $f : \mathcal{D} \to \mathcal{D}$ be a continuous function. Then, f has fixpoints, and the set of fixpoints has even a maximum $\hat{x}$ and a minimum $\check{x}$. The least fixpoint $\check{x}$ of f and the greatest fixpoint $\hat{x}$ can be characterized as follows:*

$$\check{x} = \mathsf{inf}\,(\{x \in \mathcal{D} \mid f(x) = x\}) = \mathsf{inf}\,(\{x \in \mathcal{D} \mid f(x) \sqsubseteq x\})$$
$$\hat{x} = \mathsf{sup}\,(\{x \in \mathcal{D} \mid f(x) = x\}) = \mathsf{sup}\,(\{x \in \mathcal{D} \mid x \sqsubseteq f(x)\})$$

Moreover, let $p, q \in \mathcal{D}$ be such that the following conditions hold:

$$(\mu_1)\ p \sqsubseteq f(p) \qquad (\nu_1)\ f(q) \sqsubseteq q$$
$$(\mu_2)\ p \sqsubseteq \check{x} \qquad (\nu_2)\ \hat{x} \sqsubseteq q$$

Then, the iteration p_i defined as $p_0 := p$ and $p_{i+1} := f(p_i)$ converges to $\check{x}$. Analogously , the iteration q_i defined as $q_0 := q$, $q_{i+1} := f(q_i)$ converges to $\hat{x}$.

Proof. We only consider the part for least fixpoints, the other part is proved in a completely dual manner. We first prove that the sequence p_i is monotonic, i.e., that (1) $\forall n. p_n \sqsubseteq p_{n+1}$ holds. For $n = 0$ this means that $p \sqsubseteq f(p)$ is shown as immediately following from μ_1. In the induction step, we already know by the induction hypothesis that $p_n \sqsubseteq p_{n+1}$ holds. By monotonicity of f, it therefore follows that $f(p_n) \sqsubseteq f(p_{n+1})$ holds, which means by definition of the sequence p_i that we have $p_{n+1} \sqsubseteq p_{n+2}$, so that the induction step follows. Hence, (1) holds.

Therefore, the function $c_p : \mathbb{N} \to \mathcal{D}$ defined as $c_p(n) := p_n = f^n(p)$ forms an ascending chain: $p \sqsubseteq f(p) \sqsubseteq f^2(p) \sqsubseteq f^3(p) \sqsubseteq \ldots$. As $(\mathcal{D}, \sqsubseteq)$ is a complete lattice, the set $\mathcal{C}_p := \{f^n(p) \mid n \in \mathbb{N}\}$ has a least upper bound $\mathsf{sup}\,(\mathcal{C}_p)$ (and of course, we have $p = \mathsf{inf}\,(\mathcal{C}_p)$). We now prove that

(2) $\mathsf{sup}(\mathcal{C}_p) = \mathsf{sup}\left(\{f^{n+1}(p) \mid n \in \mathbb{N}\}\right)$ holds. For this reason, we abbreviate the least upper bounds $m_1 := \mathsf{sup}(\mathcal{C}_p)$ and $m_2 := \mathsf{sup}\left(\{f^{n+1}(p) \mid n \in \mathbb{N}\}\right)$. Hence, we have the following facts due to the definition of the supremum:

$$\begin{array}{ll} (2.1)\ \forall n \in \mathbb{N}.f^n(p) \sqsubseteq m_1 & (2.2)\ \forall m \in \mathcal{D}.\forall n \in \mathbb{N}.f^n(p) \sqsubseteq m \to m_1 \sqsubseteq m \\ (2.3)\ \forall n \in \mathbb{N}.f^{n+1}(p) \sqsubseteq m_2 & (2.4)\ \forall m \in \mathcal{D}.\forall n \in \mathbb{N}.f^{n+1}(p) \sqsubseteq m \to m_2 \sqsubseteq m \end{array}$$

From (2.1), it follows that $\forall n \in \mathbb{N}.f^{n+1}(p) \sqsubseteq m_1$, so that by modus ponens with (2.4), we obtain (2.5) $m_2 \sqsubseteq m_1$. From (2.3), it follows that $f(p) \sqsubseteq m_2$, and by (μ_1), we have $p \sqsubseteq f(p)$, so that by transitivity of $\sqsubseteq$, we have $p \sqsubseteq m_2$. This supplements (2.3) to $\forall n \in \mathbb{N}.f^n(p) \sqsubseteq m_2$, so that by modus ponens with (2.2), we get (2.6) $m_1 \sqsubseteq m_2$. Hence, by (2.5) and (2.6), we have $m_1 = m_2$, to that (2) holds.

Using (2), and the assumption that f is continuous, it now follows that $\mathsf{sup}(\mathcal{C}_p)$ is a fixpoint of f:

$$\begin{aligned} (3)\ f(\mathsf{sup}(\mathcal{C}_p)) &= f(\mathsf{sup}(\{f^n(p) \mid n \in \mathbb{N}\})) = \mathsf{sup}\left(\{f^{n+1}(p) \mid n \in \mathbb{N}\}\right) \\ &\overset{(2)}{=} \mathsf{sup}(\{f^n(p) \mid n \in \mathbb{N}\}) = \mathsf{sup}(\mathcal{C}_p) \end{aligned}$$

Hence, we now know that f has fixpoints, i.e., that the set $\mathcal{F}_f := \{x \mid x \in \mathcal{D} \wedge (f(x) = x)\}$ is not empty. As $\mathcal{D}$ is a complete lattice, it follows that $\mathsf{inf}(\mathcal{F}_f)$ and $\mathsf{sup}(\mathcal{F}_f)$ exist. Moreover, $\mathsf{inf}(\mathcal{F}_f)$ and $\mathsf{sup}(\mathcal{F}_f)$ are themselves fixpoints, which is seen as follows:

$$\begin{aligned} (4)\ f(\mathsf{inf}(\mathcal{F}_f)) &= f(\mathsf{inf}(\{x \mid x \in \mathcal{D} \wedge (f(x) = x)\})) \\ &= \mathsf{inf}(\{f(x) \mid x \in \mathcal{D} \wedge (f(x) = x)\}) \\ &= \mathsf{inf}(\{x \mid x \in \mathcal{D} \wedge (f(x) = x)\}) \\ &= \mathsf{inf}(\mathcal{F}_f) \end{aligned}$$

Hence, there is a least fixpoint $\check{x} := \mathsf{inf}(\mathcal{F}_f)$ of f and a greatest fixpoint $\hat{x} := \mathsf{sup}(\mathcal{F}_f)$.

We now prove that the iteration starting with p converges to the least fixpoint $\check{x}$. For this reason, we prove by induction on n that (5) $\forall n.f^n(p) \sqsubseteq \check{x}$. The induction base follows directly from the assumption μ_2 of the theorem. In the induction step, we know by the induction hypothesis that $f^n(p) \sqsubseteq \check{x}$ holds. By monotonicity of f, it therefore follows that $f^{n+1}(p) \sqsubseteq f(\check{x}) = \check{x}$, so that the induction step is proved. Hence, (5) holds, and for this reason $\check{x}$ is an upper bound of $\mathcal{C}_p$, so that we have (6) $\mathsf{sup}(\mathcal{C}_p) \sqsubseteq \check{x}$. By (3), we know that $\mathsf{sup}(\mathcal{C}_p)$ is a fixpoint of f, so that also (7) $\check{x} \sqsubseteq \mathsf{sup}(\mathcal{C}_p)$ follows. By (6) and (7), we now obtain (8) $\check{x} = \mathsf{sup}(\mathcal{C}_p)$.

We now prove that $\check{x}$ is also the infimum of the set of prefixed points of f, i.e., that the equation $\check{x} = \mathsf{inf}(\{x \in \mathcal{D} \mid f(x) \sqsubseteq x\})$ holds. For this reason, consider an arbitrary element x_0 with the property (10) $f(x_0) \sqsubseteq x_0$ (such elements exist, since in particular $\check{x}$ has this property). Now, consider the above iteration starting with $p_0 = p = \bot$. We prove by induction on n that (11) $\forall n \in \mathbb{N}.f^n(\bot) \sqsubseteq x_0$ holds. For $n = 0$, this is trivial. For the induction step, we have $f^n(\bot) \sqsubseteq x_0$ by the induction hypothesis. Due to the monotonicity of f, it therefore follows that $f^{n+1}(\bot) \sqsubseteq f(x_0)$, and by (10) and the transitivity of $\sqsubseteq$, we hence have $f^{n+1}(\bot) \sqsubseteq x_0$. Hence, (11) holds.

For this reason, every prefixed point x_0 is an upper bound of the set $\mathcal{C}_\bot := \{f^n(\bot) \mid n \in \mathbb{N}\}$. Note now, that $p := \bot$ fulfills the requirements μ_1 and μ_2 given in the theorem, and therefore, it follows by (8) that $\mathsf{sup}(\mathcal{C}_\bot)$ is also equal to the least fixpoint of f: $\check{x} = \mathsf{sup}(\mathcal{C}_\bot)$. By (11), it moreover follows that $\mathsf{sup}(\mathcal{C}_\bot) \sqsubseteq x_0$ (since x_0 is an upper bound of $\mathcal{C}_\bot$ and $\mathsf{sup}(\mathcal{C}_\bot)$ is the least upper bound of $\mathcal{C}_\bot$). Hence, we have (12) $\check{x} \sqsubseteq x_0$.

As x_0 has been chosen arbitrarily, it follows that any element x_0 with the property (10) is greater than $\check{x}$, i.e., that $\check{x}$ is a lower bound of the set $\{x \in \mathcal{D} \mid f(x) \sqsubseteq x\}$. As $\check{x}$ itself belongs to this set, it follows that $\check{x}$ is also the minimum of the set of prefixed points: $\check{x} = \mathsf{inf}(\{x \in \mathcal{D} \mid f(x) \sqsubseteq x\})$. □

The Tarski/Knaster theorem is very important for many applications in computer science. Many semantics of programming languages, in particular the semantics of recursive functions or loops is based on this fixpoint theorem (see also Appendix B for the relationship of finite and infinite recursion and least and greatest fixpoints). In many textbooks, the iteration for computing least and greatest fixpoints due to the Tarski/Knaster theorem is formulated for the special cases $p = \bot$ and $q = \top$. As these special cases satisfy the conditions μ_1, μ_2, ν_1, and ν_2 of the above formulation, it follows that the above version of the theorem is more general.

In general, the Tarski/Knaster iteration converges to the least or greatest fixpoint. However, the fixpoint, i.e., the limit $\lim_{i\to\infty} f^i(p)$ of the above mentioned iterations may never be actually reached. For finite $\mathcal{D}$, however, there must be a value n_0 such that $f^{n_0}(p) = f^{n_0+1}(p) = \lim_{i\to\infty} f^i(p)$ holds, hence the iteration will always terminate for finite lattices. The verification of infinite state systems must however face the problem that $\lim_{i\to\infty} f^i(p)$ may never be reached.

The Tarski/Knaster computation of the least and greatest fixpoints governs most verification algorithms given in this book, in particular those for checking μ-calculus formulas. For the following, we write $\mu x.f$ and $\nu x.f$ to denote the least and greatest fixpoint of a function f, respectively (without confusing this notation with the μ-calculus formulas of the next sections).

In the following, we will sometimes have to do with compound lattices, i.e. lattices that are obtained from other lattices by computing their cartesian product: Given two partial orders $(\mathcal{D}_1, \sqsubseteq_1)$ and $(\mathcal{D}_2, \sqsubseteq_2)$, we can define a partial order $\sqsubseteq_\times$ on $\mathcal{D}_1 \times \mathcal{D}_2$ as follows:

$$(d_1, d_2) \sqsubseteq_\times (d_1', d_2') :\Leftrightarrow (d_1 \sqsubseteq_1 d_1') \wedge (d_2 \sqsubseteq_2 d_2')$$

Moreover, if $(\mathcal{D}_1, \sqsubseteq_1)$ and $(\mathcal{D}_2, \sqsubseteq_2)$ are lattices, so is $(\mathcal{D}_1 \times \mathcal{D}_2, \sqsubseteq_\times)$, and even completeness of the lattices is maintained. Hence, the computation of fixpoints of continuous functions $f : \mathcal{D}_1 \times \mathcal{D}_2 \to \mathcal{D}_1 \times \mathcal{D}_2$ can be done by the

Tarski / Knaster iteration. The following lemma shows that we can reduce this fixpoint computation to others of functions of types $\mathcal{D}_1 \to \mathcal{D}_1$ and $\mathcal{D}_2 \to \mathcal{D}_2$.

Lemma 3.7 (Bekič's Lemma on Simultaneous Fixpoints [35]). *Given complete lattices $(\mathcal{D}_1, \sqsubseteq_1)$ and $(\mathcal{D}_2, \sqsubseteq_2)$, and two continuous functions $f : \mathcal{D}_1 \times \mathcal{D}_2 \to \mathcal{D}_1$ and $g : \mathcal{D}_1 \times \mathcal{D}_2 \to \mathcal{D}_2$. We define the function $h : \mathcal{D}_1 \times \mathcal{D}_2 \to \mathcal{D}_1 \times \mathcal{D}_2$ as $h(x,y) := (f(x,y), g(x,y))$. Then, h is continuous and the least fixpoint $(\breve{x}, \breve{y})$ of h is determined as $\breve{x} := \mu x.f(x, \mu y.g(x,y))$ and $\breve{y} := \mu y.g(\breve{x}, y)$. Equivalently, the least fixpoint of h can be described as $(\breve{x}', \breve{y}')$ with $\breve{x}' := \mu x.f(x, \breve{y}')$ and $\breve{y}' := \mu y.g(\mu x.f(x,y), y)$.*

Proof. Clearly, h is continuous, and therefore h has fixpoints, in particular, a least fixpoint. Let (x_0, y_0) be the least fixpoint of h. For convenience, we define the function $g' : \mathcal{D}_1 \to \mathcal{D}_2$ as $g'(x) := \mu y.g(x,y)$. Then, the following facts immediately follow by the definitions of (x_0, y_0), $\breve{x}$, $\breve{y}$, and g':

(1) $\forall x.\forall y.g'(x) = g(x, g'(x))$
(2) $\forall x.\forall y.g(x,y) \sqsubseteq_2 y \to g'(x) \sqsubseteq_2 y$
(3) $\breve{y} = g'(\breve{x})$
(4) $\breve{x} = f(\breve{x}, g'(\breve{x}))$
(5) $\forall x.f(x, g'(x)) \sqsubseteq_1 x \to \breve{x} \sqsubseteq_1 x$
(6) $x_0 = f(x_0, y_0)$
(7) $y_0 = g(x_0, y_0)$
(8) $\forall x.\forall y.f(x,y) \sqsubseteq_1 x \wedge g(x,y) \sqsubseteq_2 y \to x_0 \sqsubseteq_1 x \wedge y_0 \sqsubseteq_2 y$

(1) and (2) are due to the definition of g', since $g'(x)$ is the least fixpoint of $\lambda y.g(x,y)$. (3) is the definition of $\breve{y}$ rewritten with the definition of g'. (4) and (5) are the definition of $\breve{x}$, where we also used the function g' for conciseness. (6), (7), and (8) formalize that (x_0, y_0) is the least fixpoint of h.

By (3) and (4) we immediately obtain (9) $\breve{x} = f(\breve{x}, \breve{y})$ and from (1) and (3) that (10) $\breve{y} = g(\breve{x}, \breve{y})$ holds. Hence, $(\breve{x}, \breve{y})$ is a fixpoint of h. Therefore, we obtain by modus ponens from (9), (10), and (8) that (11) $x_0 \sqsubseteq_1 \breve{x}$ and (12) $y_0 \sqsubseteq_2 \breve{y}$ holds.

From (7), we get $g(x_0, y_0) \sqsubseteq_2 y_0$, hence, it follows by modus ponens with (2) that (13) $g'(x_0) \sqsubseteq_2 y_0$ holds. By monotonicity of f, we therefore obtain $f(x_0, g'(x_0)) \sqsubseteq_1 f(x_0, y_0)$, which means by (6) that $f(x_0, g'(x_0)) \sqsubseteq_1 x_0$ holds. Modus ponens with (5) therefore shows us (14) $\breve{x} \sqsubseteq_2 x_0$.

Using (14) and the monotonicity of g, we now obtain $g(\breve{x}, y_0) \sqsubseteq_2 g(x_0, y_0)$, and considering (7) simplifies this to $g(\breve{x}, y_0) \sqsubseteq_2 y_0$. Modus ponens with (2) results in $g'(\breve{x}) \sqsubseteq_2 y_0$, which means by (3) that (15) $\breve{y} \sqsubseteq_2 y_0$ holds.

Summing up, by (11) and (14), it follows that $\breve{x} = x_0$ and by (12) and (15), it follows that $\breve{y} = y_0$ holds. Hence, $(\breve{x}, \breve{y})$ is the least fixpoint of h.

The second characterization of the least fixpoint of h is obtained as follows: Consider $h'(y,x) := (g(x,y), f(x,y))$. By the proven facts, h' has the least fixpoint $(\breve{y}', \breve{x}')$ where $\breve{y}'$ and $\breve{x}'$ are as described in the lemma. It is however obvious that $h(x,y) = (a,b)$ iff $h'(y,x) = (b,a)$ hold. □

The above lemma is important for the understanding of simultaneous fixpoint definitions. It moreover has some surprising consequences that we will consider in the following. For example, note that we have

$$\breve{x} := \mu x.f(x, \mu y.g(x,y)) = \mu z.f(z, \mu y.g(\mu x.f(x,y),y)) =: \breve{x}',$$

since least fixpoints are uniquely determined. In the special case where $f(x,y) := y$ holds, this reduces to $\mu x.\mu y.g(x,y) = \mu y.g(y,y))$, so that we see multiple least fixpoint operators that follow on each other can be merged to a single one.

A further result that is more important is that we can 'serialize' the computation of simultaneous fixpoints, i.e., we can reduce it to the computation of some fixpoints that are not simultaneous. This will be very important for the construction of model checking procedures for the vectorized μ-calculus.

Lemma 3.8 (Special Fixpoint Iterations). *Given two complete lattices $(\mathcal{D}_1, \sqsubseteq_1)$ and $(\mathcal{D}_2, \sqsubseteq_2)$ and the function $h : \mathcal{D}_1 \times \mathcal{D}_2 \to \mathcal{D}_1 \times \mathcal{D}_2$ defined by two continuous functions $f : \mathcal{D}_2 \to \mathcal{D}_1$ and $g : \mathcal{D}_1 \times \mathcal{D}_2 \to \mathcal{D}_2$ as $h(x,y) := (f(y), g(x,y))$. Given that h is continuous, and $\breve{y} := \mu y.g(f(y),y)$ then it follows that the least fixpoint of h is $(f(\breve{y}), \breve{y})$. Moreover, the following two iteration schemes both compute this fixpoint:*

$x_0 := \bot$	$y_0 := \bot$	$x_0 := \bot$	$y_0 := \bot$
$x_{i+1} := f(y_i)$	$y_{i+1} := g(x_{i+1}, y_i)$	$x_{i+1} := f(y_i)$	$y_{i+1} := \mu y.g(x_{i+1}, y)$

Proof. According to Lemma 3.7, the least fixpoint of h is given as $(f(\breve{y}), \breve{y})$ where $\breve{y} := \mu y.g(f(y),y)$ holds. Hence, we can compute $\breve{y}$ according to the Tarski/Knaster theorem by the iteration sequence: $y_0 := \bot$, $y_{i+1} := g(f(y_i), y_i)$. Abbreviating $x_0 := \bot$ and $x_{i+1} := f(y_i)$ transforms this iteration directly into the one that is given on the left hand side of the lemma. Note further that $\lim_{i\to\infty} x_i = \lim_{i\to\infty} x_{i+1} = \lim_{i\to\infty} f(y_i) = f(\lim_{i\to\infty} y_i) = f(\breve{y})$ holds, thus, the sequence (x_i, y_i) converges to the least fixpoint $(f(\breve{y}), \breve{y})$ of h.

Now consider the iteration given on the right hand side of the lemma. We replace x_{i+1} by $f(y_i)$ in the iteration for y_{i+1} and therefore see that $\lim_{i\to\infty} y_i = \mu z.\mu y.g(f(z), y)$. To see this, consider the Tarski iteration that is obtained for this fixpoint: $z_0 := \bot$ and $z_{i+1} := \mu y.g(f(z_i), y) = \mu y.g(x_{i+1}, y)$. We have already seen that a consequence of Lemma 3.7 is, that we can merge succeeding least fixpoint operators. Therefore, we see that $\mu z.\mu y.g(f(z), y) = \mu y.g(f(y), y) = \breve{y}$ holds. Hence, y_i converges to $\breve{y}$ and therefore, by the same argument as before, x_i converges to $f(\breve{y})$, so that the iteration also computes the least fixpoint $(f(\breve{y}), \breve{y})$ of h. □

The above iterations will be used in model checking algorithms for the modal μ-calculus that are the heart of almost all verification procedures that are presented in this book. In particular, they are used in Figure 3.8 and Figure 3.14 to optimize the model checking of vectorized fixpoint expressions.

3.2 The Basic μ-Calculus

Having established some basic notations and algorithms for fixpoints, we are now ready to consider the fragment of $\mathcal{L}_{\mathsf{spec}}$ that is usually called μ-calculus. Actually, 'calculus' is not a good name for a language, since a calculus usually consists of more than a language, namely also of some rules and axioms for that language to derive the valid theorems. The μ-calculus is a logic that is based on the computation of fixpoints of functions $f : 2^{\mathcal{S}} \to 2^{\mathcal{S}}$ that map sets of states to sets of states of a given Kripke structure. We endow the powerset $2^{\mathcal{S}}$ of $\mathcal{S}$ with the set inclusion to obtain a complete lattice $(2^{\mathcal{S}}, \subseteq)$[1]. As our Kripke structures always have finitely many states, it follows that every monotonic function $f : 2^{\mathcal{S}} \to 2^{\mathcal{S}}$ is also continuous. Hence, every monotonic function $f : 2^{\mathcal{S}} \to 2^{\mathcal{S}}$ has fixpoints, in particular it has a least fixpoint and a greatest fixpoint that can be computed with the Tarski/Knaster iterations.

The functions $f : 2^{\mathcal{S}} \to 2^{\mathcal{S}}$ are sometimes called 'state transformers'. The question is now, how these state transformers f are related to formulas of our logic. This relationship is quite simple: given a formula Φ where a variable x occurs. We can define the set of states $[\![\Phi]\!]_{\mathcal{K}}$ of a structure $\mathcal{K}$ where Φ holds. Clearly, this computation depends on the set of a states $[\![x]\!]_{\mathcal{K}}$ where x holds. So, we can make $[\![\Phi]\!]_{\mathcal{K}}$ a function in $[\![x]\!]_{\mathcal{K}}$ by changing the labels of the variable x in the Kripke structure. This means, we define for every formula Φ the function $f_\Phi : 2^{\mathcal{S}} \to 2^{\mathcal{S}}$ by $f_\Phi(Q) := [\![\Phi]\!]_{\mathcal{K}_x^Q}$, where $\mathcal{K}_x^Q$ is the structure that is obtained by changing the labels of the states such that exactly the states in Q are labeled by x. By the semantics of $\mathcal{L}_{\mathsf{spec}}$, it immediately follows that $[\![\mu x.\Phi]\!]_{\mathcal{K}}$ is the least fixpoint of f_Φ and that $[\![\nu x.\Phi]\!]_{\mathcal{K}}$ is the greatest fixpoint of f_Φ.

We are particularly interested in formulas Φ where the corresponding state transformer f_Φ is monotonic, since in this case, we know that fixpoints exist and we moreover know how to compute the least and greatest one. For this reason, we must impose some syntactic restrictions on Φ to ensure this. Before considering this restriction, we define the following subset of $\mathcal{L}_{\mathsf{spec}}$:

Definition 3.9 (Formulas of the μ-Calculus). *Given a finite set of variables V_Σ, the set of μ-calculus pre-formulas is the set of formulas that can be derived from the symbol S via the following grammar rules (where x represents any variable of V_Σ):*

$$S ::= x \mid \neg S \mid S \wedge S \mid S \vee S \mid \mathsf{E}P \mid \mathsf{A}P \mid \Diamond S \mid \Box S \mid \overleftarrow{\Diamond} S \mid \overleftarrow{\Box} S \mid \mu x.S \mid \nu x.S$$
$$P ::= S \mid \neg P \mid P \wedge P \mid P \vee P \mid \mathsf{X}P$$

The set of μ-calculus formulas $\mathcal{L}_\mu$ is the subset of pre-formulas where each subformula of the form $\mu x.\Phi$ or $\nu x.\Phi$ satisfies the constraint that all occurrences of x in Φ occur under an even number of negation symbols.

A subformula, where all X operators occur in the scope of a path quantifier (E or A) is a state formula, otherwise it is a path formula. The semantics of

[1] Clearly, we have $\inf(\{Q_i \mid i \in I\}) = \bigcap_{i \in I} Q_i$ and $\sup(\{Q_i \mid i \in I\}) = \bigcup_{i \in I} Q_i$.

state formulas is defined on states, while the semantics of path formulas is defined on paths of the Kripke structure. The μ-calculus is a logic that is merely based on state formulas, and indeed, in many textbooks and papers, the formulas of the μ-calculus are restricted such that each X operator must be directly preceded by a path quantifier and that every path quantifier must be immediately followed by a X operator. Hence, these papers consider the following subset of pre-formulas:

$$S ::= x \mid \neg S \mid S \wedge S \mid S \vee S \mid \Diamond S \mid \Box S \mid \overleftarrow{\Diamond} S \mid \overleftarrow{\Box} S \mid \mu x.S \mid \nu x.S$$

Obviously, this definition covers (syntactically!) only a strict subset of the above Definition 3.9, but we can show that every formula can be transformed to an equivalent one that obeys the above grammar. This is stated in the next lemma.

Lemma 3.10. *The following laws below hold for all path formulas φ_1 and φ_2 and all state formulas ψ, where we abbreviated $\Phi_{\mathsf{inf}} :\equiv \nu x.\Diamond x$ (cf. pages 81 and 106):*

$$\begin{array}{lll}
\mathsf{X}[\neg\varphi_1] = \neg\mathsf{X}\varphi_1 & \mathsf{E}\neg\varphi_1 = \neg\mathsf{A}\varphi_1 & \mathsf{A}\neg\varphi_1 = \neg\mathsf{E}\varphi_1 \\
\mathsf{X}[\varphi_1 \wedge \varphi_2] = \mathsf{X}\varphi_1 \wedge \mathsf{X}\varphi_2 & \mathsf{E}[\psi \wedge \varphi_1] = \psi \wedge \mathsf{E}\varphi_1 & \mathsf{A}[\varphi_1 \wedge \varphi_2] = \mathsf{A}\varphi_1 \wedge \mathsf{A}\varphi_2 \\
\mathsf{X}[\varphi_1 \vee \varphi_2] = \mathsf{X}\varphi_1 \vee \mathsf{X}\varphi_2 & \mathsf{E}[\varphi_1 \vee \varphi_2] = \mathsf{E}\varphi_1 \vee \mathsf{E}\varphi_2 & \mathsf{A}[\psi \vee \varphi_1] = \psi \vee \mathsf{E}\varphi_1 \\
\mathsf{EX}\psi = \Diamond(\psi \wedge \Phi_{\mathsf{inf}}) & \mathsf{E}\psi = \psi \wedge \Phi_{\mathsf{inf}} & \mathsf{A}\psi = \Phi_{\mathsf{inf}} \rightarrow \psi \\
\mathsf{AX}\psi = \Box(\Phi_{\mathsf{inf}} \rightarrow \psi) & \mathsf{EX}\varphi_1 = \mathsf{EXE}\varphi_1 & \mathsf{AX}\varphi_1 = \mathsf{AXA}\varphi_1
\end{array}$$

The proofs of the above laws are simple and are therefore omitted here. However, note the law $\mathsf{E}[\psi] = \psi \wedge \mathsf{E}1$. The formulas $\mathsf{E}\psi$ and ψ are not equivalent: while $(\mathcal{K}, s) \models \psi$ only states that ψ holds in state s, $(\mathcal{K}, s) \models \mathsf{E}\psi$ states that there is a path starting in s, and in the first state of this path, i.e. in s, the property ψ holds. Therefore, $(\mathcal{K}, s) \models \mathsf{E}\psi$ additionally says that an infinite path starts in s, this is exactly what is specified with Φ_{inf}. We could alternatively use $\mathsf{E}1$ or $\mathsf{EX}1$ to replace Φ_{inf}, but this would not eliminate the path quantifiers.

Theorem 3.11 (Normal Form of μ-Calculus Formulas). *For every formula of the μ-calculus as given in Definition 3.9, there is an equivalent formula of the μ-calculus where neither path quantifiers* E,A *nor* X *operators occur.*

Proof. Without loss of generality, we may assume that the given formula Φ is in negation normal form (see Definition 2.48 on page 84). Hence, negation symbols only occur in front of variables, which means that we can neglect the grammar rule $P ::= \neg P$. We now prove by induction how a reduced formula $\Theta(\Phi)$ can be obtained. For the state formulas, we simple define:

- $\Theta(x) := x$
- $\Theta(\neg x) := \neg x$
- $\Theta(\varphi \wedge \psi) = \Theta(\varphi) \wedge \Theta(\psi)$
- $\Theta(\varphi \vee \psi) = \Theta(\varphi) \vee \Theta(\psi)$

- $\Theta(\mu x.\varphi) = \mu x.\Theta(\varphi)$
- $\Theta(\nu x.\varphi) = \nu x.\Theta(\varphi)$
- $\Theta(\Diamond\varphi) = \Diamond(\Theta(\varphi))$
- $\Theta(\Box\varphi) = \Box(\Theta(\varphi))$
- $\Theta(\overleftarrow{\Diamond}\varphi) = \overleftarrow{\Diamond}(\Theta(\varphi))$
- $\Theta(\overleftarrow{\Box}\varphi) = \overleftarrow{\Box}(\Theta(\varphi))$
- $\Theta(\mathsf{A}\varphi) = \neg\Theta(\mathsf{E}(\mathsf{NNF}(\neg\varphi)))$

The only case that is missing is the definition of $\Theta(\mathsf{E}\Phi)$. These cases are also recursively defined on the structure of Φ. Due to the assumption that Φ is in negation normal form, we only have to consider the following four cases:

- $\Theta(\mathsf{E}\varphi) := \Theta(\varphi) \wedge \Phi_{\mathsf{inf}}$ for every state formula φ
- $\Theta(\mathsf{E}[\varphi \vee \psi]) := \Theta(\mathsf{E}\varphi) \vee \Theta(\mathsf{E}\psi)$
- $\Theta(\mathsf{EX}\varphi) := \Diamond(\Theta(\mathsf{E}\varphi)) \wedge \Phi_{\mathsf{inf}}$

The final case that is missing (which is the only interesting one) is the definition of $\Theta(\mathsf{E}[\varphi \wedge \psi])$. In this case, we compute the disjunctive normal form of $\varphi \wedge \psi$. If we obtain $\bigvee_{i\in I}\bigwedge_{j\in J_i}\varphi_{i,j}$, then we use the rule $\mathsf{E}[\varphi \vee \psi] = \mathsf{E}\varphi \vee \mathsf{E}\psi$ to shift the E quantifier over the disjunction. In the remaining cases, we have to define $\Theta(\mathsf{E}[\bigwedge_{j\in J_i}\varphi_{i,j}])$, where each $\varphi_{i,j}$ is either a variable, a negation of a variable, or it starts with X, $\Diamond$, $\Box$, $\overleftarrow{\Diamond}$, $\overleftarrow{\Box}$, E, A, μ or ν. We can combine the subformulas starting with X by the law $\mathsf{X}\varphi_1 \wedge \mathsf{X}\varphi_2 = \mathsf{X}[\varphi_1 \wedge \varphi_2]$. The final case is now of the form $\Theta(\mathsf{E}[\psi \wedge \mathsf{X}\varphi])$, where ψ is a conjunction of state formulas, hence, a state formula. We reduce this formula to $\Theta(\psi \wedge \mathsf{EX}\varphi)$. □

Therefore, we see that we can assume, without loss of generality, that our μ-calculus formulas are built up by only modal operators $\Diamond$, $\Box$, $\overleftarrow{\Diamond}$, $\overleftarrow{\Box}$, Boolean operators $\neg$, $\wedge$, $\vee$, and the fixpoint operators. In particular, we can neglect path quantifiers E, A, and the X operators.

The normal form can be even more restricted, as outlined in [29]: We can demand that in every fixpoint formula $\mu x.\Phi$, every occurrence of the variable x in Φ must be in the scope of a modal operator. We call such occurrences 'guarded' occurrences, others are called 'unguarded'. Hence, formulas like $\mu x.x \vee a$ or $\mu x.x \vee \Diamond[a \vee x]$ can be reduced. Although the following lemma is not required for the proof, it gives some insight into the materia.

Lemma 3.12 (Factorization of Positive Formulas). *Given a propositional formula Φ over the variables V_Σ where each occurrence of a variable x in Φ is positive. Then, the following holds:*

$$(1)\ \Phi = (x \wedge [\Phi]_x^1) \vee [\Phi]_x^0 \qquad (2)\ \Phi = (x \vee [\Phi]_x^0) \wedge [\Phi]_x^1$$

If, on the other hand, all occurrences of x in Φ are negative, then we have

$$(3)\ \Phi = (\neg x \wedge [\Phi]_x^0) \vee [\Phi]_x^1 \qquad (4)\ \Phi = (\neg x \vee [\Phi]_x^1) \wedge [\Phi]_x^0$$

The proof is done by simply considering the disjunctive and conjunctive normal form of Φ. It is easily seen that positive and negative occurrences remain positive and negative, respectively, when these normal forms are computed. They may only be copied into further occurrences of the same type (positive or negative). Hence, if x has only positive occurrences in Φ, then there will be no minterm where $\neg x$ occurs. The proof is then obtained by collecting the different minterms that either contain x or do not contain x, and by using some distributive laws. An alternative proof of the conjunction of (1) and (2) proceeds by a simultaneous induction on Φ, where Φ is assumed to be in negation normal form.

The next step to prove the existence of guarded normal forms as given in the following lemma. It contains some interesting properties of the μ-calculus like the unwinding and negation laws.

Lemma 3.13 (Unwinding and Negation Laws). *The following facts are valid:*

- *substitution law:* $[\![[\varphi]_x^\tau]\!]_\mathcal{K} = [\![\varphi]\!]_{\mathcal{K}_x^{[\![\tau]\!]_\mathcal{K}}}$
- $[\![\mu x.\varphi]\!]_\mathcal{K} = Q$ *iff* $Q = [\![\varphi]\!]_{\mathcal{K}_x^Q}$ *and for all* $Q' \subseteq \mathcal{S}$ *with* $Q' = [\![\varphi]\!]_{\mathcal{K}_x^{Q'}}$ *it follows* $Q \subseteq Q'$.
- $[\![\nu x.\varphi]\!]_\mathcal{K} = Q$ *iff* $Q = [\![\varphi]\!]_{\mathcal{K}_x^Q}$ *and for all* $Q' \subseteq \mathcal{S}$ *with* $Q' = [\![\varphi]\!]_{\mathcal{K}_x^{Q'}}$ *it follows* $Q' \subseteq Q$.
- *unwinding laws:* $\mu x.\varphi = [\varphi]_x^{\mu x.\varphi}$ *and* $\nu x.\varphi = [\varphi]_x^{\nu x.\varphi}$
- *negation laws:* $\neg\mu x.\varphi = \nu x.\neg [\varphi]_x^{\neg x}$ *and* $\neg\nu x.\varphi = \mu x.\neg [\varphi]_x^{\neg x}$
- *fixed point induction: suppose* $\psi = [\varphi]_x^\psi$ *holds, i.e.* ψ *is a fixpoint of* φ*, then also* $(\mu x.\varphi) \to \psi$ *and* $\psi \to \nu x.\varphi$ *hold (in every state of every structure).*
- *reduction laws ([289]):*
  - $\varphi \to \nu x.\psi$ *iff* $\varphi \to [\psi]_x^{\nu x.\psi\vee\varphi}$
  - $(\mu x.\psi) \to \varphi$ *iff* $[\psi]_x^{\nu x.\psi\vee\varphi} \to \varphi$

Proof. The substitution law can be proved by induction on φ. The second and third propositions are immediate consequences of the definition of the semantics ($[\![\mu x.\varphi]\!]_\mathcal{K}$ and $[\![\nu x.\varphi]\!]_\mathcal{K}$ are the least and greatest fixpoints of the corresponding state transformer $f_{x,\varphi}(Q) := [\![\varphi]\!]_{\mathcal{K}_x^Q}$).

The unwind law $\mu x.\varphi = [\varphi]_x^{\mu x.\varphi}$ is equivalent to $[\![\mu x.\varphi]\!]_\mathcal{K} = [\![\varphi]\!]_{\mathcal{K}_x^{[\![\mu x.\varphi]\!]_\mathcal{K}}}$ (by the substitution law). As $[\![\mu x.\varphi]\!]_\mathcal{K}$ is a fixpoint of the state transformer $f_{x,\varphi}(Q) := [\![\varphi]\!]_{\mathcal{K}_x^Q}$, the unwind laws follow.

To prove the negation laws, consider again the function $f_{x,\varphi}(Q) := [\![\varphi]\!]_{\mathcal{K}_x^Q}$ and its dual function $\widetilde{f}_{x,\varphi}(Q) := \mathcal{S} \setminus f_{x,\varphi}(\mathcal{S} \setminus Q)$. By the substitution law, it follows that $\widetilde{f}_{x,\varphi}(Q)$ is the state transformer of the formula $\neg [\varphi]_x^{\neg x}$. As $Q = f_{x,\varphi}(Q)$ is equivalent to $\mathcal{S}\setminus Q = \mathcal{S}\setminus f_{x,\varphi}(Q)$, and hence to $\mathcal{S}\setminus Q = \widetilde{f}_{x,\varphi}(\mathcal{S}\setminus Q)$, it follows that $\mathcal{S} \setminus Q$ is a fixpoint of $\widetilde{f}_{x,\varphi}$ iff Q is a fixpoint of $f_{x,\varphi}$. Therefore the least fixpoint of $f_{x,\varphi}$ is the greatest fixpoint of $\widetilde{f}_{x,\varphi}$ and vice versa.

The last proposition is trivial: $\psi = [\varphi]_x^\psi$ holds if and only if $[\![\psi]\!]_\mathcal{K} = \left[\!\left[[\varphi]_x^\psi \right]\!\right]_\mathcal{K}$ which is by the substitution law equivalent to $[\![\psi]\!]_\mathcal{K} = [\![\varphi]\!]_{\mathcal{K}_x^P}$ with

$P := [\![\psi]\!]_{\mathcal{K}}$. Hence, this means that $[\![\psi]\!]_{\mathcal{K}}$ is a fixpoint of $f_{x,\varphi}(P) := [\![\varphi]\!]_{\mathcal{K}_x^P}$. As $[\![\mu x.\varphi]\!]_{\mathcal{K}}$ and $[\![\nu x.\varphi]\!]_{\mathcal{K}}$ are the least and greatest fixpoint of $f_{x,\varphi}$, respectively, the proposition follows. □

We are now able to prove the following lemma that will, together with the previous one, provide the proof of the guarded normal form:

Lemma 3.14 (Reduction to Guarded Normal Form). *The following equations hold for all μ-calculus formulas:*

$$(1)\ (\nu x.\ \varphi \vee (x \wedge \psi)) = \nu x.\ \varphi \vee \psi \qquad (3)\ (\nu x.\ \varphi \vee x) = 1$$
$$(2)\ (\mu x.\ \varphi \wedge (x \vee \psi)) = \mu x.\ \varphi \wedge \psi \qquad (4)\ (\mu x.\ \varphi \wedge x) = 0$$

Proof. (3) follows immediately from (1) by instantiating $\psi = 1$. Also, (4) follows from (2) by instantiating $\psi = 0$. Moreover, (2) follows from (1) by the negation laws $\neg\mu x.\varphi = \nu x.\neg [\varphi]_x^{\neg x}$ and $\neg\nu x.\varphi = \mu x.\neg [\varphi]_x^{\neg x}$ that we proved in Lemma 3.13. So, it remains to prove (1). Therefore, we prove two implications:

- $\boxed{\Rightarrow:}$ For every Kripke structure, we have $[\![\varphi \vee (x \wedge \psi)]\!]_{\mathcal{K}} \subseteq [\![\varphi \vee \psi]\!]_{\mathcal{K}}$, so that we obtain the following inclusion $f_{x,\varphi\vee(x\wedge\psi)}(Q) \subseteq f_{x,\varphi\vee\psi}(Q)$. For this reason, we can prove by induction that $f_{x,\varphi\vee(x\wedge\psi)}(Q_i) \subseteq f_{x,\varphi\vee\psi}(P_i)$ holds for the iterations $Q_{i+1} = f_{x,\varphi\vee(x\wedge\psi)}(Q_i)$ and $P_{i+1} = f_{x,\varphi\vee\psi}(P_i)$ (starting with $P_0 = Q_0 = \{\}$). Hence, the set inclusion also holds for the finally obtained fixpoints.
- $\boxed{\Leftarrow:}$ Let $Q = [\![\nu x.\varphi \vee \psi]\!]_{\mathcal{K}}$. Then, Q is a fixpoint, i.e. we have $Q = [\![\varphi \vee \psi]\!]_{\mathcal{K}_x^Q}$. It is also easily seen then that $Q = [\![\varphi]\!]_{\mathcal{K}_x^Q} \cup (Q \cap [\![\psi]\!]_{\mathcal{K}_x^Q})$ holds (because $\varphi \vee \psi \leftrightarrow \varphi \vee (\varphi \vee \psi) \wedge \psi$ is a tautology), so that Q is also a fixpoint of $f_{x,\varphi\vee(x\wedge\psi)}$. As $[\![\nu x.\varphi \vee (x \wedge \psi)]\!]_{\mathcal{K}}$ is the greatest fixpoint of f, it therefore follows that $[\![\nu x.\varphi \vee \psi]\!]_{\mathcal{K}} \subseteq [\![\nu x.\varphi \vee (x \wedge \psi)]\!]_{\mathcal{K}}$.

□

We can use the last lemma to compute the guarded normal form, where in each subformulas $\mu x.\Phi$ and $\nu x.\Phi$, all occurrences of x must be in the scope of a modal operator (see also [289, 509]). We call such occurrences of bound variables 'guarded' occurrences, and others 'unguarded' ones.

Theorem 3.15 (Reduction to Guarded Normal Form). *For all fixpoint formulas $\mu x.\Phi$ and $\nu x.\Phi$, there are equivalent formulas $\mu x.\Psi$ and $\nu x.\Psi$ respectively, such that every occurrence of x in Ψ must be in the scope of a modal operator.*

Proof. The proof proceeds by induction along the structure of the formula. The only nontrivial cases are those for the fixpoint operators, which are furthermore dual to each other. So, consider a formula of the form $\mu x.\Phi$, where Φ has by induction hypothesis an equivalent formula Φ' in guarded normal form. Now consider the equivalent formula $\mu x.\Phi'$. Suppose Φ' contains occurrences of x that are not inside the scope of a modal operator (i.e. unguarded occurrences).

Our first transformation step will yield an equivalent formula, where all unguarded occurrences of x will be brought outside the scopes of fixpoint operators inside Φ'. To obtain this, consider a subformula $\sigma y.\Psi$ of Φ' (with $\sigma \in \{\mu, \nu\}$) where x has unguarded occurrences inside Ψ. We then replace $\sigma y.\Psi$ with the equivalent formula $[\Psi]_y^{\sigma y.\Psi}$ (see Lemma 3.13). By the induction hypothesis, all occurrences of y in Ψ are guarded and it follows that all occurrences of x in $[\Psi]_y^{\sigma y.\Psi}$ are either guarded or beyond the scope of the σy binder.

By application of the above technique, we yield a formula Φ'' equivalent to Φ where all unguarded occurrences of x are beyond the scopes of fixpoint operators. We transform Φ'' into conjunctive normal form, where we consider non-propositional subformulas (i.e. those of the forms $\Diamond\varphi$, $\Box\varphi$, $\overleftarrow{\Diamond}\varphi$, $\overleftarrow{\Box}\varphi$, $\mu y.\varphi$, and $\nu y.\varphi$) as atoms. The resulting formula looks as follows: $\mu x.(x \vee \varphi_1) \wedge \ldots (x \vee \varphi_n) \wedge \psi$, where all occurrences of x in φ_i or ψ are guarded. Note that negative occurrences of x can not occur in the conjunctive normal form, since all occurrences of x must be positive. The formula is obviously equivalent to $\mu x.(x \vee (\varphi_1 \wedge \ldots \varphi_n)) \wedge \psi$. By Lemma 3.14, the formula is furthermore equivalent to $\mu x.(\varphi_1 \wedge \ldots \varphi_n) \wedge \psi$, which is finally a formula where all occurrences of x are guarded. □

The above guarded form immediately shows that some fixpoints can be simplified. For example, the formula $\mu x.a \vee x$, which can be simplified to $\mu x.a$, is the same as a, and therefore there is no need for a Tarski / Knaster iteration.

3.3 Monotonicity of State Transformers

Recall that the Tarski / Knaster theorem (Theorem 3.6 on page 93) guarantees the existence of fixpoints, whenever the function is continuous. In our case, where the lattice is a finite one, this is equivalent to the fact that the function is monotonic. For this reason, it is important to find a criteria to ensure the monotonicity of the state transformer $f_{x,\varphi}(Q) := [\![\varphi]\!]_{\mathcal{K}_x^Q}$ of a given formula φ, a variable x, and a structure $\mathcal{K}$.

Recall that an occurrence of a subformula is positive if it is preceded by an even number of negation symbols. We have already imposed that restriction to define the set of μ-calculus formulas in Definition 3.9. We will now prove that this restriction implies that the corresponding state transformers are monotonic, so that the Tarski / Knaster theorem guarantees the existence of the fixpoints.

Note that if all occurrences of x in φ are positive, then the occurrences of x in $\neg\,[\varphi]_x^{\neg x}$ are also all positive. As we have seen in the proof of Lemma 3.13, the state transformers of φ and $\neg\,[\varphi]_x^{\neg x}$ are dual. Note further, that the monotonicity of f also implies the monotonicity of the dual function (it is not decreasing, but increasing like f).

An important consequence of Lemma 3.13 is that we can establish a negation normal form for μ-calculus formulas that has already been stated in Lemma 2.48 on page 84. This simplifies the following considerations. For example, it simplifies the proof of the following lemma that states that the fixpoint operators themselves are monotonic functions. In other words, given a function $f(x, y)$ that is monotonic in both arguments, then the functions $g(x) := \mu y.f(x, y)$ and $h(y) := \mu x.f(x, y)$ are also monotonic.

Lemma 3.16 (Monotonicity of Fixpoint Operators). *Given a Kripke structure $\mathcal{K} = (\mathcal{I}, \mathcal{S}, \mathcal{R}, \mathcal{L})$ over some variables V_Σ and a μ-calculus formula Φ where variables $x, y \in V_\Sigma$ occur such that the following properties are fulfilled:*

M1: $\forall P_1, P_2, Q \subseteq \mathcal{S}.\ P_1 \subseteq P_2 \to [\![\Phi]\!]_{K_{x,y}^{P_1,Q}} \subseteq [\![\Phi]\!]_{K_{x,y}^{P_2,Q}}$

M2: $\forall Q_1, Q_2, P \subseteq \mathcal{S}.\ Q_1 \subseteq Q_2 \to [\![\Phi]\!]_{K_{x,y}^{P,Q_1}} \subseteq [\![\Phi]\!]_{K_{x,y}^{P,Q_2}}$

Then, we have $\forall P_1, P_2 \subseteq \mathcal{S}.\ P_1 \subseteq P_2 \to [\![\mu y.\Phi]\!]_{K_x^{P_1}} \subseteq [\![\mu y.\Phi]\!]_{K_x^{P_2}} \wedge [\![\nu y.\Phi]\!]_{K_x^{P_1}} \subseteq [\![\nu y.\Phi]\!]_{K_x^{P_2}}$

Proof. Given $P_1, P_2 \subseteq \mathcal{S}$ with $P_1 \subseteq P_2$, we define $R_1 := [\![\mu y.\Phi]\!]_{K_x^{P_1}}$ and $R_2 := [\![\mu y.\Phi]\!]_{K_x^{P_2}}$. Due to reasons of readability, we define for all $P, Q \subseteq \mathcal{S}$ the function $f(P, Q) := [\![\Phi]\!]_{K_{x,y}^{P,Q}}$. Due to the Tarski/Knaster theorem, we already know that R_1 and R_2 can be computed by fixpoint iterations, i.e., $R_i := \lim_{j\to\infty} R_{i,j}$ for the iterations $R_{i,0} := \{\}$ and $R_{i,j+1} := f(P_i, R_{i,j})$ $(i \in \{1, 2\})$.

We now prove by induction on j that $\forall j \in \mathbb{N}.R_{1,j} \subseteq R_{2,j}$ holds. The induction base where $j = 0$ holds, is clear, since $R_{1,0} = \{\} \subseteq \{\} = R_{2,0}$ holds. In the induction step, we have to prove that $R_{1,j+1} \subseteq R_{2,j+1}$ holds, provided that $R_{1,j} \subseteq R_{2,j}$ holds. By our definition, $R_{1,j+1} \subseteq R_{2,j+1}$ is equivalent to $f(P_1, R_{1,j}) \subseteq f(P_2, R_{2,j})$, which we moreover reduce by the transitivity of $\subseteq$ to (1) $f(P_1, R_{1,j}) \subseteq f(P_2, R_{1,j})$ and (2) $f(P_2, R_{1,j}) \subseteq f(P_2, R_{2,j})$. (1) holds due to our assumption $P_1 \subseteq P_2$ and the property **M1**, and (2) holds due to the induction hypothesis and property **M2**. Hence, we have $\forall j \in \mathbb{N}.R_{1,j} \subseteq R_{2,j}$, and therefore also $R_1 \subseteq R_2$, i.e. $[\![\mu y.\Phi]\!]_{K_x^{P_1}} \subseteq [\![\mu y.\Phi]\!]_{K_x^{P_2}}$. The proof for the monotonicity of the greatest fixpoint operator follows the same lines. □

Using these facts, it is now possible to prove that the state transformer of every μ-calculus formula is monotonic. The important consequence is then, that the Tarski/Knaster theorem will become the heart of our model checking procedure for the μ-calculus.

Theorem 3.17 (Monotonicity of State Transformers). *Given a μ-calculus formula φ,where all occurrences of a variable $x \in V_\Sigma$ are positive. Then, for every Kripke structure $\mathcal{K}$, the corresponding state transformer $f_{x,\varphi}(Q) := [\![\varphi]\!]_{K_x^Q}$ is a monotonic function.*

Proof. From Lemma 3.13, we may assume that φ is in negation normal form. The proof is then done by induction on φ. In the following cases, we assume that $P, Q \subseteq \mathcal{S}$ are arbitrary sets with $P \subseteq Q$.

$\boxed{\Phi \in V_\Sigma:}$ In the case of $\Phi \equiv x$, we have $f_{x,x}(P) = [\![x]\!]_{\mathcal{K}_x^P} = P \subseteq Q = [\![x]\!]_{\mathcal{K}_x^Q} = f_{x,x}(Q)$. If Φ is a different variable, say y, then $f_{x,y}(P) = [\![y]\!]_{\mathcal{K}_x^P} = [\![y]\!]_{\mathcal{K}} = [\![y]\!]_{\mathcal{K}_x^Q} = f_{x,y}(Q)$.

$\boxed{\Phi \equiv \neg\varphi:}$ In this case, φ is a variable, since Φ is in negation normal form. As all occurrences of x must be positive in Φ, it follows that φ is a variable different from x, say y. Then, we have $f_{x,\neg y}(P) = [\![\neg y]\!]_{\mathcal{K}_x^P} = [\![\neg y]\!]_{\mathcal{K}} = [\![\neg y]\!]_{\mathcal{K}_x^Q} = f_{x,\neg y}(Q)$.

$\boxed{\Phi \equiv \varphi \wedge \psi \text{ and } \Phi \equiv \varphi \vee \psi:}$ All occurrences of x in φ and ψ must also be positive. Therefore, by induction hypothesis, the functions $f_{x,\varphi}$ and $f_{x,\psi}$ are monotonic. As $f_{x,\varphi\wedge\psi}(P) = f_{x,\varphi}(P) \cap f_\psi(P)$ and $f_{x,\varphi\vee\psi}(P) = f_\varphi(P) \cup f_\psi(P)$ hold, we conclude that also $f_{x,\Phi}$ is monotonic.

$\boxed{\Phi \equiv \Diamond\varphi, \Phi \equiv \Box\varphi, \Phi \equiv \overleftarrow{\Diamond}\varphi, \text{ and } \Phi \equiv \overleftarrow{\Box}\varphi:}$ By the induction hypothesis, all occurrences of x in φ are positive, and hence the induction hypothesis applies to φ. Hence, $f_{x,\varphi}$ is monotonic. The rest follows from the facts that the functions that map Q to $\mathsf{pre}_\exists^{\mathcal{R}}(Q)$, $\mathsf{pre}_\forall^{\mathcal{R}}(Q)\mathsf{suc}_\exists^{\mathcal{R}}(Q)$, and $\mathsf{suc}_\forall^{\mathcal{R}}(Q)$ are monotonic (cf. Lemma 2.6 on page 49), and that the composition of monotonic functions is also monotonic.

$\boxed{\Phi \equiv \mu y.\varphi \text{ and } \Phi \equiv \nu y.\varphi:}$ By the induction hypothesis, all occurrences of x in φ are positive. Furthermore, all occurrences of y in φ are positive, since the formula must obey the restrictions we have given. Hence, the function $f(P,Q) := [\![\varphi]\!]_{\mathcal{K}_{x,y}^{P,Q}}$ is monotonic in both arguments, and therefore it follows by the previous lemma that the function $f_{x,\mu y.\varphi}(P) := [\![\mu y.\varphi]\!]_{\mathcal{K}_x^P}$ is also monotonic.

□

By the above theorem, we now know that all state transformers that we obtain from μ-calculus formulas are monotonic. Therefore, the Tarski/Knaster theorem shows us how we can compute the semantics of the μ-calculus formulas. In particular, we obtain the following corollary from the above theorem and the Tarski/Knaster theorem:

Corollary 3.18 (Tarski-Knaster Theorem for μ-Calculus). *Let $\mathcal{K}$ be a Kripke structure over the variables V_Σ and let $\mu x.\varphi$ and $\nu x.\varphi$ be μ-calculus formulas over the variables V_Σ. Then, we consider the following iterations:*

$$\begin{array}{ll} Q_0 := \{\} & R_0 := \mathcal{S} \\ Q_{i+1} := [\![\varphi]\!]_{\mathcal{K}_x^{Q_i}} & R_{i+1} := [\![\varphi]\!]_{\mathcal{K}_x^{R_i}} \end{array}$$

It follows that there are numbers $n, m \in \mathbb{N}$ such that $Q_n = Q_{n+1}$ and $R_m = R_{m+1}$ hold. For these numbers, we have $Q_n := [\![\mu x.\varphi]\!]_{\mathcal{K}}$ and $R_m := [\![\nu x.\varphi]\!]_{\mathcal{K}}$.

With the above corollary, we have finally proved that the semantics of our μ-calculus formulas is well-defined. Moreover, the Tarski-Knaster iteration gives us an algorithm to compute the semantics (see next section). Note, however, that state transformers of formulas that do not fulfill the requirement that the bound variable has only positive occurrences, may also have fixpoints. However, this is not guaranteed. Let us now consider some examples, where we can apply the previous results.

$\boxed{\sigma x.x:}$ The state transformer is $f_{x,x}(Q) := [\![x]\!]_{\mathcal{K}_x^Q} = Q$. Clearly, every set $Q \subseteq \mathcal{S}$ is a fixpoint of $f_{x,x}$, and therefore, we conclude that $[\![\mu x.x]\!]_{\mathcal{K}} = \{\}$ and $[\![\nu x.x]\!]_{\mathcal{K}} = \mathcal{S}$.

$\boxed{\sigma x.\neg x:}$ This is not a μ-calculus formula, so the semantics need not be defined. The state transformer is $f_{x,\neg x}(Q) := [\![\neg x]\!]_{\mathcal{K}_x^Q} = \mathcal{S} \setminus Q$. If $f_{x,\neg x}$ would have a fixpoint, then there would be a set P with $P = \mathcal{S} \setminus P$, which is however not the case. Hence, the expression has no meaning.

$\boxed{\sigma x.x \vee \varphi:}$ The state transformer is $f_{x,x\vee\varphi}(Q) := [\![x \vee \varphi]\!]_{\mathcal{K}_x^Q} = Q \cup [\![\varphi]\!]_{\mathcal{K}}$. Hence, the set of fixpoints of $f_{x,x\vee\varphi}$ is $\{Q \subseteq \mathcal{S} \mid Q = Q \cup [\![\varphi]\!]_{\mathcal{K}}\}$, i.e., the set $\{Q \subseteq \mathcal{S} \mid [\![\varphi]\!]_{\mathcal{K}} \subseteq Q\}$. Therefore all supersets of $[\![\varphi]\!]_{\mathcal{K}}$ are fixpoints, and therefore, it follows that $[\![\mu x.x \vee \varphi]\!]_{\mathcal{K}} = [\![\varphi]\!]_{\mathcal{K}}$ and $[\![\nu x.x \vee \varphi]\!]_{\mathcal{K}} = \mathcal{S}$.

$\boxed{\sigma x.x \wedge \varphi:}$ The set of fixpoints of the state transformer is $\{Q \subseteq \mathcal{S} \mid Q = Q \cap [\![\varphi]\!]_{\mathcal{K}}\}$, i.e. the set $\{Q \subseteq \mathcal{S} \mid Q \subseteq [\![\varphi]\!]_{\mathcal{K}}\}$. Therefore all subsets of $[\![\varphi]\!]_{\mathcal{K}}$ are fixpoints and therefore, it follows that $[\![\mu x.x \vee \varphi]\!]_{\mathcal{K}} = \{\}$ and $[\![\nu x.x \vee \varphi]\!]_{\mathcal{K}} = [\![\varphi]\!]_{\mathcal{K}}$.

$\boxed{\sigma x.\neg x \vee \varphi:}$ This is not a μ-calculus formula, so it may not make sense. The set of fixpoints of the state transformer is $\{Q \subseteq \mathcal{S} \mid Q = (\mathcal{S}\setminus Q) \cup [\![\varphi]\!]_{\mathcal{K}}\}$. In particular, a fixpoint Q must satisfy $\mathcal{S} \setminus Q \subseteq Q$ which can not be satisfied. Therefore, no fixpoint exists and the semantics of the formula can not be defined.

$\boxed{\sigma x.\neg x \wedge \varphi:}$ The set of fixpoints is $\{Q \subseteq \mathcal{S} \mid Q = (\mathcal{S}\setminus Q) \cap [\![\varphi]\!]_{\mathcal{K}}\}$. In particular, a fixpoint Q must satisfy $Q \subseteq \mathcal{S} \setminus Q$ which can not be satisfied. Again, no fixpoint exists and the semantics of the formula can not be defined.

$\boxed{\mu x.\Diamond x:}$ The set of fixpoints is $\{Q \subseteq \mathcal{S} \mid Q = \mathsf{pre}_\exists^{\mathcal{R}}(Q)\}$. Hence, it is easily seen that $[\![\mu x.\Diamond x]\!]_{\mathcal{K}} = \{\}$ holds, since $\{\} = \mathsf{pre}_\exists^{\mathcal{R}}(\{\})$.

$\boxed{\Phi_{\mathsf{inf}} \equiv \nu x.\Diamond x:}$ We can compute this fixpoint by the iteration $Q_0 := \mathcal{S}$ and $Q_{i+1} := \mathsf{pre}_\exists^{\mathcal{R}}(Q_i)$, and we know that $\lim_{i\to\infty} Q_i = \bigcap_{i=0}^{\infty} Q_i$ holds. It is easily seen by induction that $Q_n = \{s_0 \in \mathcal{S} \mid \exists s_1, \ldots, s_n \in \mathcal{S}. \bigwedge_{i=1}^{n}(s_{i-1}, s_i) \in \mathcal{R}\}$ holds. We now define $\mathcal{S}_{\mathsf{inf}} := \{s \in \mathcal{S} \mid \mathsf{Paths}_{\mathcal{K}}(s) \neq \{\}\}$, i.e., $\mathcal{S}_{\mathsf{inf}}$ is the set of states where at least one infinite path starts, and prove $\mathcal{S}_{\mathsf{inf}} = \bigcap_{i=0}^{\infty} Q_i$. First of all, note that for every n the inclusion $\mathcal{S}_{\mathsf{inf}} \subseteq Q_n$ holds, so that $\mathcal{S}_{\mathsf{inf}} \subseteq \bigcap_{i=0}^{\infty} Q_i$ follows. To prove the converse, assume that $\bigcap_{i=0}^{\infty} Q_i \not\subseteq \mathcal{S}_{\mathsf{inf}}$ would hold, i.e., there is a state $s \in \bigcap_{i=0}^{\infty} Q_i$, but $s \notin \mathcal{S}_{\mathsf{inf}}$. Because of the latter, all paths starting in s lead to deadend states. Let n now be the maximum length of all the finite paths starting in s, then it follows that $s \notin Q_{n+1}$ and therefore $s \notin \bigcap_{i=0}^{\infty} Q_i$, which is a contradiction. Therefore, it follows that $[\![\nu x.\Diamond x]\!]_{\mathcal{K}} = \mathcal{S}_{\mathsf{inf}}$.

$\boxed{\Phi_{\mathsf{allfin}} \equiv \mu x.\Box x:}$ By the negation law, we obtain $\mu x.\Box x = \neg\nu.\Diamond x$, so this example has already been discussed. The fixpoint describes the set of states that have no infinite path.

$\boxed{\sigma x.\varphi \wedge \Diamond x:}$ All fixpoints must fulfill the condition $Q = [\![\varphi]\!]_{\mathcal{K}} \cap \mathsf{pre}_{\exists}^{\mathcal{R}}(Q)$. Therefore, it is easily seen that $[\![\mu x.\varphi \wedge \Diamond x]\!]_{\mathcal{K}} = \{\}$. By the Tarski/Knaster iteration it is seen that $[\![\nu x.\varphi \wedge \Diamond x]\!]_{\mathcal{K}} = [\![\mathsf{EG}\varphi]\!]_{\mathcal{K}}$, i.e., $[\![\nu x.\varphi \wedge \Diamond x]\!]_{\mathcal{K}}$ is the set of states where at least one (infinite) path starts whose states belong to $[\![\varphi]\!]_{\mathcal{K}}$ (the formal argumentation is similar to the one of Φ_{inf}).

$\boxed{\sigma x.\varphi \vee \Box x:}$ By the negation law, and the previous example, it follows that $[\![\nu x.\varphi \vee \Box x]\!]_{\mathcal{K}} = \mathcal{S}$ and $[\![\mu x.\varphi \vee \Box x]\!]_{\mathcal{K}} = [\![\mathsf{AF}\varphi]\!]_{\mathcal{K}}$, i.e., the set of states where all (infinite) paths visit at least once the set $[\![\varphi]\!]_{\mathcal{K}}$.

$\boxed{\sigma x.\varphi \vee \Diamond x:}$ All fixpoints must fulfill the condition $Q = [\![\varphi]\!]_{\mathcal{K}} \cup \mathsf{pre}_{\exists}^{\mathcal{R}}(Q)$, and therefore all fixpoints must contain $[\![\varphi]\!]_{\mathcal{K}}$. $[\![\mu x.\varphi \vee \Diamond x]\!]_{\mathcal{K}}$ is the set of states that have a possibly finite path that visits a state in $[\![\varphi]\!]_{\mathcal{K}}$ (check this with the Tarski/Knaster iteration: Q_{i+1} is the set of states that can reach $[\![\varphi]\!]_{\mathcal{K}}$ in at most i steps). $[\![\nu x.\varphi \vee \Diamond x]\!]_{\mathcal{K}}$ additionally contains the states that have an infinite path ($\mathcal{S}_{\mathsf{inf}}$).

$\boxed{\sigma x.\varphi \wedge \Box x:}$ By the negation law and the previous example, we conclude that $[\![\nu x.\varphi \wedge \Box x]\!]_{\mathcal{K}}$ is the set of states where all infinite and finite paths must exclusively run through $[\![\varphi]\!]_{\mathcal{K}}$. $[\![\mu x.\varphi \wedge \Box x]\!]_{\mathcal{K}}$ is obtained by removing the states $\mathcal{S}_{\mathsf{inf}}$ from $[\![\nu x.\varphi \wedge \Box x]\!]_{\mathcal{K}}$. Hence, the states in $[\![\mu x.\varphi \wedge \Box x]\!]_{\mathcal{K}}$ only have finite paths that exclusively run through $[\![\varphi]\!]_{\mathcal{K}}$.

$\boxed{\sigma x.\varphi \wedge (\nu y.\Diamond y) \vee \Diamond x:}$ According to the above examples, it immediately follows that the least fixpoint is $[\![\mathsf{EF}\varphi]\!]_{\mathcal{K}}$, i.e., the set of states that have an infinite path that visits at least once the set $[\![\varphi]\!]_{\mathcal{K}}$. The greatest fixpoint is simply $\mathcal{S}_{\mathsf{inf}} = [\![\nu y.\Diamond y]\!]_{\mathcal{K}}$.

$\boxed{\sigma x.\varphi \vee \overleftarrow{\Diamond} x:}$ $\left[\!\!\left[\mu x.\varphi \vee \overleftarrow{\Diamond} x\right]\!\!\right]_{\mathcal{K}}$ is the set of states that can be reached from a state in $[\![\varphi]\!]_{\mathcal{K}}$ by a possible finite path. $\left[\!\!\left[\nu x.\varphi \vee \overleftarrow{\Diamond} x\right]\!\!\right]_{\mathcal{K}}$ adds states that can be reached by a possible finite path from a cycle of states.

$\boxed{\mathsf{Cycle}_{\varphi} :\equiv \nu y.\varphi \wedge y \wedge \overleftarrow{\Diamond} y \wedge \Diamond y:}$ This fixpoint evaluates to the subset of states in $[\![\varphi]\!]_{\mathcal{K}}$ that belong to a cycle in $[\![\varphi]\!]_{\mathcal{K}}$. Hence, it is the union of all cycles that can be formed with states in $[\![\varphi]\!]_{\mathcal{K}}$.

$\boxed{\sigma x.\varphi \wedge \Diamond\Diamond x:}$ We have $[\![\mu x.\varphi \wedge \Diamond\Diamond x]\!]_{\mathcal{K}} = \{\}$ and $[\![\nu x.\varphi \wedge \Diamond\Diamond x]\!]_{\mathcal{K}} = \{s \in \mathcal{S} \mid \exists \pi \in \mathsf{Paths}_{\mathcal{K}}(s).\forall t \in \mathbb{N}.(\mathcal{K}, \pi^{(2t)}) \models \varphi\}$ (this is the set of states that have an infinite path where in each even state φ holds). We will see later, that this is not expressible with temporal logics.

$\boxed{\sigma x.\neg x \wedge \Box x:}$ All fixpoints must fulfill the condition $Q = (\mathcal{S} \setminus Q) \cap \mathsf{pre}_{\forall}^{\mathcal{R}}(Q)$, hence, in particular $Q \subseteq (\mathcal{S} \setminus Q)$, so that we see that no fixpoint exists.

$\boxed{\mu x.\varphi \wedge x \wedge \Diamond\neg x:}$ Any fixpoint must fulfill the condition $Q = [\![\varphi]\!]_{\mathcal{K}} \cap Q \cap \mathsf{pre}_{\exists}^{\mathcal{R}}(\mathcal{S} \setminus Q)$, which is easily seen to be equivalent to $Q \subseteq [\![\varphi]\!]_{\mathcal{K}} \cap \mathsf{pre}_{\exists}^{\mathcal{R}}(\mathcal{S} \setminus$

Q). Therefore, we easily see that $[\![\mu x.\varphi \wedge x \wedge \Diamond\neg x]\!]_{\mathcal{K}} = \{\}$. However, $\nu x.\varphi \wedge x \wedge \Diamond\neg x$ need not exist. This should be the largest set Q that satisfies the condition $Q \subseteq [\![\varphi]\!]_{\mathcal{K}} \cap \mathsf{pre}_{\exists}^{\mathcal{R}}(\mathcal{S} \setminus Q)$.

Note that in the above examples problems have occurred only when the requirement given in Definition 3.9 (that all occurrences of the bound variable must be positive) has been violated. Hence, these formulas do not belong to the set of μ-calculus formulas that we have defined before. Note however, that there are also formulas that do not fulfill our requirements, but that also have well-defined least and greatest fixpoints.

3.4 Model Checking of the Basic μ-Calculus

In this section, we present global model checking procedures for the propositional μ-calculus. The first subsection considers a naive model checking procedure that is only based on Corollary 3.18 and Lemma 3.16. We will use this naive procedure as a basis to discuss further optimizations of the model checking procedure.

In Section 3.4.2, we will then present an improvement of this procedure which is due to Emerson and Lei [174]. This improvement is based on the observation that nestings of fixpoint operators of the same kind can be much more efficiently computed than by the naive procedure since a complete restart of the computation is not necessary.

3.4.1 A Naive Model Checking Procedure

The iteration schema of Corollary 3.18 (together with Lemma 3.16) can be directly implemented in a model checking procedure for the μ-calculus as given in Figure 3.2. Although this is only a naive model checking procedure, we will consider it as a basis for further optimizations. We will see that it gives us first hints on the critical parts of the formulas that influence the complexity of the model checking procedure.

To discuss the algorithm, we need to discuss some data structures that are used by the algorithm in advance. In particular, we use an array whose indices are the states $\mathcal{S}$ of the Kripke structure $\mathcal{K} = (\mathcal{I}, \mathcal{S}, \mathcal{R}, \mathcal{L})$ or the variables V_Σ. We therefore impose a total order on the set of states and the variables so that we can inspect them by sequentially listing their elements. Hence, sets of states can be represented as Boolean arrays[2] $a[|\mathcal{S}|]$ where $a[s] = \mathsf{true}$ encodes that state s belongs to the set a. The transition relation $\mathcal{R}$ is directly given as a list of pairs (s, s'). We assume that $[\,]$ denotes the empty list, that $\mathsf{head}(\ell)$ computes the first element of the list ℓ, and that $\mathsf{tail}(\ell)$ deletes the first element of

[2] This is very much in the spirit of symbolic model checking, although we do not make use of propositional logic representations like BDDs here.

the list ℓ. Finally, the label function is implemented as an array $L[|V_\Sigma|][|\mathcal{S}|]$ such that for every variable $x \in V_\Sigma$, $L[x]$ represents the set of states of $\mathcal{S}$, where x holds. Hence, $L[x][s] = 1$ iff $x \in \mathcal{L}(s)$. Note that $L[x]$ is therefore also an array that represents the set $[\![x]\!]_\mathcal{K}$.

It is easily seen that the set operations $\cap$, $\cup$, and also the computation of the complement set can be performed in time $O(|\mathcal{S}|)$, and that the predecessor and successor functions $\mathsf{pre}_\exists^\mathcal{R}(a)$, $\mathsf{pre}_\forall^\mathcal{R}(a)$, and $\mathsf{suc}_\exists^\mathcal{R}(a)$, $\mathsf{suc}_\forall^\mathcal{R}(a)$ can be computed in time $O(|\mathcal{R}|)$. For example, the implementations of the union function, of $\mathsf{pre}_\exists^\mathcal{R}(a)$, and of $\mathsf{suc}_\exists^\mathcal{R}(a)$ are given in Figure 3.1. The local variable c is assumed to be initialized to false, which may add additional costs of order $O(|\mathcal{S}|)$. Therefore, we should be careful and compute the worst case runtime of the predecessor function as $O(|\mathcal{S}|+|\mathcal{R}|)$. For the following, we define $|\mathcal{K}| := \max\{|\mathcal{S}|, |\mathcal{R}|\}$, so that $O(|\mathcal{S}| + |\mathcal{R}|) = O(\max\{|\mathcal{S}|, |\mathcal{R}|\}) = O(|\mathcal{K}|)$ holds. The runtime complexity of the successor and predecessor computation is then determined as $O(|\mathcal{K}|)$.

```
function union(a, b)
  c : array[1..|S|] of B;
  for all s ∈ S do
    c[s] := a[s] ∨ b[s]
  end;
  return c;
end;
```

```
function pre∃^R(a)
  c : array[1..|S|] of B;
  ℓ := R;
  while ℓ ≠ [] do
    (s, s') := head(ℓ);
    ℓ := tail(ℓ);
    if a[s'] then c[s] := true;
  end;
  return c;
end;
```

```
function suc∃^R(a)
  c : array[1..|S|] of B;
  ℓ := R;
  while ℓ ≠ [] do
    (s, s') := head(ℓ);
    ℓ := tail(ℓ);
    if a[s] then c[s'] := true;
  end;
  return c;
end;
```

Fig. 3.1. Algorithms for evaluating Boolean and modal operators

Using these algorithms, we now construct a recursive procedure to evaluate a μ-calculus expression. Note that our procedure is very much in the spirit of symbolic model checking, but we still use an explicit state space representation here. This is sufficient for us to see that the number of nestings of fixpoint formulas is crucial for the runtime required to evaluate a fixpoint formula.

Theorem 3.19 (Correctness and Complexity of $\mathcal{L}_\mu$-Model-Checking (I)). *Given a μ-calculus formula Φ and a Kripke structure $\mathcal{K} = (\mathcal{I}, \mathcal{S}, \mathcal{R}, \mathcal{L})$. Then, the function* $\mathsf{States}_\mu(\cdot)$ *given in Figure 3.2 computes the set of states* $\mathsf{States}_\mu(\Phi) \subseteq \mathcal{S}$ *where Φ holds, i.e.* $\mathsf{States}_\mu(\Phi) = [\![\Phi]\!]_\mathcal{K}$.

The worst case time complexity of the algorithm is of order $O(|\mathcal{K}|\,|\Phi|\,|\mathcal{S}|^{\mathsf{nest}(\Phi)})$, *where* $\mathsf{nest}(\Phi)$ *is the maximal number of fixpoint operator nestings in Φ, formally:*

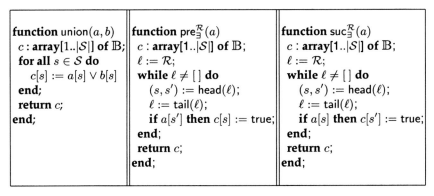

```
function States_μ(Φ)
  case Φ of
    is_var(Φ): return L[Φ];
    ¬φ       : return S \ States_μ(φ);
    φ ∧ ψ    : return States_μ(φ) ∩ States_μ(ψ);
    φ ∨ ψ    : return States_μ(φ) ∪ States_μ(ψ);
    ◇φ       : return pre∃^R(States_μ(φ));
    □φ       : return pre∀^R(States_μ(φ));
    ←◇φ      : return suc∃^R(States_μ(φ));
    ←□φ      : return suc∀^R(States_μ(φ));
    μx.φ     : L[x] := {};
               repeat
                 Q := L[x];
                 L[x] := States_μ(φ);
               until Q = L[x];
               return L[x];
    νx.φ     : return States_μ(¬μx.¬ [φ]_x^{¬x});
  end
end
```

Fig. 3.2. A simple algorithm for checking μ-calculus formulas

$\mathsf{nest}(x) := 0$	$\mathsf{nest}(\neg\varphi) := \mathsf{nest}(\varphi)$
$\mathsf{nest}(\varphi \wedge \psi) := \max(\mathsf{nest}(\varphi), \mathsf{nest}(\psi))$	$\mathsf{nest}(\varphi \vee \psi) := \max(\mathsf{nest}(\varphi), \mathsf{nest}(\psi))$
$\mathsf{nest}(\Diamond\varphi) := \mathsf{nest}(\varphi)$	$\mathsf{nest}(\Box\varphi) := \mathsf{nest}(\varphi)$
$\mathsf{nest}(\overleftarrow{\Diamond}\varphi) := \mathsf{nest}(\varphi)$	$\mathsf{nest}(\overleftarrow{\Box}\varphi) := \mathsf{nest}(\varphi)$
$\mathsf{nest}(\mu x.\varphi) := \mathsf{nest}(\varphi) + 1$	$\mathsf{nest}(\nu x.\varphi) := \mathsf{nest}(\varphi) + 1$

The correctness of the algorithm immediately follows from the semantics of the μ-calculus and Corollary 3.18 (together with Lemma 3.16). To derive its complexity, we have already seen that modal and Boolean operators can be evaluated in time $O(|\mathcal{K}|)$ and $O(|\mathcal{S}|)$, respectively. Therefore, we obtain with a suitable constant $C \in \mathbb{N}$ the following inequations for the runtime $T(\varphi)$ to evaluate the μ-calculus formula φ:

- $T(x) \leq C$
- $T(\neg\varphi) \leq C\,|\mathcal{S}| + T(\varphi)$
- $T(\varphi \wedge \psi) \leq C\,|\mathcal{S}| + T(\varphi) + T(\psi)$
- $T(\varphi \vee \psi) \leq C\,|\mathcal{S}| + T(\varphi) + T(\psi)$
- $T(\Diamond\varphi) \leq C\,|\mathcal{K}| + T(\varphi)$
- $T(\Box\varphi) \leq C\,|\mathcal{K}| + T(\varphi)$
- $T(\overleftarrow{\Diamond}\varphi) \leq C\,|\mathcal{K}| + T(\varphi)$
- $T(\overleftarrow{\Box}\varphi) \leq C\,|\mathcal{K}| + T(\varphi)$
- $T(\mu x.\varphi) \leq C\,|\mathcal{S}|\,T(\varphi)$
- $T(\nu x.\varphi) \leq C\,|\mathcal{S}|\,T(\varphi)$

It is not hard to prove by induction on Φ that $T(\Phi) \leq C\,|\mathcal{K}|\,|\Phi|\,|\mathcal{S}|^{\mathsf{nest}(\Phi)}$ holds. Recall that $|\mathcal{S}|$ is normally a very large number: State sets with more than 10^{100} states are not unusual, even after sophisticated abstractions of the systems. Therefore, by the model checking procedure given in Figure 3.2, it is only possible to check μ-calculus formulas with a small number of fixpoint nestings. The length of the μ-calculus formulas is however not so critical, as the runtime only depends linearly on it. Hence, optimizations of the algorithm should reduce the fixpoint nestings.

3.4.2 Optimization by the Alternation Depth

The algorithm given in Figure 3.2 is far from being optimal. Several optimizations have been reported in the literature that we will consider in the remainder of this chapter. To evoke the first improvement, consider what happens when nested fixpoint operators of the same kind are evaluated. For this reason, we are interested in the sequence of sets that the variables Q_0 (and Q_1) in Figure 3.2 pass through during the iterations.

If we have a nesting like $\mu x.\Phi(x, \mu y.\Psi(y))$, which means that $\mu y.\Psi(y)$ is a subformula of $\mu x.\Phi(x, \mu y.\Psi(y))$ such that the inner fixpoint $\mu y.\Psi(y)$ does not depend on the value of x that appears in the outer fixpoint formula, then this nesting is only artificial and does not contribute to the complexity: By the substitution law, it follows with a new variable ℓ that

$$[\![\mu x.\Phi(x, \mu y.\Psi(y))]\!]_{\mathcal{K}} = \left[\!\!\left[[\mu x.\Phi(x, \ell)]_{\ell}^{\mu y.\Psi(y)} \right]\!\!\right]_{\mathcal{K}} = [\![\mu x.\Phi(x, \ell)]\!]_{\mathcal{K}_{\ell}^{Q}}$$

with $Q := [\![\mu y.\Psi(y)]\!]_{\mathcal{K}}$. Hence, we need not restart the fixpoint iteration for $\ell := \mu y.\Psi(y)$ when an iteration step for the computation of $\mu x.\Phi(x, \ell)$ is performed, as the value of ℓ does not depend on x. Hence, this is a first, simple optimization of the algorithm of the previous section.

However, if $\Psi(y)$ also depends on x, this is not possible. However, another improvement can be found here. Consider the computation of such interdependent fixpoints according to the algorithm of Figure 3.2. By unrolling the function call, We will obtain a nested iteration:

$P := \{\}$;
repeat
  $R := \{\}$;
  repeat
    $R' := R$;
    $R := [\![\Psi]\!]_{\mathcal{K}_{x,y}^{P,R}}$;
  until $R' = R$; $(*R' = R = \mu y.\Psi*)$
  $P' := P$;
  $P := [\![\Phi]\!]_{\mathcal{K}_{x,y}^{P,R}}$;
until $P' = P$; $(*P' = P = \mu x.\Phi*)$

Consider how the formula $\mu x.\Phi(x, \mu y.\Psi(x,y))$ is evaluated, where $\Psi(x,y)$ denotes a formula where both x and y occurs. For convenience, we define $f_\Phi(P,Q) := [\![\Phi(x,y)]\!]_{\mathcal{K}_{x,y}^{P,Q}}$, $f_\Psi(P,Q) := [\![\Psi(x,y))]\!]_{\mathcal{K}_{x,y}^{P,Q}}$, and $g_\Psi(P) := [\![\mu y.\Psi(x,y)]\!]_{\mathcal{K}_x^P}$. Of course, f_Φ, f_Ψ and g_Ψ are monotonic in all arguments. Note that by these definitions, we have the following facts:

$$
\begin{array}{l}
M_{\Phi,1} : \forall P, P', Q \subseteq \mathcal{S}.\ P \subseteq P' \to f_\Phi(P,Q) \subseteq f_\Phi(P',Q) \\
M_{\Phi,2} : \forall P, Q, Q' \subseteq \mathcal{S}.\ Q \subseteq Q' \to f_\Phi(P,Q) \subseteq f_\Phi(P,Q') \\
M_{\Psi,1} : \forall P, P', Q \subseteq \mathcal{S}.\ P \subseteq P' \to f_\Psi(P,Q) \subseteq f_\Psi(P',Q) \\
M_{\Psi,2} : \forall P, Q, Q' \subseteq \mathcal{S}.\ Q \subseteq Q' \to f_\Psi(P,Q) \subseteq f_\Psi(P,Q') \\
M_{\Psi,3} : \forall P, P' \subseteq \mathcal{S}.\ P \subseteq P' \to g_\Psi(P) \subseteq g_\Psi(P) \\
F_\Psi : \forall P \subseteq \mathcal{S}.\ g_\Psi(P) = f_\Psi(P, g_\Psi(P))
\end{array}
$$

$M_{\Phi,1}$, $M_{\Phi,2}$, $M_{\Psi,1}$, and $M_{\Psi,2}$ are due to the assumptions that Φ and Ψ are monotonic in each argument. $M_{\Psi,3}$ follows directly from Lemma 3.16, and F_Ψ is simply due to the fact that $g_\Psi(P)$ is a fixpoint of the function that maps a set Q to $f_\Psi(P,Q)$ (where P is arbitrary, but fixed).

We already know that $[\![\mu x.\Phi(x, \mu y.\Psi(x,y))]\!]_{\mathcal{K}}$ can be computed by a fixpoint computation according to Theorem 3.18, where we start with $P_0 := \{\}$ and define $P_{i+1} := f_\Phi(P_i, g_\Psi(P_i))$. Hence, in each iteration i, we have to compute another fixpoint, namely $\widehat{R}_i := g_\Psi(P_i) := [\![\mu y.\Psi(x,y)]\!]_{\mathcal{K}_x^{P_i}}$. We do this by another iteration, where we successively compute the sets $R_{i,0} := \{\}$ and $R_{i,j+1} := f_\Psi(P_i, R_{i,j})$. For these sets, we can easily prove the following facts:

$$
\begin{array}{l}
F_1 : \forall j.\forall i.\ R_{i,j} \subseteq R_{i,j+1} \\
F_2 : \forall i.\ P_i \subseteq P_{i+1} \\
F_3 : \forall j.\forall i.\ R_{i,j} \subseteq R_{i+1,j} \\
F_4 : \forall i.\ \widehat{R}_i \subseteq f_\Psi(P_{i+1}, \widehat{R}_i), \text{ i.e. } \forall i.\ g_\Psi(P_i) \subseteq f_\Psi(P_{i+1}, g_\Psi(P_i)) \\
F_5 : \forall i.\ g_\Psi(P_i) = \lim_{j\to\infty} R_{i,j}
\end{array}
$$

F_1 and F_2 follow directly from the proof of the Tarski/Knaster theorem, but we repeat their proofs here: F_1 is proved by induction on j: The base case $j = 0$ is trivial since $R_{i,0} := \{\}$. In the induction step, we have to prove $R_{i,j+1} \subseteq R_{i,j+2}$, i.e., $f_\Psi(P_i, R_{i,j}) \subseteq f_\Psi(P_i, R_{i,j+1})$, which is reduced by modus ponens with $M_{\Psi,2}$ to the induction hypothesis $R_{i,j} \subseteq R_{i,j+1}$.

F_2 is also proved by induction: The base case, where $i = 0$ holds is again trivial due to the definition $P_0 := \{\}$. In the induction step, we have to prove $P_{i+1} \subseteq P_{i+2}$, i.e. $f_\Phi(P_i, g_\Psi(P_i)) \subseteq f_\Phi(P_{i+1}, g_\Psi(P_{i+1}))$. By induction hypothesis $P_i \subseteq P_{i+1}$, it follows by modus ponens with $M_{\Psi,3}$ that $g_\Psi(P_i) \subseteq g_\Psi(P_{i+1})$ holds, which can be used to prove with $M_{\Phi,2}$ that $f_\Phi(P_i, g_\Psi(P_i)) \subseteq f_\Phi(P_i, g_\Psi(P_{i+1}))$ holds. By $M_{\Phi,1}$ and the induction hypothesis, we obtain $f_\Phi(P_i, g_\Psi(P_{i+1})) \subseteq f_\Phi(P_{i+1}, g_\Psi(P_{i+1}))$, so that our result follows from transitivity of $\subseteq$.

F_3 is trivial for $j = 0$ since $R_{i,0} := \{\}$ holds. In the induction step, we have to prove $R_{i,j+1} \subseteq R_{i+1,j+1}$, i.e., $f_\Psi(P_i, R_{i,j}) \subseteq f_\Psi(P_{i+1}, R_{i+1,j})$. By modus ponens with the induction hypothesis and $M_{\Psi,2}$, we immediately deduce that $f_\Psi(P_i, R_{i,j}) \subseteq f_\Psi(P_i, R_{i+1,j})$ holds. The rest follows from $M_{\Psi,1}$ together with F_2.

F_4 is proved as follows: by F_Ψ, it first follows that $g_\Psi(P_i) = f_\Psi(P_i, g_\Psi(P_i))$ holds for an arbitrary i. By F_2 and $M_{\Psi,1}$, we then obtain $f_\Psi(P_i, g_\Psi(P_i)) \subseteq f_\Psi(P_{i+1}, g_\Psi(P_i))$, so that by transitivity of $\subseteq$, we conclude the result.

F_5 is clear by Tarski's theorem. Therefore, we have the following relationships between the fixpoint approximations (we have listed the iterations for P_i in a vertical column to indicate that these are influenced by the results of the iterations to compute $\widehat{R}_{i-1}$):

$$
\begin{array}{llllllll}
P_0 & & & & & & & \\
\rotatebox{90}{$\supseteq$} & \{\} = R_{0,0} \subseteq & R_{0,1} \subseteq & R_{0,2} \subseteq \ldots \subseteq & R_{0,n_0-1} = & R_{0,n_0} = & \widehat{R}_0 & \subseteq f_\Psi(P_1, \widehat{R}_0) \\
P_1 & \quad \cap\!| & \cap\!| & \cap\!| & \cap\!| & \cap\!| & \cap\!| & \\
\rotatebox{90}{$\supseteq$} & \{\} = R_{1,0} \subseteq & R_{1,1} \subseteq & R_{1,2} \subseteq \ldots \subseteq & R_{1,n_1-1} = & R_{1,n_1} = & \widehat{R}_1 & \subseteq f_\Psi(P_2, \widehat{R}_1) \\
P_2 & \quad \cap\!| & \cap\!| & \cap\!| & \cap\!| & \cap\!| & \cap\!| & \\
\rotatebox{90}{$\supseteq$} & \{\} = R_{2,0} \subseteq & R_{2,1} \subseteq & R_{2,2} \subseteq \ldots \subseteq & R_{2,n_2-1} = & R_{2,n_2} = & \widehat{R}_2 & \subseteq f_\Psi(P_3, \widehat{R}_2) \\
P_3 & \quad \cap\!| & \cap\!| & \cap\!| & \cap\!| & \cap\!| & \cap\!| & \\
\vdots & \quad \vdots & \vdots & \vdots & \vdots & \vdots & \vdots & \\
P_{m-1} & \quad \cap\!| & \cap\!| & \cap\!| & \cap\!| & \cap\!| & \cap\!| & \\
\| & \{\} = R_{m,0} \subseteq & R_{m,1} \subseteq & R_{m,2} \subseteq \ldots \subseteq & R_{m,n_m-1} = & R_{m,n_m} = & \widehat{R}_m & \subseteq f_\Psi(P_{m+1}, \widehat{R}_m) \\
P_m & & & & & & &
\end{array}
$$

The crucial observation is however fact F_4, which implies that $\widehat{R}_i$ is a prefixed point of the function that maps R to $f_\Psi(P_{i+1}, R)$. For Tarski's fixpoint iteration, *it is sufficient to start with a prefixed point, i.e., an approximation of the desired least fixpoint that is less than the fixpoint, instead of the minimal set* $\{\}$. *Therefore, there is no need to reset the variable R in the previously considered computation, instead we can retain its current value*, i.e., the last approximation we had computed for $\mu y.\Psi(x, y)$. We therefore obtain the following modification of the computation of $[\![\mu x.\Phi(x, \mu y.\Psi(x, y))]\!]_\mathcal{K}$ given on the right hand side of Figure 3.3 (for comparison, we have listed the previous algorithm on the left hand side).

The algorithms only differ in the initialization of R. The algorithm on the left hand side initializes R in each iteration of the outer loop, but the algorithm on the right hand side will keep the previous value of R instead. We will see that the modification has a dramatic impact on runtime for the computation of the fixpoints. Before we present a modified model checking procedure for the μ-calculus, we first recall that Tarski's fixpoint iteration remains correct when we start with prefixed points. This is given in the following corollary that we derive from Theorem 3.6 and Lemma 3.17:

Corollary 3.20 (Optimized Fixpoint Iteration). *Let $\mathcal{K} = (\mathcal{I}, \mathcal{S}, \mathcal{R}, \mathcal{L})$ be a Kripke structure over some variables V_Σ, Φ be a state formula and $x \in V_\Sigma$ such that all occurrences of x in Φ are positive. Moreover, let $Q_0, R_0 \subseteq \mathcal{S}$ be sets of states such that the following conditions hold:*

```
P := {};                                  P := {};
repeat                                    R := {};
    R := {};                              repeat
    repeat                                    repeat
        R' := R;                                  R' := R;
        R := [[Ψ]]_{K_{x,y}^{P,R}};               R := [[Ψ]]_{K_{x,y}^{P,R}};
    until R' = R; (*R' = R = μy.Ψ*)           until R' = R; (*R' = R = μy.Ψ*)
    P' := P;                                  P' := P;
    P := [[Φ]]_{K_{x,y}^{P,R}};               P := [[Φ]]_{K_{x,y}^{P,R}};
until P' = P; (*P' = P = μx.Φ*)           until P' = P; (*P' = P = μx.Φ*)
```

Fig. 3.3. Improvement of nested fixpoint computations of the same kind

(1) $Q_0 \subseteq [\![\Phi]\!]_{\mathcal{K}_x^{Q_0}}$	(3) $[\![\Phi]\!]_{\mathcal{K}_x^{R_0}} \subseteq R_0$
(2) $Q_0 \subseteq [\![\mu x.\Phi]\!]_{\mathcal{K}}$	(4) $[\![\mu x.\Phi]\!]_{\mathcal{K}} \subseteq R_0$

Then, the iterations $Q_{i+1} := [\![\Phi]\!]_{\mathcal{K}_x^{Q_i}}$ *and* $R_{i+1} := [\![\Phi]\!]_{\mathcal{K}_x^{R_i}}$ *starting in* Q_0 *and* R_0*, respectively converge, i.e. there are numbers* $n, m \in \mathbb{N}$ *such that* $Q_n = Q_{n+1}$ *and* $R_m = R_{m+1}$ *hold. Moreover,* $Q_n := [\![\mu x.\Phi]\!]_{\mathcal{K}}$ *and* $R_m := [\![\nu x.\Phi]\!]_{\mathcal{K}}$*.*

The above corollary is a generalization of the one we used for the construction of the algorithm in Figure 3.2, as can be seen by the choices $Q_0 := \{\}$ and $R_0 := \mathcal{S}$, it tells us that we need not necessarily start with $\{\}$ and $\mathcal{S}$, respectively. Instead, initial approximations that fulfill the above constraints were sufficient.

Using the algorithm given on the right hand side of Figure 3.3, we successively compute the sets $R'_{0,0} := \{\}$, $R'_{i+1,0} := g_\Psi(P_i)$, and $R'_{i,j+1} := f_\Psi(P_i, R'_{i,j})$. It then follows by the above theorem that the same fixpoints are computed, i.e., we can now prove the following fact F_6:

$$F_6 : \ \forall i.\ g_\Psi(P_i) = \lim_{j\to\infty} R'_{i,j}$$

Note that we have already abbreviated $\widehat{R}_i := g_\Psi(P_i)$ and know that $\widehat{R}_i = \lim_{j\to\infty} R_{i,j}$ holds. We prove F_6 by induction on i: For $i = 0$, we have for any $j \in \mathbb{N}$ the equation $R'_{0,j} = R_{0,j}$, so that everything follows from F_5. For the induction step, we first notice that by induction hypothesis, we have $g_\Psi(P_i) = \lim_{j\to\infty} R'_{i,j}$, and therefore it follows that $\widehat{R}_i = \lim_{j\to\infty} R'_{i,j}$ holds. Hence, by F_4, we have $\widehat{R}_i \subseteq f_\Psi(P_{i+1}, \widehat{R}_i)$, so that the first assumption of the above theorem is fulfilled. The second assumption, i.e., $\widehat{R}_i \subseteq \widehat{R}_{i+1}$ is also fulfilled due to $M_{\Psi,3}$ and F_2. Therefore, by the above theorem, we conclude $g_\Psi(P_{i+1}) = \lim_{j\to\infty} R'_{i+1,j}$.

While we have only considered one nesting of fixpoint formulas of the same kind, the principle can be extended to an arbitrary deep nesting of fixpoint operators of the same kind. These observations lead to a new algorithm that is given in Figure 3.4.

```
function Initialize(σ, Φ)
  case Φ of
    is_var(Φ)      : ;
    ¬φ             : Initialize(σ, φ);
    φ ∧ ψ, φ ∨ ψ   : Initialize(σ, φ); Initialize(σ, ψ);
    ◇φ, □φ         : Initialize(σ, φ);
    ←◇ φ, ←□ φ     : Initialize(σ, φ);
    μx.φ           : if σ = ν then L[x] := {} end;
    νx.φ           : if σ = μ then L[x] := S end;
  end
end

function States_μ(Φ) =
  case Φ of
    is_var(Φ): return {s ∈ S | Φ ∈ L(s)};
    ¬φ       : return S \ States_μ(φ);
    φ ∧ ψ    : return States_μ(φ) ∩ States_μ(ψ);
    φ ∨ ψ    : return States_μ(φ) ∪ States_μ(ψ);
    ◇φ       : return pre_∃^R(States_μ(φ));
    □φ       : return pre_∀^R(States_μ(φ));
    ←◇ φ     : return suc_∃^R(States_μ(φ));
    ←□ φ     : return suc_∀^R(States_μ(φ));
    σx.φ     : Initialize(σ, φ);
               repeat
                 Q := L[x];
                 L[x] := States_μ(φ);
               until Q = L[x];
               return L[x];
  end
end
```

Fig. 3.4. Improved algorithm for checking μ-calculus formulas

The algorithm uses the same data structures than the previous one. In particular, it stores for every bound variable x the current approximation in the array $L[x]$. Hence, we initialize $L[x] := \{\}$ for least fixpoints and $L[x] := \mathcal{S}$ for greatest fixpoints before starting the model checking. The algorithm then works like the one we have previously considered. The difference is that in the computation of a fixpoint $\sigma x.\varphi$ with $\sigma \in \{\mu, \nu\}$, the iterations for evaluating direct fixpoint subformulas of φ with the same fixpoint operator σ start with their previous value. If the fixpoint operator is different, we reinitialize $L[x]$ instead.

The complexity of the algorithm can be determined in terms of the *alternation depth* of the given μ-calculus formula. Several authors have given different definitions of alternation depths: Emerson and Lei used, in [174], a simple definition where the alternations of interdependent nested fixpoints were counted. This notion of alternation depth is computed as shown in Figure 3.5. Niwiński introduced a refined notion of alternation depth, which is more difficult to compute [68, 388, 515]. For example, $\mu x.\nu y.\Box y \wedge \mu z.\Box(x \vee z)$ has alternation depth 2 according to Niwiński, while the algorithm of Figure 3.5 overapproximates this as 3.

```
function ad(Φ)
  (l_Φ, g_Φ, n_Φ) := ad({}, φ);
  return n_Φ;
end

function ad(B, Φ)
  case Φ of
    is_var(Φ)     : return (0, 0, 0);
    ¬φ            : return ad(B, φ);
    φ ∧ ψ, φ ∨ ψ: (l_φ, g_φ, n_φ) := ad(B, φ); (l_ψ, g_ψ, n_ψ) := ad(B, ψ);
                    return (max{l_φ, l_ψ}, max{g_φ, g_ψ}, max{n_φ, n_ψ})
    ◇φ, □φ        : return ad(B, φ);
    ◇←φ, □←φ      : return ad(B, φ);
    σx.φ          : if x ∉ FV(φ) then return ad(B, φ)
                    elsif B ∩ FV(Φ) = {} then
                      (l_φ, g_φ, n_φ) := ad({x}, φ);
                      if σ = μ then d := max{l_φ, g_φ + 1, n_φ}
                      else d := max{l_φ + 1, g_φ, n_φ} end ;
                      return (0, 0, d)
                    else
                      (l_φ, g_φ, n_φ) := ad(B ∪ {x}, φ);
                      if σ = μ then return (max{l_φ, g_φ + 1}, 0, n_φ)
                      else return (0, max{l_φ + 1, g_φ}, n_φ)
                      end;
                    end;
  end
end
```

Fig. 3.5. Computing the alternation depth

The algorithm in Figure 3.5 gives an algorithm for the computation of $\mathsf{ad}(\Phi)$. It is mainly based on a secondary function that obtains as a further argument the set of variables B that are bound in the context of the currently considered subformula Φ. For a given set B, the function returns a triple (l_Φ, g_Φ, n_Φ), with the following meaning:

- l_Φ is the maximal alternation depth of the top-level μ-subformulas of Φ that contain free occurrences of variables in B
- g_Φ is the maximal alternation depth of the top-level ν-subformulas of Φ that contain free occurrences of variables in B

- n_Φ is the maximal alternation depth of subformulas (not necessarily top-level fixpoint subformulas) that do not contain free occurrences of variables in B.

We thereby say that a formula is a top-level μ-subformula, if it is a subformula of the form $\mu x.\varphi$ and it is not the subformula of another fixpoint formula. Moreover, a fixpoint formula depends on a set of variables B if one of these variables occurs in the fixpoint formula. Note that if Φ is a fixpoint formula, then either l_Φ or g_Φ must be 0, since the formula itself is the only top-level fixpoint formula.

The correctness of the algorithm is easily seen, just consider the case of a fixpoint subformula $\sigma x.\varphi$. Given that x does not occur in φ, we could neglect the binding, since φ is equivalent to $\sigma x.\varphi$. Otherwise, if we have $B \cap \mathsf{FV}(\Phi) = \{\}$, then this subformula is independent of the context B, and therefore, we return $l_\Phi = g_\Phi = 0$. The third one must be the alternation depth of $\sigma x.\varphi$ which is either $\max\{l_\varphi, g_\varphi + 1, n_\varphi\}$ or $\max\{l_\varphi + 1, g_\varphi, n_\varphi\}$. Finally, if the considered formula $\sigma x.\varphi$ depends on B, then the argument n_φ of the computation starting with φ is passed through, and either l_φ or g_φ must be updated.

For example, for the previously mentioned formulas, we compute

- $\mathsf{ad}(\nu y.\mu z.\Diamond y \wedge (a \vee \Diamond z)) = 2$
- $\mathsf{ad}(\nu y.\Diamond y \wedge \mu z.a \vee \Diamond z) = 1$

Formulas with an alternation depth higher than two are notoriously hard to understand and occur rarely in specifications. It is therefore natural to ask whether higher alternation depths are really needed: In other words, we ask whether the above hierarchy of fixpoint formulas collapses at a certain index, i.e., if for some n_0, every μ-calculus formula can be expressed by an equivalent one of alternation depth n_0. Arnold and Niwiński already proved in [24] that at least both $\nu\mu$ and $\mu\nu$ alternations are required. The final answer has however been given by Bradfield and Lenzi [22, 64, 65, 321], who proved the strictness of the alternation hierarchy.

Theorem 3.21 (Strictness of Alternation Hierarchy). *For every $n \in \mathbb{N}$ there is a μ-calculus formula Φ_n of alternation depth $\mathsf{ad}(\Phi_n) = n$ that can not be expressed by a μ-calculus formula with alternation depth less than n.*

We give no proof of this theorem due to lack of space, the interested reader is referred to [64, 65, 221]. The problem to determine the least alternation depth that is required to express a given μ-calculus formula has only recently been considered: Otto [393] showed in 1999 how to decide if a μ-calculus formula can be expressed without fixpoints, i.e., in modal logic ML. Küsters and Wilke [307] described in 2002 a decision procedure to decide if a property can be expressed by alternation-free μ-calculus formulas. The complexity of this problem is moreover EXPTIME-complete [307]. Recently, Kupferman and Vardi [306] proved in 2003 that a μ-calculus formula can be expressed in the alternation-free μ-calculus if and only if it can be expressed by two μ-calculus formulas of alternation depth 2, one starting with a greatest and the other with a least fixpoint operator. We will not consider these results in more detail. Instead, we now turn back to our improved model checking procedure and determine its complexity:

Theorem 3.22 (Correctness and Complexity of $\mathcal{L}_\mu$-Model-Checking (II)). *For every μ-calculus formula Φ end every Kripke structure $\mathcal{K} = (\mathcal{I}, \mathcal{S}, \mathcal{R}, \mathcal{L})$, the function* $\mathsf{States}_\mu(\cdot)$ *given in Figure 3.4 computes the set of states* $\mathsf{States}_\mu(\Phi) \subseteq \mathcal{S}$ *where Φ holds, i.e.,* $\mathsf{States}_\mu(\Phi) = [\![\Phi]\!]_\mathcal{K}$. *The time complexity of the algorithm is of order* $O(|\mathcal{K}|\,(|\Phi|\,|\mathcal{S}|)^{\mathsf{ad}(\Phi)+1})$.

The algorithm was first given in [174]. Its correctness is clear due to the previous theorems and explanations. The complexity is not too hard to prove, but we will see that similar results can be obtained more directly from the vectorized μ-calculus that we will consider in detail in the next section. Note further that the algorithm can be generalized to the computation of nested fixpoints in arbitrary lattices.

3.5 Vectorized μ-Calculus

In the previous sections, we have so-far excluded vectorized fixpoint expressions of the form $\mathsf{fix}\ E\ \mathsf{in}\ \varphi\ \mathsf{end}$. Clearly, we can replace formulas $\mathsf{fix}\ E\ \mathsf{in}\ \varphi\ \mathsf{end}$ by the equivalent fixpoint formula $E\langle\varphi\rangle$ (which is equivalent to the semantics, see page 79). In practice, this reduction is however not recommended as $E\langle\varphi\rangle$ is usually much larger than $\mathsf{fix}\ E\ \mathsf{in}\ \varphi\ \mathsf{end}$, since $\mathsf{fix}\ E\ \mathsf{in}\ \varphi\ \mathsf{end}$ makes excessive use of sharing common subformulas. This is a major advantage of the vectorized μ-calculus which allows its formulas to be exponentially more succinct.

Another advantage is that the equational form gives us more freedom for the evaluation of the different parts of the formula. We will see that this will enable us to find more efficient model checking procedures. Therefore, we will now consider the semantics and the model checking problem of vectorized fixpoint expressions in more detail.

In the next section, we will first study the corresponding state transformer of an equation system E. Recall E is a *list* (hence the order is important) of equations of the form $x \stackrel{\sigma}{=} \varphi$, where $\sigma \in \{\mu, \nu\}$ and $x \in V_\Sigma$. For a given structure $\mathcal{K}$, the state transformer will therefore be a function on tuples of state sets $(Q_1, \ldots, Q_n)$ (where n is the length of E).

For the notation, recall that $E_1 \& E_2$ denotes the concatenation of two lists E_1 and E_2 and that for an equation system $E = [x_1 \stackrel{\sigma_1}{=} \varphi_1, \ldots, x_n \stackrel{\sigma_n}{=} \varphi_n]$, we define its length as $\mathsf{length}(E) := n$, its size as $|E| := \sum_{i=1}^{n} |\varphi_i|$, and the set of defined variables by $\mathsf{defvars}(E) = \{x_1, \ldots, x_n\}$. A system $E = [x_i \stackrel{\sigma_i}{=} \varphi_i \mid i = 1..n]$ is sometimes alternatively written as $E = [x_i \stackrel{\sigma_i}{=} \varphi_i \mid i = 1..n]$. The associated substitution $\mathsf{EqSubs}(E)$, and the application $E\langle\Phi\rangle$ of an equation system E to a formula Φ or to another equation system E' (written as $E\langle E'\rangle$) have been defined on page 78. For reasons of readability, we will write the equation systems top-to-bottom instead of in left-to-right manner.

3.5.1 State Transformers of Vectorized Fixpoint Expressions

As we have defined the semantics of $\mathsf{fix}\ E\ \mathsf{in}\ \varphi\ \mathsf{end}$ by the associated substitution $\mathsf{EqSubs}(E)$ or equivalently by the application of E to φ, we have so far no direct meaning of such expressions. For this reason, we now study the corresponding state transformers of the corresponding equation system E. To this end, the following definition will be useful.

Definition 3.23 (Modification of Structures by Equation Systems). *Let $\mathcal{K} = (\mathcal{I}, \mathcal{S}, \mathcal{R}, \mathcal{L})$ be a Kripke structure over V_Σ and $\mathsf{fix}\ E\ \mathsf{in}\ \varphi\ \mathsf{end}$ be a formula of $\mathcal{L}_{\mathsf{spec}}$. Then, we define the E-modification $[\mathcal{K}|\,E]$ of $\mathcal{K}$ as $[\mathcal{K}|\,E] := \mathcal{K}_{x_1,\ldots,x_n}^{Q_1,\ldots,Q_n}$ where $Q_i := [\![E\langle x_i\rangle]\!]_\mathcal{K}$.*

This notation will make the following observation more readable, where we will show that vectorized fixpoint expressions really correspond with fixpoints computed over the complete partial order $((2^\mathcal{S})^n, \subseteq_n)$, where $\subseteq_n$ is defined pointwise, i.e. $(Q_1,\ldots,Q_n) \subseteq_n (P_1,\ldots,P_n)$ holds iff $Q_i \subseteq P_i$ holds for all $i \in \{1,\ldots,n\}$. To see this, we first need to prove the following lemma, that relates composition of associated substitution and concatenation (recall that the composition of two substitutions $\varrho = \{(x_1,\alpha_1), \ldots, (x_m,\alpha_m)\}$ and $\rho = \{(y_1,\beta_1), \ldots, (y_n,\beta_n)\}$ is defined as $\rho\circ\varrho := \{(x_1,[\alpha_1]_\rho), \ldots, (x_m,[\alpha_m]_\rho), (y_1,\beta_1), \ldots, (y_n,\beta_n)\}$, provided that the set of variables $\{x_1, \ldots, x_m\}$ and $\{y_1, \ldots, y_n\}$ are disjoint).

Lemma 3.24 (Compositional Computation of $\mathsf{EqSubs}(E)$). *For every vectorized fixpoint formula $\mathsf{fix}\ E_1\&E_2\ \mathsf{in}\ \varphi\ \mathsf{end}$, the following (equivalent) facts hold for $E_2' := E_1\langle E_2\rangle$:*

- $(E_1\&E_2)\langle\psi\rangle = E_2'\langle E_1\langle\psi\rangle\rangle$ *for every* $\psi \in \mathcal{L}_{\mathsf{spec}}$,
- $\mathsf{EqSubs}(E_1\&E_2) = \mathsf{EqSubs}(E_2') \circ \mathsf{EqSubs}(E_1)$

Moreover, if we recursively define substitutions Δ_i for $i \in \{1,\ldots,n\}$ and $E = [x_i \overset{\sigma_i}{=} \varphi_i \mid i = 1..n]$ as given below, then we have $\mathsf{EqSubs}(E) = \Delta_n$.

$$
\begin{aligned}
\Delta_1 &:= \{(x_1, \sigma_1 x_1.\varphi_1)\}\\
\Delta_{i+1} &:= \{(x_{i+1}, \sigma_{i+1} x_{i+1}.\,[\varphi_{i+1}]_{\Delta_i})\} \circ \Delta_i
\end{aligned}
$$

Proof. The lemma is proved by induction on the length of E_2. For $E_2 = [\,]$, the proposition is trivial. In the induction step, we consider $E_2\&[x \overset{\sigma}{=} \varphi]$ and abbreviate $E_2' := E_1\langle E_2\rangle$ (note the associativity of $\&$, Definition 2.40 on page 78, and the associativity of $\circ$):

$$\begin{aligned}
&\mathsf{EqSubs}\left(E_1\&(E_2\&[x \overset{\sigma}{=} \varphi])\right)\\
&= \mathsf{EqSubs}\left((E_1\&E_2)\&[x \overset{\sigma}{=} \varphi]\right)\\
&= \{(x, \sigma x.(E_1\&E_2)\langle\varphi\rangle)\} \circ \mathsf{EqSubs}\,(E_1\&E_2)\\
&= \{(x, \sigma x.E_2'\langle E_1\langle\varphi\rangle\rangle)\} \circ (\mathsf{EqSubs}\,(E_2') \circ \mathsf{EqSubs}\,(E_1))\\
&= \underbrace{(\,\{(x, \sigma x.E_2'\langle E_1\langle\varphi\rangle\rangle)\} \circ \mathsf{EqSubs}\,(E_2'))}_{\mathsf{EqSubs}\left(E_2'\&[x \overset{\sigma}{=} E_1\langle\varphi\rangle]\right)} \circ \mathsf{EqSubs}\,(E_1)
\end{aligned}$$

The second proposition is easily obtained by induction on the number of equations in E. □

The above lemma is a technical one and tells us how $\mathsf{EqSubs}\,(E)$ is related to subsequent associated substitutions $\mathsf{EqSubs}\,(E_1)$. Using this result, we can now prove the following theorem that tells us that the semantics of $\mathsf{fix}\ E\ \mathsf{in}\ \varphi\ \mathsf{end}$ indeed relies on fixpoints of vectorized functions $f_E : (2^{\mathcal{S}})^n \to (2^{\mathcal{S}})^n$.

Theorem 3.25 (Satisfying States of Vectorized Fixpoint Formulas). *Let $\mathcal{K} = (\mathcal{I}, \mathcal{S}, \mathcal{R}, \mathcal{L})$ be a Kripke structure over V_Σ and $\mathsf{fix}\ E\ \mathsf{in}\ \varphi\ \mathsf{end}$ be a formula of $\mathcal{L}_{\mathsf{spec}}$ with the equation system $E = [x_1 \overset{\sigma_1}{=} \varphi_1, \ldots, x_n \overset{\sigma_n}{=} \varphi_n]$. Define $f_E : (2^{\mathcal{S}})^n \to (2^{\mathcal{S}})^n$ as*

$$f_E(Q_1, \ldots, Q_n) := \left([\![\varphi_1]\!]_{\mathcal{K}^{Q_1,\ldots,Q_n}_{x_1,\ldots,x_n}}, \ldots, [\![\varphi_n]\!]_{\mathcal{K}^{Q_1,\ldots,Q_n}_{x_1,\ldots,x_n}} \right).$$

Then, the following holds:

- $[\![\mathsf{fix}\ E\ \mathsf{in}\ \varphi\ \mathsf{end}]\!]_{\mathcal{K}} = [\![E\langle\varphi\rangle]\!]_{\mathcal{K}} = [\![\varphi]\!]_{[\mathcal{K}|E]}$
- *$([\![E\langle x_1\rangle]\!]_{\mathcal{K}}, \ldots, [\![E\langle x_n\rangle]\!]_{\mathcal{K}})$ is a fixpoint of f_E, i.e. we have $[\![E\langle x_j\rangle]\!]_{\mathcal{K}} = [\![\varphi_j]\!]_{[\mathcal{K}|E]}$ for all $j \in \{1, \ldots, n\}$.*

Proof. The first proposition is immediate by Lemma 2.45 and Definition 3.23. To prove the second proposition for a particular j, we first split the equation system E into parts: We define $E_1 := [x_1 \overset{\sigma_1}{=} \varphi_1, \ldots, x_{j-1} \overset{\sigma_{j-1}}{=} \varphi_{j-1}]$, $\eta_j := \sigma_j x_j.E_1\langle\varphi_j\rangle$, $E_2 := [x_{j+1} \overset{\sigma_{j+1}}{=} \varphi_{j+1}, \ldots, x_n \overset{\sigma_n}{=} \varphi_n]$, and $E_2' := [x_{j+1} \overset{\sigma_{j+1}}{=} [E_1\langle\varphi_{j+1}\rangle]^{\eta_j}_{x_j}, \ldots, x_n \overset{\sigma_n}{=} [E_1\langle\varphi_n\rangle]^{\eta_j}_{x_j}]$. Note that by Lemma 3.24, we have $(*)\ E\langle\Phi\rangle = E_2'\langle[E_1\langle\Phi\rangle]^{\eta_j}_{x_j}\rangle$ for every Φ. Hence, the following holds:

$$\begin{aligned}
[\![\varphi_j]\!]_{[\mathcal{K}|E]} &= [\![E\langle\varphi_j\rangle]\!]_{\mathcal{K}} && \text{by Lemma 2.45}\\
&= \left[\!\!\left[(E_1\&[x_j \overset{\sigma_j}{=} \varphi_j]\&E_2)\langle\varphi_j\rangle\right]\!\!\right]_{\mathcal{K}} && \text{by definition of } E_1 \text{ and } E_2\\
&= \left[\!\!\left[E_2'\langle[E_1\langle\varphi_j\rangle]^{\eta_j}_{x_j}\rangle\right]\!\!\right]_{\mathcal{K}} && \text{by Lemma 3.24}\\
&= \left[\!\!\left[E_2'\langle[E_1\langle\varphi_j\rangle]^{\sigma_j x_j.E_1\langle\varphi_j\rangle}_{x_j}\rangle\right]\!\!\right]_{\mathcal{K}} && \text{by definition of } \eta_j\\
&= [\![E_2'\langle\sigma_j x_j.E_1\langle\varphi_j\rangle\rangle]\!]_{\mathcal{K}} && \text{by unwinding (Lemma 3.13))}\\
&= [\![E\langle x_j\rangle]\!]_{\mathcal{K}} && \text{by Lemma 3.24}
\end{aligned}$$

□

Therefore, the semantics of a fixpoint expression fix E in φ end with respect to a Kripke structure $\mathcal{K}$ can alternatively be explained as follows: First, we have to compute the fixpoint $(\llbracket E\langle x_1\rangle\rrbracket_{\mathcal{K}}, \ldots, \llbracket E\langle x_n\rangle\rrbracket_{\mathcal{K}})$ of the function f_E and then consider the modification of $\mathcal{K}$ where the labels of the bound variables x_i are changed such that x_i holds in exactly the states of $\llbracket E\langle x_i\rangle\rrbracket_{\mathcal{K}}$. As $(\llbracket E\langle x_1\rangle\rrbracket_{\mathcal{K}}, \ldots, \llbracket E\langle x_n\rangle\rrbracket_{\mathcal{K}})$ is therefore the key to the semantics of a vectorized fixpoint expression, we will call it the *solution of E w.r.t. $\mathcal{K}$* in the following.

In general, $(\llbracket E\langle x_1\rangle\rrbracket_{\mathcal{K}}, \ldots, \llbracket E\langle x_n\rangle\rrbracket_{\mathcal{K}})$ is neither the least nor the greatest fixpoint of f_E. Note, however, that f_E has a least and a greatest fixpoint: This is due to the requirement for equation systems $E = [x_1 \stackrel{\sigma_1}{=} \varphi_1, \ldots, x_n \stackrel{\sigma_n}{=} \varphi_n]$ that every occurrence of every variable x_i in every right hand side φ_j must be positive (this simply follows from Theorem 3.17). It is easily seen that this assures that the function f_E defined in the above theorem is monotonic w.r.t. to $\subseteq_n$, so that by the Tarski/Knaster theorem, f_E has a least fixpoint $(\check{Q}_1, \ldots, \check{Q}_n)$ and a greatest fixpoint $(\hat{Q}_1, \ldots, \hat{Q}_n)$. The above theorem additionally tells us that $(\llbracket E\langle x_1\rangle\rrbracket_{\mathcal{K}}, \ldots, \llbracket E\langle x_n\rangle\rrbracket_{\mathcal{K}})$ is another fixpoint. In general, this is neither the least nor the greatest fixpoint, but if all equations in E are of the same parity (either all μ or all ν), then the next theorem states that $(\llbracket E\langle x_1\rangle\rrbracket_{\mathcal{K}}, \ldots, \llbracket E\langle x_n\rangle\rrbracket_{\mathcal{K}})$ is the corresponding extremal fixpoint of f_E.

Theorem 3.26 (Least and Greatest Fixpoints of Equation Systems). *Let $\mathcal{K} = (\mathcal{I}, \mathcal{S}, \mathcal{R}, \mathcal{L})$ be a Kripke structure over V_Σ and* fix E in φ end *be a formula of $\mathcal{L}_{\mathsf{spec}}$ with the equation system $E = [x_1 \stackrel{\sigma}{=} \varphi_1, \ldots, x_n \stackrel{\sigma}{=} \varphi_n]$ for a particular $\sigma \in \{\mu, \nu\}$. Define $f_E : (2^{\mathcal{S}})^n \to (2^{\mathcal{S}})^n$ as*

$$f_E(Q_1, \ldots, Q_n) := \left(\llbracket\varphi_1\rrbracket_{\mathcal{K}_{x_1,\ldots,x_n}^{Q_1,\ldots,Q_n}}, \ldots, \llbracket\varphi_n\rrbracket_{\mathcal{K}_{x_1,\ldots,x_n}^{Q_1,\ldots,Q_n}}\right).$$

Then, the following holds:

- *Given that $\sigma = \mu$, then $(\llbracket E\langle x_1\rangle\rrbracket_{\mathcal{K}}, \ldots, \llbracket E\langle x_n\rangle\rrbracket_{\mathcal{K}})$ is the least fixpoint of f_E.*
- *Given that $\sigma = \nu$, then $(\llbracket E\langle x_1\rangle\rrbracket_{\mathcal{K}}, \ldots, \llbracket E\langle x_n\rangle\rrbracket_{\mathcal{K}})$ is the greatest fixpoint of f_E.*

Proof. We only prove the proposition on least fixpoints, the other one for greatest fixpoints is completely dual. By Theorem 3.25, we already know that $(\llbracket E\langle x_1\rangle\rrbracket_{\mathcal{K}}, \ldots, \llbracket E\langle x_n\rangle\rrbracket_{\mathcal{K}})$ is a fixpoint of f_E. As f_E is monotonic, it moreover follows that f_E has a unique least and a unique greatest fixpoint. Therefore, it remains to prove that $(\llbracket E\langle x_1\rangle\rrbracket_{\mathcal{K}}, \ldots, \llbracket E\langle x_n\rangle\rrbracket_{\mathcal{K}})$ is the least one. This proof is done by induction on the number of equations n. The base case is trivial.

In the induction step, we are given the equation system $E = [x_1 \stackrel{\mu}{=} \varphi_1, \ldots, x_n \stackrel{\mu}{=} \varphi_n]$ with $n > 0$. To carefully distinguish between the different functions, equation systems, fixpoints, and substitution lists, we use the following definitions:

(A) $E' = [x_1 \stackrel{\mu}{=} \varphi_1, \ldots, x_{n-1} \stackrel{\mu}{=} \varphi_{n-1}]$, hence $E\langle\Phi\rangle = (E'\&[x_n \stackrel{\mu}{=} \varphi_n])\langle\Phi\rangle = [E'\langle\Phi\rangle]_{x_n}^{\mu x_n.E'\langle\varphi_n\rangle}$

(B) $f_i(Q_1,\dots,Q_n) := [\![\varphi_i]\!]_{\mathcal{K}^{Q_1,\dots,Q_n}_{x_1,\dots,x_n}}$

(C) $f_{E'}(Q_1,\dots,Q_{n-1}) :=$

$$(f_1(Q_1,\dots,Q_{n-1},[\![x_n]\!]_{\mathcal{K}}),\dots,f_{n-1}(Q_1,\dots,Q_{n-1},[\![x_n]\!]_{\mathcal{K}}))$$

(D) Let $(\check{Q}_1,\dots,\check{Q}_n)$ be the least fixpoint of f_E, i.e.

(D1) $\bigwedge_{i=1}^{n} f_i(\check{Q}_1,\dots,\check{Q}_n) = \check{Q}_i$

(D2) $\forall Q_1\dots Q_n.\,(\bigwedge_{i=1}^{n} Q_i \subseteq f_i(Q_1,\dots,Q_n)) \to (\bigwedge_{i=1}^{n} \check{Q}_i \subseteq Q_i)$

(E) $\check{P}_n := [\![E\langle x_n\rangle]\!]_{\mathcal{K}}$

(F) Let $(\check{P}_1,\dots,\check{P}_{n-1})$ be the least fixpoint of $f_{E'}$ w.r.t. to the structure $\mathcal{K}^{\check{P}_n}_{x_n}$, i.e.

(F1) $\bigwedge_{i=1}^{n-1} f_i(\check{P}_1,\dots,\check{P}_n) = \check{P}_i$

(F2) $\forall P_1\dots P_{n-1}.\,\left(\bigwedge_{i=1}^{n-1} P_i \subseteq f_i(P_1,\dots,P_{n-1},\check{P}_n)\right) \to \left(\bigwedge_{i=1}^{n-1} \check{P}_i \subseteq P_i\right)$

We have to prove that $\check{Q}_i = [\![E\langle x_i\rangle]\!]_{\mathcal{K}}$ holds for $i = 1, \dots, n$. For this reason, we proceed by proving the following results in the mentioned order:

F_1 : $\check{Q}_i \subseteq [\![E\langle x_i\rangle]\!]_{\mathcal{K}}$ for $i = 1,\dots,n$
F_2 : $\check{P}_i := [\![E'\langle x_i\rangle]\!]_{\mathcal{K}'}$ for $i < n$, where $\mathcal{K}' := \mathcal{K}^{\check{P}_n}_{x_n}$
F_3 : $\check{P}_i = [\![E\langle x_i\rangle]\!]_{\mathcal{K}}$ for $i = 1,\dots,n$
F_4 : $\check{Q}_i \subseteq \check{P}_i$ for $i = 1,\dots,n$
F_5 : $\check{Q}_i \subseteq f_i(\check{Q}_1,\dots,\check{Q}_{n-1},\check{P}_n)$ for $i < n$
F_6 : $\check{P}_i = \check{Q}_i$ holds for $i < n$
F_7 : $\check{P}_n = \check{Q}_n$

By F_6 and F_7, it follows that $\check{P}_i = \check{Q}_i$ holds for $i = 1,\dots,n$, so that the least fixpoint of f_E is $(\check{P}_1, \dots, \check{P}_n)$. The rest follows from fact F_3. The proofs of the facts $F_1, \dots, F_7$ are as follows:

F_1 : By Theorem 3.25, we already know that $([\![E\langle x_1\rangle]\!]_{\mathcal{K}},\dots,[\![E\langle x_n\rangle]\!]_{\mathcal{K}})$ is a fixpoint of f_E. Therefore, the result follows by (D2).

F_2 : By the induction hypothesis, the tuple $([\![E'\langle x_1\rangle]\!]_{\mathcal{K}},\dots,[\![E'\langle x_{n-1}\rangle]\!]_{\mathcal{K}})$ is for every structure $\mathcal{K}$ the fixpoint of $f_{E'}$. In particular, it is the *least* fixpoint of $f_{E'}$ with respect to the structure $\mathcal{K} := \mathcal{K}^{\check{P}_n}_{x_n}$, and therefore our subgoal follows by (F).

F_3 : For $i = n$, this is given by definition (E). For $i < n$, it follows directly by F_2, definition (E), the substitution lemma, and definition (C) (note that $E\langle x_n\rangle = \mu x_n.E'\langle\varphi_n\rangle$):

$$\check{P}_i \overset{F_2}{=} [\![E'\langle x_i\rangle]\!]_{\mathcal{K}^{\check{P}_n}_{x_n}} \overset{(E)}{=} [\![E'\langle x_i\rangle]\!]_{\mathcal{K}^{[\![E\langle x_n\rangle]\!]_{\mathcal{K}}}_{x_n}} = \left[\!\left[[E'\langle x_i\rangle]^{E\langle x_n\rangle}_{x_n}\right]\!\right]_{\mathcal{K}} \overset{(A)}{=} [\![E\langle x_i\rangle]\!]_{\mathcal{K}}\,.$$

F_4 : This follows immediately by F_1 and F_3.

F_5 : We deduce $f_i(\check{Q}_1,\dots,\check{Q}_{n-1},\check{Q}_n) \subseteq f_i(\check{Q}_1,\dots,\check{Q}_{n-1},\check{P}_n)$, since $\check{Q}_n \subseteq \check{P}_n$ holds due to F_4 (note the monotonicity of f_i). The rest follows from (D1).

F_6 : We instantiate (F2) with $\check{Q}_1, \dots, \check{Q}_{n-1}$, and use modus ponens with F_5 to derive that $\check{P}_i \subseteq \check{Q}_i$ holds for $i < n$. The rest follows then by F_4.

F_7 : Consider the function $g(Q) := f_n(\check{P}_1, \ldots, \check{P}_{n-1}, Q)$. By (B), F_3, and the substitution lemma, we conclude $g(Q) = \left[\!\left[[\varphi_n]_{x_1 \ldots x_{n-1}}^{E\langle x_1 \rangle \ldots E\langle x_{n-1}\rangle} \right]\!\right]_{\mathcal{K}_{x_n}^Q}$ (note that $[\![E\langle x_i \rangle]\!]_{\mathcal{K}} = [\![E\langle x_i \rangle]\!]_{\mathcal{K}_{x_n}^Q}$ holds, since x_n does not occur free in $E\langle x_i \rangle$). By (B), (D), and F_6, we now see that $\check{Q}_n := \left[\!\left[\mu x_n . [\varphi_n]_{x_1 \ldots x_{n-1}}^{E\langle x_1 \rangle \ldots E\langle x_{n-1}\rangle} \right]\!\right]_{\mathcal{K}}$ holds, since (D1) says that $\check{Q}_n = \left[\!\left[[\varphi_n]_{x_1 \ldots x_{n-1}}^{E\langle x_1 \rangle \ldots E\langle x_{n-1}\rangle} \right]\!\right]_{\mathcal{K}_{x_n}^{\check{Q}_n}}$ holds and (D2) says that $\check{Q}_n$ is the least set that fulfills this equation.
Moreover, $\check{P}_n = [\![\mu x_n . E'\langle \varphi_n \rangle]\!]_{\mathcal{K}} = \left[\!\left[\mu x_n . [\varphi_n]_{x_1 \ldots x_{n-1}}^{E'\langle x_1 \rangle \ldots E'\langle x_{n-1}\rangle} \right]\!\right]_{\mathcal{K}}$ holds due to by (E) and (C). Hence, Tarski's theorem tells us that we can compute $\check{P}_n$ and $\check{Q}_n$ by the following iteration schemes ($[\![E\langle x_i \rangle]\!]_{\mathcal{K}} = [\![E\langle x_i \rangle]\!]_{\mathcal{K}_{x_n}^{\check{Q}_n^i}}$ holds since x_n does not occur free in $E\langle x_i \rangle$):

$$
\begin{aligned}
\check{P}_n^0 &:= \{\} \\
\check{P}_n^{i+1} &:= \left[\!\left[[\varphi_n]_{x_1 \ldots x_{n-1}}^{E'\langle x_1 \rangle \ldots E'\langle x_{n-1}\rangle} \right]\!\right]_{\mathcal{K}_{x_n}^{\check{P}_n^i}} \\
&= f_n \left([\![E'\langle x_1 \rangle]\!]_{\mathcal{K}_{x_n}^{\check{P}_n^i}}, \ldots [\![E'\langle x_{n-1} \rangle]\!]_{\mathcal{K}_{x_n}^{\check{P}_n^i}}, \check{P}_n^i \right) \\
\check{Q}_n^0 &:= \{\} \\
\check{Q}_n^{i+1} &:= \left[\!\left[[\varphi_n]_{x_1 \ldots x_{n-1}}^{E\langle x_1 \rangle \ldots E\langle x_{n-1}\rangle} \right]\!\right]_{\mathcal{K}_{x_n}^{\check{Q}_n^i}} \\
&= f_n \left([\![E\langle x_1 \rangle]\!]_{\mathcal{K}}, \ldots [\![E\langle x_{n-1} \rangle]\!]_{\mathcal{K}}, \check{Q}_n^i \right)
\end{aligned}
$$

It moreover follows that $\check{P}_n^i \subseteq \check{P}_n$ and $\check{Q}_n^i \subseteq \check{Q}_n$ for every $i \in \mathbb{N}$. We now prove by induction on i that $\forall i. \check{P}_n^i \subseteq \check{Q}_n^i$ holds. For $i = 0$ this is trivial. In the induction step, we already have by the induction hypothesis that $\check{P}_n^i \subseteq \check{Q}_n^i$ holds. As the function $h(Q) := [\![E'\langle x_i \rangle]\!]_{\mathcal{K}_{x_n}^Q}$ is monotonic (since x_n has only positive occurrences in $E'\langle x_i \rangle$), it follows that $[\![E'\langle x_i \rangle]\!]_{\mathcal{K}_{x_n}^{\check{P}_n^i}} \subseteq [\![E'\langle x_i \rangle]\!]_{\mathcal{K}_{x_n}^{\check{P}_n}} = \left[\!\left[[E'\langle x_i \rangle]_{x_n}^{E\langle x_n \rangle} \right]\!\right]_{\mathcal{K}} = [\![E\langle x_i \rangle]\!]_{\mathcal{K}}$ (note F_3, Lemma 2.45). Hence, we have the following inequation

$$
\left([\![E'\langle x_1 \rangle]\!]_{\mathcal{K}_{x_n}^{\check{P}_n^i}}, \ldots [\![E'\langle x_{n-1} \rangle]\!]_{\mathcal{K}_{x_n}^{\check{P}_n^i}}, \check{P}_n^i \right) \subseteq_n \left([\![E\langle x_1 \rangle]\!]_{\mathcal{K}}, \ldots [\![E\langle x_{n-1} \rangle]\!]_{\mathcal{K}}, \check{Q}_n^i \right),
$$

and by monotonicity of f_n, we conclude that $\check{P}_n^{i+1} \subseteq \check{Q}_n^{i+1}$ holds. Therefore $\forall i. \check{P}_n^i \subseteq \check{Q}_n^i$ holds, and therefore that $\check{P}_n \subseteq \check{Q}_n$. $\check{Q}_n \subseteq \check{P}_n$ has already been proved in F_4. □

The above theorem is quite powerful and has some remarkable consequences. One of these consequences is that the order of equations in equation systems, where all equations have the same parity, does not matter. To see why this is the case, consider an equation system $E = [x_1 \overset{\sigma}{=} \varphi_1, \ldots, x_n \overset{\sigma}{=} \varphi_n]$ and let $\pi : \{1, \ldots, n\} \to \{1, \ldots, n\}$ be any permutation of the indices $\{1, \ldots, n\}$. Define the permuted equation system $E_\pi = [x_{\pi(1)} \overset{\sigma}{=} \varphi_{\pi(1)}, \ldots, x_{\pi(n)} \overset{\sigma}{=} \varphi_{\pi(n)}]$. For the associated functions $f_E, f_{E_\pi} : (2^{\mathcal{S}})^n \to (2^{\mathcal{S}})^n$, it easily follows that $f_E(Q_1, \ldots, Q_n) = f_{E'}(Q_{\pi(1)}, \ldots, Q_{\pi(n)})$ holds, and the above theorem tells us that $(\llbracket E\langle x_1\rangle\rrbracket_{\mathcal{K}}, \ldots, \llbracket E\langle x_n\rangle\rrbracket_{\mathcal{K}})$ and $(\llbracket E_\pi\langle x_{\pi(1)}\rangle\rrbracket_{\mathcal{K}}, \ldots, \llbracket E_\pi\langle x_{\pi(n)}\rangle\rrbracket_{\mathcal{K}})$ are the least fixpoints of f_E and f_{E_π}, respectively. But then, it follows that $\llbracket E_\pi\langle x_{\pi(i)}\rangle\rrbracket_{\mathcal{K}} = \llbracket E\langle x_i\rangle\rrbracket_{\mathcal{K}}$, and we have proved the following lemma:

Lemma 3.27 (Order Invariance of Least and Greatest Fixpoint Formulas). *Given a formula* $\Phi = \mathsf{fix}\ [x_1 \stackrel{\sigma}{=} \varphi_1, \ldots, x_n \stackrel{\sigma}{=} \varphi_n]\ \mathsf{in}\ \varphi\ \mathsf{end}$ *of* $\mathcal{L}_{\mathsf{spec}}$. *Then, the order of the equations does not affect the semantics of* Φ. *More precisely, if we define* $E_\pi := [x_{\pi(i)} \stackrel{\sigma}{=} \varphi_{\pi(i)} \mid i = 1 \ldots n]$ *for a bijection* $\pi : \{1, \ldots, n\} \to \{1, \ldots, n\}$, *then we have* $\llbracket E_\pi\langle x_{\pi(i)}\rangle\rrbracket_{\mathcal{K}} = \llbracket E\langle x_i\rangle\rrbracket_{\mathcal{K}}$ *for every structure* $\mathcal{K}$.

The lemma gives us some insight into a couple of formulas whose semantics are far from being straightforwardly understood. For example, with its help, we can easily prove the following facts:

- $\mu x. [\varphi]_y^{y_0} = \mu x. [\varphi]_y^{\mu y.\psi}$ where $y_0 := \mu y. [\psi]_x^{\mu x.\varphi}$
- $\mu y. [\psi]_x^{\mu x.\varphi} = \mu y. [\psi]_x^{x_0}$ where $x_0 := \mu x. [\varphi]_y^{\mu y.\psi}$
- $\mu x. [\varphi]_y^{\mu y.\mu x.\varphi} = \mu x. [\varphi]_y^x$
- $\mu y.\mu x.\varphi = \mu x. [\varphi]_y^x$
- $\mu x_1. \ldots \mu x_n.\varphi = \mu x. [\varphi]_{x_1\ldots x_n}^{x\ldots x}$

For the proofs, consider the equation system $E = [x \stackrel{\mu}{=} \varphi, y \stackrel{\mu}{=} \psi]$ and compute $\mathsf{EqSubs}(E) = \{(x, \mu x. [\varphi]_y^{y_0}), (y, \mu y. [\psi]_x^{\mu x.\varphi})\}$ with $y_0 := \mu y. [\psi]_x^{\mu x.\varphi}$. For the reordered system $E' = [y \stackrel{\mu}{=} \psi, x \stackrel{\mu}{=} \varphi]$, we compute $\mathsf{EqSubs}(E') = \{(y, \mu y. [\psi]_x^{x_0}), (x, \mu x. [\varphi]_y^{\mu y.\psi})\}$ with $x_0 := \mu x. [\varphi]_y^{\mu y.\psi}$. By the previous lemma, both equation systems define the same least fixpoint, and therefore, the first two equations above follow. The third and fourth equations are obtained by considering the special case $\psi := x$ in the first equation. The last equation is finally obtained by an easy induction on n, where we use the third result.

Hence, $\Delta_E := \{(x, \mu x. [\varphi]_y^{\mu y.\psi}), (y, \mu y. [\psi]_x^{\mu x.\varphi})\}$ could be used instead as substitution for defining the semantics of an expression $\mathsf{fix}\ E\ \mathsf{in}\ \Phi\ \mathsf{end}$ with $E = [x \stackrel{\mu}{=} \varphi, y \stackrel{\mu}{=} \psi]$. Note that Δ_E and $\mathsf{EqSubs}(E)$ are very different substitutions, but the semantics of fixpoint expressions $\mathsf{fix}\ E\ \mathsf{in}\ \Phi\ \mathsf{end}$ remains the same no matter which of the substitutions we use.

3.5.2 Decomposing Equation Systems

In this section, we will show that the equation system E of a fixpoint expression $\mathsf{fix}\ E\ \mathsf{in}\ \Phi\ \mathsf{end}$ can sometimes be decomposed into smaller equations systems $E = C_1 \& \ldots \& C_m$, so that the fixpoint expression can be hierarchically organized as follows:

$$\mathsf{fix}\ E\ \mathsf{in}\ \Phi\ \mathsf{end} = \mathsf{fix}\ C_m\ \mathsf{in}\ \ldots \mathsf{fix}\ C_1\ \mathsf{in}\ \Phi\ \mathsf{end} \ldots \mathsf{end}$$

This will be important to reduce the complexity of model checking procedures for vectorized fixpoint expressions, since the model checking problem can now also be hierarchically organized. The first step towards this result is the following lemma:

Lemma 3.28 (Decomposing Independent Blocks). *Given equation systems E_1 and E_2, with disjoint variables* $\mathsf{defvars}(E_1) \cap \mathsf{defvars}(E_2) = \{\}$, *and a formula Φ over over the variables V_Σ. Then, the following formulas are valid:*

- $\mathsf{fix}\ E_1\ \mathsf{in}\ \mathsf{fix}\ E_2\ \mathsf{in}\ \Phi\ \mathsf{end}\ \mathsf{end} = \mathsf{fix}\ E_2\&E_1\ \mathsf{in}\ \Phi\ \mathsf{end}$
- $\neg\mathsf{fix}\ E\ \mathsf{in}\ \Phi\ \mathsf{end} = \mathsf{fix}\ E\ \mathsf{in}\ \neg\Phi\ \mathsf{end}$
- $\mathsf{fix}\ E\ \mathsf{in}\ \varphi \wedge \psi\ \mathsf{end} = \varphi \wedge \mathsf{fix}\ E\ \mathsf{in}\ \psi\ \mathsf{end}$, *provided that φ contains none of the defined variables of E*
- $\mathsf{fix}\ E\ \mathsf{in}\ \varphi \vee \psi\ \mathsf{end} = \varphi \vee \mathsf{fix}\ E\ \mathsf{in}\ \psi\ \mathsf{end}$, *provided that φ contains none of the defined variables of E*

Proof. Assume that $E_1 := [x_i \stackrel{\sigma_i}{=} \varphi_i \mid i = 1..n]$ and $E_2 := [y_i \stackrel{\varrho_i}{=} \psi_i \mid i = 1..m]$. By Lemma 3.24, it follows that $(E_2\&E_1)\langle\Phi\rangle = E_1'\langle E_2\langle\Phi\rangle\rangle$ holds, where $E_1' := [x_i \stackrel{\sigma_i}{=} E_2\langle\varphi_i\rangle \mid i = 1..n]$. Note that by the syntactic requirements of $\mathcal{L}_{\mathsf{spec}}$, none of the bound variables $\{y_1, \ldots, y_m\}$ of E_2 must occur in the φ_i's. Hence, it follows that $E_1' = E_1$, which implies $(*)$ $(E_2\&E_1)\langle\Phi\rangle = E_1\langle E_2\langle\Phi\rangle\rangle$. By the semantics, we have $[\![\mathsf{fix}\ E_1\ \mathsf{in}\ \mathsf{fix}\ E_2\ \mathsf{in}\ \Phi\ \mathsf{end}\ \mathsf{end}]\!]_{\mathcal{K}} = [\![E_1\langle E_2\langle\Phi\rangle\rangle]\!]_{\mathcal{K}}$. According to $(*)$, this is the same as $[\![(E_2\&E_1)\langle\Phi\rangle]\!]_{\mathcal{K}}$, and therefore the same as $[\![\mathsf{fix}\ E_2\&E_1\ \mathsf{in}\ \Phi\ \mathsf{end}]\!]_{\mathcal{K}}$. The other laws are simple consequences of the definition of the semantics. □

Given a fixpoint expression $\mathsf{fix}\ E_2\&E_1\ \mathsf{in}\ \Phi\ \mathsf{end}$ such that none of the bound variables of E_2 occur in E_1, then we can split the expression into two subsequent fixpoint expressions according to the above lemma. This is very important for the efficient computation of fixpoint expressions, since it enables us to compute the fixpoint $([\![E\langle x_1\rangle]\!]_{\mathcal{K}}, \ldots, [\![E\langle x_n\rangle]\!]_{\mathcal{K}})$ hierarchically: First, we compute the solution of E_1, and modify the structure $\mathcal{K}$, i.e., use $[\mathcal{K}|\, E_1]$, to solve E_2.

It is reasonable to split equation systems whenever possible to reduce the complexity of the computation of $\mathsf{EqSubs}(E_2\&E_1)$. However, the requirement that none of the bound variables of E_2 must occur in E_1 is often not fulfilled. As an example, consider the following fixpoint formula:

$$\mathsf{fix}\ \underbrace{\begin{bmatrix} x_1 \stackrel{\mu}{=} \Diamond x_2 \\ x_2 \stackrel{\nu}{=} x_1 \vee x_3 \\ x_3 \stackrel{\mu}{=} x_2 \wedge x_4 \\ x_4 \stackrel{\mu}{=} x_4 \wedge x_5 \\ x_5 \stackrel{\mu}{=} x_4 \vee x_5 \end{bmatrix}}_{=:E_1}\ \mathsf{in}\ \Phi\ \mathsf{end}$$

It seems that if there is no possibility of splitting this equation system in the required manner, and this can be easily checked by examining the four possible splitting points (between any two equations). In general, the order of the equation is important, i.e., it influences the semantics. However, in certain cases, the order of equations is not relevant, so that we can reorder them. The following lemma gives a criterion when an equation can be placed at another position.

Lemma 3.29 (Reordering Equations). *Given a fixpoint formula* fix E in φ end $\in \mathcal{L}_{\mathsf{spec}}$ *with* $E = E_0\&E_1\&[y \stackrel{\rho}{=} \psi]\&E_2$ *such that none of the left hand side variables of* E_1 *occurs in* ψ *or in a right hand side of* E_0*, then, it follows that*

$$\mathsf{EqSubs}\left(E_0\&E_1\&[y \stackrel{\rho}{=} \psi]\&E_2\right) = \mathsf{EqSubs}\left(E_0\&[y \stackrel{\rho}{=} \psi]\&E_1\&E_2\right).$$

Proof. To prove the lemma, we proceed in four steps:

(1) We show that $\mathsf{EqSubs}\left([x \stackrel{\sigma}{=} \varphi, y \stackrel{\rho}{=} \psi]\right) = \mathsf{EqSubs}\left([y \stackrel{\rho}{=} \psi, x \stackrel{\sigma}{=} \varphi]\right)$ holds, provided that $x \neq y$ and x does not occur in ψ. The proof is as follows: We first obtain

$$\begin{aligned}
&\mathsf{EqSubs}\left([x \stackrel{\sigma}{=} \varphi, y \stackrel{\rho}{=} \psi]\right) \\
&= \mathsf{EqSubs}\left([y \stackrel{\rho}{=} [\psi]_x^{\sigma x.\varphi}]\right) \circ \{(x, \sigma x.\varphi)\} && \text{by Lemma 3.24} \\
&= \mathsf{EqSubs}\left([y \stackrel{\rho}{=} \psi]\right) \circ \{(x, \sigma x.\varphi)\} && \text{since } x \text{ does not occur in } \psi \\
&= \{(y, \rho y.\psi)\} \circ \{(x, \sigma x.\varphi)\} && \text{by Definition 2.40} \\
&= \{(y, \rho y.\psi), (x, \sigma x.\, [\varphi]_y^{\rho y.\psi})\} && \text{by Lemma 2.45}
\end{aligned}$$

On the other hand, we have

$$\begin{aligned}
&\mathsf{EqSubs}\left([y \stackrel{\rho}{=} \psi, x \stackrel{\sigma}{=} \varphi]\right) \\
&= \mathsf{EqSubs}\left([x \stackrel{\sigma}{=} [\varphi]_y^{\rho y.\psi}]\right) \circ \{(y, \rho y.\psi)\} && \text{by Lemma 3.24} \\
&= \{(x, \sigma x.\, [\varphi]_y^{\rho y.\psi})\} \circ \{(y, \rho y.\psi)\} && \text{by Definition 2.40} \\
&= \{(x, \sigma x.\, [\varphi]_y^{\rho y.\psi}), (y, \rho y.\, [\psi]_x^{\sigma x.[\varphi]_y^{\rho y.\psi}})\} && \text{definition of } \circ \\
&= \{(x, \sigma x.\, [\varphi]_y^{\rho y.\psi}), (y, \rho y.\psi)\} && \text{since } x \text{ does not occur in } \psi
\end{aligned}$$

(2) $\mathsf{EqSubs}\left(E_1\&[x \stackrel{\sigma}{=} \varphi, y \stackrel{\rho}{=} \psi]\&E_2\right) = \mathsf{EqSubs}\left(E_1\&[y \stackrel{\rho}{=} \psi, x \stackrel{\sigma}{=} \varphi]\&E_2\right)$, if neither x nor a left hand side variable of E_1 occurs free in ψ. Due to this requirement, we have $E_1\langle\psi\rangle \equiv \psi$. For conciseness, we abbreviate $E_0 := [x \stackrel{\sigma}{=} E_1\langle\varphi\rangle, y \stackrel{\rho}{=} \psi]$, $E_0' := [y \stackrel{\rho}{=} \psi, x \stackrel{\sigma}{=} E_1\langle\varphi\rangle]$, and $E_2' := E_1\langle E_2\rangle$. By (1), we have $E_0\langle\Phi\rangle = E_0'\langle\Phi\rangle$. The proof of (2) can be easily reduced to (1) by successive applications of Lemma 3.24:

$$
\begin{aligned}
&\left(E_1\&[x \overset{\sigma}{=} \varphi, y \overset{\rho}{=} \psi]\&E_2\right)\langle\Phi\rangle \\
&= \left([x \overset{\sigma}{=} E_1\langle\varphi\rangle, y \overset{\rho}{=} E_1\langle\psi\rangle]\&(E_1\langle E_2\rangle)\right)\langle E_1\langle\Phi\rangle\rangle \\
&= \left([x \overset{\sigma}{=} E_1\langle\varphi\rangle, y \overset{\rho}{=} \psi]\&(E_1\langle E_2\rangle)\right)\langle E_1\langle\Phi\rangle\rangle \\
&= (E_0\&E_2')\langle E_1\langle\Phi\rangle\rangle \\
&= (E_0\langle E_2'\rangle)\langle E_0\langle E_1\langle\Phi\rangle\rangle\rangle \\
&\overset{(1)}{=} (E_0'\langle E_2'\rangle)\langle E_0'\langle E_1\langle\Phi\rangle\rangle\rangle \\
&= (E_0'\&E_2')\langle E_1\langle\Phi\rangle\rangle \\
&= \left([y \overset{\rho}{=} \psi, x \overset{\sigma}{=} E_1\langle\varphi\rangle]\&(E_1\langle E_2\rangle)\right)\langle E_1\langle\Phi\rangle\rangle \\
&= \left([y \overset{\rho}{=} E_1\langle\psi\rangle, x \overset{\sigma}{=} E_1\langle\varphi\rangle]\&(E_1\langle E_2\rangle)\right)\langle E_1\langle\Phi\rangle\rangle \\
&= \left(E_1\&[y \overset{\rho}{=} \psi, x \overset{\sigma}{=} \varphi]\&E_2\right)\langle\Phi\rangle
\end{aligned}
$$

(3) For the special case $E_0 \equiv [\,]$, it is easily seen that a repeated application of (2) allows us to shift the equation $y \overset{\rho}{=} \psi$ to the head of the equation list E_1. Hence, we have proved the result for this case, which can be more formally done by induction on the length of E_1.

(4) The final result is now a simple consequence of Lemma 3.24 and (3) (note that none of the left hand side variables of E_1 can occur in $E_0\langle\psi\rangle$ and that E_1 and $E_0\langle E_1\rangle$ have the same left hand side variables):

$$
\begin{aligned}
&\left(E_0\&E_1\&[y \overset{\rho}{=} \psi]\&E_2\right)\langle\Phi\rangle \\
&= \left((E_0\langle E_1\rangle)\&[y \overset{\rho}{=} E_0\langle\psi\rangle]\&(E_0\langle E_2\rangle)\right)\langle E_0\langle\Phi\rangle\rangle \\
&\overset{(3)}{=} \left([y \overset{\rho}{=} E_0\langle\psi\rangle]\&(E_0\langle E_1\rangle)\&(E_0\langle E_2\rangle)\right)\langle E_0\langle\Phi\rangle\rangle \\
&= \left(E_0\&[y \overset{\rho}{=} \psi]\&E_1\&E_2\right)\langle\Phi\rangle
\end{aligned}
$$

□

Reconsider now the previously example equation system E_1. Using the above lemma, we can now shift the equation for x_4 to the head of the equation system and after this, we can shift x_5 over the equations for x_1, x_2 and x_3:

$$
\mathsf{EqSubs}\left(\begin{bmatrix} x_1 \overset{\mu}{=} \Diamond x_2 \\ x_2 \overset{\nu}{=} x_1 \vee x_3 \\ x_3 \overset{\mu}{=} x_2 \wedge x_4 \\ x_4 \overset{\mu}{=} x_4 \wedge x_5 \\ x_5 \overset{\mu}{=} x_4 \vee x_5 \end{bmatrix}\right) = \mathsf{EqSubs}\left(\begin{bmatrix} x_4 \overset{\mu}{=} x_4 \wedge x_5 \\ x_5 \overset{\mu}{=} x_4 \vee x_5 \\ \hline\hline x_1 \overset{\mu}{=} \Diamond x_2 \\ x_2 \overset{\nu}{=} x_1 \vee x_3 \\ x_3 \overset{\mu}{=} x_2 \wedge x_4 \end{bmatrix}\right)
$$

Note that the latter equation system can be split up into the two parts that are separated with the double line.

The next natural question is how to determine suitable sublists E_0 and E_1 so that a maximal splitting of the equation system is achieved. For this reason, we consider the so-called dependence graph of an equation system that tells us which variables influence the other ones in that the corresponding right hand side contains that variable.

Definition 3.30 (Dependence Graph of an Equation System). *Given a vectorized fixpoint expression* fix E in φ end $\in \mathcal{L}_{\mathsf{spec}}$ *with* $E = [x_1 \stackrel{\sigma_1}{=} \varphi_1, \ldots, x_n \stackrel{\sigma_n}{=} \varphi_n]$*, the dependence graph* $\mathsf{DepG}(E)$ *of* E *is defined as a graph whose vertices are the variables* $\{x_1, \ldots, x_n\}$ *of* E*. There is an edge from* x_j *to* x_k *iff* x_j *occurs as a free variable in* φ_k*. Formally, we define*

$$\mathsf{DepG}(E) := (\{x_1, \ldots, x_n\}, \{(x_j, x_k) \mid x_j \in \mathsf{FV}(\varphi_k)\})$$

It is easily seen that at most $|\varphi_k|$ edges are leading to x_k, so that the number of edges is certainly limited by $\sum_{k=1}^{n} |\varphi_k|$. Hence, we can compute this graph in time $O(|E|)$ and with memory $O(|E|)$. If the dependence graph $\mathsf{DepG}(E)$ of E contains an edge (x_j, x_k), then this means that the value of x_j may directly influence the value of x_k. If no such edge exists, then it follows that the value of x_k is independent of the value of x_j. A change of x_j may trigger a change of x_k, but it is not guaranteed that the value of x_k will also change. In contrast, if there is no edge (x_j, x_k), then it is guaranteed that changing the value of x_j will not influence the value of x_k. Hence, we should preferably talk about the *independencies* that are considered. As an example, the dependence graph of the previously considered equation system looks as follows:

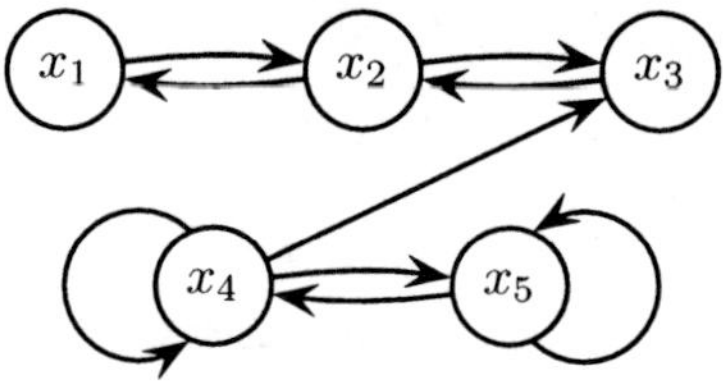

We can clearly see that the dependency graph contains two strongly connected components (SCCs) that are given by $C_1 := \{x_1, x_2, x_3\}$ and $C_2 := \{x_4, x_5\}$. We can easily check out that SCCs can never be split into two parts since all defined variables of an SCC depend at least on all other defined variables of that SCC. Hence, sublists that can not be split must completely contain the SCC of its equations.

Lemma 3.29 allows us to reorder the equations such that an equation system is partitioned into its SCCs. To see this, consider a *quotient graph* whose vertices are the SCCs and which has an edge between two such SCCs if these contain variables that are connected with such an edge. This quotient graph is clearly an acyclic graph that therefore has leaf vertices, which do not have outgoing edges, and root vertices which have no incoming edges. Consider now an arbitrary root C of this quotient graph. As there is no incoming edge, the variables that appear in C only depend on themselves. Therefore, Lemma 3.29 allows us to shift these equations at the head of the equation system (while we retain for a moment the order of these equations that they had in E). We therefore obtain $E = C\&E'$ and can split E into two parts, namely into C and E'. By the induction hypothesis, we proceed in the same manner with E'. Hence, we have proved the following theorem:

Theorem 3.31 (Decomposing Equation Systems into SCC-Blocks). *The order of the equations in an equation system E can be changed, so that E is partitioned into its strongly connected components $\{C_1, \ldots, C_m\}$, i.e. $E = C_1\&\ldots\&C_m$, where the order of the equations in a C_i is the same as in the original system E. The order of the SCCs is such that right hand sides of equations in a component C_i do not contain left hand side variables of a components C_j with $i < j$. Therefore, it follows that*

$$\mathsf{EqSubs}\,(E) = \mathsf{EqSubs}\,(C_1\&\ldots\&C_m) = \mathsf{EqSubs}\,(C_m) \circ \ldots \circ \mathsf{EqSubs}\,(C_1)$$

and moreover that

$$\mathsf{fix}\ E\ \mathsf{in}\ \Phi\ \mathsf{end} = \mathsf{fix}\ C_1\&\ldots\&C_m\ \mathsf{in}\ \Phi\ \mathsf{end} = \mathsf{fix}\ C_m\ \mathsf{in}\ \ldots \mathsf{fix}\ C_1\ \mathsf{in}\ \Phi\ \mathsf{end}\ldots\ \mathsf{end}$$

By the above lemma, we now know about the maximal splitting of an equation system into subsystems. Note that the order of the C_i's is not unique, and is obtained by a topological ordering of the quotient graph. The semantics does not rely on a particular ordering, as long as the quotient graph is respected.

How about the order of equations inside a single SCC? Can we still reorder them and benefit from this reordering or is the order inside the SCCs fixed? To clarify the situation, consider the next example that we first decompose into its four SCCs. The corresponding dependence graph is given in Figure 3.6.

$$\mathsf{EqSubs}\left(\left[\begin{array}{l} x_1 \overset{\mu}{=} \Diamond x_2 \\ x_2 \overset{\nu}{=} x_1 \vee x_3 \\ x_3 \overset{\mu}{=} x_4 \wedge x_6 \\ x_4 \overset{\mu}{=} x_4 \wedge x_5 \\ x_5 \overset{\mu}{=} x_4 \vee x_5 \\ x_6 \overset{\mu}{=} \Diamond x_7 \\ x_7 \overset{\nu}{=} \Diamond x_8 \\ x_8 \overset{\mu}{=} \Diamond x_6 \end{array}\right]\right) = \mathsf{EqSubs}\left(\left[\begin{array}{l} x_6 \overset{\mu}{=} \Diamond x_7 \\ x_7 \overset{\nu}{=} \Diamond x_8 \\ x_8 \overset{\mu}{=} \Diamond x_6 \\ \hline\hline x_4 \overset{\mu}{=} x_4 \wedge x_5 \\ x_5 \overset{\mu}{=} x_4 \vee x_5 \\ \hline\hline x_3 \overset{\mu}{=} x_4 \wedge x_6 \\ \hline\hline x_1 \overset{\mu}{=} \Diamond x_2 \\ x_2 \overset{\nu}{=} x_1 \vee x_3 \end{array}\right]\right)$$

Consider the SCC that consists of the equations with the left hand sides $\{x_6, x_7, x_8\}$. Lemma 3.29 allows us to shift the equation for x_7 over the one for x_6, so that we see with this example, that the order of equations inside an SCC is not uniquely determined.

3.5.3 Model Checking Vectorized Fixpoint Expressions

Theorem 3.31 allows us to reduce the computation of the semantics of fixpoint expressions to those where the equation system consists of a single SCC

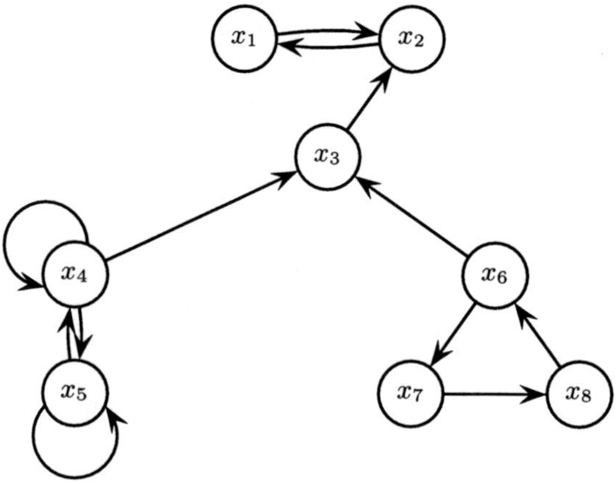

Fig. 3.6. Example dependence graph

only. This will turn out to be important for the efficiency of the model checking algorithm, since we are now able to formulate it as a *divide and conquer* algorithm. It remains to compute for equation systems $E = [x_i \stackrel{\sigma_i}{=} \varphi_i \mid i = 1..n]$ whose dependency graphs consist of a single SCC the tuple $([\![E\langle x_1\rangle]\!]_{\mathcal{K}}, \ldots, [\![E\langle x_n\rangle]\!]_{\mathcal{K}})$. Theorem 3.25 told us already that the mentioned tuple is a fixpoint of the function f_E as defined in Theorem 3.25, and Theorem 3.26 moreover added the fact that the tuple is the least or the greatest fixpoint if we have $\sigma_1 = \ldots = \sigma_n = \mu$ or $\sigma_1 = \ldots = \sigma_n = \nu$, respectively. Hence, by the Tarski/Knaster theorem, we are already able to compute the tuple in these cases.

In the general case, however, the tuple $([\![E\langle x_1\rangle]\!]_{\mathcal{K}}, \ldots, [\![E\langle x_n\rangle]\!]_{\mathcal{K}})$ is neither the least nor the greatest fixpoint of the function f_E. Therefore, the Tarski/Knaster theorem can not directly be used to compute this tuple. We therefore now generalize Theorem 3.26 for cases where not all σ_i's were the same. Instead, we consider a suffix list $E_2 := [x_i \stackrel{\sigma_i}{=} \varphi_i \mid i = m..n]$ of E where all σ_i's are the same (such a suffix trivially exists) and can therefore characterize the subtuple $([\![E\langle x_m\rangle]\!]_{\mathcal{K}}, \ldots, [\![E\langle x_n\rangle]\!]_{\mathcal{K}})$ as the least or greatest fixpoint of some function g_f.

Theorem 3.32 (Semantics of Equation Systems (I)). *Given equation systems* $E_1 = [x_i \stackrel{\sigma_i}{=} \varphi_i \mid i = 1..m]$ *and* $E_2 = [y_i \stackrel{\rho}{=} \psi_i \mid i = 1..n]$ *and a Kripke structure* $\mathcal{K}$. *We define the function* $g_f : (2^S)^n \to (2^S)^n$ *as:* $g_f(Q_1, \ldots, Q_n) := \left([\![\psi_1]\!]_{\left[\mathcal{K}_{y_1\ldots y_n}^{Q_1\ldots Q_n}\middle| E_1\right]}, \ldots, [\![\psi_n]\!]_{\left[\mathcal{K}_{y_1\ldots y_n}^{Q_1\ldots Q_n}\middle| E_1\right]}\right)$. *Then, the following holds:*

- *If* $\rho = \mu$, *then* $([\![(E_1\&E_2)\langle y_1\rangle]\!]_{\mathcal{K}}, \ldots, [\![(E_1\&E_2)\langle y_n\rangle]\!]_{\mathcal{K}})$ *is the least fixpoint of* g_f.
- *If* $\rho = \nu$, *then* $([\![(E_1\&E_2)\langle y_1\rangle]\!]_{\mathcal{K}}, \ldots, [\![(E_1\&E_2)\langle y_n\rangle]\!]_{\mathcal{K}})$ *is the greatest fixpoint of* g_f.

Proof. We only consider the case $\rho = \mu$, the case $\rho = \nu$ is completely dual to this proof. First, we note the following fact: Given an equation system E, a structure $\mathcal{K}'$, and a formula Φ, it follows directly by Definition 3.23 and the substitution Lemma 2.45 that $(*)$ $[\![\Phi]\!]_{[\mathcal{K}'|E]} = [\![E\langle\Phi\rangle]\!]_{\mathcal{K}'}$ holds.

We now define $E_2' := [y_i \overset{\rho}{=} E_1\langle\psi_i\rangle \mid i = 1..n]$, so that by the composition Lemma 3.24, it follows that $E\langle y_i\rangle = (E_1\&E_2)\langle y_i\rangle = E_2'\langle E_1\langle y_i\rangle\rangle = E_2'\langle y_i\rangle$ (note that $y_i \notin \mathsf{defvars}(E_1)$).

Therefore, we have to prove that $([\![E_2'\langle y_1\rangle]\!]_{\mathcal{K}}, \ldots, [\![E_2'\langle y_n\rangle]\!]_{\mathcal{K}})$ is the least fixpoint of g_f. By Theorem 3.26, we already know that this tuple is the least fixpoint of $f_{E_2'}(Q_1, \ldots, Q_n) := ([\![E_1\langle\psi_1\rangle]\!]_{\mathcal{K}_{y_1\ldots y_n}^{Q_1\ldots Q_n}}, \ldots, [\![E_1\langle\psi_n\rangle]\!]_{\mathcal{K}_{y_1\ldots y_n}^{Q_1\ldots Q_n}})$. Hence, the proof is complete, if we could prove that $g_f = f_{E_2'}$ holds, i.e., that $[\![\psi_i]\!]_{\left[\mathcal{K}_{y_1\ldots y_n}^{Q_1\ldots Q_n}\middle|E_1\right]} = [\![E_1\langle\psi_i\rangle]\!]_{\mathcal{K}_{y_1\ldots y_n}^{Q_1\ldots Q_n}}$ holds for $i \in \{1, \ldots, m\}$. However this follows directly from $(*)$.

□

The above theorem applies to general equation systems E, since we can split every equation system into two parts $E = E_1\&E_2$, where all equations in E_2 are of the same parity (μ or ν equations). Given that $E_1 = [x_i \overset{\sigma_i}{=} \varphi_i \mid i = 1..m]$ and $E_2 = [y_i \overset{\rho}{=} \psi_i \mid i = 1..n]$ holds, then the theorem above tells us that we can compute the part $([\![(E_1\&E_2)\langle y_1\rangle]\!]_{\mathcal{K}}, \ldots, [\![(E_1\&E_2)\langle y_n\rangle]\!]_{\mathcal{K}})$ of the fixpoint $([\![(E_1\&E_2)\langle x_1\rangle]\!]_{\mathcal{K}}, \ldots, [\![(E_1\&E_2)\langle x_m\rangle]\!]_{\mathcal{K}}, [\![(E_1\&E_2)\langle y_1\rangle]\!]_{\mathcal{K}}, \ldots, [\![(E_1\&E_2)\langle y_n\rangle]\!]_{\mathcal{K}})$ as the least or greatest fixpoint of the function g_f.

However, this does not yet help us to compute the entire fixpoint: The computation of $([\![(E_1\&E_2)\langle y_1\rangle]\!]_{\mathcal{K}}, \ldots, [\![(E_1\&E_2)\langle y_n\rangle]\!]_{\mathcal{K}})$ according to the Tarski/Knaster theorem requires us to know the values $[\![(E_1\&E_2)\langle x_i\rangle]\!]_{\mathcal{K}}$ in advance to evaluate the function g_f. For this reason, we can not simply start a Tarski/Knaster iteration to compute that fixpoint. The next theorem is therefore used to generalize this result once more: We characterize the entire fixpoint that corresponds with E as a least or greatest fixpoint of a function h.

Theorem 3.33 (Semantics of Equation Systems (II)). *Given equation systems* $E_1 = [x_i \overset{\sigma_i}{=} \varphi_i \mid i = 1..m]$ *and* $E_2 = [y_i \overset{\rho}{=} \psi_i \mid i = 1..n]$ *and a Kripke structure* $\mathcal{K}$. *For all sets* $P_1, \ldots, P_m, Q_1, \ldots, Q_n \subseteq \mathcal{S}$, *we define the structure* $\mathcal{K}' := \mathcal{K}_{x_1\ldots x_m y_1\ldots y_n}^{P_1\ldots P_m Q_1\ldots Q_n}$. *Using* $\mathcal{K}'$, *we moreover define the function* $h : (2^{\mathcal{S}})^{m+n} \to (2^{\mathcal{S}})^{m+n}$ *as follows:*

$$h(P_1, \ldots, P_m, Q_1, \ldots, Q_n) := \left([\![E_1\langle x_1\rangle]\!]_{\mathcal{K}'}, \ldots, [\![E_1\langle x_m\rangle]\!]_{\mathcal{K}'}, [\![\psi_1]\!]_{\mathcal{K}'}, \ldots, [\![\psi_n]\!]_{\mathcal{K}'}\right)$$

With the abbreviation $E := E_1\&E_2$, *the following holds:*

- *If* $\rho = \mu$, *then* $([\![E\langle x_1\rangle]\!]_{\mathcal{K}}, \ldots, [\![E\langle x_m\rangle]\!]_{\mathcal{K}}, [\![E\langle y_1\rangle]\!]_{\mathcal{K}}, \ldots, [\![E\langle y_n\rangle]\!]_{\mathcal{K}})$ *is the least fixpoint of* h.
- *If* $\rho = \nu$, *then* $([\![E\langle x_1\rangle]\!]_{\mathcal{K}}, \ldots, [\![E\langle x_m\rangle]\!]_{\mathcal{K}}, [\![E\langle y_1\rangle]\!]_{\mathcal{K}}, \ldots, [\![E\langle y_n\rangle]\!]_{\mathcal{K}})$ *is the greatest fixpoint of* h.

Proof. We first define $E_2' := [y_i \stackrel{\rho}{=} E_1\langle\psi_i\rangle \mid i = 1..m]$. Note that (1) $E\langle y_i\rangle = (E_1\&E_2)\langle y_i\rangle = E_2'\langle E_1\langle y_i\rangle\rangle = E_2'\langle y_i\rangle$ holds, since $x_i \notin \mathsf{defvars}(E_1)$. Now, we define the following functions:

$$\begin{aligned}
&f(Q_1,\ldots,Q_n) := (\llbracket E_1\langle x_1\rangle\rrbracket_{\mathcal{K}_{y_1\ldots y_n}^{Q_1\ldots Q_n}},\ldots,\llbracket E_1\langle x_m\rangle\rrbracket_{\mathcal{K}_{y_1\ldots y_n}^{Q_1\ldots Q_n}})\\
&g((P_1,\ldots,P_m),(Q_1,\ldots,Q_n)) := (\llbracket\psi_1\rrbracket_{\mathcal{K}_{x_1\ldots x_m y_1\ldots y_n}^{P_1\ldots P_m Q_1\ldots Q_n}},\ldots,\llbracket\psi_n\rrbracket_{\mathcal{K}_{x_1\ldots x_m y_1\ldots y_n}^{P_1\ldots P_m Q_1\ldots Q_n}})\\
&g_f(Q_1,\ldots,Q_n) := g(f(Q_1,\ldots,Q_n),(Q_1,\ldots,Q_n))
\end{aligned}$$

Obviously[3], the tuple $(f(Q_1,\ldots,Q_n), g((P_1,\ldots,P_m),(Q_1,\ldots,Q_n)))$ is equal to $h(P_1,\ldots,P_m,Q_1,\ldots,Q_n)$. Thus, we can use Lemma 3.8 on page 97 to compute the least fixpoint of h by the least fixpoint of g_f. Therefore, consider the function g_f in more detail. It is easily seen that the following holds, where we abbreviated $P_i' := \llbracket E_1\langle x_i\rangle\rrbracket_{\mathcal{K}_{y_1\ldots y_n}^{Q_1\ldots Q_n}}$:

$$g_f(Q_1,\ldots,Q_n) := (\llbracket\psi_1\rrbracket_{\mathcal{K}_{x_1\ldots x_m y_1\ldots y_n}^{P_1'\ldots P_m' Q_1\ldots Q_n}},\ldots,\llbracket\psi_n\rrbracket_{\mathcal{K}_{x_1\ldots x_m y_1\ldots y_n}^{P_1'\ldots P_m' Q_1\ldots Q_n}})$$

But then, it follows for all $i \in \{1,\ldots,n\}$ that the following holds, which proves that the function g_f as defined above is identical to the function g_f that has been considered in the previous theorem.

$$\llbracket\psi_i\rrbracket_{\mathcal{K}_{x_1\ldots x_m y_1\ldots y_n}^{P_1'\ldots P_m' Q_1\ldots Q_n}} = \llbracket E_1\langle\psi_i\rangle\rrbracket_{\mathcal{K}_{y_1\ldots y_n}^{Q_1\ldots Q_n}} = \llbracket\psi_i\rrbracket_{\left[\mathcal{K}_{y_1\ldots y_n}^{Q_1\ldots Q_n}\middle| E_1\right]}$$

Therefore, we know by the previous theorem, that the least fixpoint $(\check{Q}_1, \ldots, \check{Q}_n)$ of g_f is the tuple $(\llbracket E\langle y_1\rangle\rrbracket_{\mathcal{K}},\ldots,\llbracket E\langle y_n\rangle\rrbracket_{\mathcal{K}})$. Hence, we have (2) $\check{Q}_i = \llbracket E\langle y_i\rangle\rrbracket_{\mathcal{K}}$ and by (1) also (3) $\check{Q}_i = \llbracket E_2'\langle y_i\rangle\rrbracket_{\mathcal{K}}$. Now, we use Lemma 3.8 to compute the least fixpoint of h from this tuple: we simply have to supplement the tuple with $(\check{P}_1, \ldots, \check{P}_m) := f(\check{Q}_1, \ldots, \check{Q}_n)$. Note further that the following holds:

$$\check{P}_i = \llbracket E_1\langle x_i\rangle\rrbracket_{\mathcal{K}_{y_1\ldots y_n}^{\check{Q}_1\ldots\check{Q}_n}} \stackrel{(3)}{=} \llbracket E_1\langle x_i\rangle\rrbracket_{[\mathcal{K}|E_2']} = \llbracket E_2'\langle E_1\langle x_i\rangle\rangle\rrbracket_{\mathcal{K}} = \llbracket E\langle x_i\rangle\rrbracket_{\mathcal{K}}$$

□

We call E_2 a μ- and ν-block of E if all equations of E are of parity μ and ν, respectively. By the above theorem, it now follows that we can compute the solution of an equation system in a recursive manner along the μ- and ν-blocks of E. To explain in more detail how this works, assume that we can split E into $E_1\&E_2$ where E_2 is either a μ- or a ν-block. In the following, we assume that E_2 is a μ-block, the other case is completely dual. So, assume that $E_1 = [x_i \stackrel{\sigma_i}{=} \varphi_i \mid i = 1..m]$ and $E_2 = [y_i \stackrel{\mu}{=} \psi_i \mid i = 1..n]$. Then, the previous theorem states that the desired solution $(\llbracket E\langle x_1\rangle\rrbracket_{\mathcal{K}'}, \ldots, \llbracket E\langle x_n\rangle\rrbracket_{\mathcal{K}'}, \llbracket E\langle y_1\rangle\rrbracket_{\mathcal{K}'}, \ldots, \llbracket E\langle y_m\rangle\rrbracket_{\mathcal{K}})$ is the least fixpoint of the following function h where $\mathcal{K}' := \mathcal{K}_{x_1\ldots x_m y_1\ldots y_n}^{P_1\ldots P_m Q_1\ldots Q_n}$:

[3] For conciseness, we neglect here and also in the definition of g_f the tupeling which can be done more formally with additional functions.

$$h(P_1, \ldots, P_m, Q_1, \ldots, Q_n) := (\llbracket E_1\langle x_1\rangle \rrbracket_{\mathcal{K}'}, \ldots, \llbracket E_1\langle x_m\rangle \rrbracket_{\mathcal{K}'}, \llbracket \psi_1 \rrbracket_{\mathcal{K}'}, \ldots, \llbracket \psi_n \rrbracket_{\mathcal{K}'})$$

In the proof of the previous theorem, we have moreover seen that the function h can be defined as $h(x, y) = (f(y), g(x, y))$ with the following two functions f and g:

$$f(Q_1, \ldots, Q_n) := (\llbracket E_1\langle x_1\rangle \rrbracket_{\mathcal{K}_{y_1 \ldots y_n}^{Q_1 \ldots Q_n}}, \ldots, \llbracket E_1\langle x_m\rangle \rrbracket_{\mathcal{K}_{y_1 \ldots y_n}^{Q_1 \ldots Q_n}})$$
$$g(P_1, \ldots, P_m, Q_1, \ldots, Q_n) := (\llbracket \psi_1 \rrbracket_{\mathcal{K}_{x_1 \ldots x_m y_1 \ldots y_n}^{P_1 \ldots P_m Q_1 \ldots Q_n}}, \ldots, \llbracket \psi_n \rrbracket_{\mathcal{K}_{x_1 \ldots x_m y_1 \ldots y_n}^{P_1 \ldots P_m Q_1 \ldots Q_n}})$$

The next key ingredient is Lemma 3.8 on page 97. This lemma tells us that the least fixpoint of a function $h(x, y) := (f(y), g(x, y))$ is $(f(\check{y}), \check{y})$, where $\check{y} := \mu y.g(f(y), y)$ holds. Hence, the problem of finding the solution of an equation system is reduced to a simple least fixpoint computation. Since the functions f and g are monotonic, we can use the Tarski/Knaster iteration to compute this fixpoint. Note that by Lemma 3.8, we thereby have to compute the following steps (where $\perp$ is a tuple $(\{\}, \ldots, \{\})$ of the appropriate length):

$$\begin{array}{ll} x_0 := \perp & y_0 := \perp \\ x_{i+1} := f(y_i) & y_{i+1} := g(x_{i+1}, y_i), \end{array}$$

Considering the definition of f, we see that the step $x_{i+1} := f(y_i)$ in the above iteration is the computation of the solution of the equation system E_1 with the current approximations $Q_1, \ldots, Q_n$ for the variables in defvars (E_2). *According to the definition of g, the step $y_{i+1} := g(x_{i+1}, y_i)$ then simply updates the current approximations Q_i, and the entire procedure repeats until a fixpoint is found.*

Therefore, we see that the algorithm given in Figure 3.8 correctly computes the solution of an equation system E with respect to a given Kripke structure $\mathcal{K}$. We use the auxiliary functions given in Figure 3.7. Eval(Φ) evaluates a formula that consists of Boolean and modal operators. The function LastBlock splits an equation system E into two parts E_1 and E_2 such that E_2 is the largest μ- or ν-block at the end of E. This function also returns the parity. LastBlock is used to divide the model checking problem into a smaller model checking problem (according to the previous theorem).

Given an equation system $E = [x_1 \stackrel{\sigma_1}{=} \varphi_1, \ldots, x_p \stackrel{\sigma_p}{=} \varphi_p]$, the algorithm given in Figure 3.8 maintains for every variable x_i a preliminary approximation $L[x_i]$ for the value $\llbracket E\langle x_i\rangle \rrbracket_{\mathcal{K}}$. The labels of the other variables are also assumed to be given as $L[y] = \llbracket y \rrbracket_{\mathcal{K}}$. We assume that these variables are globally seen by all functions.

The function fixpoint is the main part that computes the fixpoint iteration as outlined above. This means, we compute the least fixpoint $\check{y} := \mu y.g(f(y), y)$ as outlined above. Hence, after splitting E into two lists $E = E_1 \& E_2$, we initialize the variables in defvars (E_2) according to the parity of E_2. After this, we simply perform the Tarski/Knaster iteration for $g(f(y), y)$. Note that, the assignment $x_{i+1} := f(y_i)$ corresponds with the recursive call fixpoint(E_1), and that the assignment $y_{i+1} := g(x_{i+1}, y_i)$ corresponds with the

```
function Eval(Φ)
  case Φ of
    Φ ∈ V   : return L[Φ];
    ¬φ      : return S \ Eval(φ);
    φ ∧ ψ   : return Eval(φ) ∩ Eval(ψ);
    φ ∨ ψ   : return Eval(φ) ∪ Eval(ψ);
    ◇φ      : return pre_∃^R(Eval(φ));
    □φ      : return pre_∀^R(Eval(φ));
    ←◇ φ    : return suc_∃^R(Eval(φ));
    ←□ φ    : return suc_∀^R(Eval(φ));
  end
end

function LastBlock(E)
  [x_1 =^{σ_1} φ_1, ..., x_p =^{σ_p} φ_p] ≡ E;
  ρ := σ_p;
  i := p;
  while (σ_i = ρ) ∧ (i > 0) do i := i − 1 end;
  return ([x_1 =^{σ_1} φ_1, ..., x_i =^{σ_i} φ_i], [x_{i+1} =^{σ_{i+1}} φ_{i+1}, ..., x_p =^{σ_p} φ_p], ρ);
end
```

Fig. 3.7. Auxiliary functions for the algorithm given in Figure 3.8

the call Update(E_2), which is responsible for updating the approximations of the variables of defvars (E_2).

Note that the call Update(E_2) after the computation of fixpoint(E_1) is already done with the new approximations for the variables in defvars (E_1) that have been computed by fixpoint(E_1). This is legal due to Lemma 3.8 (the first iteration). We have therefore found the correctness of the algorithm of Figure 3.8.

Theorem 3.34 (Vectorized Model Checking). *Given a Kripke structure $\mathcal{K}$ and an equation system $E = B_1\&\ldots\&B_\ell$ where $B_i = [x_{i,1} \stackrel{\sigma_i}{=} \varphi_{i,1}, \ldots, x_{i,n_i} \stackrel{\sigma_i}{=} \varphi_{i,n_i}]$ and $\sigma_i \neq \sigma_{i+1}$. Then, the algorithm* Fixpoint *given in Figure 3.8 computes the solution $(\llbracket E\langle x_{1,1}\rangle\rrbracket_{\mathcal{K}}, \ldots, \llbracket E\langle x_{\ell,n_\ell}\rangle\rrbracket_{\mathcal{K}})$ in time $O\left(\left(\frac{n_E\,|\mathcal{S}|}{\ell}\right)^\ell |\mathcal{K}|\,|E|\right)$, where $n_E := \sum_{i=1}^{\ell} n_i$ is the number of equations of E.*

Proof. The correctness of the algorithm immediately follows from the previous theorem. The complexity of the algorithm is essentially the complexity of the function fixpoint. For the following, we abbreviate $E_\ell := B_1\&\ldots\&B_\ell$ for $\ell > 0$ and $E_0 := [\,]$, and denote the number of equations of block B_i as n_i. Let $T_{\mathsf{fixpoint}}(E_\ell)$ be the time required to execute fixpoint(E_ℓ) and let

```
function InitBlock([y_1 =^ρ ψ_1, ..., y_n =^ρ ψ_n])
  if ρ = μ then S_0 := {} else S_0 := S end;
  for i := 1 to n do
    L[y_i] := S_0
  end
end

function Update([y_1 =^ρ ψ_1, ..., y_n =^ρ ψ_n])
  changed := 0;
  for i := 1 to n do
    Q_i := Eval(ψ_i);
    if Q_i ≠ L[y_i] then changed := 1 end
  end;
  for i := 1 to n do L[y_i] := Q_i end
  return changed
end

function fixpoint(E)
  if E = [ ] then return end;
  (E_1, E_2, ρ) := LastBlock(E);
  InitBlock(E_2);
  repeat
    fixpoint(E_1);
    changed := Update(E_2)
  until ¬changed
end

function Fixpoint(E)
  [x_1 =^σ1 φ_1, ..., x_p =^σp φ_p] ≡ E;
  fixpoint(E);
  return (L[x_1], ..., L[x_p])
end
```

Fig. 3.8. Fixpoint computation due to Theorem 3.33

$T_{\mathsf{InitBlock}}(B_\ell)$ and $T_{\mathsf{Update}}(B_\ell)$ be the runtimes of the functions InitBlock and Update for block B_ℓ, respectively. Then, the following holds for some C_1:

- $T_{\mathsf{fixpoint}}([\,]) := C_1$
- $T_{\mathsf{fixpoint}}(E_\ell) = T_{\mathsf{InitBlock}}(B_\ell) + (n_\ell\,|\mathcal{S}| + 1)\,(T_{\mathsf{fixpoint}}(E_{\ell-1}) + T_{\mathsf{Update}}(B_\ell))$

The above equation is easily seen as follows: in each iteration, at least one of the values $L[x_1]$, ..., $L[x_n]$ must change. As each of them either monotonically increases or monotonically decreases, there are at most $n_\ell\,|\mathcal{S}| + 1$ iterations of the **repeat** loop in function fixpoint when it is called for E_ℓ. In each iteration, we call the function fixpoint recursively for the equation system $E_{\ell-1}$, which requires time $T_{\mathsf{fixpoint}}(E_{\ell-1})$, and we call Update to update the variables in block B_ℓ. A simple induction on ℓ reveals the following:

$$\begin{aligned} T_{\mathsf{fixpoint}}(E_\ell) = & \left(\sum_{i=1}^{\ell} T_{\mathsf{InitBlock}}(B_i)\left(\prod_{j=i+1}^{\ell}(n_j\,|\mathcal{S}|+1)\right)\right)+\\ & \left(\sum_{i=1}^{\ell} T_{\mathsf{Update}}(B_i)\left(\prod_{j=i}^{\ell}(n_j\,|\mathcal{S}|+1)\right)\right)+\\ & C_1\left(\prod_{j=1}^{\ell}(n_j\,|\mathcal{S}|+1)\right)\end{aligned}$$

We now derive the asymptotic complexity of T_{fixpoint}. The inequation between the geometric and the arithmetic means assures for arbitrary numbers $\alpha_i > 0$ that the inequation $\prod_{i=1}^{\ell}\alpha_i \leq \left(\frac{1}{\ell}\sum_{i=1}^{\ell}\alpha_i\right)^{\ell}$ holds. Hence, we have $\prod_{i=1}^{\ell}(\alpha_i+1) \leq \left(1+\frac{1}{\ell}\sum_{i=1}^{\ell}\alpha_i\right)^{\ell}$, and therefore we conclude for $\ell > 0$:

$$\begin{aligned} T_{\mathsf{fixpoint}}(E_\ell) \leq\ & T_{\mathsf{InitBlock}}(B_\ell)+\\ & \left(\sum_{i=1}^{\ell-1} T_{\mathsf{InitBlock}}(B_i)\left(1+\frac{|\mathcal{S}|}{\ell-i}\sum_{j=i+1}^{\ell}n_j\right)^{\ell-i}\right)+\\ & \left(\sum_{i=1}^{\ell} T_{\mathsf{Update}}(B_i)\left(1+\frac{|\mathcal{S}|}{\ell-i+1}\sum_{j=i}^{\ell}n_j\right)^{\ell-i+1}\right)+\\ & C_1\left(1+\frac{|\mathcal{S}|}{\ell}\sum_{j=1}^{\ell}n_j\right)^{\ell}\end{aligned}$$

If we replace $\sum_{j=i+1}^{\ell}n_j$ and $\sum_{j=i}^{\ell}n_j$ by $n_E := \sum_{j=1}^{\ell}n_j$, and then the expressions $\left(1+\frac{|\mathcal{S}|n_E}{\ell-i}\right)^{\ell-i}$ and $\left(1+\frac{|\mathcal{S}|n_E}{\ell-i+1}\right)^{\ell-i+1}$ by $\left(1+\frac{|\mathcal{S}|n_E}{\ell}\right)^{\ell}$, which is legal since for all numbers $m, n \in \mathbb{N}$, $m < n$ implies[4] $\left(1+\frac{\lambda}{m}\right)^m < \left(1+\frac{\lambda}{n}\right)^n$, then we obtain the following estimation:

$$T_{\mathsf{fixpoint}}(E_\ell) \leq \left(1+\frac{|\mathcal{S}|\,n_E}{\ell}\right)^{\ell}\left[C_1+\sum_{i=1}^{\ell}\left(T_{\mathsf{InitBlock}}(B_i)+T_{\mathsf{Update}}(B_i)\right)\right]$$

We instantiate the above generic results now for our particular implementation of InitBlock and Update. $T_{\mathsf{InitBlock}}(B_p)$ is clearly of order $O(n_p\,|\mathcal{S}|)$. T_{Update}

[4] Proofs of this fact can be found in many mathematical textbooks. We just sketch some hints: $m < n$ implies $(*)$ $1-\dfrac{a}{m} < 1-\dfrac{a}{n}$ for $a > 0$, and therefore

$$\begin{aligned}\binom{m}{i}\left(\frac{\lambda}{m}\right)^i &= \frac{1}{i!}\frac{m}{m}\frac{m-1}{m}\cdots\frac{m-i+1}{m}\lambda^i = \frac{1}{i!}\left(1-\frac{1}{m}\right)\left(1-\frac{2}{m}\right)\cdots\left(1-\frac{i-1}{m}\right)\lambda^i\\ &\overset{(*)}{<} \frac{1}{i!}\left(1-\frac{1}{n}\right)\left(1-\frac{2}{n}\right)\cdots\left(1-\frac{i-1}{n}\right)\lambda^i = \frac{1}{i!}\frac{n}{n}\frac{n-1}{n}\cdots\frac{n-i+1}{n}\lambda^i = \binom{n}{i}\left(\frac{\lambda}{n}\right)^i\end{aligned}$$

This can be used to finally conclude:

$$\left(1+\frac{\lambda}{m}\right)^m = \sum_{i=0}^{m}\binom{m}{i}\left(\frac{\lambda}{m}\right)^i < \sum_{i=0}^{m}\binom{n}{i}\left(\frac{\lambda}{n}\right)^i < \sum_{i=0}^{n}\binom{n}{i}\left(\frac{\lambda}{n}\right)^i = \left(1+\frac{\lambda}{n}\right)^n$$

can be estimated as follows: The function Update evaluates each right hand side $\varphi_{p,j}$ of the last block B_p in the current environment. The latter can be done for each right hand side formula $\varphi_{i,j}$ in time $O(|\mathcal{K}|\,|\varphi_{i,j}|)$. We moreover require for each $L[x_i]$ some time of order $O(|\mathcal{S}|)$ for updating and checking possible changes, but since we have $|\mathcal{S}| \leq |\mathcal{K}|$, it follows that $T_{\mathsf{Update}}(B_p)$ is of order $O(|\mathcal{K}|\,|B_p|)$. Hence, $\sum_{i=1}^{\ell} T_{\mathsf{InitBlock}}(B_i)$ is of order $O(|\mathcal{S}|\,n_E)$, and $\sum_{i=1}^{\ell} T_{\mathsf{Update}}(B_i)$ is of order $O(|\mathcal{K}|\,|E_\ell|)$. For this reason, there are constants c_1 and c_2 so that the following holds:

$$T_{\mathsf{fixpoint}}(E_\ell) \leq \left(1 + \frac{|\mathcal{S}|\,n_E}{\ell}\right)^{\ell} [c_1\,|\mathcal{S}|\,n_E + c_2\,|\mathcal{K}|\,|E_\ell| + C_1]$$

Therefore, we see that $T_{\mathsf{fixpoint}}(E_\ell)$ is of order $O\left(\left(1 + \frac{|\mathcal{S}|n_E}{\ell}\right)^{\ell} |\mathcal{K}|\,|E_\ell|\right)$. Finally, note that for the functions $f(x) := \left(1 + \frac{\alpha x}{\ell}\right)^{\ell}$ and $g(x) := \left(\frac{\alpha x}{\ell}\right)^{\ell}$, we have $\lim_{x\to\infty} \frac{f(x)}{g(x)} = 1$. □

Having found a model checking procedure for the vectorized μ-calculus, we can now think about possible optimizations. There are a couple of improvements, which do not however affect the worst case complexity given in the previous theorem. Nevertheless, it is important for implementations to use these techniques. A first optimization is to combine the two for-loops in function Update as shown in function Update1 of Figure 3.9. The result is then not strictly the iteration sequence given in Lemma 3.8, since the updated values $L[y_i]$ are already used for subsequent updates of $L[y_j]$ with $j > i$. Note that this is correct, since all functions are monotonic, and we will therefore reach the fixpoint faster, but we can not grow beyond it (we always deal with prefixed points). Note that we also save variables, since we can do with only one auxiliary variable Q.

A similar, but more powerful improvement is to use the other iteration schema of Lemma 3.8, i.e. to proceed as follows:

$$\begin{array}{ll} x_0 := \bot & y_0 := \bot \\ x_{i+1} := f(y_i) & y_{i+1} := \mu y.g(x_{i+1}, y) \end{array}$$

This means that our update procedure should not simply perform one evaluation step for each right hand side of the equations, but should instead perform such evaluations only if there is no further change. This will save subsequent recursive calls, so that the overall runtime will be faster. An update procedure that implements this improved iteration is Update2, also given in Figure 3.9. These improvements are also important, they do not affect the overall worst case complexity. To see this, note that there may still be $n_\ell\,|\mathcal{S}|+1$ recursive calls to fixpoint, and that the repeat-loop of Update2 may iterate $n_\ell\,|\mathcal{S}| + 1$ many times, where each time Update1 is executed. An execution

```
function Update1([y_1 ≜^ρ ψ_1, ..., y_n ≜^ρ ψ_n])
  changed := 0;
  for i := 1 to n do
    Q := L[y_i];
    L[y_i] := Eval(ψ_i);
    if Q ≠ L[y_i] then changed := 1 end;
  end;
  return changed
end

function Update2(E)
  changed_1 := 0;
  repeat
    changed_0 := Update1(E);
    if changed_0 then changed_1 := 1 end;
  until ¬changed_0;
  return changed_1
end
```

Fig. 3.9. Improvements of the vector model checking procedure of Figure 3.8

of Update1 takes time $O(|\mathcal{K}|\,|B_\ell|)$, but the sum of all these calls of Update1 in Update2 is limited by $O((n_\ell\,|\mathcal{S}|+1)\,|\mathcal{K}|\,|B_\ell|)$. Therefore, we end up with essentially the same estimations and conclude that even with Update2, the worst case time complexity is still the same.

Finally, note that the Tarski/Knaster iteration for computing $y_{i+1} := \mu y.g(x_{i+1}, y)$ should start with the bottom element, so that at a first glance, we should have to reinitialize the block E in function Update2. Due to reasons of monotonicity, we can however use the previous approximation as a prefixed point to start the new fixpoint iteration. Hence, we do not have to reinitialize here. Initialisations of blocks is only necessary in the function fixpoint when a new block of different parity is entered.

3.5.4 Comparing Basic and Vectorized μ-Calculus Model Checking

In the previous section, we developed a model checking procedure for the vectorized μ-calculus. The semantics of the vectorized μ-calculus was defined by a reduction via the associated substitution to the basic μ-calculus. In this section, we consider the converse, i.e. a reduction from the basic μ-calculus to the vectorized one. We are then able to compare the model checking procedures obtained so-far w.r.t. their complexities.

Note that the complexities of the non-vectorized model checking algorithms have been given in terms of the alternation depth or the nesting depth of formulas while the algorithm given in Figure 3.8 uses the number of blocks of an equation system as a measure for the complexity. We therefore note the following lemma that relates alternation depths and SCCs of equation systems with each other.

Lemma 3.35 (Alternation Depth of Equations). *Given an equation system* $E = [x_i \stackrel{\sigma_i}{=} \varphi_i \mid i = 1 \ldots n]$ *whose dependency graph contains a single SCC. Let* $\mathsf{EqSubs}(E) = \{(x_i, \eta_i) \mid i = 1 \ldots n\}$*. Then, all* η_j *have the same alternation depth, i.e.* $\forall i, j \in \{1, \ldots, n\}.\mathsf{ad}(\eta_i) = \mathsf{ad}(\eta_j)$*.*

Proof. We prove by induction on the number of equations of E that for all indices $1 \leq i < |E|$, $\mathsf{ad}(E\langle x_i \rangle) = \mathsf{ad}(E\langle x_{i+1} \rangle)$ holds. The induction base is trivial. For the induction step, we are given the equation system $E = [x_i \stackrel{\sigma_i}{=} \varphi_i \mid i = 1 \ldots n]$ with $n > 0$. Define $E' = [x_i \stackrel{\sigma_i}{=} [\varphi_i]_{x_1}^{\sigma_1 x_1 . \varphi_1} \mid i = 2 \ldots n]$, $\Delta := \mathsf{EqSubs}(E)$, and $\Delta' := \mathsf{EqSubs}(E')$. By Lemma 3.24, we know that $\Delta = \Delta' \circ \{(x_1, \sigma_1 x_1 . \varphi_1)\}$ holds. We have to prove that $\mathsf{ad}(E\langle x_i \rangle) = \mathsf{ad}(E\langle x_{i+1} \rangle)$ for all $1 \leq i < n$. Using the equation $\Delta = \Delta' \circ \{(x_1, \sigma_1 x_1 . \varphi_1)\}$, this reduces to the following goals G_1 and G_2:

G_1:$\mathsf{ad}(E'\langle x_i \rangle) = \mathsf{ad}(E'\langle x_{i+1} \rangle)$ for all $2 \leq i < n$
G_2:$\mathsf{ad}(E'\langle \sigma_1 x_1 . \varphi_1 \rangle) = \mathsf{ad}(E'\langle x_2 \rangle)$

To prove G_1, note that the dependence graph of E' forms a single SCC. To see this, note that every edge (x_1, x_j) with $j > 1$ that occurs in the dependence graph of E is now replaced by the set of edges $\{(y, x_j) \mid y \in \mathsf{free\_vars}(\varphi_1) \setminus \{x_1\}\}$. Therefore, a path that leads over x_1, e.g. as $x_j \to x_1 \to x_k$ will now go directly from x_j to x_k. Hence, we can apply the induction hypothesis to E', so that the goal G_1 immediately follows.

To prove G_2, we abbreviate for convenience $\eta_i := E'\langle x_i \rangle$ for $i = 2 \ldots n$ and hence have $\Delta' = \{(x_i, \eta_i) \mid 2 \leq i \leq n\}$. By G_1, we have $\mathsf{ad}(\eta_2) = \mathsf{ad}(\eta_3) = \ldots = \mathsf{ad}(\eta_n)$. Thus, we have to prove that $\mathsf{ad}(\sigma_1 x_1 . [\varphi_1]_{x_2 \ldots x_n}^{\eta_2 \ldots \eta_n}) = \mathsf{ad}(\eta_j)$ for some $2 \leq j \leq n$.

Note that the subformulas η_j that will occur after substitution in $[\varphi_1]_{x_2 \ldots x_n}^{\eta_2 \ldots \eta_n}$ are independent in the sense that none of the variables x_1, …, x_n occurs free in a η_j. Therefore, we see that (note that $\mathsf{ad}(\sigma_1 x_1 . \varphi_1) = 1$ and $\mathsf{ad}(\eta_j) \geq 1$):

$$\begin{aligned} \mathsf{ad}(\sigma_1 x_1 . [\varphi_1]_{x_2 \ldots x_n}^{\eta_2 \ldots \eta_n}) &= \max\left(\{\mathsf{ad}(\sigma_1 x_1 . \varphi_1)\} \cup \{\mathsf{ad}(\eta_j) \mid 1 < j \wedge x_j \in \mathsf{FV}(\varphi_1)\}\right) \\ &= \max\{\mathsf{ad}(\eta_j) \mid 1 < j \wedge x_j \in \mathsf{FV}(\varphi_1)\} \end{aligned}$$

As the dependence graph of E forms a SCC, at least one of the variables x_2, …, x_n must occur in φ_1. No matter which one it is, say x_j, we see that $\mathsf{ad}(\sigma_1 x_1 . [\varphi_1]_{x_2 \ldots x_n}^{\eta_2 \ldots \eta_n}) = \mathsf{ad}(\eta_j)$ holds. □

By the above lemma, we see that the alternation depths $\mathsf{ad}(\eta_j)$ can not be used to further structure the equation systems. The above lemma tells us that the translation of an equation system to non-vectorized formulas, i.e., the computation of $\mathsf{EqSubs}(E)$ yields formulas of the same alternation depth for any SCC. We can therefore define the alternation depth of an SCC as the alternation depth of an arbitrary formula $E\langle x_i \rangle$. Given that we translate a non-vectorized formula Φ to an equivalent equation system E_Φ, it is moreover easily seen that $\mathsf{ad}(\Phi)$ is the maximal alternation depth of an SCC in E_Φ.

It is not too complicated to translate non-vectorized μ-calculus formulas into a vectorized form. The next theorem tells us how it can be done. Note that each fixpoint formula corresponds with an equation, and that equations for outer fixpoints are placed at the end of the equation system.

```
function Vectorize(Φ)
  case Φ of
    is_var(Φ): return ([ ],Φ);
    ¬φ       : (E_φ, φ') := Vectorize(φ);
               return (E_φ, ¬φ');
    φ ∧ ψ    : (E_φ, φ') := Vectorize(φ);
               (E_ψ, ψ') := Vectorize(ψ);
               return (E_φ&E_ψ, φ' ∧ ψ');
    φ ∨ ψ    : (E_φ, φ') := Vectorize(φ);
               (E_ψ, ψ') := Vectorize(ψ);
               return (E_φ&E_ψ, φ' ∨ ψ');
    ◇φ       : (E, ψ) := Vectorize(φ);
               return (E, ◇ψ);
    □φ       : (E, ψ) := Vectorize(φ);
               return (E, □ψ);
    ←◇ φ     : (E, ψ) := Vectorize(φ);
               return (E, ←◇ ψ);
    ←□ φ     : (E, ψ) := Vectorize(φ);
               return (E, ←□ ψ);
    σx.φ     : (E_φ, φ') := Vectorize(φ);
               return (E&[x =^σ φ'], x);
  end
end
```

Fig. 3.10. Translating non-vectorized μ-calculus formulas to equation systems

Theorem 3.36 (Translating μ-Calculus Formulas to Equation Systems). *Given a non-vectorized μ-calculus formula Φ where each bound variable is only bound once. Then, the function call* Vectorize(Φ) *with the function* Vectorize *given in Figure 3.10 computes a tuple (E, Ψ) where E is an equation system and Ψ is a formula that is built up only with variables, Boolean and modal operators, so that* $\Phi = \mathsf{fix}\ E\ \mathsf{in}\ \Psi\ \mathsf{end}$ *holds.*

The theorem is easily proved by induction on the given formula Φ, where we need Lemma 3.28 for the induction steps. Note further that in the cases for conjunctions and disjunctions, we could alternatively return the equation system $E_\psi \& E_\varphi$ instead of $E_\varphi \& E_\psi$. Therefore, the resulting equation system is not unique.

We have already considered in Theorem 3.19 and Theorem 3.22 model checking algorithms for non-vectorized μ-calculus formulas. The translation algorithm given in Figure 3.10 in combination with the algorithm given in Figure 3.8 now gives us a third alternative to check these formulas. In order to compare these variants, we now 'simulate' the algorithms mentioned in Theorem 3.19 and Theorem 3.22 in a 'vectorized form'.

It is not too hard to see that the naive approach of Theorem 3.19 performs the computations that our vectorized model checking procedure would perform, when the function LastBlock would be changed, so that only the last equation would be split up. Furthermore, the update procedure used is the simple one, i.e. function Update in Figure 3.8. If we assume that the equation system E_Φ that is obtained from a non-vector formula Φ is decomposed into its SCCs then the remaining equation systems correspond with the top-level fixpoint formulas of Φ. Furthermore, we then have $\ell \leq \mathsf{nd}(\Phi)$ for every SCC (ℓ is the number of blocks of the SCC). Consider now again the upper bound for the runtime of the vector model checking procedure that we have determined in the previous section:

$$\begin{aligned} T_{\mathsf{fixpoint}}(E_\ell) = & \left(\sum_{i=1}^{\ell} T_{\mathsf{InitBlock}}(B_i)\left(\prod_{j=i+1}^{\ell}(n_j\,|\mathcal{S}|+1)\right)\right) + \\ & \left(\sum_{i=1}^{\ell} T_{\mathsf{Update}}(B_i)\left(\prod_{j=i}^{\ell}(n_j\,|\mathcal{S}|+1)\right)\right) + \\ & C_1\left(\prod_{j=1}^{\ell}(n_j\,|\mathcal{S}|+1)\right) \end{aligned}$$

If we instantiate $n_j = 1$, $T_{\mathsf{InitBlock}}(B_i) = c_1\,|\mathcal{S}|$, $T_{\mathsf{Update}}(B_i) = c_2\,|\mathcal{K}|\,|B_i|$, we obtain the following estimation:

$$\begin{aligned} T_{\mathsf{fixpoint}}(E_\ell) = & \left(\sum_{i=1}^{\ell} c_1\,|\mathcal{S}|\,(|\mathcal{S}|+1)^{\ell-i}\right) + \\ & \left(\sum_{i=1}^{\ell} c_2\,|\mathcal{K}|\,|B_i|\,(|\mathcal{S}|+1)^{\ell-i+1}\right) + \\ & C_1\,(|\mathcal{S}|+1)^{\ell} \\ \leq & \; c_1\ell\,|\mathcal{S}|\,(|\mathcal{S}|+1)^{\ell-1} + c_2\,|E_\ell|\,|\mathcal{K}|\,(|\mathcal{S}|+1)^{\ell} + C_1\,(|\mathcal{S}|+1)^{\ell} \end{aligned}$$

and therefore see that $T_{\mathsf{fixpoint}}(E_\ell)$ is of order $O\left(|E_\ell|\,|\mathcal{K}|\,(|\mathcal{S}|+1)^{\ell}\right)$. As $|E_\ell| \leq \Phi$ and $\ell \leq \mathsf{nd}(\Phi)$, we see that the vectorized version is at least as good as the naive approach considered in Theorem 3.19.

Consider now how the improved algorithm of Figure 3.5 on page 116 is obtained from our vectorized version. We use the function LastBlock as it is, but use a special update procedure Update3 given in Figure 3.11. For a block $E_2 = [y_1 \stackrel{\varrho}{=} \psi_1, \ldots, y_n \stackrel{\varrho}{=} \psi_n])$, it first updates ψ_1. If this leads to a change of $L[y_1]$, then the update process terminates and leads to another recursive call of fixpoint. If, on the other hand, $L[y_1]$ remains the same, then the update procedure updates $L[y_2]$, and so on.

```
function Update3([y_1 =^ρ ψ_1, ..., y_n =^ρ ψ_n])
  i := 1;
  changed := 0;
  repeat
    Q := L[y_i];
    L[y_i] := Eval(ψ_i);
    if Q ≠ L[y_i] then changed := 1 end
    i := i + 1;
  until ¬changed ∨ (i > n)
  return changed
end
```

Fig. 3.11. Update procedure for simulating the non-vectorized μ-calculus model checking on page 116

Hence, we see that this algorithm is already block-oriented: Instead of splitting up only the last equation, it splits up the last block of equations E_2 with the same parity. It then initializes the approximations $L[y_i]$ for the block E_2' and will never reinitialize these approximations according to Theorem 3.4, unless a new block is split up (this block has different parity). Hence, the algorithm given in Figure 3.5 on page 116 is essentially identical to our vectorized version with the simple update procedure Update, although it tries to invoke recursive calls to fixpoint as soon as possible. In general, this is not a good idea, but the overall worst case complexity is not affected by this: We still have at most $n_\ell |S| + 1$ recursive calls to fixpoint, and a call to Update3 will run in time $O(|B|\,|\mathcal{K}|)$ for updating block B. Hence, we end up with the same estimations, yielding the same worst case complexity.

3.5.5 Dependency-Triggered Evaluations

In the previous section, we discussed model checking algorithms for the vectorized μ-calculus and so developed the vectorized fixpoint algorithm of Figure 3.8. We have also seen that this algorithm can be used to check ordinary, i.e., non-vectorized μ-calculus formulas and that the algorithms we had discussed for these non-vectorized μ-calculus formulas (Figures 3.2 and 3.4) can be simulated by the vectorized version when appropriate auxiliary functions for updating the blocks are used.

In this section, we present an improvement to the model checking algorithm of Figure 3.8 by considering the dependencies between the variables defined in the equation systems. However, the algorithm DepFixpoint that we will thereby obtain, has still the same worst case complexity. Nevertheless, it will be more efficient in practice, and it will show us the way to the Cleaveland-Steffen algorithm in the next section that has a better worst case complexity.

```
function foreign(V, σ, Φ)
  case Φ of
    is_var(Φ) : if Φ ∈ V then return ([ ], Φ)
                else y := newvar; return ([y =σ Φ], y) end;
    ¬φ        : (E_φ, y_φ) := foreign(V, σ, φ);
                return (E_φ, ¬y_φ);
    φ ∧ ψ     : (E_φ, y_φ) := foreign(V, σ, φ); (E_ψ, y_ψ) := foreign(V, σ, ψ);
                return (E_φ&E_ψ, y_φ ∧ y_ψ);
    φ ∨ ψ     : (E_φ, y_φ) := foreign(V, σ, φ); (E_ψ, y_ψ) := foreign(V, σ, ψ);
                return (E_φ&E_ψ, y_φ ∨ y_ψ);
    ◇φ        : (E_φ, y_φ) := foreign(V, σ, φ);
                return (E_φ, ◇y_φ);
    □φ        : (E_φ, y_φ) := foreign(V, σ, φ);
                return (E_φ, □y_φ);
    ←◇ φ      : (E_φ, y_φ) := foreign(V, σ, φ);
                return (E_φ, ←◇ y_φ);
    ←□ φ      : (E_φ, y_φ) := foreign(V, σ, φ);
                return (E_φ, ←□ y_φ);
  end
end

function DefForeignBlock([x_1 =σ φ_1, ..., x_n =σ φ_n])
  V := {x_1, ..., x_n};
  D := [ ]; E := [ ];
  for i := 1 to n do
    (D_φ, φ) := foreign(V, σ, φ_i);
    D := D&D_φ;
    E := E&[x_i =σ φ];
  end;
  return D&E
end
```

Fig. 3.12. Abbreviating foreign variables

The improvement of the new algorithm is motivated by the following observation of the function fixpoint of Figure 3.8: Reconsidering the proof of Theorem 3.34, we see that we have assumed that the execution of the loop in function fixpoint(E_p) requires at most $n_p\,|\mathcal{S}| + 1$ iterations where n_p is the length of the last block of E_p. Moreover, *the update procedure requires time of order $O(|\mathcal{K}|\,|B_p|)$ since each equation of B_p is evaluated in every iteration step* (we consider Update or Update1 here). In the worst case example that really requires $n_p\,|\mathcal{S}| + 1$ iteration steps, however only one variable $L[x_i]$ of the block B_p changes per iteration, so that the evaluations of the other equations are useless: their evaluations return the same value. To keep track of computations that really matter, we now consider dependencies between the equations so that we can avoid computations that have no effect.

Propagating value changes through dependencies becomes much easier when we transform the equation system such that the only interactions between blocks are given by equations of the form $x \stackrel{\sigma}{=} y$, where y is a variable that is not defined in the same block as x. We call such an equation a 'forward definition'. Every equation system can be transformed into such a form by the following two steps:

- The first step of the transformation is to *eliminate forward definitions* $x_i \stackrel{\sigma_i}{=} y$ where y is a variable (regardless whether it belongs to $\mathsf{defvars}(E)$ or not). It is clear that we can remove such an equation and replace x_i by y everywhere in the equation system.
- We now decompose E into its blocks, i.e. $E = B_1\&\ldots\&B_\ell$, and replace each block B_i by the result of the function call $\mathsf{DefForeignBlock}(B_i)$, where DefForeignBlock is defined in Figure 3.12.

Note that the function DefForeignBlock will reintroduce forward equations. The aim is that the variables of a block that do not belong to $\mathsf{defvars}(B)$ are abbreviated by forward definitions. The benefit is that we now know that for every forward definition $x_i \stackrel{\sigma_i}{=} z$, the variable z is not defined in the same block as x_i. This will be important for the propagation of values to other blocks. Clearly, we have the following result:

Lemma 3.37 (Abbreviating Foreign Variables). *Given an equation system E without forward definitions, i.e., no right hand side is a variable. Let $B_1\&\ldots\&B_\ell$ be the decomposition of E into its maximal μ- and ν-blocks, respectively. We define $B'_i := \mathsf{DefForeignBlock}(B_i)$ for $i \in \{1,\ldots,\ell\}$ and $E' := B'_1\&\ldots\&B'_\ell$.*

It follows that $|E'| \in O(|E|)$. Moreover, every solution of E' uniquely corresponds with a solution of E, i.e., we have for every structure $\mathcal{K}$ and for all $x \in \mathsf{defvars}(E)$ the equation $[\![E\langle x\rangle]\!]_{\mathcal{K}} = [\![E'\langle x\rangle]\!]_{\mathcal{K}}$.

Finally, it follows for every equation $y_i \stackrel{\sigma_i}{=} \psi_i$ of B'_i that either ψ_i is not a variable or it is not contained in $\mathsf{defvars}(B'_i)$.

The correctness is easily seen. What happens is just that forward definitions are introduced for variables that do not belong to the considered block. These equations will serve as starting points for the update procedure that follows the dependencies. It is moreover easily seen that the transformation does not affect the number of blocks: Simply note that a new introduced equation is of the same parity as the equation it stems from (which is the parity of the block). The above information about forward definitions will be used by the following algorithms for propagating values between blocks.

To propagate changes of $L[x_i]$, we need to know which variable influences another one. We already know that this information is provided by the dependence graph $\mathsf{DepG}(E)$ of an equation system E as given in Definition 3.30. Hence, if E contains an equation $x_i \stackrel{\sigma_i}{=} \varphi_i$ where φ_i contains a variable x_j, and we know that $L[x_j]$ has recently been changed, then this change has to be

```
function Propagate([x_1 =^σ φ_1, ..., x_n =^σ φ_n])
  W := [];
  for i = 1 to n do
    if is_var(φ_i) then
      if L[x_i] ≠ L[φ_i] then
        L[x_i] := L[φ_i]; W := [x_i]&W
      end
    end
  end;
  return W
end

function DepInitBlock([x_1 =^σ φ_1, ..., x_n =^σ φ_n])
  if σ = ν then S_0 := S else S_0 := {} end;
  for i = 1 to n do L[x_i] := S_0 end;
  return Propagate([x_1 =^σ φ_1, ..., x_n =^σ φ_n])
end

function DepUpdate([x_1 =^σ φ_1, ..., x_n =^σ φ_n])
  V := {x_1, ..., x_n};
  W := Propagate([x_1 =^σ φ_1, ..., x_n =^σ φ_n]);
  changed := (W ≠ [ ]);
  while W ≠ [ ] do
    [x_i]&W ≡ W;
    for (x_i, x_j) ∈ D_E ∧ x_j ∈ V do
      Q := Eval(φ_j);
      if Q ≠ L[x_j] then
        L[x_j] := Q; W := W&[x_j]
      end
    end
  end;
  return changed
end
```

Fig. 3.13. Vectorized fixpoint evaluation using dependencies

propagated to a new evaluation of φ_i to update $L[x_i]$. Recall that in the algorithm of Figure 3.8 the update mechanism is blind for variable dependencies and simply updates every equation of the block. We therefore improve the function Fixpoint of Figure 3.8 by changing the update and initialization procedures, as given in Figure 3.13, which are used by the algorithm of Figure 3.14.

Beneath the dependency graph $\mathcal{D}_E$, the algorithm also maintains worklists $\mathcal{W}$ (one for each block) to *store the variables that have been changed, but whose changes have not yet been propagated through the block.* There are two reasons why a variable x_i may be contained in a worklist: either due to the initialization, or since its value has recently been changed by the update procedure. We consider first the initialization procedure DepInitBlock. After having set the standard initial value for the Tarski / Knaster iteration, the call to function Propagate will put in the worklist every variable that has been defined by a forward definition. The reason for this is that Propagate also changes the values $L[x_i]$ in case that x_i is defined by a forward definition. This ensures that current approximations that have been computed by the other blocks are used for the evaluation of the considered block. Of course, the values of the variables that are not bound in the equation system are propagated in this way.

The update procedure also starts with a call to Propagate. This is necessary since the previous call to depfixpoint in Figure 3.14 might change some variable values that are bound in the lower blocks. For this reason, these values have to be propagated to the current block as starting points for the update procedure. Note that if Propagate will not detect changes to the previous values, it will not change a $L[x_i]$ and will return $\mathcal{W} = [\,]$. In this case, the update procedure also terminates immediately since all values now satisfy the equations. Otherwise, the update procedure computes the fixpoint starting with variables that are defined by forward definitions. The update procedure propagates these value changes until all values become stable. This is done by removing a variable x_i from the current worklist and evaluating the definition φ_i of every variable x_j that depends on x_i and that is also defined in the current block. If this evaluation differs from the current value of $L[x_j]$, we update $L[x_j]$ and put x_j into the worklist, since it has now changed. If the worklist is finally empty, then the values $(L[x_1], \ldots, L[x_n])$ contain the solution, based on the approximations of the higher blocks and the fixpoints computed in the lower blocks (the latter are not however the final results, since they are also based on the approximations of the outer blocks).

The interaction between blocks is only due to the propagation function, i.e. by forward definitions. The current values of the other blocks are propagated either when an update is called or if the block is initialized. If a block is initialized due to a new fixpoint computation, new information flows from higher blocks to the current one. If the update procedure calls the propagation function, new information flows from lower blocks to the current one.

Note that a real implementation should preferably be based on lists $D[x_i]$ that contain the variables x_j that depend on x_i and that are defined in the same block as x_i. Then, the loop **for** $(x_i, x_j) \in \mathcal{D}_E \wedge x_j \in V \ldots$ in DepUpdate is a simple iteration through the list $D[x_i]$.

It is easily seen that DepFixpoint is equivalent to Fixpoint using Update2 since it only leaves out some of the computations that are known to be worthless. Therefore, it is clear that DepFixpoint will run, in general, more efficiently than Fixpoint (with Update2), since in each step, it will update, at most, as many variables as Fixpoint would update in the same situation. The additional effort for maintaining the worklists $\mathcal{W}$ is negligible. However, in the worst case, where every variable depends on any other one, DepFixpoint

```
function InitAllBlocks(E)
  if E = [] then return end;
  (E_1, E_2, ρ) := LastBlock(E);
  E_2 ≡ [x_1 =σ φ_1, ..., x_n =σ φ_n];
  if σ = ν then S_0 := S else S_0 := {} end;
  for i = 1 to n do L[x_i] := S_0 end;
  InitAllBlocks(E_1)
end

function depfixpoint(E)
  if E = [] then return end;
  (E_1, E_2, ρ) := LastBlock(E);
  W := DepInitBlock(E_2);
  repeat
    depfixpoint(E_1);
    changed := DepUpdate(E_2)
  until ¬changed
end

function DepFixpoint(E)
  EliminateForwardDefs(E); (* eliminate forward definitions *)
  AbbrevForeigns(E); (* apply DefForeignBlock (Figure 3.12) blockwise *)
  D_E := DepG (E);
  InitAllBlocks(E);
  depfixpoint(E);
  [x_1 =σ_1 φ_1, ..., x_p =σ_p φ_p] ≡ E;
  return (L[x_1], ..., L[x_p])
end
```

Fig. 3.14. Vectorized fixpoint evaluation using dependencies

needs to update every variable and will therefore then require the same runtime. Hence, while we expect DepFixpoint to be more efficient in the average case, it has the same worst case complexity as Fixpoint, i.e., we have the following theorem.

Theorem 3.38 (Correctness and Complexity of DepFixpoint**).** *Given a Kripke structure $\mathcal{K}$ and an equation system $E = B_1\&\ldots\&B_\ell$ where $B_i = [x_{i,1} \stackrel{\sigma_i}{=} \varphi_{i,1}, \ldots, x_{i,n_i} \stackrel{\sigma_i}{=} \varphi_{i,n_i}]$ and $\sigma_i \neq \sigma_{i+1}$. Then, the algorithm* DepFixpoint *given in Figure 3.14 computes $(\llbracket E\langle x_{1,1}\rangle\rrbracket_{\mathcal{K}}, \ldots, \llbracket E\langle x_{\ell,n_\ell}\rangle\rrbracket_{\mathcal{K}})$ in time $O\left(\left(\frac{n_E\,|\mathcal{S}|}{\ell}\right)^\ell |\mathcal{K}|\,|E|\right)$, where $n_E := \sum_{i=1}^{\ell} n_i$ is the number of equations of E.*

The reason why we still have the same worst case complexity is that we still evaluate expressions that possibly do not lead to changes. We have already eliminated many of these worthless computations, but have still not eliminated all of them. The algorithm given in the next section will completely eliminate worthless computations and will therefore improve the complexity.

3.5.6 The Cleaveland-Steffen Algorithm

Based on the algorithm of the previous section, we will now refine the dependency-triggered evaluation, and will thereby obtain the Cleaveland-Steffen algorithm. The algorithm goes back to Cleaveland, Klein and Steffen, and has been developed in a couple of papers [116–119] that are refinements of the work of Arnold and Crubille [23]. Arnold and Crubille [23] presented an algorithm to compute the least fixpoint of a μ- or ν-block E for a structure $\mathcal{K}$ in time $O(|\mathcal{K}|\,|E|^2)$. This was improved by Cleaveland and Steffen in [117] so that a runtime of order $O(|\mathcal{K}|\,|E|)$ has been obtained. The same authors extended, in [118], the algorithm to handle equation systems whose SCCs were either μ- or ν-blocks (i.e., the alternation-free fragment) with the same complexity ([119] is a more detailed version of [118]). Finally, an extension to arbitrary equation systems has been presented in [116] and is discussed in detail in this section.

To motivate the data structures used by the algorithm, consider why algorithm DepFixpoint of the previous section still has the same worst case complexity than our previous version. *The problem is that we can not predict when $L[x_i]$ will actually change, and therefore, we are still in danger of performing worthless computations.* The dependencies allowed us to eliminate some of the worthless computations, but not all of them. It may still be the case that $L[x_i]$ does not change, although it depends on some x_j whose value has changed. In this case, we still evaluate the right hand side of x_i, although it does not yield any new results. If we were able to predict which changes would definitely lead to other changes *before* evaluating the corresponding formulas, we could save a significant part of the runtime. The data structures and techniques that we will discuss in this section enable us to make such predictions, and therefore allow us to reduce the complexity. It is clear that predictions of value changes are hardly possible for arbitrary equations. For this reason, we first transform a given equation system into a *simplified* form by the following steps:

- The first step is again to eliminate *forward* definitions.
- We now decompose E into its blocks, i.e. $E = B_1\&\ldots\&B_\ell$, and replace each block B_i by the result of the function call SimplifyBlock(B_i), where the function SimplifyBlock is defined in Figure 3.15.

Note that the function SimplifyBlock will reintroduce forward equations. Similar to the call to DefForeignBlock the benefit is that we now know that for every forward equation $x_i \overset{\sigma_i}{=} z$, the variable z is not defined in the same block as x_i. The propagation of values changes is done as before in

```
function abbrev(V, σ, Φ)
  if is_var(Φ) then
    if Φ ∈ V then return (Φ, [ ])
    else y := newvar; return (y, [y ≗σ Φ]) end
  else y := newvar; return (y, simplify(y ≗σ Φ))
  end;
end

function simplify(V, x ≗σ Φ)
  case Φ of
    y      : fail with 'eliminate forward definitions in advance!';
    ¬φ     : return [x ≗σ Φ] (* φ is a variable due to NNF *)
    φ ∧ ψ: (y_φ, E_φ) := abbrev(V, σ, φ); (y_ψ, E_ψ) := abbrev(V, σ, ψ);
             return E_φ&E_ψ&[x ≗σ y_φ ∧ y_ψ];
    φ ∨ ψ: (y_φ, E_φ) := abbrev(V, σ, φ); (y_ψ, E_ψ) := abbrev(V, σ, ψ);
             return E_φ&E_ψ&[x ≗σ y_φ ∨ y_ψ];
    ◇φ     : (y_φ, E_φ) := abbrev(V, σ, φ);
             return E_φ&[x ≗σ ◇y_φ];
    □φ     : (y_φ, E_φ) := abbrev(V, σ, φ);
             return E_φ&[x ≗σ □y_φ];
    ←◇ φ   : (y_φ, E_φ) := abbrev(V, σ, φ);
             return E_φ&[x ≗σ ←◇ y_φ];
    ←□φ    : (y_φ, E_φ) := abbrev(V, σ, φ);
             return E_φ&[x ≗σ ←□y_φ];
  end
end

function SimplifyBlock([x_1 ≗σ φ_1, ..., x_n ≗σ φ_n])
  V := {x_1, ..., x_n};
  E := [ ];
  for i := 1 to n do
    E := E&simplify(V, x_i ≗σ NNF(φ_i))
  end;
  return E
end
```

Fig. 3.15. Computing simple equation systems

function DepFixpoint, and therefore this property of forward definitions can be exploited in the same way. The difference between SimplifyBlock and DefForeignBlock is that the former abbreviates not only the foreign variables, but all subformulas by new equations. This restricts the right hand sides to be very small formulas, which will be important for the update procedure. We first state the following result:

Lemma 3.39 (Computing Simple Equation Systems). *Given an equation system* $E = [x_1 \stackrel{\sigma_1}{=} \varphi_1, \ldots, x_n \stackrel{\sigma_n}{=} \varphi_n]$ *without forward definitions, i.e., no* φ_i *is a variable. Let* $B_1\&\ldots\&B_\ell$ *be the decomposition of* E *into its maximal* μ*- and* ν*-blocks, respectively. We define* $E' := \mathsf{SimplifyBlock}(B_1)\&\ldots\&\mathsf{SimplifyBlock}(B_\ell)$ *to be the corresponding simple equation system. Every equation in* E' *is of one of the following forms (of course, we trivially have* $y_i \in \mathsf{defvars}(E')$*):*

- $y_i \stackrel{\sigma_i}{=} y_j \wedge y_k$ *and* $y_i \stackrel{\sigma_i}{=} y_j \vee y_k$*, where* $y_j, y_k \in \mathsf{defvars}(E')$
- $y_i \stackrel{\sigma_i}{=} \Diamond y_j$ *and* $y_i \stackrel{\sigma_i}{=} \Box y_j$*, where* $y_j \in \mathsf{defvars}(E')$
- $y_i \stackrel{\sigma_i}{=} \overleftarrow{\Diamond} y_j$ *and* $y_i \stackrel{\sigma_i}{=} \overleftarrow{\Box} y_j$*, where* $y_j \in \mathsf{defvars}(E')$
- $y_i \stackrel{\sigma_i}{=} \neg z$*, where* $z \notin \mathsf{defvars}(E')$
- $y_i \stackrel{\sigma_i}{=} z$*, where* $y_i \in \mathsf{defvars}(B_k)$ *implies* $z \notin \mathsf{defvars}(B_k)$

The size of E' *is of order* $O(|E|)$*. Moreover, a solution of* E' *uniquely corresponds with a solution of* E*, i.e., we have for every structure* $\mathcal{K}$ *and for all* $x \in \mathsf{defvars}(E)$ *the equation* $[\![E\langle x\rangle]\!]_{\mathcal{K}} = [\![E'\langle x\rangle]\!]_{\mathcal{K}}$*.*

The correctness is easily seen. Intuitively, each introduced variable corresponds with a node in the syntax tree of φ_i. It is moreover easily seen that the simplification of an equation system does not affect the number of blocks: Simply note that a newly introduced equation is of the same parity as the equation it stems from.

It does not matter for the previously discussed algorithms, whether the considered equation system is a simple one or not. The benefit of simple equation systems only comes into play when we consider not the state sets $L[x_i]$ as a whole, but instead the particular Boolean values $L[x_i][s]$ of that array. The reason is that for every simple equation system, we can precisely predict when $L[x_i][s]$ changes. For the following explanations of these predictions, we assume that a least fixpoint is to be computed; computations of greatest fixpoints are completely dual. Hence, we start with initial values $L[x_i][s] := 0$ (although we will consider a different initialization with propagations of foreign variables later on). Due to reasons of monotonicity, all variables $L[x_i][s]$ may therefore only change once from 0 to 1. The predictions of changes are then as follows:

- If an equation $x \stackrel{\mu}{=} y \vee z$ is to be updated, since we know that either $L[y][s]$ or $L[z][s]$ has been changed, then we immediately know that this will definitely set $L[x][s] := 1$. The reason is that we know that y and z belong to the same block as x, and therefore have been initialized with 0. As one of them has changed, one of them is now 1.
- The prediction of a change for an equation $x \stackrel{\mu}{=} y \wedge z$ is however not so easily possible. If we know that either $L[y][s]$ or $L[z][s]$ have been changed, then we know that at least one of them is now 1. The reason is again that we know that both y and z belong to the block as x, and therefore have been initialized with 0. A change must therefore have made one of them 1.

Without loss of generality, assume that $L[y][s]$ has recently been changed and is therefore now 1. $L[z][s]$ might still be 0, so that there will be no change of $L[x][s]$. A second attempt to update $L[x][s]$ must then succeed, since $L[y][s]$ will never change afterwards, and therefore the new attempt to update $L[x][s]$ is due to a change of $L[z][s]$.
Moreover, the first update attempt to change $L[x][s]$ must always fail, since both changes of $L[y][s]$ and $L[z][s]$ are necessary to change $L[x][s]$. Hence, we only need to keep track of the number of changes to $L[y][s]$ and $L[z][s]$, and if both have changed, we immediately change $L[x][s]$. For this reason, we simply count the 'change attempts' for $L[x][s]$.

- The prediction for equations of the form $x \stackrel{\mu}{=} \Diamond y$ is also simple: a change of $L[y][s']$ will definitely lead to a change of $L[x][s]$ whenever we have $(s, s') \in \mathcal{R}$. Similarly, for an equation $x \stackrel{\mu}{=} \overleftarrow{\Diamond} y$, we know that a change of $L[y][s]$ will lead to changes of $L[x][s']$ for all $(s, s') \in \mathcal{R}$.
- The only equations whose changes can not be so easily predicted are those of the form $x \stackrel{\mu}{=} \Box y$ and $x \stackrel{\mu}{=} \overleftarrow{\Box} y$. $L[x][s]$ changes iff all $L[y][s']$ changed for all s' with $(s, s') \in \mathcal{R}$. Hence, similar to the case $x \stackrel{\mu}{=} y \wedge z$, we therefore count the number of triggers that try to update $L[x][s]$. If this number reaches $|\{s' \in \mathcal{S} \mid (s, s') \in \mathcal{R}\}|$, we know that $L[x][s]$ must change, too. In the same way, we count triggers for $x \stackrel{\mu}{=} \overleftarrow{\Box} y$ up to $|\{s' \in \mathcal{S} \mid (s', s) \in \mathcal{R}\}|$.

Hence, to make precise predictions on the changes to the values of $L[x][s]$, we need to use counters $C[x][s]$ for equations of the types $x \stackrel{\mu}{=} y \wedge z$, $x \stackrel{\mu}{=} \Box y$, and $x \stackrel{\mu}{=} \overleftarrow{\Box} y$. Note that we have to use separate counters $C[x][s]$ for every state $s \in \mathcal{S}$, which limits the algorithm to small structures only. The data structures that are used by the Cleaveland-Steffen algorithm are thus the following ones:

- For every variable x and every state $s \in \mathcal{S}$, we use a Boolean value $L[x][s] \in \mathbb{B}$ to represent the current labels of the Kripke structure. Clearly, for every $x \in \mathsf{defvars}(E)$, we should finally have $[\![E\langle x \rangle]\!]_{\mathcal{K}} = \{s \in \mathcal{S} \mid L[x][s] = 1\}$.
- For every variable $x \in \mathsf{defvars}(E)$ and every state $s \in \mathcal{S}$, we use a counter $C[x][s] \in \mathbb{N}$. $C[x][s]$ is the number change attempts that will finally lead to a change of $L[x][s]$. We will use the counter only for equations of type $x \stackrel{\mu}{=} y \wedge z$, $x \stackrel{\mu}{=} \Box y$, and $x \stackrel{\mu}{=} \overleftarrow{\Box} y$, and the related greatest fixpoint equations.
- For every block B_p, we store in a worklist $\mathcal{W}$ the pairs (x, s) where $L[x][s]$ has recently changed, but whose change has not yet propagated through the equation system.

The Cleaveland-Steffen algorithm is a further refinement of the algorithm DepFixpoint that we have considered before. The only differences are that different initialization and update procedures are used that exploit the fact that the equation system is simple.

```
function CSInitBlock([x_1 =σ φ_1, ..., x_n =σ φ_n])
  iv := (σ = ν);
  W := [];
  for s ∈ S do
    for i = 1 to n do
      case φ_i of
        isvar(φ_i) : L[x_i][s] := L[φ_i][s];
        ¬y         : L[x_i][s] := ¬L[y][s];
        x_j ∧ x_k  : L[x_i][s] := iv; C[x_i][s] := 2;
        x_j ∨ x_k  : L[x_i][s] := iv; C[x_i][s] := 2;
        ◇x_j       : L[x_i][s] := iv;
                     if σ = ν then
                       C[x_i][s] := |{s' ∈ S | (s, s') ∈ R}|;
                       L[x_i][s] := (C[x_i][s] > 0)
                     end;
        □x_j       : L[x_i][s] := iv;
                     if σ = μ then
                       C[x_i][s] := |{s' ∈ S | (s, s') ∈ R}|;
                       L[x_i][s] := (C[x_i][s] = 0)
                     end;
        ←◇x_j      : L[x_i][s] := iv;
                     if σ = ν then
                       C[x_i][s] := |{s' ∈ S | (s', s) ∈ R}|;
                       L[x_i][s] := (C[x_i][s] > 0)
                     end;
        ←□x_j      : L[x_i][s] := iv;
                     if σ = μ then
                       C[x_i][s] := |{s' ∈ S | (s', s) ∈ R}|;
                       L[x_i][s] := (C[x_i][s] = 0)
                     end;
      end case;
      if L[x_i][s] ≠ iv then W := [(x_i, s)]&W end
    end for
  end for;
  return W
end function
```

Fig. 3.16. Initialization of blocks for the Cleaveland-Steffen algorithm

Consider first the initialization of the blocks as given in Figure 3.16 by function CSInitBlock. We have already explained the initialization of the counters $C[x_i][s]$. It remains to explain the initialization of the worklist $\mathcal{W}$ and the initial approximations $L[x_i][s]$. Clearly, for a μ-block, the initial value for $L[x_i][s]$ should be 0, but there are some cases that we want to handle differently:

- For forward definitions $x_i \overset{\sigma}{=} y$, we initialize $L[x_i][s] := L[y][s]$ to propagate the value of y for lower or higher blocks to the current block. For the same reason, equations $x_i \overset{\sigma}{=} \neg y$ with a variable y, lead to the initialization $L[x_i][s] := \neg L[y][s]$.
- For equations $x_i \overset{\mu}{=} \Box x_j$ and $x_i \overset{\mu}{=} \overleftarrow{\Box} x_j$, we initialize $L[x_i][s] := 1$ if s has no successors or predecessors, respectively. This is due to the semantics of $\Box$.
- Analogously, we initialize $L[x_i][s] := 0$ for equations $x_i \overset{\nu}{=} \Diamond x_j$ and $x_i \overset{\nu}{=} \overleftarrow{\Diamond} x_j$, when s has successors or predecessors, respectively.

It is clear, that these different initializations are also correct, since they would be obtained after an iteration anyway. As in DepFixpoint, we use them to propagate values from other blocks. In case of the modal operators, the changes are made to avoid difficult cases in the update procedures.

The benefit of simple equation systems is now seen in the update functions MinUpdate and MaxUpdate. We only discuss MinUpdate in the following, MaxUpdate works completely similarly. Any update of $L[x_i][s]$ is triggered by a previous change of some value $L[x_j][s]$ where x_j occurs in φ_i. Hence, we have to process each pair (x_j, s) of the worklist $\mathcal{W}$ since these values have recently been changed and their effect has not yet been propagated to other values $L[x_i][s]$. This propagation is done by considering for all pairs (x_j, s) in the worklist and all equations $x_i \overset{\nu}{=} \varphi_i$ of the block where x_j occurs in φ_i, i.e., where (x_j, x_i) is an edge in DepG (E). The propagation of the change from $L[x_j][s]$ to $L[x_i][s]$ depends then on the formula φ_i:

$x_i \overset{\mu}{=} x_j$: As x_j is a foreign variable, it can not be contained in $\mathcal{W}$, and therefore there will never be an update for x_i. $L[x_i][s]$ has already received the final value at initialization time.

$x_i \overset{\mu}{=} \neg x_j$: Similar to the previous case, it follows that since x_j is a foreign variable, it can not be contained in $\mathcal{W}$, and therefore there will never be an update for x_i. $L[x_i][s]$ has already received the final value at initialization time.

$x_i \overset{\mu}{=} x_j \wedge x_k$: As the block has been simplified, all variables $\{x_i, x_j, x_k\}$ are defined in this block. As $L[x_j][s]$ has recently changed, its value is therefore $L[x_j][s] = 1$. As this is not sufficient for a change of $L[x_i][s]$, we inspect the counter $C[x_i][s]$, that has been initialized with 2. Recall that $C[x_i][s]$ contains the number of change attempts that have to occur for changing $L[x_i][s]$. Hence, we have $C[x_i][s] = 1$ iff $L[x_k][s]$ has already been changed before (and therefore is now true). Hence, if $C[x_i][s] = 2$ holds, $L[x_i][s]$ does not change, and we decrement $C[x_i][s]$. On the other hand, if $C[x_i][s] = 1$ holds, $L[x_i][s]$ changes and the pair (x_i, s) is put in the worklist.

```
function MinUpdate(𝒲, [x_1 ≗^σ φ_1, ..., x_n ≗^σ φ_n])
  changed := 𝒲 ≠ [];
  while 𝒲 ≠ [] do
    [(x_j, s)]&𝒲 ≡ 𝒲;
    for (x_j, x_i) ∈ 𝒟_E do
      case φ_i of
        x_j ∧ x_k : C[x_i][s] := C[x_i][s] − 1;
                    if C[x_i][s] = 0 then
                      L[x_i][s] := 1; 𝒲 := [(x_i, s)]&𝒲;
                    end
        x_j ∨ x_k : if ¬L[x_i][s] then
                      L[x_i][s] := 1; 𝒲 := [(x_i, s)]&𝒲;
                    end
        ◇x_j      : for (s', s) ∈ ℛ do
                      if ¬L[x_i][s'] then
                        L[x_i][s'] := 1; 𝒲 := [(x_i, s')]&𝒲;
                      end
                    end
        □x_j      : for (s', s) ∈ ℛ do
                      C[x_i][s'] := C[x_i][s'] − 1;
                      if C[x_i][s'] = 0 then
                        L[x_i][s'] := 1; 𝒲 := [(x_i, s')]&𝒲;
                      end
                    end
        ←◇ x_j    : for (s, s') ∈ ℛ do
                      if ¬L[x_i][s'] then
                        L[x_i][s'] := 1; 𝒲 := [(x_i, s')]&𝒲;
                      end
                    end
        ←□ x_j    : for (s, s') ∈ ℛ do
                      C[x_i][s'] := C[x_i][s'] − 1;
                      if C[x_i][s'] = 0 then
                        L[x_i][s'] := 1; 𝒲 := [(x_i, s')]&𝒲;
                      end
                    end
      end case
    end for
  end while;
  return changed
end
```

Fig. 3.17. Updating minimal blocks for the Cleaveland-Steffen algorithm

```
function MaxUpdate((W, [x_1 =σ φ_1, ..., x_n =σ φ_n])
  changed := W ≠ [];
  while W ≠ [] do
    [(x_j, s)]&W ≡ W;
    for (x_j, x_i) ∈ D_E do
      case φ_i of
        x_j ∧ x_k : if L[x_i][s] then
                      L[x_i][s] := 0; W := [(x_i, s)]&W;
                    end
        x_j ∨ x_k : C[x_i][s] := C[x_i][s] − 1;
                    if C[x_i][s] = 0 then
                      L[x_i][s] := 0; W := [(x_i, s)]&W;
                    end
        ◇x_j      : for (s', s) ∈ R do
                      C[x_i][s'] := C[x_i][s'] − 1;
                      if C[x_i][s'] = 0 then
                        L[x_i][s'] := 0; W := [(x_i, s')]&W;
                      end
                    end
        □x_j      : for (s', s) ∈ R do
                      if L[x_i][s'] then
                        L[x_i][s'] := 0; W := [(x_i, s')]&W;
                      end
                    end
        ←◇ x_j    : for (s, s') ∈ R do
                      C[x_i][s'] := C[x_i][s'] − 1;
                      if C[x_i][s'] = 0 then
                        L[x_i][s'] := 0; W := [(x_i, s')]&W;
                      end
                    end
        ←□ x_j    : for (s, s') ∈ R do
                      if L[x_i][s'] then
                        L[x_i][s'] := 0; W := [(x_i, s')]&W;
                      end
                    end
      end case
    end for
  end while;
  return changed
end
```

Fig. 3.18. Updating maximal blocks for the Cleaveland-Steffen algorithm

$x_i \stackrel{\mu}{=} x_j \vee x_k$: As the block has been simplified, all variables $\{x_i, x_j, x_k\}$ are defined in this block. According to Figure 3.16, the initial approximation $L[x_i][s]$ for every state s is 0. As (x_j, s) belongs to $\mathcal{W}$, we know that the value of $L[x_j][s]$ has recently been changed. As x_j also belongs to this μ-block, we therefore know that $L[x_j][s]$ must have changed from 0 to 1. Consequently, we must now change the value for $L[x_i][s]$ to 1. As $L[x_i][s]$ has then changed, we must moreover add (x_i, s) to the list $\mathcal{W}$.

$x_i \stackrel{\mu}{=} \Diamond x_j$: As the block has been simplified, both x_i and x_j are defined in this block. As $L[x_j][s]$ has been changed, it is now true, and therefore we must change $L[x_i][s'] := 1$ for every predecessor state s' of s. Note, however, that only those pairs (x_i, s') are added to the worklist that have thereby actually changed.

$x_i \stackrel{\mu}{=} \Box x_j$: Recall that we established the invariant that $C[x_i][s']$ counts the number of successor states s of s' where $L[x_j][s]$ holds. Therefore, the change of $L[x_j][s]$ has first the effect that we must decrement each counter $C[x_i][s']$, where s' is a predecessor of s. If after the decrementation $C[x_i][s'] = 0$ holds, then we know that s' has no successor states s where $L[x_j][s] = 0$ holds. Consequently, we change the value of $L[x_i][s']$ to 1 and add the pair (x_i, s') to the worklist $\mathcal{W}$.

$x_i \stackrel{\mu}{=} \overleftarrow{\Diamond} x_j$ and $x_i \stackrel{\mu}{=} \overleftarrow{\Box} x_j$: These cases are handled completely analogously to the cases $x_i \stackrel{\mu}{=} \Diamond x_j$ and $x_i \stackrel{\mu}{=} \Box x_j$, respectively.

The above steps are invoked for every pair (x_j, s) of the worklist $\mathcal{W}$ until this list becomes empty. The update procedure for ν-blocks is completely dual and is given in Figure 3.18. After termination of MinUpdate and MaxUpdate, respectively, the values $L[x_i][s]$ present the least or greatest fixpoint of the considered block B_p where the values of the other blocks have been used. Note that the interaction of blocks, i.e., the transfer of preliminary approximations is exclusively done via forward definitions, just as we have done in DepFixpoint. The transfer is therefore done by the code preceding the calls to MinUpdate or MaxUpdate given in Figure 3.19.

We are now able to derive an algorithm CleaStef from our basic algorithm of Figure 3.8, or better from the already refined algorithm DepFixpoint of Figure 3.14. To this end, we exchange the functions DepInitBlock and DepUpdate by CSInitBlock and CSUpdate, respectively. Moreover, AbbrevForeigns is replaced with by a blockwise application of SimplifyBlock. The propagation of values is the same as in DepFixpoint, the only changes are in the initialization and update procedures. The correctness of the algorithm is therefore already clear. However, the complexity is different, since now *all* updates of block B_p can be done in time $O(|B_p|\,|\mathcal{K}|)$. We therefore obtain the following improved result:

```
function CSUpdate(B_p)
  [x_1 =σ φ_1, ..., x_n =σ φ_n] ≡ B_p;
  W := Propagate(B_p);
  if σ = μ then
    return MinUpdate(W, B_p)
  else
    return MaxUpdate(W, B_p)
  end
end function
```

Fig. 3.19. Update procedure for the Cleaveland-Steffen algorithm

Theorem 3.40 (Cleaveland-Steffen Algorithm). *The Cleaveland-Steffen algorithm* CleaStef *is obtained from algorithm* DepFixpoint *of Figure 3.14 by using* CSInitBlock *and* CSUpdate *as initialization and update procedures, respectively. Furthermore, we replace the call to* AbbrevForeigns *in* DepFixpoint *by a blockwise application of* SimplifyBlock. *For every equation system E and every Kripke structure $\mathcal{K}$,* CleaStef *then computes the tuple* $(\llbracket E\langle x_1\rangle\rrbracket_{\mathcal{K}}, \ldots, \llbracket E\langle x_p\rangle\rrbracket_{\mathcal{K}})$ *in time* $O\left(\left(\frac{|E|\,|\mathcal{S}|}{\ell}\right)^{\ell-1} |\mathcal{K}|\,|E|\right)$.

Proof. The correctness is clear by the previous explanations. To derive the complexity, we abbreviate $E_\ell := B_1\&\ldots\&B_\ell$ for $\ell > 0$ and $E_0 := [\,]$, and denote the number of equations of block B_i as n_i. Let $T_{\mathsf{CleaStef}}(E_\ell)$ be the time required to execute depfixpoint(E_ℓ) and let $T_{\mathsf{CSInitBlock}}(B_\ell)$ and $T_{\mathsf{CSUpdate}}(B_\ell)$ be the runtimes of the functions CSInitBlock and CSUpdate for block B_ℓ, respectively. To be precise: $T_{\mathsf{CSUpdate}}(B_\ell)$ is the sum of the runtimes required for all calls CSUpdate(B_ℓ) during the computation of CleaStef(E_ℓ). Then, the following holds for some C_1 (and all $\ell > 1$):

$$\begin{aligned}
&T_{\mathsf{CleaStef}}(E_1) \leq T_{\mathsf{CSInitBlock}}(B_1) + T_{\mathsf{CSUpdate}}(B_1)\\
&T_{\mathsf{CleaStef}}(E_\ell) \leq T_{\mathsf{CSInitBlock}}(B_\ell) + T_{\mathsf{CSUpdate}}(B_\ell) + (n_\ell\,|\mathcal{S}| + 1)T_{\mathsf{CleaStef}}(E_{\ell-1})
\end{aligned}$$

Note that this differs from the previous estimations since we now consider the sum of the runtimes of all updates during a fixpoint computation, instead of estimating one call and multiplying it by $n_\ell\,|\mathcal{S}| + 1$. The reason for this is clear, we do not know the contents of the worklist for a particular call, but we know that the sum of all calls will at most consider every pair $(x_{\ell,i}, s)$ once, since its values can only change once. If a pair $(x_{\ell,i}, s)$ is taken from the worklist $\mathcal{W}$, the required computations are handled in a time bound by $O(|\{s' \in \mathcal{S} \mid (s,s') \in \mathcal{R}\}|)$. Therefore, we obtain for some constant C:

$$T_{\mathsf{CSUpdate}}(B_\ell) \leq \sum_{s\in\mathcal{S}} \sum_{i=1}^{n_\ell} C\,|\{s' \in \mathcal{S} \mid (s,s') \in \mathcal{R}\}| = Cn_\ell\,|\mathcal{K}| \in O(n_\ell\,|\mathcal{K}|)$$

CSInitBlock consists of two nested loops, one over the set of states $s \in \mathcal{S}$, and another one over the set of defined variables $x_{\ell,i}$ of B_ℓ. In the loop body, a pair $(x_{\ell,i}, s)$ is considered, and it is handled in a time bound by $O(|\{s' \in \mathcal{S} \mid (s,s') \in \mathcal{R}\}|)$. Hence, we obtain for some constant C:

$$T_{\mathsf{CSInitBlock}}(B_\ell) \le \sum_{s\in\mathcal{S}} \sum_{i=1}^{n_\ell} C\,|\{s' \in \mathcal{S} \mid (s,s') \in \mathcal{R}\}| = Cn_\ell\,|\mathcal{K}| \in O(n_\ell\,|\mathcal{K}|)$$

Hence, CSInitBlock and CSUpdate both run in time $O(|\mathcal{K}|\,|B_\ell|)$. It is easily seen by induction on ℓ that the following holds for $\ell \ge 1$:

$$T_{\mathsf{CleaStef}}(\ell) = \sum_{i=1}^{\ell} (T_{\mathsf{CSInitBlock}}(B_i) + T_{\mathsf{CSUpdate}}(B_i)) \prod_{j=i+1}^{\ell} (n_j\,|\mathcal{S}|+1)$$

Therefore, we see that there the following holds for $\ell > 1$ ($\ell = 1$ is immediately clear):

$$\begin{aligned}
T_{\mathsf{CleaStef}}(\ell) &= \textstyle\sum_{i=1}^{\ell} (T_{\mathsf{CSInitBlock}}(B_i) + T_{\mathsf{CSUpdate}}(B_i)) \prod_{j=i+1}^{\ell} (n_j\,|\mathcal{S}|+1) \\
&\in O\left(\textstyle\sum_{i=1}^{\ell} n_i\,|\mathcal{K}| \prod_{j=i+1}^{\ell} (n_j\,|\mathcal{S}|+1)\right) \\
&= O\left(n_\ell\,|\mathcal{K}| + \textstyle\sum_{i=1}^{\ell-1} n_i\,|\mathcal{K}| \prod_{j=i+1}^{\ell} (n_j\,|\mathcal{S}|+1)\right) \\
&\subseteq O\left(n_\ell\,|\mathcal{K}| + \textstyle\sum_{i=1}^{\ell-1} n_i\,|\mathcal{K}| \left(1 + \frac{|\mathcal{S}|}{\ell-i} \sum_{j=i+1}^{\ell} n_j\right)^{\ell-i}\right) \\
&\subseteq O\left(n_\ell\,|\mathcal{K}| + \textstyle\sum_{i=1}^{\ell-1} n_i\,|\mathcal{K}| \left(1 + \frac{|E_\ell||\mathcal{S}|}{\ell-i}\right)^{\ell-i}\right) \\
&\subseteq O\left(n_\ell\,|\mathcal{K}| + \left(1 + \frac{|E_\ell||\mathcal{S}|}{\ell-1}\right)^{\ell-1} \textstyle\sum_{i=1}^{\ell-1} n_i\,|\mathcal{K}|\right) \\
&\subseteq O\left(\left(1 + \frac{|E_\ell||\mathcal{S}|}{\ell-1}\right)^{\ell-1} |\mathcal{K}| \textstyle\sum_{i=1}^{\ell} n_i\right) \\
&\subseteq O\left(\left(1 + \frac{|E_\ell||\mathcal{S}|}{\ell-1}\right)^{\ell-1} |\mathcal{K}|\,|E_\ell|\right) \subseteq O\left(\left(\frac{|E_\ell||\mathcal{S}|}{\ell}\right)^{\ell-1} |\mathcal{K}|\,|E_\ell|\right)
\end{aligned}$$

We give some remarks on the above estimations. The first estimation is due to the fact determined above that $T_{\mathsf{CSInitBlock}}(B_i)$ and $T_{\mathsf{CSUpdate}}(B_i)$ run in time $O(|\mathcal{K}|\,|B_i|)$. Note that we have simple equation systems, and therefore have $|B_i| \in O(n_i)$ and $n_i \in O(|B_i|)$. The next step is to separate the summand $n_\ell\,|\mathcal{K}|$ since it yields an empty product, which prevents us from applying the next step. This next step is to apply the inequation between the geometric and arithmetic means, which states that for arbitrary numbers $\alpha_i > 0$ that the inequation $\prod_{i=1}^{\ell} \alpha_i \le \left(\frac{1}{\ell}\sum_{i=1}^{\ell} \alpha_i\right)^{\ell}$ holds. In particular, we have $\prod_{i=1}^{\ell}(\alpha_i + 1) \le \left(1 + \frac{1}{\ell}\sum_{i=1}^{\ell} \alpha_i\right)^{\ell}$. We then replace $\sum_{j=i+1}^{\ell} n_j$ by $\sum_{j=1}^{\ell} n_j$, i.e. $|E_\ell|$. After this, we note again that $m < n$ implies $(1 + \frac{\lambda}{m})^m < (1 + \frac{\lambda}{n})^n$ (see the proof of Theorem 3.34) on page 134), and for this reason, we replace $\left(1 + \frac{|E_\ell||\mathcal{S}|}{\ell-i}\right)^{\ell-i}$ by $\left(1 + \frac{|E_\ell||\mathcal{S}|}{\ell-1}\right)^{\ell-1}$. As this no longer depends on i, we can apply distributive laws. Finally, note that for the functions $f(x) := \left(1 + \frac{\alpha x}{\ell - 1}\right)^{\ell-1}$ and $g(x) := \left(\frac{\alpha x}{\ell}\right)^{\ell-1}$, we have $\lim_{x\to\infty} \frac{f(x)}{g(x)} = \left(1 + \frac{1}{\ell - 1}\right)^{\ell-1} \in \{x \in \mathcal{R} \mid 2 < x \leq 2.718\}$.

□

Hence, the Cleaveland-Steffen algorithm improves the complexity of the previously considered algorithm given in Figure 3.8. In particular, it allows us to evaluate alternation-free equation systems, i.e., simple μ- or ν-blocks in time $O(|\mathcal{K}|\,|E|)$, i.e., in time linear to the size of the structure $\mathcal{K}$ as well as linear to the size of the equation system E.

However, the runtimes of real implementations are heavily governed by the constants that we are allowed to neglect in asymptotic complexities. In particular, algorithm DepFixpoint has the advantage that it can be implemented as a *symbolic model checking* procedure [360] based on binary decision diagrams [74]. This is not easily possible for the Cleaveland-Steffen algorithm, since that algorithm is based on very sophisticated data structures.

3.6 Reducing the Alternation Depth w.r.t. Structures

In the previous sections, we have considered several algorithms for model checking μ-calculus formulas. The most efficient algorithm (at least in theory) that we found was the Cleaveland-Steffen algorithm of the previous section. We now discuss the question of whether this algorithm is optimal, and we will see in this section that there is still room for improvements.

Long, Browne, Clarke, Jha, and Marrero [333] showed in 1994 an important improvement of the model checking procedure for the μ-calculus. The improvement is obtained for fixpoint formulas with alternation depths ≥ 3. Their idea is best understood by the alternative proof given by Seidl in [452] that we will follow in this section. The key idea is based on the following simple observation on 'finite' lattices: In a complete lattice $(\mathcal{D}, \sqsubseteq)$, where the largest chain of strictly decreasing or increasing elements has a finite length d, the Tarski/Knaster iteration can take at most d iterations. For this reason, the least fixpoint of a function is simply $f^d(\bot)$ and the greatest fixpoint is simply $f^d(\top)$. Clearly, the fixpoint is normally reached much earlier, but in theory, these values may occur.

For the vectorized μ-calculus, we consider the lattices $\left(\left(2^{\mathcal{S}}\right)^n, \subseteq_n\right)$, where the longest chain has length $d := n\,|\mathcal{S}| + 1$. Hence, we can replace a fixpoint expression $\mathsf{fix}\ x \stackrel{\mu}{=} \varphi\ \mathsf{in}\ \Phi\ \mathsf{end}$ by the following one:

$$\mathsf{fix}\left[\begin{array}{l} x_0 = [\varphi]_x^0 \\ \vdots \\ x_{i+1} = [\varphi]_x^{x_i} \\ \vdots \\ x_{|S|} = [\varphi]_x^{x_{|S|-1}} \end{array}\right] \mathsf{in}\ [\Phi]_x^{x_{|S|}}\ \mathsf{end}$$

Note that we have omitted the parities of the equations, since these are no longer of interest: The right hand sides $[\varphi]_x^{x_i}$ do not contain occurrences of the variables x_j with $j \neq i$. Therefore, the fixpoint is now simply found by computing all the right hand sides. For a single equation like the one above this gives no improvement of the complexity, since it is the worst computation that appears in the Tarski/Knaster iteration.

However, we will find an astonishing improvement, when we apply the above 'unrolling technique' to nested fixpoints. To this end, we consider an equation system $E = B_1\&\ldots\&B_\ell$, that is decomposed into its maximal blocks (equations of the same parity). Note that the algorithms that we have developed either compute the least or greatest fixpoint of the functions mentioned in Theorem 3.33 on page 131. For this reason, we can also apply the above 'unrolling technique' to their computation.

This is done by the function Expand given in Figure 3.20. This function unrolls the fixpoint iteration that is necessary to compute the fixpoint related with the last block B_ℓ, hence the expected arguments are $E = B_1\&\ldots\&B_{\ell-1}$ and $B = B_\ell$. Note, that Expand does not however eliminate the lower fixpoint expressions in the blocks B_i with $i < \ell$.

Lemma 3.41 (Expanding Equation Systems). *Given an equation system $E = B_1\&\ldots\&B_\ell$ with maximal μ- and ν-blocks B_i. Assume B_i has n_i equations. Then, for every Kripke structure $\mathcal{K}$ with state set $\mathcal{S}$, the equation system $E' :=$ $\mathsf{Expand}(n_\ell\,|\mathcal{S}|\,, B_1\&\ldots\&B_{\ell-1}, B_\ell)$ is equivalent to E and can be decomposed into $\ell - 1$ blocks. Moreover, for the size of E', we have $|E'| \leq (n_\ell\,|\mathcal{S}| + 1)\,|E|$, and the number of equations is $\mathsf{length}\,(E') = (n_\ell\,|\mathcal{S}| + 1)\,\mathsf{length}\,(E)$.*

The correctness of the lemma is easily seen: It simply unrolls the fixpoint iteration given by the Tarski/Knaster theorem. Note how the propagation of values is performed by instantiating variables with different indices. We can also apply the above expansion step to intermediate blocks B_p. In this case, we define $E_p := \mathsf{Expand}(n_p\,|\mathcal{S}|\,, B_1\&\ldots\&B_{p-1}, B_p)$ and obtain the equation system $E' := E_p\&B_{p+1}\&\ldots\&B_\ell$. The variables defined in the higher blocks $B_{p+1}, \ldots, B_\ell$ are simply treated as environment variables when the fixpoints of the lower blocks are computed. For example, given $[x \stackrel{\mu}{=} f(x,y,z), y \stackrel{\nu}{=} g(x,y,z), z \stackrel{\mu}{=} h(x,y,z)]$ is expanded as follows (the lines mark the intermediate results of the recursive function calls):

```
function expand(k, p, E, B)
  [x_1 =^{σ_1} φ_1, ..., x_m =^{σ_m} φ_m]) ≡ E;
  [y_1 =^{σ} ψ_1, ..., y_n =^{σ} ψ_n]) ≡ B;
  if k = 0 then
    α := (σ = ν);
    return [y_{1,0} = α, ..., y_{1,0} = α]
  else
    E_B := expand(k − 1, p, E, B);
    ϱ_y := {(y_1, y_{1,k−1}), ..., (y_n, y_{n,k−1})};
    ϱ_x := {(x_1, x_{1,k−1}), ..., (x_m, x_{m,k−1})};
    ϱ := ϱ_x ∪ ϱ_y;
    E' := [x_{1,k−1} =^{σ_1} [φ_1]_ϱ, ..., x_{m,k−1} =^{σ_m} [φ_m]_ϱ];
    if k = p then B' := [y_1 = [ψ_1]_ϱ, ..., y_n = [ψ_n]_ϱ]
    else B' := [y_{1,k} = [ψ_1]_ϱ, ..., y_{n,k} = [ψ_n]_ϱ]
    end;
    return E_B&B'&E'
  end
end

function Expand(k, E, B)
  E' := expand(k, k, E, B);
  return E'&B
end

function ExpandEvenBlocks(k, [B_1, ..., B_ℓ])
  i = 1;
  E := [];
  while i < ℓ do
    E := Expand(k, E&B_i, B_{i+1});
    i := i + 2
  end;
  if i = ℓ then return E&B_ℓ
  else return E end
end
```

Fig. 3.20. Expanding Equation Systems

$$
\left[
\begin{array}{l}
y_0 = 1 \\
\hline
x_0 \stackrel{\mu}{=} f(x_0, y_0, z) \\
y_1 = g(x_0, y_0, z) \\
\hline
\vdots \\
\hline
x_{k-1} \stackrel{\mu}{=} f(x_{k-1}, y_{k-1}, z) \\
y_k \stackrel{\mu}{=} g(x_{k-1}, y_{k-1}, z) \\
\hline
x_k \stackrel{\mu}{=} f(x_k, y_k, z) \\
y \stackrel{\mu}{=} g(x_k, y_k, z) \\
\hline
x \stackrel{\mu}{=} f(x, y, z) \\
z \stackrel{\mu}{=} h(x, y, z)
\end{array}
\right]
$$

There is no longer a need to distinguish between least and greatest fixpoint equations for the equations of y_i. The solutions are uniquely determined, since the right hand sides of the $y_{i,k}$ variables no longer depend on their left hand side. Hence, we can choose the parity of the first block, thus obtaining a single block after expansion.

Using the above expansion of intermediate blocks, we can reduce every equation system with respect to a given Kripke structure to an equivalent one that consists of only one block. The reduction is as follows: Given an equation system $E = B_1\&\ldots\&B_\ell$, where the blocks B_i have alternating parity, we successively expand the even numbered blocks, and then change their parity into the one of the odd numbered blocks. This is done by function ExpandEvenBlocks in Figure 3.20.

Having seen that a reduction to an alternation-free system E' is possible, we recall that the Cleaveland-Steffen algorithm can then be used to solve the remaining problem in time $O(|\mathcal{K}|\,|E'|)$. We are therefore interested in the size of E': If $|E'|$ is less than $O\left(\left(\frac{1}{\ell}|E|\,|\mathcal{S}|\right)^{\ell-1}\right)$, then the expansion step combined with the Cleaveland-Steffen algorithm would be more efficient than the Cleaveland-Steffen algorithm alone. We will see that this is indeed the case.

To analyse this carefully, we must therefore consider $|E'|$. We first consider the equation systems E_i that appear as intermediate steps of the expansion of $E = B_1\&\ldots\&B_\ell$ and upper bounds of their sizes λ_k. The precise definitions are as follows:

- $E_1 := B_1$
- $E_{2k} := \mathsf{Expand}(n_{2k}\,|\mathcal{S}|\,, E_{2k-1}, B_{2k})$
- $E_{2k+1} := E_{2k}\&B_{2k+1}$
- $\lambda_1 := |B_1|$
- $\lambda_{2k} := (n_{2k}\,|\mathcal{S}| + 1)\,(\lambda_{2k-1} + |B_{2k}|)$
- $\lambda_{2k+1} := \lambda_{2k} + |B_{2k+1}|$

Hence, the task is now to determine the asymptotic growth of λ_k in terms of the n_i, E and S. Unfortunately, the relationship is quite involved, and therefore we abbreviate $\alpha_k := n_{2k+2}\,|\mathcal{S}| + 1$, $\beta_k := (n_{2k+2}\,|\mathcal{S}| + 1)(|B_{2k+2}| + |B_{2k+1}|)$, and $\xi_k := \lambda_{2k}$. It is not hard to prove that we then have $\xi_1 = \beta_0$ and $\xi_{k+1} = \alpha_k\xi_k + \beta_k$. By induction on k, we furthermore prove that $\xi_k = \sum_{i=1}^{k} \beta_{i-1} \prod_{j=i}^{k-1} \alpha_j$ holds, and we therefore obtain the following expression for λ_{2k}:

$$\lambda_{2k} = \sum_{i=1}^{k} (n_{2i}\,|\mathcal{S}| + 1)\,(|B_{2i-1}| + |B_{2i}|) \prod_{j=i}^{k-1} (n_{2j+2}\,|\mathcal{S}| + 1)$$

Once again, we estimate the geometric by the arithmetic means, i.e. we use again the inequation $\prod_{i=1}^{\ell} a_i \leq \left(\frac{1}{\ell}\sum_{i=1}^{\ell} a_i\right)^{\ell}$, to obtain the following estimation for $k > 1$:

$$
\begin{aligned}
\lambda_{2k} &= \sum_{i=1}^{k} (n_{2i}\,|\mathcal{S}|+1)\,(|B_{2i-1}|+|B_{2i}|)\prod_{j=i}^{k-1}(n_{2j+2}\,|\mathcal{S}|+1) \\
&\subseteq O\left(\sum_{i=1}^{k} n_{2i}\,|\mathcal{S}|\,|E|\prod_{j=i}^{k-1}(n_{2j+2}\,|\mathcal{S}|+1)\right) \\
&\subseteq O\left(|\mathcal{S}|\,|E|\,n_{2k} + |\mathcal{S}|\,|E|\sum_{i=1}^{k-1} n_{2i}\prod_{j=i}^{k-1}(n_{2j+2}\,|\mathcal{S}|+1)\right) \\
&\subseteq O\left(|\mathcal{S}|\,|E|\,n_{2k} + |\mathcal{S}|\,|E|\sum_{i=1}^{k-1} n_{2i}\left(1+\tfrac{1}{k-i}\sum_{j=i}^{k-1} n_{2j+2}\,|\mathcal{S}|\right)^{k-i}\right) \\
&\subseteq O\left(|\mathcal{S}|\,|E|\,n_{2k} + |\mathcal{S}|\,|E|\sum_{i=1}^{k-1} n_{2i}\left(1+\tfrac{n_E|\mathcal{S}|}{k-i}\right)^{k-i}\right) \\
&\subseteq O\left(|\mathcal{S}|\,|E|\,n_{2k} + |\mathcal{S}|\,|E|\left(1+\tfrac{n_E|\mathcal{S}|}{k-1}\right)^{k-1}\sum_{i=1}^{k-1} n_{2i}\right) \\
&\subseteq O\left(|\mathcal{S}|\,|E|\,n_{2k} + |\mathcal{S}|\,|E|\left(1+\tfrac{n_E|\mathcal{S}|}{k-1}\right)^{k-1} n_E\right) \\
&\subseteq O\left(|\mathcal{S}|\,|E|\,n_E\left(1+\tfrac{n_E|\mathcal{S}|}{k-1}\right)^{k-1}\right) \\
&\subseteq O\left(|\mathcal{S}|\,|E|\,n_E\left(\tfrac{n_E|\mathcal{S}|}{k-1}\right)^{k-1}\right) \\
&\subseteq O\left(|E|\,k\left(\tfrac{n_E|\mathcal{S}|}{k}\right)^{k}\right)
\end{aligned}
$$

For the above proof, we note again that $m < n$ implies $\left(1+\frac{\lambda}{m}\right)^m < \left(1+\frac{\lambda}{n}\right)^n$ (see the proof of Theorem 3.34 on page 134), and that $(k-1)^{k-1} \in O(k^{k-1})$.

In case the equation system consists of an odd number of blocks, it is easily seen that the above estimation is also valid. Hence, we have the following theorem:

Theorem 3.42 (Reducing the Alternation-Depth w.r.t. Kripke Structures). *Given an equation system $E = B_1\&\ldots\&B_\ell$ where the blocks B_i have alternating parity, and a Kripke structure $\mathcal{K}$ with state set $\mathcal{S}$. Let $\ell \geq 2$ and define $k = \left\lfloor \frac{\ell}{2} \right\rfloor$. By successive expansions, we compute an alternation-free equation system E' of size $O\left(\left(\frac{1}{k} n_E\,|\mathcal{S}|\right)^k |E|\,k\right)$. For this reason, the solution of E can be computed in time $O\left(\left(\frac{n_E|\mathcal{S}|}{k}\right)^k |E|\,k\right)$.*

With the above theorem, we clearly see that even the Cleaveland-Steffen algorithm is far from being optimal. For example, we compare the complexities for a number of alternation depths:

ℓ	CleaStef	Expand
2	$O(\lvert\mathcal{K}\rvert\,\lvert E\rvert\,(\frac{1}{2}\,\lvert\mathcal{S}\rvert\,\lvert E\rvert)^1)$	$O(\lvert\mathcal{K}\rvert\,\lvert E\rvert\,(\frac{1}{1}\,\lvert\mathcal{S}\rvert\,\lvert E\rvert)^1)$
3	$O(\lvert\mathcal{K}\rvert\,\lvert E\rvert\,(\frac{1}{3}\,\lvert\mathcal{S}\rvert\,\lvert E\rvert)^2)$	$O(\lvert\mathcal{K}\rvert\,\lvert E\rvert\,(\frac{1}{1}\,\lvert\mathcal{S}\rvert\,\lvert E\rvert)^1)$
4	$O(\lvert\mathcal{K}\rvert\,\lvert E\rvert\,(\frac{1}{4}\,\lvert\mathcal{S}\rvert\,\lvert E\rvert)^3)$	$O(\lvert\mathcal{K}\rvert\,\lvert E\rvert\,(\frac{1}{2}\,\lvert\mathcal{S}\rvert\,\lvert E\rvert)^2)$
5	$O(\lvert\mathcal{K}\rvert\,\lvert E\rvert\,(\frac{1}{5}\,\lvert\mathcal{S}\rvert\,\lvert E\rvert)^4)$	$O(\lvert\mathcal{K}\rvert\,\lvert E\rvert\,(\frac{1}{2}\,\lvert\mathcal{S}\rvert\,\lvert E\rvert)^2)$
6	$O(\lvert\mathcal{K}\rvert\,\lvert E\rvert\,(\frac{1}{6}\,\lvert\mathcal{S}\rvert\,\lvert E\rvert)^5)$	$O(\lvert\mathcal{K}\rvert\,\lvert E\rvert\,(\frac{1}{3}\,\lvert\mathcal{S}\rvert\,\lvert E\rvert)^3)$
7	$O(\lvert\mathcal{K}\rvert\,\lvert E\rvert\,(\frac{1}{7}\,\lvert\mathcal{S}\rvert\,\lvert E\rvert)^6)$	$O(\lvert\mathcal{K}\rvert\,\lvert E\rvert\,(\frac{1}{3}\,\lvert\mathcal{S}\rvert\,\lvert E\rvert)^3)$

The explanation of this phenomenon is that the unrolling technique allows us to use prefixed points as starting points for the Tarski/Knaster fixpoint iteration. To see this, consider again the expansion of the equation system $[x \overset{\mu}{=} f(x,y,z), y \overset{\nu}{=} g(x,y,z), z \overset{\mu}{=} h(x,y,z)]$. When the outermost block, i.e. the equation $z \overset{\mu}{=} h(x,y,z)$ invokes a new iteration, we normally have to start the fixpoint iteration for $y \overset{\nu}{=} g(x,y,z)$ from $y = 1$. During the iteration, we would then obtain the values of the unrolled equation system, following the equations of the y_k's. However, as the right hand side g is monotonic, the values would now be greater than in the previous iteration. Hence, there is no need to restart the iteration, instead we can start from a prefixed point to evaluate the y_k's.

The effect is therefore very similar to the improvement of Theorem 3.22 where we considered the alternation of fixpoints as a criterion to restart an iteration. A complete unrolling of the fixpoints is however not useful in practice, and normally the fixpoints are reached much earlier. An implementation should therefore generate the expanded blocks on-the-fly, and should evaluate these whenever necessary.

3.7 Computing Fair States

In the previous sections, we have developed algorithms for checking μ-calculus formulas on Kripke structures. In particular, we have seen that the set of states $\mathcal{S}_{\mathsf{inf}}$ of a structure $\mathcal{K}$ that have at least one finite path can be computed by evaluation of a μ-calculus formula, namely $\Phi_{\mathsf{inf}} :\equiv \nu x.\Diamond x$ (page 106). The set $\mathcal{S}_{\mathsf{inf}}$ is important for the evaluation of many other formulas (cf. Lemma 2.43 on page 81). In particular, we have the following equations that show how EX and AX can be defined by $\Diamond$ and $\Box$, respectively:

- $[\![\mathsf{EX}\varphi]\!]_{\mathcal{K}} = \mathsf{pre}_{\exists}^{\mathcal{R}}(\mathcal{S}_{\mathsf{inf}} \cap [\![\varphi]\!]_{\mathcal{K}})$, hence, $\mathsf{EX}\varphi = \Diamond(\Phi_{\mathsf{inf}} \wedge \varphi)$
- $[\![\mathsf{AX}\varphi]\!]_{\mathcal{K}} = \mathsf{pre}_{\forall}^{\mathcal{R}}((\mathcal{S} \setminus \mathcal{S}_{\mathsf{inf}}) \cup [\![\varphi]\!]_{\mathcal{K}})$, hence, $\mathsf{AX}\varphi = \Box(\Phi_{\mathsf{inf}} \rightarrow \varphi)$

Using the modified transition relation $\mathcal{R}_{\mathsf{inf}} := \mathcal{R} \cap (\mathcal{S} \times \mathcal{S}_{\mathsf{inf}})$, we can equivalently use the following equations:

- $[\![\mathsf{EX}\varphi]\!]_{\mathcal{K}} = \mathsf{pre}_{\exists}^{\mathcal{R}_{\mathsf{inf}}}([\![\varphi]\!]_{\mathcal{K}})$
- $[\![\mathsf{AX}\varphi]\!]_{\mathcal{K}} = \mathsf{pre}_{\forall}^{\mathcal{R}_{\mathsf{inf}}}([\![\varphi]\!]_{\mathcal{K}})$

The difference between EX and $\Diamond$ is therefore that EX considers only states that have at least one infinite path, while $\Diamond$ considers all states, including those that only have finite paths. The restriction of EX is due to the semantics of the path quantifiers: recall that $\mathsf{E}\varphi$ holds in a state s iff there is an infinite path starting in s such that φ holds on that path.

In general, it is possible to further restrict the set of paths that should be considered for quantification by particular path formulas Φ: we simply have to replace $\mathsf{E}\varphi$ with $\mathsf{E}(\Phi \wedge \varphi)$. We then often write $\mathsf{E}_\Phi\varphi$ and $\mathsf{A}_\Phi\varphi$ as abbreviations for $\mathsf{E}(\Phi \wedge \varphi)$ and $\mathsf{A}(\Phi \rightarrow \varphi)$, respectively (cf. Theorem 5.13 on page 300).

The most important restriction of this kind is thereby the restriction to fair paths. Recall that a path π is fair w.r.t. a set of fairness constraints $\mathcal{F} = \{F_1, \ldots, F_f\}$ iff every $F_i \in \mathcal{F}$ contains a state that appears infinitely often on π (cf. Definition 2.3 on page 47). Moreover, the set of fair states $\mathcal{S}_{\mathsf{fair}}$ is the set of states that have at least one fair path.

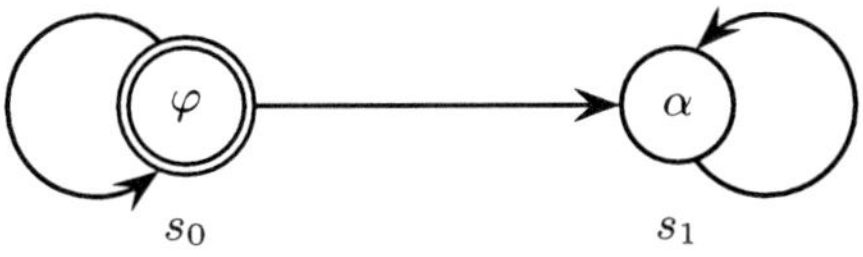

Fig. 3.21. Existence of unfair paths after restriction to $\mathcal{S}_{\mathsf{fair}}$

The computation of fair states is a fundamental problem for the verification of reactive systems. In particular, model checking of temporal logics can be reduced to this problem. Unlike the restriction to infinite paths, the restriction to fair paths can not be simply solved by restricting the Kripke structure to the fair states. This can be seen by the example in Figure 3.21, where we assume that state s_1 should be infinitely often visited. The path that remains in the initial state s_0 is certainly an unfair one, but nevertheless we have $\mathcal{S}_{\mathsf{fair}} = \{s_0, s_1\} = \mathcal{S}$. For this reason, the formula $\mathsf{EG}\varphi$ holds in the structure of Figure 3.21, but is false when we add the fairness constraint $\{s_1\}$ (which equivalently means that we change the formula to $\mathsf{E}_{\mathsf{GF}\alpha}\mathsf{G}\varphi$).

In the remainder of this section, we consider several algorithms to compute $\mathcal{S}_{\mathsf{fair}}$. We describe these algorithms by means of μ-calculus formulas. To this end, we consider a given structure $\mathcal{K} = (\mathcal{I}, \mathcal{S}, \mathcal{R}, \mathcal{L})$ together with a set of fairness constraints $\mathcal{F} = \{\alpha_1, \ldots, \alpha_f\}$ where all α_i are propositional formulas. A path is then fair iff it satisfies the formula $\bigwedge_{i=1}^{f} \mathsf{GF}\alpha_i$, and therefore we have $\mathcal{S}_{\mathsf{fair}} = \left[\!\left[\mathsf{E}\bigwedge_{i=1}^{f} \mathsf{GF}\alpha_i\right]\!\right]_{\mathcal{K}}$. The following lemma therefore shows how $\mathcal{S}_{\mathsf{fair}}$ can be computed by means of the μ-calculus:

Lemma 3.43 (Computing $\mathcal{S}_{\mathsf{fair}}$ [174, 175]). *Given a structure $\mathcal{K} = (\mathcal{I}, \mathcal{S}, \mathcal{R}, \mathcal{L})$ over V_Σ with $\mathcal{F} = \{\alpha_1, \ldots, \alpha_f\}$. Then, the following holds:*

- $$\mathsf{E}\left[(\mathsf{G}\beta) \wedge \bigwedge_{i=1}^{f} \mathsf{GF}\alpha_i\right] = \mathsf{fix}\begin{bmatrix} x_1 \stackrel{\mu}{=} y \wedge \alpha_1 \vee \beta \wedge \Diamond x_1 \\ \vdots \\ x_f \stackrel{\mu}{=} y \wedge \alpha_f \vee \beta \wedge \Diamond x_f \\ y \stackrel{\nu}{=} \beta \wedge \bigwedge_{i=1}^{f} \Diamond x_i \end{bmatrix} \mathsf{in}\ y\ \mathsf{end}$$
- $$\mathsf{E}\left[(\mathsf{G}\beta) \wedge \bigwedge_{i=1}^{f} \mathsf{GF}\alpha_i\right] = \nu y.\beta \wedge \bigwedge_{i=1}^{f} \Diamond[\mu x_i.y \wedge \alpha_i \vee \beta \wedge \Diamond x_i]$$

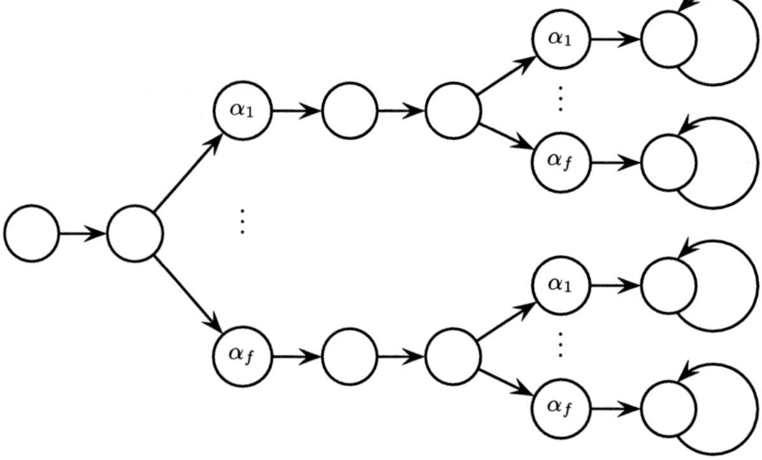

Fig. 3.22. Illustrating the computation of fair states

Proof. Abbreviate $F_i := \llbracket \alpha_i \rrbracket_{\mathcal{K}}$, $\mathcal{F} := \{F_1, \ldots, F_f\}$, and $B := \llbracket \beta \rrbracket_{\mathcal{K}}$. It is easily seen that $\llbracket \mu x_i.y \wedge \alpha_i \vee \beta \wedge \Diamond x_i \rrbracket_{\mathcal{K}}$ is the set of states that have a possibly finite path that runs through states of $\llbracket \beta \rrbracket_{\mathcal{K}}$ to finally reach a state in $\llbracket y \wedge \alpha_i \rrbracket_{\mathcal{K}}$. Consider the Tarski / Knaster iteration for $\nu y.\beta \wedge \bigwedge_{i=1}^{f} \Diamond[\mu x_i.y \wedge \alpha_i \vee \beta \wedge \Diamond x_i]$: we iterate $Q_{k+1} := B \cap \bigcap_{i=1}^{f} \mathsf{pre}_{\exists}^{\mathcal{R}}(\llbracket \mu x_i.y \wedge \alpha_i \vee \beta \wedge \Diamond x_i \rrbracket)_{\mathcal{K}_y^{Q_k}}$ starting from $Q_0 := \mathcal{S}$.

Let $\mathcal{K}_B$ be the structure that is obtained by restricting the set of states of $\mathcal{K}$ to B and the transition relation to $\mathcal{R}_\beta := \{(s, s') \in \mathcal{R} \mid s \in B \wedge s' \in B\}$. Then, we prove by induction on k that Q_k is the set of states that have a possibly finite path π through $\mathcal{K}_B$ that can visit every F_i at least k times. The proof is simple, just consider Figure 3.22. But then $\lim_{k\to\infty} Q_k$ is the set of states where an infinite path through $\mathcal{K}_B$ starts that infinitely often visits every F_i. Hence, $\lim_{k\to\infty} Q_k = \left\llbracket \mathsf{E}\left[(\mathsf{G}\beta) \wedge \bigwedge_{i=1}^{f} \mathsf{GF}\alpha_i\right] \right\rrbracket_{\mathcal{K}}$. The equivalence with the vectorized fixpoint expression is trivial since this is exactly what is obtained by the algorithm of Figure 3.10 from the non-vectorized μ-calculus formula. □

The above fixpoint formula does even more than just computing $\mathcal{S}_{\mathsf{fair}}$: additionally, it checks that another formula β must invariantly hold on the fair path. We will need that in the temporal logic chapter, and may omit β by instantiating $\beta := 1$ to compute $\mathcal{S}_{\mathsf{fair}}$.

As an example, consider how the formula is evaluated on the Kripke structure given in Figure 3.23, where we have just one fairness constraint that is given by the states labeled with α. We thus have to evaluate the μ-calculus formula $\nu y.\Diamond[\mu x.y \wedge \alpha \vee \Diamond x]$, which is done by the following Tarski / Knaster iterations:

- $Y_0 := \{s_0, \ldots, s_9\}$ yields

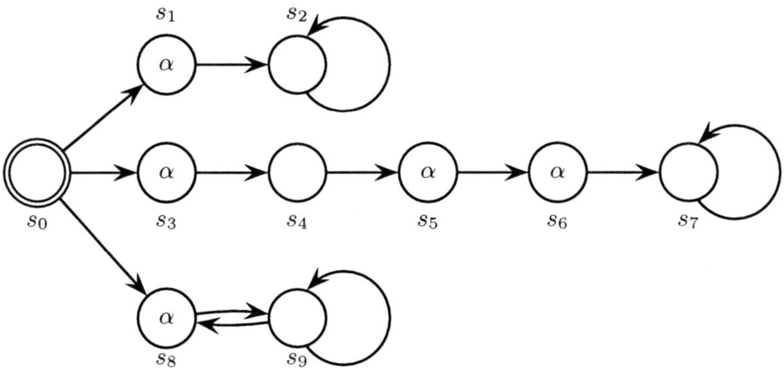

Fig. 3.23. Example Structure to Compute $\mathcal{S}_{\mathsf{fair}}$

  - $X_{0,0} := \{\}$
  - $X_{0,1} := \{s_1, s_3, s_5, s_6, s_8\}$
  - $X_{0,2} := \{s_0, s_1, s_3, s_4, s_5, s_6, s_8, s_9\}$
  - $X_{0,3} := X_{0,2}$
- $Y_1 := \mathsf{pre}_{\exists}^{\mathcal{R}}(X_{0,3}) = \{s_0, s_3, s_4, s_5, s_8, s_9\}$ yields
  - $X_{1,0} := \{\}$
  - $X_{1,1} := \{s_3, s_5, s_8\}$
  - $X_{1,2} := \{s_0, s_3, s_4, s_5, s_8, s_9\}$
  - $X_{1,3} := X_{1,2}$
- $Y_2 := \mathsf{pre}_{\exists}^{\mathcal{R}}(X_{1,3}) = \{s_0, s_3, s_4, s_8, s_9\}$ yields
  - $X_{2,0} := \{\}$
  - $X_{2,1} := \{s_3, s_8\}$
  - $X_{2,2} := \{s_0, s_3, s_8, s_9\}$
  - $X_{2,3} := X_{2,2}$
- $Y_3 := \mathsf{pre}_{\exists}^{\mathcal{R}}(X_{2,3}) = \{s_0, s_8, s_9\}$ yields
  - $X_{3,0} := \{\}$
  - $X_{3,1} := \{s_8\}$
  - $X_{3,2} := \{s_0, s_8, s_9\}$
  - $X_{3,3} := X_{3,2}$
- $Y_4 := Y_3 = \mathcal{S}_{\mathsf{fair}}$

As can be seen, Y_i contains the set of states that have a successor such that states where α holds are visited at least i times. The condition $Y_i = Y_{i+1}$ (for $i > n_0$ for some n_0) is therefore satisfied by the set of states that can visit α infinitely often.

The above computation to determine $\mathcal{S}_{\mathsf{fair}}$ goes back to Emerson and Lei [174, 175]. For one fairness constraint and $\beta = 1$, this reduces to the formula $\nu y.\Diamond[\mu x.y \wedge \alpha \vee \Diamond x]$. This formula can be rewritten in several ways to obtain equivalent variants: for example, Emerson uses $\nu y.\mu x.\Diamond[y \wedge \alpha \vee x]$ in [159], and Walukiewicz uses $\nu y.\mu x.\Diamond y \wedge \alpha \vee \Diamond x$ in [510].

In the meantime, other methods have been developed that have been compared by Somenzi et. al. in [423]. To describe these fixpoints in a more readable form, we abbreviate first the following macros:

- $\mathsf{CanGoTo}(\psi) := \mu y.\ \psi \vee \mathsf{EX}y$
- $\mathsf{CanComeFrom}(\psi) := \mu y.\ \psi \vee \overleftarrow{\Diamond}\, y$
- $\mathsf{CanGoToOver}(\varphi, \psi) := \mu y.\ \psi \vee \varphi \wedge \mathsf{EX}y$
- $\mathsf{CanComeFromOver}(\varphi, \psi) := \mu y.\ \psi \vee \varphi \wedge \overleftarrow{\Diamond}\, y$
- $\mathsf{CanStayIn}(\varphi) := \nu y.\ \varphi \wedge \overleftarrow{\Diamond}\, y$
- $\mathsf{Cycle}(\varphi) := \nu y.\ \varphi \wedge y \wedge \overleftarrow{\Diamond}\, y \wedge \mathsf{EX}y$
- $\mathsf{CanFromTo}(\varphi) := \mathsf{CanGoTo}(\varphi) \wedge \mathsf{CanComeFrom}(\varphi)$

Note that $\mathsf{CanGoTo}(\psi)$ holds on the set of states that have a possibly finite path that leads to a state where ψ holds. $\mathsf{CanGoToOver}(\varphi, \psi)$ additionally requires that φ must hold on every state of the (possibly finite) path up to the state where ψ holds. Similarly, $\mathsf{CanComeFrom}(\psi)$ corresponds with the set of states that can be reached from a state where ψ holds, and $\mathsf{CanComeFromOver}(\varphi, \psi)$ additionally requires that φ must hold on every state of the path from the state where ψ held. $\mathsf{CanStayIn}(\varphi)$ holds on the set of states that have an infinite path through the states where φ holds. $\mathsf{Cycle}(\varphi)$ is the union of all states that lie on a cycle where φ holds. Finally, $\mathsf{CanFromTo}(\varphi)$ holds on the set of states that can both reach a state where φ holds and can be reached from such a state. Using these macros, formulas to compute $\mathcal{S}_{\mathsf{fair}}$ are as follows:

Emerson-Lei [174, 175]: $\nu y.\ \bigwedge_{i=1}^{f} \Diamond\mathsf{CanGoTo}(y \wedge \alpha_i)$
Emerson-Lei [174, 175]: $\nu y.\ \bigwedge_{i=1}^{f} \Diamond\mathsf{CanGoToOver}(y, y \wedge \alpha_i)$
Hojati-Kesten [249, 281]: $\nu y.\mathsf{CanStayIn}\left(\bigwedge_{i=1}^{f} \mathsf{CanComeFromOver}(y, y \wedge \alpha_i)\right)$
Hojati-Hardin [234, 249]: $\nu y.\mathsf{Cycle}\left(\bigwedge_{i=1}^{f} y \wedge \mathsf{CanFromTo}(y \wedge \alpha_i)\right)$

In [423], the runtimes of these algorithms have been compared by some experimental benchmarks. As a result, [423] states that none of the newer algorithms performs better than the old Emerson-Lei approach on a significant number of examples.

Considering the complexity analysis of the Cleaveland-Steffen algorithm, we easily find out that the Emerson-Lei formulas can be evaluated in time $O(f\,|\mathcal{S}|\,|\mathcal{K}|)$. In [423], the complexity of this formula is studied in a the more general context of SCC-hull algorithms. The complexity is therefore determined as $O(f\,|\mathcal{S}|\,h)$, where h is the length of the longest path through SCCs of the Kripke structure (actually $|\mathcal{S}|$ can be replaced with the diameter of the structure, which is the length of the longest path without cycles).

To conclude this section, consider how the Hojati-Hardin algorithm works for Figure 3.23 (note however that the steps themselves contain fixpoint iterations whose computations we have omitted):

- $Y_0 := \{s_0, \dots, s_9\}$ yields
  - $U_0 := [\![\mathsf{CanGoTo}(\alpha)]\!]_{\mathcal{K}} = \{s_0, s_1, s_3, s_4, s_5, s_6, s_8, s_9\}$
  - $V_0 := [\![\mathsf{CanComeFrom}(\alpha)]\!]_{\mathcal{K}} = \{s_1, s_2, s_3, s_4, s_5, s_6, s_8, s_9\}$
  - $W_0 := Y_0 \cap U_0 \cap V_0 = \{s_1, s_3, s_4, s_5, s_6, s_8, s_9\}$
  - $X_0 := \mathsf{Cycle}(W_0) = \{s_8, s_9\}$
- $Y_1 := \{s_8, s_9\}$

3.8 Final Remarks on Completeness and Expressiveness

We conclude this chapter with final remarks on the μ-calculus. Fixpoints are manyfold in mathematics, and in particular, in computer science, and therefore there are a lot of applications for the μ-calculus. We only list some of them to show the role of the μ-calculus, not only as machinery for verifying reactive systems, but also for other fields in computer science.

The first remarkable point is that the model checking problem for the μ-calculus is in $\mathsf{NP} \cap \mathsf{coNP}$ [40, 169, 337]. This means that a nondeterministic machine is able to solve every μ-calculus model checking problem in polynomial time (see Appendix B.3). As for every formula φ, its negation $\neg\varphi$ is also a μ-calculus formula, it follows that the μ-calculus model checking problem is also in coNP. The interesting point here is that there are only a few problems in $\mathsf{NP} \cap \mathsf{coNP}$, where no deterministic polynomial algorithm is known. For examples, checking the primality of a given number is such a problem that has been recently shown [5] to have a polynomial decision procedure. Hence, there is still a hope that we can find more efficient model checking algorithms in the future. The latest improvement was that made by Jurdziński [270] in that he showed that the upper bound can be improved to $\mathsf{UP} \cap \mathsf{coUP}$ [270], which seems to be sharper than $\mathsf{NP} \cap \mathsf{coNP}$. UP is the class of problems that can be solved in polynomial time by an unambiguous Turing machine. An unambiguous Turing machine may have several runs for an input, but only one of these runs is accepting. Hence, this machine is not too nondeterministic.

Having seen that the μ-calculus is also of interest for complexity theory, we consider three further related fields in this section. In the next section, we consider the relationship of bisimulation relations and the μ-calculus, then the relationship to alternating tree automata and games, and finally the historical origins of the μ-calculus, namely dynamic logic and the Hoare calculus.

3.8.1 Bisimilarity and the Future Fragment

In this section, we derive two important results: First, we establish a relationship between bisimulation relations and the μ-calculus, and second we prove that the future fragment is strictly less powerful than the full μ-calculus. The future fragment is thereby the set of μ-calculus formulas that do not contain occurrences of the past modalities $\overleftarrow{\Diamond}$ and $\overleftarrow{\Box}$. We denote the future fragment as $\mathcal{L}_\mu^f$ in the following.

Theorem 3.44 (Bisimilarity and the μ-Calculus). *Given two Kripke structures $\mathcal{K}_1 = (\mathcal{I}_1, \mathcal{S}_1, \mathcal{R}_1, \mathcal{L}_1)$ and $\mathcal{K}_2 = (\mathcal{I}_2, \mathcal{S}_2, \mathcal{R}_2, \mathcal{L}_2)$ over the variables V_Σ and the greatest bisimulation relation $\approx$ between $\mathcal{K}_1$ and $\mathcal{K}_2$. Then, the following holds for all states $s_1 \in \mathcal{S}_1$ and $s_2 \in \mathcal{S}_2$:*

$$s_1 \approx s_2 \Leftrightarrow \forall \varphi \in \mathcal{L}_\mu^f . s_1 \in [\![\varphi]\!]_{\mathcal{K}_1} \Leftrightarrow s_2 \in [\![\varphi]\!]_{\mathcal{K}_2}$$

We even have $s_1 \approx s_2 \Leftrightarrow \forall \varphi \in \mathcal{L}_\mu^{f,0} . s_1 \in [\![\varphi]\!]_{\mathcal{K}_1} \Leftrightarrow s_2 \in [\![\varphi]\!]_{\mathcal{K}_2}$, where $\mathcal{L}_\mu^{f,0}$ is the subset of $\mathcal{L}_\mu^f$ without fixpoints.

Proof. We first prove the $\Rightarrow$ direction. The proof is done by induction on the alternation depth of φ. The induction base is also proved by induction, this time by induction on the structure of φ (we only list the relevant cases):

$\boxed{\varphi \in V_\Sigma:}$ $s_1 \in [\![\varphi]\!]_{\mathcal{K}_1}$ is equivalent to $\varphi \in \mathcal{L}_1(s_1)$ which implies $\varphi \in \mathcal{L}_2(s_2)$ by **SIM1**, and therefore $s_2 \in [\![\varphi]\!]_{\mathcal{K}_2}$. The analogous argumentation can be used to prove the converse direction.

$\boxed{\varphi \equiv \neg\psi:}$ $s_1 \in [\![\neg\psi]\!]_{\mathcal{K}_1}$ holds iff $s_1 \notin [\![\psi]\!]_{\mathcal{K}_1}$, which is by induction hypothesis equivalent to $s_2 \notin [\![\psi]\!]_{\mathcal{K}_2}$, i.e., to $s_2 \in [\![\neg\psi]\!]_{\mathcal{K}_2}$.

$\boxed{\varphi \equiv \varphi_1 \wedge \varphi_2:}$ $s_1 \in [\![\varphi_1 \wedge \varphi_2]\!]_{\mathcal{K}_1}$ holds iff $s_1 \in [\![\varphi_1]\!]_{\mathcal{K}_1}$ and $s_1 \in [\![\varphi_2]\!]_{\mathcal{K}_1}$ holds. By induction hypothesis, this is equivalent to $s_2 \in [\![\varphi_1]\!]_{\mathcal{K}_2}$ and $s_2 \in [\![\varphi_2]\!]_{\mathcal{K}_2}$, and hence, equivalent to $s_2 \in [\![\varphi_1 \wedge \varphi_2]\!]_{\mathcal{K}_2}$.

$\boxed{\varphi \equiv \Diamond\psi:}$ $s_1 \in [\![\Diamond\psi]\!]_{\mathcal{K}_1}$ holds iff $s_1 \in \mathsf{pre}_\exists^{\mathcal{R}_1}([\![\psi]\!]_{\mathcal{K}_1})$. Hence, there is a state $s_1' \in \mathcal{S}_1$ with $(s_1, s_1') \in \mathcal{R}_1$, such that $s_1' \in [\![\psi]\!]_{\mathcal{K}_1}$. By **SIM2** and the assumption $s_1 \approx s_2$, it follows that there must be a state $s_2' \in \mathcal{S}_2$ with $(s_2, s_2') \in \mathcal{R}_2$, such that $s_1' \approx s_2'$. Hence, by induction hypothesis, it follows that $s_2' \in [\![\psi]\!]_{\mathcal{K}_2}$. Finally, we conclude $s_2 \in [\![\Diamond\psi]\!]_{\mathcal{K}_2}$.

Hence, we have already proved the proposition for μ-calculus formulas without fixpoint operators. In the induction step, we already know that the proposition holds for formulas with alternation depth less than $n+1$, and have to prove the proposition for formulas with alternation depth $n+1$. The cases for Boolean connectives and modal operators are proved in the same manner as in the above induction base.

It remains to consider a formula $\varphi \equiv \mu x.\psi$, where ψ has alternation depth n (the ν-case can be reduced to this case). As Kripke structures are finite lattices, we can replace $[\![\mu x.\psi]\!]_{\mathcal{K}_1}$ by $[\![\psi_{|\mathcal{S}_1|+1}]\!]_{\mathcal{K}_1}$, where ψ_i is recursively defined as follows: $\psi_0 := 0$, and $\psi_{i+1} := [\psi]_x^{\psi_i}$. Similarly, we can replace $[\![\mu x.\psi]\!]_{\mathcal{K}_2}$ by $[\![\psi_{|\mathcal{S}_2|+1}]\!]_{\mathcal{K}_2}$. Proceeding this way with the outermost fixpoint operators, yields formulas with alternation depth $\leq n$, so that we can use the induction hypothesis to derive our result.

For the other direction, we construct for given states $s_1 \in \mathcal{S}_1$, $s_2 \in \mathcal{S}_2$ with $s_1 \approx s_2$ a μ-calculus formula φ such that $(\mathcal{K}_1, s_1) \models \varphi \not\Leftrightarrow (\mathcal{K}_2, s_2) \models \varphi$. For this reason, we construct the following formulas $\Phi_i(s_1)$ for a given state $s_1 \in \mathcal{S}_1$:

- $\Phi_0(s_1) = \bigwedge_{x \in \mathcal{L}_1(s_1)} x \wedge \bigwedge_{x \in V_\Sigma \setminus \mathcal{L}_1(s_1)} \neg x$
- $\Phi_{i+1}(s_1) = \Phi_i(s_1) \wedge \bigwedge_{(s_1, s_1') \in \mathcal{R}_1} \Diamond \Phi_i(s_1') \wedge \Box \bigvee_{(s_1, s_1') \in \mathcal{R}_1} \Phi_i(s_1')$

Clearly, $(\mathcal{K}_1, s_1) \models \Phi_i(s_1)$ holds for each $i \in \mathbb{N}$ and each state $s_1 \in \mathcal{S}_1$. Recall now that the following sequence of relations converges to the largest bisimulation relation (see Lemma 2.22 on page 60):

- $(s_1, s_2) \in \mathcal{B}_0 :\Leftrightarrow \mathcal{L}_1(s_1) = \mathcal{L}_2(s_2)$
- $(s_1, s_2) \in \mathcal{B}_{i+1} :\Leftrightarrow \left(\begin{array}{l} (s_1, s_2) \in \mathcal{B}_i \wedge \\ \forall s_1' \in \mathcal{S}_1.(s_1, s_1') \in \mathcal{R}_1 \rightarrow \\ \qquad \exists s_2' \in \mathcal{S}_2.(s_2, s_2') \in \mathcal{R}_2 \wedge (s_1', s_2') \in \mathcal{B}_i \wedge \\ \forall s_2' \in \mathcal{S}_2.(s_2, s_2') \in \mathcal{R}_2 \rightarrow \\ \qquad \exists s_1' \in \mathcal{S}_1'.(s_1, s_1') \in \mathcal{R}_1 \wedge (s_1', s_2') \in \mathcal{B}_i \end{array}\right)$

We have already seen that there is a $n \in \mathbb{N}$ such that $\mathcal{B}_n$ is the greatest bisimulation relation, i.e., $\approx$ by our assumption. We show now by induction on i that $(\mathcal{K}_2, s_2) \models \Phi_i(s_1)$ holds if and only if $(s_1, s_2) \in \mathcal{B}_i$.

$\boxed{\text{i=0:}}$ $(\mathcal{K}_2, s_2) \models \Phi_0(s_1) \Leftrightarrow [\![\Phi_0(s_1)]\!]_{\mathcal{L}_2(s_2)} \Leftrightarrow \mathcal{L}_1(s_1) = \mathcal{L}_2(s_2) \Leftrightarrow (s_1, s_2) \in \mathcal{B}_0$

$\boxed{\text{i>0:}}$ $(\mathcal{K}_2, s_2) \models \Phi_{i+1}(s_1)$

$$\begin{array}{l}
\Leftrightarrow (\mathcal{K}_2, s_2) \models \Phi_i(s_1) \wedge \bigwedge_{(s_1, s_1') \in \mathcal{R}_1} \Diamond \Phi_i(s_1') \wedge \Box \bigvee_{(s_1, s_1') \in \mathcal{R}_1} \Phi_i(s_1') \\
\Leftrightarrow (\mathcal{K}_2, s_2) \models \Phi_i(s_1) \wedge \\
\quad \forall s_1' \in \mathcal{S}_1.(s_1, s_1') \in \mathcal{R}_1 \rightarrow (\mathcal{K}_2, s_2) \models \Diamond \Phi_i(s_1') \wedge \\
\quad \forall s_2' \in \mathcal{S}_2.(s_2, s_2') \in \mathcal{R}_2 \rightarrow (\mathcal{K}_2, s_2) \models \bigvee_{(s_1, s_1') \in \mathcal{R}_1} \Phi_i(s_1') \\
\Leftrightarrow (s_1, s_2) \in \mathcal{B}_i \wedge \\
\quad \forall s_1' \in \mathcal{S}_1.(s_1, s_1') \in \mathcal{R}_1 \rightarrow \exists s_2' \in \mathcal{S}_2.(s_2, s_2') \in \mathcal{R}_2 \wedge (s_1', s_2') \in \mathcal{B}_i \wedge \\
\quad \forall s_2' \in \mathcal{S}_2.(s_2, s_2') \in \mathcal{R}_2 \rightarrow \exists s_1' \in \mathcal{S}_1'.(s_1, s_1') \in \mathcal{R}_1 \wedge (s_1', s_2') \in \mathcal{B}_i \\
\Leftrightarrow (s_1, s_2) \in \mathcal{B}_{i+1}
\end{array}$$

The convergence of $\mathcal{B}_i$ has now the following effect: there must be a $i_0 \in \mathbb{N}$ such that $(\mathcal{K}_2, s_2) \not\models \Phi_{i_0}(s_1)$ iff $s_1 \not\approx s_2$. As $(\mathcal{K}_1, s_1) \models \Phi_{i_0}(s_1)$ holds, we can use the formula $\varphi := \Phi_{i_0}(s_1)$ to conclude that there are even fixpoint-free μ-calculus formulas that can distinguish states that are not bisimilar. □

Hence, we see that the future fragment of the μ-calculus can not distinguish between bisimilar states. For this reason, given a structure $\mathcal{K}$ and a μ-calculus future formula φ, we can compute the quotient structure with the greatest bisimulation relation on $\mathcal{K}$ before model checking φ. The result will be the same.

However, the full μ-calculus, including the past modalities can distinguish certain bisimilar state as shown in Figure 3.24. The largest bisimulation relation between the structures $\mathcal{K}_1$ and $\mathcal{K}_2$ is obviously the one that relates the states of the structures with the same labels. However, the formula $\overleftarrow{\Diamond}(\overleftarrow{\Diamond} b \wedge \overleftarrow{\Diamond} c)$ holds only in the initial state of $\mathcal{K}_1$, but not in the initial state of $\mathcal{K}_2$ (which is the only bisimilar counterpart of the initial state of $\mathcal{K}_1$). Therefore the formula $\overleftarrow{\Diamond}(\overleftarrow{\Diamond} b \wedge \overleftarrow{\Diamond} c)$ can distinguish between the initial states of the structures, which is not possible for any formula of the future fragment of the μ-calculus due to our previous theorem.

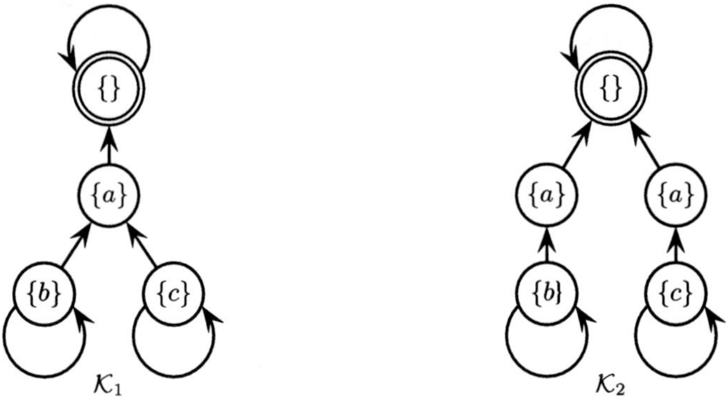

Fig. 3.24. Example for the weaker expressiveness of the future fragment of $\mathcal{L}_\mu$

Of course, we can derive in a completely analogous manner that the past fragment is also less expressive than the full language (simply reverse the transitions and replace $\Diamond$ with $\overleftarrow{\Diamond}$). To derive a relationship between bisimulation and the full μ-calculus, we add a property **PSIM2** to the properties of simulation relations as follows:

Definition 3.45 (Pre/Post-Simulation Relations). *Given two structures $\mathcal{K}_1 = (\mathcal{I}_1, \mathcal{S}_1, \mathcal{R}_1, \mathcal{L}_1)$, $\mathcal{K}_2 = (\mathcal{I}_2, \mathcal{S}_2, \mathcal{R}_2, \mathcal{L}_2)$ over variables V_{Σ_1} and V_{Σ_2}, respectively, with $V_{\Sigma_1} \subseteq V_{\Sigma_2}$. A relation $\sigma \subseteq \mathcal{S}_1 \times \mathcal{S}_2$ is called a pre/post-simulation relation between $\mathcal{K}_1$ and $\mathcal{K}_2$ iff the following holds:*

- **SIM1:** $(s_1, s_2) \in \sigma$ *implies* $\mathcal{L}_1(s_1) = \mathcal{L}_2(s_2) \cap V_{\Sigma_1}$
- **SIM2:** *for states $s_1, s_1' \in \mathcal{S}_1$ and $s_2 \in \mathcal{S}_2$ with $(s_1, s_2) \in \sigma$ and $(s_1, s_1') \in \mathcal{R}_1$, there is a state $s_2' \in \mathcal{S}_2$ such that $(s_1', s_2') \in \sigma$ and $(s_2, s_2') \in \mathcal{R}_2$ holds.*
- **PSIM2:** *for states $s_1, s_1' \in \mathcal{S}_1$ and $s_2' \in \mathcal{S}_2$ with $(s_1', s_2') \in \sigma$ and $(s_1, s_1') \in \mathcal{R}_1$, there is a state $s_2 \in \mathcal{S}_2$ such that $(s_1, s_2) \in \sigma$ and $(s_2, s_2') \in \mathcal{R}_2$ holds.*
- **SIM3:** *for any $s_1 \in \mathcal{I}_1$, there is a $s_2 \in \mathcal{I}_2$ with $(s_1, s_2) \in \sigma$.*

Equivalently, we could define for a structure $\mathcal{K}_i = (\mathcal{I}_i, \mathcal{S}_i, \mathcal{R}_i, \mathcal{L}_i)$ its mirrored structure $\mathcal{K}_i^{-1} = (\mathcal{I}_i, \mathcal{S}_i, \mathcal{R}_i^{-1}, \mathcal{L}_i)$ with $(s_1, s_1') \in \mathcal{R}_i^{-1} :\Leftrightarrow (s_1', s_1) \in \mathcal{R}_i$. Then, we could replace **PSIM2** by **SIM2** with the mirrored structures. Moreover, we can define pre / post-bisimulation relations, and then have the following result [241]:

Theorem 3.46 (Pre/Post-Bisimilarity and the μ-Calculus [241]). *Given two Kripke structures $\mathcal{K}_1 = (\mathcal{I}_1, \mathcal{S}_1, \mathcal{R}_1, \mathcal{L}_1)$ and $\mathcal{K}_2 = (\mathcal{I}_2, \mathcal{S}_2, \mathcal{R}_2, \mathcal{L}_2)$ over the variables V_Σ and the greatest pre-post-bisimulation relation $\approx$ between $\mathcal{K}_1$ and $\mathcal{K}_2$. Then, the following holds for all states $s_1 \in \mathcal{S}_1$ and $s_2 \in \mathcal{S}_2$:*

$$s_1 \approx s_2 \Leftrightarrow \forall \varphi \in \mathcal{L}_\mu . s_1 \in [\![\varphi]\!]_{\mathcal{K}_1} \Leftrightarrow s_2 \in [\![\varphi]\!]_{\mathcal{K}_2}$$

The greatest pre / post-(bi)simulation relation can be computed similar to the greatest (bi)simulation relation. For this reason, given a structure $\mathcal{K}$ and an arbitrary μ-calculus formula φ, we can compute the quotient structure with the greatest pre / post-bisimulation relation on $\mathcal{K}$ before model checking φ.

A further reduction is possible if the given formula belongs to the existential $\mathcal{L}^{\mathsf{E}}$ or universal fragment $\mathcal{L}^{\mathsf{A}}$ of $\mathcal{L}$: In $\mathcal{L}^{\mathsf{E}}$, all occurrences of subformulas $\Diamond\varphi$, $\overleftarrow{\Diamond}\varphi$, $\Box\varphi$, and $\overleftarrow{\Box}\varphi$ must be positive, positive, negative, and negative, respectively. $\mathcal{L}^{\mathsf{E}}$ and $\mathcal{L}^{\mathsf{A}}$ are preserved under simulation relations:

Theorem 3.47 (Simulation Relations and the μ-Calculus [37]). *Given two Kripke structures $\mathcal{K}_1 = (\mathcal{I}_1, \mathcal{S}_1, \mathcal{R}_1, \mathcal{L}_1)$ and $\mathcal{K}_2 = (\mathcal{I}_2, \mathcal{S}_2, \mathcal{R}_2, \mathcal{L}_2)$ with a pre/post-simulation relation ζ between $\mathcal{K}_1$ and $\mathcal{K}_2$. Then, the following holds:*

- $(s_1, s_2) \in \zeta \;\Leftrightarrow\; \forall \varphi \in \mathcal{L}^{\mathsf{A}}.\ (\mathcal{K}_2, s_2) \models \varphi \Rightarrow (\mathcal{K}_1, s_1) \models \varphi$
- $(s_1, s_2) \in \zeta \;\Leftrightarrow\; \forall \varphi \in \mathcal{L}^{\mathsf{E}}.\ (\mathcal{K}_1, s_1) \models \varphi \Rightarrow (\mathcal{K}_2, s_2) \models \varphi$

Again, we may also restrict $\mathcal{L}^{\mathsf{A}}$ and $\mathcal{L}^{\mathsf{E}}$ to fixpoint-free formulas without destroying the above equivalences.

Formalisms that can be embedded in the μ-calculus, like temporal logics, can often be divided into their existential and universal fragments (see Theorem 5.97 on page 402). Moreover, appendix C considers the construction of structures that simulate a given structure that can be used for this purpose.

There are some interesting properties that can be easily computed by fixpoints using past modal operators. For example, the set of states that are reachable (by possibly finite paths) from a property φ is given by $\mu x.\varphi \vee \overleftarrow{\Diamond} x$. As a further example, the set of states that are on a circle with a state belonging to φ is computed as $\left(\mu x.\varphi \vee \overleftarrow{\Diamond} x\right) \wedge (\mu x.\varphi \vee \Diamond x)$.

3.8.2 Relationship to ω-Tree Automata and Games

The μ-calculus is closely related to the theory of ω-tree automata, and therefore to the theory of games (or better winning strategies). In particular, every μ-calculus formula φ can be translated to an equivalent ω-tree automaton $\mathcal{A}_\varphi$, where equivalent means that $\mathcal{A}_\varphi$ accepts exactly the structures that satisfy

φ (see Appendix B.3). In particular, the consideration of *alternating* tree automata is advantageous for this relationship [167]. The relationship to games is established in that the emptiness problem of alternating tree automata can be reduced to the winner problem of parity games.

It is beyond the scope of this book to describe these related fields in detail. The interested reader is referred to [24, 165, 167, 168, 388, 390] for literature on the relationship between (alternating) tree automata and $\mathcal{L}_\mu$. The further connection to the theory of winning strategies is established in [224, 270, 271]. A comprehensive survey of these results is given in [514] and in the new book of Grädel, Thomas, and Wilke [221]. We will therefore just list an example for computing the winner states of a simple game with the help of the μ-calculus.

Winning strategies are nice examples that show the power of the μ-calculus. To see how such strategies can be derived, we list a simple example that is taken from [526]. The NIM game is played with some objects (often matches) that are placed in several rows as follows: The first row contains one element, the second row contains 3 elements, and so on (the n-th row contains $2n + 1$ elements):

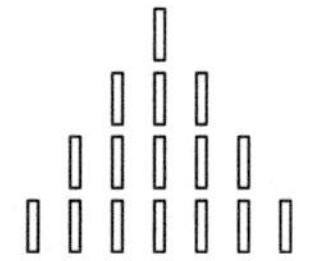

Two players A and B successively choose a row and take an arbitrary number of elements from that row. We assume that player A has the first choice. The player who takes away the last element looses the game. Clearly, there will always be a winner. In the following, we denote the NIM game with n rows as NIM_n. We immediately see that player B always wins NIM_1, since player A must take away the only element. NIM_2, on the other hand, can always be won by player A by taking away all three elements of row 2.

The Kripke structure for NIM_2 is given in Figure 3.25, where state A_{ij} is the state where player A has the choice, and the first and second row contain i and j matches, respectively. B_{ij} is defined analogously, but here player B has to take a match. Hence, the game is over in states A_{00} and B_{00}, where player A has won in state A_{00} and player B has won in state B_{00} (note that the structure has only finite paths).

The states where A can win the game, no matter what B will do, are called the winning states for A. Clearly, A_{00} belongs to this set. Moreover, if a state s belongs to this set, then all states in $\mathsf{pre}_\exists^{\mathcal{R}}(\mathsf{pre}_\forall^{\mathcal{R}}(s))$ belong to this set, since A can take a transition such that all the following transitions taken by B will lead to s. Hence, the winning states of A can be computed by evaluating $\mu x.A_{00} \vee \Diamond(\Diamond x \wedge \Box x)$.

Note that if a state has no successors, then $\Box\varphi$ trivially holds on this state, but $\Diamond\varphi$ will not hold on it. Hence, the conjunction $\Diamond x \wedge \Box x$ will hold on every state that has successors, and whose successors all belong to $[\![x]\!]_\mathcal{K}$. The computation for the structure of Figure 3.25 is as follows:

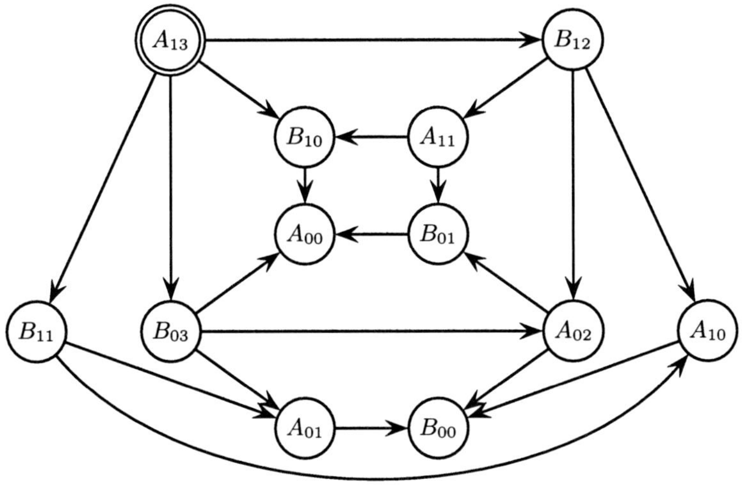

Fig. 3.25. Kripke structure of the NIM game

- $Q_0 = \{\}$
- $Q_1 = \{A_{00}\} \cup \mathsf{pre}_{\exists}^{\mathcal{R}}((\mathsf{pre}_{\exists}^{\mathcal{R}}(\{\}) \cap \mathsf{pre}_{\forall}^{\mathcal{R}}(\{\}))) = \{A_{00}\}$
- $Q_2 = \{A_{00}\} \cup \mathsf{pre}_{\exists}^{\mathcal{R}}((\mathsf{pre}_{\exists}^{\mathcal{R}}(\{A_{00}\}) \cap \mathsf{pre}_{\forall}^{\mathcal{R}}(\{A_{00}\}))) = \{A_{00}, A_{02}, A_{11}, A_{13}\}$
- $Q_3 = Q_2$

Hence, it follows that player A can always win, since the initial state A_{13} belongs to the set of states $\{A_{00}, A_{11}, A_{02}, A_{13}\}$ where A has a winning strategy. To find out what A has to do in which state, simply note that A has to proceed to one of the states $\mathsf{pre}_{\exists}^{\mathcal{R}}(Q_2) \cap \mathsf{pre}_{\forall}^{\mathcal{R}}(Q_2) = \{B_{01}, B_{10}\}$.

In a similar way, we can compute the set of states where player B has a winning strategy. This is determined by the analog formula $\mu x.B_{00} \vee \Diamond(\Diamond x \wedge \Box x)$. Its evaluation yields the set $\{B_{00}, B_{11}, B_{03}, B_{12}\}$. As the initial state does not belong to this set, player B can not win in any case. However, if B manages to reach the set $\{B_{00}, B_{11}, B_{03}, B_{12}\}$, B can win.

3.8.3 Dynamic Logic

We have already emphasized that the μ-calculus had its origins in program logics that are used to reason about the correctness of programs. The research in program verification began in the late 1960s, and landmark results are the papers of Floyd [196] 1967 and Hoare [248] 1969. As it has been realized that first order predicate logic is not powerful enough to express properties like reachability (see Theorem 6.6 on page 412), there was a need for more powerful logics that endow first order logic with a transitive closure operator or a fixpoint operator (see page 414).

Dynamic logic is such an extension that has been introduced by Pratt [411, 412] in 1976. Dynamic logics and Hoare's calculus are often called *exogenous logics* since programs are explicitly given in the logic formulas, while in *endogenous logics* the programs are not given inside the formulas. Dynamic logic is a special form of modal logic, where truth is not fixed, instead it depends on the current instant of time. Modal logics like the μ-calculus have special (modal) operators like $\Diamond$, $\Box$ to reason about the next possible interpretation. We will see that dynamic logic can be used as foundation of Hoare's calculus since the latter can be defined in terms of dynamic logic. Moreover, we will see that propositional dynamic logic PDL (introduced by Fischer and Ladner in 1979 [192]) and its extension PDL-Δ by the looping operator Δ, can both be seen as fragments of the propositional μ-calculus. We will give an embedding of PDL and PDL-Δ in the μ-calculus.

Although dynamic logic is therefore in some way only a forerunner of the μ-calculus, it is still an important means for reasoning about the semantics of programs (see [291] for a survey on dynamic logic). We therefore briefly consider the propositional dynamic logic PDL, and its extension PDL-Δ [476]:

Definition 3.48 (Propositional Dynamic Logic PDL-Δ). *Given a set of variables V_Σ and action symbols $\mathcal{A}_\Sigma$, the sets of PDL programs and formulas are defined as the least sets that satisfy the following mutually exclusive rules:*

Programs:

- *every action $\alpha \in \mathcal{A}_\Sigma$ is a program*
- *α^- is a program, for every action $\alpha \in \mathcal{A}_\Sigma$*
- *$P;Q$ is a program, provided that P and Q are programs*
- *$P \cup Q$ is a program, provided that P and Q are programs*
- *P^* is a program, provided that P is a program*
- *$\Phi?$ is a program provided that Φ is a formula*

Formulas:

- *every variable $x \in V_\Sigma$ is a formula*
- *$\neg\Phi$, $\Phi \wedge \Psi$, $\Phi \vee \Psi$ are formulas, provided that Φ and Ψ are formulas*
- *$\langle P\rangle\Phi$ is a formula provided that P is a program and*
- *$[P]\Phi$ is a formula provided that P is a program and Φ is a formula*
- *ΔP is a formula provided that P is a program*

Intuitively, $P;Q$ is the sequential composition of the programs P and Q, i.e., we first execute P and after termination of P, we execute Q. $P \cup Q$ denotes the nondeterministic choice between the programs P and Q, i.e., executing $P \cup Q$ means either executing P or Q, which is decided at runtime. An important construct is P^* which means that we finitely often execute P in sequence. The number of iterations is not limited, but must be finite. The program $\Phi?$ tests whether Φ holds; if Φ is true, the program continues, otherwise the program is abnormally aborted. Note that the presence of the test construct makes the sets of programs and formulas mutually recursive. The original version of

PDL does not have the test construct, and therefore the above language of PDL defines actually what is normally called *PDL with tests*.

The formulas are easily understood: $\langle P\rangle\Phi$ means that it is possible to execute P, such that the execution terminates, and that after execution of P the formula Φ holds (note that the nondeterministic choice $P \cup Q$ between programs P and Q gives different possibilities for execution). $[P]\Phi$ means that after *every execution* of P the formula Φ holds, provided that the execution of P terminates. The iteration formula $\langle P^*\rangle\Phi$ holds in a state iff there is a computation path where we can execute P for some finite number of times, so that afterwards Φ holds. Therefore, this construct resembles to loops of programming languages that are forced to terminate. The 'converse execution' $\langle\alpha^-\rangle\Phi$ means that the current situation can be reached by executing α from a situation where Φ held. It is possible to extend the converse execution to combined programs: $(P;Q)^- := (Q^-;P^-)$, $(P \cup Q)^- := (P^- \cup Q^-)$, and $(P^*)^- := (P^-)^*$. We will however consider only formulas, where the converse operator is applied to atomic actions.

Finally, ΔP holds in all states where the program P can be executed infinitely often. The Δ operator is therefore interesting for reactive systems. It is in some way the dual of P^* since the termination is not included here. PDL-Δ is often called *PDL with looping*. The Δ operator has been introduced by Streett [476] to reason about nonterminating behaviors of programs. We have already given the intuitive semantics of PDL-Δ, and the formal definition of the constructs over Kripke structures is given as follows:

Definition 3.49 (Semantics of PDL-Δ). *Given a set of variables V_Σ, a set of action symbols $\mathcal{A}_\Sigma$, and a labeled Kripke structure $\mathcal{K} = (\mathcal{I}, \mathcal{S}, \mathcal{R}, \mathcal{L})$ over V_Σ where $\mathcal{R} \subseteq \mathcal{S} \times \mathcal{A}_\Sigma \times \mathcal{S}$. Then, the semantics $[\![P]\!]_\mathcal{K}$ of a PDL-Δ program P is a subset of $\mathcal{S} \times \mathcal{S}$, and the semantics $[\![\Phi]\!]_\mathcal{K}$ of a PDL-Δ formula Φ is a subset of $\mathcal{S}$. Both $[\![P]\!]_\mathcal{K}$ and $[\![\Phi]\!]_\mathcal{K}$ are defined by the following rules:*

Programs:
- $[\![\alpha]\!]_\mathcal{K} := \{(s,s') \in \mathcal{S} \times \mathcal{S} \mid (s,\alpha,s') \in \mathcal{R}\}$ *for every action* $\alpha \in \mathcal{A}_\Sigma$
- $[\![\alpha^-]\!]_\mathcal{K} := \{(s',s) \in \mathcal{S} \times \mathcal{S} \mid (s,\alpha,s') \in \mathcal{R}\}$ *for every action* $\alpha \in \mathcal{A}_\Sigma$
- $[\![P;Q]\!]_\mathcal{K} := \{(s,s') \in \mathcal{S} \times \mathcal{S} \mid \exists s'' \in \mathcal{S}.(s,s'') \in [\![P]\!]_\mathcal{K} \wedge (s'',s') \in [\![Q]\!]_\mathcal{K}\}$
- $[\![P \cup Q]\!]_\mathcal{K} := [\![P]\!]_\mathcal{K} \cup [\![Q]\!]_\mathcal{K}$
- $[\![P^*]\!]_\mathcal{K}$ *is the reflexive and transitive closure of* $[\![P]\!]_\mathcal{K}$
- $[\![\Phi?]\!]_\mathcal{K} := \{(s,s) \in \mathcal{S} \times \mathcal{S} \mid s \in [\![\Phi]\!]_\mathcal{K}\}$

Formulas:
- $[\![x]\!]_\mathcal{K} := \{s \in \mathcal{S} \mid x \in \mathcal{L}(s)\}$ *for every* $x \in V_\Sigma$
- $[\![\neg\Phi]\!]_\mathcal{K} := \mathcal{S} \setminus [\![\Phi]\!]_\mathcal{K}$
- $[\![\Phi \wedge \Psi]\!]_\mathcal{K} := [\![\Phi]\!]_\mathcal{K} \cap [\![\Psi]\!]_\mathcal{K}$
- $[\![\Phi \vee \Psi]\!]_\mathcal{K} := [\![\Phi]\!]_\mathcal{K} \cup [\![\Psi]\!]_\mathcal{K}$
- $[\![\langle P\rangle\Phi]\!]_\mathcal{K} := \mathsf{pre}_\exists^{[\![P]\!]_\mathcal{K}}([\![\Phi]\!]_\mathcal{K})$
- $[\![[P]\Phi]\!]_\mathcal{K} := \mathsf{pre}_\forall^{[\![P]\!]_\mathcal{K}}([\![\Phi]\!]_\mathcal{K})$
- $[\![\Delta P]\!]_\mathcal{K}$ *is the greatest set* $S \subseteq \mathcal{S}$ *such that* $S = \mathsf{pre}_\exists^{[\![P]\!]_\mathcal{K}}(S)$ *holds*

The semantics of PDL-Δ is given over labeled Kripke structures that differ from usual Kripke structures in that their transitions are labeled with action symbols. Hence, these structures do have several transition relations $\mathcal{R}_\alpha$, one for each action symbol $\alpha \in \mathcal{A}_\Sigma$. In principle, it is possible to define the μ-calculus over labeled Kripke structures, in that we endow the modal operators $\Diamond$, $\overleftarrow{\Diamond}$, $\Box$, and $\overleftarrow{\Box}$ with action symbols, so that we have operators $\Diamond^\alpha$, $\overleftarrow{\Diamond}^\alpha$, $\Box^\alpha$, and $\overleftarrow{\Box}^\alpha$. The semantics refers then to the relation $\mathcal{R}_\alpha$, i.e., $[\![\Diamond^\alpha\varphi]\!]_\mathcal{K} = \mathsf{pre}_\exists^{\mathcal{R}_\alpha}([\![\varphi]\!]_\mathcal{K})$, $\left[\!\left[\overleftarrow{\Diamond}^\alpha\varphi\right]\!\right]_\mathcal{K} = \mathsf{suc}_\exists^{\mathcal{R}_\alpha}([\![\varphi]\!]_\mathcal{K})$, $[\![\Box^\alpha\varphi]\!]_\mathcal{K} = \mathsf{pre}_\forall^{\mathcal{R}_\alpha}([\![\varphi]\!]_\mathcal{K})$, and $\left[\!\left[\overleftarrow{\Box}^\alpha\varphi\right]\!\right]_\mathcal{K} = \mathsf{suc}_\forall^{\mathcal{R}_\alpha}([\![\varphi]\!]_\mathcal{K})$.

In a first order dynamic logic, we may consider atomic programs that manipulate data such as assignments, as e.g. $x := y + 1$. These assignments change the current state of the program since the value of x is changed. In propositional dynamic logic, we do not consider these higher order statements, but only model that their execution provokes some change in the state. This is the intuitive understanding of actions.

We now show how PDL-Δ formulas can be translated to equivalent μ-calculus formulas. As μ-calculus formulas are evaluated as state sets, it is not possible to translate PDL programs to μ-calculus formulas. Therefore the translation can only be done recursively over the PDL formulas. Hence, we eliminate the combined programs in PDL formulas according to the following laws:

- $\langle P;Q\rangle\Phi = \langle P\rangle\langle Q\rangle\Phi$
- $\langle P\cup Q\rangle\Phi = \langle P\rangle\Phi \vee \langle Q\rangle\Phi$
- $\langle P^*\rangle\Phi = \bigvee_{i=0}^{\infty} \underbrace{\langle P\rangle\ldots\langle P\rangle}_{\text{i times}}\Phi$
- $\langle\Psi?\rangle\Phi = \Psi\wedge\Phi$
- $[P]\varphi = \neg\langle P\rangle\neg\varphi$

After the above reductions, combined programs can therefore only occur after the Δ operator. According to the semantics of the Δ operator, it describes the greatest set of states that satisfies the condition $x = \langle P\rangle x$. As we are able to reduce the right hand side for combined programs according to the above laws, we end up with the translation given in Figure 3.26 that applies the above laws on-the-fly.

Theorem 3.50 (Translating PDL-Δ to μ-Calculus). *Given a PDL-Δ formula Φ over the variables V_Σ and the actions $\mathcal{A}_\Sigma$. Then, the function given in Figure 3.26 translates Φ to an equivalent μ-calculus formula with length $|\mathsf{PDL}_\mu(\Phi)| \in O(|\Phi|)$.*

The theorem can be proved by structural induction on Φ. For the size of $\mathsf{PDL}_\mu(\Phi)$, we have to note that for the translation of $\langle P\cup Q\rangle\varphi$, we have to share φ by abbreviating φ in a let term (or better by an abbreviation in a translation to the vectorized μ-calculus).

```
function PDL_μ(Φ)
  case Φ of
    is_var(Φ)   : return Φ;
    ¬φ          : return ¬PDL_μ(φ);
    φ ∧ ψ       : return PDL_μ(φ) ∧ PDL_μ(ψ);
    φ ∨ ψ       : return PDL_μ(φ) ∨ PDL_μ(ψ);
    ΔP          : return νx.PDL_μ(⟨P⟩x);
    ⟨P;Q⟩φ      : return PDL_μ(⟨P⟩⟨Q⟩φ);
    ⟨P ∪ Q⟩φ    : return PDL_μ(⟨P⟩φ) ∨ PDL_μ(⟨Q⟩φ);
    ⟨P*⟩φ       : return μx.PDL_μ(φ) ∨ PDL_μ(⟨P⟩x);
    ⟨ψ?⟩φ       : return PDL_μ(ψ) ∧ PDL_μ(φ);
    [P]φ        : return PDL_μ(P)(¬⟨P⟩¬φ)
    ⟨α⟩φ        : return ◇^α(PDL_μ(φ));
    ⟨α⁻⟩φ       : return ←◇^α(PDL_μ(φ));
  end
end
```

Fig. 3.26. Algorithm for translating PDL-Δ to μ-calculus

It can be furthermore seen that PDL (without Δ) can be translated to the alternation-free μ-calculus. Hence, PDL is at most as expressive as the alternation free μ-calculus. Kozen [289] has proved in 1983 that formulas like $\mu x.a \vee \Box x$ can not be expressed in PDL, and therefore PDL is strictly less expressive than the alternation-free μ-calculus.

Similarly, we can easily see that every PDL-Δ formula can be translated to equivalent μ-calculus formulas of alternation depth ≤ 2. On the other hand, Niwiński proved, in 1984 [387], that the formula $\nu x.(a \wedge \Diamond x) \vee (b \wedge \Diamond x)$ can not be expressed in PDL-Δ, and therefore PDL-Δ is strictly less expressive than the μ-calculus of alternation depth 2.

The converse operator also adds an interesting feature: In 1982 Streett showed [476] that PDL-Δ with the converse operator is elementarily decidable. This is remarkable, since this logic no longer has the finite model property (cf. page 521). For example, the formula $(\Delta\alpha) \wedge \neg\langle\alpha^*\rangle\Delta(\alpha^-)$ is only satisfiable in infinite models [476] (cf. page 504). Clearly, this implies that the full μ-calculus with future and past modalities does also not have the finite model property. However, the future fragment, i.e., the subset without past modalities has the finite model property (cf. page 521).

We do not consider further variants of dynamic logic here, and refer instead to [291]. Instead, we now consider how dynamic logic can be used as a foundation of Hoare's calculus for program verification. Hoare's calculus was formulated for imperative programming languages in the form of triples $\{\Phi\}P\{\Psi\}$ where Φ and Ψ are predicate logic formulas, and P is a program. We therefore consider a simple programming language that consist of basic programs α (i.e., actions), sequential composition $P_1; P_2$, conditionals **if** B **then** P_1 **else** P_2 **end**, and loops **while** B **do** S **end**. There are two further basic statements, namely the empty statement **nothing** which does nothing, and **exit** to abnormally terminate the program. For convenience, we moreover introduce the guarded command **guard** $\varphi_1 : P_1 \,[\!]\, \ldots \,[\!]\, \varphi_n : P_n$ **else** P_0 **end**, which means that one of those P_i's is executed whose guard φ_i holds. If no guard φ_i holds, then P_0 is executed. It is not hard to see that the additional statements can be defined in PDL as well:

- **nothing** $:= 1?$
- **exit** $:= 0?$
- **if** B **then** P_1 **else** P_2 **end** $:= (B?; P_1) \cup (\neg B?; P_2)$
- **while** B **do** S **end** $:= (B?; S)^*; (\neg B)?$
- **guard** $\varphi_1 : P_1 \,[\!]\, \ldots \,[\!]\, \varphi_n : P_n$ **else** P_0 **end** $:=$
  $(\varphi_1?; P_1) \cup \ldots \cup (\varphi_n?; P_n) \cup (\neg\varphi_1 \wedge \ldots \wedge \neg\varphi_n?; P_0)$

To understand the above definitions, note that the PDL program $B?; S$ executes S if B holds, and fails if B does not hold (failure is indicated by our translation that the formula translates to 0). This behavior is repeated for a finite number of times to define the loop, and after that it is required that $\neg B$ holds.

Using these abbreviations, Hoare's calculus is formulated on triples of the form $\{\Phi\}P\{\Psi\}$ with a program P and formulas Φ and Ψ. Φ is the precondition and Ψ is the postcondition of the triple. The postcondition is the formula that is usually given as the specification of the program, while the precondition specifies only what kind of data may be given as input to the program P, so that it fulfills its task correctly. Therefore, the meaning of a Hoare triple is defined in PDL as $\Phi \rightarrow [P]\Psi$, which means that, if initially Φ holds and P is executed and (normally) terminates, then Ψ must hold. We say that P normally terminates if the termination is not provoked by the execution of the **exit** command. If termination is also taken into account, some authors use triples of the form $\langle\Phi\rangle P\langle\Psi\rangle$ which are defined as $\Phi \rightarrow \langle P\rangle\Psi$. In Hoare's original calculus, termination has however not been considered, and therefore Hoare's celebrated rules are essentially as given in Figure 3.27.

Using our embedding of the Hoare calculus into PDL, and the embedding of PDL into the μ-calculus, we can prove the correctness of Hoare's rules. For example, take the conditional statement: $\{\Phi \wedge B\}P_1\{\Psi\}$ abbreviates the PDL formula $\Phi \wedge B \rightarrow [P_1]\Psi$ which is translated to $\Phi \wedge B \wedge P_1 \rightarrow \Box\Psi$, and analogously, $\{\Phi \wedge \neg B\}P_1\{\Psi\}$ is translated to $\Phi \wedge \neg B \wedge P_1 \rightarrow \Box\Psi$. The conclusion of the Hoare rule $\{\Phi\}$**if** B **then** P_1 **else** P_2 **end**$\{\Psi\}$ abbreviates the PDL formula $\Phi \rightarrow [(B?P_1) \cup (\neg B?P_2)]\Psi$ which is translated to the μ-calculus formula $(\Phi \wedge B \wedge P_1 \rightarrow \Box\Psi) \wedge (\Phi \wedge \neg B \wedge P_2 \rightarrow \Box\Psi)$. It is obvious that the rule is correct.

The rule for the loops is of particular interest. The proposition Φ_I is thereby called an invariant since it invariantly holds before and after the execution of the loops body P (provided that before execution of P also the loop condition B holds). The application of the rule therefore depends on the choice of a suitable invariant Φ_I.

$$\frac{\Phi \rightarrow \Psi}{\{\Phi\}\mathbf{nothing}\{\Psi\}} \qquad \frac{}{\{\Phi\}\mathbf{exit}\{\Psi\}}$$

$$\frac{\Phi \wedge \alpha \rightarrow \Box\Psi}{\{\Phi\}\alpha\{\Psi\}} \qquad \frac{\{\Phi\}P_1\{\Phi'\} \qquad \{\Phi'\}P_2\{\Psi\}}{\{\Phi\}P_1; P_2\{\Psi\}}$$

$$\frac{\{\Phi \wedge B\}P_1\{\Psi\} \qquad \{\Phi \wedge \neg B\}P_2\{\Psi\}}{\{\Phi\}\mathbf{if}\ B\ \mathbf{then}\ P_1\ \mathbf{else}\ P_2\ \mathbf{end}\{\Psi\}} \quad \frac{\Phi \rightarrow \Phi_I \quad \{\Phi_I \wedge B\}P\{\Phi_I\} \quad \Phi_I \wedge \neg B \rightarrow \Psi}{\{\Phi\}\mathbf{while}\ B\ \mathbf{do}\ P\ \mathbf{end}\{\Psi\}}$$

$$\frac{\{\Phi \wedge \varphi_1\}P_1\{\Psi\} \quad \ldots \quad \{\Phi \wedge \varphi_n\}P_n\{\Psi\} \qquad \{\Phi \wedge \bigwedge_{i=1}^{n} \neg\varphi_i\}P_0\{\Psi\}}{\{\Phi\}\mathbf{guard}\ \varphi_1 : P_1 \ [] \ldots [] \ \varphi_n : P_n\ \mathbf{else}\ P_0\ \mathbf{end}\{\Psi\}}$$

Fig. 3.27. Hoare's calculus

Another way to define program semantics is to compute weakest preconditions $wp(P, \Psi)$ of a program P and a postcondition Ψ. The weakest precondition $wp(P, \Psi)$ is thereby defined as the formula that is implied by any other formula Φ with the property $\{\Phi\}P\{\Psi\}$. As the latter is only an abbreviation for $\Phi \rightarrow [P]\Psi$, it is easily seen that the weakest precondition is simply the formula $[P]\Psi$ itself. Hence, our translation of this PDL formula to the μ-calculus gives us a μ-calculus formulas to compute the weakest preconditions. Alternatively, we can directly define the weakest preconditions as follows:

$$
\begin{aligned}
&wp(\mathbf{nothing}, \Psi) := \Psi\\
&wp(\mathbf{exit}, \Psi) := 1\\
&wp(\alpha, \Psi) := x_\alpha \wedge \Box(y_\alpha \rightarrow \Psi)\\
&wp(P_1; P_2, \Psi) := wp(P_1; wp(P_2, \Psi))\\
&wp(\mathbf{if}\ B\ \mathbf{then}\ P_1\ \mathbf{else}\ P_2\ \mathbf{end}, \Psi) := B \wedge wp(P_1, \Psi) \vee \neg B \wedge wp(P_2, \Psi)\\
&wp(\mathbf{while}\ B\ \mathbf{do}\ S\ \mathbf{end}, \Psi) := \mu x.(\neg B \wedge \Psi) \vee (B \wedge wp(S, x))\\
&wp(\mathbf{guard}\ \varphi_1 : P_1 \ [] \ldots [] \ \varphi_n : P_n\ \mathbf{else}\ P_0\ \mathbf{end}, \Psi) :=\\
&\qquad (\bigvee_{i=1}^{n} \varphi_i \wedge wp(P_i, \Psi)) \vee (\bigwedge_{i=1}^{n} \neg\varphi_i) \wedge wp(P_0, \Psi)
\end{aligned}
$$

By definition, the triple $\{wp(P, \Psi)\}P\{\Psi\}$ holds for every program P and every formula Ψ, and $wp(P, \Psi)$ is the weakest precondition for that triple. PDL and Hoare's calculus are not considered in more detail in this book. The interested reader is referred to [237, 291] for a reference on dynamic logic, and to [19] for a survey on Hoare's calculus.

4

Finite Automata

Many types of automata have been developed in computer science to study different ways of computations. In particular, Turing machines, pushdown automata and finite state automata form a hierarchy that is in a beautiful correspondence to the Chomsky hierarchy of formal languages [251]. Common to all of these machines is that they have a finite set of internal states that determine their behavior, and that they read an input word from a tape. The input word is formed from symbols of a finite alphabet Σ. At each point of time, the automaton is in exactly one of the possible internal states, and reads an input from the tape. Thereby, the internal state is changed according to the transition relation of the automaton, which may be viewed as its program. The sequence of internal states that is induced by an input word is called a run over the corresponding input word.

According to the transition relation, we can distinguish between *partial and total transition relations*: the former class allows us that there can be input words such that there is no run over the word, since an internal state may be reached where no successor state is defined for the current input symbol. Total transition relations, on the other hand, define at least one successor state for each reachable internal state and each possible input symbol. We can furthermore distinguish between *deterministic and nondeterministic* transition relations: The former class has at most one successor state for every reachable state and every input symbol, while the the latter class may define more than one successor state. Clearly, we can talk about partial deterministic, total deterministic, and total nondeterministic transition relations having at most one run, exactly one run, and at least one run, respectively. Moreover, we may also have partial nondeterministic transition relations, which may or may not have runs for certain input words. If they have a run for an input word, there may be another run, too. In the following, we assume that a deterministic transition relation is always total, and that a nondeterministic transition relation may be partial, unless otherwise stated.

In general, one distinguishes further between *acceptors and transducers*. An acceptor is a machine that reads a word from the tape and decides then whether the word should be accepted or not. Therefore these acceptors can be used to define languages, which are the sets of words that are accepted by the machine. There are several notions of acceptance conditions that are defined as properties that must be fulfilled by the runs that are possible for a given input word. Transducers, on the other hand, do not accept or reject input words. Instead, they produce an output word that is recursively defined by the run and the input word: at each point of time, an output function defines which output symbol is emitted in terms of the current internal state and the currently read input. Clearly, we can map every transducer to an acceptor in that we consider the combination of the input and the output word that would have been generated by the transducer. The acceptor will then accept the input/output combination iff they match together. For this reason, acceptors are somewhat more general and therefore, we will only consider acceptors in this chapter.

Some machines like Turing machines or pushdown automata may use an *additional memory for their computations*. In this memory, the machines can read and write words to store intermediate computations. Unlike the set of control states, the memory need not be finite, and therefore it increases the computational power of the machine. In the most general form, the Turing machines, the access to the memory's entries is totally unrestricted: Symbols can be read and written to every position on the tape. Pushdown automata, on the other hand, have limited access to their memory: they can only read the last symbol they have written. Hence, their memory is organized as a stack of unlimited size. Finite state machines, finally, have no additional memory, and therefore must encode all intermediate results of their computations in their finitely many control states. We will only consider finite state automata in this book, but want to note that other types of automata may also be used for verification [357].

A further distinction is the length of the input, i.e., whether the machine works on *input words of finite or infinite lengths*. A finite word over the input symbols is accepted by a finite state machine if and only if there is a run of the machine such that after having processed the entire word, the machine will be in one of some designated states. Hence, these states are often called the final states of the automaton. Finite automata that read words of infinite length are called ω-automata. The acceptance of ω-automata is more complicated, because an infinite word is read. We will see that there are several different ways to define the acceptance of a word; and not all of them are equivalent to each other.

The study of ω-automata started in 1960 [80], when Büchi proved the decidability of second order monadic theories (see Chapter 6). He found out that formulas of the second order arithmetic of one successor can be reduced to nondeterministic finite state ω-automata whose acceptance condition requires that there must be a run over the word such that at least one of a designated set of final states is visited infinitely often. These ω-automata are named after Büchi (*Büchi automata*).

It was soon determined that the deterministic form of Büchi automata was not closed under complement and is therefore strictly less expressive than the nondeterministic form. Therefore, several other forms of ω-automata have been considered after the pioneering work of Büchi. The first results of deterministic ω-automata that have the same expressiveness as Büchi's nondeterministic ω-automata were introduced by Muller [380] in 1963. The acceptance condition of *Muller automata* is defined by a finite number of state sets $F_0,\ldots,F_n$. To be accepted by a Muller automaton, an input word must have at least one run such that the set of infinitely visited states is exactly one of the sets F_i. However, Muller's proof of the fact that his deterministic ω-automata are as expressive as Büchi's nondeterministic ω-automata contained an error. A correct proof was found later by McNaughton [363] in 1966.

In the time that followed, *other acceptance conditions* were considered [252, 312, 376, 469, 491, 504, 505]. A summary of these results can be found in [506], where moreover, measures of complexities for the languages that are defined by accepting ω-automata are defined. There are different ways for the definition of such complexity measures that have strong relationships with topology, in particular with the Borel hierarchy (see Section 4.6).

Besides deterministic and nondeterministic automata, their generalization to *alternating finite state automata* [82, 96] has also been considered for ω-automata [374, 381–383]. The transition relations of deterministic and nondeterministic automata may be viewed as partial functions $\delta : \mathcal{S} \times \Sigma \to \mathcal{S}$ and $\delta : \mathcal{S} \times \Sigma \to 2^{\mathcal{S}}$, respectively. The transition relation of an alternating automaton is a function $\delta : \mathcal{S} \times \Sigma \to 2^{2^{\mathcal{S}}}$ that maps the current state $s \in \mathcal{S}$ and the current input symbol $a \in \Sigma$ to a set of sets of possible next states. If the machine is in state $s \in \mathcal{S}$ and reads the input $a_0 \in \Sigma$, and $\delta(s, a_0) = \{Q_1, \ldots, Q_m\}$ holds, where $Q_i \subseteq \mathcal{S}$, then the machine accepts the finite word $a_0 \ldots a_l$ if and only if there is a $Q_i \in \delta(s, a_0)$ such that for each state of $s_i \in Q_i$ there is a run over $a_1 \ldots a_l$ starting in $s_i \in Q_i$ that is accepted. Hence, nondeterministic automata are special forms of alternating automata where each Q_i is a singleton set. Alternating ω-automata are considered in [374, 381–383], and Vardi shows in [494] how temporal logics can be translated to alternating finite state ω-automata of linear size in terms of the input formula (see also [262]). The enriched possibilities of the transition relation of alternating automata makes them (exponentially) more succinct, and they often give rise to simpler translations.

While the automata mentioned so far are automata on finite or infinite words, it is also natural to consider *automata that read finite or infinite trees* instead of words. Tree automata have also an internal state and read an input symbol from a k-ary branching input tree. A deterministic transition relation will then map a state $s \in \mathcal{S}$ and an input symbol $a \in \Sigma$ to a tuple $(s_1, \ldots, s_k)$ of successor states. Hence, each k-ary branching input tree induces a run that is also a k-ary branching tree labeled with the states of the automaton. Again, we can distinguish between deterministic, nondeterministic, and alternating transition relations for tree automata. We will almost neglect tree automata, except for Appendix B.3.

In the previous section, we considered the μ-calculus as a basic means for the recursive definition of state properties. In some way, we can view ω-automata on words as a recursive way to define path properties, so that both formalisms form different basic dimensions of our specification language. We will also see that all decision problems for ω-automata can be reduced to equivalent μ-calculus problems, so we can use the algorithms for the μ-calculus given in the previous section to solve these problems.

This chapter is organized as follows: in the following two sections, we consider different kinds of ω-automata with their closure properties under Boolean operations and the relationship between the deterministic and non-deterministic variants. After that, we investigate the relationship with the Borel hierarchy that is known from topology theory. We will see that this relationship gives us strong results on the expressiveness of the considered ω-automata. After that, we consider decision procedures that can be used to verify specifications given as ω-automata. In particular, we investigate for the translation of ω-automata into equivalent μ-calculus formulas. We do however neither consider alternating ω-automata nor ω-automata on infinite trees, although both of the automaton classes are interesting topics. The reason for this is simply lack of space.

4.1 Regular Languages, Regular Expressions and Automata

Let Σ be a finite set of 'input symbols' that are not further specified. The set of finite strings over Σ is denoted by Σ^* and the set of infinite strings over Σ is denoted with Σ^ω. Each subset of Σ^* or Σ^ω is called a *language* over the alphabet Σ and each member of such a language is called a word over the alphabet Σ. The concatenation of a finite word $\alpha \in \Sigma^*$ with a finite or infinite word $\beta \in \Sigma^* \cup \Sigma^\omega$ is written as $\alpha\beta$. Moreover, for languages $L_1 \subseteq \Sigma^*$ and $L_2 \subseteq \Sigma^* \cup \Sigma^\omega$, we define $L_1 \cdot L_2 := \{\alpha\beta \mid \alpha \in L_1, \beta \in L_2\}$.

Moreover, given a language of finite words $L_1 \subseteq \Sigma^*$, the language $L_1^* \subseteq \Sigma^*$ is the set of all finite concatenations of the words of L_1. Analogously, L_1^ω is the set of all infinite concatenations of the words of L_1. In the following, we consider infinite words $\alpha \in \Sigma^\omega$ as functions $\alpha : \mathbb{N} \to \Sigma$, the symbol at the $i+1$-th position in the word α is therefore $\alpha^{(i)}$; hence, we have $\alpha = \alpha^{(0)}\alpha^{(1)}\alpha^{(2)}\ldots$. The segment $\alpha^{(n)}\alpha^{(n+1)}\ldots\alpha^{(m)}$ of a finite or infinite word is denoted as $\alpha^{(n..m)}$. Hence, the prefix of length n of the word α is $\alpha^{(0..n-1)}$. Finally, given $L \subseteq \Sigma^*$, we define $\mathsf{Lim}(L) := \{\alpha \in \Sigma^\omega \mid \left|\{n \in \mathbb{N} \mid \alpha^{(0..n)} \in L\}\right| = \infty\}$, as the set of all infinite words where infinitely many prefixes belong to L.

Regular languages are conveniently described with regular expressions. Over a set of variables V_Σ, the regular expressions are defined as follows.

Definition 4.1 (General Regular Expressions). *The set of general regular expressions* REG_Σ *over the alphabet* Σ *is defined as the smallest set, that satisfies the following properties:*

- $\emptyset \in \mathsf{REG}_\Sigma$ *and* $1 \in \mathsf{REG}_\Sigma$
- $\Sigma \subseteq \mathsf{REG}_\Sigma$
- *for* $\alpha, \beta \in \mathsf{REG}_\Sigma$*, we also have* $\alpha + \beta \in \mathsf{REG}_\Sigma$
- *for* $\alpha, \beta \in \mathsf{REG}_\Sigma$*, we also have* $\alpha\beta \in \mathsf{REG}_\Sigma$
- *for* $\alpha \in \mathsf{REG}_\Sigma$*, we also have* $\alpha^* \in \mathsf{REG}_\Sigma$
- *for* $\alpha, \beta \in \mathsf{REG}_\Sigma$*, we also have* $\alpha\&\beta \in \mathsf{REG}_\Sigma$
- *for* $\alpha \in \mathsf{REG}_\Sigma$*, we also have* $\overline{\alpha} \in \mathsf{REG}_\Sigma$

Moreover, we define the set of star-free regular expressions SFREG_Σ *over the alphabet* Σ *as the subset of* REG_Σ *where no* $*$ *operator occurs, except for* $\overline{\emptyset}^*$.

We will define the 'semantics' of the above regular expressions in the next definition where we map the regular expressions to languages over Σ. In particular, $\overline{\alpha}$, $\alpha\&\beta$, and $\alpha + \beta$ will correspond with the set operations on the associated languages. We use the notion of 'general' regular expressions, since the operations $\alpha\&\beta$ and $\overline{\alpha}$ can be eliminated in every regular expression. This is easily shown by translating a regular expression to an equivalent finite state automaton and then translating the automaton back to a regular expression [251]. Well-known algorithms for those translations do not use intersection $\alpha\&\beta$ and complement $\overline{\alpha}$. For the semantics of regular expressions, we define the associated language $\mathsf{Lang}(\alpha)$ of a regular expression $\alpha \in \mathsf{REG}_\Sigma$ as given below (moreover we use an empty word ε that consists of no letter).

Definition 4.2 (Associated Language of a Regular Expression). *We define for every general regular expression in* REG_Σ *the language* $\mathsf{Lang}(\alpha) \subseteq \Sigma^*$ *as follows:*

- $\mathsf{Lang}(\emptyset) := \{\}$ *and* $\mathsf{Lang}(1) = \{\varepsilon\}$
- $\mathsf{Lang}(a) := \{a\}$ *for every letter* $a \in \Sigma$
- $\mathsf{Lang}(\alpha + \beta) := \mathsf{Lang}(\alpha) \cup \mathsf{Lang}(\beta)$
- $\mathsf{Lang}(\alpha\beta) := \mathsf{Lang}(\alpha)\mathsf{Lang}(\beta)$
- $\mathsf{Lang}(\alpha^*) := \mathsf{Lang}(\alpha)^*$
- $\mathsf{Lang}(\alpha\&\beta) = \mathsf{Lang}(\alpha) \cap \mathsf{Lang}(\beta)$
- $\mathsf{Lang}(\overline{\alpha}) := \Sigma^* \setminus \mathsf{Lang}(\alpha)$

One can show that the following equations hold, which shows that the regular expressions have the algebraic structure of an idempotent semiring:

$$\begin{array}{ll}
\alpha + \beta = \beta + \alpha & \alpha + \alpha = \alpha \\
\alpha(\beta + \gamma) = \alpha\beta + \alpha\gamma & (\beta + \gamma)\alpha = \beta\alpha + \gamma\alpha \\
\alpha(\beta\gamma) = (\alpha\beta)\gamma & \emptyset + \alpha = \alpha + \emptyset = \alpha \\
1\alpha = \alpha 1 = \alpha & \emptyset\alpha = \alpha\emptyset = \emptyset
\end{array}$$

Note that there are regular expressions with a * operation that have equivalent star-free expressions. For example, for $\Sigma = \{a\}$, the expression $(a\overline{a})^*$ is equivalent to the star-free expression $1+(a\overline{\emptyset}^*\&\overline{\emptyset}^*\overline{a})\&\overline{\overline{\emptyset}^*(aa+\overline{aa})\overline{\emptyset}^*}$ (note that $\mathsf{Lang}(\overline{\emptyset}) = \Sigma$).

There are two ways to extend regular expressions to ω-regular expressions denoting languages of infinite words. The first one is by adding the limes operator $\mathsf{Lim}(\alpha)$ which represents the set of all infinite words that have infinitely many prefixes in the set $\mathsf{Lang}(\alpha)$. The second one is by adding an operation α^ω which means an infinite concatenation of the language $\mathsf{Lang}(\alpha)$. In the following definition, we use both ways and we also define the associated language of an ω-regular expression.

Definition 4.3 (ω-Regular Expressions and ω-Regular Languages). *For the alphabet Σ, we define the set of ω-regular expressions $\mathsf{REG}_\Sigma^\omega$ over Σ as the smallest set such that the following holds:*

- $\emptyset \in \mathsf{REG}_\Sigma^\omega$
- *for every $\alpha \in \mathsf{REG}_\Sigma$ and $\beta \in \mathsf{REG}_\Sigma^\omega$, we have $\alpha\beta \in \mathsf{REG}_\Sigma^\omega$*
- *for $\alpha, \beta \in \mathsf{REG}_\Sigma^\omega$, we also have $\alpha + \beta \in \mathsf{REG}_\Sigma^\omega$*
- *for every $\alpha \in \mathsf{REG}_\Sigma$, we have $\alpha^\omega \in \mathsf{REG}_\Sigma^\omega$*
- *for every $\alpha \in \mathsf{REG}_\Sigma$, we have $\mathsf{Lim}(\alpha) \in \mathsf{REG}_\Sigma^\omega$*
- *for $\alpha, \beta \in \mathsf{REG}_\Sigma^\omega$, we also have $\alpha\&\beta \in \mathsf{REG}_\Sigma^\omega$*
- *for $\alpha \in \mathsf{REG}_\Sigma^\omega$, we also have $\overline{\alpha} \in \mathsf{REG}_\Sigma^\omega$*

For every ω-regular expression over Σ, we define an associated language of infinite words $\mathsf{Lang}(\alpha) \subseteq \Sigma^\omega$ as follows:

- $\mathsf{Lang}(\emptyset) := \{\}$
- $\mathsf{Lang}(\alpha\beta) := \mathsf{Lang}(\alpha)\mathsf{Lang}(\beta)$
- $\mathsf{Lang}(\alpha + \beta) := \mathsf{Lang}(\alpha) \cup \mathsf{Lang}(\beta)$
- $\mathsf{Lang}(\alpha^\omega) := (\mathsf{Lang}(\alpha))^\omega$
- $\mathsf{Lang}(\mathsf{Lim}(\alpha))$ *is the set of all $\alpha \in \Sigma^\omega$ that have infinitely many prefixes in* $\mathsf{Lang}(\alpha)$
- $\mathsf{Lang}(\alpha\&\beta) = \mathsf{Lang}(\alpha) \cap \mathsf{Lang}(\beta)$
- $\mathsf{Lang}(\overline{\alpha}) := \Sigma^\omega \setminus \mathsf{Lang}(\alpha)$

Regular and ω-regular languages can be characterized by finite automata and ω-automata, respectively. Unlike classical automata, ω-automata run over the given infinite word. The acceptance of a given infinite word is defined via an acceptance condition on the infinite run of the word. So, let us first define what is common to all automata types.

Definition 4.4 (Semiautomaton). *A semiautomaton $\mathfrak{A} = (\Sigma, \mathcal{S}, \mathcal{I}, \mathcal{R})$ is a tuple where $\mathcal{S}$ is the finite set of states, Σ a finite alphabet, $\mathcal{I} \subseteq \mathcal{S}$ is the set of initial states, and $\mathcal{R} \subseteq \mathcal{S} \times \Sigma \times \mathcal{S}$ is the transition relation of $\mathfrak{A}$.*

We see that Kripke structures are similar to semiautomata. The differences are that transitions of Kripke structures are not labeled with input letters, and that states of the Kripke structures are labeled with propositional variable assignments. Semiautomata that are endowed with an output function $\zeta : \mathcal{S} \times \Sigma \to \Gamma$, where Γ is the output alphabet, may therefore be viewed as Kripke structures, when we use a singleton set as input alphabet, so that the inputs are of no interest.

Moreover, semiautomata are closely related to the theory of monoids and semigroups. Original work is found in [151, 209], more recent work has been done by Perrin and Pin in [120, 401–404] and by Straubing [475]. We will consider that relationship in Section 4.7. To define acceptance conditions, we have to define the set of runs of a word.

Definition 4.5 (Run of an Infinite Word). *Given a semiautomaton $\mathfrak{A} = (\Sigma, \mathcal{S}, \mathcal{I}, \mathcal{R})$ and an infinite word $\alpha : \mathbb{N} \to \Sigma$ over Σ. Then, each infinite word $\beta : \mathbb{N} \to \mathcal{S}$ with $\beta^{(0)} \in \mathcal{I}$ and $\forall t.(\beta^{(t)}, \alpha^{(t)}, \beta^{(t+1)}) \in \mathcal{R}$ is called a run of α through $\mathfrak{A}$. The set of all runs of α through $\mathfrak{A}$ is hence defined as follows:*

$$\mathsf{RUN}_{\mathfrak{A}}(\alpha) := \{\beta : \mathbb{N} \to \mathcal{S} \mid \beta^{(0)} \in \mathcal{I} \ \wedge \ \forall t.(\beta^{(t)}, \alpha^{(t)}, \beta^{(t+1)}) \in \mathcal{R}\}$$

Finally, the set of states that are reached infinitely often by a run $\beta \in \mathsf{RUN}_{\mathfrak{A}}(\alpha)$ is denoted as $\mathsf{INF}(\beta)$, i.e. $\mathsf{INF}(\beta) := \left\{s \in \mathcal{S} \mid \forall t_1.\exists t_2.\beta^{(t_1+t_2)} = s\right\}$.

The acceptance of a word is then specified with the set of its runs. Manna and Pnueli considered in [348, 349] $\forall$-automata that have an acceptance condition that must be fulfilled by *all* runs of a word. Usually, however, automata are considered that only require that a word has *at least* one run that fulfills the specified acceptance condition. We will consider different types of acceptance conditions in detail in the next sections.

4.2 The Logic of Automaton Formulas

As the set of states $\mathcal{S}$ and the set of input symbols Σ of a semiautomaton must be finite sets, we can encode these sets by sets of Boolean variables. In the following, we therefore assume without loss of generality that $\mathcal{S} = 2^{\{q_1,\ldots,q_m\}}$ and $\Sigma = 2^{\{i_1,\ldots,i_n\}}$. This means that in the following, a state is a subset of the state variables $\{q_1, \ldots, q_m\}$; a state variable may or may not belong to a state. Similarly, inputs are encoded as subsets of the input variables $\{i_1, \ldots, i_n\}$. Sets of states can therefore be encoded as propositional formulas Φ over the state variables $\{q_1, \ldots, q_m\}$ as follows: a state $\vartheta \subseteq \{q_1, \ldots, q_m\}$ belongs to the set Φ if and only if $\vartheta \in \mathsf{models}_{\{q_1,\ldots,q_m\}}(\Phi)$. In a similar manner, we can encode the transition relation as a propositional formula over $\{q_1, \ldots, q_m\} \cup \{i_1, \ldots, i_n\} \cup \{\mathsf{X}q_1, \ldots, \mathsf{X}q_m\}$, where the $\mathsf{X}q_i$ encode the successor state.

Using these encodings, we can easily describe semiautomata with the automaton formulas that we have already introduced. In general, an automaton formula $\mathcal{A}_\exists\,(Q, \Phi_\mathcal{I}, \Phi_\mathcal{R}, \Phi_\mathcal{F})$ describes an automaton with the state set 2^Q (i.e., a state that is a subset of Q). The initial states are those subsets of Q that satisfy $\Phi_\mathcal{I}$, i.e., $\vartheta \subseteq Q$ is an initial state iff $[\![\Phi_\mathcal{I}]\!]_\vartheta = \mathsf{true}$ holds. The transition relation is encoded in a similar manner: $(\vartheta, \sigma, \vartheta')$ is a transition for $\vartheta, \vartheta' \subseteq Q$ and $\sigma \subseteq V_\Sigma$ iff $[\![\Phi_\mathcal{R}]\!]_{\vartheta \cup \sigma \cup \{\mathsf{X}q \mid q \in \vartheta'\}} = \mathsf{true}$ holds.

When we draw state transition diagrams, we often label the transitions with propositional formulas Φ over V_Σ, which means that the transition is enabled for each input $\sigma \in \mathsf{models}_{V_\Sigma}(\Phi)$. Hence, in case that the transition is enabled for every input, we label it with 1.

For example, consider the automaton formula $\mathcal{A}_\exists(Q, \Phi_\mathcal{I}, \Phi_\mathcal{R}, \Phi_\mathcal{F})$ with $Q := \{p, q\}$, $\Phi_\mathcal{I} := \neg p \wedge \neg q$, and the transition relation $\Phi_\mathcal{R} := (p \to \mathsf{X}p) \wedge (\mathsf{X}p \to q \vee \neg q) \wedge (\mathsf{X}q \leftrightarrow (p \wedge \neg q \wedge \neg a) \vee (p \wedge q))$. To determine a state transition graph, we first note that the possible states are $\{\}, \{p\}, \{q\}, \{p, q\}$. The only initial state is $\{\}$. To determine the transition relation, we consider it in each of the states and obtain the following simplifications. For this reason, we simply assume that $V_\Sigma = \{a\}$ holds, so that we have only two possible inputs, namely $\{\}$ and $\{a\}$. Clearly, we would obtain the same consideration for every set of variables V_Σ that is finite and that would contain a if we consider two classes of inputs, namely those that contain a and those that do not contain a. However, for reasons of simplicity, just consider $V_\Sigma = \{a\}$:

state $\{\}$: Here, we have $p = q = 0$ so that $\Phi_\mathcal{R}$ reduces to $\Phi_\mathcal{R} = (\mathsf{X}q \leftrightarrow 0)$. This means regardless of the input, that the next state is one that does not contain the variable q. As there are two such states, namely $\{\}$ and $\{p\}$, both of them become successors for every input of this state.

state $\{p\}$: In this case, the transition relation simplifies to $\Phi_\mathcal{R} = \mathsf{X}p \wedge (\mathsf{X}q \leftrightarrow \neg a)$. Hence, if the input $\{a\}$ is read the next state will be state $\{p\}$ and if $\{\}$ is read, the next state will be $\{p, q\}$.

state $\{q\}$: We will later see that this state can not be reached, so that we need not consider it. Nevertheless, it is instructive, to consider the complete example here. In this state, the transition relation yields in $\Phi_\mathcal{R} = \neg\mathsf{X}p \wedge \neg\mathsf{X}q$, so that the next state does not depend on the input and is in any case the state $\{\}$.

state $\{p, q\}$: In this state, we have the transitions $\Phi_\mathcal{R} = \mathsf{X}p \wedge \mathsf{X}q$, so that the only successor state is the state $\{p, q\}$ itself.

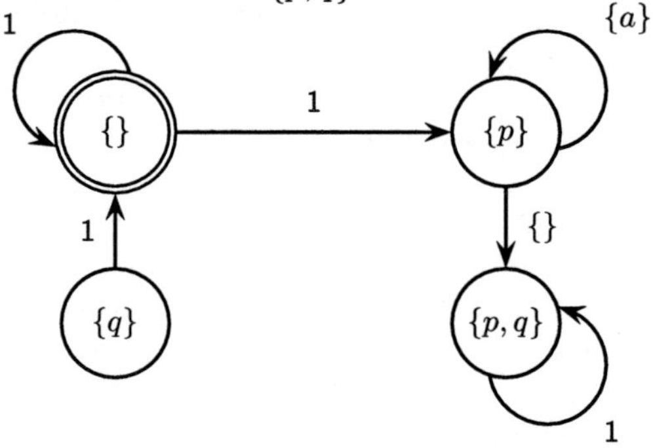

Fig. 4.1. State transition diagram of an ω-automaton

The above discussion of the automaton leads to the state transition diagram given in Figure 4.1. It can be easily seen that the state $\{q\}$ is not reachable from the single initial state $\{\}$.

One might think that an automaton formula $\mathcal{A}_{\exists}(Q, \Phi_{\mathcal{I}}, \Phi_{\mathcal{R}}, \Phi_{\mathcal{F}})$ could be replaced by the quantified formula $\exists q_1 \ldots \exists q_m.\Phi_{\mathcal{I}} \land \mathsf{G}\Phi_{\mathcal{R}} \land \Phi_{\mathcal{F}}$. Indeed, if the quantification is defined correctly, such a relationship holds (see Section 6.3). However, the quantification over subsets of a Kripke structure as introduced in Section 2.2, and used by the μ-calculus is not the correct semantics for this relationship (cf. the example in Figure 2.10 on page 83).

So far, we have said nothing about the acceptance conditions. A word is accepted of an automaton of the form $\mathcal{A}_{\exists}(Q, \Phi_{\mathcal{I}}, \Phi_{\mathcal{R}}, \Phi_{\mathcal{F}})$ iff there is at least one infinite run through this automaton of the word such that the acceptance condition $\Phi_{\mathcal{F}}$ is fulfilled. *Note that this implies in particular that there is at least an infinite run of the word through the automaton.* The following definition of our logic of automaton formulas explains which formulas may be used as acceptance conditions.

Definition 4.6 (The Language $\mathcal{L}_{\omega}$ of Automaton Formulas). *Given a finite set of variables $\mathcal{Q}$ that is distinct from the variables V_{Σ}, the language $\mathcal{L}_{\omega}$ is derived from the symbol S by the following grammar rules (we furthermore assume Q to represent a subset of $\mathcal{Q}$):*

$$\begin{aligned}
I &::= V_{\Sigma} \mid \mathcal{Q} \mid \neg I \mid I \land I \mid I \lor I \\
P &::= \mathcal{Q} \mid \neg P \mid P \land P \mid P \lor P \\
R &::= V_{\Sigma} \mid \mathcal{Q} \mid \neg R \mid R \land R \mid R \lor R \mid \mathsf{X}P \\
T &::= V_{\Sigma} \mid \mathcal{Q} \mid \neg T \mid T \land T \mid T \lor T \mid \mathsf{G}T \mid \mathsf{F}T \\
A &::= T \mid \mathcal{A}_{\exists}(Q, I, R, A) \mid \mathcal{A}_{\forall}(Q, I, R, A) \mid \neg A \mid A \land A \mid A \lor A \\
S &::= V_{\Sigma} \mid \neg S \mid S \land S \mid S \lor S \mid \mathsf{E}A \mid \mathsf{A}A
\end{aligned}$$

We furthermore assume that the sets of state variables of nested automaton formulas are pairwise disjoint, i.e., in an automaton formula $\mathcal{A}_{\exists}(Q, I, R, A)$, the variables contained in Q can not be bound twice as state variables by automaton formulas occurring in A (but they may occur in A, of course).

As can be seen, I and P represent the set of propositional formulas over the variables $V_{\Sigma} \cup \mathcal{Q}$ and $\mathcal{Q}$, respectively, T extends this by allowing the use of the temporal operators G and F with arbitrary nestings, and R extends I by allowing the application of the temporal operator X to a propositional formula over the variables $\mathcal{Q}$. Finally, A is the set of automaton formulas which contains nestings of automaton formulas and also their Boolean closure. Note, that we allow the initial condition $\Phi_{\mathcal{I}}$ and the acceptance condition $\Phi_{\mathcal{F}}$ of an automaton formula $\mathcal{A}_{\exists}(Q, \Phi_{\mathcal{I}}, \Phi_{\mathcal{R}}, \Phi_{\mathcal{F}})$ to use the input variables V_{Σ}. This does not extend the expressive power, but will make some constructions simpler. However, in general, we can do without this extension.

The acceptance for an existential automaton $\mathcal{A}_{\exists}(Q, \Phi_{\mathcal{I}}, \Phi_{\mathcal{R}}, \Phi_{\mathcal{F}})$ is then defined as follows: there must be a run of the input word through the automaton that satisfies the condition $\Phi_{\mathcal{F}}$. We have already formalized this by the semantics in Definition 2.42 on page 79. In the following, we will consider the classic acceptance conditions:

Definition 4.7 (Classes of Acceptance Conditions). *Let Φ_i and Ψ_i for all $i \in \{0,\ldots,f\}$ be propositional formulas over the state and input variables, then we define the following classes of acceptance conditions [352]:*

$$
\begin{aligned}
\textit{Safety condition: } & \mathsf{G}\Phi_0 \\
\textit{Liveness condition: } & \mathsf{F}\Phi_0 \\
\textit{Büchi condition [80, 81]: } & \mathsf{GF}\Phi_0 \\
\textit{Persistence condition [352]: } & \mathsf{FG}\Phi_0 \\
\textit{Rabin condition [420]: } & \bigvee_{j=0}^{f} \mathsf{GF}\Phi_j \wedge \mathsf{FG}\Psi_j \\
\textit{Streett condition [476]: } & \bigwedge_{j=0}^{f} \mathsf{FG}\Phi_j \vee \mathsf{GF}\Psi_j \\
\textit{Prefix condition (1.kind) [352, 433]: } & \bigwedge_{j=0}^{f} \mathsf{G}\Phi_j \vee \mathsf{F}\Psi_j \\
\textit{Prefix condition (2.kind) [352, 433]: } & \bigvee_{j=0}^{f} \mathsf{G}\Phi_j \wedge \mathsf{F}\Psi_j
\end{aligned}
$$

The above conditions define corresponding automaton classes. We denote the set of (nondeterministic) safety, liveness, Büchi, persistence, Prefix-1, Prefix-2, Rabin, and Streett automata with $\mathsf{NDet}_{\mathsf{G}}$, $\mathsf{NDet}_{\mathsf{F}}$, $\mathsf{NDet}_{\mathsf{GF}}$, $\mathsf{NDet}_{\mathsf{FG}}$, $\mathsf{NDet}_{\mathsf{Prefix1}}$, $\mathsf{NDet}_{\mathsf{Prefix2}}$, $\mathsf{NDet}_{\mathsf{Rabin}}$, *and* $\mathsf{NDet}_{\mathsf{Streett}}$, *respectively. The corresponding deterministic classes are denoted as* $\mathsf{Det}_{\mathsf{G}}$, $\mathsf{Det}_{\mathsf{F}}$, $\mathsf{Det}_{\mathsf{GF}}$, $\mathsf{Det}_{\mathsf{FG}}$, $\mathsf{Det}_{\mathsf{Prefix1}}$, $\mathsf{Det}_{\mathsf{Prefix2}}$, $\mathsf{Det}_{\mathsf{Rabin}}$, *and* $\mathsf{Det}_{\mathsf{Streett}}$, *respectively. The universal counterparts of these automaton classes are denoted as* $\mathsf{(N)Det}^{\forall}_{\mathsf{G}}$, $\mathsf{(N)Det}^{\forall}_{\mathsf{F}}$, $\mathsf{(N)Det}^{\forall}_{\mathsf{GF}}$, $\mathsf{(N)Det}^{\forall}_{\mathsf{FG}}$, $\mathsf{(N)Det}^{\forall}_{\mathsf{Prefix1}}$, $\mathsf{(N)Det}^{\forall}_{\mathsf{Prefix2}}$, $\mathsf{(N)Det}^{\forall}_{\mathsf{Rabin}}$, *and* $\mathsf{(N)Det}^{\forall}_{\mathsf{Streett}}$, *respectively.*

The subformulas Φ_j and Ψ_j are thereby propositional formulas over the input variables and the state variables. It should be noted that in the literature the conditions Φ_j and Ψ_j often do not depend on the inputs. Hence, these formulas represent situations, i.e., pairs composed of a state and an input. Clearly, for finite sets of input and state variables, there are only finitely many situations.

Safety automata require that a word must have at least one infinite run through the automaton so that the condition Φ_0 invariantly holds. Liveness automata, on the other hand, require that there must be a run of the word such that the condition Φ_0 holds at least once. The acceptance condition $\mathsf{GF}\Phi_0$ of a Büchi automaton requires that the condition Φ_0 must hold infinitely often, and the condition $\mathsf{FG}\Phi_0$ of a persistence automaton requires that Φ_0 must always hold from a certain position on.

While the four kinds of ω-automata above are the basic ones, the others are more complicated. To be accepted by a Rabin automaton, there must be an index $j \in \{0, \ldots, f\}$ such that the run infinitely often satisfies Φ_j and after some time always satisfies Ψ_j. In other words, for some j, the run must satisfy infinitely often Φ_j and may only finitely often violate the condition $\neg\Psi_j$. Note further that for every Rabin automaton, we can demand that $\Phi_j \rightarrow \Psi_j$ is valid: In particular, we can replace Φ_j by $\Phi_j \wedge \Psi_j$. The acceptance condition of Streett automata is dual to the one of Rabin automata.

An important special case of Rabin automata are *parity automata* [376]. Their acceptance is defined as follows: All situations, i.e., pairs of states and inputs, are partitioned into $f+1$ different classes. To this end, often a coloring function Ω is used that assigns one of the colors $0, \ldots, f$ to every situation. Hence, a parity condition can be represented with $f+1$ disjoint conditions $\Phi_0, \ldots, \Phi_f$, i.e., $\Phi_i \wedge \Phi_j$ is unsatisfiable for $i \neq j$ and $\bigvee_{j=0}^{f} \Phi_j$ is valid (at least when these formulas are restricted to the reachable states). Hence, every input word and every suitable run for this input word must satisfy at least one of the conditions Φ_j infinitely often. The acceptance is defined as follows: an input is accepted if it has a run such that the condition Φ_j with the least index j that is infinitely often satisfied must have an even index. In terms of a Rabin condition this is expressed as follows (where $k := \left\lfloor \frac{f}{2} \right\rfloor$):

$$\bigvee_{j=0}^{k} \mathsf{GF}\Phi_{2j} \wedge \mathsf{FG} \bigvee_{i=2j}^{f} \Phi_i$$

Note that the condition $\mathsf{GF}\Phi_{2j} \wedge \mathsf{FG} \bigvee_{i=2j}^{f} \Phi_i$ means that Φ_{2j} is infinitely often satisfied, and the conditions $\Phi_0, \ldots, \Phi_{2j-1}$ are only finitely often satisfied. Hence, Φ_{2j} is the least condition (in terms of the index) that is infinitely often satisfied, and its index is even. It is also possible to convert every (deterministic) Rabin automaton to a (deterministic) parity automaton.

Another equally expressive automaton class are *Muller automata* [380]. Muller automata define the acceptance via conditions $\Phi_0, \ldots, \Phi_f$ such that one of these conditions represents *exactly* the set of situations that appear infinitely often. Given that $\Phi_j = \bigvee_{i=1}^{n_j} \varphi_{i,j}$ is an explicit enumeration of the situations $\varphi_{i,j}$ represented by Φ_j, this is expressed as follows:

$$\bigvee_{j=0}^{f} \left(\bigwedge_{i=1}^{n_j} \mathsf{GF}\varphi_{i,j} \right) \wedge \mathsf{FG}\Phi_j$$

Hence, *every* situation $\varphi_{i,j}$ represented by Φ_j must be satisfied infinitely often, and no situation not represented by Φ_j must be satisfied infinitely often.

Deterministic parity automata can be easily complemented by incrementing the indices of the conditions Φ_j. Boolean operations on deterministic Muller automata easily translate to Boolean operations on the accepting conditions of the Muller automata. The simplicity of these operations makes parity and Muller automata attractive from a theoretical viewpoint. However, the translation to equivalent fixpoint expressions for verification is more complicated than for Rabin or Streett acceptance conditions. Section 4.4 of this book and Chapter 1 of [221] considers translations between automaton classes and also lower bounds for the complexities of converting acceptance conditions into each other.

Prefix automata, also called Staiger-Wagner automata [469], come in two forms that correspond in some ways to simplifications of Streett and Rabin automata. A word is accepted by a Prefix automaton of the first kind, iff there is at least one run through the automaton such that for all $j \in \{0, \ldots, f\}$ either the run satisfies on all positions the condition Φ_j or it satisfies Ψ_j at least once. The acceptance condition of Prefix automata of the second kind is dual.

Büchi automata are sometimes further classified into *weak* and *terminal* Büchi automata [40, 52, 221, 381]. We will discuss these special classes on page 370.

4.3 Boolean Closure

The language given in Definition 4.6 contains Boolean combinations and nestings of automaton formulas. We will now show that these connectives can be removed, so that we can concentrate on flat existential automaton formulas $\mathcal{A}_\exists(Q, \mathcal{I}, \mathcal{R}, \Phi)$ where Φ does not contain automaton formulas, and is instead one of the classic acceptance condition. To additionally establish the equivalence to regular and ω-regular expressions, we start with the following lemma:

Lemma 4.8 (Concatenation and Star Operation). *Concatenation and star operation can be transformed on automaton formulas as follows, where we assume* $P \cap Q = \{\}$*:*

- $\mathsf{concat}(\mathcal{A}_\exists(P, \Phi_\mathcal{I}, \Phi_\mathcal{R}, \Phi_\mathcal{F}), \mathcal{A}_\exists(Q, \Psi_\mathcal{I}, \Psi_\mathcal{R}, \Psi_\mathcal{F}))$
$$= \mathcal{A}_\exists\left(\begin{array}{l} P \cup Q \cup \{q\}, \\ \neg q \wedge \Phi_\mathcal{I} \vee q \wedge \Phi_\mathcal{I} \wedge \Phi_\mathcal{F} \wedge \Psi_\mathcal{I}, \\ \neg q \wedge \Phi_\mathcal{R} \wedge \neg \mathsf{X}q \vee \neg q \wedge \Phi_\mathcal{R} \wedge \mathsf{X}q \wedge \mathsf{X}\Phi_\mathcal{F} \wedge \mathsf{X}\Psi_\mathcal{I} \vee q \wedge \Psi_\mathcal{R} \wedge \mathsf{X}q, \\ q \wedge \Psi_\mathcal{F} \end{array}\right)$$
- $\mathsf{star}(\mathcal{A}_\exists(P, \Phi_\mathcal{I}, \Phi_\mathcal{R}, \Phi_\mathcal{F}))$
$$= \mathcal{A}_\exists\left(\begin{array}{l} Q \cup Q' \cup \{p\}, \\ \neg p \wedge \Phi_\mathcal{I}, \\ \neg p \wedge \Phi_\mathcal{R} \wedge \neg \mathsf{X}p \vee \neg p \wedge \Phi_\mathcal{R} \wedge \mathsf{X}p \wedge \mathsf{X}\Phi_\mathcal{F} \wedge \mathsf{X}\Phi'_\mathcal{I} \vee \\ \quad p \wedge \Phi'_\mathcal{R} \wedge \mathsf{X}p \vee p \wedge \Phi'_\mathcal{R} \wedge \neg \mathsf{X}p \wedge \mathsf{X}\Phi'_\mathcal{F} \wedge \mathsf{X}\Phi_\mathcal{I}, \\ \neg p \wedge \Phi_\mathcal{I} \vee \neg p \wedge \Phi_\mathcal{F} \vee p \wedge \Phi'_\mathcal{F} \end{array}\right),$$
where $Q' := \{q' \mid q \in Q\}$ *are copies of the state variables in* Q, $p \notin Q$, *and* $\Phi'_\mathcal{I}$, $\Phi'_\mathcal{R}$, $\Phi'_\mathcal{F}$ *are obtained from* $\Phi_\mathcal{I}$, $\Phi_\mathcal{R}$, $\Phi_\mathcal{F}$ *by replacing any occurrence of a state variable* $q \in Q$ *by its copy* $q' \in Q'$.

While the above lemma looks rather like a definition, its intention is to state that the mentioned operations correspond with the concatenation and star operation on regular expressions. The acceptance conditions $\Phi_{\mathcal{F}}$ and $\Psi_{\mathcal{F}}$ are thereby propositional formulas that are used to define the set of finite words having a path from $\Phi_{\mathcal{I}}$ to $\Phi_{\mathcal{F}}$ through $\Phi_{\mathcal{R}}$. Note that the new state variable q is used to enable one or the other automaton, and that in the star-operation, we have to use copies of the state variables to satisfy $\mathsf{X}\Phi_{\mathcal{F}} \wedge \mathsf{X}\Phi'_{\mathcal{I}}$ also in cases where initial states are not final states. Furthermore, we have $\mathsf{Lim}(\mathcal{A}_{\exists}(P, \Phi_{\mathcal{I}}, \Phi_{\mathcal{R}}, \Phi_{\mathcal{F}})) = \mathcal{A}_{\exists}(P, \Phi_{\mathcal{I}}, \Phi_{\mathcal{R}}, \mathsf{GF}\Phi_{\mathcal{F}})$, so that the only missing operations are Boolean combinations. The next lemma shows that Boolean combinations of automaton formulas can be reduced to Boolean combinations of acceptance conditions:

Lemma 4.9 (Boolean Operations of Automaton Formulas). *Boolean operations can be easily eliminated as follows if $P \cap Q = \{\}$:*

- $\mathcal{A}_{\exists}(\{\}, 1, 1, \Phi_{\mathcal{F}}) = \Phi_{\mathcal{F}}$
- $\mathcal{A}_{\forall}(\{\}, 1, 1, \Phi_{\mathcal{F}}) = \Phi_{\mathcal{F}}$
- $\mathcal{A}_{\exists}(P, \Phi_{\mathcal{I}}, \Phi_{\mathcal{R}}, \mathcal{A}_{\exists}(Q, \Psi_{\mathcal{I}}, \Psi_{\mathcal{R}}, \Phi_{\mathcal{F}})) = \mathcal{A}_{\exists}(P \cup Q, \Phi_{\mathcal{I}} \wedge \Psi_{\mathcal{I}}, \Phi_{\mathcal{R}} \wedge \Psi_{\mathcal{R}}, \Phi_{\mathcal{F}})$
- $\neg\mathcal{A}_{\forall}(Q, \Phi_{\mathcal{I}}, \Phi_{\mathcal{R}}, \Phi_{\mathcal{F}}) = \mathcal{A}_{\exists}(Q, \Phi_{\mathcal{I}}, \Phi_{\mathcal{R}}, \neg\Phi_{\mathcal{F}})$
- $(\mathcal{A}_{\exists}(P, \Phi_{\mathcal{I}}, \Phi_{\mathcal{R}}, \Phi_{\mathcal{F}}) \ \wedge \ \mathcal{A}_{\exists}(Q, \Psi_{\mathcal{I}}, \Psi_{\mathcal{R}}, \Psi_{\mathcal{F}}))$
  $= \mathcal{A}_{\exists}(P \cup Q, \Phi_{\mathcal{I}} \wedge \Psi_{\mathcal{I}}, \Phi_{\mathcal{R}} \wedge \Psi_{\mathcal{R}}, \Phi_{\mathcal{F}} \wedge \Psi_{\mathcal{F}})$
- *Given that each input word has at least one run through $\mathcal{A}_{\exists}(P, \Phi_{\mathcal{I}}, \Phi_{\mathcal{R}}, \Phi_{\mathcal{F}})$ and $\mathcal{A}_{\exists}(Q, \Psi_{\mathcal{I}}, \Psi_{\mathcal{R}}, \Psi_{\mathcal{F}})$, then the following holds:*

$$\begin{array}{l}(\mathcal{A}_{\exists}(P, \Phi_{\mathcal{I}}, \Phi_{\mathcal{R}}, \Phi_{\mathcal{F}}) \ \vee \ \mathcal{A}_{\exists}(Q, \Psi_{\mathcal{I}}, \Psi_{\mathcal{R}}, \Psi_{\mathcal{F}})) \\ \quad = \mathcal{A}_{\exists}(P \cup Q, \Phi_{\mathcal{I}} \wedge \Psi_{\mathcal{I}}, \Phi_{\mathcal{R}} \wedge \Psi_{\mathcal{R}}, \Phi_{\mathcal{F}} \vee \Psi_{\mathcal{F}})\end{array}$$

- *In general, the disjunction can be computed as follows, where q is a new state variable:*

$$\begin{array}{l}(\mathcal{A}_{\exists}(P, \Phi_{\mathcal{I}}, \Phi_{\mathcal{R}}, \Phi_{\mathcal{F}}) \ \vee \ \mathcal{A}_{\exists}(Q, \Psi_{\mathcal{I}}, \Psi_{\mathcal{R}}, \Psi_{\mathcal{F}})) \\ = \mathcal{A}_{\exists}\left(\begin{array}{l}P \cup Q \cup \{q\}, \\ \neg q \wedge \Phi_{\mathcal{I}} \vee q \wedge \Psi_{\mathcal{I}}, \\ \neg q \wedge \Phi_{\mathcal{R}} \wedge \neg\mathsf{X}q \vee q \wedge \Psi_{\mathcal{R}} \wedge \mathsf{X}q, \\ \neg q \wedge \Phi_{\mathcal{F}} \vee q \wedge \Psi_{\mathcal{F}}\end{array}\right)\end{array}$$

- *Given that $\mathcal{A}_{\exists}(Q, \Phi_{\mathcal{I}}, \Phi_{\mathcal{R}}, \Phi_{\mathcal{F}})$ is deterministic, i.e., for each input word there is exactly one run through the automaton, then we moreover have*

$$\mathcal{A}_{\exists}(Q, \Phi_{\mathcal{I}}, \Phi_{\mathcal{R}}, \Phi_{\mathcal{F}}) = \mathcal{A}_{\forall}(Q, \Phi_{\mathcal{I}}, \Phi_{\mathcal{R}}, \Phi_{\mathcal{F}})$$

The proofs of the above facts are straightforward, and are mostly based on the construction of the product automaton. However, we should give some explanations for the disjunction. Here, we must face the problem that for a given input word, there might be no run through one of the automata. For example, assume there is an input word α that is accepted by $\mathcal{A}_{\exists}(P, \Phi_{\mathcal{I}}, \Phi_{\mathcal{R}}, \Phi_{\mathcal{F}})$, but there is no run through $\mathcal{A}_{\exists}(Q, \Psi_{\mathcal{I}}, \Psi_{\mathcal{R}}, \Psi_{\mathcal{F}})$ of this word. Hence, the product automaton $\mathcal{A}_\exists\left(P \cup Q, \Phi_\mathcal{I} \wedge \Psi_\mathcal{I}, \Phi_\mathcal{R} \wedge \Psi_\mathcal{R}, \ldots\right)$ has also no run for α, so that there is no chance to define an appropriate acceptance condition. So, the first equivalence only holds when both automata are total, i.e., for each input word, we have at least one run.

In the general case, where the automata may be partially defined, we use the following trick: we add a new state variable q that is constantly false or constantly true, depending on its initial value. Depending on this, the initial value of q nondeterministically chooses between one of the given automata. As q is constantly false or true, the following equations are valid and show that we can already compute the disjunction for certain classes of automata:

- $\neg q \wedge \mathsf{G}\varphi \vee q \wedge \mathsf{G}\psi = \mathsf{G}\left(\neg q \wedge \varphi \vee q \wedge \psi\right)$
- $\neg q \wedge \mathsf{F}\varphi \vee q \wedge \mathsf{F}\psi = \mathsf{F}\left(\neg q \wedge \varphi \vee q \wedge \psi\right)$
- $\neg q \wedge \mathsf{FG}\varphi \vee q \wedge \mathsf{FG}\psi = \mathsf{FG}\left(\neg q \wedge \varphi \vee q \wedge \psi\right)$
- $\neg q \wedge \mathsf{GF}\varphi \vee q \wedge \mathsf{GF}\psi = \mathsf{GF}\left(\neg q \wedge \varphi \vee q \wedge \psi\right)$
- $\neg q \wedge \left(\bigvee_{i=1}^{n} \mathsf{G}\alpha_i \wedge \mathsf{F}\beta_i\right) \vee q \wedge \left(\bigvee_{i=1}^{m} \mathsf{G}\gamma_i \wedge \mathsf{F}\delta_i\right)$
  $= \left(\bigvee_{i=1}^{n} \mathsf{G}(\neg q \wedge \alpha_i) \wedge \mathsf{F}(\neg q \wedge \beta_i)\right) \vee \left(\bigvee_{i=1}^{m} \mathsf{G}(q \wedge \gamma_i) \wedge \mathsf{F}(q \wedge \delta_i)\right)$
- $\neg q \wedge \left(\bigvee_{i=1}^{n} \mathsf{GF}\alpha_i \wedge \mathsf{FG}\beta_i\right) \vee q \wedge \left(\bigvee_{i=1}^{m} \mathsf{GF}\gamma_i \wedge \mathsf{FG}\delta_i\right)$
  $= \left(\bigvee_{i=1}^{n} \mathsf{GF}(\neg q \wedge \alpha_i) \wedge \mathsf{FG}(\neg q \wedge \beta_i)\right) \vee \left(\bigvee_{i=1}^{m} \mathsf{GF}(q \wedge \gamma_i) \wedge \mathsf{FG}(q \wedge \delta_i)\right)$
- $\neg q \wedge \left(\bigwedge_{i=1}^{n} \mathsf{G}\alpha_i \vee \mathsf{F}\beta_i\right) \vee q \wedge \left(\bigwedge_{i=1}^{m} \mathsf{G}\gamma_i \vee \mathsf{F}\delta_i\right)$
  $= \left(\bigwedge_{i=1}^{n} \mathsf{G}(\neg q \wedge \alpha_i) \vee \mathsf{F}(\neg q \wedge \beta_i)\right) \vee \left(\bigwedge_{i=1}^{m} \mathsf{G}(q \wedge \gamma_i) \vee \mathsf{F}(q \wedge \delta_i)\right)$
- $\neg q \wedge \left(\bigwedge_{i=1}^{n} \mathsf{GF}\alpha_i \vee \mathsf{FG}\beta_i\right) \vee q \wedge \left(\bigwedge_{i=1}^{m} \mathsf{GF}\gamma_i \vee \mathsf{FG}\delta_i\right)$
  $= \left(\bigwedge_{i=1}^{n} \mathsf{GF}(\neg q \wedge \alpha_i) \vee \mathsf{FG}(\neg q \wedge \beta_i)\right) \vee \left(\bigwedge_{i=1}^{m} \mathsf{GF}(q \wedge \gamma_i) \vee \mathsf{FG}(q \wedge \delta_i)\right)$

For example, consider the disjunction of two Büchi automata: For the Büchi automata $\mathfrak{A}_1 := \mathcal{A}_\exists\left(P, \Phi_\mathcal{I}, \Phi_\mathcal{R}, \mathsf{GF}\varphi\right)$ and $\mathfrak{A}_2 := \mathcal{A}_\exists\left(Q, \Psi_\mathcal{I}, \Psi_\mathcal{R}, \mathsf{GF}\psi\right)$, we obtain:

$$\mathfrak{A}_1 \vee \mathfrak{A}_2 = \mathcal{A}_\exists \begin{pmatrix} P \cup Q \cup \{q\}, \\ \neg q \wedge \Phi_\mathcal{I} \vee q \wedge \Psi_\mathcal{I}, \\ \neg q \wedge \Phi_\mathcal{R} \wedge \neg \mathsf{X}q \vee q \wedge \Psi_\mathcal{R} \wedge \mathsf{X}q, \\ \mathsf{GF}(\neg q \wedge \varphi \vee q \wedge \psi) \end{pmatrix}$$

Some of the conjunctions can also be combined: for example, we have $\mathsf{G}\varphi \wedge \mathsf{G}\psi = \mathsf{G}(\varphi \wedge \psi)$ and $\mathsf{FG}\varphi \wedge \mathsf{FG}\psi = \mathsf{FG}(\varphi \wedge \psi)$. However, there is no simple way to combine conjunctions of like $\mathsf{F}\varphi \wedge \mathsf{F}\psi$ and $\mathsf{GF}\varphi \wedge \mathsf{GF}\psi$. Also, disjunctions of Streett automata and Prefix-1 automata can not be directly obtained by the above laws. However, we obtain the following corollary.

Corollary 4.10. *Let* $\kappa \in \{\mathsf{G}, \mathsf{F}, \mathsf{GF}, \mathsf{FG}, \mathsf{Prefix1}, \mathsf{Prefix2}, \mathsf{Rabin}, \mathsf{Streett}\}$. *Every class* NDet_κ *is closed under disjunction and conjunction iff the disjunction and conjunction of the corresponding acceptance conditions can be expressed as a* NDet_κ *automaton. Furthermore, the class* Det_κ *is closed under negation iff the negation of the acceptance condition can be expressed as a* Det_κ *automaton.*

Hence, we need some further laws to express Boolean combinations of the acceptance conditions by means of the corresponding automata. The next lemma will show how we can combine all disjunctions and conjunctions of the four basic acceptance conditions, and therefore we will see that all basic automaton classes are closed under disjunction and conjunction.

Lemma 4.11 (Boolean Combination of Acceptance Conditions). *For all propositional formulas φ and ψ over the variables V_Σ and all variables $p, q \notin V_\Sigma$, the following laws are valid:*

Boolean Combination of G*:*

1. $\varphi = \mathcal{A}_\exists\left(\{p\}, \neg p, \mathsf{X}p, \mathsf{G}[p \vee \varphi]\right)$
2. $\neg\mathsf{G}\varphi = \mathsf{F}\neg\varphi$
3. $\mathsf{G}\varphi \wedge \mathsf{G}\psi = \mathsf{G}[\varphi \wedge \psi]$
4. $\mathsf{G}\varphi \vee \mathsf{G}\psi = \mathcal{A}_\exists\left(\{p, q\}, p \wedge q, [\mathsf{X}p \leftrightarrow p \wedge \varphi] \wedge [\mathsf{X}q \leftrightarrow q \wedge \psi], \mathsf{G}[p \vee q]\right)$

Boolean Combination of F*:*

1. $\varphi = \mathcal{A}_\exists\left(\{p\}, \neg p, \mathsf{X}p, \mathsf{F}[\neg p \wedge \varphi]\right)$
2. $\neg\mathsf{F}\varphi = \mathsf{G}\neg\varphi$
3. $\mathsf{F}\varphi \wedge \mathsf{F}\psi = \mathcal{A}_\exists\left(\{p, q\}, \neg p \wedge \neg q, [\mathsf{X}p \leftrightarrow p \vee \varphi] \wedge [\mathsf{X}q \leftrightarrow q \vee \psi], \mathsf{F}[p \wedge q]\right)$
4. $\mathsf{F}\varphi \vee \mathsf{F}\psi = \mathsf{F}[\varphi \vee \psi]$

Boolean Combination of FG*:*

1. $$\varphi = \mathcal{A}_\exists\left(\begin{array}{l}\{p, q\},\\ \neg p \wedge \neg q,\\ (\mathsf{X}p \leftrightarrow 1) \wedge (\mathsf{X}q \leftrightarrow (\neg p \wedge \neg q \wedge \varphi) \vee (p \wedge q)),\\ \mathsf{FG}q\end{array}\right)$$
2. $\neg\mathsf{FG}\varphi = \mathsf{GF}\neg\varphi$
3. $\mathsf{FG}\varphi \wedge \mathsf{FG}\psi = \mathsf{FG}[\varphi \wedge \psi]$
4. $\mathsf{FG}\varphi \vee \mathsf{FG}\psi = \mathcal{A}_\exists\left(\{q\}, \neg q, \mathsf{X}q \leftrightarrow (q \Rightarrow \psi | \neg\varphi), \mathsf{FG}[\neg q \vee \psi]\right)$

Boolean Combination of GF*:*

1. $$\varphi = \mathcal{A}_\exists\left(\begin{array}{l}\{p, q\},\\ \neg p \wedge \neg q,\\ (\mathsf{X}p \leftrightarrow 1) \wedge (\mathsf{X}q \leftrightarrow (\neg p \wedge \neg q \wedge \varphi) \vee (p \wedge q)),\\ \mathsf{GF}q\end{array}\right)$$
2. $\neg\mathsf{GF}\varphi = \mathsf{FG}\neg\varphi$
3. $\mathsf{GF}\varphi \wedge \mathsf{GF}\psi = \mathcal{A}_\exists\left(\{q\}, \neg q, \mathsf{X}q \leftrightarrow (q \Rightarrow \neg\psi | \varphi), \mathsf{GF}[q \wedge \psi]\right)$
4. $\mathsf{GF}\varphi \vee \mathsf{GF}\psi = \mathsf{GF}[\varphi \vee \psi]$

For each basic acceptance condition, we have listed four equations. The first equation allows us to express every propositional formula as an automaton of the corresponding class, and the second one shows that certain classes are dual to each other, i.e., they can be transformed into each other by negations. The third and fourth equations determine the conjunction and disjunction of the acceptance conditions as automata of the corresponding class. Consider the combination of $\mathsf{F}\varphi \wedge \mathsf{F}\psi$ to a Det_F automaton. The state transition diagram is shown on the left hand side of Figure 4.2. As can be seen, the state variables p and q are initially 0, and become true when φ and ψ, respectively, are true for the first time. Once, p is true, it remains so, independent of the later values of φ (the same holds for q and ψ). We call state variables that observe a condition 'watchdogs' for that condition. The reduction of $\mathsf{G}\varphi \vee \mathsf{G}\psi$ is obtained in the same way by the use of dual watchdogs.

The state transition diagram of the $\mathsf{Det}_{\mathsf{GF}}$ automaton used to express $\mathsf{GF}\varphi \wedge \mathsf{GF}\psi$ is given on the right hand side of Figure 4.2. It is easily seen that the states $\{\}$ and $\{q\}$ wait for the conditions φ and ψ, respectively, and change the state in that case. Hence, if $q \wedge \psi$ holds infinitely often, then we infinitely often switch from state $\{q\}$ to $\{\}$. As the only way to return to state $\{q\}$ is for φ to hold again, it follows that infinitely often φ and infinitely often ψ must hold. The converse is also true.

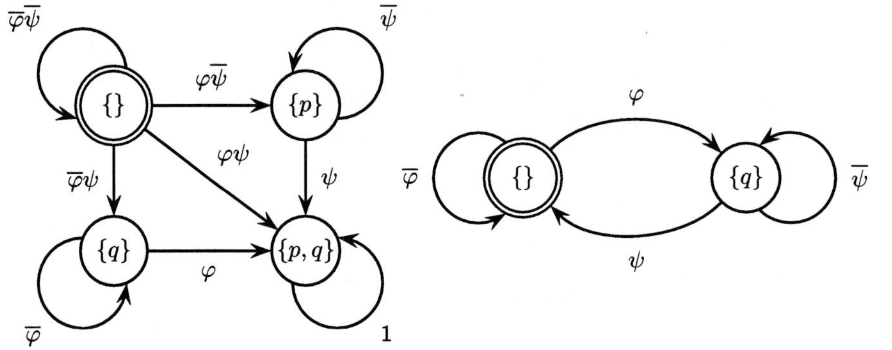

Fig. 4.2. Automata for the reduction of $\mathsf{F}\varphi \wedge \mathsf{F}\psi$ and $\mathsf{GF}\varphi \wedge \mathsf{GF}\psi$

Therefore, by the last two lemmas, it immediately follows that that automaton classes $\mathsf{Det}_{\mathsf{G}}$, $\mathsf{Det}_{\mathsf{F}}$, $\mathsf{Det}_{\mathsf{GF}}$, $\mathsf{Det}_{\mathsf{FG}}$, and also $\mathsf{NDet}_{\mathsf{G}}$, $\mathsf{NDet}_{\mathsf{F}}$, $\mathsf{NDet}_{\mathsf{GF}}$, $\mathsf{NDet}_{\mathsf{FG}}$ are all closed under conjunction and disjunction. Moreover, the complements of $\mathsf{Det}_{\mathsf{G}}$, $\mathsf{Det}_{\mathsf{F}}$, $\mathsf{Det}_{\mathsf{GF}}$, and $\mathsf{Det}_{\mathsf{FG}}$ are exactly the classes $\mathsf{Det}_{\mathsf{F}}$, $\mathsf{Det}_{\mathsf{G}}$, $\mathsf{Det}_{\mathsf{FG}}$, and $\mathsf{Det}_{\mathsf{GF}}$, respectively. It remains to consider the Boolean combinations of the acceptance conditions of Prefix, Rabin and Streett automata. We start with Prefix automata, and obtain the following lemma.

Lemma 4.12 (Boolean Closure of Safety and Liveness). *Given the variables V_Σ, the Boolean closure of safety and liveness formulas is defined as the following subset of $\mathcal{L}_{\mathsf{spec}}$ where the start symbol is T:*

$$\begin{aligned} I &::= V_\Sigma \mid \neg I \mid I \wedge I \mid I \vee I \\ T &::= \neg T \mid T \wedge T \mid T \vee T \mid \mathsf{G}I \mid \mathsf{F}I \end{aligned}$$

For every formula that can be derived from T, there are equivalent formulas in the following normal forms:

$$\bigwedge_{i=0}^{f} \left(\mathsf{F}\Psi_i \vee \bigvee_{j=0}^{n_i} \mathsf{G}\Phi_{i,j} \right) \qquad\qquad \bigvee_{i=0}^{f} \left(\mathsf{G}\Phi_i \wedge \bigwedge_{j=0}^{n_i} \mathsf{F}\Psi_{i,j} \right)$$

The proof of the above lemma is straightforward, we just compute the negation normal form and then the disjunctive or conjunctive normal forms where the formulas starting with G or F are treated as atomic propositions. After this, we use the laws $\mathsf{G}\varphi \wedge \mathsf{G}\psi = \mathsf{G}(\varphi \wedge \psi)$ and $\mathsf{F}\varphi \vee \mathsf{F}\psi = \mathsf{F}(\varphi \wedge \psi)$ to combine one type of formula.

By the above lemma, we can already see that the Boolean closure of Det_G and Det_F is the class of deterministic ω-automata that have an acceptance condition in either one of the above mentioned normal forms. The next theorem will restrict these normal forms so that $n_i = 0$ holds, i.e., to Prefix1 and Prefix2 automata. The key to this restriction is simply given by the rules of Lemma 4.11 that tell us that a conjunction of liveness properties and a disjunction of safety properties can be reduced to a Det_F and Det_G automaton, respectively.

Theorem 4.13 (Boolean Closure of $\mathsf{Det}_\mathsf{Prefix}$). *For every formula that is a Boolean combination of Det_G and Det_F formulas, there are equivalent automaton formulas in both $\mathsf{Det}_\mathsf{Prefix1}$ and $\mathsf{Det}_\mathsf{Prefix2}$. In particular, it follows that both $\mathsf{Det}_\mathsf{Prefix1}$ and $\mathsf{Det}_\mathsf{Prefix2}$ are closed under all Boolean operations. Moreover, for every formula of $\mathsf{Det}_\mathsf{Prefix1}$, there is an equivalent one in $\mathsf{Det}_\mathsf{Prefix2}$, and vice versa.*

Proof. Given a Boolean combination of safety and liveness properties, we first compute the normal form $\bigwedge_{i=0}^{f} \mathsf{F}\Psi_i \vee \bigvee_{j=0}^{n_i} \mathsf{G}\Phi_{i,j}$ as given by the above lemma. Now, note that the following holds, which is a generalization of the rule given in Lemma 4.11:

$$\bigvee_{j=0}^{n_i} \mathsf{G}\Phi_{i,j} = \mathcal{A}_\exists \left(\begin{array}{l} \{q_{i,0}, \ldots, q_{i,n_i}\}, \\ \bigwedge_{j=0}^{n_i} q_{i,j}, \\ \bigwedge_{j=0}^{n_i} \mathsf{X}q_{i,j} = q_{i,j} \wedge \Phi_{i,j}, \\ \mathsf{G} \bigvee_{j=0}^{n_i} q_{i,j} \end{array} \right)$$

We use the above equation to replace the subformulas $\bigvee_{j=0}^{n_i} \mathsf{G}\Phi_{i,j}$ in our normal form by the corresponding automaton formulas and then use the disjunction rule for $\exists$-automata given in Lemma 4.9 to obtain (note that the transition relations of the automata are all total):

$$\bigwedge_{i=0}^{f} \mathcal{A}_\exists \left(\begin{array}{l} \{q_{i,0}, \ldots, q_{i,n_i}\}, \\ \bigwedge_{j=0}^{n_i} q_{i,j}, \\ \bigwedge_{j=0}^{n_i} \mathsf{X}q_{i,j} = q_{i,j} \wedge \Phi_{i,j}, \\ \mathsf{F}\Psi_i \vee \mathsf{G} \bigvee_{j=0}^{n_i} q_{i,j} \end{array} \right)$$

The rest is obtained by the conjunction rule of Lemma 4.9. The proof for $\mathsf{Det}_\mathsf{Prefix2}$ automata is obtained in a completely analogous manner. □

In particular, the above theorem implies that the classes $\mathsf{Det}_\mathsf{Prefix1}$ and $\mathsf{Det}_\mathsf{Prefix2}$ are closed under complement, since the complement of a $\mathsf{Det}_\mathsf{Prefix1}$ automaton is (by Lemma 4.9) a $\mathsf{Det}_\mathsf{Prefix2}$ automaton, and the complement of a $\mathsf{Det}_\mathsf{Prefix2}$

automaton is a $\mathsf{Det}_{\mathsf{Prefix1}}$ automaton. Moreover, we also see that we would define an automaton class where the acceptance condition $\Phi_{\mathcal{F}}$ is an arbitrary Boolean combination of safety and liveness properties, this class would then be equally expressive as $\mathsf{Det}_{\mathsf{Prefix1}}$ and $\mathsf{Det}_{\mathsf{Prefix2}}$. As for every formula of $\mathsf{Det}_{\mathsf{Prefix1}}$, there is an equivalent one in $\mathsf{Det}_{\mathsf{Prefix2}}$, and vice versa, we do not always distinguish between $\mathsf{Det}_{\mathsf{Prefix1}}$ and $\mathsf{Det}_{\mathsf{Prefix2}}$, and simply write $\mathsf{Det}_{\mathsf{Prefix}}$ whenever the special kind of prefix automaton is of no interest.

The above language of Boolean closed safety and liveness properties does not allow nestings of G and F operators. Clearly, there are some trivial cases, like $\mathsf{GG}\varphi$ and $\mathsf{FF}\varphi$ that are equivalent to $\mathsf{G}\varphi$ and $\mathsf{F}\varphi$, respectively. However, in the general case, we can also obtain the formulas $\mathsf{GF}\varphi$ and $\mathsf{FG}\varphi$ that can not be reduced to a safety or liveness property (this will be proved in Theorem 4.19). We can now proceed in the same manner with these classes:

Lemma 4.14 (Boolean Closure of Persistence and Fairness). *Given variables V_Σ, the Boolean closure of persistence and fairness formulas is defined as the following subset of $\mathcal{L}_{\mathsf{spec}}$ where the start symbol is T:*

$$\begin{aligned} I &::= V_\Sigma \mid \neg I \mid I \wedge I \mid I \vee I \\ T &::= \neg T \mid T \wedge T \mid T \vee T \mid \mathsf{GF}I \mid \mathsf{FG}I \end{aligned}$$

For every formula that can be derived from T, there are equivalent formulas in the following normal forms:

$$\bigwedge_{i=0}^{f}\left(\mathsf{GF}\Psi_i \vee \bigvee_{j=0}^{n_i} \mathsf{FG}\Phi_{i,j}\right) \qquad \bigvee_{i=0}^{f}\left(\mathsf{FG}\Phi_i \wedge \bigwedge_{j=0}^{n_i} \mathsf{GF}\Psi_{i,j}\right)$$

The proof is again done by shifting negation symbols inwards, computing disjunctive or conjunctive normal forms, where the subformulas starting with either FG or GF are treated as atomic propositions. After this, the laws $\mathsf{FG}\varphi \wedge \mathsf{FG}\psi = \mathsf{FG}(\varphi \wedge \psi)$ and $\mathsf{GF}\varphi \vee \mathsf{GF}\psi = \mathsf{GF}(\varphi \vee \psi)$ are used to combine one type of formula.

By the above theorem, we can already see that the Boolean closure of $\mathsf{Det}_{\mathsf{GF}}$ and $\mathsf{Det}_{\mathsf{FG}}$ is the class of deterministic ω-automata that have an acceptance condition in either one of the above mentioned normal forms. Similar to Theorem 4.13, the next theorem shows that we can restrict these normal forms so that $n_i = 0$ holds, i.e., to Rabin and Streett automata. The key to this restriction is also given by the rules of Lemma 4.11 that tell us that a conjunction of fairness properties and a disjunction of persistence properties can be reduced to a $\mathsf{Det}_{\mathsf{FG}}$ and $\mathsf{Det}_{\mathsf{GF}}$ automaton, respectively.

Theorem 4.15 (Boolean Closure of $\mathsf{Det}_{\mathsf{Rabin}}$ and $\mathsf{Det}_{\mathsf{Streett}}$). *For every formula that is a Boolean combination of $\mathsf{Det}_{\mathsf{GF}}$ and $\mathsf{Det}_{\mathsf{FG}}$ formulas, there are equivalent automaton formulas in both $\mathsf{Det}_{\mathsf{Rabin}}$ and $\mathsf{Det}_{\mathsf{Streett}}$. Hence, it follows that both $\mathsf{Det}_{\mathsf{Rabin}}$ and $\mathsf{Det}_{\mathsf{Streett}}$ are closed under all Boolean operations. Moreover, for every formula of $\mathsf{Det}_{\mathsf{Rabin}}$, there is an equivalent one in $\mathsf{Det}_{\mathsf{Streett}}$, and vice versa.*

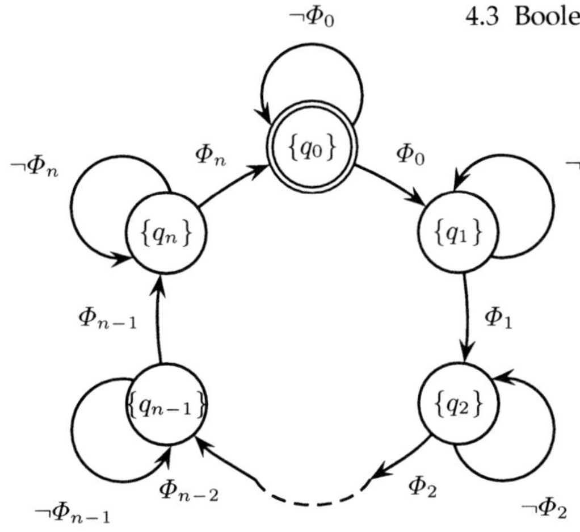

Fig. 4.3. Automaton for the conjunction of finitely many fairness properties

Proof. The proof runs on the same lines as the proof of Theorem 4.13, where we use the following generalizations of the rules of Lemma 4.11:

$$\bigwedge_{j=0}^{n} \mathsf{GF}\Phi_j = \mathcal{A}_\exists \left(\begin{array}{l} \{q_0, \ldots, q_n\}, \\ q_0 \wedge \bigwedge_{j=1}^{n} \neg q_j, \\ [\mathsf{X}q_0 = (q_n \wedge \Phi_n) \vee (q_0 \wedge \neg\Phi_0)] \wedge \\ \bigwedge_{j=1}^{n} [\mathsf{X}q_j = (q_{j-1} \wedge \Phi_{j-1}) \vee (q_j \wedge \neg\Phi_j)], \\ \mathsf{GF}q_0 \end{array} \right)$$

$$\bigvee_{j=0}^{n} \mathsf{FG}\Phi_j = \mathcal{A}_\exists \left(\begin{array}{l} \{q_0, \ldots, q_n\}, \\ q_0 \wedge \bigwedge_{j=1}^{n} \neg q_j, \\ [\mathsf{X}q_0 = (q_n \wedge \neg\Phi_n) \vee (q_0 \wedge \Phi_0)] \wedge \\ \bigwedge_{j=1}^{n} [\mathsf{X}q_j = (q_{j-1} \wedge \neg\Phi_{j-1}) \vee (q_j \wedge \Phi_j)], \\ \mathsf{FG}\neg q_0 \end{array} \right)$$

Both formulas are dual to each other. To see how they are constructed, consider Figure 4.3. Figure 4.3 shows the state transition diagram of the automaton formula that we use to replace $\bigwedge_{j=0}^{n} \mathsf{GF}\Phi_j$. The automaton has $n+1$ states, hence the state variables form a 'one-hot' encoding, i.e., each state is a singleton set that consists of exactly one state variable. In state $\{q_i\}$ we wait for Φ_i, and remain in $\{q_i\}$ as long as this event did not occur. Hence, if $\{q_0\}$ (or any other $\{q_i\}$) holds infinitely often, each of the events Φ_i must occur infinitely often. □

Hence, we have already seen that all of the mentioned automaton classes are closed under conjunction and disjunction. Moreover, $\mathsf{Det}_{\mathsf{Prefix1}}$, $\mathsf{Det}_{\mathsf{Prefix2}}$, $\mathsf{Det}_{\mathsf{Rabin}}$, and $\mathsf{Det}_{\mathsf{Streett}}$, are closed under all Boolean combination (including the negation), while the complements of $\mathsf{Det}_{\mathsf{G}}$, $\mathsf{Det}_{\mathsf{F}}$, $\mathsf{Det}_{\mathsf{GF}}$, and $\mathsf{Det}_{\mathsf{FG}}$ are exactly the classes $\mathsf{Det}_{\mathsf{F}}$, $\mathsf{Det}_{\mathsf{G}}$, $\mathsf{Det}_{\mathsf{FG}}$, and $\mathsf{Det}_{\mathsf{GF}}$, respectively. Hence, we already know all about the Boolean combinations of the deterministic automaton classes. Complementing nondeterministic automata is difficult; we will reduce this problem by determinization of the automata.

4.4 Converting Automaton Classes

Beneath the computation of conjunctions and disjunctions of automata of the same class, and complements of deterministic automata, we can already transform deterministic Streett and Rabin automata into each other, and also deterministic prefix automata of different kinds into each other. Hence, we already know that $\mathsf{Det}_{\mathsf{Prefix1}} \approx \mathsf{Det}_{\mathsf{Prefix2}}$, $\mathsf{Det}_{\mathsf{Rabin}} \approx \mathsf{Det}_{\mathsf{Streett}}$, $\mathsf{NDet}_{\mathsf{Prefix1}} \approx \mathsf{NDet}_{\mathsf{Prefix2}}$ and $\mathsf{NDet}_{\mathsf{Rabin}} \approx \mathsf{NDet}_{\mathsf{Streett}}$ hold. We consider now the conversion of other types of ω-automata into each other. First of all, note that every Büchi automaton is already a special Streett and also a special Rabin automaton. Hence, we have $\mathsf{Det}_{\mathsf{GF}} \precapprox \mathsf{Det}_{\mathsf{Streett}}$, $\mathsf{Det}_{\mathsf{GF}} \precapprox \mathsf{Det}_{\mathsf{Rabin}}$, $\mathsf{NDet}_{\mathsf{GF}} \precapprox \mathsf{NDet}_{\mathsf{Streett}}$ and $\mathsf{NDet}_{\mathsf{GF}} \precapprox \mathsf{NDet}_{\mathsf{Rabin}}$.

The transformation of a Büchi automaton with acceptance condition condition $\mathsf{GF}\varphi$ to an equivalent Muller automaton is straightforward: while the Büchi automaton's acceptance condition only requires that the situations represented by the propositional part φ are satisfied infinitely often, the Muller automaton's acceptance condition requires that the situations satisfied infinitely often is *exactly* one of its accepting sets. To obtain a Muller automaton, we may therefore use the state transition system of the Büchi automaton and replace its acceptance condition with those formulas φ_i such that $\varphi \wedge \varphi_i$ is satisfiable. Recall here the relationship between sets and propositional formulas, and note that there are only finitely many different propositional formulas over finitely many variables.

Hence, we also have $\mathsf{Det}_{\mathsf{GF}} \precapprox \mathsf{Det}_{\mathsf{Muller}}$ and $\mathsf{NDet}_{\mathsf{GF}} \precapprox \mathsf{NDet}_{\mathsf{Muller}}$. In general, it is however not possible to transform Büchi automata to safety, liveness, persistence or prefix automata. We will prove in Theorems 4.19 and 4.33 that these are strictly less expressive, and mention in Section 4.6 procedures to decide whether such reductions are possible. The following lemma shows how the basic acceptance conditions can be reduced to each other, if possible (most automata are weak and terminal Büchi automata, see page 370).

Lemma 4.16 (Transforming Acceptance Conditions). *Given a propositional formula φ over the variables V_Σ. Then, the following equations are valid:*

Reducing G:

1. $\mathsf{G}\varphi = \mathcal{A}_\exists\left(\{q\}, q, \varphi \wedge q \wedge \mathsf{X}q, \mathsf{F}q\right)$
2. $\mathsf{G}\varphi = \mathcal{A}_\exists\left(\{q\}, q, \mathsf{X}q \leftrightarrow q \wedge \varphi, \mathsf{FG}q\right)$
3. $\mathsf{G}\varphi = \mathcal{A}_\exists\left(\{q\}, q, \mathsf{X}q \leftrightarrow q \wedge \varphi, \mathsf{GF}q\right)$

Reducing F:

1. $\mathsf{F}\varphi$ *can not be reduced to an existential automaton with* G *acceptance*
2. $\mathsf{F}\varphi = \mathcal{A}_\exists\left(\{q\}, \neg q, \mathsf{X}q \leftrightarrow q \vee \varphi, \mathsf{FG}q\right)$
3. $\mathsf{F}\varphi = \mathcal{A}_\exists\left(\{q\}, \neg q, \mathsf{X}q \leftrightarrow q \vee \varphi, \mathsf{GF}q\right)$

Reducing FG*:*

1. $\mathsf{FG}\varphi$ *can not be reduced to an existential automaton with* G *acceptance*
2. $\mathsf{FG}\varphi = \mathcal{A}_\exists\left(\{q\}, \neg q, q \rightarrow \varphi \wedge \mathsf{X}q, \mathsf{F}q\right)$
3. $$\mathsf{FG}\varphi = \mathcal{A}_\exists\left(\begin{array}{l}\{p,q\},\\ \neg p \wedge \neg q,\\ \left[\begin{array}{l}(p \rightarrow \mathsf{X}p) \wedge (\mathsf{X}p \rightarrow p \vee \neg q)\wedge\\ (\mathsf{X}q \leftrightarrow (p \wedge \neg q \wedge \neg\varphi) \vee (p \wedge q))\end{array}\right],\\ \mathsf{G}\neg q \wedge \mathsf{F}p\end{array}\right)$$
4. $$\mathsf{FG}\varphi = \mathcal{A}_\exists\left(\begin{array}{l}\{p,q\},\\ \neg p \wedge \neg q,\\ \left[\begin{array}{l}(p \rightarrow \mathsf{X}p) \wedge (\mathsf{X}p \rightarrow p \vee \neg q)\wedge\\ (\mathsf{X}q \leftrightarrow (p \wedge \neg q \wedge \neg\varphi) \vee (p \wedge q))\end{array}\right],\\ \mathsf{GF}[p \wedge \neg q]\end{array}\right)$$

Reducing GF*:*

1. $\mathsf{GF}\varphi$ *can not be reduced to an existential automaton with* G *acceptance*
2. $\mathsf{GF}\varphi$ *can not be reduced to an existential automaton with* F *acceptance*
3. $\mathsf{GF}\varphi$ *can not be reduced to an existential automaton with* FG *acceptance*

Proof. The impossibilities of expressiveness listed in the above lemma are proved later on. The above facts are easily seen to be true when we consider the state transition diagrams of the automata. For the equation $\mathsf{G}\varphi = \mathcal{A}_\exists\left(\{q\}, q, \varphi \wedge q \wedge \mathsf{X}q, \mathsf{F}q\right)$, consider the automaton below:

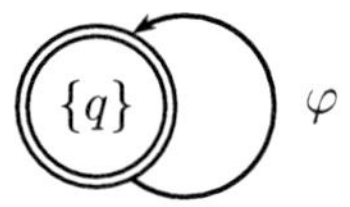

Clearly, the automaton has only an infinite run when φ holds all the time. In this case, clearly the only state is reached, hence, the automaton formula is equivalent to $\mathsf{G}\varphi$. For the reduction of G to FG and GF, we could use the same automaton with the acceptance condition $\mathsf{FG}q$ and $\mathsf{GF}q$, respectively. However, using the other automaton formulas given in the lemma, we also prove that there are $\mathsf{Det}_{\mathsf{FG}}$ and $\mathsf{Det}_{\mathsf{GF}}$ automata that can be used to replace a safety property. Both automata have the following state transition diagram:

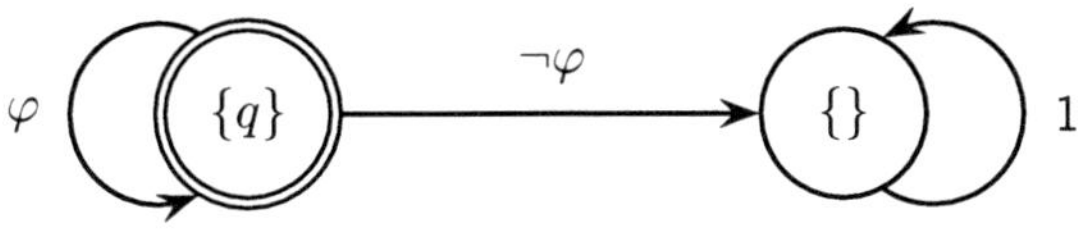

It is easily seen that this automaton is deterministic and that it remains in its initial state as long as φ is satisfied. If there is however a point of time, where φ is not satisfied, then the automaton switches to state $\{\}$, where it is then caught for ever. Therefore, $\mathsf{G}\varphi$ holds if and only if the automaton never reaches state $\{\}$, which means that we are always in state $\{q\}$, which is in turn equivalent to being infinitely often in state $\{q\}$ and also to being always in $\{q\}$ from a certain point on. The reduction of liveness properties to persistence and fairness properties follows from the reduction of safety properties to fairness and persistence properties, respectively, by negation of both sides of the equation.

For the reduction of $\mathsf{FG}\varphi$ to NDet_F we have used the following transition relation:

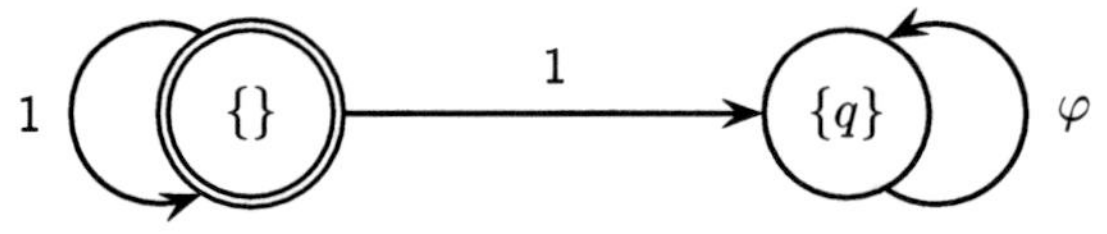

The automaton has for every word at least one run, in particular the one that remains for ever in the initial state. The acceptance condition does not however allow this, and requires that at least once the state $\{q\}$ must be reached. It is easily seen that once this state has been reached, every infinite run must remain in this state and must read φ from that point of time on. Hence, the automaton is equivalent to $\mathsf{FG}\varphi$. We will see later that $\mathsf{FG}\varphi$ can not be reduced to a NDet_F automaton with a total transition relation.

For the reduction of $\mathsf{FG}\varphi$ to $\mathsf{NDet}_\mathsf{Prefix}$ and $\mathsf{NDet}_\mathsf{GF}$ we have used the following (total) transition relation:

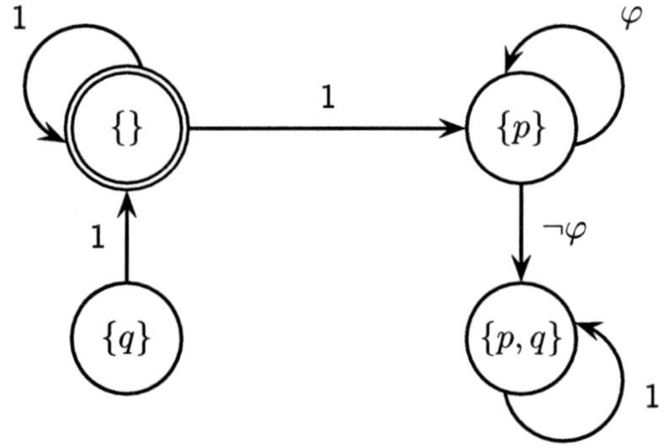

First consider the Prefix automaton that is given in the above lemma for $\mathsf{FG}\varphi$. Its acceptance condition requires that every path to be accepted must exclusively run through the states $\{\}$ and $\{p\}$, and must visit at least once one of the states $\{p\}$ or $\{p,q\}$. Clearly, this is only achieved by runs that remain for a finite time in state $\{\}$ and switch then to state $\{p\}$. All other runs are not accepted. It is easily seen that these runs do belong to input words that satisfy after some finite point of time the propositional formula φ.

The Büchi automaton requires that the state $\{p\}$ must be visited infinitely often. As there is no transition from state $\{p,q\}$ back to $\{p\}$, this implies that we must never reach state $\{p, q\}$, and therefore must remain in state $\{p\}$ after some point of time. Hence, this is also equivalent to the acceptance condition of the prefix automaton. □

Hence, we can easily convert Rabin and Streett automata to equivalent nondeterministic Büchi automata. All we have to do is to replace the persistence conditions by nondeterministic Büchi automata as shown above and to use the combination laws of the previous section to eliminate the conjunctions and disjunctions. As Büchi automata are special cases of Rabin and Streett automata, we therefore have $\mathsf{NDet}_{\mathsf{GF}} \approx \mathsf{NDet}_{\mathsf{Rabin}} \approx \mathsf{NDet}_{\mathsf{Streett}}$. Further facts on expressiveness are given in the following theorem:

Theorem 4.17 (Hierarchy of ω-Automata (I)). *By Lemma 4.11 and Lemma 4.16, the following expressiveness results hold:*

- $\mathsf{Det}_{\mathsf{Prefix1}} \approx \mathsf{Det}_{\mathsf{Prefix2}} \precapprox \mathsf{Det}_{\mathsf{Rabin}} \approx \mathsf{Det}_{\mathsf{Streett}}$
- $\mathsf{NDet}_{\mathsf{G}} \precapprox \mathsf{NDet}_{\mathsf{F}} \approx \mathsf{NDet}_{\mathsf{Prefix}} \approx \mathsf{NDet}_{\mathsf{FG}} \precapprox \mathsf{NDet}_{\mathsf{GF}} \approx \mathsf{NDet}_{\mathsf{Rabin}} \approx \mathsf{NDet}_{\mathsf{Streett}}$

According to Lemma 4.16, we can replace every safety and liveness condition by $\mathsf{NDet}_{\mathsf{FG}}$ and $\mathsf{NDet}_{\mathsf{GF}}$ automata. Hence, this transforms prefix automata to equivalent Rabin or Streett automata, where the determinism is not disturbed. The equal expressiveness between $\mathsf{Det}_{\mathsf{Prefix1}} \approx \mathsf{Det}_{\mathsf{Prefix2}}$ and $\mathsf{Det}_{\mathsf{Rabin}} \approx \mathsf{Det}_{\mathsf{Streett}}$ has already been shown in the previous section.

The equivalence $\mathsf{NDet}_{\mathsf{F}} \approx \mathsf{NDet}_{\mathsf{FG}}$ immediately follows from the above lemma, since we can replace every formula $\mathsf{FG}\varphi$ by an equivalent automaton of $\mathsf{NDet}_{\mathsf{F}}$ and we can also replace every formula $\mathsf{F}\varphi$ by an equivalent automaton of $\mathsf{NDet}_{\mathsf{FG}}$.

Moreover, $\mathsf{NDet}_{\mathsf{F}} \precapprox \mathsf{NDet}_{\mathsf{Prefix}}$ is clear, since $\mathsf{F}\varphi$ is a special form of the Prefix acceptance condition. The converse follows when we replace all safety properties of a given prefix automaton of the first kind by an equivalent $\mathsf{NDet}_{\mathsf{F}}$ automaton according to the above lemma. Shifting out the transition relations according to Lemma 4.9, and combining disjunctions of the liveness properties yields in a nondeterministic ω-automaton with acceptance condition of the form $\bigwedge_{j=0}^{n} \mathsf{F}\Psi_j$. This is reduced to a $\mathsf{NDet}_{\mathsf{F}}$ automaton using watchdogs by the following rule:

$$\bigwedge_{j=0}^{n} \mathsf{F}\Psi_j = \mathcal{A}_{\exists}\left(\begin{array}{l}\{q_0, \ldots, q_n\}, \\ \bigwedge_{j=0}^{n} \neg q_j, \\ \bigwedge_{j=0}^{n} \mathsf{X}q_j \leftrightarrow q_i \vee \Phi_j, \\ \mathsf{F} \bigwedge_{j=0}^{n} q_j\end{array}\right)$$

However, we have not yet a connection between $\mathsf{NDet}_{\mathsf{Rabin}}$ and $\mathsf{Det}_{\mathsf{Rabin}}$. We will see later on that these classes are the same. However, this is not the case for Büchi automata. Note that by Lemma 4.16, the formula $\mathsf{FG}a$ can be expressed as an equivalent Büchi automaton and also as an equivalent Prefix automaton. Also note that both automata are nondeterministic. We will now prove that it is not possible to find for $\mathsf{FG}a$ an equivalent deterministic Büchi automaton. This has some consequences for the strictness of some expressiveness results and the determinization of ω-automata that we will discuss in the next section.

Lemma 4.18 (Complements of Deterministic Büchi Automata). *Given a propositional formula φ over the variables V_Σ. There is no formula in* $\mathsf{Det}_{\mathsf{GF}}$ *that is equivalent to* $\mathsf{FG}\varphi$*. Consequently, there is no formula in* $\mathsf{Det}_{\mathsf{FG}}$ *that is equivalent to* $\mathsf{GF}\varphi$ *and hence, both* $\mathsf{Det}_{\mathsf{GF}}$ *and* $\mathsf{Det}_{\mathsf{FG}}$ *are not closed under complement.*

Proof. We give a proof by contradiction that can be found in many texts on ω-automata e.g. [312, 486]. It is sufficient to prove the lemma for propositional variables φ. Hence, assume that $a \in V_\Sigma$ is given and that $\mathfrak{A} := \mathcal{A}_\exists(Q, \Phi_\mathcal{I}, \Phi_\mathcal{R}, \mathsf{GF}\Phi_\mathcal{F})$ would be a deterministic Büchi automaton formula equivalent to $\mathsf{FG}a$. We first consider the word $\alpha_0 := a^\omega$. Clearly, this word satisfies $\mathsf{FG}a$, and therefore it must be accepted by the automaton $\mathfrak{A}$. Thus, the uniquely determined run ξ_0 must infinitely often satisfy $\Phi_\mathcal{F}$. Let t_0 be the first point of time, where ξ_0 satisfies $\Phi_\mathcal{F}$. We then construct the word α_1 as $\alpha_1^{(t)} := a$ if $t \neq t_0$, and $\alpha_1^{(t_0)} := \neg a$.

Clearly, α_1 also satisfies $\mathsf{FG}a$, and therefore, α_1 also has an accepting run ξ_1 through the automaton $\mathfrak{A}$, that must also satisfy infinitely often $\Phi_\mathcal{F}$. Note that by construction, we have $\xi_0^{(t)} = \xi_1^{(t)}$ for $t \leq t_0$, so that t_0 is still the first point of time, where ξ_1 satisfies $\Phi_\mathcal{F}$. Let now be t_1 the first point of time after t_0, where ξ_1 satisfies $\Phi_\mathcal{F}$. We then construct the word α_2 as $\alpha_1^{(t)} := a$ if $t \notin \{t_0, t_1\}$, and $\alpha_1^{(t)} := \neg a$ if $t \in \{t_0, t_1\}$.

We continue the construction, obtaining words α_i, corresponding runs ξ_i and points of time t_i. α_i obtaining the form $\alpha_i^{(t)} := a$ if $t \notin \{t_0, \ldots, t_i\}$, and $\alpha_i^{(t)} := \neg a$ if $t \in \{t_0, \ldots, t_i\}$. Its run ξ_i satisfies $\Phi_\mathcal{F}$ at the points $\{t_0, \ldots, t_i\}$ (and infinitely often afterwards).

We consider now the sets of states $\mathcal{S}_i := \{\xi_i^{(t_0)}, \ldots, \xi_i^{(t_i)}\}$. As $\mathfrak{A}$ only has a finite number of states, it follows that there is a least number i, such that two states $\xi_i^{(t_j)}$ and $\xi_i^{(t_k)}$ are the same. But then, a word is accepted where infinitely often $\neg a$ occurs (see Figure 4.4). □

Therefore, neither $\mathsf{Det}_{\mathsf{GF}}$ nor $\mathsf{Det}_{\mathsf{FG}}$ is closed under complement, as especially $\mathsf{GF}a \in \mathsf{Det}_{\mathsf{GF}}$ and $\mathsf{FG}a \in \mathsf{Det}_{\mathsf{FG}}$ have no complement in the corresponding class. However, the class $\mathsf{NDet}_{\mathsf{GF}}$ is closed under complement, which is however difficult to prove. Büchi's original construction for this result requires difficult combinatorial facts (Ramsey's theorem [422]), but better constructions are known today. For example, we can obtain an optimal procedure by determinization, which will be proved on page 236.

The above lemma has some consequences for the closure under complement and the determinization of some other types of ω-automata. These results are given in the following theorem that is a refinement of the results we have already proved in Theorem 4.17.

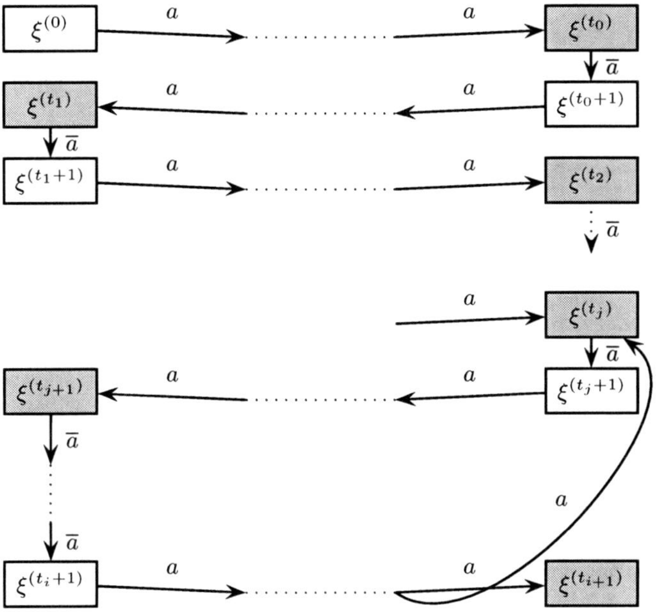

Fig. 4.4. Structure $\mathcal{K}_i$ for the proof of Lemma 4.18

Theorem 4.19 (Hierarchy of ω-Automata (II)). *The following expressiveness results hold for deterministic ω-automata:*

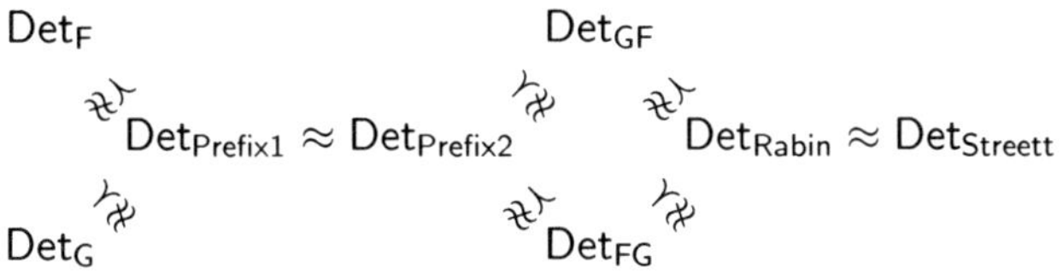

Proof. $\mathsf{Det_F} \precnapprox \mathsf{Det_{Prefix}}$ and $\mathsf{Det_G} \precnapprox \mathsf{Det_{Prefix}}$ do trivially hold, since $\mathsf{Det_F}$ and $\mathsf{Det_G}$ automata are only special forms of $\mathsf{Det_{Prefix}}$ automata. Similarly, $\mathsf{Det_{GF}} \precnapprox \mathsf{Det_{Rabin}}$ and $\mathsf{Det_{FG}} \precnapprox \mathsf{Det_{Rabin}}$ hold since $\mathsf{Det_{GF}}$ and $\mathsf{Det_{FG}}$ automata are special forms of $\mathsf{Det_{Rabin}}$ automata. $\mathsf{Det_{Prefix}} \precnapprox \mathsf{Det_{GF}}$ and $\mathsf{Det_{Prefix}} \precnapprox \mathsf{Det_{FG}}$ hold by the equations of Lemma 4.16. The equal expressiveness of $\mathsf{Det_{Rabin}} \approx \mathsf{Det_{Streett}}$ and $\mathsf{Det_{Prefix1}} \approx \mathsf{Det_{Prefix2}}$ has already been proved.

It remains to prove the strictness of the mentioned relations. The strictness of $\mathsf{Det_{Prefix}} \precnapprox \mathsf{Det_{FG}}$ is seen as follows: Assume $\mathsf{Det_{Prefix}} \approx \mathsf{Det_{FG}}$ would hold. In particular, there would then be an automaton in $\mathsf{Det_{Prefix}}$ that would be equivalent to $\mathsf{FG}a$. As each automaton of $\mathsf{Det_{Prefix}}$ can be transformed to an equivalent automaton of $\mathsf{Det}_{\mathsf{GF}}$ (cf. Lemma 4.16), this would contradict Lemma 4.18. Hence, $\mathsf{Det}_{\mathsf{Prefix}} \precnapprox \mathsf{Det}_{\mathsf{FG}}$ holds.

The strictness of $\mathsf{Det}_{\mathsf{Prefix}} \precnapprox \mathsf{Det}_{\mathsf{GF}}$ is seen as follows: Assume $\mathsf{Det}_{\mathsf{Prefix}} \approx \mathsf{Det}_{\mathsf{GF}}$ would hold. As $\mathsf{Det}_{\mathsf{Prefix}}$ is closed under complement, this would imply that $\mathsf{Det}_{\mathsf{Prefix}} \approx \mathsf{Det}_{\mathsf{FG}}$. However, we have proved above that this is not the case. Hence, $\mathsf{Det}_{\mathsf{Prefix}} \precnapprox \mathsf{Det}_{\mathsf{GF}}$ holds.

The strictness of $\mathsf{Det}_{\mathsf{FG}} \precnapprox \mathsf{Det}_{\mathsf{Rabin}}$ is seen as follows: Assume $\mathsf{Det}_{\mathsf{FG}} \approx \mathsf{Det}_{\mathsf{Rabin}}$ would hold. As in particular $\mathsf{GF}a \in \mathsf{Det}_{\mathsf{Rabin}}$ holds, this immediately contradicts Lemma 4.18. Hence, we have $\mathsf{Det}_{\mathsf{FG}} \precnapprox \mathsf{Det}_{\mathsf{Rabin}}$. The strictness of $\mathsf{Det}_{\mathsf{GF}} \precnapprox \mathsf{Det}_{\mathsf{Rabin}}$ follows immediately by Lemma 4.18, since $\mathsf{FG}a$ is a special deterministic Rabin automaton.

We will prove in Theorem 4.25 that $\mathsf{Det}_{\mathsf{G}} \approx \mathsf{NDet}_{\mathsf{G}}$ holds. Hence, if $\mathsf{Det}_{\mathsf{G}} \approx \mathsf{Det}_{\mathsf{Prefix}}$ would hold, it would follow that $\mathsf{NDet}_{\mathsf{G}} \approx \mathsf{NDet}_{\mathsf{Prefix}}$, since we could replace the acceptance condition of a prefix automaton by a $\mathsf{Det}_{\mathsf{G}}$ automaton. Thus, it would follow that $\mathsf{Det}_{\mathsf{G}} \approx \mathsf{NDet}_{\mathsf{Prefix}}$ would hold, and we see by Theorem 4.17 that $\mathsf{Det}_{\mathsf{G}} \approx \mathsf{NDet}_{\mathsf{FG}}$ would also follow. Because of this, there would be an automaton in $\mathsf{Det}_{\mathsf{G}}$ that is equivalent to $\mathsf{FG}a$ for a variable $a \in V_{\Sigma}$. But as we have already seen that $\mathsf{Det}_{\mathsf{G}} \precnapprox \mathsf{Det}_{\mathsf{GF}}$ holds, this would again contradict Lemma 4.18. Hence, we have $\mathsf{Det}_{\mathsf{G}} \precnapprox \mathsf{Det}_{\mathsf{Prefix}}$.

Finally, if $\mathsf{Det}_{\mathsf{F}} \approx \mathsf{Det}_{\mathsf{Prefix}}$ holds, we could conclude by the Boolean closure of $\mathsf{Det}_{\mathsf{Prefix}}$ that $\mathsf{Det}_{\mathsf{F}} \approx \mathsf{Det}_{\mathsf{G}} \approx \mathsf{Det}_{\mathsf{Prefix}}$ would hold. However, we have seen above that $\mathsf{Det}_{\mathsf{G}} \precnapprox \mathsf{Det}_{\mathsf{Prefix}}$ holds, and therefore $\mathsf{Det}_{\mathsf{F}} \precnapprox \mathsf{Det}_{\mathsf{Prefix}}$ must also hold. □

The above theorem lists all expressiveness results for the deterministic versions of ω-automata. We have moreover seen some expressiveness results of nondeterministic ω-automata in Theorem 4.17. To relate the expressiveness of deterministic and nondeterministic automata, we have to consider the determinization of ω-automata in the next section.

We conclude this section with the final remark that Rabin and Streett automata are powerful enough to express all acceptance conditions of our language $\mathcal{L}_\omega$ as given in Definition 4.6 on page 191. According to that definition, the acceptance condition $\Phi_{\mathcal{F}}$ of an automaton formula $\mathcal{A}_\exists(Q, \Phi_{\mathcal{I}}, \Phi_{\mathcal{R}}, \Phi_{\mathcal{F}})$ obeys the grammar rules of the nonterminal A of Definition 4.6. Hence, we can use arbitrary combinations of Boolean operators and the temporal operators G and F, together with automaton formulas. Using arbitrary combinations of Boolean operators and the temporal operators G and F as acceptance conditions, the obtained automaton formulas are as expressive as Rabin or Streett automata.

Theorem 4.20 (Completeness of Rabin- and Streett Conditions). *Every deterministic automaton formula whose acceptance condition is derived from the grammar below can be reduced to equivalent* $\mathsf{Det}_{\mathsf{Rabin}}$ *and* $\mathsf{Det}_{\mathsf{Streett}}$ *automata:*

$$I ::= V_{\Sigma} \mid \neg I \mid I \wedge I \mid I \vee I$$
$$T ::= \mathsf{G}I \mid \mathsf{F}I \mid \neg T \mid T \wedge T \mid T \vee T \mid \mathsf{G}T \mid \mathsf{F}T$$

The proof is deferred to the temporal logic chapter, where we prove that every linear time temporal logic formula (which is more than the above subset) can be translated to $\mathsf{Det}_{\mathsf{Rabin}}$ and $\mathsf{Det}_{\mathsf{Streett}}$ automata.

For the understanding of the above theorem, we note the following: we call a formula φ prefix-closed when $\mathsf{G}(\varphi \rightarrow \overleftarrow{\mathsf{G}}\varphi)$ holds, and suffix-closed when $\mathsf{G}(\varphi \rightarrow \mathsf{G}\varphi)$ holds. Hence, φ is prefix-closed iff φ holding somewhere in the future implies that it must hold from the initial point of time until that point. Similarly, if φ is suffix-closed, then its holds from a certain point of time to forever. Now, note the following:

	prefix-closed	suffix-closed
$\mathsf{G}\varphi$	no	yes
$\mathsf{F}\varphi$	yes	no
$\mathsf{FG}\varphi$	yes	yes
$\mathsf{GF}\varphi$	yes	yes

The sets of prefix-closed and suffix-closed formulas are furthermore closed under conjunction and disjunction. Therefore, we obtain the following:

- $\mathsf{G}\left(\bigwedge_{i=0}^{f} \mathsf{GF}\varphi_i \vee \mathsf{FG}\psi_i\right) = \bigwedge_{i=0}^{f} \mathsf{GF}\varphi_i \vee \mathsf{FG}\psi_i$
- $\mathsf{F}\left(\bigwedge_{i=0}^{f} \mathsf{GF}\varphi_i \vee \mathsf{FG}\psi_i\right) = \bigwedge_{i=0}^{f} \mathsf{GF}\varphi_i \vee \mathsf{FG}\psi_i$
- $\mathsf{G}\left(\bigvee_{i=0}^{f} \mathsf{GF}\varphi_i \wedge \mathsf{FG}\psi_i\right) = \bigvee_{i=0}^{f} \mathsf{GF}\varphi_i \wedge \mathsf{FG}\psi_i$
- $\mathsf{F}\left(\bigvee_{i=0}^{f} \mathsf{GF}\varphi_i \wedge \mathsf{FG}\psi_i\right) = \bigvee_{i=0}^{f} \mathsf{GF}\varphi_i \wedge \mathsf{FG}\psi_i$

Prefix-closedness and suffix-closedness are exploited by Etessami and Holzmann [185] for speeding up the verification of temporal properties.

4.5 Determinization and Complementation

Determinization and complementation of finite state automata are closely related to each other: By Lemma 4.9, it is simple to complement deterministic automata, as only the acceptance condition has to be negated. If the negated acceptance condition can itself be expressed as a deterministic automaton of the same class, we can easily derive an algorithm for complementation.

However, we have already seen that not all classes of ω-automata are closed under complement (see Lemma 4.18). In particular, we can not compute the complement of a nondeterministic Büchi automaton by determinizing it. Nevertheless, we will see in this section, that for every nondeterministic automaton class NDet_κ with $\kappa \in \{\mathsf{G}, \mathsf{F}, \mathsf{GF}, \mathsf{FG}, \mathsf{Prefix1}, \mathsf{Prefix2}, \mathsf{Rabin},$

Streett}, there is an equally expressive deterministic class. For this reason, we can always compute the complement by first computing an equivalent deterministic automaton (of possibly another class). Therefore, we consider in this section the determinization of ω-automata. To this end, we do not make use of the symbolic description of automaton formulas, and instead use the explicit representations.

4.5.1 The Rabin-Scott Subset Construction

It is well-known that nondeterministic automata on finite words can be made deterministic, i.e., for every nondeterministic automaton on finite words there is an equivalent deterministic one. Moreover, this deterministic counterpart can be effectively computed by the so-called subset construction that goes back to Rabin and Scott [421]. The basic idea of this construction is to simultaneously collect all possible runs of an input word, i.e., we begin with the set of all initial states, and consider which states can be reached when a certain input symbol is read. This defines a new set of states that is obtained by following the transitions from the initial states under the considered input. The procedure is applied as long as new states are obtained. Note that a state of the thereby computed semiautomaton is a set of states of the given transition system. Hence, there may be an exponential blow-up when we compute a corresponding deterministic automaton. The subset construction is formally defined as follows:

```
function RabinScott(Σ, S, I, R)
  front := {I};
  S̃ := {};
  R̃ := {};
  while front ≠ {} do
    S := selectfrom(front);
    S̃ := S̃ ∪ {S};
    front := front \ {S};
    for σ ∈ Σ do
      S' := suc_∃^{R_σ}(S);
      R̃ := R̃ ∪ {(S, σ, S')};
      if S' ∉ S̃ then front := front ∪ {S'} end
    end
  end;
  return (Σ, S̃, {I}, R̃)
end
```

Fig. 4.5. Rabin-Scott subset construction

Definition 4.21 (Rabin-Scott Subset Construction). *Given a semiautomaton* $\mathfrak{A} = (\Sigma, \mathcal{S}, \mathcal{I}, \mathcal{R})$, *we define for every* $\sigma \in \Sigma$ *the relation* $\mathcal{R}_\sigma := \{(s, s') \in \mathcal{S} \times \mathcal{S} \mid (s, \sigma, s') \in \mathcal{R}\}$. *Then, we define the corresponding semiautomaton* $\widetilde{\mathfrak{A}} = (\Sigma, 2^{\mathcal{S}}, \{\mathcal{I}\}, \widetilde{\mathcal{R}})$ *with the following transition relation:* $\widetilde{\mathcal{R}} := \{(S, \sigma, \mathsf{suc}_\exists^{\mathcal{R}_\sigma}(S)) \mid \sigma \in \Sigma \wedge S \subseteq \mathcal{S}\}$. $\widetilde{\mathfrak{A}}$ *may have* $2^{|\mathcal{S}|}$ *states which is the lower bound of the problem.*

By definition of $\widetilde{\mathcal{R}}$, it is easily seen that $\widetilde{\mathfrak{A}}$ is deterministic. The implementation given in Figure 4.5 is even a bit more efficient, since it only considers reachable states of $\widetilde{\mathfrak{A}}$.

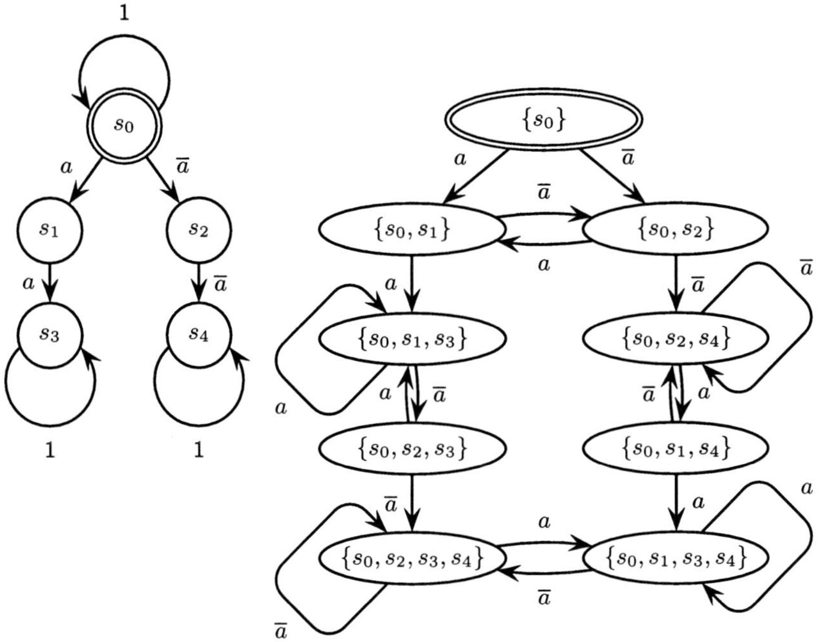

Fig. 4.6. Application of the subset construction

As an example, consider the semiautomata given in Figure 4.6. The computation starts with the set of initial states $S_0 := \mathcal{I} = \{s_0\}$. Next, we compute the successor states of S_0 under the inputs a and $\overline{a}$. We obtain $S_1 := \mathsf{suc}_\exists^{\mathcal{R}_a}(S_0) = \{s_0, s_1\}$ and $S_2 := \mathsf{suc}_\exists^{\mathcal{R}_{\overline{a}}}(S_0) = \{s_0, s_2\}$. For these two new states, we compute again the successors and obtain $S_3 := \mathsf{suc}_\exists^{\mathcal{R}_a}(S_1) = \{s_0, s_1, s_3\}$, $\mathsf{suc}_\exists^{\mathcal{R}_{\overline{a}}}(S_1) = S_2$, $\mathsf{suc}_\exists^{\mathcal{R}_a}(S_2) = S_1$, $S_4 := \mathsf{suc}_\exists^{\mathcal{R}_{\overline{a}}}(S_2) = \{s_0, s_2, s_4\}$. The computation of successor sets is repeated as long new states are generated. The final result is given on the right hand side of Figure 4.6.

It can be seen that the subset construction does not yield optimal results in terms of the minimality of the automata. For example, if we take $\{s_3, s_4\}$ as final states in Figure 4.6, and require with our acceptance condition that at least one of these states should be reached once, then it is easily seen that the given automaton accepts all words that contain two succeeding occurrences of a or $\overline{a}$. Therefore, it can be easily seen that the automaton that is obtained by the subset construction is rather wasteful (in fact, four states are sufficient for an automaton to accept this language).

A worst-case example that requires an exponential blow-up is given by the languages $\{a,b\}^*a\{a,b\}^n$ for constants $n \in \mathbb{N}$. It is simple to construct a nondeterministic automaton with $n+2$ states accepting this language, but every deterministic automaton requires $2^{O(n)}$ states.

Note that our definition of $\widetilde{\mathfrak{A}}$ does not include acceptance conditions. To answer the question of which acceptance conditions should be defined for the deterministic transition system, we must consider in more detail what is behind the subset construction. This is given in the next lemma.

Lemma 4.22 (Subset Construction). *Given a semiautomaton* $\mathfrak{A} = (\Sigma, \mathcal{S}, \mathcal{I}, \mathcal{R})$ *and the corresponding deterministic semiautomaton* $\widetilde{\mathfrak{A}} = (\Sigma, 2^{\mathcal{S}}, \{\mathcal{I}\}, \widetilde{\mathcal{R}})$ *as given in Definition 4.21. Then, for every infinite word* $\alpha : \mathbb{N} \to \Sigma$*, the following holds:*

1. $\mathsf{RUN}_{\widetilde{\mathfrak{A}}}(\alpha)$ *is a singleton set, i.e.,* $\widetilde{\mathfrak{A}}$ *is total and deterministic.*
2. *For every* $t_0 \in \mathbb{N}$*, the set* $\widetilde{\pi}^{(t_0)}$ *fulfills the following equation:*

$$s \in \widetilde{\pi}^{(t_0)} \Leftrightarrow \left(\begin{array}{l} \exists \xi : \mathbb{N} \to \mathcal{S}. \\ \quad [\xi^{(0)} \in \mathcal{I}] \wedge [\xi^{(t_0)} = s] \wedge \\ \quad [\forall t < t_0 . (\xi^{(t)}, \alpha^{(t)}, \xi^{(t+1)}) \in \mathcal{R}] \end{array}\right)$$

3. $\widetilde{\pi} \in \mathsf{RUN}_{\widetilde{\mathfrak{A}}}(\alpha) \wedge \xi \in \mathsf{RUN}_{\mathfrak{A}}(\alpha) \to \forall t \in \mathbb{N}.\xi^{(t)} \in \widetilde{\pi}^{(t)}$

Proof. The first proposition is trivial by the construction of $\widetilde{\mathfrak{A}}$: for every macro state $S \subseteq \mathcal{S}$, we define its successor state for every input $\sigma \in \Sigma$ as $\mathsf{suc}_{\exists}^{\mathcal{R}_\sigma}(S)$. Hence, every state of $\widetilde{\mathfrak{A}}$ has for each $\sigma \in \Sigma$ exactly one successor state, namely $\mathsf{suc}_{\exists}^{\mathcal{R}_\sigma}(S)$. Therefore, for every word α, there is exactly one run on $\mathfrak{A}$.

The second proposition is proved by induction on t_0. In the induction base, the proposition means that (note $\forall t < 0.\Phi$ holds for every Φ) $\widetilde{\pi}^{(0)} := \{s \in \mathcal{S} \mid \exists s' \in \mathcal{S}.s' \in \mathcal{I} \wedge [s' = s]\} = \{s \in \mathcal{S} \mid s \in \mathcal{I}\} = \mathcal{I}$. Clearly, this holds by construction of $\widetilde{\mathfrak{A}}$ since the run $\widetilde{\pi}$ must start in the initial state of $\widetilde{\mathfrak{A}}$ which is by construction the set $\mathcal{I}$. For the induction step, note first that by construction of $\widetilde{\mathcal{R}}$, it follows from $\widetilde{\pi}^{(t_0+1)} = \mathsf{suc}_{\exists}^{\mathcal{R}_a}(\widetilde{\pi}^{(t_0)})$ (with $a = \alpha^{(t_0)}$) that $\widetilde{\pi}^{(t_0+1)} = \{s' \in \mathcal{S} \mid \exists s \in \widetilde{\pi}^{(t_0)} \wedge (s, \alpha^{(t_0)}, s') \in \mathcal{R}\}$. By induction hypothesis we also know that $\widetilde{\pi}^{(t_0)}$ is exactly the set of states that can be reached by some finite sequence ξ from one of the initial states $\mathcal{I}$ of $\mathfrak{A}$ while reading the inputs from α. So, it is easily seen that the induction step holds since we can extend every such finite sequence of length t_0 by a transition leading from a state in $\widetilde{\pi}^{(t_0)}$ to a state in $\widetilde{\pi}^{(t_0+1)}$ to obtain a finite sequence of length t_0+1. Conversely, every sequence of length t_0+1 through $\mathfrak{A}$ over α can be split into a sequence of length t_0 so that it follows that $\xi^{(t_0)} \in \widetilde{\pi}^{(t_0)}$ and hence that $\xi^{(t_0+1)} \in \widetilde{\pi}^{(t_0+1)}$.

The third proposition is shown by induction on t. $\xi^{(0)} \in \widetilde{\pi}^{(0)}$ holds since $\widetilde{\pi}^{(0)} = \mathcal{I}$ and $\xi^{(0)} \in \mathcal{I}$ holds. In the induction step, we must prove $\xi^{(t+1)} \in \widetilde{\pi}^{(t+1)}$. By construction, we know that $\widetilde{\pi}^{(t+1)} = \mathsf{suc}_{\exists}^{\mathcal{R}_a}(\widetilde{\pi}^{(t)})$ with $a = \alpha^{(t)}$ and also that $(\xi^{(t)}, \xi^{(t+1)}) \in \mathcal{R}_a$. Hence, it follows by the induction hypothesis that $\xi^{(t+1)} \in \widetilde{\pi}^{(t+1)}$ holds. □

The main proposition of the lemma is the second one: it essentially says that in the states of the determinized transition system, we have collected the states that can be reached from one of the initial states by reading a finite word. The third proposition extends this to infinite runs: if there is an infinite run over the word, then the states of this run must belong pointwise to the states that form the run over the determinized transition system. Note, however that the converse does not hold, i.e., we can not pick arbitrarily states from the states $\widetilde{\pi}^{(t)}$ to construct a run through $\mathfrak{A}$.

4.5.2 Determinization of NDet_F

We now turn to the question how acceptance conditions have to be defined for $\widetilde{\mathfrak{A}}$ so that equivalent deterministic automata are obtained. For this reason, we consider first NDet_F automata. So, assume we have constructed $\widetilde{\mathfrak{A}}$ for the semiautomaton that corresponds with a NDet_F automaton with designated states $\mathcal{S}_\mathcal{F}$. A first attempt could be to define $\exists t.\widetilde{\pi}^{(t)} \cap \mathcal{S}_\mathcal{F} \neq \{\}$ as the acceptance condition. However, Figure 4.7 shows that this is not sufficient: If the semiautomaton given in the upper part of Figure 4.7 is extended to a NDet_F automaton with the set of designated states $\mathcal{S}_\mathcal{F} := \{s_1, s_2\}$, then the automaton accepts exactly the two words, namely a^ω and $\overline{a}^\omega$, i.e., it is equivalent to $\mathsf{G}a \vee \mathsf{G}\neg a$.

The semiautomaton that is obtained by the subset construction is given in the lower part of Figure 4.7. The acceptance condition $\exists t.\widetilde{\pi}^{(t)} \cap \mathcal{S}_\mathcal{F} \neq \{\}$ requires that at least one of the states $\{s_1\}$ or $\{s_2\}$ is traversed. Therefore, the automaton accepts all words and is therefore not equivalent to the given one. The problem is seen when we consider the word $\overline{a}a^\omega$ that should not be accepted by the deterministic automaton. Consider first what happens in the given automaton: Reading the first symbol $\overline{a}$ will first turn the automaton from the initial state s_0 to state s_2 such that a designated state is visited, but then there is no possibility to extend this run. Hence, there is no infinite run of $\overline{a}a^\omega$, and therefore this word is not accepted. Consider now what happens in the determinized semiautomaton: starting in state $\{s_0\}$, the automaton switches to state $\{s_2\}$ and then to state $\{\}$, where it finally remains. Hence, there is an infinite run over $\widetilde{\mathfrak{A}}$ for this word, and this run moreover satisfies our acceptance condition. Hence, the automaton erroneously accepts the word $\overline{a}a^\omega$.

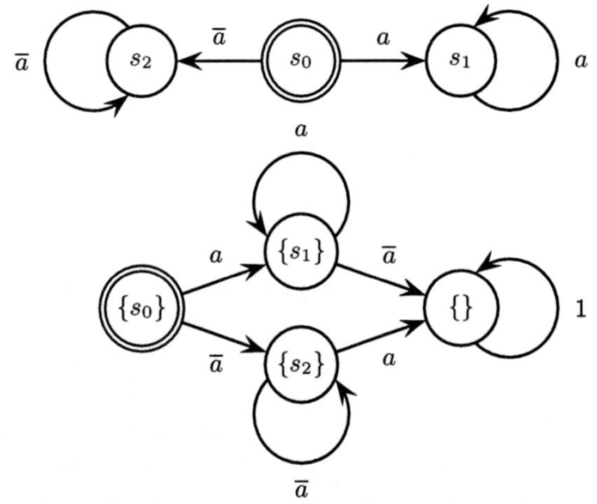

Fig. 4.7. A problem for the acceptance condition of the subset construction

This means that we must face the problem that there can be a finite input sequence of a given input word α that turns the automaton to one of its designated states, but then there is no possibility to extend this run to an infinite one for the considered input word. According to Lemma 4.22, this is exactly the case when the state $\{\}$ is reachable in $\widetilde{\mathfrak{A}}$. Hence, our next attempt is to add a further criterion that says that for the run through $\widetilde{\mathfrak{A}}$ there is also an infinite run through $\mathfrak{A}$. An attempt to do this would be to add the safety condition $\forall t.\widetilde{\pi}^{(t)} \neq \{\}$, but the example in Figure 4.8 shows that even this does not work.

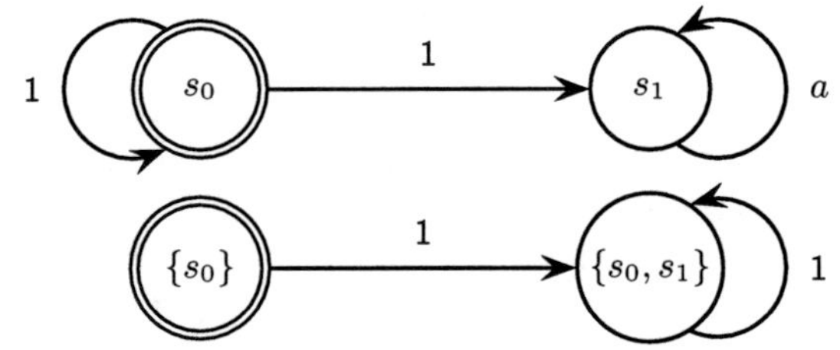

Fig. 4.8. Another problem for the acceptance condition of the subset construction

The upper half of Figure 4.8 shows the transition diagram of an automaton with the acceptance condition that the state s_1 must be visited at least once. We have used this automaton already in the proof of Lemma 4.16, and showed there that it is equivalent to the formula $\mathsf{FG}a$. It is however easily seen that the 'determinized' automaton given in the lower part of Figure 4.8 accepts every word. The problem is again that there are runs over the original automaton that lead to the designated state s_1, but these runs can not be extended to infinite runs. Note however, that every word has a run in both automata given in Figure 4.8.

Hence, it seems at this point that there is no simple way to define an appropriate acceptance condition such that $\mathsf{NDet_F}$ automata could be reduced to $\mathsf{Det_F}$ with the subset construction. One might think that we have to use another algorithm, but we will prove later that both classes are in fact different, and hence there is no such algorithm. However, as all problems we mentioned are due to the fact that runs leading to the designated states could not be extended to infinite ones, it is natural to consider the restriction to $\mathsf{NDet_F}$ automata that have a total transition relation. In these automata, every word has an infinite run, and therefore, the mentioned problems can not occur. We can easily prove the following theorem:

Theorem 4.23 (Subset Construction for $\mathsf{NDet_F^{total}}$). *Given a semiautomaton $\mathfrak{A} = (\Sigma, \mathcal{S}, \mathcal{I}, \mathcal{R})$ with a total transition relation $\mathcal{R}$, and the corresponding deterministic semiautomaton $\widetilde{\mathfrak{A}} = (\Sigma, 2^{\mathcal{S}}, \{\mathcal{I}\}, \widetilde{\mathcal{R}})$. Let $\mathcal{S}_\mathcal{F} \subseteq \mathcal{S}$ be a set of designated states. Then, for every infinite word $\alpha : \mathbb{N} \to \Sigma$, the following are equivalent:*

- $\exists \xi \in \mathsf{RUN}_\mathfrak{A}(\alpha).\ \exists t \in \mathbb{N}.\ \xi^{(t)} \in \mathcal{S}_\mathcal{F}$
- $\exists \widetilde{\pi} \in \mathsf{RUN}_{\widetilde{\mathfrak{A}}}(\alpha).\ \exists t \in \mathbb{N}.\ \widetilde{\pi}^{(t)} \cap \mathcal{S}_\mathcal{F} \neq \{\}$

Hence, if $\mathsf{NDet_F^{total}}$ denotes the subclass of $\mathsf{NDet_F}$ with total transition relations, then we have $\mathsf{Det_F} \approx \mathsf{NDet_F^{total}}$.

Proof. The equivalence is split into two implications:

[$\Rightarrow$:] Given $\xi \in \mathsf{RUN}_\mathfrak{A}(\alpha)$ and $t_0 \in \mathbb{N}$ with $\xi^{(t_0)} \in \mathcal{S}_\mathcal{F}$. By the previous lemma, we have $\xi^{(t)} \in \widetilde{\pi}^{(t)}$ (for every $t \in \mathbb{N}$) for the unique run $\widetilde{\pi} \in \mathsf{RUN}_{\widetilde{\mathfrak{A}}}(\alpha)$. In particular, it follows that $\widetilde{\pi}^{(t_0)} \cap \mathcal{S}_\mathcal{F} \neq \{\}$.

[$\Leftarrow$:] Assume $\widetilde{\pi} \in \mathsf{RUN}_{\widetilde{\mathfrak{A}}}(\alpha)$ and for some $t_0 \in \mathbb{N}$, we have $\widetilde{\pi}^{(t_0)} \cap \mathcal{S}_\mathcal{F} \neq \{\}$. This means that there is a state $s \in \widetilde{\pi}^{(t_0)} \cap \mathcal{S}_\mathcal{F}$ that is the end of a finite run over α through $\mathfrak{A}$, i.e., we have ξ with $\xi^{(0)} \in \mathcal{I}$, $\xi^{(t_0)} = s$, and $\forall t < t_0.(\xi^{(t)}, \alpha^{(t)}, \xi^{(t+1)}) \in \mathcal{R}$. As $\mathcal{R}$ is total, this finite run ξ can be extended to an infinite one over α through $\mathfrak{A}$. So, the proposition holds.

□

It was shown in 1970 [491] by Trachtenbrot et. al. that $\mathsf{NDet_F}$ is more powerful than $\mathsf{Det_F}$ when the transition relation is allowed to be partial. In particular, we have already seen in Theorem 4.17 that $\mathsf{NDet_F} \approx \mathsf{NDet_{FG}}$ holds, which is also shown in [491]. In the same year, Hossley showed in [252] that things are different when the transition relation must be total, so that the above theorem was obtained.

4.5.3 Determinization of $\mathsf{NDet_G}$

In this section, we show how the Rabin-Scott subset construction can be used for the determinization of $\mathsf{NDet_G}$. To see how this can be achieved, simply note that a run of an $\mathsf{NDet_G}$ automaton with admissible states $\mathcal{S_F}$ is accepted if and only if it traverses exclusively states that belong to $\mathcal{S_F}$. We can easily establish this by removing all states of the automaton that do not belong to $\mathcal{S_F}$. Clearly, the set of accepting runs does not thereby change, even if we remove the acceptance condition, since the latter now becomes trivial. Instead, it is now sufficient to demand that a run must exist for an input word. It is easily seen that if a word has no run, then the state $\{\}$ belongs to the determinized transition system $\widetilde{\mathfrak{A}}$ and the word will bring $\widetilde{\mathfrak{A}}$ to this state (where it would remain). Hence, it is natural to use the acceptance condition $\forall t.\widetilde{\pi}^{(t)} \neq \{\}$. The next theorem states that this does in fact work.

Lemma 4.24 (Subset Construction for $\mathsf{NDet_G}$). *Given a semiautomaton $\mathfrak{A} = (\Sigma, \mathcal{S}, \mathcal{I}, \mathcal{R})$ and a set of admissible states $\mathcal{S_F} \subseteq \mathcal{S}$. Let $\widetilde{\mathfrak{A}}_1 = (\Sigma, 2^{\mathcal{S}}, \{\mathcal{I}\}, \widetilde{\mathcal{R}})$ be the result of the application of the subset construction as given in Definition 4.21 to the restricted transition system $\mathfrak{A}_1 := (\Sigma, \mathcal{S_F}, \mathcal{I} \cap \mathcal{S_F}, \mathcal{R} \cap (\mathcal{S_F} \times \mathcal{S_F}))$. Then, for every infinite word $\alpha : \mathbb{N} \to \Sigma$, the following holds:*

1. *for all $\sigma \in \Sigma$ and $S_1 \subseteq \mathcal{S_F}$, we have $(S_1, \sigma, S_2) \in \widetilde{\mathcal{R}} \Leftrightarrow S_2 = \mathsf{suc}_{\exists}^{\mathcal{R}_\sigma}(S_1) \cap \mathcal{S_F}$*
2. *For the run $\widetilde{\pi} \in \mathsf{RUN}_{\widetilde{\mathfrak{A}}_1}(\alpha)$ and every $t_0 \in \mathbb{N}$, the following equivalence holds:*

$$s \in \widetilde{\pi}^{(t_0)} \Leftrightarrow \left(\begin{array}{l} \exists \xi : \mathbb{N} \to \mathcal{S}. \\ \quad [\xi^{(0)} \in \mathcal{I} \cap \mathcal{S_F}] \wedge [\xi^{(t_0)} = s] \wedge \\ \quad [\forall t < t_0.(\xi^{(t)}, \alpha^{(t)}, \xi^{(t+1)}) \in \mathcal{R}] \wedge \\ \quad [\forall t \leq t_0.\xi^{(t)} \in \mathcal{S_F}] \end{array}\right)$$

3. *$\widetilde{\pi} \in \mathsf{RUN}_{\widetilde{\mathfrak{A}}_1}(\alpha) \wedge \xi \in \mathsf{RUN}_{\mathfrak{A}}(\alpha) \wedge [\forall t \in \mathbb{N}.\xi^{(t)} \in \mathcal{S_F}] \to \forall t \in \mathbb{N}.\xi^{(t)} \in \widetilde{\pi}^{(t)}$*
4. *$\widetilde{\pi} \in \mathsf{RUN}_{\widetilde{\mathfrak{A}}_1}(\alpha) \to \forall t \in \mathbb{N}.\widetilde{\pi}^{(t)} \subseteq \mathcal{S_F}$*

Proof. The first proposition follows immediately by construction of $\widetilde{\mathfrak{A}}_1$:

$$\begin{aligned} (S_1, \sigma, S_2) \in \widetilde{\mathcal{R}} &\Leftrightarrow S_2 = \mathsf{suc}_{\exists}^{\mathcal{R}_{1,\sigma}}(S_1) \\ &\Leftrightarrow S_2 = \{s' \mid \exists s \in S_1.(s, \sigma, s') \in \mathcal{R}_1\} \\ &\Leftrightarrow S_2 = \{s' \mid \exists s \in S_1.(s, \sigma, s') \in \mathcal{R} \wedge s \in \mathcal{S_F} \wedge s' \in \mathcal{S_F}\} \\ &\Leftrightarrow S_2 = \{s' \mid \exists s \in S_1.(s, \sigma, s') \in \mathcal{R} \wedge s' \in \mathcal{S_F}\} \\ &\Leftrightarrow S_2 = \{s' \mid \exists s \in S_1.(s, \sigma, s') \in \mathcal{R}\} \cap \mathcal{S_F} \\ &\Leftrightarrow S_2 = \mathsf{suc}_{\exists}^{\mathcal{R}_a}(S_1) \cap \mathcal{S_F} \end{aligned}$$

The second proposition is proved by induction on t_0.

$\boxed{t_0 = 0:}$ In this case, the following holds:

$$\begin{aligned} &\exists \xi : \mathbb{N} \to \mathcal{S}.[\xi^{(0)} \in \mathcal{I} \cap \mathcal{S_F}] \wedge [\xi^{(0)} = s] \wedge \underbrace{[\forall t < 0.\ldots]}_{=:1} \wedge \underbrace{[\forall t \leq 0.\xi^{(t)} \in \mathcal{S_F}]}_{=:\xi^{(0)} \in \mathcal{S_F}} \\ &\Leftrightarrow \exists \xi : \mathbb{N} \to \mathcal{S}.[\xi^{(0)} \in \mathcal{I} \cap \mathcal{S_F}] \wedge [\xi^{(0)} = s] \wedge [\xi^{(0)} \in \mathcal{S_F}] \\ &\Leftrightarrow \exists \xi : \mathbb{N} \to \mathcal{S}.[s \in \mathcal{I} \cap \mathcal{S_F}] \wedge [\xi^{(0)} = s] \\ &\Leftrightarrow s \in \mathcal{I} \cap \mathcal{S_F} \\ &\Leftrightarrow s \in \widetilde{\pi}^{(0)} \end{aligned}$$

$t_0 > 0$: The induction step is seen as follows, where we used the induction hypothesis at step (*):

$$
\begin{aligned}
& s \in \widetilde{\pi}^{(t_0+1)} \\
& \overset{(1)}{\Leftrightarrow} \exists s_1 \in \mathcal{S}.(s_1, \alpha^{(t_0)}, s) \in \mathcal{R} \wedge s_1 \in \widetilde{\pi}^{(t_0)} \wedge s \in \mathcal{S_F} \\
& \overset{(*)}{\Leftrightarrow} \exists s_1 \in \mathcal{S}.\exists \xi : \mathbb{N} \to \mathcal{S}. \\
& \qquad (s_1, \alpha^{(t_0)}, s) \in \mathcal{R} \wedge s \in \mathcal{S_F} \wedge [\xi^{(0)} \in \mathcal{I} \cap \mathcal{S_F}] \wedge [\xi^{(t_0)} = s_1] \wedge \\
& \qquad [\forall t < t_0.(\xi^{(t)}, \alpha^{(t)}, \xi^{(t+1)}) \in \mathcal{R}] \wedge \\
& \qquad [\forall t \leq t_0.\xi^{(t)} \in \mathcal{S_F}] \\
& \overset{(2)}{\Leftrightarrow} \exists \xi_1 : \mathbb{N} \to \mathcal{S}. \\
& \qquad [\xi_1^{(0)} \in \mathcal{I} \cap \mathcal{S_F}] \wedge [\xi_1^{(t_0+1)} = s] \wedge \\
& \qquad [\forall t < t_0 + 1.(\xi_1^{(t)}, \alpha^{(t)}, \xi_1^{(t+1)}) \in \mathcal{R}] \wedge \\
& \qquad [\forall t \leq t_0 + 1.\xi_1^{(t)} \in \mathcal{S_F}]
\end{aligned}
$$

Step (1) follows by the first proposition of the lemma, that we have already proved. The correctness of the last step is seen as follows: the direction $\Leftarrow$ is seen by instantiating $s_1 := \xi_1^{(t_0)}$ and $\xi := \xi_1$ and the direction $\Rightarrow$ is seen by instantiating $\xi_1 := \lambda t. \left(t \leq t_0 \Rightarrow \xi^{(t)} \middle| s\right)$.

Proposition 4 and 5 are easily proved by induction on t, so we skip the proof here. □

The above lemma essentially says that a state obtained by the subset construction (applied to the semiautomaton that only contains the admissible states) is exactly the set of states that are endings of a *finite* path from an initial state over some finite prefix of the considered input word. So, it is immediately seen that if there is an accepting run over α through $\mathfrak{A}$, then each state of the uniquely determined run $\widetilde{\pi}$ over α through $\widetilde{\mathfrak{A}}$ must be different from $\{\}$. The converse also holds, but to see why this is the case, we need to consider the proof of the theorem below:

Theorem 4.25 (Subset Construction for $\mathsf{NDet_G}$**).** *Given a semiautomaton* $\mathfrak{A} = (\Sigma, \mathcal{S}, \mathcal{I}, \mathcal{R})$ *and a set of admissible states* $\mathcal{S_F} \subseteq \mathcal{S}$. *Let* $\widetilde{\mathfrak{A}}_1 = (\Sigma, 2^{\mathcal{S}}, \{\mathcal{I}\}, \widetilde{\mathcal{R}})$ *be the result of the application of subset construction as given in Definition 4.21 to the modified transition system* $\mathfrak{A}_1 := (\Sigma, \mathcal{S_F}, \mathcal{I} \cap \mathcal{S_F}, \mathcal{R} \cap (\mathcal{S_F} \times \mathcal{S_F}))$. *Then, for every infinite word* $\alpha : \mathbb{N} \to \Sigma$, *the following is equivalent:*

- $\exists \xi \in \mathsf{RUN}_{\mathfrak{A}}(\alpha).\forall t \in \mathbb{N}.\ \xi^{(t)} \in \mathcal{S_F}$
- $\exists \widetilde{\pi} \in \mathsf{RUN}_{\widetilde{\mathfrak{A}}_1}(\alpha).\forall t \in \mathbb{N}.\ \widetilde{\pi}^{(t)} \neq \{\}$

Therefore, we can construct for every automaton $\mathsf{NDet_G}$ *an equivalent automaton* $\mathsf{Det_G}$.

Proof. The equivalence is split into two implications:

$\boxed{\Rightarrow:}$ Is clear, by the previous lemma, since it follows that $\forall t.\xi^{(t)} \in \widetilde{\pi}^{(t)}$.

$\boxed{\Leftarrow:}$ Given that $\forall t \in \mathbb{N}.\widetilde{\pi}^{(t)} \neq \{\}$ holds, we obtain from proposition 3 of the previous lemma the following:

$$
\begin{array}{l}
\forall t_0.\exists \xi : \mathbb{N} \to \mathcal{S}. \\
\quad [\xi^{(0)} \in \mathcal{I} \cap \mathcal{S}_{\mathcal{F}}] \wedge \\
\quad [\forall t < t_0.(\xi^{(t)}, \alpha^{(t)}, \xi^{(t+1)}) \in \mathcal{R}] \wedge \\
\quad [\forall t \leq t_0.\xi^{(t)} \in \mathcal{S}_{\mathcal{F}}]
\end{array}
$$

Now, consider the tree of all runs for the word α that start in a state $s_0 \in \mathcal{S}_{\mathcal{F}}$. The root of this tree is labeled with s_0, and if a node at level t_0 is labeled with a state s, then the successor nodes in the tree are labeled with the states $\mathsf{suc}_{\exists}^{\mathcal{R}}(\{s\})$. By the above condition, this tree has for every number t_0, a path of a length greater or equal to t_0. For this reason, the tree has an infinite number of nodes, and as it is finitely branching (because $\mathsf{suc}_{\exists}^{\mathcal{R}}(\{s\})$ is finite), it follows by König's lemma that the tree has an infinite path. Therefore, the proposition holds.

□

The proof of the direction $\Leftarrow$ makes use of König's Lemma[1] and is not constructive, i.e., we can not construct from the run $\widetilde{\pi}$ a run ξ through $\mathfrak{A}$. Instead, we just know that such a run must exist.

So, we have $\mathsf{Det}_\mathsf{G} \approx \mathsf{NDet}_\mathsf{G}$, even if we allow that the transition relations in NDet_G may be partial. One might think that this allows us to determinize $\mathsf{NDet}_\mathsf{Prefix}$ automata due to the rules given in Lemma 4.16, since we could apply the rules for conjunction and disjunction in a backward manner as follows:

$$
\begin{array}{l}
\mathcal{A}_{\exists}\left(Q, \Phi_{\mathcal{I}}, \Phi_{\mathcal{R}}, \bigwedge_{j=0}^{f} \mathsf{G}\Phi_j \vee \mathsf{F}\Psi_j\right) \\
\qquad \stackrel{?}{=} \bigwedge_{j=0}^{f} \mathcal{A}_{\exists}\left(Q, \Phi_{\mathcal{I}}, \Phi_{\mathcal{R}}, \mathsf{G}\Phi_j\right) \vee \mathcal{A}_{\exists}\left(Q, \Phi_{\mathcal{I}}, \Phi_{\mathcal{R}}, \mathsf{F}\Psi_j\right)
\end{array}
$$

Note that Lemma 4.9 *does not allow to do that* since it would be necessary to partition the set of state variables Q into disjoint subsets. In fact, the above equation need not hold: as an example, consider the prefix automaton we have given for the formula $\mathsf{FG}a$ in Lemma 4.16. If we distribute the transition relation over the safety and liveness conditions, the resulting automata would accept every word.

Hence, we can not yet determinize prefix automata. In fact, we will prove later that nondeterministic prefix automata are strictly stronger than the deterministic variants, even if we restrict the nondeterministic transition relations to total ones. As an example, consider the nondeterministic prefix automaton we have given for the formula $\mathsf{FG}a$ in Lemma 4.16. Lemma 4.16 already proves that $\mathsf{NDet}_\mathsf{Prefix} \approx \mathsf{NDet}_\mathsf{FG}$ holds, and even $\mathsf{NDet}_\mathsf{Prefix}^\mathsf{total} \approx \mathsf{NDet}_\mathsf{FG}$

[1] König's lemma says that every finitely branching tree with infinitely many nodes has at least one infinite path.

holds. Hence, it is in general not possible to reduce a nondeterministic prefix automaton to a deterministic one.

4.5.4 Determinization of NDet$_{\mathsf{FG}}$

In this section, we consider the determinization of the equally expressive classes NDet$_{\mathsf{FG}}$, NDet$_{\mathsf{F}}$, and NDet$_{\mathsf{Prefix}}$. Surprisingly, or not, we will see that we can compute for every NDet$_{\mathsf{FG}}$ automaton an equivalent Det$_{\mathsf{FG}}$ automaton with at most exponentially many states. The equal expressiveness of NDet$_{\mathsf{FG}}$ and Det$_{\mathsf{FG}}$ was shown for the first time by Wagner in [504], however the construction of this section follows related constructions given in [302, 374].

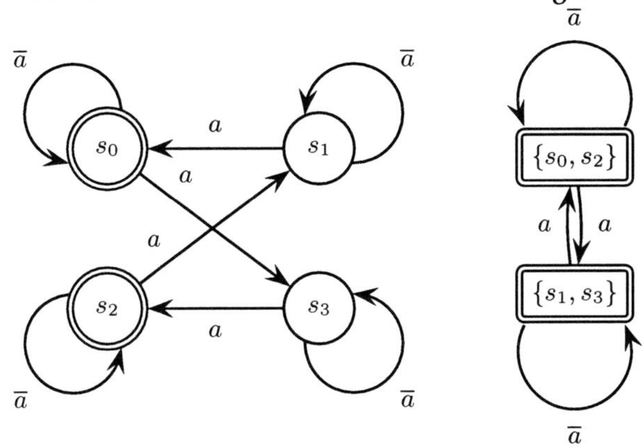

Fig. 4.9. A problem for the determinization of FG automata

To see why the Rabin-Scott subset construction can not be used to determinize NDet$_{\mathsf{FG}}$, consider the example given in Figure 4.9. The semiautomaton given on the left hand side is nondeterministic, since there are two initial states s_0 and s_2 (but for every state and every input symbol, there is exactly one successor state). On the right hand side of Figure 4.9, the result of the Rabin-Scott subset construction is given.

We now extend the semiautomaton to a NDet$_{\mathsf{FG}}$ automaton with the designated state set $\mathcal{S_F} := \{s_2, s_3\}$. It is therefore easily seen that this automaton formula is equivalent to $\mathsf{FG}\neg a$. A run is accepting iff it remains in the designated state set $\mathcal{S_F}$ after some point of time. Consider now the transition diagram given on the right hand side that is obtained by the subset construction. We must impose an acceptance condition for the 'subset' path $\widetilde{\pi}$ such that this condition holds iff there is an accepting run 'inside' $\widetilde{\pi}$. However, if we take the acceptance condition $\exists t_1.\forall t_2.\widetilde{\pi}^{(t_1+t_2)} \subseteq \mathcal{S_F}$, then no word is accepted by this automaton. On the other hand, if we take the acceptance condition $\exists t_1.\forall t_2.\widetilde{\pi}^{(t_1+t_2)} \cap \mathcal{S_F} \neq \{\}$, then every word is accepted. Hence, both automata would not be equivalent in either case.

The problem is that we have not distinguished between transitions that enter the set of designated states $\mathcal{S_F}$ and those that move inside $\mathcal{S_F}$. As can

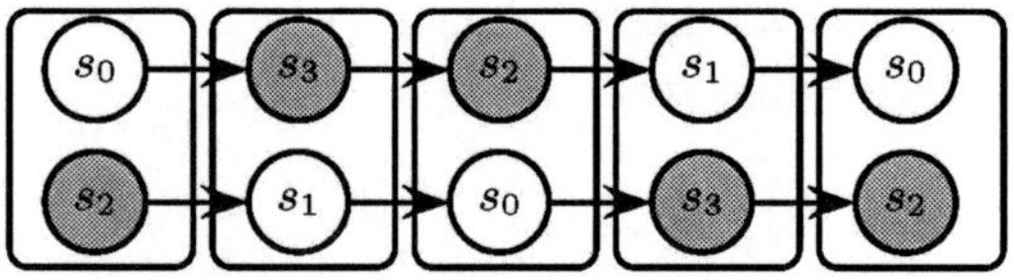

Fig. 4.10. A path through the determinized automaton of Figure 4.9

be seen in Figure 4.10 the two runs of the word a^ω enter and leave the set of designated states infinitely often. In their combination, however, one of the two will always be in the designated states, and the other one is not. To detect this, we must refine the subset construction. The key idea is to keep track of the states in $\widetilde{\pi}^{(t)}$ that may have a path that will stay in $\mathcal{S}_\mathcal{F}$ forever in a second state set. This is essentially done by the following breakpoint construction [302, 374].

function Breakpoint$(\Sigma, \mathcal{S}, \mathcal{I}, \mathcal{R}, \mathcal{S}_\mathcal{F})$
  front $:= \{(\mathcal{I}, \{\})\}$;
  $\widetilde{\mathcal{S}} := \{\}$;
  $\widetilde{\mathcal{R}} := \{\}$;
  while *front* $\neq \{\}$ **do**
    $(S_1, S_2) :=$ **selectfrom**(*front*);
    $\widetilde{\mathcal{S}} := \widetilde{\mathcal{S}} \cup \{(S_1, S_2)\}$;
    front $:=$ *front* $\setminus \{(S_1, S_2)\}$;
    for $\sigma \in \Sigma$ **do**
      $S_1' := \mathsf{suc}_\exists^{\mathcal{R}_\sigma}(S_1)$;
      if $S_2 = \{\}$ **then** $S_2' := S_1' \cap \mathcal{S}_\mathcal{F}$ **else** $S_2' := \mathsf{suc}_\exists^{\mathcal{R}_\sigma}(S_2) \cap \mathcal{S}_\mathcal{F}$ **end**;
      $\widetilde{\mathcal{R}} := \widetilde{\mathcal{R}} \cup \{((S_1, S_2), \sigma, (S_1', S_2'))\}$;
      if $(S_1', S_2') \notin \widetilde{\mathcal{S}}$ **then** *front* $:=$ *front* $\cup \{(S_1', S_2')\}$ **end**
    end
  end;
  return $(\Sigma, \widetilde{\mathcal{S}}, \{(\mathcal{I}, \{\})\}, \widetilde{\mathcal{R}})$
end

Fig. 4.11. Breakpoint construction

Definition 4.26 (Breakpoint Construction). *Given a semiautomaton* $\mathfrak{A} = (\Sigma, \mathcal{S}, \mathcal{I}, \mathcal{R})$*, and a set of designated states* $\mathcal{S}_\mathcal{F} \subseteq \mathcal{S}$*. We define for every* $\sigma \in \Sigma$ *the relation* $\mathcal{R}_\sigma := \{(s, s') \in \mathcal{S} \times \mathcal{S} \mid (s, \sigma, s') \in \mathcal{R}\}$*. Then, the semiautomaton* $\widetilde{\mathfrak{A}} = (\Sigma, 2^\mathcal{S} \times 2^\mathcal{S}, \{(\mathcal{I}, \{\})\}, \widetilde{\mathcal{R}})$ *is obtained with the following transition relation* $\widetilde{\mathcal{R}}$*:*

$$\{((S_1, S_2),\ \sigma,\ (\mathsf{suc}_\exists^{\mathcal{R}_\sigma}(S_1), \mathsf{suc}_\exists^{\mathcal{R}_\sigma}(S_2) \cap \mathcal{S}_\mathcal{F}) \mid \sigma \in \Sigma \wedge \{\} \neq S_2 \subseteq S_1 \subseteq \mathcal{S}\} \cup$$
$$\{((S_1, \{\}),\ \sigma,\ (\mathsf{suc}_\exists^{\mathcal{R}_\sigma}(S_1), \mathsf{suc}_\exists^{\mathcal{R}_\sigma}(S_1) \cap \mathcal{S}_\mathcal{F}) \mid \sigma \in \Sigma \wedge S_1 \subseteq \mathcal{S}\}$$

Every state (S_1, S_2) *with* $S_2 = \{\}$ *is called a breakpoint.* $\widetilde{\mathfrak{A}}$ *has at most* $3^{|\mathcal{S}|}$ *states.*

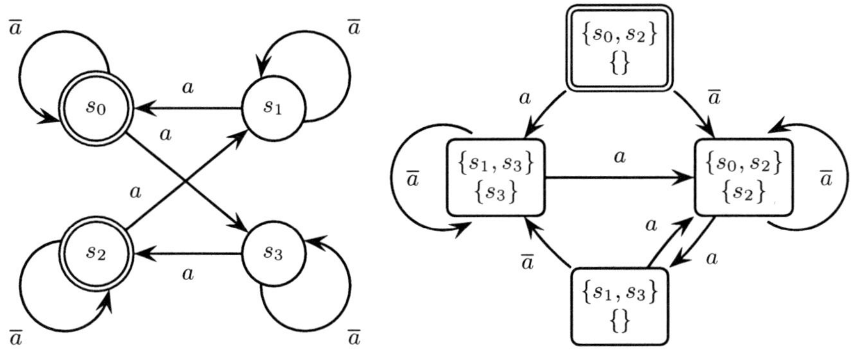

Fig. 4.12. Example for the breakpoint construction (Definition 4.26)

The key idea of the breakpoint construction is to store in the first component S_1 of a state (S_1, S_2) the set of states that can be reached by reading the same input sequence. This is exactly what is computed in the Rabin-Scott subset construction. The second component S_2 contains the states of S_1 that have a run that did not leave the designated states $\mathcal{S}_{\mathcal{F}}$ after the last breakpoint. For example, Figure 4.12 shows an application of the breakpoint construction with $\mathcal{S}_{\mathcal{F}} = \{s_2, s_3\}$, where the pairs (S_1, S_2) are drawn in a stacked manner, i.e., S_1 is put on top of S_2.

The resulting transition system $\widetilde{\mathfrak{A}}$ obtained by the breakpoint construction is clearly deterministic. To estimate its size in the worst case, note that for every state (S_1, S_2) of $\widetilde{\mathfrak{A}}$, we have $S_2 \subseteq S_1 \cap \mathcal{S}_{\mathcal{F}}$. Hence, the number of states is of order $O(3^{|\mathcal{S}|})$, which is seen by the equation $3^n = (1+2)^n = \sum_{i=0}^{n} \binom{n}{i} 2^i$ and the observation that there are $\binom{|\mathcal{S}|}{i}$ subsets of $\mathcal{S}$ with i elements (which are candidates for the first component S_1) that can have in turn 2^i subsets (which are candidates for the second component S_2). Hence, the construction is exponential in $|\mathcal{S}|$ like the Rabin-Scott subset construction (whose resulting automaton may have $2^{|\mathcal{S}|}$ states). The correctness of the breakpoint construction for the determinization of $\mathsf{NDet}_{\mathsf{FG}}$ is given in the next theorem, where we use the projections $\mathsf{fst}((a, b)) := a$ and $\mathsf{snd}((a, b)) := b$.

Theorem 4.27 (Breakpoint Construction). *Given a semiautomaton $\mathfrak{A} = (\Sigma, \mathcal{S}, \mathcal{I}, \mathcal{R})$, and a set of designated states $\mathcal{S}_{\mathcal{F}} \subseteq \mathcal{S}$. Let $\widetilde{\mathfrak{A}} = (\Sigma, 2^{\mathcal{S}} \times 2^{\mathcal{S}}, \{(\mathcal{I}, \{\})\}, \widetilde{\mathcal{R}})$ be the semiautomaton obtained by the breakpoint construction as given in Definition 4.26. Then, for every infinite word $\alpha : \mathbb{N} \to \Sigma$, the following propositions are equivalent:*

- $\exists \xi \in \mathsf{RUN}_{\mathfrak{A}}(\alpha).\ \exists t_1 \in \mathbb{N}. \forall t_2 \in \mathbb{N}.\ \xi^{(t_1+t_2)} \in \mathcal{S}_{\mathcal{F}}$
- $\forall \widetilde{\pi} \in \mathsf{RUN}_{\widetilde{\mathfrak{A}}}(\alpha).\ \exists t_1 \in \mathbb{N}. \forall t_2 \in \mathbb{N}.\ \mathsf{snd}(\widetilde{\pi}^{(t_1+t_2)}) \neq \{\}$
- $\exists \widetilde{\pi} \in \mathsf{RUN}_{\widetilde{\mathfrak{A}}}(\alpha).\ \exists t_1 \in \mathbb{N}. \forall t_2 \in \mathbb{N}.\ \mathsf{snd}(\widetilde{\pi}^{(t_1+t_2)}) \neq \{\}$

Proof. The last two propositions are easily seen to be equivalent since $\widetilde{\mathfrak{A}}$ is deterministic. For the equivalence between the first and the second proposition, we first note that the following two facts hold and can be proved by induction on t_0: Given that $\widetilde{\pi}$ is the run of an arbitrary input word α, then the following holds for every $t_0 \in \mathbb{N}$:

$$s \in \mathsf{fst}(\widetilde{\pi}^{(t_0)}) \Leftrightarrow \left(\begin{array}{l} \exists \xi : \mathbb{N} \to \mathcal{S}. \\ \quad [\xi^{(0)} \in \mathcal{I}] \wedge [\xi^{(t_0)} = s] \wedge \\ \quad [\forall t < t_0 . (\xi^{(t)}, \alpha^{(t)}, \xi^{(t+1)}) \in \mathcal{R}] \end{array}\right)$$

$$s \in \mathsf{snd}(\widetilde{\pi}^{(t_0)}) \Leftrightarrow \left(\begin{array}{l} \exists \xi : \mathbb{N} \to \mathcal{S}. \\ \quad [\xi^{(0)} \in \mathcal{I}] \wedge [\xi^{(t_0)} = s] \wedge \\ \quad [\forall t < t_0 . (\xi^{(t)}, \alpha^{(t)}, \xi^{(t+1)}) \in \mathcal{R}] \wedge \\ \quad \exists t_1 < t_0 . \\ \quad\quad [\mathsf{snd}(\widetilde{\pi}^{(t_1)}) = \{\}] \wedge \\ \quad\quad [\forall t . t_1 < t \leq t_0 \to \mathsf{snd}(\widetilde{\pi}^{(t)}) \neq \{\}] \wedge \\ \quad\quad [\forall t . t_1 < t \leq t_0 \to \xi^{(t)} \in \mathsf{snd}(\widetilde{\pi}^{(t)})] \end{array}\right)$$

The first fact is already known from the Rabin-Scott subset construction and simply says that for every t_0 the set $\mathsf{fst}(\pi^{(t_0)})$ contains the set of states that are reachable via the finite input sequence $\alpha^{(0)}, \ldots, \alpha^{(t_0-1)}$. *The second fact states that* $\mathsf{snd}(\pi^{(t_0)})$ *contains the set of states that are endpoints of a path* ξ *that had never left the designated state set since the last breakpoint* ($\pi^{(t_1)}$). Note that for every state (S_1, S_2) of $\widetilde{\mathfrak{A}}$, we have $S_2 \subseteq S_1 \cap \mathcal{S}_{\mathcal{F}}$.

Using these two facts, the above theorem is easily seen to hold: suppose that $\widetilde{\pi}$ contains only finitely many breakpoints. Then there must be a run ξ through $\mathfrak{A}$ for the word α such that after some point of time, we always have $\xi^{(t)} \in \mathsf{snd}(\widetilde{\pi}^{(t)})$. Hence, ξ never leaves $\mathcal{S}_{\mathcal{F}}$ after some point of time, and therefore ξ is accepting.

Conversely, assume that there is a run ξ of α that never leaves the designated states $\mathcal{S}_{\mathcal{F}}$ after some point of time. Then, $\widetilde{\pi}$ clearly contains only finitely many breakpoints, since after some point of time, we always have $\xi^{(t)} \in \mathsf{snd}(\widetilde{\pi}^{(t)})$. □

Hence, the breakpoint construction can be used to compute equivalent automata in $\mathsf{Det}_{\mathsf{FG}}$ of given automata in $\mathsf{NDet}_{\mathsf{FG}}$. *All we have to do is to apply the breakpoint construction to the given* $\mathsf{NDet}_{\mathsf{FG}}$ *automaton and have to set up the acceptance condition that after some point of time, the second component will never be empty.*

Similar to the Rabin-Scott subset construction, the breakpoint construction is exponential in the worst case in terms of the number of states of the given automaton. Moreover, the construction is optimal, since there are automata that lead in fact to the exponential blow-up. So, the determinization procedures of the automaton classes $\mathsf{NDet}_{\mathsf{G}}$, $\mathsf{NDet}_{\mathsf{F}}^{\mathsf{total}}$, and $\mathsf{NDet}_{\mathsf{FG}}$, have an increasing complexity, which matches with their expressiveness.

4.5.5 Reducing $\mathsf{NDet}_{\mathsf{GF}}$ to $\mathsf{Det}_{\mathsf{Rabin}}$

In the previous section, we have seen that the Rabin-Scott subset construction that is well-known from the determinization of finite state machines on finite words can be used to determinize the classes $\mathsf{NDet}_{\mathsf{G}}$ and $\mathsf{NDet}_{\mathsf{F}}^{\mathsf{total}}$. Moreover, we have seen that the breakpoint construction, which is an extension of the Rabin-Scott subset construction can be used to determinize the class $\mathsf{NDet}_{\mathsf{FG}}$.

There is one basic modality left: Therefore, we consider the determinization of $\mathsf{NDet}_{\mathsf{GF}}$ in this section. We already know that there is no automaton in $\mathsf{Det}_{\mathsf{GF}}$ that is equivalent to $\mathsf{FG}a$ (cf. Lemma 4.18). However, there are automata in $\mathsf{NDet}_{\mathsf{GF}}$ that can express this formula (cf. Lemma 4.16). Therefore, we see that $\mathsf{Det}_{\mathsf{GF}} \precnapprox \mathsf{NDet}_{\mathsf{GF}}$ holds, i.e., we can not reduce $\mathsf{NDet}_{\mathsf{GF}}$ to $\mathsf{Det}_{\mathsf{GF}}$.

This result is quite old, and Büchi already showed that his automata ($\mathsf{NDet}_{\mathsf{GF}}$) are nevertheless closed under complement (while $\mathsf{Det}_{\mathsf{GF}}$ is not closed under complement). As this situation is somewhat disturbing, several researchers searched for other types of deterministic ω-automata that reach the expressive power of $\mathsf{NDet}_{\mathsf{GF}}$. Clearly, any such class of automata must be closed under all Boolean operations since $\mathsf{NDet}_{\mathsf{GF}}$ is closed under all Boolean operations. The first automaton class with that property was presented by Muller [380]. His proof was corrected by McNaughton [363] who used a specialized form of the Muller acceptance condition. This acceptance condition was later used by Rabin [418], and thus it was named after Rabin (we also call that class $\mathsf{Det}_{\mathsf{Rabin}}$). However, the construction given by McNaughton required a doubly exponential blow-up, i.e., from a nondeterministic Büchi automaton with n states, the algorithm computes a deterministic automaton with c^{c^n} states for some $c > 1$. Therefore, better determinization and complementation algorithms have been searched for some time. Sistla, Vardi, and Wolper presented, in 1987, a new algorithm for the complementation of Büchi automata that involved only a blow-up by $O(16^{n^2})$, so that only a single exponential blow-up was sufficient [458, 459]. Pécuchet presented in [399] a simplified presentation of this algorithm inspired by group theory. An optimal result was however found by Safra [428] in 1988. Safra's construction involves only a blow-up by $2^{O(n \log n)}$ and it can be proved that this is optimal [367, 428, 487]. Therefore, Safra's construction is the most important algorithm for the conversion of nondeterministic ω-automata into deterministic ones. Note that we have already seen how to convert the classes $\mathsf{Det}_{\mathsf{Rabin}}$ and $\mathsf{Det}_{\mathsf{Streett}}$ into each other. Also, we already know how to convert the classes $\mathsf{NDet}_{\mathsf{GF}}$, $\mathsf{NDet}_{\mathsf{Rabin}}$, and $\mathsf{NDet}_{\mathsf{Streett}}$ into each other. Therefore, Safra's construction is a bridge between the nondeterministic classes and the deterministic ones, as it enables us to convert any of the classes $\mathsf{Det}_{\mathsf{Rabin}}$, $\mathsf{Det}_{\mathsf{Streett}}$, $\mathsf{NDet}_{\mathsf{GF}}$, $\mathsf{NDet}_{\mathsf{Rabin}}$, and $\mathsf{NDet}_{\mathsf{Streett}}$ into each other. So, we consider in this section Safra's algorithm in detail.

To explain Safra's construction, we first consider how we would like to modify the breakpoint construction for the determinization of $\mathsf{NDet}_{\mathsf{GF}}$ and why this does not work. We first recall the breakpoint construction of Definition 4.26. The run $\widetilde{\pi}$ of a given input word α contains at each stage $t_0 \in \mathbb{N}$ in its first component $\mathsf{fst}(\widetilde{\pi}^{(t_0)})$ the set of states that can be reached via the prefix of length t_0 of α (cf. Lemma 4.22). The second component $\mathsf{snd}(\widetilde{\pi}^{(t_0)})$ contains the subset of $\mathsf{fst}(\widetilde{\pi}^{(t_0)}) \cap \mathcal{S}_{\mathcal{F}}$ where a path ends that exclusively went through the states of $\mathcal{S}_{\mathcal{F}}$ since the last breakpoint was visited. A new breakpoint is declared whenever the second component becomes empty.

Given a Büchi automaton with designated state set $\mathcal{S}_{\mathcal{F}}$, we apply the breakpoint construction with $\mathcal{S} \setminus \mathcal{S}_{\mathcal{F}}$ to its state transition system. Hence, the second components $\mathsf{snd}(\widetilde{\pi}^{(t_0)})$ of a path $\widetilde{\pi}$ contain the subsets of $\mathsf{fst}(\widetilde{\pi}^{(t_0)}) \cap (\mathcal{S} \setminus \mathcal{S}_{\mathcal{F}})$ where a path ends that exclusively went through the states of $\mathcal{S} \setminus \mathcal{S}_{\mathcal{F}}$ since the last breakpoint was visited.

Clearly, every run has at least the initial state $\widetilde{\pi}^{(0)}$ as breakpoint. However, except for this one, it is not guaranteed that any other breakpoint will exist on the run. However, if there are several breakpoints, then it is clear by definition of the breakpoints that between two breakpoints $\widetilde{\pi}^{(t_i)}$ and $\widetilde{\pi}^{(t_{i+1})}$, *every* run $\xi \in \mathsf{RUN}_{\mathfrak{A}}(\alpha, t_{i+1})$ must visit, at least once, the designated states $\mathcal{S}_{\mathcal{F}}$ of the Büchi automaton somewhere between t_i and t_{i+1}. If the run $\widetilde{\pi}$ contains infinitely many breakpoints, then there must be a run $\xi \in \mathsf{RUN}_{\mathfrak{A}}(\alpha)$ that visits at least one designated state infinitely often.

It is not difficult to define a modified breakpoint construction so that between two breakpoints $\widetilde{\pi}^{(t_i)}$ and $\widetilde{\pi}^{(t_{i+1})}$, *there is a* run $\xi \in \mathsf{RUN}_{\mathfrak{A}}(\alpha, t_{i+1})$ that must visit, at least once, the designated states $\mathcal{S}_{\mathcal{F}}$ of the Büchi automaton somewhere between t_i and t_{i+1}. Hence, if we use the acceptance condition that a word is accepted if and only if its run $\widetilde{\pi}$ contains infinitely many breakpoints, then it follows that every word accepted by the determinized automaton is also accepted by the original automaton, i.e., we have $\mathsf{Lang}(\widehat{\mathfrak{A}}) \subseteq \mathsf{Lang}(\mathfrak{A})$. However, the converse need not hold.

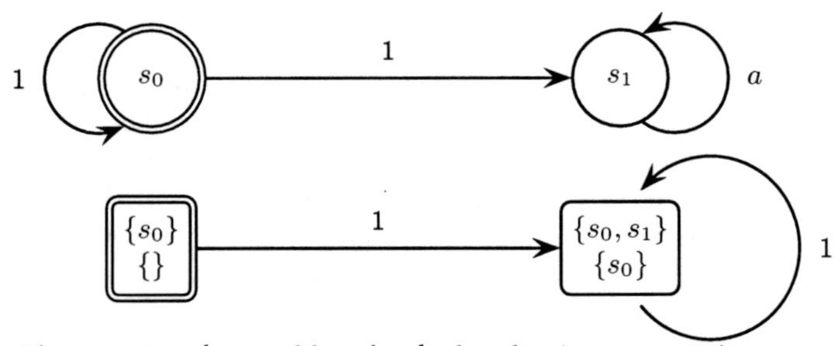

Fig. 4.13. Another problem for the breakpoint construction

If we were to define the acceptance condition in a different manner, namely that a run $\widetilde{\pi}$ is accepted iff there are infinitely many states that contain *at least one* marked state, then this would also not lead to an equivalent automaton. To see this, consider Figure 4.13. We endow the semiautomaton shown in the upper part of Figure 4.13 with the designated state set $\mathcal{S}_{\mathcal{F}} := \{s_1\}$ and the

Büchi acceptance condition. We have already seen that this $\mathsf{NDet}_{\mathsf{GF}}$ automaton is equivalent to $\mathsf{FG}a$.

The lower part of Figure 4.13 gives the result of the breakpoint construction with designated state set $\{s_0, s_1\} \setminus \{s_1\} = \{s_0\}$. Now, assume we establish the acceptance condition that a word is accepted iff its run contains infinitely many states that contain at least one designated state. Then, it is easily seen that with this acceptance condition, the automaton in the lower part of Figure 4.13 accepts every word. On the other hand, if a word should be accepted iff its run contains infinitely many states which contain only designated states, then the automaton in the lower part of Figure 4.13 accepts no word at all.

Hence, the breakpoint construction of Definition 4.26 is not of much use here. We have only considered it for motivating Safra's construction, since the latter is a refinement of the breakpoint construction. To see where we have to refine the construction, consider again the breakpoint construction where we wish to use the following acceptance condition: a word is accepted iff its run contains infinitely many breakpoints. We have already seen that $\mathsf{Lang}(\widetilde{\mathfrak{A}}) \subseteq \mathsf{Lang}(\mathfrak{A})$ holds, but in general the converse is not true. Consider now, why the converse is not true. If a word α has an accepting run $\xi_1 \in \mathsf{RUN}_{\mathfrak{A}}(\alpha)$, but also a run $\xi_2 \in \mathsf{RUN}_{\mathfrak{A}}(\alpha)$, that is not accepting, then after some time t_0, the second component $\mathsf{snd}(\widetilde{\pi}^{(t+t_0)})$ of the run $\widetilde{\pi} \in \mathsf{RUN}_{\widetilde{\mathfrak{A}}}(\alpha)$ contains at least one state, namely $\xi_1^{(t+t_0)}$, but not every state that is contained in the first component $\mathsf{fst}(\widetilde{\pi}^{(t+t_0)})$, since $\xi_2^{(t+t_0)}$ is missing.

Therefore, we must consider breakpoints with a finer granulation: Instead of defining breakpoints by the entire set of states reachable with a finite word, we now define subsequent breakpoints, i.e., subsets of the set of reachable states. These *subsequent breakpoints* are defined as follows:

- each subset of the initial state $\widetilde{\pi}^{(0)}$ is a breakpoint
- $S_{i+1} \subseteq \widetilde{\pi}^{(t_{i+1})}$ is a successor breakpoint for the breakpoint $S_i \subseteq \widetilde{\pi}^{(t_i)}$ with $t_i < t_{i+1}$ iff for each state $s \in S_{i+1}$, there is a ξ such that the following holds:
  1. $\xi^{(t_i)} \in S_i$
  2. $\xi^{(t_{i+1})} = s$
  3. $\forall t. t_i \leq t < t_{i+1} \rightarrow (\xi^{(t)}, \alpha^{(t)}, \xi^{(t+1)}) \in \mathcal{R}$
  4. $\exists t. t_i < t \leq t_{i+1} \wedge \xi^{(t)} \in \mathcal{S}_{\mathcal{F}}$

This is essentially the main idea of Safra's construction. The acceptance condition requires then that the run $\widetilde{\pi}$ must contain an infinite sequence $S_0 := \widetilde{\pi}^{(0)}$, $S_1 \subseteq \widetilde{\pi}^{(t_1)}$, $S_2 \subseteq \widetilde{\pi}^{(t_2)}$ ... such that $S_{i+1} \subseteq \widetilde{\pi}^{(t_{i+1})}$ is a successor breakpoint of $S_i \subseteq \widetilde{\pi}^{(t_i)}$. As between two breakpoints, each run traversing the two breakpoints visits, at least once, the designated states $\mathcal{S}_{\mathcal{F}}$, it is clear that there must then be a run that visits the designated states $\mathcal{S}_{\mathcal{F}}$ infinitely often. Conversely, if there is a run $\xi \in \mathsf{RUN}_{\mathfrak{A}}(\alpha)$ that visits $\mathcal{S}_{\mathcal{F}}$ infinitely often, then there must be a sequence of subsequent breakpoints *in $\widetilde{\pi}$. To see this, let $t_0, t_1, \ldots$ be the points of time where $\xi^{(t_i)} \in \mathcal{S}_\mathcal{F}$ holds. Simply define $S_i := \{\xi^{(t_i+1)}\}$ to see that there is a sequence of subsequent breakpoints.*

Using subsequent breakpoints, we can handle the case when a word α has accepting and non-accepting runs. The problem is now to find a data structure and an algorithm for the computation of these breakpoints. For this reason, let us observe the run $\widetilde{\pi}$ for a given input word α. Assume, t_0 is the first point of time where $\widetilde{\pi}^{(t_0)} \cap \mathcal{S}_\mathcal{F} \neq \{\}$ holds. Clearly, it may be the case that *all* states of $\widetilde{\pi}^{(t_0)}$ can be extended to an infinite accepting run ξ. Nevertheless, we distinguish in the following between the sets $\widetilde{\pi}^{(t_0)} \cap \mathcal{S}_\mathcal{F}$ and $\widetilde{\pi}^{(t_0)} \setminus \mathcal{S}_\mathcal{F}$, since we already know that the states $\widetilde{\pi}^{(t_0)} \cap \mathcal{S}_\mathcal{F}$ have visited $\mathcal{S}_\mathcal{F}$, while the runs ending in the states $\widetilde{\pi}^{(t_0)} \setminus \mathcal{S}_\mathcal{F}$ have not so far visited $\mathcal{S}_\mathcal{F}$.

Note that it would be wrong to simply declare $\widetilde{\pi}^{(t_0)} \cap \mathcal{S}_\mathcal{F}$ as a next breakpoint, since the definition of breakpoints requires that runs leading from one breakpoint to the next one must visit $\mathcal{S}_\mathcal{F}$ *between* the breakpoints. Also, it would be wrong to declare $\mathsf{suc}_\exists^{\mathcal{R}_a}(\widetilde{\pi}^{(t_0)} \cap \mathcal{S}_\mathcal{F})$ (with $a = \alpha^{(t_0)}$) to be the next breakpoint, since there might be transitions leading from $\widetilde{\pi}^{(t_0)} \setminus \mathcal{S}_\mathcal{F}$ to $\mathsf{suc}_\exists^{\mathcal{R}_a}(\widetilde{\pi}^{(t_0)} \cap \mathcal{S}_\mathcal{F})$, such that a run from the previous breakpoint $\widetilde{\pi}^{(t_0)}$ to $\mathsf{suc}_\exists^{\mathcal{R}_a}(\widetilde{\pi}^{(t_0)} \cap \mathcal{S}_\mathcal{F})$ could exist that does not visit $\mathcal{S}_\mathcal{F}$ between the points 0 and t_0.

Hence, at this point of time, we do not have enough information to declare a next breakpoint. In order to obtain this information for future points of time, we therefore distinguish between the set of states that are reached from $\widetilde{\pi}^{(t_0)} \cap \mathcal{S}_\mathcal{F}$ and the others. Therefore, we consider a subsequent run $\widetilde{\pi}_1$ from $t_0 + 1$ on, that is defined as $\widetilde{\pi}_1^{(t_0+1)} := \mathsf{suc}_\exists^{\mathcal{R}_{\alpha^{(t_0)}}}(\widetilde{\pi}_0^{(t_0)} \cap \mathcal{S}_\mathcal{F})$ and $\widetilde{\pi}_1^{(t+t_0+1)} := \mathsf{suc}_\exists^{\mathcal{R}_{\alpha^{(t+t_0)}}}(\widetilde{\pi}_1^{(t+t_0)})$.

Let now be t_1 the next point of time where $\widetilde{\pi}^{(t_1)} \cap \mathcal{S}_\mathcal{F} \neq \{\}$ holds. Consider first the case that $\widetilde{\pi}_1^{(t_1)} \subseteq \mathcal{S}_\mathcal{F}$. This means that we can declare $\widetilde{\pi}_1^{(t_1)}$ as the next breakpoint since all states of $\widetilde{\pi}_1^{(t_1)}$ are endings of runs that (1) lead from the previous breakpoint $\widetilde{\pi}^{(0)}$ to $\widetilde{\pi}_1^{(t_1)}$ and (2) visited at some intermediate point $\mathcal{S}_\mathcal{F}$. Hence, a subsequent breakpoint has been obtained.

If, on the other hand $\widetilde{\pi}_1^{(t_1)} \subseteq \mathcal{S}_\mathcal{F}$ does not hold, then we have to consider the set of states that are reached from $\widetilde{\pi}_1^{(t_1)} \cap \mathcal{S}_\mathcal{F}$, $\widetilde{\pi}_1^{(t_1)} \setminus \mathcal{S}_\mathcal{F}$, $\widetilde{\pi}^{(t_1)} \cap \mathcal{S}_\mathcal{F}$, and $\widetilde{\pi}^{(t_1)} \setminus \mathcal{S}_\mathcal{F}$. The reason for splitting $\widetilde{\pi}_1^{(t_1)}$ into two subsequent threads is the same as for splitting $\widetilde{\pi}^{(t_0)}$ before: there might be a non-accepting run starting in either $\widetilde{\pi}^{(t_1)} \cap \mathcal{S}_\mathcal{F}$ or $\widetilde{\pi}^{(t_1)} \setminus \mathcal{S}_\mathcal{F}$ that would not allow one of these threads to have a breakpoint in the future at all. Hence, we distinguish between these two sets and hope that at least one of them will have a future breakpoint.

Hence, we split off a new thread $\widetilde{\pi}^{(t_1)} \cap \mathcal{S}_\mathcal{F}$ from $\widetilde{\pi}$ for the same reason. As it can be seen, this splitting into subsequent threads leads to a tree structure that is used in Safra's construction. For a precise formulation of Safra's construction, we will use the following (general) definition of labeled trees:

Definition 4.28 ($\mathcal{S}$-Labeled Trees). *Given a set $\mathcal{S}$, a $\mathcal{S}$-labeled tree is given as a tuple $\mathcal{T} = (\mathcal{V}, \mathcal{V}_{\mathcal{F}}, r, \chi, \ell)$, where $\mathcal{V}$, $\mathcal{V}_{\mathcal{F}}$, r, χ, and ℓ have the following meaning:*

- *$\mathcal{V} = \{\nu_1, \ldots, \nu_n\}$ is a finite set of vertices.*
- *$\mathcal{V}_{\mathcal{F}} \subseteq \mathcal{V}$ is the set of marked vertices.*
- *$r \in \mathcal{V}$ is a distinguished vertex called the root of $\mathcal{T}$.*
- *χ is a function that maps every vertex $\nu \in \mathcal{V}$ to a list $\chi(\nu)$ of vertices. Each vertex ν_i in $\chi(\nu)$ is called a child of ν and ν is called the parent vertex of each vertex ν_i in $\chi(\nu)$. The following constraints must be fulfilled for χ*
  - $\forall \nu_1, \nu_2 \in \mathcal{V}.\ \nu_1 \neq \nu_2 \rightarrow \chi(\nu_1) \cap \chi(\nu_2) = \{\}$
  - *each vertex except the root vertex appears in exactly one child list*
- *$\ell : \mathcal{V} \rightarrow 2^{\mathcal{S}}$ is the label function that maps each vertex ν to a set $\ell(\nu) \subseteq \mathcal{S}$.*

Note that the list of children $\chi(\nu)$ of a vertex ν defines an order on the children. Given that $\chi(\nu) = [\nu_1, \ldots, \nu_k]$ holds, we say that ν_j is on the right of ν_i iff $i < j$ holds and we say that ν_1 and ν_k is the leftmost and the rightmost child of ν, respectively. Moreover, ν_1 is called an ancestor of ν_2 if ν_2 is either a member of $\chi(\nu_1)$ or there is a child of ν_1 that is an ancestor of ν_2.

Safra's construction essentially starts with a tree with only one vertex labeled with the initial states. To construct a run $\widehat{\pi}$ for α whose states are labeled with $\mathcal{S}$-labeled trees, we compute the label of $\widehat{\pi}^{(t+1)}$ from the label of $\widehat{\pi}^{(t)}$ as follows: for each vertex ν of the tree, we replace the label $\ell(\nu)$ by the new label $\mathsf{suc}_{\exists}^{\mathcal{R}_a}(\ell(\nu))$ with $a = \alpha^{(t)}$. Also, whenever $\ell(\nu) \cap \mathcal{S}_{\mathcal{F}} \neq \{\}$ holds for a vertex ν, we split off a new thread by adding a rightmost child ν' of ν that is labeled (at the next point of time) with $\mathsf{suc}_{\exists}^{\mathcal{R}_a}(\ell(\nu) \cap \mathcal{S}_{\mathcal{F}})$ because both $\ell(\nu) \setminus \mathcal{S}$ and $\ell(\nu) \cap \mathcal{S}_{\mathcal{F}}$ could contains states which are starting points of non-accepting runs.

Breakpoints are now defined relative to a vertex ν, so that we can talk about ν-breakpoints. These are now defined as follows: Assume a vertex ν is introduced at a certain point of time t_ν of a run[2]. Then, ν is a breakpoint in the tree that is the label of the state $\widehat{\pi}^{(t_\nu)}$. Given points of time $t_\nu \leq t_0 < t_1$, so that $\widehat{\pi}^{(t_0)}$ and $\widehat{\pi}^{(t_1)}$ were labeled with trees $\mathcal{T}_{t_0}$ and $\mathcal{T}_{t_1}$ (note that both $\mathcal{T}_{t_0}$ and $\mathcal{T}_{t_1}$ contain ν). Let S_0 and S_1 be the labels of ν in $\mathcal{T}_{t_0}$ and $\mathcal{T}_{t_1}$, respectively. Then, ν is declared as the next breakpoint $\mathcal{T}_{t_1}$ if ν is a breakpoint in $\mathcal{T}_{t_0}$, and if every run leading to S_1 visits the designated states $\mathcal{S}_{\mathcal{F}}$ at least once at some point of time t with $t_0 < t < t_1$, and visits the set S_0 at time t_0.

How do we detect these breakpoints in the trees? Denote for every vertex ν the point of time where ν is added to the tree with t_ν. Note that all runs ending in $\ell^{(t_\nu)}(\nu)$ visit $\mathcal{S}_{\mathcal{F}}$ since we have, in particular, $\ell^{(t_\nu)}(\nu) \subseteq \mathcal{S}_{\mathcal{F}}$ (this is the reason for adding ν to the tree). Moreover, denote the sequence of labels of ν with $\ell^{(t)}(\nu)$. Consider now a vertex ν that has no child at a certain point of time t_0. Assume at some point of time t_1 with $t_0 < t_1$, that the equation $\ell^{(t_1)}(\nu) = \bigcup_{\nu' \in \chi(\nu)} \ell^{(t_1)}(\nu')$ holds and let t_1 be the first point of time after t_0

[2] At this stage of the explanation of Safra's construction, we always retain the vertices in the tree. Later, we will define rules for removing vertices.

where this holds. Then, for each state $s \in \ell^{(t_1)}(\nu)$ there is a finite run from a state $s' \in \ell^{(t_\nu)}(\nu)$ that visited $\mathcal{S}_\mathcal{F}$ at least once, since (1) it holds for at least one $\nu' \in \chi(\nu)$ that $s \in \ell^{(t_1)}(\nu')$, (2) that $\ell^{(t_1)}(\nu')$ contains the set of states that come from $\ell^{(t_{\nu'})}(\nu')$, (3) $\ell^{(t_{\nu'})}(\nu') \subseteq \mathcal{S}_\mathcal{F}$, and that (4) $t_0 < t_{\nu'} < t_1$ holds. Therefore, we can declare ν at time t_1 to be the first ν-breakpoint after t_0.

As this information 'overwrites' the need for distinguishing between $\ell^{(t)}(\nu)$ and $\ell^{(t)}(\nu')$ for $\nu' \in \chi(\nu)$, we can now drop all children $\nu' \in \chi(\nu)$ of ν. Recall that children are only introduced because we are afraid of having a state in $\ell(\nu)$ that does not visit $\mathcal{S}_\mathcal{F}$ any more. As we see at this point of time that this is not the case for ν, we can eliminate all its children. This is called the *vertical merge rule*. However, ν may have new children in the future run.

As the vertical merge rule eliminates vertices, we have rules that introduce vertices and rules that eliminate them. Note that the vertical merge rule guarantees that for all trees that occur as labels, we have for each vertex the proper inclusion $\ell^{(t)}(\nu) \supsetneq \bigcup_{\nu' \in \chi(\nu)} \ell^{(t)}(\nu')$. All states in $\ell^{(t)}(\nu) \setminus \bigcup_{\nu' \in \chi(\nu)} \ell^{(t)}(\nu')$ are specific to ν, since they do not appear in the labels of the children of ν. Hence, it follows that every state that appears in the label of the root vertex r must be specific to some vertex, and therefore the tree can never have more than $|\ell(r)| \leq |\mathcal{S}|$ vertices.

In order to establish a bound for the branching of the trees, Safra's construction also considers a horizontal merge rule: Let $\chi(\nu) = [\nu_1, \ldots, \nu_n]$ be the children of a vertex ν and let $\ell(\nu_i) \cap \ell(\nu_j) \neq \{\}$ for $i < j$. It is unnecessary to consider the states $\ell(\nu_i) \cap \ell(\nu_j)$ twice and therefore we remove them from the $\ell(\nu_j)$.

Due to these two rules, we can see that we can reuse vertices to deal with a finite number of vertices for the entire construction. While the explanations so far only give the principles of Safra's construction where we have omitted some technical details, the following definition now gives the construction in full detail.

The procedure defined in the following definition constructs a semiautomaton whose states are $\mathcal{S}$-labeled trees. We therefore use some set of vertices $\mathcal{V}^*$, and by construction, we know that the cardinality of $|\mathcal{V}^*| = 2\,|\mathcal{S}|$ will be sufficient. Using the functions of Figure 4.14, the construction is as follows (the marking defines the breakpoints):

Definition 4.29 (Safra's Construction). *Given a semiautomaton $\mathfrak{A} = (\Sigma, \mathcal{S}, \mathcal{I}, \mathcal{R})$ together with a set of designated states $\mathcal{S}_\mathcal{F} \subseteq \mathcal{S}$. Let $\mathcal{V}^*$ be an arbitrary set of cardinality $|\mathcal{V}^*| = 2\,|\mathcal{S}|$. Then, we define the corresponding state transition system $\widehat{\mathfrak{A}} = (\Sigma, \widehat{\mathcal{S}}, \{\mathcal{I}\}, \widehat{\mathcal{R}})$ as follows: States $\widehat{\mathcal{S}}$ are finite $\mathcal{S}$-labeled trees whose vertices are a subset of $\mathcal{V}^*$. The construction involves the computation of the successor tree $\mathcal{T}_\sigma$ of a tree $\mathcal{T}$ for an input $\sigma \in \Sigma$. This is done by the following steps (cf. Figure 4.14), where we assume $\mathcal{T} = (\mathcal{V}, \mathcal{V}_\mathcal{F}, r, \chi, \ell)$:*

1. *Remove all marks, i.e., set $\mathcal{V}_\mathcal{F} := \{\}$.*

```
function split(v)
begin
    for ν' in χ(ν) do
        split(ν');
    end;
    Q := ℓ(ν) ∩ S_F;
    vl := χ(ν);
    if Q ≠ {} then
        ν' := choose_some(V* \ V);
        χ := χ_ν^(vl◁ν');
        ℓ := ℓ_ν'^Q;
        χ := χ_ν'^[];
    end
end
```

```
function successor(ν, a)
begin
    Q := suc_∃^(R_a)(ℓ(ν));
    ℓ := ℓ_ν^Q;
    vl := χ(ν);
    while vl ≠ [] do
        successor(hd(vl), a);
        vl := tl(vl);
    end
end
```

```
function remove(Q, vl)
begin
    vl' := [];
    while vl ≠ [] do
        ν := hd(vl);
        vl := tl(vl);
        Q' := ℓ(ν);
        if Q' ⊆ Q then
            V := V \ {ν};
            V_F := V_F \ {ν};
        else
            vl' := (v;' ◁ν)
        end;
        ℓ := ℓ_ν^(Q'\Q);
        Q := Q ∪ Q';
    end
    return vl'
end
```

```
function horizontal_merge(ν)
begin
    vl := χ(ν);
    vl := remove(ℓ(hd(vl)), tl(vl);
    χ := χ_ν^(vl');
end
```

```
function vertical_merge(ν)
begin
    vl := χ(ν);
    Q := {};
    while vl ≠ [] do
        Q := Q ∪ ℓ(hd(vl));
        vertical_merge(hd(vl));
        vl := tl(vl);
    end
    if ℓ(ν) = Q then
        V := V \ χ(ν);
        V_F := V_F \ χ(ν);
        χ := χ_ν^[];
        V_F := V_F ∪ {ν};
end
```

Fig. 4.14. Algorithm's for Safra's construction

2. ***Splitting Rule:*** *If there is a vertex* $\nu \in \mathcal{T}$ *that is labeled with a set* $\ell(\nu)$ *with* $\ell(\nu) \cap \mathcal{S}_{\mathcal{F}} \neq \{\}$*, then take some vertex* ν' *from* $\mathcal{V}^* \setminus \mathcal{V}$ *and add* ν' *to* $\mathcal{V}$ *such that* ν' *becomes the rightmost child of* ν*.* ν' *is labeled with* $\ell(\nu) \cap \mathcal{S}_{\mathcal{F}}$*.*
3. ***Subset Construction:*** *We define for every* $\sigma \in \Sigma$ *the relation* $\mathcal{R}_\sigma := \{(s, s') \in \mathcal{S} \times \mathcal{S} \mid (s, \sigma, s') \in \mathcal{R}\}$*. Replace the labels* $\ell(\nu)$ *of every vertex* $\nu \in \mathcal{V}$ *by* $\mathsf{suc}_{\exists}^{\mathcal{R}_\sigma}(S_\nu)$*.*
4. ***Horizontal Merge Rule:*** *If there is a vertex* $\nu \in \mathcal{V}$ *with the children* $\chi(\nu) = [\nu_1, \ldots, \nu_n]$ *and if there is a state* $s \in \mathcal{S}$ *such that* $s \in \ell(\nu_i) \cap \ell(\nu_j)$ *where* $i < j$*, then remove* s *from* $\ell(\nu_j)$*. If the label* $\ell(\nu_i)$ *becomes empty, remove the node* ν_i*.*
5. ***Vertical Merge Rule:*** *If the vertex* ν *has the children* $\chi(\nu) = [\nu_1, \ldots, \nu_n]$ *and we have* $\ell(\nu) = \bigcup_{i=1}^{n} \ell(\nu_i)$*, then remove all sons* $\nu_1, \ldots, \nu_n$ *and add* ν *to the set of marked vertices.*

The construction starts now with an initial state s_0 *that is labeled with a tree* $\mathcal{T}_0$ *with only a root vertex* r_0*. The label of* r_0 *is* $\ell_0(r_0) := \mathcal{S}_{\mathcal{F}}$*. No vertex of* $\mathcal{T}_0$ *is marked. Given that* s *is a so far obtained state with label* $\mathcal{T}$ *and* $\sigma \in \Sigma$*, then we first compute the successor tree* $\mathcal{T}_\sigma$ *of* $\mathcal{T}$ *by the above steps. If there is already a state* s_σ *that is labeled with* $\mathcal{T}_\sigma$*, then we add* (s, σ, s_σ) *to* $\widehat{\mathcal{R}}$*. Otherwise a new state* s_σ *is created with label* $\mathcal{T}_\sigma$ *and we also add* (s, σ, s_σ) *to* $\widehat{\mathcal{R}}$*. This is repeated as long as new states are obtained.*

As can be seen, Safra's construction is more complicated than the Rabin-Scott construction or the breakpoint construction that we have previously considered. It can be easily seen that the roots of the $\mathcal{S}$-labeled trees are exactly the sets of states that are obtained by the Rabin-Scott subset construction. However, there may be states labeled with trees that are different, but that have the same root node. Hence, we see that Safra's construction is a refinement of the Rabin-Scott subset construction.

Now, let us analyse what is behind the construction. Clearly, a deterministic transition system is obtained. Therefore every input word α has a uniquely determined run through $\widehat{\mathfrak{A}}$. Moreover, we have already seen that Safra's construction is a refinement of the Rabin-Scott subset construction as the root vertices of the trees are labeled with the subsets of states that were obtained by the subset construction.

We have already seen that the subset construction does not work with the example given in Figure 4.9. The reason for this was that at every point of time, one of the two runs of a word was entering the set of designated states, while the other run was leaving the set of designated states. The splitting rule is used to control which run either enters or leaves the set of designated states in that each run is assigned a new son.

We have also seen the usage of the vertical merge rule: if we reach a state that is labeled with a tree $\mathcal{T}$, where for a vertex ν of $\mathcal{T}$ the equation $\ell^{(t_1)}(\nu) = \bigcup_{\nu' \in \chi(\nu)} \ell^{(t_1)}(\nu')$ holds, then we have already proved that each run ξ ending in a state $q \in \ell(\nu)$ must have visited $\mathcal{S}_{\mathcal{F}}$ at least once since that last ν-breakpoint. Therefore, we have found a new ν-breakpoint whenever

$\ell^{(t_1)}(\nu) = \bigcup_{\nu' \in \chi(\nu)} \ell^{(t_1)}(\nu')$ holds. For example, in Figure 4.15, the lowest state contains the only ν_1 breakpoint.

Lemma 4.30 (Safra's Construction). *Given a semiautomaton $\mathfrak{A} = (\Sigma, \mathcal{S}, \mathcal{I}, \mathcal{R})$, a set of designated states $\mathcal{S}_\mathcal{F} \subseteq \mathcal{S}$ and the corresponding deterministic semiautomaton $\widehat{\mathfrak{A}} = (\Sigma, \widehat{\mathcal{S}}, s_0, \widehat{\mathcal{R}})$ as given in Definition 4.29. Then, for every infinite word $\alpha : \mathbb{N} \to \Sigma$, the following holds:*

1. *If $\mathcal{T} = (\mathcal{V}, \mathcal{V}_\mathcal{F}, r, \chi, \ell)$ is the label of a state, then the following two properties are satisfied:*
   a) *For all $\nu \in \mathcal{V}$, we have $\bigcup_{\nu' \in \chi(\nu)} \ell(\nu') \subsetneq \ell(\nu)$*
   b) *If ν_1 and ν_2 are not ancestors of each other, then $\ell(\nu_1) \cap \ell(\nu_2) = \{\}$.*
   c) *For all $\nu \in \mathcal{V}$, we have $\ell(\nu) \neq \{\}$.*
2. *For every $t_0 \in \mathbb{N}$, let S_{t_0} be the label of the root node of the tree that is the label of $\widehat{\pi}^{(t_0)}$. Then, the following holds:*

$$s \in S_{t_0} \Leftrightarrow \left(\begin{array}{l} \exists \xi : \mathbb{N} \to \mathcal{S}. \\ \quad [\xi^{(0)} \in \mathcal{I}] \wedge [\xi^{(t_0)} = s] \wedge \\ \quad [\forall t < t_0.(\xi^{(t)}, \alpha^{(t)}, \xi^{(t+1)}) \in \mathcal{R}] \end{array} \right)$$

3. ***Correctness of the Vertical Merge Rule:** If $\widehat{\pi} \in \mathsf{RUN}_{\widehat{\mathfrak{A}}}(\alpha)$ holds, denote with $\mathcal{T}^{(t)}$ the sequence of trees that form the labels of $\widehat{\pi}$ and with $\ell^{(t)}(\nu)$ the sequence of labels of a vertex ν. For all numbers $t_0 < t_1$ such that (1) the vertex ν occurs in all trees from $\mathcal{T}^{(t_0)}, \ldots, \mathcal{T}^{(t_1)}$, and (2) ν has no children in $\mathcal{T}^{(t_0)}$, and (3) $\mathcal{T}^{(t_1)}$ is the first tree in the sequence where the equation $\ell^{(t_1)}(\nu) = \bigcup_{\nu' \in \chi(\nu)} \ell^{(t_1)}(\nu')$ holds, the following holds: each finite run ξ ending in a state $s \in \ell^{(t_1)}(\nu)$ with $\xi^{(t_0)} \in \ell^{(t_0)}(\nu)$ must have visited $\mathcal{S}_\mathcal{F}$ at least once since t_0.*

Proof. The first proposition is seen to be invariant for the construction given in Definition 4.29: (a) holds due to the splitting, the subset, and the vertical merge rule; (b) and (c) follow directly from the horizontal merge rule. The second proposition is immediately seen by noting that the Safra's construction is a refinement of the Rabin-Scott construction.

The correctness of the vertical merge rules was explained on page 227: Denote for every vertex ν the point of time where ν is added to the tree with t_ν. Then, for each state $s \in \ell^{(t_1)}(\nu)$ there is a finite run from a state $s' \in \ell^{(t_\nu)}(\nu)$ that visited at least once $\mathcal{S}_\mathcal{F}$, since (1) it holds for at least one $\nu' \in \chi(\nu)$ that $s \in \ell^{(t_1)}(\nu')$, (2) that $\ell^{(t_1)}(\nu')$ contains the set of states that come from $\ell^{(t_{\nu'})}(\nu')$, (3) $\ell^{(t_{\nu'})}(\nu') \subseteq \mathcal{S}_\mathcal{F}$, and since (4) $t_0 < t_{\nu'} < t_1$ holds.

As there is no longer a need to distinguish between $\ell^{(t)}(\nu)$ and $\ell^{(t)}(\nu')$ for $\nu' \in \chi(\nu)$, we can now remove all children $\nu' \in \chi(\nu)$ of ν. Recall that children are only introduced because we are afraid of having a state in $\ell(\nu)$ that does not visit $\mathcal{S}_\mathcal{F}$ any more. As we can see at this point, this is not the case for ν, and thus we can eliminate all its children. □

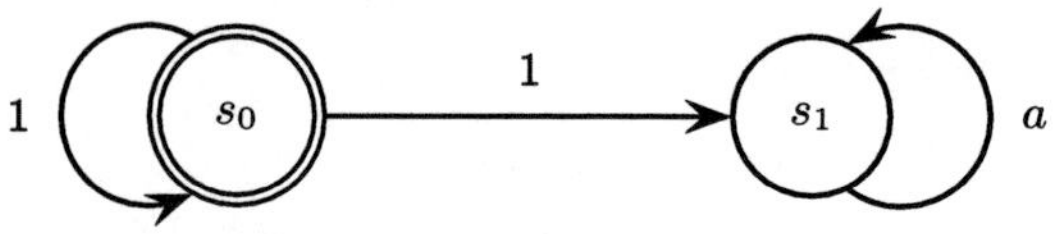

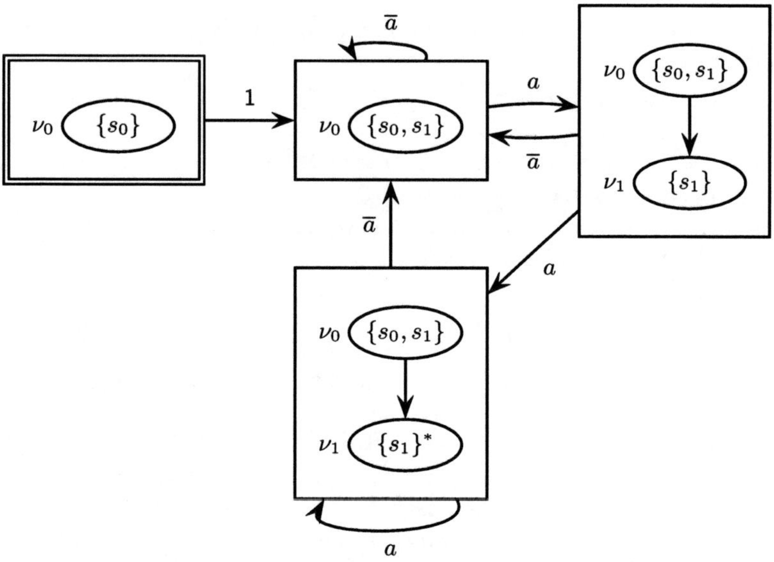

Fig. 4.15. Example for Safra's construction

By the first proposition, the number of different trees is limited. In particular, for every vertex $\nu \in \mathcal{V}$, there must be a specific state $s \in \mathcal{S}$, i.e., a state that belongs to $\ell(\nu)$, but not to a label of the children of ν. Therefore, the number of vertices of each tree is bound by $|\ell(r)| - 1$ where $r \in \mathcal{V}$ is the root of the tree, and hence by $|\mathcal{S}|$.

Moreover, it follows that the depth of the tree is limited to $|\ell(r)|-1$, where $r \in \mathcal{V}$ is again the root of the tree. Also the number of children is limited since each label $\ell(\nu)$ is nonempty and the inclusion $\bigcup_{\nu' \in \chi(\nu)} \ell(\nu') \subsetneq \ell(\nu)$ holds. Therefore, there are at least $|\ell(\nu)|$ children for a vertex $\nu \in \mathcal{V}$.

Due to these properties, we can now prove that the set $\mathcal{V}^*$, where we take vertices from is large enough. Note that the splitting rule must take vertices from $\mathcal{V}^* \setminus \mathcal{V}$ to add new vertices in a tree. As this may happen for every vertex and as there are at most $|\ell(r)| - 1 < |\mathcal{S}|$ vertices, the set $\mathcal{V}^* \setminus \mathcal{V}$ must always have enough vertices.

We still have not said how the acceptance condition of the deterministic automaton obtained by Safra's construction is defined. Clearly, the run $\widehat{\pi}$ must have infinitely many subsequent breakpoints. However, *as vertices come* *and go, we must furthermore demand that the vertex that occurs infinitely often as a breakpoint on $\widehat{\pi}$ is always the same 'instance', i.e., it is not removed and introduced infinitely often.* For example, in Figure 4.15, the run for $a(aa\overline{a})^\omega$ introduces and removes the vertex ν_1 infinitely often and therefore contains infinitely many ν_1 breakpoints. So, the following theorem shows that this yields an acceptance condition in form of the Rabin acceptance.

Theorem 4.31 (Reduction of $\mathsf{NDet_{GF}}$ to $\mathsf{Det_{Rabin}}$). *Given a semiautomaton $\mathfrak{A} = (\Sigma, \mathcal{S}, \mathcal{I}, \mathcal{R})$ with the designated state set $\mathcal{S_F}$, and the semiautomaton $\widehat{\mathfrak{A}} = (\Sigma, \widehat{\mathcal{S}}, s_0, \widehat{\mathcal{R}})$ as given in Definition 4.29. Then, the deterministic Rabin automaton with the state transition system $\widehat{\mathfrak{A}}$ and the following acceptance condition is equivalent to $\mathfrak{A}$:*

$$\bigvee_{\nu \in \mathcal{V}^*} \mathsf{FG}\, \Phi_\nu \wedge \mathsf{GF}\, \Psi_\nu$$

where Φ_ν represents the set of states that are labeled with a tree that contains the vertex ν and Ψ_ν represents the subset of Φ_ν where the vertex ν is even marked.

Proof. Let $\widehat{\mathfrak{A}}$ be the deterministic Rabin automaton as described in the theorem. Then, the correctness is proved in two steps:

$\boxed{\mathsf{Lang}(\widehat{\mathfrak{A}}) \subseteq \mathsf{Lang}(\mathfrak{A})\text{:}}$ Let $\alpha \in \mathsf{Lang}(\widehat{\mathfrak{A}})$ be any input word that is accepted by $\widehat{\mathfrak{A}}$ and let $\widehat{\pi} \in \mathsf{RUN}_{\widehat{\mathfrak{A}}}(\alpha)$ be its run through $\widehat{\mathfrak{A}}$. Consider the sequence of trees $\mathcal{T}^{(0)}$, $\mathcal{T}^{(1)}$, ...that are the labels of $\widehat{\pi}^{(0)}$, $\widehat{\pi}^{(1)}$, ... Let $\mathcal{V}^{(i)}$ be the set of vertices of $\mathcal{T}^{(i)}$ and $\mathcal{V}_\mathcal{F}^{(i)}$ be the set of marked vertices of $\mathcal{T}^{(i)}$.
As α is accepted, there must be a vertex $\nu \in \mathcal{V}^*$ such that (1) $\exists t_1 \in \mathbb{N}.\forall t_2 \in \mathbb{N}.\nu \in \mathcal{V}^{(t_1+t_2)}$ and (2) $\forall t_1 \in \mathbb{N}.\exists t_2 \in \mathbb{N}.\nu \in \mathcal{V}_\mathcal{F}^{(t_1+t_2)}$. We have to prove that there is an accepting run $\xi \in \mathsf{RUN}_\mathfrak{A}(\alpha)$. Let $0 < t_1 < t_2$ ...be the ν-breakpoints, i.e., positions where $\nu \in \mathcal{V}_\mathcal{F}^{(t_i)}$ holds. Define additionally $t_0 := 0$. Let $Q^{(0)} := \mathcal{I}$ and $Q^{(i)} := \ell_i(\nu)$ where ℓ_{t_i} is the label function of tree $\mathcal{T}^{(t_i)}$. By the previous lemma (correctness of the vertical merge rule), it follows that for every $q \in Q^{(i+1)}$ and each run $\xi \in \mathsf{RUN}_\mathfrak{A}(\alpha, t_i+1)$ with $\xi^{(t_i)} \in Q^{(i)}$, there is some t with $t_i < t < t_{i+1}$ such that $\xi^{(t)} \in \mathcal{S_F}$.
We now construct for any initial state q_0 an infinite tree as follows: the vertices are taken from the set $\{(q,i) \mid q \in Q^{(i)}\}$. As the parent of $(q, i+1)$ (with $q \in Q^{(i+1)}$), we pick one of the pairs (p,i), such that $p \in Q^{(i)}$ holds and that there is a run $\xi \in \mathsf{RUN}_\mathfrak{A}(\alpha, t_i + 1)$ as described above. Clearly, these trees are finitely branching, since each vertex ν is labeled with a finite set $\ell(\nu)$. Moreover, for at least one initial state q_0 the corresponding tree must have an infinite number of vertices, because we have an infinite sequence of breakpoints. Therefore, we conclude by König's lemma that there is an initial state q_0 such that there is an infinite path $(q_0, 0)$, $(q_1, 1)$, ..., through the tree we have constructed for q_0. Recall now that there are finite runs from q_i to q_{i+1} that consume the word $\alpha^{(t_i)}$, ..., $\alpha^{(t_{i+1}-1)}$ and visit, at least once, the designated states between t_i and t_{i+1}. Any infinite

concatenation of these segments gives an infinite run $\xi \in \mathsf{RUN}_{\mathfrak{A}}(\alpha)$ that visits $\mathcal{S}_{\mathcal{F}}$ infinitely often.

$\boxed{\mathsf{Lang}(\mathfrak{A}) \subseteq \mathsf{Lang}(\widehat{\mathfrak{A}}):}$ Given a word $\alpha \in \mathsf{Lang}(\mathfrak{A})$ with an accepting run $\xi \in \mathsf{RUN}_{\mathfrak{A}}(\alpha)$. We must prove that the run $\widehat{\pi} \in \mathsf{RUN}_{\widehat{\mathfrak{A}}}(\alpha)$ is also accepting, i.e., contains an infinite number of subsequent breakpoints. Consider again the sequence of trees $\mathcal{T}^{(i)}$ that are the labels of $\widehat{\pi}^{(i)}$. Again let $\mathcal{V}^{(i)}$ be the set of vertices of $\mathcal{T}^{(i)}$ and and $\mathcal{V}_{\mathcal{F}}^{(i)}$ be the set of marked vertices of $\mathcal{T}^{(i)}$. Then, we have to show that there is a vertex $\nu \in \mathcal{V}^*$ such that (1) $\exists t_1 \in \mathbb{N}.\forall t_2 \in \mathbb{N}.\nu \in \mathcal{V}^{(t_1+t_2)}$ and (2) $\forall t_1 \in \mathbb{N}.\exists t_2 \in \mathbb{N}.\nu \in \mathcal{V}_{\mathcal{F}}^{(t_1+t_2)}$.
To see this, note that $\xi^{(t)}$ is, for each $t \in \mathbb{N}$, a member of the label of the root vertices. Therefore, the labels of the roots are never empty, and therefore, the roots are never removed. If the roots of the trees $\mathcal{T}^{(i)}$ are marked infinitely often, then we are done. Otherwise, there must be another run over α that is not accepting. Consider now the first visit of ξ in $\mathcal{S}_{\mathcal{F}}$ after the last time the root of $\mathcal{T}^{(i)}$ was marked. At that point t_0, $\xi^{(t_0)}$ is placed somewhere in the children of $\mathcal{T}^{(i)}$: The splitting rule will create a new vertex that will have at an intermediate state a label that contains $\xi^{(t_0)}$, but due to the horizontal merge rule, $\xi^{(t_0)}$ may be deleted from the label of the newly added vertex. However, $\xi^{(t_0)}$ must then be a member of a left child ν_1 of this vertex. This child is then never removed, otherwise (due to the splitting rule) the root node would become marked, which is not the case due to our assumption.
Now, the same arguments are applied to ν_1. We consider again two cases: It either follows that (1) ν_1 is infinitely often marked, and we can take ν_1 to prove that the Rabin acceptance condition holds, or (2) it will never be marked after some point t_1 on. But by the same arguments as above, it then follows that there must be a vertex ν_2 which is a child of ν_1 whose label contains the current state of ξ. Additionally, ν_2 can not be removed in the future, as ν_1 would otherwise be marked.
Repeating this argumentation n times, we obtain vertices $\nu_1, \ldots, \nu_n$ such that $\xi^{(t)} \in \ell(\nu_i)$ holds for $i \in \{1, \ldots, n\}$ and $\nu_{i+1} \in \chi(\nu_i)$ holds for $i \in \{1, \ldots, n-1\}$. If ν_n is marked infinitely often, i.e., the first case holds, we are done. Otherwise, note that the depth of the trees is limited by $|\mathcal{S}|$, so that it follows that our sequence $\nu_1, \ldots, \nu_n$ must finally end up with a leaf vertex ν_n so that we can not make the second case distinction. Therefore, the first case must hold for ν_n which means that ν_n is infinitely often marked.

□

The complexity of the above algorithm that is able to convert a $\mathsf{NDet_{GF}}$ automaton to an equivalent $\mathsf{NDet_{Rabin}}$ automaton is of special interest for a lot of decision procedures (e.g. the one that converts monadic second order formulas to $\mathsf{NDet_{GF}}$ automata, see Chapter 6). Therefore, consider now, how many Safra trees can exists for a given set of states $\mathcal{S}$. Therefore, consider a Safra tree $\mathcal{T} = (\mathcal{V}, \mathcal{V}_{\mathcal{F}}, r, \chi, \ell)$. We have already seen that each tree has less than $|\mathcal{S}|$ vertices, hence we have $|\mathcal{V}| \leq |\mathcal{S}|$. Now let $f_\ell : \mathcal{S} \to \mathcal{V} \cup \{\bot\}$ be the function that maps a state $s \in \mathcal{S}$ to the last vertex ν in $\mathcal{T}$ where it occurs, i.e., we have $s \in \ell(f_\ell(s))$, but $s \notin \nu$ for every $\nu \in \chi(f_\ell(s))$. If s does not occur in any label of any vertex, we map s to $\bot$. f_ℓ encodes the label function ℓ of the tree $\mathcal{T}$: We can re-establish ℓ from f_ℓ, and vice versa. Now, note that if A and B are finite sets, then there are $|B|^{|A|}$ many functions from A to B. Therefore, we have at most $|\mathcal{S}|^{|\mathcal{V}|+1} \leq |\mathcal{S}|^{|\mathcal{S}|+1}$ different labels for a tree. Moreover, $\mathcal{V}_{\mathcal{F}}$ can be any subset of $\mathcal{V}$, and therefore we additionally have $2^{|\mathcal{V}|}$ possibilities for $\mathcal{V}_{\mathcal{F}}$. Finally, the child function χ gives us another factor of $|\mathcal{V}|^{|\mathcal{V}|}$, so that we end up with $|\mathcal{S}|^{O(|\mathcal{S}|)}) = 2^{O(|\mathcal{S}| \log |\mathcal{S}|)}$ different trees. Without doubt this is a large number, but it is significantly better than previously known constructions that obtained $2^{2^{O(|\mathcal{S}|)}}$ states.

Therefore, we obtain a deterministic Rabin automaton with $2^{O(|\mathcal{S}| \log(|\mathcal{S}|))}$ states and $O(|\mathcal{S}|)$ acceptance pairs[3]. Michel has shown [367, 428, 487] that this is essentially optimal, since we can construct, for every $n \in \mathbb{N}$, an ω-regular language L_n such that L_n is recognized by a $\mathsf{NDet_{GF}}$ automaton with $n+2$ states, while any $\mathsf{NDet_{GF}}$ automaton that recognizes the complement of L_n must have more than $n!$ states. The language L_n is thereby the one that is recognized by the automaton given in Figure 4.16, where $\mathcal{S}_{\mathcal{F}} = \{s_i\}$.

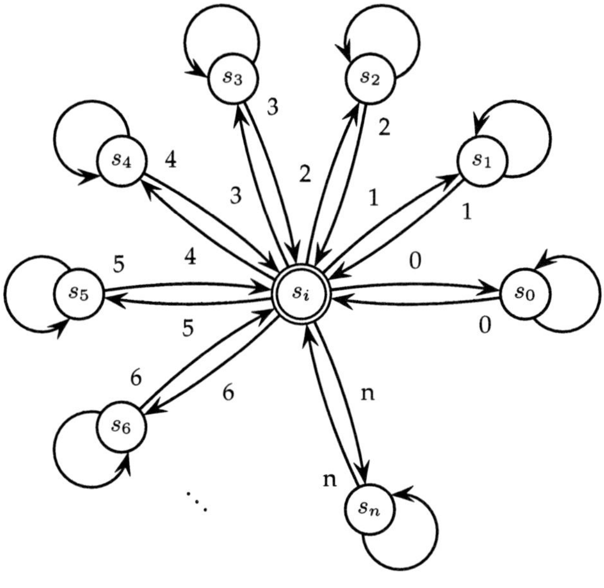

Fig. 4.16. A worst case example for Safra's construction

[3] As we have taken $\mathcal{V}^*$ with cardinality $|\mathcal{V}^*| = 2|\mathcal{S}|$, we have $2|\mathcal{S}|$ acceptance pairs.

As we have already remarked the relationship between complementation and determinization, we can now give the following theorem on the complementation of $\mathsf{NDet}_{\mathsf{GF}}$ automata.

Theorem 4.32 (Complementation of $\mathsf{NDet}_{\mathsf{GF}}$). *Given a nondeterministic Büchi automaton $\mathfrak{A} \in \mathsf{NDet}_{\mathsf{GF}}$, there is an automaton $\overline{\mathfrak{A}} \in \mathsf{NDet}_{\mathsf{GF}}$ such that $\mathfrak{A} \leftrightarrow \neg\overline{\mathfrak{A}}$ holds on every path of every structure. Moreover, if $\mathfrak{A}$ has the set of states $\mathcal{S}$, then $\overline{\mathfrak{A}}$ has $2^{O(|\mathcal{S}| \log(|\mathcal{S}|))}$ states.*

The proof of the previous theorem is immediate. We first transform $\mathfrak{A}$ to an equivalent $\mathfrak{D} \in \mathsf{Det}_{\mathsf{Rabin}}$, and negate $\mathfrak{D}$. According to Lemma 4.9, this transforms $\mathfrak{D}$ to an equivalent deterministic Streett automaton with the same set of states, the same initial states, the same transition relation, and the same number of acceptance pairs. The rest follows from the fact, that we can transform any $\mathfrak{S} \in \mathsf{Det}_{\mathsf{Streett}}$ with n states and f acceptance pairs to an equivalent $\overline{\mathfrak{A}} \in \mathsf{NDet}_{\mathsf{GF}}$ automaton with $n \cdot 2^{O(f)}$ states.

There are also algorithms for complementing Büchi automata that avoid the determinization. In fact, Büchi's early work in 1960 contained such a construction [80] based on Ramsey's combinatorial theorem [422]. However, Büchi's construction is doubly exponential, i.e., the complement may have $2^{2^{O(|\mathcal{S}|)}}$ states. Sistla, Vardi, and Wolper [458] presented in 1985 an improvement that required at most $2^{O(|\mathcal{S}|^2)}$ states, hence, only a single exponential blow-up. Similar constructions are given by Pécuchet [399] and Emerson and Jutla [166]. By Safra's determinization procedure of 1988, it became then possible to complement Büchi automata with only a blow up of $2^{O(|\mathcal{S}| \log(|\mathcal{S}|))}$ states.

After that, Klarlund [284] presented a complementation procedure without determinization in 1991 that also requires only a blow-up to $2^{O(|\mathcal{S}| \log(|\mathcal{S}|))}$ states. Recently, Kupferman and Vardi described a complementation algorithm that goes through weak alternating automata [302] whose implementation has been recently refined in [225].

To conclude this section, consider Figure 4.17 as another example of Safra's construction (applied to the automaton of Figure 4.12).

4.6 The Hierarchy of ω-Automata and the Borel Hierarchy

In this section, we reconsider the hierarchy results of ω-automata in terms of a language-oriented view. We will see that the set of infinite words over an alphabet Σ can be endowed with a metric. Hence, we obtain an elegant bridge to already existing mathematical theories. In particular, we will discuss the relationship between the hierarchy of ω-automata and the Borel hierarchy of topology. Before presenting these facts, let us first summarize the expressiveness results we have proved in the previous sections.

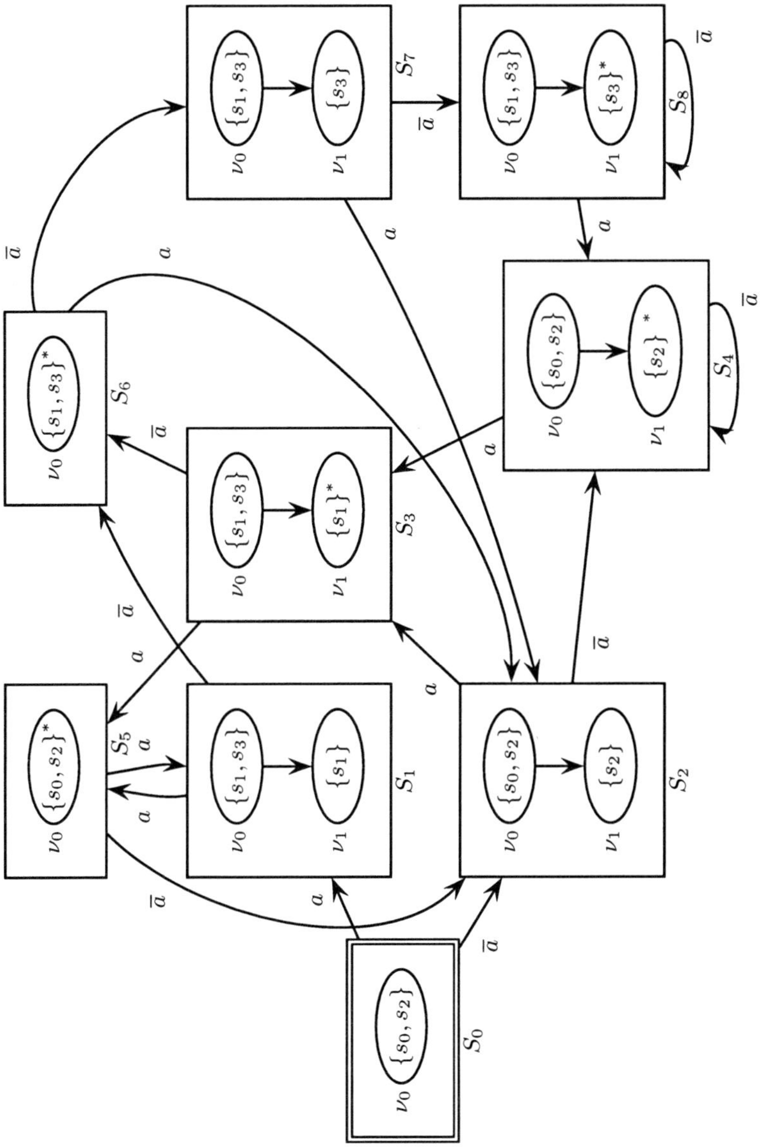

Fig. 4.17. Another example of Safra's construction

Theorem 4.33 (Hierarchy of ω-Automata (III)). *The following expressiveness results hold for the ω-automata:*

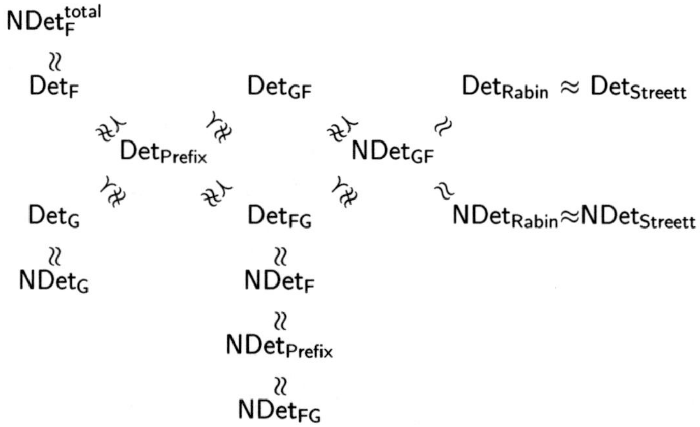

As can be seen, there are six different classes, and each class contains a deterministic representative. Note that the above result implies furthermore that none of the classes Det_G, Det_F, Det_FG, nor Det_FG is closed under complement. Assuming that Det_G or Det_F would be closed under complement, would imply that the class would be closed under all Boolean connectives, and hence would be equivalent to $\mathsf{Det}_\mathsf{Prefix}$. Similarly, neither Det_FG nor Det_GF is closed under complement. Note, however, that every class is closed under union and intersection.

Based on the results of this section, we will deepen the relationship of these classes and will characterize them in terms of topology. We will see that open and closed sets correspond with the classes Det_F and Det_G, respectively. Sometimes, also *clopen sets* are considered that are both open and closed [305, 481, 489], i.e., properties that can be expressed by Det_F and Det_G automata. It can be shown [305, 481, 489] that such properties can be expressed by deterministic automata whose acceptance condition can be expressed by propositional connectives and X. The corresponding languages are of the form $\{\alpha_1, \ldots, \alpha_n\}\Sigma^\omega$ with finitely many finite words $\alpha_1, \ldots, \alpha_n$.

Moreover, the above hierarchy can be refined in that we consider in the classes $\mathsf{Det}_\mathsf{Rabin}$ and $\mathsf{Det}_\mathsf{Prefix}$ those automata with at most f acceptance pairs, i.e., those automata with *Rabin index* f. The resulting hierarchy, the Rabin index hierarchy proposed by Wagner [506] in 1979 is known to be strict. Furthermore, it can be decided how many acceptance pairs are required for a given property [506].

To reason about such results, we now consider the above hierarchy of ω-automata in more detail. In particular, we will discuss how the different classes can be obtained from each other. We already know that the classes Det_G and Det_F, and also the classes Det_FG and Det_GF are dual, i.e., can be obtained from each other by complementation. Moreover, we have already seen that $\mathsf{Det}_{\mathsf{Prefix}}$ is the Boolean closure of the classes $\mathsf{Det}_{\mathsf{G}}$ and $\mathsf{Det}_{\mathsf{F}}$, and analogously, that $\mathsf{Det}_{\mathsf{Rabin}}/\mathsf{Det}_{\mathsf{Streett}}$ is the Boolean closure of $\mathsf{Det}_{\mathsf{GF}}$ and $\mathsf{Det}_{\mathsf{FG}}$. $\mathsf{Det}_{\mathsf{GF}}$ can be obtained from $\mathsf{Det}_{\mathsf{F}}$ by the limes-operation (Definition 4.3).

We will now consider these operations in a different setting, namely in a topological one. Similar constructions are used in topology to establish a similar hierarchy, namely the Borel hierarchy [356, 489]. In general, the Borel hierarchy can be defined for every topology. We do however restrict our discussion to metric spaces[4]. For this reason, we first introduce some basic notions of metric spaces and then define the Borel hierarchy in this general setting. After this, we will discuss how ω-regular languages are related to this.

Definition 4.34 (Metric Spaces). *Every pair $\langle M, \delta \rangle$ with a set M and a function $\delta : M \times M \to \mathbb{R}$ is a metric space if the following properties are satisfied:*

- $\forall x, y \in M.\, 0 \leq \delta(x, y)$
- $\forall x, y \in M.\, 0 = \delta(x, y) \Leftrightarrow x = y$
- $\forall x, y \in M.\, \delta(x, y) = \delta(y, x)$
- $\forall x, y, z \in M.\, \delta(x, z) \leq \delta(x, y) + \delta(y, z)$

For every $\varepsilon \in \mathbb{R}$ with $0 < \varepsilon$ and every $x \in M$, we define $\mathfrak{S}_\varepsilon(x) := \{y \in M \mid \delta(x, y) < \varepsilon\}$ as the ε-sphere around x.

Intuitively, $\delta(x, y)$ denotes the distance between two elements $x, y \in M$. Therefore, metric spaces consider the neighborhood of elements. In particular, an ε-sphere contains the elements of M whose distance to x is less than ε. These ε-spheres are used for a variety of purposes. For example, ε-spheres are used to define convergence of a function $f : \mathbb{N} \to M$: we define $x = \lim_{n\to\infty} f(n)$ iff $\forall \varepsilon > 0.\exists n_0 \in \mathbb{N}.\forall n > n_0.f(n) \in \mathfrak{S}_\varepsilon(x)$. This means, no matter how small we choose an ε-sphere around x, it will contain almost all values $f(n)$.

Some important properties of sets $A \subseteq M$ are coupled with convergent functions. A set $A \subseteq M$ is closed if for every convergent function $f : \mathbb{N} \to A$, the limes $\lim_{n\to\infty} f(n)$ belongs to M. Open and closed sets can also be defined in the following equivalent manner:

Definition 4.35 (Open and Closed Sets). *Given a metric space $\langle M, \delta \rangle$. Then, a set $A \subseteq M$ is open if for all $x \in A$ there is a $\varepsilon \in \mathbb{R}$ with $0 < \varepsilon$ and $\mathfrak{S}_\varepsilon(x) \subseteq A$. $A \subseteq M$ is closed if its complement $M \setminus A$ is open, i.e., if for each $x \in M \setminus A$, there is a $\varepsilon \in \mathbb{R}$ with $0 < \varepsilon$ and $\mathfrak{S}_\varepsilon(x) \subseteq M \setminus A$.*

This means that open sets $A \subseteq M$ contain with every element x also some ε-sphere of x, and therefore some neighborhood of the element, and not only the element itself. In particular $\{\}$ and M are open sets. Note that there are sets that are neither closed nor open: For example, the real numbers are a

[4] Note that every metric space induces a topology, but that there are topologies that are not induced by a metric space.

metric space with the usual distance function $\delta(x,y) := |x-y|$. The set $\{x \mid 1 < x < 3\}$ is open, the set $\{x \mid 4 \leq x \leq 5\}$ is closed, but $\{x \mid 1 < x < 3\} \cup \{x \mid 4 \leq x \leq 5\}$ is neither open nor closed.

According to the above definition, the complements of the open sets are the closed sets, and vice versa. Hence, these sets are dual to each other. Moreover, the union of arbitrary many open sets is open, and also the intersection of finitely many open sets is open. Analogously, the intersection of arbitrary many closed sets is closed, and the union of finitely many closed sets is closed. Hence, we have a similar situation as in the automaton hierarchy, since the first two classes $\mathsf{Det_G}$ and $\mathsf{Det_F}$ are dual to each other, closed under intersection and union, but not under complement.

The Borel hierarchy is now obtained by successively defining new classes from countable intersections and unions of already known classes. Formally, the Borel hierarchy for a metric space is defined as follows (the notation of the sets F_i and G_i is due to historical reasons: F_i is due to the French word fermé):

Definition 4.36 (Borel Hierarchy). *Given a metric space $\langle M, \delta \rangle$, the Borel hierarchy is defined as follows:*

- $G_1 := \{L \subseteq M \mid L \text{ is open}\}$
- $F_1 := \{L \subseteq M \mid L \text{ is closed}\}$
- $G_{n+1} := \{L \subseteq M \mid L = \bigcup_{i=0}^{\infty} L_i \text{ with } L_i \in F_n\}$
- $F_{n+1} := \{L \subseteq M \mid L = \bigcap_{i=0}^{\infty} L_i \text{ with } L_i \in G_n\}$

In the literature, some different notations are used for the classes that form the Borel hierarchy. For example, [486] denotes the open sets as G, the closed sets as F, and adds then for every countable union the suffix σ, and for every countable intersection the suffix δ. Hence, the sets F_σ, G_δ, $G_{\delta\sigma}$, $F_{\sigma\delta}$, and so on, are obtained. Landweber [312] uses our notation, except that for even numbers, G_{2n} and F_{2n} are switched. We do not follow this notations since they make the formal proofs more complicated as we would then have to distinguish whether the index is an odd or even number to see if the class is obtained from a countable union or intersection of the class at the next lower level. The following theorem on the relationship of the sets G_n and F_n of the Borel hierarchy shows a first connection to the hierarchy we have already found for the ω-automata.

Theorem 4.37 (Borel Hierarchy). *Given a metric space $\langle M, \delta \rangle$ with its Borel hierarchy G_n, F_n for $n \in \mathbb{N}$. Then, the following holds for every $n \in \mathbb{N}$:*

1. *$A \in G_n$ iff $M \setminus A \in F_n$.*
2. *G_n and F_n are both closed under finite union and intersection.*
3. *Any set $G_n \cap F_n$ is closed under complement, finite union and finite intersection.*

If M is countable, then we moreover have the following:

4. *$G_n \cup F_n \subseteq G_{n+1} \cap F_{n+1}$.*

Proof. The first proposition is proved by induction on n. For $n = 0$, it immediately holds by definition of closed and open sets. For $n + 1$, we have by induction hypothesis that $A \in G_n$ iff $M \setminus A \in F_n$ holds for every set $A \subseteq M$. Now consider a set $A \in G_{n+1}$. By definition of G_{n+1}, A is the countable union $A = \bigcup_{i=0}^{\infty} A_i$ of sets $A_i \in F_n$. Hence, we have $M \setminus A = M \setminus \bigcup_{i=0}^{\infty} A_i = \bigcap_{i=0}^{\infty} M \setminus A_i$, i.e., $M \setminus A$ is a countable intersection of sets $M \setminus A_i$ that belong by our induction hypothesis to F_n, and hence, it follows that $M \setminus A \in F_{n+1}$.

To prove the second proposition, it is sufficient to prove it for G_n, since the result follows by the first proposition for F_n. The proof for G_n is done by induction on n. For $n = 0$, we have to prove that the union and intersection of two open sets is again an open set. Assume that A_1 and A_2 are open sets and $x \in A_1 \cap A_2$. As A_1 and A_2 are open, there are a $\varepsilon > 0$ and $\varrho > 0$ such that $\mathfrak{S}_\varepsilon(x) \subseteq A_1$ and $\mathfrak{S}_\varrho(x) \subseteq A_2$. Let $\vartheta = \min\{\varepsilon, \varrho\}$, then it follows that $\mathfrak{S}_\vartheta(x) \subseteq A_1 \cap A_2$. Hence, $A_1 \cap A_2$ is open. The proof of for $A_1 \cup A_1$ is similar.

For proving the induction step, assume we have $A, B \in G_{n+1}$, i.e., $A = \bigcup_{i=0}^{\infty} A_i$ and $B = \bigcup_{i=0}^{\infty} B_i$ with $A_i, B_i \in F_n$. Hence, $A \cup B = \bigcup_{i=0}^{\infty} A_i \cup B_i$, and by the induction hypothesis we have $A_i \cup B_i \in F_n$, it immediately follows that $A \cup B \in G_{n+1}$. For proving $A \cap B \in G_{n+1}$, consider the following:

$$\begin{aligned}
\alpha \in A \cap B &\Leftrightarrow \alpha \in (\textstyle\bigcup_{i=0}^{\infty} A_i) \cap (\bigcup_{i=0}^{\infty} B_i) \Leftrightarrow (\alpha \in \bigcup_{i=0}^{\infty} A_i) \wedge (\alpha \in \bigcup_{i=0}^{\infty} B_i) \\
&\Leftrightarrow (\exists i \in \mathbb{N}.\alpha \in A_i) \wedge (\exists j \in \mathbb{N}.\alpha \in B_j) \Leftrightarrow \exists i, j \in \mathbb{N}.\alpha \in A_i \wedge \alpha \in B_j \\
&\Leftrightarrow \exists i, j \in \mathbb{N}.\alpha \in A_i \cap B_j \Leftrightarrow \alpha \in \textstyle\bigcup_{i=0}^{\infty} \bigcup_{j=0}^{\infty} A_i \cap B_j
\end{aligned}$$

Hence, we have $A \cap B = \bigcup_{i=0}^{\infty} \bigcup_{j=0}^{\infty} A_i \cap B_j$, such that $A \cap B$ is also a countable union of sets that belong to F_n. Hence, $A \cap B \in G_{n+1}$.

As a consequence of the first two propositions, every set $G_n \cap F_n$ is Boolean closed: for $A, B \in G_n \cap F_n$, it follows by our first proposition that $M \setminus A \in G_n \cap F_n$, and by our second proposition that $A \cup B, A \cap B \in G_n \cap F_n$.

Next, we turn to the fourth proposition. Instead of proving $G_n \cup F_n \subseteq G_{n+1} \cap F_{n+1}$ directly, we prove instead the four propositions (1) $G_n \subseteq G_{n+1}$, (2) $G_n \subseteq F_{n+1}$, (3) $F_n \subseteq G_{n+1}$, and (4) $F_n \subseteq F_{n+1}$, which imply our proposition. (2) and (3) hold trivially by definition of G_{n+1} and F_{n+1}: simply represent $A \in G_{n+1}$ as $A = \bigcup_{i=1}^{\infty} A$, and $B \in F_{n+1}$ as $B = \bigcap_{i=1}^{\infty} B$. (1) and (4) are proved by simultaneous induction on n: To prove $G_0 \subseteq G_1$, simply represent $A \in G_0$ as $A = \bigcup_{a \in A}\{a\}$. As M is countable, so is A. Moreover, $\{a\}$ is clearly a closed set, hence we have $\{a\} \in F_0$. Therefore, it follows $A \in G_1$, and hence $G_0 \subseteq G_1$. Similarly, to prove $F_0 \subseteq F_1$, simply represent $A \in F_0$ as $A = \bigcap_{a \in A} M \setminus \{a\}$. All sets $M \setminus \{a\}$ are open sets, hence $M \setminus \{a\} \in G_0$ holds, and therefore $A \in F_1$.

For the induction step, we have to prove $G_{n+1} \subseteq G_{n+2}$ and $F_{n+1} \subseteq F_{n+2}$. Consider an arbitrary set $A \in G_{n+1}$ with the representation $A = \bigcup_{i=0}^{\infty} A_i$ where $A_i \in F_n$ for all $i \in \mathbb{N}$. As we already know by the induction hypothesis, $G_n \subseteq G_{n+1}$ and $F_n \subseteq F_{n+1}$ hold, and it follows for all $i \in \mathbb{N}$ that $A_i \in F_{n+1}$ holds, and thus $A \in G_{n+2}$ holds. Similarly, we prove $F_{n+1} \subseteq F_{n+2}$. □

The above theorem lists the essential results on the Borel hierarchy. The relationships between the sets G_n and F_n are thus pictorially given as follows, where G_n contains the complements of the sets of F_n and vice versa, and the sets $G_n \cap F_n$ are Boolean closed.

$$
\begin{array}{ccccccccc}
G_1 & & & G_2 & & & G_3 & & \\
 & \searrow\subseteq & \subseteq\nearrow & & \searrow\subseteq & \subseteq\nearrow & & \searrow\subseteq & \\
 & & G_1 \cup F_1 \subseteq G_2 \cap F_2 & & & G_2 \cup F_2 \subseteq G_3 \cap F_3 & & & G_3 \cup F_3 \subseteq \dots \\
 & \subseteq\nearrow & \searrow\subseteq & & \subseteq\nearrow & \searrow\subseteq & & \subseteq\nearrow & \\
F_1 & & & F_2 & & & F_3 & &
\end{array}
$$

It is apparent that the above diagram resembles the hierarchy of ω-automata that we have already stated in Theorem 4.33. To establish this correspondence at a formal level, we have to endow the set of infinite words with a metric.

Definition 4.38 (Metric of ω-Regular Words). *Given a finite alphabet Σ, we define the function $\delta_\omega : \Sigma^\omega \times \Sigma^\omega \to \mathbb{R}$ as follows:*

$$
\delta_\omega(\alpha, \beta) := \begin{cases} 0 & : \alpha = \beta \\ \dfrac{1}{i+1} & : \alpha^{(i)} \neq \beta^{(i)} \quad \wedge \quad \forall j < i.\, \alpha^{(j)} = \beta^{(j)} \end{cases}
$$

It is easily seen that $\langle \Sigma^\omega, \delta_\omega \rangle$ is a metric space. The longer the common prefix of two words α and β is, the closer are the words α and β to each other, i.e., the smaller is their distance $\delta_\omega(\alpha, \beta)$. In particular, it is easily seen that $\mathfrak{S}_\varepsilon(\alpha) = \{\beta \in \Sigma^\omega \mid \forall i < \left\lceil \frac{1}{\varepsilon} - 1 \right\rceil . \alpha^{(i)} = \beta^{(i)}\}$, where $\lceil x \rceil \in \mathbb{Z}$ denotes the smallest integer that is larger than $x \in \mathbb{R}$. We therefore have the following characterization of a sphere $\mathfrak{S}_\varepsilon(\alpha) = \{\alpha^{(0..n)}\}\Sigma^\omega$ with $n = \left\lceil \frac{1}{\varepsilon} - 1 \right\rceil$.

Now, the next natural question at this stage is to ask what it means for a language $L \subseteq \Sigma^\omega$ to be closed or open? Due to the definition of the metric δ_ω, it immediately follows that a language $L \subseteq \Sigma^\omega$ is open iff for every $\alpha \in L$ there is a $n \in \mathbb{N}$ such that $\{\alpha^{(0..n)}\}\Sigma^\omega \subseteq L$ holds.

Before considering what the correspondence between the classes of the Borel hierarchy and the automaton classes is, we must first restrict our considerations to ω-regular languages L, i.e., languages that are accepted by a ω-automaton. Clearly, there are subsets of infinite words that are not ω-regular. For example, if we have the alphabet $\Sigma = \{0, \dots, 9\}$, then the closed set $\{14142\dots\}$ (the decimal representation of $\sqrt{2}$) is not ω-regular. This is easily seen since every ω-regular language is non-empty iff it contains a ultimately periodic word, i.e., a word of the form $\alpha\beta^\omega$ (which implies that both α and β are finite words over Σ). This is a simple consequence of the fact that every finite automaton that accepts such a language has only a finite number of states and therefore, we can construct such a word by detecting a cycle in the state transition diagram. For the ω-regular subsets of F_i and G_i, Landweber gave, in 1969, the following result [312]:

Theorem 4.39 (Borel Hierarchy of ω-Regular Languages). *Given a finite alphabet Σ, and the metric space $\langle \Sigma^\omega, \delta_\omega \rangle$ as given in Definition 4.38. Let G_n and F_n be the classes occurring in the Borel hierarchy for $\langle \Sigma^\omega, \delta_\omega \rangle$, then define the ω-regular subsets $\mathcal{G}_i$ and $\mathcal{F}_i$ of these classes as follows:*

$$\mathcal{G}_i := \{L \subseteq \Sigma^\omega \mid L \in G_i \wedge \exists \mathfrak{A} \in \mathsf{Det}_{\mathsf{Rabin}}.\, \mathsf{Lang}(\mathfrak{A}) = L\}$$
$$\mathcal{F}_i := \{L \subseteq \Sigma^\omega \mid L \in F_i \wedge \exists \mathfrak{A} \in \mathsf{Det}_{\mathsf{Rabin}}.\, \mathsf{Lang}(\mathfrak{A}) = L\}$$

For the sets $\mathcal{G}_n$ and $\mathcal{F}_n$, the following holds:

- *$\mathcal{G}_1$ is the set of languages accepted by Det_F automata.*
- *$\mathcal{F}_1$ is the set of languages accepted by Det_G automata.*
- *$\mathcal{G}_2 \cap \mathcal{F}_2$ is the set of languages accepted by $\mathsf{Det}_\mathsf{Prefix}$ automata.*
- *$\mathcal{G}_2$ is the set of languages accepted by Det_FG automata.*
- *$\mathcal{F}_2$ is the set of languages accepted by Det_GF automata.*
- *$\mathcal{G}_3 \cap F_3$ is the set of languages accepted by $\mathsf{Det}_\mathsf{Rabin}$ automata.*

This result of Landweber [312] shows the correspondence between the Det_κ classes and the Borel hierarchy. The proof of the above theorem is quite complicated; we will prove it by considering two directions: One direction, namely the 'inclusion' of Det_κ in the classes $\mathcal{G}_n$ and $\mathcal{F}_n$ can be proved by showing that the languages that are accepted by the classes Det_κ can be characterized by ω-regular expressions, so that we can determine their Borel class.

For example, note that a word α is accepted by an automaton Det_F iff there is a prefix $\alpha^{(0..n)}$ of α, such that every infinite word $\alpha^{(0..n)}\beta$ is accepted by Det_F. The run of $\alpha^{(0..n)}$ leads from the initial state to one of the designated states. Hence, the language accepted by a Det_F automaton is of the form $L_{\mathsf{reg}}\Sigma$, where L_{reg} is the set of finite words that have a path from the initial state to one of the designated states. As the sphere $\mathfrak{S}_\varepsilon(\alpha)$ around a word α is the set of words of the form $\{\alpha^{(0..n)}\}\Sigma^\omega$, it follows that the languages of the form $L_{\mathsf{reg}}\Sigma$ are open, and hence the languages accepted by automata of the class Det_F are open. Due to the duality between Det_F and Det_G, this immediately implies that the languages accepted by automata of the class Det_G are closed.

Lemma 4.40 (Characterizing Det_κ by ω-Regular Expressions). *For every ω-regular language $L \subseteq \Sigma^\omega$, the following holds:*

- *$L = \mathsf{Lang}(\mathfrak{A})$ for some $\mathfrak{A} \in \mathsf{Det}_\mathsf{F}$ iff there is a regular language L_{reg} with $L = L_{\mathsf{reg}}\Sigma^\omega$*
- *$L = \mathsf{Lang}(\mathfrak{A})$ for some $\mathfrak{A} \in \mathsf{Det}_\mathsf{G}$ iff there is a regular language L_{reg} with $L = \Sigma^\omega \setminus L_{\mathsf{reg}}\Sigma^\omega$*
- *$L = \mathsf{Lang}(\mathfrak{A})$ for some $\mathfrak{A} \in \mathsf{Det}_\mathsf{Prefix}$ iff there are regular languages $K_{\mathsf{reg}}^{(i)}$ and $L_{\mathsf{reg}}^{(i)}$ with $L = \bigcup_{i=0}^{f} K_{\mathsf{reg}}^{(i)}\Sigma^\omega \cap (\Sigma^\omega \setminus L_{\mathsf{reg}}^{(i)}\Sigma^\omega)$*
- *$L = \mathsf{Lang}(\mathfrak{A})$ for some $\mathfrak{A} \in \mathsf{Det}_\mathsf{GF}$ iff there is a regular language L_{reg} with $L = \mathsf{Lim}(L_{\mathsf{reg}})$*

- $L = \mathsf{Lang}(\mathfrak{A})$ *for some* $\mathfrak{A} \in \mathsf{Det}_{\mathsf{FG}}$ *iff there is a regular language* L_{reg} *with* $L = \Sigma^\omega \setminus \mathsf{Lim}(L_{\mathsf{reg}})$
- $L = \mathsf{Lang}(\mathfrak{A})$ *for some* $\mathfrak{A} \in \mathsf{Det}_{\mathsf{Rabin}}$ *iff there are regular languages* $K_{\mathsf{reg}}^{(i)}$ *and* $L_{\mathsf{reg}}^{(i)}$ *with* $L = \bigcup_{i=0}^{f} \mathsf{Lim}(K_{\mathsf{reg}}^{(i)}) \cap (\Sigma^\omega \setminus \mathsf{Lim}(L_{\mathsf{reg}}^{(i)}))$
- $L = \mathsf{Lang}(\mathfrak{A})$ *for some* $\mathfrak{A} \in \mathsf{Det}_{\mathsf{GF}}$ *implies that there are regular languages* $L_{\mathsf{reg}}^{(i)}$ *with* $L = \bigcap_{i=0}^{\infty} L_{\mathsf{reg}}^{(i)} \Sigma^\omega$

Proof. We have already explained the first two equivalences, the third one is a direct consequence of the first two ones.

The fourth proposition is obtained in a similar manner. Given $\mathfrak{A} \in \mathsf{Det}_{\mathsf{GF}}$, we construct L_{reg} as the set of finite words that have a path starting in the initial state, leading to a cycle that has a nonempty intersection with the designated states. The equivalence for $\mathsf{Det}_{\mathsf{FG}}$ is dual to this, and the one for $\mathsf{Det}_{\mathsf{Rabin}}$ easily follows.

To prove the last proposition, define the regular languages $L_{\mathsf{reg}}^{(i)}$ for the given automaton $\mathfrak{A} \in \mathsf{Det}_{\mathsf{GF}}$ as follows:

$$L_{\mathsf{reg}}^{(i)} := \{\alpha \in \Sigma^* \mid \exists \pi \in \mathsf{RUN}_{\mathfrak{A}}(\alpha). \left|\{t \in \mathbb{N} \mid \pi^{(t)} \in \mathcal{S}_{\mathcal{F}}\}\right| \geq i\}.$$

Hence, $L_{\mathsf{reg}}^{(i)}$ contains exactly those finite words whose run π visits the designated states at least i times. Clearly, we have $L_{\mathsf{reg}}^{(i+1)} \subseteq L_{\mathsf{reg}}^{(i)}$, and therefore $L_{\mathsf{reg}}^{(k)} \Sigma^\omega = \bigcap_{i=0}^{k} L_{\mathsf{reg}}^{(i)} \Sigma^\omega$. Hence, the latter set contains the ω-words whose infinite run π visits the designated states at least i times. Therefore, the set $\lim_{k\to\infty} L_{\mathsf{reg}}^{(k)} \Sigma^\omega = \bigcap_{i=0}^{\infty} L_{\mathsf{reg}}^{(i)} \Sigma^\omega$ is exactly the set $\mathsf{Lang}(\mathfrak{A})$. □

As a consequence of the above lemma, it immediately follows that the languages accepted by $\mathsf{Det}_{\mathsf{F}}$ and $\mathsf{Det}_{\mathsf{G}}$ are open and closed, respectively. This is easily seen since languages of the form $L_{\mathsf{reg}}\Sigma^\omega$ and $\Sigma^\omega \setminus L_{\mathsf{reg}}\Sigma^\omega$ are easily identified as open and closed sets, respectively. From the last point, it follows that the languages accepted by $\mathsf{Det}_{\mathsf{GF}}$ automata are countable intersections of open sets, and hence, they belong to $\mathcal{F}_2$. Since, $\mathcal{G}_2$ and $\mathcal{F}_2$, and $\mathsf{Det}_{\mathsf{FG}}$ and $\mathsf{Det}_{\mathsf{GF}}$ are dual, it follows that the languages accepted by $\mathsf{Det}_{\mathsf{FG}}$ automata belong to $\mathcal{G}_2$. This explains the four basic acceptance classes.

We have already proved that $\mathsf{Det}_{\mathsf{Prefix}} \precnapprox \mathsf{Det}_{\mathsf{FG}}$ and $\mathsf{Det}_{\mathsf{Prefix}} \precnapprox \mathsf{Det}_{\mathsf{GF}}$ (see Lemma 4.16). Hence, it follows that the languages accepted by $\mathsf{Det}_{\mathsf{Prefix}}$ automata must belong to $\mathcal{G}_2 \cap \mathcal{F}_2$. The result for $\mathsf{Det}_{\mathsf{Prefix}}$ and $\mathsf{Det}_{\mathsf{Rabin}}$ may also be obtained from the fact that we already know that these classes are the Boolean closures of $\mathsf{Det}_{\mathsf{F}}$ and $\mathsf{Det}_{\mathsf{GF}}$, respectively (we have already seen that $\mathcal{G}_{n+1} \cap \mathcal{F}_{n+1}$ contains $\mathcal{G}_n \cup \mathcal{F}_n$ and is closed under all Boolean operations).

Hence, we have shown that the languages accepted by $\mathsf{Det}_{\mathsf{F}}$, $\mathsf{Det}_{\mathsf{G}}$, $\mathsf{Det}_{\mathsf{FG}}$, $\mathsf{Det}_{\mathsf{GF}}$, $\mathsf{Det}_{\mathsf{Prefix}}$, and $\mathsf{Det}_{\mathsf{Rabin}}$ automata belong to the classes $\mathcal{G}_1$, $\mathcal{F}_1$, $\mathcal{G}_2$, $\mathcal{F}_2$, $\mathcal{G}_2 \cap \mathcal{F}_2$, and $\mathcal{G}_3 \cap \mathcal{F}_3$ respectively.

The other inclusions are proved by answering the following question: Given a $\mathsf{Det}_{\mathsf{Rabin}}$ automaton, is there an equivalent Det_κ automaton for $\kappa \in$

{G, F, GF, FG, Prefix}? To answer this question, we again follow the results and proofs given in [293, 312].

For the following considerations, we have to introduce some new notations. These are given formally in the definition below. Informally, $\mathsf{reach}(s, s')$ holds if s' is reachable from s, and s is reachable from some initial state. $\mathsf{loop}(S)$ holds iff the states of S form a cycle and one of them (and hence all of them) is reachable from an initial state. Finally, $\mathsf{Loops}(s)$ contains all reachable cycles where s belongs to. Note that $\mathsf{Loops}(s)$ is always a finite set since $\mathsf{Loops}(s) \subseteq 2^{\mathcal{S}}$.

Definition 4.41 (Reachable Loops of a State). *Given a deterministic automaton $\mathfrak{A} \in \mathsf{Det}_\kappa$ with the states $\mathcal{S}$, we introduce the following definitions for $s, s' \in \mathcal{S}$ and $S \subseteq \mathcal{S}$:*

$$\mathsf{reach}(s, s') \Leftrightarrow \exists \alpha \in \Sigma^\omega . \exists \pi \in \mathsf{RUN}_{\mathfrak{A}}(\alpha). \exists n, m \in \mathbb{N}. (\pi^{(n)} = s) \wedge (\pi^{(n+m)} = s')$$

$$\mathsf{loop}(S) \Leftrightarrow \left(\begin{array}{l} \exists \alpha \in \Sigma^\omega . \exists \pi \in \mathsf{RUN}_{\mathfrak{A}}(\alpha). \\ \quad \left(\exists n \in \mathbb{N}. \forall t \in \mathbb{N}. \pi^{(t+n)} = \pi^{((t \bmod \ell)+n)}\right) \wedge \\ \quad S = \{\pi^{(n)}, \ldots, \pi^{(\ell-1+n)}\} \end{array} \right)$$

$$\mathsf{Loops}(s) = \{S \subseteq \mathcal{S} \mid s \in S \wedge \mathsf{loop}(S)\}$$

With the above notations, we can now set up criteria for given ω-regular languages that hold iff the language can be accepted by some Det_κ automaton. To this end, we first assume that the ω-regular language is given as an accepted language of a $\mathsf{Det}_{\mathsf{Muller}}$ automaton. We recall that such an automaton has a set of designated sets of states $\mathcal{S}_{\mathcal{F}} = \{S_1, \ldots, S_f\}$ to define the acceptance condition as follows: a run is accepted iff one of the S_i in $\mathcal{S}_{\mathcal{F}}$ is exactly the set of states that the run visits infinitely often.

Theorem 4.42 (Checking Openess of ω-Regular Languages). *For every $\mathfrak{A} \in \mathsf{Det}_{\mathsf{Muller}}$ with the states $\mathcal{S}$ and the designated sets of states $\mathcal{S}_{\mathcal{F}} = \{S_1, \ldots, S_f\}$, the following is equivalent:*

(1) $\mathsf{Lang}(\mathfrak{A})$ *is open, i.e., it belongs to* $\mathcal{G}_1$
(2) $\forall s, s' \in \mathcal{S}. \mathsf{reach}(s, s') \wedge (\mathsf{Loops}(s) \cap \mathcal{S}_{\mathcal{F}} \neq \{\}) \to \mathsf{Loops}(s') \subseteq \mathcal{S}_{\mathcal{F}}$

If the latter holds, then the automaton $\mathfrak{A}_{\mathsf{F}} \in \mathsf{Det}_{\mathsf{F}}$ with $\mathcal{S}'_{\mathcal{F}} := \bigcup_{i=1}^{f} S_i$ is equivalent to $\mathfrak{A}$.

Proof. First note that for $\mathsf{Lang}(\mathfrak{A}) = \{\}$ the theorem is trivial, since $\forall s \in \mathcal{S}. \mathsf{Loops}(s) \cap \mathcal{S}_{\mathcal{F}} = \{\}$ must hold. Hence, assume now that $\mathsf{Lang}(\mathfrak{A}) \neq \{\}$. We split the equivalence in two implications:

$\boxed{\Rightarrow:}$ Assume $\mathsf{Lang}(\mathfrak{A})$ is open. Consider an arbitrary word $\gamma \in \mathsf{Lang}(\mathfrak{A})$. Since $\mathsf{Lang}(\mathfrak{A})$ is open, there must be a $n \in \mathbb{N}$ such that $\{\gamma^{(0..n-1)}\}\Sigma^\omega \subseteq \mathsf{Lang}(\mathfrak{A})$. Let now be s_0 the state that is reached after reading $\gamma^{(0..n-1)}$ from the initial state of $\mathfrak{A}$ and let $r_0 \in \mathcal{S}$ be an arbitrary state with $\mathsf{reach}(s_0, r_0)$. Furthermore, assume we have $\mathsf{Loops}(s_0) \cap \mathcal{S}_{\mathcal{F}} \neq \{\}$. We

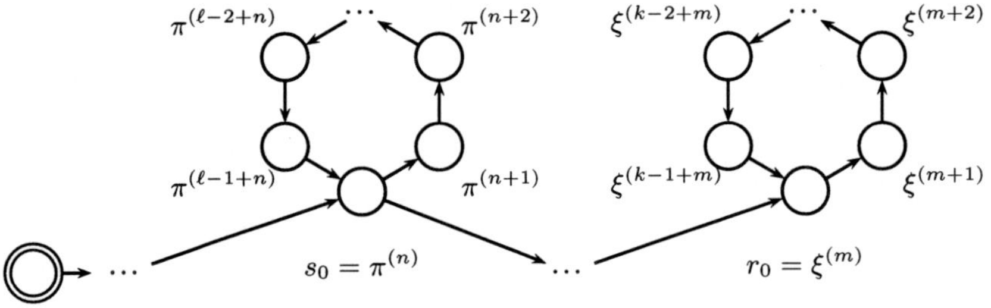

Fig. 4.18. The situation given in the proof of Theorem 4.42.

therefore have to prove that $\mathsf{Loops}(r_0) \subseteq \mathcal{S}_\mathcal{F}$ holds (in particular, this also implies that $\mathsf{Loops}(s_0) \subseteq \mathcal{S}_\mathcal{F}$ holds).

By the definition of Loops, there is a word $\alpha \in \mathsf{Lang}(\mathfrak{A})$ with run π and a number $n \in \mathbb{N}$ such that $\forall t \in \mathbb{N}.\pi^{(t+n)} = \pi^{((t \bmod \ell)+n)}$ holds. Clearly, α is also periodic: $\forall t.\alpha^{(t+n)} = \alpha^{((t \bmod \ell)+n)}$. Let now $C \in \mathsf{Loops}(r_0)$ be an arbitrary cycle of r_0. We must show that $C \in \mathcal{S}_\mathcal{F}$ holds. By definition of reach and Loops, there must be a word $\alpha^{(0..n-1)}\beta \in \Sigma^\omega$ with run ξ such that for some $k, m \in \mathbb{N}$ with $n \leq m$, we have $\forall t.\xi^{(t+m)} = \xi^{((t \bmod k)+m)}$, $C = \{\xi^{(m)}, \ldots, \xi^{(k-1+m)}\}$, $r_0 = \xi^{(t+m)}$, and $\forall t \leq n.\xi^{(t)} = \pi^{(t)}$. The situation is depicted in Figure 4.18. As we clearly have $\alpha^{(0..n-1)}\beta \in \{\alpha^{(0..n-1)}\}\Sigma^\omega$ it follows that $\alpha^{(0..n-1)}\beta \in \mathsf{Lang}(\mathfrak{A})$ and hence that $C \in \mathcal{S}_\mathcal{F}$.

$\boxed{\Leftarrow:}$ Given a finite word $\alpha \in \Sigma^*$, denote with $s_\alpha \in \mathcal{S}$ the state this is reached from the initial state of $\mathfrak{A}$ after reading α. Define $L = \{\alpha \in \Sigma^* \mid \mathsf{Loops}(s_\alpha) \cap \mathcal{S}_\mathcal{F} \neq \{\}\}$. We show that $\mathsf{Lang}(\mathfrak{A}) = L\Sigma^\omega$ holds, and therefore $\mathsf{Lang}(\mathfrak{A})$ is open.

Let $\alpha \in \mathsf{Lang}(\mathfrak{A})$ be arbitrarily given and let $S \subseteq \mathcal{S}$ be the set of states that appear infinitely often on the run over α. Let $n \in \mathbb{N}$ be an arbitrary number such that reading $\alpha^{(0..n)}$ leads to a state in $s_0 \in S$ that is visited infinitely often. Clearly, we then have $S \in \mathsf{Loops}(s_0) \cap \mathcal{S}_\mathcal{F}$, and thus $\alpha^{(0..n)} \in L$. Hence, it follows by the condition (2), that is the assumption of this part of the proof that for every r_0 with $\mathsf{reach}(s_0, r_0)$ that $\mathsf{Loops}(r_0) \subseteq \mathcal{S}_\mathcal{F}$ holds.

Consider now a word $\alpha^{(0..n)}\beta \in \Sigma^\omega$ together with its run ξ. As we have $\forall t.\mathsf{reach}(s_0, \xi^{(t+n)})$ it follows by the above facts that $\forall t.\mathsf{Loops}(\xi^{(t+n)}) \subseteq \mathcal{S}_\mathcal{F}$ holds. But this means that $\alpha^{(0..n)}\beta \in \mathsf{Lang}(\mathfrak{A})$, and hence we see that $\{\alpha^{(0..n)}\}\Sigma^\omega \subseteq \mathsf{Lang}(\mathfrak{A})$ so that $\mathsf{Lang}(\mathfrak{A})$ is open.

Finally, assume that $\mathfrak{A} \in \mathsf{Det}_{\mathsf{Muller}}$ satisfies condition (2). Let π be the run of an arbitrary word α and let $\mathsf{inf}(\pi)$ be the set of states that appear infinitely often on π. If π reaches some state r at time t_r of a designated set of states $S_i \in \mathcal{S}_\mathcal{F}$, then we have $S_i \in \mathsf{Loops}(r) \cap \mathcal{S}_\mathcal{F}$. Let now be $s \in \mathsf{inf}(\pi)$ that appears after t_r on π, so that we have $\mathsf{reach}(r, s)$. By condition (2), it therefore follows that $\mathsf{Loops}(s) \subseteq \mathcal{S}_\mathcal{F}$ holds, and therefore that in particular $\mathsf{inf}(\pi) \in \mathcal{S}_\mathcal{F}$ holds.

Hence, we have $\mathsf{Lang}(\mathfrak{A}_\mathsf{F}) \subseteq \mathsf{Lang}(\mathfrak{A})$. The converse is trivial, since if $\mathsf{inf}(\pi)$ is the set of states that appear infinitely often on π, then π trivially reaches $\mathsf{inf}(\pi)$. □

Hence, the above theorem gives us a computable criterion to decide for a given automaton $\mathfrak{A} \in \mathsf{Det}_\mathsf{Muller}$, if its accepted language $\mathsf{Lang}(\mathfrak{A})$ belongs to $\mathcal{G}_1$ or not. In the case where it does, we can even compute an equivalent automaton $\mathfrak{A}_\mathsf{F} \in \mathsf{Det}_\mathsf{F}$. As $\mathsf{Det}_\mathsf{Muller}$ is closed under complement[5], we can also check if $\mathsf{Lang}(\mathfrak{A})$ belongs to $\mathcal{F}_1$ or not. In the case that $\mathsf{Lang}(\mathfrak{A})$ belongs to $\mathcal{F}_1$, we can compute an equivalent automaton $\mathfrak{A}_\mathsf{G} \in \mathsf{Det}_\mathsf{G}$. Hence, it is decidable for a given ω-regular language, if it belongs to $\mathcal{F}_1$ and $\mathcal{G}_1$. Note that this also implies that every ω-regular open set is accepted by some automaton in Det_F and that every ω-regular closed set is accepted by some automaton in Det_G. We now consider a similar approach for level 2.

Theorem 4.43 (Checking for Membership in $\mathcal{F}_2$). *Given an automaton $\mathfrak{A} \in \mathsf{Det}_\mathsf{Muller}$ with the states $\mathcal{S}$ and the designated sets of states $\mathcal{S}_\mathcal{F} = \{S_1, \ldots, S_f\}$. Using the functions* reach, loop, *and* Loops *given in Theorem 4.42, the following are equivalent:*

(1) $\exists \mathfrak{A}_\mathsf{GF} \in \mathsf{Det}_\mathsf{GF}.\ \mathsf{Lang}(\mathfrak{A}) = \mathsf{Lang}(\mathfrak{A}_\mathsf{GF})$
(2) $\forall s \in \mathcal{S}. \forall C_1, C_2 \in \mathsf{Loops}(s).\ C_1 \in \mathcal{S}_\mathcal{F} \rightarrow C_1 \cup C_2 \in \mathcal{S}_\mathcal{F}$

Proof. We split the equivalence in two implications:

$\boxed{\Rightarrow:}$ Assume that $\mathsf{Lang}(\mathfrak{A}) = \mathsf{Lang}(\mathfrak{A}_\mathsf{GF})$ holds. It follows that $\mathsf{Lang}(\mathfrak{A}) = \mathsf{Lim}(L_\mathsf{reg})$ for the regular language L_reg that is accepted by $\mathfrak{A}_\mathsf{GF}$ when it is interpreted as a finite automaton on finite words. Equivalently, we have $\mathsf{Lang}(\mathfrak{A}) = \bigcap_{i=0}^{\infty} L_i$ for the open languages $L_i \in \mathcal{G}_1$ that contain the infinite words that have at least i prefixes in L_reg. Let $s \in S$ with $C_1, C_2 \in \mathsf{Loops}(s)$ be arbitrarily chosen, such that $C_1 \in \mathcal{S}_\mathcal{F}$ holds. We must prove that $C_1 \cup C_2 \in \mathcal{S}_\mathcal{F}$ holds. This is done by constructing a word $\varrho \in \mathsf{Lang}(\mathfrak{A})$ such that the set of states that appear infinitely often on its run π is $C_1 \cup C_2$.
To this end, choose α, β, and γ such that after reading α we have reached state s. Reading β from s will traverse the states C_1 and then finally returns to state s; analogously, reading γ from s will traverse the states C_2 and then finally returns to state s. Note that α, β, and γ exist, since $C_1, C_2 \in \mathsf{Loops}(s)$ holds; hence, s is reachable and there are loops C_1 and C_2 that both contain s.
It follows that $\alpha\beta^\omega \in \mathsf{Lang}(\mathfrak{A})$, since the set of states that are visited infinitely often by its run is C_1 and we have $C_1 \in \mathcal{S}_\mathcal{F}$. Therefore, the run of $\alpha\beta^\omega$ through $\mathfrak{A}_\mathsf{GF}$ will visit the designated states of $\mathfrak{A}_\mathsf{GF}$ infinitely often. Hence, there is a prefix $\alpha\beta^{i_1}$ of $\alpha\beta^\omega$ that visits the designated states

[5] The complement of $\mathfrak{A} \in \mathsf{Det}_\mathsf{Muller}$ with $\mathcal{S}_\mathcal{F}$ is simply obtained by replacing $\mathcal{S}_\mathcal{F}$ by $2^\mathcal{S} \setminus \mathcal{S}_\mathcal{F}$.

of $\mathfrak{A}_{\mathsf{GF}}$ at least once, so that we have $\{\alpha\beta^{i_1}\gamma\}\Sigma^\omega \subseteq L_1$. Now, observe that $\alpha\beta^{i_1}\gamma\beta^\omega \in \mathsf{Lang}(\mathfrak{A})$ holds, since this word also visits exactly the states C_1 of $\mathfrak{A}$ infinitely often. Hence, we repeat the procedure and obtain the fact that $\{\alpha\beta^{i_1}\gamma\ldots\beta^{i_k}\gamma\}\Sigma^\omega \subseteq L_k$ holds for every $k \in \mathbb{N}$. It follows that the word $\varrho = \alpha\beta^{i_1}\gamma\ldots\beta^{i_k}\gamma\ldots$ belongs to all L_k and hence to $\mathsf{Lang}(\mathfrak{A})$. As this word visits the states $C_1 \cup C_2$ infinitely often, it follows that $C_1 \cup C_2 \in \mathcal{S}_{\mathcal{F}}$.

$\boxed{\Leftarrow:}$ The proof for this direction is done by constructing a $\mathfrak{A}_{\mathsf{GF}} \in \mathsf{Det}_{\mathsf{GF}}$ automaton that is equivalent to the given $\mathfrak{A} \in \mathsf{Det}_{\mathsf{Muller}}$, provided that (2) holds. $\mathfrak{A}_{\mathsf{GF}}$ is constructed as follows: The states are taken from the set $\mathcal{S} \times 2^{\mathcal{S}}$, and the transition relation is defined as

$$((s,S),\sigma,(s',S')) \in \mathcal{R}' :\Leftrightarrow \begin{cases} (s,\sigma,s') \in \mathcal{R} \wedge S' = \{\} & : \text{if } S \in \mathcal{S}_{\mathcal{F}} \\ (s,\sigma,s') \in \mathcal{R} \wedge S' = S \cup \{s'\} & : \text{otherwise} \end{cases}$$

This means that the transition relation is essentially the same, but the states are further equipped with a memory where all the states are kept that have been traversed so far from the last reset of the memory (this is some sort of subset construction). The initial state is $(s_0, \{\})$, where s_0 is the initial state of $\mathfrak{A}$, and the final states are $\mathcal{S}'_{\mathcal{F}} := \{(s,\{\}) \mid s \in \mathcal{S}\}$.

As $\mathfrak{A}_{\mathsf{GF}}$ accepts a word α iff a final state $(s,\{\})$ is visited infinitely often, it follows by construction of $\mathfrak{A}_{\mathsf{GF}}$ that the run over α through $\mathfrak{A}_{\mathsf{GF}}$ visited some designated state sets $S_i \in \mathcal{S}_{\mathcal{F}}$ infinitely often. Due to our assumption the union of these also belongs to $\mathcal{S}_{\mathcal{F}}$, and it follows that $\mathfrak{A}$ accepts α.

Conversely, if $\mathfrak{A}$ accepts a word α, then the states that appear infinitely often on the run over α through $\mathfrak{A}$ is one of the designated state sets $S_i \in \mathcal{S}_{\mathcal{F}}$. Hence, there must be a $s \in \mathcal{S}$ such that the run over α through $\mathfrak{A}_{\mathsf{GF}}$ visits infinitely often (s, S_i), hence, $\mathfrak{A}_{\mathsf{GF}}$ accepts $\mathfrak{A}$.

□

Hence, we have also a criterion for testing whether a given Muller automaton $\mathfrak{A} \in \mathsf{Det}_{\mathsf{Muller}}$ is equivalent to a Büchi automaton, and the proof also gives a construction of such a Büchi automaton $\mathfrak{A}_{\mathsf{GF}}$. In contrast to the reduction to $\mathsf{Det}_{\mathsf{F}}$, we can not use the same semiautomaton (see an example at the end of this section). We already know that the languages accepted by deterministic Büchi automata belong to $\mathcal{F}_2$. The converse is also true [312, 486], so that the above criterion is actually a criterion for testing membership in $\mathcal{F}_2$. By complementing $\mathfrak{A}$ first, we also obtain a method for testing whether there is an equivalent $\mathfrak{A}_{\mathsf{FG}} \in \mathsf{Det}_{\mathsf{FG}}$ for $\mathfrak{A}$, and we can also construct such an automaton.

As Muller automata are inconvenient in practice, we describe in the following similar criteria for checking membership in the Borel classes for $\mathsf{Det}_{\mathsf{Rabin}}$ and $\mathsf{Det}_{\mathsf{Streett}}$ automata. This is fairly easy, since we can effectively transform every given $\mathsf{Det}_{\mathsf{Rabin}}$ and $\mathsf{Det}_{\mathsf{Streett}}$ automaton to an equivalent $\mathsf{Det}_{\mathsf{Muller}}$ automaton using the same underlying semiautomaton: Given $\mathfrak{A} \in \mathsf{Det}_{\mathsf{Rabin}}$ with the acceptance condition $\bigvee_{i=0}^{n} \mathsf{GF}\Phi_i \wedge \mathsf{FG}\Psi_i$, an equivalent Muller automaton $\mathfrak{A}_{\mathsf{Muller}}$ is obtained with the following accepting sets (we view Φ_i and Ψ_i directly as sets of states):

$$\mathcal{S}_{\mathcal{F}} := \{\Delta \subseteq \mathcal{S} \mid \exists i \leq n.\ \Delta \cap \Phi_i \neq \{\} \wedge \Delta \subseteq \Psi_i\}$$

It is easily seen that $\mathsf{Lang}(\mathfrak{A}_{\mathsf{Rabin}}) = \mathsf{Lang}(\mathfrak{A}_{\mathsf{Muller}})$ holds. As both automata are based on the same semiautomaton, it suffices to prove that every run ξ_α accepted by $\mathfrak{A}_{\mathsf{Rabin}}$ is also accepted by $\mathfrak{A}_{\mathsf{Muller}}$. So, assume that ξ_α is accepted by $\mathfrak{A}_{\mathsf{Rabin}}$, i.e., there is an $i \leq n$ with $\mathsf{inf}(\xi_\alpha) \cap \Phi_i \neq \{\} \wedge \mathsf{inf}(\xi_\alpha) \subseteq \Psi_i$. But then $\mathsf{inf}(\xi_\alpha) \in \mathcal{S}_{\mathcal{F}}$, so that ξ_α is also accepted by $\mathfrak{A}_{\mathsf{Muller}}$. Conversely, if $\mathsf{inf}(\xi_\alpha) \in \mathcal{S}_{\mathcal{F}}$ holds, then by construction of $\mathcal{S}_{\mathcal{F}}$, there must be an $i \leq n$ with $\mathsf{inf}(\xi_\alpha) \cap \Phi_i \neq \{\} \wedge \mathsf{inf}(\xi_\alpha) \subseteq \Psi_i$, so that ξ_α is also accepted by $\mathfrak{A}_{\mathsf{Rabin}}$.

Similarly, given $\mathfrak{A} \in \mathsf{Det}_{\mathsf{Streett}}$ with the acceptance condition $\bigwedge_{i=0}^{n} \mathsf{GF}\Phi_i \vee \mathsf{FG}\Psi_i$, an equivalent Muller automaton $\mathfrak{A}_{\mathsf{Muller}}$ is obtained with the following accepting sets (we view Φ_i and Ψ_i directly as sets of states):

$$\mathcal{S}_{\mathcal{F}} := \{\Delta \subseteq \mathcal{S} \mid \forall i \leq n.\ \Delta \cap \Phi_i \neq \{\} \vee \Delta \subseteq \Psi_i\}$$

Using the reductions from $\mathfrak{A}_{\mathsf{Rabin}}$ and $\mathfrak{A}_{\mathsf{Streett}}$ to $\mathfrak{A}_{\mathsf{Muller}}$, and the duality between $\mathsf{Det}_{\mathsf{Rabin}}$ and $\mathsf{Det}_{\mathsf{Streett}}$, we can rephrase the previous two theorems (see also [293, 312, 350]):

Theorem 4.44 (Determining Borel Classes for $\mathsf{Det}_{\mathsf{Rabin}}$). *Given $\mathfrak{A}_{\mathsf{Rabin}} \in \mathsf{Det}_{\mathsf{Rabin}}$ with the acceptance sets $\{(\Phi_1, \Psi_1), \ldots, (\Phi_f, \Psi_f)\}$. We assume the same definitions as given in Theorem 4.42, and split the loops of a state into the disjoint partitions of accepting ones $\mathsf{SCA}_{\mathsf{Rabin}}(s)$ and rejecting ones $\mathsf{SCR}_{\mathsf{Rabin}}(s)$:*

- $\mathsf{SCA}_{\mathsf{Rabin}}(s) := \{C \in \mathsf{Loops}(s) \mid \bigvee_{i=1}^{n} C \cap \Phi_i \neq \{\} \wedge C \subseteq \Psi_i\}$
- $\mathsf{SCR}_{\mathsf{Rabin}}(s) := \{C \in \mathsf{Loops}(s) \mid \neg \bigvee_{i=1}^{n} C \cap \Phi_i \neq \{\} \wedge C \subseteq \Psi_i\}$

Then, the following criteria show when a reduction to lower Borel classes is possible, and how it is obtained:

Reduction to $\mathsf{Det}_{\mathsf{G}}$: The following facts are equivalent:

(1) $\exists \mathfrak{A}_{\mathsf{G}} \in \mathsf{Det}_{\mathsf{G}}.\ \mathsf{Lang}(\mathfrak{A}_{\mathsf{Rabin}}) = \mathsf{Lang}(\mathfrak{A}_{\mathsf{G}})$

(2) $\forall s_1, s_2 \in \mathcal{S}.\ \mathsf{reach}(s_1, s_2) \wedge \mathsf{SCR}_{\mathsf{Rabin}}(s_1) \neq \{\} \rightarrow \mathsf{SCA}_{\mathsf{Rabin}}(s_2) = \{\}$

If (2) holds, an equivalent $\mathsf{Det}_{\mathsf{G}}$ automaton is obtained by changing the acceptance condition of $\mathfrak{A}_{\mathsf{Rabin}}$ to a safety condition where the designated state set is the intersection of the sets in $\{\Delta \subseteq \mathcal{S} \mid \exists i \leq n.\ \Delta \cap \Phi_i \neq \{\} \wedge \Delta \subseteq \Psi_i\}$.

Reduction to $\mathsf{Det}_{\mathsf{F}}$: The following facts are equivalent:

(1) $\exists \mathfrak{A}_{\mathsf{F}} \in \mathsf{Det}_{\mathsf{F}}.\ \mathsf{Lang}(\mathfrak{A}_{\mathsf{Rabin}}) = \mathsf{Lang}(\mathfrak{A}_{\mathsf{F}})$

(2) $\forall s_1, s_2 \in \mathcal{S}.\ \mathsf{reach}(s_1, s_2) \wedge \mathsf{SCA}_{\mathsf{Rabin}}(s_1) \neq \{\} \rightarrow \mathsf{SCR}_{\mathsf{Rabin}}(s_2) = \{\}$

If (2) holds, an equivalent $\mathsf{Det}_{\mathsf{F}}$ automaton is obtained by changing the acceptance condition of $\mathfrak{A}_{\mathsf{Rabin}}$ to a liveness condition where the designated state set is the union of the sets in $\{\Delta \subseteq \mathcal{S} \mid \exists i \leq n.\ \Delta \cap \Phi_i \neq \{\} \wedge \Delta \subseteq \Psi_i\}$.

Reduction to $\mathsf{Det}_{\mathsf{FG}}$: The following facts are equivalent:

(1) $\exists \mathfrak{A}_{\mathsf{FG}} \in \mathsf{Det}_{\mathsf{FG}}.\ \mathsf{Lang}(\mathfrak{A}_{\mathsf{Rabin}}) = \mathsf{Lang}(\mathfrak{A}_{\mathsf{FG}})$

(2) $\forall s \in \mathcal{S}.\ \forall C_1, C_2 \in \mathsf{Loops}(s).\ C_1 \in \mathsf{SCR}_{\mathsf{Rabin}}(s) \rightarrow C_1 \cup C_2 \in \mathsf{SCR}_{\mathsf{Rabin}}(s)$

In the case that (2) holds, it is not always possible to define an FG *acceptance condition on the semiautomaton of* $\mathfrak{A}_{\mathsf{Rabin}}$ *to obtain an equivalent* $\mathfrak{A}_{\mathsf{FG}}$ *automaton.*

Reduction to $\mathsf{Det}_{\mathsf{GF}}$*: Here, the following facts are equivalent:*

(1) $\exists \mathfrak{A}_{\mathsf{GF}} \in \mathsf{Det}_{\mathsf{GF}}.\ \mathsf{Lang}(\mathfrak{A}_{\mathsf{Rabin}}) = \mathsf{Lang}(\mathfrak{A}_{\mathsf{GF}})$

(2) $\forall s \in \mathcal{S}.\ \forall C_1, C_2 \in \mathsf{Loops}(s).\ C_1 \in \mathsf{SCA}_{\mathsf{Rabin}}(s) \rightarrow C_1 \cup C_2 \in \mathsf{SCA}_{\mathsf{Rabin}}(s)$

If (2) holds, an equivalent $\mathsf{Det}_{\mathsf{GF}}$ *automaton is obtained by changing the acceptance condition of* $\mathfrak{A}_{\mathsf{Rabin}}$ *to a fairness condition with* $\{s \in \mathcal{S} \mid \mathsf{SCR}_{\mathsf{Rabin}}(s) = \{\}\}$ *as designated states.*

Theorem 4.45 (Determining Borel Classes for $\mathsf{Det}_{\mathsf{Streett}}$**).** *Given* $\mathfrak{A}_{\mathsf{Streett}} \in \mathsf{Det}_{\mathsf{Streett}}$ *with the acceptance sets* $\{(\Phi_1, \Psi_1), \ldots, (\Phi_f, \Psi_f)\}$*. We assume the same definitions as given in Theorem 4.42, and split the loops of a state into the disjoint partitions of accepting ones* $\mathsf{SCA}_{\mathsf{Streett}}(s)$ *and rejecting ones* $\mathsf{SCR}_{\mathsf{Streett}}(s)$*:*

- $\mathsf{SCA}_{\mathsf{Streett}}(s) := \{C \in \mathsf{Loops}(s) \mid \bigwedge_{i=1}^{n} C \cap \Phi_i \neq \{\} \vee C \subseteq \Psi_i\}$
- $\mathsf{SCR}_{\mathsf{Streett}}(s) := \{C \in \mathsf{Loops}(s) \mid \neg \bigwedge_{i=1}^{n} C \cap \Phi_i \neq \{\} \vee C \subseteq \Psi_i\}$

Then, the following criteria show when a reduction to lower Borel classes is possible, and how it is obtained:

Reduction to $\mathsf{Det}_{\mathsf{G}}$*: The following facts are equivalent:*

(1) $\exists \mathfrak{A}_{\mathsf{G}} \in \mathsf{Det}_{\mathsf{G}}.\ \mathsf{Lang}(\mathfrak{A}_{\mathsf{Streett}}) = \mathsf{Lang}(\mathfrak{A}_{\mathsf{G}})$

(2) $\forall s_1, s_2 \in \mathcal{S}.\ \mathsf{reach}(s_1, s_2) \wedge \mathsf{SCA}_{\mathsf{Streett}}(s_1) \neq \{\} \rightarrow \mathsf{SCR}_{\mathsf{Streett}}(s_2) = \{\}$

If (2) holds, an equivalent $\mathsf{Det}_{\mathsf{G}}$ *automaton is obtained by changing the acceptance condition of* $\mathfrak{A}_{\mathsf{Streett}}$ *to a safety condition where the designated state set is the intersection of the sets in* $\{\Delta \subseteq \mathcal{S} \mid \forall i \leq n.\ \Delta \cap \Phi_i \neq \{\} \vee \Delta \subseteq \Psi_i\}$.

Reduction to $\mathsf{Det}_{\mathsf{F}}$*: The following facts are equivalent:*

(1) $\exists \mathfrak{A}_{\mathsf{F}} \in \mathsf{Det}_{\mathsf{F}}.\ \mathsf{Lang}(\mathfrak{A}_{\mathsf{Streett}}) = \mathsf{Lang}(\mathfrak{A}_{\mathsf{F}})$

(2) $\forall s_1, s_2 \in \mathcal{S}.\ \mathsf{reach}(s_1, s_2) \wedge \mathsf{SCA}_{\mathsf{Streett}}(s_1) \neq \{\} \rightarrow \mathsf{SCR}_{\mathsf{Streett}}(s_2) = \{\}$

If (2) holds, an equivalent $\mathsf{Det}_{\mathsf{F}}$ *automaton is obtained by changing the acceptance condition of* $\mathfrak{A}_{\mathsf{Streett}}$ *to a liveness condition where the designated state set is the union of the sets in* $\{\Delta \subseteq \mathcal{S} \mid \forall i \leq n.\ \Delta \cap \Phi_i \neq \{\} \vee \Delta \subseteq \Psi_i\}$.

Reduction to $\mathsf{Det}_{\mathsf{FG}}$*: The following facts are equivalent:*

(1) $\exists \mathfrak{A}_{\mathsf{FG}} \in \mathsf{Det}_{\mathsf{FG}}.\ \mathsf{Lang}(\mathfrak{A}_{\mathsf{Streett}}) = \mathsf{Lang}(\mathfrak{A}_{\mathsf{FG}})$

(2) $\forall s \in \mathcal{S}.\ \forall C_1, C_2 \in \mathsf{Loops}(s).\ C_1 \in \mathsf{SCR}_{\mathsf{Streett}}(s) \rightarrow C_1 \cup C_2 \in \mathsf{SCR}_{\mathsf{Streett}}(s)$

If (2) holds, an equivalent $\mathsf{Det}_{\mathsf{FG}}$ *automaton is obtained by changing the acceptance condition of* $\mathfrak{A}_{\mathsf{Streett}}$ *to a persistence condition with the states* $\{s \in \mathcal{S} \mid \mathsf{SCA}_{\mathsf{Streett}}(s) = \{\}\}$ *as designated states.*

Reduction to $\mathsf{Det}_{\mathsf{GF}}$*: Here, the following facts are equivalent:*

(1) $\exists \mathfrak{A}_{\mathsf{GF}} \in \mathsf{Det}_{\mathsf{GF}}.\ \mathsf{Lang}(\mathfrak{A}_{\mathsf{Streett}}) = \mathsf{Lang}(\mathfrak{A}_{\mathsf{GF}})$

(2) $\forall s \in \mathcal{S}.\ \forall C_1, C_2 \in \mathsf{Loops}(s).\ C_1 \in \mathsf{SCA}_{\mathsf{Streett}}(s) \rightarrow C_1 \cup C_2 \in \mathsf{SCA}_{\mathsf{Streett}}(s)$

In the case that (2) holds, it is not always possible to define an GF *acceptance condition on the semiautomaton of* $\mathfrak{A}_{\mathsf{Streett}}$ *to obtain an equivalent* $\mathfrak{A}_{\mathsf{GF}}$ *automaton.*

Automata that satisfy the condition that the union $C_1 \cup C_2$ of a reachable accepting cycle $C_1 \in \mathsf{SCA}(s)$ with a possibly not accepting reachable cycle C_2 must belong to $\mathsf{SCA}(s)$, are often said to be *full*. Hence, $\mathsf{Det}_{\mathsf{Muller}}$, $\mathsf{Det}_{\mathsf{Rabin}}$, and $\mathsf{Det}_{\mathsf{Streett}}$ can be translated to equivalent $\mathsf{Det}_{\mathsf{GF}}$ automata iff they are full. Note that for $C_1, C_2 \in \mathsf{Loops}(s)$, we always have $C_1 \cup C_2 \in \mathsf{Loops}(s)$. Hence, it follows that the conditions $C_1 \in \mathsf{SCR}(s) \to C_1 \cup C_2 \in \mathsf{SCR}(s)$ are equivalent to $C_1 \cup C_2 \in \mathsf{SCA}(s) \to C_1 \in \mathsf{SCA}(s)$ by contraposition (this formulation has been used in [350]).

The construction of equivalent $\mathsf{Det}_{\mathsf{G}}$ and $\mathsf{Det}_{\mathsf{F}}$ automata is achieved according to Theorem 4.42. The result for the $\mathsf{Det}_{\mathsf{G}}$ reduction for $\mathsf{Det}_{\mathsf{Rabin}}$ is thereby obtained from the $\mathsf{Det}_{\mathsf{F}}$ reduction for $\mathsf{Det}_{\mathsf{Streett}}$, which in turn is directly obtained from Theorem 4.42. In a similar way, the $\mathsf{Det}_{\mathsf{G}}$ reduction for $\mathsf{Det}_{\mathsf{Streett}}$ is obtained from the $\mathsf{Det}_{\mathsf{F}}$ reduction for $\mathsf{Det}_{\mathsf{Rabin}}$, which is a direct consequence of Theorem 4.42.

In an analogous way, we have derived the other reduction criteria from Theorem 4.43. In Theorem 4.43, we constructed an equivalent $\mathsf{Det}_{\mathsf{GF}}$ automaton with a different semiautomaton from the given $\mathsf{Det}_{\mathsf{Muller}}$ automaton. This is necessary, as the example given in Figure 4.19 shows (the example is taken from [293]). If we endow the upper semiautomaton of Figure 4.19 with the acceptance condition $\{\{s_1, s_2\}\}$ to a $\mathsf{Det}_{\mathsf{Muller}}$ automaton, it accepts the language of infinite words over $\{a, b\}$ where infinitely many a's and infinitely many b's occur. We can also use $\mathsf{GF}s_1 \wedge \mathsf{GF}s_2$ as a Streett condition to define the same language.

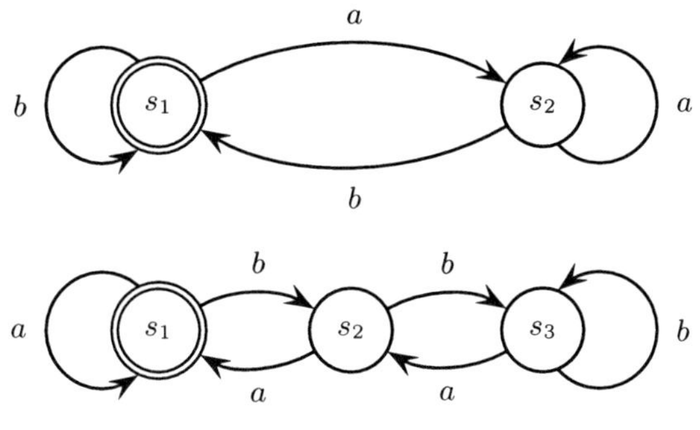

Fig. 4.19. Necessity for constructing new semiautomata

It can be easily verified that we can not find a state set so that the same semiautomaton extended to a $\mathsf{Det}_{\mathsf{GF}}$ automaton would define the same language. The four possibilities $\{\}$, $\{s_1\}$, $\{s_2\}$, and $\{s_1, s_2\}$ define different languages. However, there is an equivalent $\mathsf{Det}_{\mathsf{GF}}$ automaton: for example, the semiautomaton in the lower part of Figure 4.19 with designated states $\{s_2\}$ is an equivalent $\mathsf{Det}_{\mathsf{GF}}$ automaton.

Hence, even if an equivalent $\mathsf{Det}_{\mathsf{GF}}$ automaton exists, it is not always possible to redefine the acceptance condition of $\mathsf{Det}_{\mathsf{Muller}}$ and $\mathsf{Det}_{\mathsf{Streett}}$ automata so that an equivalent $\mathsf{Det}_{\mathsf{GF}}$ automaton is obtained. In [293], it is however proved that the reduction from $\mathsf{Det}_{\mathsf{Rabin}}$ to $\mathsf{Det}_{\mathsf{GF}}$ (if possible) can always reuse the semiautomaton of the given $\mathsf{Det}_{\mathsf{Rabin}}$ automaton, and that the $\mathsf{Det}_{\mathsf{GF}}$ automaton mentioned in the theorem is then equivalent. An analog situation holds for the reduction from $\mathsf{Det}_{\mathsf{Streett}}$ to $\mathsf{Det}_{\mathsf{FG}}$.

4.7 Automata and Monoids

In the previous section, we have outlined the relationship between ω-regular languages and metric spaces. These considerations gave new insight in the languages that are accepted by Det_κ automata. In particular, we also found algorithms to determine whether a language can be accepted by an automaton of a certain class Det_κ.

There is also a tight relationship between automata and algebraic structures. In this section, we will briefly describe this relationship, that will give us a further insight into the subsets of automata that are equivalent to temporal logic properties that are the topic of the next chapter. The interested reader is referred to [151, 209], and for more recent work to [120, 401–404, 475].

4.7.1 Finite Semigroups and Monoids

In this section, we list basic definitions and theorems about simple algebraic structures called semigroups and monoids. In general, an algebraic structure is a pair $\langle M, \odot\rangle$ where M is a set, and $\odot$ is a binary operation on M, thus mapping two elements of M to another element of M. According to certain properties of $\odot$, we distinguish different algebraic structures $\langle M, \odot\rangle$:

Definition 4.46 (Semigroups, Monoids and Groups). *Given a function $\odot : G \times G \to G$ on a set G, we define the following properties:*

$$\begin{aligned} \textit{Associativity: } & \forall g_1, g_2, g_3 \in G.(g_1 \odot g_2) \odot g_3 = g_1 \odot (g_2 \odot g_3) \\ \textit{Identity: } & \exists e \in G.\forall g \in G.e \odot g = g \wedge g \odot e = g \\ \textit{Inverse Elements: } & \forall g \in G.\exists g^{-1} \in G.g \odot g^{-1} = e \wedge g^{-1} \odot g = e \\ \textit{Commutativity: } & \forall g_1, g_2 \in G.g_1 \odot g_2 = g_2 \odot g_1 \end{aligned}$$

$\langle G, \odot\rangle$ is a semigroup, if $\langle G, \odot\rangle$ is associative; a semigroup $\langle G, \odot\rangle$ with an identity $e \in G$ is a monoid, and a monoid $\langle G, \odot\rangle$ with inverse elements is a group. A group where additionally the commutative law holds is a commutative group (sometimes also called an abelian group).

An important example of a monoid is $\langle \Sigma^*, \cdot\rangle$, i.e., the set of finite words Σ^* over an alphabet Σ with the word concatenation as the operation. Clearly, word concatenation is associative and concatenating the empty word does not change a word. However, there are no inverse elements and hence, $\langle \Sigma^*, \cdot\rangle$

is not a group. Moreover, the set of Boolean square matrices is a monoid with the following multiplication operation:

$$\begin{pmatrix} \alpha_{1,1} & \cdots & \alpha_{1,n} \\ \vdots & & \vdots \\ \alpha_{n,1} & \cdots & \alpha_{n,n} \end{pmatrix} \times \begin{pmatrix} \beta_{1,1} & \cdots & \beta_{1,n} \\ \vdots & & \vdots \\ \beta_{n,1} & \cdots & \beta_{n,n} \end{pmatrix} = \begin{pmatrix} \bigvee_{k=1}^{n} \alpha_{1,k} \wedge \beta_{k,1} & \cdots & \bigvee_{k=1}^{n} \alpha_{1,k} \wedge \beta_{k,n} \\ \vdots & & \vdots \\ \bigvee_{k=1}^{n} \alpha_{n,k} \wedge \beta_{k,1} & \cdots & \bigvee_{k=1}^{n} \alpha_{n,k} \wedge \beta_{k,n} \end{pmatrix}$$

The identity is the Boolean square matrix with entries $e_{i,j}$ such that $e_{i,j} = 1$ iff $i = j$ holds. Before considering further examples, we prove some simple properties of monoids and groups:

Lemma 4.47 (Simple Properties of Monoids and Groups).

- *In every monoid $\langle G, \odot \rangle$, $\forall g \in G.x \odot g = g$ implies that x is the identity.*
- *In every group $\langle G, \odot \rangle$, $\exists g \in G.x \odot g = g$ implies that x is the identity.*
- *The inverse elements are uniquely determined in every group.*
- *$(a \odot b)^{-1} = b^{-1} \odot a^{-1}$ holds in every group.*
- *In every group, the following uniqueness laws hold:*
  - *$a \odot b = a \odot c$ implies $b = c$ for all $a, b, c \in G$*
  - *$b \odot a = c \odot a$ implies $b = c$ for all $a, b, c \in G$*

Proof. We assume that id is the identity of the monoid/group:

- Instantiating $g := id$ yields $x \odot id = id$, and by the axiom for the identity, we furthermore have $x \odot id = x$, and hence $x = id$.
- Given $x, g \in G$ with $x \odot g = g \odot x = g$, we have the following equivalence:

$$\begin{aligned} x \odot g = g &\Leftrightarrow (x \odot g) \odot g^{-1} = g \odot g^{-1} \\ &\Leftrightarrow x \odot (g \odot g^{-1}) = g \odot g^{-1} \\ &\Leftrightarrow x \odot id = id \\ &\Leftrightarrow x = id \end{aligned}$$

- Uniqueness of inverse elements is seen as follows:

$$\begin{aligned} a \odot b = id &\Leftrightarrow (a \odot b) \odot b^{-1} = id \odot b^{-1} \\ &\Leftrightarrow a \odot (b \odot b^{-1}) = id \odot b^{-1} \\ &\Leftrightarrow a \odot id = b^{-1} \\ &\Leftrightarrow a = b^{-1} \end{aligned}$$

- The next proof is also simple (when the above property is considered):

$$\begin{aligned} (a \odot b) \odot (b^{-1} \odot a^{-1}) &= a \odot ((b \odot b^{-1}) \odot a^{-1}) \\ &= a \odot (id \odot a^{-1}) \\ &= a \odot a^{-1} \\ &= id \end{aligned}$$

- Assume (1) $a \odot b = d$ and (2) $a \odot c = d$. Then, we have $b \odot d^{-1} \overset{(1)}{=} b \odot (a \odot b)^{-1} = a^{-1}$, and $c \odot d^{-1} \overset{(2)}{=} c \odot (a \odot c)^{-1} = a^{-1}$, hence, $b \odot d^{-1} = c \odot d^{-1}$. As inverse elements are uniquely determined, it follows $b = c$. The other point is proved analogously.

□

It is noteworthy that the last properties in the above lemma assure that the rows and columns of a group table are permutations of the group elements. Hence, there are no elements $b \neq c$ such that $a \odot b = a \odot c$ or $b \odot a = c \odot a$ holds.

For the following, we need more knowledge of finite semigroups. To this end, it is convenient to define an exponentiation operation as follows: $g^1 := g$ and $g^{n+1} := g^n \odot g$. Obviously, this exponentiation operation has simple properties like $g^n \odot g^m = g^{m+n} = g^m \odot g^n$, and in monoids, we additionally define $g^0 = id$.

The following theorem lists a couple of important properties of finite semigroups, in particular, it introduces the notion of index, period, and exponent of semigroup elements. These notions are then extended in the next theorem to the whole semigroup.

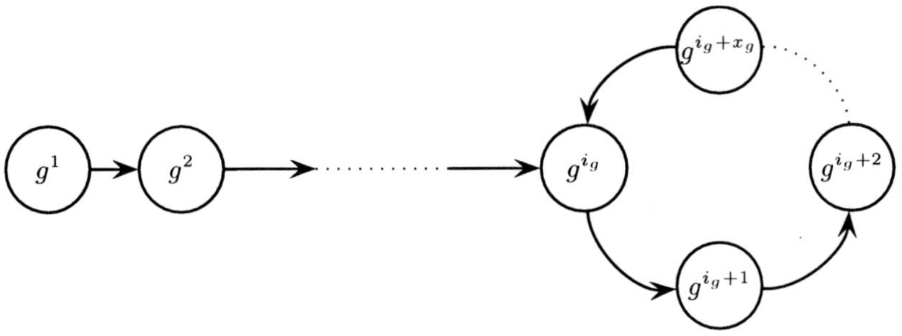

Fig. 4.20. Index and period of an element $g \in G$ ($x_g := p_g - 1$)

Theorem 4.48 (Properties of Finite Semigroups (I)). *For every element $g \in G$ of a finite semigroup $\langle G, \odot \rangle$, there are numbers $\mathsf{idx}(g)$, $\mathsf{prd}(g) \in \mathbb{N}$ such that the following hold:*

1. $g, g^2, \ldots, g^{\mathsf{idx}(g)+\mathsf{prd}(g)-1}$ *are pairwise distinct*
2. $\forall j, k. g^{\mathsf{idx}(g)+k} = g^{\mathsf{idx}(g)+j\mathsf{prd}(g)+k}$
3. $\forall k. g^{\mathsf{idx}(g)+k} = g^{\mathsf{idx}(g)+(k \bmod \mathsf{prd}(g))}$
4. *Every element of a finite semigroup has an idempotent power, i.e., for any $g \in G$ there is a smallest number $\mathsf{exp}(g) \in \mathbb{N}$ such that $g^{\mathsf{exp}(g)} \odot g^{\mathsf{exp}(g)} = g^{\mathsf{exp}(g)}$.*
5. *Every finite semigroup has an idempotent element.*
6. $(\{g^{\mathsf{idx}(g)+(k \bmod \mathsf{prd}(g))} \mid k \in \mathbb{N}\}, \odot)$ *is a commutative subgroup of $\langle G, \odot \rangle$.*

Proof. The proof is straightforward. Consider for an arbitrary element $g \in G$ the sequence of powers $g, g^2, g^3, \ldots$. Since G is finite, it follows that there are numbers i_g and p_g such that $g^{i_g} = g^{i_g+p_g}$ holds. The smallest numbers i_g and p_g with these properties are $\mathsf{idx}(g)$ and $\mathsf{prd}(g)$, respectively.

We prove by induction on k that even $\forall k. g^{i_g+k} = g^{i_g+p_g+k}$ holds, and with a further induction on j that even $\forall j, k. g^{i_g+k} = g^{i_g+jp_g+k}$ holds.

We define $\mathsf{exp}(g) := j_g\mathsf{prd}(g)$ with the smallest number j_g such that $j_g\mathsf{prd}(g) \geq \mathsf{idx}(g)$ holds. Clearly, we then have $j_g\mathsf{prd}(g) = \mathsf{idx}(g) + j$ with $j := j_g\mathsf{prd}(g) - \mathsf{idx}(g)$, and therefore:

$$\begin{aligned} g^{j_g\mathsf{prd}(g)} \odot g^{j_g\mathsf{prd}(g)} &= g^{j_g\mathsf{prd}(g)+j_g\mathsf{prd}(g)} \\ &= g^{\mathsf{idx}(g)+j+j_g\mathsf{prd}(g)} \\ &= g^{\mathsf{idx}(g)+j} \\ &= g^{j_g\mathsf{prd}(G)} \end{aligned}$$

Consider now the set $G_g := \{g^{i_g+(k \bmod p_g)} \mid k \in \mathbb{N}\}$. Endowed with $\odot$, G_g is a commutative group:

- G_g is closed under $\odot$; for $j, k < \mathsf{prd}(g)$, we have:

$$\begin{aligned} g^{\mathsf{idx}(g)+j} \odot g^{\mathsf{idx}(g)+k} &= g^{\mathsf{idx}(g)+\mathsf{idx}(g)+j+k} \\ &= g^{\mathsf{idx}(g)+((\mathsf{idx}(g)+j+k) \bmod \mathsf{prd}(g))} \end{aligned}$$

- $\odot$ is associative on G, and hence also associative on G_g.
- Let j_0 be the smallest number such that $j_0\mathsf{prd}(g) \geq \mathsf{idx}(g)$ holds. Then, with $k_0 := (j_0\mathsf{prd}(g) - \mathsf{idx}(g)) \bmod \mathsf{prd}(g)$, the element $g^{\mathsf{idx}(g)+k_0}$ is the identity of G_g, since we have $g^{\mathsf{idx}(g)+k_0} = g^{j_0\mathsf{prd}(g)}$, and therefore, it follows for any $j < \mathsf{prd}(g)$:

$$\begin{aligned} g^{\mathsf{idx}(g)+j} \odot g^{\mathsf{idx}(g)+k_0} &= g^{\mathsf{idx}(g)+j} \odot g^{j_0\mathsf{prd}(g)} \\ &= g^{\mathsf{idx}(g)+j+j_0\mathsf{prd}(g)} \\ &= g^{\mathsf{idx}(g)+j} \end{aligned}$$

- Each element $g^{\mathsf{idx}(g)+j}$ has an inverse element:

$$\begin{aligned} g^{\mathsf{idx}(g)+j} \odot g^{\mathsf{idx}(g)+j'} &= g^{(\mathsf{idx}(g)+j)+(\mathsf{idx}(g)+j')} \\ &= g^{\mathsf{idx}(g)+(j+\mathsf{idx}(g)+j')} \end{aligned}$$

  It is obvious that we can choose j' such that $j + \mathsf{idx}(g) + j'$ is equivalent to k_0 modulo $\mathsf{prd}(g)$.
- Furthermore, we find the commutative law on G_g:

$$\begin{aligned} g^{\mathsf{idx}(g)+j} \odot g^{\mathsf{idx}(g)+k} &= g^{(\mathsf{idx}(g)+j)+(\mathsf{idx}(g)+k)} \\ &= g^{(\mathsf{idx}(g)+k)+(\mathsf{idx}(g)+j)} \\ &= g^{\mathsf{idx}(g)+k} \odot g^{\mathsf{idx}(g)+j} \end{aligned}$$

□

The interesting fact of the above lemma is that every finite semigroup has commutative subgroups. However, these subgroups may not be interesting, since they could be trivial, i.e., they may consist of only the identity. The existence of idempotent elements, regardless of the existence of trivial subgroups, is also guaranteed by the above lemma.

In the above lemma, we have shown the existence of the index $\mathsf{idx}(g)$, the period $\mathsf{prd}(g)$, and the exponent $\mathsf{exp}(g)$ of an element $g \in G$. These definitions can be extended to the whole semigroup G, as shown by the next lemma:

Lemma 4.49 (Properties of Finite Semigroups (II)). *The following facts hold for finite semigroups $\langle G, \odot \rangle$:*

1. *There are (smallest) numbers $\mathsf{idx}(G)$, $\mathsf{prd}(G) \in \mathbb{N}$ such that for all elements $g \in G$, we have $\forall k.g^{\mathsf{idx}(G)+k} = g^{\mathsf{idx}(G)+(k \bmod \mathsf{prd}(G))}$.*
2. *There is a (smallest) number $\mathsf{exp}(G) \in \mathbb{N}$, such that $\forall g \in G.g^{\mathsf{exp}(G)} \odot g^{\mathsf{exp}(G)} = g^{\mathsf{exp}(G)}$.*
3. *Let $\langle G, \odot \rangle$ be a finite semigroup with $|G| = n$. For every sequence $g_1, \ldots, g_n$ of elements of G, there is an index $i \in \{1, \ldots, n\}$ and an $g_0 \in G$ such that $g_0 \odot g_0 = g_0$ and $g_1 \odot \ldots \odot g_i \odot g_0 = g_1 \odot \ldots \odot g_i$.*

Proof. To prove the first statement, we choose $\mathsf{idx}(G) := \max\{\mathsf{idx}(g) \mid g \in G\}$ and for $\mathsf{prd}(G)$ the least common multiple of the numbers $\{\mathsf{prd}(g) \mid g \in G\}$. Analogously, we define $\mathsf{exp}(G)$ as the least common multiple of the numbers $\{\mathsf{exp}(g) \mid g \in G\}$.

To prove the third statement, abbreviate $x_1 := g_1$, $x_2 := g_1 \odot g_2$, ..., $x_n := g_1 \odot \ldots \odot g_n$. If all x_i's are distinct, then it follows that $G = \{x_1, \ldots, x_n\}$ and by the previous lemma, it follows that one of the x_i's must be idempotent, so that we can choose that element for g_0. On the other hand, if the x_i's are not distinct, then at least two of them are equal, say x_i and x_{i+p}. Now abbreviate $y_{i,p} := g_{i+1} \odot \ldots \odot g_{i+p}$, so that $x_i = x_i \odot y_{i,p}$ holds. Hence, we have $x_i = x_i \odot y_{i,p} = x_i \odot y_{i,p} \odot \ldots \odot y_{i,p}$, and in particular $x_i = x_i \odot y_{i,p}^{\mathsf{exp}(G)}$. Since $y_{i,p}^{\mathsf{exp}(G)}$ is idempotent, everything follows. □

For the relationship between temporal logics, star-free languages, first-order logic on linear orders, finite automata and monoids, the following definition will be important.

Definition 4.50 (Aperiodic Semigroups). *A semigroup $\langle G, \odot \rangle$ is aperiodic if $\mathsf{prd}(G) = 1$, i.e., if $\forall g \in G.g^{\mathsf{idx}(G)} = g^{\mathsf{idx}(G)+1}$ holds.*

Clearly, we then have $\forall g \in G.\forall k \in \mathbb{N}.g^{\mathsf{idx}(G)} = g^{\mathsf{idx}(G)+k}$ as a simple consequence of every aperiodic semigroup. Moreover, we get the following result for aperiodic semigroups:

Theorem 4.51. *A semigroup is aperiodic iff it only contains trivial subgroups, i.e., singleton subgroups.*

Proof. Assume first that all subgroups of $\langle G, \odot \rangle$ are singletons. As a consequence, the commutative subgroups $G_g := (\{g^{\mathsf{idx}(g)+(k \bmod \mathsf{prd}(g))} \mid k \in \mathbb{N}\}, \odot)$ must be singletons, too. But then, it follows that $\mathsf{prd}(G) = 1$.

Conversely, assume that $\langle G, \odot \rangle$ has a nontrivial subgroup G'. We have to show that $\mathsf{prd}(G) > 1$, which follows if we find one element g with $\mathsf{prd}(g) > 1$. Now let g be an arbitrary element of G' that is not the identity of G'. Hence, we have $g \neq id$, and by repeated application of the last fact of Lemma 4.47, it follows that $g^2 \neq g$, $g^3 \neq g^2$, ..., and by induction that $\forall k \in \mathbb{N} \setminus \{0\}. g^{k+1} \neq g^k$. As a consequence, $\mathsf{prd}(g) \neq 1$, and hence, $\langle G, \odot \rangle$ is aperiodic. □

4.7.2 Automata and Their Monoids

Having presented some basic facts about monoids, we now establish the desired relationship between automata and monoids. In particular, we define for a semiautomaton $\mathfrak{A}$ its transition monoid $\mathsf{TM}(\mathfrak{A})$, and for a language L its syntactic monoid $\mathsf{SM}(L)$. For a finite state automaton on finite words, we can furthermore define its syntactic monoid as the monoid of its accepted language. We start with the definition of the transition monoid.

To this end, consider a semiautomaton $\mathfrak{A} = (\Sigma, \mathcal{S}, \mathcal{I}, \mathcal{R})$ and the relations $\mathcal{R}_\sigma := \{(s, s') \in \mathcal{S} \times \mathcal{S} \mid (s, \sigma, s') \in \mathcal{R})\}$ that we define for every $\sigma \in \Sigma$. We moreover define for every word $\alpha \in \Sigma^*$ a relation $\mathcal{R}_\alpha \subseteq \mathcal{S} \times \mathcal{S}$ as follows:

- $\mathcal{R}_\varepsilon := \{(s, s) \mid s \in \mathcal{S}\}$
- $\mathcal{R}_{\sigma\alpha} := \mathcal{R}_\sigma \circ \mathcal{R}_\alpha$, hence $\mathcal{R}_{\sigma\alpha} = \{(s_1, s_2) \mid \exists s' \in \mathcal{S}. (s_1, s') \in \mathcal{R}_\sigma \wedge (s', s_2) \in \mathcal{R}_\alpha\}$ for every $\sigma \in \Sigma$ and every $\alpha \in \Sigma^*$

Intuitively, we have $(s_1, s_2) \in \mathcal{R}_\alpha$ iff the state s_2 can be reached from s_1 by reading the word α. It is not difficult to prove that we have for arbitrary words $\alpha, \beta \in \Sigma^*$ the equation $\mathcal{R}_\alpha \circ \mathcal{R}_\beta = \mathcal{R}_{\alpha\beta}$, so that the relational product operation maps two relations $\mathcal{R}_\beta$ and $\mathcal{R}_\alpha$ to another one ($\mathcal{R}_{\alpha\beta}$). Moreover, $\circ$ is associative, and $\mathcal{R}_\varepsilon$ is the identity. Hence, we come to the following definition:

Definition 4.52 (Transition Monoid). *For every semiautomaton $\mathfrak{A} = (\Sigma, \mathcal{S}, \mathcal{I}, \mathcal{R})$, we define for each input $\sigma \in \Sigma$ the relation $\mathcal{R}_\sigma := \{(s, s') \in \mathcal{S} \times \mathcal{S} \mid (s, \sigma, s') \in \mathcal{R})\}$. The transition monoid $\mathsf{TM}(\mathfrak{A})$ of $\mathfrak{A}$ is the set of binary relations on $\mathcal{S} \times \mathcal{S}$ generated by $\{\mathcal{R}_\sigma \mid \sigma \in \Sigma\}$ under the relational product $\circ$ plus the identity relation $\mathcal{R}_\varepsilon := \{(s, s) \mid s \in \mathcal{S}\}$.*

The transition monoid is sometimes defined in terms of the following Boolean square matrices $\mathcal{M}_\sigma$ with the Boolean matrix multiplication as operation:

$$\mathcal{M}_\sigma := \begin{pmatrix} (s_1, \sigma, s_1) \in \mathcal{R} & \cdots & (s_1, \sigma, s_n) \in \mathcal{R} \\ \vdots & & \vdots \\ (s_n, \sigma, s_1) \in \mathcal{R} & \cdots & (s_n, \sigma, s_n) \in \mathcal{R} \end{pmatrix}$$

Using the Boolean matrix multiplication, we define $\mathcal{M}_{\alpha\beta} := \mathcal{M}_\beta \times \mathcal{M}_\alpha$, thus obtaining another Boolean square matrix. It is not hard to see that there is a bijection $\hbar$ between $\mathcal{R}_\alpha$ and $\mathcal{M}_\alpha$ that is even a homomorphism since we have $\hbar(\mathcal{R}_{\alpha\beta}) = \hbar(\mathcal{R}_\alpha \circ \mathcal{R}_\beta) = \hbar(\mathcal{R}_\alpha) \times \hbar(\mathcal{R}_\beta) = \mathcal{M}_\alpha \times \mathcal{M}_\beta = \mathcal{M}_{\alpha\beta}$. Hence, it is only a matter of taste whether we define $\mathsf{TM}(\mathfrak{A})$ with Boolean square matrices or binary relations.

Beyond the different representation of $\mathsf{TM}(\mathfrak{A})$ with Boolean square matrices, we can also characterize $\mathsf{TM}(\mathfrak{A})$ as the set of classes of an equivalence relation on $\Sigma^* \times \Sigma^*$.

Definition 4.53 (Induced Equivalence). *For every semiautomaton $\mathfrak{A} = (\Sigma, \mathcal{S}, \mathcal{I}, \mathcal{R})$, we define the binary relation $\equiv_\mathfrak{A}$ on Σ^* as $\alpha \equiv_\mathfrak{A} \beta :\Leftrightarrow \mathcal{R}_\alpha = \mathcal{R}_\beta$.*

It is easily seen that $\equiv_\mathfrak{A}$ is an equivalence relation and moreover a congruence relation w.r.t. word concatenation, since we have $\alpha \equiv_\mathfrak{A} \beta$ iff $\alpha\gamma \equiv_\mathfrak{A} \beta\gamma$ and $\alpha \equiv_\mathfrak{A} \beta$ iff $\gamma\alpha \equiv_\mathfrak{A} \gamma\beta$. Moreover, $\Sigma^*_{/\equiv_\mathfrak{A}}$ is closely related to $\mathsf{TM}(\mathfrak{A})$, in particular, it is finite.

Theorem 4.54 (Induced Equivalence). *Given a semiautomaton $\mathfrak{A} = (\Sigma, \mathcal{S}, \mathcal{I}, \mathcal{R})$, the induced relation $\equiv_\mathfrak{A}$ is an equivalence relation on Σ^*, and even more a congruence relation w.r.t. concatenation. Moreover, the monoid $(\Sigma^*_{/\equiv_\mathfrak{A}}, \cdot)$ is isomorphic to $\mathsf{TM}(\mathfrak{A})$.*

Proof. We easily see that $\equiv_\mathfrak{A}$ is an equivalence relation, i.e., that $\equiv_\mathfrak{A}$ is reflexive, symmetric, and transitive. Moreover, it is easily seen that $\equiv_\mathfrak{A}$ is a congruence relation since $[\alpha\beta]_{\equiv_\mathfrak{A}} = [\alpha]_{\equiv_\mathfrak{A}} \cdot [\beta]_{\equiv_\mathfrak{A}}$ (note that the left operation is word concatenation and the right one is a language concatenation). It remains to define an isomorphism between $(\Sigma^*_{/\equiv_\mathfrak{A}}, \cdot)$ and $\mathsf{TM}(\mathfrak{A})$. To this end, we define $\hbar : \Sigma^*_{/\equiv_\mathfrak{A}} \to \mathsf{TM}(\mathfrak{A})$ by $\hbar([\alpha]_{\equiv_\mathfrak{A}}) := \mathcal{R}_\alpha$. Then, note the following:

- $\hbar$ is well-defined since $\alpha \equiv_\mathfrak{A} \beta$ implies $\mathcal{R}_\alpha = \mathcal{R}_\beta$
- $\hbar$ is injective: $\alpha \not\equiv_\mathfrak{A} \beta$ holds iff there are states $s, s' \in \mathcal{S}$ with $(s, s') \in \mathcal{R}_\alpha \Leftrightarrow (s, s') \in \mathcal{R}_\beta$, and this in turn holds iff $\mathcal{R}_\alpha \neq \mathcal{R}_\beta$
- $\hbar$ is surjective: any $\mathcal{R} \in \mathsf{TM}(\mathfrak{A})$ is generated by a word $\alpha \in \Sigma^*$, and for that word, we have $\hbar([\alpha]_{\equiv_\mathfrak{A}}) := \mathcal{R}$
- $\hbar$ is a homomorphism: $\hbar([\alpha]_{\equiv_\mathfrak{A}} \cdot [\beta]_{\equiv_\mathfrak{A}}) = \hbar([\alpha\beta]_{\equiv_\mathfrak{A}}) = \mathcal{R}_{\alpha\beta} = \mathcal{R}_\alpha \circ \mathcal{R}_\beta = \hbar([\alpha]_{\equiv_\mathfrak{A}}) \circ \hbar([\beta]_{\equiv_\mathfrak{A}})$

□

As $(\Sigma^*_{/\equiv_\mathfrak{A}}, \cdot)$ is isomorphic to $\mathsf{TM}(\mathfrak{A})$, we need not really distinguish between the two monoids and could use either one for any purpose. It is just a matter of taste which of these monoids is used to define the transition monoid of a semiautomaton.

We now come to the second monoid that is related with automata. This monoid is defined for languages $L \subseteq \Sigma^*$ on finite words.

Definition 4.55 (Syntactic Congruence of a Language). *For every language $L \subseteq \Sigma^*$ over an alphabet Σ, we define the equivalence relation $\equiv_L$ on $\Sigma^* \times \Sigma^*$ as follows:*

$$\alpha \equiv_L \beta :\Leftrightarrow \forall \delta, \gamma \in \Sigma^*.\ \delta\alpha\gamma \in L \Leftrightarrow \delta\beta\gamma \in L$$

It is easily seen that for every language $L \subseteq \Sigma^*$, its syntactic congruence $\equiv_L$ is an equivalence relation. As furthermore, $\alpha \equiv_L \beta$ implies for any $\gamma \in \Sigma^*$ that also $\alpha\gamma \equiv_L \beta\gamma$ and $\gamma\alpha \equiv_L \gamma\beta$ holds, it is a congruence relation on the monoid $(\Sigma^*, \cdot)$. We can therefore endow the set of equivalence classes $\Sigma^*_{/\equiv_L}$ with the concatenation operation to obtain a monoid:

Definition 4.56 (Syntactic Monoid of a Language). *For every language $L \subseteq \Sigma^*$ over an alphabet Σ, we define the syntactic monoid $\mathsf{SM}(L)$ of L as $(\Sigma^*_{/\equiv_L}, \cdot)$, where $\Sigma^*_{/\equiv_L}$ is the set of equivalence classes obtained by the syntactic congruence $\equiv_L$ of L. Furthermore, the function $\eta_L : \Sigma^* \to \Sigma^*_{/\equiv_L}$ that maps a word $\alpha \in \Sigma^*$ to its equivalence class $[\alpha]_L$ is called the syntactic morphism of L.*

We have already mentioned that $\equiv_L$ is a congruence relation, and that $\mathsf{SM}(L)$ is really a monoid. This is straightforward to prove, and therefore, we just list the following proposition:

Theorem 4.57 (Syntactic Monoid of a Language). *For every language $L \subseteq \Sigma^*$ over an alphabet Σ, the relation $\equiv_L$ is a congruence relation on the monoid $(\Sigma^*, \cdot)$. Therefore, $\mathsf{SM}(L)$ is a monoid, and the syntactic morphism $\eta_L : \Sigma^* \to \Sigma^*_{/\equiv_L}$ is a monoid morphism between $(\Sigma^*, \cdot)$ and $\mathsf{SM}(L)$.*

Hence, we have seen that we can construct for every language $L \subseteq \Sigma^*$ a monoid, namely its syntactic monoid $\mathsf{SM}(L)$. The converse is also possible, i.e., for every monoid $\langle G, \odot \rangle$ and every alphabet Σ, there is a regular language L such that there is a homomorphism from $\mathsf{SM}(L)$ to $\langle G, \odot \rangle$ [475]. Hence, the theory of regular languages is very closely related to the theory of monoids.

We already know that extending a semiautomaton $\mathfrak{A} = (\Sigma, \mathcal{S}, \mathcal{I}, \mathcal{R})$ by a state set $\mathcal{F} \subseteq \mathcal{S}$ yields an acceptor $\mathfrak{A} = (\Sigma, \mathcal{S}, \mathcal{I}, \mathcal{R}, \mathcal{F})$ that defines a regular language $\mathsf{Lang}(\mathfrak{A})$: This is the set of finite words that can be read from an initial state $\mathcal{I}$ such that the automaton can be in a final state $\mathcal{F}$ after reading the word. For languages, we have furthermore defined the syntactic monoid. This raises the question of how the $\mathsf{TM}(\mathfrak{A})$ and $\mathsf{SM}(\mathsf{Lang}(\mathfrak{A}))$ are related.

The next fundamental theorem answers this question completely. It will turn out that $\equiv_{\mathfrak{A}}$ is a refinement of $\equiv_{\mathsf{Lang}(\mathfrak{A})}$, i.e., that the equivalence classes of $\equiv_{\mathsf{Lang}(\mathfrak{A})}$ are coarser and consist of classes of $\equiv_{\mathfrak{A}}$. Moreover, the minimal automaton accepting a regular language can be defined in terms of $\equiv_{\mathsf{Lang}(\mathfrak{A})}$. The minimal automaton of a regular language L is up to isomorphism uniquely determined, and its induced equivalence relation is $\equiv_L$.

Theorem 4.58 (Transition Monoid and Syntactic Monoid). *Given a finite state automaton $\mathfrak{A} = (\Sigma, \mathcal{S}, \mathcal{I}, \mathcal{R}, \mathcal{F})$, and its accepted language $L := \mathsf{Lang}(\mathfrak{A})$, with the induced congruence relations $\equiv_{\mathfrak{A}}$ and $\equiv_L$. Then, we have:*

- $\alpha \equiv_{\mathfrak{A}} \beta$ *implies* $\alpha \equiv_L \beta$
- $[\alpha]_{\equiv_{\mathfrak{A}}} \subseteq [\alpha]_{\equiv_L}$, *hence,* $[\alpha]_{\equiv_L}$ *is a finite union of classes* $[\alpha_i]_{\equiv_{\mathfrak{A}}}$, *i.e., for every word* $\alpha \in \Sigma^*$ *there are words* $\alpha_1, \ldots, \alpha_n \in \Sigma^*$ *such that* $[\alpha]_{\equiv_L} = \bigcup_{i=1}^n [\alpha_i]_{\equiv_{\mathfrak{A}}}$.
- $\mathsf{Lang}(\mathfrak{A})$ *is a finite union of classes* $[\alpha]_{\equiv_{\mathfrak{A}}}$, *in particular, let* $[\alpha_1]_{\equiv_{\mathfrak{A}}}, \ldots, [\alpha_n]_{\equiv_{\mathfrak{A}}}$ *be the classes, where* $\mathcal{R}_{\alpha_i} \cap (\mathcal{I} \times \mathcal{F}) \neq \{\}$ *holds, then we have* $\mathsf{Lang}(\mathfrak{A}) = \bigcup_{i=1}^n [\alpha_i]_{\equiv_{\mathfrak{A}}}$.
- *The function* $\hbar : \Sigma^*_{/\equiv_{\mathfrak{A}}} \to \Sigma^*_{/\equiv_L}$ *defined by* $\hbar([\alpha]_{\equiv_{\mathfrak{A}}}) := [\alpha]_{\equiv_L}$ *is a homomorphism between* $(\Sigma^*_{/\equiv_{\mathfrak{A}}}, \cdot)$ *and* $(\Sigma^*_{/\equiv_L}, \cdot)$.
- *If* $\mathfrak{A}$ *is the minimal automaton that accepts* L, *then* $\alpha \equiv_{\mathfrak{A}} \beta$ *is equivalent to* $\alpha \equiv_L \beta$, *and* $\hbar$ *is an isomorphism, so that* $\mathsf{TM}(\mathfrak{A})$ *and* $\mathsf{SM}(L)$ *are then isomorphic.*
- *If* $\mathsf{TM}(\mathfrak{A})$ *is aperiodic, so is* $\mathsf{SM}(L)$. *Moreover, if* $\mathfrak{A}$ *is the minimal automaton that accepts* L, *then aperiodicity of* $\mathsf{SM}(L)$ *also implies aperiodicity of* $\mathsf{TM}(\mathfrak{A})$.

The proofs are immediate, note that a word α is accepted by $\mathfrak{A}$ iff $\mathcal{R}_\alpha \cap (\mathcal{I} \times \mathcal{F}) \neq \{\}$ holds. For example, $\alpha \equiv_{\mathfrak{A}} \beta$ implies $\mathcal{R}_\alpha = \mathcal{R}_\beta$. Hence, it follows for all words γ and δ that $\mathcal{R}_{\gamma\alpha\delta} = \mathcal{R}_{\gamma\beta\delta}$. Hence, $\mathcal{R}_{\gamma\alpha\delta} \cap (\mathcal{I} \times \mathcal{F})$ is equivalent to $\mathcal{R}_{\gamma\beta\delta} \cap (\mathcal{I} \times \mathcal{F})$, which implies $\alpha \equiv_L \beta$.

Note that by the last point, it follows that for every regular language $L \subseteq \Sigma^*$ with aperiodic syntactic monoid $\mathsf{SM}(L)$, there is an automaton $\mathfrak{A}$ with $L = \mathsf{Lang}(\mathfrak{A})$ whose transition monoid $\mathsf{TM}(\mathfrak{A})$ is aperiodic. However, there may be another automaton $\mathfrak{A}'$ with periodic $\mathsf{TM}(\mathfrak{A})$ that nevertheless accepts L.

Moreover, it can be shown that a language is regular, i.e., can be described by means of a finite state automaton if and only if the equivalence relation $\equiv_L$ has a finite index (number of equivalence classes).

Theorem 4.59 (Myhill-Nerode Theorem). *The equivalence relation* $\equiv_L$ *of a language* $L \subseteq \Sigma^*$ *has finitely many equivalence classes if and only if there is a finite state automaton* $\mathfrak{A}$ *with* $L = \mathsf{Lang}(\mathfrak{A})$.

For the proof, note that we have already seen above that the equivalence relation $\equiv_{\mathsf{Lang}}$ $(\mathfrak{A})$of the accepted language $\mathsf{Lang}(\mathfrak{A})$ of an automaton $\mathfrak{A}$ has finitely many equivalence classes (since $\equiv_{\mathfrak{A}}$ has only finitely many equivalence classes). For the converse, assume the relation $\equiv_L$ for a language $L \subseteq \Sigma^*$ has a finite index: let $[\alpha_1]_{\equiv_L}$, ..., $[\alpha_n]_{\equiv_L}$ be the equivalence classes of $L \subseteq \Sigma^*$, and let without loss of generality be $L = \bigcup_{i=1}^f [\alpha_i]_{\equiv_L}$ (with some $f \leq n$).

We construct an automaton $\mathfrak{A}^L = (\Sigma, \Sigma^*_{/\equiv_L}, \mathcal{I}^L, \mathcal{R}^L, \mathcal{F}^L)$ as follows: the states $\Sigma^*_{/\equiv_L}$ are the classes $[\alpha_1]_{\equiv_L}$, ..., $[\alpha_1]_{\equiv_L}$, the (deterministic and complete) transition relation is defined as follows:

$$\left([\alpha_i]_{\equiv_L}, \sigma, [\alpha_j]_{\equiv_L}\right) \in \mathcal{R}^L :\Leftrightarrow \left([\alpha_i\sigma]_{\equiv_L} = [\alpha_j]_{\equiv_L}\right)$$

The only initial state is moreover $[\varepsilon]_{\equiv_L}$, i.e., the class of the empty word. The final states are clearly $\mathcal{F} := \{[\alpha_1]_{\equiv_L}, \ldots, [\alpha_f]_{\equiv_L}\}$. By construction, it follows for every $\alpha \in \Sigma^*$ that the state $[\alpha\sigma]_{\equiv_L}$ is the only one that is reached by reading the word α from the initial state $[\varepsilon]_{\equiv_L}$. Hence, it is not hard to see that $L = \mathsf{Lang}(\mathfrak{A}^L)$. It is moreover well-known that the automaton $\mathfrak{A}^L$ is the minimal automaton that accepts L (it is uniquely determined up to isomorphism).

Having seen that we can construct for each semiautomaton $\mathfrak{A}$ a monoid, namely its transition monoid $\mathsf{TM}(\mathfrak{A})$, we can now transfer the notions of index, period and exponent from monoids to semiautomata:

Definition 4.60 (Index, Period and Exponent of Semiautomata). *The index, period, and exponent of a semiautomaton $\mathfrak{A}$ is the index, period, and exponent of its transition monoid* $\mathsf{TM}(\mathfrak{A})$.

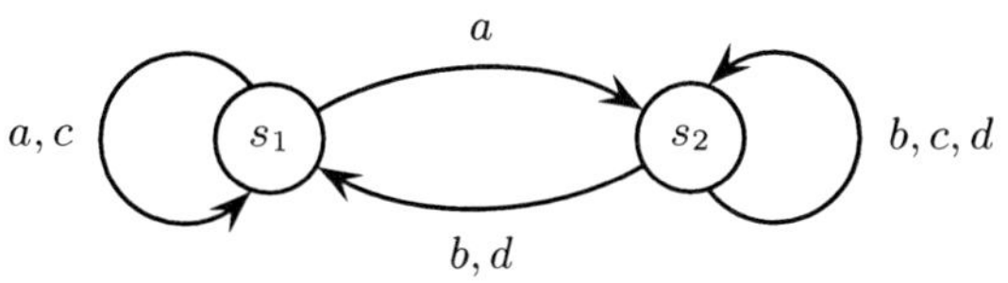

Fig. 4.21. Example of a noncounting semiautomaton $\mathfrak{A}$

As an example, consider the semiautomaton $\mathfrak{A}$ given in Figure 4.21. The automaton has the input alphabet $\Sigma = \{a, b, c, d\}$ that induce the following Boolean square matrices that generate $\mathsf{TM}(\mathfrak{A})$.

$$\mathcal{M}_a = \begin{pmatrix} 1\,1 \\ 0\,0 \end{pmatrix} \; \mathcal{M}_b = \begin{pmatrix} 0\,0 \\ 1\,1 \end{pmatrix} \; \mathcal{M}_c = \begin{pmatrix} 1\,0 \\ 0\,1 \end{pmatrix} \; \mathcal{M}_d = \mathcal{M}_b$$

Clearly, we could instead, also represent the transition monoid by the relations $\mathcal{R}_a$, $\mathcal{R}_b = \mathcal{R}_d$, and $\mathcal{R}_c$; we have chosen the matrix representation here since it is a bit more readable. Hence, the transition monoid $\mathsf{TM}(\mathfrak{A})$ of $\mathfrak{A}$ consists of three matrices, since we have the following operation table:

$\times$	$\mathcal{M}_c$	$\mathcal{M}_a$	$\mathcal{M}_b$
$\mathcal{M}_c$	$\mathcal{M}_c$	$\mathcal{M}_a$	$\mathcal{M}_b$
$\mathcal{M}_a$	$\mathcal{M}_a$	$\mathcal{M}_a$	$\mathcal{M}_a$
$\mathcal{M}_b$	$\mathcal{M}_b$	$\mathcal{M}_b$	$\mathcal{M}_b$

As neither each row nor each column is a permutation of the monoid's elements, it follows that this monoid is not a group, and therefore, not every matrix has an inverse element. As the monoid has three elements, it follows by Theorem 4.54 that $\Sigma^*_{/\equiv_{\mathfrak{A}}}$ has three classes $[a]_{\equiv_{\mathfrak{A}}}$, $[b]_{\equiv_{\mathfrak{A}}}$, and $[c]_{\equiv_{\mathfrak{A}}}$. Furthermore, it is not too difficult to see that the three equivalence classes are the following languages $[a]_{\equiv_{\mathfrak{A}}} = c^* a \Sigma^*$, $[b]_{\equiv_{\mathfrak{A}}} = c^*(b + d)\Sigma^*$, and $[c]_{\equiv_{\mathfrak{A}}} = [d]_{\equiv_{\mathfrak{A}}} = c^*$. Hence, if we want to extend the semiautomaton to an acceptor by choosing initial and final states $\mathcal{I}$ and $\mathcal{F}$, respectively, then the accepted languages are corresponding unions of the classes $[a]_{\equiv_{\mathfrak{A}}}$, $[b]_{\equiv_{\mathfrak{A}}}$, and $[c]_{\equiv_{\mathfrak{A}}}$. The semiautomaton can not accept other languages.

For the semiautomaton $\mathfrak{A}$ of Figure 4.21, it follows that $\exp(\mathsf{TM}(\mathfrak{A})) = 1$, $\mathsf{idx}(\mathsf{TM}(\mathfrak{A})) = 0$, and $\mathsf{prd}(\mathsf{TM}(\mathfrak{A})) = 1$. Hence, $\mathsf{TM}(\mathfrak{A})$ is aperiodic. Automata whose transition monoid is aperiodic are called noncounting automata. This class of automata was first studied in [364], and since then a lot of interesting characterizations have been found (see page 386). We will list some simple properties of noncounting automata after the following definition.

Definition 4.61 (Noncounting Semiautomata). $\mathfrak{A} = (\Sigma, \mathcal{S}, \mathcal{I}, \mathcal{R})$ *is noncounting, if there is a number* $n \in \mathbb{N}$ *such that for every word* $\alpha \in \Sigma^*$, *we have* $\mathcal{R}_{\alpha^n} = \mathcal{R}_{\alpha^{n+1}}$.

We remark that since $\mathcal{R}_{\alpha\beta} = \mathcal{R}_\alpha \circ \mathcal{R}_\beta$ holds, it follows that $\mathcal{R}_{\alpha^n} = (\mathcal{R}_\alpha)^n$. Therefore, we immediately see that $\mathfrak{A}$ is noncounting if and only if $\mathsf{TM}(\mathfrak{A})$ is aperiodic. The next proposition lists two further characterizations for noncounting semiautomata. The equivalences of these properties are all straightforward to prove, but they nevertheless enhance our understanding. In particular, the second one establishes the relationship with the theory of aperiodic monoids.

Theorem 4.62 (Noncounting Semiautomata). *The following properties are all equivalent for a semiautomaton* $\mathfrak{A} = (\Sigma, \mathcal{S}, \mathcal{I}, \mathcal{R})$ *and therefore characterize noncounting semiautomata:*

(1) $\mathfrak{A}$ *is noncounting*
(2) $\mathsf{TM}(\mathfrak{A})$ *is aperiodic*
(3) *there is a number* $n \in \mathbb{N}$ *such that for each word* $\alpha\beta\gamma \in \Sigma^*$, *and each* $k \in \mathbb{N}$, *we have* $\mathcal{R}_{\alpha\beta^n\gamma} = \mathcal{R}_{\alpha\beta^{n+k}\gamma}$
(4) *for every word* $\alpha\beta\gamma \in \Sigma^*$, *there is a number* $n \in \mathbb{N}$ *such that for every* $k \in \mathbb{N}$, *we have* $\mathcal{R}_{\alpha\beta^n\gamma} = \mathcal{R}_{\alpha\beta^{n+k}\gamma}$

Proof. To prove (1) $\Leftrightarrow$ (2), note that $\mathcal{R}_{\alpha^n} = \mathcal{R}_\alpha^n$ holds. Hence, if $\mathfrak{A}$ is noncounting, it follows that there is a $n \in \mathbb{N}$ such that for all words $\alpha \in \Sigma^*$, we have $\mathcal{R}_\alpha^n = \mathcal{R}_\alpha^{n+1}$, which means that $\mathsf{TM}(\mathfrak{A})$ is aperiodic. Conversely, if $\mathsf{TM}(\mathfrak{A})$ is aperiodic, it follows that there is a $n \in \mathbb{N}$ such that for each word $\alpha \in \Sigma^*$, we have $\mathcal{R}_\alpha^n = \mathcal{R}_\alpha^{n+1}$, hence $\mathcal{R}_{\alpha^n} = \mathcal{R}_{\alpha^{n+1}}$, and therefore $\mathfrak{A}$ is noncounting.

The equivalence (1) $\Leftrightarrow$ (3) is also simple: for (3) $\Rightarrow$ (1) simply instantiate the empty word for α and γ and set $k := 1$; for (1) $\Rightarrow$ (3) prove first by induction (on k) that (1′) for each $k \in \mathbb{N}$ and each $\beta \in \Sigma^*$, $\mathcal{R}_{\beta^n} = \mathcal{R}_{\beta^{n+k}}$ holds. The result then easily follows by product computation with $\mathcal{R}_\alpha$ and $\mathcal{R}_\gamma$.

To prove (3) $\Leftrightarrow$ (4), first note that (3) $\Rightarrow$ (4) is trivial since $\exists y.\forall x.P(x,y)$ implies $\forall x.\exists y.P(x,y)$ for all predicates P. For the other implication, it first follows from (4) that $\mathcal{R}_\beta$ is for each word β aperiodic. Hence, $\mathsf{TM}(\mathfrak{A})$ is aperiodic, so that (4) $\Rightarrow$ (2) follows. The rest follows from (2) $\Leftrightarrow$ (1) and and (1) $\Leftrightarrow$ (3). □

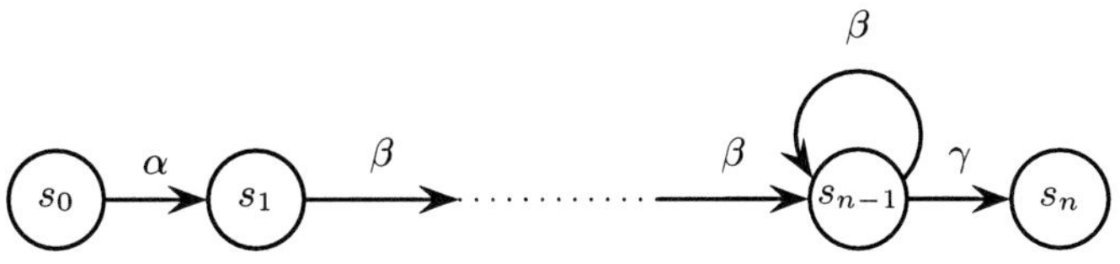

Fig. 4.22. Path in a deterministic noncounting semiautomaton (cf. Theorem 4.63)

In the previous section, we have seen that we can compute for every nondeterministic automaton an equivalent deterministic one (of a possible different class). Noncounting deterministic automata can be characterized by further properties that are more closely related to their state transition diagram. For deterministic automata, the noncounting property can be characterized in the following way:

Theorem 4.63 (Deterministic Noncounting Semiautomata). *For every deterministic semiautomaton $\mathfrak{A} = (\Sigma, \mathcal{S}, \mathcal{I}, \mathcal{R})$, the following facts are equivalent:*

(1) *$\mathfrak{A}$ is noncounting*
(2) *there is a $n \in \mathbb{N}$ such that for all $\alpha\beta\gamma \in \Sigma^*$, all $k \in \mathbb{N}$, and all $s_1, s_2, s_3 \in \mathcal{S}$ with $(s_1, s_2) \in \mathcal{R}_{\alpha\beta^n\gamma}$, and $(s_1, s_3) \in \mathcal{R}_{\alpha\beta^{n+k}\gamma}$, it follows $s_2 = s_3$.*
(3) *there is no word α and there are no pairwise different states $s_0, \ldots, s_{n-1} \in \mathcal{S}$ (with $n > 1$) such that $(s_i, s_{(i+1) \bmod n}) \in \mathcal{R}_\alpha$ (i.e., the states $s_0, \ldots, s_{n-1}$ form a cycle)*
(4) $\forall \alpha \in \Sigma^*. \forall s_1, s_2 \in \mathcal{S}.\ s_1 \neq s_2 \wedge (s_1, s_2) \in \mathcal{R}_\alpha \rightarrow \neg\exists n \geq 1.(s_2, s_1) \in \mathcal{R}_{\alpha^n}$
(5) $\forall \alpha \in \Sigma^*. \forall s \in \mathcal{S}.\ (s, s) \in \mathcal{R}_\alpha \rightarrow \neg\exists \beta \in \Sigma^*. \exists n > 1. \alpha = \beta^n$
(6) $\forall S \subseteq \mathcal{S}. \forall \alpha \in \Sigma^*.\ \mathsf{suc}_\exists^{\mathcal{R}_\alpha}(S) = S \rightarrow\ \forall s \in S.\ \mathsf{suc}_\exists^{\mathcal{R}_\alpha}(\{s\}) = \{s\}$

Proof. Since $\mathfrak{A}$ is deterministic, it follows for every word α that $(s_1, s_2) \in \mathcal{R}_\alpha$ and $(s_1, s_3) \in \mathcal{R}_\alpha$ implies $s_2 = s_3$. Hence, the equivalence of (1) and (2) easily follows from the previous theorem.

We prove (1) $\Rightarrow$ (3) as follows: if $\mathsf{TM}(\mathfrak{A})$ is aperiodic, then there is a n such that $\mathcal{R}_{\alpha^n} = \mathcal{R}_{\alpha^{n+1}}$. Hence, $(s_0, s_n) \in \mathcal{R}_{\alpha^n}$ holds iff $(s_0, s_n) \in \mathcal{R}_{\alpha^{n+1}}$ holds. Given that $(s_0, s_n) \in \mathcal{R}_{\alpha^n}$ holds, it follows that $(s_0, s_n) \in \mathcal{R}_{\alpha^{n+1}}$, and as $\mathfrak{A}$ is deterministic, we conclude that $(s_n, s_n) \in \mathcal{R}_\alpha$. But then, the sequence of states s_1, s_2, …that can be reached by reading α, α^2, …from a state s_0 ends in a 'α-cycle' of length 1, and hence (3) holds. Conversely, assume that (3) holds. We consider again the sequence of states s_1, s_2, …that can be reached by reading α, α^2, …from a state s_0. Clearly, the sequence must end in a cycle, i.e., there must be smallest numbers i and p with $s_i = s_{i+p}$. As (3) holds, it follows that $p = 1$. As this holds for every state s_0, it follows that there is a number n such that $\mathcal{R}_\alpha^n = \mathcal{R}_\alpha^{n+1}$, and hence $\mathsf{TM}(\mathfrak{A})$ is aperiodic. The equivalence of (4), (5) and (6) to (3) is obvious. □

Hence, if a deterministic semiautomaton is not noncounting, then there is a word α and states $s_0, \ldots, s_{n-1}$ with $(s_i, s_{(i+1) \bmod n}) \in \mathcal{R}_\alpha$, i.e., these states form a cycle where α is read between two states s_i and $s_{(i+1) \bmod n}$. In other words, in a noncounting deterministic automaton, *every sequence of states s_i with $(s_i, s_{i+1}) \in \mathcal{R}_\alpha$ ends in a self-loop*. This is expressed by $(4-6)$ in different ways: (4) says that if s_2 can be reached from s_1 by reading α, then it is not possible to reach s_1 from s_2 by reading a word α^n (otherwise we would have a cycle that is not a self-loop). (5) expresses this in another way: if we have a self-loop, i.e., if a state s can be reached from itself by reading α, then the word α is not of the form β^n with $n > 1$, since otherwise we would have a β-cycle of length $n > 1$.

Finally, consider the formulation (6): if $\mathsf{suc}_{\exists}^{\mathcal{R}_\alpha}(S) = S$ holds, then the functions that maps a state s to its 'successor state' under $\mathcal{R}_\alpha$ is a permutation of S. If we do not have $(s, s) \in \mathcal{R}_\alpha$, then we could form an α-cycle of length > 1. This observation leads then to decomposition theorems like the Krohn-Rhodes theorem [151, 209, 309, 341, 342, 475] (see also page 383).

The noncounting restriction for deterministic automata is therefore, that a noncounting semiautomaton can not distinguish between the words $\alpha\beta^n\gamma$, $\alpha\beta^{n+1}\gamma, \ldots, \alpha\beta^{n+k}\gamma$, i.e., either none or all of these words is accepted, since they all connect the same states. The automaton can therefore only count in a limited way, namely up to n occurrences of β. The only way to distinguish further words would be to count the number of repetitions of β modulo $n > 2$ which is something the automaton cannot do.

It is easily seen that the above equivalences do not remain valid for nondeterministic semiautomata. For example, the semiautomaton given in Figure 4.23 has states s_0 and s_1 that form a cycle with the input φ, but the automaton is nevertheless noncounting.

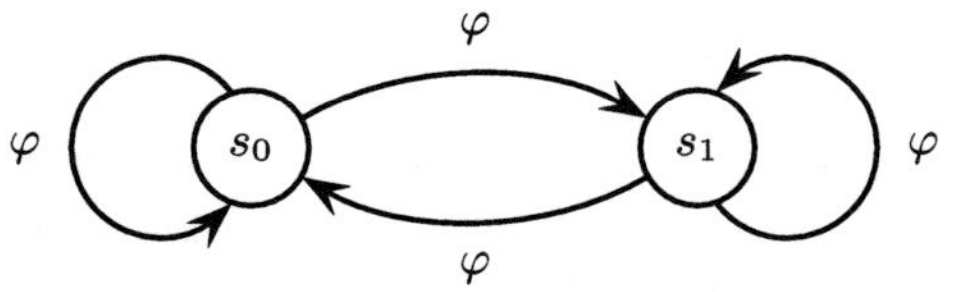

Fig. 4.23. Counterexample for nondeterministic semiautomata

4.8 Decision Procedures for ω-Automata

In the previous sections, we have defined the logic $\mathcal{L}_\omega$ of ω-automata. In particular, we have considered the expressiveness of the classes Det_κ, have proved their relationship to the Borel hierarchy and in the previous section, we have moreover considered the relationship to algebraic structures. In this section, we will consider the verification of $\mathcal{L}_\omega$ formulas, i.e., for a Kripke structure $\mathcal{K}$ and a formula $\Phi \in \mathcal{L}_\omega$, we want to compute the satisfying states $[\![\Phi]\!]_{\mathcal{K}}$.

To this end, we will first prove in Section 4.8.1 that we can restrict our considerations to formulas of the form $\mathsf{E}\mathfrak{A}$, where $\mathfrak{A}$ is an automaton formula whose acceptance condition neither contains further automaton formulas nor path quantifiers. As we already know that these automaton formulas can be restricted to the classes $(\mathsf{N})\mathsf{Det}_\kappa$, we will consider the verification of these particular classes in detail. We will thereby consider two different approaches: In Section 4.8.2, we will first reduce the model checking problem $(\mathcal{K}, s) \models \mathsf{E}\mathfrak{A}$ to an equivalent problem, namely to check whether there is a state $s_\mathfrak{A} \in \mathcal{I}$ such that $(\mathcal{K} \times \mathsf{Struct}(\mathfrak{A}), (s, s_\mathfrak{A})) \models \mathsf{E}\Phi_\mathcal{F}$ holds. The latter problem is finally solved in that we translate the 'acceptance conditions' $\mathsf{E}\Phi_\mathcal{F}$ to equivalent μ-calculus formulas. The second approach given in Section 4.8.3 is more rigorous: we will show how formulas of the form $\mathsf{E}\mathfrak{A}$ can be translated to equivalent μ-calculus formulas $\Phi_{\mathsf{E}\mathfrak{A}}$ so that the model checking problem of $\mathcal{L}_\omega$ is again reduced to a model checking problem of the μ-calculus.

Both solutions for the model checking problem of $\mathcal{L}_\omega$ have their advantages and disadvantages. The translation of $\mathsf{E}\mathfrak{A}$ to equivalent μ-calculus formulas $\Phi_{\mathsf{E}\mathfrak{A}}$ suffers from the fact, that the size of $\Phi_\mathfrak{A}$ grows linearly with the number of states and transitions of $\mathfrak{A}$. This can be a limitation in practice when large automata have to be checked. The evaluation of the 'acceptance' condition $\mathsf{E}\Phi_\mathcal{F}$ in the product structure $\mathcal{K} \times \mathsf{Struct}(\mathfrak{A})$ does not have this limitation, since it can be done with an implicit representation of the automaton in form of propositional formulas.

4.8.1 Flattening ω-Automata

In this section, we will briefly explain that the model checking problem of $\mathcal{L}_\omega$ can be reduced to checking formulas of the form $\mathsf{E}\mathfrak{A}$, where $\mathfrak{A} \in \mathsf{NDet}_\kappa$ holds for $\kappa \in \{\mathsf{G}, \mathsf{F}, \mathsf{Prefix}, \mathsf{GF}, \mathsf{FG}, \mathsf{Rabin}\}$. To show this, first reconsider the language of automaton formulas $\mathcal{L}_\omega$ that has been given in Definition 4.6. The formulas are derived from the nonterminal S according to the following grammar rules:

$$
\begin{aligned}
I &::= V_\Sigma \mid \mathcal{Q} \mid \neg I \mid I \wedge I \mid I \vee I \\
P &::= \mathcal{Q} \mid \neg P \mid P \wedge P \mid P \vee P \\
R &::= V_\Sigma \mid \mathcal{Q} \mid \neg R \mid R \wedge R \mid R \vee R \mid \mathsf{X}P \\
T &::= V_\Sigma \mid \mathcal{Q} \mid \neg T \mid T \wedge T \mid T \vee T \mid \mathsf{G}T \mid \mathsf{F}T \\
A &::= T \mid \mathcal{A}_\exists (Q, I, R, A) \mid \mathcal{A}_\forall (Q, I, R, A) \mid \neg A \mid A \wedge A \mid A \vee A \\
S &::= V_\Sigma \mid \neg S \mid S \wedge S \mid S \vee S \mid \mathsf{E}A \mid \mathsf{A}A
\end{aligned}
$$

Using the prenex normal form as introduced in Theorem 2.49 on page 85, we can reduce every formula to an equivalent one in the following normal form, where the Φ_i are formulas that are derived from the nonterminal A, and Ψ is derived from I (hence propositional):

$$\mathsf{let}\begin{pmatrix}\vartheta_1 = \mathsf{E}\Phi_1\\ \vdots\\ \vartheta_n = \mathsf{E}\Phi_n\end{pmatrix}\mathsf{in}\ \Psi\ \mathsf{end}$$

Furthermore, the formulas Φ_i can be brought into negation normal form, so that negation symbols only occur in front of variables.

We have furthermore already seen in Theorem 4.33 that all acceptance conditions can be restricted to Büchi conditions, i.e., we could replace the grammar rules for the nonterminal T in Definition 4.6 by $T ::= \mathsf{GF}I$. We may however also retain the other κ classes, they are simply redundant. As we will see, some of these classes can be more efficiently checked since they can be reduced to alternation-free μ-calculus formulas, and it is reasonable to still consider them in the restricted language. Hence, we can change the grammar rules to $T ::= \mathsf{G}I \mid \mathsf{F}I \mid \mathsf{GF}I \mid \mathsf{FG}I$ (and if desired some of the others to allow Rabin-, Streett- and Prefix-conditions).

As we have proved that $\mathsf{NDet}_{\mathsf{GF}}$ is at least closed under all Boolean combinations, we can furthermore eliminate the Boolean combinations of automaton formulas. It may thereby be necessary to convert $\mathsf{(N)Det}_\kappa$ automata to equivalent $\mathsf{NDet}_{\mathsf{GF}}$ automata for computing the Boolean combinations, but we have already seen how this can be done.

A more severe problem is to compute conjunctions, disjunctions and nestings of automata of different (universal/existential) quantification type. We have to apply a determinization step to convert the universal automaton to a deterministic one, so that we can change its quantification type. After this, we can easily apply the results of the Lemmas 4.9, 4.11, and 4.16 to compute the final existential automaton that is then again converted to a $\mathsf{(N)Det}_\kappa$ class. Hence, after all translations, we obtain the following result (see [107, 485, 500] for similar logics):

Theorem 4.64 (Normal Form for $\mathcal{L}_\omega$). *For every formula $\Phi \in \mathcal{L}_\omega$, we can compute an equivalent formula in the following form, where the $\mathfrak{A}_i \in \mathsf{NDet}_\kappa$ for $\kappa \in \{\mathsf{G}, \mathsf{F}, \mathsf{GF}, \mathsf{FG}, \mathsf{Prefix}, \mathsf{Rabin}, \mathsf{Streett}\}$ holds, and Ψ is propositional.*

$$\mathsf{let}\begin{pmatrix}\vartheta_1 = \mathsf{E}\mathfrak{A}_1\\ \vdots\\ \vartheta_n = \mathsf{E}\mathfrak{A}_n\end{pmatrix}\mathsf{in}\ \Psi\ \mathsf{end}$$

The size of the above formula is nonelementary in the size of Φ.

A function $f : \mathbb{N} \to \mathbb{N}$ is thereby nonelementary, if it grows larger than all functions $e_k(n)$ that are defined as $e_1(n) := 2^n$ and $e_{k+1}(n) := 2^{e_k(n)}$. The nonelementary growth is due to several determinization steps. Each determinization step may yield an exponential growth, and a formula of size n may yield $O(n)$ such determinization steps, therefore the size of the above normal form may grow faster than $e_n(n)$.

4.8.2 Translating $\mathcal{L}_\omega$ Model Checking to $\mathcal{L}_\mu$ Model Checking

Having seen that we can restrict the model checking problem of $\mathcal{L}_\omega$ to formulas of the form $\mathsf{E}\mathfrak{A}$ where $\mathfrak{A} \in \mathsf{NDet}_\kappa$ for $\kappa \in \{\mathsf{G}, \mathsf{F}, \mathsf{GF}, \mathsf{FG}, \mathsf{Prefix}, \mathsf{Rabin}, \mathsf{Streett}\}$, we now propose a first approach to solve these remaining problems. In this section, we will show how these problems can be reduced to simple μ-calculus model checking problems on the product structure $\mathcal{K} \times \mathsf{Struct}(\mathfrak{A})$. As we will see, we will thereby only have to translate the acceptance conditions (endowed with a path quantifier) to the μ-calculus. The algorithms of the next section translate the entire formula $\mathsf{E}\mathfrak{A}$ to the μ-calculus.

The model checking problem $(\mathcal{K}, s) \models \mathsf{E}\mathfrak{A}$ is thereby interpreted as a *language inclusion problem* (often also called language containment problem). On the one hand, we have the language $L_\mathcal{K}(s)$ of infinite words of the form $\lambda t.\mathcal{L}(\pi^{(t)})$ where π is a path of $\mathcal{K}$ starting in s, and on the other hand we have the language $\mathsf{Lang}(\mathfrak{A})$ that is accepted by $\mathfrak{A}$. We obviously have $(\mathcal{K}, s) \models \mathsf{E}\mathfrak{A}$ iff $L_\mathcal{K}(s) \cap \mathsf{Lang}(\mathfrak{A}) \neq \{\}$ holds. The notion 'language inclusion problem' might be a bit misleading at this stage, but note $L_1 \cap L_2 \neq \{\}$ holds if and only if $L_1 \not\subseteq (\Sigma^\omega \setminus L_2)$ holds.

In addition to the model checking problem $(\mathcal{K}, s) \models \mathsf{E}\mathfrak{A}$, which is related to a language inclusion problem of ω-regular languages, one may also consider the *satisfiability problem of automata* $\mathfrak{A}$: We ask whether a structure $\mathcal{K}$ and a state s exists, so that $(\mathcal{K}, s) \models \mathsf{E}\mathfrak{A}$ holds. This problem is obviously related with the *nonemptiness problem* of $\mathsf{Lang}(\mathfrak{A})$, since for every word in $\mathsf{Lang}(\mathfrak{A})$, we can construct a structure containing just this path, and therefore would satisfy $\mathsf{E}\mathfrak{A}$. Note here that a language $\mathsf{Lang}(\mathfrak{A})$ is nonempty if and only if it contains an ultimately periodic path. It is obvious how to construct a Kripke structure of such a word. Finally, the *universality problem of a language*, i.e., to check whether $\mathsf{Lang}(\mathfrak{A}) = \Sigma^\omega$ holds, is dual to the nonemptiness problem. For automata formulas, this means that we have to check if the automaton formula $\mathfrak{A}$ is equivalent to 1. This is equivalent to checking if $\neg\mathfrak{A}$ is equivalent to 0, i.e., to check whether $\mathsf{Lang}(\neg\mathfrak{A})$ is empty. Since $\mathcal{L}_\omega$ is closed under negation, we can handle every problem iff we can handle the dual problem. Hence, we can also provide solutions to the universality problem.

We will now show that all of these problems can be reduced to equivalent μ-calculus model checking problems so that they can be solved with the model checking procedures we have considered so far. The reductions are as follows:

Theorem 4.65 (Model Checking of Automaton Formulas). *Given an automaton formula $\mathfrak{A} = \mathcal{A}_\exists(Q, \Phi_\mathcal{I}, \Phi_\mathcal{R}, \Phi_\mathcal{F})$ and a structure $\mathcal{K} = (\mathcal{I}, \mathcal{S}, \mathcal{R}, \mathcal{L})$ over some variables V_Σ. Let $\mathcal{K}_\mathfrak{A} = \mathsf{Struct}(\mathfrak{A})$ be the associated Kripke structure of $\mathfrak{A}$ as given in Definition 2.39. Then, the following are equivalent:*

- $(\mathcal{K}, s) \models \mathsf{E}\mathfrak{A}$
- *there is a $\vartheta \subseteq Q \cup V_\Sigma$ so that $(\mathcal{K} \times \mathcal{K}_\mathfrak{A}, (s, \vartheta)) \models \Phi_\mathcal{I} \wedge \mathsf{E}\Phi_\mathcal{F}$*

For special kinds of automaton formulas, we can translate the latter to equivalent μ-calculus formulas by the following laws:

- $\mathsf{EG}\varphi = \nu y.\, \varphi \wedge \Diamond y$
- $\mathsf{EF}\varphi = \mu y.\, \varphi \wedge (\nu x.\, \Diamond x) \vee \Diamond y = \mathsf{fix}\begin{bmatrix} x \overset{\nu}{=} \Diamond x \\ y \overset{\mu}{=} \varphi \wedge x \vee \Diamond y \end{bmatrix} \mathsf{in}\ y\ \mathsf{end}$
- $\mathsf{EFG}\varphi = \mu y.\, (\nu x.\varphi \wedge \Diamond x) \vee \Diamond y = \mathsf{fix}\begin{bmatrix} x \overset{\nu}{=} \varphi \wedge \Diamond x \\ y \overset{\mu}{=} x \vee \Diamond y \end{bmatrix} \mathsf{in}\ y\ \mathsf{end}$
- $\mathsf{EGF}\varphi = \nu y.\, \Diamond[\mu x.\, y \wedge \varphi \vee \Diamond x] = \mathsf{fix}\begin{bmatrix} x \overset{\mu}{=} y \wedge \varphi \vee \Diamond x \\ y \overset{\nu}{=} \Diamond x \end{bmatrix} \mathsf{in}\ y\ \mathsf{end}$
- $\mathsf{E}\left[\mathsf{G}\beta \wedge \bigwedge_{i=1}^{f} \mathsf{GF}\alpha_i\right] = \mathsf{fix}\begin{bmatrix} x_1 \overset{\mu}{=} y \wedge \alpha_1 \vee \beta \wedge \Diamond x_1 \\ \vdots \\ x_f \overset{\mu}{=} y \wedge \alpha_f \vee \beta \wedge \Diamond x_f \\ y \overset{\nu}{=} \beta \wedge \bigwedge_{i=1}^{f} \Diamond x_i \end{bmatrix} \mathsf{in}\ y\ \mathsf{end}$
- $\mathsf{E}\bigvee_{j=0}^{f} \mathsf{G}\varphi_j \wedge \mathsf{F}\psi_j = \bigvee_{j=0}^{f} \mathsf{fix}\begin{bmatrix} x \overset{\nu}{=} \varphi_j \wedge \Diamond x \\ y \overset{\mu}{=} \psi_j \wedge x \vee \varphi_j \wedge \Diamond y \end{bmatrix} \mathsf{in}\ y\ \mathsf{end}$
- $\mathsf{E}\bigvee_{j=0}^{f} \mathsf{GF}\varphi_j \wedge \mathsf{FG}\psi_j = \bigvee_{j=0}^{f} \mathsf{fix}\begin{bmatrix} x \overset{\mu}{=} y \wedge \varphi_j \vee \psi_j \wedge \Diamond x \\ y \overset{\nu}{=} \psi_j \wedge \Diamond x \\ z \overset{\mu}{=} y \vee \Diamond z \end{bmatrix} \mathsf{in}\ z\ \mathsf{end}$
- $\mathsf{E}\bigwedge_{j=0}^{f} \mathsf{GF}\varphi_j \vee \mathsf{FG}\psi_j = \mathsf{fix}\begin{bmatrix} x_1 \overset{\mu}{=} y \wedge \varphi_1 \vee y \wedge \Diamond x_1 \\ \vdots \\ x_f \overset{\mu}{=} y \wedge \varphi_f \vee y \wedge \Diamond x_f \\ y \overset{\nu}{=} \bigwedge_{j=0}^{f} \Diamond x_j \vee \psi_j \wedge \Diamond y \\ z \overset{\mu}{=} y \vee \Diamond z \end{bmatrix} \mathsf{in}\ z\ \mathsf{end}$

Proof. The proofs for the classes $\mathsf{EG}\varphi$ and $\mathsf{EF}\varphi$ are simple. Note that $\mu y.\varphi \vee \Diamond y$ would not be correct, since this formula would also consider finite paths (adding the formula $\Phi_{\mathsf{inf}} :\equiv \nu x.\Diamond x$ corrects this since this formula holds exactly in the states that have an infinite path). Using the restriction of $\mathcal{R}$ to $\mathcal{R}_{\mathsf{inf}}$, as shown in Section 3.7, is an alternative solution.

For the proof of $\mathsf{EFG}\varphi$ simply note that $\mathsf{EFG}\varphi = \mathsf{EFEG}\varphi$ holds so that two independent fixpoint iterations are obtained. As the $\mathsf{EG}\varphi$ fixpoint already neglects finite paths, we need not add a correction term as in the case for $\mathsf{EF}\varphi$.

Shifting a path quantifier inwards is not possible for $\mathsf{EGF}\varphi$. The fixpoint for this formula is obtained as a special case of $\mathsf{E}\left[\mathsf{G}\beta \wedge \bigwedge_{i=1}^{f} \mathsf{GF}\alpha_i\right]$ that we already considered in detail on page 165, and that we have also listed for completeness in the above theorem.

In the case of $\mathsf{E}\bigvee_{j=0}^{f} \mathsf{G}\varphi_j \wedge \mathsf{F}\psi_j$, we first shift the quantifier E inside to obtain $\bigvee_{j=0}^{f} \mathsf{E}[\mathsf{G}\varphi_j \wedge \mathsf{F}\psi_j]$. Then, we make use of the equivalences $\mathsf{G}\varphi_j \wedge \mathsf{F}\psi_j =$

$[\varphi_j\ \underline{\mathsf{U}}\ (\psi_j \wedge \mathsf{G}\varphi_j)]$ and $\mathsf{E}[\varphi_j\ \underline{\mathsf{U}}\ \psi_j] = \mathsf{E}[\varphi_j\ \underline{\mathsf{U}}\ \mathsf{E}\psi_j]$ for state formulas φ_j and ψ_j. These equations are formally proved in Lemma 5.18 and Theorem 5.22.

In the case $\mathsf{E}\bigvee_{j=0}^{f} \mathsf{GF}\varphi_j \wedge \mathsf{FG}\psi_j$, we first shift the quantifier inwards to obtain $\bigvee_{j=0}^{f} \mathsf{E}[\mathsf{GF}\varphi_j \wedge \mathsf{FG}\psi_j]$. The crucial observation is now that infinite occurrences of φ_j need not be considered on finite prefixes of a path, i.e., $\mathsf{E}[\mathsf{GF}\varphi_j \wedge \mathsf{FG}\psi_j]$ is equivalent to $\mathsf{EF}[\mathsf{GF}\varphi_j \wedge \mathsf{G}\psi_j]$. We will see in Theorem 5.22 that $\mathsf{EF}a = \mathsf{EFE}a$ holds. Hence, it remains to find a μ-calculus formula for $\mathsf{E}[\mathsf{GF}\varphi_j \wedge \mathsf{G}\psi_j]$, which is again a special case of $\mathsf{E}\left[\mathsf{G}\beta \wedge \bigwedge_{i=1}^{f} \mathsf{GF}\alpha_i\right]$ that we considered in detail on page 165.

Finally, for $\mathsf{E}\bigwedge_{j=0}^{f} \mathsf{GF}\varphi_j \vee \mathsf{FG}\psi_j$, we note again that infinite occurrences need not be checked on finite prefixes of paths, which means here that $\mathsf{E}\bigwedge_{j=0}^{f} \mathsf{GF}\varphi_j \vee \mathsf{FG}\psi_j = \mathsf{EFE}\bigwedge_{j=0}^{f} \mathsf{GF}\varphi_j \vee \mathsf{G}\psi_j$ holds. Hence, we only need to find a μ-calculus formula for $\mathsf{E}\bigwedge_{j=0}^{f} \mathsf{GF}\varphi_j \vee \mathsf{G}\psi_j$. To see that y is equivalent to this, note that the x_j are equivalent to $\mathsf{E}[\varphi_j\ \underline{\mathsf{B}}\ (\neg y)]$ (see next chapter), and that the iteration is a generalization of that we used for $\mathsf{E}\left[\bigwedge_{i=1}^{f} \mathsf{GF}\alpha_i\right]$ that we already considered in detail on page 165 (see also [174]). □

In general, $[\![\mathsf{E}[\psi \wedge \mathsf{G}\varphi]]\!]_{\mathcal{K}}$ can be evaluated as follows: first compute $S_\varphi := [\![\mathsf{EG}\varphi]\!]_{\mathcal{K}}$, and then compute $S_\psi := [\![\mathsf{E}\psi]\!]_{\mathcal{K}_\psi}$, where $\mathcal{K}_\psi$ is the structure $\mathcal{K}$ restricted to the states S_φ. We then have $[\![\mathsf{E}[\psi \wedge \mathsf{G}\varphi]]\!]_{\mathcal{K}} = S_\varphi \cap S_\psi$ [168].

By the above theorem, we obtain a procedure for checking automaton formulas, in that we perform the fixpoint iteration on the product structure. As the acceptance conditions of NDet_G, NDet_F, $\mathsf{NDet}_\mathsf{Prefix}$, and $\mathsf{NDet}_\mathsf{FG}$ can be translated to the alternation-free μ-calculus, it follows that the runtime for checking these automaton formulas is of order $O(|\mathcal{K}|\ 2^{2|Q|}\ |\varphi|)$ (since the product structure may have $2^{2|Q|}\ |\mathcal{R}|$ transitions). However, the fixpoints for $\mathsf{NDet}_\mathsf{GF}$, Rabin and Streett conditions are of alternation depth 2, and therefore require $O(|\mathcal{S}|\ |\mathcal{K}|\ 2^{3|Q|}\ |\varphi|)$ since the set of states of the product structure is of order $O(|\mathcal{S}|\ 2^{|Q|})$ and their transitions are of order $O(|\mathcal{R}|\ 2^{2|Q|})$.

Theorem 4.66 (Satisfiability of Automaton Formulas). *Given an automaton formula $\mathfrak{A} = \mathcal{A}_\exists(Q, \Phi_\mathcal{I}, \Phi_\mathcal{R}, \Phi_\mathcal{F})$ and its associated Kripke structure $\mathcal{K}_\mathfrak{A} = \mathsf{Struct}(\mathfrak{A})$ as given in Definition 2.39. Then the following is equivalent:*

- *there is a structure $\mathcal{K}$ and a state s with $(\mathcal{K}, s) \models \mathsf{E}\mathfrak{A}$*
- *there is a $\vartheta \subseteq Q \cup V_\Sigma$ such that $(\mathcal{K}_\mathfrak{A}, \vartheta) \models \Phi_\mathcal{I} \wedge \mathsf{E}\Phi_\mathcal{F}$ holds*
- *the language accepted by $\mathfrak{A}$ is not empty*

Consequently, satisfiability checking of (un-nested) automaton formulas can be reduced to the corresponding model checking problem.

In the next section, we will see how temporal logic formulas can be translated to automaton formulas, so that the above theorem allows us to check the satisfiability of temporal logic formulas.

It was shown in [172, 173] that checking the nonemptiness of a Büchi automaton (i.e., the problem to decide whether there is a structure $\mathcal{K}$ and a state s such that $(\mathcal{K}, s) \models \mathsf{E}\mathfrak{A}$ holds) is decidable in linear time. In contrast, the algorithms we have developed by the reduction to μ-calculus do not reach that efficiency, apart from the 'alternation-free' classes NDet_G, NDet_F, $\mathsf{NDet}_\mathsf{Prefix}$, and $\mathsf{NDet}_\mathsf{FG}$. Moreover, [386] proves that the same problem is NLOGSPACE-complete. [459] proves that the universality problem for Büchi automata is decidable in exponential time and is PSPACE-complete.

4.8.3 Translating Automata to Vectorized μ-Calculus

Dam [135] gives a translation of $\mathsf{NDet}_\mathsf{GF}$ automata to the equivalent (non-vectorized) μ-calculus. The size of the resulting μ-calculus formulas is however exponential in terms of the size of the given automaton which limits the usefulness of his translation. We will now construct alternative translations to the vectorized μ-calculus and will thereby improve the result of [135]. In particular, we will see that the basic automaton classes NDet_G, NDet_F, and $\mathsf{NDet}_\mathsf{FG}$ can be translated to equivalent alternation-free μ-calculus formulas of only linear size w.r.t. to the number of transitions of the given automaton.

As a consequence, it follows that the model checking problems $(\mathcal{K}, s) \models \mathsf{E}\mathfrak{A}$ where $\mathfrak{A}$ belongs to either NDet_G, NDet_F, or $\mathsf{NDet}_\mathsf{FG}$, are solvable in linear time w.r.t. to the size of $\mathfrak{A}$ (which may be exponential in the size of the formula $|\mathfrak{A}|$) and $|\mathcal{R}|$. Hence, these automaton classes are particularly interesting for specification and verification as they can be very efficiently checked.

The translations of the mentioned classes are remarkably simple. Given a Kripke structure $\mathcal{K}$ and an automaton $\mathfrak{A}$, the idea behind the translations is that we simulate the product structure $\mathcal{K} \times \mathsf{Struct}(\mathfrak{A})$ without computing it. This is done by labeling the states of $\mathcal{K}$ with new variables y_σ for every reachable situation σ of the automaton $\mathfrak{A}$. Exactly those states s of $\mathcal{K}$ should be labeled with y_σ that have a product state (s, σ) in $\mathcal{K} \times \mathsf{Struct}(\mathfrak{A})$ where at least one path starts that satisfies the acceptance condition of $\mathfrak{A}$.

We illustrate this translation principle by the class NDet_G and briefly give translations for other automaton classes. Suppose $\mathfrak{A} \equiv \mathcal{A}_\exists(Q, \Phi_\mathcal{I}, \Phi_\mathcal{R}, \mathsf{G}\Phi) \in \mathsf{NDet}_\mathsf{G}$ is given over the variables V_Σ together with a Kripke structure $\mathcal{K} = (\mathcal{S}, \mathcal{I}, \mathcal{R}, \mathcal{L}, \{\})$ over the variables V_Σ. Recall that the product structure $\mathcal{K} \times \mathsf{Struct}(\mathfrak{A}) = (\mathcal{S}_\times, \mathcal{I}_\times, \mathcal{R}_\times, \mathcal{L}_\times)$ is defined as follows:

- $\mathcal{S}_\times := \{(s, \sigma) \mid s \in \mathcal{S} \wedge \sigma \subseteq Q \cup V_\Sigma \wedge \mathcal{L}(s) = \sigma \cap V_\Sigma\}$
- $\mathcal{I}_\times := \{(s, \sigma) \in \mathcal{S}_\times \mid s \in \mathcal{I} \wedge [\![\Phi_\mathcal{I}]\!]_\sigma = \mathsf{true}\}$
- $\mathcal{R}_\times := \{((s, \sigma), (s', \sigma')) \in \mathcal{S}_\times \times \mathcal{S}_\times \mid (s, s') \in \mathcal{R} \wedge [\![\Phi_\mathcal{R}]\!]_{\sigma,\sigma'} = \mathsf{true}\}$
- $\mathcal{L}_\times((s, \sigma)) := \mathcal{L}(s) \cup \sigma$

Note that states of the automaton are sets of state variables Q and inputs are sets of input variables V_Σ. Hence, the states of $\mathsf{Struct}(\mathfrak{A})$ are sets $\sigma \subseteq Q \cup V_\Sigma$. Moreover, states of $\mathcal{K} \times \mathsf{Struct}(\mathfrak{A})$ are pairs (s, σ), whose first component s

stems from the structure $\mathcal{K}$ and whose second component σ stems from the structure Struct $(\mathfrak{A})$. A product state (s, σ) must furthermore be consistent, i.e., it must satisfy the condition $\mathcal{L}(s) = \sigma \cap V_\Sigma$.

Next, we aim at computing the set of states of $\mathcal{K}$ that have a product state in $\mathcal{K} \times$ Struct $(\mathfrak{A})$ where an infinite path π starts. Note that every path through the product structure $\mathcal{K} \times$ Struct $(\mathfrak{A})$ consists of a path through $\mathcal{K}$ and of a path through Struct $(\mathfrak{A})$. The acceptance condition of $\mathfrak{A}$ demands that the 'component path' that runs through Struct $(\mathfrak{A})$ will only visit states of the safety set Φ.

For the construction of the formulas, we have to explicitly construct the semiautomaton that is implicitly encoded in an automaton formula $\mathfrak{A}$. To this end, we introduce some notations for reasons of readability and conciseness. Given an automaton formula $\mathfrak{A} \equiv \mathcal{A}_\exists(Q, \Phi_\mathcal{I}, \Phi_\mathcal{R}, \Phi_\mathcal{F})$ over the variables V_Σ, we define for every set $\vartheta \subseteq V_\Sigma \cup Q \cup \{\mathsf{X}q \mid q \in Q\}$ the following formulas:

- $\iota(\vartheta) := \vartheta \cap V_\Sigma$ describes the current input
- $\kappa(\vartheta) := \vartheta \cap Q$ describes the current state
- $\aleph(\vartheta) := \{q \in Q \mid \mathsf{X}q \in \vartheta\}$ describes the next state
- $\varphi_\iota(\vartheta) := \mathsf{minterm}_{V_\Sigma}(\vartheta \cap V_\Sigma)$ describes the current input as a formula
- $\mathcal{T} := \{\vartheta \subseteq V_\Sigma \cup Q \cup \{\mathsf{X}q \mid q \in Q\} \mid [\![\Phi_\mathcal{R}]\!]_{\iota(\vartheta)\cup\kappa(\vartheta),\aleph(\vartheta)}\}$
- $\mathcal{T}_\sigma := \{\vartheta \in \mathcal{T} \mid \kappa(\vartheta) = \sigma\}$

Note that a set $\vartheta \subseteq V_\Sigma \cup Q \cup \{\mathsf{X}q \mid q \in Q\}$ denotes a transition of $\mathfrak{A}$ from state $\kappa(\vartheta) \subseteq Q$ under the input $\iota(\vartheta) \subseteq V_\Sigma$ to the successor state $\aleph(\vartheta)$, whenever ϑ 'satisfies' $\Phi_\mathcal{R}$. For reasons of readability, we abbreviate the set of transitions encoded by $\Phi_\mathcal{R}$ as $\mathcal{T}$ and the transition of $\mathfrak{A}$ that start in state σ as $\mathcal{T}_\sigma$.

The labeling procedure works in an iterative manner until a fixpoint is reached. If we denote the set of states which are labeled with y_σ in the i-th iteration by $\mathcal{S}_{\sigma,i}$, the labeling procedure is described as follows:

- $\mathcal{S}_{\sigma,0} := \mathcal{S}$ which defines $\mathcal{K}_0$ by changing the label function $\mathcal{L}$ of $\mathcal{K}$ for the variables y_σ such that $[\![y_\sigma]\!]_{\mathcal{K}_0} := \mathcal{S}_{\sigma,0}$ holds for every $\sigma \subseteq Q$
- $\mathcal{S}_{\sigma,i+1} := [\![\bigvee_{\vartheta\in\mathcal{T}_\sigma} \varphi_\iota(\vartheta) \wedge \Diamond y_{\aleph(\vartheta)}]\!]_{\mathcal{K}_i}$ which moreover defines $\mathcal{K}_{i+1}$ by changing the label function $\mathcal{L}_i$ of $\mathcal{K}_i$ for the variables y_σ to such that $[\![y_\sigma]\!]_{\mathcal{K}_{i+1}} := \mathcal{S}_{\sigma,i+1}$ for every $\sigma \subseteq Q$

Intuitively, $s \in \mathcal{S}_{\sigma,i}$ holds iff $(s, \sigma \cup \mathcal{L}(s))$ is a product state in $\mathcal{K} \times$ Struct $(\mathfrak{A})$ where a path $(s, \sigma \cup \mathcal{L}(s)), (s_1, \sigma_1 \cup \mathcal{L}(s_1)), \ldots, (s_i, \sigma_i \cup \mathcal{L}(s_i))$ with at least i transitions is starting. The situation is depicted in Figure 4.24, where a product path of $\mathcal{K} \times$ Struct $(\mathfrak{A})$ is drawn. The upper part is the corresponding path through $\mathcal{K}$, and the lower part is the corresponding path through Struct $(\mathfrak{A})$. We suppose that $s_1 \in \mathcal{S}_{\sigma',i}$ holds for some states σ' of Struct $(\mathfrak{A})$, which means that there is a product path with at least i transitions leaving the product state $(s_1, \sigma' \cup \mathcal{L}(s_1))$. Hence, to establish $s \in \mathcal{S}_{\sigma,i+1}$, it is enough to demand that there is a $\vartheta_1 \in \mathcal{T}$ with $\sigma = \kappa(\vartheta_1)$, $\mathcal{L}(s) = \iota(\vartheta_1)$, and $\sigma' = \aleph(\vartheta_1)$. To be more precise, we now claim that the following is an invariant of the construction:

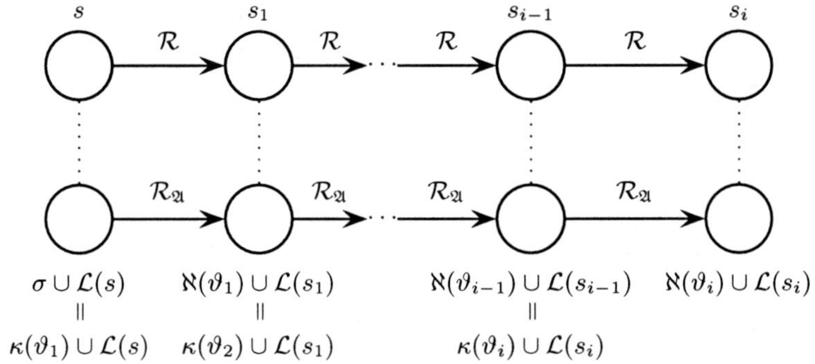

Fig. 4.24. Illustration of the fixpoint iteration

$$\mathcal{S}_{\sigma,i} := \left\{ s \in \mathcal{S} \,\middle|\, \begin{array}{l} \exists \vartheta_1, \ldots, \vartheta_i \in \mathcal{T}. \exists s_1, \ldots, s_i \in \mathcal{S}. \\ \quad \kappa(\vartheta_1) = \sigma \wedge \iota(\vartheta_1) = \mathcal{L}(s) \wedge (s, s_1) \in \mathcal{R} \wedge \\ \quad \forall j \in \{1, \ldots, i-1\}. \\ \qquad \kappa(\vartheta_{j+1}) = \aleph(\vartheta_j) \wedge \iota(\vartheta_{j+1}) = \mathcal{L}(s_j) \wedge (s_j, s_{j+1}) \in \mathcal{R} \end{array} \right\}$$

The proof of the invariance is done by induction on i. The induction base, where $i = 0$ holds is trivial. For the induction step, consider the following:

$$\begin{array}{l} s \in \mathcal{S}_{\sigma,i+1} \Leftrightarrow s \in \left[\!\left[\bigvee_{\vartheta \in \mathcal{T}_\sigma} \varphi_\iota(\vartheta) \wedge \Diamond y_{\aleph(\vartheta)} \right]\!\right]_{\mathcal{K}_i} \\ \quad \Leftrightarrow (\mathcal{K}_i, s) \models \bigvee_{\vartheta \in \mathcal{T}_\sigma} \varphi_\iota(\vartheta) \wedge \Diamond y_{\aleph(\vartheta)} \\ \quad \Leftrightarrow \exists \vartheta \in \mathcal{T}. \kappa(\vartheta) = \sigma \wedge (\mathcal{K}_i, s) \models \varphi_\iota(\vartheta) \wedge (\mathcal{K}_i, s) \models \Diamond y_{\aleph(\vartheta)} \\ \quad \Leftrightarrow \exists \vartheta \in \mathcal{T}. \kappa(\vartheta) = \sigma \wedge \iota(\vartheta) = \mathcal{L}_i(s) \wedge \exists s' \in \mathcal{S}.(s, s') \in \mathcal{R} \wedge (\mathcal{K}_i, s') \models y_{\aleph(\vartheta)} \\ \quad \Leftrightarrow \exists \vartheta \in \mathcal{T}. \exists s' \in \mathcal{S}. \kappa(\vartheta) = \sigma \wedge \iota(\vartheta) = \mathcal{L}_i(s) \wedge (s, s') \in \mathcal{R} \wedge s' \in \left[\!\left[y_{\aleph(\vartheta)} \right]\!\right]_{\mathcal{K}_i} \\ \quad \Leftrightarrow \exists \vartheta \in \mathcal{T}. \exists s' \in \mathcal{S}. \kappa(\vartheta) = \sigma \wedge \iota(\vartheta) = \mathcal{L}_i(s) \wedge (s, s') \in \mathcal{R} \wedge s' \in \mathcal{S}_{\aleph(\vartheta),i} \end{array}$$

It is now easy to see that the induction step holds, when we use the induction hypothesis for $s' \in \mathcal{S}_{\aleph(\vartheta),i}$. Therefore, our invariant is proved to hold for every σ and every i.

Moreover, it is easily seen that for every i and every σ, we have $\mathcal{S}_{\sigma,i+1} \subseteq \mathcal{S}_{\sigma,i}$ for every $\sigma \subseteq Q$. Therefore, these sequences converge to a limit set $\mathcal{S}_{\sigma,\infty}$, and by the Tarski/Knaster theorem, it follows that $\mathcal{S}_{\sigma,\infty}$ is the greatest fixpoint of the iteration function. Clearly, $\mathcal{S}_{\sigma,\infty}$ contains the set of states of $\mathcal{K}$ that have product state $(s, \sigma \cup \mathcal{L}(s))$ where an infinite path starts. If we restrict the states of $\mathfrak{A}$ to only states of the safety set Φ, we furthermore obtain the following theorem:

Theorem 4.67 (Translating $\mathsf{NDet_G}$-Automata to $\mathcal{L}_\mu$). *Given an automaton formula $\mathfrak{A} \equiv \mathcal{A}_\exists(Q, \Phi_\mathcal{I}, \Phi_\mathcal{R}, \mathsf{G}\Phi)$ over the variables V_Σ with the reachable states $\{\sigma_1, \ldots, \sigma_n\} \subseteq 2^Q$. Let $\mathcal{T}_{\sigma_i}^{\Phi}$ be the set of transitions leaving state $\sigma_i \subseteq Q$ that satisfy Φ and define $\Theta_\mathcal{I} := \mathsf{models}_{Q \cup V_\Sigma}(\Phi_\mathcal{I})$. Then, the following holds:*

$$\mathsf{E}\mathfrak{A} = \mathsf{fix}\left[\begin{array}{l} y_{\sigma_1} \overset{\nu}{=} \bigvee_{\vartheta \in \mathcal{T}^{\Phi}_{\sigma_1}} \varphi_\iota(\vartheta) \wedge \Diamond y_{\aleph(\vartheta)} \\ \vdots \\ y_{\sigma_n} \overset{\nu}{=} \bigvee_{\vartheta \in \mathcal{T}^{\Phi}_{\sigma_n}} \varphi_\iota(\vartheta) \wedge \Diamond y_{\aleph(\vartheta)} \end{array}\right] \text{in} \bigvee_{\vartheta \subseteq \Theta_{\mathcal{I}}} y_{\kappa(\vartheta)} \wedge \varphi_\iota(\vartheta) \text{ end}$$

Note that the above μ-calculus formula is alternation-free and can therefore be checked in a structure $\mathcal{K}$ with transition relation $\mathcal{R}$ in time $O(|\mathcal{R}|\,|\Phi|)$, where Φ is the above formula.

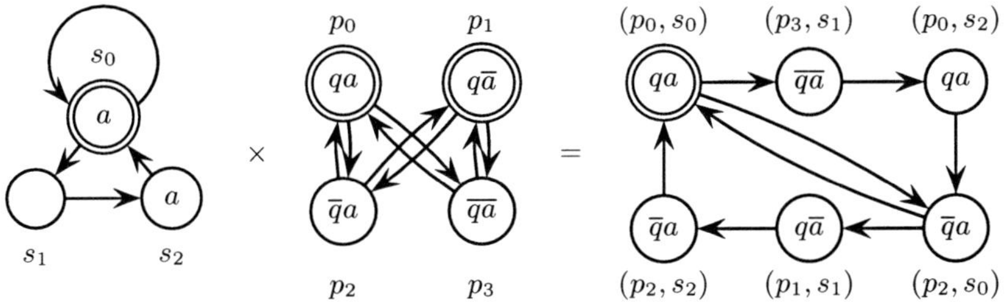

Fig. 4.25. Example of the translation of $\mathcal{L}_\omega$ to $\mathcal{L}_\mu$

Before presenting the other translations, we illustrate the method with an example. For this reason, consider Figure 4.25, which we already considered in Figure 2.10 on page 83. On the left hand side of Figure 4.25 we have given an example structure $\mathcal{K}$, where we want to check the formula $\mathsf{E}\mathfrak{A}$ with the automaton formula $\mathfrak{A} := \mathcal{A}_\exists(\{q\}, q, \mathsf{X}q \leftrightarrow \neg q, \mathsf{G}[q \rightarrow a])$. The structure given in the middle of Figure 4.25 is the associated structure $\mathsf{Struct}(\mathfrak{A})$. The structure on the right hand side is the product structure of $\mathcal{K} \times \mathsf{Struct}(\mathfrak{A})$.

Now, let us compute the set of states of $\mathcal{K}$ where $\mathsf{E}\mathfrak{A}$ holds, i.e., the states of $\mathcal{K}$ that have a path such that a holds on every even position. For the translation of $\mathfrak{A}$ to an equivalent μ-calculus formula, we first note that $\mathfrak{A}$ has the following transitions[6]: $\mathcal{T} := \{\{q, a\}, \{q\}, \{a, \mathsf{X}q\}, \{\mathsf{X}q\}\}$. Moreover, we have $\mathcal{T}^{\Phi}_{\{\}} = \{\{a, \mathsf{X}q\}, \{\mathsf{X}q\}\}$ and $\mathcal{T}^{\Phi}_{\{q\}} = \{\{q, a\}\}$. Hence, the translation of $\mathsf{E}\mathfrak{A}$ to an equivalent μ-calculus formula according to the above rules is as follows:

$$\mathsf{fix}\left[\begin{array}{l} y_{\{\}} \overset{\nu}{=} \neg a \wedge \Diamond y_{\{q\}} \vee a \wedge \Diamond y_{\{q\}} \\ y_{\{q\}} \overset{\nu}{=} a \wedge \Diamond y_{\{\}} \end{array}\right] \text{in } y_{\{q\}} \text{ end}$$

For the model checking, we have to compute the greatest fixpoint of the vector $(y_{\{\}}, y_{\{q\}})$ by a simultaneous fixpoint iteration over both equations. The intermediate results of this fixpoint iteration are given in the following table,

[6] Note that a set like $\{q, a\}$ means that q and a is true, but $\mathsf{X}q$ is false.

where the i-th column gives the values of $\mathcal{S}_{\{\},i}$ in the first row and $\mathcal{S}_{\{q\},i}$ in the second row.

	$i=0$	$i=1$	$i\geq 2$
$\mathcal{S}_{\{\},i}$	$\{s_0,s_1,s_2\}$	$\{s_0,s_1,s_2\}$	$\{s_0,s_1,s_2\}$
$\mathcal{S}_{\{q\},i}$	$\{s_0,s_1,s_2\}$	$\{s_0,s_2\}$	$\{s_0,s_2\}$

As $\{q\}$ is the only initial state of $\mathfrak{A}$, this means that $[\![\mathsf{E}\mathfrak{A}]\!]_{\mathcal{K}} = \{s_0, s_2\}$. Note that for checking $(\mathcal{K}, s_0) \models \mathsf{E}\mathfrak{A}$, $(\mathcal{K}, s_1) \models \mathsf{E}\mathfrak{A}$, $(\mathcal{K}, s_2) \models \mathsf{E}\mathfrak{A}$ according to the semantics, i.e., by computing the product structure $\mathcal{K} \times \mathsf{Struct}(\mathfrak{A})$, we have to start from the product states (p_0, s_0), (p_1, s_1), and (p_0, s_2), respectively, since the path in question must start from an initial state of $\mathfrak{A}$.

In a similar way as $\mathsf{NDet_G}$ automata, we can also translate other classes of ω-automata. The translation principle is in all cases the same and is based on a dynamic programming approach to compute certain sets of states. The translation for the automaton class $\mathsf{NDet_F}$ is given in the next theorem.

Theorem 4.68 (Translating $\mathsf{NDet_F}$ to μ-Calculus). *Given an automaton formula $\mathfrak{A} \equiv \mathcal{A}_\exists(Q, \Phi_\mathcal{I}, \Phi_\mathcal{R}, \mathsf{F}\Phi_\mathcal{F})$ over the variables V_Σ with the reachable states $\{\sigma_1, \ldots, \sigma_n\}$. Define $\Theta_\mathcal{I} := \mathsf{models}_{Q\cup V_\Sigma}(\Phi_\mathcal{I})$ and $\Theta_\mathcal{F} := \mathsf{models}_{Q\cup V_\Sigma}(\Phi_\mathcal{F})$. Then, the following holds:*

$$
\mathsf{E}\mathfrak{A} = \mathsf{fix}\left[\begin{array}{l}
y_{\sigma_1} \stackrel{\nu}{=} \bigvee_{\vartheta\in\mathcal{T}_{\sigma_1}} \varphi_\iota(\vartheta) \wedge \Diamond y_{\aleph(\vartheta)} \\
\vdots \\
y_{\sigma_n} \stackrel{\nu}{=} \bigvee_{\vartheta\in\mathcal{T}_{\sigma_n}} \varphi_\iota(\vartheta) \wedge \Diamond y_{\aleph(\vartheta)} \\
\hline
u \stackrel{\nu}{=} \bigvee_{\vartheta\in\Theta_\mathcal{F}} y_{\kappa(\vartheta)} \wedge \varphi_\iota(\vartheta) \\
\hline
z_{\sigma_1} \stackrel{\mu}{=} u \vee \bigvee_{\vartheta\in\mathcal{T}_{\sigma_1}} \varphi_\iota(\vartheta) \wedge \Diamond z_{\aleph(\vartheta)} \\
\vdots \\
z_{\sigma_n} \stackrel{\mu}{=} u \vee \bigvee_{\vartheta\in\mathcal{T}_{\sigma_n}} \varphi_\iota(\vartheta) \wedge \Diamond z_{\aleph(\vartheta)}
\end{array}\right] \mathsf{in} \bigvee_{\vartheta\in\Theta_\mathcal{I}} z_{\kappa(\vartheta)} \wedge \varphi_\iota(\vartheta)\ \mathsf{end}
$$

At a first glance, the formula might be more complicated than necessary, since one would have expected only the lower half of the equation system. The upper half computes the set of states y_{σ_i} that have a product state $(s, \sigma_i \cup \mathcal{L}(s))$ where an infinite path is starting through the product structure. Hence, u is the union of all of the states s that have a product state $(s, \sigma \cup \mathcal{L}(s))$, so that an infinite product path is starting there such that the liveness condition $\Phi_\mathcal{F}$ is satisfied. The lower part of the equation system is responsible for reaching u.

If we can assure that the Kripke structure $\mathcal{K}$ has no finite paths, e.g. in that we use its restriction $\mathcal{K}_{\mathsf{inf}}$ as defined in section 164, then the equations for y_σ are unnecessary. They are only responsible for guaranteeing that after the liveness condition $\Phi_{\mathcal{F}}$ is satisfied the path can be extended to an infinite one. The same solution was used when we translated the formula $\mathsf{EF}\varphi$ to an equivalent μ-calculus formula. An intuitive approach would be to use the formula $\mu y.\varphi \vee \Diamond y$, but this is not always correct. The difference between both formulas is that $\mathsf{EF}\varphi$ holds only in a state if there is an *infinite* path starting where at least once φ holds, while $\mu y.\varphi \vee \Diamond y$ holds even if the state has only a *finite* path where φ holds (at least once). A correct translation of $\mathsf{EF}\varphi$ is therefore $\mu y.([\nu z.\Diamond z] \wedge \varphi) \vee \Diamond y$, where $\nu z.\Diamond z$ holds in the set of states where an infinite path starts. As already mentioned, we could alternatively omit the subformula $\nu z.\Diamond z$ if we can guarantee that there are no finite paths, e.g., by using the restricted structure restriction $\mathcal{K}_{\mathsf{fair}}$.

The translation of $\mathsf{NDet}_{\mathsf{FG}}$ is done in the same spirit (note that the fixpoints for $\mathsf{EFG}\varphi$ and $\mathsf{EF}\varphi$ as given in Theorem 4.65 are also related). This means that we first collect the states that reach a certain state set and then search the states that run forever in the persistence property. Similar to the equation system for $\mathsf{NDet}_{\mathsf{G}}$ automata, we guarantee the latter by only considering the transitions that 'satisfy' the persistence property. Note that $\mathsf{EFG}\varphi$ is equivalent to $\mathsf{EFEG}\varphi$, so the obtained fixpoint is alternation free. The same holds for the equation system that we obtain for $\mathsf{NDet}_{\mathsf{FG}}$ automata:

Theorem 4.69 (Translating $\mathsf{NDet}_{\mathsf{FG}}$ to μ-Calculus). *Given an automaton formula $\mathfrak{A} \equiv \mathcal{A}_\exists(Q, \Phi_{\mathcal{I}}, \Phi_{\mathcal{R}}, \mathsf{FG}\Phi)$ over the variables V_Σ with the reachable states $\{\sigma_1, \ldots, \sigma_n\} \subseteq 2^Q$. Let $\mathcal{T}_{\sigma_i}^{\Phi}$ be the set of transitions leaving state $\sigma_i \subseteq Q$ that satisfy Φ and define $\Theta_{\mathcal{I}} := \mathsf{models}_{Q \cup V_\Sigma}(\Phi_{\mathcal{I}})$. Then, the following holds:*

$$\mathsf{E}\mathfrak{A} = \mathsf{fix} \left[\begin{array}{l} y_{\sigma_1} \stackrel{\nu}{=} \bigvee_{\vartheta \in \mathcal{T}_{\sigma_1}^{\Phi}} \varphi_\iota(\vartheta) \wedge \Diamond y_{\aleph(\vartheta)} \\ \vdots \\ y_{\sigma_n} \stackrel{\nu}{=} \bigvee_{\vartheta \in \mathcal{T}_{\sigma_n}^{\Phi}} \varphi_\iota(\vartheta) \wedge \Diamond y_{\aleph(\vartheta)} \\ \hline u \stackrel{\nu}{=} \bigvee_{i=1}^{n} y_{\sigma_i} \\ \hline z_{\sigma_1} \stackrel{\mu}{=} u \vee \bigvee_{\vartheta \in \mathcal{T}_{\sigma_1}} \varphi_\iota(\vartheta) \wedge \Diamond z_{\aleph(\vartheta)} \\ \vdots \\ z_{\sigma_n} \stackrel{\mu}{=} u \vee \bigvee_{\vartheta \in \mathcal{T}_{\sigma_n}} \varphi_\iota(\vartheta) \wedge \Diamond z_{\aleph(\vartheta)} \end{array}\right] \mathsf{in} \bigvee_{\vartheta \in \Theta_{\mathcal{I}}} z_{\mathcal{K}(\vartheta)} \wedge \varphi_\iota(\vartheta) \ \mathsf{end}$$

The formula is similar to the one from the previous theorem. The difference is that when we search for the existence of an infinite path in the upper part of the equation system, we now impose the further restriction that the persistence condition Φ of the automaton must be satisfied. The rest of the formulas are the same. Comparing the equation systems obtained so-far with the fixpoint on page 267, it becomes clear how $\mathsf{NDet}_{\mathsf{GF}}$ should be translated:

Theorem 4.70 (Translating $\mathsf{NDet}_{\mathsf{GF}}$ to μ-Calculus). *Given an automaton formula $\mathfrak{A} \equiv \mathcal{A}_{\exists}(Q, \Phi_{\mathcal{I}}, \Phi_{\mathcal{R}}, \mathsf{FG}\Phi_{\mathcal{F}})$ over the variables V_{Σ} with the reachable states $\{\sigma_1, \ldots, \sigma_n\} \subseteq 2^Q$. Let $\mathcal{T}^{\Phi}_{\sigma_i}$ be the set of transitions leaving state $\sigma_i \subseteq Q$ and define $\Theta_{\mathcal{I}} := \mathsf{models}_{Q \cup V_{\Sigma}}(\Phi_{\mathcal{I}})$ and $\Theta_{\mathcal{F}} := \mathsf{models}_{Q \cup V_{\Sigma}}(\Phi_{\mathcal{F}})$. Then, the following holds:*

$$
\mathsf{E}\mathfrak{A} = \mathsf{fix} \left[\begin{array}{l} y_{\sigma_1} \stackrel{\mu}{=} u \vee \bigvee_{\vartheta \in \mathcal{T}_{\sigma_1}} \varphi_{\iota}(\vartheta) \wedge \Diamond y_{\aleph(\vartheta)} \\ \vdots \\ y_{\sigma_n} \stackrel{\mu}{=} u \vee \bigvee_{\vartheta \in \mathcal{T}_{\sigma_n}} \varphi_{\iota}(\vartheta) \wedge \Diamond y_{\aleph(\vartheta)} \\ \hline u \stackrel{\nu}{=} \bigvee_{\vartheta \in \Theta_{\mathcal{F}}} z_{\kappa(\vartheta)} \wedge \varphi_{\iota}(\vartheta) \\ \hline z_{\sigma_1} \stackrel{\nu}{=} \bigvee_{\vartheta \in \mathcal{T}_{\sigma_1}} \varphi_{\iota}(\vartheta) \wedge \Diamond y_{\aleph(\vartheta)} \\ \vdots \\ z_{\sigma_n} \stackrel{\nu}{=} \bigvee_{\vartheta \in \mathcal{T}_{\sigma_n}} \varphi_{\iota}(\vartheta) \wedge \Diamond y_{\aleph(\vartheta)} \end{array} \right] \mathsf{in} \bigvee_{\vartheta \in \Theta_{\mathcal{I}}} z_{\kappa(\vartheta)} \wedge \varphi_{\iota}(\vartheta) \ \mathsf{end}
$$

We have therefore seen that the classes $\mathsf{NDet}_{\mathsf{G}}$, $\mathsf{NDet}_{\mathsf{F}}$, $\mathsf{NDet}_{\mathsf{FG}}$, and $\mathsf{NDet}_{\mathsf{GF}}$ can be translated to equivalent vectorized μ-calculus formulas. The size of the μ-calculus formula grows only linearly with the number of states and transitions of the given ω-automaton. However, the latter may grow exponentially in terms of $|Q|$ and therefore the approach suffers from an exponential blow-up from the formula $\mathfrak{A}$ to the equivalent μ-calculus formula. Nevertheless, the complexity is in general comparable to the product structure approach. However, the latter has the advantage that it can be done in a completely symbolic manner, i.e., without explicitly enumerating the states and transitions of the automata.

Conclusions

In this chapter, we have introduced different classes of automata on infinite words. We have considered their expressiveness both for deterministic and nondeterministic variants, and have shown conversions to translate different classes into each other, whenever this is possible. We have also studied the automaton hierarchy and its relationship to the Borel hierarchy of metric spaces. Besides the topological characterizations we have thereby found, we have moreover considered algebraic characterizations of automata, and have considered automata with aperiodic monoids, i.e., noncounting automata.

Moreover, we have defined a logic $\mathcal{L}_\omega$ that is a temporal logic whose temporal modalities are arbitrary ω-automata. The language allows us to nest automaton formulas, and we have seen that all these nestings can be removed as well as the Boolean combinations between ω-automata. As a result, the model checking problem for $\mathcal{L}_\omega$ can be reduced to formulas of the form $\mathsf{E}\mathfrak{A}$ for existential ω-automata $\mathfrak{A}$. The reduction of $\mathcal{L}_\omega$ to these flat existential ω-automata is however nonelementary. We will use this result in Chapter 6, when we will reveal that our automaton formulas are a monadic second order predicate logic.

We have given two solutions for model checking flat automaton formulas $\mathsf{E}\mathfrak{A}$ for existential ω-automata $\mathfrak{A}$: firstly, we have shown how $\mathsf{E}\mathfrak{A}$ can be translated to an equivalent μ-calculus formula $\Phi_{\mathfrak{A}}$ whose size grows linear in terms of the number of states and transitions of $\mathfrak{A}$. Secondly, we have shown that $(\mathcal{K}, s) \models \mathsf{E}\mathfrak{A}$ is equivalent to the existence of an initial state ϑ, such that $(\mathcal{K} \times \mathcal{K}_{\mathfrak{A}}, (s, \vartheta)) \models \Phi_{\mathcal{I}} \wedge \mathsf{E}\Phi_{\mathcal{F}}$ holds, where $\Phi_{\mathcal{I}}$ and $\Phi_{\mathcal{F}}$ are the initial and the acceptance condition of $\mathfrak{A}$, respectively. We have given translations to the μ-calculus of the formula $\mathsf{E}\Phi_{\mathcal{F}}$ for most types of ω-automata, so that also these problems can be finally solved by the μ-calculus machinery.

Based on the theory of ω-automata, we have therefore seen in this section how decision problems of ω-automata, and also the model checking problem of our automaton based logic $\mathcal{L}_\omega$ can be reduced to equivalent μ-calculus model checking problems. Therefore, it is reasonable to view the μ-calculus as a basic machinery to also prove ω-automaton problems. In the next chapter, we will see how temporal logics can be translated to equivalent ω-automaton problems and hence, that the μ-calculus machinery can also solve these problems.

We have furthermore seen that for the translation of $\mathcal{L}_\omega$ to $\mathcal{L}_\mu$ formulas of alternation depth 2 were sufficient. Hence, it follows that $\mathcal{L}_\mu$ is more expressive than $\mathcal{L}_\omega$, and even the μ-calculus formulas of alternation depth ≤ 2 are more expressive (e.g. consider winning strategies with alternating predecessor-successor computations). However, we have already outlined that there are automata that reach the same expressiveness as $\mathcal{L}_\mu$, namely alternating ω-automata on trees (see Appendix B.3).

5

Temporal Logics

5.1 Introduction

In the previous two chapters we have introduced μ-calculus and ω-automata as basic formalisms for the specification and verification of reactive systems. We have already seen that every formula of our logic of ω-automata $\mathcal{L}_\omega$ can be translated to an equivalent μ-calculus formula, but that the converse is, in general, not possible. The reason for this is that μ-calculus formulas of alternation depth 2 were sufficient to capture $\mathcal{L}_\omega$, and hence, there are μ-calculus formulas of higher alternation depth that can not be described with $\mathcal{L}_\omega$. Nevertheless, specifications in $\mathcal{L}_\omega$ are, in general, more readable than μ-calculus formulas and are therefore better suited for the specification of reactive systems. Their expressiveness is still sufficient for most applications, and their ability to be used as graphical specification formalisms is advantageous for obtaining readable specifications.

However, if the size of automata grows (even less than ten states are sometimes enough) then it becomes, in many cases, difficult to figure out what is expressed by an ω-automaton. For this reason, more readable specification logics like temporal logics have been developed. The advantage of nesting temporal formulas into each other provides a natural way to write down structured specifications, whereas ω-automata are mostly based on flat, i.e., unstructured state transition diagrams (unless statechart-like approaches are used [236]).

Temporal logics are therefore convenient formalisms for specifying systems with a complex temporal behavior. They have been first proposed in 1977 for the specification of reactive systems by Pnueli [407, 408] (Kröger [294] used temporal logic in the same year for specifying sequential programs). Other authors that used temporal logics around the early eighties as specification language are Hailpern [228], Owicki [229], and Lamport [311].

There is, however, not a single temporal logic, since there are lot of ways a temporal logic can be defined. For example, some temporal logics consider the future as well as the past [274, 315, 326], while others only have future time temporal operators. Some use temporal operators that include the present point of time, while others exclude it. Another distinction is the modeling of time: usually discrete points of time are considered, and it is assumed that every transition in the Kripke structure requires one unit of time. However, for special purposes, there are real-time temporal logics that are based on a continuous time model [9, 12, 30, 90, 91], and others that are based on a discrete time model where transitions may however require more than one unit of time [10, 11, 95, 238, 243, 316, 329, 330, 392, 427]. Furthermore, there are other variants such as first order temporal logics [1, 345], partial order temporal logics [406], and interval temporal logics [377, 450].

Throughout this chapter and this book, we will only consider propositional temporal logics with a discrete model of time. It is assumed that a transition in the Kripke structure requires one unit of time. Temporal logics of this kind are the most popular ones and have seen many success stories in the past [112, 114]. The mentioned criteria do not yet fix a particular temporal logic. There is still freedom for the set of temporal operators and the way these operators can be combined. In general, one distinguishes between *temporal* operators that express a temporal relationship along a computation path of a structure, and *path quantifiers* E and A that can be used to quantify over computation paths: We already know that $\mathsf{E}\varphi$ means that there is a path starting in the considered state that satisfies φ, and $\mathsf{A}\varphi$ means that for all paths starting in this state, the property φ holds. Examples for temporal operators are the ones that have been introduced in Section 2.2, i.e., X, G, F, U, W, B, $\underline{\mathsf{U}}$, $\underline{\mathsf{W}}$, and $\underline{\mathsf{B}}$, with the semantics as given in Section 2.2.

We briefly list some historical remarks and start with the genealogy of temporal operators. Kamp [274] used, in 1968, only one temporal operator and its corresponding past operator, namely the $[\cdot\ \underline{\mathsf{XU}}\ \cdot]$ operator that we can define as $[\varphi\ \underline{\mathsf{XU}}\ \psi] := \mathsf{X}\,[\varphi\ \underline{\mathsf{U}}\ \psi]$. Kamp proved that his logic is more expressive than previous ones that were only based on G and F. Moreover, he showed that his temporal logic is expressively equivalent to the first order theory of linear order (cf. Chapter 6). The same was proved in 1980 for the future time fragment by Gabbay, Pnueli, Shelah, and Stavi in [203], so that past time operators have been considered as unnecessary since then. Recently, past time operators have gained new attention, since it turned out that their usage makes temporal logic exponentially more succinct [316, 355].

Further temporal operators, such as the next-time X operator, the precede operator, and the weak U operator were introduced by Manna and Pnueli in 1979, 1982, and 1982, respectively in [343, 345, 346]. Despite the fact that different temporal operators may be used, the resulting logics will all be called LTL, if they can express Kamp's $[\cdot\ \underline{\mathsf{XU}}\ \cdot]$ operator. In 1985, it has been shown by Sistla and Clarke that the complexity of the LTL model checking problem is PSPACE-complete [143, 456]. Lichtenstein, Pnueli, and Zuck presented in the same year a model checking procedure that ran in time $O(|\mathcal{K}|\,2^{c|\Phi|})$ (with some constant c) for every structure $\mathcal{K}$ and every LTL formula Φ [325].

In 1980, Emerson and Clarke [160], and in 1981, Ben-Ari, Manna, and Pnueli [36] explicitly used for the first time the path operators E and A. In [36] this was used to define a simple branching time temporal logic called UB (Unified system of Branching time) which is presented in detail in this chapter. In UB, path quantifiers and temporal operators occur in pairs. UB only used the temporal operators X, G, and F and provided hence the 'macro' operators EX, EG, EF, AX, AG, and AF. In the same year, Emerson and Clarke [160, 161] pointed out that UB can be interpreted as a fragment of the alternation-free μ-calculus. Moreover, they added the $\underline{\mathsf{U}}$ operator and thus defined the temporal logic CTL which, although being strictly more expressive than UB, may still be interpreted as a fragment of the alternation-free μ-calculus. The expressiveness and complexity of CTL was investigated by Emerson and Halpern [162] and Sistla and Clarke [456] in 1985. In particular, it turned out that every CTL formula Φ can be checked on a structure $\mathcal{K}$ in time $O(|\mathcal{K}|\,|\Phi|)$. One year later, Emerson and Halpern defined the more powerful temporal logic CTL* [163] and proved in [165] that its model checking problem is PSPACE-complete.

After the introduction of linear time and branching time temporal logics, there has been an extensive debate [163, 172, 176, 310, 324, 497] on whether branching time logics like CTL and CTL* or linear time temporal logics like LTL are more suited to the specification and verification of reactive systems. In general, a linear time temporal logic consists of formulas of the form AΦ, where Φ does not contain path quantifiers at all, while branching time temporal logics allow nested path quantifiers. Depending on the choice of temporal operators and the way they are allowed to be nested, different linear time and branching-time temporal logics can be defined. We will consider some of them in the next section in more detail.

In [163], it was argued in favor of the linear time approach that for the verification of already existing systems, it is normally not necessary to reason about the existence of computation paths (this is something that can be specified in branching time temporal logics, but not in linear time temporal logics). [163] further argued that the usual specifications only require a property to hold for *all* computation paths, and hence linear time temporal logics are sufficient for that purpose. In comparison to CTL, linear time specifications tend to be more readable, since complex temporal properties require arbitrary nested temporal operators. Nested temporal operators are also allowed in CTL, but the syntax of CTL requires us to insert a path quantifier E or A in front of every temporal operator. This restricts the expressiveness and the readability of the formulas [434, 497].

After this, 'branching-time stroked back' [176]: Clearly, every linear time temporal logic can be extended to a corresponding branching time temporal logic by simply allowing path quantifiers to occur everywhere. Emerson and Lei showed in 1987 [176] that every model checking procedure for a linear time temporal logic can be extended to a model checking procedure for the corresponding branching time logic without changing the complexity of the procedure. It is a powerful argument to prefer branching time temporal logics, since these contain the linear time logics as fragments, but do not increase the complexity of the verification procedure. Since then, the debate has continued, and beneath readability, expressiveness, and complexity other features like modular verification have also been considered. The interested reader is referred to Vardi's recent survey [497] for more pros and cons in this debate and also to Emerson's survey [158] that is still a rich source of interesting results.

Independent on the usage of a linear time or a branching time logic, a lack of expressiveness was seen by Wolper [519] in 1983. He pointed out that there are some simple properties that can not be expressed by temporal logics. For example, you can not express that a property holds *at least* for all even points of time. These properties can however be expressed in the μ-calculus and also by ω-automata. In fact, the result was known a long time before Wolper's remark: McNaughton and Papert had already shown in 1971 that the monadic first order theory of linear orders $\mathsf{MFO}_<$ (see Chapter 6) can be translated to noncounting automata (see Section 5.5.1) [364], and due to Kamp's result [274] (see Section 6.4), the same holds for temporal logic formulas. Wolper therefore suggested to extend temporal logics by grammar operators which essentially yields the flattened fragment of the logic $\mathcal{L}_\omega$ of the previous chapter. However, while it does no harm to extend temporal logics with automaton formulas to increase their expressiveness, the use of temporal operators is still recommended to increase the readability of specifications. Such hybrid logics are nowadays discussed for industrial usage like ForSpec [21] logic or Sugar logic [2, 20, 33].

Hence, with this and the previous two chapters, we now have three different formalisms: μ-calculus, ω-automata, and temporal logic (CTL*). The expressiveness of these formalisms is strictly decreasing in this order, but the readability of the formalisms is strictly increasing. The expressiveness of CTL* is sufficient for most applications. The additional expressiveness provided by ω-automata and the μ-calculus is rarely necessary. Hence, temporal logics like CTL* are usually sufficient, and due to their better readability, their use is strongly recommended.

As the model checking problem of CTL* is PSPACE-complete, a lot of researchers considered sublogics of CTL* to find a good compromise between complexity and expressiveness. An extreme example is the computation tree logic CTL that is not very expressive, but very efficient (it is P-complete). In the next section, we will therefore discuss some sublanguages of CTL* and compare them w.r.t. to their expressiveness and complexity. These sublanguages of CTL* either restrict the set of available temporal operators or the possible combinations of these operators. To see which combinations can be removed without loosing expressive power, we will discuss two important transformations of CTL* formulas: the 'elimination of quantified Boolean subformulas' (Section 5.3.3) and the 'duplication of path quantifiers' (Section 5.3.4). The first transformation allows us to eliminate applications of path quantifiers to Boolean operators (for example $\mathsf{E}[\varphi \wedge \psi]$). The other transformation inserts path quantifiers at certain subformulas without changing the truth value (for example the LTL formula $\mathsf{AGF}\varphi$ is equivalent to the CTL formula $\mathsf{AGAF}\varphi$; however, note that even $\mathsf{EXEG}\varphi$ is equivalent to $\mathsf{EXG}\varphi$ and $\mathsf{EGX}\varphi$, but not equivalent to $\mathsf{EGEX}\varphi$).

Beyond proving the expressiveness of sublanguages of CTL*, the two transformations have a direct impact on the construction of verification procedures. Using these transformations, a direct translation to the temporal logic CTL, and hence to the alternation-free μ-calculus is possible for some CTL* formulas. Hence, these transformations are of practical importance, since they allow us to formulate specifications in syntactically richer logics, that are expressively equivalent to syntactically weaker logics. In particular, we will define the logic LeftCTL* and prove that LeftCTL* can be reduced by the mentioned transformations to CTL. As an example, the formula $\mathsf{E}[\mathsf{F}a \wedge \mathsf{FG}b]$ is a LeftCTL* formula, but not a CTL formula. The formula states that there is a computation in the system where a holds at least once, and from a certain point of time b must hold. By the transformations given in Section 5.3.3 and Section 5.3.4, we can translate this formula to the equivalent CTL formula given below:

$$\mathsf{EF}[a \wedge \mathsf{EFEG}b] \vee \mathsf{EFE}[b \ \underline{\mathsf{U}} \ (a \wedge \mathsf{EG}b)]$$

The above example clearly shows that LeftCTL* specifications can be more readable and more succinct than equivalent CTL specifications. In fact, by a recent result of Wilke [513], it follows that there are LeftCTL* specifications that require an exponential blow-up in the translation to CTL (a similar blow-up appears in the elimination of past temporal operators [316, 355]; see page 392). Adler and Immerman [4] improved this result in 2001 to a lower bound $|\varphi|!$. In fact, the translation of LeftCTL* to exponentially sized 'CTL' formulas given in Section 5.3.5 translates the formulas to CTL formulas where common subterms are shared. For this reason only a blow-up $O(|\Phi|\, 2^{2|\Phi|})$ is sufficient. Recently, Johannsen and Lange [266] proved that satisfiability checking of CTL^+ is 2EXPTIME-complete. As satisfiability checking of CTL is only EXPTIME-complete (as well as the sat-problem of the μ-calculus), it follows that every translation from CTL^+ to CTL (or to the μ-calculus) must necessarily have an exponential blow-up.

However, both logics, LeftCTL* and CTL, are expressively equivalent. The transformations in Section 5.3.3 and Section 5.3.4 are therefore important front-ends for CTL model checking tools so that specifications can be given in richer logics like LeftCTL*, while the model checking machinery can still be based on CTL.

In Section 5.4, we follow another approach: *instead of translating temporal logics to equivalent μ-calculus formulas, we translate them to equivalent ω-automata*, i.e., to formulas of $\mathcal{L}_\omega$. Of course, the obtained automata can in turn be translated to μ-calculus, but we need not necessarily do so since we can also check the acceptance conditions in the product structures (Section 4.8.2).

In general, there are two different kinds of translations to ω-automata: procedures that construct the automata explicitly like [138, 185, 207, 208, 324, 386, 468, 501, 520], and others that derive a symbolic description of the automata like [89, 105, 131, 281, 437, 439]. The latter have the advantage that they run with linear runtime and memory requirements w.r.t. the length of the formulas, and that their result can be directly used for symbolic model checking. However, the different classes of translation are related as we will point out in Section 5.4.

While LeftCTL* and CTL can be translated to alternation-free μ-calculus formulas, the translation of CTL* to $\mathcal{L}_\omega$ requires to use the most powerful automaton class; for example, our translations yield $\mathsf{NDet}_{\mathsf{Streett}}$ automata. The translation of these automata to the μ-calculus requires alternation depth 2, which follows from results in [40, 381, 419]. The same holds for the reduction of the model checking problem with the help of the product structure (Section 4.8.2).

It is therefore natural to ask for (quantifier-free) temporal logics TL_κ such that every formula of TL_κ can be translated to an equivalent Det_κ automaton for $\kappa \in \{\mathsf{G}, \mathsf{F}, \mathsf{Prefix}, \mathsf{GF}, \mathsf{FG}, \mathsf{Streett}\}$. Hence, these logics completely correspond with the automata hierarchy that we have discovered in the previous chapter. Based on previous work of Manna and Pnueli [350–352], we will define temporal logics TL_κ, and show their translateability to Det_κ [437]. Moreover, we show their completeness, and their equal expressiveness to the classes of safety, guarantee, obligation, recurrence, persistence, and reactivity properties [350–352]. We will thereby also find a sublogic AFCTL* of CTL* that is strictly stronger than CTL and LeftCTL*, but that can still be translated to the alternation-free μ-calculus.

5.2 Branching Time Logics – Sublanguages of CTL*

In this section, we start with the definition of the most prominent logics CTL, LTL and CTL*, that are still the topic of many research projects. As already outlined, CTL and LTL were independently developed, and after a long debate, have been merged to the logic CTL* to overcome the disadvantages of CTL and LTL.

In particular, we explain in this section the different expressiveness of CTL and LTL and of the underlying temporal operators. CTL is still supported and favored by a lot of verification tools because it has the nice property that it can be checked in linear time. However, the logic has some limitations that makes its practical use inconvenient. Having seen the limitations of CTL that are not only due to the lack of expressiveness, but also due to a very limited syntax, we will consider, in Section 5.2.2, further temporal logics like

LeftCTL* that are equally expressive as CTL, but whose model checking problem is more complex. At first glance, this may sound as a disadvantage, but it is indeed an advantage: The higher complexity enables logics like LeftCTL* to be exponentially more succinct than CTL [4, 266, 513]. Moreover, we will see that every CTL formula is also a LeftCTL* formula, so that relying to the CTL subset leads to the same efficiency.

5.2.1 CTL, LTL and CTL*

We now start with the definition of CTL, LTL and CTL*. Although their origins are from a historical point of view very different, we will present CTL and LTL as subsets of CTL* (historically, CTL* has been obtained by combining CTL and LTL). The definition of these logics, and also of the forerunner UB of CTL, are given formally in the next definition.

Definition 5.1 (Sublanguages of CTL* (I)). *Given a finite set of variables V_Σ, the following grammar rules define the temporal logics* CTL*, UB, CTL, *and* LTL:

$$
\begin{array}{lll}
\mathsf{CTL}^*: & S ::= & V_\Sigma \mid \neg S \mid S \wedge S \mid S \vee S \mid \mathsf{E}P \mid \mathsf{A}P \\
& P ::= & S \mid \neg P \mid P \wedge P \mid P \vee P \mid \mathsf{X}P \mid \mathsf{G}P \mid \mathsf{F}P \\
& & \mid [P\ \mathsf{W}\ P] \mid [P\ \mathsf{U}\ P] \mid [P\ \mathsf{B}\ P] \\
& & \mid [P\ \underline{\mathsf{W}}\ P] \mid [P\ \underline{\mathsf{U}}\ P] \mid [P\ \underline{\mathsf{B}}\ P] \\
\mathsf{LTL}: & S ::= & \mathsf{A}P \\
& P ::= & V_\Sigma \mid \neg P \mid P \wedge P \mid P \vee P \mid \mathsf{X}P \mid \mathsf{G}P \mid \mathsf{F}P \\
& & \mid [P\ \mathsf{W}\ P] \mid [P\ \mathsf{U}\ P] \mid [P\ \mathsf{B}\ P] \\
& & \mid [P\ \underline{\mathsf{W}}\ P] \mid [P\ \underline{\mathsf{U}}\ P] \mid [P\ \underline{\mathsf{B}}\ P] \\
\mathsf{CTL}: & S ::= & V_\Sigma \mid \neg S \mid S \wedge S \mid S \vee S \mid \mathsf{E}P \mid \mathsf{A}P \\
& P ::= & \mathsf{X}S \mid \mathsf{G}S \mid \mathsf{F}S \\
& & \mid [S\ \mathsf{W}\ S] \mid [S\ \mathsf{U}\ S] \mid [S\ \mathsf{B}\ S] \\
& & \mid [S\ \underline{\mathsf{W}}\ S] \mid [S\ \underline{\mathsf{U}}\ S] \mid [S\ \underline{\mathsf{B}}\ S] \\
\mathsf{UB}: & S ::= & V_\Sigma \mid \neg S \mid S \wedge S \mid S \vee S \mid \mathsf{E}P \mid \mathsf{A}P \\
& P ::= & \mathsf{X}S \mid \mathsf{G}S \mid \mathsf{F}S
\end{array}
$$

In the above grammars, the formulas that are generated from the nonterminals S and P are state and path formulas, respectively. As can be seen, CTL* has no restrictions on its syntax: Temporal operators can be nested in an arbitrary manner to formulate temporal properties of paths. State formulas can be obtained by Boolean combination of other state formulas or by quantification of path formulas. LTL provides a powerful set of path formulas, however, state formulas of LTL are restricted to the very limited form AP, where P must not contain further path quantifiers. CTL has other restrictions: temporal operators and path quantifiers have to occur in pairs, i.e., every path quantifier must be followed by a temporal operator, and conversely, every temporal operator must be preceded by a path quantifier. Finally, UB is the sublanguage of CTL that has only the temporal operators X, G, and F.

The choice among the binary temporal operators is thereby rather arbitrary. To reach the expressive power of $\mathsf{MFO}_<$, the monadic first order theory of linear orders, we only need the X operator and one of the binary operators. For example, the $\underline{\mathsf{U}}$ operator can define the other operators as follows:

$$\begin{array}{ll} \mathsf{G}\varphi = \neg\,[1\ \underline{\mathsf{U}}\ (\neg\varphi)] & \mathsf{F}\varphi = [1\ \underline{\mathsf{U}}\ \varphi] \\ [\varphi\ \mathsf{W}\ \psi] = \neg\,[(\neg\varphi \vee \neg\psi)\ \underline{\mathsf{U}}\ (\neg\varphi \wedge \psi)] & [\varphi\ \underline{\mathsf{W}}\ \psi] = [(\neg\psi)\ \underline{\mathsf{U}}\ (\varphi \wedge \psi)] \\ [\varphi\ \mathsf{B}\ \psi] = \neg\,[(\neg\varphi)\ \underline{\mathsf{U}}\ \psi] & [\varphi\ \underline{\mathsf{B}}\ \psi] = [(\neg\psi)\ \underline{\mathsf{U}}\ (\varphi \wedge \neg\psi)] \\ [\varphi\ \mathsf{U}\ \psi] = \neg\,[(\neg\psi)\ \underline{\mathsf{U}}\ (\neg\varphi \wedge \neg\psi)] & \end{array}$$

Analogously, each one of the binary temporal operators can define $\underline{\mathsf{U}}$:

$$\begin{array}{ll} [\varphi\ \underline{\mathsf{U}}\ \psi] = \neg\,[(\neg\psi)\ \mathsf{U}\ (\neg\varphi \wedge \neg\psi)] & \\ [\varphi\ \underline{\mathsf{U}}\ \psi] = \neg\,[(\neg\psi)\ \mathsf{W}\ (\varphi \rightarrow \psi)] & [\varphi\ \underline{\mathsf{U}}\ \psi] = [\psi\ \underline{\mathsf{W}}\ (\varphi \rightarrow \psi)] \\ [\varphi\ \underline{\mathsf{U}}\ \psi] = \neg\,[(\neg\varphi)\ \mathsf{B}\ \psi] & [\varphi\ \underline{\mathsf{U}}\ \psi] = [\psi\ \underline{\mathsf{B}}\ (\neg\varphi \wedge \neg\psi)] \end{array}$$

It is worthwhile noting that the until-operator that excludes the present, i.e., Kamp's version which is defined as $[\varphi\ \underline{\mathsf{XU}}\ \psi] := \mathsf{X}\,[\varphi\ \underline{\mathsf{U}}\ \psi]$, can express all other operators:

$$[\varphi\ \underline{\mathsf{U}}\ \psi] = \psi \vee \varphi \wedge [\varphi\ \underline{\mathsf{XU}}\ \psi] \qquad \mathsf{X}\varphi = [0\ \underline{\mathsf{XU}}\ \varphi]$$

Hence, we could define temporal logics with the only temporal operator $[\cdot\ \underline{\mathsf{XU}}\ \cdot]$. We have also the choice among the temporal operators for defining CTL. The classical definition is normally based on $\mathsf{E}\underline{\mathsf{U}}$, EG, and EX, which can be obtained due to the following rules:

$$\begin{array}{l} \mathsf{EF}\varphi = \mathsf{E}[1\ \underline{\mathsf{U}}\ \varphi] \\ \mathsf{E}[\varphi\ \mathsf{U}\ \psi] = \mathsf{E}[\varphi\ \underline{\mathsf{U}}\ \psi] \vee \mathsf{EG}\varphi \\ \mathsf{E}[\varphi\ \underline{\mathsf{B}}\ \psi] = \mathsf{E}[(\neg\psi)\ \underline{\mathsf{U}}\ (\varphi \wedge \neg\psi)] \\ \mathsf{E}[\varphi\ \underline{\mathsf{W}}\ \psi] = \mathsf{E}[(\neg\psi)\ \underline{\mathsf{U}}\ (\varphi \wedge \psi)] \\ \mathsf{E}[\varphi\ \mathsf{B}\ \psi] = \mathsf{E}[(\neg\psi)\ \underline{\mathsf{U}}\ (\varphi \wedge \neg\psi)] \vee \mathsf{EG}\neg\psi \\ \mathsf{E}[\varphi\ \mathsf{W}\ \psi] = \mathsf{E}[(\neg\psi)\ \underline{\mathsf{U}}\ (\varphi \wedge \psi)] \vee \mathsf{EG}\neg\psi \\ \mathsf{AX}\varphi = \neg\mathsf{EX}\neg\varphi \\ \mathsf{AG}\varphi = \neg\mathsf{E}[1\ \underline{\mathsf{U}}\ \neg\varphi] \\ \mathsf{AF}\varphi = \neg\mathsf{EG}\neg\varphi \\ \mathsf{A}[\varphi\ \mathsf{U}\ \psi] = \neg\mathsf{E}[(\neg\psi)\ \underline{\mathsf{U}}\ (\neg\varphi \wedge \neg\psi)] \\ \mathsf{A}[\varphi\ \mathsf{B}\ \psi] = \neg\mathsf{E}[(\neg\varphi)\ \underline{\mathsf{U}}\ \psi] \\ \mathsf{A}[\varphi\ \mathsf{W}\ \psi] = \neg\mathsf{E}[(\neg\psi)\ \underline{\mathsf{U}}\ (\neg\varphi \wedge \psi)] \\ \mathsf{A}[\varphi\ \underline{\mathsf{U}}\ \psi] = \neg\mathsf{E}[(\neg\psi)\ \underline{\mathsf{U}}\ (\neg\varphi \wedge \neg\psi)] \wedge \neg\mathsf{EG}\neg\psi \\ \mathsf{A}[\varphi\ \underline{\mathsf{B}}\ \psi] = \neg\mathsf{E}[(\neg\varphi)\ \underline{\mathsf{U}}\ \psi] \wedge \neg\mathsf{EG}\neg\varphi \\ \mathsf{A}[\varphi\ \underline{\mathsf{W}}\ \psi] = \neg\mathsf{E}[(\neg\psi)\ \underline{\mathsf{U}}\ (\neg\varphi \wedge \psi)] \wedge \neg\mathsf{EG}\neg\psi \end{array}$$

The above reduction to the basic operator sets $\mathsf{E}\underline{\mathsf{U}}$, EG, and EX has the disadvantage that in some cases two fixpoints are generated. Therefore, we recommend the following reductions to the basic operators $\mathsf{E}\underline{\mathsf{U}}$, EU, and EX:

$$
\begin{array}{ll}
 & \mathsf{AX}\varphi = \neg\mathsf{EX}\neg\varphi \\
\mathsf{EG}\varphi = \mathsf{E}[\varphi\ \mathsf{U}\ 0] & \mathsf{AG}\varphi = \neg\mathsf{E}[1\ \underline{\mathsf{U}}\ \neg\varphi] \\
\mathsf{EF}\varphi = \mathsf{E}[1\ \underline{\mathsf{U}}\ \varphi] & \mathsf{AF}\varphi = \neg\mathsf{E}[(\neg\varphi)\ \mathsf{U}\ 0] \\
 & \mathsf{A}[\varphi\ \mathsf{U}\ \psi] = \neg\mathsf{E}[(\neg\psi)\ \underline{\mathsf{U}}\ (\neg\varphi\wedge\neg\psi)] \\
 & \mathsf{A}[\varphi\ \underline{\mathsf{U}}\ \psi] = \neg\mathsf{E}[(\neg\psi)\ \mathsf{U}\ (\neg\varphi\wedge\neg\psi)] \\
\mathsf{E}[\varphi\ \mathsf{B}\ \psi] = \mathsf{E}[(\neg\psi)\ \mathsf{U}\ (\varphi\wedge\neg\psi)] & \mathsf{A}[\varphi\ \mathsf{B}\ \psi] = \neg\mathsf{E}[(\neg\varphi)\ \underline{\mathsf{U}}\ \psi] \\
\mathsf{E}[\varphi\ \underline{\mathsf{B}}\ \psi] = \mathsf{E}[(\neg\psi)\ \underline{\mathsf{U}}\ (\varphi\wedge\neg\psi)] & \mathsf{A}[\varphi\ \underline{\mathsf{B}}\ \psi] = \neg\mathsf{E}[(\neg\varphi)\ \mathsf{U}\ \psi] \\
\mathsf{E}[\varphi\ \mathsf{W}\ \psi] = \mathsf{E}[(\neg\psi)\ \mathsf{U}\ (\varphi\wedge\psi)] & \mathsf{A}[\varphi\ \mathsf{W}\ \psi] = \neg\mathsf{E}[(\neg\psi)\ \underline{\mathsf{U}}\ (\neg\varphi\wedge\psi)] \\
\mathsf{E}[\varphi\ \underline{\mathsf{W}}\ \psi] = \mathsf{E}[(\neg\psi)\ \underline{\mathsf{U}}\ (\varphi\wedge\psi)] & \mathsf{A}[\varphi\ \underline{\mathsf{W}}\ \psi] = \neg\mathsf{E}[(\neg\psi)\ \mathsf{U}\ (\neg\varphi\wedge\psi)]
\end{array}
$$

Hence, we see that the choice among the binary operators is absolutely a matter of taste, both for LTL and CTL. One might ask at this point whether we can also express one of the binary operators also with G and F. Kamp has shown in his thesis that this is not the case [274]. We will also present a short proof for this fact below (see also page 450).

Consider a state s of an arbitrary structure $\mathcal{K} = (\mathcal{S}, \mathcal{I}, \mathcal{R}, \mathcal{L})$, and an arbitrary path $\pi \in \mathsf{Paths}_{\mathcal{K}}(s)$ through $\mathcal{K}$ that starts in s. Consider the corresponding sequence of labels, i.e., the infinite sequence $\lambda t.\mathcal{L}(\pi^{(t)})$. As V_Σ is finite, there is only a finite number of subsets of V_Σ, and hence only finitely many different possibilities to label a state in the structure. For this reason, it must be the case that at least one $\vartheta \subseteq V_\Sigma$ occurs infinitely often on $\lambda t.\mathcal{L}(\pi^{(t)})$, while others may occur only finitely often. Hence, among the labels $L_\pi := \{\mathcal{L}(\pi^{(t)}) \mid t \in \mathbb{N}\}$ there are some that occur infinitely often, and others that occur only finitely often. Let L_π^{fin} be the subset of L_π that consists of those $\vartheta \subseteq V_\Sigma$ that occur only finitely often on $\lambda t.\mathcal{L}(\pi^{(t)})$, and let L_π^{inf} be the remaining labels.

It is then clear that there is a number $j \in \mathbb{N}$ such that $\forall t \geq j.\, \mathcal{L}(\pi^{(t)}) \in L_\pi^{\mathsf{inf}}$ holds. The same holds for every $j' > j$, but not necessarily for all $j' < j$. So, let $j_\pi \in \mathbb{N}$ be the least number such that $\forall t \geq j_\pi.\, \mathcal{L}(\pi^{(t)}) \in L_\pi^{\mathsf{inf}}$ holds. We will see in the following lemma that the formulas that are build up with only the temporal operators G and F can not distinguish the order of states after the position j_π:

Lemma 5.2 (Temporal Logic without Binary Temporal Operators). *Given a structure $\mathcal{K} = (\mathcal{S}, \mathcal{I}, \mathcal{R}, \mathcal{L})$ over a set of variables V_Σ, a state $s \in \mathcal{S}$, and a path $\pi \in \mathsf{Paths}_{\mathcal{K}}(s)$. Let $j_\pi \in \mathbb{N}$ be the smallest number such that $\{\mathcal{L}(\pi^{(t)}) \mid t \geq j_\pi\} = \{\vartheta \subseteq V_\Sigma \mid \forall t_1.\exists t_2.\mathcal{L}(\pi^{(t_1+t_2)}) = \vartheta\}$ holds. Moreover, let $\mathsf{A}\varphi$ be a LTL formula that is built up only with Boolean operators and the temporal operators G and F. Then, the following holds for all positions $t_1, t_2 \geq j_\pi$ with $\mathcal{L}(\pi^{(t_1)}) = \mathcal{L}(\pi^{(t_2)})$:*

$$
(\mathcal{K}, \pi, t_1) \models \varphi \quad \textit{iff} \quad (\mathcal{K}, \pi, t_2) \models \varphi
$$

Proof. The proof is done by induction on the structure of φ. We only list the relevant cases (every formula can be reduced to an equivalent one using only these operators by rewriting with $\mathsf{G}\varphi = \neg\mathsf{F}\neg\varphi$ and $\varphi \vee \psi = \neg(\neg\varphi \wedge \neg\psi)$).

$\boxed{\varphi \in V_\Sigma:}$ By the semantics of variables, we have $(\mathcal{K}, \pi, t_1) \models \varphi$ iff $\varphi \in \mathcal{L}(\pi^{(t_1)})$. By the assumption of the lemma, we have $\mathcal{L}(\pi^{(t_1)}) = \mathcal{L}(\pi^{(t_2)})$, so that the proposition holds for variables.

$\boxed{\neg\varphi:}$ This case follows directly from the induction hypothesis.

$\boxed{\varphi \wedge \psi:}$ This case follows directly from the induction hypothesis.

$\boxed{\mathsf{F}\varphi:}$ Given $t_1, t_2 \geq j_\pi$ with $\mathcal{L}(\pi^{(t_1)}) = \mathcal{L}(\pi^{(t_2)})$, we have to prove that $(\mathcal{K}, \pi, t_1) \models \mathsf{F}\varphi$ holds iff $(\mathcal{K}, \pi, t_2) \models \mathsf{F}\varphi$ holds. We only show that $(\mathcal{K}, \pi, t_1) \models \mathsf{F}\varphi$ implies $(\mathcal{K}, \pi, t_2) \models \mathsf{F}\varphi$, since the other direction is symmetric. So, assuming that $(\mathcal{K}, \pi, t_1) \models \mathsf{F}\varphi$ holds, this means that there must be a $\delta_1 \in \mathbb{N}$ such that $(\mathcal{K}, \pi, t_1 + \delta_1) \models \varphi$ holds. We must now show that there is a $\delta_2 \in \mathbb{N}$, such that $(\mathcal{K}, \pi, t_2 + \delta_2) \models \varphi$ holds.
If $t_2 \leq t_1 + \delta_1$ holds, we can use $\delta_2 := (t_1 - t_2 + \delta_1)$ to satisfy the condition. In the remaining case, we have $t_2 < t_1 + \delta$. As $t_1 > j_\pi$ holds, it also follows that $t_1 + \delta_1 > j_\pi$ holds, which means that there are infinitely many states on the path with the same label $\mathcal{L}(\pi^{(t_1+\delta_1)})$. Hence, there are infinitely many k_i where $\mathcal{L}(\pi^{(t_1+\delta_1)}) = \mathcal{L}(\pi^{(t_1+k_i)})$ holds. By the induction hypothesis, it therefore follows that $(\mathcal{K}, \pi, t_1 + k_i) \models \varphi$ holds at these positions. Moreover, there is a $n \in \mathbb{N}$ such that $t_1 + k_n > t_2$ holds. Therefore, we can use $\delta_2 := t_1 + k_n - t_2$ to see that there is a δ_2 with $(\mathcal{K}, \pi, t_2 + \delta_2) \models \varphi$.
□

The above lemma essentially says that the quantifier-free kernels φ of LTL formulas $\mathsf{A}\varphi$, that are build up only with Boolean operators and the temporal operators G and F, can not distinguish states $\pi^{(t_1)}$ and $\pi^{(t_2)}$ that have the same labels and are after a certain position on the path π. In particular, this means that these formulas can not distinguish between the order of such states on the path.

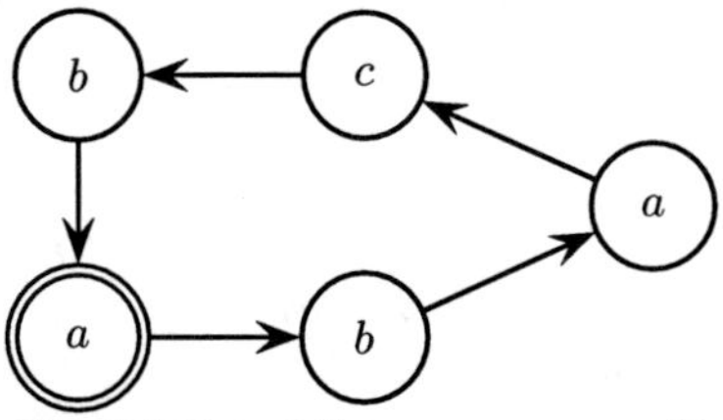

Fig. 5.1. G and F can not express U

The lemma does not hold for the binary temporal operators since these can distinguish the order of events. As an example, consider the structure given in Figure 5.1. There is only one path π leaving the initial state and all states on this path repeat infinitely often, hence, we have $j_\pi = 0$. Now, note that we have $(\mathcal{K}, \pi, 2) \not\models [a \underline{\mathsf{U}} b]$, but $(\mathcal{K}, \pi) \models [a \underline{\mathsf{U}} b]$. Moreover, we have $(\mathcal{K}, \pi, 2) \not\models \mathsf{X}b$, but $(\mathcal{K}, \pi) \models \mathsf{X}b$, so that we also see that the lemma can not be extended to X operators.

However, we can shift X operators inside so that they are finally applied to variables (or to other X operators). Abbreviating the formulas $\mathsf{X}^k x$ by a new variable x_k then allows us to derive the following result:

Theorem 5.3. *None of the binary operators* U, B, W, $\underline{\mathsf{U}}$, $\underline{\mathsf{B}}$, $\underline{\mathsf{W}}$ *can be expressed by the unary temporal operators* X, G *and* F.

It therefore follows immediately that UB is strictly less expressive than CTL, since the formula $\mathsf{E}[b\ \underline{\mathsf{U}}\ a]$ can not be expressed in UB. Conversely, it is clear that every UB formula is also a CTL formula.

To compare CTL and LTL, we note that there are CTL formulas that can not be expressed in LTL, and there are LTL formulas that can not be expressed in CTL. For example, no CTL formula is equivalent to $\mathsf{EGF}\varphi$, and no LTL formula is equivalent to $\mathsf{AXEX}\varphi$. It is furthermore well-known which formulas can be expressed in these logics. We briefly list some essential results for the consideration of these facts, and start with an inherent property of LTL formulas:

Lemma 5.4 (Invariance under Language Equivalence). *Given two structures* $\mathcal{K}_1 = (\mathcal{I}_1, \mathcal{S}_1, \mathcal{R}_1, \mathcal{L}_1)$ *and* $\mathcal{K}_2 = (\mathcal{I}_2, \mathcal{S}_2, \mathcal{R}_2, \mathcal{L}_2)$ *over* V_Σ*, two states* $s_1 \in \mathcal{S}_1$*,* $s_2 \in \mathcal{S}_2$*, and two paths* $\pi_1 \in \mathsf{Paths}_{\mathcal{K}_1}(s_1)$ *and* $\pi_2 \in \mathsf{Paths}_{\mathcal{K}_2}(s_2)$ *with* $\forall t.\mathcal{L}_1(\pi_1^{(t)}) = \mathcal{L}_2(\pi_2^{(t)})$*. For every* LTL *formula* $\mathsf{A}\varphi$*, the following holds for every* $t \in \mathbb{N}$*:*

$$(\mathcal{K}_1, \pi_1, t) \models \varphi \textit{ iff } (\mathcal{K}_2, \pi_2, t) \models \varphi$$

The proof is by induction on φ, where it is sufficient to consider the cases $\neg\varphi$, $\varphi \wedge \psi$, $\mathsf{X}\varphi$, $[\varphi\ \underline{\mathsf{U}}\ \psi]$. We omit the proof, since it is very simple. The lemma says that for evaluating quantifier-free formulas only the sequence of labels is of interest. In other words, these formulas can not be used to describe the branching behavior of a structure, which is intuitively clear. Note that the same holds for automaton formulas $\mathcal{A}_\exists(Q, \Phi_\mathcal{I}, \Phi_\mathcal{R}, \Phi_\mathcal{F})$.

We will see in Section 5.4 that every LTL formula φ can be translated to an equivalent ω-automaton $\mathfrak{A}_\varphi \in \mathsf{NDet}_\mathsf{GF}$. Hence, we have $(\mathcal{K}, \pi, t) \models \varphi$ iff $(\mathcal{K}, \pi, t) \models \mathfrak{A}_\varphi$, and this in turn holds if the ω-word $\lambda t.\mathcal{L}(\pi^{(t)})$ is accepted by the automaton. However, as Kripke structures and automata are finite, we immediately find the following lemma that is a variant of the fact that ω-regular languages are not empty, iff they contain a rational word.

Lemma 5.5 (Satisfiability by Rational Paths). *Given a Kripke structure* $\mathcal{K} = (\mathcal{I}, \mathcal{S}, \mathcal{R}, \mathcal{L})$ *over* V_Σ *and a states* $s \in \mathcal{S}$*. Then, the following holds for every* LTL *formula* $\mathsf{A}\varphi$*:*

- $(\mathcal{K}, s) \models \mathsf{A}\varphi$ *iff for all* $\pi \in \mathsf{RatFairPaths}_\mathcal{K}(s)$ *we have* $(\mathcal{K}, \pi, 0) \models \varphi$
- $(\mathcal{K}, s) \models \mathsf{E}\varphi$ *iff there is a* $\pi \in \mathsf{RatFairPaths}_\mathcal{K}(s)$ *with* $(\mathcal{K}, \pi, 0) \models \varphi$

The previous two lemmas can now be used to prove the following theorem due to Clarke and Draghicescu [101]. This theorem provides a criterion to test whether a given CTL* formula can be expressed in LTL. If it can be expressed in LTL, the theorem even constructs such a formula:

Theorem 5.6 (Criterion for Reducibility from CTL* to LTL). *For every CTL* formula Φ, the following are equivalent:*

- *there is a LTL formula $\mathsf{A}\varphi$ that is equivalent to Φ*
- *Φ is equivalent to $\mathsf{A}(\mathsf{remove}_{\mathsf{E,A}}(\Phi))$, where $\mathsf{remove}_{\mathsf{E,A}}(\Phi)$ is obtained from Φ by deleting all path quantifiers.*

Proof. One direction is simple: given that $\Phi = \mathsf{A}(\mathsf{remove}_{\mathsf{E,A}}(\Phi))$ holds, then there is a LTL formula that is equivalent to Φ, namely $\mathsf{A}(\mathsf{remove}_{\mathsf{E,A}}(\Phi))$. To prove the other direction, suppose there is a LTL formula $\mathsf{A}\varphi$ that is equivalent to Φ. This means that $(*)$ for any state s of any structure $\mathcal{K}$, we have $(\mathcal{K}, s) \models \Phi$ iff $(\mathcal{K}, s) \models \mathsf{A}\varphi$. We then also have to show that $(\mathcal{K}, s) \models \mathsf{A}(\mathsf{remove}_{\mathsf{E,A}}(\Phi))$ holds.

We construct, for a rational path π with $\forall t.\pi^{(t+n)} = \pi^{((t \bmod \ell)+n)}$, a structure $\mathcal{K}_\pi = (\mathcal{I}_\pi, \mathcal{S}_\pi, \mathcal{R}_\pi, \mathcal{L}_\pi)$ as follows:

- $\mathcal{S}_\pi := \{0, \ldots, \ell - 1 + n\} \subseteq \mathbb{N}$
- $\mathcal{I}_\pi := \{0\}$
- $\mathcal{R}_\pi := \{(i, i+1) \mid i \in \{0, \ldots, \ell - 2 + n\}\} \cup \{(\ell - 1 + n, n)\}$
- $\mathcal{L}_\pi(i) := \mathcal{L}(\pi^{(i)})$ for $i \in \{0, \ldots, \ell - 1 + n\}$

Clearly, the structure has only one path, that is furthermore language equivalent to the original path π. Hence, it is easily seen that we have $(**)$ $(\mathcal{K}_\pi, 0) \models \Phi$ if and only if $(\mathcal{K}_\pi, 0) \models \mathsf{A}(\mathsf{remove}_{\mathsf{E,A}}(\Phi))$, which can be proved by induction. Therefore, given any structure $\mathcal{K}$ and any state s of it, the following equivalences hold:

$$
\begin{aligned}
(\mathcal{K}, s) \models \Phi &\overset{(*)}{\Leftrightarrow} (\mathcal{K}, s) \models \mathsf{A}\varphi \\
&\overset{(1)}{\Leftrightarrow} \forall \pi \in \mathsf{RatFairPaths}_{\mathcal{K}}(s).\ (\mathcal{K}, \pi, 0) \models \varphi \\
&\overset{(2)}{\Leftrightarrow} \forall \pi \in \mathsf{RatFairPaths}_{\mathcal{K}}(s).\ (\mathcal{K}_\pi, \pi, 0) \models \varphi \\
&\overset{(3)}{\Leftrightarrow} \forall \pi \in \mathsf{RatFairPaths}_{\mathcal{K}}(s).\ (\mathcal{K}_\pi, 0) \models \mathsf{A}\varphi \\
&\overset{(*)}{\Leftrightarrow} \forall \pi \in \mathsf{RatFairPaths}_{\mathcal{K}}(s).\ (\mathcal{K}_\pi, 0) \models \Phi \\
&\overset{(**)}{\Leftrightarrow} \forall \pi \in \mathsf{RatFairPaths}_{\mathcal{K}}(s).\ (\mathcal{K}_\pi, 0) \models \mathsf{A}(\mathsf{remove}_{\mathsf{E,A}}(\Phi)) \\
&\overset{(4)}{\Leftrightarrow} \forall \pi \in \mathsf{RatFairPaths}_{\mathcal{K}}(s).\ (\mathcal{K}_\pi, \pi, 0) \models \mathsf{remove}_{\mathsf{E,A}}(\Phi)) \\
&\overset{(5)}{\Leftrightarrow} \forall \pi \in \mathsf{RatFairPaths}_{\mathcal{K}}(s).\ (\mathcal{K}, \pi, 0) \models \mathsf{remove}_{\mathsf{E,A}}(\Phi) \\
&\overset{(6)}{\Leftrightarrow} (\mathcal{K}, s) \models \mathsf{A}(\mathsf{remove}_{\mathsf{E,A}}(\Phi))
\end{aligned}
$$

Step $(*)$ is due to our assumption, (1) is due to Lemma 5.5, and (2) due to Lemma 5.4. (3) holds since $\mathcal{K}_\pi$ has only one path. The next step is again due to our assumption $(*)$, this time applied to the single path structures $\mathcal{K}_\pi$. The next step $(**)$ is by construction of $\mathcal{K}_\pi$ as mentioned above. (4) holds since $\mathcal{K}_\pi$ has only the path π. (5) is clear by construction of $\mathcal{K}_\pi$, and (6) holds finally due to Lemma 5.5. □

The theorem can be used in two ways: Firstly, if we know that a given CTL* formula has an equivalent LTL formula, then we can determine an equivalent LTL formula very easily. Secondly, to decide whether a given CTL* formula Φ has an equivalent LTL formula or not, we have to check whether Φ and $\mathsf{A}(\mathsf{remove}_{\mathsf{E,A}}(\Phi))$ are equivalent. In particular, to show that a CTL* formula Φ is not expressible in LTL, we have to present a Kripke structure that interprets Φ and $\mathsf{A}(\mathsf{remove}_{\mathsf{E,A}}(\Phi))$ differently. For example, the CTL formula $\mathsf{AFAG}a$ is not equivalent to any LTL formula. To prove this, simply check that the structure given in Figure 5.2 satisfies $\mathsf{AFAG}a$, but not $\mathsf{AFG}a$.

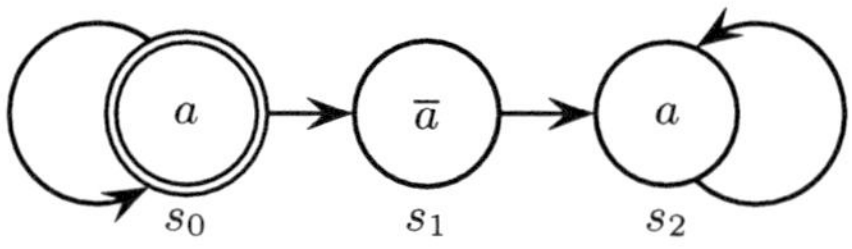

Fig. 5.2. Counterexample for $\mathsf{AFG}a = \mathsf{AFAG}a$

It is easily seen that $(\mathcal{K}, s_0) \models \mathsf{AFG}a$ holds, since every path starting in s_0 must either stay forever in s_0 or must leave s_0 via s_1 such that it must stay after that point of time forever in s_2. However, we have $(\mathcal{K}, s_0) \not\models \mathsf{AFAG}a$, since $[\![\mathsf{AG}a]\!]_{\mathcal{K}} = \{s_2\}$, and hence, $[\![\mathsf{AFAG}a]\!]_{\mathcal{K}} = \{s_1, s_2\}$. Hence, this structure shows that the LTL formula $\mathsf{AFG}a$ is not equivalent to the CTL formula $\mathsf{AFAG}a$, and the above theorem tells us additionally that no other LTL formula can therefore be equivalent to $\mathsf{AFAG}a$.

The structure given in Figure 5.2 shows also that $\mathsf{EGF}\varphi$ is not equivalent to $\mathsf{EGEF}\varphi$ and $\mathsf{EGX}\varphi$ is not equivalent to $\mathsf{EGEX}\varphi$. Note that $[\![\mathsf{EGF}\neg a]\!]_{\mathcal{K}} = \{\}$, $[\![\mathsf{EGEF}\neg a]\!]_{\mathcal{K}} = \{s_0\}$, $[\![\mathsf{EGX}\neg a]\!]_{\mathcal{K}} = \{\}$, and $[\![\mathsf{EGEX}\neg a]\!]_{\mathcal{K}} = \{s_0\}$. In a similar way, it is possible to show with another simple structure that $\mathsf{EXAX}\varphi$ can not be expessed in LTL.

Hence, we have obtained a criterion to check whether a CTL* formula, and hence, whether a CTL formula can be expressed in LTL. The opposite problem, namely to check if a LTL formula can be expressed in CTL turned out to be much harder and was unsolved for quite a long time. A breakthrough in that direction was obtained in 1998 by Kupferman and Vardi [303] who characterized the fragment of LTL that can be translated to the alternation-free μ-calculus:

Theorem 5.7 (LTL and Alternation-Free μ-Calculus). *A formula* $\mathsf{A}\varphi \in \mathsf{LTL}$ *is equivalent to an alternation-free μ-calculus formula iff φ is equivalent to some* $\mathfrak{A} \in \mathsf{Det}_{\mathsf{GF}}$.

We can not present the proof here since it requires some knowledge about tree automata. The above theorem characterizes the subset of LTL formulas that can be translated to the alternation-free μ-calculus, which is a superset of

CTL (as we will see in the next section). A tight characterization was finally obtained in 2000 by Maidl [338]. In particular, she defined the following logic:

Definition 5.8 (Semantic Intersection of CTL and LTL). *We define the logic* $\mathsf{LTL}_{\mathsf{det}}$ *as the least subset of* LTL *that satisfies the following rules:*

- $V_\Sigma \subseteq \mathsf{LTL}_{\mathsf{det}}$
- $\varphi \wedge \psi \in \mathsf{LTL}_{\mathsf{det}}$ *if* $\varphi, \psi \in \mathsf{LTL}_{\mathsf{det}}$
- $x \wedge \psi \vee \neg x \wedge \varphi \in \mathsf{LTL}_{\mathsf{det}}$ *if* $\varphi, \psi \in \mathsf{LTL}_{\mathsf{det}}$ *and* $x \in V_\Sigma$
- $\mathsf{X}\varphi \in \mathsf{LTL}_{\mathsf{det}}$ *if* $\varphi \in \mathsf{LTL}_{\mathsf{det}}$
- $[(x \wedge \varphi)\ \underline{\mathsf{U}}\ (\neg x \wedge \psi)] \in \mathsf{LTL}_{\mathsf{det}}$ *if* $\varphi, \psi \in \mathsf{LTL}_{\mathsf{det}}$ *and* $x \in V_\Sigma$
- $[(x \wedge \varphi)\ \mathsf{U}\ (\neg x \wedge \psi)] \in \mathsf{LTL}_{\mathsf{det}}$ *if* $\varphi, \psi \in \mathsf{LTL}_{\mathsf{det}}$ *and* $x \in V_\Sigma$

The idea is thereby to eliminate some 'overlaps': for example, to satisfy a formula $[\varphi\ \underline{\mathsf{U}}\ \psi]$ we must have a path where φ holds up to position t and where ψ holds at position $t+1$. It may be the case that φ also holds at $t+1$, which is an overlap that is eliminated in $\mathsf{LTL}_{\mathsf{det}}$. The same holds for disjunctions: the variable x selects one of the two subformulas to be satisfied. Maidl then proved the following result [338] and presented an algorithm to test whether for a $\mathsf{A}\varphi \in \mathsf{LTL}$, there is an equivalent $\mathsf{LTL}_{\mathsf{det}}$ formula.

Theorem 5.9 (Semantic Intersection of CTL and LTL). *A formula* $\mathsf{A}\varphi \in \mathsf{LTL}$ *is equivalent to a* CTL *formula iff* φ *is equivalent to a* $\mathsf{LTL}_{\mathsf{det}}$ *formula.*

5.2.2 Adding Syntactic Sugar to CTL

In the previous section, we have considered the temporal logics CTL, LTL, and CTL* and have compared their expressiveness. As CTL* includes both logics, it is clearly the best choice if we require maximal expressiveness. The model checking problem for CTL* is however PSPACE-complete [103, 172, 176], the same holds for the LTL model checking problem [456], while CTL model checking can be solved in polynomial time [103, 116, 443].

However, complexity and expressiveness are not the only issues. From a practical point of view, the readability of a specification logic is also a major criterion. Considering the readability, several authors claimed that CTL suffers from restrictions that limit its practical usage. These restrictions are not only due to a limited expressiveness, but also due to a unnecessarily hard restrictive syntax. For example, consider the following formula:

$$\mathcal{H}_n :\equiv \mathsf{E}\left[\left(\bigwedge_{i=0}^{n} \mathsf{F}\varphi_i\right) \wedge \bigwedge_{i=0}^{n} \mathsf{G}\left(\varphi_i \rightarrow \mathsf{XG}\neg\varphi_i\right)\right]$$

The formula $\mathcal{H}_n$ states that there must be a path that visits every set $[\![\varphi_i]\!]_{\mathcal{K}}$ exactly once. Hence, checking the formula on a structure (that is appropriately labeled) is equivalent to finding Hamilton paths in the structure which is known to be NP-complete [204].

We will define below the logic LeftCTL*, and will then see that $\mathcal{H}_n$ belongs to LeftCTL*. We already know that $\mathcal{H}_n$ is not a CTL formula, but in the next section we will develop techniques to translate every LeftCTL* formula to an equivalent CTL formula. Hence, it follows that there are formulas in CTL that are equivalent to $\mathcal{H}_n$, but these formulas are very large. In general, our transformations will generate, for a given LeftCTL* formula Φ, an equivalent CTL formula of size $O(|\Phi|!)$ and or $O(|\Phi|\, 2^{2|\Phi|})$ if common subterms are shared, so there may be an exponential blow-up. As LeftCTL* satisfiability checking is 2EXPTIME-complete [266], but CTL satisfiability checking is only EXPTIME-complete, it follows that the exponential blow-up can not be avoided. See also [4, 513] for lower bounds of this translation.

Hence, we see that not only the expressiveness itself is an issue, but also the succinctness and hence, the readability of a logic. This is clearly due to a higher complexity of the model checking problem: If a logic like LeftCTL* is exponentially more succinct than CTL, then it can no longer have a polynomial model checking procedure. In fact, the model checking problem of LeftCTL* is NP-hard (Section 5.6) and Δ_2^p-complete [103, 314, 443], hence better than the model checking problems of CTL* and LTL. Moreover, there are further good reasons to prefer LeftCTL* (if the expressiveness allows this), since in contrast to LTL or CTL*, LeftCTL* can be translated to CTL so that available model checking tools for CTL can also be used for model checking LeftCTL*. Furthermore, in Section 5.4.5, we will integrate the LeftCTL* to CTL translation in the translations for LTL and CTL*, so that LTL and CTL* model checking also benefits from this reduction.

Therefore, it is interesting to define sublogics of CTL* that can be reduced to CTL, but that allow more succinct specifications. To this end, a lot of other sublogics of CTL* have been considered [158, 163, 300, 434] in order to find a good compromise between readability, expressiveness, and complexity. From a theoretical point of view, these logics may be uninteresting, since most of them are equivalent to CTL. However, from a practical point of view, it is necessary to make specifications more readable and (even exponentially) more succinct, as the above example formula $\mathcal{H}_n$ has shown.

In this section, we therefore list further sublogics to motivate the translations from these logics to CTL, which may be used here as synonym for the alternation-free μ-calculus. The translations themselves are given in the following sections (Section 5.3.3 and Section 5.3.4). For a systematic classification of sublogics [163] introduced a hierarchy of branching time temporal logics. These are given in the following definition (see also [158]):

Definition 5.10 (Sublanguages of CTL* (II)). *Given a finite set of variables V_Σ, the following grammar rules define the state formulas for all branching time sublanguages of CTL* given below:*

$$S ::= V_\Sigma \mid \neg S \mid S \wedge S \mid S \vee S \mid \mathsf{E}P \mid \mathsf{A}P$$

Depending on the grammar rules for the path formulas, the following branching time sublanguages are defined:

$$
\begin{array}{ll}
\mathsf{B}(\mathsf{X}): & P ::= \mathsf{X}S \\
\mathsf{B}(\mathsf{F}): & P ::= \mathsf{F}S \\
\mathsf{B}(\mathsf{X},\mathsf{F}): & P ::= \mathsf{X}S \mid \mathsf{F}S \\
\mathsf{B}(\neg,\wedge,\mathsf{X},\mathsf{F}): & P ::= \neg P \mid P \wedge P \mid \mathsf{X}S \mid \mathsf{F}S \\
\mathsf{B}(\mathsf{X},\mathsf{F},\underline{\mathsf{U}}): & P ::= \mathsf{X}S \mid \mathsf{F}S \mid [S\ \underline{\mathsf{U}}\ S] \\
\mathsf{B}(\neg,\wedge,\mathsf{X},\mathsf{F},\underline{\mathsf{U}}): & P ::= \neg P \mid P \wedge P \mid \mathsf{X}S \mid \mathsf{F}S \mid [S\ \underline{\mathsf{U}}\ S] \\
\mathsf{B}(\neg,\wedge,\mathsf{X},\mathsf{F},\underline{\mathsf{U}},\mathsf{GF}): & P ::= \neg P \mid P \wedge P \mid \mathsf{X}S \mid \mathsf{F}S \mid [S\ \underline{\mathsf{U}}\ S] \mid \mathsf{GF}S
\end{array}
$$

Hence, $\mathsf{B}(M)$ allows, after a path quantifier, exactly formulas that start with an operator of the set M. As a further restriction, the arguments of temporal operators must be state formulas. Hence, temporal operators are not allowed to be nested without separating the nesting with a path quantifier. In the logic $\mathsf{B}(\neg,\wedge,\mathsf{X},\mathsf{F},\underline{\mathsf{U}},\mathsf{GF})$, we consider GF as a single macro operator, although it is composed of two temporal operators. Some authors, e.g. [158], write F^∞ and G^∞ instead of GF and FG, respectively, to stress that these macros should be treated as a single operators. We already know that $\mathsf{GF}a$ means that a holds infinitely often, while $\mathsf{FG}a$ means that a holds from a certain point of time on.

Hence, in the above terminology, $\mathsf{B}(\{\mathsf{X},\mathsf{G},\mathsf{F},\mathsf{W},\mathsf{U},\mathsf{B},\underline{\mathsf{W}},\underline{\mathsf{U}},\underline{\mathsf{B}}\})$ is our CTL logic, and the logic UB is $\mathsf{B}(\{\mathsf{X},\mathsf{G},\mathsf{F}\})$. LTL and CTL* can not be expressed in this terminology, since these logics allow the nesting of temporal operators in an arbitrary manner. For the above logics, expressiveness and complexity results have been derived in [163] (cf. Figure 5.3). We list these results in this section and also list some simple remarks that prove some of these results. Other results are however deeper and require certain transformations that we will develop in Section 5.3.3 and Section 5.3.4. The following remarks are however easily seen:

1. For two logics $\mathsf{B}(M_1)$ and $\mathsf{B}(M_2)$ with $M_1 \subseteq M_2$ we trivially have $\mathsf{B}(M_1) \subseteq \mathsf{B}(M_2)$, and hence $\mathsf{B}(M_1) \precsim \mathsf{B}(M_2)$.
2. For every set of operators M, we have $\mathsf{B}(\{\neg,\wedge\} \cup M) \approx \mathsf{B}(\{\neg,\wedge,\vee\} \cup M)$. Similar to the previous point, we can derive $\neg(\neg P \wedge \neg P)$ from P by the rules of $\mathsf{B}(\{\neg,\wedge\} \cup M)$.
3. $\mathsf{B}(\{\neg,\mathsf{F}\} \cup M) \approx \mathsf{B}(\{\neg,\mathsf{F},\mathsf{G}\} \cup M)$, since $\mathsf{G}\varphi = \neg\mathsf{F}\neg\varphi$ holds, and we can derive $\neg\mathsf{F}\neg S$ from P in $\mathsf{B}(\{\neg,\mathsf{F}\} \cup M)$.
4. For every set of operators M with $\{\neg,\wedge,\vee,\underline{\mathsf{U}}\} \subseteq M$, we have $\mathsf{B}(M) \approx \mathsf{B}(M \setminus \{\mathsf{G},\mathsf{F},\mathsf{W},\mathsf{U},\mathsf{B},\underline{\mathsf{W}},\underline{\mathsf{B}}\})$, since we have already seen that we can define these temporal operators with $\underline{\mathsf{U}}$. Alternatively, we can also use any of the binary temporal operators, since each of them can express $\underline{\mathsf{U}}$.
5. We will see in the next section that for every set of operators M with $\underline{\mathsf{U}} \in M$, we have $\mathsf{B}(M) \approx \mathsf{B}(M \setminus \{\neg,\wedge\})$ and also $\mathsf{B}(M) \approx \mathsf{B}(M \setminus \{\neg,\wedge,\vee\})$, i.e., we can eliminate applications of path quantifiers to subformulas starting with Boolean operators.

The above remarks already show that we have some freedom for the construction of equally expressive logics. One thing that was discovered quite early was that Boolean operations may occur after path quantifiers, even in an arbitrary nesting depth (Section 5.3.3). This lead to the definition of UB^+ and CTL^+ that are defined in the above terminology as $\mathsf{B}(\{\neg, \wedge, \vee, \mathsf{X}, \mathsf{G}, \mathsf{F}\})$ and $\mathsf{B}(\{\neg, \wedge, \vee, \mathsf{X}, \mathsf{G}, \mathsf{F}, \mathsf{W}, \mathsf{U}, \mathsf{B}, \underline{\mathsf{W}}, \underline{\mathsf{U}}, \underline{\mathsf{B}}\})$. It can be shown that this transformation may require an exponential increase of the size of the formulas [4, 266, 513]. Note that this is not only a criterion on the complexity of a logic, but also a criterion on the succinctness.

Also, it has been known for a long time, that path quantifiers can be shifted inwards over some temporal operators, e.g., the formulas $\mathsf{AGF}a$ and $\mathsf{AGAF}a$ are equivalent. In contrast to the previous transformation, this transformation only requires a linear increase of the size of the formulas.

The author has defined a temporal logic called LeftCTL* [434] that was designed as a superset of CTL^+ such that all available laws are exploited to eliminate Boolean operations that occur after path quantifiers (Section 5.3.3) and to shift path quantifiers inwards (see Section 5.3.4). A formal definition of the languages LeftCTL* and CTL^+ amongst others is given by the following definition in form of BNF grammars:

Definition 5.11 (Sublanguages of CTL* (III)). *Given a finite set of variables V_Σ, the following grammars define the logics UB^+, CTL^+, CTL^{++}, $\mathsf{LeftCTL}^{++}$, and LeftCTL*:*

$$
\begin{array}{lll}
\mathsf{LeftCTL}^*: & S ::= & V_\Sigma \mid \neg S \mid S \wedge S \mid S \vee S \mid \mathsf{E}P_E \mid \mathsf{A}P_A \\
& P_E ::= & S \mid \neg P_A \mid P_E \wedge P_E \mid P_E \vee P_E \mid \mathsf{X}P_E \mid \mathsf{G}S \mid \mathsf{F}P_E \\
& & \mid [P_E\ \mathsf{W}\ S] \mid [S\ \mathsf{U}\ P_E] \mid [P_E\ \mathsf{B}\ S] \\
& & \mid [P_E\ \underline{\mathsf{W}}\ S] \mid [S\ \underline{\mathsf{U}}\ P_E] \mid [P_E\ \underline{\mathsf{B}}\ S] \\
& P_A ::= & S \mid \neg P_E \mid P_A \wedge P_A \mid P_A \vee P_A \mid \mathsf{X}P_A \mid \mathsf{G}P_A \mid \mathsf{F}S \\
& & \mid [P_A\ \mathsf{W}\ S] \mid [P_A\ \mathsf{U}\ S] \mid [S\ \mathsf{B}\ P_E] \\
& & \mid [P_A\ \underline{\mathsf{W}}\ S] \mid [P_A\ \underline{\mathsf{U}}\ S] \mid [S\ \underline{\mathsf{B}}\ P_E] \\
\mathsf{LeftCTL}^{++}: & S ::= & V_\Sigma \mid \neg S \mid S \wedge S \mid S \vee S \mid \mathsf{E}P_E \mid \mathsf{A}P_A \\
& P_E ::= & S \mid \mathsf{X}P_E \mid \mathsf{G}S \mid \mathsf{F}P_E \\
& & \mid [P_E\ \mathsf{W}\ S] \mid [S\ \mathsf{U}\ P_E] \mid [P_E\ \mathsf{B}\ S] \\
& & \mid [P_E\ \underline{\mathsf{W}}\ S] \mid [S\ \underline{\mathsf{U}}\ P_E] \mid [P_E\ \underline{\mathsf{B}}\ S] \\
& P_A ::= & S \mid \mathsf{X}P_A \mid \mathsf{G}P_A \mid \mathsf{F}S \\
& & \mid [P_A\ \mathsf{W}\ S] \mid [P_A\ \mathsf{U}\ S] \mid [S\ \mathsf{B}\ P_E] \\
& & \mid [P_A\ \underline{\mathsf{W}}\ S] \mid [P_A\ \underline{\mathsf{U}}\ S] \mid [S\ \underline{\mathsf{B}}\ P_E] \\
\mathsf{CTL}^{++}: & S ::= & V_\Sigma \mid \neg S \mid S \wedge S \mid S \vee S \mid \mathsf{E}P_1 \mid \mathsf{A}P_1 \\
& P_1 ::= & \mathsf{X}P \mid \mathsf{G}P \mid \mathsf{F}P \\
& & \mid [P\ \mathsf{W}\ P] \mid [P\ \mathsf{U}\ P] \mid [P\ \mathsf{B}\ P] \\
& & \mid [P\ \underline{\mathsf{W}}\ P] \mid [P\ \underline{\mathsf{U}}\ P] \mid [P\ \underline{\mathsf{B}}\ P] \\
& P ::= & S \mid \neg P \mid P \wedge P \mid P \vee P \mid P_1 \\
\mathsf{CTL}^{+}: & S ::= & V_\Sigma \mid \neg S \mid S \wedge S \mid S \vee S \mid \mathsf{E}P \mid \mathsf{A}P \\
& P ::= & \neg P \mid P \wedge P \mid P \vee P \mid \mathsf{X}S \mid \mathsf{G}S \mid \mathsf{F}S \\
& & \mid [S\ \mathsf{W}\ S] \mid [S\ \mathsf{U}\ S] \mid [S\ \mathsf{B}\ S] \\
& & \mid [S\ \underline{\mathsf{W}}\ S] \mid [S\ \underline{\mathsf{U}}\ S] \mid [S\ \underline{\mathsf{B}}\ S] \\
\mathsf{UB}^{+}: & S ::= & V_\Sigma \mid \neg S \mid S \wedge S \mid S \vee S \mid \mathsf{E}P \mid \mathsf{A}P \\
& P ::= & \neg P \mid P \wedge P \mid P \vee P \mid \mathsf{X}S \mid \mathsf{G}S \mid \mathsf{F}S
\end{array}
$$

As in the grammars before, the nonterminals S and P with or without indices describe sets of state or path formulas, respectively. LeftCTL* formulas allow arbitrary deep nested Boolean operators after path quantifiers, and also certain arbitrary deep nestings of temporal operators. However, the nesting of temporal operators is only allowed on one argument of the binary temporal operators. As the logic has been developed from a strictly weaker logic, given in [433], that only considers the W operator, and as the nestings are allowed only for the left hand arguments of W operators, the logic has been named as LeftCTL*. Note that the nesting side of U and B operators depends on whether the formula occurs after an E or A quantifier. Therefore, the grammar distinguishes between path formulas that occur after an E or A quantifier by the nonterminals P_E and P_A, respectively.

CTL^{++} contains all formulas of CTL* where no path quantifier is applied to an expression with a Boolean operator on top, i.e., each path quantifier in CTL^{++} must be followed by a temporal operator. Hence, we must distinguish in CTL^{++} between path formulas P_1 beginning with a temporal operator and general path formulas P.

LeftCTL^{++} is the intersection of LeftCTL* and CTL^{++}, i.e., the subset of LeftCTL*, where it is not allowed for Boolean operators to occur immediately after a path quantifier. Finally, CTL$^+$ is the generalization of CTL that allows arbitrary deep nestings of Boolean operators after path quantifiers. Path formulas of CTL$^+$ that start with a temporal operator are however, exactly the same as in CTL.

Note that we distinguish between the sets of formulas and the expressiveness of the logic. For the above logics, we have syntactically the following inclusion diagram (expressiveness results are given in Figure 5.3):

$$
\begin{array}{ccccc}
\text{UB}^+ & \subseteq & \text{CTL}^+ & \subseteq & \text{LeftCTL}^* \\
\cup\! & & \cup\! & & \cap \\
\text{UB} & \subseteq \text{CTL} & & & \text{CTL}^* \\
& \cap & & & \cup \\
& & \text{LeftCTL}^{++} & \subseteq & \text{CTL}^{++}
\end{array}
$$

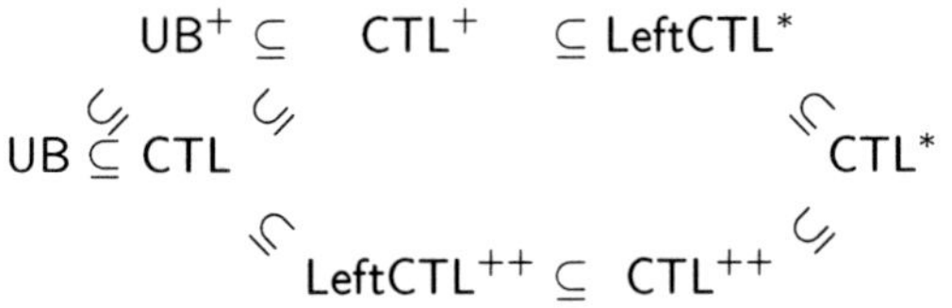

We have already noted that efficient verification tools are available for CTL, so that logics weaker than CTL are not of much interest. We have already mentioned (and will prove in detail later) that LeftCTL* is as expressive as CTL, but the logics differ dramatically in their succinctness.

Considering the expressiveness of the logics CTL and LeftCTL*, we can say that it is sufficient for most practical applications. However, there is one aspect that is sometimes required in practice that can not be specified in CTL, and hence not in LeftCTL*: There is no CTL formula that is equivalent to the CTL* formula EGFφ which states that there is a path where φ holds infinitely often [160, 163, 310]. However, for some applications, specifications of the form E[(GFφ) $\wedge$ Φ] or A[(GFφ) $\rightarrow$ Φ] occur naturally. For example, $\neg$E[(GFreq) $\wedge$ G$\neg ack$] means that there is no computation path where a request *req* is given infinitely often without acknowledge *ack*. Another example involves the fairness of an arbiter that administrates the access of n components to a shared resource. For a correct function of such a system, it is required that each component releases the shared resource after some time. The specification $\mathsf{A}\left[(\bigwedge_{i=0}^{n} \neg\mathsf{FG}own_i) \rightarrow (\bigwedge_{i=0}^{n} \neg\mathsf{FG}[req_i \wedge \neg ack_i])\right]$ means that it is not the case that a component requests access while never being granted access (provided that each component releases the shared resource after some time).

Properties of this kind are therefore expressed by restricting the path quantifiers by *fairness constraints*, as the set of computation paths where the quantification is applied on is restricted only to certain *fair* paths instead of the set of all paths. We can alternatively express such restrictions in our Kripke structures by adding appropriate fairness constraints to the structure. If the fair sets $F_1, \ldots, F_f \subseteq \mathcal{S}$ that have to be visited infinitely often by a fair path can be identified with propositional formula α_i such that $[\![\alpha_i]\!]_{\mathcal{K}'} = F_i$ holds (where $\mathcal{K}'$ is the corresponding structure without fairness constraints), then some logics can express the restrictions by fairness constraints directly in their formulas. For example, in CTL* we just have to replace every subformula $\mathsf{E}\varphi$ by $\mathsf{E}\left[\left(\bigwedge_{i=1}^{f}\right) \wedge \varphi\right]$, and analogously, we replace every subformula $\mathsf{A}\varphi$ by $\mathsf{A}\left[\left(\bigwedge_{i=1}^{f}\right) \rightarrow \varphi\right]$. As these are also CTL* formulas, we see that CTL* can directly express fairness constraints.

CTL, and hence all expressively equivalent logics like LeftCTL*, are however not powerful enough to do this [160, 163, 310]. As such fairness constraints can not be expressed in CTL, an extension to fairness constraints of CTL has been proposed in [175] which on the one hand, extends the expressiveness of CTL, but on the other hand still retains a polynomial model checking algorithm. We will see this in the next section and list here an adaption of the last definition.

Definition 5.12 (Sublanguages of CTL* (IV)). *Given propositional formulas* $\alpha_1, \ldots, \alpha_f$, *we define* $\Phi := \bigwedge_{i=1}^{f} \mathsf{GF}\alpha_i$ *and the macros* $\mathsf{E}_\Phi\varphi := \mathsf{E}(\Phi \wedge \varphi)$ *and* $\mathsf{A}_\Phi\varphi := \mathsf{A}(\Phi \rightarrow \varphi)$. *The logics* FairCTL, FairCTL$^+$, FairLeftCTL^{++}, FairLeftCTL* *are obtained by changing the grammar rules for* CTL, CTL$^+$, LeftCTL^{++}, *and* LeftCTL* *in that all occurrences of* E *and* A *are replaced with* E_Φ *and* A_Φ, *respectively.*

The diagram for expressivenesses of the different logics we have encountered so far is given in Figure 5.3. We will prove the equal expressiveness results by the transformations in the following sections. For the strictness of the listed $\precsim\!\!\!\!/\,$ relations, we just note here without proof that the following example formulas can be expressed in some of the logics, but not in the other ones below in the hierarchy (see [162]).

$$
\begin{array}{ccccc}
 & & \mathsf{CTL}^* & & \\
 & & \rotatebox{90}{$\approx$} & & \\
 & & \mathsf{CTL}^{++} & & \\
 & & \rotatebox{90}{$\precnapprox$} & & \\
\mathsf{FairLeftCTL}^{+} & \approx & \mathsf{FairCTL}^{+} & \approx & \mathsf{FairLeftCTL}^* \\
 & & \rotatebox{90}{$\approx$} & & \\
 & & \mathsf{FairCTL} & & \\
 & & \rotatebox{90}{$\precnapprox$} & & \\
 & & \mathsf{LeftCTL}^* & \approx & \mathsf{LeftCTL}^{++} \\
 & & \rotatebox{90}{$\approx$} & & \\
\mathsf{B}(\neg,\wedge,\mathsf{X},\underline{\mathsf{U}}) & \approx & \mathsf{CTL}^{+} & \approx & \mathsf{B}(\neg,\wedge,\mathsf{X},\mathsf{F},\mathsf{G},\mathsf{B},\underline{\mathsf{U}}) \\
 & & \rotatebox{90}{$\approx$} & & \\
\mathsf{B}(\mathsf{X},\underline{\mathsf{U}}) & \approx & \mathsf{CTL} & \approx & \mathsf{B}(\mathsf{X},\mathsf{F},\mathsf{G},\mathsf{B},\underline{\mathsf{U}}) \\
 & & \rotatebox{90}{$\precnapprox$} & & \\
\mathsf{B}(\neg,\wedge,\mathsf{X},\mathsf{F}) & \approx & \mathsf{UB}^{+} & \approx & \mathsf{B}(\neg,\wedge,\mathsf{X},\mathsf{F},\mathsf{G}) \\
 & & \rotatebox{90}{$\precnapprox$} & & \\
\mathsf{B}(\mathsf{X},\mathsf{F}) & \approx & \mathsf{UB} & \approx & \mathsf{B}(\mathsf{X},\mathsf{F},\mathsf{G}) \\
 & & \rotatebox{90}{$\precnapprox$} & & \\
 & & \mathsf{B}(\mathsf{F}) & &
\end{array}
$$

Fig. 5.3. Sublanguages of CTL* and their expressiveness

formula ($a, b \in V_\Sigma$)	expressible in	but not in
$\mathsf{E}[\mathsf{G}a \wedge \mathsf{F}b]$	UB^+	UB
$\mathsf{E}[a\ \underline{\mathsf{U}}\ b]$	CTL	UB^+
$\mathsf{EGF}a$	FairCTL	CTL
$\mathsf{AF}[a \wedge \mathsf{X}a]$	CTL*	FairCTL

Note that $\mathsf{E}[\mathsf{G}a \wedge \mathsf{F}b] = \mathsf{E}[a\ \underline{\mathsf{U}}\ (b \wedge \mathsf{EG}a)]$ holds, so that this formula can be expressed in CTL as well. Note further that $\mathsf{AF}[a \wedge \mathsf{X}a]$ can be translated to the alternation-free μ-calculus: $\mathsf{G}[\varphi \vee \mathsf{X}\varphi]$ can be easily translated to the ω-automaton $\mathcal{A}_\exists(\{q\}, \neg q, \Phi_\mathcal{R}, 1)$ with $\Phi_\mathcal{R} := \neg q \wedge \neg\varphi \wedge \mathsf{X}q \vee \varphi \wedge \neg\mathsf{X}q$ (see Figure 5.4). Hence, according to Theorem 4.67, we obtain the following μ-calculus formula for $\mathsf{EG}[\varphi \vee \mathsf{X}\varphi]$:

$$
\mathsf{fix}\begin{bmatrix} y_{\{\}} \stackrel{\nu}{=} \varphi \wedge \Diamond y_{\{\}} \vee \neg\varphi \wedge \Diamond y_{\{q\}} \\ y_{\{q\}} \stackrel{\nu}{=} \varphi \wedge \Diamond y_{\{\}} \end{bmatrix} \mathsf{in}\ y_{\{\}}\ \mathsf{end}
$$

Hence, we find the following equivalences:

- $\mathsf{EG}[\varphi \vee \mathsf{X}\varphi] = \nu y.\ \varphi \wedge \Diamond y \vee \neg\varphi \wedge \Diamond(\varphi \wedge \Diamond y)$
- $\mathsf{AF}[\varphi \wedge \mathsf{X}\varphi] = \mu y.\ (\varphi \vee \Box y) \wedge (\neg\varphi \vee \Box(\varphi \vee \Box y))$

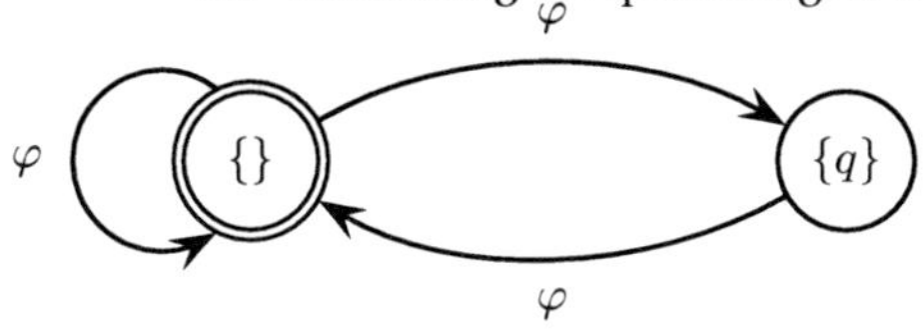

Fig. 5.4. State transition diagram of the automaton for $\mathsf{G}[\varphi \vee \mathsf{X}\varphi]$

Moreover, it is easily seen that the above formulas can be simplied as follows:

- $\mathsf{EG}[\varphi \vee \mathsf{X}\varphi] = \nu y.\ \varphi \wedge \Diamond y \vee \neg\varphi \wedge \Diamond(\varphi \wedge y)$
- $\mathsf{AF}[\varphi \wedge \mathsf{X}\varphi] = \mu y.\ (\varphi \vee \Box y) \wedge (\neg\varphi \vee \Box(\varphi \vee y))$

To formally prove the equivalence, one needs to have a decision procedure for the satisfiabilty of μ-calculus formulas as described in Section B.3.

5.3 Translating Temporal Logics to the μ-Calculus

As expected, we can translate every formula of CTL^* to an equivalent μ-calculus formula. For example, a direct translation is given in [135], where a CTL^* formula Φ is translated to an equivalent μ-calculus formula Ψ of length $O(2^{2^{|\Phi|}})$ and alternation depth 2. We will not follow this approach, and will only show in this section the translation of some simpler sublogics of CTL^* to equivalent μ-calculus formulas. However, in Section 5.4, we will show how we can compute for arbitrary LTL formulas $\mathsf{A}\varphi$ an ω-automaton $\mathfrak{A}_\varphi$ that is equivalent to φ. The further translations of $\mathfrak{A}_\varphi$ according to the theorems of Section 4.8.3 will then show that we can translate every LTL formula $\mathsf{A}\varphi$ to an equivalent μ-calculus formula Φ of size $O(|\varphi|\, 2^{|\varphi|})$ and an alternation depth not higher than 2. Moreover, using the PQNF normal form of Definition 2.49 on page 85 allows us to apply these results to CTL^* formulas. Hence, it follows that for every CTL^* formula φ we can compute an equivalent μ-calculus formula Φ of single exponential size.

Hence, our translation of CTL^* or LTL to the μ-calculus is done indirectly via an intermediate translation to ω-automata. We will present these procedures in detail in Section 5.4. In this section, we consider instead the direct translation of sublogics of CTL^* to the μ-calculus. In particular, we will consider in this section the logics CTL, $\mathsf{FairCTL}$, CTL^2 [300], and $\mathsf{LeftCTL}^*$ [434]. The reason for this is that these logics can be translated in a very intuitive way to the μ-calculus. In fact, as these logics all refer to CTL, and CTL can be directly interpreted as fragment of the μ-calculus, we may also view the mentioned logics as fragments of the μ-calculus. However, while the translation of CTL, $\mathsf{FairCTL}$, and CTL^2 yield linear sized μ-calculus formulas, the translation of $\mathsf{LeftCTL}^*$ may result in an exponential blow-up. In contrast to the other mentioned logics, $\mathsf{LeftCTL}^*$ is therefore not in a one-to-one correspondence with the μ-calculus.

The outline of this section is as follows: in the next section, we show that CTL and FairCTL formulas can be translated in linear time to equivalent μ-calculus formulas of alternation depth 1 and 2, respectively. In Section 5.3.2, we consider the temporal logic CTL^2 [300] of Kupferman and Grumberg. The idea of this logic is roughly as follows: while CTL provides macro operators that consist of pairs of a path quantifier and a temporal operator, CTL^2 provides macro operators that consist of a path quantifier and two nested temporal operators. In [300], it has been shown how CTL^2 can be translated to linear-sized μ-calculus formulas of alternation depth 2. We will follow these ideas in Section 5.3.2. Hence, the model checking algorithms we have already presented for the μ-calculus can be applied more or less directly to CTL, FairCTL, and CTL^2 and give polynomial time verification procedures.

The translation of LeftCTL* requires a bit more effort: In Section 5.3.3, we will describe how applications of path quantifiers to subformulas starting with Boolean operators can be eliminated. In Section 5.3.4, we moreover see that path quantifiers also induce the presence of path quantifiers in their subformulas, so that we can add path quantifiers at certain positions. These two transformations are sufficient to prove all of the equal expressiveness results of Figure 5.3. However, a naive use of our results would transform given LeftCTL* formulas to equivalent CTL formulas of size $O(|\Phi| \cdot |\Phi|!)$. We will therefore show in Section 5.3.5 that the translation can be improved by sharing subformulas in that we translate to the vectorized μ-calculus. As a result, we will obtain formulas of size $O(|\Phi|\, 2^{2|\Phi|})$, which will be a great improvement. We therefore obtain an exponential time verification procedure for LeftCTL*.

5.3.1 CTL and FairCTL as Fragments of the μ-Calculus

CTL and FairCTL are subsets of CTL*, but they can also be viewed as subsets of the μ-calculus. This was pointed out by Clarke and Emerson in [102, 160], and in fact, they designed CTL as a macro language for the μ-calculus. Hence, the translation of CTL and FairCTL to equivalent μ-calculus formulas is done by replacing the CTL and FairCTL operators with their definitions:

Theorem 5.13 (Translating CTL and FairCTL to μ-Calculus). *Given a fairness constraint $\Phi = \bigwedge_{i=1}^{n} \mathsf{GF}\alpha_i$ (with propositional formulas α_i), define*[1] *$\Phi_{\mathsf{fair}} = \nu z. \bigwedge_{i=1}^{f} \Diamond[\mu x.z \wedge \alpha_i \vee \Diamond x]$. The following equations rewrite every FairCTL formula φ to an equivalent μ-calculus formula of size $O(|\varphi|)$ and alternation depth 2:*

- $\mathsf{E}_{\Phi}\mathsf{X}\varphi = \Diamond(\Phi_{\mathsf{fair}} \wedge \varphi)$
- $\mathsf{E}_{\Phi}\mathsf{G}\varphi = \nu z.\ \varphi \wedge \bigwedge_{i=1}^{n} \Diamond[\mu x.z \wedge \alpha_i \vee \varphi \wedge \Diamond x]$
- $\mathsf{E}_{\Phi}\mathsf{F}\varphi = \mu x.\ \Phi_{\mathsf{fair}} \wedge \varphi \vee \Diamond x$

[1] Of course, every other μ-calculus formula to compute the fair states can be used as well for this purpose (cf. Section 3.7).

- $\mathsf{E}_\Phi [\varphi\ \underline{\mathsf{U}}\ \psi] = \mu x.\ \Phi_{\mathsf{fair}} \wedge \psi \vee \varphi \wedge \Diamond x$
- $\mathsf{E}_\Phi [\varphi\ \underline{\mathsf{W}}\ \psi] = \mu x.\ \Phi_{\mathsf{fair}} \wedge \psi \wedge \varphi \vee \neg(\Phi_{\mathsf{fair}} \wedge \psi) \wedge \Diamond x$
- $\mathsf{E}_\Phi [\varphi\ \underline{\mathsf{B}}\ \psi] = \mu x.\ \neg\psi \wedge ((\Phi_{\mathsf{fair}} \wedge \varphi) \vee \Diamond x)$
- $\mathsf{E}_\Phi [\varphi\ \mathsf{U}\ \psi] = \mathsf{E}_\Phi [\varphi\ \underline{\mathsf{U}}\ \psi] \vee \mathsf{E}_\Phi \mathsf{G}\varphi$
- $\mathsf{E}_\Phi [\varphi\ \mathsf{W}\ \psi] = \mathsf{E}_\Phi [\varphi\ \underline{\mathsf{W}}\ \psi] \vee \mathsf{E}_\Phi \mathsf{G}\neg\psi$
- $\mathsf{E}_\Phi [\varphi\ \mathsf{B}\ \psi] = \mathsf{E}_\Phi [\varphi\ \underline{\mathsf{B}}\ \psi] \vee \mathsf{E}_\Phi \mathsf{G}(\neg\varphi \wedge \neg\psi)$

For the other operators, note that the following negation laws hold:

$$
\begin{array}{ll}
\mathsf{A}_\Phi \mathsf{X}\varphi = \neg\mathsf{E}_\Phi \mathsf{X}(\neg\varphi) & \\
\mathsf{A}_\Phi \mathsf{G}\varphi = \neg\mathsf{E}_\Phi \mathsf{F}(\neg\varphi) & \mathsf{A}_\Phi \mathsf{F}\varphi = \neg\mathsf{E}_\Phi \mathsf{G}(\neg\varphi) \\
\mathsf{A}_\Phi [\varphi\ \mathsf{U}\ \psi] = \neg\mathsf{E}[(\neg\varphi)\ \underline{\mathsf{B}}\ \psi] & \mathsf{A}_\Phi [\varphi\ \underline{\mathsf{U}}\ \psi] = \neg\mathsf{E}[(\neg\varphi)\ \mathsf{B}\ \psi] \\
\mathsf{A}_\Phi [\varphi\ \mathsf{B}\ \psi] = \neg\mathsf{E}_\Phi [(\neg\varphi)\ \underline{\mathsf{U}}\ \psi] & \mathsf{A}_\Phi [\varphi\ \underline{\mathsf{B}}\ \psi] = \neg\mathsf{E}_\Phi [(\neg\varphi)\ \mathsf{U}\ \psi] \\
\mathsf{A}_\Phi [\varphi\ \mathsf{W}\ \psi] = \neg\mathsf{E}_\Phi [(\neg\varphi)\ \underline{\mathsf{W}}\ \psi] & \mathsf{A}_\Phi [\varphi\ \underline{\mathsf{W}}\ \psi] = \neg\mathsf{E}_\Phi [(\neg\varphi)\ \mathsf{W}\ \psi]
\end{array}
$$

For checking a CTL *formula, i.e. the special case where $\Phi :\equiv 1$ holds, we use the above equations with $\Phi_{\mathsf{fair}} := \Phi_{\mathsf{inf}} := \nu z.\Diamond z$, except for*

- $\mathsf{E}_\Phi \mathsf{G}\varphi = \nu z.\ \varphi \wedge \Diamond x$

Hence, the translation of CTL *yields alternation-free μ-calculus formulas.*

The fixpoints are rather clear: for example, consider $\mathsf{E}_\Phi [\varphi\ \underline{\mathsf{U}}\ \psi]$. By the semantics, a state satisfies this formula if it either satisfies ψ or if it satisfies φ and has a successor state that satisfies $\mathsf{E}_\Phi [\varphi\ \underline{\mathsf{U}}\ \psi]$. However, we have to be sure that the path that is thereby followed is a fair one. This is done by reaching out for $\Phi_{\mathsf{fair}} \wedge \psi$ instead of reaching out for only ψ. Note that the satisfaction of fairness constraints can be postponed for an arbitrary long (finite) time. The other fixpoints can be explained in the same manner; the only one that is more difficult is the one for $\mathsf{E}_\Phi \mathsf{G}\varphi$ which was discussed on page 165.

The situation is simplified for CTL, when no fairness constraints have to be considered. In principle, we could then use the same equations as before with $f = 1$ and $\alpha_1 = 1$. Hence, we would have $\Phi_{\mathsf{fair}} = \nu z.\Diamond[\mu x.z \vee \Diamond x]$, which is equivalent to $\nu z.\Diamond z$: both fixpoints determine the set of states that have at least one infinite path. In the case, where every state of the Kripke structure has at least one successor state, we can even use $\Phi_{\mathsf{fair}} = 1$, so that the situation is even simpler. This can be achieved by replacing $\mathcal{R}$ with the relation $\mathcal{R}_{\mathsf{inf}}$ as explained in Section 3.7.

Hence, by our previous results on the μ-calculus, we see that FairCTL formulas can be checked, at least in time $O(|\mathcal{K}|\,|\mathcal{S}|\,|\Phi|^2)$, according to Theorem 3.40, and even in time $O(|\mathcal{K}|\,|\mathcal{S}|\,f\,|\Phi|)$ with our remarks after Theorem 3.43 on page 165. [103] even shows that it can be done in time $O(|\mathcal{K}|\,|\mathcal{S}_{\mathsf{fair}}|\,|\Phi|)$, where $\mathcal{S}_{\mathsf{fair}}$ is the set of fair states, i.e. those that satisfy Φ_{fair}.

Model checking CTL formulas in Kripke structures with fairness constraints can obviously be reduced to checking the corresponding FairCTL formulas in the same structure without fairness constraints, so that we obtain the same results. However, the model checking problem is simpler when there are no fairness constraints: In this case, we use the alternation-free formula $\Phi_{\mathsf{fair}} = \nu z.\Diamond z$ and $\mathsf{E}_{\Phi}\mathsf{G}\varphi = \nu z.\ \varphi \wedge \Diamond x$, so that an alternation-free formula is obtained. We therefore know that the complexity is $O(|\mathcal{K}|\,|\Phi|)$.

Theorem 5.14 (Complexity of CTL Model Checking). *For every Kripke structure $\mathcal{K} = (\mathcal{I}, \mathcal{S}, \mathcal{R}, \mathcal{L})$ and every* CTL *formula Φ, the computation of $[\![\Phi]\!]_{\mathcal{K}}$ can be done in time $O(|\mathcal{K}|\,|\Phi|)$. Given propositional formulas $\alpha_1, \ldots, \alpha_f$ as fairness constraints for a* FairCTL *formula Φ, the states where Φ holds can be computed in time $O(|\mathcal{K}|\,|\mathcal{S}|\,f\,|\Phi|)$.*

Note that we have assumed that the same fairness constraints were used for all path quantifiers. In principle, every occurrence of a path quantifier could have its own fairness constraints which would then require to compute the corresponding sets of fair states for every particular fixpoint iteration (due to a CTL operator). Moreover, we could consider different kinds of fairness constraints. Above, we considered the generalized Büchi constraints, where all sets $[\![\alpha_i]\!]_{\mathcal{K}}$ must be visited infinitely often. Instead, we could replace these constraints with the more general Streett condition $\bigwedge_{i=1}^{n} \mathsf{GF}\alpha_i \vee \mathsf{FG}\beta_i$. We have already seen in Theorem 4.65 on page 267 how the corresponding fair states can be computed.

5.3.2 CTL^2 as a Fragment of the μ-Calculus

In [300], Kupferman and Grumberg proposed another interesting logic called CTL^2 which is a strict superset of CTL, and a strict subset of CTL* (both in terms of expressiveness as well as in terms of syntax). The idea is inspired by generalizing the restrictions of CTL. Recall that CTL requires that path quantifiers and temporal operators occur in pairs, i.e., after a path quantifier there is exactly one temporal operator that is not within the scope of another path quantifier.

The idea of Kupferman and Grumberg was then to consider a similar logic that provides macro operators that consist of pairs of a path quantifier and one or two nested temporal operators (they also allowed a Boolean operator instead of a temporal operator). For this reason, it is clear that CTL is a strict subset of CTL^2. In particular, Kupferman and Grumberg considered the following logic:

$$
\begin{aligned}
S &::= V_{\Sigma} \mid \neg S \mid S \wedge S \mid S \vee S \mid \mathsf{E}P \mid \mathsf{A}P \\
P &::= P_1 \mid P_2 \\
P_1 &::= \mathsf{X}S \mid [S\ \underline{\mathsf{U}}\ S] \mid \neg P_1 \\
P_2 &::= \mathsf{X}P_1 \mid [P_1\ \underline{\mathsf{U}}\ S] \mid [S\ \underline{\mathsf{U}}\ P_1] \mid \neg P \mid S \wedge P_1 \mid P_1 \wedge S
\end{aligned}
$$

In the above grammar, the formulas derived from S are again the state formulas and those derived from P are the path formulas. There are path formulas of degree 1 or 2, meaning path formulas that are derived from P_1 or P_2.

Those that are derived from P_1 start with a temporal operator whose arguments must be state formulas. Path formulas derived from P_2 allow instead one more operator, i.e., either a Boolean or another temporal operator.

The overall idea is better understood by discussing the following equivalent logic (we have however already eliminated the applications of the path quantifiers to Boolean operators):

$$
\begin{array}{rl}
S ::= & V_\Sigma \mid \neg S \mid S \wedge S \mid S \vee S \mid \mathsf{E}[S \vee T] \mid \mathsf{E}[S \wedge T] \\
T ::= & \mid \mathsf{EX}S \mid \mathsf{E}[S \,\underline{\mathsf{U}}\, S] \mid \mathsf{E}[S \,\mathsf{B}\, S] \\
& \mid \mathsf{EXX}S \mid \mathsf{EX}\,[S \,\underline{\mathsf{U}}\, S] \mid \mathsf{EX}\,[S \,\mathsf{B}\, S] \\
& \mid \mathsf{E}\,[\mathsf{X}S \,\underline{\mathsf{U}}\, S] \mid \mathsf{E}\,[[S \,\underline{\mathsf{U}}\, S] \,\underline{\mathsf{U}}\, S] \mid \mathsf{E}\,[[S \,\mathsf{B}\, S] \,\underline{\mathsf{U}}\, S] \\
& \mid \mathsf{E}\,[S \,\underline{\mathsf{U}}\, \mathsf{X}S] \mid \mathsf{E}\,[S \,\underline{\mathsf{U}}\, [S \,\underline{\mathsf{U}}\, S]] \mid \mathsf{E}\,[S \,\underline{\mathsf{U}}\, [S \,\mathsf{B}\, S]] \\
& \mid \mathsf{E}\,[\mathsf{X}S \,\mathsf{B}\, S] \mid \mathsf{E}\,[[S \,\underline{\mathsf{U}}\, S] \,\mathsf{B}\, S] \mid \mathsf{E}\,[[S \,\mathsf{B}\, S] \,\mathsf{B}\, S] \\
& \mid \mathsf{E}\,[S \,\mathsf{B}\, \mathsf{X}S] \mid \mathsf{E}\,[S \,\mathsf{B}\, [S \,\underline{\mathsf{U}}\, S]] \mid \mathsf{E}\,[S \,\mathsf{B}\, [S \,\mathsf{B}\, S]]
\end{array}
$$

As can be seen CTL^2 allows us to nest after a path quantifier at most two temporal operators, and in the same way, we could define CTL^3, CTL^4, and so on. The surprising fact is that most of these macro operators can be reduced to simple CTL formulas according to the following equations, where α, β, and γ are arbitrary state formulas:

- $\mathsf{EXX}\alpha = \mathsf{EXEX}\alpha$
- $\mathsf{EX}\,[\alpha \,\underline{\mathsf{U}}\, \beta] = \mathsf{EXE}\,[\alpha \,\underline{\mathsf{U}}\, \beta]$
- $\mathsf{EX}\,[\alpha \,\mathsf{B}\, \beta] = \mathsf{EXE}\,[\alpha \,\mathsf{B}\, \beta]$
- $\mathsf{E}\,[(\mathsf{X}\alpha) \,\underline{\mathsf{U}}\, \beta] = \beta \vee \mathsf{EXE}[\alpha \,\underline{\mathsf{U}}\, (\alpha \wedge \beta)]$
- $\mathsf{E}\,[[\alpha \,\underline{\mathsf{U}}\, \beta] \,\underline{\mathsf{U}}\, \gamma] = \gamma \vee \mathsf{E}[(\alpha \vee \beta) \,\underline{\mathsf{U}}\, (\beta \wedge \mathsf{EX}\gamma \vee \gamma \wedge \mathsf{E}[\alpha \,\underline{\mathsf{U}}\, \beta])]$
- $\mathsf{E}\,[[\alpha \,\mathsf{B}\, \beta] \,\underline{\mathsf{U}}\, \gamma] = \gamma \vee \mathsf{E}[(\neg\beta) \,\underline{\mathsf{U}}\, (\alpha \wedge \neg\beta \wedge \mathsf{EX}\gamma \vee \gamma \wedge \mathsf{E}[\alpha \,\mathsf{B}\, \beta])]$
- $\mathsf{E}\,[\alpha \,\underline{\mathsf{U}}\, \mathsf{X}\beta] = \mathsf{E}\,[\alpha \,\underline{\mathsf{U}}\, (\mathsf{EX}\beta)]$
- $\mathsf{E}\,[\alpha \,\underline{\mathsf{U}}\, [\beta \,\underline{\mathsf{U}}\, \gamma]] = \mathsf{E}\,[\alpha \,\underline{\mathsf{U}}\, (\mathsf{E}\,[\beta \,\underline{\mathsf{U}}\, \gamma])]$
- $\mathsf{E}\,[\alpha \,\underline{\mathsf{U}}\, [\beta \,\mathsf{B}\, \gamma]] = \mathsf{E}\,[\alpha \,\underline{\mathsf{U}}\, (\mathsf{E}\,[\beta \,\mathsf{B}\, \gamma])]$
- $\mathsf{E}\,[\mathsf{X}\alpha \,\mathsf{B}\, \beta] = \mathsf{E}\,[(\mathsf{EX}\alpha) \,\mathsf{B}\, \beta]$
- $\mathsf{E}\,[[\alpha \,\underline{\mathsf{U}}\, \beta] \,\mathsf{B}\, \gamma] = \mathsf{E}\,[(\mathsf{E}\,[\alpha \,\underline{\mathsf{U}}\, \beta]) \,\mathsf{B}\, \gamma]$
- $\mathsf{E}\,[[\alpha \,\mathsf{B}\, \beta] \,\mathsf{B}\, \gamma] = \mathsf{E}\,[(\mathsf{E}\,[\alpha \,\mathsf{B}\, \beta]) \,\mathsf{B}\, \gamma]$
- $\mathsf{E}\,[\alpha \,\mathsf{B}\, \mathsf{X}\beta] = \alpha \wedge \neg\mathsf{AX}\beta \vee \mathsf{EXE}[(\neg\beta) \,\mathsf{U}\, (\alpha \wedge \neg\beta \wedge \neg\mathsf{AX}\beta)]$
- $\mathsf{E}\,[\alpha \,\mathsf{B}\, [\beta \,\underline{\mathsf{U}}\, \gamma]] = \mathsf{E}[(\neg\gamma) \,\mathsf{U}\, (\alpha \wedge \mathsf{E}[(\neg\beta) \,\mathsf{B}\, \gamma])]$
- $\mathsf{E}\,[\alpha \,\mathsf{B}\, [\beta \,\mathsf{B}\, \gamma]] = \mathsf{E}[(\neg\beta \vee \gamma) \,\underline{\mathsf{U}}\, (\alpha \wedge \mathsf{E}[(\neg\beta) \,\underline{\mathsf{U}}\, \gamma])] \vee \mathsf{EG}\,[(\neg\beta) \,\underline{\mathsf{U}}\, \gamma]$

Hence, all macro operators of CTL^2 can be reduced to simple CTL formulas apart from the last equation that contains the subformula $\mathsf{EG}\,[\alpha \,\underline{\mathsf{U}}\, \beta]$. It is not difficult to see that $\mathsf{EG}\,[\alpha \,\underline{\mathsf{U}}\, \beta]$ is equivalent to $\mathsf{E}(\mathsf{G}(\alpha \vee \beta) \wedge \mathsf{GF}\beta)$, so that we once more encounter the fixpoint that we have considered in Theorem 3.43 on page 165. Therefore, we obtain the following result:

Theorem 5.15 (Translating CTL^2 to μ-Calculus). *Every formula $\Phi \in \mathsf{CTL}^2$ can be translated to an equivalent μ-calculus formula Ψ of alternation depth not higher than 2 and size $O(|\Phi|)$.*

In fact, most formulas can be translated to the alternation-free μ-calculus. Only the nesting $\mathsf{E}\,[\alpha\ \mathsf{B}\ [\beta\ \mathsf{B}\ \gamma]]$ requires to generate a fixpoint of alternation depth 2. For this reason, CTL^2 is powerful enough to express $\mathsf{EGF}\varphi = \mathsf{E}[0\ \mathsf{B}\ [0\ \mathsf{B}\ \varphi]]$, which is not possible in CTL.

It is natural to consider generalizations CTL^n of CTL^2 that provide macro operators where at most n temporal operators can appear after a path quantifier. Clearly, we can do the same with CTL^n, i.e., we could list all possible macro operators, and translate them to the μ-calculus. We will thereby obtain μ-calculus formulas of alternation depth ≤ 2 and of a size that is determined by n. No matter what the relationship between the size of the fixpoint formulas is, it is constant for a fixed n. Hence, all logics CTL^n have a polynomial model checking procedure.

5.3.3 Eliminating Quantified Boolean Expressions

One distinction between the temporal logics that we have considered is that some allow Boolean operators to occur after a path quantifier, while other logics do not allow this. In this section, we prove that logics that differ in this kind of formulas have the same expressiveness, provided they have one binary temporal operator like $\underline{\mathsf{U}}$. Hence, for example, the logics, CTL^* and CTL^{++}, CTL^{+} and CTL, as well as $\mathsf{LeftCTL}^*$ and $\mathsf{LeftCTL}^{++}$, have the same expressiveness.

It must be noted however, that the transformation from the syntactically richer language to the weaker one gives a potentially enormous blow-up in the length of the formulas. The transformation we present here will turn a given formula of length n to an equivalent one of length $O(nn!)$. It can however be improved so that only an exponential blow-up occurs when common subformulas are shared.

The essential problem that has to be solved is that conjunctions can appear after a E quantifier. To see this, reduce any given temporal logic formula $\Phi \in \mathsf{CTL}^*$ first to the normal form $\mathsf{PQNF}(\Phi)$ (cf. 85), so that we only need to consider subformulas of the form $\mathsf{E}\Psi$ where Ψ contains no path quantifier. Computing further $\mathsf{TDNF}(\Psi)$ allows us then to shift the E quantifier over the eventually arising disjunctions by the law $\mathsf{E}[\varphi \vee \psi] = \mathsf{E}\varphi \vee \mathsf{E}\psi$. Some other laws of this kind are given in the next lemma.

Lemma 5.16. *Given arbitrary path formulas $\varphi, \psi, \Phi \in \mathsf{PF}_\Sigma$, and a state formula α, the following equations hold, where $\mathsf{E}_\Phi\varphi$ and $\mathsf{A}_\Phi\varphi$ are abbreviations for $\mathsf{E}[\Phi \wedge \varphi]$ and $\mathsf{A}[\Phi \rightarrow \varphi]$, respectively.*

$\models \mathsf{E}_\Phi\neg\varphi = \neg\mathsf{A}_\Phi\varphi$	$\models \mathsf{A}_\Phi\neg\varphi = \neg\mathsf{E}_\Phi\varphi$
$\models \mathsf{E}_\Phi\alpha = \mathsf{E}\Phi \wedge \alpha$	$\models \mathsf{A}_\Phi\alpha = \mathsf{E}\Phi \rightarrow \alpha$
$\models \mathsf{E}_\Phi(\alpha \wedge \varphi) = \alpha \wedge \mathsf{E}_\Phi\varphi$	$\models \mathsf{A}_\Phi(\alpha \wedge \varphi) = \alpha \wedge \mathsf{A}_\Phi\varphi$
$\models \mathsf{E}_\Phi(\varphi \vee \psi) = \mathsf{E}_\Phi\varphi \vee \mathsf{E}_\Phi\psi$	$\models \mathsf{A}_\Phi(\varphi \wedge \psi) = \mathsf{A}_\Phi\varphi \wedge \mathsf{A}_\Phi\psi$

Note that the special case $\Phi := 1$ does not allow us to replace $\mathsf{E}1$ with 1: $\mathsf{E}1$ holds in a given state iff there is an infinite path starting in that state. Hence, we could replace $\mathsf{E}1$ with Φ_{inf} (cf. page 106).

Hence, we only have to consider the problem that E may be applied to a conjunction of formulas that start with temporal operators. The next lemma is one of the major steps that are used to handle this problem. It shows that both top-level conjunctions and disjunctions of a temporal operator can be eliminated.

Lemma 5.17 (Eliminating Homogeneous Conjunctions and Disjunctions). *The equations below can be used to eliminate top-level conjunctions or disjunctions of a temporal operator. The conjunction or disjunction is replaced by an equivalent formula that has as top-level operator the corresponding temporal operator. Corresponding theorems also hold for the strong versions of the temporal operators (cf. Lemma 2.48).*

- $\bigwedge_{i=1}^{n} \mathsf{X}\varphi_i = \mathsf{X}\left(\bigwedge_{i=1}^{n} \varphi_i\right)$ *and* $\bigvee_{i=1}^{n} \mathsf{X}\varphi_i = \mathsf{X}\left(\bigvee_{i=1}^{n} \varphi_i\right)$
- $\bigwedge_{i=1}^{n} \mathsf{G}\varphi_i = \mathsf{G}\left(\bigwedge_{i=1}^{n} \varphi_i\right)$ *and* $\bigvee_{i=1}^{n} \mathsf{G}\psi_i = \mathsf{G}\left(\bigwedge_{i=1}^{n} \psi_i \vee \bigvee_{k=1,k\neq i}^{n} \mathsf{G}\psi_k\right)$
- $\bigwedge_{i=1}^{n} \mathsf{F}\psi_i = \mathsf{F}\left(\bigvee_{i=1}^{n} \psi_i \wedge \bigwedge_{k=1,k\neq i}^{n} \mathsf{F}\psi_k\right)$ *and* $\bigvee_{i=1}^{n} \mathsf{F}\varphi_i = \mathsf{F}\left(\bigvee_{i=1}^{n} \varphi_i\right)$
- $\bigwedge_{i=1}^{n} [\varphi_i \mathrel{\mathsf{W}} \psi_i] = \left[\left(\bigvee_{i=1}^{n} \varphi_i \wedge \psi_i \wedge \bigwedge_{k=1,k\neq i}^{n} [\varphi_k \mathrel{\mathsf{W}} \psi_k]\right) \mathrel{\mathsf{W}} \left(\bigvee_{k=1}^{n} \psi_k\right)\right]$
- $\bigvee_{i=1}^{n} [\varphi_i \mathrel{\mathsf{W}} \psi_i] = \left[\left(\bigwedge_{i=1}^{n} \varphi_i \vee \neg\psi_i \vee \bigvee_{k=1,k\neq i}^{n} [\varphi_k \mathrel{\mathsf{W}} \psi_k]\right) \mathrel{\mathsf{W}} \left(\bigvee_{k=1}^{n} \psi_k\right)\right]$
- $\bigwedge_{i=1}^{n} [\varphi_i \mathrel{\mathsf{U}} \psi_i] = \left[\left(\bigwedge_{k=1}^{n} \varphi_k\right) \mathrel{\mathsf{U}} \left(\bigvee_{i=1}^{n} \psi_i \wedge \bigwedge_{k=1,k\neq i}^{n} [\varphi_k \mathrel{\mathsf{U}} \psi_k]\right)\right]$
- $\bigvee_{i=1}^{n} [\varphi_i \mathrel{\mathsf{U}} \psi_i] = \left[\left(\bigwedge_{i=1}^{n} \varphi_i \vee \bigvee_{k=1,k\neq i}^{n} [\varphi_k \mathrel{\mathsf{U}} \psi_k]\right) \mathrel{\mathsf{U}} \left(\bigvee_{k=1}^{n} \psi_k\right)\right]$
- $\bigwedge_{i=1}^{n} [\psi_i \mathrel{\mathsf{B}} \varphi_i] = \left[\left(\bigvee_{i=1}^{n} \psi_i \wedge \bigwedge_{k=1,k\neq i}^{n} [\psi_k \mathrel{\mathsf{B}} \varphi_k]\right) \mathrel{\mathsf{B}} \left(\bigvee_{k=1}^{n} \varphi_k\right)\right]$
- $\bigvee_{i=1}^{n} [\psi_i \mathrel{\mathsf{B}} \varphi_i] = \left[\left(\bigvee_{k=1}^{n} \psi_k\right) \mathrel{\mathsf{B}} \left(\bigvee_{i=1}^{n} \varphi_i \wedge \neg \bigvee_{k=1,k\neq i}^{n} [\psi_k \mathrel{\mathsf{B}} \varphi_k]\right)\right]$

Note that the right hand sides can also be written as conjunctions or disjunctions by applying the rules below (again, corresponding rules do also hold for the strong ver-

sions of the temporal operators). This allows us to replace homogeneous conjunctions by disjunctions and homogeneous disjunctions by conjunctions of the same operator.

$$
\begin{aligned}
[\varphi_1\ \mathsf{W}\ \psi] \vee [\varphi_2\ \mathsf{W}\ \psi] &= [(\varphi_1 \vee \varphi_2)\ \mathsf{W}\ \psi] \\
[\varphi_1\ \mathsf{W}\ \psi] \wedge [\varphi_2\ \mathsf{W}\ \psi] &= [(\varphi_1 \wedge \varphi_2)\ \mathsf{W}\ \psi] \\
[\varphi\ \mathsf{U}\ \psi_1] \vee [\varphi\ \mathsf{U}\ \psi_2] &= [\varphi\ \mathsf{U}\ (\psi_1 \vee \psi_2)] \\
[\varphi_1\ \mathsf{U}\ \psi] \wedge [\varphi_2\ \mathsf{U}\ \psi] &= [(\varphi_1 \wedge \varphi_2)\ \mathsf{U}\ \psi] \\
[\varphi_1\ \mathsf{B}\ \psi] \vee [\varphi_2\ \mathsf{B}\ \psi] &= [(\varphi_1 \vee \varphi_2)\ \mathsf{B}\ \psi] \\
[\varphi\ \mathsf{B}\ \psi_1] \wedge [\varphi\ \mathsf{B}\ \psi_2] &= [\varphi\ \mathsf{B}\ (\psi_1 \vee \psi_2)]
\end{aligned}
$$

Proof. The rules for eliminating conjunctions are dual to the rules for eliminating disjunctions, as can be easily seen by negating both sides of the equations and producing negation normal form afterwards. Hence, it is sufficient to prove only the rules for conjunctions. These proofs follow the same scheme that is mainly based on case distinctions on which one of the signals ψ_i will occur first. For example, consider the equation of the W-operator. In the first case, consider the case that none of the ψ_i's will ever hold. Then all W-expressions on the left and on the right hand side evaluate to 1 such that the equation holds. Now, consider the case that at least one of the ψ_i's will hold at least once, and assume that ψ_{i_0} ($i_0 \in \{1, \ldots, n\}$) is the one that holds first and that t_0 is the first point of time where ψ_{i_0} holds. First, the implication from left to right is shown. Clearly, at t_0 both φ_{i_0} and ψ_{i_0} must hold, otherwise $[\varphi_{i_0}\ \mathsf{W}\ \psi_{i_0}]$ would not hold. Moreover $\bigwedge_{k=1,k\neq i_0}^{n} [\varphi_i\ \mathsf{W}\ \psi_i]$ must hold since, the other ψ_k's have not occurred so far. The implication from right to left is similarly proved. The subterm $\Phi_{i_0} := \varphi_{i_0} \wedge \psi_{i_0} \wedge \bigwedge_{k=1,k\neq i_0}^{n} [\varphi_k\ \mathsf{W}\ \psi_k]$ of the disjunction on the right hand side is sufficient for the proof: clearly, $\bigvee_{k=1}^{n} \psi_k$ also holds at t_0 and from Φ_{i_0} it can then be concluded that φ_{i_0} has to hold. Hence, $[\varphi_{i_0}\ \mathsf{W}\ \psi_{i_0}]$ holds. Moreover, from Φ_{i_0} it can be concluded that $\bigwedge_{k=1,k\neq i_0}^{n} [\varphi_k\ \mathsf{W}\ \psi_k]$ holds. As none of the events ψ_k with $k \neq i_0$ have occurred before t_0, this is equivalent to the left hand side. □

The complexity of the transformations in the above lemma is however not harmless: For example, the left hand side of the rule for the W-operator has a length of $O(\sum_{i=1}^{n} |\varphi_i| + |\psi_i|)$, but the right hand side has the size $O(n \cdot \sum_{i=1}^{n} |\varphi_i| + |\psi_i|)$. This does not seem to be a problem as only a linear factor n has been added. However, the rules must be applied repeatedly to shift an E quantifier inwards and the right hand side contains n subproblems of the same problem of size $n-1$. Hence, if all conjunctions are to be removed by recursively applying the equations of Lemma 5.17, then a formula of size n results in a formula of size $O(n \cdot n!)$. Better algorithms that keep track of common subformulas are given in Section 5.3.5.

The above rules can be used to combine conjunctions of formulas that start with the same temporal operators to a single formula that starts with that operator. It is also possible to combine *heterogeneous conjunctions*. This can be done by converting the binary operators into one and use the combination laws of the previous lemma. The only additional point is to keep track of the operator strength.

For example, to find a combination law for conjunctions of B and $\underline{\mathsf{U}}$, we first express $[\gamma_j \mathsf{B}\, \delta_j]$ as $[(\neg\delta_j) \mathsf{U} (\gamma_j \wedge \neg\delta_j)]$, and then use the combination law for $\underline{\mathsf{U}}$. If there are no $\underline{\mathsf{U}}$ operators, we simply obtain (by the combination law for U):

$$\bigwedge_{j=1}^{n} [\gamma_j \mathsf{B}\, \delta_j] = \left[\left(\bigwedge_{k=1}^{n} \neg\delta_k\right) \mathsf{U} \left(\bigvee_{k\in J} \gamma_k \wedge \neg\delta_k \wedge \bigwedge_{j=1,j\neq k}^{n} [\gamma_j \mathsf{B}\, \delta_j]\right)\right]$$

Hence, we obtain the following lemma for combining heterogeneous conjunctions:

Lemma 5.18 (Eliminating Heterogeneous Conjunctions). *Given* CTL* *path formulas* $\{\alpha_i \mid i \in I\}$, $\{\beta_i \mid i \in I\}$, $\{\gamma_j \mid j \in J\}$, *and* $\{\delta_j \mid j \in J\}$ *where* $I \neq \{\}$, *the following formula is equivalent to* $\left(\bigwedge_{i\in I} [\alpha_i \underline{\mathsf{U}}\, \beta_i]\right) \wedge \left(\bigwedge_{j\in J} [\gamma_j \mathsf{B}\, \delta_j]\right)$, *where we abbreviate* $\Phi_I := \bigwedge_{i\in I} \alpha_i$ *and* $\Psi_J := \bigwedge_{j\in J} \neg\delta_j$:

$$\left[(\Phi_I \wedge \Psi_J)\, \underline{\mathsf{U}} \left(\begin{array}{l} \bigvee_{k\in I} \beta_k \wedge \left(\bigwedge_{i\in I\setminus\{k\}} [\alpha_i \underline{\mathsf{U}}\, \beta_i]\right) \wedge \left(\bigwedge_{j\in J} [\gamma_j \mathsf{B}\, \delta_j]\right) \vee \\ \bigvee_{k\in J} \gamma_k \wedge \neg\delta_k \wedge \left(\bigwedge_{i\in I} [\alpha_i \underline{\mathsf{U}}\, \beta_i]\right) \wedge \left(\bigwedge_{j\in J\setminus\{k\}} [\gamma_j \mathsf{B}\, \delta_j]\right) \end{array}\right)\right]$$

In the case $I = \{\}$, *the following equation holds:*

$$\bigwedge_{j\in J} [\gamma_j \mathsf{B}\, \delta_j] = \left[\Psi_J \mathsf{U} \left(\bigvee_{k\in J} \gamma_k \wedge \neg\delta_k \wedge \bigwedge_{j\in J\setminus\{k\}} [\gamma_j \mathsf{B}\, \delta_j]\right)\right]$$

Using the above lemma, we will now prove that CTL*, LeftCTL*, CTL$^+$, and UB$^+$ can be translated to CTL^{++}, LeftCTL^{++}, CTL, and UB, respectively. All of these translations are based on the same principle that is given in the above lemmas, namely to make successive case distinctions on the order of the events that are awaited.

A first observation that is used for that transformation is that the logics CTL*, LeftCTL*, CTL$^+$, and UB$^+$ are robust w.r.t. to negation normal form computation, i.e., if the function given in Lemma 2.48 is applied to a formula Φ of one of these logics, it yields a formula NNF(Φ) of the same logic. The same holds for the extensions of these logics by fairness constraints, which is a more general result, which can be seen by choosing one fairness constraint that is simply 1.

Lemma 5.19 (NNF Robustness). *The logics defined in Definition 5.11, as well as their extensions by fairness constraints according to Definition 5.12 are closed with respect to negation normal form computation.*

For the proof, it is sufficient to notice that the rules given in Lemma 2.48 preserve membership in the mentioned logics, which can be straightforwardly done by case distinctions. The above lemma allows us therefore to assume in the following that the given formulas are in negation normal form, i.e., negations can be neglected.

The next step reduces the temporal operators G, F, W, U, $\underline{\mathsf{W}}$, $\underline{\mathsf{B}}$ to $\underline{\mathsf{U}}$ and B. This is straightforwardly done for the logics except for $\mathsf{FairLeftCTL}^{++}$, $\mathsf{LeftCTL}^{++}$, $\mathsf{FairLeftCTL}^{*}$ and $\mathsf{LeftCTL}^{*}$. For these logics, the replacement has to be done with some care: The problem is with the W and the $\underline{\mathsf{W}}$ operators. We have two rules for replacing W and the $\underline{\mathsf{W}}$ operators, as the following equations are valid:

$$[\varphi\ \mathsf{W}\ \psi] = [\psi\ \mathsf{B}\ (\neg\varphi \wedge \psi)] \qquad [\varphi\ \mathsf{W}\ \psi] = [(\neg\psi)\ \underline{\mathsf{U}}\ (\varphi \wedge \psi)] \vee [0\ \mathsf{B}\ \psi]$$

However, if $[\varphi\ \mathsf{W}\ \psi]$ is derivable from P_E, then the right hand side of the first equation is no $\mathsf{LeftCTL}^{*}$ formula, and if $[\varphi\ \mathsf{W}\ \psi]$ is derivable from P_A, then the right hand side of the second equation is no $\mathsf{LeftCTL}^{*}$ formula. Therefore, we have to consider for the replacement of W formulas, whether we have to replace a formula that is derived from the nonterminal P_E or from P_A. This is essentially shown in the next lemma.

Lemma 5.20 (Temporal Bases for $\mathsf{FairLeftCTL}^{*}$). *The following temporal operator bases can be used for $\mathsf{FairLeftCTL}^{*}$:*

1. *For each $\mathsf{FairLeftCTL}^{*}$ formula there is an equivalent $\mathsf{FairLeftCTL}^{*}$ formula in NNF where only the temporal operators $\mathsf{X}\cdot$, $[\cdot\ \underline{\mathsf{U}}\ \cdot]$ and $[\cdot\ \mathsf{B}\ \cdot]$ occur.*
2. *For each $\mathsf{FairLeftCTL}^{*}$ formula there is an equivalent $\mathsf{FairLeftCTL}^{*}$ formula in NNF where only the temporal operators $\mathsf{X}\cdot$, $[\cdot\ \mathsf{U}\ \cdot]$ and $[\cdot\ \underline{\mathsf{B}}\ \cdot]$ occur.*

Proof. The first item is proved by the following rules that can be used to replace some grammar rules for P_A and P_E:

$P_A ::= \{[\cdot\ \underline{\mathsf{U}}\ \cdot], [\cdot\ \mathsf{B}\ \cdot]\}$	$P_E ::= \{[\cdot\ \underline{\mathsf{U}}\ \cdot], [\cdot\ \mathsf{B}\ \cdot]\}$
$\mathsf{G}P_A = [0\ \mathsf{B}\ (\neg P_A)]$	$\mathsf{G}S = [0\ \mathsf{B}\ (\neg S)]$
$\mathsf{F}S = [1\ \underline{\mathsf{U}}\ S]$	$\mathsf{F}P_E = [1\ \underline{\mathsf{U}}\ P_E]$
$[P_A\ \mathsf{W}\ S] = [S\ \mathsf{B}\ (\neg P_A \wedge S)]$	$[P_E\ \mathsf{W}\ S] = [(\neg S)\ \underline{\mathsf{U}}\ (P_E \wedge S)] \vee [0\ \mathsf{B}\ S]$
$[P_A\ \underline{\mathsf{W}}\ S] = [S\ \mathsf{B}\ (\neg P_A \wedge S)] \wedge [1\ \underline{\mathsf{U}}\ S]$	$[P_E\ \underline{\mathsf{W}}\ S] = [(\neg S)\ \underline{\mathsf{U}}\ (P_E \wedge S)]$
$[P_A\ \mathsf{U}\ S] = [P_A\ \underline{\mathsf{U}}\ S] \vee [0\ \mathsf{B}\ (\neg P_A)]$	$[S\ \mathsf{U}\ P_E] = [S\ \underline{\mathsf{U}}\ P_E] \vee [0\ \mathsf{B}\ (\neg S)]$
$[S\ \underline{\mathsf{B}}\ P_E] = [S\ \mathsf{B}\ P_E] \wedge [1\ \underline{\mathsf{U}}\ S]$	$[P_E\ \underline{\mathsf{B}}\ S] = [P_E\ \mathsf{B}\ S] \wedge [1\ \underline{\mathsf{U}}\ P_E]$

The second item is proved by the following rules that can be used to replace some grammar rules for P_A and P_E such that only $[\cdot\ \mathsf{U}\ \cdot]$ and $[\cdot\ \underline{\mathsf{B}}\ \cdot]$ occur apart from X:

$P_A ::= \{[\cdot\ \mathsf{U}\ \cdot], [\cdot\ \underline{\mathsf{B}}\ \cdot]\}$	$P_E ::= \{[\cdot\ \mathsf{U}\ \cdot], [\cdot\ \underline{\mathsf{B}}\ \cdot]\}$
$\mathsf{G}P_A = [P_A\ \mathsf{U}\ 0]$	$\mathsf{G}S = [S\ \mathsf{U}\ 0]$
$\mathsf{F}S = [S\ \underline{\mathsf{B}}\ 0]$	$\mathsf{F}P_E = [P_E\ \underline{\mathsf{B}}\ 0]$
$[P_A\ \mathsf{W}\ S] = [S\ \underline{\mathsf{B}}\ (\neg P_A \wedge S)] \vee [(\neg S)\ \mathsf{U}\ 0]$	$[P_E\ \mathsf{W}\ S] = [(\neg S)\ \mathsf{U}\ (P_E \wedge S)]$
$[P_A\ \underline{\mathsf{W}}\ S] = [S\ \underline{\mathsf{B}}\ (\neg P_A \wedge S)]$	$[P_E\ \underline{\mathsf{W}}\ S] = [(\neg S)\ \mathsf{U}\ (P_E \wedge S)] \wedge [S\ \underline{\mathsf{B}}\ 0]$
$[P_A\ \underline{\mathsf{U}}\ S] = [P_A\ \mathsf{U}\ S] \wedge [S\ \underline{\mathsf{B}}\ 0]$	$[S\ \underline{\mathsf{U}}\ P_E] = [S\ \mathsf{U}\ P_E] \wedge [P_E\ \underline{\mathsf{B}}\ 0]$
$[S\ \mathsf{B}\ P_E] = [S\ \underline{\mathsf{B}}\ P_E] \vee [(\neg P_E)\ \mathsf{U}\ 0]$	$[P_E\ \mathsf{B}\ S] = [P_E\ \underline{\mathsf{B}}\ S] \vee [(\neg S)\ \mathsf{U}\ 0]$

Using these rules, every occurrence of the other temporal operators can be eliminated. Note that if the left hand side in the above rules belongs to P_A or P_E, then the right hand side also belongs to P_A or P_E, respectively. As $\neg [a\ \underline{\mathsf{U}}\ b] = [(\neg a)\ \mathsf{B}\ b]$, $\neg [a\ \mathsf{B}\ b] = [(\neg a)\ \underline{\mathsf{U}}\ b]$, $\neg [a\ \mathsf{U}\ b] = [(\neg a)\ \underline{\mathsf{B}}\ b]$, and $\neg [a\ \underline{\mathsf{B}}\ b] = [(\neg a)\ \mathsf{U}\ b]$ hold, the negation normal form computation does not reintroduce one of the eliminated operators. □

Using the above lemmas, we can now to prove that CTL*, FairLeftCTL*, LeftCTL*, FairCTL$^+$, and CTL$^+$, are as expressive as the corresponding logics CTL^{++}, FairLeftCTL^{++}, LeftCTL^{++}, FairCTL, and CTL, respectively.

Theorem 5.21. *The logics* CTL*, FairLeftCTL*, LeftCTL*, FairCTL$^+$, *and* CTL$^+$ *can be reduced to the corresponding subsets* CTL^{++}, FairLeftCTL^{++}, LeftCTL^{++}, FairCTL, *and* CTL, *respectively.*

Proof. We use the following replacement laws to remove the temporal operators $\mathsf{G}\cdot$, $\mathsf{F}\cdot$, $[\cdot\ \mathsf{U}\ \cdot]$, $[\cdot\ \mathsf{W}\ \cdot]$, $[\cdot\ \underline{\mathsf{W}}\ \cdot]$, $[\cdot\ \underline{\mathsf{B}}\ \cdot]$ (in case of FairLeftCTL* and LeftCTL*, we take special care in case of the W and $\underline{\mathsf{W}}$ operators, as given in the previous theorem):

$$\begin{array}{ll}
\mathsf{G}\varphi = [0\ \mathsf{B}\ (\neg\varphi)] & \mathsf{F}\varphi = [1\ \underline{\mathsf{U}}\ \varphi] \\
[\varphi\ \mathsf{U}\ \psi] = [\varphi\ \underline{\mathsf{U}}\ \psi] \vee [0\ \mathsf{B}\ (\neg\varphi)] & [\varphi\ \underline{\mathsf{B}}\ \psi] = [\varphi\ \mathsf{B}\ \psi] \wedge [1\ \underline{\mathsf{U}}\ \varphi] \\
[\varphi\ \mathsf{W}\ \psi] = [(\neg\psi)\ \underline{\mathsf{U}}\ (\varphi\wedge\psi)] \vee [0\ \mathsf{B}\ \psi] & [\varphi\ \underline{\mathsf{W}}\ \psi] = [(\neg\psi)\ \underline{\mathsf{U}}\ (\varphi\wedge\psi)] \\
[\varphi\ \mathsf{W}\ \psi] = [\psi\ \mathsf{B}\ (\neg\varphi\wedge\psi)] & [\varphi\ \underline{\mathsf{W}}\ \psi] = [\psi\ \mathsf{B}\ (\neg\varphi\wedge\psi)] \wedge [1\ \underline{\mathsf{U}}\ \psi]
\end{array}$$

The resulting formula Φ belongs still to the same logic. After this, we compute $\mathsf{PQNF}(\Phi)$ of the obtained formula Φ, so that *it remains to consider formulas* $\mathsf{E}\varphi$ *(or* $\mathsf{E}_\Phi\varphi$*) of the same logic where* φ *does not contain any path quantifier. For these formulas, we prove the transformation by an induction over the maximal number of nestings of temporal operators in* φ. The base case, where φ is propositional is handled by Lemma 5.16: $\mathsf{E}_\Phi\varphi = \varphi\wedge\mathsf{E}_\Phi 1$. In this case, there are $n+1$ temporal operators in φ, and we compute $\mathsf{TDNF}(\varphi)$ and shift E (or E_Φ) over possibly obtained disjunctions. Hence, we have now obtained a formula of the following form, where for CTL*, LeftCTL*, and CTL$^+$ the fairness constraint Φ is not apparent and the formulas e_j are state formulas (as no path quantifier can occur in e_j, it even follows that e_j is propositional):

$$\mathsf{E}_\Phi\left(\bigwedge_{j=1}^{n_1}[a_j\ \underline{\mathsf{U}}\ b_j]\wedge\bigwedge_{j=1}^{n_2}[c_j\ \mathsf{B}\ d_j]\wedge\bigwedge_{j=1}^{n_3}e_j\wedge\bigwedge_{j=1}^{n_4}\mathsf{X}f_j\right)$$

We now shift the X operator over the conjunction, and abbreviate $e := \bigwedge_{j=1}^{n_3} e_j$ and $f := \bigwedge_{j=1}^{n_4} f_j$. Moreover, we use Lemma 5.16 to obtain the following formula:

$$e\wedge\mathsf{E}_\Phi\left(\bigwedge_{j=1}^{n_1}[a_j\ \underline{\mathsf{U}}\ b_j]\wedge\bigwedge_{j=1}^{n_2}[c_j\ \mathsf{B}\ d_j]\wedge\mathsf{X}f\right)$$

Note that we can still not apply the induction hypothesis, since it may be the case that the maximal nesting of temporal operators is still the same. We now use Lemma 5.18 to convert the subformula $\bigwedge_{j=1}^{n_1} [a_j \ \underline{\mathsf{U}}\ b_j] \wedge \bigwedge_{j=1}^{n_2} [c_j \ \mathsf{B}\ d_j]$ to an equivalent one of the form $\left[\varphi \ \underline{\mathsf{U}}\ \left(\bigvee_{i\in I} \psi_i\right)\right]$ (in case $n_1 > 0$) or of the form $\left[\varphi \ \mathsf{U}\ \left(\bigvee_{i\in I} \psi_i\right)\right]$ (in case $n_1 = 0$ and $n_2 > 0$). In both cases, we proceed in the same manner (we only list one case):

In the case $n_1 > 0$, we have to convert $\mathsf{E}_\Phi \left(\left[\varphi \ \underline{\mathsf{U}}\ \left(\bigvee_{i\in I} \psi_i\right)\right] \wedge \mathsf{X} f\right)$. We use the distributive law $\left[\varphi \ \underline{\mathsf{U}}\ \left(\bigvee_{i\in I} \psi_i\right)\right] = \bigvee_{i\in I} [\varphi \ \underline{\mathsf{U}}\ \psi_i]$ and the recursion law $[\varphi \ \underline{\mathsf{U}}\ \psi_i] = \psi_i \vee \varphi \wedge \mathsf{X}\, [\varphi \ \underline{\mathsf{U}}\ \psi_i]$, distributive laws of $\wedge$ and $\vee$, and once again Lemma 5.16 to obtain:

$$
\begin{aligned}
&\mathsf{E}_\Phi \left(\left[\varphi \ \underline{\mathsf{U}}\ \left(\textstyle\bigvee_{i\in I} \psi_i\right)\right] \wedge \mathsf{X} f\right)\\
&\quad \Leftrightarrow \mathsf{E}_\Phi \textstyle\bigvee_{i\in I} \left([\varphi \ \underline{\mathsf{U}}\ \psi_i] \wedge \mathsf{X} f\right)\\
&\quad \Leftrightarrow \textstyle\bigvee_{i\in I} \mathsf{E}_\Phi \left([\varphi \ \underline{\mathsf{U}}\ \psi_i] \wedge \mathsf{X} f\right)\\
&\quad \Leftrightarrow \textstyle\bigvee_{i\in I} \mathsf{E}_\Phi \left(\psi_i \wedge \mathsf{X} f\right) \vee \mathsf{E}_\Phi \left(\varphi \wedge \mathsf{X}\left[[\varphi \ \underline{\mathsf{U}}\ \psi_i] \wedge f\right]\right)
\end{aligned}
$$

Hence, the repeated application of the above transformation steps eliminate each conjunction that appears after an E quantifier. □

We remark here that it is not possible to use the transformation that is used in the above proof for transforming the logic UB^+ to the corresponding logic UB. We can apply similar transformation steps as given in the above proof and obtain then formulas of the form $\mathsf{E}\left(\bigwedge_{j=1}^{n} \mathsf{F} a_j \wedge \mathsf{G} b \wedge \mathsf{X} f\right)$, where a_j, b, and f is propositional. Using Lemma 5.17, we can now replace $\bigwedge_{j=1}^{n_1} \mathsf{F} a_j$ by a disjunction of F formulas, and using distributive laws and, once more, Lemma 5.16 will reduce the problem further to subproblems of the form $\mathsf{E}[\mathsf{F} a \wedge \mathsf{G} b \wedge \mathsf{X} f]$. The problem is now that we can neither combine $\mathsf{F} a \wedge \mathsf{G} b$ to a F nor to a G formula. However, we can reduce it as follows: $\mathsf{F} a \wedge \mathsf{G} b = [b \ \underline{\mathsf{U}}\ (a \wedge \mathsf{G} b)]$, and prove thus that UB^+ can be reduced to CTL which is however subsumed by the above theorem since $\mathsf{UB}^+ \subseteq \mathsf{CTL}^+$ holds.

5.3.4 Adding Path Quantifiers

In the previous section, we have solved one of the problems that distinguishes some temporal logics, by presenting a transformation that allows us to eliminate Boolean operators that occur directly after a path quantifier. The remaining problem is that some logics allow only state formulas as arguments of temporal operators, and not general path formulas. For example, in CTL^{++} each path quantifier precedes a temporal operator, but not vice versa, while in CTL the converse is also true. $\mathsf{LeftCTL}^{++}$ is even more restricted than CTL^{++} since path formulas are only allowed on one side of a temporal binary operator. The following theorem is the background for the definition of the languages $\mathsf{LeftCTL}^{++}$, $\mathsf{LeftCTL}^*$, and $\mathsf{FairLeftCTL}^*$:

Theorem 5.22 (Adding Path Quantifiers). *For all path formulas φ and all state formulas ψ, the following equations hold for any fairness constraint $\Phi := \bigwedge_{i=1}^{n} \mathsf{GF}\alpha_i$ with propositional α_i:*

(1) $\models \mathsf{E}_\Phi\mathsf{X}\varphi = \mathsf{E}_\Phi\mathsf{X}\mathsf{E}_\Phi\varphi$	(2) $\models \mathsf{A}_\Phi\mathsf{X}\varphi = \mathsf{A}_\Phi\mathsf{X}\mathsf{A}_\Phi\varphi$
(3) $\models \mathsf{E}_\Phi\mathsf{F}\varphi = \mathsf{E}_\Phi\mathsf{F}\mathsf{E}_\Phi\varphi$	(4) $\models \mathsf{A}_\Phi\mathsf{G}\varphi = \mathsf{A}_\Phi\mathsf{G}\mathsf{A}_\Phi\varphi$
(5) $\models \mathsf{E}_\Phi\,[\varphi\ \mathsf{W}\ \psi] = \mathsf{E}_\Phi\,[(\mathsf{E}_\Phi\varphi)\ \mathsf{W}\ \psi]$	(6) $\models \mathsf{A}_\Phi\,[\varphi\ \mathsf{W}\ \psi] = \mathsf{A}_\Phi\,[(\mathsf{A}_\Phi\varphi)\ \mathsf{W}\ \psi]$
(7) $\models \mathsf{E}_\Phi\,[\varphi\ \underline{\mathsf{W}}\ \psi] = \mathsf{E}_\Phi\,[(\mathsf{E}_\Phi\varphi)\ \underline{\mathsf{W}}\ \psi]$	(8) $\models \mathsf{A}_\Phi\,[\varphi\ \underline{\mathsf{W}}\ \psi] = \mathsf{A}_\Phi\,[(\mathsf{A}_\Phi\varphi)\ \underline{\mathsf{W}}\ \psi]$
(9) $\models \mathsf{E}_\Phi\,[\psi\ \mathsf{U}\ \varphi] = \mathsf{E}_\Phi\,[\psi\ \mathsf{U}\ (\mathsf{E}_\Phi\varphi)]$	(10) $\models \mathsf{A}_\Phi\,[\varphi\ \mathsf{U}\ \psi] = \mathsf{A}_\Phi\,[(\mathsf{A}_\Phi\varphi)\ \mathsf{U}\ \psi]$
(11) $\models \mathsf{E}_\Phi\,[\psi\ \underline{\mathsf{U}}\ \varphi] = \mathsf{E}_\Phi\,[\psi\ \underline{\mathsf{U}}\ (\mathsf{E}_\Phi\varphi)]$	(12) $\models \mathsf{A}_\Phi\,[\varphi\ \underline{\mathsf{U}}\ \psi] = \mathsf{A}_\Phi\,[(\mathsf{A}_\Phi\varphi)\ \underline{\mathsf{U}}\ \psi]$
(13) $\models \mathsf{E}_\Phi\,[\varphi\ \mathsf{B}\ \psi] = \mathsf{E}_\Phi\,[(\mathsf{E}_\Phi\varphi)\ \mathsf{B}\ \psi]$	(14) $\models \mathsf{A}_\Phi\,[\psi\ \mathsf{B}\ \varphi] = \mathsf{A}_\Phi\,[\psi\ \mathsf{B}\ (\mathsf{E}_\Phi\varphi)]$
(15) $\models \mathsf{E}_\Phi\,[\varphi\ \underline{\mathsf{B}}\ \psi] = \mathsf{E}_\Phi\,[(\mathsf{E}_\Phi\varphi)\ \underline{\mathsf{B}}\ \psi]$	(16) $\models \mathsf{A}_\Phi\,[\psi\ \underline{\mathsf{B}}\ \varphi] = \mathsf{A}_\Phi\,[\psi\ \underline{\mathsf{B}}\ (\mathsf{E}_\Phi\varphi)]$

The equations (10) and (12) do also hold if ψ is a path formula.

The proof of the equations is straightforward. In case of binary temporal operators the preceding path quantifier can be shifted to one of the arguments, so that this subformula is converted to a state formula. The logics $\mathsf{LeftCTL}^{++}$, $\mathsf{LeftCTL}^*$, and $\mathsf{FairLeftCTL}^*$ are defined in such a way that the above laws can be applied, i.e., that one of the arguments of the binary temporal operators is a state formula. Hence, together with the transformation of the previous section, the rewriting with the equations of Theorem 5.22 yields in pure CTL or FairCTL formulas.

Note that it is not possible to generalize the above equations. In particular, it is not possible to shift the path quantifier to both arguments. Otherwise we could transform every CTL^* formula into an equivalent CTL formula, which is however not possible since CTL^* is more expressive than CTL. Also, it is important to see that the condition in Theorem 5.22 that the formula ψ has to be a state formula is necessary. In particular, the following lemma holds:

Lemma 5.23. *In general, the following formulas are not valid:*

(1) $\not\models \mathsf{E}[(\mathsf{E}\varphi)\ \mathsf{W}\ \psi] \rightarrow \mathsf{E}[\varphi\ \mathsf{W}\ \psi]$	(2) $\not\models \mathsf{A}[\varphi\ \mathsf{W}\ \psi] \rightarrow \mathsf{A}[(\mathsf{A}\varphi)\ \mathsf{W}\ \psi]$
(3) $\not\models \mathsf{E}[(\mathsf{E}\varphi)\ \underline{\mathsf{W}}\ \psi] \rightarrow \mathsf{E}[\varphi\ \underline{\mathsf{W}}\ \psi]$	(4) $\not\models \mathsf{A}[\varphi\ \underline{\mathsf{W}}\ \psi] \rightarrow \mathsf{A}[(\mathsf{A}\varphi)\ \underline{\mathsf{W}}\ \psi]$
(5) $\not\models \mathsf{E}[\varphi\ \mathsf{U}\ (\mathsf{E}\psi)] \rightarrow \mathsf{E}[\varphi\ \mathsf{U}\ \psi]$	(6) $\not\models \mathsf{E}[\varphi\ \underline{\mathsf{U}}\ (\mathsf{E}\psi)] \rightarrow \mathsf{E}[\varphi\ \underline{\mathsf{U}}\ \psi]$
(7) $\not\models \mathsf{EGE}\varphi \rightarrow \mathsf{EG}\varphi$	(8) $\not\models \mathsf{AF}\varphi \rightarrow \mathsf{AFA}\varphi$
(9) $\not\models \mathsf{E}[\varphi\ \mathsf{W}\ (\mathsf{E}\psi)] \rightarrow \mathsf{E}[\varphi\ \mathsf{W}\ \psi]$	(10) $\not\models \mathsf{E}[\varphi\ \underline{\mathsf{W}}\ (\mathsf{E}\psi)] \rightarrow \mathsf{E}[\varphi\ \underline{\mathsf{W}}\ \psi]$
(11) $\not\models \mathsf{E}[\varphi\ \mathsf{W}\ \psi] \rightarrow \mathsf{E}[\varphi\ \mathsf{W}\ (\mathsf{E}\psi)]$	(12) $\not\models \mathsf{E}[\varphi\ \underline{\mathsf{W}}\ \psi] \rightarrow \mathsf{E}[\varphi\ \underline{\mathsf{W}}\ (\mathsf{E}\psi)]$

(11) and (12) do not even hold under the additional restriction that φ is a state formula, but (9) and (10) hold in this case.

Proof. Consider state s_0 in the Kripke structure $\mathcal{K}$ in Figure 5.5. There are exactly two paths starting in state s_0. It is easy to see that on the one hand $(\mathcal{K}, s_0) \not\models \mathsf{E}[(\mathsf{F}a)\ \mathsf{W}\ (\mathsf{G}b)]$ holds, but on the other hand we have $(\mathcal{K}, s_0) \models \mathsf{E}[(\mathsf{EF}a)\ \mathsf{W}\ (\mathsf{G}b)]$ since $(\mathcal{K}, s_0) \models \mathsf{EF}a$ holds. This is due to the fact that the E path quantifier inside the W-expression allows us to choose the right path

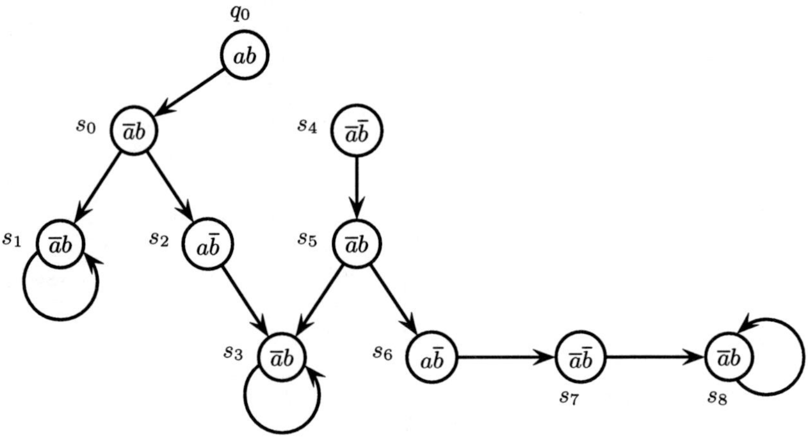

Fig. 5.5. A Kripke structure for disproving some formulas.

in state s_0 while the entire formula holds on the left hand path of s_0. Hence, (1) is disproved. We can disprove (3) by exchanging W by $\underline{\mathsf{W}}$ in the previous argumentation. (2) and (4) can be reduced to (3) and (1), respectively by the identity $\neg [\varphi \;\mathsf{W}\; \psi] = [(\neg\varphi) \;\underline{\mathsf{W}}\; \psi]$.

Now, consider state s_4 in Figure 5.5. Again there are two paths starting in state s_4. It can easily be seen that $(\mathcal{K}, s_4) \not\models \mathsf{E}[(\mathsf{F}a) \;\mathsf{U}\; (\mathsf{G}b)]$, but on the other hand $(\mathcal{K}, s_4) \models \mathsf{E}[(\mathsf{F}a) \;\mathsf{U}\; (\mathsf{EG}b)]$. The latter holds since we can choose in state s_5 the left alternative to validate $(\mathcal{K}, s_5) \models \mathsf{EG}b$, while the right alternative is chosen to satisfy the entire formula. Hence, (6) is disproved and the same argumentation also disproves (5).

Clearly, $\mathsf{EG}\varphi \rightarrow \mathsf{EGE}\varphi$ does hold. Hence, if (7) also holds then we could reduce $\mathsf{EGF}a$ to $\mathsf{EGEF}a$. However, this is a CTL formula, which contradicts the fact that no CTL formula is equivalent to $\mathsf{EGF}a$ [162]. (8) can be reduced to (7) by contraposition and pushing negation symbols inwards and outwards.

To disprove (11) and (12) consider state q_0: $(\mathcal{K}, q_0) \models \mathsf{E}[(\neg a) \;\mathsf{W}\; (\mathsf{G}b)]$ holds, since $[(\neg a) \;\mathsf{W}\; (\mathsf{G}b)]$ holds on the path $(q_0, s_0, s_2, s_3, \ldots)$. On the other hand, $(\mathcal{K}, q_0) \not\models \mathsf{E}[(\neg a) \;\mathsf{W}\; (\mathsf{EG}b)]$, since $(\mathcal{K}, q_0) \models \mathsf{EG}b$ holds (because of $(\mathcal{K}, (q_0, s_0, s_1, \ldots) \models \mathsf{G}b)$, but $(\mathcal{K}, q_0) \not\models \neg a)$. The same argumentation disproves (12) when W is exchanged by $\underline{\mathsf{W}}$.

To disprove (9) and (10), note again that $(\mathcal{K}, s_0) \not\models \mathsf{E}[(\mathsf{F}a) \;\mathsf{W}\; (\mathsf{G}b)]$. On the other hand $(\mathcal{K}, s_0) \models \mathsf{E}[(\mathsf{F}a) \;\mathsf{W}\; (\mathsf{EG}b)]$ holds, since $[(\mathsf{F}a) \;\mathsf{W}\; (\mathsf{EG}b)]$ holds along the path $s_0, s_2, s_3, \ldots$ (because $(\mathcal{K}, s_0) \models \mathsf{EG}b$ and $(\mathcal{K}, (s_0, s_2, s_3, \ldots)) \models \mathsf{F}a$). The same argumentation disproves (10) when W is exchanged by $\underline{\mathsf{W}}$. □

As the above formulas do not hold, path quantifiers can not be added on both sides of a binary temporal operator and the restriction that ψ must be a state formula is necessary in Theorem 5.22. It is also not possible to add a path quantifier on the right side of the W-operator as shown by the formulas (9), (10), (11) and (12).

We have used fairness constraints of the form $\bigwedge_{j=1}^{f} \mathsf{GF}\alpha_i$ in our logics. We can even extend the above results to more general fairness constraints, namely to Boolean combinations of formulas $\mathsf{GF}\alpha_i$ with propositional formulas α_i. In this case, we proceed as follows: Given a formula $\Phi \in \mathsf{FairLeftCTL}^*$, we compute $\mathsf{PQNF}(\Phi)$ (cf. Figure 2.11), so that we only have to consider subformulas of the form $\mathsf{E}_\Phi\Psi$ of that logic where Ψ contains no path quantifiers. We now replace $\mathsf{E}_\Phi\Psi$ by $\mathsf{E}(\Phi \wedge \Psi)$, i.e., no longer treat E_Φ as a special path quantifier, and instead shift the fairness constraint to the quantified formula. We now transform Φ into $\mathsf{TDNF}(\Phi)$ (cf. Figure 2.12), and apply Lemma 5.16, so that we obtain a formula of the following form:

$$\bigvee_{i=0}^{n} \mathsf{E}\left(\bigwedge_{j=0}^{p_i} \mathsf{GF}\varphi_{i,j} \wedge \bigwedge_{j=0}^{q_i} \mathsf{FG}\psi_{i,j} \wedge \Psi\right)$$

Using the law $\bigwedge_{j=0}^{q_i} \mathsf{FG}\psi_{i,j} = \mathsf{FG} \bigwedge_{j=0}^{q_i} \psi_{i,j}$, we combine the negated fairness constraints $\mathsf{FG}\psi_{i,j}$ and obtain the following formula:

$$\bigvee_{i=0}^{n} \mathsf{E}\left(\underbrace{\left(\bigwedge_{j=0}^{p_i} \mathsf{GF}\varphi_{i,j}\right)}_{=:\Phi'} \wedge \underbrace{\left(\mathsf{FG} \bigwedge_{j=0}^{q_i} \psi_{i,j} \wedge \Psi\right)}_{=:\Psi'}\right)$$

With the above abbreviations, we have therefore obtained a formula $\mathsf{E}_{\Phi'}\Psi'$ with fairness constraints Φ' in the normal form $\bigwedge_{j=0}^{p_i} \mathsf{GF}\varphi_{i,j}$. Note now that Ψ' is a P_E formula if and only if Ψ is a P_E formula. Hence, this proves that we can convert any $\mathsf{FairLeftCTL}^*$ formula with general fairness constraints to one with fairness constraints in the mentioned normal form. For these formulas, we can then apply the rules given in Theorem 5.22.

For the logic FairCTL the same reduction can be performed. However, we then obtain a formula $\mathsf{E}_{\Phi'}\Psi'$, where Ψ' does not belong to a legal path formula of FairCTL, since it may start with a conjunction. In the previous section, we have however seen, that these conjunctions can be removed so that we finally end up with a FairCTL formula.

5.3.5 Translating LeftCTL* to Vectorized μ-Calculus

We have already seen how $\mathsf{LeftCTL}^*$ can be reduced to $\mathsf{LeftCTL}^+$ and even to CTL. Hence, we can use CTL model checking tools to construct a model checking tool for $\mathsf{LeftCTL}^*$. However, the complexity of the presented transformation has a big drawback: in each one of the rules of Lemma 5.17, the right hand side contains n subproblems of the same kind of size $n-1$. Therefore, the rules have to be applied $n-1$ times for the formulas on the left hand sides such that a formula larger than $O(n!)$ is obtained. The combination of the presented transformation procedure with a CTL model checking procedure yields therefore a LeftCTL* model checking procedure whose complexity is also higher than $O(n!)$.

In this section, we therefore consider an optimization of the transformation from LeftCTL* to CTL. In particular, we will prove that the factorial blow-up of the naive transformation can be avoided by sharing subformulas in the generated formulas. The resulting transformation has then a complexity of $O(n2^{2n})$, i.e., it is exponential and therefore a strong improvement on the naive approach. Sharing of subformulas can be 'implemented' by translating to the vectorized μ-calculus instead of translating to CTL. Nevertheless, we will use the CTL operators in the following equation systems, even when we call them μ-calculus formulas.

The outline of this section is as follows: first, we will illustrate the drawback of the naive transformation by an example that leads to a factorial blow-up. After this, we define the new transformation procedure and prove its correctness in detail.

Illustrating Example

Consider the transformation of the LeftCTL* formula $\mathsf{E}\bigwedge_{i=1}^{n} \mathsf{F}a_i$ to an equivalent CTL formula according to the transformations presented so far. The problem is to shift the path quantifier E over the conjunction to the temporal operators. The essential idea of Lemma 5.17 in solving this problem was to make case distinctions on *all possible orders* of the events a_i. The conjunction is thereby turned into a disjunction where all permutations of $\{a_1, \ldots, a_n\}$ have to be considered. Having transformed the conjunction into a disjunction, the preceding E path quantifier can then be shifted inwards and duplicated for each F operator. For this reason, the following formula can be seen as a naive result of the transformation of $\mathsf{E}\bigwedge_{i=1}^{n} \mathsf{F}a_i$, where P_n is the set of all permutations of the numbers $1, \ldots, n$:

$$\mathsf{E}\bigwedge_{i=1}^{n} \mathsf{F}a_i = \bigvee_{\pi \in P_n} \mathsf{EF}\left(a_{\pi(1)} \wedge \mathsf{EF}\left(a_{\pi(2)} \wedge \ldots \wedge \mathsf{EF}\left(a_{\pi(n-1)} \wedge \mathsf{EF}a_{\pi(n)}\right) \ldots\right)\right)$$

It is easily seen that the length of the right hand size is of order $O(n \cdot n!)$. For this reason, the translation procedure from LeftCTL* to CTL has a worst case complexity that is higher than the exponential complexity obtained from corresponding translations to ω-automata (next section). This different complexity is due to the fact that automata benefit from sharing common situations in the form of separate states. We will show now that we can do the same by abbreviating common subformulas. Let us therefore consider where common subformulas arise in the translation procedure. The procedure repeatedly applies the following rule (cf. Lemma 5.17):

$$\bigwedge_{i=1}^{n} \mathsf{F} a_i = \mathsf{F} \bigvee_{i=1}^{n} \left(a_i \wedge \bigwedge_{l=1, l \neq i}^{n} \mathsf{F} a_l \right)$$

After the first application of the rule, n different subproblems of the size $n - 1$ are obtained. Multiple rule applications of this rule generate equivalent subformulas. To see this, consider two successive rule applications:

$$\bigwedge_{i=1}^{n} \mathsf{F} a_i = \mathsf{F} \left(\bigvee_{i=1}^{n} a_i \wedge \mathsf{F} \left(\bigvee_{j=1, j \neq i}^{n} a_j \wedge \bigwedge_{l=1, l \notin \{i,j\}}^{n} \mathsf{F} a_l \right) \right)$$

Let us abbreviate for every subset $I \subseteq \{1, \ldots, n\}$ the subformula $\bigwedge_{k=1, k \notin I}^{n} \mathsf{F} a_k$ as φ_I. It is easily seen that each $\varphi_{\{p,q\}}$ occurs twice on the right hand side, for the values $(i, j) = (p, q)$ and $(i, j) = (q, p)$, since the order of the previous events a_i and a_j does not matter for this term. Hence, the interleaving of the previous event history can be neglected; all that matters is which of the events occurred. Sharing the subformula $\varphi_{\{p,q\}}$ would halve the size of the formula.

The procedure has to be recursively applied to the subformulas $\varphi_{\{p,q\}}$. The application to different formulas $\varphi_{\{p,q\}}$ and $\varphi_{\{p,r\}}$ will then generate more common subformulas, namely $\varphi_{\{p,q,r\}}$. Hence, the procedure has to consider common subformulas that are generated in different recursion calls, which makes a recursive treatment rather complicated.

Having seen where the factorial blow-up stems from, we now consider how it can be avoided by sharing *all* common subterms. For this reason, consider first an ω-automaton equivalent to $\bigwedge_{i=1}^{n} \mathsf{F} a_i$. A typical, intuitively obtained automaton uses a hypercube as transition relation. For example, the case $n = 2$ yields the automaton that is given in Figure 5.6.

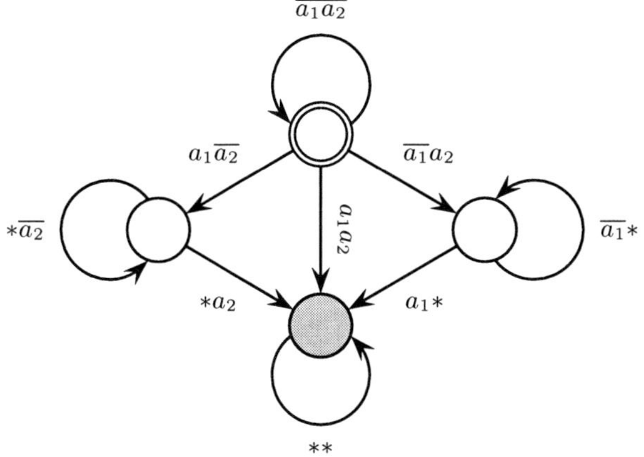

Fig. 5.6. State transition diagram of an automaton waiting concurrently for events a_1 and a_2.

In general, the states s_M of the automaton are associated with the set of events $M \subseteq \{a_1, \ldots, a_n\}$ that are awaited in that state. Hence, the initial state is $s_{\{1,\ldots,n\}}$ (drawn with double lines in Figure 5.6) and the final state is $s_{\{\}}$ (gray-shaded in Figure 5.6). From state s_M, there are transitions to each state s_N with $N \subseteq M$. The transition from s_M to s_N is taken if all events $\{a_k \mid k \in M \setminus N\}$ occur at once. The transitions at state s_M are independent of the events $\{a_k \mid k \in \{1, \ldots, n\} \setminus M\}$, since these events have already occurred before and are therefore no longer of interest. The acceptance condition of the automaton requires that the final state $s_{\{\}}$ must be visited at least once. This is equivalent to visiting it infinitely often and also to staying in it from a certain point of time on, since the only transition leaving from this state leads to the state itself.

Obviously, the automaton for $\bigwedge_{i=1}^{n} \mathsf{F} a_i$ has 2^n states, as the set $\{a_1, \ldots, a_n\}$ has 2^n subsets. Moreover, there are $\binom{n}{k}$ states s_M with $|M| = k$ and from each one of these 2^k transitions are leaving as M has 2^k subsets. Hence, there are $\sum_{k=0}^{n} \binom{n}{k} 2^k = (1+2)^n = 3^n$ edges.

We now represent the automaton in form of a shared temporal formula, where each state s_M of the automaton is represented by a subformula φ_M. In order to share these subformulas, we abbreviate them by a unique variable ϱ_M. We obtain the following shared temporal logic formula for the automaton:

$$\mathsf{E} \bigwedge_{i=1}^{n} \mathsf{F} a_i = \left(\begin{array}{l} \mathsf{let}\ \ \varrho_{\{\}} := 1 \\ \mathsf{and}\ \varrho_M := \bigvee_{i \in M} \mathsf{F}\left(a_i \wedge \varrho_{M \setminus \{i\}}\right)\ \mathsf{for}\ \{\} \neq M \subseteq \{1, \ldots, n\} \\ \mathsf{in}\ \ \ \mathsf{E}\varrho_{\{1,\ldots,n\}} \\ \mathsf{end} \end{array} \right)$$

A simple induction proof over $|M|$ shows that $\varrho_M = \bigwedge_{i \in M} \mathsf{F} a_i$ holds (just consider Lemma 5.17). The length of the above formula can be easily computed: the length of the definition of ϱ_M is $O(|M|)$. As there are $\binom{n}{k}$ subsets with k elements of a set with n elements, we obtain for the length $D(n)$ of all definitions and hence the formula itself $D(n) \leq \sum_{k=0}^{n} k\binom{n}{k} = \sum_{k=1}^{n} k\binom{n}{k} = n2^{n-1}$. Therefore, the size of the above shared formula is even less than the size of the automaton that grows with $O(3^n)$. The reason for this is that the F operator includes the present, and therefore we can restrict the 'recursive calls' for ϱ_M to subsets $M \setminus \{i\}$. Hence, we have only $|M|$ recursive calls instead of $2^{|M|}$ (which is the number of transitions leaving a corresponding state in the automaton).

It is clear how the latter formula can be translated to CTL: We can now duplicate the path quantifier E for the inner temporal operators. Hence, the following shared CTL formula is obtained:

$$\mathsf{E}\bigwedge_{i=1}^{n}\mathsf{F}a_i = \left(\begin{array}{l} \text{let } \varrho_{\{\}} := 1 \\ \text{and } \varrho_M := \bigvee_{i\in M} \mathsf{EF}\left(a_i \wedge \varrho_{M\setminus\{i\}}\right) \text{ for } \{\} \neq M \subseteq \{1,\ldots,n\} \\ \text{in } \varrho_{\{1,\ldots,n\}} \\ \text{end} \end{array}\right)$$

Note that the length is still of order $O(|\Phi|\, 2^{|\Phi|})$ and that our model checking procedure for CTL can directly make use of the shared formula by successively computing the sets of states where ϱ_M holds for increasing sets M. Therefore, we can check the formula $\mathsf{E}\bigwedge_{i=1}^{n}\mathsf{F}a_i$ in time $O(|\mathcal{K}|\, n2^n)$.

Transformation of LeftCTL* to Disjunctive Normal Form

Having seen the essential idea of the use of shared subformulas, we now start with the construction of an exponential-time translation procedure of arbitrary LeftCTL* formulas. We first replace all temporal operators by $\underline{\mathsf{U}}$, B and X according to Theorem 5.20 on page 308. After this, we separate the path quantified subformulas by computing the PQNF normal form by the algorithm given in Figure 2.49 such that, without loss of generality, we can consider in the following, LeftCTL* formulas of the form $\mathsf{E}\Phi$, where Φ contains only the temporal operators $\underline{\mathsf{U}}$, B and X and no path quantifier.

The first step of our transformation is to transform these formulas into a normal form. To explain how this normal form looks, we need some definitions in advance. In particular, we must be able to handle arbitrary deep nestings of $\underline{\mathsf{U}}$ and B. In order to write these nestings in a more concise manner, we use the following definitions for nested operators:

$$\begin{array}{l} [\langle\rangle\ \underline{\mathsf{U}}\ b] := b \\ [\langle a_1,\ldots,a_{p+1}\rangle\ \underline{\mathsf{U}}\ b] := [\langle a_1,\ldots,a_p\rangle\ \underline{\mathsf{U}}\ [a_{p+1}\ \underline{\mathsf{U}}\ b]] \\ [a\ \mathsf{B}\ \langle\rangle] := a \\ [a\ \mathsf{B}\ \langle b_1,\ldots,b_{p+1}\rangle] := [[a\ \mathsf{B}\ \langle b_1,\ldots,b_p\rangle]\ \mathsf{B}\ b_{p+1}] \end{array}$$

This means that $[\langle a_1,\ldots,a_p\rangle\ \underline{\mathsf{U}}\ b]$ abbreviates $[a_1\ \underline{\mathsf{U}}\ [a_2\ \underline{\mathsf{U}}\ \ldots [a_p\ \underline{\mathsf{U}}\ b]\ldots]]$ and $[a\ \mathsf{B}\ \langle b_1,\ldots,b_p\rangle]$ abbreviates $[\ldots[[a\ \mathsf{B}\ b_1]\ \mathsf{B}\ b_2]\ldots\ \mathsf{B}\ b_p]$. For an intuitive understanding of these formulas, note that $(\mathcal{K},\pi) \models [\langle a_1,\ldots,a_p\rangle\ \underline{\mathsf{U}}\ b]$ holds iff the following situation is found on π: let t_p be the first point on π where b holds, i.e., $(\mathcal{K},\pi,t_p) \models \neg b$ holds for $t < t_p$ and $(\mathcal{K},\pi,t_p) \models b$ holds. Then there must be numbers $0 = t_0 \leq t_1 \leq \ldots \leq t_p$ such that $(\mathcal{K},\pi,t) \models a_i$ for $t_{i-1} \leq t < t_i$. This means that the interval $\{t \mid 0 \leq t < t_p\}$ is divided into p intervals where the formulas a_i hold in sequence. Note, however, that some of these intervals may be empty.

$[a\ \mathsf{B}\ \langle b_1,\ldots,b_p\rangle]$ holds on a path π if there are points $t_0 < t_1 < \ldots < t_p$ on the path such that $(\mathcal{K},\pi,t_0) \models a$ and $(\mathcal{K},\pi,t_i) \models b_i$ holds. Alternatively, it may be the case that one of the b_i's never holds on the path. In this case, $[a\ \mathsf{B}\ \langle b_1,\ldots,b_i\rangle]$ trivially holds, and therefore the entire formula also holds.

Neither B nor $\underline{\mathsf{U}}$ is associative, i.e., neither $[[a\ \mathsf{B}\ b]\ \mathsf{B}\ c] = [a\ \mathsf{B}\ [b\ \mathsf{B}\ c]]$ nor $[[a\ \underline{\mathsf{U}}\ b]\ \underline{\mathsf{U}}\ c] = [a\ \underline{\mathsf{U}}\ [b\ \underline{\mathsf{U}}\ c]]$ holds. Therefore the order of the nestings is important. However, we have the following equations which can be easily proved by induction on p:

$$[\langle a_1, \ldots, a_{p+1}\rangle\ \underline{\mathsf{U}}\ b] = [a_1\ \underline{\mathsf{U}}\ [\langle a_2, \ldots, a_{p+1}\rangle\ \underline{\mathsf{U}}\ b]]$$
$$[a\ \mathsf{B}\ \langle b_1, \ldots, b_{p+1}\rangle] = [[a\ \mathsf{B}\ b_1]\ \mathsf{B}\ \langle b_2, \ldots, b_p\rangle]$$

Using the above shorthand notation for nestings, we can now define the following classes of temporal logic formulas:

Definition 5.24 (CUB Formulas). *Given propositional formulas $\alpha_{i,k}$, β_i for $i \in \{1, \ldots, n\}$ and $k \in \{1, \ldots, p_i\}$ and γ_j, $\delta_{j,k}$ for $j \in \{1, \ldots, m\}$ and $k \in \{1, \ldots, q_j\}$, then each* CTL^* *path formula of the following form is a CUB formula of order 0:*

$$\left(\bigwedge_{i=1}^{n} [\langle \alpha_{i,1}, \ldots, \alpha_{i,p_i}\rangle\ \underline{\mathsf{U}}\ \beta_i]\right) \wedge \left(\bigwedge_{j=1}^{m} [\gamma_j\ \mathsf{B}\ \langle \delta_{j,1}, \ldots, \delta_{j,q_j}\rangle]\right)$$

CUB formulas of order $n+1$ have the same form, where β_i and γ_j are CUB formulas of order n.

It is easily seen that every CUB formula can be derived from the nonterminal P_E with the grammar rules of $\mathsf{LeftCTL}^*$, *hence, for every CUB formula Φ, we have* $\mathsf{E}\Phi \in \mathsf{LeftCTL}^*$. *Moreover, the set of CUB formulas is closed with respect to conjunction.* Note that the definition of CUB formulas does not directly allow propositional formulas to occur in the conjunction. However, as $\varphi = [0\ \underline{\mathsf{U}}\ \varphi]$ holds, each propositional formula can be given as a $\underline{\mathsf{U}}$ formula. This means that for convenience, we do not explicitly treat propositional formulas, but embed them as temporal logic formulas of the form $[0\ \underline{\mathsf{U}}\ \varphi]$.

We are now ready to explain the normal form that is established in this section. It handles the propositional logic part of the $\mathsf{LeftCTL}^*$ formula by transforming it into a disjunctive normal form similar to the one given in Figure 2.12 on page 88. The difference is however, that also right hand arguments of $\underline{\mathsf{U}}$ and left hand arguments of B are recursively transformed into this normal form. The algorithm is given in Figure 5.7; it does not however apply explicitly associative laws for $\wedge$ and $\vee$ (in the cases for $\varphi \wedge \psi$ and $\varphi \vee \psi$, respectively) which is also necessary.

Note that in the cases for $[\varphi\ \underline{\mathsf{U}}\ \psi]$ and $[\varphi\ \mathsf{B}\ \psi]$, the subformula φ is copied in the above algorithm for each minterm ψ_j. By the grammar of $\mathsf{LeftCTL}^*$, φ must be a state formula, and by our assumptions that no path quantifier must occur, it follows that φ is propositional. Hence, for our translation from $\mathsf{LeftCTL}^*$ to CTL we can leave this formula unchanged. For this reason, is is not necessary to copy this formula for each factor, instead we should abbreviate φ by a new variable ϑ and copy ϑ instead of φ. Implementations of our translation procedure need to consider this, but the asymptotic complexities that are proved in this section are not influenced by this fact.

function $\mathsf{DeepDNF}(\Phi)$
  (* Φ *should be in negation normal form* *)
  case Φ **of**
    $\mathsf{is\_var}(\Phi)$: **return** Φ;
    $\neg\varphi$: **return** $\neg\varphi$; (* *since* $\varphi \in V_\Sigma$ *)
    $\varphi \wedge \psi$: $\bigvee_{i\in I} \varphi_i \equiv \mathsf{DeepDNF}(\varphi)$;
      $\bigvee_{i\in J} \psi_j \equiv \mathsf{DeepDNF}(\psi)$;
      : **return** $\bigvee_{i\in I} \bigvee_{i\in J} \varphi_i \wedge \psi_j$;
    $\varphi \vee \psi$: **return** $\mathsf{DeepDNF}(\varphi) \vee \mathsf{DeepDNF}(\psi)$;
    $\mathsf{X}\varphi$: $\bigvee_{i\in I} \varphi_i \equiv \mathsf{DeepDNF}(\varphi)$; **return** $\bigvee_{i\in I} \mathsf{X}\varphi_i$;
    $[\varphi \,\underline{\mathsf{U}}\, \psi]$: $\bigvee_{j\in J} \psi_j \equiv \mathsf{DeepDNF}(\psi)$; **return** $\bigvee_{j\in J} [\varphi \,\underline{\mathsf{U}}\, \psi_j]$;
    $[\varphi \,\mathsf{B}\, \psi]$: $\bigvee_{i\in I} \varphi_i \equiv \mathsf{DeepDNF}(\varphi)$; **return** $\bigvee_{i\in I} [\varphi_i \,\mathsf{B}\, \psi]$;
  end
end

Fig. 5.7. Transformation into temporal disjunctive normal form

Theorem 5.25 (DeepDNF). *Given any* LeftCTL* *formula* $\mathsf{E}\Phi$, *where* Φ *contains no path quantifiers. There is an equivalent* LeftCTL* *formula* $\mathsf{E}\Phi_\vee$ *such that* $\Phi_\vee := \bigvee_{k\in M} \Phi_k$ *where* $\Phi_k := \bigwedge_{j=0}^{m_k} \mathsf{X}^k \varphi_{j,k}$ *with CUB formulas* $\varphi_{j,k}$. *Moreover,* $|\Phi_\vee| \in O(|\Phi|\, 2^{|\Phi|})$, *and in particular* $|M| \in O(2^{|\Phi|})$ *and* $|\Phi_k| \in O(|\Phi|)$ *hold.*

The proof of the above theorem is done by induction on Φ along the algorithm given in Figure 5.7. The correctness is clear, the only interesting laws that are used are $[a \,\underline{\mathsf{U}}\, (b_1 \vee b_2)] = [a \,\underline{\mathsf{U}}\, b_1] \vee [a \,\underline{\mathsf{U}}\, b_2]$ and $[(a_1 \vee a_2) \,\mathsf{B}\, b] = [a_1 \,\mathsf{B}\, b] \vee [a_2 \,\mathsf{B}\, b]$ and the distributivity of X over $\wedge$ and $\vee$. Note that also $[(a_1 \wedge a_2) \,\underline{\mathsf{U}}\, b] = [a_1 \,\underline{\mathsf{U}}\, b] \wedge [a_2 \,\underline{\mathsf{U}}\, b]$ and $[a \,\underline{\mathsf{B}}\, (b_1 \vee b_2)] = [a \,\underline{\mathsf{B}}\, b_1] \wedge [a \,\underline{\mathsf{B}}\, b_2]$ hold, but these laws are not used in Figure 5.7. The reason for not using the latter ones is that the conjunctions that would thereby be split are propositional formulas. Hence, our transformations would not benefit from these additional expansions.

Now, consider the lengths of the formulas. All cases apart from $\Phi \equiv \varphi \wedge \psi$ are non-critical, hence, we only consider this one here. By the induction hypothesis, we can compute $\mathsf{DeepDNF}(\varphi) = \bigvee_{i\in K_1} \varphi_i$ and $\mathsf{DeepDNF}(\psi) = \bigvee_{j\in K_2} \psi_j$ where $|K_1| \in O(2^{|\varphi|})$, $|\varphi_i| \in O(|\varphi|)$, $|K_2| \in O(2^{|\psi|})$, and $|\psi_j| \in O(|\psi|)$ holds. The result of the algorithm given in Figure 5.7 is then the formula $\bigvee_{i\in K_1} \bigvee_{j\in K_2} \varphi_i \wedge \psi_j$, which consists of $O(2^{|\varphi|} 2^{|\psi|}) = O(2^{|\Phi|})$ factors of lengths $O(|\varphi| + |\psi|) = O(\Phi)$.

Having computed $\mathsf{DeepDNF}(\Phi)$ for a given formula $\mathsf{E}\Phi$, we can shift the path quantifier inwards such that in the following, we only need to translate LeftCTL* formulas of the form $\mathsf{E} \bigwedge_{k=0}^{\ell} \mathsf{X}^k \Phi_k$ to CUB formulas Φ_k. In the next section, we will show, how X-free CUB formulas can be translated which means that we will handle the case $\ell = 0$. The results are then extended to arbitrary ℓ in the final subsection of this section.

Transformation of X-Free LeftCTL*

In this section, we show how CUB formulas of arbitrary order can be translated into a shared form such that an outermost E path quantifier could be shifted inwards without problem, i.e., whenever it is applied to a conjunction, then one of the arguments of the conjunction is a propositional formula. Hence, we can use the law $\mathsf{E}(\varphi \wedge \psi) = \varphi \wedge \mathsf{E}\psi$ (where φ is propositional). The essential lemma of this transformation is again the elimination of conjunctions that are quantified by an E path quantifier as given by Lemma 5.18.

Lemma 5.18 is essential for the transformation of CUB formulas. It corresponds to the rule $\bigwedge_{i=1}^{n} \mathsf{F}a_i = \mathsf{F}\left(\bigvee_{i=1}^{n} a_i \wedge \bigwedge_{l=1,l\neq i}^{n} \mathsf{F}a_l\right)$ we need for transforming the illustrative example. It is also easily seen that on the right hand side of the equations common subformulas occur. It is now important to describe how all of these common subterms can be collected. For this reason, first consider the transformation of a CUB formula of order 0, i.e., formulas of the form $(\bigwedge_{i=1}^{n} [\langle \alpha_{i,1}, \ldots, \alpha_{i,p_i}\rangle \; \underline{\mathsf{U}} \; \beta_i]) \wedge \left(\bigwedge_{j=1}^{m} \left[\gamma_j \; \mathsf{B} \; \langle \delta_{j,1}, \ldots, \delta_{j,q_j}\rangle\right]\right)$, where $\alpha_{i,k}$, β_i, γ_j, and $\delta_{j,k}$ are propositional.

In general, the problem is that several events are concurrently awaited, and we do not know which of them will be the first to occur. The solution is therefore based on making successive case distinctions on which of these events is the first one (or among the first ones) to occur. Up to the point of time where one of the events occurs, some other condition must hold. Additionally, we must deal with the fact that when one event occurs, it generates another event that is then awaited. The dependencies of the events that are awaited in the above formula are given in Figure 5.8.

Initially, the events of the first row in Figure 5.8 are awaited and until one of them occurs $\bigwedge_{i=1}^{n} \alpha_{i,1}$ and $\bigwedge_{j=1}^{m} \neg\delta_{j,q_j}$ must hold. If one of the events listed in the first row occurs, then this event is replaced by its successor event, i.e., the event in the same column directly below it. If more than one event occurs at the same point of time, then these are all replaced by their successor events. If finally, b_k or c_k occur, then the 'event family' of column k is released and only the events of the other columns are awaited. Hence, choosing from each column in Figure 5.8, at most one node leads to a situation where the events of that nodes are concurrently awaited.

Figure 5.8 precisely specifies the order in which the events are awaited: Events on the same column must occur in the order given by the column, while events on different columns may occur in an arbitrary order. The aim is now to represent the situations along with their dependencies as given in Figure 5.8 for arbitrary CUB formulas. For this reason, we must first find some representation of the 'event structure' of these formulas and represent the shared formula directly with the event structure. The extension of Figure 5.8 to an event structure for a CUB formula of order $k \geq 0$ is formally defined as follows (recall that PF_Σ is the set of path formulas):

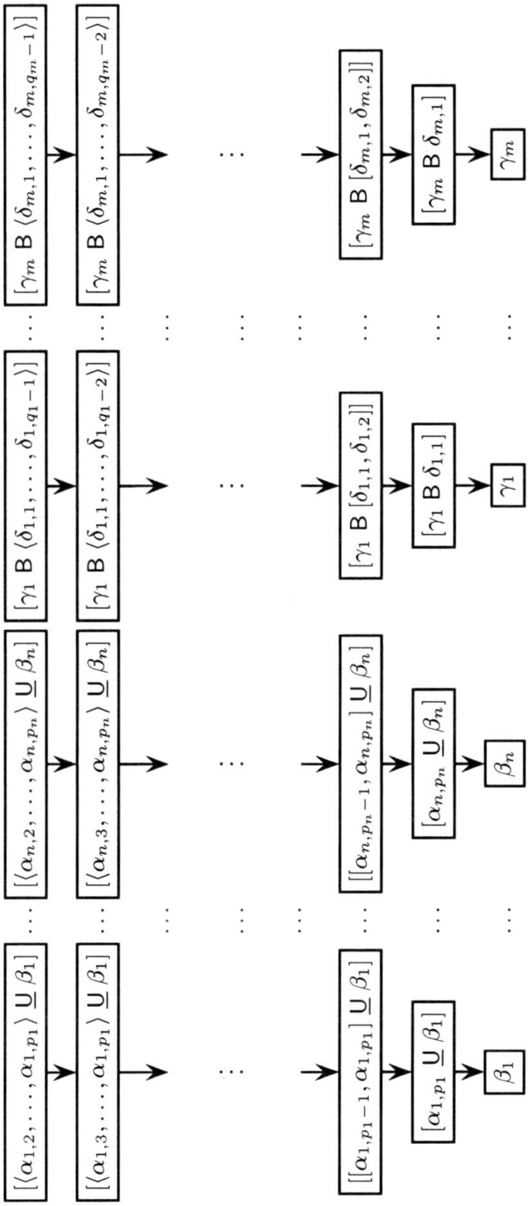

Fig. 5.8. Event structure for CUB formulas

Definition 5.26 (Event Structure of a CUB Formula). *An event structure for a CUB formula is a tuple $(\mathcal{I}, \mathcal{B}, \mathcal{S}, \mathcal{R}, \iota, \epsilon)$, where $\mathcal{S}$ is a finite set of states, $\mathcal{I} \subseteq \mathcal{S}$ is the set of initial states, and $\mathcal{R} \subseteq \mathcal{S} \times \mathcal{S}$ is the set of edges that is an acyclic relation. $\iota : \mathcal{S} \to \mathsf{PF}_\Sigma$ maps each state $s \in \mathcal{S}$ to a propositional formula $\iota(s)$ that is called the invariant of s. $\epsilon : \mathcal{S} \to \mathsf{PF}_\Sigma$ maps each state $s \in \mathcal{S}$ to a CUB formula $\epsilon(s)$ that is called the event of s. Finally, $\mathcal{B} \subseteq \mathcal{S}$ is the set of* B*-states of the structure. The event structure* $\mathsf{EVS}(\Phi)$ *for a particular CUB formula Φ is defined by the algorithm in Figure 5.9.*

```
function EVS(Φ)
  case Φ of
   is_prop(Φ):
        return ({}, {}, {}, {}, {}, {});
   [⟨α_1, ..., α_p⟩ U̲ φ]:
        (I_1, B_1, S_1, R_1, ι_1, ε_1) := EVS(φ);
        S := S_1 ∪ {s_1, ..., s_p};
        R_2 := R_1 ∪ {(s_i, s_{i+1}) | i ∈ {1, ..., p−1}};
        R := R_2 ∪ {(s_p, q) | q ∈ I_1};
        ι := ι_1 ∪ {(s_i, α_i) | i ∈ {1, ..., p}};
        ε := ε_1 ∪ {(s_i, [⟨α_{i+1}, ..., α_p⟩ U̲ φ]) | i ∈ {1, ..., p}};
        return ({s_1}, B_1, S, R, ι, ε);
   [φ B ⟨δ_1, ..., δ_p⟩]:
        (I_1, B_1, S_1, R_1, ι_1, ε_1) := EVS(φ);
        B := B_1 ∪ {s_1, ..., s_p};
        S := S_1 ∪ {s_1, ..., s_p};
        R_2 := R_1 ∪ {(s_i, s_{i+1}) | i ∈ {1, ..., p−1}};
        R := R_2 ∪ {(s_p, q) | q ∈ I_1};
        ι := ι_1 ∪ {(s_i, ¬δ_{p−i+1}) | i ∈ {1, ..., p}};
        ε := ε_1 ∪ {(s_i, ¬δ_{p−i+1} ∧ [φ B ⟨δ_1, ..., δ_{p−i}⟩]) | i ∈ {1, ..., p}};
        return ({s_1}, B, S, R, ι, ε);
   ⋀_{i∈M} φ_i :
        (I_i, B_i, S_i, ι_i, ε_i) := EVS(φ_i);
        return (⋃_{i∈M} I_i, ⋃_{i∈M} B_i, ⋃_{i∈M} S_i, ⋃_{i∈M} ι_i, ⋃_{i∈M} ε_i);
  end
end
```

Fig. 5.9. Computation of the event structure of a CUB formula

The size of $\mathsf{EVS}(\Phi)$ *is linear in terms of $|\Phi|$, i.e. in particular $|\mathcal{S}|, |\mathcal{R}| \in O(|\Phi|)$.* In general the intention is that the event structure formalizes a *partial order* on the events that occur in a formula: whenever we know from the structure of the formula that an event e_1 is awaited after another event e_2 then there is a path through the event structure from a state s_1 to a state s_2 such that $\epsilon(s_1) = e_1$ and $\epsilon(s_2) = e_2$ holds. Hence, $\epsilon(s)$ is the event that is awaited when the structure is in state s. Until this event occurs, the formula $\iota(s)$ must hold.

The event structures of $[\langle\alpha_1,\ldots,\alpha_p\rangle\ \underline{\mathsf{U}}\ \varphi]$ and $[\varphi\ \mathsf{B}\ \langle\delta_1,\ldots,\delta_p\rangle]$ are obtained from the event structure of φ by adding new states $s_1,\ldots,s_p$ that are connected as a chain. s_1 is the new initial state and s_p is connected with each initial state of the event structure of φ. *Therefore, it is easily seen that the event structure of a CUB formula is a finite set of trees.* Figure 5.8 shows the event structure of a CUB formula of order 0, where each state is labeled with its event $\epsilon(s)$.

Each tree of the event structure of a CUB formula stems from a top-level formula of the form $[\langle\alpha_1,\ldots,\alpha_p\rangle\ \underline{\mathsf{U}}\ \varphi]$ or $[\varphi\ \mathsf{B}\ \langle\delta_1,\ldots,\delta_p\rangle]$ respectively. As the events in these formulas are, in general, independent of each other, we must consider all possible combinations of these basic events to form global events. For this reason, we need the following definition:

Definition 5.27 (Consistent Situations of an Event Structure). *Let $\mathcal{E} = (\mathcal{I}, \mathcal{B}, \mathcal{S}, \mathcal{R}, \iota, \epsilon)$ be an event structure. The set of consistent situations of $\mathcal{E}$ is defined as the least set that satisfies the following properties:*

1. *$\mathcal{I}$ is a consistent situation*
2. *if χ is a consistent situation, and $s \in \chi$, then $(\chi \setminus \{s\}) \cup \mathsf{suc}_{\exists}^{\mathcal{R}}(\{s\})$ is a consistent situation*

The set of consistent situations of $\mathcal{E}$ is denoted by $\mathfrak{S}(\mathcal{E})$.

The set of consistent situations $\mathfrak{S}(\mathcal{E})$ are those subsets of $\mathcal{S}$ that are obtained from the initial situation by replacing a state by its successor states. *It has to be noted, that switching from one situation to its successor situation does not necessarily need to consume time. This means that even in the first instant of time, each consistent situation may occur.* In the previous lemma, the consistent situations have been encoded by the tuples $(i_1,\ldots,i_n)$ and $(j_1,\ldots,j_m)$, where the event structure has been represented by incrementing one component of the tuples. As the consistent situations correspond to horizontal cuts through the event structure, the set of consistent situations can also be characterized as given in the following lemma:

Lemma 5.28 (Consistent Situations of an Event Structure). *Let $\mathcal{E} = (\mathcal{I}, \mathcal{B}, \mathcal{S}, \mathcal{R}, \iota, \epsilon)$ be an event structure and let $\prec$ be the partial order induced by $\mathcal{E}$ (i.e., the reflexive and transitive closure of $\mathcal{R}$). A set of states $\chi \subseteq \mathcal{S}$ is consistent iff $\forall s_1, s_2 \in \chi.\ s_1 \not\prec s_2 \wedge s_2 \not\prec s_1$.*

The consistency condition means that a consistent situation must not contain two states that lie on the same path of the structure. On the other hand, it is not required that a consistent situation must be complete, i.e., it need not necessarily contain states of all path of the structure. To determine an upper bound for the number of consistent situations of the event structure $\mathsf{EVS}(\Phi)$ of a CUB formula, we prove the following lemma:

Lemma 5.29. *Given a CUB formula Φ of an arbitrary order k and its event structure $\mathsf{EVS}(\Phi) = (\mathcal{I}, \mathcal{B}, \mathcal{S}, \mathcal{R}, \iota, \epsilon)$. There are at most $2^{|\Phi|}$ consistent situations of $\mathsf{EVS}(\Phi)$. Moreover, for each $\chi \in \mathfrak{S}(\mathcal{E})$ the inequation $|\chi| \leq |\Phi|$ holds.*

The proof is done inductively on the structure of Φ. The proof is easy, once it is seen that the following equations hold:

- $|\mathfrak{S}(\mathsf{EVS}(b))| = 1$ for each propositional formula b
- $|\mathfrak{S}(\mathsf{EVS}([\langle\alpha_1,\ldots,\alpha_p\rangle\ \underline{\mathsf{U}}\ \varphi]))| = p + |\mathfrak{S}(\mathsf{EVS}(\varphi))|$
- $|\mathfrak{S}(\mathsf{EVS}([\varphi\ \mathsf{B}\ \langle\delta_1,\ldots,\delta_p\rangle]))| = p + |\mathfrak{S}(\mathsf{EVS}(\varphi))|$
- $\left|\mathfrak{S}(\mathsf{EVS}(\bigwedge_{i\in M}\varphi_i))\right| = \prod_{i\in M}|\mathfrak{S}(\mathsf{EVS}(\varphi_i))|$

Moreover, if we define $m(\mathcal{E}) := \max\{|\chi| \mid \chi \in \mathfrak{S}(\mathcal{E})\}$ as the least upper bound of the size of the consistent situations, then it is also easily seen that the following equations hold:

- $m(\mathsf{EVS}(b)) = 0$ for each propositional formula b
- $m(\mathsf{EVS}([\langle\alpha_1,\ldots,\alpha_p\rangle\ \underline{\mathsf{U}}\ \varphi])) = m(\mathsf{EVS}(\varphi))$
- $m(\mathsf{EVS}([\varphi\ \mathsf{B}\ \langle\delta_1,\ldots,\delta_p\rangle])) = m(\mathsf{EVS}(\varphi))$
- $m(\mathsf{EVS}(\bigwedge_{i\in M}\varphi_i)) = \sum_{i\in M} m(\mathsf{EVS}(\varphi_i))$

The remaining proof is then done by induction on the order of the CUB formula.

We now show the translation of $\mathsf{E}\Phi$ for a CUB formula Φ to an equivalent alternation-free μ-calculus formula. Based on the construction of the event structure $\mathsf{EVS}(\Phi)$, we proceed as follows:

Theorem 5.30 (Translating CUB to Vectorized μ-Calculus). *Given a CUB formula Φ of an arbitrary order k and its event structure $\mathsf{EVS}(\Phi) = (\mathcal{I},\mathcal{B},\mathcal{S},\mathcal{R},\iota,\epsilon)$. We define for each consistent situation χ an equation to define a variable ϱ_χ as follows:*

$$\varrho_\chi := \begin{cases} \left[\left(\bigwedge_{s\in\chi}\iota(s)\right)\ \underline{\mathsf{U}}\ \left(\bigvee_{s\in\chi}\xi_\chi(s)\right)\right] & : \textit{if } \chi \not\subseteq \mathcal{B} \\ \left[\left(\bigwedge_{s\in\chi}\iota(s)\right)\ \mathsf{U}\ \left(\bigvee_{s\in\chi}\xi_\chi(s)\right)\right] & : \textit{if } \chi \subseteq \mathcal{B} \end{cases}$$

$$\textit{where } \xi_\chi(s) := \begin{cases} \varrho_{(\chi\setminus\{s\})\cup\mathsf{suc}_\exists^{\mathcal{R}}(\{s\})} & : \textit{if } \mathsf{suc}_\exists^{\mathcal{R}}(\{s\}) \neq \{\} \\ \epsilon(s) \wedge \varrho_{\chi\setminus\{s\}} & : \textit{otherwise} \end{cases}$$

Under these recursive definitions, Φ is equivalent to $\varrho_{\mathcal{I}}$. Hence, for each CUB formula Φ there is an alternation-free μ-calculus formula of size $O(|\Phi|\,2^{|\Phi|})$ that is equivalent to $\mathsf{E}\Phi$.

Proof. It can be easily seen that all situations χ that are used as indices are consistent situations. First of all, one has to note that for each CUB formula Ψ with $\mathsf{EVS}(\Psi) = (\mathcal{I},\mathcal{B},\mathcal{S},\mathcal{R},\iota,\epsilon)$, we have

$$(*)\ \ \Psi = \left(\bigwedge_{s\in\mathcal{I}\setminus\mathcal{B}}[\iota(s)\ \underline{\mathsf{U}}\ \epsilon(s)]\right) \wedge \left(\bigwedge_{s\in\mathcal{I}\cap\mathcal{B}}[\iota(s)\ \mathsf{U}\ \epsilon(s)]\right)$$

This is easily seen since for each $\underline{\mathsf{U}}$ formula φ_i new states $s_{i,1}$, ..., s_{i,p_1} are introduced where $\varphi_i = [\iota(s_{i,1})\ \underline{\mathsf{U}}\ \epsilon(s_{i,1})]$. Similarly, for each B formula ψ_j new states $s_{j,1}, \ldots, s_{j,q_j}$ are introduced with $\psi_j = [\iota(s_{j,1})\ \mathsf{U}\ \epsilon(s_{j,1})]$. As $\mathcal{I}$ consists exactly of the states $s_{i,1}$ and $s_{j,1}$, the above equation holds.

Now, we can prove that for each event structure computed by the algorithm given in Figure 5.9 for a CUB formula, the following holds[2]:

$$(**)\ \forall s \in \mathcal{S}.\ \mathsf{suc}_{\exists}^{\mathcal{R}}(\{s\}) \neq \{\} \rightarrow \left[\epsilon(s) = \left(\bigwedge_{t\in\mathsf{suc}_{\exists}^{\mathcal{R}}(\{s\})\setminus\mathcal{B}} [\iota(t)\ \underline{\mathsf{U}}\ \epsilon(t)]\right) \wedge \left(\bigwedge_{t\in\mathsf{suc}_{\exists}^{\mathcal{R}}(\{s\})\cap\mathcal{B}} [\iota(t)\ \mathsf{U}\ \epsilon(t)]\right)\right]$$

To see that it holds, note that states are introduced in the algorithm for computing $\mathsf{EVS}(\Phi)$ in Figure 5.9 only for formulas that start with a temporal operator $\underline{\mathsf{U}}$ or B. Assume that the states $s_1, \ldots, s_p$ are introduced for $[\langle\alpha_1,\ldots,\alpha_p\rangle\ \underline{\mathsf{U}}\ \varphi]$. Then we have by definition of Figure 5.9 for $i \in \{1,\ldots,p\}$ that $\iota(s_i) := \alpha_i$, $\epsilon(s_i) := [\langle\alpha_{i+1},\ldots,\alpha_p\rangle\ \underline{\mathsf{U}}\ \varphi]$ holds. Moreover, for $1 \leq i < p$, we have $\mathsf{suc}_{\exists}^{\mathcal{R}}(\{s_i\}) := \{s_{i+1}\}$, and hence, $\epsilon(s_i) = [\iota(s_{i+1})\ \underline{\mathsf{U}}\ \epsilon(s_{i+1})]$ such that $(**)$ holds for $1 \leq i < p$. For s_p, we need equation $(*)$ above: firstly, we have $\mathsf{suc}_{\exists}^{\mathcal{R}}(\{s_p\}) := \mathcal{I}_\varphi$, where $\mathcal{I}_\varphi$ are the initial states of $\mathsf{EVS}(\varphi)$. The rest follows as $\epsilon(s_p) := \varphi$, hence by $(*)$, we have $\epsilon(s_p) = \bigwedge_{s\in\mathcal{I}_\varphi\setminus\mathcal{B}_\varphi} [\iota(s)\ \underline{\mathsf{U}}\ \epsilon(s)] \wedge \bigwedge_{s\in\mathcal{I}_\varphi\cap\mathcal{B}_\varphi} [\iota(s)\ \mathsf{U}\ \epsilon(s)]$.

Having seen that $(**)$ holds, we can now use it for proving the following equation by induction on the order of the consistent situations χ:

$$(***)\ \varrho_\chi = \bigwedge_{s\in\chi\setminus\mathcal{B}} [\iota(s)\ \underline{\mathsf{U}}\ \epsilon(s)] \wedge \bigwedge_{s\in\chi\cap\mathcal{B}} [\iota(s)\ \mathsf{U}\ \epsilon(s)]$$

The induction base is clear since for the maximal situation $\{\}$, we have $\varrho_{\{\}} = [1\ \mathsf{U}\ 0] = 1$. In the induction step, we first consider the case $\chi \not\subseteq \mathcal{B}$, such that we can apply the first equation of Lemma 5.18 to transform $(***)$ as follows: $\varrho_\chi = \left[\left(\bigwedge_{s\in\chi}\iota(s)\right)\ \underline{\mathsf{U}}\ \left(\bigvee_{s\in\chi}\epsilon(s)\wedge\varrho_{\chi\setminus\{s\}}\right)\right]$. In case $\chi \subseteq \mathcal{B}$, we use the second equation of Lemma 5.18 to obtain the same proof goal where $\underline{\mathsf{U}}$ is replaced with U. In each case, it therefore remains to show that for every state $s \in \chi$ of any consistent situation χ the equation $\xi_\chi(s) = \epsilon(s)\wedge\varrho_{\chi\setminus\{s\}}$ holds. For the case $\mathsf{suc}_{\exists}^{\mathcal{R}}(\{s\}) = \{\}$, this holds by definition of $\xi_\chi(s)$. In case $\mathsf{suc}_{\exists}^{\mathcal{R}}(\{s\}) \neq \{\}$, we argue as follows (where we need the induction hypothesis):

$$\begin{aligned}\xi_\chi(s) &\overset{def}{=} \varrho_{(\chi\setminus\{s\})\cup\mathsf{suc}_{\exists}^{\mathcal{R}}(\{s\})}\\ &\overset{(***)}{=} \textstyle\bigwedge_{s\neq t\in\chi\setminus\mathcal{B}} [\iota(t)\ \underline{\mathsf{U}}\ \epsilon(t)] \wedge \bigwedge_{s\neq t\in\chi\cap\mathcal{B}} [\iota(t)\ \mathsf{U}\ \epsilon(t)] \wedge\\ &\qquad \textstyle\bigwedge_{t\in\mathsf{suc}_{\exists}^{\mathcal{R}}(\{s\})\setminus\mathcal{B}} [\iota(t)\ \underline{\mathsf{U}}\ \epsilon(t)] \wedge \bigwedge_{t\in\mathsf{suc}_{\exists}^{\mathcal{R}}(\{s\})\cap\mathcal{B}} [\iota(t)\ \mathsf{U}\ \epsilon(t)]\\ &\overset{(**)}{=} \varrho_{\chi\setminus\{s\}}\wedge\epsilon(s)\end{aligned}$$

□

[2] Note that by construction of $\mathsf{EVS}(\Phi)$, we have that $\mathsf{suc}_{\exists}^{\mathcal{R}}(\{s\}) = \{\}$ holds iff Φ is propositional. However, we only need to prove $(**)$.

The construction of the definitions ϱ_χ implies that in the situation χ, all formulas $\iota(s)$ for $s \in \chi$ must hold until one of the events $\bigvee_{s\in\chi} \xi_\chi(s)$ occurs. If $\xi_\chi(s)$ occurs then χ is replaced by its successor event of the tree where s stems from. If no successor event of that tree is available, then this tree is released, i.e., removed from χ. Therefore, the construction is a generalization of the construction given in Figure 2.12.

The given upper bound is tight, i.e., there are examples that really match it (for example, take the order 0 for the CUB formula with one nesting of temporal operators). Note further that it is easily possible to shift an outermost E path quantifier inside the formula: the only cases where conjunctions occur are the subformulas $\epsilon(s) \wedge \varrho_{\chi\setminus\{s\}}$, which are generated as events $\xi_\chi(s)$ when $\mathsf{suc}_\exists^\mathcal{R}(\{s\}) = \{\}$. We have already noted in the proof of the above theorem that in this case, $\epsilon(s)$ is propositional. Therefore, we can shift E over $\epsilon(s)$ with the rule $\mathsf{E}\epsilon(s) \wedge \varrho_{\chi\setminus\{s\}} = \epsilon(s) \wedge \mathsf{E}\varrho_{\chi\setminus\{s\}}$.

Theorem 5.25 together with Theorem 5.30 allows the transformation of arbitrary LeftCTL* formulas Φ without X operators to alternation-free μ-calculus formulas of size $O(|\Phi|\, 2^{2|\Phi|})$. We will not prove this here, since this result is proved for general LeftCTL* formulas in the next subsection.

Transformation of Full LeftCTL*

In order to develop a transformation of full LeftCTL* to vectorized μ-calculus formulas, we must additionally handle the X-operator. Recall that the computation of the DeepDNF(Φ) as given in Theorem 5.25 of a given LeftCTL* formula Φ is a disjunction of at most $2^{|\Phi|}$ formulas of the form $\bigwedge_{k=0}^{\ell} \mathsf{X}^k\Phi_k$ where each Φ_k is a CUB formula of an arbitrary order. We will now show, how a vectorized μ-calculus formula for the subformulas $\bigwedge_{k=0}^{\ell} \mathsf{X}^k\Phi_k$ can be computed. The idea of that computation is best explained by considering the simple case where two CUB formulas $\Phi_i \wedge \mathsf{X}\Phi_{i+1}$ are to be combined. It is important to see that in the first instant of time, only the ι conditions of Φ_i must be satisfied and only the ϵ-conditions of Φ_i are awaited. Hence, in the first instant of time, Φ_{i+1} is totally neglected. Depending on the events that hold in the first instant of time, the situation of the event structure EVS(Φ_i) can be an arbitrary one, since the transition from one situation to a successive one does not necessarily consume time. In the second instant of time, we must hence combine *all* situations of EVS(Φ_i) with *all* situations of EVS(Φ_{i+1}). For this reason, we need to compute the event structure EVS($\Phi_i \wedge \Phi_{i+1}$), and for the general case EVS($\bigwedge_{k=0}^{\ell} \Phi_k$).

The next theorem shows how this can be established for an arbitrary conjunction $\bigwedge_{k=0}^{\ell} \mathsf{X}^k\Phi_k$ of CUB formulas Φ_k. The key is that beginning with EVS(Φ_0), we unroll the definitions of the substitution variables by applying the recursion laws $[a\ \underline{\mathsf{U}}\ b] = b \vee a \wedge \mathsf{X}\,[a\ \underline{\mathsf{U}}\ b]$ and $[a\ \mathsf{U}\ b] = b \vee a \wedge \mathsf{X}\,[a\ \mathsf{U}\ b]$. Inside the scope of the thereby generated X operator, we know that one instant of time has been consumed and therefore we must consider there also the situations of Φ_1. The same procedure is repeated until we have reached the ℓ-th point of time, where all situations of $\mathsf{EVS}(\Phi_0)$, ..., $\mathsf{EVS}(\Phi_\ell)$ are considered. The detailed construction is given in the following theorem:

Theorem 5.31. *Given CUB formulas $\Phi_0, \ldots, \Phi_\ell$ of arbitrary order and their event structures $\mathsf{EVS}(\Phi_k) = (\mathcal{I}_k, \mathcal{B}_k, \mathcal{S}_k, \mathcal{R}_k, \iota_k, \epsilon_k)$. Define $\Phi := \bigwedge_{k=0}^{\ell} \Phi_k$ and $\Psi := \bigwedge_{k=0}^{\ell} \mathsf{X}^k \Phi_k$. Moreover, let $(\mathcal{I}, \mathcal{B}, \mathcal{S}, \mathcal{R}, \iota, \epsilon) := \mathsf{EVS}(\Phi)$. Then we define equations for variables ϱ_χ^k for $k \in \{0, \ldots, \ell\}$ and for $\chi \in \bigcup_{i=0}^{k} \mathfrak{S}(\mathsf{EVS}(\Phi_i))$ as follows:*

$$\varrho_\chi^k := \begin{cases} \left(\bigvee_{s\in\chi} \xi_\chi^k(s)\right) \vee \left(\bigwedge_{s\in\chi} \iota(s)\right) \wedge \mathsf{X}\varrho_{\chi\cup\mathcal{I}_{k+1}}^{k+1} & : \text{if } k < \ell \\ \left[\left(\bigwedge_{s\in\chi} \iota(s)\right) \underline{\mathsf{U}} \left(\bigvee_{s\in\chi} \xi_\chi^k(s)\right)\right] & : \text{if } k = \ell \text{ and } \chi \not\subseteq \mathcal{B} \\ \left[\left(\bigwedge_{s\in\chi} \iota(s)\right) \mathsf{U} \left(\bigvee_{s\in\chi} \xi_\chi^k(s)\right)\right] & : \text{if } k = \ell \text{ and } \chi \subseteq \mathcal{B} \end{cases}$$

$$\text{where for each } k\ \xi_\chi^k(s) := \begin{cases} \varrho^k_{(\chi\setminus\{s\})\cup\mathsf{suc}_\exists^{\mathcal{R}}(\{s\})} & : \text{if } \mathsf{suc}_\exists^{\mathcal{R}}(\{s\}) \neq \{\} \\ \epsilon(s) \wedge \varrho^k_{\chi\setminus\{s\}} & : \text{otherwise} \end{cases}$$

Under these recursive definitions, Ψ is equivalent to $\varrho^0_{\mathcal{I}_0}$. Moreover, the size of all of the above definitions is of order $O(|\Psi|\, 2^{|\Psi|})$.

Proof. The proof is done by induction on ℓ. For $\ell = 0$, the theorem is equivalent to Theorem 5.30. Moreover, from the proof of Theorem 5.30 it follows that $\varrho^\ell_{\mathcal{I}_k} = \Phi_k$ holds for each $\ell \in \mathbb{N}$. For $\ell > 0$, we prove by recursion on j that the following holds:

$$(*)\quad \varrho_\chi^{\ell-k} = \varrho_\chi^\ell \wedge \bigwedge_{j=1}^{k} \mathsf{X}^j \varrho^\ell_{\mathcal{I}_{j+\ell-k}} \text{ for } k \in \{0, \ldots, \ell\} \text{ and } \chi \in \bigcup_{j=0}^{\ell-k} \mathfrak{S}(\mathsf{EVS}(\Phi_j))$$

Note that $\xi_\chi^{\ell-k}(s) = \xi_\chi^\ell(s) \wedge \bigwedge_{j=1}^{k} \mathsf{X}^j \varrho^\ell_{\mathcal{I}_{j+\ell-k}}$ can be directly derived from $(*)$ (this is easily seen by the definition of $\xi_\chi^{\ell-j}(s)$). Before proving $(*)$, we show that the theorem can indeed be derived from it. For this reason, instantiate $(*)$ with $k = \ell$ and $\chi = \mathcal{I}_0$, such that it takes the form $\varrho^0_{\mathcal{I}_0} = \bigwedge_{j=0}^{\ell} \mathsf{X}^j \varrho^\ell_{\mathcal{I}_j}$. The rest follows from the fact $\varrho^\ell_{\mathcal{I}_k} = \Phi_k$, which we have already showed in the proof of Theorem 5.30.

Consider now the proof of $(*)$ that starts with induction on k: for $k = 0$ the equation degenerates to $\varrho_\chi^\ell = \varrho_\chi^\ell$, which is clearly true for each χ. In the induction step, we have to show $(*)$ where we can use the following induction hypothesis:

$$(**)\quad \varrho_\chi^{\ell-k+1} = \varrho_\chi^\ell \wedge \bigwedge_{j=1}^{k-1} \mathsf{X}^j \varrho^\ell_{\mathcal{I}_{j+\ell-k+1}} \text{ for each } \chi \in \bigcup_{j=0}^{\ell-k+1} \mathfrak{S}(\mathsf{EVS}(\Phi_j))$$

We proceed with another induction, this time on χ. In the induction base, we have to prove $(*)$ for $\chi = \{\}$, i.e. we have to prove $\varrho_{\{\}}^{\ell-k} = \bigwedge_{j=1}^{k} \mathsf{X}^j \varrho_{\mathcal{I}_{j+\ell-k}}^{\ell}$ (note that $\varrho_{\{\}}^{\ell} = [1 \,\mathsf{U}\, 0] = 1$). This is proved with our induction hypothesis $(**)$ as follows:

$$\begin{aligned}
\varrho_{\{\}}^{\ell-k} &\overset{def}{=} \left(\bigvee_{s\in\{\}} \xi_{\{\}}^{\ell-k}(s)\right) \vee \left(\bigwedge_{s\in\{\}} \iota(s)\right) \wedge \mathsf{X}\varrho_{\{\}\cup\mathcal{I}_{\ell-k+1}}^{\ell-k+1} \\
&= 0 \vee 1 \wedge \mathsf{X}\varrho_{\{\}\cup\mathcal{I}_{\ell-k+1}}^{\ell-k+1} \\
&= \mathsf{X}\varrho_{\mathcal{I}_{\ell-k+1}}^{\ell-k+1} \overset{(**)}{=} \mathsf{X}\left[\varrho_{\mathcal{I}_{\ell-k+1}}^{\ell} \wedge \bigwedge_{j=1}^{k-1} \mathsf{X}^j \varrho_{\mathcal{I}_{j+\ell-k+1}}^{\ell}\right] \\
&= \mathsf{X}\left[\bigwedge_{j=0}^{k-1} \mathsf{X}^j \varrho_{\mathcal{I}_{j+\ell-k+1}}^{\ell}\right] \\
&= \bigwedge_{j=0}^{k-1} \mathsf{X}^{j+1} \varrho_{\mathcal{I}_{j+\ell-k+1}}^{\ell} \\
&= \bigwedge_{j=1}^{k} \mathsf{X}^{j} \varrho_{\mathcal{I}_{j+\ell-k}}^{\ell}
\end{aligned}$$

In the induction step, it remains to prove $(*)$ for our fixed $k > 0$ and a consistent situation $\chi \neq \{\}$, where we can additionally use the following induction hypothesis $(***)$:

$$(***)\quad \varrho_X^{\ell-k} = \varrho_X^{\ell} \wedge \bigwedge_{j=1}^{k} \mathsf{X}^j \varrho_{\mathcal{I}_{j+\ell-k}}^{\ell} \text{ for each } X \prec \chi$$

The remaining proof is then established as follows, where $k > 0$ and $\chi \neq \{\}$ holds and the assumptions $(**)$ and $(***)$ are used:

$$\begin{aligned}
\varrho_\chi^{\ell-k} &\overset{def}{=} \left(\bigvee_{s\in\chi} \xi_\chi^{\ell-k}(s)\right) \vee \left(\bigwedge_{s\in\chi} \iota(s)\right) \wedge \mathsf{X}\varrho_{\chi\cup\mathcal{I}_{\ell-k+1}}^{\ell-k+1} \\
&\overset{(**)}{=} \left(\bigvee_{s\in\chi} \xi_\chi^{\ell-k}(s)\right) \vee \left(\bigwedge_{s\in\chi} \iota(s)\right) \wedge \mathsf{X}\left[\varrho_{\chi\cup\mathcal{I}_{\ell-k+1}}^{\ell} \wedge \bigwedge_{j=1}^{k-1} \mathsf{X}^j \varrho_{\mathcal{I}_{j+\ell-k+1}}^{\ell}\right] \\
&= \left(\bigvee_{s\in\chi} \xi_\chi^{\ell-k}(s)\right) \vee \left(\bigwedge_{s\in\chi} \iota(s)\right) \wedge \mathsf{X}\left[\varrho_\chi^{\ell} \wedge \varrho_{\mathcal{I}_{\ell-k+1}}^{\ell} \wedge \bigwedge_{j=1}^{k-1} \mathsf{X}^j \varrho_{\mathcal{I}_{j+\ell-k+1}}^{\ell}\right] \\
&= \left(\bigvee_{s\in\chi} \xi_\chi^{\ell-k}(s)\right) \vee \left(\bigwedge_{s\in\chi} \iota(s)\right) \wedge \mathsf{X}\left[\varrho_\chi^{\ell} \wedge \bigwedge_{j=0}^{k-1} \mathsf{X}^j \varrho_{\mathcal{I}_{j+\ell-k+1}}^{\ell}\right] \\
&= \left(\bigvee_{s\in\chi} \xi_\chi^{\ell-k}(s)\right) \vee \left(\bigwedge_{s\in\chi} \iota(s)\right) \wedge \mathsf{X}\varrho_\chi^{\ell} \wedge \bigwedge_{j=1}^{k} \mathsf{X}^j \varrho_{\mathcal{I}_{j+\ell-k}}^{\ell} \\
&\overset{(***)}{=} \left(\bigvee_{s\in\chi} \xi_\chi^{\ell}(s) \wedge \bigwedge_{j=1}^{k} \mathsf{X}^j \varrho_{\mathcal{I}_{j+\ell-k}}^{\ell}\right) \vee \left(\bigwedge_{s\in\chi} \iota(s)\right) \wedge \mathsf{X}\varrho_\chi^{\ell} \wedge \bigwedge_{j=1}^{k} \mathsf{X}^j \varrho_{\mathcal{I}_{j+\ell-k}}^{\ell} \\
&= \left[\left(\bigvee_{s\in\chi} \xi_\chi^{\ell}(s)\right) \vee \left(\bigwedge_{s\in\chi} \iota(s)\right) \wedge \mathsf{X}\varrho_\chi^{\ell}\right] \wedge \bigwedge_{j=1}^{k} \mathsf{X}^j \varrho_{\mathcal{I}_{j+\ell-k}}^{\ell} \\
&= \varrho_\chi^{\ell} \wedge \bigwedge_{j=1}^{k} \mathsf{X}^j \varrho_{\mathcal{I}_{j+\ell-k}}^{\ell}
\end{aligned}$$

The last step holds due to the recursion laws of $\underline{\mathsf{U}}$ and U (note that ϱ_χ^{ℓ} is either a $\underline{\mathsf{U}}$ or a U formula). Now, consider the length of the definitions and let $\Psi = \bigwedge_{k=0}^{\ell} \mathsf{X}^k \Phi_k$. Clearly, Ψ is a CUB formula and the application of Theorem 5.31 results in the definitions for ϱ_χ^{ℓ}. According to Lemma 5.29 we know that there are at most $2^{|\Psi|}$ consistent situations of a CUB formula Ψ and moreover $|\chi| \leq |\Psi|$ holds. However, we have additional costs in the above constructions, as possibly $\ell + 1$ definitions $\varrho_\chi^0, \ldots, \varrho_\chi^{\ell}$ for a single situation χ are necessary. Hence, we have in the above construction at most $(\ell+1)2^{|\Psi|}$ definitions of length $O(|\Psi|)$ resulting in a complexity of order $O((\ell+1)\,|\Psi|\,2^{|\Psi|})$. This is certainly not greater than $O(|\Psi|\, 2^{\ell} 2^{|\Psi|})$ and this in turn is not greater than $O((\ell+|\Psi|)2^{\ell+|\Psi|})$. The latter is the same as $O(|\Phi|\, 2^{|\Phi|})$, since we have $O(|\Phi|) = O(\ell + |\Psi|)$. □

This completes the translation of LeftCTL* to vectorized alternation-free μ-calculus. The following theorem summarizes the results which improve the complexity of the former naive transformation.

Theorem 5.32 (Translating LeftCTL* to Alternation-Free μ-Calculus). *Given an arbitrary LeftCTL* formula Φ, there is an equivalent vectorized alternation-free μ-calculus formula of length $O(|\Phi|\, 2^{2|\Phi|})$. This implies that there is a model checking procedure for LeftCTL* formulas that runs in time $O(|\mathcal{K}|\, |\Phi|\, 2^{2|\Phi|})$ and a satisfiability checking procedure that runs in time $2^{O(|\Phi| 2^{2|\Phi|})}$.*

Proof. We first compute PQNF(Φ) of the given formula Φ and therefore only need to consider LeftCTL* formulas of the form EΦ' where Φ' does not contain any path quantifier at all. To handle these formulas, we compute DeepDNF(Φ') of Φ' by the algorithm given in Figure 5.7. Hence, we obtain a formula $\bigvee_{i\in M} \Phi_i$ with $|M| \in O(2^{\Phi})$, where each Φ_i has a length of order $O(|\Phi|)$ and is of the form $\bigwedge_{k=0}^{\ell_i} \mathsf{X}^k \varphi_{i,k}$ for some CUB formulas $\varphi_{i,k}$. The last theorem can be used to translate each Φ_i in a shared form of size $O(|\Phi_i|\, 2^{|\Phi_i|})$ such that the E path quantifiers can be shifted inwards with only a linear increase of the size. Hence, the overall costs are of order $O(|M|\, |\Phi_i|\, 2^{|\Phi_i|}) = O(|M|\, |\Phi|\, 2^{|\Phi|}) = O(|\Phi|\, 2^{2|\Phi|})$.

The proposition for the complexity of the satisfiability check is to due to satisfiability checking of CTL formulas that can be done in time $2^{O(|\Phi|)}$ [158]. □

We note that the upper bound of the transformation does not seem not to be tight, i.e., no example has been found that leads to an increase of $O(|\Phi|\, 2^{2|\Phi|})$. However, as our illustrating example of Subsection 5.3.5 showed, there are examples that lead to an increase of $O(|\Phi|\, 2^{|\Phi|})$. In either case however, the result shown in this section proves that the transformation from LeftCTL* can become exponential if vectorized μ-calculus formulas are used. Note, however, the lower bounds established in [4, 266, 513].

5.4 Translating Temporal Logics to ω-Automata

In the previous section, we have considered translations of the logics CTL, CTL^2, LeftCTL*, FairCTL, and FairLeftCTL* to the μ-calculus, so that we have obtained efficient decision procedures for these logics. There are however more powerful temporal logics whose model checking problems we have not considered so far. We will therefore consider in this section model checking algorithms for more general logics, in particular for CTL*. However, we will not directly translate to the μ-calculus. Instead, we will show how quantifier-free formulas (even with past time temporal operators) can be efficiently translated to equivalent ω-automata. As we already know how to translate the branching time logic $\mathcal{L}_\omega$ of ω-automata to the μ-calculus, we can also translate arbitrary branching time temporal logic formulas to the μ-calculus.

The ω-automaton $\mathfrak{A}_\Phi$ that is computed for a given formula Φ has, at most, $O(2^{|\Phi|})$ states. Nevertheless, our translation procedure is able to compute that automaton in linear time $O(|\Phi|)$ because it generates a *symbolic representation* in terms of our ω-automaton formulas (it is easy to see that we can write for every $i \in \mathbb{N}$ an ω-automaton formula $\mathfrak{A}_i = \mathcal{A}_\exists(Q, \Phi_\mathcal{I}, \Phi_\mathcal{R}, \Phi_\mathcal{F})$ of size $O(i)$ with $O(2^i)$ reachable states). The translation from ω-automata to the μ-calculus can not however benefit from the symbolic representation of the ω-automata. Hence, we get an exponential blow-up there: given an arbitrary temporal logic formula Φ, we can compute an equivalent μ-calculus formula of exponential size in terms of $|\Phi|$.

This blow-up can probably not be avoided due to complexity results: CTL* model checking is PSPACE-complete (Section 5.6). We have already seen that model checking of alternation-free μ-calculus formulas can be done in linear time. So, if there were a polynomial translation from a temporal logic to equivalent alternation-free μ-calculus formulas, this would result in a polynomial time model checking procedure for that logic. Hence, for temporal logics like LeftCTL*, LTL, and CTL*, it is probably not possible to obtain μ-calculus formulas of polynomial size (in general), since their model checking problems are NP-hard (even Δ_2^p-complete) and PSPACE-complete (Section 5.6), respectively.

Similar to the automaton hierarchy (cf. Figure 4.33), we will also define a corresponding hierarchy for temporal logics. Recall that any of the automaton classes has a deterministic representative: For example, we can choose the classes $\mathsf{Det_G}$, $\mathsf{Det_F}$, $\mathsf{Det_{Prefix}}$, $\mathsf{Det_{FG}}$, $\mathsf{Det_{GF}}$, and $\mathsf{Det_{Streett}}$ as representatives. We have also seen that our translation from $\mathsf{Det_{GF}}$, and $\mathsf{Det_{Streett}}$ to the μ-calculus results in μ-calculus formulas with alternation depth 2, while the classes $\mathsf{Det_G}$, $\mathsf{Det_F}$, $\mathsf{Det_{Prefix}}$, $\mathsf{Det_{FG}}$ can be translated to the alternation-free μ-calculus. Therefore, we are interested in temporal logics $\mathsf{TL_G}$, $\mathsf{TL_F}$, $\mathsf{TL_{Prefix}}$, and $\mathsf{TL_{FG}}$ that correspond with the automaton classes $\mathsf{Det_G}$, $\mathsf{Det_F}$, $\mathsf{Det_{Prefix}}$, and $\mathsf{Det_{FG}}$ because these formulas can be translated to the alternation-free μ-calculus and can therefore be checked more efficiently.

The outline of this section is therefore as follows: in the next subsection, we will present a simple translation from quantifier-free temporal logic formulas to equivalent $\mathsf{NDet_{Streett}}$ automata. We will then show in Section 5.4.2 how this translation can be improved by considering the monotonicity of temporal operators. This observation necessitates the definition of the temporal logics $\mathsf{TL_G}$, $\mathsf{TL_F}$, $\mathsf{TL_{Prefix}}$, $\mathsf{TL_{FG}}$, $\mathsf{TL_{GF}}$, and $\mathsf{TL_{Streett}}$ in Section 5.4.3. We construct efficient procedures for translation of these logics to their corresponding automaton class in Section 5.4.4. We then investigate the tight relationship between the logic LeftCTL* and the logics $\mathsf{TL_{FG}}$ and $\mathsf{TL_{GF}}$ in Section 5.4.5 and show there that the *model checking problems* of these logics can be directly translated to equivalent CTL model checking problems. For this reason, we will also define a logic AFCTL* that can be translated to the alternation-free μ-calculus. In Section 5.4.5, we collect all these results in a final translation procedure that is able to translate CTL* model checking problems to equivalent FairCTL model checking problems.

In the following, we will often consider the quantifier-free fragment of CTL*, and often we furthermore allow past temporal operators. Hence, for reasons of conciseness, we will define the following temporal logic LTL_p:

Definition 5.33 (Temporal Path Formulas LTL_p). *Given a finite set of variables V_Σ, the following grammar rules define the temporal logic LTL_p:*

$$\begin{aligned} P ::= {} & S \mid \neg P \mid P \wedge P \mid P \vee P \\ & \mid \mathsf{X}P \mid \mathsf{G}P \mid \mathsf{F}P \\ & \mid \overleftarrow{\mathsf{X}}P \mid \overleftarrow{\underline{\mathsf{X}}}P \mid \overleftarrow{\mathsf{G}}P \mid \overleftarrow{\mathsf{F}}P \\ & \mid [P\ \mathsf{U}\ P] \mid [P\ \mathsf{B}\ P] \mid [P\ \underline{\mathsf{U}}\ P] \mid [P\ \underline{\mathsf{B}}\ P] \\ & \mid [P\ \overleftarrow{\mathsf{U}}\ P] \mid [P\ \overleftarrow{\mathsf{B}}\ P] \mid [P\ \overleftarrow{\underline{\mathsf{U}}}\ P] \mid [P\ \overleftarrow{\underline{\mathsf{B}}}\ P] \end{aligned}$$

We have excluded the W and $\underline{\mathsf{W}}$ operators, to reduce the number of cases. Clearly, we could do the same with some other operators, but want to retain the others to show up some similarities. The algorithms in the remainder of this section do also only consider the above set of temporal operators, sometimes even further restricted to the next and previous operators, the strong-until and the weak-before (or the weak until).

5.4.1 The Basic Translation from LTL_p to $\mathsf{NDet}_{\mathsf{Streett}}$

Translations from temporal logics to equivalent ω-automata have been intensively studied. Early research, as done by Vardi and Wolper considered translations to equivalent Büchi automata, where the automaton has been explicitly constructed [386]. For that reason, Vardi and Wolper have defined the set of *elementary subformulas* of a given formula Φ which is the set of all subformulas of Φ that start with a temporal operator. The procedure has been refined in a couple of further papers [138, 185, 207, 208, 468, 520]. We will not directly present Vardi and Wolper's procedure, but its underlying ideas are still contained in the procedures that we will present.

Assume that Φ has the elementary formulas $\{\varphi_1, \ldots, \varphi_n\}$. The states of the ω-automaton that is to be constructed consist of the truth values of these elementary formulas. For this reason, we need n state variables $\{q_1, \ldots, q_n\}$ to encode the state set, and therefore we already see where the exponential blow-up comes from. Clearly, for any run through the automaton, we want $q_i \leftrightarrow \varphi_i$ to hold. For this reason, the transition relation of the automaton must respect the semantics of the temporal operators that occur in φ_i. Having this view, we will describe in this section how to define a transition relation for the ω-automaton such that the desired equivalences $q_i \leftrightarrow \varphi_i$ hold for all elementary subformulas of the given LTL_p formula Φ. In particular, we are able to define a transition relation of size $O(|\Phi|)$ so that our translation procedure will also run in time $O(|\Phi|)$, which is not possible for explicit constructions of the automaton. Procedures that translate temporal logic formulas to symbolic descriptions have been considered in [88, 89, 105, 131, 281, 439].

For example, consider the formula $\mathsf{FG}a \rightarrow \mathsf{GF}a$. The elementary subformulas are abbreviated as follows: $q_1 = \mathsf{G}a$, $q_2 = \mathsf{F}q_1$, $q_3 = \mathsf{F}a$, $q_4 = \mathsf{G}q_3$, so that the resulting formula is $\Psi \equiv q_2 \rightarrow q_4$. Therefore, our ω-automaton will be constructed with the state variables $\{q_1, q_2, q_3, q_4\}$, and its transitions should be such that the above equations are respected. For this reason, the following recursion laws must be respected by the transition relation of our automaton:

Lemma 5.34 (Recursion Laws of Temporal Operators). *The following equations are generally valid for all formulas φ and ψ:*

$$
\begin{array}{ll}
\mathsf{G}\varphi = \varphi \wedge \mathsf{X}\mathsf{G}\varphi & \mathsf{F}\varphi = \varphi \vee \mathsf{X}\mathsf{F}\varphi \\
[\varphi\ \mathsf{U}\ \psi] = \psi \vee \varphi \wedge \mathsf{X}\,[\varphi\ \mathsf{U}\ \psi] & [\varphi\ \underline{\mathsf{U}}\ \psi] = \psi \vee \varphi \wedge \mathsf{X}\,[\varphi\ \underline{\mathsf{U}}\ \psi] \\
[\varphi\ \mathsf{B}\ \psi] = \neg\psi \wedge (\varphi \vee \mathsf{X}\,[\varphi\ \mathsf{B}\ \psi] & [\varphi\ \underline{\mathsf{B}}\ \psi] = \neg\psi \wedge (\varphi \vee \mathsf{X}\,[\varphi\ \underline{\mathsf{B}}\ \psi] \\
\overleftarrow{\mathsf{G}}\varphi = \varphi \wedge \overleftarrow{\mathsf{X}}\,\overleftarrow{\mathsf{G}}\varphi & \overleftarrow{\mathsf{F}}\varphi = \varphi \vee \underline{\overleftarrow{\mathsf{X}}}\,\overleftarrow{\mathsf{F}}\varphi \\
[\varphi\ \overleftarrow{\mathsf{U}}\ \psi] = \psi \vee \varphi \wedge \overleftarrow{\mathsf{X}}\,[\varphi\ \overleftarrow{\mathsf{U}}\ \psi] & [\varphi\ \underline{\overleftarrow{\mathsf{U}}}\ \psi] = \psi \vee \varphi \wedge \underline{\overleftarrow{\mathsf{X}}}\,[\varphi\ \underline{\overleftarrow{\mathsf{U}}}\ \psi] \\
[\varphi\ \overleftarrow{\mathsf{B}}\ \psi] = \neg\psi \wedge (\varphi \vee \overleftarrow{\mathsf{X}}\,[\varphi\ \overleftarrow{\mathsf{B}}\ \psi] & [\varphi\ \underline{\overleftarrow{\mathsf{B}}}\ \psi] = \neg\psi \wedge (\varphi \vee \underline{\overleftarrow{\mathsf{X}}}\,[\varphi\ \underline{\overleftarrow{\mathsf{B}}}\ \psi]
\end{array}
$$

It is to be noted that the strong and weak operators share exactly the same recursion laws and that the recursion laws of the past time modalities correspond with the recursion laws of the corresponding future time modality. Furthermore, for the past time modalities, we must use the strong previous operator in the recursion laws for the strong operators and the weak one for the recursion laws of the weak operators.

Hence, given that both φ and ψ would be propositional formulas, we could built an ω-automaton by simply substituting a new state variable q for the elementary subformula that should be abbreviated by q. For example, for the formula $[\varphi\ \underline{\mathsf{U}}\ \psi]$, the transition relation should then be $q \leftrightarrow \psi \vee \varphi \wedge \mathsf{X}q$. Using this transition relation, we know that q is a solution of the fixpoint equation $x \leftrightarrow \psi \vee \varphi \wedge \mathsf{X}x$.

However, this does not help much at the moment: We already know that $[\varphi\ \mathsf{U}\ \psi]$ and $[\varphi\ \underline{\mathsf{U}}\ \psi]$ are also solutions of this equation, and therefore there is more than one solution. However, it could be the case that there could possibly be other solutions, too. For this reason, we now consider the solutions of the above fixpoint equations in detail. The following lemma lists the essential properties of the fixpoint equation $q \leftrightarrow \psi \vee \varphi \wedge \mathsf{X}q$ and will be of important use for a lot of theorems in this section. We will see that besides $[\varphi\ \mathsf{U}\ \psi]$ and $[\varphi\ \underline{\mathsf{U}}\ \psi]$, there are no further solutions, and this will make the automata even unambiguous, i.e., every accepted word has exactly one accepting run.

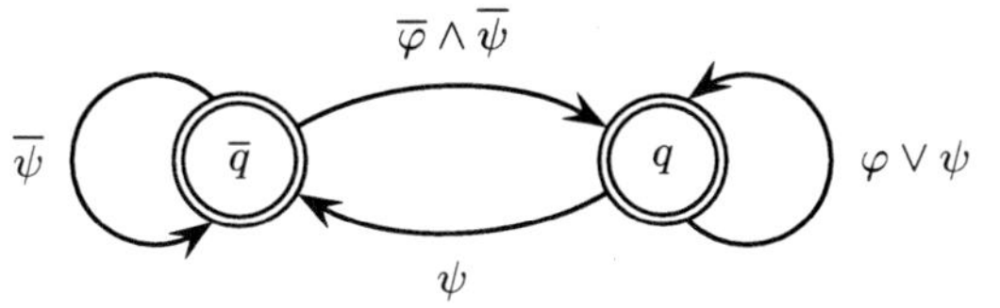

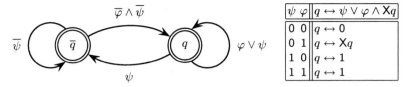

ψ	φ	$q \leftrightarrow \psi \vee \varphi \wedge \mathsf{X}q$
0	0	$q \leftrightarrow 0$
0	1	$q \leftrightarrow \mathsf{X}q$
1	0	$q \leftrightarrow 1$
1	1	$q \leftrightarrow 1$

Fig. 5.10. ω-automaton for discussing the fixpoint equation $q \leftrightarrow \psi \vee \varphi \wedge \mathsf{X}q$

Lemma 5.35 (Solutions of $q \leftrightarrow \psi \vee \varphi \wedge \mathsf{X}q$). *Assuming that* $\mathsf{G}\,[q \leftrightarrow \psi \vee \varphi \wedge \mathsf{X}q]$ *initially holds, then the following facts can be derived (for the initial point of time):*

(1) $\mathsf{G}\,[\psi \rightarrow q] \wedge \mathsf{G}\,[\neg\varphi \wedge \neg\psi \rightarrow \neg q] \wedge \mathsf{G}\,[\varphi \wedge \neg\psi \rightarrow (q \leftrightarrow \mathsf{X}q)]$
(2) $\mathsf{G}\,[\mathsf{F}(\varphi \rightarrow \psi) \rightarrow (q \leftrightarrow [\varphi\ \underline{\mathsf{U}}\ \psi])]$
(3) $\mathsf{G}\left(\mathsf{F}(\varphi \rightarrow \psi) \Rightarrow \overleftarrow{\mathsf{G}}\,(q \leftrightarrow [\varphi\ \underline{\mathsf{U}}\ \psi]) \middle|\ \mathsf{G}q \vee \mathsf{G}\neg q\right)$
(4) $\mathsf{G}\,[q \leftrightarrow [\varphi\ \underline{\mathsf{U}}\ \psi]] \vee \mathsf{G}\,[q \leftrightarrow [\varphi\ \mathsf{U}\ \psi]]$
(5) $\mathsf{G}\left(\mathsf{F}(q \rightarrow \psi) \Rightarrow \overleftarrow{\mathsf{G}}\,(q \leftrightarrow [\varphi\ \underline{\mathsf{U}}\ \psi]) \middle|\ \mathsf{G}(q \wedge \varphi \wedge \neg\psi)\right)$
(6) $\mathsf{G}\left(\mathsf{F}(q \rightarrow \psi) \Rightarrow \overleftarrow{\mathsf{G}}\,(q \leftrightarrow [\varphi\ \underline{\mathsf{U}}\ \psi]) \middle|\ \mathsf{G}(q \leftrightarrow [\varphi\ \mathsf{U}\ \psi])\right)$
(7) $\mathsf{G}\left(\mathsf{F}(q \rightarrow \psi) \Rightarrow \overleftarrow{\mathsf{G}}\,(q \leftrightarrow [\varphi\ \underline{\mathsf{U}}\ \psi]) \middle|\ \overleftarrow{\mathsf{G}}\,(q \leftrightarrow [\varphi\ \mathsf{U}\ \psi]) \wedge \mathsf{G}(q \leftrightarrow [\varphi\ \mathsf{U}\ \psi])\right)$
(8) $\mathsf{G}\left[(q \leftrightarrow [\varphi\ \underline{\mathsf{U}}\ \psi]) \leftrightarrow \overleftarrow{\mathsf{G}}\,(q \leftrightarrow [\varphi\ \underline{\mathsf{U}}\ \psi])\right]$
(9) $\mathsf{G}\,[(q \leftrightarrow [\varphi\ \underline{\mathsf{U}}\ \psi]) \leftrightarrow \mathsf{F}(q \rightarrow \psi)]$
(10) $\mathsf{G}\,[(q \leftrightarrow [\varphi\ \mathsf{U}\ \psi]) \leftrightarrow \mathsf{F}(\varphi \rightarrow q)]$

Before turning to the proof, we first discuss some of the above facts. (1) means that the truth value of any solution q of the fixpoint equation is immediately and uniquely determined at any point of time where either ψ or $\neg\varphi \wedge \neg\psi$ holds. In the remaining case, where $\varphi \wedge \neg\psi$ holds, the truth value is the same as that of the next point of time.

(2) details this in that it additionally says that whenever $\varphi \rightarrow \psi$ holds (note that $\neg(\varphi \wedge \neg\psi)$ is equivalent to $\varphi \rightarrow \psi$) at some point of time, then we definitely have $q \leftrightarrow [\varphi\ \underline{\mathsf{U}}\ \psi]$ (and also $q \leftrightarrow [\varphi\ \mathsf{U}\ \psi]$). The same holds if only $\mathsf{F}(\varphi \rightarrow \psi)$ holds at some point of time. (3) gives even more details: if $\mathsf{F}(\varphi \rightarrow \psi)$ holds at some point of time, then we have $q \leftrightarrow [\varphi\ \underline{\mathsf{U}}\ \psi]$ (and also $q \leftrightarrow [\varphi\ \mathsf{U}\ \psi]$) for now and all previous moments of time. (3) also states what happens if $\mathsf{F}(\varphi \rightarrow \psi)$ does not hold: then there are two solutions for q: one that is constantly 1, the other one is constantly 0. (4) specifies the set of all solutions of the fixpoint equations: we either have $q \leftrightarrow [\varphi\ \underline{\mathsf{U}}\ \psi]$ or $q \leftrightarrow [\varphi\ \mathsf{U}\ \psi]$ for all moments of time. *Hence, the equation $q \leftrightarrow \psi \vee \varphi \wedge \mathsf{X}q$ has exactly two solutions!* (5 – 7) specifies in more detail in which case we have $q \leftrightarrow [\varphi\ \underline{\mathsf{U}}\ \psi]$ or $q \leftrightarrow [\varphi\ \mathsf{U}\ \psi]$, respectively, and (8 – 10) are further reformulations of (5). Now, consider the proofs of these facts:

Proof. We prove the facts in the listed order, where we consider an arbitrary path π of an arbitrary Kripke structure $\mathcal{K}$. As a shorthand notation, we simply write $\varphi^{(t)}$ instead of $(\mathcal{K}, \pi, t) \models \varphi$ to be more concise in the following proofs:

(1): These facts are obtained by propositional simplifications of the fixpoint equation: For example, if $\varphi \wedge \neg\psi$ holds, then $q \leftrightarrow \psi \vee \varphi \wedge \mathsf{X}q$ simplifies to $q \leftrightarrow \mathsf{X}q$.

(2): Let t_0 be an arbitrary point of time, where $\mathsf{F}(\varphi \rightarrow \psi)$ holds. Then, there is a number t_1 such that (2.1) $\varphi \rightarrow \psi$ holds at time $t_0 + t_1$. In particular, we can choose t_1 to be the smallest number with this property, so that we additionally have (2.2) $\forall t < t_1.\varphi^{(t_0+t)} \wedge \neg\psi^{(t_0+t)}$. By (1), it then follows that (2.3) $\forall t < t_1. \rightarrow q^{(t_0+t)} = q^{(t_0+t+1)}$. This means that the truth value of any solution of the fixpoint equation remains constant until $\varphi \wedge \neg\psi$ is read. Hence, the truth value of $q^{(t_0+t_1)}$ determines the truth value for all $q^{(t_0+t)}$ with $t < t_1$, i.e., we have (2.4) $\forall t \leq t_1.q^{(t_0+t)} = q^{(t_0+t_1)}$, and in particular that (2.5) $q^{(t_0)} = q^{(t_0+t_1)}$ ((2.5) can be proved without (2.4) by induction on t_1). Now, we consider two cases according to (2.1):
In the first case, we have (2.1.1) $\psi^{(t_0+t_1)}$, and hence obtain by (1) that $q^{(t_0+t_1)}$ holds, and hence, by (2.5) that $q^{(t_0)}$ holds. By (2.2), (2.1.1), and the semantics of the temporal operators, we also have $[\varphi \ \underline{\mathsf{U}}\ \psi]^{(t_0)}$, so that the equation $q^{(t_0)} = [\varphi \ \underline{\mathsf{U}}\ \psi]^{(t_0)}$ holds.
In the second case, we have (2.1.2) $\neg\varphi^{(t_0+t_1)} \wedge \neg\psi^{(t_0+t_1)}$, and hence obtain by (1) that $\neg q^{(t_0+t_1)}$ holds, and hence, by (2.5) that $\neg q^{(t_0)}$ holds. By (2.2), (2.1.2), and the semantics of the temporal operators, we also have $\neg [\varphi \ \underline{\mathsf{U}}\ \psi]^{(t_0)}$, so that the equation $q^{(t_0)} = [\varphi \ \underline{\mathsf{U}}\ \psi]^{(t_0)}$ holds.

(3): We have to prove the implications $\mathsf{G}\left[\mathsf{F}(\varphi \rightarrow \psi) \rightarrow \overleftarrow{\mathsf{G}}(q \leftrightarrow [\varphi \ \underline{\mathsf{U}}\ \psi])\right]$ and $\mathsf{G}[\neg\mathsf{F}(\varphi \rightarrow \psi) \rightarrow (\mathsf{G}q \vee \mathsf{G}\neg q)]$. The first implication follows more or less directly from (2): Assume that t_0 is an arbitrary point of time where $[\mathsf{F}(\varphi \rightarrow \psi)]^{(t_0)}$ holds, then we also have for all t_1 with $t_1 \leq t_0$ that $[\mathsf{F}(\varphi \rightarrow \psi)]^{(t_1)}$ holds. Thus we can use (2) to derive for all t_1 with $t_1 \leq t_0$ that $[q \leftrightarrow [\varphi \ \underline{\mathsf{U}}\ \psi]]^{(t_1)}$ holds.
To prove $\mathsf{G}[\neg\mathsf{F}(\varphi \rightarrow \psi) \rightarrow (\mathsf{G}q \vee \mathsf{G}\neg q)]$, assume that at some point of time t_0, we would have $\neg[\mathsf{F}(\varphi \rightarrow \psi)]^{(t_0)}$, i.e. (3.1) $\forall t.\varphi^{(t_0+t)} \wedge \neg\psi^{(t_0+t)}$. From the fixpoint equation, it then follows that (3.2) $\forall t.q^{(t_0+t)} = q^{(t_0+t+1)}$, so that we conclude by induction on t that (3.3) $\forall t.q^{(t_0+t)} = q^{(t_0)}$. Depending on $q^{(t_0)}$, we thus have either $[\mathsf{G}q]^{(t_0)}$ or $[\mathsf{G}\neg q]^{(t_0)}$.

(4) We consider two cases: In the first case, we assume that $\mathsf{GF}(\varphi \rightarrow \psi)^{(0)}$ holds. Thus, we have $\mathsf{F}(\varphi \rightarrow \psi)^{(t_0)}$ for all t_0, and hence by (2) that $q^{(t_0)} = [\varphi \ \underline{\mathsf{U}}\ \psi]^{(t_0)}$ holds. In the second case, we have $\mathsf{FG}(\varphi \wedge \neg\psi)^{(0)}$, hence there must be a point of time t_0, with (4.1) $\forall t \geq t_0.\varphi^{(t_0+t)} \wedge \neg\psi^{(t_0+t)}$. By (3), it therefore follows that (4.2) $[\mathsf{G}q]^{(t_0)}$ or $[\mathsf{G}\neg q]^{(t_0)}$ holds. Combining (4.1) and (4.2) results in (4.3) $[\mathsf{G}(q \wedge \varphi \wedge \neg\psi)]^{(t_0)}$ or $[\mathsf{G}(\neg q \wedge \varphi \wedge \neg\psi)]^{(t_0)}$. Hence, we consider two cases according to (4.3.1): If $[\mathsf{G}(q \wedge \varphi \wedge \neg\psi)]^{(t_0)}$ holds, then it follows by the semantics of the temporal operators that

$[\mathsf{G}(q \leftrightarrow [\varphi \mathsf{U} \psi])]^{(t_0)}$, and if $[\mathsf{G}(\neg q \wedge \varphi \wedge \neg\psi)]^{(t_0)}$ holds, then it follows by the semantics of the temporal operators that $[\mathsf{G}(q \leftrightarrow [\varphi \underline{\mathsf{U}} \psi])]^{(t_0)}$.

(5): We first prove that $\mathsf{G}[\neg\mathsf{F}(q \rightarrow \psi) \rightarrow \mathsf{G}(q \wedge \varphi \wedge \neg\psi]$ holds: Let t_0 be an arbitrary point of time, where $\neg[\mathsf{F}(q \rightarrow \psi)]^{(t_0)}$ holds. Then, we have $[\mathsf{G}(q \wedge \neg\psi)]^{(t_0)}$, so that by our fixpoint equation $[\mathsf{G}\varphi]^{(t_0)}$ follows, which already proves our second implication.
Now we prove that $\mathsf{G}[\mathsf{F}(q \rightarrow \psi) \rightarrow (q \leftrightarrow [\varphi \underline{\mathsf{U}} \psi])]$ holds: Let t_0 be an arbitrary point of time, where $[\mathsf{F}(q \rightarrow \psi)]^{(t_0)}$ holds. This is obviously equivalent to (5.1) $[\mathsf{F}\neg q]^{(t_0)} \vee [\mathsf{F}\psi]^{(t_0)}$, so that we make a case distinction: In the first case, we have (5.1.1) $[\mathsf{F}\psi]^{(t_0)}$, and thus also (5.1.2) $[\mathsf{F}(\varphi \rightarrow \psi)]^{(t_0)}$. Hence, our proposition follows from (2).
In the second case, we have (5.1.2) $[\mathsf{F}\neg q]^{(t_0)} \wedge \neg[\mathsf{F}\psi]^{(t_0)}$. Hence, there is a number t_1 such that (5.1.3) $\neg q^{(t_0+t_1)}$ holds. In particular, we can choose t_1 to be the least number with this property, so that we additionally have (5.1.4) $\forall t < t_1 . q^{(t_0+t)}$. By (5.1.2), (5.1.4) and our fixpoint equation, we now obtain (5.1.5) $\forall t < t_1 . \varphi^{(t_0+t)} \wedge \neg\psi^{(t_0+t)} \wedge q^{(t_0+t)} \wedge q^{(t_0+t+1)}$. But then, it follows that $t_1 = 0$ must hold: If $0 < t_1$ holds, then we could instantiate $t := t_1 - 1$ in (5.1.5), so that we obtain $q^{(t_0+t_1)}$, and hence a contradiction to (5.1.3). Therefore, we have (5.1.6) $t_1 = 0$, and thus by (5.1.3) that (5.1.7) $\neg q^{(t_0)}$. We now make a case distinction on (4): In the first case, we have $\mathsf{G}[q \leftrightarrow [\varphi \underline{\mathsf{U}} \psi]]$, and therefore our proposition does trivially hold. In the second case, we have $\mathsf{G}[q \leftrightarrow [\varphi \mathsf{U} \psi]]$, and thus by (5.1.7) that $\neg[\varphi \mathsf{U} \psi]^{(t_0)}$. As strong operators imply the weak ones, this implies by contraposition $\neg[\varphi \underline{\mathsf{U}} \psi]^{(t_0)}$ which also proves our proposition in this case.
It is now straightforward to prove that our first implication holds: Just note that if $\mathsf{F}\Phi$ holds at some point of time t_0 then it also holds at any point of time t_1 with $t_1 \leq t_0$.

(6): The first implication follows immediately from (5). For the second one, let t_0 be arbitrarily chosen. We obtain from (5) that $[\mathsf{G}(q \wedge \varphi \wedge \neg\psi)]^{(t_0)}$ holds, and this implies by the semantics of the temporal operators that also $[\mathsf{G}(q \leftrightarrow [\varphi \mathsf{U} \psi])]^{(t_0)}$ holds.

(7): We only prove $\mathsf{G}\left(\neg\mathsf{F}[q \rightarrow \psi] \rightarrow \overleftarrow{\mathsf{G}}(q \leftrightarrow [\varphi \underline{\mathsf{U}} \psi])\right)$, the rest follows immediately from (6). Assume first that (7.1) $[\mathsf{GF}[q \rightarrow \psi]]^{(0)}$ holds. Then, it follows by (5) that $[\mathsf{G}[q \leftrightarrow [\varphi \underline{\mathsf{U}} \psi]]]^{(0)}$ must hold for any solution q of the fixpoint equation. As $[\varphi \mathsf{U} \psi]$ is by (4) a solution of the fixpoint equation, we thus have $[\mathsf{G}[[\varphi \mathsf{U} \psi] \leftrightarrow [\varphi \underline{\mathsf{U}} \psi]]]^{(0)}$, so that our proposition holds.
If, on the other hand, (7.2) $[\mathsf{FG}[q \wedge \neg\psi]]^{(0)}$ holds, then there is a point of time t_0 where (7.3) $[\mathsf{G}[q \wedge \neg\psi]]^{(t_0)}$ holds. We consider the least t_0 with that property, i.e. we have (7.4) $\forall t < t_0 . [\mathsf{F}[q \rightarrow \psi]]^{(t)}$. If $t_0 = 0$ holds, then our proposition follows by (7.3) and (6). Hence, assume further (7.5) $0 < t_0$, so that we can instantiate $t := t_0 - 1$ in (7.4) to obtain (7.6) $[\mathsf{F}[q \rightarrow \psi]]^{(t_0-1)}$, and thus together with (5) that $[\overleftarrow{\mathsf{G}}[q \leftrightarrow [\varphi \underline{\mathsf{U}} \psi]]]^{(t_0-1)}$ holds for any solution of the fixpoint equation. As $[\varphi \mathsf{U} \psi]$ is by (4) a solution of the

fixpoint equation, we thus have $[\overleftarrow{\mathsf{G}}[[\varphi\ \mathsf{U}\ \psi] \leftrightarrow [\varphi\ \underline{\mathsf{U}}\ \psi]]]^{(t_0-1)}$, and hence $[\overleftarrow{\mathsf{G}}[q \leftrightarrow [\varphi\ \underline{\mathsf{U}}\ \psi]]]^{(t_0-1)}$.

(8) and (9): These are just simple consequences of (5).

(10): The implication from left to right is simple: Assume that (10.1) $q^{(t_0)} = [\varphi\ \mathsf{U}\ \psi]^{(t_0)}$ holds, but $\mathsf{F}[\varphi \rightarrow q]$ will not hold at some point of time t_0. Hence, this means that (10.2) $\mathsf{G}[\varphi \wedge \neg q]$ must hold at t_0. But then, due to (10.1) and (10.2) we have that (10.3) $\neg[\varphi\ \mathsf{U}\ \psi]^{(t_0)}$, and hence, (10.4) $[(\neg\varphi)\ \underline{\mathsf{B}}\ \psi]^{(t_0)}$. This implies however that (10.5) $\mathsf{F}(\neg\varphi)^{(t_0)}$, which contradicts (10.2). Hence, (10.1) and (10.2) can not both hold, so that (10.1) implies the negation of (10.2).

For the implication from right to left, we first note that by fact (4) of the lemma, we already know that either $\mathsf{G}[q \leftrightarrow [\varphi\ \underline{\mathsf{U}}\ \psi]]$ or $\mathsf{G}[q \leftrightarrow [\varphi\ \mathsf{U}\ \psi]]$ hold. In the latter case, there is nothing to prove, so consider the former one, i.e., we have (10.6) $\mathsf{G}[q \leftrightarrow [\varphi\ \underline{\mathsf{U}}\ \psi]]$. Consider an arbitrary point of time t_0. Given that $q^{(t_0)}$ holds, we have by (10.6) that $[\varphi\ \underline{\mathsf{U}}\ \psi]^{(t_0)}$, and as strong operators imply the weak ones, we also have $[\varphi\ \mathsf{U}\ \psi]^{(t_0)}$. So, consider the remaining case where (10.7) $\neg q^{(t_0)}$ holds. By (10.6), we also have (10.8) $\neg[\varphi\ \underline{\mathsf{U}}\ \psi]^{(t_0)}$ and have to prove that $\neg[\varphi\ \mathsf{U}\ \psi]^{(t_0)}$ holds. It is sufficient to show that $[\mathsf{F}\neg\varphi]^{(t_0)}$ holds, since under this assumption (10.8) implies $\neg[\varphi\ \mathsf{U}\ \psi]^{(t_0)}$. By our assumption, we have (10.9) $[\mathsf{F}(\varphi \rightarrow q)]^{(t_0)}$, so that we consider two cases:

$[\mathsf{F}\neg\varphi]^{(t_0)}$: As our case assumption is identical to the goal of our proof, there is nothing to prove.

$[\mathsf{F}q]^{(t_0)}$: Let t_1 be the least point of time after t_0 where $q^{(t_0+t_1)}$ holds. Due to the fixpoint equation of q, it follows that we can only move from $\neg q$ to q when $\neg\varphi \wedge \neg\psi$ is read. Hence, we have $\neg\varphi^{(t_0+t_1)}$, which implies $[\mathsf{F}\neg\varphi]^{(t_0)}$.

The previous lemma is quite powerful. We will see that it provides us with the main hints for many improvements of the translation from temporal logics to ω-automata. At the moment, only fact (4) of the lemma is of interest for us since it precisely specifies the set of solutions of our fixpoint equations. We can also determine in the same manner the set of solutions of the other fixpoint equations. As a result, we will see in the next theorem that the fixpoint equations for the past time operators have a unique solution[3] and that the fixpoint equations for the future time operators have exactly two solutions that are given by the strong and weak variant of the operator (for G and F, we view 0 and 1 as counterparts).

[3] This is due to the fact that all past time operators can be defined by primitive recursion: For example, $[\varphi\ \overleftarrow{\underline{\mathsf{U}}}\ \psi]^{(0)} := 0$ and $[\varphi\ \overleftarrow{\underline{\mathsf{U}}}\ \psi]^{(t+1)} := \psi^{(t)} \vee \varphi^{(t)} \wedge [\varphi\ \overleftarrow{\underline{\mathsf{U}}}\ \psi]^{(t)}$. Note that each primitive recursive definition has a unique solution.

Theorem 5.36 (Temporal Fixpoint Equations). *The following equivalences are generally valid for all formulas φ and $\psi \in \mathsf{LTL}_p$. These equivalences determine the set of solutions of the fixpoint equations of Lemma 5.34:*

$$
\begin{aligned}
\mathsf{G}[q \leftrightarrow \varphi \wedge \mathsf{X}q] &\Leftrightarrow \mathsf{G}[q \leftrightarrow \mathsf{G}\varphi] \vee \mathsf{G}[q \leftrightarrow 0] \\
\mathsf{G}[q \leftrightarrow \varphi \vee \mathsf{X}q] &\Leftrightarrow \mathsf{G}[q \leftrightarrow \mathsf{F}\varphi] \vee \mathsf{G}[q \leftrightarrow 1] \\
\mathsf{G}[q \leftrightarrow \psi \vee \varphi \wedge \mathsf{X}q] &\Leftrightarrow \mathsf{G}[q \leftrightarrow [\varphi\ \mathsf{U}\ \psi]] \vee \mathsf{G}[q \leftrightarrow [\varphi\ \underline{\mathsf{U}}\ \psi]] \\
\mathsf{G}[q \leftrightarrow \neg\psi \wedge (\varphi \vee \mathsf{X}q)] &\Leftrightarrow \mathsf{G}[q \leftrightarrow [\varphi\ \mathsf{B}\ \psi]] \vee \mathsf{G}[q \leftrightarrow [\varphi\ \underline{\mathsf{B}}\ \psi]] \\
\mathsf{G}[q \leftrightarrow \varphi \wedge \overleftarrow{\mathsf{X}}q] &\Leftrightarrow \mathsf{G}[q \leftrightarrow \overleftarrow{\mathsf{G}}\varphi] \\
\mathsf{G}[q \leftrightarrow \varphi \vee \overleftarrow{\underline{\mathsf{X}}}q] &\Leftrightarrow \mathsf{G}[q \leftrightarrow \overleftarrow{\mathsf{F}}\varphi] \\
\mathsf{G}[q \leftrightarrow \psi \vee \varphi \wedge \overleftarrow{\mathsf{X}}q] &\Leftrightarrow \mathsf{G}[q \leftrightarrow [\varphi\ \overleftarrow{\mathsf{U}}\ \psi]] \\
\mathsf{G}[q \leftrightarrow \psi \vee \varphi \wedge \overleftarrow{\underline{\mathsf{X}}}q] &\Leftrightarrow \mathsf{G}[q \leftrightarrow [\varphi\ \overleftarrow{\underline{\mathsf{U}}}\ \psi]] \\
\mathsf{G}[q \leftrightarrow \neg\psi \wedge (\varphi \vee \overleftarrow{\mathsf{X}}q)] &\Leftrightarrow \mathsf{G}[q \leftrightarrow [\varphi\ \overleftarrow{\mathsf{B}}\ \psi]] \\
\mathsf{G}[q \leftrightarrow \neg\psi \wedge (\varphi \vee \overleftarrow{\underline{\mathsf{X}}}q)] &\Leftrightarrow \mathsf{G}[q \leftrightarrow [\varphi\ \overleftarrow{\underline{\mathsf{B}}}\ \psi]]
\end{aligned}
$$

Proof. All implications from right to the left follow simply from Lemma 5.34, since we can replace q with the corresponding temporal subformula. The implications from left to the right for the past time temporal operators simply follow from the uniqueness of primitive recursion. The remaining implications from left to right of the future time operators are more challenging. For the equation $\mathsf{G}[q \leftrightarrow \psi \vee \varphi \wedge \mathsf{X}q]$, we have already given the proof in the previous lemma. We now instantiate $p := \neg q$ in fact (4) of the previous lemma. It then says that if $\mathsf{G}[\neg p \leftrightarrow \neg\psi \wedge (\varphi \vee \neg\mathsf{X}p)]$ holds, then we have either $\mathsf{G}[\neg p \leftrightarrow [\varphi\ \underline{\mathsf{U}}\ \psi]]$ or $\mathsf{G}[\neg p \leftrightarrow [\varphi\ \mathsf{U}\ \psi]]$. Driving the negations first to the right hand side and then inwards, then results in our proposition for the B operator. In the same manner we can reduce the remaining equations to (4) of the previous lemma.

Hence, if the transition relation of an automaton implies for a state variable q that $q \leftrightarrow \psi \vee \varphi \wedge \mathsf{X}q$ invariantly holds, then we can immediately conclude that q behaves either like $[\varphi\ \underline{\mathsf{U}}\ \psi]$ or as $[\varphi\ \mathsf{U}\ \psi]$. Moreover, if the transition relation assures that $\mathsf{G}[q \leftrightarrow \psi \vee \varphi \wedge \overleftarrow{\underline{\mathsf{X}}}q]$ holds, then q will definitely behave exactly as $[\varphi\ \overleftarrow{\underline{\mathsf{U}}}\ \psi]$.

However, there are three problems for our translation procedure: first, the subformulas φ and ψ must be propositional, so that the discussed equations can be used as part of a transition relation of an ω-automaton. This can always be achieved when we work in a bottom-up manner through the syntax tree of the given formula. The second problem is that we are not allowed to use the operators $\overleftarrow{\mathsf{X}}$ and $\overleftarrow{\underline{\mathsf{X}}}$ in the transition relation of an ω-automaton. However, the fixpoint equations for the past time operators, use these operators. Hence, if we reach a subformula $[\varphi\ \overleftarrow{\mathsf{U}}\ \psi]$ with propositional arguments φ and ψ, we need to define a new state variable with the transition relation $q \leftrightarrow \psi \vee \varphi \wedge \overleftarrow{\mathsf{X}}q$ and replace $[\varphi\ \overleftarrow{\mathsf{U}}\ \psi]$ by q. As $\overleftarrow{\mathsf{X}}$ should not occur in the transition relation, we are not allowed to do this. Instead, we 'delay' our state variable q by one point of time, by using $\mathsf{X}q \leftrightarrow \psi \vee \varphi \wedge q$ in the transition relation. The question is now, what solutions does this new fixpoint equation have. We will see in the next theorem that there are two solutions of this equation, namely $[\varphi\ \overleftarrow{\mathsf{U}}\ \psi]$ and $[\varphi\ \overleftarrow{\underline{\mathsf{U}}}\ \psi]$. The uniqueness of the solution is now lost, since the equation $\mathsf{X}q \leftrightarrow \psi \vee \varphi \wedge q$ allows us to define q differently at the initial point of time. Before presenting a theorem that states all these facts, we introduce a concise notation for substitution that makes the remainder more readable.

Definition 5.37 (Formula Templates). *Given a formula Φ with some occurrences of a variable x, we abbreviate for convenience $\Phi\langle\varphi\rangle_x := [\Phi]_x^{\varphi}$.*

The main reason for the introduction of the above abbreviation is to make the following formulas more readable in that a lot of subscripts and superscripts with complex formulas are avoided.

Note that the notation allows us to single out *some* of the occurrences of a subformula: For example, given the formula $\mathsf{G}a \vee \neg\mathsf{G}a$, we can use the templates $\Phi_1 := x \vee \neg\mathsf{G}a$, $\Phi_2 := \mathsf{G}a \vee \neg x$, or $\Phi_3 := x \vee \neg x$ for one or both occurrences of the subformula $\mathsf{G}a$. For example, we then have $\Phi_1\langle\mathsf{F}a\rangle_x := \mathsf{F}a \vee \neg\mathsf{G}a$, $\Phi_2\langle\mathsf{F}a\rangle_x := \mathsf{G}a \vee \neg\mathsf{F}a$, and $\Phi_3\langle\mathsf{F}a\rangle_x := \mathsf{F}a \vee \neg\mathsf{F}a$.

Theorem 5.38 (Defining Past Time Modalities by ω-Automata). *Given a formula $\Phi \in \mathsf{LTL}_p$ with some occurrences of a variable x, and propositional formulas φ and ψ, the following equations are initially valid (we use the notation of Definition 5.37):*

$$
\begin{aligned}
\Phi\langle\overleftarrow{\mathsf{X}}\varphi\rangle_x &\Leftrightarrow \mathcal{A}_\exists\left(\{q\}, q, \mathsf{X}q \leftrightarrow \varphi, \Phi\langle q\rangle_x\right)\\
\Phi\langle\overleftarrow{\underline{\mathsf{X}}}\varphi\rangle_x &\Leftrightarrow \mathcal{A}_\exists\left(\{q\}, \neg q, \mathsf{X}q \leftrightarrow \varphi, \Phi\langle q\rangle_x\right)\\
\Phi\langle\overleftarrow{\mathsf{G}}\varphi\rangle_x &\Leftrightarrow \mathcal{A}_\exists\left(\{q\}, q, \mathsf{X}q \leftrightarrow \varphi \wedge q, \Phi\langle\varphi \wedge q\rangle_x\right)\\
\Phi\langle\overleftarrow{\mathsf{F}}\varphi\rangle_x &\Leftrightarrow \mathcal{A}_\exists\left(\{q\}, \neg q, \mathsf{X}q \leftrightarrow \varphi \vee q, \Phi\langle\varphi \vee q\rangle_x\right)\\
\Phi\langle[\varphi\ \overleftarrow{\mathsf{U}}\ \psi]\rangle_x &\Leftrightarrow \mathcal{A}_\exists\left(\{q\}, q, \mathsf{X}q \leftrightarrow \psi \vee \varphi \wedge q, \Phi\langle\psi \vee \varphi \wedge q\rangle_x\right)\\
\Phi\langle[\varphi\ \overleftarrow{\underline{\mathsf{U}}}\ \psi]\rangle_x &\Leftrightarrow \mathcal{A}_\exists\left(\{q\}, \neg q, \mathsf{X}q \leftrightarrow \psi \vee \varphi \wedge q, \Phi\langle\psi \vee \varphi \wedge q\rangle_x\right)\\
\Phi\langle[\varphi\ \overleftarrow{\mathsf{B}}\ \psi]\rangle_x &\Leftrightarrow \mathcal{A}_\exists\left(\{q\}, q, \mathsf{X}q \leftrightarrow \neg\psi \wedge (\varphi \vee q), \Phi\langle\neg\psi \wedge (\varphi \vee q)\rangle_x\right)\\
\Phi\langle[\varphi\ \overleftarrow{\underline{\mathsf{B}}}\ \psi]\rangle_x &\Leftrightarrow \mathcal{A}_\exists\left(\{q\}, \neg q, \mathsf{X}q \leftrightarrow \neg\psi \wedge (\varphi \vee q), \Phi\langle\neg\psi \wedge (\varphi \vee q)\rangle_x\right)
\end{aligned}
$$

Using the above equations in a bottom-up traversal over the syntax tree of a given formula allows us already to translate any temporal logic formula without future time modalities into an equivalent ω-automaton. It is remarkable that all transitions are *deterministic* and that the (intermediate) acceptance condition is only formed by the abbreviated formula $\Phi\langle q\rangle_x$ alone. Using the flattening law below (cf. Lemma 4.9), shows that at the end of our traversal, we end up with an ω-automaton of the form $\mathcal{A}_\exists\left(\{q_1, \ldots, q_n\}, \Phi_{\mathcal{I}}, \Phi_{\mathcal{R}}, \Phi\right)$ where Φ is a propositional formula.

$$
\mathcal{A}_\exists\left(Q_\Phi, \Phi_{\mathcal{I}}, \Phi_{\mathcal{R}}, \mathcal{A}_\exists\left(Q_\Psi, \Psi_{\mathcal{I}}, \Psi_{\mathcal{R}}, \Psi_{\mathcal{F}}\right)\right) \Leftrightarrow \mathcal{A}_\exists\left(Q_\Phi \cup Q_\Psi, \Phi_{\mathcal{I}} \wedge \Psi_{\mathcal{I}}, \Phi_{\mathcal{R}} \wedge \Psi_{\mathcal{R}}, \Psi_{\mathcal{F}}\right)
$$

Note further that $\Phi_{\mathcal{I}}$ is thereby a conjunction of possibly negated state variables q_i and therefore determines exactly one initial state. *Hence, we can translate any temporal logic formula without future time operators into a deterministic ω-automaton with a propositional acceptance condition Φ.* What restrictions are there for an input sequence to be accepted by such an automaton? Clearly, as the automaton is deterministic, a corresponding run through the transition system of the automaton exists, and it is even unique. Hence, the input sequence and its run only need to fulfill the acceptance condition $\Psi_{\mathcal{F}}$ of the automaton, and as $\Psi_{\mathcal{F}}$ is propositional, it only refers to the initial input of the sequence. This is not surprising: as we do not have future operators, we can only refer to the initial point of time, and at that point of time, any formula with past operators is equivalent to a propositional formula (hence, we do not need ω-automata at all in this case).

To extend our translation procedure to more interesting cases, we need to handle future time operators in a similar way, and must therefore face the following problem: Simply abbreviating a subformula as e.g. $[\varphi \mathsf{U} \psi]$ by a new state formula q in that we add the transition relation $q \leftrightarrow \psi \vee \varphi \wedge \mathsf{X}q$ is not enough: According to Theorem 5.36, q can then either behave as $[\varphi \mathsf{U} \psi]$ or as $[\varphi \underline{\mathsf{U}} \psi]$. As the truth value of the formula normally depends on the strength of the temporal operators, we must additionally fix the strength of the temporal expression that has been abbreviated. The next theorem shows that this can be done by adding a suitable fairness constraint of the form $\mathsf{GF}\Psi$.

Theorem 5.39 (Defining Future Time Modalities by ω-Automata). *Given a formula $\Phi \in \mathsf{LTL}_p$ with some occurrences of a variable x, and propositional formulas φ and ψ, the following equations are initially valid (we use the notation of Definition 5.37):*

$$\begin{aligned}
\Phi\langle \mathsf{X}\varphi\rangle_x &\Leftrightarrow \mathcal{A}_\exists(\{q\}, 1, q \leftrightarrow \mathsf{X}\varphi, \Phi\langle q\rangle_x)\\
\Phi\langle \mathsf{X}\varphi\rangle_x &\Leftrightarrow \mathcal{A}_\exists(\{q_0, q_1\}, 1, (q_0 \leftrightarrow \varphi) \wedge (q_1 \leftrightarrow \mathsf{X}q_0), \Phi\langle q_1\rangle_x)\\
\Phi\langle \mathsf{G}\varphi\rangle_x &\Leftrightarrow \mathcal{A}_\exists(\{q\}, 1, q \leftrightarrow \varphi \wedge \mathsf{X}q, \Phi\langle q\rangle_x \wedge \mathsf{GF}[\varphi \rightarrow q])\\
\Phi\langle \mathsf{F}\varphi\rangle_x &\Leftrightarrow \mathcal{A}_\exists(\{q\}, 1, q \leftrightarrow \varphi \vee \mathsf{X}q, \Phi\langle q\rangle_x \wedge \mathsf{GF}[q \rightarrow \varphi])\\
\Phi\langle [\varphi \mathsf{U} \psi]\rangle_x &\Leftrightarrow \mathcal{A}_\exists(\{q\}, 1, q \leftrightarrow \psi \vee \varphi \wedge \mathsf{X}q, \Phi\langle q\rangle_x \wedge \mathsf{GF}[\varphi \rightarrow q])\\
\Phi\langle [\varphi \underline{\mathsf{U}} \psi]\rangle_x &\Leftrightarrow \mathcal{A}_\exists(\{q\}, 1, q \leftrightarrow \psi \vee \varphi \wedge \mathsf{X}q, \Phi\langle q\rangle_x \wedge \mathsf{GF}[q \rightarrow \psi])\\
\Phi\langle [\varphi \mathsf{B} \psi]\rangle_x &\Leftrightarrow \mathcal{A}_\exists(\{q\}, 1, q \leftrightarrow \neg\psi \wedge (\varphi \vee \mathsf{X}q), \Phi\langle q\rangle_x \wedge \mathsf{GF}[q \vee \psi])\\
\Phi\langle [\varphi \underline{\mathsf{B}} \psi]\rangle_x &\Leftrightarrow \mathcal{A}_\exists(\{q\}, 1, q \leftrightarrow \neg\psi \wedge (\varphi \vee \mathsf{X}q), \Phi\langle q\rangle_x \wedge \mathsf{GF}[q \rightarrow \varphi])
\end{aligned}$$

Proof. All implications from the left to the right are simple: Instantiate for q the subformula to be abbreviated and use Lemma 5.34 to prove the transition relation. The formulas that result from the fairness constraints can be easily proved by considering suitable instances of points of time. Hence, consider now the implications from the right to the left. The implications for $\Phi\langle \mathsf{X}\varphi\rangle_x$ are simple. The equations for $\Phi\langle [\varphi \mathsf{U} \psi]\rangle_x$ and $\Phi\langle [\varphi \underline{\mathsf{U}} \psi]\rangle_x$ follow directly from facts (10) and (9) of Lemma 5.35, respectively. The equation for $\Phi\langle [\varphi \underline{\mathsf{B}} \psi]\rangle_x$ and $\Phi\langle [\varphi \mathsf{B} \psi]\rangle_x$ can be reduced to the equations for $\Phi\langle [\varphi \mathsf{U} \psi]\rangle_x$ and $\Phi\langle [\varphi \underline{\mathsf{U}} \psi]\rangle_x$, respectively, by replacing $q := \neg p$ and driving the negation inwards.

The equations of the above theorem show how we can assure that the newly generated variables q_i can be fixed as either the strong or the weak version of an operator by adding additional fairness constraints. These fairness constraints distinguish between the two solutions of the fixpoint equation and safely select one of the two solutions.

While the choice of the transition relation is uniquely determined, we can choose different fairness constraints that might be more or less efficient to check. For example, we could also use $\mathsf{GF}[\neg q \vee \neg\varphi \vee \psi]$ instead of $\mathsf{GF}[q \rightarrow \psi]$ for the abbreviation of $\Phi\langle[\varphi\ \underline{\mathsf{U}}\ \psi]\rangle_x$. Also, we could use $\mathsf{GF}[q \vee \neg\varphi \vee \psi]$ instead of $\mathsf{GF}[\varphi \rightarrow q]$ for the abbreviation of $\Phi\langle[\varphi\ \mathsf{U}\ \psi]\rangle_x$. It can not be predicted which version of the fairness constraint will be more efficient to prove, but one might speculate that it is a good strategy to choose them as small as possible. This advocates the versions we have chosen.

Another point has to be noted concerning the X operator: Intuitively, one would like to use the first equation $\Phi\langle \mathsf{X}\varphi\rangle_x \Leftrightarrow \mathcal{A}_\exists\left(\{q\}, 1, q \leftrightarrow \mathsf{X}\varphi, \Phi\langle q\rangle_x\right)$, which is also valid. However, as φ might also contain occurrences of input variables, we would then refer to the next input in the transition relation of the automaton. In this case, the formula $\mathcal{A}_\exists\left(\{q\}, 1, q \leftrightarrow \mathsf{X}\varphi, \Phi\langle q\rangle_x\right)$ is not well-formed. To circumvent this, we introduce two state variables q_0 and q_1 to store the information of the previous input we need to fix the transition relation appropriately.

The last two theorems can be used to translate an arbitrary LTL_p formula Φ to an equivalent ω-automaton $\mathfrak{A}_\Phi$ as given in Figure 5.11. The function implements a bottom-up traversal over the syntax tree and applies the rules of Theorem 5.38 and Theorem 5.39 during this traversal. As we must add fairness constraints, it is unnecessarily difficult to handle them with the intermediate acceptance condition. We have therefore added for convenience another argument to our automaton formulas:

Definition 5.40 (Automaton Formulas with Constraints). *For any finite set of temporal logic formulas $\mathcal{F} \subseteq \mathsf{LTL}_q$, we define*

- $\mathcal{A}_\exists\left(\mathcal{Q}, \mathcal{I}, \mathcal{R}, \mathcal{F}, \Phi\right) := \mathcal{A}_\exists\left(\mathcal{Q}, \mathcal{I}, \mathcal{R}, \Phi \wedge \bigwedge_{\xi\in\mathcal{F}} \xi\right)$
- $\mathcal{A}_\forall\left(\mathcal{Q}, \mathcal{I}, \mathcal{R}, \mathcal{F}, \Phi\right) := \mathcal{A}_\forall\left(\mathcal{Q}, \mathcal{I}, \mathcal{R}, \left(\bigwedge_{\xi\in\mathcal{F}} \xi\right) \rightarrow \Phi\right)$

According to the above definition, the set of constraints $\mathcal{F}$ belongs to the acceptance condition, so that nothing new is achieved by the above definition. For the following, it is however convenient to use the above definition in order to split the acceptance condition into two parts. It is moreover straightforward to define a product operation on automaton formulas with constraints:

Definition 5.41 (Product of Constrained Automaton Formulas). *Given two automaton formulas $\mathcal{A}_\exists(\mathcal{Q}_1, \mathcal{I}_1, \mathcal{R}_1, \mathcal{F}_1, \mathcal{A}_1)$ and $\mathcal{A}_\exists(\mathcal{Q}_2, \mathcal{I}_2, \mathcal{R}_2, \mathcal{F}_2, \mathcal{A}_2)$, we define their product as follows:*

$$\begin{aligned}&\mathcal{A}_\exists(\mathcal{Q}_1, \mathcal{I}_1, \mathcal{R}_1, \mathcal{F}_1, \mathcal{A}_1) \times \mathcal{A}_\exists(\mathcal{Q}_2, \mathcal{I}_2, \mathcal{R}_2, \mathcal{F}_2, \mathcal{A}_2)\\ &\qquad := \mathcal{A}_\exists(\mathcal{Q}_1 \cup \mathcal{Q}_2, \mathcal{I}_1 \wedge \mathcal{I}_2, \mathcal{R}_1 \wedge \mathcal{R}_2, \mathcal{F}_1 \cup \mathcal{F}_2, \mathcal{A}_1 \wedge \mathcal{A}_2)\end{aligned}$$

We can easily prove that $\mathfrak{A}_1 \times \mathfrak{A}_1 = \mathfrak{A}_1 \wedge \mathfrak{A}_2$ holds. Using this definition, we can now implement our basic translation algorithm as given in Figure 5.11. Obviously, this implementation merely applies the rules of Theorem 5.38 and Theorem 5.39 in a recursive manner. It is thereby important that the algorithm translates the formulas in a bottom-up manner, i.e., it translates first the subformulas of a considered formula into equivalent ω-automata and then constructs an automaton for the entire formula using the equations of Theorem 5.38 and Theorem 5.39. For example, consider how the formula $\left[a\ \underline{\mathsf{U}}\ \left(\overleftarrow{\mathsf{G}}\ [b\ \mathsf{U}\ c]\right)\right]$ is translated by successively applying the rules of the previous theorems:

$$\begin{aligned}&\left[a\ \underline{\mathsf{U}}\ \overleftarrow{\mathsf{G}}\ [b\ \mathsf{U}\ c]\right]\\ &= \mathcal{A}_\exists\left(\{q_1\}, 1, q_1 \leftrightarrow c \vee b \wedge \mathsf{X}q_1, \{\mathsf{GF}[b \rightarrow q_1]\}, \left[a\ \underline{\mathsf{U}}\ \overleftarrow{\mathsf{G}}\, q_1\right]\right)\\ &= \mathcal{A}_\exists\left(\begin{array}{l}\{q_1, q_2\}, q_2, [q_1 \leftrightarrow c \vee b \wedge \mathsf{X}q_1] \wedge [\mathsf{X}q_2 \leftrightarrow q_1 \wedge q_2],\\ \{\mathsf{GF}[b \rightarrow q_1]\}, [a\ \underline{\mathsf{U}}\ q_2]\end{array}\right)\\ &= \mathcal{A}_\exists\left(\begin{array}{l}\{q_1, q_2, q_3\}, q_2,\\ [q_1 \leftrightarrow c \vee b \wedge \mathsf{X}q_1] \wedge [\mathsf{X}q_2 \leftrightarrow q_1 \wedge q_2] \wedge [q_3 \leftrightarrow q_2 \vee a \wedge \mathsf{X}q_3],\\ \{\mathsf{GF}[b \rightarrow q_1], \mathsf{GF}[q_3 \rightarrow q_2],\}, q_3\end{array}\right)\end{aligned}$$

Hence, we see that our translation yields for every future temporal operator (apart from X) one fairness constraint for the $\mathsf{NDet}_{\mathsf{Streett}}$ automaton. Moreover, the acceptance condition that is finally obtained is propositional, but of course the generated fairness constraints must also be considered. The following theorem shows that the resulting automata are really $\mathsf{NDet}_{\mathsf{Streett}}$ automata.

Theorem 5.42 (Translating Temporal Logic to ω-Automata). *Given any LTL_p formula Φ, and $\mathcal{A}_\exists(\mathcal{Q}, \mathcal{I}, \mathcal{R}, \mathcal{F}, \Phi_0) = \mathsf{Streett}(\Phi)$, where Streett is defined as in Figure 5.11, then the following holds:*

(1) $\mathsf{Streett}(\Phi)$ *runs in time $O(|\Phi|)$.*
(2) Φ_0 *is propositional*
(3) *each $\xi \in \mathcal{F}$ is of the form $\mathsf{GF}\xi'$ with a propositional ξ'*
(4) $\Phi \leftrightarrow \mathcal{A}_\exists\left(\mathcal{Q}, \mathcal{I} \wedge \Phi_0, \mathcal{R}, \bigwedge_{\xi \in \mathcal{F}} \xi\right)$ *is initially valid*

Proof. The proof of (1) and (2) easily follow by induction along the structure of Φ. For (1), just note that $|\mathcal{Q}| \leq |\Phi|$, $|\mathcal{I}| \leq |\Phi|$, $|\mathcal{R}| \leq |\Phi|$, $|\mathcal{F}| \leq |\Phi|$,

```
function Streett(Φ)
  case Φ of
    is_prop(Φ): return A∃ ({}, 1, 1, {}, Φ);
    ¬φ        : A∃ (Q_φ, I_φ, R_φ, F_φ, φ') ≡ Streett(φ);
                return A∃ (Q_φ, I_φ, R_φ, F_φ, ¬φ');
    φ ∧ ψ     : A∃ (Q_Φ, I_Φ, R_Φ, F_Φ, φ' ∧ ψ') ≡ Streett(φ) × Streett(ψ);
                return A∃ (Q_Φ, I_Φ, R_Φ, F_Φ, φ' ∧ ψ');
    φ ∨ ψ     : A∃ (Q_Φ, I_Φ, R_Φ, F_Φ, φ' ∧ ψ') ≡ Streett(φ) × Streett(ψ);
                return A∃ (Q_Φ, I_Φ, R_Φ, F_Φ, φ' ∨ ψ');
    Xφ        : A∃ (Q_φ, I_φ, R_φ, F_φ, φ') ≡ Streett(φ); q := new_var;
                return A∃ (Q_φ ∪ {q}, I_φ, R_φ ∧ (q ↔ Xφ'), F_φ, q);
    [φ U̲ ψ]   : A∃ (Q_Φ, I_Φ, R_Φ, F_Φ, φ' ∧ ψ') ≡ Streett(φ) × Streett(ψ);
                q := new_var; R_q := [q ↔ ψ' ∨ φ' ∧ Xq]; F_q := {GF[q → ψ']};
                return A∃ (Q_Φ ∪ {q}, I_Φ, R_Φ ∧ R_q, F_Φ ∪ F_q, q);
    [φ B ψ]   : A∃ (Q_Φ, I_Φ, R_Φ, F_Φ, φ' ∧ ψ') ≡ Streett(φ) × Streett(ψ);
                q := new_var; R_q := [q ↔ ¬ψ' ∧ (φ' ∨ Xq)]; F_q := {GF[q ∨ ψ']};
                return A∃ (Q_Φ ∪ {q}, I_Φ, R_Φ ∧ R_q, F_Φ ∪ F_q, q);
    X⃖φ        : A∃ (Q_φ, I_φ, R_φ, F_φ, φ') ≡ Streett(φ); q := new_var;
                return A∃ (Q_φ ∪ {q}, I_φ ∧ q, R_φ ∧ (Xq ↔ φ'), F_φ, q);
    X̲⃖φ        : A∃ (Q_φ, I_φ, R_φ, F_φ, φ') ≡ Streett(φ); q := new_var;
                return A∃ (Q_φ ∪ {q}, I_φ ∧ ¬q, R_φ ∧ (Xq ↔ φ'), F_φ, q);
    [φ U̲⃖ ψ]   : A∃ (Q_Φ, I_Φ, R_Φ, F_Φ, φ' ∧ ψ') ≡ Streett(φ) × Streett(ψ);
                q := new_var; r_q := ψ' ∨ φ' ∧ q; R_q := [Xq ↔ r_q]; I_q := ¬q;
                return A∃ (Q_Φ ∪ {q}, I_Φ ∧ I_q, R_Φ ∧ R_q, F_Φ, r_q);
    [φ B⃖ ψ]   : A∃ (Q_Φ, I_Φ, R_Φ, F_Φ, φ' ∧ ψ') ≡ Streett(φ) × Streett(ψ);
                q := new_var; r_q := ¬ψ' ∧ (φ' ∨ q); R_q := [Xq ↔ r_q]; I_q := q;
                return A∃ (Q_Φ ∪ {q}, I_Φ ∧ I_q, R_Φ ∧ R_q, F_Φ, r_q);
  end case
end function
```

Fig. 5.11. The basic translation from temporal logic to ω-Automata

$\forall \xi \in \mathcal{F}. |\xi| \leq |\Phi|$, and $|\Phi_0| \leq |\Phi|$ holds. (3) is directly seen by observing that the algorithm does only add constraints of the mentioned form to the constraints set. (4) is the essential property to be proved. As already explained in the explanations for the implementation of Streett, it can be simply proved by consulting the equations of Theorem 5.38 and Theorem 5.39 in a recursive manner. Note that the initial validity is sufficient for this purpose. To prove (4), simply recall that there the added transition relations are fixpoint equations with exactly two solutions and that our constraints choose exactly one of these solutions. Hence, any input sequence has exactly one *accepting* run. In general, there may however be further runs that do not satisfy the fairness constraints.

The acceptance condition $\Phi_0 \wedge \bigwedge_{i=1}^{n} \mathsf{GF}\varphi_i$ used in fact (3) is somewhat disturbing since it does not directly fit into the automaton classes we have considered in the previous chapter. As Φ_0 is however a propositional formula, it only adds an additional restriction for the initial point of time on the input sequence and its run. Hence, it is natural to add it to the initial condition, as shown in the above theorem.

To illustrate the algorithm once more, let us apply the procedure to another example: We want to translate the formula $\mathsf{FG}a \rightarrow \mathsf{GF}a$ to an equivalent ω-automaton.

$$\mathsf{FG}a \rightarrow \mathsf{GF}a = \mathcal{A}_\exists \left(\begin{array}{l} \{q_1, q_2, q_3, q_4\}, q_2 \rightarrow q_4, \\ [q_1 \leftrightarrow a \wedge \mathsf{X}q_1] \wedge [q_2 \leftrightarrow q_1 \vee \mathsf{X}q_2] \wedge \\ [q_3 \leftrightarrow a \vee \mathsf{X}q_3] \wedge [q_4 \leftrightarrow q_3 \wedge \mathsf{X}q_4], \\ [\mathsf{GF}[a \rightarrow q_1]] \wedge [\mathsf{GF}[q_2 \rightarrow q_1]] \wedge \\ [\mathsf{GF}[q_3 \rightarrow a]] \wedge [\mathsf{GF}[q_3 \rightarrow q_4]] \end{array}\right)$$

Our algorithm therefore translates any temporal logic formula to an equivalent $\mathsf{NDet}_{\mathsf{Streett}}$ automaton with a special acceptance condition of the form $\bigwedge_{i=0}^{n} \mathsf{GF}\xi_i$. These automata are sometimes also called generalized Büchi automata, but we prefer to view them as special $\mathsf{NDet}_{\mathsf{Streett}}$ automata. As we have already seen, $\mathsf{NDet}_{\mathsf{Streett}}$ is equal expressive as $\mathsf{NDet}_{\mathsf{GF}}$, we could also reduce the result to $\mathsf{NDet}_{\mathsf{GF}}$. From the viewpoint of verification, the reduction to a Büchi automaton with a single fairness constraint is however not necessary, and even expensive. According to Theorem 3.43 on page 165, we can check the $\bigwedge_{i=0}^{n} \mathsf{GF}\xi_i$ with a fixpoint formula of alternation depth 2 in time $O(f\,|\mathcal{K}|\,|\mathcal{S}|)$.

5.4.2 Exploitation of Monotonicity

The abbreviation rules given in Theorems 5.38 and 5.39 allow us to successively abbreviate elementary subformulas by a new variable that will be used as a state variable of the desired ω-automaton. The state transition relation of these variables is chosen such that the state variable obeys the recursion laws of the corresponding temporal operator, and therefore, as we have already seen by Theorem 5.36 the state variable will either behave like the strong or weak variant of the temporal expression. To fix the operator strength, we have used suitable initial conditions in case of past temporal operators (cf. Theorem 5.38), and fairness constraints in case of future temporal operators (cf. Theorem 5.39). Based on these theorems, the algorithm in Figure 5.11 is therefore able to compute for any LTL_p formula an equivalent $\mathsf{NDet}_{\mathsf{Streett}}$ automaton. *Although this automaton is not deterministic, we emphasize that any input sequence has a unique accepting run. In particular, Φ and $\neg\Phi$ yield in very similar automata, that differ only in their initial conditions (we obtain $\neg\Phi_0$ instead of Φ_0 in Theorem 5.42).* The basic translation procedure as given in Figure 5.11 has however the drawback that it introduces for *every* future time temporal operator (apart from X) a fairness constraint. We will now see that there are situations where the fairness constraint is not necessary, and in the following section, we will furthermore see that the fairness constraints can often be replaced with simpler reachability constraints.

We have already seen by Theorems 5.36 and 5.39 that the fairness constraints are added to fix the strength of the temporal operators that are abbreviated. Consequently, if we simply omit the fairness constraints, then we leave it unspecified whether the abbreviated operator was a weak or strong one. This immediately proves the following equivalences[4]:

$$\begin{aligned}
\mathcal{A}_{\exists}\left(\{q\}, 1, q \leftrightarrow \varphi \wedge \mathsf{X}q, \Phi\langle q\rangle_x\right) &\Leftrightarrow \Phi\langle \mathsf{G}\varphi\rangle_x \vee \Phi\langle 0\rangle_x \\
\mathcal{A}_{\exists}\left(\{q\}, 1, q \leftrightarrow \varphi \vee \mathsf{X}q, \Phi\langle q\rangle_x\right) &\Leftrightarrow \Phi\langle \mathsf{F}\varphi\rangle_x \vee \Phi\langle 1\rangle_x \\
\mathcal{A}_{\exists}\left(\{q\}, 1, q \leftrightarrow \psi \vee \varphi \wedge \mathsf{X}q, \Phi\langle q\rangle_x\right) &\Leftrightarrow \Phi\langle [\varphi \ \mathsf{U} \ \psi]\rangle_x \vee \Phi\langle [\varphi \ \underline{\mathsf{U}} \ \psi]\rangle_x \\
\mathcal{A}_{\exists}\left(\{q\}, 1, q \leftrightarrow \neg\psi \wedge (\varphi \vee \mathsf{X}q), \Phi\langle q\rangle_x\right) &\Leftrightarrow \Phi\langle [\varphi \ \mathsf{B} \ \psi]\rangle_x \vee \Phi\langle [\varphi \ \underline{\mathsf{B}} \ \psi]\rangle_x
\end{aligned}$$

Hence, whenever the strength of the temporal operator that is on top of the subformula Ψ that is to be abbreviated in $\Phi\langle\Psi\rangle_x$ does not influence the truth value of the entire formula, then we can omit the fairness constraints. The question now is when will this be the case.

Note that the propositional formula $(p \rightarrow q) \rightarrow (p \vee q \leftrightarrow q)$ is a tautology and that each strong operator implies the corresponding weak version. Therefore, we conclude by modus ponens that the equations $[\varphi \ \mathsf{U} \ \psi] \vee [\varphi \ \underline{\mathsf{U}} \ \psi] = [\varphi \ \mathsf{U} \ \psi]$ and $[\varphi \ \mathsf{B} \ \psi] \vee [\varphi \ \underline{\mathsf{B}} \ \psi] = [\varphi \ \mathsf{B} \ \psi]$ hold. However, this is not yet sufficient for our purpose, as we should establish equations where formulas as $[\varphi \ \mathsf{U} \ \psi]$ or $[\varphi \ \mathsf{B} \ \psi]$ occur as subformulas in a surrounding formula.

Again regarding the tautology $(p \rightarrow q) \rightarrow (p \vee q \leftrightarrow q)$, we must find criteria that assure that from $\mathsf{G}[y \rightarrow z]$ it follows (1) $\mathsf{G}[\Phi\langle y\rangle_x \rightarrow \Phi\langle z\rangle_x]$ and (2) $\mathsf{G}[\Phi\langle z\rangle_x \rightarrow \Phi\langle y\rangle_x]$. In the first case, we could then conclude that $\Phi\langle [\varphi \ \mathsf{U} \ \psi]\rangle_x \vee \Phi\langle [\varphi \ \underline{\mathsf{U}} \ \psi]\rangle_x = \Phi\langle [\varphi \ \mathsf{U} \ \psi]\rangle_x$ holds and in the second case, we have $\Phi\langle [\varphi \ \mathsf{U} \ \psi]\rangle_x \vee \Phi\langle [\varphi \ \underline{\mathsf{U}} \ \psi]\rangle_x = \Phi\langle [\varphi \ \underline{\mathsf{U}} \ \psi]\rangle_x$ (similar for the other operators). Hence, we must study the monotonicity of the temporal logic operators as given in the next lemma:

Lemma 5.43 (Monotonicity of Temporal Operators). *Given that* $\mathsf{G}[\alpha \rightarrow \underline{\alpha}]$ *and* $\mathsf{G}[\beta \rightarrow \underline{\beta}]$ *holds on a path, then the following implications hold on the path:*

[4] For reasons of completeness, we also mention that the following equations hold for the past operators. These equations show that the initialization of the corresponding state variables are used here to fix the strength of the temporal operators. However, as we already mentioned, there is no need to modify the translation of past time operators.

$$\begin{aligned}
\mathcal{A}_{\exists}\left(\{q\}, 1, \mathsf{X}q \leftrightarrow \varphi \wedge q, \Phi\langle q\rangle_x\right) &\Leftrightarrow \Phi\langle \overleftarrow{\mathsf{X}}\,\overleftarrow{\mathsf{G}}\varphi\rangle_x \vee \Phi\langle 0\rangle_x \\
\mathcal{A}_{\exists}\left(\{q\}, 1, \mathsf{X}q \leftrightarrow \varphi \vee q, \Phi\langle q\rangle_x\right) &\Leftrightarrow \Phi\langle \overleftarrow{\underline{\mathsf{X}}}\,\overleftarrow{\mathsf{F}}\varphi\rangle_x \vee \Phi\langle 1\rangle_x \\
\mathcal{A}_{\exists}\left(\{q\}, 1, \mathsf{X}q \leftrightarrow \psi \vee \varphi \wedge q, \Phi\langle q\rangle_x\right) &\Leftrightarrow \Phi\langle \overleftarrow{\mathsf{X}}[\varphi \ \overleftarrow{\mathsf{U}} \ \psi]\rangle_x \vee \Phi\langle \overleftarrow{\underline{\mathsf{X}}}[\varphi \ \overleftarrow{\underline{\mathsf{U}}} \ \psi]\rangle_x \\
\mathcal{A}_{\exists}\left(\{q\}, 1, \mathsf{X}q \leftrightarrow \neg\psi \wedge (\varphi \vee q), \Phi\langle q\rangle_x\right) &\Leftrightarrow \Phi\langle \overleftarrow{\mathsf{X}}[\varphi \ \overleftarrow{\mathsf{B}} \ \psi]\rangle_x \vee \Phi\langle \overleftarrow{\underline{\mathsf{X}}}[\varphi \ \overleftarrow{\underline{\mathsf{B}}} \ \psi]\rangle_x
\end{aligned}$$

$$
\begin{array}{ll}
\mathsf{G}[\neg\underline{\alpha} \rightarrow \neg\alpha] & \mathsf{G}[\mathsf{X}\alpha \rightarrow \mathsf{X}\underline{\alpha}] \\
\mathsf{G}[\alpha \wedge \beta \rightarrow \underline{\alpha} \wedge \underline{\beta}] & \mathsf{G}[\alpha \vee \beta \rightarrow \underline{\alpha} \vee \underline{\beta}] \\
\mathsf{G}[\mathsf{G}\alpha \rightarrow \mathsf{G}\underline{\alpha}] & \mathsf{G}[\mathsf{F}\alpha \rightarrow \mathsf{F}\underline{\alpha}] \\
\mathsf{G}[[\alpha\ \mathsf{U}\ \beta] \rightarrow [\underline{\alpha}\ \mathsf{U}\ \underline{\beta}]] & \mathsf{G}[[\alpha\ \underline{\mathsf{U}}\ \beta] \rightarrow [\underline{\alpha}\ \underline{\mathsf{U}}\ \underline{\beta}]] \\
\mathsf{G}[[\alpha\ \mathsf{B}\ \underline{\beta}] \rightarrow [\underline{\alpha}\ \mathsf{B}\ \beta]] & \mathsf{G}[[\alpha\ \underline{\mathsf{B}}\ \underline{\beta}] \rightarrow [\underline{\alpha}\ \underline{\mathsf{B}}\ \beta]] \\
\mathsf{G}[\overleftarrow{\mathsf{X}}\alpha \rightarrow \overleftarrow{\mathsf{X}}\underline{\alpha}] & \mathsf{G}[\overleftarrow{\underline{\mathsf{X}}}\alpha \rightarrow \overleftarrow{\underline{\mathsf{X}}}\underline{\alpha}] \\
\mathsf{G}[\overleftarrow{\mathsf{G}}\alpha \rightarrow \overleftarrow{\mathsf{G}}\underline{\alpha}] & \mathsf{G}[\overleftarrow{\mathsf{F}}\alpha \rightarrow \overleftarrow{\mathsf{F}}\underline{\alpha}] \\
\mathsf{G}[[\alpha\ \overleftarrow{\mathsf{U}}\ \beta] \rightarrow [\underline{\alpha}\ \overleftarrow{\mathsf{U}}\ \underline{\beta}]] & \mathsf{G}[[\alpha\ \overleftarrow{\underline{\mathsf{U}}}\ \beta] \rightarrow [\underline{\alpha}\ \overleftarrow{\underline{\mathsf{U}}}\ \underline{\beta}]] \\
\mathsf{G}[[\alpha\ \overleftarrow{\mathsf{B}}\ \underline{\beta}] \rightarrow [\underline{\alpha}\ \overleftarrow{\mathsf{B}}\ \beta]] & \mathsf{G}[[\alpha\ \overleftarrow{\underline{\mathsf{B}}}\ \underline{\beta}] \rightarrow [\underline{\alpha}\ \overleftarrow{\underline{\mathsf{B}}}\ \beta]]
\end{array}
$$

We can now use the above laws in a recursive manner to establish our criteria (1) and (2) above. To be precise and concise, we introduce the following notion of positive and negative subformulas in a temporal logic formula.

Definition 5.44 (Positive and Negative Occurrences). *The following rules define the signum of an occurrence of a subformula in a surrounding formula Φ (we furthermore add the fact that Φ itself occurs positively in Φ):*

- *Given that one of the formulas $\mathsf{X}\varphi$, $\mathsf{G}\varphi$, $\mathsf{F}\varphi$, $\overleftarrow{\mathsf{X}}\varphi$, $\overleftarrow{\underline{\mathsf{X}}}\varphi$, $\overleftarrow{\mathsf{G}}\varphi$, and $\overleftarrow{\mathsf{F}}\varphi$ has a positive/negative occurrence in Φ, then the occurrence of φ is positive/negative.*
- *Given that $\neg\varphi$ has a positive/negative occurrence in Φ, then the occurrence of φ is negative/positive.*
- *Given that one of the formulas $\varphi \wedge \psi$, $\varphi \vee \psi$, $\mathsf{X}\varphi$, $\mathsf{G}\varphi$, $\mathsf{F}\varphi$, $[\varphi\ \mathsf{U}\ \psi]$, $[\varphi\ \underline{\mathsf{U}}\ \psi]$, $\overleftarrow{\mathsf{X}}\varphi$, $\overleftarrow{\underline{\mathsf{X}}}\varphi$, $\overleftarrow{\mathsf{G}}\varphi$, $\overleftarrow{\mathsf{F}}\varphi$, $[\varphi\ \overleftarrow{\mathsf{U}}\ \psi]$, $[\varphi\ \overleftarrow{\underline{\mathsf{U}}}\ \psi]$ has a positive/negative occurrence in Φ, then both occurrences of φ and ψ are positive/negative.*
- *Given that one of the formulas $[\varphi\ \mathsf{B}\ \psi]$, $[\varphi\ \underline{\mathsf{B}}\ \psi]$, $[\varphi\ \overleftarrow{\mathsf{B}}\ \psi]$, and $[\varphi\ \overleftarrow{\underline{\mathsf{B}}}\ \psi]$ has a positive/negative occurrence in Φ, then the occurrence of φ is positive/negative, and the occurrence of ψ is negative/positive.*

If all occurrences of a variable x in a template formula Φ are positive/negative, then we write $\Phi\langle\varphi\rangle_x^+/\Phi\langle\varphi\rangle_x^-$ for $\Phi\langle\varphi\rangle_x$.

Using the notion of positive and negative occurrences of subformulas, we can now use the previous lemma in a recursive manner to prove the following important lemma:

Lemma 5.45 (Substitution Lemma). *Given a formula Φ that contains a variable x, the following equations are valid for every path of every structure:*

- *In any case, $\mathsf{G}[\varphi \leftrightarrow \psi]$ implies $\mathsf{G}[\Phi\langle\varphi\rangle_x \leftrightarrow \Phi\langle\psi\rangle_x]$.*
- *If x has only positive occurrences in Φ, then $\mathsf{G}[\varphi \rightarrow \psi]$ implies $\mathsf{G}[\Phi\langle\varphi\rangle_x \rightarrow \Phi\langle\psi\rangle_x]$.*
- *If x has only negative occurrences in Φ, then $\mathsf{G}[\varphi \rightarrow \psi]$ implies $\mathsf{G}[\Phi\langle\psi\rangle_x \rightarrow \Phi\langle\varphi\rangle_x]$.*

The proof of all facts can be obtained by a straightforward induction on the structure of $\Phi\langle x\rangle_x$.

The key observation is therefore that every positive occurrence of a weak temporal future operator and every negative occurrence of a strong temporal future operator can be simply translated into a transition relation without adding initial conditions or further parts for an acceptance condition. Therefore, positive occurrences of weak temporal operators and negative occurrences strong future temporal operators are completely harmless for a translation to equivalent ω-automata: The translation procedure of the previous section can be modified such that, in these cases, no fairness constraint is added. This means that the transformation rules given in Theorem 5.39 for the future time operators are now refined by the following theorem (the rules for the past time operators given in Theorem 5.38 remain unchanged):

Theorem 5.46 (Defining Future Time Modalities w.r.t. Positive and Negative Occurrences). *Given a formula $\Phi \in \mathsf{LTL}_p$ where a variable x has only positive occurrences, and propositional formulas φ and ψ, the following equations are generally valid:*

$$\begin{aligned}
\Phi\langle \mathsf{G}\varphi\rangle_x^+ &\Leftrightarrow \mathcal{A}_\exists\left(\{q\}, 1, q \leftrightarrow \varphi \wedge \mathsf{X}q, \Phi\langle q\rangle_x^+\right)\\
\Phi\langle [\varphi \;\mathsf{U}\; \psi]\rangle_x^+ &\Leftrightarrow \mathcal{A}_\exists\left(\{q\}, 1, q \leftrightarrow \psi \vee \varphi \wedge \mathsf{X}q, \Phi\langle q\rangle_x^+\right)\\
\Phi\langle [\varphi \;\mathsf{B}\; \psi]\rangle_x^+ &\Leftrightarrow \mathcal{A}_\exists\left(\{q\}, 1, q \leftrightarrow \neg\psi \wedge (\varphi \vee \mathsf{X}q), \Phi\langle q\rangle_x^+\right)\\
\Phi\langle [\varphi \;\mathsf{W}\; \psi]\rangle_x^+ &\Leftrightarrow \mathcal{A}_\exists\left(\{q\}, 1, q \leftrightarrow \psi \wedge \varphi \vee \neg\psi \wedge \mathsf{X}q), \Phi\langle q\rangle_x^+\right)
\end{aligned}$$

Given a formula $\Phi \in \mathsf{LTL}_p$ where a variable x has only negative occurrences, and propositional formulas φ and ψ, the following equations are valid:

$$\begin{aligned}
\Phi\langle \mathsf{F}\varphi\rangle_x^- &\Leftrightarrow \mathcal{A}_\exists\left(\{q\}, 1, q \leftrightarrow \varphi \vee \mathsf{X}q, \Phi\langle q\rangle_x^-\right)\\
\Phi\langle [\varphi \;\underline{\mathsf{U}}\; \psi]\rangle_x^- &\Leftrightarrow \mathcal{A}_\exists\left(\{q\}, 1, q \leftrightarrow \psi \vee \varphi \wedge \mathsf{X}q, \Phi\langle q\rangle_x^-\right)\\
\Phi\langle [\varphi \;\underline{\mathsf{B}}\; \psi]\rangle_x^- &\Leftrightarrow \mathcal{A}_\exists\left(\{q\}, 1, q \leftrightarrow \neg\psi \wedge (\varphi \vee \mathsf{X}q), \Phi\langle q\rangle_x^-\right)\\
\Phi\langle [\varphi \;\underline{\mathsf{W}}\; \psi]\rangle_x^- &\Leftrightarrow \mathcal{A}_\exists\left(\{q\}, 1, q \leftrightarrow \psi \wedge \varphi \vee \neg\psi \wedge \mathsf{X}q), \Phi\langle q\rangle_x^-\right)
\end{aligned}$$

Proof. We only consider $\Phi\langle [\varphi \;\mathsf{U}\; \psi]\rangle_x^+ \Leftrightarrow \mathcal{A}_\exists\left(\{q\}, 1, q \leftrightarrow \psi \vee \varphi \wedge \mathsf{X}q, \Phi\langle q\rangle_x^+\right)$ in case that any occurrence of x in Φ is positive. By Lemma 5.45, it therefore follows from $\mathsf{G}[\alpha \rightarrow \beta]$ that $\mathsf{G}[\Phi\langle\alpha\rangle_x^+ \rightarrow \Phi\langle\beta\rangle_x^+]$ holds. This, in turn implies by the tautology $(p \rightarrow q) \rightarrow (p \vee q \leftrightarrow q)$ that $\mathsf{G}[\Phi\langle\alpha\rangle_x^+ \vee \Phi\langle\beta\rangle_x^+ = \Phi\langle\beta\rangle_x^+]$ holds. Using $\alpha := [\varphi \;\underline{\mathsf{U}}\; \psi]$ and $\beta := [\varphi \;\mathsf{U}\; \psi]$ allows us therefore to immediately conclude that $\mathsf{G}[\Phi\langle[\varphi \;\underline{\mathsf{U}}\; \psi]\rangle_x^+ \vee \Phi\langle[\varphi \;\mathsf{U}\; \psi]\rangle_x^+ = \Phi\langle[\varphi \;\mathsf{U}\; \psi]\rangle_x^+]$ holds. The rest follows from Theorem 5.36, because this theorem implies the following equation: $\mathcal{A}_\exists\left(\{q\}, 1, q \leftrightarrow \psi \vee \varphi \wedge \mathsf{X}q, \Phi\langle q\rangle_x^+\right) \Leftrightarrow \Phi\langle[\varphi \;\mathsf{U}\; \psi]\rangle_x^+ \vee \Phi\langle[\varphi \;\underline{\mathsf{U}}\; \psi]\rangle_x^+$. Considering whether the occurrence of a subformula that is to be abbreviated by a new state variable q is positive or negative allows us therefore to omit the addition of fairness constraints in the above cases. In the other cases, namely when weak operators occur negatively or strong operators occur positively, we still use the rules of Theorem 5.39. Hence, in these cases, fairness constraints are still added. A refinement of the algorithm Figure 5.11 is therefore given in Figure 5.12.

```
function TopProp_σ(Φ)
 case Φ of
 isProp(Φ): return A∃({},1,1,{},Φ);
 ¬φ       : A∃(Q_φ,I_φ,R_φ,F_φ,φ') ≡ TopProp_¬σ(φ);
            return A∃(Q_φ,I_φ,R_φ,F_φ,¬φ');
 φ ∧ ψ    : A∃(Q_Φ,I_Φ,R_Φ,F_Φ,φ' ∧ ψ') ≡ TopProp_σ(φ) × TopProp_σ(ψ);
            return A∃(Q_Φ,I_Φ,R_Φ,F_Φ,φ' ∧ ψ');
 φ ∨ ψ    : A∃(Q_Φ,I_Φ,R_Φ,F_Φ,φ' ∧ ψ') ≡ TopProp_σ(φ) × TopProp_σ(ψ);
            return A∃(Q_Φ,I_Φ,R_Φ,F_Φ,φ' ∨ ψ');
 Xφ       : A∃(Q_φ,I_φ,R_φ,F_φ,φ') ≡ TopProp_σ(φ); q := new_var;
            return A∃(Q_φ ∪ {q},I_φ,R_φ ∧ (q ↔ Xφ'),F_φ,q);
 [φ U̲ ψ]  : A∃(Q_Φ,I_Φ,R_Φ,F_Φ,φ' ∧ ψ') ≡ TopProp_σ(φ) × TopProp_σ(ψ);
            q := new_var; R_q := [q ↔ ψ' ∨ φ' ∧ Xq];
            F_q := if σ then {GF[q → ψ']} else {};
            return A∃(Q_Φ ∪ {q},I_Φ,R_Φ ∧ R_q,F_Φ ∪ F_q,q);
 [φ B ψ]  : A∃(Q_Φ,I_Φ,R_Φ,F_Φ,φ' ∧ ψ') ≡ TopProp_σ(φ) × TopProp_¬σ(ψ);
            q := new_var; R_q := [q ↔ ¬ψ' ∧ (φ' ∨ Xq)];
            F_q := if σ then {} else {GF[q ∨ ψ']};
            return A∃(Q_Φ ∪ {q},I_Φ,R_Φ ∧ R_q,F_Φ ∪ F_q,q);
 ←Xφ      : A∃(Q_φ,I_φ,R_φ,F_φ,φ') ≡ TopProp_σ(φ); q := new_var;
            return A∃(Q_φ ∪ {q},I_φ ∧ q,R_φ ∧ (Xq ↔ φ'),F_φ,q);
 ←X̲φ      : A∃(Q_φ,I_φ,R_φ,F_φ,φ') ≡ TopProp_σ(φ); q := new_var;
            return A∃(Q_φ ∪ {q},I_φ ∧ ¬q,R_φ ∧ (Xq ↔ φ'),F_φ,q);
 [φ ←U̲ ψ] : A∃(Q_Φ,I_Φ,R_Φ,F_Φ,φ' ∧ ψ') ≡ TopProp_σ(φ) × TopProp_σ(ψ);
            q := new_var; r_q := ψ' ∨ φ' ∧ q; R_q := [Xq ↔ r_q];
            return A∃(Q_Φ ∪ {q},I_Φ ∧ ¬q,R_Φ ∧ R_q,F_Φ,r_q);
 [φ ←B ψ] : A∃(Q_Φ,I_Φ,R_Φ,F_Φ,φ' ∧ ψ') ≡ TopProp_σ(φ) × TopProp_¬σ(ψ);
            q := new_var; r_q := ¬ψ' ∧ (φ' ∨ q); R_q := [Xq ↔ r_q];
            return A∃(Q_Φ ∪ {q},I_Φ ∧ q,R_Φ ∧ R_q,F_Φ,r_q);
 end case
end function
```

Fig. 5.12. Translation of LTL_p improved by monotonicity laws

Theorem 5.47 (Correctness of $\mathsf{TopProp}_\sigma(\Phi)$**).** *Given any formula* $\Phi \in \mathsf{LTL}_p$*, and the automaton formula* $\mathcal{A}_\exists(\mathcal{Q},\mathcal{I},\mathcal{R},\mathcal{F},\Phi_0) = \mathsf{TopProp}_\sigma(\Phi)$ *obtained by the algorithm* TopProp *given in Figure 5.12, then the following holds:*

(1) $\mathsf{TopProp}_\sigma(\Phi)$ *runs in time* $O(|\Phi|)$.
(2) Φ_0 *is propositional*
(3) *Each* $\xi \in \mathcal{F}$ *is of the form* $\mathsf{GF}\xi'$ *where* ξ' *is propositional.*
(4) *For* $\sigma = 1$*, the equation* $\Phi \leftrightarrow \mathcal{A}_\exists\left(\mathcal{Q}, \Phi_0 \wedge \mathcal{I}, \mathcal{R}, \bigwedge_{\xi\in\mathcal{F}} \xi\right)$ *is initially valid.*
(5) *For* $\sigma = 0$*, the equation* $\neg\Phi \leftrightarrow \mathcal{A}_\exists\left(\mathcal{Q}, \neg\Phi_0 \wedge \mathcal{I}, \mathcal{R}, \bigwedge_{\xi\in\mathcal{F}} \xi\right)$ *is initially valid.*

Note that the refined algorithm given in Figure 5.12 differs from the one given in Figure 5.11 only in that the signum of the currently considered subformula is given as a further argument σ, and that the fairness constraints for the future time temporal operators are added only when necessary according to the above theorem. The proof is essentially the same as for the Streett algorithm, however for fact (4), we additionally consult Theorem 5.46. (5) is easily seen by considering what the algorithm does with negations: One can easily see that $\mathcal{A}_\exists(\mathcal{Q}, \mathcal{I}, \mathcal{R}, \mathcal{F}, \neg\Phi_0) = \mathsf{TopProp}_\sigma(\neg\Phi)$ holds iff $\mathcal{A}_\exists(\mathcal{Q}, \mathcal{I}, \mathcal{R}, \mathcal{F}, \Phi_0) = \mathsf{TopProp}_{\neg\sigma}(\Phi)$ holds.

5.4.3 Borel Classes of Temporal Logic

We have seen in the last two sections how arbitrary LTL_p formulas can be translated to equivalent $\mathsf{NDet}_{\mathsf{Streett}}$ automata. We already know that there are weaker classes of ω-automata, but we also know that the temporal logic formula $\mathsf{GF}\varphi \vee \mathsf{FG}\psi$ can not be expressed by the lower Borel classes. Hence, for the translation of arbitrary LTL_p formulas, we really need the most powerful Borel class $\mathsf{NDet}_{\mathsf{Streett}}$. It is nevertheless reasonable to ask for temporal logics that correspond with the lower Borel classes. In particular, it is important to know the logics that correspond with the classes Det_G, Det_F, $\mathsf{Det}_{\mathsf{Prefix}}$, and $\mathsf{Det}_{\mathsf{FG}}$, because these classes can be translated to the alternation-free μ-calculus, while the remaining classes $\mathsf{Det}_{\mathsf{GF}}$ and $\mathsf{NDet}_{\mathsf{Streett}}$ require μ-calculus formulas of alternation depth 2.

In this section, we will therefore define temporal logics TL_κ in analogy to the automaton classes Det_κ for $\kappa \in \{\mathsf{G}, \mathsf{F}, \mathsf{Prefix}, \mathsf{FG}, \mathsf{GF}, \mathsf{Streett}\}$. After this, we will prove some simple properties of these logics. For example, we will see that TL_G and TL_F, and that also $\mathsf{TL}_{\mathsf{GF}}$ and $\mathsf{TL}_{\mathsf{FG}}$ are dual to each other (this means that the negations of one class are in the dual class). Moreover, we will see that $\mathsf{TL}_{\mathsf{Prefix}}$ is the Boolean closure of both TL_G and TL_F, and that $\mathsf{TL}_{\mathsf{Streett}}$ is the Boolean closure of both $\mathsf{TL}_{\mathsf{GF}}$ and $\mathsf{TL}_{\mathsf{FG}}$.

Furthermore, we will see that our translation function TopProp is already able to translate TL_G to NDet_G. As TL_F is dual to TL_G, and as NDet_G is equally expressive to Det_G, this immediately implies that TL_F can be translated to Det_F. However, this indirect translation of TL_F to Det_F requires an exponential runtime due to the determinization step. In the next section, we will also develop further techniques to construct a linear time translation procedure from TL_F to NDet_F.

To conclude this section, we consider extraction procedures that are able to split any temporal logic formula into a part that belongs to one of the classes TL_κ, and another part that is translated with TopProp. These extraction procedures work roughly as follows: They follow the grammar rules of the sublogics TL_κ, and abbreviate each subformula that violates these grammar rules by applying the function TopProp to that subformula. This also explains the name of the previous function TopProp. It is also an extraction procedure that extracts the largest top-level propositional part. The other extraction functions are defined in a similar way.

To start with, consider the following definition of the temporal logic Borel classes that are defined in analogy to the automaton hierarchy:

Definition 5.48 (Temporal Borel Classes). *We define the logics* TL_G *and* TL_F *by the following grammar rules, where* TL_G *and* TL_F *is the set of formulas that can be derived from the nonterminal* P_G *and* P_F*, respectively:*

$$\begin{array}{llll}
P_\mathsf{G} ::= V_\Sigma & & & \\
\mid \neg P_\mathsf{F} & \mid P_\mathsf{G} \wedge P_\mathsf{G} & \mid P_\mathsf{G} \vee P_\mathsf{G} \\
\mid \mathsf{X} P_\mathsf{G} & \mid [P_\mathsf{G}\ \mathsf{U}\ P_\mathsf{G}] & \mid [P_\mathsf{G}\ \mathsf{B}\ P_\mathsf{F}] \\
\mid \overleftarrow{\underline{\mathsf{X}}} P_\mathsf{G} & \mid [P_\mathsf{G}\ \overleftarrow{\underline{\mathsf{U}}}\ P_\mathsf{G}] & \mid [P_\mathsf{G}\ \overleftarrow{\underline{\mathsf{B}}}\ P_\mathsf{F}] \\
\mid \overleftarrow{\mathsf{X}} P_\mathsf{G} & \mid [P_\mathsf{G}\ \overleftarrow{\mathsf{U}}\ P_\mathsf{G}] & \mid [P_\mathsf{G}\ \overleftarrow{\mathsf{B}}\ P_\mathsf{F}]
\end{array}
\qquad
\begin{array}{llll}
P_\mathsf{F} ::= V_\Sigma & & & \\
\mid \neg P_\mathsf{G} & \mid P_\mathsf{F} \wedge P_\mathsf{F} & \mid P_\mathsf{F} \vee P_\mathsf{F} \\
\mid \mathsf{X} P_\mathsf{F} & \mid [P_\mathsf{F}\ \underline{\mathsf{U}}\ P_\mathsf{F}] & \mid [P_\mathsf{F}\ \underline{\mathsf{B}}\ P_\mathsf{G}] \\
\mid \overleftarrow{\underline{\mathsf{X}}} P_\mathsf{F} & \mid [P_\mathsf{F}\ \overleftarrow{\underline{\mathsf{U}}}\ P_\mathsf{F}] & \mid [P_\mathsf{F}\ \overleftarrow{\underline{\mathsf{B}}}\ P_\mathsf{G}] \\
\mid \overleftarrow{\mathsf{X}} P_\mathsf{F} & \mid [P_\mathsf{F}\ \overleftarrow{\mathsf{U}}\ P_\mathsf{F}] & \mid [P_\mathsf{F}\ \overleftarrow{\mathsf{B}}\ P_\mathsf{G}]
\end{array}$$

The temporal logic $\mathsf{TL}_\mathsf{Prefix}$ *is the set of temporal logic formulas that can be derived from the nonterminal* P_Prefix *with the following additional grammar rules:*

$$P_\mathsf{Prefix} ::= P_\mathsf{G} \mid P_\mathsf{F} \mid \neg P_\mathsf{Prefix} \mid P_\mathsf{Prefix} \wedge P_\mathsf{Prefix} \mid P_\mathsf{Prefix} \vee P_\mathsf{Prefix}$$

Moreover, we define the logics TL_GF *and* TL_FG *by the following grammar rules, where* TL_GF *and* TL_FG *are the set of formulas that can be derived from the nonterminal* P_GF *and* P_FG*, respectively:*

$$\begin{array}{llll}
P_\mathsf{GF} ::= V_\Sigma & & & \\
\mid \neg P_\mathsf{FG} & \mid P_\mathsf{GF} \wedge P_\mathsf{GF} & \mid P_\mathsf{GF} \vee P_\mathsf{GF} \\
\mid \mathsf{X} P_\mathsf{GF} & \mid [P_\mathsf{GF}\ \underline{\mathsf{U}}\ P_\mathsf{F}] & \mid [P_\mathsf{F}\ \underline{\mathsf{B}}\ P_\mathsf{FG}] \\
 & \mid [P_\mathsf{GF}\ \mathsf{U}\ P_\mathsf{GF}] & \mid [P_\mathsf{GF}\ \mathsf{B}\ P_\mathsf{FG}] \\
\mid \overleftarrow{\underline{\mathsf{X}}} P_\mathsf{GF} & \mid [P_\mathsf{GF}\ \overleftarrow{\underline{\mathsf{U}}}\ P_\mathsf{GF}] & \mid [P_\mathsf{GF}\ \overleftarrow{\underline{\mathsf{B}}}\ P_\mathsf{FG}] \\
\mid \overleftarrow{\mathsf{X}} P_\mathsf{GF} & \mid [P_\mathsf{GF}\ \overleftarrow{\mathsf{U}}\ P_\mathsf{GF}] & \mid [P_\mathsf{GF}\ \overleftarrow{\mathsf{B}}\ P_\mathsf{FG}]
\end{array}
\qquad
\begin{array}{llll}
P_\mathsf{FG} ::= V_\Sigma & & & \\
\mid \neg P_\mathsf{GF} & \mid P_\mathsf{FG} \wedge P_\mathsf{FG} & \mid P_\mathsf{FG} \vee P_\mathsf{FG} \\
\mid \mathsf{X} P_\mathsf{FG} & \mid [P_\mathsf{FG}\ \underline{\mathsf{U}}\ P_\mathsf{FG}] & \mid [P_\mathsf{FG}\ \underline{\mathsf{B}}\ P_\mathsf{GF}] \\
 & \mid [P_\mathsf{G}\ \mathsf{U}\ P_\mathsf{FG}] & \mid [P_\mathsf{FG}\ \mathsf{B}\ P_\mathsf{F}] \\
\mid \overleftarrow{\underline{\mathsf{X}}} P_\mathsf{FG} & \mid [P_\mathsf{FG}\ \overleftarrow{\underline{\mathsf{U}}}\ P_\mathsf{FG}] & \mid [P_\mathsf{FG}\ \overleftarrow{\underline{\mathsf{B}}}\ P_\mathsf{GF}] \\
\mid \overleftarrow{\mathsf{X}} P_\mathsf{FG} & \mid [P_\mathsf{FG}\ \overleftarrow{\mathsf{U}}\ P_\mathsf{FG}] & \mid [P_\mathsf{FG}\ \overleftarrow{\mathsf{B}}\ P_\mathsf{GF}]
\end{array}$$

Finally, $\mathsf{TL}_\mathsf{Streett}$ *is the set of temporal logic formulas that can be derived from the nonterminal* P_Streett *with the following additional grammar rules:*

$$P_\mathsf{Streett} ::= P_\mathsf{GF} \mid P_\mathsf{FG} \mid \neg P_\mathsf{Streett} \mid P_\mathsf{Streett} \wedge P_\mathsf{Streett} \mid P_\mathsf{Streett} \vee P_\mathsf{Streett}$$

It is easily seen that every occurrence of a subformula of a TL_G formula that is derived from the nonterminal P_G has a positive occurrence. Analogously, any occurrence of a subformula that is derived from the nonterminal P_F in a TL_G formula is negative. This is easily verified by induction on the structure of TL_G and TL_F formulas. Moreover, we have the following properties:

Lemma 5.49 (Relationship between Borel Classes). *The following properties hold for the temporal Borel classes:*

(1) $\Phi \in \mathsf{TL}_\mathsf{F}$ *iff* $\neg\Phi \in \mathsf{TL}_\mathsf{G}$ *and* $\Phi \in \mathsf{TL}_\mathsf{G}$ *iff* $\neg\Phi \in \mathsf{TL}_\mathsf{F}$
(2) $\Phi \in \mathsf{TL}_\mathsf{FG}$ *iff* $\neg\Phi \in \mathsf{TL}_\mathsf{GF}$ *and* $\Phi \in \mathsf{TL}_\mathsf{GF}$ *iff* $\neg\Phi \in \mathsf{TL}_\mathsf{FG}$

(3) $\mathsf{TL_F} \subseteq \mathsf{TL_{FG}}$ *and* $\mathsf{TL_G} \subseteq \mathsf{TL_{GF}}$
(4) $\mathsf{TL_G} \subseteq \mathsf{TL_{FG}}$ *and* $\mathsf{TL_F} \subseteq \mathsf{TL_{GF}}$
(5) $\mathsf{TL_{Prefix}} \subseteq \mathsf{TL_{FG}}$ *and* $\mathsf{TL_{Prefix}} \subseteq \mathsf{TL_{GF}}$*, hence* $\mathsf{TL_{Prefix}} \subseteq \mathsf{TL_{FG}} \cap \mathsf{TL_{GF}}$

Proof. (1), (2), (3), and (4) can be easily proved by induction along the formulas. Using (3) and (4), a further induction along the grammar of $\mathsf{TL_{Prefix}}$ then proves that (5) holds. □

(1) states the duality of the logics $\mathsf{TL_F}$ and $\mathsf{TL_G}$, and (2) states the duality of the logics $\mathsf{TL_{FG}}$ and $\mathsf{TL_{GF}}$. (3) and (4) shows that $\mathsf{TL_G} \cup \mathsf{TL_F} \subseteq \mathsf{TL_{FG}} \cap \mathsf{TL_{GF}}$ holds. Moreover, it is easily seen that $\mathsf{TL_{Prefix}}$ is the Boolean closure of both $\mathsf{TL_F}$ and $\mathsf{TL_G}$, and (5) states that even $\mathsf{TL_{Prefix}}$ is contained in $\mathsf{TL_{FG}} \cap \mathsf{TL_{GF}}$. In a similar way, it is easily seen that $\mathsf{TL_{Streett}}$ is the Boolean closure of both $\mathsf{TL_{FG}}$ and $\mathsf{TL_{GF}}$. Therefore, we have the following lemma:

Lemma 5.50 (Boolean Closures of TL_κ). *Each of the logics* TL_κ *for* $\kappa \in \{\mathsf{G}, \mathsf{F}, \mathsf{Prefix}, \mathsf{GF}, \mathsf{FG}, \mathsf{Streett}\}$ *is closed under conjunction and disjunction. Moreover,* $\mathsf{TL_{Prefix}}$ *and* $\mathsf{TL_{Streett}}$ *are closed under negation, and are therefore the Boolean closures of* $\mathsf{TL_G}/\mathsf{TL_F}$ *and* $\mathsf{TL_{FG}}/\mathsf{TL_{GF}}$*, respectively.*

The proofs are immediately seen by considering the grammar rules of the logics. It is furthermore remarkable that we can convert each formula of any of the classes into negation normal form without leaving the considered class. This property may be used to eliminate the mutual recursive definition of the classes.

Lemma 5.51 (Robustness of TL_κ under Negation Normal Form). *For any formula from the logics* TL_κ *for* $\kappa \in \{\mathsf{G}, \mathsf{F}, \mathsf{Prefix}, \mathsf{GF}, \mathsf{FG}, \mathsf{Streett}\}$ *there is an equivalent formula of the same class in negation normal form.*

We now turn to the translation of the logics TL_κ to their corresponding automaton classes Det_κ. For this reason, note again that any occurrence of a subformula of a $\mathsf{TL_G}$ formula that is derived from the nonterminal P_G has a positive occurrence, and that any occurrence of a subformula that is derived from the nonterminal P_F in a $\mathsf{TL_G}$ formula is negative. Therefore, it immediately follows that each $\mathsf{TL_G}$ will be translated by function TopProp of Figure 5.12 to an ω-automaton without any fairness or other constraint. This, together with the previous lemmas yield the following result on the translateability:

Theorem 5.52 (Temporal Borel Classes (I)). *The following holds for the temporal logics* $\mathsf{TL_G}$*,* $\mathsf{TL_F}$*, and* $\mathsf{TL_{Prefix}}$*:*

- *For any formula* $\Phi \in \mathsf{TL_G}$*, there is an equivalent* ω*-automaton* $\mathfrak{A}_\Phi \in \mathsf{Det_G}$.
- *For any formula* $\Phi \in \mathsf{TL_F}$*, there is an equivalent* ω*-automaton* $\mathfrak{A}_\Phi \in \mathsf{Det_F}$.
- *For any formula* $\Phi \in \mathsf{TL_{Prefix}}$*, there is an equivalent* ω*-automaton* $\mathfrak{A}_\Phi \in \mathsf{Det_{Prefix}}$.

Proof. The first proposition is easily shown by induction on the given $\mathsf{TL_G}$ formula, where we can assume by the previous lemma that the given formula is given in negation normal form. Moreover, we can replace B operators by corresponding U operators and still preserve membership in $\mathsf{TL_G}$. The same holds for the strong before and the past time before operators. According to Theorem 5.47, we can use the algorithm of Figure 5.12, to obtain an automaton formula $\mathcal{A}_\exists\left(Q, \mathcal{I} \wedge \Phi_0, \Phi_\mathcal{R}, \bigwedge_{i=0}^{n} \xi_i\right)$. Due to the grammar rules of $\mathsf{TL_G}$, we can however easily see that $n = 0$ holds, i.e., that no fairness constraints were generated. Hence, the automaton formula is a (special) $\mathsf{NDet_G}$ automaton (one might add the 'constraint' $\mathsf{G}1$). Note finally, that $\mathsf{NDet_G}$ is equally expressive as $\mathsf{Det_G}$.

The second proposition follows by duality of $\mathsf{TL_G}$ and $\mathsf{TL_F}$, and the duality of $\mathsf{Det_G}$ with $\mathsf{Det_F}$. The third proposition is then proved by an easy induction on the given $\mathsf{TL_{Prefix}}$ formula Φ: The base cases where $\Phi \in \mathsf{TL_G}$ or $\Phi \in \mathsf{TL_F}$ holds follow immediately from the first two propositions, since $\mathsf{Det_G} \cup \mathsf{Det_F} \subset \mathsf{Det_{Prefix}}$ holds. The remaining cases follow by the Boolean closure of $\mathsf{Det_{Prefix}}$. □

Hence, we have already seen the correspondence of the logics $\mathsf{TL_G}$, $\mathsf{TL_F}$, and $\mathsf{TL_{Prefix}}$ with the automaton classes $\mathsf{Det_G}$, $\mathsf{Det_F}$, and $\mathsf{Det_{Prefix}}$. Using the function TopProp of Figure 5.12, gives us an algorithm for translating $\mathsf{TL_G}$ to $\mathsf{NDet_G}$. However, our translation from $\mathsf{TL_F}$ to $\mathsf{Det_F}$ is still indirect: We translate the negated formula which belongs to $\mathsf{TL_G}$, determinize the automaton and negate it. Clearly, this procedures suffers from an exponential blow-up due to the determinization. We will find another algorithm for directly translating $\mathsf{TL_F}$ to $\mathsf{NDet_F}$ within only linear runtime that is similar to TopProp in the next section.

Consider now the logics $\mathsf{TL_{FG}}$ and $\mathsf{TL_{GF}}$. These logics have been defined similar to the logics $\mathsf{TL_F}$ and $\mathsf{TL_G}$. To make this correspondence more apparent, note that we could first replace the rules $P_{\mathsf{GF}} ::= V_\Sigma$ and $P_{\mathsf{FG}} ::= V_\Sigma$ with $P_{\mathsf{GF}} ::= P_{\mathsf{Prefix}}$ and $P_{\mathsf{FG}} ::= P_{\mathsf{Prefix}}$, since $\mathsf{TL_{Prefix}} \subseteq \mathsf{TL_{FG}} \cap \mathsf{TL_{GF}}$. After this, we can eliminate the rules $P_{\mathsf{FG}} ::= [P_\mathsf{G}\ \mathsf{U}\ P_{\mathsf{FG}}]$ and $P_{\mathsf{FG}} ::= [P_{\mathsf{FG}}\ \mathsf{B}\ P_\mathsf{F}]$ as shown below:

- $[P_\mathsf{G}\ \mathsf{U}\ P_{\mathsf{FG}}] = \underbrace{[P_\mathsf{G}\ \underline{\mathsf{U}}\ P_{\mathsf{FG}}]}_{\in \mathsf{TL_{FG}}} \vee \underbrace{[P_\mathsf{G}\ \mathsf{U}\ 0]}_{\in \mathsf{TL_G} \subseteq \mathsf{TL_{Prefix}}}$
- $[P_{\mathsf{FG}}\ \mathsf{B}\ P_\mathsf{F}] = \underbrace{[P_{\mathsf{FG}}\ \underline{\mathsf{B}}\ P_\mathsf{F}]}_{\in \mathsf{TL_{FG}}} \vee \underbrace{[(\neg P_\mathsf{F})\ \mathsf{U}\ 0]}_{\in \mathsf{TL_G} \subseteq \mathsf{TL_{Prefix}}}$

Eliminating these rules (and the corresponding two of the grammar rules of P_{GF}) shows the correspondence between $\mathsf{TL_{FG}}$ and $\mathsf{TL_{GF}}$ with $\mathsf{TL_F}$ and $\mathsf{TL_G}$, respectively. The difference is then that only P_{FG} and P_{GF} accept P_{Prefix} formulas where P_F and P_G require variables.

Hence, $\mathsf{TL_{FG}}$ allows arbitrary positive nestings with strong future and arbitrary past operators, but not with weak future operators: once a weak future operator is used in a positive occurrence, this must be $\mathsf{TL_G}$ formula, where only weak future and arbitrary past operators may be nested. Note that if we were to allow strong operators to appear as arguments of weak operators, we could express the formula $\mathsf{GF}\varphi$ that can not be expressed by any $\mathsf{Det}_{\mathsf{FG}}$ automaton.

Analogously, $\mathsf{TL}_{\mathsf{GF}}$ allows arbitrary positive nestings with weak future and arbitrary past operators, but not with strong future operators: once a strong future operator is used in a positive occurrence, this must be a TL_{F} formula, where only strong future and arbitrary past operators may be nested. In particular, these restriction do not allow us to generate the formula $\mathsf{FG}\varphi$ that can not be expressed by any $\mathsf{Det}_{\mathsf{GF}}$ automaton.

Before considering the efficient translations of all the logics TL_κ to NDet_κ, we consider how top-level formulas of these classes can be extracted from arbitrary LTL_p formulas. For this reason, we implement the functions TopFG and TopG as given in Figures 5.14 and 5.13. The principle of these functions is the same: They follow the grammar rules of the sublogics, and abbreviate each subformula that violates these grammar rules by applying the function TopProp. Hence, the functions TopFG, TopG, and TopProp are closely related to each other in that they extract the largest top-level $\mathsf{TL}_{\mathsf{FG}}$, TL_{G}, and propositional formulas. The precise specification of the functions TopFG and TopG is given in the following theorem.

Theorem 5.53 (Correctness of TopFG and TopG). *Given any formula $\Phi \in \mathsf{LTL}_p$, and the resulting automaton formula $\mathcal{A}_\exists(\mathcal{Q},\mathcal{I},\mathcal{R},\mathcal{F},\Phi_0) = \mathsf{TopG}_\sigma(\Phi)$ obtained by the algorithm given in Figure 5.13, then the following holds:*

(1) $\mathsf{TopG}_\sigma(\Phi)$ *runs in time* $O(|\Phi|)$.
(2) *If* $\sigma = 1$ *holds, we have* $\Phi_0 \in \mathsf{TL}_{\mathsf{G}}$*, otherwise, we have* $\Phi_0 \in \mathsf{TL}_{\mathsf{F}}$.
(3) *Each* $\xi \in \mathcal{F}$ *is of the form* $\mathsf{GF}\xi'$ *where* ξ' *is propositional.*
(4) *For* $\sigma = 1$*, the equation* $\Phi = \mathcal{A}_\exists\left(\mathcal{Q},\mathcal{I},\mathcal{R},\Phi_0 \wedge \bigwedge_{\xi\in\mathcal{F}} \xi\right)$ *is initially valid.*
(5) *For* $\sigma = 0$*, the equation* $\neg\Phi = \mathcal{A}_\exists\left(\mathcal{Q},\mathcal{I},\mathcal{R},\neg\Phi_0 \wedge \bigwedge_{\xi\in\mathcal{F}} \xi\right)$ *is initially valid.*

Given any formula $\Phi \in \mathsf{LTL}_p$, and the automaton formula $\mathcal{A}_\exists(\mathcal{Q},\mathcal{I},\mathcal{R},\mathcal{F},\Phi_0) = \mathsf{TopFG}_\sigma(\Phi)$ obtained by the algorithm given in Figure 5.14, then the following holds:

(1) $\mathsf{TopFG}_\sigma(\Phi)$ *runs in time* $O(|\Phi|)$.
(2) *If* $\sigma = 1$ *holds, we have* $\Phi_0 \in \mathsf{TL}_{\mathsf{FG}}$*, otherwise, we have* $\Phi_0 \in \mathsf{TL}_{\mathsf{GF}}$.
(3) *Each* ξ_i *is of the form* $\mathsf{GF}\xi'$ *where* ξ' *is propositional.*
(4) *For* $\sigma = 1$*, the equation* $\Phi = \mathcal{A}_\exists\left(\mathcal{Q},\mathcal{I},\mathcal{R},\Phi_0 \wedge \bigwedge_{\xi\in\mathcal{F}} \xi\right)$ *is initially valid.*
(5) *For* $\sigma = 0$*, the equation* $\neg\Phi = \mathcal{A}_\exists\left(\mathcal{Q},\mathcal{I},\mathcal{R},\neg\Phi_0 \wedge \bigwedge_{\xi\in\mathcal{F}} \xi\right)$ *is initially valid.*

function $\mathsf{TopG}_\sigma(\Phi)$
  case Φ **of**
  $\mathsf{is\_prop}(\Phi)$: **return** $\mathcal{A}_\exists(\{\}, 1, 1, \{\}, \Phi)$;
  $\neg\varphi$: $\mathcal{A}_\exists(\mathcal{Q}_\varphi, \mathcal{I}_\varphi, \mathcal{R}_\varphi, \mathcal{F}_\varphi, \varphi') \equiv \mathsf{TopG}_{\neg\sigma}(\varphi)$;
    return $\mathcal{A}_\exists(\mathcal{Q}_\varphi, \mathcal{I}_\varphi, \mathcal{R}_\varphi, \mathcal{F}_\varphi, \neg\varphi')$;
  $\varphi \wedge \psi$: $\mathcal{A}_\exists(\mathcal{Q}_\varphi, \mathcal{I}_\varphi, \mathcal{R}_\varphi, \mathcal{F}_\varphi, \varphi') \equiv \mathsf{TopG}_\sigma(\varphi)$;
    $\mathcal{A}_\exists(\mathcal{Q}_\psi, \mathcal{I}_\psi, \mathcal{R}_\psi, \mathcal{F}_\psi, \psi') \equiv \mathsf{TopG}_\sigma(\psi)$;
    return $\mathcal{A}_\exists(\mathcal{Q}_\varphi \cup \mathcal{Q}_\psi, \mathcal{I}_\varphi \wedge \mathcal{I}_\psi, \mathcal{R}_\varphi \wedge \mathcal{R}_\psi, \mathcal{F}_\varphi \cup \mathcal{F}_\psi, \varphi' \wedge \psi')$;
  $\varphi \vee \psi$: $\mathcal{A}_\exists(\mathcal{Q}_\varphi, \mathcal{I}_\varphi, \mathcal{R}_\varphi, \mathcal{F}_\varphi, \varphi') \equiv \mathsf{TopG}_\sigma(\varphi)$;
    $\mathcal{A}_\exists(\mathcal{Q}_\psi, \mathcal{I}_\psi, \mathcal{R}_\psi, \mathcal{F}_\psi, \psi') \equiv \mathsf{TopG}_\sigma(\psi)$;
    return $\mathcal{A}_\exists(\mathcal{Q}_\varphi \cup \mathcal{Q}_\psi, \mathcal{I}_\varphi \wedge \mathcal{I}_\psi, \mathcal{R}_\varphi \wedge \mathcal{R}_\psi, \mathcal{F}_\varphi \cup \mathcal{F}_\psi, \varphi' \vee \psi')$;
  $\mathsf{X}\varphi$: $\mathcal{A}_\exists(\mathcal{Q}_\varphi, \mathcal{I}_\varphi, \mathcal{R}_\varphi, \mathcal{F}_\varphi, \varphi') \equiv \mathsf{TopG}_\sigma(\varphi)$;
    return $\mathcal{A}_\exists(\mathcal{Q}_\varphi, \mathcal{I}_\varphi, \mathcal{R}_\varphi, \mathcal{F}_\varphi, \mathsf{X}\varphi')$;
  $[\varphi\ \underline{\mathsf{U}}\ \psi]$: **if** σ **then return** $\mathsf{TopProp}_\sigma(\Phi)$ **end**;
    $\mathcal{A}_\exists(\mathcal{Q}_\varphi, \mathcal{I}_\varphi, \mathcal{R}_\varphi, \mathcal{F}_\varphi, \varphi') \equiv \mathsf{TopG}_\sigma(\varphi)$;
    $\mathcal{A}_\exists(\mathcal{Q}_\psi, \mathcal{I}_\psi, \mathcal{R}_\psi, \mathcal{F}_\psi, \psi') \equiv \mathsf{TopG}_\sigma(\psi)$;
    return $\mathcal{A}_\exists(\mathcal{Q}_\varphi \cup \mathcal{Q}_\psi, \mathcal{I}_\varphi \wedge \mathcal{I}_\psi, \mathcal{R}_\varphi \wedge \mathcal{R}_\psi, \mathcal{F}_\varphi \cup \mathcal{F}_\psi, [\varphi'\ \underline{\mathsf{U}}\ \psi'])$;
  $[\varphi\ \mathsf{B}\ \psi]$: **if** $\neg\sigma$ **then return** $\mathsf{TopProp}_\sigma(\Phi)$ **end**;
    $\mathcal{A}_\exists(\mathcal{Q}_\varphi, \mathcal{I}_\varphi, \mathcal{R}_\varphi, \mathcal{F}_\varphi, \varphi') \equiv \mathsf{TopG}_\sigma(\varphi)$;
    $\mathcal{A}_\exists(\mathcal{Q}_\psi, \mathcal{I}_\psi, \mathcal{R}_\psi, \mathcal{F}_\psi, \psi') \equiv \mathsf{TopG}_{\neg\sigma}(\psi)$;
    return $\mathcal{A}_\exists(\mathcal{Q}_\varphi \cup \mathcal{Q}_\psi, \mathcal{I}_\varphi \wedge \mathcal{I}_\psi, \mathcal{R}_\varphi \wedge \mathcal{R}_\psi, \mathcal{F}_\varphi \cup \mathcal{F}_\psi, [\varphi'\ \mathsf{B}\ \psi'])$;
  $\overleftarrow{\mathsf{X}}\varphi$: $\mathcal{A}_\exists(\mathcal{Q}_\varphi, \mathcal{I}_\varphi, \mathcal{R}_\varphi, \mathcal{F}_\varphi, \varphi') \equiv \mathsf{TopG}_\sigma(\varphi)$;
    return $\mathcal{A}_\exists\left(\mathcal{Q}_\varphi, \mathcal{I}_\varphi, \mathcal{R}_\varphi, \mathcal{F}_\varphi, \overleftarrow{\mathsf{X}}\varphi'\right)$;
  $\overleftarrow{\underline{\mathsf{X}}}\varphi$: $\mathcal{A}_\exists(\mathcal{Q}_\varphi, \mathcal{I}_\varphi, \mathcal{R}_\varphi, \mathcal{F}_\varphi, \varphi') \equiv \mathsf{TopG}_\sigma(\varphi)$;
    return $\mathcal{A}_\exists\left(\mathcal{Q}_\varphi, \mathcal{I}_\varphi, \mathcal{R}_\varphi, \mathcal{F}_\varphi, \overleftarrow{\underline{\mathsf{X}}}\varphi'\right)$;
  $[\varphi\ \overleftarrow{\underline{\mathsf{U}}}\ \psi]$: $\mathcal{A}_\exists(\mathcal{Q}_\varphi, \mathcal{I}_\varphi, \mathcal{R}_\varphi, \mathcal{F}_\varphi, \varphi') \equiv \mathsf{TopG}_\sigma(\varphi)$;
    $\mathcal{A}_\exists(\mathcal{Q}_\psi, \mathcal{I}_\psi, \mathcal{R}_\psi, \mathcal{F}_\psi, \psi') \equiv \mathsf{TopG}_\sigma(\psi)$;
    return $\mathcal{A}_\exists\left(\mathcal{Q}_\varphi \cup \mathcal{Q}_\psi, \mathcal{I}_\varphi \wedge \mathcal{I}_\psi, \mathcal{R}_\varphi \wedge \mathcal{R}_\psi, \mathcal{F}_\varphi \cup \mathcal{F}_\psi, [\varphi'\ \overleftarrow{\underline{\mathsf{U}}}\ \psi']\right)$;
  $[\varphi\ \overleftarrow{\mathsf{B}}\ \psi]$: $\mathcal{A}_\exists(\mathcal{Q}_\varphi, \mathcal{I}_\varphi, \mathcal{R}_\varphi, \mathcal{F}_\varphi, \varphi') \equiv \mathsf{TopG}_\sigma(\varphi)$;
    $\mathcal{A}_\exists(\mathcal{Q}_\psi, \mathcal{I}_\psi, \mathcal{R}_\psi, \mathcal{F}_\psi, \psi') \equiv \mathsf{TopG}_{\neg\sigma}(\psi)$;
    return $\mathcal{A}_\exists\left(\mathcal{Q}_\varphi \cup \mathcal{Q}_\psi, \mathcal{I}_\varphi \wedge \mathcal{I}_\psi, \mathcal{R}_\varphi \wedge \mathcal{R}_\psi, \mathcal{F}_\varphi \cup \mathcal{F}_\psi, [\varphi'\ \overleftarrow{\mathsf{B}}\ \psi']\right)$;
  end case
end function

Fig. 5.13. Extraction of top-level $\mathsf{TL_G}$ ($\sigma = 1$) and $\mathsf{TL_F}$ ($\sigma = 0$) formulas

The proof of the above theorem is not too difficult: Properties $(1-3)$ are easily proved by induction. Properties $(4-5)$ are proved in the same manner as the correctness of TopProp was proved, i.e., by means of Theorems 5.38, 5.39, and 5.46.

One might wonder whether in the definition of $\mathsf{TL_{FG}}$, the grammar rules $P_{\mathsf{FG}} := [P_{\mathsf{G}}\ \mathsf{U}\ P_{\mathsf{FG}}]$ and $P_{\mathsf{FG}} := [P_{\mathsf{FG}}\ \mathsf{B}\ P_{\mathsf{F}}]$ could be generalized to $P_{\mathsf{FG}} := [P_{\mathsf{FG}}\ \mathsf{U}\ P_{\mathsf{FG}}]$ and $P_{\mathsf{FG}} := [P_{\mathsf{FG}}\ \mathsf{B}\ P_{\mathsf{FG}}]$. This is not possible since the formula $[[1\ \underline{\mathsf{U}}\ \varphi]\ \mathsf{U}\ 0]$ would then belong to $\mathsf{TL_{FG}}$. However, as this formula is equiva-

function $\mathsf{TopFG}_\sigma(\Phi)$
case Φ **of**
$\mathsf{is\_prop}(\Phi)$: **return** $\mathcal{A}_\exists(\{\}, 1, 1, \{\}, \Phi)$;
$\neg\varphi$: $\mathcal{A}_\exists(\mathcal{Q}_\varphi, \mathcal{I}_\varphi, \mathcal{R}_\varphi, \mathcal{F}_\varphi, \varphi') \equiv \mathsf{TopFG}_{\neg\sigma}(\varphi)$;
return $\mathcal{A}_\exists(\mathcal{Q}_\varphi, \mathcal{I}_\varphi, \mathcal{R}_\varphi, \mathcal{F}_\varphi, \neg\varphi')$;
$\varphi \wedge \psi$: $\mathcal{A}_\exists(\mathcal{Q}_\varphi, \mathcal{I}_\varphi, \mathcal{R}_\varphi, \mathcal{F}_\varphi, \varphi') \equiv \mathsf{TopFG}_\sigma(\varphi)$;
$\mathcal{A}_\exists(\mathcal{Q}_\psi, \mathcal{I}_\psi, \mathcal{R}_\psi, \mathcal{F}_\psi, \psi') \equiv \mathsf{TopFG}_\sigma(\psi)$;
return $\mathcal{A}_\exists(\mathcal{Q}_\varphi \cup \mathcal{Q}_\psi, \mathcal{I}_\varphi \wedge \mathcal{I}_\psi, \mathcal{R}_\varphi \wedge \mathcal{R}_\psi, \mathcal{F}_\varphi \cup \mathcal{F}_\psi, \varphi' \wedge \psi')$;
$\varphi \vee \psi$: $\mathcal{A}_\exists(\mathcal{Q}_\varphi, \mathcal{I}_\varphi, \mathcal{R}_\varphi, \mathcal{F}_\varphi, \varphi') \equiv \mathsf{TopFG}_\sigma(\varphi)$;
$\mathcal{A}_\exists(\mathcal{Q}_\psi, \mathcal{I}_\psi, \mathcal{R}_\psi, \mathcal{F}_\psi, \psi') \equiv \mathsf{TopFG}_\sigma(\psi)$;
return $\mathcal{A}_\exists(\mathcal{Q}_\varphi \cup \mathcal{Q}_\psi, \mathcal{I}_\varphi \wedge \mathcal{I}_\psi, \mathcal{R}_\varphi \wedge \mathcal{R}_\psi, \mathcal{F}_\varphi \cup \mathcal{F}_\psi, \varphi' \vee \psi')$;
$\mathsf{X}\varphi$: $\mathcal{A}_\exists(\mathcal{Q}_\varphi, \mathcal{I}_\varphi, \mathcal{R}_\varphi, \mathcal{F}_\varphi, \varphi') \equiv \mathsf{TopFG}_\sigma(\varphi)$;
return $\mathcal{A}_\exists(\mathcal{Q}_\varphi, \mathcal{I}_\varphi, \mathcal{R}_\varphi, \mathcal{F}_\varphi, \mathsf{X}\varphi')$;
$[\varphi\ \underline{\mathsf{U}}\ \psi]$: $\mathcal{A}_\exists(\mathcal{Q}_\varphi, \mathcal{I}_\varphi, \mathcal{R}_\varphi, \mathcal{F}_\varphi, \varphi') \equiv \mathsf{TopFG}_\sigma(\varphi)$;
if σ **then** $\mathcal{A}_\exists(\mathcal{Q}_\psi, \mathcal{I}_\psi, \mathcal{R}_\psi, \mathcal{F}_\psi, \psi') \equiv \mathsf{TopFG}_\sigma(\psi)$
else $\mathcal{A}_\exists(\mathcal{Q}_\psi, \mathcal{I}_\psi, \mathcal{R}_\psi, \mathcal{F}_\psi, \psi') \equiv \mathsf{TopG}_\sigma(\psi)$ **end**;
return $\mathcal{A}_\exists(\mathcal{Q}_\varphi \cup \mathcal{Q}_\psi, \mathcal{I}_\varphi \wedge \mathcal{I}_\psi, \mathcal{R}_\varphi \wedge \mathcal{R}_\psi, \mathcal{F}_\varphi \cup \mathcal{F}_\psi, [\varphi'\ \underline{\mathsf{U}}\ \psi'])$;
$[\varphi\ \mathsf{B}\ \psi]$: $\mathcal{A}_\exists(\mathcal{Q}_\varphi, \mathcal{I}_\varphi, \mathcal{R}_\varphi, \mathcal{F}_\varphi, \varphi') \equiv \mathsf{TopFG}_\sigma(\varphi)$;
if σ **then** $\mathcal{A}_\exists(\mathcal{Q}_\psi, \mathcal{I}_\psi, \mathcal{R}_\psi, \mathcal{F}_\psi, \psi') \equiv \mathsf{TopG}_{\neg\sigma}(\psi)$
else $\mathcal{A}_\exists(\mathcal{Q}_\psi, \mathcal{I}_\psi, \mathcal{R}_\psi, \mathcal{F}_\psi, \psi') \equiv \mathsf{TopFG}_{\neg\sigma}(\psi)$ **end**;
return $\mathcal{A}_\exists(\mathcal{Q}_\varphi \cup \mathcal{Q}_\psi, \mathcal{I}_\varphi \wedge \mathcal{I}_\psi, \mathcal{R}_\varphi \wedge \mathcal{R}_\psi, \mathcal{F}_\varphi \cup \mathcal{F}_\psi, [\varphi'\ \mathsf{B}\ \psi'])$;
$\overleftarrow{\mathsf{X}}\varphi$: $\mathcal{A}_\exists(\mathcal{Q}_\varphi, \mathcal{I}_\varphi, \mathcal{R}_\varphi, \mathcal{F}_\varphi, \varphi') \equiv \mathsf{TopFG}_\sigma(\varphi)$;
return $\mathcal{A}_\exists\left(\mathcal{Q}_\varphi, \mathcal{I}_\varphi, \mathcal{R}_\varphi, \mathcal{F}_\varphi, \overleftarrow{\mathsf{X}}\varphi'\right)$;
$\overleftarrow{\underline{\mathsf{X}}}\varphi$: $\mathcal{A}_\exists(\mathcal{Q}_\varphi, \mathcal{I}_\varphi, \mathcal{R}_\varphi, \mathcal{F}_\varphi, \varphi') \equiv \mathsf{TopFG}_\sigma(\varphi)$;
return $\mathcal{A}_\exists\left(\mathcal{Q}_\varphi, \mathcal{I}_\varphi, \mathcal{R}_\varphi, \mathcal{F}_\varphi, \overleftarrow{\underline{\mathsf{X}}}\varphi'\right)$;
$[\varphi\ \overleftarrow{\underline{\mathsf{U}}}\ \psi]$: $\mathcal{A}_\exists(\mathcal{Q}_\varphi, \mathcal{I}_\varphi, \mathcal{R}_\varphi, \mathcal{F}_\varphi, \varphi') \equiv \mathsf{TopFG}_\sigma(\varphi)$;
$\mathcal{A}_\exists(\mathcal{Q}_\psi, \mathcal{I}_\psi, \mathcal{R}_\psi, \mathcal{F}_\psi, \psi') \equiv \mathsf{TopFG}_\sigma(\psi)$;
return $\mathcal{A}_\exists\left(\mathcal{Q}_\varphi \cup \mathcal{Q}_\psi, \mathcal{I}_\varphi \wedge \mathcal{I}_\psi, \mathcal{R}_\varphi \wedge \mathcal{R}_\psi, \mathcal{F}_\varphi \cup \mathcal{F}_\psi, [\varphi'\ \overleftarrow{\underline{\mathsf{U}}}\ \psi']\right)$;
$[\varphi\ \overleftarrow{\mathsf{B}}\ \psi]$: $\mathcal{A}_\exists(\mathcal{Q}_\varphi, \mathcal{I}_\varphi, \mathcal{R}_\varphi, \mathcal{F}_\varphi, \varphi') \equiv \mathsf{TopFG}_\sigma(\varphi)$;
$\mathcal{A}_\exists(\mathcal{Q}_\psi, \mathcal{I}_\psi, \mathcal{R}_\psi, \mathcal{F}_\psi, \psi') \equiv \mathsf{TopFG}_{\neg\sigma}(\psi)$;
return $\mathcal{A}_\exists\left(\mathcal{Q}_\varphi \cup \mathcal{Q}_\psi, \mathcal{I}_\varphi \wedge \mathcal{I}_\psi, \mathcal{R}_\varphi \wedge \mathcal{R}_\psi, \mathcal{F}_\varphi \cup \mathcal{F}_\psi, [\varphi'\ \overleftarrow{\mathsf{B}}\ \psi']\right)$;
end case
end function

Fig. 5.14. Extraction of top-level $\mathsf{TL}_{\mathsf{FG}}$ ($\sigma = 1$) and $\mathsf{TL}_{\mathsf{GF}}$ ($\sigma = 0$) formulas

lent to $\mathsf{GF}\varphi$, and the latter can not be expressed by $\mathsf{Det}_{\mathsf{FG}}$ automata, this generalization would really extend the expressiveness of $\mathsf{TL}_{\mathsf{FG}}$, so that it could no longer be translated to $\mathsf{Det}_{\mathsf{FG}}$. The same holds for the impossible generalizations $P_{\mathsf{FG}} := [P_{\mathsf{Prefix}}\ \mathsf{U}\ P_{\mathsf{FG}}]$ and $P_{\mathsf{FG}} := [P_{\mathsf{FG}}\ \mathsf{B}\ P_{\mathsf{Prefix}}]$.

In fact, we will prove in Section 5.5.3 that our definitions are complete in some sense, i.e., the logics that we have defined are essentially the strongest that can be translated to the desired automaton classes. Before we proceed with considerations of the completeness, we should however construct further translation procedures for the remaining classes.

5.4.4 Reducing Temporal Borel Classes to Borel Automata

We have seen in Section 5.4.2 that the basic translation as given in Section 5.4.1 can be improved when the monotonicity of operators is taken into account. In the previous section, we have moreover defined a hierarchy of temporal logics TL_κ that is analogous with the automaton hierarchy. Moreover, we have already seen in the previous section that the logics TL_G, TL_F, and $\mathsf{TL}_\mathsf{Prefix}$ can be translated to equivalent Det_G, Det_F, and $\mathsf{Det}_\mathsf{Prefix}$ automata. Moreover, the function TopProp translates any TL_G formula in linear time to an equivalent NDet_G automaton, so that we have an efficient translation for this logic. Our current translation from TL_F to NDet_F is, however, indirect: We first negate the TL_F formula Φ to obtain the TL_G formula $\neg\Phi$, which is then translated by the function TopProp to a NDet_G automaton $\mathfrak{A}_{\neg\Phi}$. Up to this point, all computations are done within $O(|\Phi|)$ time, but now our current translation needs to determinize $\mathfrak{A}_{\neg\Phi}$, so that we can compute its complement. This complement is then our desired Det_F automaton. The translation of $\mathsf{TL}_\mathsf{Prefix}$ to $\mathsf{Det}_\mathsf{Prefix}$ is done in the same spirit, where we have to additionally compute the Boolean closures of the obtained Det_G and Det_F automata.

In this section, we will develop another translation that does not suffer from the exponential blow-up due to the determinization. This translation however, only translates TL_F to NDet_F instead of translating it to Det_F, but this is completely sufficient for verification purposes. The translation that we will now develop is a modification of the function TopProp. Recall that the key idea of TopProp is to abbreviate elementary subformulas by state variables of the ω-automaton to be constructed. As the abbreviations of the future operators are only determined up to the operator strength with the transition relations, the function TopProp uses fairness constraints to fix the desired operator strength when necessary.

We will now see that for TL_F formulas, a simper *reachability constraint* of the form $\mathsf{F}\varphi$ can be used instead of a fairness constraint to fix the operator strength. The key idea is as follows: Assume that $[\varphi \ \underline{\mathsf{U}}\ \psi]$ holds at some point of time t_0. To check this, we must only inspect finitely many points of time, namely those from t_0 up to the first point of time after t_0, where ψ holds. In this interval, we must evaluate the subformulas φ and ψ, and need to check if the semantics of $[\varphi \ \underline{\mathsf{U}}\ \psi]$ are respected. Hence, it is *not necessary* to define state variables q_φ and q_ψ such that we have $\mathsf{G}[q_\varphi \leftrightarrow \varphi]$ and $\mathsf{G}[q_\psi \leftrightarrow \psi]$. Instead, it would be sufficient if the equations $q_\varphi \leftrightarrow \varphi$ would *hold long enough* so that we can evaluate the formula $[\varphi \ \underline{\mathsf{U}}\ \psi]$. The syntax of TL_F and TL_FG guarantees that no outer operator requires the infinitely often checking of truth values. It is sufficient to evaluate the subformulas in a finite interval.

For example, consider a formula of the form $[(\Phi\langle[\varphi \ \underline{\mathsf{U}}\ \psi]\rangle_x) \ \underline{\mathsf{U}}\ \gamma]$, where the formulas φ and ψ are propositional. Furthermore, assume that x does not occur in the scope of a future temporal operator inside the formula Φ. As in the previous algorithms, we abbreviate the subformula $[\varphi\ \underline{\mathsf{U}}\ \psi]$ with a new state variable q by using the transition relation $q \leftrightarrow \psi \vee \varphi \wedge \mathsf{X}q$. We already know (cf. Theorem 5.36) that this restricts q so that either $\mathsf{G}[q \leftrightarrow [\varphi\ \mathsf{U}\ \psi]]$ or $\mathsf{G}[q \leftrightarrow [\varphi\ \underline{\mathsf{U}}\ \psi]]$ holds, and thus the behavior of q is not yet uniquely fixed. As already outlined above, the crucial observation is that it is not necessary to determine the unique behavior of q for *all points of time*. Instead, it is *sufficient to uniquely determine it up to the point of time where γ holds for the first time.* Note that the latter would not be sufficient if x would occur in the scope of a future temporal operator, as e.g., in $[(\mathsf{G}x)\ \underline{\mathsf{U}}\ \gamma]$.

How can we do this without adding fairness constraints? According to fact (6) of Lemma 5.35 (on page 333), we already know that if $\mathsf{F}[q \rightarrow \psi]$ holds at some point of time t_0, then all solutions of the fixpoint equation $\mathsf{G}[q \leftrightarrow \psi \vee \varphi \wedge \mathsf{X}q]$ have the same truth value at least up to this point of time t_0. In particular, we then have $\overleftarrow{\mathsf{G}}\,[q \leftrightarrow [\varphi\ \underline{\mathsf{U}}\ \psi]]$. Let t_1 be the first point of time where γ becomes true. Hence, we must establish in some way that $\mathsf{F}[q \rightarrow \psi]$ holds at t_1 (or after t_1, which implies that it will also hold at t_1). A simple attempt could therefore be to use the formula $[(\Phi\langle q\rangle_x)\ \underline{\mathsf{U}}\ (\gamma \wedge \mathsf{F}[q \rightarrow \psi])]$, and a detailed proof will show that it is correct.

We note again that it is necessary that x must not occur in the scope of a future time temporal operator in Φ: The key idea of the above theorem is that we need to evaluate q only in a finite interval, i.e., up to some point of time. However, iff x were to occur in the scope of a future time temporal operator in Φ, then we require it to correct the operator strength for all times, which must then be done by a fairness constraint instead.

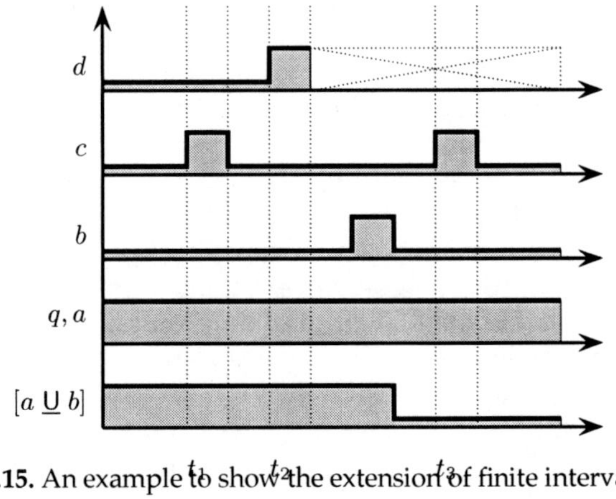

Fig. 5.15. An example to show the extension of finite intervals of interest

However, even if the interval of interest remains finite, it may be extended by operator nestings. To see this, consider the formula $[[[a\ \underline{\mathsf{U}}\ b]\ \underline{\mathsf{U}}\ c]\ \underline{\mathsf{U}}\ d]$ where we assume that a, b, c, and d are variables. Of course, we start by abbreviating $[a\ \underline{\mathsf{U}}\ b]$ with a new state variable q in that we add the transition relation $q \leftrightarrow b \vee a \wedge \mathsf{X}q$. To fix the operator strength, we must now establish that the constraint $\mathsf{F}[q \rightarrow b]$ holds at the end of the finite interval where we need the truth value of q. Now, note that it is not sufficient to add the constraint that follows:

$$\mathcal{A}_{\exists}\left(\{q\}, 1, q \leftrightarrow b \vee a \wedge \mathsf{X}q, [[q\ \underline{\mathsf{U}}\ c]\ \underline{\mathsf{U}}\ (d \wedge \mathsf{F}[q \rightarrow b])]\right)$$

Our constraint has been put at the first point of time where d holds, and therefore, we can guarantee that $q \leftrightarrow [a\ \underline{\mathsf{U}}\ b]$ holds up to this point of time. However, the further nesting in another temporal operator shows that this is not sufficient: If we assume that a, b, c, and d, have the values as given in the timing diagram of Figure 5.15, then we see that $q \leftrightarrow [a\ \underline{\mathsf{U}}\ b]$ holds up to the first point after t_2 where b holds, but after that, we only have $q \leftrightarrow [a\ \mathsf{U}\ b]$. The equation $q \leftrightarrow [a\ \underline{\mathsf{U}}\ b]$ should however hold up to t_3, so that we see that we must place the constraint at point t_3. Therefore, the constraint $\mathsf{F}[q \rightarrow b]$ must be put in the next upper event that is awaited, i.e., our intermediate result should be the following automaton formula:

$$\mathcal{A}_{\exists}\left(\{q\}, 1, q \leftrightarrow b \vee a \wedge \mathsf{X}q, [[q\ \underline{\mathsf{U}}\ (c \wedge \mathsf{F}[q \rightarrow b])]\ \underline{\mathsf{U}}\ d]\right)$$

After that, we would like to further abbreviate $[q\ \underline{\mathsf{U}}\ (c \wedge \mathsf{F}[q \rightarrow b])]$ with another state variable. As the subformulas are not propositional, we would need to abbreviate $\mathsf{F}[q \rightarrow b]$ in advance, which yields in an infinite loop (we abbreviate a reachability constraint by another reachability constraint that also needs to be abbreviated, and so on).

We will see in the following that this problem can be circumvented. The key idea is thereby the same as the one used by function TopProp, i.e., we traverse the syntax tree of the formula in a bottom-up manner. This means, we first translate the subformulas of a formula to an equivalent ω-automaton and construct then the entire automaton. However, we can not simply drop the G operators of the GF-constraints of Theorem 5.39 and use the resulting equations. As we have seen by the above example, we must nest the generated constraints in the same way as the formulas are nested where they stem from.

Hence, a first attempt is to assume that we already have proved that the equations $\varphi \leftrightarrow \mathcal{A}_{\exists}(\mathcal{Q}_{\varphi}, \mathcal{I}_{\varphi}, \mathcal{R}_{\varphi}, \mathcal{F}_{\varphi}, \varphi')$ and $\psi \leftrightarrow \mathcal{A}_{\exists}(\mathcal{Q}_{\psi}, \mathcal{I}_{\psi}, \mathcal{R}_{\psi}, \mathcal{F}_{\psi}, \psi')$, where we may assume that the constraint sets $\mathcal{F}_{\varphi}$ and $\mathcal{F}_{\psi}$ contain reachability constraints of the form $\mathsf{F}\xi'$ with propositional ξ'. The task is now to generate an automaton that is equivalent to $[\varphi\ \underline{\mathsf{U}}\ \psi]$ out of the already available automata. Due to the presence of past operators we will only be able to generate automata that are initially equivalent to the original formula. This is sufficient for verification purposes, but prevents us from nesting the automata: To translate the formula $[\varphi\ \underline{\mathsf{U}}\ \psi]$, we need to establish the equivalence of φ to an automaton not only for the initial point of time, but for a finite interval that is determined by ψ. Also, the initial equivalence of ψ with an automaton is not of much use, since we need the equation for later points of time.

We are therefore interested in proving the initial validity of automaton formulas whose acceptance condition is of the form $\zeta_\Phi \to \overleftarrow{\mathsf{G}}[\Phi_0 \leftrightarrow \Phi]$, where ζ_Φ is an appropriate reachability constraint. This will allow us to generate, more or less, the same automata with the acceptance condition ζ_Φ. For a detailed proof, we will however need to construct universal automata. As universal automaton formulas may however trivially hold in the case where there is no product path in the product structure, we must additionally prove the existence of product paths. Therefore, we need the following lemma to establish the invariants of our algorithm:

Lemma 5.54 (Fixing Operator Strength by F-Constraints (I)). *The following implications are initially valid and show how one can recursively construct universal ω-automata from $\mathsf{TL_F}$ formulas:*

- $$\left(\begin{array}{l} \mathsf{G}(\varphi \to \varphi_0) \wedge \mathcal{A}_\exists\left(\mathcal{Q}_\varphi, \mathcal{I}_\varphi, \mathcal{R}_\varphi, \mathsf{G}\zeta_\varphi\right) \wedge \\ \mathsf{G}(\psi \to \psi_0) \wedge \mathcal{A}_\exists\left(\mathcal{Q}_\psi, \mathcal{I}_\psi, \mathcal{R}_\psi, \mathsf{G}\zeta_\psi\right) \wedge \\ \mathcal{A}_\forall\left(\mathcal{Q}_\varphi, \mathcal{I}_\varphi, \mathcal{R}_\varphi, \mathsf{G}\left(\zeta_\varphi \to \overleftarrow{\mathsf{G}}[\varphi_0 \leftrightarrow \varphi]\right)\right) \wedge \\ \mathcal{A}_\forall\left(\mathcal{Q}_\psi, \mathcal{I}_\psi, \mathcal{R}_\psi, \mathsf{G}\left(\zeta_\psi \to \overleftarrow{\mathsf{G}}[\psi_0 \leftrightarrow \psi]\right)\right) \wedge \\ \to \mathcal{A}_\forall\left(\begin{array}{l} \mathcal{Q}_\varphi \cup \mathcal{Q}_\psi \cup \{q\}, \mathcal{I}_\varphi \wedge \mathcal{I}_\psi, \\ \mathcal{R}_\varphi \wedge \mathcal{R}_\psi \wedge (q \leftrightarrow \psi_0 \vee \varphi_0 \wedge \mathsf{X}q), \\ \mathsf{G}\left(\mathsf{F}([q \to \psi_0] \wedge \zeta_\varphi \wedge \zeta_\psi) \to \overleftarrow{\mathsf{G}}(q \leftrightarrow [\varphi\ \underline{\mathsf{U}}\ \psi])\right) \end{array}\right) \end{array}\right)$$
- $$\left(\begin{array}{l} \mathsf{G}(\varphi_0 \to \varphi) \wedge \mathcal{A}_\exists\left(\mathcal{Q}_\varphi, \mathcal{I}_\varphi, \mathcal{R}_\varphi, \mathsf{G}\zeta_\varphi\right) \wedge \\ \mathsf{G}(\psi_0 \to \psi) \wedge \mathcal{A}_\exists\left(\mathcal{Q}_\psi, \mathcal{I}_\psi, \mathcal{R}_\psi, \mathsf{G}\zeta_\psi\right) \wedge \\ \mathcal{A}_\forall\left(\mathcal{Q}_\varphi, \mathcal{I}_\varphi, \mathcal{R}_\varphi, \mathsf{G}\left(\zeta_\varphi \to \overleftarrow{\mathsf{G}}[\varphi_0 \leftrightarrow \varphi]\right)\right) \wedge \\ \mathcal{A}_\forall\left(\mathcal{Q}_\psi, \mathcal{I}_\psi, \mathcal{R}_\psi, \mathsf{G}\left(\zeta_\psi \to \overleftarrow{\mathsf{G}}[\psi_0 \leftrightarrow \psi]\right)\right) \wedge \\ \to \mathcal{A}_\forall\left(\begin{array}{l} \mathcal{Q}_\varphi \cup \mathcal{Q}_\psi \cup \{q\}, \mathcal{I}_\varphi \wedge \mathcal{I}_\psi, \\ \mathcal{R}_\varphi \wedge \mathcal{R}_\psi \wedge (q \leftrightarrow \psi_0 \vee \varphi_0 \wedge \mathsf{X}q), \\ \mathsf{G}\left(\mathsf{F}([q \vee \neg\varphi_0] \wedge \zeta_\varphi \wedge \zeta_\psi) \to \overleftarrow{\mathsf{G}}(q \leftrightarrow [\varphi\ \mathsf{U}\ \psi])\right) \end{array}\right) \end{array}\right)$$
- $$\left(\begin{array}{l} \mathsf{G}(\varphi \to \varphi_0) \wedge \mathcal{A}_\exists\left(\mathcal{Q}_\varphi, \mathcal{I}_\varphi, \mathcal{R}_\varphi, \mathsf{G}\zeta_\varphi\right) \wedge \\ \mathsf{G}(\psi_0 \to \psi) \wedge \mathcal{A}_\exists\left(\mathcal{Q}_\psi, \mathcal{I}_\psi, \mathcal{R}_\psi, \mathsf{G}\zeta_\psi\right) \wedge \\ \mathcal{A}_\forall\left(\mathcal{Q}_\varphi, \mathcal{I}_\varphi, \mathcal{R}_\varphi, \mathsf{G}\left(\zeta_\varphi \to \overleftarrow{\mathsf{G}}[\varphi_0 \leftrightarrow \varphi]\right)\right) \wedge \\ \mathcal{A}_\forall\left(\mathcal{Q}_\psi, \mathcal{I}_\psi, \mathcal{R}_\psi, \mathsf{G}\left(\zeta_\psi \to \overleftarrow{\mathsf{G}}[\psi_0 \leftrightarrow \psi]\right)\right) \wedge \\ \to \mathcal{A}_\forall\left(\begin{array}{l} \mathcal{Q}_\varphi \cup \mathcal{Q}_\psi \cup \{q\}, \mathcal{I}_\varphi \wedge \mathcal{I}_\psi, \\ \mathcal{R}_\varphi \wedge \mathcal{R}_\psi \wedge (q \leftrightarrow \neg\psi_0 \wedge (\varphi_0 \wedge \mathsf{X}q)), \\ \mathsf{G}\left(\mathsf{F}([q \to \varphi_0] \wedge \zeta_\varphi \wedge \zeta_\psi) \to \overleftarrow{\mathsf{G}}(q \leftrightarrow [\varphi\ \underline{\mathsf{B}}\ \psi])\right) \end{array}\right) \end{array}\right)$$

- $$\left(\begin{array}{l}
\mathsf{G}(\varphi_0 \rightarrow \varphi) \wedge \mathcal{A}_\exists\left(\mathcal{Q}_\varphi, \mathcal{I}_\varphi, \mathcal{R}_\varphi, \mathsf{G}\zeta_\varphi\right) \wedge \\
\mathsf{G}(\psi \rightarrow \psi_0) \wedge \mathcal{A}_\exists\left(\mathcal{Q}_\psi, \mathcal{I}_\psi, \mathcal{R}_\psi, \mathsf{G}\zeta_\psi\right) \wedge \\
\mathcal{A}_\forall\left(\mathcal{Q}_\varphi, \mathcal{I}_\varphi, \mathcal{R}_\varphi, \mathsf{G}\left(\zeta_\varphi \rightarrow \overleftarrow{\mathsf{G}}\left[\varphi_0 \leftrightarrow \varphi\right]\right)\right) \wedge \\
\mathcal{A}_\forall\left(\mathcal{Q}_\psi, \mathcal{I}_\psi, \mathcal{R}_\psi, \mathsf{G}\left(\zeta_\psi \rightarrow \overleftarrow{\mathsf{G}}\left[\psi_0 \leftrightarrow \psi\right]\right)\right) \wedge \\
\rightarrow \mathcal{A}_\forall\left(\begin{array}{l}
\mathcal{Q}_\varphi \cup \mathcal{Q}_\psi \cup \{q\}, \mathcal{I}_\varphi \wedge \mathcal{I}_\psi, \\
\mathcal{R}_\varphi \wedge \mathcal{R}_\psi \wedge (q \leftrightarrow \neg\psi_0 \wedge (\varphi_0 \wedge \mathsf{X}q)), \\
\mathsf{G}\left(\mathsf{F}\left([q \vee \psi_0] \wedge \zeta_\varphi \wedge \zeta_\psi\right) \rightarrow \overleftarrow{\mathsf{G}}\left(q \leftrightarrow [\varphi\ \mathsf{B}\ \psi]\right)\right)
\end{array}\right)
\end{array}\right)$$

The above implications are used in the following to develop an algorithm for translating $\mathsf{TL_F}$ formulas to equivalent $\mathsf{NDet_F}$ automata. This algorithm (given in Figure 5.16) will recursively apply the above implications to end up with an equivalent ω-automaton. One should not be bothered about the universal automata that are used in the above equations. The algorithm will generate existential automata, but to prove its correctness, the above formulas are used as they stand. For the proof of these implications, we only note that they can be easily reduced to formulas where no automaton formulas occur. For example, the first implication can be reduced to the following 'automaton-free' implication:

$$\left(\begin{array}{l}
\mathsf{G}(\varphi \rightarrow \varphi_0) \wedge \mathsf{G}(\zeta_\varphi \rightarrow \overleftarrow{\mathsf{G}}\left[\varphi_0 \leftrightarrow \varphi\right]) \wedge \\
\mathsf{G}(\psi \rightarrow \psi_0) \wedge \mathsf{G}(\zeta_\psi \rightarrow \overleftarrow{\mathsf{G}}\left[\psi_0 \leftrightarrow \psi\right]) \wedge \\
\mathsf{G}(q \leftrightarrow \psi_0 \vee \varphi_0 \wedge \mathsf{X}q) \\
\rightarrow \mathsf{G}\left(\mathsf{F}\left([q \rightarrow \psi_0] \wedge \zeta_\varphi \wedge \zeta_\psi\right) \rightarrow \overleftarrow{\mathsf{G}}\left(q \leftrightarrow [\varphi\ \underline{\mathsf{U}}\ \psi]\right)\right)
\end{array}\right)$$

The remaining proofs of these implications all run in the same lines, and rely again on the important Lemma 5.35 of page 333 (the proofs are however rather technical and tedious, so that we skip them here). The implications of the lemma required as assumptions that the subsequent automata have product paths with any Kripke structure that satisfy their constraints. This was established by adding existential ω-automata as preconditions of the implications. In order to apply the above implications in a recursive algorithm, we also need to establish these formulas as invariants. For this reason, we will now prove the following lemma:

Lemma 5.55 (Fixing Operator Strength by F-Constraints (II)). *The following implications are initially valid, and show that for any path π in any structure $\mathcal{K}$, there is a product path that satisfies the constraint used in Lemma 5.54:*

- $$\left(\begin{array}{l}
\mathcal{A}_\exists\left(\mathcal{Q}_\varphi, \mathcal{I}_\varphi, \mathcal{R}_\varphi, \mathsf{G}\zeta_\varphi\right) \wedge \mathcal{A}_\exists\left(\mathcal{Q}_\psi, \mathcal{I}_\psi, \mathcal{R}_\psi, \mathsf{G}\zeta_\psi\right) \wedge \\
\rightarrow \mathcal{A}_\exists\left(\begin{array}{l}
\mathcal{Q}_\varphi \cup \mathcal{Q}_\psi \cup \{q\}, \mathcal{I}_\varphi \wedge \mathcal{I}_\psi, \\
\mathcal{R}_\varphi \wedge \mathcal{R}_\psi \wedge (q \leftrightarrow \psi_0 \vee \varphi_0 \wedge \mathsf{X}q), \\
\mathsf{GF}\left([q \rightarrow \psi_0] \wedge \zeta_\varphi \wedge \zeta_\psi\right)
\end{array}\right)
\end{array}\right)$$
- $$\left(\begin{array}{l}
\mathcal{A}_\exists\left(\mathcal{Q}_\varphi, \mathcal{I}_\varphi, \mathcal{R}_\varphi, \mathsf{G}\zeta_\varphi\right) \wedge \mathcal{A}_\exists\left(\mathcal{Q}_\psi, \mathcal{I}_\psi, \mathcal{R}_\psi, \mathsf{G}\zeta_\psi\right) \wedge \\
\rightarrow \mathcal{A}_\exists\left(\begin{array}{l}
\mathcal{Q}_\varphi \cup \mathcal{Q}_\psi \cup \{q\}, \mathcal{I}_\varphi \wedge \mathcal{I}_\psi, \\
\mathcal{R}_\varphi \wedge \mathcal{R}_\psi \wedge (q \leftrightarrow \psi_0 \vee \varphi_0 \wedge \mathsf{X}q), \\
\mathsf{GF}\left([q \vee \neg\varphi_0] \wedge \zeta_\varphi \wedge \zeta_\psi\right)
\end{array}\right)
\end{array}\right)$$

- $\left(\begin{array}{l}\mathcal{A}_{\exists}\left(\mathcal{Q}_{\varphi},\mathcal{I}_{\varphi},\mathcal{R}_{\varphi},\mathsf{G}\zeta_{\varphi}\right)\wedge\mathcal{A}_{\exists}\left(\mathcal{Q}_{\psi},\mathcal{I}_{\psi},\mathcal{R}_{\psi},\mathsf{G}\zeta_{\psi}\right)\wedge\\ \rightarrow\mathcal{A}_{\exists}\left(\begin{array}{l}\mathcal{Q}_{\varphi}\cup\mathcal{Q}_{\psi}\cup\{q\},\mathcal{I}_{\varphi}\wedge\mathcal{I}_{\psi},\\ \mathcal{R}_{\varphi}\wedge\mathcal{R}_{\psi}\wedge(q\leftrightarrow\neg\psi_0\wedge(\varphi_0\wedge\mathsf{X}q)),\\ \mathsf{GF}\left([q\rightarrow\varphi_0]\wedge\zeta_{\varphi}\wedge\zeta_{\psi}\right)\end{array}\right)\end{array}\right)$
- $\left(\begin{array}{l}\mathcal{A}_{\exists}\left(\mathcal{Q}_{\varphi},\mathcal{I}_{\varphi},\mathcal{R}_{\varphi},\mathsf{G}\zeta_{\varphi}\right)\wedge\mathcal{A}_{\exists}\left(\mathcal{Q}_{\psi},\mathcal{I}_{\psi},\mathcal{R}_{\psi},\mathsf{G}\zeta_{\psi}\right)\wedge\\ \rightarrow\mathcal{A}_{\exists}\left(\begin{array}{l}\mathcal{Q}_{\varphi}\cup\mathcal{Q}_{\psi}\cup\{q\},\mathcal{I}_{\varphi}\wedge\mathcal{I}_{\psi},\\ \mathcal{R}_{\varphi}\wedge\mathcal{R}_{\psi}\wedge(q\leftrightarrow\neg\psi_0\wedge(\varphi_0\wedge\mathsf{X}q)),\\ \mathsf{GF}\left([q\vee\psi_0]\wedge\zeta_{\varphi}\wedge\zeta_{\psi}\right)\end{array}\right)\end{array}\right)$

Proof. The proof of the implications is straightforward. Just note that the added transition relation for the new variable q determines q to behave like either a weak or strong temporal future operator. The constraints that are introduced moreover imply the fairness constraints used to fix the operator strengths of the mentioned temporal future operator. Therefore, we may simply identify q with the mentioned temporal expression ($[\varphi_0 \ \underline{\mathsf{U}}\ \psi_0]$ for the first implication). □

The above two lemmas are essential in the construction of an algorithm that will translate TL_F to NDet_F by the abbreviation technique. The main part of this translation is done by the algorithm given in Figure 5.16. We will furthermore see in Theorem 5.57 that the same algorithm can also be applied to TL_FG with the same effect: It does not translate to NDet_F or $\mathsf{NDet}_\mathsf{FG}$, but to automata with a more complicated acceptance condition that we can easily reduce to NDet_F or $\mathsf{NDet}_\mathsf{FG}$. As $\mathsf{TL}_\mathsf{Prefix} \subseteq \mathsf{TL}_\mathsf{FG}$ holds, the algorithm is furthermore able to handle $\mathsf{TL}_\mathsf{Prefix}$ formulas.

The previous lemmas are sufficient the prove the essential step towards an algorithm for efficiently translating TL_F to NDet_F. For this reason, consider the algorithm given in Figure 5.16. We will see that this algorithm is our desired translation algorithm. To formally prove its correctness, we will however first prove the following lemma:

Lemma 5.56 (Correctness of $\mathsf{Borel}_\sigma(\Phi)$). *Given an arbitrary formula $\Phi \in \mathsf{TL}_\mathsf{FG}$, and the automaton $\mathcal{A}_{\exists}(\mathcal{Q},\mathcal{I},\mathcal{R},\mathcal{F},\Phi_0) = \mathsf{Borel}_1(\Phi)$ obtained by the algorithm given in Figure 5.16. Then, the following formulas are initially valid, where we abbreviate $\zeta_\Phi := \bigwedge_{\xi\in\mathcal{F}}\xi$ for conciseness:*

(1) $\mathcal{A}_{\exists}(\mathcal{Q},\mathcal{I},\mathcal{R},\mathsf{G}\zeta_\Phi)$
(2) $\mathcal{A}_{\forall}\left(\mathcal{Q},\mathcal{I},\mathcal{R},\mathsf{G}\left(\zeta_\Phi\rightarrow\overleftarrow{\mathsf{G}}[\Phi_0\leftrightarrow\Phi]\right)\right)$
(3) $\mathcal{A}_{\exists}(\mathcal{Q},\mathcal{I},\mathcal{R},\mathsf{G}(\zeta_\Phi\wedge[\Phi_0\leftrightarrow\Phi]))$

Of course, this implies that also the following formulas are initially valid:

(1′) $\mathcal{A}_{\exists}(\mathcal{Q},\mathcal{I},\mathcal{R},\zeta_\Phi)$
(2′) $\mathcal{A}_{\forall}(\mathcal{Q},\mathcal{I},\mathcal{R},(\zeta_\Phi\rightarrow[\Phi_0\leftrightarrow\Phi]))$
(3′) $\mathcal{A}_{\exists}(\mathcal{Q},\mathcal{I},\mathcal{R},\zeta_\Phi\wedge[\Phi_0\leftrightarrow\Phi])$

```
function Borel_σ(Φ)
  case Φ of
    is_prop(Φ): return A∃({}, 1, 1, {}, Φ);
    ¬φ        : A∃(Q_φ, I_φ, R_φ, F_φ, φ') ≡ Borel_¬σ(φ);
                return A∃(Q_φ, I_φ, R_φ, F_φ, ¬φ');
    φ ∧ ψ     : return Borel_σ(φ) × Borel_σ(ψ);
    φ ∨ ψ     : A∃(Q_Φ, I_Φ, R_Φ, F_Φ, φ' ∧ ψ') ≡ Borel_σ(φ) × Borel_σ(ψ);
                return A∃(Q_Φ, I_Φ, R_Φ, F_Φ, φ' ∨ ψ');
    Xφ        : A∃(Q_φ, I_φ, R_φ, F_φ, φ') ≡ Borel_σ(φ); q := new_var;
                if F_Φ ≠ {} then F_Φ := {X ⋀_{ξ∈F_Φ} ξ} end;
                return A∃(Q_φ ∪ {q}, I_φ, R_φ ∧ (q ↔ Xφ'), F_φ, q);
    [φ U̲ ψ]   : A∃(Q_Φ, I_Φ, R_Φ, F_Φ, φ' ∧ ψ') ≡ Borel_σ(φ) × Borel_σ(ψ);
                q := new_var; R_q := [q ↔ ψ' ∨ φ' ∧ Xq];
                if σ then F_Φ := {F[(q → ψ') ∧ ⋀_{ξ∈F_Φ} ξ]} end;
                return A∃(Q_Φ ∪ {q}, I_Φ, R_Φ ∧ R_q, F_Φ, q);
    [φ B ψ]   : A∃(Q_Φ, I_Φ, R_Φ, F_Φ, φ' ∧ ψ') ≡ Borel_σ(φ) × Borel_¬σ(ψ);
                q := new_var; R_q := [q ↔ ¬ψ' ∧ (φ' ∨ Xq)];
                if ¬σ then F_Φ := {F[(q ∨ ψ') ∧ ⋀_{ξ∈F_Φ} ξ]} end;
                return A∃(Q_Φ ∪ {q}, I_Φ, R_Φ ∧ R_q, F_Φ, q);
    X⃖φ        : A∃(Q_φ, I_φ, R_φ, F_φ, φ') ≡ Borel_σ(φ); q := new_var;
                return A∃(Q_φ ∪ {q}, I_φ ∧ q, R_φ ∧ (Xq ↔ φ'), F_φ, q);
    X̲⃖φ        : A∃(Q_φ, I_φ, R_φ, F_φ, φ') ≡ Borel_σ(φ); q := new_var;
                return A∃(Q_φ ∪ {q}, I_φ ∧ ¬q, R_φ ∧ (Xq ↔ φ'), F_φ, q);
    [φ U̲⃖ ψ]   : A∃(Q_Φ, I_Φ, R_Φ, F_Φ, φ' ∧ ψ') ≡ Borel_σ(φ) × Borel_σ(ψ);
                q := new_var; r_q := ψ' ∨ φ' ∧ q; R_q := [Xq ↔ r_q];
                return A∃(Q_Φ ∪ {q}, I_Φ ∧ ¬q, R_Φ ∧ R_q, F_Φ, r_q);
    [φ B⃖ ψ]   : A∃(Q_Φ, I_Φ, R_Φ, F_Φ, φ' ∧ ψ') ≡ Borel_σ(φ) × Borel_¬σ(ψ);
                q := new_var; r_q := ¬ψ' ∧ (φ' ∨ q); R_q := [Xq ↔ r_q];
                return A∃(Q_Φ ∪ {q}, I_Φ ∧ q, R_Φ ∧ R_q, F_Φ, r_q);
  end case
end function
```

Fig. 5.16. Translation of $\mathsf{TL_{FG}}$ to $\mathsf{NDet_{FG}}$ (first part)

Proof. The proof of (1) is done by a simple induction on Φ, where we only need to consider the implications of Lemma 5.55. Using this, we can prove (2) by another induction on Φ, where the induction steps are proved by application of the implications of Lemma 5.54. The required assumptions are proved by (1). Note that we have not listed implications for the past operators in Lemma 5.54 and 5.55, since no constraints are generated there. However, the induction steps require similar implications for these cases, which are straightforward to prove. (3) is a simple consequence of (1) and (2): Consider an arbitrary path π of an arbitrary structure $\mathcal{K}$. By (1), it follows that there is at least one product path ξ that satisfies ζ_Φ on all of its states. Hence, we can derive by (2) that $\mathsf{G}[\Phi_0 \leftrightarrow \Phi]$ holds on ξ, so that we obtain (3). (1'),

(2′), and (3′) are simple consequences of (1), (2), and (3), respectively, where we only consider the first point of the path. □

The previous lemma is the essential part required to prove the correctness of our translation. It almost directly implies the correctness of our translation procedure Borel for all $\mathsf{TL}_{\mathsf{FG}}$ formulas. There is only one point that has to be considered: We have to eliminate the following 'grammar rules':

$$P_{\mathsf{GF}} ::= [P_{\mathsf{GF}}\ \underline{\mathsf{U}}\ P_{\mathsf{F}}] \mid [P_{\mathsf{F}}\ \underline{\mathsf{B}}\ P_{\mathsf{FG}}]\ P_{\mathsf{FG}} ::= [P_{\mathsf{G}}\ \mathsf{U}\ P_{\mathsf{FG}}] \mid [P_{\mathsf{FG}}\ \mathsf{B}\ P_{\mathsf{F}}]$$

We have already seen that this can be done by rewriting the formulas with the following equivalences:

- $[P_{\mathsf{GF}}\ \underline{\mathsf{U}}\ P_{\mathsf{F}}] = [P_{\mathsf{GF}}\ \mathsf{U}\ P_{\mathsf{F}}] \wedge [P_{\mathsf{F}}\ \underline{\mathsf{B}}\ 0]$
- $[P_{\mathsf{F}}\ \underline{\mathsf{B}}\ P_{\mathsf{FG}}] = [P_{\mathsf{F}}\ \mathsf{B}\ P_{\mathsf{FG}}] \wedge [P_{\mathsf{F}}\ \underline{\mathsf{B}}\ 0]$
- $[P_{\mathsf{G}}\ \mathsf{U}\ P_{\mathsf{FG}}] = [P_{\mathsf{G}}\ \underline{\mathsf{U}}\ P_{\mathsf{FG}}] \vee [P_{\mathsf{G}}\ \mathsf{U}\ 0]$
- $[P_{\mathsf{FG}}\ \mathsf{B}\ P_{\mathsf{F}}] = [P_{\mathsf{FG}}\ \underline{\mathsf{B}}\ P_{\mathsf{F}}] \vee [(\neg P_{\mathsf{F}})\ \mathsf{U}\ 0]$

It is however not recommended to rewrite the formulas with the above equations in advance, since this could provoke a blow-up of the formula. Instead, the above equations should be considered while using the algorithm given in Figure 5.16. Therefore, we can state the following theorem:

Theorem 5.57 (Translating $\mathsf{TL}_{\mathsf{FG}}$ with Borel). *Given any formula $\Phi \in \mathsf{TL}_{\mathsf{FG}}$ that does not require the following rules for its derivation with the grammar of Definition 5.48:*

$$P_{\mathsf{GF}} ::= [P_{\mathsf{GF}}\ \underline{\mathsf{U}}\ P_{\mathsf{F}}] \mid [P_{\mathsf{F}}\ \underline{\mathsf{B}}\ P_{\mathsf{FG}}]\ P_{\mathsf{FG}} ::= [P_{\mathsf{G}}\ \mathsf{U}\ P_{\mathsf{FG}}] \mid [P_{\mathsf{FG}}\ \mathsf{B}\ P_{\mathsf{F}}]$$

For the ω-automaton $\mathcal{A}_\exists(\mathcal{Q},\mathcal{I},\mathcal{R},\mathcal{F},\Phi_0) := \mathsf{Borel}_\sigma(\Phi)$ that is obtained by the algorithm Borel *as implemented in Figure 5.16, the following holds:*

(1) $\mathsf{Borel}_\sigma(\Phi)$ *runs in time $O(|\Phi|)$.*
(2) *Φ_0 is propositional.*
(3) *Each $\xi \in \mathcal{F}$ can be derived from the nonterminal C_{F} by the following grammar rules:*

$$P_{\mathsf{Prop}} ::= V_\Sigma \mid \neg P_{\mathsf{Prop}} \mid P_{\mathsf{Prop}} \wedge P_{\mathsf{Prop}} \mid P_{\mathsf{Prop}} \vee P_{\mathsf{Prop}} \mid P_{\mathsf{Prop}} \rightarrow P_{\mathsf{Prop}}$$
$$C_{\mathsf{F}} ::= \mathsf{F}P_{\mathsf{Prop}} \mid \mathsf{F}\,(P_{\mathsf{Prop}} \wedge C_{\mathsf{F}}) \mid \mathsf{X}C_{\mathsf{F}} \mid C_{\mathsf{F}} \wedge C_{\mathsf{F}}$$

(4) *For $\sigma = 1$, the equation $\Phi = \mathcal{A}_\exists\left(\mathcal{Q},\mathcal{I},\mathcal{R},\Phi_0 \wedge \bigwedge_{\xi\in\mathcal{F}} \xi\right)$ is initially valid.*

(5) *For $\sigma = 0$, the equation $\Phi = \mathcal{A}_\exists\left(\mathcal{Q},\mathcal{I},\mathcal{R},\neg\Phi_0 \wedge \bigwedge_{\xi\in\mathcal{F}} \xi\right)$ is initially valid.*

(6) *For $\sigma = 1$ and $\Phi \in \mathsf{TL}_{\mathsf{G}}$, we have $\mathcal{F} = \{\}$, and thus $\mathsf{Borel}_1(\Phi) = \mathsf{TopProp}_1(\Phi)$.*
(7) *For $\sigma = 0$ and $\Phi \in \mathsf{TL}_{\mathsf{F}}$, we have $\mathcal{F} = \{\}$, and thus $\mathsf{Borel}_0(\Phi) = \mathsf{TopProp}_0(\Phi)$.*

Proof. (1 – 3) are easily seen by inspecting the algorithm. To prove (4), we split the equation into two implications, where we abbreviate $\zeta_\Phi := \bigwedge_{\xi\in\mathcal{F}}\xi$ in the following. The first subgoal requires us to prove that $\Phi \rightarrow \mathcal{A}_\exists(\mathcal{Q},\mathcal{I},\mathcal{R},\zeta_\Phi\wedge\Phi_0)$ is initially valid. This is equivalent to the initial validity of $\mathcal{A}_\exists(\mathcal{Q},\mathcal{I},\mathcal{R},\Phi\rightarrow\zeta_\Phi\wedge\Phi_0)$. As $\zeta_\Phi\wedge[\Phi_0=\Phi]\rightarrow(\Phi\rightarrow\zeta_\Phi\wedge\Phi_0)$ is a propositional tautology, our subgoal follows immediately from fact $(3)'$ of Lemma 5.56.

It remains to prove that $\mathcal{A}_\exists(\mathcal{Q},\mathcal{I},\mathcal{R},\zeta_\Phi\wedge\Phi_0)\rightarrow\Phi$ is initially valid. Again, we can easily verify that this is equivalent to the initial validity of the formula $\mathcal{A}_\forall(\mathcal{Q},\mathcal{I},\mathcal{R},[\zeta_\Phi\wedge\Phi_0]\rightarrow\Phi)$. Note that we now have obtained a universal automaton formula. As $[\zeta_\Phi\wedge\Phi_0]\rightarrow\Phi$ is equivalent to $\zeta_\Phi\rightarrow(\Phi_0\rightarrow\Phi)$, this can be concluded from fact $(2')$ of Lemma 5.56. The other facts are easily seen by inspection of the algorithm. □

To be precise, property (3) above does not hold as it stands. There are cases, where empty conjunctions are added as a constraint, i.e., when $\mathcal{F}_\Phi=\{\}$ holds. In these cases, the algorithm generates a constraint of the form $\mathsf{F}[\zeta\wedge 1]$ (where ζ is propositional), but we assume that this will be immediately simplified to $\mathsf{F}\zeta$.

Hence, we almost have an efficient algorithm to translate the logics TL_F, $\mathsf{TL}_\mathsf{Prefix}$, and TL_FG. However, the result is not yet a NDet_κ automaton, as the acceptance condition is not yet of the desired form.

We will now show that the generated acceptance condition can be converted to an equivalent NDet_F or $\mathsf{NDet}_\mathsf{FG}$ automaton. To this end, we call the formulas that appear as acceptance conditions of the automata that are constructed by the Borel algorithm C_F formulas. It is not hard to see that the equations of the following lemma can be used to compute for any C_F formula an equivalent $\mathsf{NDet}_\mathsf{FG}$ automaton:

Lemma 5.58 (Translating C_F to $\mathsf{NDet}_\mathsf{FG}$). *Given a propositional formula φ, and the two $\mathsf{NDet}_\mathsf{FG}$ automaton formulas $\mathfrak{A}_\Phi=\mathcal{A}_\exists(Q_\Phi,\Phi_\mathcal{I},\Phi_\mathcal{R},\mathsf{FG}\Phi_\mathcal{F})$, and $\mathfrak{A}_\Psi=\mathcal{A}_\exists(Q_\Psi,\Psi_\mathcal{I},\Psi_\mathcal{R},\mathsf{FG}\Psi_\mathcal{F})$, the following equations hold:*

- $\mathsf{F}\varphi=\mathcal{A}_\exists(\{q\},\neg q,\neg q\wedge\neg\varphi\wedge\neg\mathsf{X}q\vee\neg q\wedge\varphi\wedge\mathsf{X}q\vee q\wedge\mathsf{X}q,\mathsf{FG}q)$
- $\mathsf{F}(\varphi\wedge\mathfrak{A}_\Phi)=\mathcal{A}_\exists\left(\begin{array}{l}Q\cup\{p\},\neg p\vee\Phi_\mathcal{I},\\ [\neg p\wedge\neg\mathsf{X}p]\vee\\ [\neg p\wedge\mathsf{X}(p\wedge\Phi_\mathcal{I}\wedge\varphi)]\vee\\ [p\wedge\Phi_\mathcal{R}\wedge\mathsf{X}p],\\ \mathsf{FG}(p\wedge\Phi_\mathcal{F})\end{array}\right)$
- $\mathsf{X}[\mathfrak{A}_\Phi]=\mathcal{A}_\exists\left(\begin{array}{l}Q\cup\{p\},\\ \neg p,\\ [\neg p\wedge\mathsf{X}p\wedge\mathsf{X}\Phi_\mathcal{I}]\vee[p\wedge\Phi_\mathcal{R}\wedge\mathsf{X}p],\\ \mathsf{FG}\Phi_\mathcal{F}\end{array}\right)$
- $\varphi\wedge\mathfrak{A}_\Phi=\mathcal{A}_\exists(Q_\Phi,\Phi_\mathcal{I}\wedge\varphi,\Phi_\mathcal{R},\mathsf{FG}\Phi_\mathcal{F})$
- $\mathfrak{A}_\Phi\wedge\mathfrak{A}_\Psi=\mathcal{A}_\exists(Q_\Phi\cup Q_\Psi,\Phi_\mathcal{I}\wedge\Psi_\mathcal{I},\Phi_\mathcal{R}\wedge\Psi_\mathcal{R},\mathsf{FG}(\Phi_\mathcal{F}\wedge\Psi_\mathcal{F}))$

Obviously, the equations correspond with the grammar rules of C_{F}: The idea is to compute within a bottom-up traversal over the C_{F} formulas an equivalent $\mathsf{NDet_{FG}}$ automaton out of previously computed $\mathsf{NDet_{FG}}$ automata for its subformulas. This is quite different from our previous translation procedures, which are best understood as extraction procedures that extract some sort of largest top-level formulas: Subformulas that violate some grammar rules are abbreviated by new state variables.

Hence, we are now able to translate within linear runtime any $\mathsf{TL_{FG}}$ formula to an equivalent one of $\mathsf{NDet_{FG}}$. The above lemma can also be formulated with $\mathsf{NDet_F}$ automata; which is not surprising since we already know that $\mathsf{NDet_{FG}} \approx \mathsf{NDet_F}$ holds. However, one has to take care with the following problem: We can efficiently compute the conjunction of $\mathsf{NDet_{FG}}$ automata due to the following equivalence $\mathsf{FG}\varphi \wedge \mathsf{FG}\psi = \mathsf{FG}(\varphi \wedge \psi)$. In general, the equation $\mathsf{F}\varphi \wedge \mathsf{F}\psi = \mathsf{F}(\varphi \wedge \psi)$ is not valid, and we therefore used watchdogs to compute the conjunction of $\mathsf{NDet_F}$ automata in Lemma 4.11.

However, this additional effort is not necessary for the automata that are computed for the C_{F} formulas, as these $\mathsf{NDet_F}$ automata have a special property: Their acceptance condition is of the form $\mathsf{F}\Phi_{\mathcal{F}}$ and it is equivalent to $\mathsf{FG}\Phi_{\mathcal{F}}$, which means that once a run satisfies the formula $\Phi_{\mathcal{F}}$, then all its remaining states satisfy $\Phi_{\mathcal{F}}$, too. Hence, the acceptance conditions are suffix-closed (cf. page 209). For this reason, we have the following lemma for the reduction of C_{F} formulas to $\mathsf{NDet_F}$ automata:

Lemma 5.59 (Translating C_{F} to $\mathsf{NDet_F}$). *Given a propositional formula φ, and the two $\mathsf{NDet_F}$ automaton formulas $\mathfrak{A}_\Phi = \mathcal{A}_\exists(Q_\Phi, \Phi_\mathcal{I}, \Phi_\mathcal{R}, \mathsf{F}\Phi_\mathcal{F})$, and $\mathfrak{A}_\Psi = \mathcal{A}_\exists(Q_\Psi, \Psi_\mathcal{I}, \Psi_\mathcal{R}, \mathsf{F}\Psi_\mathcal{F})$ which are equivalent to the $\mathsf{NDet_{FG}}$ automaton formulas $\mathcal{A}_\exists(Q_\Phi, \Phi_\mathcal{I}, \Phi_\mathcal{R}, \mathsf{FG}\Phi_\mathcal{F})$ and $\mathcal{A}_\exists(Q_\Psi, \Psi_\mathcal{I}, \Psi_\mathcal{R}, \mathsf{FG}\Psi_\mathcal{F})$, respectively, then the following equations hold:*

- $\mathsf{F}\varphi = \mathcal{A}_\exists(\{q\}, \neg q, \neg q \wedge \neg\varphi \wedge \neg \mathsf{X}q \vee \neg q \wedge \varphi \wedge \mathsf{X}q \vee q \wedge \mathsf{X}q, \mathsf{F}q)$
- $\mathsf{F}(\varphi \wedge \mathfrak{A}_\Phi) = \mathcal{A}_\exists\left(\begin{array}{l} Q \cup \{p\}, \neg p \vee \Phi_\mathcal{I}, \\ [\neg p \wedge \neg \mathsf{X}p] \vee \\ [\neg p \wedge \mathsf{X}(p \wedge \Phi_\mathcal{I} \wedge \varphi)] \vee \\ [p \wedge \Phi_\mathcal{R} \wedge \mathsf{X}p], \\ \mathsf{F}(p \wedge \Phi_\mathcal{F}) \end{array}\right)$
- $\mathsf{X}[\mathfrak{A}_\Phi] = \mathcal{A}_\exists\left(\begin{array}{l} Q \cup \{p\}, \\ \neg p, \\ [\neg p \wedge \mathsf{X}p \wedge \mathsf{X}\Phi_\mathcal{I}] \vee [p \wedge \Phi_\mathcal{R} \wedge \mathsf{X}p], \\ \mathsf{F}\Phi_\mathcal{F} \end{array}\right)$
- $\varphi \wedge \mathfrak{A}_\Phi = \mathcal{A}_\exists(Q_\Phi, \Phi_\mathcal{I} \wedge \varphi, \Phi_\mathcal{R}, \mathsf{F}\Phi_\mathcal{F})$
- $\mathfrak{A}_\Phi \wedge \mathfrak{A}_\Psi = \mathcal{A}_\exists(Q_\Phi \cup Q_\Psi, \Phi_\mathcal{I} \wedge \Psi_\mathcal{I}, \Phi_\mathcal{R} \wedge \Psi_\mathcal{R}, \mathsf{F}(\Phi_\mathcal{F} \wedge \Psi_\mathcal{F}))$

Furthermore, the acceptance conditions $\mathsf{F}\mathcal{F}$ of all automata on the right hand sides can also be replaced with $\mathsf{FG}\mathcal{F}$.

Unfortunately, we still have to apply the first equation to the C_{F} formulas that are generated by the grammar rule $C_{\mathsf{F}} ::= \mathsf{F}P_{\mathsf{Prop}}$, since the reachability constraints that are introduced by our algorithms do not have the terminal property (which means that F could be replaced with FG). Nevertheless, we now have the following extension of Theorem 5.52:

Corollary 5.60 (Temporal Borel Classes). *For any formula* $\Phi \in \mathsf{TL}_\kappa$ *with* $\kappa \in \{\mathsf{G}, \mathsf{F}, \mathsf{Prefix}, \mathsf{GF}, \mathsf{FG}, \mathsf{Streett}\}$, *there is an equivalent* ω*-automaton* $\mathfrak{A}_\Phi \in \mathsf{Det}_\kappa$.

5.4.5 Reductions to CTL/LeftCTL* Model Checking

The algorithms of the previous sections enable us to translate any temporal logic formula to an equivalent existential ω-automaton. We are therefore able to solve the model checking problem for all temporal logics, and even the satisfiability problem for linear time temporal logics. The following two lemmas show how these problems are handled. First of all, the *model checking problem* can be reduced to an automaton problem:

Lemma 5.61 (Temporal Logic Model Checking). *Given any* LTL_p *formula* Φ, *an automaton* $\mathfrak{A}_\Phi = \mathcal{A}_\exists(\mathcal{Q}_\Phi, \mathcal{I}_\Phi, \mathcal{R}_\Phi, \mathcal{F}_\Phi)$ *that is initially equivalent to* Φ, *and a further automaton* $\mathfrak{A}_{\neg\Phi} := \mathcal{A}_\exists(\mathcal{Q}_{\neg\Phi}, \mathcal{I}_{\neg\Phi}, \mathcal{R}_{\neg\Phi}, \mathcal{F}_{\neg\Phi})$ *that is initially equivalent to* $\neg\Phi$. *Moreover, let* $\mathcal{K}_\Phi = \mathsf{Struct}(\mathfrak{A}_\Phi)$ *and* $\mathcal{K}_{\neg\Phi} = \mathsf{Struct}(\mathfrak{A}_{\neg\Phi})$ *be the associated Kripke structures of* $\mathfrak{A}_\Phi$ *and* $\mathfrak{A}_{\neg\Phi}$, *respectively, then the following hold:*

- $[\![\mathsf{E}\Phi]\!]_\mathcal{K} = [\![\mathsf{E}\mathfrak{A}_\Phi]\!]_\mathcal{K} = \{s \in \mathcal{S} \mid \exists\vartheta \subseteq \mathcal{Q}_\Phi \cup V_\Sigma.(\mathcal{K} \times \mathcal{K}_\Phi, (s,\vartheta)) \models \mathcal{I}_\Phi \wedge \mathsf{E}\mathcal{F}_\Phi\}$
- $[\![\mathsf{A}\Phi]\!]_\mathcal{K} = \{s \in \mathcal{S} \mid \forall\vartheta \subseteq \mathcal{Q}_{\neg\Phi} \cup V_\Sigma.(\mathcal{K} \times \mathcal{K}_{\neg\Phi}, (s,\vartheta)) \models \mathcal{I}_{\neg\Phi} \rightarrow \mathsf{A}\neg\mathcal{F}_{\neg\Phi}\}$

If the above lemma is used in connection with the PQNF normal form (page 85), it is also possible to extend it to CTL* formulas. To prove its correctness, simply recall how we reduced ω-automata model checking to equivalent μ-calculus problems in Theorem 4.65: *Given an automaton formula* $\mathfrak{A} = \mathcal{A}_\exists(\mathcal{Q}, \mathcal{I}, \mathcal{R}, \mathcal{F})$, *then the following are equivalent for any structure* $\mathcal{K}$, *and any state* s *of* $\mathcal{K}$:

- $(\mathcal{K}, s) \models \mathsf{E}\mathcal{A}_\exists(\mathcal{Q}_\Phi, \mathcal{I}_\Phi, \mathcal{R}_\Phi, \mathcal{F})$
- *there is a* $\vartheta \subseteq \mathcal{Q} \cup \mathcal{V}$ *such that* $(\mathcal{K} \times \mathcal{K}_\mathfrak{A}, (s,\vartheta)) \models \mathcal{I} \wedge \mathsf{E}\mathcal{F}$ *and* $\mathcal{L}(s) = \vartheta \cap \mathcal{V}$

Hence, we see that our translations allow us to efficiently solve the model checking problems. The next lemma shows how the validity and satisfiability problems for linear time temporal logic can be solved:

Lemma 5.62 (Satisfiability Problem of LTL_p). *Given any* LTL_p *formula* Φ *over the variables* V_Σ, *an automaton* $\mathfrak{A}_\Phi = \mathcal{A}_\exists(\mathcal{Q}_\Phi, \mathcal{I}_\Phi, \mathcal{R}_\Phi, \mathcal{F}_\Phi)$ *that is initially equivalent to* Φ, *and a further automaton* $\mathfrak{A}_{\neg\Phi} := \mathcal{A}_\exists(\mathcal{Q}_{\neg\Phi}, \mathcal{I}_{\neg\Phi}, \mathcal{R}_{\neg\Phi}, \mathcal{F}_{\neg\Phi})$ *that is initially equivalent to* $\neg\Phi$. *Moreover, let* $\mathcal{K}_\Phi = \mathsf{Struct}(\mathfrak{A}_\Phi)$ *and* $\mathcal{K}_{\neg\Phi} = \mathsf{Struct}(\mathfrak{A}_{\neg\Phi})$ *be the associated Kripke structures of* $\mathfrak{A}_\Phi$ *and* $\mathfrak{A}_{\neg\Phi}$, *respectively, then the following hold:*

- Φ *is valid iff* $[\![\mathcal{I}_{\neg\Phi} \wedge \mathsf{E}\mathcal{F}_{\neg\Phi}]\!]_{\mathcal{K}_{\neg\Phi}} = \{\}$
- Φ *is satisfiable iff* $[\![\mathcal{I}_\Phi \wedge \mathsf{E}\mathcal{F}_\Phi]\!]_{\mathcal{K}_\Phi} \neq \{\}$

The PQNF normal form does not however help us to construct a satisfiability checking procedure for CTL*. Satisfiability checking can be obtained by reductions to ω-tree automata (see Appendix B.3). The satisfiability checking problem for CTL* is, moreover, 2EXPTIME-complete [165, 177].

Moreover, we have already shown in Theorem 4.65 how the standard acceptance conditions of the ω-automata of the Borel hierarchy are reduced to equivalent μ-calculus formulas. Some of them can even be reduced to the alternation-free μ-calculus, and some even to CTL.

Having this view, we see that it is not problematic when an acceptance condition is a larger CTL formula than simple ones like $\mathsf{EG}\Phi$, $\mathsf{EF}\Phi$, or $\mathsf{EFEF}\Phi$ (with propositional Φ). For this reason, the primary goal in efficiently solving the model checking problem for temporal logics is not a reduction to simple ω-automata. Instead, a reduction to 'some' automaton formula with acceptance condition $\mathcal{F}$, so that $\mathsf{E}\mathcal{F}$ can be reduced to a CTL formula, will do. Now, recall that we have already found a temporal logic, namely LeftCTL*, that can be translated to CTL, and that has nontrivial path formulas.

Hence, a translation to ω-automata with acceptance condition $\mathcal{F}$, so that $\mathsf{E}\mathcal{F} \in$ LeftCTL holds, is more interesting for practice than a reduction to standard automata.* This way we can save states for the automaton construction and generate rather larger acceptance conditions instead. For this reason, note that it was completely superfluous to reduce the C_{F} formulas that appeared as intermediate acceptance conditions to equivalent $\mathsf{NDet}_{\mathsf{FG}}$ automata, since for any C_{F} formula Φ, we have $\mathsf{E}\Phi \in$ LeftCTL*. Our translation from LeftCTL* to CTL can then be used for the final translation to a CTL model checking problem.

Hence, we should extract LeftCTL* formulas instead of $\mathsf{TL}_{\mathsf{FG}}$ formulas. To be more precise, we now define the following linear-time temporal logics $\mathsf{TL}_{\mathsf{PA}}$ and $\mathsf{TL}_{\mathsf{PE}}$ that are obviously related to LeftCTL*:

Definition 5.63 (The Logics $\mathsf{TL}_{\mathsf{PE}}$ and $\mathsf{TL}_{\mathsf{PA}}$). *We define the logics $\mathsf{TL}_{\mathsf{PE}}$ and $\mathsf{TL}_{\mathsf{PA}}$ by the following grammar rules, where $\mathsf{TL}_{\mathsf{PE}}$ and $\mathsf{TL}_{\mathsf{PA}}$ are the sets of formulas that can be derived from the nonterminals P_{PE} and P_{PA}, respectively:*

$$P_{\mathsf{Prop}} ::= V_\Sigma \mid \neg P_{\mathsf{Prop}} \mid P_{\mathsf{Prop}} \wedge P_{\mathsf{Prop}} \mid P_{\mathsf{Prop}} \vee P_{\mathsf{Prop}}$$

$$\begin{array}{ll}
P_{\mathsf{PA}} ::= P_{\mathsf{Prop}} & P_{\mathsf{PE}} ::= P_{\mathsf{Prop}} \\
\quad \mid \neg P_{\mathsf{PE}} \mid P_{\mathsf{PA}} \wedge P_{\mathsf{PA}} \mid P_{\mathsf{PA}} \vee P_{\mathsf{PA}} & \quad \mid \neg P_{\mathsf{PA}} \mid P_{\mathsf{PE}} \wedge P_{\mathsf{PE}} \mid P_{\mathsf{PE}} \vee P_{\mathsf{PE}} \\
\quad \mid \mathsf{X}P_{\mathsf{PA}} \mid \mathsf{G}P_{\mathsf{PA}} \mid \mathsf{F}P_{\mathsf{Prop}} & \quad \mid \mathsf{X}P_{\mathsf{PE}} \mid \mathsf{G}P_{\mathsf{Prop}} \mid \mathsf{F}P_{\mathsf{PE}} \\
\quad \mid [P_{\mathsf{PA}}\ \underline{\mathsf{U}}\ P_{\mathsf{Prop}}] \mid [P_{\mathsf{Prop}}\ \underline{\mathsf{B}}\ P_{\mathsf{PE}}] & \quad \mid [P_{\mathsf{Prop}}\ \underline{\mathsf{U}}\ P_{\mathsf{PE}}] \mid [P_{\mathsf{PE}}\ \underline{\mathsf{B}}\ P_{\mathsf{Prop}}] \\
\quad \mid [P_{\mathsf{PA}}\ \mathsf{U}\ P_{\mathsf{Prop}}] \mid [P_{\mathsf{Prop}}\ \mathsf{B}\ P_{\mathsf{PE}}] & \quad \mid [P_{\mathsf{Prop}}\ \mathsf{U}\ P_{\mathsf{PE}}] \mid [P_{\mathsf{PE}}\ \mathsf{B}\ P_{\mathsf{Prop}}]
\end{array}$$

The logics $\mathsf{TL}_{\mathsf{PE}}$ and $\mathsf{TL}_{\mathsf{PA}}$ are closely related to the branching time temporal logic LeftCTL* that we have already studied: It is not hard to see that for any $\mathsf{TL}_{\mathsf{PE}}$ formula Φ the formula $\mathsf{E}\Phi$ belongs to LeftCTL*, and analogously, that for any $\mathsf{TL}_{\mathsf{PA}}$ formula Φ the formula $\mathsf{A}\Phi$ belongs to LeftCTL*. It is furthermore not difficult to see that the logics $\mathsf{TL}_{\mathsf{PE}}$ and $\mathsf{TL}_{\mathsf{PA}}$ are subsets of the logics $\mathsf{TL}_{\mathsf{FG}}$ and $\mathsf{TL}_{\mathsf{GF}}$, respectively, and that $\mathsf{TL}_{\mathsf{PE}}$ and $\mathsf{TL}_{\mathsf{PA}}$ are dual to each other.

Lemma 5.64 (Relationship between $\mathsf{TL}_{\mathsf{PE}}/\mathsf{TL}_{\mathsf{PA}}$ and $\mathsf{TL}_{\mathsf{FG}}/\mathsf{TL}_{\mathsf{GF}}$).

- $\mathsf{TL}_{\mathsf{PE}} \subseteq \mathsf{TL}_{\mathsf{FG}}$ *and* $\mathsf{TL}_{\mathsf{PA}} \subseteq \mathsf{TL}_{\mathsf{GF}}$
- *For any* $\Phi \in \mathsf{TL}_{\mathsf{PE}}$, *we have* $\neg\Phi \in \mathsf{TL}_{\mathsf{PA}}$, *and for any* $\Phi \in \mathsf{TL}_{\mathsf{PA}}$, *we have* $\neg\Phi \in \mathsf{TL}_{\mathsf{PE}}$.

However, $\mathsf{TL}_{\mathsf{PE}}$ is significantly weaker than $\mathsf{TL}_{\mathsf{FG}}$, in particular, neither TL_{G} nor TL_{F} is a subset of $\mathsf{TL}_{\mathsf{PE}}$. For example, we have already mentioned that $\mathsf{AF}[a \wedge \mathsf{X}a]$ can neither be expressed in CTL nor in FairCTL [162], hence, this formula can also not be expressed in LeftCTL*. However, the formula $\mathsf{F}[a \wedge \mathsf{X}a]$ is a $\mathsf{TL}_{\mathsf{GF}}$ formula.

LeftCTL* has however the advantage of a relatively simple translation to the alternation-free μ-calculus, even a translation to CTL. For this reason, we will now define an extraction procedure TopPE similar to TopFG, but assume that we start the extraction from a $\mathsf{TL}_{\mathsf{FG}}$ formula (this formula may be obtained by TopFG). With that assumption, we can abbreviate the subformulas without generating fairness constraints as shown in Figure 5.17.

Theorem 5.65 (Correctness of $\mathsf{TopPE}_\sigma(\Phi)$). *Given any formula $\Phi \in \mathsf{TL}_{\mathsf{FG}}$, and the resulting automaton formula $\mathcal{A}_\exists(\mathcal{Q}, \mathcal{I}, \mathcal{R}, \Phi_0) = \mathsf{TopPE}_1(\Phi)$ obtained by the algorithm given in Figure 5.17, then the following hold:*

(1) $\mathsf{TopPE}_\sigma(\Phi)$ *runs in time* $O(|\Phi|)$.
(2) $\Phi_0 \in \mathcal{P}_{\mathsf{PE}}$
(3) $\Phi = \mathcal{A}_\exists(\mathcal{Q}, \mathcal{I}, \mathcal{R}, \Phi_0)$ *is initially valid.*

The proof is not too complicated. In particular, the same explanations as given in the correctness proof of Borel hold, i.e., the introduced abbreviations must hold long enough as controlled by the generated $\mathcal{C}_{\mathsf{F}}$ constraints. These constraints can now however be integrated into the remaining $\mathsf{TL}_{\mathsf{PE}}/\mathsf{TL}_{\mathsf{PA}}$ formulas. Note that we do not have the problem that we had in translating $\mathsf{TL}_{\mathsf{FG}}$ formulas: Algorithm Borel could not be used to handle these formulas since it was not clear where to put the reachability constraints for the subformulas that have been generated by the 'asymmetric' grammar rules of $\mathsf{TL}_{\mathsf{FG}}$. The problem does not occur here since we no longer need to abbreviate the until operators, even if weak ones occur positively.

A possible translation procedure could now work as follows: we first extract the largest $\mathsf{TL}_{\mathsf{FG}}$ formula by generating fairness constraints. After that, we further extract the largest $\mathsf{TL}_{\mathsf{PE}}$ formula, and translate the remaining automaton problem to an equivalent CTL model checking problem. *For this reason, as much as possible is kept in the acceptance condition, and as less as possible is translated into states and state transitions.*

However, this will not always be the best solution: Recall that the translation from LeftCTL* to CTL requires an exponential runtime in the worst case. So, there might be cases, where a translation to 'state variables' can be more efficient. Nevertheless, it is reasonable to still extract $\mathsf{TL}_{\mathsf{PE}}$ formulas even if

function $\mathsf{TopPE}_\sigma(\Phi)$

case Φ **of**

$\mathsf{is\_prop}(\Phi)$: **return** $\mathcal{A}_\exists(\{\}, 1, 1, \Phi)$;

$\neg\varphi$: $\mathcal{A}_\exists(\mathcal{Q}_\varphi, \mathcal{I}_\varphi, \mathcal{R}_\varphi, \varphi') \equiv \mathsf{TopPE}_{\neg\sigma}(\varphi)$;
return $\mathcal{A}_\exists(\mathcal{Q}_\varphi, \mathcal{I}_\varphi, \mathcal{R}_\varphi, \neg\varphi')$;

$\varphi \wedge \psi$: $\mathcal{A}_\exists(\mathcal{Q}_\varphi, \mathcal{I}_\varphi, \mathcal{R}_\varphi, \varphi') \equiv \mathsf{TopPE}_\sigma(\varphi)$;
$\mathcal{A}_\exists(\mathcal{Q}_\psi, \mathcal{I}_\psi, \mathcal{R}_\psi, \psi') \equiv \mathsf{TopPE}_\sigma(\psi)$;
return $\mathcal{A}_\exists(\mathcal{Q}_\varphi \cup \mathcal{Q}_\psi, \mathcal{I}_\varphi \wedge \mathcal{I}_\psi, \mathcal{R}_\varphi \wedge \mathcal{R}_\psi, \varphi' \wedge \psi')$;

$\varphi \vee \psi$: $\mathcal{A}_\exists(\mathcal{Q}_\varphi, \mathcal{I}_\varphi, \mathcal{R}_\varphi, \varphi') \equiv \mathsf{TopPE}_\sigma(\varphi)$;
$\mathcal{A}_\exists(\mathcal{Q}_\psi, \mathcal{I}_\psi, \mathcal{R}_\psi, \psi') \equiv \mathsf{TopPE}_\sigma(\psi)$;
return $\mathcal{A}_\exists(\mathcal{Q}_\varphi \cup \mathcal{Q}_\psi, \mathcal{I}_\varphi \wedge \mathcal{I}_\psi, \mathcal{R}_\varphi \wedge \mathcal{R}_\psi, \varphi' \vee \psi')$;

$\mathsf{X}\varphi$: $\mathcal{A}_\exists(\mathcal{Q}_\varphi, \mathcal{I}_\varphi, \mathcal{R}_\varphi, \varphi') \equiv \mathsf{TopPE}_\sigma(\varphi)$;
return $\mathcal{A}_\exists(\mathcal{Q}_\varphi, \mathcal{I}_\varphi, \mathcal{R}_\varphi, \mathsf{X}\varphi')$;

$[\varphi\ \mathsf{U}\ \psi]$: **if** σ **then** $\mathcal{A}_\exists(\mathcal{Q}_\varphi, \mathcal{I}_\varphi, \mathcal{R}_\varphi, \mathcal{F}_\varphi, \varphi') \equiv \mathsf{Borel}_\sigma(\varphi)$;
$\mathcal{A}_\exists(\mathcal{Q}_\psi, \mathcal{I}_\psi, \mathcal{R}_\psi, \psi') \equiv \mathsf{TopPE}_\sigma(\psi \wedge \bigwedge_{\xi \in \mathcal{F}_\varphi} \xi)$;
else $\mathcal{A}_\exists(\mathcal{Q}_\psi, \mathcal{I}_\psi, \mathcal{R}_\psi, \mathcal{F}_\psi, \psi') \equiv \mathsf{Borel}_\sigma(\psi)$;
$\mathcal{A}_\exists(\mathcal{Q}_\varphi, \mathcal{I}_\varphi, \mathcal{R}_\varphi, \varphi') \equiv \mathsf{TopPE}_\sigma(\varphi \wedge \bigwedge_{\xi \in \mathcal{F}_\psi} \xi)$;
end;
return $\mathcal{A}_\exists(\mathcal{Q}_\varphi \cup \mathcal{Q}_\psi, \mathcal{I}_\varphi \wedge \mathcal{I}_\psi, \mathcal{R}_\varphi \wedge \mathcal{R}_\psi, [\varphi'\ \mathsf{U}\ \psi'])$;

$[\varphi\ \underline{\mathsf{U}}\ \psi]$: **if** σ **then** $\mathcal{A}_\exists(\mathcal{Q}_\varphi, \mathcal{I}_\varphi, \mathcal{R}_\varphi, \mathcal{F}_\varphi, \varphi') \equiv \mathsf{Borel}_\sigma(\varphi)$;
$\mathcal{A}_\exists(\mathcal{Q}_\psi, \mathcal{I}_\psi, \mathcal{R}_\psi, \psi') \equiv \mathsf{TopPE}_\sigma(\psi \wedge \bigwedge_{\xi \in \mathcal{F}_\varphi} \xi)$;
else $\mathcal{A}_\exists(\mathcal{Q}_\psi, \mathcal{I}_\psi, \mathcal{R}_\psi, \mathcal{F}_\psi, \psi') \equiv \mathsf{Borel}_\sigma(\psi)$;
$\mathcal{A}_\exists(\mathcal{Q}_\varphi, \mathcal{I}_\varphi, \mathcal{R}_\varphi, \varphi') \equiv \mathsf{TopPE}_\sigma(\varphi \wedge \bigwedge_{\xi \in \mathcal{F}_\psi} \xi)$;
end;
return $\mathcal{A}_\exists(\mathcal{Q}_\varphi \cup \mathcal{Q}_\psi, \mathcal{I}_\varphi \wedge \mathcal{I}_\psi, \mathcal{R}_\varphi \wedge \mathcal{R}_\psi, [\varphi'\ \underline{\mathsf{U}}\ \psi'])$;

$[\varphi\ \mathsf{B}\ \psi]$: **if** σ **then** $\mathcal{A}_\exists(\mathcal{Q}_\psi, \mathcal{I}_\psi, \mathcal{R}_\psi, \mathcal{F}_\psi, \psi') \equiv \mathsf{Borel}_{\neg\sigma}(\psi)$;
$\mathcal{A}_\exists(\mathcal{Q}_\varphi, \mathcal{I}_\varphi, \mathcal{R}_\varphi, \varphi') \equiv \mathsf{TopPE}_\sigma(\varphi \wedge \bigwedge_{\xi \in \mathcal{F}_\psi} \xi)$;
else $\mathcal{A}_\exists(\mathcal{Q}_\varphi, \mathcal{I}_\varphi, \mathcal{R}_\varphi, \mathcal{F}_\varphi, \varphi') \equiv \mathsf{Borel}_\sigma(\varphi)$;
$\mathcal{A}_\exists(\mathcal{Q}_\psi, \mathcal{I}_\psi, \mathcal{R}_\psi, \psi') \equiv \mathsf{TopPE}_{\neg\sigma}(\psi \wedge \bigwedge_{\xi \in \mathcal{F}_\varphi} \xi)$;
end;
return $\mathcal{A}_\exists(\mathcal{Q}_\varphi \cup \mathcal{Q}_\psi, \mathcal{I}_\varphi \wedge \mathcal{I}_\psi, \mathcal{R}_\varphi \wedge \mathcal{R}_\psi, [\varphi'\ \mathsf{B}\ \psi'])$;

$[\varphi\ \underline{\mathsf{B}}\ \psi]$: **if** σ **then** $\mathcal{A}_\exists(\mathcal{Q}_\psi, \mathcal{I}_\psi, \mathcal{R}_\psi, \mathcal{F}_\psi, \psi') \equiv \mathsf{Borel}_{\neg\sigma}(\psi)$;
$\mathcal{A}_\exists(\mathcal{Q}_\varphi, \mathcal{I}_\varphi, \mathcal{R}_\varphi, \varphi') \equiv \mathsf{TopPE}_\sigma(\varphi \wedge \bigwedge_{\xi \in \mathcal{F}_\psi} \xi)$;
else $\mathcal{A}_\exists(\mathcal{Q}_\varphi, \mathcal{I}_\varphi, \mathcal{R}_\varphi, \mathcal{F}_\varphi, \varphi') \equiv \mathsf{Borel}_\sigma(\varphi)$;
$\mathcal{A}_\exists(\mathcal{Q}_\psi, \mathcal{I}_\psi, \mathcal{R}_\psi, \psi') \equiv \mathsf{TopPE}_{\neg\sigma}(\psi \wedge \bigwedge_{\xi \in \mathcal{F}_\varphi} \xi)$;
end;
return $\mathcal{A}_\exists(\mathcal{Q}_\varphi \cup \mathcal{Q}_\psi, \mathcal{I}_\varphi \wedge \mathcal{I}_\psi, \mathcal{R}_\varphi \wedge \mathcal{R}_\psi, [\varphi'\ \underline{\mathsf{B}}\ \psi'])$;

otherwise: $\mathcal{A}_\exists(\mathcal{Q}_\Phi, \mathcal{I}_\Phi, \mathcal{R}_\Phi, \mathcal{F}_\Phi, \Phi') \equiv \mathsf{Borel}_\sigma(\Phi)$;
return $\mathcal{A}_\exists\left(\mathcal{Q}_\Phi, \mathcal{I}_\Phi \wedge \Phi', \mathcal{R}_\Phi, \bigwedge_{\xi \in \mathcal{F}_\Phi} \xi\right)$;

end case

end function

Fig. 5.17. Extraction of top-level $\mathsf{LeftCTL}^*$ $\mathsf{TL}_{\mathsf{PE}}$ ($\sigma = 1$) and $\mathsf{TL}_{\mathsf{PA}}$ ($\sigma = 0$) formulas

no further translation to a CTL model checking problem is desired. The reason for this is as follows: *Temporal operators that are abbreviated by* Borel *using a reachability constraint introduce a state variable to abbreviate the subformula, and a reachability constraint. A later translation using the closure theorems of Lemma 5.58, will then add further state variables.* Therefore, one temporal operator may introduce more than one state variable with this approach.

To circumvent this overhead, we now show that this is not necessary for $\mathsf{TL_{PE}}$ formulas in that we develop a translation from $\mathsf{TL_{PE}}$ to $\mathsf{NDet_{FG}}$ that is independent of the function Borel. Our alternative translation is based on closure theorems just like the translation of the C_{F} formulas, i.e., we construct in a bottom-up manner $\mathsf{NDet_{FG}}$ from the $\mathsf{NDet_{FG}}$ automaton that has been generated by one of the subformulas. This computation is done with the following closure theorems.

Lemma 5.66 (Translating $\mathsf{TL_{PE}}$ to $\mathsf{NDet_{FG}}$). *Given a propositional formula φ, and the $\mathsf{NDet_{FG}}$ automaton formulas $\mathfrak{A}_\Phi = \mathcal{A}_\exists(Q_\Phi, \Phi_\mathcal{I}, \Phi_\mathcal{R}, \mathsf{FG}\Phi_\mathcal{F})$, and $\mathfrak{A}_\Psi = \mathcal{A}_\exists(Q_\Psi, \Psi_\mathcal{I}, \Psi_\mathcal{R}, \mathsf{FG}\Psi_\mathcal{F})$, the following equations hold:*

- $\mathfrak{A}_\Phi \wedge \mathfrak{A}_\Psi = \mathcal{A}_\exists(Q_\Phi \cup Q_\Psi, \Phi_\mathcal{I} \wedge \Psi_\mathcal{I}, \Phi_\mathcal{R} \wedge \Psi_\mathcal{R}, \mathsf{FG}(\Phi_\mathcal{F} \wedge \Psi_\mathcal{F}))$
- $\mathfrak{A}_\Phi \vee \mathfrak{A}_\Psi = \mathcal{A}_\exists\begin{pmatrix} Q_\Phi \cup Q_\Psi \cup \{p\}, \\ \neg p \wedge \Phi_\mathcal{I} \vee p \wedge \Psi_\mathcal{I}, \\ \neg p \wedge \Phi_\mathcal{R} \wedge \neg \mathsf{X}p \vee p \wedge \Psi_\mathcal{R} \wedge \mathsf{X}p, \\ \mathsf{FG}(\neg p \wedge \Phi_\mathcal{F} \vee p \wedge \Psi_\mathcal{F}) \end{pmatrix}$
- $\mathsf{X}[\mathfrak{A}_\Phi] = \mathcal{A}_\exists\begin{pmatrix} Q \cup \{p\}, \\ \neg p, \\ [\neg p \wedge \mathsf{X}p \wedge \mathsf{X}\Phi_\mathcal{I}] \vee [p \wedge \Phi_\mathcal{R} \wedge \mathsf{X}p], \\ \mathsf{FG}\Phi_\mathcal{F} \end{pmatrix}$
- $[\varphi\ \underline{\mathsf{U}}\ \mathfrak{A}_\Phi] = \mathcal{A}_\exists\begin{pmatrix} Q \cup \{p\}, \neg p \vee \Phi_\mathcal{I}, \\ [\neg p \wedge \varphi \wedge \neg \mathsf{X}p] \vee \\ [\neg p \wedge \varphi \wedge \mathsf{X}p \wedge \mathsf{X}\Phi_\mathcal{I}] \vee \\ [p \wedge \Phi_\mathcal{R} \wedge \mathsf{X}p], \\ \mathsf{FG}(p \wedge \Phi_\mathcal{F}) \end{pmatrix}$
- $[\varphi\ \mathsf{U}\ \mathfrak{A}_\Phi] = \mathcal{A}_\exists\begin{pmatrix} Q \cup \{p\}, \neg p \vee \Phi_\mathcal{I}, \\ [\neg p \wedge \varphi \wedge \neg \mathsf{X}p] \vee \\ [\neg p \wedge \varphi \wedge \mathsf{X}p \wedge \mathsf{X}\Phi_\mathcal{I}] \vee \\ [p \wedge \Phi_\mathcal{R} \wedge \mathsf{X}p], \\ \mathsf{FG}(\neg p \vee \Phi_\mathcal{F}) \end{pmatrix}$
- $[\mathfrak{A}_\Phi\ \underline{\mathsf{B}}\ \varphi] = \mathcal{A}_\exists\begin{pmatrix} Q \cup \{p\}, \neg\varphi \wedge (\neg p \vee \Phi_\mathcal{I}), \\ [\neg p \wedge \neg\varphi \wedge \neg \mathsf{X}p] \vee \\ [\neg p \wedge \neg\varphi \wedge \mathsf{X}p \wedge \mathsf{X}\Phi_\mathcal{I} \wedge \neg\mathsf{X}\varphi] \vee \\ [p \wedge \Phi_\mathcal{R} \wedge \mathsf{X}p], \\ \mathsf{FG}(p \wedge \Phi_\mathcal{F}) \end{pmatrix}$

- $$[\mathfrak{A}_\Phi\ \mathsf{B}\ \varphi] = \mathcal{A}_\exists\left(\begin{array}{l} Q \cup \{p\}, \neg\varphi \wedge (\neg p \vee \Phi_\mathcal{I}),\\ [\neg p \wedge \neg\varphi \wedge \neg \mathsf{X} p] \vee \\ [\neg p \wedge \neg\varphi \wedge \mathsf{X} p \wedge \mathsf{X}\Phi_\mathcal{I} \wedge \neg\mathsf{X}\varphi] \vee \\ [p \wedge \Phi_\mathcal{R} \wedge \mathsf{X} p],\\ \mathsf{FG}(\neg p \vee \Phi_\mathcal{F}) \end{array}\right)$$

The rationale behind the above equations is as follows: in case of disjunctions, we add an additional state variable p that may initially be either 1 or 0. According to the transition relation, p will always maintain its initial value. Hence, depending on the initial value of p the automaton obtained for the disjunctive closure collapses to either one of the given automata.

In the closure for the X operator, the additional state variable will initially be 0 and will be 1 for all $t > 0$. Hence, the transition relation formalizes that at time $t = 1$, we are in an initial state, i.e. a state satisfying $\Phi_\mathcal{I}$, and for all points of time $t \geq 1$, the transitions encoded by $\Phi_\mathcal{R}$ are enabled.

The closure of $\underline{\mathsf{U}}$ is constructed as follows: We add new initial states encoded by $\neg p$ (note that $\neg p \vee \Phi_\mathcal{I} = \neg p \vee p \wedge \Phi_\mathcal{I}$ is valid) and retain also the previous initial states (that are extended by a true value of p). We may loop in the new initial states $\neg p$ whenever φ holds, but may also leave these states with the same input to reach an initial state of $p \wedge \Phi_\mathcal{I}$. The second alternative then enables the automaton $\mathfrak{A}$. The closures for $[\mathfrak{A}\ \mathsf{B}\ \varphi]$ and $[\mathfrak{A}\ \underline{\mathsf{B}}\ \varphi]$ are similar, just note that $[\varphi\ \mathsf{B}\ \psi] = [(\neg\psi)\ \mathsf{U}\ (\varphi \wedge \neg\psi)]$ and $[\varphi\ \underline{\mathsf{B}}\ \psi] = [(\neg\psi)\ \underline{\mathsf{U}}\ (\varphi \wedge \neg\psi)]$ are valid.

Büchi automata are sometimes further classified into *weak* and *terminal* Büchi automata [40, 52, 221, 381]. A Büchi automaton is weak iff there exists a partition of its states into classes $Q_0, \ldots, Q_{f+n}$ that are partially ordered so that the transitions of the automaton never move from Q_i to Q_j unless $Q_j \preceq Q_i$ holds. Thus, every cycle is completely contained in a class Q_i. Given that Ψ_i represents the situations of Q_i, it is furthermore assumed that the acceptance condition $\mathsf{GF}\Phi_0$ is given as a disjunction $\Phi_0 = \bigvee_{i \in \mathcal{F}} \Psi_i$ of classes Q_i. Furthermore, a weak Büchi automaton is terminal if the classes Ψ_i contained in the acceptance condition Φ_0 correspond with minimal state sets Q_i or direct successors of minimal state sets w.r.t. $\preceq$, i.e., $\Phi_0 = \bigvee_{i=0}^{f} \Psi_i$. It is easily seen that weak and terminal Büchi automata are special forms of $\mathsf{NDet}_\mathsf{FG}$ and NDet_F automata [52, 502], respectively: one can simply replace the acceptance condition $\mathsf{GF}\Phi_0$ by $\mathsf{FG}\Phi_0$ and $\mathsf{F}\Phi_0$, respectively [52]. Conversely, one can construct for every $\mathsf{NDet}_\mathsf{FG}$ and NDet_F automaton a weak and terminal Büchi automaton [502]. Note that the automata obtained by the closure theorems fulfill the terminal condition.

Recall that the idea of our new translation procedure for TL_PE is to compute ω-automata in a bottom-up traversal through the syntax tree of the formula, where the ω-automaton of an elementary formula is obtained from the ω-automata of its arguments by application of a corresponding closure operation. For example, consider the formula $[\Phi\ \mathsf{U}\ \Psi]$ where Φ is propositional and we already have translated Ψ to an equivalent $\mathsf{NDet}_\mathsf{FG}$ automaton for $\mathfrak{A}_\Psi$.

We then use the above closure theorems to construct an $\mathsf{NDet}_{\mathsf{FG}}$ automaton for $[\Phi \; \mathsf{U} \; \Psi]$ out of $\mathfrak{A}_\Psi$. *It is important to note that by the above closure theorems, every temporal operator is replaced with only a single state variable!* This makes it, in general, more efficient than Borel.

In order to complete this translation, we must show how the base cases of our recursive treatment are obtained. This means that we have to show how only the $\mathsf{TL}_{\mathsf{PE}}$ formulas that have only propositional subformulas (apart from themselves) are translated. These cases are very simple and can, for example, be solved as shown in the following lemma.

Lemma 5.67. *Given that φ and ψ are propositional formulas, then the following rules can be used for a translation to* $\mathsf{NDet}_{\mathsf{FG}}$*:*

- $[\varphi \; \mathsf{U} \; \psi] = \mathcal{A}_\exists \left(\{q\}, \neg q, \neg q \wedge \varphi \wedge \neg\psi \wedge \neg \mathsf{X} q \vee \neg q \wedge \psi \wedge \mathsf{X} q \vee q \wedge \mathsf{X} q, \mathsf{FG}1\right)$
- $[\varphi \; \underline{\mathsf{U}} \; \psi] = \mathcal{A}_\exists \left(\{q\}, \neg q, \neg q \wedge \varphi \wedge \neg\psi \wedge \neg \mathsf{X} q \vee \neg q \wedge \psi \wedge \mathsf{X} q \vee q \wedge \mathsf{X} q, \mathsf{FG} q\right)$
- $[\varphi \; \mathsf{B} \; \psi] = [(\neg\psi) \; \mathsf{U} \; (\varphi \wedge \neg\psi)]$
- $[\varphi \; \underline{\mathsf{B}} \; \psi] = [(\neg\psi) \; \underline{\mathsf{U}} \; (\varphi \wedge \neg\psi)]$
- $\mathsf{X}\varphi = \mathcal{A}_\exists \begin{pmatrix} \{p, q\}, \\ \neg p \wedge \neg q, \\ \neg p \wedge \neg q \wedge \mathsf{X} p \wedge \neg \mathsf{X} q \vee \\ p \wedge \neg q \wedge \varphi \wedge \mathsf{X} p \wedge \mathsf{X} q \vee \\ p \wedge q \wedge \mathsf{X} p \wedge \mathsf{X} q, \\ \mathsf{FG}1 \end{pmatrix}$

The reader may draw the state transition diagrams of the above mentioned automata to see that these automata are indeed equivalent to the mentioned temporal logic formulas.

Hence, having extracted $\mathsf{TL}_{\mathsf{FG}}$ formulas, and having furthermore extracted $\mathsf{TL}_{\mathsf{PE}}$ formulas, we have the choice of whether we would like to translate the $\mathsf{TL}_{\mathsf{PE}}$ formulas to a 'CTL formula' or to a $\mathsf{NDet}_{\mathsf{FG}}$ automaton using the above closures.

Hence, we now have many possibilities at hand to translate LTL_p model checking problems to equivalent fixpoint problems. A simple algorithm that combines all of these procedures is listed in Figure 5.18. We assume that BorelFG is the function that consists of the removal of the 'asymmetric' grammar rules as explained in Theorem 5.57 on page 362. The algorithm has three Boolean valued parameters *OnlyMono*, *useBorel*, and *toCTL* to control the translation. If *OnlyMono* is true, then the algorithm will simply use the function TopProp to compute an equivalent $\mathsf{NDet}_{\mathsf{Streett}}$ automaton for Φ. Note, that this function considers the monotonicity improvement and will therefore already translate TL_{G} formulas to equivalent $\mathsf{NDet}_{\mathsf{G}}$ automata. However, for any positive/negative occurrence of a weak/strong future temporal operator, a fairness constraint is generated.

If this is not wanted, we have to set *OnlyMono* $= 1$. In this case, we first use the function TopFG to extract the largest top-level $\mathsf{TL}_{\mathsf{FG}}$ Φ_0 of Φ. The remaining parts are thereby translated by generating fairness constraints as it

```
function Automaton(OnlyMono, useBorel, toCTL, Φ)
  if OnlyMono then return TopProp₁(Φ) end;
  A∃ (Q0, I0, R0, F0, Φ0) ≡ TopFG₁(Φ);
  if useBorel then (* translate to reachability automaton *)
    A∃ (Q1, I1, R1, F1, Φ1) ≡ BorelFG1(Φ0);
    I1 := I1 ∧ Φ1;
    Φ1 := ⋀_{ξ∈F1} ξ
  else (* extract top-level TL_PE formula *)
    A∃ (Q1, I1, R1, Φ1) ≡ TopPE₁(Φ0)
  end;
  (* in any case, we now have Φ1 ∈ TL_PE *)
  if toCTL then (* translate to CTL *)
    Φ2 := LeftCTL2CTL(Φ1);
    return A∃ (Q0 ∪ Q1, I0 ∧ I1, R0 ∧ R1, F0, Φ2)
  else (* apply closure theorems *)
    A∃ (Q2, I2, R2, Φ_FG) ≡ close(Φ1);
    return A∃ (Q0 ∪ Q1 ∪ Q2, I0 ∧ I1 ∧ I2, R0 ∧ R1 ∧ R2, F0, Φ_FG)
  end
end function
```

Fig. 5.18. The final translation from LTL_p to ω-Automata or CTL model checking

would have been done in TopProp. The extracted $\Phi_0 \in \mathsf{TL}_{\mathsf{FG}}$, however, can be further translated without the introduction of fairness constraints. Depending on the other parameters *useBorel* and *toCTL* this is done as follows: if *useBorel* is true, we apply the function BorelFG to reduce Φ_0 to a reachability automaton; otherwise we reduce Φ_0 by TopPE to an ω-automaton whose acceptance condition Φ_0 belongs to $\mathsf{TL}_{\mathsf{PE}}$. Of course, the latter will leave more parts of Φ_0 in the acceptance condition, while the function BorelFG will introduce more state variables and a smaller acceptance condition.

Since we replace Φ_1 with the conjunction of the reachability constraints in case *useBorel* is true, it then follows (independent of the value of *useBorel*) that $\Phi_1 \in \mathsf{TL}_{\mathsf{PE}}$. We therefore have two possibilities for the further translation: If *toCTL* is true, we translate $\mathsf{E}\Phi_1$ to an equivalent CTL formula, and drop all path quantifiers in the result (a later translation to a CTL model checking problem will then only have to add these path quantifiers again). If, on the other hand, *toCTL* is false, then we use the closure theorems to compute an equivalent $\mathsf{NDet}_{\mathsf{FG}}$ automaton for Φ_1. After that, we collect the different automaton parts, so that finally the desired ω-automaton is obtained.

Hence, the function given in Figure 5.18 summarizes all of the previous translations in that these can be obtained by using particular instances. In general, it is not clear in advance, which parameters will finally lead to a model checking problem that can be efficiently solved. For this reason, it is necessary in practice to be able to use different translations. To conclude this section, we embed our temporal logics TL_κ in CTL^* so that we obtain the following 'alternation-free' fragment of CTL^*:

Definition 5.68 (The Logic AFCTL^*). *We define the logic AFCTL^* as the set of formulas that can be derived from the nonterminal S by the following grammar rules:*

$$S ::= V_\Sigma \mid \neg S \mid S \wedge S \mid S \vee S \mid \mathsf{E}P_{\mathsf{FG}} \mid \mathsf{A}P_{\mathsf{GF}}$$

$$\begin{array}{llll}
P_{\mathsf{G}} ::= S & & & \\
\mid \neg P_{\mathsf{F}} & \mid P_{\mathsf{G}} \wedge P_{\mathsf{G}} & \mid P_{\mathsf{G}} \vee P_{\mathsf{G}} & \\
\mid \mathsf{X} P_{\mathsf{G}} & \mid [P_{\mathsf{G}}\ \mathsf{U}\ P_{\mathsf{G}}] & \mid [P_{\mathsf{G}}\ \mathsf{B}\ P_{\mathsf{F}}] & \\
\mid \overleftarrow{\underline{\mathsf{X}}} P_{\mathsf{G}} & \mid [P_{\mathsf{G}}\ \overleftarrow{\underline{\mathsf{U}}}\ P_{\mathsf{G}}] & \mid [P_{\mathsf{G}}\ \overleftarrow{\underline{\mathsf{B}}}\ P_{\mathsf{F}}] & \\
\mid \overleftarrow{\mathsf{X}} P_{\mathsf{G}} & \mid [P_{\mathsf{G}}\ \overleftarrow{\mathsf{U}}\ P_{\mathsf{G}}] & \mid [P_{\mathsf{G}}\ \overleftarrow{\mathsf{B}}\ P_{\mathsf{F}}] &
\end{array}
\qquad
\begin{array}{llll}
P_{\mathsf{F}} ::= S & & & \\
\mid \neg P_{\mathsf{G}} & \mid P_{\mathsf{F}} \wedge P_{\mathsf{F}} & \mid P_{\mathsf{F}} \vee P_{\mathsf{F}} & \\
\mid \mathsf{X} P_{\mathsf{F}} & \mid [P_{\mathsf{F}}\ \underline{\mathsf{U}}\ P_{\mathsf{F}}] & \mid [P_{\mathsf{F}}\ \underline{\mathsf{B}}\ P_{\mathsf{G}}] & \\
\mid \overleftarrow{\underline{\mathsf{X}}} P_{\mathsf{F}} & \mid [P_{\mathsf{F}}\ \overleftarrow{\underline{\mathsf{U}}}\ P_{\mathsf{F}}] & \mid [P_{\mathsf{F}}\ \overleftarrow{\underline{\mathsf{B}}}\ P_{\mathsf{G}}] & \\
\mid \overleftarrow{\mathsf{X}} P_{\mathsf{F}} & \mid [P_{\mathsf{F}}\ \overleftarrow{\mathsf{U}}\ P_{\mathsf{F}}] & \mid [P_{\mathsf{F}}\ \overleftarrow{\mathsf{B}}\ P_{\mathsf{G}}] &
\end{array}$$

$$\begin{array}{lll}
P_{\mathsf{GF}} ::= S & & \\
\mid \neg P_{\mathsf{FG}} & \mid P_{\mathsf{GF}} \wedge P_{\mathsf{GF}} & \mid P_{\mathsf{GF}} \vee P_{\mathsf{GF}} \\
\mid \mathsf{X} P_{\mathsf{GF}} & \mid [P_{\mathsf{GF}}\ \underline{\mathsf{U}}\ P_{\mathsf{F}}] & \mid [P_{\mathsf{F}}\ \underline{\mathsf{B}}\ P_{\mathsf{FG}}] \\
 & \mid [P_{\mathsf{GF}}\ \mathsf{U}\ P_{\mathsf{GF}}] & \mid [P_{\mathsf{GF}}\ \mathsf{B}\ P_{\mathsf{FG}}] \\
\mid \overleftarrow{\underline{\mathsf{X}}} P_{\mathsf{GF}} & \mid [P_{\mathsf{GF}}\ \overleftarrow{\underline{\mathsf{U}}}\ P_{\mathsf{GF}}] & \mid [P_{\mathsf{GF}}\ \overleftarrow{\underline{\mathsf{B}}}\ P_{\mathsf{FG}}] \\
\mid \overleftarrow{\mathsf{X}} P_{\mathsf{GF}} & \mid [P_{\mathsf{GF}}\ \overleftarrow{\mathsf{U}}\ P_{\mathsf{GF}}] & \mid [P_{\mathsf{GF}}\ \overleftarrow{\mathsf{B}}\ P_{\mathsf{FG}}]
\end{array}
\qquad
\begin{array}{lll}
P_{\mathsf{FG}} ::= S & & \\
\mid \neg P_{\mathsf{GF}} & \mid P_{\mathsf{FG}} \wedge P_{\mathsf{FG}} & \mid P_{\mathsf{FG}} \vee P_{\mathsf{FG}} \\
\mid \mathsf{X} P_{\mathsf{FG}} & \mid [P_{\mathsf{FG}}\ \underline{\mathsf{U}}\ P_{\mathsf{FG}}] & \mid [P_{\mathsf{FG}}\ \underline{\mathsf{B}}\ P_{\mathsf{GF}}] \\
 & \mid [P_{\mathsf{G}}\ \mathsf{U}\ P_{\mathsf{FG}}] & \mid [P_{\mathsf{FG}}\ \mathsf{B}\ P_{\mathsf{F}}] \\
\mid \overleftarrow{\underline{\mathsf{X}}} P_{\mathsf{FG}} & \mid [P_{\mathsf{FG}}\ \overleftarrow{\underline{\mathsf{U}}}\ P_{\mathsf{FG}}] & \mid [P_{\mathsf{FG}}\ \overleftarrow{\underline{\mathsf{B}}}\ P_{\mathsf{GF}}] \\
\mid \overleftarrow{\mathsf{X}} P_{\mathsf{FG}} & \mid [P_{\mathsf{FG}}\ \overleftarrow{\mathsf{U}}\ P_{\mathsf{FG}}] & \mid [P_{\mathsf{FG}}\ \overleftarrow{\mathsf{B}}\ P_{\mathsf{GF}}]
\end{array}$$

Intuitively, AFCTL^* formulas are those CTL^* formulas where any subformula of the form $\mathsf{E}\Phi$ with quantifier-free Φ 'correspond' to $\mathsf{TL}_{\mathsf{FG}}$. This 'correspondence' is exactly the same as the correspondence between $\mathsf{LeftCTL}^*$ and the formulas $\mathsf{E}\Phi$ with $\Phi \in \mathsf{TL}_{\mathsf{PE}}$. To make this 'correspondence' more precise, we convert the formulas into PQNF normal form (cf. Theorem 2.49):

Theorem 5.69 (The Logic AFCTL^*). *Any formula Φ of the logic AFCTL^* over the variables V_Σ can be reduced in linear time to its PQNF normal form, where $\varphi_i \in \mathsf{TL}_{\mathsf{FG}}$ holds and Ψ is a propositional formula over $V_\Sigma \cup \{x_1, \ldots, x_n\}$:*

$$\Phi = \mathsf{let} \begin{bmatrix} x_1 = \mathsf{E}\varphi_1 \\ \vdots \\ x_n = \mathsf{E}\varphi_n \end{bmatrix} \mathsf{in}\ \Psi\ \mathsf{end}$$

Hence, any formula Φ of the logic AFCTL^* over the variables V_Σ can be reduced in linear time into a formula of the form below, where $\mathfrak{A}_i \in \mathsf{NDet}_{\mathsf{FG}}$ holds and Ψ is a propositional formula over $V_\Sigma \cup \{x_1, \ldots, x_n\}$:

$$\Phi = \mathsf{let} \begin{bmatrix} x_1 = \mathsf{E}\mathfrak{A}_1 \\ \vdots \\ x_n = \mathsf{E}\mathfrak{A}_n \end{bmatrix} \mathsf{in}\ \Psi\ \mathsf{end}$$

Hence, the model checking problem for AFCTL^* can be reduced to the alternation-free μ-calculus.

The above defined logic AFCTL* has some interesting properties from both the practical and the theoretical side. For the practice, it is clearly a very interesting logic, since it can be efficiently checked: Using the algorithm BorelFG and then the translation by the closure theorems, allows us to compute the normal form mentioned in the above theorem in time $O(|\Phi|)$. Note that this implies that the size of the formula is also linear w.r.t. $|\Phi|$.

Therefore, the logic is interesting from the practical side. For the theoretical side, it is closely related with Kupferman and Vardi's result [303] that $\mathsf{E}\Phi$ with $\Phi \in \mathsf{LTL}_p$ can be translated to the alternation-free μ-calculus iff Φ can be translated to $\mathsf{Det}_{\mathsf{FG}}$. However, this does not imply that AFCTL* is the alternation-free fragment of the CTL*, even though we prove in the next section that if $\Phi \in \mathsf{LTL}_p$ can be translated to $\mathsf{Det}_{\mathsf{FG}}$, then there is an equivalent formula in $\mathsf{TL}_{\mathsf{FG}}$. Hence, the classes TL_κ are complete with respect to the classes Det_κ. However, this is not sufficient to prove that AFCTL* is equally expressive as the alternation-free fragment of CTL*.

Let us now compare LeftCTL* and AFCTL*, which is equivalent to comparing $\mathsf{TL}_{\mathsf{PE}}$ with $\mathsf{TL}_{\mathsf{FG}}$. Of course, it immediately follows from the syntactical inclusion $\mathsf{TL}_{\mathsf{PE}} \subseteq \mathsf{TL}_{\mathsf{FG}}$ that AFCTL* is at least as expressive as LeftCTL* and hence, as CTL. Clearly, this need not necessarily mean that AFCTL* is more expressive than LeftCTL*.

However, as the formula $\mathsf{E}[[p \vee \mathsf{X}p]\ \mathsf{U}\ 0]$ belongs to AFCTL*, but it is well-known not to be expressible in CTL, it immediately follows that LeftCTL* $\precnapprox$ AFCTL* holds (just note that $\mathsf{E}[[p \vee \mathsf{X}p]\ \mathsf{U}\ 0]$ is equivalent to $\mathsf{EG}[p \vee \mathsf{X}p]$, which is the negation of $\mathsf{AF}[\neg p \wedge \neg \mathsf{X}p]$, whose inequivalence to CTL formulas is shown in [162]). We therefore have the following result:

Theorem 5.70. *The logics* $\mathsf{TL}_{\mathsf{PE}}$, $\mathsf{TL}_{\mathsf{PA}}$, *and* LeftCTL* *are strictly less expressive than the logics* $\mathsf{TL}_{\mathsf{FG}}$, $\mathsf{TL}_{\mathsf{GF}}$, *and* AFCTL*, *respectively.*

Of course, some AFCTL* formulas that are syntactically not LeftCTL* formulas can be replaced by equivalent LeftCTL* formulas. For example, the following is such a reduction:

$$[[\alpha\ \underline{\mathsf{U}}\ \beta]\ \underline{\mathsf{U}}\ \gamma] = \left(\begin{array}{l} \gamma \vee \\ [(\alpha \vee \beta)\ \underline{\mathsf{U}}\ (\beta \wedge [\beta\ \underline{\mathsf{U}}\ \gamma])] \vee \\ [(\alpha \vee \beta)\ \underline{\mathsf{U}}\ [(\alpha \wedge \neg\beta)\ \underline{\mathsf{U}}\ (\gamma \wedge [\alpha\ \underline{\mathsf{U}}\ \beta])]] \end{array}\right)$$

Further examples of that kind are the reductions that we used to translate CTL^2 to CTL (cf. Section 5.3.2). Dams has shown in [136] that the formula $[(r \vee [p\ \underline{\mathsf{U}}\ (q \wedge [q\ \underline{\mathsf{U}}\ r])])\ \underline{\mathsf{U}}\ (s \wedge [s\ \underline{\mathsf{U}}\ (t \wedge [t\ \underline{\mathsf{U}}\ u])])]$ can not be written without a left nesting of until operators (and has explained that this is somehow the simplest example). However, it is easily seen that this formula belongs to TL_{F} and can thus be translated to a $\mathsf{Det}_{\mathsf{F}}$ automaton.

As further related work, Etessami and Wilke considered in [188] the until hierarchy of temporal logic, i.e., the sets of temporal logic formulas where k until operators are nested, and proved that this hierarchy of formulas is strictly increasing in its expressiveness. So, it is not always possible to eliminate nestings of until operators.

Hence, not any formula of AFCTL* can be translated to CTL, but it can nevertheless be translated to the alternation-free μ-calculus. Please note that the difference between AFCTL* and LeftCTL* is that AFCTL* does allow P_{G} formulas, where LeftCTL* needs to have a state formula S. This allows us to construct formulas such as the ones above that are not expressible in $\mathsf{TL}_{\mathsf{PE}}$.

5.5 Completeness and Expressiveness of Temporal Logic

In the previous section, we have developed translation procedures from temporal logics to ω-automata. In particular, we have seen that the classes TL_κ can be translated to the corresponding classes Det_κ. We now turn to the question of completeness, i.e., whether Det_κ automata can be translated to TL_κ. We will see that this is not the case, which immediately follows from various well-known results that imply that temporal logic is in general not as expressive as ω-automata, since the latter provide some form of second order quantification (see next chapter). However, we will see that the classes TL_κ are complete w.r.t. noncounting Det_κ automata (cf. Definition 4.61), which are those Det_κ automata that do not have this second order capability.

To this end, we will first list some well-known results on the expressiveness of temporal logics in Section 5.5.1. The expressiveness of LTL_p has many characterizations, and is still a topic of research. Unfortunately, most proofs of this issue are highly complex and are often obtained indirectly by other formalisms (cf. Theorem 5.76 and 5.82). In general, there are two techniques to prove these results: One is based on the Krohn-Rhodes theorem [151, 209, 309, 341, 342, 475], which concerns the decomposition theory of semigroups. The other follows Schützenberger's proof [402, 444, 445] that is based on a certain induction over the syntactic monoids of languages. In Section 5.5.1, we will follow Wilke's direct proof [512] of the fact that every deterministic noncounting automaton can be translated to LTL_p. The proof is constructive and provides an algorithm to compute temporal logic formulas for given automata.

In Section 5.5.2, we show the completeness of the logics TL_κ with respect to noncounting Det_κ automata. To this end, we show that the 'past fragments' of our logics TL_κ correspond with Manna and Pnueli's normal forms for safety, guarantee, obligation, recurrence, persistence, and reactivity properties. By the techniques of Section 5.5.2, it also follows that noncounting deterministic ω-automata can be translated to LTL_p.

Finally, we will prove the completeness of the future time fragments of the logics TL_κ in Section 5.5.3, in that we show that the logics TL_κ have the separation property: Every formula with future and past temporal operators can be converted in a normal form where future and past operators are separated. In particular, all past operators can therefore be eliminated in these logics (w.r.t. initial validity).

5.5.1 Noncounting Automata and Temporal Logic

We have already mentioned that ω-automata are strictly more expressive than temporal logics. The reason for this will become clearer in the next chapter where we will prove that LTL_p corresponds with the first order theory of linear order, while ω-automata correspond with the second order theory of linear order. Hence, ω-automata provide means for second order quantification, which is not available in LTL_p. For example, there is no LTL_p formula that can express that a proposition φ should hold at every even point of time [518, 519]. In general, automata have the ability to store information in their states which enables them to 'count modulo a constant number n'. This is not possible in any of the temporal logics we consider in this book.

The inability of temporal logics to 'count' has been known for a long time. In 1960, Büchi proved that the monadic second order logic of one successor S1S can be reduced to $\mathsf{NDet}_{\mathsf{GF}}$ automata [80, 81, 455] (see next Chapter), and thereby initiated research in the field of ω-automata. It is immediately seen that S1S is equal expressive as the monadic second order logic of linear orders $\mathsf{MSO}_<$ (cf. next Chapter). Hence, it was a major achievement of Büchi to show that the mathematical theories S1S and $\mathsf{MSO}_<$ are both decidable, and that decision procedures can be obtained by a suitable reduction to automata problems. At that time, an important problem was finding characterizations for the *first* order logic of linear orders $\mathsf{MFO}_<$. In 1968, Kamp [274] proved that $\mathsf{MFO}_<$ is equal expressive as our logic LTL_p and therefore presented a predicate logic characterization of temporal logic. Hence, it became clear that LTL_p is the subset of $\mathsf{MSO}_<$ that is restricted to first order quantification. But still a characterization of the subset of ω-automata that correspond with $\mathsf{MFO}_<$ was unknown. The question was then answered by McNaughton and Papert [364] in 1971. They introduced the notion of 'noncounting' automata and proved the equal expressiveness of $\mathsf{MFO}_<$ and star-free regular expressions.

Therefore, considering again the issue of completeness of the logics TL_κ, we must refine our question in that we ask *whether it is possible to translate any noncounting* Det_κ *automaton to an equivalent* TL_κ *formula.* We will see in this section, that the answer to that question is 'yes' for all classes κ, and therefore we have our desired completeness results for the logics TL_κ. To establish this result, we will not directly pose our considerations on noncounting Det_κ automata. Instead, we will consider another characterization of these automata which is directly related to temporal logic. We will consider temporally defined automata as introduced by Lichtenstein, Pnueli, and Zuck [326], and later used by Maler and Pnueli [342] in 1990, and Manna and Pnueli [352] in 1992.

The intuitive idea of temporally defined automata is that we first forget about their acceptance conditions, thus we consider semiautomata $\mathfrak{A} = (\Sigma, \mathcal{S}, \mathcal{I}, \mathcal{R})$. We then consider the *regular languages* $L_{s,s'}$ whose words have a run leading from state s to state s'. *A semiautomaton* $\mathfrak{A}$ *is then temporally defined iff all languages* $L_{s,s'}$ *can be characterized by temporal logic formulas*. Of course, we have to make precise how 'characterized' is to be understood. To this end, we restrict our consideration to automata whose input alphabet is encoded by Boolean variables V_Σ that we furthermore use to build formulas of LTL_p. As we are only interested in finite words at the moment, we only consider LTL_p formulas that do not contain future temporal operators:

Definition 5.71 (End-Satisfiability of Past Formulas). *Given a pure past formula* φ*, we define the following set* $\mathsf{ESat}(\varphi)$ *of finite words over* 2^{V_Σ}*:*

$$\mathsf{ESat}(\varphi) := \left\{ (\alpha^{(0)}, \ldots, \alpha^{(\ell)}) \in (2^{V_\Sigma})^* \;\middle|\; \begin{array}{l} \exists \mathcal{K}. \exists \pi \in \mathsf{Paths}_\mathcal{K}(\pi^{(0)}). \\ \quad (\mathcal{K}, \pi, \ell) \models \varphi \wedge \\ \quad \forall t \leq \ell.\ \alpha^{(t)} = \mathcal{L}(\pi^{(t)}) \end{array} \right\}$$

We write $(\alpha^{(0)}, \ldots, \alpha^{(\ell)}) \models \varphi$ *to denote that* $(\alpha^{(0)}, \ldots, \alpha^{(\ell)}) \in \mathsf{ESat}(\varphi)$ *holds.*

For example, for $V_\Sigma = \{a, b, c\}$, we have $(\{\}, \{b\}, \{a, c\}, \{a\}, \{a, c\}) \models [a\ \overleftarrow{\underline{\mathsf{U}}}\ b]$. It is not complicated to determine $\mathsf{ESat}(\varphi)$ for a given formula LTL_p where only past temporal operators occur: We construct the automaton $\mathfrak{A}_\varphi$ that is obtained for a pure past formula φ by the repeated application of the laws of Theorem 5.38 on page 338. We thereby obtain an automaton formula $\mathfrak{A}_\varphi = \mathcal{A}_\exists(Q, \varphi_\mathcal{I}, \varphi_\mathcal{R}, \varphi_\mathcal{F})$, where $\varphi_\mathcal{F}$ is propositional. Moreover, the automaton has a deterministic and complete transition relation $\varphi_\mathcal{R}$, and exactly one initial state ι. $\mathsf{ESat}(\varphi)$ is then obtained as the union of languages $L_{\iota,s'}$ where $L_{\iota,s'}$ is the set of finite words that are read by $\mathfrak{A}_\varphi$ from the initial state ι such that the computation ends in a state where with the last letter of the word the condition $\varphi_\mathcal{F}$ holds.

Proceeding this way, it is not difficult to see that the syntactic monoid $\mathsf{SM}(\mathsf{ESat}(\varphi))$ of the language $\mathsf{ESat}(\varphi)$ is aperiodic. We can prove this by induction on the number of temporal operators in φ. The induction base is thereby trivial, since for propositional formulas φ, we obtain the automaton $\mathcal{A}_\exists(\{\}, \varphi, 1, 1)$ with no state variables, and hence, only one state. The induction step follows from the following lemma, where we also introduce the *cascade product* of two automata:

Lemma 5.72 (Aperiodicity of Cascade Product). *Given semiautomata* $\mathfrak{A} = (\Sigma, \mathcal{S}^\mathfrak{A}, \mathcal{I}^\mathfrak{A}, \mathcal{R}^\mathfrak{A})$ *and* $\mathcal{B} = (\Sigma \times \mathcal{S}^\mathfrak{A}, \mathcal{S}^\mathfrak{B}, \mathcal{I}^\mathfrak{B}, \mathcal{R}^\mathfrak{B})$*, whose transition monoids* $\mathsf{TM}(\mathfrak{A})$ *and* $\mathsf{TM}(\mathfrak{B})$ *are aperiodic. Then, the transition monoid* $\mathsf{TM}(\mathfrak{C})$ *of any*[5] *semiautomaton* $\mathfrak{C} := (\Sigma, \mathcal{S}^\mathfrak{A} \times \mathcal{S}^\mathfrak{B}, \mathcal{I}^\mathfrak{C}, \mathcal{R}^\mathfrak{C})$ *with* $\mathcal{R}^\mathfrak{C}$ *defined as below (called the cascade product of* $\mathfrak{A}$ *and* $\mathfrak{B}$*) is also aperiodic:*

$$((s_1, s_2), \sigma, (s_1', s_2')) \in \mathcal{R}^\mathfrak{C} :\Leftrightarrow (s_1, \sigma, s_1') \in \mathcal{R}^\mathfrak{A} \wedge (s_2, (\sigma, s_1), s_2') \in \mathcal{R}^\mathfrak{B}$$

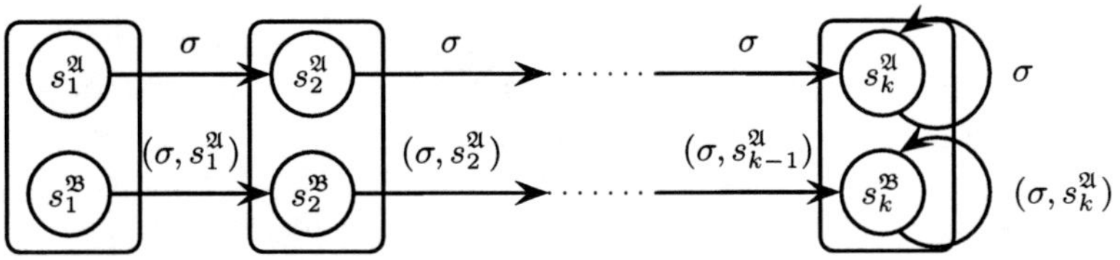

Fig. 5.19. A path through the cascade product of two automata $\mathfrak{A}$ and $\mathfrak{B}$

Proof. For the proof, we consider what happens when we repeatedly read a letter $\sigma \in \Sigma$ in the cascade product $\mathfrak{C}$. The corresponding run is given in Figure 5.19. As $\mathsf{TM}(\mathfrak{A})$ is aperiodic, there is a number n such that $\mathcal{R}_{\sigma^n}^{\mathfrak{A}} = \mathcal{R}_{\sigma^{n+1}}^{\mathfrak{A}}$ holds. Hence, after having read n times σ, we end in a self-loop in the semiautomaton $\mathfrak{A}$. Up to this point, we have read different letters $(\sigma, s_1^{\mathfrak{A}})$, $(\sigma, s_2^{\mathfrak{A}})$, ...in the semiautomaton $\mathfrak{B}$, but after this point, we only read $(\sigma, s_n^{\mathfrak{A}})$, since $\mathfrak{A}$ is now caught in a self-loop. As $\mathsf{TM}(\mathfrak{B})$ is also aperiodic, it follows that after some further transitions, also $\mathfrak{B}$ must be caught in a self-loop, so that it follows that $\mathsf{TM}(\mathfrak{C})$ is also aperiodic. □

We can moreover apply the above lemma to the $\mathsf{NDet}_{\mathsf{Streett}}$ automata that are obtained by our translations of LTL_p by function Streett of Figure 5.11 on page 342 and function TopProp of Figure 5.12 on page 347. *Indeed, the automata that are constructed by these procedures are cascade products of automata with only two states (every temporal operator of the formula corresponds with such a two-state automaton.* This decomposition is closely related with the decomposition stated by the Krohn-Rhodes decomposition theorem [151, 209, 309, 475].

We can therefore conclude that we can translate every $\varphi \in \mathsf{LTL}_p$ to an equivalent ω-automaton $\mathfrak{A}_\varphi$ whose transition monoid $\mathsf{TM}(\mathfrak{A})$ is aperiodic. Hence, it follows by Theorem 4.58 on page 259 that the syntactic monoids of the languages $L_{s,s'}$ for every pair (s, s') are aperiodic.

In the following, regular languages with aperiodic syntactic monoid are called 'star-free'. This notion is due to the further characterization that these languages can be described with star-free regular expressions. Hence, we obtain the following result for the regular languages $\mathsf{ESat}(\varphi)$:

Theorem 5.73 (LTL_p and Noncounting Automata). *For every formula φ of the past fragment of LTL_p, the syntactic monoid $\mathsf{SM}(\mathsf{ESat}(\varphi))$ of the language $\mathsf{ESat}(\varphi)$ is aperiodic. In particular, the automata constructed by function* Streett *of Figure 5.11 on page 342 and function* TopProp *of Figure 5.12 on page 347 are noncounting.*

The above theorem establishes one part of the relationship between noncounting automata and temporal logic. The other part is more complicated: We have to show that for a noncounting automaton $\mathfrak{A}$ the languages $L_{s,s'}$ can be described by pure past temporal logic formulas $\varphi_{s,s'}$ such that $L_{s,s'} =$

[5] We have the choice for $\mathcal{I}^{\mathfrak{C}}$.

$\mathsf{ESat}(\varphi_{s,s'})$ holds. To this end, we first note that we have the following relationship between the languages $L_{s,s'}$ and the classes of the transition monoid (note that the union is a finite one):

$$L_{s,s'} := \bigcup_{(s,s')\in\mathcal{R}_\alpha} [\alpha]_{\equiv_{\mathfrak{A}}}$$

Hence, it is obviously enough to characterize the finitely many classes $[\alpha]_{\equiv_{\mathfrak{A}}}$ by pure past formulas, i.e., to define pure past formulas φ_α such that $[\alpha]_{\equiv_{\mathfrak{A}}} = \mathsf{ESat}(\varphi_\alpha)$ holds. This is shown in the following theorem, whose proof has been taken from [512]:

Theorem 5.74 (Translating Noncounting Automata to LTL_p). *If a deterministic and complete semiautomaton $\mathfrak{A} = (\Sigma, \mathcal{S}, \mathcal{I}, \mathcal{R})$ is noncounting, then every class $[\alpha]_{\equiv_{\mathfrak{A}}}$ of its transition monoid can be characterized by a pure past temporal logic formula φ_α, i.e., φ_α satisfies the equation $[\alpha]_{\equiv_{\mathfrak{A}}} = \mathsf{ESat}(\varphi_\alpha)$.*

Proof. Given a deterministic and complete semiautomaton $\mathfrak{A} = (\Sigma, \mathcal{S}, \mathcal{I}, \mathcal{R})$ that is noncounting, we will construct a temporal logic formula φ_α to describe $[\alpha]_{\equiv_{\mathfrak{A}}}$. To simplify the notation, we use the letters of the alphabet Σ as atomic propositions of the temporal logic. The correct form would require that Σ is the powerset of the variables of the temporal logic, and that a letter ϑ is translated to $\mathsf{minterm}_{V_\Sigma}(\vartheta)$.

The following proof is done by a well-founded induction over all deterministic complete noncounting semiautomata. For this purpose, we define the following binary relation on semiautomata:

$$\begin{array}{l}(\Sigma^{\mathfrak{A}}, \mathcal{S}^{\mathfrak{A}}, \mathcal{I}^{\mathfrak{A}}, \mathcal{R}^{\mathfrak{A}}) \preceq (\Sigma^{\mathfrak{B}}, \mathcal{S}^{\mathfrak{B}}, \mathcal{I}^{\mathfrak{B}}, \mathcal{R}^{\mathfrak{B}}) \\ \quad :\Leftrightarrow \left|\mathcal{S}^{\mathfrak{A}}\right| < \left|\mathcal{S}^{\mathfrak{B}}\right| \vee \left|\mathcal{S}^{\mathfrak{A}}\right| = \left|\mathcal{S}^{\mathfrak{B}}\right| \wedge \left|\Sigma^{\mathfrak{A}}\right| \leq \left|\Sigma^{\mathfrak{B}}\right|\end{array}$$

It is easily seen that $\preceq$ is reflexive and transitive, and will be antisymmetric when we identify semiautomata with the same number of states and inputs. Furthermore, there is then a least semiautomaton (up to isomorphism) that has only one state and one input letter. Hence, $\preceq$ is a well-founded ordering that can be used for a well-founded induction. In the induction base, we consider a semiautomaton $\mathfrak{A} = (\Sigma, \mathcal{S}, \mathcal{I}, \mathcal{R})$ with $|\mathcal{S}| = |\Sigma| = 1$. This is trivial: if $\Sigma = \{\sigma\}$, then define $\varphi_\alpha := \overleftarrow{\mathsf{G}}\sigma$.

For the induction step, we consider two cases: in the first case, assume that there is no $\sigma \in \Sigma$ such that $\mathsf{suc}_{\exists}^{\mathcal{R}_\sigma}(\mathcal{S}) \subsetneq \mathcal{S}$. Hence, for all $\sigma \in \Sigma$, we have $\mathsf{suc}_{\exists}^{\mathcal{R}_\sigma}(\mathcal{S}) = \mathcal{S}$, which implies due to the noncounting property (cf. Theorem 4.63 on page 263) that $\mathsf{suc}_{\exists}^{\mathcal{R}_\sigma}(\{s\}) = \{s\}$ holds. Hence, all transitions under all input letters $\sigma \in \Sigma$ are self-loops, and hence we have for each word $\alpha \in \Sigma^*$ the equation $[\alpha]_{\equiv_{\mathfrak{A}}} = \Sigma^*$. The language Σ^* is characterized by the formula $\overleftarrow{\mathsf{G}} \bigvee_{\sigma\in\Sigma} \sigma$.

The remaining case of the induction step is more difficult. Here, we have at least one input $\sigma \in \Sigma$ where $\mathsf{suc}_{\exists}^{\mathcal{R}_\sigma}(\mathcal{S}) \subsetneq \mathcal{S}$. This means, there is at least one state $s \in \mathcal{S}$ that can not be reached from any other state by reading σ. We use this input letter to construct other automata with either fewer states or the same states, but fewer inputs. To this end, it will be convenient to abbreviate $\Sigma_\sigma := \Sigma \setminus \{\sigma\}$ and $\mathcal{S}_\sigma := \mathsf{suc}_\exists^{\mathcal{R}_\sigma}(\mathcal{S})$. Using this, we define two further semiautomata (we ignore the initial sets since they do not matter):

- $\mathfrak{B} := (\Sigma_\sigma, \mathcal{S}, \{(s, a, s') \in \mathcal{R} \mid a \in \Sigma_\sigma\})$
- $\mathfrak{C} := (\Sigma^{\mathfrak{C}}, \mathcal{S}_\sigma, \mathcal{R}^{\mathfrak{C}})$ with input alphabet $\Sigma^{\mathfrak{C}} := \{[\gamma\sigma]_{\equiv_{\mathfrak{A}}} \mid \gamma \in \Sigma_\sigma^*\}$ and transition relation $(s, [\gamma\sigma]_{\equiv_{\mathfrak{A}}}, s') \in \mathcal{R}^{\mathfrak{C}} :\Leftrightarrow (s, s') \in \mathcal{R}_{\gamma\sigma}^{\mathfrak{A}}$

The semiautomata $\mathfrak{B}$ and $\mathfrak{C}$ are used in the following to construct the formula φ_α. Note that the input letters of $\mathfrak{C}$ are classes $[\gamma\sigma]_{\equiv_{\mathfrak{A}}}$ with $\gamma \in \Sigma_\sigma^*$, i.e., classes of words on Σ that end with the letter σ. Hence, we have to consider finite words of these classes for $\mathfrak{C}$, i.e., words $[\gamma_1\sigma]_{\equiv_{\mathfrak{A}}} [\gamma_2\sigma]_{\equiv_{\mathfrak{A}}} \ldots [\gamma_n\sigma]_{\equiv_{\mathfrak{A}}}$ with $\gamma_i \in \Sigma_\sigma^*$. We first list some facts of these semiautomata that obviously hold:

Fact 1: $\mathfrak{B} \preceq \mathfrak{A}$ and $\mathfrak{C} \preceq \mathfrak{A}$, and both $\mathfrak{B}$ and $\mathfrak{C}$ are deterministic, complete and noncounting, so that the induction hypothesis can be applied both to $\mathfrak{B}$ and $\mathfrak{C}$. Therefore, we can find by the induction hypothesis for all classes $[\beta]_{\equiv_{\mathfrak{B}}}$ and $[\gamma\sigma]_{\equiv_{\mathfrak{C}}}$, characterizing formulas φ_β and $\varphi_{\gamma\sigma}$.

Fact 2: for every word $\alpha \in \Sigma_\sigma^*$, we have $[\alpha]_{\equiv_{\mathfrak{A}}} \cap \Sigma_\sigma^* = [\equiv_\alpha]_{\mathfrak{B}}$

Fact 3: for every word $\gamma_1\sigma\gamma_2\sigma\ldots\gamma_n\sigma$ with $\gamma_i \in \Sigma_\sigma^*$, we have $\mathcal{R}_{\gamma_1\sigma\ldots\gamma_n\sigma}^{\mathfrak{A}} = \mathcal{R}_{[\gamma_1\sigma]_{\equiv_{\mathfrak{A}}}\ldots[\gamma_n\sigma]_{\equiv_{\mathfrak{A}}}}^{\mathfrak{C}}$

Fact 4: for all words $\gamma_1, \ldots, \gamma_n \in \Sigma_\sigma^*$, we have the following:

$$
\begin{aligned}
&\left[[\gamma_1\sigma]_{\equiv_{\mathfrak{A}}} \ldots [\gamma_n\sigma]_{\equiv_{\mathfrak{A}}}\right]_{\mathfrak{C}} \\
&= \{[\delta_1\sigma]_{\equiv_{\mathfrak{A}}} \ldots [\delta_n\sigma]_{\equiv_{\mathfrak{A}}} \mid [\gamma_1\sigma]_{\equiv_{\mathfrak{A}}} \ldots [\gamma_n\sigma]_{\equiv_{\mathfrak{A}}} \equiv_{\mathfrak{C}} [\delta_1\sigma]_{\equiv_{\mathfrak{A}}} \ldots [\delta_n\sigma]_{\equiv_{\mathfrak{A}}}\} \\
&= \{[\delta_1\sigma]_{\equiv_{\mathfrak{A}}} \ldots [\delta_n\sigma]_{\equiv_{\mathfrak{A}}} \mid \mathcal{R}^{\mathfrak{C}}_{[\gamma_1\sigma]_{\equiv_{\mathfrak{A}}}\ldots[\gamma_n\sigma]_{\equiv_{\mathfrak{A}}}} = \mathcal{R}^{\mathfrak{C}}_{[\delta_1\sigma]_{\equiv_{\mathfrak{A}}}\ldots[\delta_n\sigma]_{\equiv_{\mathfrak{A}}}}\} \\
&= \{[\delta_1\sigma]_{\equiv_{\mathfrak{A}}} \ldots [\delta_n\sigma]_{\equiv_{\mathfrak{A}}} \mid \mathcal{R}^{\mathfrak{A}}_{\gamma_1\sigma\ldots\gamma_n\sigma} = \mathcal{R}^{\mathfrak{A}}_{\delta_1\sigma\ldots\delta_n\sigma}\} \\
&= \{[\delta_1\sigma]_{\equiv_{\mathfrak{A}}} \ldots [\delta_n\sigma]_{\equiv_{\mathfrak{A}}} \mid [\gamma_1\sigma \ldots \gamma_n\sigma]_{\equiv_{\mathfrak{A}}} = [\delta_1\sigma \ldots \delta_n\sigma]_{\equiv_{\mathfrak{A}}}\} \\
&= \{[\delta_1\sigma \ldots \delta_n\sigma]_{\equiv_{\mathfrak{A}}} \mid [\gamma_1\sigma \ldots \gamma_n\sigma]_{\equiv_{\mathfrak{A}}} = [\delta_1\sigma \ldots \delta_n\sigma]_{\equiv_{\mathfrak{A}}}\} \\
&= \{[\gamma_1\sigma \ldots \gamma_n\sigma]_{\equiv_{\mathfrak{A}}}\}
\end{aligned}
$$

We next consider a particular language $[\alpha]_{\equiv_{\mathfrak{A}}}$ and partition it into the set of words with none, one, or more than one occurrences of the letter $\sigma \in \Sigma$:

$$
[\alpha]_{\equiv_{\mathfrak{A}}} = \underbrace{\left([\alpha]_{\equiv_{\mathfrak{A}}} \cap \Sigma_\sigma^*\right)}_{L_0} \cup \underbrace{\left([\alpha]_{\equiv_{\mathfrak{A}}} \cap \Sigma_\sigma^*\sigma\Sigma_\sigma^*\right)}_{L_1} \cup \underbrace{\left([\alpha]_{\equiv_{\mathfrak{A}}} \cap \Sigma_\sigma^*\sigma\Sigma^*\sigma\Sigma_\sigma^*\right)}_{L_{>1}}
$$

Now, note the following:

- $L_0 := [\alpha]_{\equiv_{\mathfrak{A}}} \cap \Sigma_\sigma^*$ is the set of words of $[\alpha]_{\equiv_{\mathfrak{A}}}$ that do not contain the letter σ. As by fact 2, $[\alpha]_{\equiv_{\mathfrak{A}}} \cap \Sigma_\sigma^* = [\alpha]_{\equiv_{\mathfrak{B}}}$ holds, we can characterize this language by a pure past formula according to the induction hypothesis for $\mathfrak{B}$.

- $L_1 := [\alpha]_{\equiv_{\mathfrak{A}}} \cap \Sigma_\sigma^* \sigma \Sigma_\sigma^*$ is the set of words of $[\alpha]_{\equiv_{\mathfrak{A}}}$ that contain exactly one occurrence of the letter σ. Hence, we have $[\alpha]_{\equiv_{\mathfrak{A}}} \cap \Sigma_\sigma^* \sigma \Sigma_\sigma^* = \{\gamma\sigma\gamma' \mid \gamma, \gamma' \in \Sigma_\sigma^* \wedge \gamma\sigma\gamma' \equiv_{\mathfrak{A}} \alpha\}$. We can transform this infinite description of L_1 into a finite one by showing that L_1 is the following *finite* union:

$$[\alpha]_{\equiv_{\mathfrak{A}}} \cap \Sigma_\sigma^* \sigma \Sigma_\sigma^* = \bigcup_{\substack{\gamma, \gamma' \in \Sigma_\sigma^*, \\ \gamma\sigma\gamma' \equiv_{\mathfrak{A}} \alpha}} [\gamma]_{\equiv_{\mathfrak{B}}} \sigma \Sigma_\sigma^* \cap \Sigma_\sigma^* \sigma [\gamma']_{\equiv_{\mathfrak{B}}}$$

  For the proof, simply consider the two inclusions $\subseteq$ and $\supseteq$: Given that $\gamma\sigma\gamma' \in L_1$ with $\gamma, \gamma' \in \Sigma_\sigma^*$ and $\gamma\sigma\gamma' \equiv_{\mathfrak{A}} \alpha$, then $\gamma\sigma\gamma'$ also belongs the the set on the right hand side. In particular, $\gamma\sigma\gamma'$ belongs to $[\gamma]_{\equiv_{\mathfrak{B}}} \sigma \Sigma_\sigma^*$ and also to $\Sigma_\sigma^* \sigma [\gamma']_{\equiv_{\mathfrak{B}}}$. For the converse, consider a word that belongs to the set on the right hand side. It is obviously of the form $\gamma\sigma\gamma'$ with $\gamma, \gamma' \in \Sigma_\sigma^*$ and $\gamma\sigma\gamma' \equiv_{\mathfrak{A}} \alpha$ and therefore belongs to L_1.
  By the induction hypothesis, we already have formulas $\Psi_\gamma^{\mathfrak{B}}$ and $\Psi_{\gamma'}^{\mathfrak{B}}$ that characterize the languages $[\gamma]_{\equiv_{\mathfrak{B}}}$ and $[\gamma']_{\equiv_{\mathfrak{B}}}$, respectively. Hence, it is not too complicated to construct a characterizing formula for L_1 in that we construct characterizing formulas for $[\gamma]_{\equiv_{\mathfrak{B}}} \sigma \Sigma_\sigma^*$ and $\Sigma_\sigma^* \sigma [\gamma']_{\equiv_{\mathfrak{B}}}$ (see [512] for the formulas).
- $L_{>1} := [\alpha]_{\equiv_{\mathfrak{A}}} \cap \Sigma_\sigma^* \sigma \Sigma^* \sigma \Sigma_\sigma^*$ is the set of words of $[\alpha]_{\equiv_{\mathfrak{A}}}$ that contain at least two occurrences of the letter σ. These words are of the form $\beta\sigma\gamma\beta'$ with $\beta, \beta' \in \Sigma_\sigma^*$ and a word γ ending with the letter σ. By fact 4 that we mentioned before, we have already seen that for words $\gamma \in \Sigma^*\sigma$, we have $\left[[\gamma]_{\equiv_{\mathfrak{A}}}\right]_{\equiv_{\mathfrak{C}}} = \{[\gamma]_{\equiv_{\mathfrak{A}}}\}$. The classes of $\mathsf{TM}(\mathfrak{C})$ are therefore singleton sets that consist of those classes $[\gamma]_{\equiv_{\mathfrak{A}}}$ of $\mathsf{TM}(\mathfrak{A})$, where the word γ ends with the letter σ. If we therefore define the mapping $\hbar$ such that $\hbar(\left[[\gamma]_{\equiv_{\mathfrak{A}}}\right]_{\equiv_{\mathfrak{C}}}) := [\gamma]_{\equiv_{\mathfrak{A}}}$ holds, then we have $[\beta\sigma\gamma\beta']_{\equiv_{\mathfrak{A}}} = [\beta]_{\equiv_{\mathfrak{A}}} [\sigma]_{\equiv_{\mathfrak{A}}} [\gamma]_{\equiv_{\mathfrak{A}}} [\beta']_{\equiv_{\mathfrak{A}}} = [\beta]_{\equiv_{\mathfrak{A}}} [\sigma]_{\equiv_{\mathfrak{A}}} \hbar(\left[[\gamma]_{\equiv_{\mathfrak{A}}}\right]_{\equiv_{\mathfrak{C}}}) [\beta']_{\equiv_{\mathfrak{A}}}$, and therefore:

$$[\alpha]_{\equiv_{\mathfrak{A}}} \cap \Sigma_\sigma^* \sigma \Sigma^* \sigma \Sigma_\sigma^* = \bigcup_{\substack{\beta, \beta' \in \Sigma_b^*, \\ \gamma \in \Sigma^*\sigma, \\ \beta\sigma\gamma\beta' \equiv_{\mathfrak{A}} \alpha}} [\beta]_{\equiv_{\mathfrak{B}}} \sigma \Sigma^* \cap \Sigma_\sigma^* \sigma \hbar(\left[[\gamma]_{\equiv_{\mathfrak{A}}}\right]_{\equiv_{\mathfrak{C}}}) \Sigma_\sigma^* \cap \Sigma^* \sigma [\beta']_{\equiv_{\mathfrak{B}}}$$

  The proof of the above equation is again simply obtained by considering the two set inclusions of the sets on the left hand side and on the right hand side. Note that the union is again finite since $\mathsf{TM}(\mathfrak{B})$ and $\mathsf{TM}(\mathfrak{C})$ are finite monoids. It now follows by induction hypothesis that we can find characterizing pure past formulas to characterize all the classes $[\beta]_{\equiv_{\mathfrak{B}}}$ and $\left[[\gamma]_{\equiv_{\mathfrak{A}}}\right]_{\equiv_{\mathfrak{C}}}$ of the monoids $\mathsf{TM}(\mathfrak{B})$ and $\mathsf{TM}(\mathfrak{C})$. It is then again not too difficult to construct characterizing formulas for $[\beta]_{\equiv_{\mathfrak{B}}} \sigma \Sigma^*$, $\Sigma^* \sigma [\beta']_{\equiv_{\mathfrak{B}}}$, and $\Sigma_\sigma^* \sigma \hbar(\left[[\gamma]_{\equiv_{\mathfrak{A}}}\right]_{\equiv_{\mathfrak{C}}}) \Sigma_\sigma^*$ (see [512] for these formulas).

□

The above two theorems establish therefore the close relationship between temporal logic and noncounting automata. The above proof is a variant of Schützenberger's proof that avoids, however, group theory. An indirect translation from noncounting automata to $\mathsf{MFO}_<$ and then to temporal logic is even simpler. The reader may rework the above proof for a translation to $\mathsf{MFO}_<$. The final translation from $\mathsf{MFO}_<$ to temporal logic is shown in the next chapter.

Theorem 5.75 (LTL_p and Noncounting Automata). *For every regular language $L \subseteq \Sigma^*$, the following is equivalent:*

- *there is a pure past formula φ with $L = \mathsf{ESat}(\varphi)$*
- *there is a temporally defined automaton that accepts L*
- *there is a noncounting automaton that accepts L*
- *$\mathsf{SM}(L)$ is aperiodic*

Note however, that there are counting automata that are nevertheless equivalent to LTL_p formulas, but then there are equivalent noncounting automata. For example, consider the automaton given in Figure 5.20. It is easily seen that its transition monoid is aperiodic with period 2. Nevertheless, the set of words that have a run through the automaton is $\mathsf{ESat}(\overleftarrow{\mathsf{G}}\,\varphi)$.

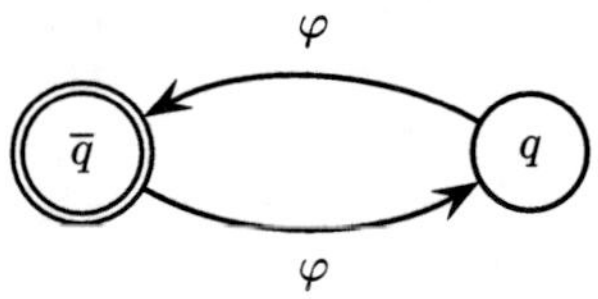

Fig. 5.20. A counting NDet_G automaton that is equivalent to $\mathsf{G}\varphi$

Beneath the above characterizations of the languages whose syntactic monoid is aperiodic, a variety of different other characterizations has been found in the past. It is beyond the scope of this book to give complete proofs for all of these characterizations, but we will prove a further one in the next chapter, namely the relationship with the monadic first order theory of linear order $\mathsf{MFO}_<$. Other characterizations are listed in the following theorem without proof:

Theorem 5.76 (Characterization of Temporal Logic on Finite Words). *For every regular language $L \subseteq \Sigma^*$, the following properties are equivalent:*

(1) there is a pure past formula Φ with $L = \mathsf{ESat}(\Phi)$
(2) there is a temporally defined automaton that accepts L
(3) there is a noncounting automaton that accepts L
(4) there is a star-free regular expression that describes L
(5) there is a $n > 0$ such that for all $\alpha, \beta, \gamma \in \Sigma^*$, $\alpha\beta^n\gamma \in L$ iff $\alpha\beta^{n+1}\gamma \in L$
(6) there is a $\mathsf{MFO}_<$ formula that describes L

We have already proved the equivalences (1)=(2) and (1)=(3). Equivalences (3)=(4)=(6) are due to McNaughton and Papert [364], and a revised proof of the equivalence between (4) and (6) has been published by Perrin and Pin in [403]. Equivalence (1)=(6) is due to Kamp [274] and Gabbay, Pnueli, Shelah and Stavi [203]. The equivalence between (2) and (3) is also proved in Zuck [326, 527], a further proof sketch can also be found in [351, 352]. Further direct translation from noncounting automata to temporal logic can be found in [120, 341, 342, 511]. The equivalence between (4) and (5) is known as Schützenberger's theorem [402, 444, 445].

A completely different approach to prove Schützenberger's result is obtained by the Krohn-Rhodes decomposition theorem which is beyond the scope of this book The interested reader may consult [151, 209, 309, 341, 342, 475]. We can however prove the following corollary of the Krohn-Rhodes theorem:

Theorem 5.77 (Krohn-Rhodes Decomposition). *Let $\mathfrak{A}$ be an acceptor such that $\mathsf{SM}(\mathsf{Lang}(\mathfrak{A}))$ is aperiodic. Then there are automata $\mathfrak{A}_1, \ldots, \mathfrak{A}_n$ with $\mathfrak{A}_i = (\Sigma, \{s_1^i, s_2^i\}, \mathcal{I}^i, \mathcal{R}^i)$ such that $\mathfrak{A}$ is equivalent to the cascade product of these automata. Furthermore, the transitions $\mathcal{R}_\sigma^i$ of any letter σ fall into one of the two following categories:*

- *Reset Inputs: There is a state s_j^i in $\mathfrak{A}_i$ such that $\mathsf{suc}_\exists^{\mathcal{R}_\sigma}(\{s_1^i, s_2^i\}) = \{s_j^i\}$.*
- *Identity Inputs: $\mathsf{suc}_\exists^{\mathcal{R}_\sigma}(\{s_1^i\}) = \{s_1^i\}$ and $\mathsf{suc}_\exists^{\mathcal{R}_\sigma}(\{s_2^i\}) = \{s_2^i\}$*

Due to our previous results, the proof is remarkably simple: We translate the automaton $\mathfrak{A}$ to a pure past formula $\varphi_\mathfrak{A}$ and use our translation procedure TopProp to translate $\varphi_\mathfrak{A}$ back to an automaton. We have already seen that this automaton is a cascade product of simple automata having two states. Inspecting the automata used in Theorem 5.38 and Theorem 5.39 shows that all their inputs are either resets or identities.

5.5.2 Completeness of the Borel Classes

In the previous section, we have developed translations that allowed us to translate the temporal logics TL_κ to the corresponding automaton classes Det_κ. In the previous subsection, we have moreover seen that the converse is not possible, since each class Det_κ contains counting automata that can not be translated to LTL_p, and hence neither to TL_κ. However, we can now consider the *subsets* TDet_κ *of* Det_κ *that consists of the noncounting automata.* Equivalently, we can characterize TDet_κ *as the set of temporally defined* Det_κ *automata.*

We now prove the completeness of the temporal logics TL_κ, which means that we have to show that we can translate every TDet_κ automaton to an equivalent TL_κ formula.

Theorem 5.78. *For any class $\kappa \in \{\mathsf{G}, \mathsf{F}, \mathsf{Prefix}, \mathsf{GF}, \mathsf{FG}, \mathsf{Streett}\}$, we have $\mathsf{TDet}_\kappa \approx \mathsf{TL}_\kappa$. Moreover, we have $\mathsf{LTL}_p \approx \mathsf{TL}_{\mathsf{Streett}}$.*

Proof. The direction $\mathsf{TL}_\kappa \precsim \mathsf{TDet}_\kappa$ has already been proved, so that it remains to prove $\mathsf{TDet}_\kappa \precsim \mathsf{TL}_\kappa$ here. Given a TDet_κ automaton $\mathfrak{A}$, we show how an equivalent formula $\Phi_\mathfrak{A} \in \mathsf{TL}_\kappa$ can be constructed. For example, consider the case $\kappa = \mathsf{FG}$ (all other cases are proved in an analogous manner). Hence, we have $\mathfrak{A} = \mathcal{A}_\exists(Q, \Phi_\mathcal{I}, \Phi_\mathcal{R}, \mathsf{FG}\Phi_\mathcal{F})$ where we can assume that $\Phi_\mathcal{I}$ and $\Phi_\mathcal{F}$ are propositional formulas over Q. Hence, these formulas encode subsets of states $Q_\mathcal{I} \subseteq 2^Q$ and $Q_\mathcal{F} \subseteq 2^Q$.

As $\mathfrak{A}$ is temporally defined, it follows that for all $\iota, \vartheta \subseteq Q$ there is a pure past formula $\varphi_{\iota,\vartheta}$ such that $L_{\iota,\vartheta} = \mathsf{ESat}(\varphi_{\iota,\vartheta})$ holds. We define

$$\Phi_\mathfrak{A} := \mathsf{FG} \bigvee_{\iota \in Q_\mathcal{I}, \vartheta \in Q_\mathcal{F}} \varphi_{\iota,\vartheta}$$

It is obvious that $\Phi_\mathfrak{A}$ and $\mathfrak{A}$ are equivalent, i.e., for any structure $\mathcal{K}$ and any path π through $\mathcal{K}$, we have $(\mathcal{K}, \pi) \models \mathfrak{A} \leftrightarrow \Phi_\mathfrak{A}$.

In the same manner, we construct formulas of the form $\mathsf{G}\psi$, $\mathsf{F}\psi$, $\mathsf{FG}\psi$, $\mathsf{GF}\psi$, $\bigwedge_{i=1}^f \mathsf{G}\varphi \vee \mathsf{F}\psi$, and $\bigwedge_{i=1}^f \mathsf{GF}\varphi \vee \mathsf{FG}\psi$ to construct TL_κ formulas of given TDet_κ automata for all mentioned classes κ.

The equal expressiveness $\mathsf{LTL}_p \approx \mathsf{TL}_\mathsf{Streett}$ follows from the fact that we can translate every LTL_p formula via our translation TopProp on page 347 to an equivalent noncounting $\mathsf{NDet}_\mathsf{Streett}$ automaton. The rest follows by the translation to $\mathsf{TL}_\mathsf{Streett}$ as indicated above. □

The above theorem allows us furthermore to prove the strictness of the expressivenesses of the TL_κ logics, since we can now transfer these results from the corresponding results of the automaton hierarchy to the logics TL_κ. In particular, we have the following theorem that establishes the analogon of the Borel hierarchy as a hierarchy of temporal logics:

Theorem 5.79 (Equal Expressiveness of TL_κ and TDet_κ). *For any $\kappa \in \{\mathsf{G}, \mathsf{F}, \mathsf{Prefix}, \mathsf{FG}, \mathsf{GF}, \mathsf{Streett}\}$, we have $\mathsf{TL}_\kappa \approx \mathsf{TDet}_\kappa$, and therefore the following hierarchy of these logics:*

$$\begin{array}{ccccccc}
\mathsf{TDet}_\mathsf{G} \approx \mathsf{TL}_\mathsf{G} & & & & \mathsf{TDet}_\mathsf{FG} \approx \mathsf{TL}_\mathsf{FG} & & \\
& \precnapprox & & \succnapprox & & \precnapprox & \\
& & \mathsf{TDet}_\mathsf{Prefix} \approx \mathsf{TL}_\mathsf{Prefix} & & & & \mathsf{TDet}_\mathsf{Streett} \approx \mathsf{TL}_\mathsf{Streett} \\
& \succnapprox & & \precnapprox & & \succnapprox & \approx \\
\mathsf{TDet}_\mathsf{F} \approx \mathsf{TL}_\mathsf{F} & & & & \mathsf{TDet}_\mathsf{GF} \approx \mathsf{TL}_\mathsf{GF} & & \mathsf{LTL}_p
\end{array}$$

Hence, the six classes TL_κ form the same hierarchy as the automata, and correspond with the Borel hierarchy. Considering the construction in the proof of Theorem 5.78 reveals that we only constructed TL_κ formulas of a very special form: The formulas that we constructed had the form of the acceptance condition of the corresponding automaton, where propositional formulas were replaced with pure past formulas.

It therefore follows that these formulas are also expressively complete w.r.t. TDet_κ, i.e., every formula in TDet_κ can be rewritten in such a restricted form. We therefore give the following definition which is due to Manna and Pnueli who were the first who investigated the temporal logic hierarchy in [350–352].

Definition 5.80 (Normal Forms for the Classes TL_κ). *Given that φ_i and ψ_i are pure past formulas for $i = 0, \ldots, n$, we define the classes of safety, liveness, obligation, persistence, fairness, and reactivity formulas as follows:*

name of normal form	*abbreviation*	*syntactic representation*
safety	NF_G	$\mathsf{G}\varphi_0$
guarantee	NF_F	$\mathsf{F}\varphi_0$
obligation	$\mathsf{NF}_\mathsf{Prefix}$	$\bigwedge_{i=0}^{n} \mathsf{G}\varphi_i \vee \mathsf{F}\varphi_i$
persistence	NF_FG	$\mathsf{FG}\varphi_0$
recurrence	NF_GF	$\mathsf{GF}\varphi_0$
reactivity	$\mathsf{NF}_\mathsf{Streett}$	$\bigwedge_{i=0}^{n} \mathsf{FG}\varphi_i \vee \mathsf{GF}\varphi_i$

It is easily seen that safety, guarantee, obligation, persistence, fairness, and reactivity formulas are syntactic subsets of TL_G, TL_F, $\mathsf{TL}_\mathsf{Prefix}$, TL_FG, TL_GF, and $\mathsf{TL}_\mathsf{Streett}$, respectively. The converse is obviously not true, since the logics TL_κ are syntactically much richer than the corresponding set NF_κ. By the proof of Theorem 5.78, we moreover have the following result:

Corollary 5.81. *For any class $\kappa \in \{\mathsf{G}, \mathsf{F}, \mathsf{Prefix}, \mathsf{GF}, \mathsf{FG}, \mathsf{Streett}\}$, we have $\mathsf{NF}_\kappa \approx \mathsf{TL}_\kappa$. In particular, we have $\mathsf{NF}_\mathsf{Streett} \approx \mathsf{LTL}_p$*

Due to the closures of the logics TL_κ, it follows that also all logics NF_κ must be closed under disjunction and conjunction. Moreover, $\mathsf{NF}_\mathsf{Streett}$ and $\mathsf{NF}_\mathsf{Prefix}$ must be closed under all Boolean operations. This can also be shown directly:

$$
\begin{array}{ll}
\mathsf{G}\varphi \wedge \mathsf{G}\psi = \mathsf{G}\,[\varphi \wedge \psi] & \mathsf{FG}\varphi \wedge \mathsf{FG}\psi = \mathsf{FG}\,[\varphi \wedge \psi] \\
\mathsf{G}\varphi \vee \mathsf{G}\psi = \mathsf{G}\left[\overleftarrow{\mathsf{G}}\varphi \vee \overleftarrow{\mathsf{G}}\psi\right] & \mathsf{FG}\varphi \vee \mathsf{FG}\psi = \mathsf{FG}\left[\psi \vee \overleftarrow{\underline{\mathsf{X}}}[\varphi\ \overleftarrow{\underline{\mathsf{U}}}\ (\varphi \wedge \neg\psi)]\right] \\
\mathsf{F}\varphi \wedge \mathsf{F}\psi = \mathsf{F}\left[\overleftarrow{\mathsf{F}}\varphi \wedge \overleftarrow{\mathsf{F}}\psi\right] & \mathsf{GF}\varphi \wedge \mathsf{GF}\psi = \mathsf{GF}\left[\psi \wedge \overleftarrow{\underline{\mathsf{X}}}[(\neg\psi)\ \overleftarrow{\underline{\mathsf{U}}}\ \varphi]\right] \\
\mathsf{F}\varphi \vee \mathsf{F}\psi = \mathsf{F}\,[\varphi \vee \psi] & \mathsf{GF}\varphi \vee \mathsf{GF}\psi = \mathsf{GF}\,[\varphi \vee \psi]
\end{array}
$$

None of the classes of safety, guarantee, persistence, and fairness formulas are however closed under negation: The closure under negation would immediately imply that the some corresponding ω-automaton classes would coincide and therefore would contradict Theorem 4.33.

Finally, consider now what happens if a NF_κ formula is translated by TopProp to an equivalent ω-automaton: as the formulas mainly consist of pure past temporal logic subformulas, the rules of Theorem 5.38 are sufficient for the translation. These rules, replace the pure past temporal logic subformulas by propositional ones and therefore introduce new state variables that correspond with the elementary subformulas of the given formula. Hence, given a formula $\Phi \in \mathsf{NF}_\kappa$, we obtain a *deterministic* TDet_κ-automaton. Hence, the formulas NF_κ can be viewed in some way as determinizations of TL_κ.

We conclude this section with related results on the characterization of the star-free ω-regular languages. These results are summarized as follows:

Theorem 5.82 (Characterization of Temporal Logic on Infinite Words). *For every ω-regular language $L \subseteq \Sigma^\omega$, the following properties are equivalent:*

(1) there is a LTL_p formula Φ whose models are the words in L
(2) there is a temporally defined Streett automaton that accepts L
(3) there is a noncounting Streett automaton that accepts L
(4) there are a star-free regular expressions $\alpha_1, \ldots, \alpha_n$ and $\beta_1, \ldots, \beta_n$ such that $L = \mathsf{Lang}(\sum_{i=1}^n \alpha_i \beta_i^\omega)$ and $\mathsf{Lang}(\beta_i\beta_i) \subseteq \mathsf{Lang}(\beta_i)$
(5) there are a star-free regular expressions $\alpha_1, \ldots, \alpha_n$ and $\beta_1, \ldots, \beta_n$ such that $L = \mathsf{Lang}(\sum_{i=1}^n \mathsf{Lim}(\alpha_i) \& \overline{\mathsf{Lim}(\beta_i)})$
(6) there are no words $\alpha, \beta, \gamma, \delta \in \Sigma^*$ such that for infinitely many n we have $\alpha\beta^n\gamma\delta^\omega \in L$ and also for infinitely many n we have $\alpha\beta^n\gamma\delta^\omega \notin L$
(7) there is a $\mathsf{MFO}_<$ formula that describes Φ

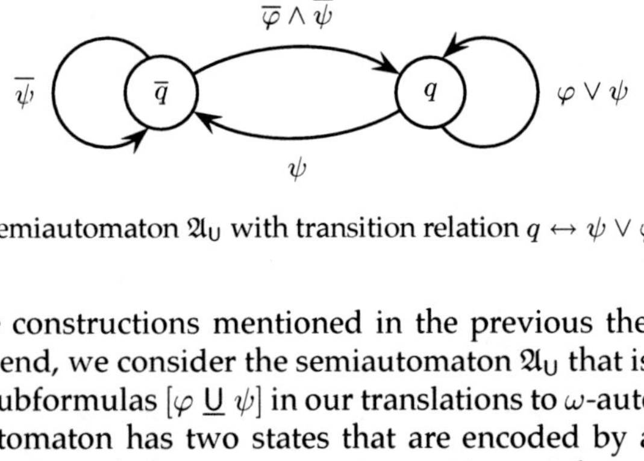

Fig. 5.21. Semiautomaton $\mathfrak{A}_\mathsf{U}$ with transition relation $q \leftrightarrow \psi \vee \varphi \wedge \mathsf{X}q$

We illustrate the constructions mentioned in the previous theorems by an example. To this end, we consider the semiautomaton $\mathfrak{A}_\mathsf{U}$ that is used for the abbreviation of subformulas $[\varphi \ \underline{\mathsf{U}}\ \psi]$ in our translations to ω-automata. Recall that this semiautomaton has two states that are encoded by a single state variable q. The transition relation is $q \leftrightarrow \psi \vee \varphi \wedge \mathsf{X}q$, and the state transition diagram is shown in Figure 5.21.

We first compute the transition monoid $\mathsf{TM}(\mathfrak{A}_\mathsf{U})$ of $\mathfrak{A}_\mathsf{U}$ and then characterize its classes with pure past LTL_p formulas. To this end, note first that we have to consider four inputs that constitute our alphabet Σ_U, namely $\overline{\varphi}\overline{\psi}$, $\overline{\varphi}\psi$, $\varphi\overline{\psi}$, and $\varphi\psi$, and therefore we obtain the following matrices:

$\mathcal{M}_{\overline{\varphi}\overline{\psi}} = \begin{pmatrix} 1\,1 \\ 0\,0 \end{pmatrix}$	$\mathcal{M}_{\overline{\varphi}\psi} = \begin{pmatrix} 0\,0 \\ 1\,1 \end{pmatrix}$	$\mathcal{M}_{\varphi\overline{\psi}} = \begin{pmatrix} 1\,0 \\ 0\,1 \end{pmatrix}$	$\mathcal{M}_{\varphi\psi} = \begin{pmatrix} 0\,0 \\ 1\,1 \end{pmatrix}$
$q = 0$	$q = 1$	$q = \mathsf{X}q$	$q = 1$

Computing their closure under matrix multiplications reveals that $\mathsf{TM}(\mathfrak{A}_\mathsf{U})$ consists of three matrices, and furthermore, we have the following operation table:

$\times$	$\mathcal{M}_{\varphi\overline{\psi}}$	$\mathcal{M}_{\overline{\varphi}\overline{\psi}}$	$\mathcal{M}_{\overline{\varphi}\psi}$
$\mathcal{M}_{\varphi\overline{\psi}}$	$\mathcal{M}_{\varphi\overline{\psi}}$	$\mathcal{M}_{\overline{\varphi}\overline{\psi}}$	$\mathcal{M}_{\overline{\varphi}\psi}$
$\mathcal{M}_{\overline{\varphi}\overline{\psi}}$	$\mathcal{M}_{\overline{\varphi}\overline{\psi}}$	$\mathcal{M}_{\overline{\varphi}\overline{\psi}}$	$\mathcal{M}_{\overline{\varphi}\overline{\psi}}$
$\mathcal{M}_{\overline{\varphi}\psi}$	$\mathcal{M}_{\overline{\varphi}\psi}$	$\mathcal{M}_{\overline{\varphi}\psi}$	$\mathcal{M}_{\overline{\varphi}\psi}$

We furthermore know by Theorem 4.54 of page 258 that the elements of $\mathsf{TM}(\mathfrak{A}_{\mathsf{U}})$ correspond with the classes $[\beta]_{\mathfrak{A}_{\mathsf{U}}}$ of the induced equivalence relation $\equiv_{\mathfrak{A}_{\mathsf{U}}}$ of $\mathfrak{A}_{\mathsf{U}}$. Hence, we have to characterize these three classes by pure past LTL_p formulas. This can be done by the algorithm indicated in the proof of Theorem 5.74, but it is not too hard to see that the following hold:

- $[\varphi\psi]_{\equiv_{\mathfrak{A}_{\mathsf{U}}}} = \{\alpha \in \Sigma_{\mathsf{U}}^* \mid \mathcal{M}_\alpha = \mathcal{M}_{\varphi\psi}\} = \mathsf{ESat}(\overleftarrow{\mathsf{F}}(\psi \wedge \overleftarrow{\mathsf{X}}\overleftarrow{\mathsf{G}}(\varphi \wedge \neg\psi)))$
- $[\overline{\varphi}\psi]_{\equiv_{\mathfrak{A}_{\mathsf{U}}}} = \{\alpha \in \Sigma_{\mathsf{U}}^* \mid \mathcal{M}_\alpha = \mathcal{M}_{\overline{\varphi}\psi}\} = [\varphi\psi]_{\equiv_{\mathfrak{A}_{\mathsf{U}}}}$
- $[\varphi\overline{\psi}]_{\equiv_{\mathfrak{A}_{\mathsf{U}}}} = \{\alpha \in \Sigma_{\mathsf{U}}^* \mid \mathcal{M}_\alpha = \mathcal{M}_{\varphi\overline{\psi}}\} = \mathsf{ESat}(\overleftarrow{\mathsf{G}}(\varphi \wedge \neg\psi))$
- $[\overline{\varphi}\overline{\psi}]_{\equiv_{\mathfrak{A}_{\mathsf{U}}}} = \{\alpha \in \Sigma_{\mathsf{U}}^* \mid \mathcal{M}_\alpha = \mathcal{M}_{\overline{\varphi}\overline{\psi}}\} = \mathsf{ESat}(\overleftarrow{\mathsf{F}}(\neg\varphi \wedge \neg\psi \wedge \overleftarrow{\mathsf{X}}\overleftarrow{\mathsf{G}}(\varphi \wedge \neg\psi)))$

Using these characterizations, we can now characterize the regular languages $L_{s,s'}$ by pure past formulas (recall that these languages are the unions of those classes $[\alpha]_{\equiv_{\mathfrak{A}}}$ with $(s,s') \in \mathcal{R}_\alpha$):

- $L_{\overline{q},\overline{q}} = [\varphi\overline{\psi}]_{\equiv_{\mathfrak{A}_{\mathsf{U}}}} \cup [\overline{\varphi}\overline{\psi}]_{\equiv_{\mathfrak{A}_{\mathsf{U}}}} = \mathsf{ESat}(\overleftarrow{\mathsf{G}}(\varphi\wedge\neg\psi)\vee\overleftarrow{\mathsf{F}}(\neg\varphi\wedge\neg\psi\wedge\overleftarrow{\mathsf{X}}\overleftarrow{\mathsf{G}}(\varphi\wedge\neg\psi)))$
- $L_{\overline{q},q} = [\overline{\varphi}\overline{\psi}]_{\equiv_{\mathfrak{A}_{\mathsf{U}}}} = \mathsf{ESat}(\overleftarrow{\mathsf{F}}(\neg\varphi \wedge \neg\psi \wedge \overleftarrow{\mathsf{X}}\overleftarrow{\mathsf{G}}(\varphi \wedge \neg\psi)))$
- $L_{q,\overline{q}} = [\psi]_{\equiv_{\mathfrak{A}_{\mathsf{U}}}} = \mathsf{ESat}(\overleftarrow{\mathsf{F}}(\psi \wedge \overleftarrow{\mathsf{X}}\overleftarrow{\mathsf{G}}(\varphi \wedge \neg\psi)))$
- $L_{q,q} = [\psi]_{\equiv_{\mathfrak{A}_{\mathsf{U}}}} \cup [\varphi\overline{\psi}]_{\equiv_{\mathfrak{A}_{\mathsf{U}}}} = \mathsf{ESat}(\overleftarrow{\mathsf{F}}(\psi \wedge \overleftarrow{\mathsf{X}}\overleftarrow{\mathsf{G}}(\varphi \wedge \neg\psi)) \vee \overleftarrow{\mathsf{G}}(\varphi \wedge \neg\psi))$

We obtain $[\varphi\ \mathsf{U}\ \psi] \leftrightarrow \mathcal{A}_\exists(\{q\}, q, q \leftrightarrow \psi \vee \varphi \wedge \mathsf{X}q, \mathsf{G}1)$ according to our translations. Hence, $[\varphi\ \mathsf{U}\ \psi]$ is satisfied by all 'words' that start in q, i.e., by $L_{q,\overline{q}} \cup L_{q,q}$ (which is $L_{q,q}$), and therefore we finally conclude:

$$[\varphi\ \mathsf{U}\ \psi] \leftrightarrow \mathsf{G}\left(\overleftarrow{\mathsf{F}}(\psi \wedge \overleftarrow{\mathsf{X}}\overleftarrow{\mathsf{G}}(\varphi \wedge \neg\psi)) \vee \overleftarrow{\mathsf{G}}(\varphi \wedge \neg\psi)\right)$$

In [342], Maler and Pnueli describe another translation from temporally defined automata to temporal logic that is however based on the Krohn-Rhodes decomposition theorem.

5.5.3 Completeness of the Future Fragments

In the following, we consider the question whether the past operators are really required in the logics TL_κ, i.e., we will answer the question of whether there is for any TL_κ formula an equivalent one where no past operator occurs. In fact, we will see that the past operators can be eliminated and we will present an algorithm for the elimination of the past operators. The key to this algorithm is the so-called separation property.

In general, a temporal logic has the separation property, iff for any formula Φ of that logic, there is an equivalent formula of the form $\bigwedge_{i=1}^{n} \varphi_i \vee \psi_i$ so that no future operator occurs in φ_i and no past operator occurs in ψ_i. Hence, the future and past operators are separated in the formulas φ_i and ψ_i, respectively. As any temporal logic formula where only past operators occur is initially equivalent to a propositional one, it follows that if a temporal logic has the separation property, then its future time fragment is expressively complete.

The separation property can often be used to reason about the completeness of a logic. For example, in [202] the following fact is proved: Given that a temporal logic contains the formula $\mathsf{F}(a \wedge \overleftarrow{\mathsf{X}}\,\overleftarrow{\mathsf{G}}\, b)$, then this logic can express the formula $[a\ \underline{\mathsf{U}}\ b]$, because of the following equivalence[6]: $[a\ \underline{\mathsf{U}}\ b] \leftrightarrow_i \mathsf{F}(a \wedge \overleftarrow{\mathsf{X}}\,\overleftarrow{\mathsf{G}}\, b)$. As F and G can not express U (see [274] and Theorem 5.3 on page 289), it follows that the temporal logic with the monadic temporal operators X, G, F, $\overleftarrow{\mathsf{X}}$, $\overleftarrow{\underline{\mathsf{X}}}$, $\overleftarrow{\mathsf{G}}$, and $\overleftarrow{\mathsf{F}}$ does not have the separation property.

We will now show that the logics TL_κ for any of the mentioned classes κ have the separation property. We will show this by proving a couple of separation theorems that eliminate a particular nesting of a future operator in a past operator, or conversely the nesting of a past operator in a future time temporal operator. We use these theorems to rewrite a given TL_κ formula so that finally a separated formula is obtained. The crucial observation is that for any of these separation theorems, the right hand side belongs to TL_κ iff the left hand side belongs to TL_κ. Hence, the rewrite procedure preserves membership in the logics TL_κ, which implies that TL_κ has the separation property.

We now present a complete list of the required separation theorems. To reduce the number of cases that must be considered, we assume that the given formula is in negation normal form and that only the temporal operators $\overleftarrow{\mathsf{X}}$, $\overleftarrow{\underline{\mathsf{X}}}$, $\overleftarrow{\underline{\mathsf{U}}}$, $\overleftarrow{\mathsf{B}}$, X, $\underline{\mathsf{U}}$, and B are used. We have already seen that this is possible. Then, the following laws are sufficient:

Lemma 5.83 (Separation Laws for X). *The following equations are valid and can be used for separation of the* X *operator:*

- $\mathsf{X}[\alpha \wedge \overleftarrow{\mathsf{X}}\beta] \leftrightarrow \beta \wedge \mathsf{X}\alpha$
- $\mathsf{X}[\alpha \wedge \overleftarrow{\underline{\mathsf{X}}}\beta] \leftrightarrow \beta \wedge \mathsf{X}\alpha$
- $\mathsf{X}[\alpha \wedge [\beta\ \overleftarrow{\underline{\mathsf{U}}}\ \gamma]] \leftrightarrow \mathsf{X}[\alpha \wedge \gamma] \vee [\beta\ \overleftarrow{\underline{\mathsf{U}}}\ \gamma] \wedge \mathsf{X}[\alpha \wedge \beta]$
- $\mathsf{X}[\alpha \wedge [\beta\ \overleftarrow{\mathsf{B}}\ \gamma]] \leftrightarrow \mathsf{X}[\alpha \wedge \beta \wedge \neg\gamma] \vee [\beta\ \overleftarrow{\mathsf{B}}\ \gamma] \wedge \mathsf{X}[\alpha \wedge \neg\gamma]$
- $\mathsf{X}[\alpha \vee \overleftarrow{\mathsf{X}}\beta] \leftrightarrow \beta \vee \mathsf{X}\alpha$
- $\mathsf{X}[\alpha \vee \overleftarrow{\underline{\mathsf{X}}}\beta] \leftrightarrow \beta \vee \mathsf{X}\alpha$
- $\mathsf{X}[\alpha \vee [\beta\ \overleftarrow{\underline{\mathsf{U}}}\ \gamma]] \leftrightarrow \mathsf{X}[\alpha \vee \gamma] \vee [\beta\ \overleftarrow{\underline{\mathsf{U}}}\ \gamma] \wedge \mathsf{X}\beta$
- $\mathsf{X}[\alpha \vee [\beta\ \overleftarrow{\mathsf{B}}\ \gamma]] \leftrightarrow \mathsf{X}[\alpha \vee \neg\gamma] \wedge \left([\beta\ \overleftarrow{\mathsf{B}}\ \gamma] \vee \mathsf{X}[\alpha \vee \beta]\right)$

[6] This equation does however only hold at the initial point of time.

Lemma 5.84 (Separation Laws for $\underline{\mathsf{U}}$). *The following equations are valid and can be used for separation of the $\underline{\mathsf{U}}$ operator:*

- $[(\alpha \wedge \beta)\ \underline{\mathsf{U}}\ \gamma] \leftrightarrow [\alpha\ \underline{\mathsf{U}}\ \gamma] \wedge [\beta\ \underline{\mathsf{U}}\ \gamma]$
- $[\alpha\ \underline{\mathsf{U}}\ (\beta \vee \gamma)] \leftrightarrow [\alpha\ \underline{\mathsf{U}}\ \beta] \vee [\alpha\ \underline{\mathsf{U}}\ \gamma]$
- $\left[\alpha\ \underline{\mathsf{U}}\ (\beta \wedge \overleftarrow{\mathsf{X}}\gamma)\right] \leftrightarrow \beta \wedge \overleftarrow{\mathsf{X}}\gamma \vee \alpha \wedge [(\mathsf{X}\alpha)\ \underline{\mathsf{U}}\ (\gamma \wedge \mathsf{X}\beta)]$
- $\left[\alpha\ \underline{\mathsf{U}}\ (\beta \wedge \overleftarrow{\underline{\mathsf{X}}}\gamma)\right] \leftrightarrow \beta \wedge \overleftarrow{\underline{\mathsf{X}}}\gamma \vee \alpha \wedge [(\mathsf{X}\alpha)\ \underline{\mathsf{U}}\ (\gamma \wedge \mathsf{X}\beta)]$
- $\left[\alpha\ \underline{\mathsf{U}}\ (\beta \wedge [\gamma\ \overleftarrow{\underline{\mathsf{U}}}\ \delta])\right] \leftrightarrow \left(\begin{array}{l} [\gamma\ \overleftarrow{\underline{\mathsf{U}}}\ \delta] \wedge [(\alpha \wedge \mathsf{X}\gamma)\ \underline{\mathsf{U}}\ \beta] \vee \\ [\alpha\ \underline{\mathsf{U}}\ (\delta \wedge [(\alpha \wedge \mathsf{X}\gamma)\ \underline{\mathsf{U}}\ \beta])] \end{array}\right)$
- $\left[\alpha\ \underline{\mathsf{U}}\ (\beta \wedge [\gamma\ \overleftarrow{\mathsf{B}}\ \delta])\right] \leftrightarrow \left(\begin{array}{l} [\gamma\ \overleftarrow{\mathsf{B}}\ \delta] \wedge [(\alpha \wedge \neg\mathsf{X}\delta)\ \underline{\mathsf{U}}\ \beta] \vee \\ [\alpha\ \underline{\mathsf{U}}\ (\gamma \wedge \neg\delta \wedge [(\alpha \wedge \neg\mathsf{X}\delta)\ \underline{\mathsf{U}}\ \beta])] \end{array}\right)$
- $\left[(\alpha \vee \overleftarrow{\mathsf{X}}\beta)\ \underline{\mathsf{U}}\ \gamma\right] \leftrightarrow \gamma \vee (\alpha \vee \overleftarrow{\mathsf{X}}\beta) \wedge [(\beta \vee \mathsf{X}\alpha)\ \underline{\mathsf{U}}\ (\mathsf{X}\gamma)]$
- $\left[(\alpha \vee \overleftarrow{\underline{\mathsf{X}}}\beta)\ \underline{\mathsf{U}}\ \gamma\right] \leftrightarrow \gamma \vee (\alpha \vee \overleftarrow{\underline{\mathsf{X}}}\beta) \wedge [(\beta \vee \mathsf{X}\alpha)\ \underline{\mathsf{U}}\ (\mathsf{X}\gamma)]$
- $\left[(\alpha \vee [\beta\ \overleftarrow{\underline{\mathsf{U}}}\ \gamma])\ \underline{\mathsf{U}}\ \delta\right] \leftrightarrow \left(\begin{array}{l} \left([\beta\ \overleftarrow{\underline{\mathsf{U}}}\ \gamma] \vee [\alpha\ \underline{\mathsf{U}}\ (\gamma \vee \delta)]\right) \wedge \\ [(\beta \vee \gamma \vee [\alpha\ \underline{\mathsf{U}}\ (\gamma \vee \delta)])\ \underline{\mathsf{U}}\ \delta] \end{array}\right)$
- $\left[(\alpha \vee [\beta\ \overleftarrow{\mathsf{B}}\ \gamma])\ \underline{\mathsf{U}}\ \delta\right] \leftrightarrow \left(\begin{array}{l} \left([\beta\ \overleftarrow{\mathsf{B}}\ \gamma] \vee [\alpha\ \underline{\mathsf{U}}\ (\beta \vee \delta)]\right) \wedge \\ [(\neg\gamma \vee \alpha \wedge \mathsf{X}\,[\alpha\ \underline{\mathsf{U}}\ (\beta \vee \delta)])\ \underline{\mathsf{U}}\ \delta] \end{array}\right)$

Finally, the following laws are derived by the equality $[\varphi\ \mathsf{B}\ \psi] \leftrightarrow \neg\,[(\neg\varphi)\ \underline{\mathsf{U}}\ \psi]$ for the separation of the B operator:

Lemma 5.85 (Separation Laws for B). *The following equations are valid and can be used for separation of the B operator:*

- $[(\alpha \vee \beta)\ \mathsf{B}\ \gamma] \leftrightarrow [\alpha\ \mathsf{B}\ \gamma] \vee [\beta\ \mathsf{B}\ \gamma]$
- $[\alpha\ \mathsf{B}\ (\beta \vee \gamma)] \leftrightarrow [\alpha\ \mathsf{B}\ \beta] \wedge [\alpha\ \mathsf{B}\ \gamma]$
- $\left[\alpha\ \mathsf{B}\ (\beta \wedge \overleftarrow{\mathsf{X}}\gamma)\right] \leftrightarrow \neg(\beta \wedge \overleftarrow{\mathsf{X}}\gamma) \wedge (\alpha \vee [(\mathsf{X}\alpha)\ \mathsf{B}\ (\gamma \wedge \mathsf{X}\beta)])$
- $\left[\alpha\ \mathsf{B}\ (\beta \wedge \overleftarrow{\underline{\mathsf{X}}}\gamma)\right] \leftrightarrow \neg(\beta \wedge \overleftarrow{\underline{\mathsf{X}}}\gamma) \wedge (\alpha \vee [(\mathsf{X}\alpha)\ \mathsf{B}\ (\gamma \wedge \mathsf{X}\beta)])$
- $\left[\alpha\ \mathsf{B}\ (\beta \wedge [\gamma\ \overleftarrow{\underline{\mathsf{U}}}\ \delta])\right] \leftrightarrow \left(\begin{array}{l} \left[[(\neg\gamma)\ \overleftarrow{\mathsf{B}}\ \delta] \vee [(\alpha \vee \neg\mathsf{X}\gamma)\ \mathsf{B}\ \beta]\right] \wedge \\ [\alpha\ \mathsf{B}\ (\delta \wedge [(\neg\alpha \wedge \mathsf{X}\gamma)\ \underline{\mathsf{U}}\ \beta])] \end{array}\right)$
- $\left[\alpha\ \mathsf{B}\ (\beta \wedge [\gamma\ \overleftarrow{\mathsf{B}}\ \delta])\right] \leftrightarrow \left(\begin{array}{l} \left[[(\neg\gamma)\ \overleftarrow{\underline{\mathsf{U}}}\ \delta] \vee [(\alpha \vee \mathsf{X}\delta)\ \mathsf{B}\ \beta]\right] \wedge \\ [\alpha\ \mathsf{B}\ (\gamma \wedge \neg\delta \wedge [(\neg\alpha \wedge \neg\mathsf{X}\delta)\ \underline{\mathsf{U}}\ \beta])] \end{array}\right)$
- $\left[(\alpha \wedge \overleftarrow{\mathsf{X}}\beta)\ \mathsf{B}\ \gamma\right] \leftrightarrow \neg\gamma \wedge \left(\alpha \wedge \overleftarrow{\mathsf{X}}\beta \vee [(\beta \wedge \mathsf{X}\alpha)\ \mathsf{B}\ (\mathsf{X}\gamma)]\right)$
- $\left[(\alpha \wedge \overleftarrow{\underline{\mathsf{X}}}\beta)\ \mathsf{B}\ \gamma\right] \leftrightarrow \neg\gamma \wedge \left(\alpha \wedge \overleftarrow{\underline{\mathsf{X}}}\beta \vee [(\beta \wedge \mathsf{X}\alpha)\ \mathsf{B}\ (\mathsf{X}\gamma)]\right)$
- $\left[(\alpha \wedge [\beta\ \overleftarrow{\underline{\mathsf{U}}}\ \gamma])\ \mathsf{B}\ \delta\right] \leftrightarrow \left(\begin{array}{l} [\beta\ \overleftarrow{\underline{\mathsf{U}}}\ \gamma] \wedge [\alpha\ \mathsf{B}\ (\neg\beta \vee \delta)] \vee \\ [(\gamma \wedge [(\mathsf{X}[\beta \wedge \neg\delta])\ \underline{\mathsf{U}}\ \alpha])\ \mathsf{B}\ \delta] \end{array}\right)$
- $\left[(\alpha \wedge [\beta\ \overleftarrow{\mathsf{B}}\ \gamma])\ \mathsf{B}\ \delta\right] \leftrightarrow \left(\begin{array}{l} [\beta\ \overleftarrow{\mathsf{B}}\ \gamma] \wedge [\alpha\ \mathsf{B}\ (\gamma \vee \delta)] \vee \\ [(\beta \wedge \neg\gamma \wedge [\alpha\ \mathsf{B}\ (\gamma \vee \delta)])\ \mathsf{B}\ \delta] \end{array}\right)$

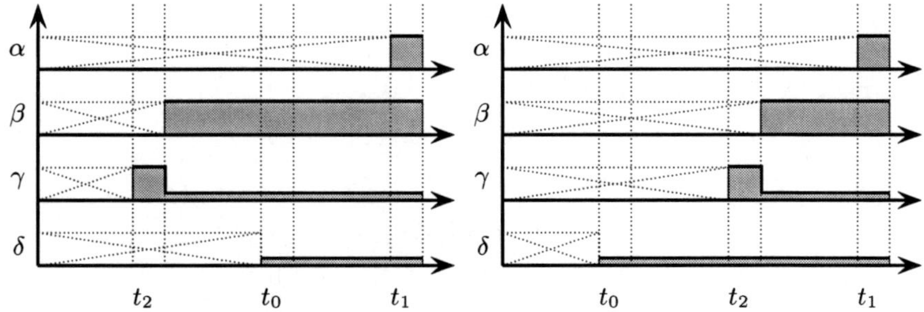

Fig. 5.22. Timing diagrams for the proof of the separation rule for B

The proofs of the above equations are all done in the same manner. For example, consider the separation law for $\left[(\alpha \wedge [\beta\ \overleftarrow{\underline{\mathsf{U}}}\ \gamma])\ \mathsf{B}\ \delta\right]$. To prove the equivalence from left to right, we assume that $\left[(\alpha \wedge [\beta\ \overleftarrow{\underline{\mathsf{U}}}\ \gamma])\ \mathsf{B}\ \delta\right]$ is evaluated along a path π at time t_0. Hence, we may assume that the event that is awaited, namely $\alpha \wedge [\beta\ \overleftarrow{\underline{\mathsf{U}}}\ \gamma]$, holds at some time t_1 with $t_0 \leq t_1$, which means that there is another point of time t_2 with $t_2 \leq t_1$ where γ held the last time before t_1. Depending on whether $t_2 \leq t_0$ or $t_0 \leq t_2$ holds, we consider then two cases that are depicted in Figure 5.22. The timing diagram given on the left hand side corresponds with the first disjunct, where $[\beta\ \overleftarrow{\underline{\mathsf{U}}}\ \gamma]$ describes the relationship of the signals in the past of t_0 and $[\alpha\ \mathsf{B}\ (\neg\beta \vee \delta)]$ describes the relationship of the signals in the future of t_0 (both formulas overlap at the present point of time). The diagram on the right hand side corresponds with the second disjunct, i.e., with the formula $[(\gamma \wedge [(\mathsf{X}[\beta \wedge \neg\delta])\ \underline{\mathsf{U}}\ \alpha])\ \mathsf{B}\ \delta]$.

For the other implication, we have to show that both disjuncts of the right hand side imply the left hand side. In both cases, this is easily seen by the timing diagrams in Figure 5.22.

Recall that we can replace any future time temporal operator by $\underline{\mathsf{U}}$ and X. Hence, the above laws allow us to eliminate all past operators that occur in the scope of any future operator. Actually, this is sufficient to prove that every temporal logic formula is initial equivalent to a temporal logic formula where only future operators occur. All we have to do is to eliminate the nestings of past operators in the future operators. The remaining occurrences of the past temporal operators are reduced to propositional logic according to their initial conditions.

To achieve the full separation property, we have to show that the converse is also true, i.e., that any occurrence of a future time temporal operator in the scope of a past operator can also be eliminated. We first consider the 'previous' operators $\overleftarrow{\mathsf{X}}$ and $\overleftarrow{\underline{\mathsf{X}}}$:

Lemma 5.86 (Separation Laws for $\overleftarrow{\mathsf{X}}$). *The following equations are valid and can be used for separation of the $\overleftarrow{\mathsf{X}}$ operator, where we abbreviated* $\mathsf{Init} := \overleftarrow{\mathsf{X}}\,0$*:*

- $\overleftarrow{\mathsf{X}}\,[\alpha \wedge \mathsf{X}\beta] \leftrightarrow \mathsf{Init} \vee \beta \wedge \overleftarrow{\mathsf{X}}\,\alpha$
- $\overleftarrow{\mathsf{X}}\,[\alpha \wedge [\beta\ \underline{\mathsf{U}}\ \gamma]] \leftrightarrow \overleftarrow{\mathsf{X}}\,[\alpha \wedge \gamma] \vee [\beta\ \underline{\mathsf{U}}\ \gamma] \wedge \overleftarrow{\mathsf{X}}\,[\alpha \wedge \beta]$
- $\overleftarrow{\mathsf{X}}\,[\alpha \wedge [\beta\ \mathsf{B}\ \gamma]] \leftrightarrow \overleftarrow{\mathsf{X}}\,[\alpha \wedge \beta \wedge \neg\gamma] \vee [\beta\ \mathsf{B}\ \gamma] \wedge \overleftarrow{\mathsf{X}}\,[\alpha \wedge \neg\gamma]$
- $\overleftarrow{\mathsf{X}}\,[\alpha \vee \mathsf{X}\beta] \leftrightarrow \beta \vee \overleftarrow{\mathsf{X}}\,\alpha$
- $\overleftarrow{\mathsf{X}}\,[\alpha \vee [\beta\ \underline{\mathsf{U}}\ \gamma]] \leftrightarrow \overleftarrow{\mathsf{X}}\,[\alpha \vee \gamma] \vee [\beta\ \underline{\mathsf{U}}\ \gamma] \wedge \overleftarrow{\mathsf{X}}\,\beta$
- $\overleftarrow{\mathsf{X}}\,[\alpha \vee [\beta\ \mathsf{B}\ \gamma]] \leftrightarrow \overleftarrow{\mathsf{X}}\,[\alpha \vee \neg\gamma] \wedge \left([\beta\ \mathsf{B}\ \gamma] \vee \overleftarrow{\mathsf{X}}\,[\alpha \vee \beta]\right)$

Similar theorems hold for the separation of the $\overleftarrow{\underline{\mathsf{X}}}$ operator:

- $\overleftarrow{\underline{\mathsf{X}}}\,[\alpha \wedge \mathsf{X}\beta] \leftrightarrow \neg\mathsf{Init} \wedge \beta \wedge \overleftarrow{\underline{\mathsf{X}}}\,\alpha$
- $\overleftarrow{\underline{\mathsf{X}}}\,[\alpha \wedge [\beta\ \underline{\mathsf{U}}\ \gamma]] \leftrightarrow \overleftarrow{\underline{\mathsf{X}}}\,[\alpha \wedge \gamma] \vee [\beta\ \underline{\mathsf{U}}\ \gamma] \wedge \overleftarrow{\underline{\mathsf{X}}}\,[\alpha \wedge \beta]$
- $\overleftarrow{\underline{\mathsf{X}}}\,[\alpha \wedge [\beta\ \mathsf{B}\ \gamma]] \leftrightarrow \overleftarrow{\underline{\mathsf{X}}}\,[\alpha \wedge \beta \wedge \neg\gamma] \vee [\beta\ \mathsf{B}\ \gamma] \wedge \overleftarrow{\underline{\mathsf{X}}}\,[\alpha \wedge \neg\gamma]$
- $\overleftarrow{\underline{\mathsf{X}}}\,[\alpha \vee \mathsf{X}\beta] \leftrightarrow \beta \vee \overleftarrow{\underline{\mathsf{X}}}\,\alpha$
- $\overleftarrow{\underline{\mathsf{X}}}\,[\alpha \vee [\beta\ \underline{\mathsf{U}}\ \gamma]] \leftrightarrow \overleftarrow{\underline{\mathsf{X}}}\,[\alpha \vee \gamma] \vee [\beta\ \underline{\mathsf{U}}\ \gamma] \wedge \overleftarrow{\underline{\mathsf{X}}}\,\beta$
- $\overleftarrow{\underline{\mathsf{X}}}\,[\alpha \vee [\beta\ \mathsf{B}\ \gamma]] \leftrightarrow \overleftarrow{\underline{\mathsf{X}}}\,[\alpha \vee \neg\gamma] \wedge \left([\beta\ \mathsf{B}\ \gamma] \vee \overleftarrow{\underline{\mathsf{X}}}\,[\alpha \vee \beta]\right)$

It is not surprising that the rules for $\overleftarrow{\mathsf{X}}$ and $\overleftarrow{\underline{\mathsf{X}}}$ are very similar and differ only at the initial point of time. Finally, we have to consider the cases where nestings of future operators occur in the scope of a binary temporal past operator, e.g. in the scope of a $[\ \overleftarrow{\underline{\mathsf{U}}}\ ]$ operator.

Lemma 5.87 (Separation Laws for $[\ \overleftarrow{\underline{\mathsf{U}}}\ ]$). *The following equations are valid and can be used for separation of the $[\ \overleftarrow{\underline{\mathsf{U}}}\ ]$ operator:*

- $[(\alpha \wedge \beta)\ \overleftarrow{\underline{\mathsf{U}}}\ \gamma] \leftrightarrow [\alpha\ \overleftarrow{\underline{\mathsf{U}}}\ \gamma] \wedge [\beta\ \overleftarrow{\underline{\mathsf{U}}}\ \gamma]$
- $[\alpha\ \overleftarrow{\underline{\mathsf{U}}}\ (\beta \wedge \mathsf{X}\gamma)] \leftrightarrow \beta \wedge \mathsf{X}\gamma \vee [\alpha\ \overleftarrow{\underline{\mathsf{U}}}\ (\alpha \wedge \gamma \wedge \overleftarrow{\underline{\mathsf{X}}}\beta)]$
- $[\alpha\ \overleftarrow{\underline{\mathsf{U}}}\ (\beta \wedge [\gamma\ \underline{\mathsf{U}}\ \delta])] \leftrightarrow \left(\begin{array}{l}[\gamma\ \underline{\mathsf{U}}\ \delta] \wedge [(\alpha \wedge \overleftarrow{\mathsf{X}}\gamma)\ \overleftarrow{\underline{\mathsf{U}}}\ \beta] \vee \\ [\alpha\ \overleftarrow{\underline{\mathsf{U}}}\ (\delta \wedge [(\alpha \wedge \overleftarrow{\mathsf{X}}\gamma)\ \overleftarrow{\underline{\mathsf{U}}}\ \beta])]\end{array}\right)$
- $[\alpha\ \overleftarrow{\underline{\mathsf{U}}}\ (\beta \wedge [\gamma\ \mathsf{B}\ \delta])] \leftrightarrow \left(\begin{array}{l}[\gamma\ \mathsf{B}\ \delta] \wedge [(\alpha \wedge \neg\overleftarrow{\mathsf{X}}\delta)\ \overleftarrow{\underline{\mathsf{U}}}\ \beta] \vee \\ [\alpha\ \overleftarrow{\underline{\mathsf{U}}}\ (\gamma \wedge \neg\delta \wedge [(\alpha \wedge \neg\overleftarrow{\mathsf{X}}\delta)\ \overleftarrow{\underline{\mathsf{U}}}\ \beta])]\end{array}\right)$
- $[\alpha\ \overleftarrow{\underline{\mathsf{U}}}\ (\beta \vee \gamma)] \leftrightarrow [\alpha\ \overleftarrow{\underline{\mathsf{U}}}\ \beta] \vee [\alpha\ \overleftarrow{\underline{\mathsf{U}}}\ \gamma]$
- $[(\alpha \vee \mathsf{X}\beta)\ \overleftarrow{\underline{\mathsf{U}}}\ \gamma] \leftrightarrow \gamma \vee (\alpha \vee \mathsf{X}\beta) \wedge [(\beta \vee \overleftarrow{\mathsf{X}}\alpha)\ \overleftarrow{\underline{\mathsf{U}}}\ (\overleftarrow{\underline{\mathsf{X}}}\gamma)]$
- $[(\alpha \vee [\beta\ \underline{\mathsf{U}}\ \gamma])\ \overleftarrow{\underline{\mathsf{U}}}\ \delta] \leftrightarrow \left(\begin{array}{l}\left[[\beta\ \underline{\mathsf{U}}\ \gamma] \vee [(\delta \vee \overleftarrow{\mathsf{X}}\gamma)\ \overleftarrow{\mathsf{B}}\ (\neg\alpha \wedge \neg\delta)]\right] \wedge \\ \left[\left(\beta \vee \gamma \vee [(\delta \vee \overleftarrow{\mathsf{X}}\gamma)\ \overleftarrow{\mathsf{B}}\ (\neg\alpha \wedge \neg\delta)]\right)\ \overleftarrow{\underline{\mathsf{U}}}\ \delta\right]\end{array}\right)$
- $[(\alpha \vee [\beta\ \mathsf{B}\ \gamma])\ \overleftarrow{\underline{\mathsf{U}}}\ \delta] \leftrightarrow \left(\begin{array}{l}\left[[\beta\ \mathsf{B}\ \gamma] \vee [(\delta \vee \overleftarrow{\mathsf{X}}\beta)\ \overleftarrow{\mathsf{B}}\ (\neg\alpha \wedge \neg\delta)]\right] \wedge \\ \left[\left(\neg\gamma \vee [(\delta \vee \overleftarrow{\mathsf{X}}\beta)\ \overleftarrow{\mathsf{B}}\ (\neg\alpha \wedge \neg\delta)]\right)\ \overleftarrow{\underline{\mathsf{U}}}\ \delta\right]\end{array}\right)$

It is not surprising that the above equations for the separation of $[\overleftarrow{\underline{\mathsf{U}}}]$ operator are similar to those of $[\underline{\mathsf{U}}]$ that have been given in Lemma 5.84. Moreover, negating both the left hand and the right hand sides give separation laws for the $[\overleftarrow{\mathsf{B}}]$ operator which are analogous to the rules in Lemma 5.85.

Note that there is a plethora of ways how one temporal operator can be expressed by another one. Therefore, there are many ways to formulate the above separation laws. For example, consider the following laws to generate further ones (that also have analogous past versions):

- $[e \ \mathsf{B}\ x] \leftrightarrow \neg [(\neg e)\ \underline{\mathsf{U}}\ x]$
- $[e \ \mathsf{B}\ x] \leftrightarrow \neg x \wedge [(\neg \mathsf{X} x)\ \mathsf{U}\ e]$
- $[e \ \mathsf{B}\ x] \leftrightarrow [(\neg x)\ \mathsf{U}\ (e \wedge \neg x)])$
- $[x \ \mathsf{U}\ e] \leftrightarrow \neg [(\neg x)\ \underline{\mathsf{B}}\ e]$
- $[x \ \mathsf{U}\ e] \leftrightarrow e \vee [(\mathsf{X} e)\ \mathsf{B}\ (\neg x)]$
- $[x \ \mathsf{U}\ e] \leftrightarrow [e\ \mathsf{B}\ (\neg e \wedge \neg x)])$

The above lemmas now give enough rules to separate the past and future temporal operators in any LTL_p formula. We remark here, that the rules of Lemma 5.84 for the separation of the $[\underline{\mathsf{U}}]$ operator remain true, if we replace any occurrence of $[\underline{\mathsf{U}}]$ by $[\mathsf{U}]$. It is moreover remarkable that for any class $\kappa \in \{\mathsf{G}, \mathsf{F}, \mathsf{Prefix}, \mathsf{GF}, \mathsf{FG}, \mathsf{Streett}\}$, all of the rules preserve membership in the logic TL_κ, which means that we now have the following theorem:

Theorem 5.88 (Expressive Completeness of the Future Fragments of TL_κ). *For every $\kappa \in \{\mathsf{G}, \mathsf{F}, \mathsf{Prefix}, \mathsf{GF}, \mathsf{FG}, \mathsf{Streett}\}$, the logic TL_κ has the separation property, i.e., it can be written in the form $\bigvee_{i=1}^{n} \Phi_i^{<} \wedge \Phi_i^{=} \wedge \Phi_i^{>}$ with formulas $\Phi_i^{<}$, $\Phi_i^{=}$, $\Phi_i^{>}$ of the same class $\Phi \in \mathsf{TL}_\kappa$. Hence, for any formula $\Phi \in \mathsf{TL}_\kappa$, there is a formula $\Psi \in \mathsf{TL}_\kappa$ where no past operator occurs which is initially equivalent to Φ. In particular, LTL_p has the separation property.*

Recall that initially equivalent means that for any structure $\mathcal{K}$ and any path π through that structure, we have $(\mathcal{K}, \pi, 0) \models \Phi$ iff $(\mathcal{K}, \pi, 0) \models \Psi$. This is the same as stating that the formula $\mathsf{G}[\Phi_{\mathsf{init}} \rightarrow (\Phi \leftrightarrow \Psi)]$ is valid, where $\Phi_{\mathsf{init}} := \overleftarrow{\mathsf{X}}\, 0$. Clearly, the past time fragment of TL_κ can not be as expressive as the entire logic TL_κ, since any formula that does not have future time operators is initially equivalent to a propositional formula.

The separation property allows us to construct for every LTL_p formula φ a LTL_p formula without past operators that is initially equivalent. For this reason, past operators are often viewed to be unnecessary. However, separating the formula into past, present, and future parts yields an exponential blow-up in the formula size. In [355, 443], it has been shown that this is unavoidable (compare this with the construction on page 451:

Theorem 5.89 (Succinctness of LTL_p with Past Operators). *There are LTL_p formulas (with past operators) of length n, such that all initial equivalent temporal logic formulas without past operators are of size $\Omega(2^n)$.*

Proof. The mentioned LTL_p formulas (with past operators) of length n are the following ones, where $\Phi_{\mathsf{init}} :\equiv \overleftarrow{\underline{\mathsf{X}}}\, 0$:

$$\mathsf{G}\left[\left(\bigwedge_{i=1}^{n}\left(x_i \leftrightarrow \overleftarrow{\mathsf{F}}\,(x_i \wedge \Phi_{\mathsf{init}})\right)\right) \rightarrow \left(y \leftrightarrow \overleftarrow{\mathsf{F}}\,(y \wedge \Phi_{\mathsf{init}})\right)\right]$$

The formula memorizes the values of the variables $x_1,\ldots,x_n$, and y at the initial point of time. For every point of time, it is then required that whenever the variables $x_1,\ldots,x_n$ have the value they had at the initial point of time, also y must have its initial value.

As past operators can look back, and can identify the initial point of time, e.g., with the formula Φ_{init} above, it is possible to refer to the initial values at any point of time. Without past operators, however, this is not possible. Instead, we have to make a case distinction depending on the initial values that yields 2^{n+1} different cases. □

For this reason, there are properties that can be expressed exponentially more succinct in with the help of past operators. Adding past does neither increase the expressive power, nor the complexity of the translation and decision procedures. For this reason, the use of past operators in temporal logics is not necessary, but recommended.

5.6 Complexities of the Model Checking Problems

In the previous sections, we have considered several temporal logics that are all subsets of CTL*. We have already discussed the expressiveness of these logics, and we will now consider the complexity classes of the corresponding model checking problems. Clearly, the more expressive a logic is, the more complex is its model checking problem. However, this is not necessarily so: there are logics with different expressivenesses, but with the same complexity. For example, model checking of LTL with or without past operators is PSPACE-complete as well as CTL* model checking. This is remarkable since CTL* is more expressive than LTL, and although LTL with past operators has the same expressiveness as LTL without past operators, it is exponentially more succinct. Moreover, LeftCTL* is not PSPACE-complete, but only Δ_2^p-complete. Finally, LeftCTL* and CTL are equal expressive, but model checking of CTL is only P-complete. Considering the satisfiabilty problem, it turns out that the sat-problem of LeftCTL* is 2EXPTIME-complete, while the sat-problem of CTL is only 2EXPTIME-complete. This explains why an exponential blow-up in the translation from LeftCTL* to CTL can not be avoided. This has been shown initially by Wilke [513]. Adler and Immerman have improved the lower bound of this translation in 2001 to even $\Omega(|\varphi|!)$. Johannsen and Lange [266] have recently proved that the sat-problem of CTL$^+$ is 2EXPTIME-complete and gave therefore another explanation.

In the following, we consider therefore some important complexity classes of model-checking problems. To this end, recall that for any function $f : \mathbb{N} \rightarrow \mathbb{N}$, the sets $\mathsf{DTime}(f(n))$/$\mathsf{NTime}(f(n))$ are the sets of problems of size n that can be solved with a deterministic/nondeterministic Turing machine in time $O(f(n))$. Analogously, $\mathsf{DSpace}(f(n))/\mathsf{NSpace}(f(n))$ are the sets of problems of size n that can be solved with a deterministic/nondeterministic Turing machine with space $O(f(n))$. Using this notation, we moreover have (see also page 427):

- $\mathsf{P} := \bigcup_{k\in\mathbb{N}} \mathsf{DTime}(n^k)$
- $\mathsf{NP} := \bigcup_{k\in\mathbb{N}} \mathsf{NTime}(n^k)$
- $\mathsf{PSPACE} := \bigcup_{k\in\mathbb{N}} \mathsf{DSpace}(n^k) = \bigcup_{k\in\mathbb{N}} \mathsf{NSpace}(n^k)$
- $\mathsf{EXPTIME} := \bigcup_{k\in\mathbb{N}} \mathsf{DTime}(2^{kn})$
- $\mathsf{2EXPTIME} := \bigcup_{k\in\mathbb{N}} \mathsf{DTime}(2^{2^{kn}})$

Clearly, we have $\mathsf{P} \subseteq \mathsf{NP} \subseteq \mathsf{PSPACE} \subseteq \mathsf{EXPTIME} \subseteq \mathsf{2EXPTIME}$. Besides membership in one of these classes, which gives us an *upper bound* of the complexity, one also considers *lower bounds* that are given by hardness results. If both bounds match, we even have a *completeness* result of the problem. The hardness w.r.t. a class $\mathcal{C}$-complete is shown by reduction of an arbitrary problem in $\mathcal{C}$-complete to the considered problem. The reduction must also be in class $\mathcal{C}$. Hence, due to this reductions, solving one problem in $\mathcal{C}$-complete gives also algorithms for all of the other problems in that class.

We now start with establishing a lower bound for some model checking problems by a reduction of 3SAT to a model checking problem [103]. In particular, we prove that the model checking problem $(\mathcal{K}, s) \models \mathsf{E}\bigwedge_{i=1}^{n} \mathsf{F}a_i$ is NP-hard, i.e., every NP-complete problem can be reduced to a model checking problem of the form $(\mathcal{K}, s) \models \mathsf{E}\bigwedge_{i=1}^{n} \mathsf{F}a_i$ in polynomial time [103, 456]:

Theorem 5.90. *The model checking problem $(\mathcal{K}, s) \models \mathsf{E}\bigwedge_{i=1}^{n} \mathsf{F}a_i$ is* NP*-complete (with variables a_i). Hence, the model checking problems for* LeftCTL* *and* CTL$^+$ *are both* NP*-hard and* coNP*-hard.*

Proof. The proof is obtained by reducing an arbitrary NP-complete problem in polynomial time to a model checking problem of the form $(\mathcal{K}, s) \models \mathsf{E}\bigwedge_{i=1}^{n} \mathsf{F}a_i$. As the latter formula belongs to CTL$^+$, and also to LeftCTL*, and as these logics are closed under complement, the above result follows.

We use 3SAT [204] for the reduction: consider an arbitrary propositional formula in conjunctive normal form over the variables $\{x_1, \ldots, x_n\}$, where each minterm consists of exactly three literals, i.e., $\Phi \equiv \bigwedge_{i=1}^{m}(a_i \vee b_i \vee c_i)$ (this means each a_i, b_i, c_i is a variable or a negated variable x_k). We define a Kripke structure $\mathcal{K}_\Phi = (\mathcal{I}_\Phi, \mathcal{S}_\Phi, \mathcal{R}_\Phi, \mathcal{L}_\Phi)$ as follows: we use m variables $\vartheta_1, \ldots, \vartheta_m$, one for each minterm of Φ. The set of states $\mathcal{S}_\Phi$ is given as $\mathcal{S}_\Phi := \{p_i \mid 0 \leq i \leq n\} \cup \{q_{i,1} \mid 0 \leq i \leq n\} \cup \{q_{i,2} \mid 0 \leq i \leq n\}$, the only initial state is p_0 and the labeling function is given as $\mathcal{L}_\Phi(p_i) := \{\}$, $\mathcal{L}_\Phi(q_{i,1}) := \{\vartheta_j \mid x_i \in \{a_j, b_j, c_j\}\}$, and $\mathcal{L}_\Phi(q_{i,2}) := \{\vartheta_j \mid \neg x_i \in \{a_j, b_j, c_j\}\}$. This means that each state $q_{i,1}$ satisfies all minterms ϑ_j that have x_i as one of its literals and $q_{i,2}$ satisfies all minterms ϑ_j that have $\neg x_i$ as one of its literals. For this reason, the state $q_{i,1}$

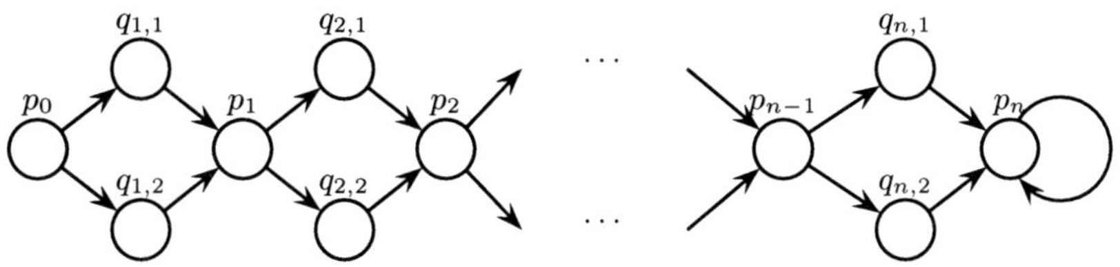

Fig. 5.23. Reducing 3SAT to CTL$^+$ / LeftCTL* model checking

is associated with the variable x_i, while $q_{i,2}$ is associated with the negation of x_i. The transition relation $\mathcal{R}_\Phi$ is given in Figure 5.23.

Clearly, for every assignment of truth values to $\{x_1, \ldots, x_n\}$, we have a unique path through the structure $\mathcal{K}_\Phi$, since each of the 2^n paths from p_0 to p_n corresponds uniquely to such an assignment. Moreover, Φ is satisfiable iff there is a path from p_0 to p_n such that $\bigwedge_{j=1}^{m} \mathsf{F}\vartheta_j$ holds on that path. Consequently, Φ is satisfiable iff $(\mathcal{K}_\Phi, p_0) \models \mathsf{E}\bigwedge_{j=1}^{m} \mathsf{F}\vartheta_j$ holds. Finally, note that $\mathcal{K}_\Phi$ has $3n+1$ states and $4n+1$ transitions, so that the model checking problem $(\mathcal{K}_\Phi, p_0) \models \mathsf{E}\bigwedge_{j=1}^{m} \mathsf{F}\vartheta_j$ is of size $O(n)$.

Membership in NP is easily seen: The nondeterministic algorithm guesses a path through $\mathcal{K}$ and checks if every variable a_i occurs on this path. □

In [443, 456] a nondeterministic model checking algorithm has been given to decide the first of these model checking problems. We will now extend this result to arbitrary LeftCTL* model checking problems of the form $\mathsf{E}\varphi$, where φ must not contain a path quantifier. Since $\mathsf{E}\bigwedge_{i=1}^{m} \mathsf{F}\vartheta_i$ is of this form, NP-hardness is already shown. The NP-completeness follows by a nondeterministic polynomial-time reduction to CTL. Our algorithm therefore guesses a permutation π of the numbers $\{1, \ldots, n\}$ and constructs then the following CTL formula:

$$\mathsf{EF}(\vartheta_{\pi(1)} \wedge \mathsf{EF}(\vartheta_{\pi(2)} \wedge \ldots \mathsf{EF}(\vartheta_{\pi(n-1)} \wedge \mathsf{EF}\vartheta_{\pi(n)}) \ldots))$$

The CTL model checking algorithm solves this remaining problem in polynomial time.

In the same way, we obtain a nondeterministic algorithm for checking LeftCTL* formulas $\mathsf{E}\varphi$ where φ contains no path quantifiers. We assume that the formula is in negation normal form and is based on the temporal operators U, $\underline{\mathsf{U}}$, and X. We reduce it by a nondeterministic algorithm to a CTL formula that implies $\mathsf{E}\varphi$. The code is given in Figure 5.24, where only the case of conjunctions is interesting. Whenever we encounter a disjunction in the formula, we nondeterministically choose one of the disjuncts. After this it follows that conjunctions are only conjunctions of formulas of the form $[\alpha_i \,\underline{\mathsf{U}}\, \beta_i]$, $[\gamma_i \,\mathsf{U}\, \delta_i]$, $\mathsf{X}\varphi_i$ and state formulas η_i. We therefore sort these conjuncts by their top-level operator.

After this, we guess a permutation to combine the $[\alpha_i \,\underline{\mathsf{U}}\, \beta_i]$ and $[\gamma_i \,\mathsf{U}\, \delta_i]$ subformulas according to that permutation, similar to the above reduction of

$\bigwedge_{i=1}^{m} \mathsf{F}\vartheta_i$ (see Lemma 5.18 on page 307). We thereby obtain a formula $[\alpha\ \underline{\mathsf{U}}\ \beta]$ or $[\alpha\ \mathsf{U}\ \beta]$ of a size linear to the conjunction of the $[\alpha_i\ \underline{\mathsf{U}}\ \beta_i]$ and $[\gamma_i\ \mathsf{U}\ \delta_i]$ subformulas. We only consider the strong-until case in the following, the weak-until case is obviously done in the same manner. Hence, our entire formula for the conjunct is now $[\alpha\ \underline{\mathsf{U}}\ \beta] \wedge \mathsf{X}\xi \wedge \eta$, where we combined also the X-subformulas to a formula $\mathsf{X}\xi$ and the state formulas to a single state formula η. Applying the recursion law $[\alpha\ \underline{\mathsf{U}}\ \beta] = \beta \vee \alpha \wedge \mathsf{X}\,[\alpha\ \underline{\mathsf{U}}\ \beta]$ shows that our nondeterministic algorithm can choose one more between $\eta \wedge \beta \wedge \mathsf{X}\xi$ and $\eta \wedge \alpha \wedge \mathsf{X}(\xi \wedge [\alpha\ \underline{\mathsf{U}}\ \beta])$.

Our nondeterministic algorithm given in Figure 5.24 is therefore able to compute a linear-sized CTL formula that implies $\mathsf{E}\varphi$. We therefore have the following result:

Theorem 5.91 (Complexity of LeftCTL* Model Checking). *Model checking* LeftCTL* *formulas of the form* $\mathsf{E}\varphi$*, where* φ *is quantifier-free is* NP*-complete. Analogously, checking* LeftCTL* *formulas of the form* $\mathsf{A}\varphi$*, where* φ *is quantifier-free is* coNP*-complete.*

This does not however imply that LeftCTL* model checking is NP-complete. If we could find a NP-algorithm for solving the general LeftCTL* model checking problem, this would mean that the problem is NP-complete. Furthermore, as it is closed under negation, the problem would also be coNP-complete. This would answer the so-far open question of whether the complexity classes NP-complete and coNP-complete are the same. Hence, it turns out that the construction of a NP model checking algorithm for LeftCTL* seems to be a basic problem of todays computer science.

The precise complexity class of LeftCTL$^+$ and LeftCTL* model checking is Δ_2^p-complete. Δ_2^p is the set of problems that can be solved in polynomial time by a deterministic Turing machine that is allowed to delegate subproblems to a nondeterministic Turing machine that must solve these subproblems in polynomial time. Hence, a problem in Δ_2^p contains polynomially many problems of NP. It is easily seen that LeftCTL* model checking can be solved by a Δ_2^p-algorithm by computing the PQNF normal form of page 85 (see also [103]). The hardness of the problem, whch closes the gap between the lower bounds NP and coNP and the upper bound Δ_2^p, has been recently shown in [314] (see also [443]):

Theorem 5.92. *The model checking problems for* LeftCTL* *and* CTL$^+$ *are* Δ_2^p*-complete.*

We will now show that the model checking problems for LTL and CTL*, are more complex, namely PSPACE-complete.

Theorem 5.93. *The model checking problems for* CTL* *and* LTL *are* PSPACE*-complete.*

```
function Conjuncts(Φ)
(* all disjunctions in Φ are under a temporal operator or form a state formula *)
  case Φ of
    φ ∧ ψ      : return Conjuncts(φ) ∪ Conjuncts(ψ);
    else       : return {Φ};
  end case
end function

function CombineU(i, π, I, C_U)
  if i = 0 then return 1
  else
    η := CombineU(i − 1, π, I \ {π(i)}, C_U);
    return [(⋀_{i∈I} α_i) U̲ (β_{π(i)} ∧ η)]
  end
end function

function SelectCTL(Φ)
(* Φ ∈ TL_PE is in negation normal form *)
  case Φ of
    is_prop(Φ): return Φ;
    ¬φ         : return Φ;
    φ ∨ ψ      : α := choose {φ, ψ};
                 return SelectCTL(α);
    φ ∧ ψ      : φ' := SelectCTL(φ); ψ' := SelectCTL(ψ);
                 C := Conjuncts(φ' ∧ ψ');
                 C_U := getU(C); C_X := getX(C); C_State := C \ (C_U ∪ C_X);
                 π_U := choose Perm({1, ..., |C_U|});
                 Φ_U := CombineU(|C_U|, π_U, {1, ..., |C_U|}, C_U);
                 Xξ ≡ CombineX(C_X); η := ⋀_{φ∈C_State} φ;
                 case Φ_U of
                   [α U̲ β] : Ψ := choose {η ∧ β ∧ Xξ, η ∧ α ∧ X(ξ ∧ [α U̲ β])};
                   [α U β] : Ψ := choose {η ∧ β ∧ Xξ, η ∧ α ∧ X(ξ ∧ [α U β])};
                 end;
                 return SelectCTL(Ψ);
    Xφ         : return X(SelectCTLφ);
    [φ U̲ ψ]    : ψ' := SelectCTL(ψ);
                 return [φ U̲ ψ'];
    [φ U ψ]    : ψ' := SelectCTL(ψ);
                 return [φ U ψ'];
  end case
end function
```

Fig. 5.24. Nondeterministic reduction from $\mathsf{TL_{PE}}$ to CTL

To prove PSPACE-completeness, we need to show that (i) the problem can be solved with a nondeterministic algorithm that runs with polynomial space requirements and (ii) that each PSPACE-complete problem can be reduced in polynomial time to a corresponding model checking problem.

Proof. Proving membership in PSPACE for LTL model checking is easy. Simply guess a path through the structure and check that the given formula holds on that path. This can be easily implemented with a nondeterministic machine.

To prove PSPACE-hardness, we give a polynomial reduction of an arbitrary PSPACE-complete problem to a model checking problem. For this reason, we consider a Turing machine $P = (\Sigma, Q, q_0, F, \Delta)$ where Σ is the alphabet, Q the set of states of P, $q_0 \in Q$ is the initial state and F are the final states. $\Delta \subseteq Q \times \Sigma \times \{-1, 0, 1\} \times Q \times \Sigma$ is the transition relation of P. A tuple $(q_i, a_i, m, q_j, a_j) \in \Delta$ has therefore the following meaning: if P is in state q_i and reads the input a_i, then it will write a_j, and will move its head by m and switches then to state q_j.

Let now P be an arbitrary Turing machine that runs for an input of length n with at most $S(n)$ memory cells such that $S(n)$ is bound by a polynomial in n. It is clear that the runtime $T(n)$ is then bound by an exponential, i.e., $T(n) \in O(2^{cn})$ for some $c \in \mathbb{N}$. We construct the computation table of P as follows:

	1	2	$\dots$	n	$n+1$	$\dots$	$S(n)$
0	(a_1, q_a)	a_2	$\dots$	a_n	β	$\dots$	β
$\vdots$	$\vdots$	$\vdots$	$\dots$	$\vdots$	$\vdots$	$\dots$	$\vdots$
$T(n)$	(β, q_e)	β	$\dots$	β	β	$\dots$	β

Each row in the above table corresponds to the description of an intermediate configuration of the Turing machine P. In particular, each row directly shows the contents of the tape, and of course, there is exactly one cell that is in $\Sigma \times Q$. This cell indicates the current position of the head of the Turing machine. Hence, the entries of the table are members of the set $\Sigma' := \Sigma \cup (\Sigma \times Q)$. The computation starts at time 0 with the tape $a_1 \dots a_n \beta \dots \beta$, where β is the blank symbol and $a_1 \dots a_n$ the input of length n that we consider. The input is accepted iff there is a computation of the machine that yields in the empty tape (filled with blank symbols β) such that the machine is in a final state $q_e \in F$.

Now, we consider the structure $\mathcal{K}_P = (\mathcal{I}_P, \mathcal{S}_P, \mathcal{R}_P, \mathcal{L}_P)$ as given in Figure 5.25, where $s := S(n)$ and $\delta = |\Sigma \cup (\Sigma \times Q)|$. The structure has the states $\mathcal{S} = \{p_i \mid 0 \leq i \leq s\} \cup \{q_{i,j} \mid 1 \leq i \leq s, 1 \leq j \leq \delta\}$, the initial states are $\mathcal{I}_P := \{p_0\}$ and the transition relation $\mathcal{R}_P$ is as given in Figure 5.25, i.e. $(p_i, q_{i+1,j}) \in \mathcal{R}_P$, $(q_{i,j}, p_i) \in \mathcal{R}_P$ and $(p_s, p_0) \in \mathcal{R}$. We enumerate the elements of $\Sigma \cup (\Sigma \times Q)$ such that $\Sigma \cup (\Sigma \times Q) := \{\sigma_1, \dots, \sigma_\delta\}$ and $\Sigma = \{\sigma_1, \dots, \sigma_d\}$. The variables of our temporal logic are $V_\Sigma := \{x_\sigma \mid \sigma \in \Sigma \cup (\Sigma \times Q)\} \cup \{y_i \mid 0 \leq i \leq s\}$, and the labeling function is given as $\mathcal{L}_P(p_i) := \{y_i\}$ and $\mathcal{L}_P(q_{i,j}) := \{x_j\}$.

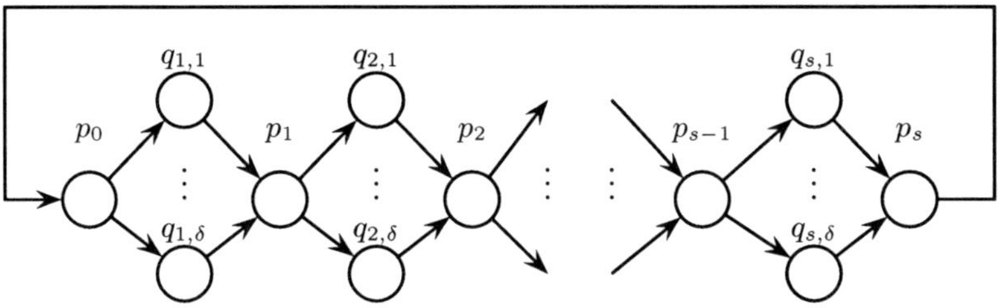

Fig. 5.25. Kripke structure for proving PSPACE-completeness

The aim of the construction of $\mathcal{K}_P$ is to model configurations of P by paths from p_0 to p_s. However, not each path p_0 to p_s corresponds to a configuration, as it is required that there is exactly one state q_{i_0,j_0} on the path such that $\sigma_{j_0} \in \Sigma \times Q$ while for all other states $q_{i,j}$ on the path $\sigma_j \in \Sigma$ holds. Each path that satisfies the following formula IsConfig corresponds to a configuration of a Turing machine P:

$$\mathsf{IsHead} := \bigvee_{i=d+1}^{\delta} x_i \qquad \mathsf{OneHead} := \bigvee_{i=1}^{s} \mathsf{X}^{2i-1}\mathsf{IsHead}$$
$$\mathsf{AtmostOneHead} := \bigvee_{i=1}^{s} \mathsf{X}^{2i-1}\mathsf{IsHead} \rightarrow \neg \bigvee_{j=1,j\neq i}^{s} \mathsf{X}^{2j-1}\mathsf{IsHead}$$
$$\mathsf{IsConfig} := \mathsf{OneHead} \wedge \mathsf{AtmostOneHead}$$

The length of the formula IsHead grows linearly in δ, and the lengths of OneHead and AtmostOneHead grow with $O(s^2)$ and $O(s^3)$, respectively. The initial and final configuration of a computation of P can also be easily specified with a temporal formula using only X operators. The following formula $\mathsf{isInitial}_a$ holds on a path starting in p_0 iff the paths corresponds to the initial configuration of P with the input $a := a_1 \ldots a_n$ and the formula isFinal describes the final configuration of P (where only the s relevant space cells are considered):

$$\mathsf{isInitial}_a := \mathsf{X}x_{(a_1,q_a)} \wedge \left(\bigwedge_{i=2}^{n} \mathsf{X}^{2i-1}x_{a_i}\right) \wedge \left(\bigwedge_{i=n+1}^{s} \mathsf{X}^{2i-1}x_{\beta}\right)$$
$$\mathsf{isFinal} := \bigvee_{q_e \in F} \mathsf{X}x_{(\beta,q_e)} \wedge \left(\bigwedge_{i=2}^{s} \mathsf{X}^{2i-1}x_{\beta}\right)$$

It is easy to see that the lengths of both formulas are again polynomial. Also, one can easily define a formula IsSucc that holds exactly on those paths π starting in p_0 where the part $\pi^{(1)}, \pi^{(3)}, \ldots, \pi^{(2s-1)}$ is a configuration such that $\pi^{(2s+2)}, \pi^{(2s+4)}, \ldots, \pi^{(4s)}$ is a succeeding configuration according to the transition function Δ of the Turing machine. Using IsSucc, the following formula states that a path π corresponds to a legal computation of P:

$$\mathsf{Run}_P := \mathsf{isInitial}_a \wedge [(y_0 \rightarrow \mathsf{IsSucc})\ \underline{\mathsf{U}}\ \mathsf{isFinal}]$$

Clearly, the length of Run_P also grows polynomially in s and Run_P holds on a path π through $\mathcal{K}_P$ iff this path starts with an initial configuration for P with input a, and finally yields in the final configuration while all intermediate path sequences starting in p_0 describe succeeding configurations according to P. Hence, we have

$$(\mathcal{K}_P, p_0) \models \mathsf{ERun}_P \text{ iff } P \text{ accepts } a$$

Therefore, the problem to decide whether P accepts a or not can be transformed in polynomial time in $s = S(n)$ and therefore in polynomial time in n to a LTL model checking problem of polynomial size in n. □

Note that Run_P as given in the proof can neither be expressed in CTL, nor with the subset of LTL where only the operators X, G, and F are allowed. In the original proof given in [456], it is also shown how the formulas required for the reduction can be described with only the $[\cdot\ \underline{\mathsf{U}}\ \cdot]$ operator. Moreover, it is not possible to express the above property in LeftCTL*. However, we immediately obtain the following result:

Theorem 5.94 (Complexity of AFCTL*). *The model checking problem of* AFCTL* *is* PSPACE-*complete.*

The upper bound, i.e., the existence of a PSPACE-algorithm for model checking AFCTL* follows from the PSPACE-algorithm for CTL* model checking. The hardness can be proved as shown above, since the formulas used there are also AFCTL* formulas.

5.7 Reductions by Simulation and Bisimulation Relations

In Section 3.8.1, we have already proved that μ-calculus formulas (without past modalities) can not distinguish between bisimilar states of a structure. For this reason, we can reduce the complexity of a μ-calculus model checking problem by computing the quotient structure with the largest bisimulation relation. As CTL* can be translated to the μ-calculus, it is also not possible to distinguish bisimilar states by CTL* formulas, and for this reason, the same reduction of the model checking problem via bisimulation relations is possible.

The converse relation needs however some care: In fact, in case of the μ-calculus, even fixpoint-free formulas are powerful enough to distinguish states that are not bisimilar. However, the same does not hold for temporal logic, when deadend states appear in the Kripke structure. For example, consider the two Kripke structures $\mathcal{K}_1$ and $\mathcal{K}_2$ given in Figure 5.26. The states s_0 and t_0 can be distinguished by the μ-calculus formula $\Diamond\Box 0$, since we have

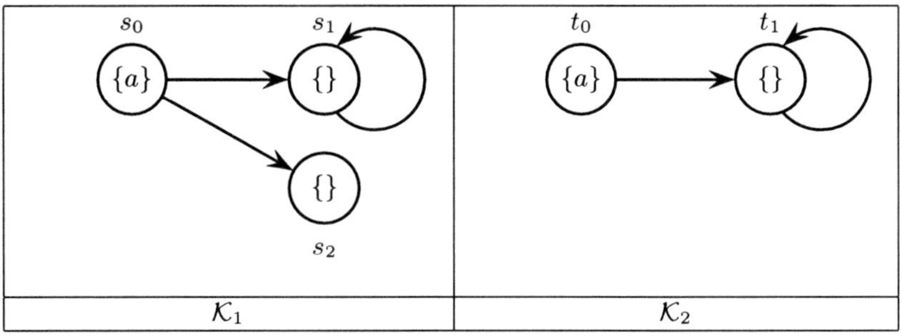

Fig. 5.26. Non-bisimilar structures that can not be distinguished by CTL^*

$(\mathcal{K}_1, s_0) \models \Diamond\Box 0$, but $(\mathcal{K}_2, t_0) \not\models \Diamond\Box 0$ (note that $\Box 0$ holds in a state iff this state has no successors). As two states are bisimilar if and only if they satisfy the same μ-calculus formulas, it follows that s_0 and t_0 are not bisimilar.

However, s_0 and t_0 satisfy the same CTL^* formulas. *The problem is that temporal logics ignore finite paths*, which is the reason why some authors set up the restriction that every state of a Kripke structure should have a successor state. Only with this restriction, the translation of $\mathsf{EF}\varphi$ is $\mu x.\varphi \vee \Diamond x$, otherwise, we need the slightly more complex version $\mu x.\varphi \wedge (\nu y.\Diamond y) \vee \Diamond x$.

This is due to the definition of the path quantifiers E and A, which consider only infinite paths. Changing this definition causes trouble in the relationship between ω-automata and temporal logic. The deadend states are the only problem, since once we remove them, the desired relationship between bisimulation and satisfiability of the same CTL^* formulas becomes valid: The restricted structures that obtained by removing the deadend states, i.e., the states in $[\![\mu x.\Box x]\!]_{\mathcal{K}}$ (cf. pages 81 and 106), are bisimilar iff they satisfy the same CTL^* formulas. The same can even be stated for CTL:

Theorem 5.95 (Bisimulation Equivalence for CTL^* and CTL). *Given two structures $\mathcal{K}_1$ and $\mathcal{K}_2$ over a the variables V_Σ. Compute $\mathcal{S}_{\mathsf{inf}}^{(1)} = [\![\nu x.\Diamond x]\!]_{\mathcal{K}_1}$ and $\mathcal{S}_{\mathsf{inf}}^{(2)} = [\![\nu x.\Diamond x]\!]_{\mathcal{K}_2}$, and let $\mathcal{K}_1^{\mathsf{inf}}$ and $\mathcal{K}_2^{\mathsf{inf}}$ be the restrictions of $\mathcal{K}_1$ and $\mathcal{K}_2$ to $\mathcal{S}_{\mathsf{inf}}^{(1)}$ and $\mathcal{S}_{\mathsf{inf}}^{(2)}$, respectively. Moreover, assume that $\approx$ is the largest bisimulation relation between $\mathcal{K}_1^{\mathsf{inf}}$ and $\mathcal{K}_2^{\mathsf{inf}}$. Then, the following holds:*

- $s_1 \approx s_2 \Leftrightarrow \forall \varphi \in \mathsf{CTL}.(\mathcal{K}_1, s_1) \models \varphi \Leftrightarrow (\mathcal{K}_2, s_2) \models \varphi$
- $s_1 \approx s_2 \Leftrightarrow \forall \varphi \in \mathsf{CTL}^*.(\mathcal{K}_1, s_1) \models \varphi \Leftrightarrow (\mathcal{K}_2, s_2) \models \varphi$

This result has been originally proved in [72]. The proof of the above theorem is similar to the proof of Theorem 3.44 on page 170, except that $\Diamond$ and $\Box$ are replaced with EX and AX in the construction of the formulas $\Phi_i(s_j)$.

On page 173, we have also established the relationship between simulation relations and the existential or the universal fragment of the μ-calculus.

The above theorem can also be stated for simulation relations and the existential / universal fragments of ACTL^* and ACTL:

$$
\begin{array}{rrl}
\mathsf{ACTL}^*: & S ::= & S_A \\
& S_A ::= & V_\Sigma \mid \neg S_E \mid S_A \wedge S_A \mid S_A \vee S_A \mid \mathsf{A}P_A \\
& S_E ::= & V_\Sigma \mid \neg S_A \mid S_E \wedge S_E \mid S_E \vee S_E \mid \mathsf{E}P_E \\
& P_E ::= & S_E \mid \neg P_A \mid P_E \wedge P_E \mid P_E \vee P_E \mid \mathsf{X}P_E \mid \mathsf{G}P_E \mid \mathsf{F}P_E \\
& & \mid [P_E\ \mathsf{W}\ P_E] \mid [P_E\ \mathsf{U}\ P_E] \mid [P_E\ \mathsf{B}\ P_A] \\
& & \mid [P_E\ \underline{\mathsf{W}}\ P_E] \mid [P_E\ \underline{\mathsf{U}}\ P_E] \mid [P_E\ \underline{\mathsf{B}}\ P_A] \\
& P_A ::= & S_A \mid \neg P_E \mid P_A \wedge P_A \mid P_A \vee P_A \mid \mathsf{X}P_A \mid \mathsf{G}P_A \mid \mathsf{F}P_A \\
& & \mid [P_A\ \mathsf{W}\ P_A] \mid [P_A\ \mathsf{U}\ P_A] \mid [P_A\ \mathsf{B}\ P_E] \\
& & \mid [P_A\ \underline{\mathsf{W}}\ P_A] \mid [P_A\ \underline{\mathsf{U}}\ P_A] \mid [P_A\ \underline{\mathsf{B}}\ P_E] \\
\mathsf{ACTL}: & S ::= & S_A \\
& S_A ::= & V_\Sigma \mid \neg S_E \mid S_A \wedge S_A \mid S_A \vee S_A \mid \mathsf{A}P_A \\
& S_E ::= & V_\Sigma \mid \neg S_A \mid S_E \wedge S_E \mid S_E \vee S_E \mid \mathsf{E}P_E \\
& P_E ::= & \mathsf{X}S_E \mid \mathsf{G}S_E \mid \mathsf{F}S_E \\
& & \mid [S_E\ \mathsf{W}\ S_E] \mid [S_E\ \mathsf{U}\ S_E] \mid [S_E\ \mathsf{B}\ S_A] \\
& & \mid [S_E\ \underline{\mathsf{W}}\ S_E] \mid [S_E\ \underline{\mathsf{U}}\ S_E] \mid [S_E\ \underline{\mathsf{B}}\ S_A] \\
& P_A ::= & \mathsf{X}S_A \mid \mathsf{G}S_A \mid \mathsf{F}S_A \\
& & \mid [S_A\ \mathsf{W}\ S_A] \mid [S_A\ \mathsf{U}\ S_A] \mid [S_A\ \mathsf{B}\ S_E] \\
& & \mid [S_A\ \underline{\mathsf{W}}\ S_A] \mid [S_A\ \underline{\mathsf{U}}\ S_A] \mid [S_A\ \underline{\mathsf{B}}\ S_E]
\end{array}
$$

Fig. 5.27. Definition of the temporal logics ACTL^* and ACTL

Definition 5.96 (ACTL^*). *Given a finite set of variables V_Σ, the grammars given in Figure 5.27 define the sublanguages ACTL^* and ACTL of CTL^*.*

ACTL^* is the set of CTL^* formulas where each occurrence of a path quantifier A is positive and each occurrence of a path quantifier E is negative. Analogously, ACTL is the subset of CTL where the occurrences of all A and E path quantifiers are positive and negative, respectively. Note that $\mathsf{LTL} \subseteq \mathsf{ACTL}^*$ holds, but the other direction does of course, not hold.

Theorem 5.97 (Simulation Reduction for ACTL**).** *Given two structures $\mathcal{K}_1$ and $\mathcal{K}_2$ over a the variables V_Σ. Compute $\mathcal{S}_{\mathsf{inf}}^{(1)} = [\![\nu x.\Diamond x]\!]_{\mathcal{K}_1}$ and $\mathcal{S}_{\mathsf{inf}}^{(2)} = [\![\nu x.\Diamond x]\!]_{\mathcal{K}_2}$, and let $\mathcal{K}_1^{\mathsf{inf}}$ and $\mathcal{K}_2^{\mathsf{inf}}$ be the restrictions of $\mathcal{K}_1$ and $\mathcal{K}_2$ to $\mathcal{S}_{\mathsf{inf}}^{(1)}$ and $\mathcal{S}_{\mathsf{inf}}^{(2)}$, respectively. Moreover, assume that ζ is the largest simulation relation between $\mathcal{K}_1^{\mathsf{inf}}$ and $\mathcal{K}_2^{\mathsf{inf}}$. Then, the following holds:*

- $(s_1, s_2) \in \zeta \Leftrightarrow \forall \varphi \in \mathsf{ACTL}.(\mathcal{K}_2, s_2) \models \varphi \Rightarrow (\mathcal{K}_1, s_1) \models \varphi$
- $(s_1, s_2) \in \zeta \Leftrightarrow \forall \varphi \in \mathsf{ACTL}^*.(\mathcal{K}_2, s_2) \models \varphi \Rightarrow (\mathcal{K}_1, s_1) \models \varphi$

Proof. We have already proved the direction from left to right, since ACTL formulas can be reduced to $\mathcal{L}_\mu^{\mathsf{A}}$ (and negations of ACTL to $\mathcal{L}_\mu^{\mathsf{E}}$). For the other direction, we construct for all states $s_1 \in \mathcal{S}_1$, $s_2 \in \mathcal{S}_2$ with $(s_1, s_2) \notin \zeta$ a ACTL formula that holds in s_2, but not in s_1. To this end, we construct the following formulas $\Phi_i(s_1)$ for a given state $s_1 \in \mathcal{S}_1$:

- $\Phi_0(s_1) = \bigwedge_{x \in \mathcal{L}_1(s_1)} x \wedge \bigwedge_{x \in V_\Sigma \setminus \mathcal{L}_1(s_1)} \neg x$
- $\Phi_{i+1}(s_1) = \Phi_i(s_1) \wedge \bigwedge_{(s_1, s_1') \in \mathcal{R}_1} \mathsf{EX}\Phi_i(s_1')$

It is obvious that $\Phi_i(s_1)$ is the negation of a ACTL formula and that $(\mathcal{K}_1, s_1) \models \Phi_i(s_1)$ holds for all i. Recall now that the following sequence of relations converges to the largest simulation relation (see Lemma 2.15 on page 56):

- $(s_1, s_2) \in \mathcal{H}_0 :\Leftrightarrow \mathcal{L}_1(s_1) = \mathcal{L}_2(s_2)$
- $(s_1, s_2) \in \mathcal{H}_{i+1} :\Leftrightarrow \left(\begin{array}{l} (s_1, s_2) \in \mathcal{H}_i \wedge \\ \forall s_1' \in \mathcal{S}_1.(s_1, s_1') \in \mathcal{R}_1 \rightarrow \\ \qquad \exists s_2' \in \mathcal{S}_2.(s_2, s_2') \in \mathcal{R}_2 \wedge (s_1', s_2') \in \mathcal{H}_i \end{array} \right)$

We have already seen that there is a $n \in \mathbb{N}$ such that $\zeta = \mathcal{H}_n$. We show now by induction on i that $(\mathcal{K}_2, s_2) \models \Phi_i(s_1)$ holds if and only if $(s_1, s_2) \in \mathcal{H}_i$.

i=0: $(\mathcal{K}_2, s_2) \models \Phi_0(s_1) \Leftrightarrow \mathcal{L}_1(s_1) = \mathcal{L}_2(s_2) \Leftrightarrow (s_1, s_2) \in \mathcal{H}_0$

i>0: $(\mathcal{K}_2, s_2) \models \Phi_{i+1}(s_1)$

$\Leftrightarrow (\mathcal{K}_2, s_2) \models \Phi_i(s_1) \wedge \bigwedge_{(s_1, s_1') \in \mathcal{R}_1} \mathsf{EX}\Phi_i(s_1')$

$\Leftrightarrow (\mathcal{K}_2, s_2) \models \Phi_i(s_1) \wedge$

$\qquad \forall s_1' \in \mathcal{S}_1.(s_1, s_1') \in \mathcal{R}_1 \rightarrow (\mathcal{K}_2, s_2) \models \mathsf{EX}\Phi_i(s_1')$

$\Leftrightarrow (s_1, s_2) \in \mathcal{H}_i \wedge$

$\qquad \forall s_1' \in \mathcal{S}_1.(s_1, s_1') \in \mathcal{R}_1 \rightarrow \exists s_2' \in \mathcal{S}_2.(s_2, s_2') \in \mathcal{R}_2 \wedge (s_1', s_2') \in \mathcal{H}_i$

$\Leftrightarrow (s_1, s_2) \in \mathcal{H}_{i+1}$

Note that due to the assumption that there are no deadend states, we have $\Diamond\varphi = \mathsf{EX}\varphi$. Moreover, note that for all i, $\neg\Phi_i(s_1)$ is a ACTL formula with $(\mathcal{K}_1, s_1) \not\models \neg\Phi_i(s_1)$. Finally, it follows that whenever there are two states $(s_1, s_2) \notin \zeta$, then there is a $n \in \mathbb{N}$ such that $(s_1, s_2) \notin \mathcal{H}_n$, and therefore by the above result, that $(\mathcal{K}_2, s_2) \models \neg\Phi_n(s_1)$ holds. Choosing n large enough (so that $\mathcal{H}_n = \zeta$ holds) shows then the result. □

Simulation relations are interesting means to reduce the complexity of a model checking problem. According to the above result, the greatest simulation relation is the coarsest abstraction that preserves all universal temporal properties. Constructions of abstract structures by simulation relation are given in Appendix C. Moreover, due its local definition, the greatest simulation relation can be computed in polynomial time, in contrast to trace containment. Extensions to fairness restrictions are considered in [26], and different variants are compared in [242].

6

Predicate Logic

6.1 Introduction

As mentioned in Chapter 1, the origins of formal logic are due to Frege [198] who invented in his 'Begriffsschrift' a formalism that we now call first order logic. In the meantime, numerous specializations and extensions have been developed. For example the extension to higher order logics [17, 100, 216] can be used to formalize the entire mathematics that we know today. Hence, predicate logic is a very general formalism.

Domain-specific applications require to consider theories of special structures like groups or linear orders. In general, such special theories are obtained by setting up a finite of axioms which are predicate logic formulas that are assumed to be valid. This means, that only interpretation of formulas are considered that satisfy the given axioms. Clearly, we have to find axioms that characterize the models (up to isomorphism) w.r.t. the desired structures. For example, predicate logics can be used to reason about natural numbers, when the following axioms due to Peano are assumed to be true:

$$\begin{aligned}
&\mathsf{Peano1}: \forall n.\ \neg 0 \doteq \mathsf{SUC}(n)\\
&\mathsf{Peano2}: \forall m.\forall n.\ (\mathsf{SUC}(m) \doteq \mathsf{SUC}(n)) \rightarrow (m \doteq n)\\
&\mathsf{Peano3}: \forall p.\ (\forall n.p(n)) \leftrightarrow p(0) \wedge \forall n.p(n) \rightarrow p(\mathsf{SUC}(n))
\end{aligned}$$

Assuming these axioms enables predicate logic to reason about natural numbers and arithmetic operations like $+$ and relations like $<$. The third axiom, Peano3, is a formula of second order logic, since it quantifies over sets (represented by the monadic predicate p). It can be shown that Peano3 can not be expressed by any finite set of first order formulas. Hence, reasoning about natural numbers requires second order logic. As discrete time, as used in Kripke structures, can be modeled by natural numbers, we conclude that the same holds for temporal properties.

However, we may also consider first order formulas over the natural numbers. In this case, we must still use Peano's axioms to restrict the models such that they are (at least isomorphic to) the natural numbers. For this reason, we still need second order logic, but as we will only consider first order formulas (except for Peano's axioms), we nevertheless speak about first order logic. Although this is not precisely correct, it is the generally accepted notation.

In this chapter, we therefore consider first and second order predicate logics, mainly interpreted over the natural numbers. There are two ways one may look at these logics, depending on whether one emphasizes the arithmetics or the ordering of the natural numbers. For the comparison with temporal logics, the ordering of the natural numbers is more important, and therefore we will, in particular, consider logics with the linear ordering (over the naturals). We will also consider some restricted classes that correspond to ω-regular languages and temporal logics. We will see that there is a strong relationship between ω-automata, temporal logics, and certain fragments of predicate logic.

The most frequently used formalisms for specifying and verifying reactive systems are temporal logics, though we already know by the previous chapter that temporal logics are less expressive than μ-calculus and ω-automata. The reason for the widespread use of temporal logics is that they are in general more readable than μ-calculus or ω-automata specifications. For some properties, however, the formalization with temporal logics is not obvious since temporal logics have an event-oriented view of time, i.e., they can not *directly refer to different points* of time or intervals. Instead, they have to use signals for referring to certain points of time where an event related to these signals holds. Predicate logics, on the other hand, can directly refer to several points of time, relate them via equations and inequations, and hence can directly refer to intervals. This makes them especially useful for the formalization of timing diagrams [14, 193, 432], which are traditionally used in the design of digital circuits. Hence, predicate logics on numbers are somehow closer to traditional design methods than other formalisms. Moreover, they are not limited to the verification of temporal properties [31, 54, 240, 296, 446, 522]. We will see that only three variables for points of time will be necessary to express all facts that can be expressed in temporal logic, and we will also consider the two-variable fragment, which is strictly weaker.

As all logics we have considered in the previous chapters for the specification of reactive systems have decidable model-checking and satisfiability checking problems, it follows that the corresponding fragments of first and second order logic must also have decidable problems. Hence, we are particularly interested in decidable fragments of predicate logic. The results are not only important for a better understanding of the logics, but also to reason about decidable or undecidable extensions.

Logicians have considered several fragments predicate logic to search for *decidable classes* (see Section 6.2.3): the first classes were defined by *quantifier prefixes*, e.g., the $\mathsf{FO}(\exists^*\forall^*)$ class contains the first order formulas that start with (possible none) existential quantifiers, then a sequence of universal quantifiers and a quantifier-free formula. Another way to restrict the formulas is to only use a finite *number of variables*. It turns out that three variables retain still the full power of first order logic, but two variables yield a decidable fragment. Two-variable fragments are of interest, since the embedding of modal logic in predicate logic only requires two variables. Vardi [495] therefore posed the question if this is the reason for the robust decidability of modal logics. We will therefore briefly consider these fragments in Section 6.2.3, and recommend Börger, Grädel, and Gurevich's book [56] for further reading. A quite new branch of decidable logic fragments is formed by *guarded logics* [15, 217, 221] that are strongly related with modal logics like the μ-calculus.

A further way to obtain decidable fragments is to restrict the signature, i.e., the available predicate and function symbols. First order logic is already a restriction of second order logic, where second order variables are forbidden. Relational logics forbid function symbols, which is often necessary to obtain decidable classes. Presburger arithmetic [191, 336, 415] is a decidable subset of (Peano's) arithmetic, where only $+$ and $<$ is allowed. Another decidable subset of arithmetic is Skolem arithmetic [336, 463], where only multiplication is allowed. Note that the full Peano arithmetic is well-known to be undecidable [212].

Of particular interest are furthermore *monadic predicate logics*, where predicate symbols of arity greater than 1 are forbidden. The decidability of *monadic second order theory of one successor* (S1S) has been proved by Büchi [80, 455, 486]. For this result, Büchi developed the theory of ω-automata and proved that ω-regular languages are closed under complementation. The first order variant of this logic seemed not to have an interesting counterpart. However, it is well-known that in second order logic, the successor can be defined by the ordering $<$ of the natural numbers and vice versa. Hence, S1S is equivalent to the *monadic second order logic over linear order* $\mathsf{MSO}_<$ (see Section 6.3). The same does not hold for the corresponding first order counterparts, since the definition of $<$ by SUC requires a second order quantification. Thomas [484] characterized the first order fragment of S1S as *locally threshold testable sets* (see also [405, 475]).

Having this view, Kamp [274] showed that the *monadic first order logic of linear order* $\mathsf{MFO}_<$ is equivalent expressive to linear time temporal logic LTL_p. McNaughton and Papert [364], and Thomas [483], furthermore added the fact that the corresponding fragment of automata is the set of noncounting automata (see Theorem 5.82 on page 386). Kamp also proved that the fragment of LTL_p where only unary temporal operators are used, is strictly less expressive than LTL_p (see Theorem 5.2 on page 287). Etessami, Vardi, and Wilke [186, 187] have furthermore shown that this fragment of LTL_p corresponds to the restriction $\mathsf{MFO}^2_<$ of $\mathsf{MFO}_<$, where only two variables are allowed. $\mathsf{MFO}_<$ with three variables, in contrast, is as expressive as $\mathsf{MFO}_<$ itself, and is therefore sufficient to capture full LTL_p.

The outline of this chapter is as follows: in Section 6.2, we consider first and second order predicate logic, in particular, the syntax and semantics in Section 6.2.1, general results on these logics in Section 6.2.2, and some decidable classes in Section 6.2.3. In Section 6.2.4, we emphasize the relationship between modal logics and two-variable fragments of predicate logic. Moreover, we consider the relevance of predicate logic over linear orders for complexity theory in Section 6.2.5 and linear time (temporal) logics. This relationship is further detailed in Section 6.3, where we show the equivalence between the monadic second order logics S1S and $\mathsf{MSO}_<$, and also between the ω-regular languages. In addition, we consider in Section 6.3.3 Büchi's original decision procedure. Although Büchi's original procedure is more difficult, it still contains transformations that are interesting in their own right.

In Section 6.4, we consider the first order fragment $\mathsf{MFO}_<$ of $\mathsf{MSO}_<$, and prove the equal expressiveness to linear time temporal logic. We also consider the two-variable fragment $\mathsf{MFO}^2_<$ of $\mathsf{MFO}_<$, which is equivalent to LTL_p where only unary operators are allowed. Finally, we consider in Section 6.5 new results that have been established to characterize regular languages with non-monadic second order logics.

Beneath the usage presented in this chapter, it has to be noted that decidable classes of predicate logic have found many other applications. For example, [296, 446] exploit the fact that the transition relation of register machines can be described with Presburger arithmetic. Therefore, it can be represented by means of finite state automata (see end of Section 6.3.1). As the same holds for most reasonable subsets of reachable states of the register machine, it follows that finite state automata can serve as a finite representation of infinite sets of states. The papers [54, 296, 446, 522] among many others [488] describe therefore the *verification of systems with infinitely many states*. Of course, decision procedures are also used as tactics in interactive theorem provers like HOL or PVS [216, 396]. In particular, S1S has been used [31, 240, 354, 442] for the *automatic verification of recursively defined regular structures*.

6.2 Predicate Logics

6.2.1 Syntax and Semantics

The syntax of any predicate logic depends on a signature $\Sigma = (C_\Sigma, V_\Sigma, \mathsf{typ}_\Sigma)$ that determines the set of constants C_Σ, the set of variables V_Σ, and a typing function typ_Σ. The latter is a function from $C_\Sigma \cup V_\Sigma$ to the set of types of the logic. For higher order logics, the set of types can be defined with a type structure, but as we will only consider first and second order logics with very simple types, we can directly define the set of types.

The syntax of a predicate logic is then determined by the signature according to the type constraints. The basic type is the set of *individuals* $\mathbb{I}$. In a *first order logic*, every variable x of the set V_Σ has this type, hence, we have

$\mathsf{typ}_\Sigma(x) = \mathbb{I}$ for every variable $x \in V_\Sigma$. The constants $c \in C_\Sigma$ of first order logic may have types of the form $\mathsf{typ}_\Sigma(c) = \mathbb{I}^n \to \mathbb{I}$ or $\mathsf{typ}_\Sigma(c) = \mathbb{I}^n \to \mathbb{B}$, where we abbreviate the cartesian product $\mathbb{I} \times \ldots \times \mathbb{I}$ with n types as $\mathbb{I}^n$. Hence, any syntactical object in first order logic has one of the following types: $\mathbb{I}$, $\mathbb{B}$, $\mathbb{I}^n \to \mathbb{I}$, or $\mathbb{I}^n \to \mathbb{B}$. In *second order logic*, we add also variables of types $\mathbb{B}$ and $\mathbb{I}^n \to \mathbb{B}$, so it is possible to quantify over sets of individuals. In general, one defines the set of terms and the set of formulas by the following recursive steps[1]:

Definition 6.1 (Syntax of First and Second Order Predicate Logic). *Given a signature $\Sigma = (C_\Sigma, V_\Sigma, \mathsf{typ}_\Sigma)$, we define the set of terms* Term_Σ *as the smallest set that satisfies the following rules:*

- $x \in \mathsf{Term}_\Sigma$ *for* $x \in V_\Sigma \cup C_\Sigma$ *with* $\mathsf{typ}_\Sigma(x) = \mathbb{I}$
- $f(\tau_1, \ldots, \tau_n) \in \mathsf{Term}_\Sigma$ *for* $f \in V_\Sigma \cup C_\Sigma$ *with* $\mathsf{typ}_\Sigma(f) = \mathbb{I}^n \to \mathbb{I}$ *and* $\tau_i \in \mathsf{Term}_\Sigma$

The set of formulas is defined as the smallest set SO *that satisfies the following rules:*

- $\tau_1 \doteq \tau_2 \in \mathsf{SO}$ *for all* $\tau_1, \tau_2 \in \mathsf{Term}_\Sigma$
- $p \in \mathsf{SO}$ *for* $p \in V_\Sigma \cup C_\Sigma$ *with* $\mathsf{typ}_\Sigma(x) = \mathbb{B}$
- $p(\tau_1, \ldots, \tau_n) \in \mathsf{SO}$ *for* $p \in V_\Sigma \cup C_\Sigma$ *with* $\mathsf{typ}_\Sigma(p) = \mathbb{I}^n \to \mathbb{B}$ *and* $\tau_i \in \mathsf{Term}_\Sigma$
- $\neg\varphi$, $\varphi \wedge \psi$, $\varphi \vee \psi \in \mathsf{SO}$ *for all* $\varphi, \psi \in \mathsf{SO}$
- $\forall x.\, \varphi \in \mathsf{SO}$ *for all* $x \in V_\Sigma$ *and* $\varphi \in \mathsf{SO}$
- $\exists x.\, \varphi \in \mathsf{SO}$ *for all* $x \in V_\Sigma$ *and* $\varphi \in \mathsf{SO}$

The above set of formulas defines second order logic SO*, the restriction where quantification over variables is only allowed for variables of type* $\mathsf{typ}_\Sigma(x) = \mathbb{I}$ *is first order logic* FO.

For the semantics, one has to choose a *domain* $\mathcal{D}$ whose members are interpreted as the individuals, hence, $\mathbb{I}$ corresponds with $\mathcal{D}$. In the following, we denote the set of total functions from a set A to a set B as $\mathfrak{F}(A, B)$. Constants of C_Σ are interpreted with an *interpretation* $\mathcal{J} : C_\Sigma \to \mathcal{D}^*$, where $\mathcal{D}^* := \mathcal{D} \cup \{\mathfrak{F}(\mathcal{D}^n, \mathcal{D}) \mid n \in \mathbb{N}\} \cup \{\mathfrak{F}(\mathcal{D}^n, \{\mathsf{true}, \mathsf{false}\}) \mid n \in \mathbb{N}\}$. Clearly, $\mathcal{J}$ must obey the typing constraints, i.e., any constant $c \in C_\Sigma$ of type $\mathbb{I}$, $\mathbb{I}^n \to \mathbb{I}$, $\mathbb{B}$, and $\mathbb{I}^n \to \mathbb{B}$ must be mapped to an element of $\mathcal{D}$, $\mathfrak{F}(\mathcal{D}^n, \mathcal{D})$, $\{\mathsf{true}, \mathsf{false}\}$, and $\mathfrak{F}(\mathcal{D}^n, \{\mathsf{true}, \mathsf{false}\})$, respectively. Variables are interpreted with a *variable assignment* ξ that is, analogously to $\mathcal{J}$, a function from $\xi : V_\Sigma \to \mathcal{D}$ that must obey the same typing constraints.

The only reason, why variables and constants are interpreted by different functions is that the mapping of variables to $\mathcal{D}$ must be modified when quantified formulas have to be evaluated. In particular, we then use the modification ξ_x^d of the variable assignment ξ for a variable x and an element $d \in \mathcal{D}$. Except for the variable x, ξ_x^d has for each variable the same value as ξ. For the variable x, we have $\xi_x^d(x) := d$, regardless of the value $\xi(x)$.

[1] In higher order logics, this distinction is usually not made.

The semantics $[\![\tau]\!]_{\mathcal{D},\mathcal{J},\xi}$ of a term $\tau \in \mathsf{Term}_\Sigma$ is then an element of $\mathcal{D}$, and the semantics $[\![\varphi]\!]_{\mathcal{D},\mathcal{J},\xi}$ of a formula $\varphi \in \mathsf{SO}$ is a Boolean value.

Definition 6.2 (Semantics of First and Second Order Predicate Logic). *Given a signature $\Sigma = (C_\Sigma, V_\Sigma, \mathsf{typ}_\Sigma)$, a domain $\mathcal{D}$, an interpretation $\mathcal{J}$, and a variable assignment ξ, the semantics $[\![\tau]\!]_{\mathcal{D},\mathcal{J},\xi}$ of a term $\tau \in \mathsf{Term}_\Sigma$ is a member of $\mathcal{D}$ that is determined as follows:*

- $[\![x]\!]_{\mathcal{D},\mathcal{J},\xi} := \xi(x)$ *for* $x \in V_\Sigma$ *with* $\mathsf{typ}_\Sigma(x) = \mathbb{I}$
- $[\![c]\!]_{\mathcal{D},\mathcal{J},\xi} := \mathcal{J}(c)$ *for* $c \in C_\Sigma$ *with* $\mathsf{typ}_\Sigma(c) = \mathbb{I}$
- $[\![f(\tau_1,\ldots,\tau_n)]\!]_{\mathcal{D},\mathcal{J},\xi} := \xi(f)([\![\tau_1]\!]_{\mathcal{D},\mathcal{J},\xi},\ldots,[\![\tau_n]\!]_{\mathcal{D},\mathcal{J},\xi})$ *for* $f \in V_\Sigma$
- $[\![f(\tau_1,\ldots,\tau_n)]\!]_{\mathcal{D},\mathcal{J},\xi} := \mathcal{J}(f)([\![\tau_1]\!]_{\mathcal{D},\mathcal{J},\xi},\ldots,[\![\tau_n]\!]_{\mathcal{D},\mathcal{J},\xi})$ *for* $f \in C_\Sigma$

The semantics $[\![\varphi]\!]_{\mathcal{D},\mathcal{J},\xi}$ of a formula φ is a Boolean value that is recursively determined as follows:

- $[\![\tau_1 \doteq \tau_2]\!]_{\mathcal{D},\mathcal{J},\xi} := \begin{cases} \mathsf{true} : & \textit{if } [\![\tau_1]\!]_{\mathcal{D},\mathcal{J},\xi} = [\![\tau_1]\!]_{\mathcal{D},\mathcal{J},\xi} \\ \mathsf{false} : & \textit{otherwise} \end{cases}$
- $[\![p]\!]_{\mathcal{D},\mathcal{J},\xi} := \xi(p)$ *for* $p \in V_\Sigma$
- $[\![p]\!]_{\mathcal{D},\mathcal{J},\xi} := \mathcal{J}(p)$ *for* $p \in C_\Sigma$
- $[\![p(\tau_1,\ldots,\tau_n)]\!]_{\mathcal{D},\mathcal{J},\xi} := \xi(p)\left([\![\tau_1]\!]_{\mathcal{D},\mathcal{J},\xi},\ldots,[\![\tau_n]\!]_{\mathcal{D},\mathcal{J},\xi}\right)$ *for* $p \in V_\Sigma$
- $[\![p(\tau_1,\ldots,\tau_n)]\!]_{\mathcal{D},\mathcal{J},\xi} := \mathcal{J}(p)\left([\![\tau_1]\!]_{\mathcal{D},\mathcal{J},\xi},\ldots,[\![\tau_n]\!]_{\mathcal{D},\mathcal{J},\xi}\right)$ *for* $p \in C_\Sigma$
- $[\![\neg\varphi]\!]_{\mathcal{D},\mathcal{J},\xi} := \neg\, [\![\varphi]\!]_{\mathcal{D},\mathcal{J},\xi}$
- $[\![\varphi \wedge \psi]\!]_{\mathcal{D},\mathcal{J},\xi} := [\![\varphi]\!]_{\mathcal{D},\mathcal{J},\xi} \wedge [\![\psi]\!]_{\mathcal{D},\mathcal{J},\xi}$
- $[\![\varphi \vee \psi]\!]_{\mathcal{D},\mathcal{J},\xi} := [\![\varphi]\!]_{\mathcal{D},\mathcal{J},\xi} \vee [\![\psi]\!]_{\mathcal{D},\mathcal{J},\xi}$
- $[\![\exists x.\varphi]\!]_{\mathcal{D},\mathcal{J},\xi} := \begin{cases} \mathsf{true} : & \textit{if there exists } d \in \mathcal{D} \textit{ with } [\![\varphi]\!]_{\mathcal{D},\mathcal{J},\xi_x^d} = \mathsf{true} \\ \mathsf{false} : & \textit{otherwise} \end{cases}$
- $[\![\forall x.\varphi]\!]_{\mathcal{D},\mathcal{J},\xi} := \begin{cases} \mathsf{true} : & \textit{if for all } d \in \mathcal{D}, [\![\varphi]\!]_{\mathcal{D},\mathcal{J},\xi_x^d} = \mathsf{true} \textit{ holds} \\ \mathsf{false} : & \textit{otherwise} \end{cases}$

We have used the symbols $\neg$, $\wedge$ and $\vee$ also in our meta language, instead of rewriting the facts in natural (English) language. We use the notions of bound and free occurrences of variables, and the substitution of variables as intuitively given.

6.2.2 Basics of Predicate Logic

In this section, we briefly consider some basic results for first and second order predicate logic. For further details, the interested reader is referred to [56, 149, 184, 195, 334, 464]. The satisfiability problem of FO (first order logic) is undecidable [99, 492]. However, the set of unsatisfiable FO formulas is recursively enumerable, i.e., there is an algorithm that can prove in finite time every valid FO sentence, but may run into an infinite loop when the given sentence is not valid. The main ingredients for this algorithm are as follows: First of all, FO formulas can be brought into special normal forms, in particular into prenex and Skolem normal forms.

Theorem 6.3 (Prenex Normal Form). *Every* SO *formula can be rewritten such that all quantifiers appear on top of the syntax tree of the formula, i.e., the formula is of the form* $\Theta_1 x_1 \ldots . \Theta_n x_n.\varphi$ *with* $\Theta_i \in \{\exists, \forall\}$ *and a quantifier-free formula* φ. *To this end, one can use the following valid formulas (provided that* x *does not occur in* ψ*):*

$$(\forall x.\varphi) \wedge \psi \Leftrightarrow \forall x.\varphi \wedge \psi \qquad (\forall x.\varphi) \vee \psi \Leftrightarrow \forall x.\varphi \vee \psi$$
$$(\exists x.\varphi) \wedge \psi \Leftrightarrow \exists x.\varphi \wedge \psi \qquad (\exists x.\varphi) \vee \psi \Leftrightarrow \exists x.\varphi \vee \psi$$
$$(\forall x.\varphi) \wedge (\forall y.\psi) \Leftrightarrow \forall x.\varphi \wedge [\psi]_y^x \qquad (\exists x.\varphi) \vee (\exists y.\psi) \Leftrightarrow \exists x.\varphi \vee [\psi]_y^x$$

Theorem 6.4 (Skolemization [461]). *Every* FO *formula (with equality) of the form* $\forall x_1 \ldots \forall x_n.\exists y.\Phi$ *is equivalent to the formula* $\exists f.\forall x_1 \ldots \forall x_n. [\Phi]_y^{f(x_1,\ldots,x_n)}$, *where* f *is a function symbol that does not occur in* Φ. *Hence,* $\forall x_1 \ldots \forall x_n.\exists y.\Phi$ *is satisfiable iff the* FO *formula* $\forall x_1 \ldots \forall x_n. [\Phi]_y^{f(x_1,\ldots,x_n)}$ *is satisfiable.*

Hence, the satisfiability problem of FO can be reduced to universally quantified formulas. The key idea of skolemization is that a quantifier alternation of the form $\forall^*\exists$ induces a functional relationship that can be made explicit by the use of a function symbol. Note that $\exists f.\forall x_1 \ldots \forall x_n. [\Phi]_y^{f(x_1,\ldots,x_n)}$ is a SO formula, but can be satisfied iff the FO formula $\forall x_1 \ldots \forall x_n. [\Phi]_y^{f(x_1,\ldots,x_n)}$ can be satisfied. The two interpretations may only differ in that f must be given a meaning.

The above two theorems can be used to compute for every FO formula an equivalent SO formula of the form $\exists f_1 \ldots \exists f_m.\forall x_1 \ldots \forall x_n.\Phi$. For this reason, *satisfiability of* FO *can be reduced to satisfiability of the fragment with only universal quantifiers*. However, even this syntactically very restricted fragment is well-known to be undecidable, which has been shown independently by Church and Turing [99, 492].

Nevertheless, the reduction to Skolem normal form has an important advantage: the search for a potential model can be restricted to so-called Herbrand models. The domain of these models is the set of terms Term_Σ itself, so that a completely syntactic treatment of the satisfiability problem is possible. The search for a model is therefore reduced to determine a suitable interpretation $\mathcal{J}$ over the domain $\mathcal{D} := \mathsf{Term}_\Sigma$:

Theorem 6.5 (Herbrand Expansion). *A* FO *formula in Skolem normal form is satisfiable iff it is satisfiable in a Herbrand model, i.e., a model whose domain is* Term_Σ. *Hence,* $\forall x_1 \ldots . \forall x_n.\varphi$ *with quantifier-free* φ *is satisfiable iff the Herbrand expansion* $\{[\varphi]_{x_1 \ldots x_n}^{\tau_1 \ldots \tau_n} \mid \tau_1, \ldots, \tau_n \in \mathsf{Term}_\Sigma\}$ *is satisfiable. Moreover, it follows that every satisfiable* FO *formula has a countable model.*

Actually, the theorem already appeared in Skolem's article [462] of 1928, but the above theorem is nevertheless attributed to Herbrand who also used these models in his dissertation in 1930. Note that the above theorems have the consequence, that uncountably infinite sets like the real numbers can not be characterized in FO. On the other hand, this property is one of the major keys to a semi-decision procedure. Due to the above theorem, we can replace a formula $\forall x_1.\dots\forall x_n.\varphi$ with quantifier-free φ with its Herbrand expansion $\{[\varphi]_{x_1\dots x_n}^{\tau_1\dots\tau_n} \mid \tau_1,\dots,\tau_n \in \mathsf{Term}_\Sigma\}$. The latter is in principle a propositional problem, except for the fact that the Herbrand expansion is usually an infinite set. The final ingredient is therefore the following fundamental theorem:

Theorem 6.6 (Compactness Theorem). *A (possible infinite) set of* FO *formulas is unsatisfiable iff there is a finite subset of this set that is unsatisfiable. Equivalently: a (possible infinite) set of* FO *formulas is satisfiable iff all finite subsets of this set are is satisfiable.*

For this reason, a semi-decision procedure for FO is obtained as follows: Firstly, transform the given formula into Skolem normal form. After this, generate instances to enumerate the Herbrand expansion, and check by a decision procedure for propositional logic (like BDDs) the consistency (satisfiability) of the so-far generated finite approximation of the Herbrand expansion. If the given formula was unsatisfiable, then the procedure will after some time have made enough instances, so that an inconsistent set is obtained. The above compactness theorem guarantees that such a finite unsatisfiable subset must exist, and if our instantiation procedure is systematic, we will find this finite subset of the Herbrand expansion after finitely many steps. Clearly, good strategies for instantiations are required to find an inconsistent finite set as soon as possible, and a lot of work in automated theorem proving has been devoted to solve this problem [47, 51, 85, 195, 334].

Hence, if the formula is unsatisfiable, the above procedure will detect this after some finite time. However, if the formula is satisfiable, the procedure may run into an infinite loop. The problem is that there are formulas that only have infinite models like the following formula (Dedekind's definition of infinity: there is a function f that is injective, but not surjective):

$$\Phi_{\mathsf{Dedekind}} :\equiv (\forall x.\forall y.f(x) \doteq f(y) \to x \doteq y) \land \neg (\forall y.\exists x.y \doteq f(x))$$

Hence, FO does not have the *finite model property*, which would make the sat-problem of FO decidable. However, there are decidable logics that do not have the finite model property (for example the full μ-calculus [476, 496] (cf. page 504) or FO with two variables and counting quantifiers [219]). Before discussing decidable fragments of FO that have the finite model property, we consider, how FO can express facts about the cardinality of the underlying domain $\mathcal{D}$. An important source is thereby the presence of the equality symbol:

Theorem 6.7 (Increasing Expressiveness by Equality). FO *with equality is more expressive than* FO *without equality: There is a formula $\Phi_{\leq n}$ in* FO *with equality that is satisfied in $(\mathcal{D}, \mathcal{J})$ iff the domain $\mathcal{D}$ has at most n elements. In contrast, if a formula in* FO *without equality is satisfied in a model $(\mathcal{D}, \mathcal{J})$ with $|\mathcal{D}| = n$, then there is also a model of cardinality $|\mathcal{D}| = n + m$ for every $m \in \mathbb{N}$.*

Proof. It is straightforward to define $\Phi_{\leq n}$ in FO with equality by using $n+1$ variables as follows:

$$\Phi_{\leq n} :\equiv \exists x_1 \ldots \exists x_n . \forall y. \bigvee_{i=1}^{n} x_i \doteq y$$

Hence, we can define $\Phi_{>n}$ as $\neg\Phi_{\leq n}$ and $\Phi_{\geq n}$ as $\neg\Phi_{\leq n-1}$, and therefore, we can also define $\Phi_{=n}$ as $\Phi_{\leq n} \wedge \Phi_{\geq n}$. Without equality, it is not possible to express these formulas, since every finite model can be extended (even to an infinite model): Given a model $(\mathcal{D}, \mathcal{J})$ with $|\mathcal{D}| = n$, the essential idea is to extend $\mathcal{D}$ by new individuals to a domain $\mathcal{D}'$ of desired cardinality. Although we can not prohibit the quantifiers to consider all elements of $\mathcal{D}'$, it is possible to ignore the new elements in some sense.

To this end, we fix an arbitrary element $d \in \mathcal{D}$ to define the projection $\pi_d : \mathcal{D}' \to \mathcal{D}$ such that $\pi_d(x) = x$ for $x \in \mathcal{D}$ and $\pi_d(x) = d$ for $x \notin \mathcal{D}$. We then define for every predicate p and every function symbol f the new interpretation $\mathcal{J}'$ as follows:

- $\mathcal{J}'(f)(d_1', \ldots, d_n') := \mathcal{J}(f)(\pi_d(d_1'), \ldots, \pi_d(d_n'))$
- $(d_1', \ldots, d_n') \in \mathcal{J}'(p)$ iff $(\pi_d(d_1'), \ldots, \pi_d(d_n')) \in \mathcal{J}(p)$

By a simple induction, it then follows that for every term τ and every formula φ without equality, we have

- $\pi_d(\llbracket \tau \rrbracket_{\mathcal{D}',\mathcal{J}',\xi'}) = \llbracket \tau \rrbracket_{\mathcal{D},\mathcal{J},\pi_d \circ \xi}$
- $\llbracket \varphi \rrbracket_{\mathcal{D}',\mathcal{J}',\xi'} = \llbracket \varphi \rrbracket_{\mathcal{D},\mathcal{J},\pi_d \circ \xi}$

In particular, it follows for every sentence φ without equality that $\llbracket \varphi \rrbracket_{\mathcal{D}',\mathcal{J}'} = \llbracket \varphi \rrbracket_{\mathcal{D},\mathcal{J}}$ holds. □

As a consequence, it follows that it is not possible to define $\doteq$ in FO, and therefore, FO with equality is more expressive than the fragment without equality. It is possible to define equality in SO, for example $x \doteq y \leftrightarrow \forall p.p(x) \leftrightarrow p(y)$ is valid.

Many fragments of FO that behave differently when equality is added. The presence of equality may influence the decidability or the complexity. For example, $\mathsf{FO}(\exists^*\forall^2\exists^*)$ in only decidable without equality [213, 214, 273, 448]. $\mathsf{FO}(\exists^*\forall\exists^*)$ is decidable with or without equality, but the complexity is different for these fragments [218].

The compactness theorem is a deeply rooted restriction for FO that leads on the one hand to the semi-decidability of FO, but restricts on the other hand the expressiveness of FO. We show some important restrictions:

Corollary 6.8 (Restrictions of First Order Logic (I)). *There is no* FO *formula Φ_{fin} such that Φ_{fin} holds in an interpretation $(\mathcal{D}, \mathcal{J})$ iff $\mathcal{D}$ is finite.*

Proof. We have already seen that for every number $n \in \mathbb{N}$, formulas $\Phi_{\geq n}$ exist that hold *iff* the domain $\mathcal{D}$ has at least n elements. These formulas do not exist without equality, but even without equality, it is possible to state formulas $\Psi_{\geq n}$ that are only satisfied when the domain $\mathcal{D}$ has at least n elements (the other implication of the *iff* may not hold). For example, it is possible to state that a binary predicate p is an equivalence relation with at least n classes:

$$\Psi_{\geq n} := \left(\begin{array}{l} \forall x.p(x,x)\wedge \\ \forall x.\forall y.p(x,y) \to p(y,x)\wedge \\ \forall x.\forall y.\forall z.p(x,y) \wedge p(y,z) \to p(x,z)\wedge \\ \exists x_1.\ldots.\exists x_n.\bigwedge_{i=1}^{n}\bigwedge_{j=i+1}^{n} \neg p(x_i,x_j) \end{array}\right)$$

It is easily seen that $[\![\Psi_{\geq n}]\!]_{\mathcal{D},\mathcal{J}} = \mathsf{true}$ implies $|\mathcal{D}| \geq n$. Hence, *all* formulas in the set $M_{\mathsf{inf}} := \{\Psi_{\geq n} \mid n \in \mathbb{N}\}$ are satisfied by $(\mathcal{D},\mathcal{J})$ iff $\mathcal{D}$ is infinite.

Now, assume there would be a formula Φ_{fin} that is satisfied iff $\mathcal{D}$ is finite. The set $\{\Phi_{\mathsf{fin}}\} \cup M_{\mathsf{inf}}$ would then be unsatisfiable. However, every finite subset of it has a model, and therefore, due to the compactness theorem, the entire set must also have a model. Hence, the existence of Φ_{fin} is not possible. □

Note that Dedekind's definition of infinity that we gave on page 412 is no contradiction to the above corollary. The above corollary states that there is no formula that holds *iff* $|\mathcal{D}|$ is finite. The formula Φ_{Dedekind} on page 412 only holds if $|\mathcal{D}|$ is infinite, but there are interpretations with infinite set $\mathcal{D}$ where this formula is false.

Corollary 6.9 (Restrictions of First Order Logic (II)). *The transitive closure of a binary relation can not be expressed in* FO *logic. More precisely, given binary predicate symbols $p, q \in C_\Sigma$, there is no* FO *sentence* $\mathsf{TC}(p,q)$ *such that for every interpretation* $(\mathcal{D},\mathcal{J})$, $[\![\mathsf{TC}(p,q)]\!]_{\mathcal{D},\mathcal{J}} = \mathsf{true}$ *holds iff* $\mathcal{J}(q)$ *is the transitive closure of* $\mathcal{J}(p)$.

Proof. Assume there would be a FO sentence $\mathsf{TC}(p,q)$ with the above property. The transitive closure of a binary relation R is obtained by closing the relation under relational product, i.e., the transitive closure is $R \cup R^2 \cup \ldots$. It is easily seen that the following formula φ_n holds in $(\mathcal{D},\mathcal{J},\xi)$ iff $(\xi(x),\xi(y)) \in (\mathcal{J}(p))^{n+1}$:

$$\varphi_n :\equiv \exists z_1.\ldots.\exists z_n.p(x,z_1) \wedge \left(\bigwedge_{i=1}^{n-1} p(z_i,z_{i+1})\right) \wedge p(z_n,y)$$

Consider now the set $M := \{\mathsf{TC}(p,q), q(x,y), \neg p(x,y)\} \cup \{\neg\varphi_{n+1} \mid n \in \mathbb{N}\}$. It is clearly not satisfiable, since on the one hand, $\{\mathsf{TC}(p,q), q(x,y)\}$ asserts that $(\xi(x),\xi(y))$ belongs to the transitive closure of $\mathcal{J}(p)$, hence to some relation $(\mathcal{J}(p))^n$, but the other formulas contradict that statement. However, every finite subset of M is satisfiable, and therefore, we have a contradiction to the compactness theorem. □

For this reason, Immerman [258, 259] proposed to extend FO by a transitive closure operator to the logic FO(TC) (see page 422). However, the logic FO(TC) looses fundamental properties of FO like the compactness theorem and the semi-decidability.

6.2.3 Fragments with Decidable Satisfiability Problem

A lot of fragments of FO have been considered to find sublogics with a decidable satisfiability problem (sat-problem for short). Note that *a decision procedure for the sat-problem of a fragment* $\mathfrak{L} \subseteq \mathsf{FO}$ *can also be used as a decision procedure for the validity problem of the dual class* $\overline{\mathfrak{L}} := \{\neg\varphi \mid \varphi \in \mathfrak{L}\}$, but in general not as a decision procedure for the sat-problem of the dual class (unless the class is closed under complementation).

Many fragments of FO that have been considered in the past are defined by the quantifier prefixes that may occur in their prenex normal form [56, 146, 323]. To this end, a regular expression α over the alphabet $\{\forall, \exists\}$ is used to describe such a quantifier prefix class $\mathsf{FO}(\alpha)$. Every word in that language is then a quantifier prefix that may occur in a in prenex normal form formula of that class. For example, $\mathsf{FO}(\exists^*\forall\forall\exists^*)$ describes the set of formulas with arbitrarily many (even zero) $\exists$-quantifiers, followed by two $\forall$-quantifiers, and a possibly empty sequence of $\exists$-quantifiers. As $\forall x.\varphi$, $\exists x.\varphi$, and φ are all equivalent if x does not occur in φ, such a prefix class also contains quantifier prefixes where some of the mentioned quantifiers are deleted. For example, $\mathsf{FO}(\exists^*\forall\forall\exists^*)$ contains the fragments $\mathsf{FO}(\exists^*\forall\exists^*)$, $\mathsf{FO}(\exists^*)$ and $\mathsf{FO}(\forall\forall)$. One is therefore interested in *maximal decidable prefix classes* and *minimal undecidable prefix classes*.

Furthermore, it has to be noted that the quantifier prefix classes listed below do not allow us to use function symbols. We will see below that even the presence of a single function symbol will make the sat-problem of $\mathsf{FO}(\forall)$ undecidable. Hence, *the following prefix classes are given over signatures without function symbols.*

It is easily seen that the sat-problem of $\mathsf{FO}(\exists^*)$ is decidable. To this end, simply note that this problem can be reduced to the sat-problem of propositional logic when all of the $\exists$-quantifiers are eliminated, and the different atoms $p(\ldots)$ are viewed as different propositional variables. Having seen the decidability of $\mathsf{FO}(\exists^*)$, one now naturally asks how this fragment can be extended without loosing decidability of the sat-problem. Possible extensions are to add $\forall$-quantifiers before or after the existential quantifiers. However, Skolem [461] showed in 1920, that the class $\mathsf{FO}(\forall^*\exists^*)$ is undecidable, since one can construct for every FO formula a sat-equivalent formula in $\mathsf{FO}(\forall^*\exists^*)$.

In 1928, a couple of fragments $\mathsf{FO}(\alpha)$ with decidable sat-problem have been found: Bernays and Schönfinkel [39] showed that the sat-problem of $\mathsf{FO}(\exists^*\forall^*)$ without equality is decidable. In the same year, Ramsey [422] extended this result to $\mathsf{FO}(\exists^*\forall^*)$ with equality. Hence, $\mathsf{FO}(\exists^*\forall^*)$ is often called the Bernays-Schönfinkel-Ramsey class. Also in 1928, Ackermann [3, 201, 323] showed that the class $\mathsf{FO}(\exists^*\forall\exists^*)$ has a decidable sat-problem (even with equality), so this class is often called the Ackermann class. The decidability of $\mathsf{FO}(\exists^*\forall^2\exists^*)$ without equality has then been independently shown by Gödel [213] (1932), Kalmár [273] (1933) and Schütte [448] (1934). Inspecting the automaton given in the upper half of Figure 6.1 shows that there are two minimal classes left that may be undecidable, namely $\mathsf{FO}(\forall\exists\forall)$ and $\mathsf{FO}(\forall^3\exists)$. The undecidability of $\mathsf{FO}(\forall^3\exists)$ has been shown by Surányi [479] in 1959, and the undecidability of $\mathsf{FO}(\forall\exists\forall)$ has been shown be Kahr, Wang, and Moore [272] in 1962. Hence, the prefix classes $\mathsf{FO}(\alpha)$ were almost completely solved in 1962. Only a decision procedure for $\mathsf{FO}(\exists^*\forall^2\exists^*)$ with equality was missing. Gödel remarked that he believed that also this class is decidable, but finally Goldfarb [214] has shown in 1984 that this is not the case. He showed that even the class $\mathsf{FO}(\forall^2\exists)$ is undecidable when equality is allowed.

Goldfarb's result completed the classification of prefix classes $\mathsf{FO}(\alpha)$ with respect to decidable sat-problems. All results about decidable prefix classes are summarized in the following tables, where only maximal decidable and minimal undecidable classes are listed. For further reading, we refer to the original literature, and excellent books on this topic like [56, 146, 323].

sat without equality is	
decidable	undecidable
$\mathsf{FO}(\exists^*\forall^*)$	$\mathsf{FO}(\forall\exists\forall)$
$\mathsf{FO}(\exists^*\forall\exists^*)$	$\mathsf{FO}(\forall^3\exists)$
$\mathsf{FO}(\exists^*\forall^2\exists^*)$	

sat with equality is	
decidable	undecidable
$\mathsf{FO}(\exists^*\forall^*)$	$\mathsf{FO}(\forall\exists\forall)$
$\mathsf{FO}(\exists^*\forall\exists^*)$	$\mathsf{FO}(\forall^2\exists)$

The table is to be read as follows: the sat-problem of a prefix class $\mathsf{FO}(\alpha)$ without equality is undecidable if it contains formulas with either the prefix $\forall\exists\forall$ or $\forall^3\exists$. For example, $\mathsf{FO}(\forall^2\exists^3\forall)$ is undecidable, since it contains $\mathsf{FO}(\forall\exists\forall)$. On the other hand, $\mathsf{FO}(\forall^*)$ is decidable, since it is contained in $\mathsf{FO}(\exists^*\forall^*)$.

A probably better description of the set of decidable quantifier-prefixes α in the cases with or without equality is given by regular expressions, or equivalently by accepting automata: The automaton given in the upper part of Figure 6.1 accepts a quantifier prefix α iff the sat-problem of the corresponding class $\mathsf{FO}(\alpha)$ is undecidable. The lower part is an acceptor for the prefixes α of the undecidable classes $\mathsf{FO}(\alpha)$ with equality.

Theorem 6.10 (Decidable Prefix Classes of FO). *The sat-problem of a prefix class $\mathsf{FO}(\alpha)$ without function symbols, but with equality is undecidable iff α is accepted by the automaton given in the lower half of Figure 6.1. The automaton given in the upper half of Figure 6.1 accepts exactly the prefixes of the undecidable classes $\mathsf{FO}(\alpha)$ when additionally equality is forbidden.*

As already remarked before, function symbols introduce a major difficulty for decision procedures. Due to skolemization, many undecidable classes can be reduced to classes that are decidable without function symbols, so that it is easily seen that the presence of function symbols makes most decidable classes undecidable. For example, formulas with prefix $\forall\exists\forall$ can be reduced to satisfiability-equivalent formulas with prefix $\forall^2$ by introducing a unary function symbol. Hence, the class $\mathsf{FO}(\forall^2)$ becomes undecidable if a unary function symbol is added.

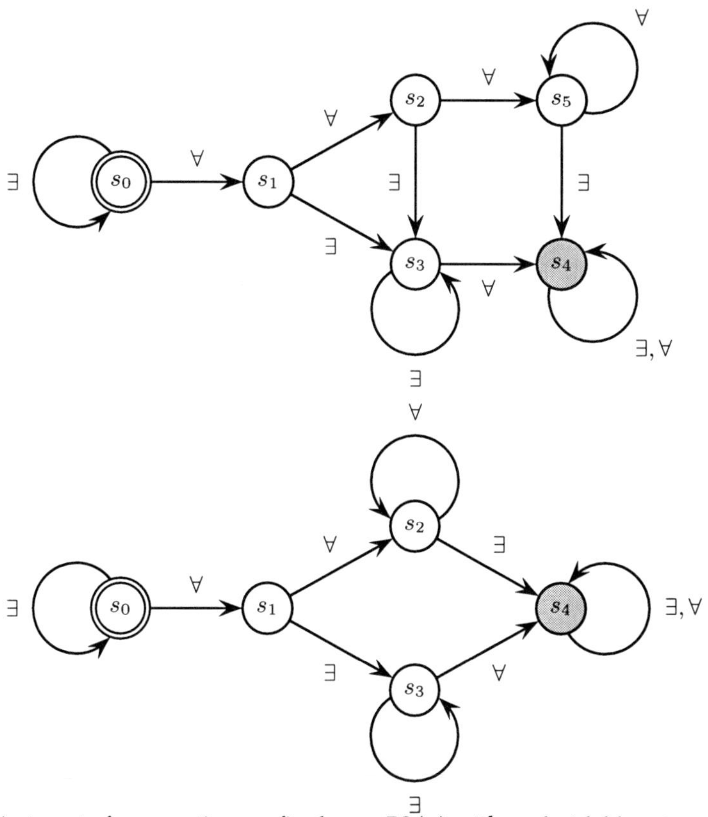

Fig. 6.1. Automata for accepting prefix classes $\mathsf{FO}(\alpha)$ with undecidable sat-problems (upper half without equality, lower half with equality)

Goldfarb's result completed the map of the prefix classes. He even proved that in the presence of equality, $\mathsf{FO}(\forall^2\exists)$ remains undecidable when only one binary predicate and some unary predicates are used. If only a binary predicate is used, then at least $\mathsf{FO}(\forall^2\exists^*)$ is undecidable. Hence, we can see that not only prefix classes have an impact on the decidability of the sat-problem. Other factors are the number of variables used and the arities of the predicate symbols. In the extreme case of MFO, where all predicate symbols have to be monadic, i.e., of arity 1, we obtain the following result [56]:

Theorem 6.11 (Small Model Theorem for MFO). *If a formula of monadic FO predicate logic (MFO) in prenex normal form $\Theta_1 x_1 \ldots . \Theta_m x_m . \varphi$ ($\Theta_i \in \{\forall, \exists\}$) with monadic predicate symbols $p_1, \ldots, p_n$ (with equality, but without function symbols) is satisfiable, then it is satisfiable in a model with no more than $m2^n$ elements. Hence, MFO is decidable.*

Proof. Assume there is a domain $\mathcal{D}$ with interpretation $\mathcal{J}$ such that φ is satisfied. We construct a new model with at most $m2^n$ elements by a quotient construction as follows: We define $d_1 \sim d_2$ iff for all predicate symbols p_i, we have $d_1 \in \mathcal{J}(p_i)$ iff $d_2 \in \mathcal{J}(p_i)$. This means the predicate symbols can not distinguish between d_1 and d_2. It is easily seen that $\sim$ is an equivalence relation on $\mathcal{D}$ so that we can consider the set of equivalence classes $\mathcal{D}_{|\sim}$, and define $\mathcal{J}_{|\sim}(p_i) = \{\widetilde{d} \in \mathcal{D}_{|\sim} \mid \exists d' \in \mathcal{D}.d' \sim d \wedge d' \in \mathcal{J}(p_i)\}$. A simple induction shows that, without equality, all formulas are interpreted in the same way in $(\mathcal{D}, \mathcal{J})$ and $(\mathcal{D}_{|\sim}, \mathcal{J}_{|\sim})$. Moreover, it is easily seen that $\mathcal{D}_{|\sim}$ has at most 2^n equivalence classes.

Adding equality forces us to make the domain larger: Having computed the equivalence classes, we choose from every class $\widetilde{d}$ at most m elements (classes with $\leq m$ elements are unchanged). The new domain is now the union of the chosen elements of the classes, which has at most $m2^n$ elements. It can be shown that satisfiability is preserved in this new domain. □

Due to the above theorem, it therefore follows that the sat-problem of MFO is decidable. A simple decision procedure would be to enumerate all models for checking the satisfiability.

The above set of formulas is often called the *Löwenheim* class with or without equality [56, 335]. Without equality, we even have 2^n as an upper bound, but the presence of m variables with equality allows us to state that the domain has more than m elements (see the formulas $\Phi_{\geq n}$ used in the proof of Theorem 6.7). The presence of function symbols also allows us to express formulas that only hold if the domain has more than m elements. To this end, even a single unary function symbol is sufficient:

$$\bigwedge_{i=1}^{m} \left(\left(\bigwedge_{j=0}^{i-1} \neg p(f^j(x_i)) \right) \wedge p(f^i(x_i)) \wedge \left(\bigwedge_{j=i+1}^{m} \neg p(f^j(x_i)) \right) \right)$$

If two of the m variables would be mapped to the same individual $d \in \mathcal{D}$, say $\xi(x_i) = \xi(x_j)$, then the formula will be false: On the one hand, we have $\neg p(f^j(x_i))$, on the other hand, we have $p(f^i(x_i))$, which should however be the same. Hence, the formula can only be satisfied when the domain has at least m elements. Nevertheless, adding a unary function symbol still yields a decidable fragment, the *Rabin class* [56], provided that we exclude equality.

The examples show that the small model property is influenced by the number of variables. It is therefore natural to consider fragments of FO where the number of variables is limited. The fragment with at most k variables is usually denoted as FO^k. We have the following results:

Theorem 6.12 (Decidability of FO^k [218, 219, 375]). FO *with only two variables* FO^2 *without function symbols, but with equality, is decidable [375]. The complexity of the problem is* NEXPTIME*-complete [218].* FO^k *with* $k > 2$*, even without equality, is undecidable [56, 323]. Moreover,* FO^2 *with only a unary function symbol is undecidable, even without equality [218].*

The undecidability of FO^k with $k > 2$ follows from the undecidability of the Kahr-Wang-Moore class $\mathsf{FO}(\forall\exists\forall)$. The decidability of FO^2 without equality has been shown by Scott [451] who showed in 1962 how FO^2 can be reduced to $\mathsf{FO}(\forall^2\exists)$. At that time, it was believed due to a remark of Gödel of 1932 that the class $\mathsf{FO}(\forall^2\exists^*)$ is decidable even if equality is added. Gödel only gave a proof for the case without equality, but claimed that the result would also hold when equality is added. However, Goldfarb [214] showed in 1984 that this claim is not true, i.e., $\mathsf{FO}(\forall^2\exists^*)$ becomes undecidable if equality is added. For this reason, Scott's reduction only proves the decidability of the class without equality. The decidability of FO^2 with equality has been shown by Mortimer [375]. Furthermore, he proved that FO^2 has the finite model property. This result has been improved by Grädel, Kolaitis, and Vardi [218] in 1997. They showed that FO^2 has the small model property with a single exponential bound. We briefly sketch their proof of the decidability of FO^2. Following [218], it essentially consists of two parts:

- establishing Scott's normal form [218, 219, 451]
- small model property of formulas in Scott's normal form [218, 219]

In the following, we assume that FO^2 only has the two variables $V_\Sigma = \{x, y\}$. The first step in the proof of [218] is to establish Scott's normal form is to eliminate predicate symbols of arity > 2. To this end, consider an atomic expression $p(x_1, \ldots, x_n)$ and note that the variables x_i are either x or y, since we have no function symbols and only these two variables. The idea is now to use for every of the possible 2^n argument lists of the n-ary predicate a new binary or unary predicate symbol. To this end, we encode the argument list as a set $\vartheta \subseteq \{1, \ldots, n\}$ such that $i \in \vartheta$ iff $x_i \equiv x$ holds. For example $p(x, y, x)$ yields the set $\vartheta = \{1, 3\}$. Then, we replace $p(x_1, \ldots, x_n)$ with either $p_\vartheta(x, y)$, $p_\vartheta(x)$, or $p_\vartheta(y)$ depending on the occurrences of the variables x and y in $p(x_1, \ldots, x_n)$. Hence, the replaced atom has the same free variables as the original atom. We have to construct further formulas to establish the relationship of the different predicates p_ϑ when arguments are unified. In particular, we add the conjunction of the following formulas, where $\overline{\vartheta} := \{1, \ldots, n\} \setminus \vartheta$ holds:

- $\forall x.\forall y.p_\vartheta(x, y) \leftrightarrow p_{\overline{\vartheta}}(y, x)$ if both for p_ϑ and $p_{\overline{\vartheta}}$ occur in the formula
- $\forall x.p_\vartheta(x, x) \leftrightarrow p_{\{1,\ldots,n\}}(x)$ if p_ϑ occurs in the formula
- $\forall y.p_\vartheta(y, y) \leftrightarrow p_{\{\}}(y)$ if p_ϑ occurs in the formula

As only those formulas are added where the corresponding predicates occur in the formula, the result is kept in polynomial size [218].

Having established that all predicate symbols are now of arity 1 or 2, we apply the algorithm given in Figure 6.2. The result is a tuple $(\Phi, M_{\forall\forall}, M_{\forall\exists}, V)$ such that Φ is quantifier-free, $M_{\forall\forall}$ contains formulas $\forall x.\forall y.\alpha_i(x, y)$, and $M_{\forall\exists}$ contains formulas $\forall x.\exists y.\beta_i(x, y)$ such that all formulas $\alpha_i(x, y)$ and $\beta_i(x, y)$ are quantifier-free and that moreover $|M_{\forall\forall}| = |M_{\forall\exists}|$ holds.

```
function Scott(Ψ)
 case Ψ of
  ¬φ         : (φ′, M∀∀, M∀∃, V) ≡ Scott(φ);
               return (¬φ′, M∀∀, M∀∃, V);
  φ ∧ ψ      : (φ′, M∀∀, M∀∃, V) ≡ Scott(φ); (ψ′, N∀∀, N∀∃, W) ≡ Scott(ψ);
               return (φ′ ∧ ψ′, M∀∀ ∪ N∀∀, M∀∃ ∪ N∀∃, V ∪ W);
  φ ∨ ψ      : (φ′, M∀∀, M∀∃, V) ≡ Scott(φ); (ψ′, N∀∀, N∀∃, W) ≡ Scott(ψ);
               return (φ′ ∨ ψ′, M∀∀ ∪ N∀∀, M∀∃ ∪ N∀∃, V ∪ W);
  ∃x.φ       : (φ′, M∀∀, M∀∃, V) ≡ Scott(φ);
               q ≡ newvar();
               M∀∀ := M∀∀ ∪ {∀y.∀x.φ → q(y)};
               M∀∃ := M∀∃ ∪ {∀y.∃x.q(y) → φ};
               return (q(y), M∀∀, M∀∃, V ∪ {q});
  ∀x.φ       : (φ′, M∀∀, M∀∃, V) ≡ Scott(φ);
               q ≡ newvar();
               M∀∀ := M∀∀ ∪ {∀y.∀x.q(y) → φ};
               M∀∃ := M∀∃ ∪ {∀y.∃x.φ → q(y)};
               return (q(y), M∀∀, M∀∃, V ∪ {q});
  ∃y.φ       : (φ′, M∀∀, M∀∃, V) ≡ Scott(φ);
               q ≡ newvar();
               M∀∀ := M∀∀ ∪ {∀x.∀y.φ → q(x)};
               M∀∃ := M∀∃ ∪ {∀x.∃y.q(x) → φ};
               return (q(x), M∀∀, M∀∃, V ∪ {q});
  ∀y.φ       : (φ′, M∀∀, M∀∃, V) ≡ Scott(φ);
               q ≡ newvar();
               M∀∀ := M∀∀ ∪ {∀x.∀y.q(x) → φ};
               M∀∃ := M∀∃ ∪ {∀x.∃y.φ → q(x)};
               return (q(x), M∀∀, M∀∃, V ∪ {q});
  otherwise  : return (Ψ, {}, {}, {});
 end
end
```

Fig. 6.2. Transformation into Scott's normal form

The idea of the algorithm given in Figure 6.2 is to successively abbreviate quantified subformulas $\forall y.\varphi$, $\exists y.\varphi$, $\forall x.\varphi$, and $\exists x.\varphi$ as soon as they are detected in a bottom-up traversal on the syntax tree. Note that these formulas may only have free occurrences for the remaining variable. For example, consider the subformula $\exists y.\varphi$. As the only free variable that can occur in $\exists y.\varphi$ is x, we abbreviate this formula by a new monadic predicate q in that we define $\forall x.q(x) \leftrightarrow \exists y.\varphi$. It is easily seen that this formula is equivalent to the following conjunction, whose parts are distributed to the sets $M_{\forall\forall}$ and $M_{\forall\exists}$, respectively:

$$(\forall x.\forall y.\varphi \rightarrow q(x)) \land (\forall x.\exists y.q(x) \rightarrow \varphi)$$

Hence, it follows that for a given formula Ψ of FO^2 with only monadic and binary predicate symbols, the result $\mathsf{Scott}(\Psi) = (\Phi, M_{\forall\forall}, M_{\forall\exists}, \{q_1,\ldots,q_n\})$ represents the following equivalence:

$$\Psi \Leftrightarrow \exists q_1.\ldots\exists q_n.\Phi \wedge \bigwedge_{\alpha\in M_{\forall\forall}} \alpha \wedge \bigwedge_{\beta\in M_{\forall\exists}} \beta$$

This result can be further reduced by combining the $\forall$-quantifiers of the α's and moreover shifting them over the variable-free subformula Φ:

Theorem 6.13 (Scott Normal Form of FO^2). *For every formula $\Phi \in \mathsf{FO}^2$, there is a formula $\Psi \in \mathsf{FO}^2$ in the following normal form such that Φ is satisfiable iff Ψ is satisfiable (even in models of the same cardinality):*

$$\Psi \equiv (\forall x.\forall y.\alpha(x,y)) \wedge \left(\bigwedge_{i=1}^{n} \forall x.\exists y.\beta_i(x,y)\right)$$

Formulas of the above form have the small model property: If Ψ is satisfiable, then it has a finite model with at most $3\,|\Psi|\,2^r$ elements, where r is the number of relation symbols occurring in Ψ.

Hence, FO^2 has the small model property: there is a constant c such that every satisfiable FO^2 sentence Φ has a model of cardinality at most $2^{c|\Phi|}$. Moreover, decidability of FO^2 is $\mathsf{NEXPTIME}$-complete.

Constructing a prenex normal form of formulas in Scott normal form shows that every FO^2 formula can be reduced to an equivalent formula of $\mathsf{FO}(\forall^2\exists)$ or alternatively of $\mathsf{FO}(\forall\exists\forall)$. However, both classes are undecidable, if $\doteq$ occurs in Φ. If $\doteq$ does not occur in Φ, this already proves the decidability of the Scott fragment, since at least $\mathsf{FO}(\forall^2\exists)$ is decidable in this case. A decision procedure for the general case with $\doteq$ is described in detail in [218].

6.2.4 Embedding Modal Logics in Predicate Logic

As predicate logic is the most general logic, it is interesting to answer the question if and how modal logics can be embedded in it. To this end, we first consider how propositional modal logic, i.e., the fragment of $\mathcal{L}_\mu$ without fixpoint operators can be embedded in predicate logic. To this end, we have to describe Kripke structures and the modal operators by corresponding FO formulas. Given a Kripke structure $\mathcal{K} = (\mathcal{I}, \mathcal{S}, \mathcal{R}, \mathcal{L})$ over the variables V_Σ, we consider the domain $\mathcal{D} := \mathcal{S}$, i.e., the individuals are the states of the Kripke structure. The signature of our predicate logic contains a binary predicate symbol R that represents the transition relation $\mathcal{R}$ of $\mathcal{K}$, a unary predicate symbol ι that represents the initial states, and for every variable $x \in V_\Sigma$, there is a monadic predicate p_x. Clearly, $p_x(s)$ holds if the state that is meant with the variable s is labeled with x. Hence, the FO interpretation $\mathcal{J}$ that is induced by a Kripke structure is as follows:

- $\mathcal{J}(R) := \mathcal{R}$
- $\mathcal{J}(\iota) := \mathcal{I}$
- $\mathcal{J}(p_x) := [\![x]\!]_{\mathcal{K}} = \{s \in \mathcal{S} \mid x \in \mathcal{L}(s)\}$

Variables are interpreted as usual by a variable assignment ξ that maps the FO variables to states. Hence, we may view a Kripke structure as a FO interpretation $(\mathcal{D}, \mathcal{J})$. It is straightforward to embed propositional modal logic by the translation rules shown in Figure 6.3.

- $\mathsf{FOL}_\mu(s, x) := p_x(s)$
- $\mathsf{FOL}_\mu(s, \neg\varphi) := \neg\mathsf{FOL}_\mu(s, \varphi)$
- $\mathsf{FOL}_\mu(s, \varphi \wedge \psi) := \mathsf{FOL}_\mu(s, \varphi) \wedge \mathsf{FOL}_\mu(s, \psi)$
- $\mathsf{FOL}_\mu(s, \varphi \vee \psi) := \mathsf{FOL}_\mu(s, \varphi) \vee \mathsf{FOL}_\mu(s, \psi)$
- $\mathsf{FOL}_\mu(s, \Diamond\varphi) := \exists s'.\mathcal{R}(s, s') \wedge \mathsf{FOL}_\mu(s', \varphi)$
- $\mathsf{FOL}_\mu(s, \Box\varphi) := \forall s'.\mathcal{R}(s, s') \rightarrow \mathsf{FOL}_\mu(s', \varphi)$
- $\mathsf{FOL}_\mu(s, \overleftarrow{\Diamond}\varphi) := \exists s'.\mathcal{R}(s', s) \wedge \mathsf{FOL}_\mu(s', \varphi)$
- $\mathsf{FOL}_\mu(s, \overleftarrow{\Box}\varphi) := \forall s'.\mathcal{R}(s', s) \rightarrow \mathsf{FOL}_\mu(s', \varphi)$

Fig. 6.3. Translating propositional modal logic to FO^2

Note that $\mathsf{FOL}_\mu(s, \varphi)$ is a FO formula with the only free variable s. The meaning of $\mathsf{FOL}_\mu(s, \varphi)$ is that it encodes a state set such that s belongs to that set iff $\mathsf{FOL}_\mu(s, \varphi)$ holds. For example, we have

$$\mathsf{FOL}_\mu(s, \Box\overleftarrow{\Diamond}a) = \forall s'.\mathcal{R}(s, s') \rightarrow \exists s''.\mathcal{R}(s'', s') \wedge a(s'')$$

Hence, every modal formula can be easily translated to FO. Moreover, it is easily observed that the existential modal operators $\Diamond$ and $\overleftarrow{\Diamond}$ introduce existential quantifiers and that the universal modal operators $\Box$ and $\overleftarrow{\Box}$ introduce universal quantifiers. Finally, it can be seen that by suitable renaming of quantified variables, it is possible to obtain a FO^2 formula:

Theorem 6.14 (Embedding Modal Logic in FO^2). *For every propositional modal logic formula φ, there is an equivalent FO^2 sentence ψ of length $O(|\varphi|)$. The formula ψ can be obtained as $\psi :\equiv \forall s.\iota(s) \rightarrow \mathsf{FOL}_\mu(s, \varphi)$, where $\mathsf{FOL}_\mu(s, \varphi)$ is defined as given in Figure 6.3.*

Based on the embedding of propositional modal logic in FO^2, we now consider how more powerful logics can be embedded in predicate logic. However, we have already seen in Corollary 6.9 that FO can not express temporal operators. Similar to the nondefinability of the transitive closure, we can also show that reachability can not be defined in FO.

For this reason, Immerman [258, 259] proposed to extend FO by a transitive closure operator to the logic FO(TC). Hence, FO(TC) is constructed by the usual rules, extended by the following one: for any formula φ and variables x, y, and for terms τ, π, the formula $\mathsf{TC}_{x,y}^{\varphi}(\tau, \pi)$ is an atomic formula. Intuitively, φ is viewed as a binary relation, namely as $\{(a,b) \in \mathcal{D}^2 \mid [\![\varphi]\!]_{\mathcal{D},\mathcal{J},\xi_{x,y}^{a,b}} = \mathsf{true}\}$, and $\mathsf{TC}_{x,y}^{\varphi}$ is interpreted as its transitive closure. Note that $\mathsf{TC}_{x,y}^{\varphi}$ can not be expressed in FO (see corollary 6.9), but it can be axiomatized in SO:

$$\left(\begin{array}{l} \forall x.\forall y.\varphi \rightarrow \mathsf{TC}_{x,y}^{\varphi}(x,y) \wedge \\ \forall x.\forall y.\forall z.\mathsf{TC}_{x,y}^{\varphi}(x,y) \wedge \mathsf{TC}_{x,y}^{\varphi}(y,z) \rightarrow \mathsf{TC}_{x,y}^{\varphi}(x,z) \wedge \\ \forall q. \left(\begin{array}{l} \forall x.\forall y.\varphi \rightarrow q(x,y) \wedge \\ \forall x.\forall y.\forall z.q(x,y) \wedge q(y,z) \rightarrow q(x,z) \\ \rightarrow \forall x.\forall y.\mathsf{TC}_{x,y}^{\varphi}(x,y) \rightarrow q(x,y) \end{array}\right) \end{array}\right)$$

It is also possible to define the *reflexive transitive closure* as $\mathsf{RTC}_{x,y}^{\varphi}(v,w) :\Leftrightarrow (v \doteq w) \vee \mathsf{TC}_{x,y}^{\varphi}(v,w)$. Of course, FO(TC) is more expressive than FO (see corollary 6.9), since it contains due to TC a piece of SO. For example, we can express that a state s' can be reached from a state s by $\mathsf{RTC}_{x,y}^{R(x,y)}(s,s')$. Moreover, we can express that state s is on a cycle and that an infinite path starts in s as follows (note that our Kripke structures have only finitely many states):

- $\mathsf{Cycle}(s) := \mathsf{TC}_{x,y}^{R(x,y)}(s,s)$
- $\mathsf{Inf}(s) := \exists s'.\mathsf{RTC}_{x,y}^{R(x,y)}(s,s') \wedge \mathsf{TC}_{x,y}^{R(x,y)}(s',s')$

Immerman and Vardi have shown in [259] that CTL and even CTL* can be translated to FO(TC). For example, we can extend the translation given in Figure 6.3 by the following rules to capture CTL:

- $\mathsf{FOL}_\mu(s, \mathsf{EX}\varphi) := \exists s'.R(s,s') \wedge \mathsf{FOL}_\mu(s',\varphi) \wedge \mathsf{Inf}(s')$
- $\mathsf{FOL}_\mu(s, \mathsf{EF}\varphi) := \exists s'.\mathsf{RTC}_{x,y}^{R(x,y)}(s,s') \wedge \mathsf{FOL}_\mu(s',\varphi) \wedge \mathsf{Inf}(s')$
- $\mathsf{FOL}_\mu(s, \mathsf{E}[\varphi \, \underline{\mathsf{U}} \, \psi]) := \left(\begin{array}{l} \exists s'. \\ \quad \mathsf{RTC}_{x,y}^{\mathsf{FOL}_\mu(x,\varphi) \wedge R(x,y)}(s,s') \wedge \\ \quad \mathsf{FOL}_\mu(s',\psi) \wedge \\ \quad \mathsf{Inf}(s') \end{array}\right)$
- $\mathsf{FOL}_\mu(s, \mathsf{EG}\varphi) := \left(\begin{array}{l} \exists s'. \\ \quad \mathsf{RTC}_{x,y}^{\mathsf{FOL}_\mu(x,\varphi) \wedge R(x,y)}(s,s') \wedge \\ \quad \mathsf{TC}_{x,y}^{\mathsf{FOL}_\mu(x,\varphi) \wedge R(x,y)}(s',s') \end{array}\right)$

It is however not possible to translate μ-calculus formulas to FO(TC). For this reason, Immerman [258] extended FO by a least fixpoint operator to the logic FO(LFP): for any formula φ, any unary predicate x, any first order variable s, and any term τ, the formula $\mathsf{LFP}_{x,s}^{\varphi}(\tau)$ is an atomic formula. Note that unary predicates x correspond with subsets of the domain $\mathcal{D}$. $\mathsf{LFP}_{x,s}^{\varphi}$ is the least fixpoint of the function $f_{x,s}^{\varphi} : 2^{\mathcal{D}} \rightarrow 2^{\mathcal{D}}$ defined as $f_{x,s}^{\varphi}(D) := \{d \in \mathcal{D} \mid [\![\varphi]\!]_{\mathcal{D},\mathcal{J},\xi_{x,s}^{D,d}} = \mathsf{true}\}$. In SO, this can be defined as follows:

$$\left(\begin{array}{l}\forall s.\mathsf{LFP}^{\varphi}_{x,s}(s) \leftrightarrow [\varphi]_x^{\mathsf{LFP}^{\varphi}_{x,s}} \wedge \\ \forall q.\left(\begin{array}{l}(\forall s.q(s) \leftrightarrow [\varphi]_x^q) \\ \rightarrow (\forall s.\mathsf{LFP}^{\varphi}_x(s) \rightarrow q(s))\end{array}\right)\end{array}\right)$$

Of course, we must guarantee that a least fixpoint exists, and therefore, x must not have negative occurrences in φ, so that $f^{\varphi}_{x,s}$ is monotonic. It is now straightforward to extend our translation to FO(LFP) to the μ-calculus:

- $\mathsf{FOL}_{\mu}(s, \mu x.\varphi) := \mathsf{LFP}_{x,s}^{\mathsf{FOL}_{\mu}(s,\varphi)}(s)$

Again, a remarkable issue is that the embedding only requires two FO variables, one for the current state and another one for the next or previous state. This raised the question how modal logics are related to two variable fragments of predicate logic [495]. However, the decidability of CTL*, $\mathcal{L}_{\mu}$, and FO^2 do neither carry over to $\mathsf{FO}^2(\mathsf{TC})$ nor to $\mathsf{FO}^2(\mathsf{LFP})$.

The restriction to two variables is however not the only restriction. Furthermore, the quantification is always guarded, i.e., with the transition relation R, the quantification is always of the following forms $\exists s'.R(s,s') \wedge \varphi$, $\exists s'.R(s',s) \wedge \varphi$, $\forall s'.R(s,s') \rightarrow \varphi$, and $\forall s'.R(s',s) \rightarrow \varphi$. This has drawn the attention to *guarded logics* [15, 217, 221] as another fragment of predicate logic.

6.2.5 Predicate Logic on Linearly Ordered Domains (on $\mathbb{N}$)

Many domains used as interpretations $(\mathcal{D}, \mathcal{J})$ for predicate logic are ordered. For example, paths of a Kripke structure, or the input for a Turing machine or other kinds of automata are finite or infinite strings. In order to *specify the language that is accepted by a particular machine $\mathfrak{A}$ in terms of a logical formula $\Phi_{\mathfrak{A}}$*, it is therefore necessary to state that the domain is a string. This is a general statement, and for a particular machine $\mathfrak{A}$, the specification $\Phi_{\mathfrak{A}}$ should hold exactly on those models that correspond with an input word σ iff σ is accepted by $\mathfrak{A}$. Following these ideas revealed interesting relationships between complexity theory and logic on linearly ordered structures.

To this end, it is however necessary, to axiomatize that the domain is a finite or infinite string (see [152]). A first step towards this axiomatization is to state that the elements of the domain are totally ordered, and for this reason, we use a binary relation $\prec$ that should be a strict total order. However, as we will see below, this is not sufficient, since we want that all elements of the domain $\mathcal{D}$ should be enumerated in a linear chain. For this reason, the domain is of the form $\mathcal{D} := \{d_i \mid i \in \mathbb{N}\}$ with $\mathcal{J}(\prec) := \{(d_i, d_j) \mid i < j\}$. It follows that $(\mathcal{D}, \prec)$ is isomorphic to $(\mathbb{N}, <)$.

However, it is not possible to achieve with a finite set of axioms that $(\mathcal{D}, \prec)$ is isomorphic to $(\mathbb{N}, <)$. We explain some erroneous attempts to illustrate this. To start with, it is possible to describe in FO with the following sentences O_1, O_2 and O_3 that a binary predicate symbol $\preceq$ is a partial order, and adding O_4 that $\preceq$ is a total order:

O_1: $\forall x.x \preceq x$
O_2: $\forall x.\forall y.x \preceq y \wedge y \preceq x \rightarrow x \doteq y$
O_3: $\forall x.\forall y.\forall z.x \preceq y \wedge y \preceq z \rightarrow x \preceq z$
O_4: $\forall x.\forall y.x \preceq y \vee y \preceq x$

It is possible to define for every partial order $\preceq$ a corresponding strict partial order $\prec$ by the following definition: $\forall x.\forall y.x \prec y \rightarrow x \preceq y \wedge \neg x \doteq y$. For the corresponding strict order $\prec$, it is then straightforward to prove the following properties:

SO_1: $\forall x.\forall y.x \prec y \rightarrow y \not\prec x$
SO_2: $\forall x.\forall y.\forall z.x \prec y \wedge y \prec z \rightarrow y \prec z$
SO_3: $\forall x.\forall y.x \prec y \vee x \doteq y \vee y \prec x$

Alternatively, it is also possible to start with the strict order $\prec$, give SO_1, SO_2, and SO_3 as axioms, define then $\preceq$ as $\forall x.\forall y.x \preceq y \rightarrow x \prec y \vee x \doteq y$ and prove O_1, O_2, O_3, and O_4. It is therefore only a matter of taste whether one starts with axioms for $\preceq$ or for $\prec$, and then defines the other symbol and proves the remaining 'axioms' that characterize the remaining symbol. In any case, we end up with the same theory.

One important definition in this theory is the successor relation. Note that for every linear order $\preceq$, we can define 'the successor relation' $\mathsf{succ}_{\preceq}$ as follows: $\forall x.\forall y.\mathsf{succ}_{\preceq}(x,y) :\leftrightarrow x \prec y \wedge \forall z.x \prec z \rightarrow y \preceq z$. This means that the successor y of x is the least element that is greater than x. If the infimum exists, it is unique, and for this reason, the relation $\mathsf{succ}_{\preceq}$ is a function. However, the above definition may not always be meaningful, since the infimum need not exist. For example, for the real numbers $\mathcal{D} := \mathbb{R}$, we would have $\forall x.\forall y.\neg\mathsf{succ}_{\preceq}(x,y)$.

For this reason, one might think of adding $\forall x.\exists y.\mathsf{succ}_{\preceq}(x,y)$ as a further axiom to guarantee the existence of successors. Moreover, one can add $\forall x.\mathsf{min} \preceq x$ to axiomatize the existence of a least element. *However, it is not possible to determine by finitely many* FO *axioms that a total order is isomorphic to the natural numbers or the integers*, i.e., that the elements are listed in a linear chain. This is a fundamental source of confusion that the notion 'linear' order suggerates.

We give two examples to illustrate this: As a first example, consider the set $\mathbb{N} \times \mathbb{N}$ with the following relation:

$$(a_1, b_1) \preceq (a_2, b_2) :\Leftrightarrow (b_1 \doteq b_2 \Rightarrow a_1 \leq a_2 | \, b_1 \leq b_2)$$

It can be easily verified that this relation $\preceq$ is a total order. Moreover, $(0,0)$ is the minimal element, and every pair (a,b) has the successor $(a+1,b)$. However, as it is not the case that $\forall x.x \doteq \mathsf{min} \vee \exists y.\mathsf{succ}(y,x)$ holds, since the elements $(0,b)$ do not have predecessors. For this reason, this total order is not isomorphic to the natural numbers. For the second example, we add $\forall x.x \doteq \mathsf{min} \vee \exists y.\mathsf{succ}(y,x)$ as further axiom. However, this does also not help, since then one can extend the chains with first component > 0 to the left with negative numbers. We still have not fixed linear domains, i.e., the natural numbers. What is essentially missing is that every element is obtained by a finite number of successor applications from the minimal element. Alternatively, we could state that every element belongs to $\mathsf{succ}^*_{\preceq}(\mathsf{min}, x)$, where $\mathsf{succ}^*_{\preceq}$ is the reflexive-transitive closure of the successor relation. However, neither finiteness nor transitive closure can be expressed in FO.

Indeed, it is well-known that the natural numbers can not be characterized by a decidable set of FO axioms, and hence, not by a finite set of axioms. This would be in contradiction to Gödel's [212] incompleteness theorem, since this would imply that the the set of theorems of the theory of the naturals would be recursively enumerable. However, the natural numbers can be characterized (up to isomorphism) by Peano's axioms:

Definition 6.15 (Predicate Logics on Linear Orders $\mathfrak{L}_<$). *Given a predicate logic $\mathfrak{L}$ with a binary relation $<$. The restriction of the semantics to consider only interpretations with domain $\mathcal{D} := \mathbb{N}$, where $\mathcal{J}(<)$ is the ordering relation on $\mathbb{N}$ is denoted as $\mathfrak{L}_<$. Equivalently, this means that the following axioms are assumed to hold:*

$\mathsf{Peano1} : \forall n.\ \neg 0 \doteq \mathsf{SUC}(n)$
$\mathsf{Peano2} : \forall m.\forall n.\ (\mathsf{SUC}(m) \doteq \mathsf{SUC}(n)) \rightarrow (m \doteq n)$
$\mathsf{Peano3} : \forall p.\ (\forall n.p(n)) \leftrightarrow p(0) \wedge \forall n.p(n) \rightarrow p(\mathsf{SUC}(n))$
$\mathsf{Order1} : \forall n.0 < \mathsf{SUC}(n)$
$\mathsf{Order2} : \forall n.\neg(n < 0)$
$\mathsf{Order3} : \forall m.\forall n.\mathsf{SUC}(m) < \mathsf{SUC}(n) \leftrightarrow m < n$

Let $\Phi_{\mathbb{N}}$ be the conjunction of the above axioms. Then, $\varphi \in \mathfrak{L}$ is valid in $\mathfrak{L}_<$ iff $\Phi_{\mathbb{N}} \rightarrow \varphi$ is valid in $\mathfrak{L}$, and $\varphi \in \mathfrak{L}$ is satisfiable in $\mathfrak{L}_<$ iff $\Phi_{\mathbb{N}} \wedge \varphi$ is satisfiable in $\mathfrak{L}$.

In particular, we consider first order logic $\mathsf{FO}_<$, monadic first order logic $\mathsf{MFO}_<$, second order logic $\mathsf{SO}_<$, monadic second order logic $\mathsf{MSO}_<$, as well as their restrictions $\mathsf{FO}^k_<$, $\mathsf{MFO}^k_<$, $\mathsf{SO}^k_<$, and $\mathsf{MSO}^k_<$ to k variables. We may also consider prefix classes $\mathsf{FO}^k_<(\alpha)$, $\mathsf{FO}_<(\alpha)$. In particular, we consider the fragment $\mathsf{ESO}_<$ of second order logic where only existential second order quantifiers are allowed, i.e., formulas of the form $\exists p_1.\dots\exists p_m.\varphi$, where φ is a FO formula. If φ belongs to a certain fragment of FO, we denote the fragment accordingly, e.g., $\mathsf{ESO}_<(\exists^*\forall^*)$ or $\mathsf{ESO}^2_<$.

It is straightforward to prove that the above axioms imply the properties SO_1, SO_2, and SO_3, and further well-known properties of the natural numbers. Due to Peano3, which is a second order formula, we have strictly speaking a second order logic, whenever we talk about linear orders. However, the commonly accepted terminology is to say that $\mathsf{FO}_<$ is also first order logic.

Having clarified the notation and axioms we assume to be true, we consider now several results on logics $\mathfrak{L}_<$ on linear orders. For example, we specify the task of a Turing machine that should accept the context-free language $\{a^n b^n \mid n \in \mathbb{N}\}$. This means that we have to find a formula Φ of some logic $\mathfrak{L}_<$ such that Φ holds iff the input stream of the Turing machine contains a

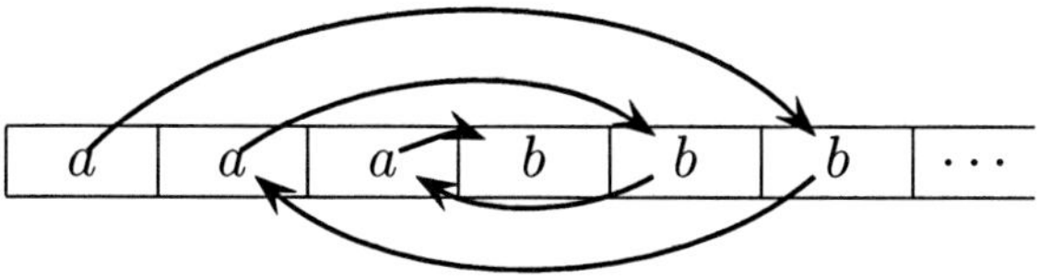

Fig. 6.4. Example for describing the language $\{a^n b^n \mid n \in \mathbb{N}\}$

word of the form $a^n b^n$. It is not hard to see that the following $\mathsf{SO}_<$ formula fulfills our requirements [154], where max is assumed to be the length of the input string:

$$\begin{aligned}
&\exists p.\forall x.\forall y.\exists z. \\
&\quad p(0, \mathsf{max}) \wedge \\
&\quad a(0) \wedge \\
&\quad [p(x, y) \rightarrow \neg p(y, x)] \wedge \\
&\quad [p(x, y) \rightarrow (a(x) \leftrightarrow b(y))] \wedge \\
&\quad [a(x) \wedge p(x, y) \wedge \neg y \doteq \mathsf{SUC}(x) \rightarrow p(y, \mathsf{SUC}(x))] \wedge \\
&\quad [b(x) \wedge p(x, y) \rightarrow x \doteq \mathsf{SUC}(z) \wedge p(y, z)] \wedge
\end{aligned}$$

The formula states that there exists a binary relation p with certain properties that are specified by the different parts of the formula. The only possibility for p for the word *aaabbb* is illustrated in Figure 6.4: lines represent the relation p.

Describing problems that are solved by Turing machines with logics, revealed a lot of interesting connections between logic and complexity theory [258]. In general, the expressiveness of a logic corresponds with the complexity of the problems that can be described with that logic. In particular, complexity theory considers the following classes (see also page 394):

LogSpace : deterministic Turing machine with logarithmic space
NLogSpace : nondeterministic Turing machine with logarithmic space
P : deterministic Turing machine with polynomial time
NP : nondeterministic Turing machine with polynomial time
PH : polynomial time hierarchy [474]
PSPACE : (non)deterministic Turing machine with polynomial space

It is well-known that the following inclusions hold, but the strictness is unclear:

$$\mathsf{LogSpace} \subseteq \mathsf{NLogSpace} \subseteq \mathsf{P} \subseteq \mathsf{NP} \subseteq \mathsf{PH} \subseteq \mathsf{PSPACE}$$

All of these classes have found logical characterizations [148, 189, 190, 258]. Hence, questions about complexity classes can be rephrased in terms of logics. For example, the famous $\mathsf{P} = \mathsf{NP}$ problem means to ask whether $\mathsf{ESO}_<$ can be reduced to $\mathsf{FO}_<(\mathsf{SUC}, \mathsf{LFP})$. This is due to the following characterizations (w.r.t. structure complexity, see page 454):

- a problem is in LogSpace iff it can be specified in $\mathsf{FO}_<(\mathsf{SUC}, \mathsf{DRTC})$, where DRTC is a deterministic reflexive transitive closure operator [258]
- a problem is in NLogSpace iff it can be specified in $\mathsf{FO}_<(\mathsf{SUC}, \mathsf{RTC})$, where RTC is the reflexive transitive closure operator [258]
- a problem is in P iff it can be specified in $\mathsf{FO}_<(\mathsf{SUC}, \mathsf{LFP})$, where LFP is the least fixpoint operator [258]
- a problem is in NP iff it can be specified in existential second order logic $\mathsf{ESO}_<$ [189]
- a problem is in PH iff it can be specified in second order logic $\mathsf{SO}_<$ [474]
- a problem is in PSPACE iff it can be specified by second order logic $\mathsf{SO}_<(\mathsf{RTC})$ with reflexive transitive closure operator [258]

In the following sections, we consider logical characterizations of the set of ω-regular languages, which are very low in the above hierarchy, since a finite state automaton can check the membership of a word in a regular language. The automaton requires linear time and no additional space.

6.3 Monadic Second Order Logic of Linear Order $\mathsf{MSO}_<$

We will consider in this section two special second order predicate logics, namely the monadic second order logic of linear order $\mathsf{MSO}_<$, and the monadic second order logic of one successor S1S. $\mathsf{MSO}_<$ is the second order logic that is obtained by the signature $C_\Sigma = \{<\}$ and only unary predicate variables. S1S is the second order logic that is obtained by the signature $C_\Sigma = \{0, \mathsf{SUC}\}$ and only unary predicate variables. We use a successor function, while some authors prefer a successor relation. This is only a matter of taste, since the relational description can be obtained as $\mathsf{succ}(x, y) :\Leftrightarrow y \doteq \mathsf{SUC}(x)$. We will see that the converse is also possible.

Note that due to Definition 6.15 on page 426, these logics are only interpreted over the natural numbers, i.e., we have $\mathcal{D} := \mathbb{N}$. We therefore replace the symbol $\mathbb{I}$ for the individuals with $\mathbb{N}$. Also the constants 0, SUC, and $<$, if available, have the standard semantics that is fixed by the axioms of Definition 6.15.

In the next section, we will see that S1S and $\mathsf{MSO}_<$ are expressively equivalent. We will also briefly mention that Presburger logic can be embedded in these monadic logics. After this, we will give a simple translation from $\mathsf{MSO}_<$ to ω-automata in Section 6.3.2. Due to the equivalence to S1S, this also gives a translation from S1S to ω-automata. Nevertheless, we present in Section 6.3.3 a direct translation that is Büchi's original translation procedure. This will require special normal forms that are interesting in their own right.

6.3.1 Equivalence of S1S and $\mathsf{MSO}_<$

S1S is the second order logic with the constants $\{0, \mathsf{SUC}\}$ and only unary predicate variables. Hence, we have the following formal definition:

Definition 6.16 (Monadic Second Order Logic of One Successor S1S). *The logic S1S is the second order predicate logic over the signature Σ with $C_\Sigma = \{0, \mathsf{SUC}\}$ where $\mathsf{typ}_\Sigma(0) = \mathbb{N}$ and $\mathsf{typ}_\Sigma(\mathsf{SUC}) = \mathbb{N} \to \mathbb{N}$ holds. Moreover, there are arbitrarily many variables of type $\mathbb{N}$ and $\mathbb{N} \to \mathbb{B}$. In more detail: the set of terms $\mathsf{Term}_{\mathsf{S1S}}$ of S1S is the least set that satisfies the following properties:*

- $0 \in \mathsf{Term}_{\mathsf{S1S}}$
- $t \in \mathsf{Term}_{\mathsf{S1S}}$ *for each variable* $t \in V_\Sigma$ *with* $\mathsf{typ}_\Sigma(t) = \mathbb{N}$
- *if* $\tau \in \mathsf{Term}_{\mathsf{S1S}}$, *then* $\mathsf{SUC}(\tau) \in \mathsf{Term}_{\mathsf{S1S}}$

The set of formulas of S1S is the least set that satisfies:

- $\tau \doteq \pi$ *for terms* $\tau, \pi \in \mathsf{Term}_{\mathsf{S1S}}$
- $p^{(\tau)} \in \mathsf{S1S}$ *for each variable* $p \in V_\Sigma$ *with* $\mathsf{typ}_\Sigma(p) = \mathbb{N} \to \mathbb{B}$ *and each term* $\tau \in \mathsf{Term}_{\mathsf{S1S}}$
- $\neg\varphi, \varphi \wedge \psi \in \mathsf{S1S}$ *if* $\varphi \in \mathsf{S1S}$ *and* $\psi \in \mathsf{S1S}$
- *for all* $t \in V_\Sigma$ *with* $\mathsf{typ}_\Sigma(t) = \mathbb{N}$ *and* $\varphi \in \mathsf{S1S}$, *we have* $\exists t.\ \varphi \in \mathsf{S1S}$
- *for all* $p \in V_\Sigma$ *with* $\mathsf{typ}_\Sigma(p) = \mathbb{N} \to \mathbb{B}$ *and* $\varphi \in \mathsf{S1S}$, *we have* $\exists p.\ \varphi \in \mathsf{S1S}$

Note that every term $\tau \in \mathsf{Term}_{\mathsf{S1S}}$ is either of the form $\mathsf{SUC}^n(0)$ or $\mathsf{SUC}^n(t)$ for some $t \in V_\Sigma$ with $\mathsf{typ}_\Sigma(t) = \mathbb{N}$. For convenience, we often write $t + n$ for $\mathsf{SUC}^n(t)$ and n for $\mathsf{SUC}^n(0)$ and introduce, thus, the numerals $0, 1, 2, \ldots$. It is furthermore needless to say that we may also define macro operators like $\forall t.\ \varphi$ and $\varphi \vee \psi$.

The semantics is clear, we only have to recall that the only domain of interest is $\mathcal{D} := \mathbb{N}$, and that 0 and SUC have the intended meaning, i.e., there is only one interpretation $\mathcal{J}$. For this reason, we will neglect the domain and the interpretation function $\mathcal{J}$ in the following. Instead, we simply have:

- $[\![0]\!]_\xi := 0$
- $[\![t]\!]_\xi := \xi(t)$ for every $t \in V_\Sigma$ with $\mathsf{typ}_\Sigma(t) = \mathbb{N}$
- $[\![\mathsf{SUC}(\tau)]\!]_\xi := [\![\tau]\!]_\xi + 1$
- $[\![p^{(\tau)}]\!]_\xi := \begin{cases} \mathsf{true} : [\![\tau]\!]_\xi \in \xi(p) \\ \mathsf{false} : [\![\tau]\!]_\xi \notin \xi(p) \end{cases}$
- $[\![\neg\varphi]\!]_\xi := \begin{cases} \mathsf{true} : [\![\varphi]\!]_\xi = \mathsf{false} \\ \mathsf{false} : [\![\varphi]\!]_\xi = \mathsf{true} \end{cases}$
- $[\![\varphi \wedge \psi]\!]_\xi := \begin{cases} \mathsf{true} : [\![\varphi]\!]_\xi = \mathsf{true} \text{ and } [\![\psi]\!]_\xi = \mathsf{true} \\ \mathsf{false} : \text{otherwise} \end{cases}$
- $[\![\exists t.\varphi]\!]_\xi := \begin{cases} \mathsf{true} : \exists n \in \mathbb{N}.\ [\![\varphi]\!]_{\xi_t^n} = \mathsf{true} \\ \mathsf{false} : \text{otherwise} \end{cases}$
- $[\![\exists p.\varphi]\!]_\xi := \begin{cases} \mathsf{true} : \exists M \subseteq \mathbb{N}.\ [\![\varphi]\!]_{\xi_p^M} = \mathsf{true} \\ \mathsf{false} : \text{otherwise} \end{cases}$

Before considering possible syntactic extensions of S1S that do not increase the expressiveness, we consider another variant of S1S, namely the *monadic second order logic of linear order* $\mathsf{MSO}_<$. The formal definition of $\mathsf{MSO}_<$ is as follows:

Definition 6.17 (Monadic Second Order Logic of Linear Order $\mathsf{MSO}_<$). *The logic $\mathsf{MSO}_<$ is the second order predicate logic over the signature Σ with $C_\Sigma = \{<\}$ with $\mathsf{typ}_\Sigma(<) = \mathbb{N} \times \mathbb{N} \to \mathbb{B}$. Moreover, there are arbitrarily many variables of type $\mathbb{N}$ and $\mathbb{N} \to \mathbb{B}$. In more detail, the set of formulas of $\mathsf{MSO}_<$ is the smallest set that satisfies the following rules:*

- *for all $t_1, t_2 \in V_\Sigma$ with $\mathsf{typ}_\Sigma(t_1) = \mathsf{typ}_\Sigma(t_2) = \mathbb{N}$, we have $t_1 \doteq t_2 \in \mathsf{MSO}_<$*
- *for all $t_1, t_2 \in V_\Sigma$ with $\mathsf{typ}_\Sigma(t_1) = \mathsf{typ}_\Sigma(t_2) = \mathbb{N}$, we have $t_1 < t_2 \in \mathsf{MSO}_<$*
- *for all $t, p \in V_\Sigma$ with $\mathsf{typ}_\Sigma(t) = \mathbb{N}$ and $\mathsf{typ}_\Sigma(p) = \mathbb{N} \to \mathbb{B}$, we have $p^{(t)} \in \mathsf{MSO}_<$*
- *for all $\varphi, \psi \in \mathsf{MSO}_<$, we have $\neg\varphi$, $\varphi \wedge \psi \in \mathsf{MSO}_<$*
- *for all $t \in V_\Sigma$ with $\mathsf{typ}_\Sigma(t) = \mathbb{N}$ and $\varphi \in \mathsf{MSO}_<$, we have $\exists t.\varphi \in \mathsf{MSO}_<$*
- *for all $p \in V_\Sigma$ with $\mathsf{typ}_\Sigma(p) = \mathbb{N} \to \mathbb{B}$ and $\varphi \in \mathsf{MSO}_<$, we have $\exists p.\varphi \in \mathsf{MSO}_<$*

While in S1S the two classes of terms $\mathsf{SUC}^n(t)$ and $\mathsf{SUC}^n(0)$ may occur, the only first order terms of $\mathsf{MSO}_<$ are variables. Again, the semantics of $\mathsf{MSO}_<$ is clear, the only domain is $\mathcal{D} := \mathbb{N}$ due to the axioms of Definition 6.15, and the only interpretation of $<$ is the ordering relation over $\mathbb{N} \times \mathbb{N}$. Again, we neglect the domain $\mathbb{N}$ and $\mathcal{J}$, and only write $[\![\varphi]\!]_\xi$. Hence, we have

$$[\![\tau_1 < \tau_2]\!]_\xi := \begin{cases} \mathsf{true} : [\![\tau_1]\!]_\xi < [\![\tau_2]\!]_\xi \\ \mathsf{false} : \text{otherwise} \end{cases}$$

We now compare the logics S1S and $\mathsf{MSO}_<$ in that we present translations from each one of the logics to the other one. This is formally stated in the following theorem.

Theorem 6.18 (Equal Expressiveness of S1S and $\mathsf{MSO}_<$).
The algorithm $\mathsf{MSO}_<$_S1S given in Figure 6.5 translates every formula in $\mathsf{MSO}_<$ to an equivalent formula in S1S. Analogously, the algorithm S1S_$\mathsf{MSO}_<$ given in Figure 6.5 translates every formula $\Phi \in$ S1S to an equivalent one of $\mathsf{MSO}_<$.

Proof. It is clear that the result of the functions $\mathsf{MSO}_<$_S1S and S1S_$\mathsf{MSO}_<$ belongs, in any case, to S1S and $\mathsf{MSO}_<$, respectively. Therefore, it only remains to prove the correctness of the translations. We first show the correctness of $\mathsf{MSO}_<$_S1S by induction on the structure of a given formula $\Phi \in \mathsf{MSO}_<$. In the base case, note that $t_1 \doteq t_2$ holds iff $\forall p.p^{(t_1)} \leftrightarrow p^{(t_2)}$ holds (which is actually due to Leibniz). The implication $(t_1 \doteq t_2) \to \forall p.p^{(t_1)} \leftrightarrow p^{(t_2)}$ is clearly true, the other direction is seen with singleton p's. Similarly, we have $t_1 < t_2 \Leftrightarrow \exists p. \left[\forall t.p^{(t)} \to p^{(t+1)}\right] \wedge \neg p^{(t_1)} \wedge p^{(t_2)}$. This is seen once one has figured out that p must be a set that contains any number above some threshold n. Hence, if $\xi(t_1)$ does not belong to $\xi(p)$, but $\xi(t_2)$ does, it easily follows that $t_1 < t_2$ must hold. The converse is proved by instantiating p with the set $\{n \in \mathbb{N} \mid n \geq \xi(t_2)\}$. The remaining cases follow immediately by the induction hypothesis, so that the correctness of $\mathsf{MSO}_<$_S1S follows.

We now consider the correctness of S1S_$\mathsf{MSO}_<$. First note that 0 is the only natural number t_1 that satisfies the law $\forall t_2.t_1 \leq t_2$ since 0 is the smallest

```
function MSO<_S1S(Φ)
  case Φ of
    t1 ≐ t2  : return ∀p.p^(t1) ↔ p^(t2);
    t1 < t2  : return ∃p. [∀t.p^(t) → p^(t+1)] ∧ ¬p^(t1) ∧ p^(t2);
    p^(t)    : return p^(t);
    ¬φ       : return ¬MSO<_S1S(φ);
    φ ∧ ψ    : return MSO<_S1S(φ) ∧ MSO<_S1S(ψ);
    φ ∨ ψ    : return MSO<_S1S(φ) ∨ MSO<_S1S(ψ);
    ∃t. φ    : return ∃t. MSO<_S1S(φ);
    ∃p. φ    : return ∃p. MSO<_S1S(φ);
  end
end

function S1S_MSO<(Φ)
  case Φ of
    p^(n)      : return ∃t1. S1S_MSO<(p^(t1+n)) ∧ (∀t2. t1 < t2 ∨ t1 ≐ t2);
    p^(t0+n)   : return ∃t1 ... tn. p^(tn) ∧ ⋀_{i=0}^{n-1} [ti < t(i+1) ∧ ∀t3.ti < t3 → t(i+1) ≤ t3];
    ¬φ         : return ¬S1S_MSO<(φ);
    φ ∧ ψ      : return S1S_MSO<(φ) ∧ S1S_MSO<(ψ);
    φ ∨ ψ      : return S1S_MSO<(φ) ∨ S1S_MSO<(ψ);
    ∃t. φ      : return ∃t. S1S_MSO<(φ);
    ∃p. φ      : return ∃p. S1S_MSO<(φ);
  end
end
```

Fig. 6.5. Translating $\mathsf{MSO}_<$ to S1S and vice versa

natural number. Therefore, we have $(t_1 \doteq 0) \Leftrightarrow \forall t_2.t_1 \leq t_2$, and also $p^{(n)} \leftrightarrow \exists t_1.(t_1 \doteq 0) \wedge p^{(t_1+n)}$, which proves the case for $p^{(n)}$. For $p^{(t_0+n)}$, we first note that $p^{(t_0+n)} \Leftrightarrow \exists t_1 \ldots t_n. \left(\bigwedge_{i=0}^{n-1} [t_{i+1} \doteq \mathsf{SUC}(t_i)] \wedge p^{(t_n)}\right)$ holds, which can be seen by an easy induction on n. It then remains to translate the equations $t_{i+1} \doteq \mathsf{SUC}(t_i)$ to $\mathsf{MSO}_<$. For this reason, note that $\mathsf{SUC}(t_i)$ is the least natural number that is larger than t_i, hence, we have $t_{i+1} \doteq \mathsf{SUC}(t_i)$ if and only if $t_i < t_{i+1} \wedge \forall t_3.t_i < t_3 \rightarrow t_{i+1} \leq t_3$ holds, which proves the correctness of the translation of $p^{(t+n)}$. The remaining cases follow immediately by the induction hypothesis. □

Hence, we see that S1S and $\mathsf{MSO}_<$ are just two variants of the same logic that differ on the set of atomic formulas. While S1S is based on 0 and SUC, $\mathsf{MSO}_<$ is based on the ordering relation $<$.

We just note here that for the translations given in Figure 6.5 we can freely choose whether we wish to have a universal or an existential quantification in the case $p^{(t_0+n)}$ of function S1S_$\mathsf{MSO}_<$. This is due to the following equations (as we see below, the same holds for the translation of $t_1 \doteq t_2$ and $t_1 < t_2$):

- $p^{(t_0+n))} \leftrightarrow \exists t_1 \ldots t_n. \left(\bigwedge_{i=0}^{n-1} [t_{i+1} \doteq \mathsf{SUC}(t_i)] \wedge p^{(t_n)} \right)$
- $p^{(t_0+n))} \leftrightarrow \forall t_1 \ldots t_n. \left(\bigwedge_{i=0}^{n-1} [t_{i+1} \doteq \mathsf{SUC}(t_i)] \right) \rightarrow p^{(t_n)}$

Therefore, we can alternatively consider S1S or $\mathsf{MSO}_<$ for our further investigations. Before we turn to the translation procedures, we list some possible macro extensions of the logics S1S and $\mathsf{MSO}_<$. By the above theorem, it is clear that we can also use the union of both languages and are then able to reduce any formula of that logic to either S1S or $\mathsf{MSO}_<$. Hence, we can add the following abbreviations:

- Adding Boolean variables $p \in V_\Sigma$ with $\mathsf{typ}_\Sigma(p) = \mathbb{B}$. Given a formula Φ where such a Boolean variable p occurs, we can prove that Φ is equivalent to $[\Phi]_p^{p^{(0)}} \wedge \forall t.p^{(t)} \leftrightarrow p^{(t+1)}$. In the latter formula we have changed the type of p, while possible quantifications over p remain unchanged.
- We add equations and inequations of terms, where we have the choice on the type of quantification when the macro is replaced:
  - $(t_1 \doteq t_2) := \forall p.p^{(t_1)} \leftrightarrow p^{(t_2)}$
  - $(t_1 \doteq t_2) := \exists pq. \left(\begin{array}{l} \left[\forall t.p^{(t)} \rightarrow p^{(t+1)}\right] \wedge p^{(t_2)} \wedge \neg p^{(t_1)} \wedge \\ \left[\forall t.q^{(t)} \rightarrow q^{(t+1)}\right] \wedge q^{(t_1+1)} \wedge \neg q^{(t_2)} \end{array} \right)$
  - $(t_1 < t_2) := \exists p. \left[\forall t.p^{(t)} \rightarrow p^{(t+1)}\right] \wedge \neg p^{(t_1)} \wedge p^{(t_2)}$
  - $(t_1 < t_2) := \forall p. \left[\forall t.p^{(t)} \rightarrow p^{(t+1)}\right] \rightarrow \left[p^{(t_1+1)} \rightarrow p^{(t_2)}\right]$
  - $(t_1 \leq t_2) := \exists p. \left[\forall t.p^{(t)} \rightarrow p^{(t+1)}\right] \wedge \neg p^{(t_1)} \wedge p^{(t_2+1)}$
  - $(t_1 \leq t_2) := \forall p. \left[\forall t.p^{(t)} \rightarrow p^{(t+1)}\right] \rightarrow \left[p^{(t_1)} \rightarrow p^{(t_2)}\right]$
  - $(t_1 > t_2) := t_2 < t_1$
  - $(t_1 \geq t_2) := t_2 \leq t_1$

  As can be seen, we have two possibilities in defining the above relations. On the one hand, by universally quantified formulas, and on the other hand by existentially quantified formulas. It is important to have these alternatives to minimize quantifier alternation.
- We can also use sums of points of times $\sum_{i=1}^{n} \tau_i$, with $\tau_i \in \mathsf{Term}^{\mathsf{S1S}}$, provided that all variables of the sum are bound. As every term is of the form $\mathsf{SUC}^n(0)$ or $\mathsf{SUC}^n(t)$, it follows that every such sum can be brought into a form $\mathsf{SUC}^k(0) + \sum_{i=1}^{n} t_i$, where the t_i are variables. We now abbreviate the partial sums by new variables, i.e., $x_1 := t_1$, and $x_{i+1} := x_i + t_{i+1}$. Due to these definitions, it follows that the new variables are ordered $x_i \leq x_{i+1}$. Hence, we can replace the partial sums by the variables x_i, and just note their ordering in the quantifiers. For example, consider the following reduction of such a sum:

$$\forall t_1.\exists t_2.\forall t_3.p^{(t_1+t_2+t_3)} \Leftrightarrow \forall x_1.[\exists x_2.x_1 \leq x_2 \wedge [\forall x_3.x_2 \leq x_3 \rightarrow p^{(x_3)}]]$$

However, sums with more than three variables are not necessary, as the following equivalences hold:
- $\forall x.\exists y.\varphi(x+y) \Leftrightarrow \forall x.\exists y.x \leq y \wedge \varphi(y)$
- $\exists x.\forall y.\varphi(x+y) \Leftrightarrow \exists x.\forall y.x \leq y \rightarrow \varphi(y)$
- $\forall x.\forall y.\varphi(x+y) \Leftrightarrow \forall x.\varphi(x)$
- $\exists x.\exists y.\varphi(x+y) \Leftrightarrow \exists x.\varphi(x)$
- $\forall x.\exists y.\forall z.\varphi(x+y+z) \Leftrightarrow \exists y.\forall z.\varphi(y+z)$
- $\exists x.\forall y.\exists z.\varphi(x+y+z) \Leftrightarrow \forall y.\exists z.\varphi(y+z)$

- Elgot and Rabin [157] showed that one may also add the unary functions 'factorial' or 'is a power of k' for some fixed $k \geq 2$ without destroying decidability. However, the addition of the unary function $\lambda x.x+x$ destroys the decidability.

It is also interesting to see how Presburger logic can be embedded in $\mathsf{MSO}_<$ or S1S. Presburger logic is the first order logic $\mathsf{FO}_<$ over the natural numbers with the constants $C_\Sigma = \{0, \mathsf{SUC}, +\}$. Due to the presence of $+$, it is furthermore possible to define $<$ by the following equivalence: $x < y :\Leftrightarrow \exists z.x + \mathsf{SUC}(z) \doteq y$. The idea of embedding Presburger logic in S1S is as follows: natural numbers are considered in their binary representation (which is unique):

$$n = \sum_{i=0}^{\lceil \log_2(n) \rceil} b_i \cdot 2^i, \text{ where } b_i := \left\lfloor \frac{n}{2^i} \right\rfloor \bmod 2$$

Numbers are first order objects in Presburger logic, but due to the binary representation, we can represent every number as a monadic predicate p_x that is true iff the corresponding digit of x is true. This observation is the key[2] to the embedding in S1S. Every formula of Presburger logic can be brought into a normal form, where every atomic formula is of the form $x + y \doteq z$ (see [446]). This formula can be represented with the following formula in S1S that describes a serial adder:

$$\mathsf{ADD}(x,y,z) :\Leftrightarrow \left(\begin{array}{l} \neg c^{(0)} \wedge \\ \exists c. \\ \qquad \left(\forall t.c^{(t+1)} \leftrightarrow x^{(t)} \wedge y^{(t)} \vee c^{(t)} \wedge \left(x^{(t)} \vee y^{(t)}\right)\right) \wedge \\ \qquad \left(\forall t.z^{(t)} \leftrightarrow x^{(t)} \oplus y^{(t)} \oplus c^{(t)}\right) \end{array} \right)$$

This immediately converts every Presburger formula to an equivalent S1S formula. The translation of S1S to ω-automata can then also be used to translate every formula of Presburger logic to an equivalent ω-automaton. To this end, one has to compute the intersection, union, complements, and projections of these automata [54, 296, 446, 522]. Note further, that $\mathsf{ADD}(x,y,z)$ can also be translated to LTL_p: it is equivalent to $\mathsf{G}[z \leftrightarrow x \oplus y \oplus \overleftarrow{\underline{\mathsf{X}}}\,[(x \oplus y)\ \overleftarrow{\underline{\mathsf{U}}}\ (x \wedge y)]]$.

[2] However, since the binary representation has only finitely many 1's, we have to add the conjunct $\mathsf{FG}\neg x$ for every number x. For the integers, we have to add the conjunct $\mathsf{FG}[x \leftrightarrow \mathsf{X}x]$, which is equivalent to $\mathsf{FG}\neg x \vee \mathsf{FG}x$.

6.3.2 Translating $\mathsf{MSO}_<$ to ω-Automata

We now turn to the translation of the logics $\mathsf{MSO}_<$ and S1S to equivalent ω-automata. We therefore present a translation procedure of $\mathsf{MSO}_<$ as given in [487], which is surprisingly simple. However, before presenting this translation procedure, we have to discuss some points concerning the semantics of variables, second order quantification in Kripke structures, and the predicate logic interpretations $\mathcal{J}$.

We have already noted on page 83, by the example given in Figure 2.10, that automaton formulas and the quantified formulas of our specification language provide some different means of quantification. We have already pointed out that state variables $q \in Q$ of an automaton formula $\mathcal{A}_\exists(Q, \Phi_\mathcal{I}, \Phi_\mathcal{R}, \Phi_\mathcal{F})$ are used for quantification over *occurrences of states on a path*, i.e, they corresponds with a subset $M_q \subseteq \mathbb{N}$. Therefore, one occurrence of a state may belong to the set M_q, and another occurrence of the same state may not belong to M_q.

In contrast, quantification over q in a $\mathcal{L}_{\mathsf{spec}}$ formula $\exists q.\varphi$ quantifies over subsets of the set of states $\mathcal{S}$ of the structure. Hence, q is associated with a set of states $Q_q \subseteq \mathcal{S}$. The difference is made explicit by the formulas $\mathcal{A}_\exists(\{q\}, q, \mathsf{X}q \leftrightarrow \neg q, \mathsf{G}[q \to a])$ and $\exists q.q \wedge \mathsf{G}[\mathsf{X}q \leftrightarrow \neg q] \wedge \mathsf{G}[q \to a]$ in the structure given in Figure 2.10 on page 83. The logics $\mathsf{MSO}_<$ and S1S also provide means of quantification, where both first and second order quantification is available. The question is now, how this form of quantification is related to the quantification provided by automaton formulas and quantified formulas of $\mathcal{L}_{\mathsf{spec}}$. To this end, we should compare the S1S formula $\exists q.q^{(0)} \wedge \left(\forall t.q^{(t+1)} \leftrightarrow \neg q^{(t)}\right) \wedge \left(\forall t.q^{(t)} \to a^{(t)}\right)$ with the above two formulas.

To answer these questions, we first have to establish a relationship between the semantics, i.e., we have to clarify what it should mean that a formula of $\mathcal{L}_{\mathsf{spec}}$ is equivalent to a formula of $\mathsf{MSO}_<$ or S1S. Note that formulas of $\mathcal{L}_{\mathsf{spec}}$ are interpreted over Kripke structures, while $\mathsf{MSO}_<$ and S1S formulas are interpreted over the natural numbers with a variable assignment ξ. Therefore, the latter semantics maps the second order variables p to a set of natural numbers $[\![p]\!]_\xi \subseteq \mathbb{N}$. Therefore, the quantification of S1S or $\mathsf{MSO}_<$ is exactly the quantification that is made by automaton formulas. We will make this more precise:

Definition 6.19 (Induced Assignment ξ_π of a Path). *Given a Kripke structure $\mathcal{K} = (\mathcal{I}, \mathcal{S}, \mathcal{R}, \mathcal{L})$ over V_Σ, an arbitrary state $s \in \mathcal{S}$, and a path $\pi \in \mathsf{Paths}_\mathcal{K}(s)$. We then define the induced assignment ξ_π of the path π as follows:*

$$\xi_\pi(p) = \{t \in \mathbb{N} \mid p \in \mathcal{L}(\pi^{(t)})\}$$

Note that the variables in V_Σ are viewed as monadic predicates and that ξ_π is not defined for first order variables (denoting natural numbers).

Note that the *variables of the Kripke structure are actually the second order variables of* S1S *or* $\mathsf{MSO}_<$. For this reason, we can also interpret S1S/$\mathsf{MSO}_<$ formulas on a path of the structure $\mathcal{K}$, provided that the S1S/$\mathsf{MSO}_<$ formulas have no free first order variables. We may therefore interpret S1S/ MSO$_<$ formulas on paths π of a Kripke structure $\mathcal{K}$, and write therefore $(\mathcal{K},\pi) \models \varphi$ for $\varphi \in$ S1S or $\varphi \in$ MSO$_<$ if $[\![\varphi]\!]_{\xi_\pi}$ holds (note the different meaning of $[\![\cdot]\!]$ here).

It is also possible to define a Kripke structure $\mathcal{K}_\xi$ and a path π_ξ for a given assignment ξ. Note that V_Σ is finite, and hence, we can take 2^{V_Σ} as set of states of $\mathcal{K}_\xi$. The transition relation connects any state with any other, i.e., $\mathcal{R}_\xi := 2^{V_\Sigma} \times 2^{V_\Sigma}$, and $\mathcal{L}_\xi(s) := s$. The path π_ξ is then obviously defined as $\pi_\xi^{(t)} := \{p \in V_\Sigma \mid t \in \xi(p)\}$. This construction is actually done by our automaton formulas, which is seen by the following extension of Lemma 2.47.

```
function BuechiS1S(𝔄)
  A∃ ({q1,...,qm}, ΦI, ΦR, GFΦF) ≡ 𝔄;
  ΨI := XProp2S1S(0, ΦI);
  ΨR := XProp2S1S(t, ΦR);
  ΨF := XProp2S1S(t2, ΦF);
  return ∃q1. ... ∃qm.ΨI ∧ [∀t.ΨR] ∧ ∀t1.∃t2.t1 < t2 ∧ ΨF;
end

function XProp2S1S(t, Φ)
  case Φ of
    Xp         : return p^(t+1);
    is_var(Φ)  : return Φ^(t);
    ¬φ         : return ¬XProp2S1S(t, φ);
    φ ∧ ψ      : return XProp2S1S(t, φ) ∧ XProp2S1S(t, ψ);
    φ ∨ ψ      : return XProp2S1S(t, φ) ∨ XProp2S1S(t, ψ);
  end
end
```

Fig. 6.6. Translating NDet$_{GF}$ to S1S

Lemma 6.20 (ω-Automata and S1S). *Given* $\mathfrak{A} = \mathcal{A}_\exists(\{q_1,\ldots,q_m\}, \Phi_\mathcal{I}, \Phi_\mathcal{R}, \Phi_\mathcal{F}) \in$ NDet$_{GF}$, *we define the* S1S *formula* BuechiS1S($\mathfrak{A}$) *as shown in Figure 6.6. For every path π of every Kripke structure $\mathcal{K}$, we then have:*

$$(\mathcal{K},\pi) \models \mathfrak{A} \textit{ iff } [\![\mathsf{BuechiS1S}(\mathfrak{A})]\!]_{\xi_\pi} = \mathsf{true}$$

Therefore, we see that Büchi automata, and hence, all ω-automata can be represented in S1S. We now turn to the converse translation, namely the translation of the logics MSO$_<$ and S1S to equivalent ω-automata. In this section, we present the translation procedure of MSO$_<$ as given in [487], which consists of two steps: The first step is the elimination of the first order variables, and thus of first order quantifiers. The idea is thereby to represent a number as a singleton set, i.e., we introduce for every first order variable t a monadic predicate p_t such that p_t is a singleton that only contains the number associated with t. Quantification over t is therefore replaced by quantification over p_t. The entire elimination procedure given in Figure 6.7 will moreover require macros for singleton, successor, and subsets:

```
function ElimFO(Φ)
  case Φ of
    t1 ≐ t2: return Subset(q_t1, q_t2) ∧ Subset(q_t2, q_t1);
    t1 < t2: Ψ :≡ ∀q1.∀q2.S2(q1, q2) → [Subset(q1, p) → Subset(q2, p)];
           : return ∃p.Ψ ∧ ¬Subset(q_t1, p) ∧ Subset(q_t2, p);
    p^(t)  : return Subset(q_t, p);
    ¬φ     : return ¬ElimFO(φ);
    φ ∧ ψ  : return ElimFO(φ) ∧ ElimFO(ψ);
    φ ∨ ψ  : return ElimFO(φ) ∨ ElimFO(ψ);
    ∃t.φ   : return ∃q_t.Sing(q_t) ∧ ElimFO(φ);
    ∃p.φ   : return ∃p.ElimFO(φ);
  end
end
```

Fig. 6.7. Eliminationg first order variables in $\mathsf{MSO}_<$

Theorem 6.21 (Elimination of First Order Variables in $\mathsf{MSO}_<$ and S1S). *For every formula $\Phi \in \mathsf{MSO}_<$ without free first order variables, the algorithm given in Figure 6.7 computes an equivalent formula without first order variables. Instead, the resulting formula* $\mathsf{ElimFO}(\Phi)$ *contains only atomic formulas of the forms* $\mathsf{Subset}(p, q)$, $\mathsf{Sing}(p)$, *and* $\mathsf{S}_2(p, q)$, *which are defined as follows:*

- $\mathsf{Subset}(p, q) :\Leftrightarrow \forall t.p^{(t)} \to q^{(t)}$
- $\mathsf{Sing}(p) :\Leftrightarrow [\exists t_1.p^{(t_1)}] \wedge [\forall t_1 t_2.p^{(t_1)} \wedge p^{(t_2)} \to t_1 \doteq t_2]$
- $\mathsf{S}_2(p, q) :\Leftrightarrow \mathsf{Sing}(p) \wedge \mathsf{Sing}(q) \wedge \forall t.p^{(t)} \to q^{(t+1)}$

Proof. The proof follows directly from algorithm ElimFO given in Figure 6.7 by induction on Φ. The arguments are similar to the ones for the translation of $\mathsf{MSO}_<$ to S1S. For the induction, note that the variables q_{t_i} are introduced by the elimination of a first order quantification, and therefore represent singleton sets. For the replacement of $<$, note that the new predicate p does not hold at t_1, but at t_2. Moreover, once p holds, it remains true forever. □

Hence, we can replace first order quantification in $\mathsf{MSO}_<$ with the macros $\mathsf{Subset}(p, q)$, $\mathsf{Sing}(p)$, and $\mathsf{S}_2(p, q)$, where numbers are viewed as singleton sets that obviously represent these numbers. The translation to ω-automata is now simple: We essentially have to construct automata for $\mathsf{Subset}(p, q)$, $\mathsf{Sing}(p)$, and $\mathsf{S}_2(p, q)$. The remaining operators, namely, Boolean operations and second order quantification are directly performed as automaton operations.

It is possible to express the macros $\mathsf{Subset}(p,q)$, $\mathsf{Sing}(p)$, and $\mathsf{S}_2(p,q)$ by equivalent temporal logic formulas, and even $\mathsf{TL}_{\mathsf{Prefix}}$ formulas are sufficient. Since we already know how to translate temporal logic to automata, this can be used to construct the desired automata. To this end, we use the following equivalences:

- $\mathsf{Subset}(p,q) :\Leftrightarrow \mathsf{G}[p \to q]$
- $\mathsf{Sing}(p) :\Leftrightarrow \mathsf{G}[p \to \mathsf{XG}\neg p] \wedge \mathsf{F}p$
- $\mathsf{S}_2(p,q) :\Leftrightarrow \mathsf{G}[p \to \mathsf{X}q \wedge \mathsf{XG}\neg p] \wedge \mathsf{F}p \wedge \mathsf{G}[q \to \mathsf{XG}\neg q]$

Translating these temporal logic formulas to equivalent automata yields our final translation to ω-automata for the atomic formulas. Alternatively, we can use the following $\mathsf{Det}_{\mathsf{Prefix}}$ automata ($\mathsf{Subset}(p,q)$ is trivial):

- $\mathsf{Sing}(p)$ can be replaced by a prefix automaton with the following state transition diagram and the acceptance condition that state s_2 is never reached, but state s_1 must be reached:

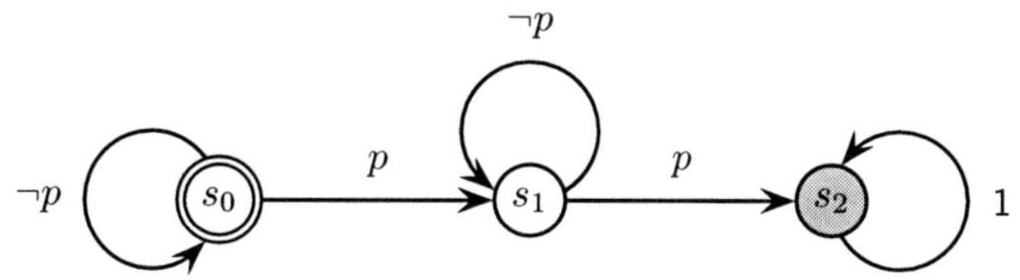

- $\mathsf{S}_2(p,q)$ can be replaced by a prefix automaton with the following state transition diagram and the acceptance condition that state s_2 must be reached, but state s_3 must not be reached:

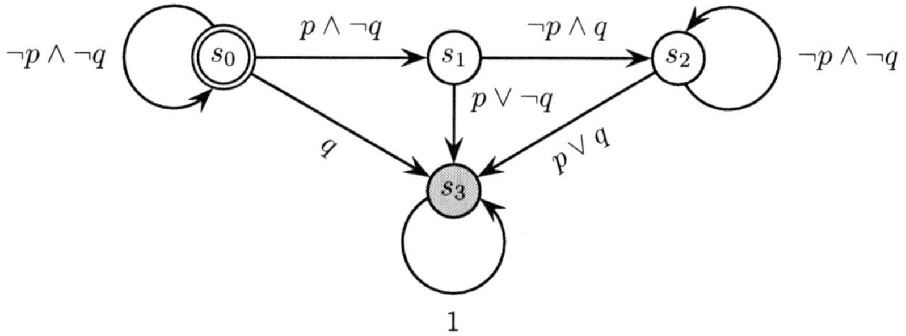

In the complete translation procedure, that is given in Figure 6.8, we use the replacement by the above temporal logic formulas. Note that this is a special case of an automaton formula, since we can write $\mathcal{A}_\exists(\{\},1,1,\varphi)$ instead of φ. Boolean operations are executed as Boolean operations on automaton formulas, and second order quantification is performed by adding the quantified variable as a new state variable of the automaton. However, the problem is that the kind of quantification, i.e., existential or universal, corresponds with the type of automaton. Hence, quantifier alternations in $\mathsf{MSO}_<$ will lead to

```
function MSO_Omega(Φ)
  case Φ of
    Subset(p,q) : return G[p → q];
    Sing(p)     : return G[p → XG¬p] ∧ Fp;
    S2(p,q)     : return ( G[p → Xq ∧ XG¬p] ∧ Fp∧ ) ;
                         ( G[q → XG¬q]             )
    ¬φ          : return ¬MSO_Omega(φ);
    φ ∧ ψ       : return MSO_Omega(φ) ∧ MSO_Omega(ψ);
    φ ∨ ψ       : return MSO_Omega(φ) ∨ MSO_Omega(ψ);
    ∃p.φ        : return A∃ ({p}, 1, 1, MSO_Omega(φ));
    ∀p.φ        : return A∀ ({p}, 1, 1, MSO_Omega(φ));
  end
end
```

Fig. 6.8. Translating $\mathsf{MSO}_<$ to ω-automata

quantifier alternations in the automaton formulas that will be generated by the algorithm of Figure 6.8.

We already know that those alternations can all be eliminated by determinization of the automaton. If the automaton is deterministic, we can exchange the universal or existential type, since every word has then exactly one run. Note, however, that this means that every quantifier alternation results in a determinization step that may in turn yield an exponential blow-up of the automaton. We have therefore proved the following theorem, which is the fundamental result of Büchi and gives us a decision procedure for the logics $\mathsf{MSO}_<$ and S1S:

Theorem 6.22 (Translating $\mathsf{MSO}_<$ and S1S to ω-Automata). *Every formula of $\mathsf{MSO}_<$, and hence, every formula of S1S, can be translated to an equivalent ω-automaton. The complexity of the translation is nonelementary [221, 473].*

To show the relationship between Presburger logic and $\mathsf{MSO}_<$/S1S, we note that we can alternatively reduce $\mathsf{MSO}_<$/S1S to the following atomic predicates [73] ([73] lists also further possibilities):

- $\mathsf{Bit}_1(x,y) :\Leftrightarrow \mathsf{Sing}(y) \wedge \mathsf{Subset}(y,x)$
- $\mathsf{Bit}_0(x,y) :\Leftrightarrow \mathsf{Sing}(y) \wedge \neg\mathsf{Subset}(y,x)$
- $\mathsf{ADD}(x,y,z) :\Leftrightarrow \mathcal{A}_\exists \left(\begin{array}{l}\{c\}, \neg c,\\ (\mathsf{X}c \leftrightarrow x \wedge y \vee c \wedge (x \vee y)),\\ \mathsf{G}\,(z \leftrightarrow x \oplus y \oplus c)\end{array}\right)$

The reason for this is that we can use the following equations (bytheway, $\mathsf{Sing}(x)$ is redundant, but still convenient: $\mathsf{Sing}(x) \leftrightarrow \exists y.\mathsf{S}_2(x,y)$):

- $\mathsf{Subset}(x,y) \leftrightarrow \forall z.\mathsf{Bit}_1(x,z) \rightarrow \mathsf{Bit}_1(y,z)$
- $\mathsf{Sing}(x) \leftrightarrow \exists y.\mathsf{Bit}_1(y,x)$
- $\mathsf{S}_2(x,y) \leftrightarrow \mathsf{Sing}(x) \wedge \mathsf{ADD}(x,x,y)$

6.3.3 Büchi's Decision Procedure: Normal Forms for S1S

The key of Büchi's transformation of S1S into equivalent automaton formulas is based on three normals forms that we consider in this section. The first one says that we can eliminate terms of the form $q^{(t+n)}$ where $n > 1$.

Lemma 6.23 (Single SUC Normal Form for S1S). *Given any formula $\Phi \in$ S1S, there is an equivalent formula $\Psi \in$ S1S, where only atomic formulas of the form $q^{(0)}$, $q^{(t)}$ or $q^{(t+1)}$ occur.*

Proof. The idea is to use first order variables $t_1, \ldots, t_n$ with the meaning $t_1 \doteq t+1, t_2 \doteq t_1+1, \ldots, t_n \doteq t_{n-1}+1$, and hence, $t_i \doteq t+i$. For this reason, we first obtain the following formulas:

- $q^{(t+n+1)} \leftrightarrow \exists t_1 \ldots t_n. \left(t_1 \doteq t+1 \wedge \left(\bigwedge_{i=1}^{n-1} t_{i+1} \doteq t_i + 1\right)\right) \wedge q^{(t_n+1)}$
- $q^{(t+n+1)} \leftrightarrow \forall t_1 \ldots t_n. \left(t_1 \doteq t+1 \wedge \left(\bigwedge_{i=1}^{n-1} t_{i+1} \doteq t_i + 1\right)\right) \rightarrow q^{(t_n+1)}$

Now, recall that $t_1 \doteq t_2 \Leftrightarrow \forall p.p^{(t_1)} \leftrightarrow p^{(t_2)}$ holds, and therefore, we obtain:

- $q^{(t+n+1)} \leftrightarrow \exists t_1 \ldots t_n.\forall p. \left(\begin{array}{l} [p^{(t_1)} \leftrightarrow p^{(t+1)}] \wedge \\ \left(\bigwedge_{i=1}^{n-1} p^{(t_{i+1})} \leftrightarrow p^{(t_i+1)}\right) \wedge \\ q^{(t_n+1)} \end{array}\right)$
- $q^{(t+n+1)} \leftrightarrow \forall t_1 \ldots t_n.\exists p. \left(\begin{array}{l} [p^{(t_1)} \leftrightarrow p^{(t+1)}] \wedge \\ \left(\bigwedge_{i=1}^{n-1} p^{(t_{i+1})} \leftrightarrow p^{(t_i+1)}\right) \\ \rightarrow q^{(t_n+1)} \end{array}\right)$

□

The next normal form is very important for the translation of S1S to equivalent automaton formulas. It is one cornerstone in the *elimination of first order variables* (and quantifications) and is used to separate between first and second order quantification.

Theorem 6.24 (Separated Prenex Normal Form for S1S). *Given any formula $\Phi \in$ S1S, there is an equivalent formula $\Theta_1 p_1 \ldots . \Theta_n p_n . \Theta_{n+1} t_1 \ldots . \Theta_{n+m} t_m . \Psi \in$ S1S, where $\Theta_i \in \{\forall, \exists\}$, and $\mathsf{typ}_\Sigma(p_i) = \mathbb{N} \rightarrow \mathbb{B}$ and $\mathsf{typ}_\Sigma(t_i) = \mathbb{N}$*

Proof. The transformation into the described normal form is given by the following rules.

- Computation of prenex normal form by the following rules (it may be necessary to rename bound variables to fulfill the proviso):
  - $[\forall t.P(t)] \wedge Q \Leftrightarrow \forall t.[P(t) \wedge Q]$, provided that t does not occur in Q
  - $[\exists t.P(t)] \wedge Q \Leftrightarrow \exists t.[P(t) \wedge Q]$, provided that t does not occur in Q
  - $[\forall t.P(t)] \vee Q \Leftrightarrow \forall t.[P(t) \vee Q]$, provided that t does not occur in Q
  - $[\exists t.P(t)] \vee Q \Leftrightarrow \exists t.[P(t) \vee Q]$, provided that t does not occur in Q

- It remains to reorder the quantifiers such that all quantifiers over variables of type $\mathbb{N} \to \mathbb{B}$ precede quantifiers over numeric variables. This transformation is based on the following theorems [156], where $\mathsf{typ}_\Sigma(p) = \mathbb{N} \to \mathbb{B}$ and $\mathsf{typ}_\Sigma(t) = \mathsf{typ}_\Sigma(t') = \mathbb{N}$:
  1. $(\exists t.\exists p.\varphi(p,t)) \Leftrightarrow (\exists p.\exists t.\varphi(p,t))$
  2. $(\forall t.\forall p.\varphi(p,t)) \Leftrightarrow (\forall p.\forall t.\varphi(p,t))$
  3. $(\exists t.\forall p.\varphi(p,t)) \Leftrightarrow (\exists q.\forall p.\forall t.\exists t'.[q(t) \to \varphi(p,t)] \wedge q(t'))$
  4. $(\forall t.\exists p.\varphi(p,t)) \Leftrightarrow (\forall q.\exists p.\exists t.\forall t'.q(t') \to [\varphi(p,t) \wedge q(t)])$

□

Büchi's decision procedure starts with the elimination of multiple SUC terms such that the only atomic formulas are of the form $q^{(t)}$ and $q^{(t+1)}$. After this step, the resulting formula is transformed into the separated normal form $\Theta_1 p_1.\ldots.\Theta_n p_n.\Theta_{n+1} t_1.\ldots.\Theta_{n+m} t_m.\Psi \in \mathsf{S1S}$. Now, we consider the first order kernel $\Theta_{n+1} t_1.\ldots.\Theta_{n+m} t_m.\Psi \in \mathsf{S1S}$. This one is converted to the last important normal form that is due to Behmann [34].

Behmann's normal form [34] which is the only transformation step of Büchi's translation procedure that makes use of the fact, that S1S contains only *monadic* symbols. Due to this fact, each term and each atomic formula contains either no or exactly one numeric variable. As a consequence, it is possible to transform each formula of S1S without second order quantifiers such that all scopes are disjoint.

Lemma 6.25 (Behmann's Normal Form [34]). *For each formula $\Phi \in \mathsf{S1S}$ without second order quantification, i.e., without quantification over variables of type $\mathbb{N} \to \mathbb{B}$, there is an equivalent $\Psi \in \mathsf{S1S}$ that is a Boolean combination of subformulas of the following kinds:*

- *$\forall t.\varphi$ where φ does not contain any quantifier at all*
- *$\exists t.\varphi$ where φ does not contain any quantifier at all*

The normal form implies that there is no intersection of scopes of quantifiers, i.e., all scopes of quantifiers are disjoint.

Proof. We first transform the considered formula into a prenex normal form: $Q_1 t_1 \ldots Q_n t_n.\varphi$ where $Q_i \in \{\forall, \exists\}$ and φ does not contain quantifiers. If $Q_n = \forall$ then φ is converted into conjunctive normal form, i.e.

$$\varphi = \bigwedge_{j=1}^{c} \left[\bigvee_{k=1}^{d_j} p_{j,k}^{(t_n + d_{j,k})} \right] \vee \left[\bigvee_{k=d_j+1}^{e_j} p_{j,k}^{(y_{j,k}+d_{j,k})} \right]$$

where $y_{j,k} \in \{0, t_1, \ldots, t_{n-1}\}$ holds. Hence, we have arranged the atomic formulas such that those containing t_n are singled out. According to the law $[\forall t.P(t) \vee Q] = [\forall t.P(t)] \vee Q$, the quantifier $Q_n = \forall$ is now shifted inwards:

$$\bigwedge_{j=1}^{c} \left[\forall t_n. \bigvee_{k=1}^{d_j} p_{j,k}^{(t_n + d_{j,k})} \right] \vee \left[\bigvee_{k=d_j+1}^{e_j} p_{j,k}^{(y_{j,k}+d_{j,k})} \right]$$

The subformulas $\bigvee_{k=1}^{d_j} p_{j,k}^{(t_n+d_{j,k})}$ for $j = 1,\ldots,c$ are the minimal scopes for the variable t_n and do not contain any other numeric variable.

If, on the other hand, $Q_n = \exists$, then φ is transformed into a disjunctive normal form and the dual transformation is done, i.e., Q_n is shifted inwards by the theorem $[\exists t.P(t) \wedge Q] = [\exists t.P(t)] \wedge Q$. These steps are recursively applied until all quantifiers have been shifted inwards. □

The above proof is constructive, i.e., it gives an algorithm for computing Behmann's normal form. However, the algorithm is complex, since it requires multiple switches from CNF to DNF and vice versa. Each time we have to minimize the resulting DNF and CNF, respectively, otherwise the length of the formula could grow each time. In order to overcome this drawback, Schneider and Weindel showed in [442] how binary decision diagrams can be used to efficiently implement this transformation.

The importance of Behmann's normal form is that it can be used to eliminate any first order quantification by a direct translation to temporal logic formulas: Given a formula in Behmann's normal form, an equivalent temporal logic formula can be computed in a bottom-up traversal on the syntax tree of the formula as follows: the leaf nodes $p^{(n)}$ and $p^{(t+n)}$ (where $t \in V_\Sigma$ and $n \in \mathbb{N}$) are both replaced with $\mathsf{X}^n p$. Of course, the two atomic formulas are not equivalent to each other, but since the entire formula is in Behmann's normal form, we know that $p^{(n)}$ is not in the scope of any quantifier and $p^{(t+n)}$ is in the scope of a quantifier binding t. In the latter case, the quantifiers $\forall$ and $\exists$ will be replaced afterwards by G and F, respectively. Boolean connectives are not changed during the bottom-up traversal. This translation is given by the function Behm_Tmp in Figure 6.9.

Figure 6.9 also gives the translation procedure of S1S to equivalent ω-automata that essentially implements Büchi's decision procedure. Similar to the function MSO_Omega, the function S1S_Omega does not convert a given formula not to a flat automaton formula. Instead, a nested automaton formula is obtained. By the results of Chapter 4, we know, however, how to convert these formulas to flat ω-automata. For this reason, it follows again that the final reduction to a flat ω-automaton formula requires as many determinization steps as there are quantifier alternations. For this reason, the runtime of the translation can not be bounded by any finite stack of exponentiations $2^{\cdot^{\cdot^{\cdot^{2^{|\varphi|}}}}}$ [221, 366, 455], i.e., it is *nonelementary* [6, 366, 473]. Results from Stockmeyer and Meyer [6, 366, 473] show that this nonelementary runtime of the decision problem of S1S can not be avoided [221, 366, 455]. However, this result can also be interpreted differently: since S1S is as expressive as ω-automata, but has a more complex decision procedure, it can be concluded that some facts can be expressed with S1S more succinctly than in comparable formalisms.

```
function Behm_Tmp(Φ)
  case Φ of
    p^(n)     : return X^n p;
    p^(t+n)   : return X^n p;
    ¬φ        : return ¬Behm_Tmp(φ);
    φ ∧ ψ     : return Behm_Tmp(φ) ∧ Behm_Tmp(ψ);
    φ ∨ ψ     : return Behm_Tmp(φ) ∨ Behm_Tmp(ψ);
    ∃t.φ      : return Fφ;
    ∀t.φ      : return Gφ;
  end
end

function S1S_Omega(Φ)
  Θ_1 p_1. ... Θ_n p_n.Θ_{n+1} t_1. ... Θ_{n+m} t_m.Φ_1 := SeparatePrenexNF(Φ);
  Φ_2 := Behmann(Θ_{n+1} t_1. ... Θ_{n+m} t_m.Φ_1);
  Φ_3 := Behm_Tmp(Φ_2);
  for i = n downto 1 do
        if Θ_i ≡ ∃ then Φ_3 := A_∃ ({p_i}, 1, 1, Φ_3)
        else Φ_3 := A_∀ ({p_i}, 1, 1, Φ_3)
        end;
  end
  return Φ_3;
end
```

Fig. 6.9. Translating S1S to ω-automata

6.4 Monadic First Order Logic of Linear Order $\mathsf{MFO}_<$

In the previous section, we have seen that the logics S1S and $\mathsf{MSO}_<$ are equal expressive, and are moreover equivalent to the ω-regular languages. Hence, we can translate every automaton formula to an equivalent formula in $\mathsf{MSO}_<$ (S1S) and vice versa. We have already pointed out that S1S is the original language considered by Büchi that lead to the introduction of ω-automata by Büchi. The introduction of $\mathsf{MSO}_<$ arose in the investigations of fragments of predicate logic which should be equally expressive as linear time temporal logic LTL_p.

We will see in this section, that the first order fragment of $\mathsf{MSO}_<$, i.e., the monadic first order logic of linear orders $\mathsf{MFO}_<$ is equal expressive as linear time temporal logic LTL_p. Therefore, we can precisely distinguish properties that can be characterized by ω-automata and those that can be expressed by temporal logic: Temporal logic corresponds with $\mathsf{MFO}_<$, while ω-automata correspond with $\mathsf{MSO}_<$.

Two remarks have to be made here: first, recall that due to Definition 6.15 on page 426, $\mathsf{MFO}_<$ is strictly speaking a second order logic, since we need to formalize that the domain is isomorphic to the natural numbers. Hence, we need Peano's induction axiom, which can not be replaced by a finite set of first order formulas. As, except for this axiom, we never use second order quantification, the commonly accepted terminology is still that we speak of a first order logic. Secondly, we have to remark that the first order fragment of S1S is not equivalent to $\mathsf{MFO}_<$, but strictly weaker: Thomas [484] characterized the first order fragment of S1S as *locally threshold testable sets* (see also [405, 475]).

By the definitions in Section 6.2, it is already clear, which formulas belong to $\mathsf{MFO}_<$, but for reasons of completeness, we list its definition directly.

Definition 6.26 (Monadic First Order Logic of Linear Order $\mathsf{MFO}_<$). *The logic $\mathsf{MFO}_<$ is the first order predicate logic over the signature Σ with $C_\Sigma = \{<\}$ with $\mathsf{typ}_\Sigma(<) = \mathbb{N} \times \mathbb{N} \to \mathbb{B}$, which is interpreted over the naturals $\mathbb{N}$ (see Definition 6.15 on page 426). Moreover, there are variables of types $\mathbb{N}$ and $\mathbb{N} \to \mathbb{B}$, but in contrast to $\mathsf{MSO}_<$, we can not quantify over the variables with type $Nat \to \mathbb{B}$. In more detail, the set of formulas of $\mathsf{MFO}_<$ is the least set that satisfies the following rules:*

- *for all $t_1, t_2 \in V_\Sigma$ with $\mathsf{typ}_\Sigma(t_1) = \mathsf{typ}_\Sigma(t_2) = \mathbb{N}$, we have $t_1 \doteq t_2 \in \mathsf{MFO}_<$*
- *for all $t_1, t_2 \in V_\Sigma$ with $\mathsf{typ}_\Sigma(t_1) = \mathsf{typ}_\Sigma(t_2) = \mathbb{N}$, we have $t_1 < t_2 \in \mathsf{MFO}_<$*
- *for all $t, p \in V_\Sigma$ with $\mathsf{typ}_\Sigma(t) = \mathbb{N}$ and $\mathsf{typ}_\Sigma(p) = \mathbb{N} \to \mathbb{B}$, we have $p^{(t)} \in \mathsf{MFO}_<$*
- *for all $\varphi, \psi \in \mathsf{MFO}_<$, we have $\neg\varphi$, $\varphi \wedge \psi \in \mathsf{MFO}_<$*
- *for all $t \in V_\Sigma$ with $\mathsf{typ}_\Sigma(t) = \mathbb{N}$ and $\varphi \in \mathsf{MFO}_<$, we have $\exists t.\varphi \in \mathsf{MFO}_<$*

Note that in contrast to $\mathsf{MSO}_<$, it is not permitted to quantify over variables p of type $\mathbb{N} \to \mathbb{B}$. The above language is more powerful than it might look at a first glance. Clearly, we can define further operators like $\forall t.\varphi :\Leftrightarrow \neg\exists t.\neg\varphi$, and further relations like $t_1 \leq t_2$, $t_1 > t_2$, and $t_1 \geq t_2$, and we can even add numeric constants, and the successor function:

- $t_1 \doteq 0 :\Leftrightarrow \forall t_2.t_1 \leq t_2$
- $t_2 \doteq \mathsf{SUC}(t_1) :\Leftrightarrow t_1 < t_2 \wedge \forall t_3.t_1 < t_3 \to t_2 \leq t_3$
- We use $\exists t.(t \doteq 0) \wedge \Phi$ as an expansion for $[\Phi]_t^0$.
- Analogously, we use $\exists t_2.(t_2 \doteq \mathsf{SUC}(t_1)) \wedge \Phi$ as an expansion for $[\Phi]_{t_2}^{\mathsf{SUC}(t_1)}$.
- We moreover abbreviate $1 := \mathsf{SUC}(0)$, $2 := \mathsf{SUC}(1) = \mathsf{SUC}(\mathsf{SUC}(0)), \ldots$.

Hence, $\mathsf{MFO}_<$ is at least as expressive as the first order fragment of S1S. The converse is however not true, i.e., the first order fragment of S1S is strictly less expressive as $\mathsf{MFO}_<$ [405, 475, 484].

As a first observation, we can easily see that any LTL_p formula can be transformed into $\mathsf{MFO}_<$ by the function given in Figure 6.10. The function call $\mathsf{LTL2MFO}(t_0, \varphi)$ computes for a given variable t_0 with type $\mathsf{typ}_\Sigma(t_0) = \mathbb{N}$ and a given LTL_p formula φ an equivalent $\mathsf{MFO}_<$ formula $\mathsf{LTL2MFO}(t_0, \varphi)$ where t_0 is the only free variable of type $\mathbb{N}$. Therefore, it is easily seen that $\mathsf{MFO}_<$ is at least as expressive as LTL_p:

```
function interval(I, φ)
  case I of
    (t0,0,t1,0) : return ∀t2. t0 < t2 ∧ t2 < t1 → LTL2MFO(t2, φ);
    (t0,0,t1,1) : return ∀t2. t0 < t2 ∧ t2 ≤ t1 → LTL2MFO(t2, φ);
    (t0,1,t1,0) : return ∀t2. t0 ≤ t2 ∧ t2 < t1 → LTL2MFO(t2, φ);
    (t0,1,t1,1) : return ∀t2. t0 ≤ t2 ∧ t2 ≤ t1 → LTL2MFO(t2, φ);
  end
end

function LTL2MFO(t0, φ)
  case Φ of
    is_var(Φ): Ψ := Φ^(t0);
    ¬φ       : Ψ := ¬LTL2MFO(t0, φ);
    φ ∧ ψ    : Ψ := LTL2MFO(t0, φ) ∧ LTL2MFO(t0, ψ);
    φ ∨ ψ    : Ψ := LTL2MFO(t0, φ) ∨ LTL2MFO(t0, ψ);
    Xφ       : Ψ := ∃t1. (t0 < t1) ∧ (∀t2.t0 < t2 → t1 ≤ t2) ∧ LTL2MFO(t1, φ);
    Gφ       : Ψ := ∀t1. t0 ≤ t1 → LTL2MFO(t1, φ);
    Fφ       : Ψ := ∃t1. t0 ≤ t1 ∧ LTL2MFO(t1, φ);
    [φ U̲ ψ]  : Ψ := ∃t1. t0 ≤ t1 ∧ LTL2MFO(t1, ψ) ∧ interval((t0,1,t1,0), φ);
    [φ B̲ ψ]  : Ψ := ∃t1. t0 ≤ t1 ∧ LTL2MFO(t1, φ) ∧ interval((t0,1,t1,1), ¬ψ);
    [φ U ψ]  : Ψ := ∀t1. t0 ≤ t1 ∧ interval((t0,1,t1,1), ¬ψ) → LTL2MFO(t1, φ);
    [φ B ψ]  : Ψ := ∀t1. t0 ≤ t1 ∧ interval((t0,1,t1,0), ¬φ) → LTL2MFO(t1, ¬ψ);
    ←Xφ      : Ψ := ∀t1. (t1 < t0) ∧ (∀t2.t2 < t0 → t2 ≤ t1) → LTL2MFO(t1, φ);
    ←X̲φ      : Ψ := ∃t1. (t1 < t0) ∧ (∀t2.t2 < t0 → t2 ≤ t1) ∧ LTL2MFO(t1, φ);
    ←Gφ      : Ψ := ∀t1. t1 ≤ t0 → LTL2MFO(t1, φ);
    ←Fφ      : Ψ := ∃t1. t1 ≤ t0 ∧ LTL2MFO(t1, φ);
    [φ ←U̲ ψ] : Ψ := ∃t1. t1 ≤ t0 ∧ LTL2MFO(t1, ψ) ∧ interval((t1,0,t0,1), φ);
    [φ ←B̲ ψ] : Ψ := ∃t1. t1 ≤ t0 ∧ LTL2MFO(t1, φ) ∧ interval((t1,1,t0,1), ¬ψ);
    [φ ←U ψ] : Ψ := ∀t1. t1 ≤ t0 ∧ interval((t1,1,t0,1), ¬ψ) → LTL2MFO(t1, φ);
    [φ ←B ψ] : Ψ := ∀t1. t1 ≤ t0 ∧ interval((t1,0,t0,1), ¬φ) → LTL2MFO(t1, ¬ψ);
  end;
  return Ψ
end
```

Fig. 6.10. Translating LTL_p to $\mathsf{MFO}_<$

Lemma 6.27 (LTL_p and $\mathsf{MFO}_<$). *Given an arbitrary LTL_p formula Φ, and a variable t_0 of type $\mathbb{N}$, the algorithm given in Figure 6.10 computes a formula $\mathsf{LTL2MFO}(t_0, \Phi)$ of $\mathsf{MFO}_<$ where t_0 is the only free variable of type $\mathbb{N}$ such that the following holds for every structure $\mathcal{K}$, every state s, and every path $\pi \in \mathsf{FairPaths}_{\mathcal{K}}(s)$:*

$$(\mathcal{K}, \pi, 0) \models \Phi \quad \textit{iff} \quad \left[\!\left[[\mathsf{LTL2MFO}(t_0, \Phi)]_{t_0}^{0} \right]\!\right]_{\xi_\pi} = \mathsf{true}$$

Hence, it follows that $\mathsf{MFO}_<$ is at least as expressive as LTL_p.

ξ_π is thereby the assignment that corresponds to π as given in Definition 6.19. It is remarkable that the computation of the formula $\mathsf{LTL2MFO}(t_0, \varphi)$ can be performed with just three first order variables: Just note that in the algorithm given in Figure 6.10 only the variables t_0, t_1, and t_2 are used. In following function calls, we can reuse these variables. Hence, we can translate temporal logic formulas, even to $\mathsf{MFO}^3_<$, i.e., the restriction to three first order variables.

The above lemma is not too surprising, since $\mathsf{MFO}_<$ is a quite powerful language. What is more surprising is that the other direction also holds, i.e., any formula of $\mathsf{MFO}_<$ with a free variable t_0 of type $\mathbb{N}$ can be translated to an equivalent LTL_p formula. This translation is quite important when the specification language is directly based on $\mathsf{MFO}_<$, as e.g., timing diagrams that are often used in the design of digital hardware circuits. In these cases, the semantics can be directly given in $\mathsf{MFO}_<$ and translated to temporal logic formulas so that we are then able to apply our decision procedure for them. Note further that a translation from $\mathsf{MFO}_<$ to LTL_p and back to $\mathsf{MFO}^3_<$ shows that $\mathsf{MFO}_<$ is equal expressive as $\mathsf{MFO}^3_<$.

The translation from $\mathsf{MFO}_<$ to LTL_p has to consider past temporal operators, at least for intermediate stages. The reason for this is that the translation makes use of the so-called *separation property*. Intuitively, this property is based on the theorem $\forall t_0.\forall t_1.t_1 < t_0 \lor t_1 \doteq t_0 \lor t_0 < t_1$, that essentially says that, relative to a number t_0, the set of natural numbers can be divided into three subsets, namely the past $\{t \in \mathbb{N} \mid t < t_0\}$, the present $\{t_0\}$, and the infinite future $\{t \in \mathbb{N} \mid t_0 < t\}$. Therefore, for proving a property as $\forall t.\Phi$, we can make a case distinction on these intervals and therefore replace $\forall t.\Phi$ by $[\forall t.t < t_0 \to \Phi] \land [\Phi]_t^{t_0} \land [\forall t.t_0 < t \to \Phi]$. This separates the property Φ into three parts, regarding the past, the present, and the future. Analogously, we can replace $\exists t.\Phi$ by $[\exists t.t < t_0 \land \Phi] \land [\Phi]_t^{t_0} \land [\exists t.t_0 < t \land \Phi]$.

Therefore, the quantifiers in the part concerning the past are of the forms $\exists t_1.t_1 < t_0 \land \Phi$ and $\forall t_1.t_1 < t_0 \to \Phi$, and in the future part of the forms $\exists t_1.t_0 < t_1 \land \Phi$ and $\forall t_1.t_0 < t_1 \to \Phi$. For the part for the present, we do not need quantifiers. In principle, we could use the formulas $\exists t_1.t_1 \doteq t_0 \land \Phi$ and $\forall t_1.t_1 \doteq t_0 \to \Phi$, but both are equivalent to $[\Phi]_t^{t_0}$, so that we can eliminate these quantifiers.

So far, we have considered the separation property directly in $\mathsf{MFO}_<$. Gabbay showed in [202] that linear time temporal logic with past operators has also the separation property. We have already shown this result in Section 5.5.3, by eliminating all possible nestings of past and future temporal operators. Amir [13] showed in 1985 that the separation property even holds for arbitrary flows of time, i.e., even in nonlinear ones, and Gabbay showed in [202] that the separation property is equivalent to the expressive completeness w.r.t. $\mathsf{MFO}_<$ on dense flows of time. The separation property of our temporal logic with past operators is given in the next theorem.

Theorem 6.28 (Separation Property of LTL_p). *Given an arbitrary formula $\Phi \in \mathsf{LTL}_p$, there is an equivalent LTL_p formula of the form $\bigvee_{i=1}^{n} \Phi_i^{<} \wedge \Phi^{=} \wedge \Phi_i^{>}$ such that the following holds:*

- *$\Phi_i^{<}$ contains no future temporal operators*
- *$\Phi_i^{=}$ contains no temporal operators*
- *$\Phi_i^{>}$ contains no past temporal operators*

To prove the above theorem, reconsider the separation rules that we have listed in Section 5.5.3 in the Lemmas 5.83, 5.84, 5.85, 5.86, and 5.87 on pages 388 – 391. These lemmas allow us to eliminate all nestings of future and past operators. To obtain a formula as mentioned in the above theorem, we then only have to apply recursive laws of the temporal operators, to obtain parts for the present, the strict past and the strict future.

Another important fact is that we can slightly generalize Behmann's normal form as shown in the next lemma. Note that we can not make use of Behmann's normal form as we did in Lemma 6.25, since $\mathsf{MFO}_<$ has binary relation symbols, namely the numeric relations[3] $\doteq, <, \leq, >$, and $\geq$. Hence, in contrast to S1S, $\mathsf{MSO}_<$ and $\mathsf{MFO}_<$ are not really monadic logics. For $\mathsf{MSO}_<$, this is no problem, since we can reduce $\mathsf{MSO}_<$ to S1S, which is a monadic logic. However, $\mathsf{MFO}_<$ is strictly more expressive than the first order fragment of S1S, and therefore, we have to proceed differently. In the transformation below, we will therefore replace numeric relations like $t_1 < t_0$, $t_1 \doteq t_0$, and $t_0 \leq t_1$ by monadic predicates $p_{t_0}(t_1)$, $n_{t_0}(t_1)$, and $f_{t_0}(t_1)$, denoting that t_1 is in the past, the present, or in the future of t_0, respectively. However, we can do this only relative to one variable t_0, and therefore, we establish the following variant of Behmann's normal form:

Lemma 6.29 (General Behmann's Normal Form). *Given a formula $\Phi \in \mathsf{FO}$ and a variable x, such that all atomic subformulas of Φ do either not contain free occurrences of x or they contain only x and no other first order variable. Then, the following holds:*

- *There is a formula equivalent to Φ that is of the form $\bigvee_{i=1}^{n} \varphi_i \wedge \psi_i$ where x occurs not in ψ_i, and φ_i is a Boolean combination of atoms that only contain x as first order variable.*
- *There is a formula equivalent to Φ that is of the form $\bigwedge_{i=1}^{n} \varphi_i \vee \psi_i$ where x occurs not in ψ_i, and φ_i is a Boolean combination of atoms that only contain x as first order variable.*

The formulas can be computed by $\mathsf{OneBehm}(\vee, x, \Phi)$ and $\mathsf{OneBehm}(\wedge, x, \Phi)$ as given in Figure 6.11, respectively, where y is a variable different[4] from x. The functions DNF and CNF compute disjunctive and conjunctive normal forms, respectively, where subformulas φ_i, $\forall y.\psi_i$, and $\exists y.\psi_i$ are viewed as atoms.

[3] Clearly, we can reduce all these atomic formulas so that only $\leq$ will be used, but we can not eliminate all binary relation symbols.

[4] Otherwise, rename the bound variable.

function $\mathsf{OneBehm}(f, x, \Phi)$
  if $f \equiv \vee$ **then** (* *compute* $\bigvee_{i=1}^{n} \varphi_i \wedge \psi_i$ *)
    case Φ of
      $\neg\varphi$: $\bigwedge_{i=1}^{n} \varphi_i \vee \psi_i \equiv \mathsf{OneBehm}(\wedge, x, \varphi)$;
        return $\bigvee_{i=1}^{n} \neg\varphi_i \wedge \neg\psi_i$;
      $\varphi \wedge \psi$: $\bigvee_{i=1}^{n} \varphi_{1,i} \wedge \psi_{1,i} \equiv \mathsf{OneBehm}(\vee, x, \varphi)$;
        $\bigvee_{j=1}^{m} \varphi_{2,j} \wedge \psi_{2,j} \equiv \mathsf{OneBehm}(\vee, x, \psi)$;
        return $\bigvee_{i=1}^{n} \bigvee_{j=1}^{m} (\varphi_{1,i} \wedge \varphi_{2,j}) \wedge (\psi_{1,i} \wedge \psi_{2,j})$;
      $\varphi \vee \psi$: **return** $\mathsf{OneBehm}(\vee, x, \varphi) \vee \mathsf{OneBehm}(\vee, x, \psi)$;
      $\exists y.\varphi$: $\bigvee_{i=1}^{n} \varphi_i \wedge \psi_i \equiv \mathsf{OneBehm}(\vee, x, \varphi)$;
        return $\bigvee_{i=1}^{n} \varphi_i \wedge \exists y.\psi_i$;
      $\forall y.\varphi$: $\bigwedge_{i=1}^{n} \varphi_i \vee \psi_i \equiv \mathsf{OneBehm}(\wedge, x, \varphi)$;
        return $\mathsf{DNF}(\bigwedge_{i=1}^{n} \varphi_i \vee \forall y.\psi_i)$;
      otherwise **if** $\mathsf{VAR}(\Phi) = \{x\}$ **then return** $\Phi \wedge 1$
        else return $1 \wedge \Phi$ **end**;
    end
  else (* *compute* $\bigwedge_{i=1}^{n} \varphi_i \vee \psi_i$ *)
    case Φ of
      $\neg\varphi$: $\bigvee_{i=1}^{n} \varphi_i \wedge \psi_i \equiv \mathsf{OneBehm}(\vee, x, \varphi)$;
        return $\bigwedge_{i=1}^{n} \neg\varphi_i \vee \neg\psi_i$;
      $\varphi \wedge \psi$: **return** $\mathsf{OneBehm}(\wedge, x, \varphi) \wedge \mathsf{OneBehm}(\wedge, x, \psi)$;
      $\varphi \vee \psi$: $\bigwedge_{i=1}^{n} \varphi_{1,i} \vee \psi_{1,i} \equiv \mathsf{OneBehm}(\wedge, x, \varphi)$;
        $\bigwedge_{j=1}^{m} \varphi_{2,j} \vee \psi_{2,j} \equiv \mathsf{OneBehm}(\wedge, x, \psi)$;
        return $\bigwedge_{i=1}^{n} \bigwedge_{j=1}^{m} (\varphi_{1,i} \vee \varphi_{2,j}) \vee (\psi_{1,i} \vee \psi_{2,j})$;
      $\exists y.\varphi$: $\bigvee_{i=1}^{n} \varphi_i \wedge \psi_i \equiv \mathsf{OneBehm}(\vee, x, \varphi)$;
        return $\mathsf{CNF}(\bigvee_{i=1}^{n} \varphi_i \wedge \forall y.\psi_i)$;
      $\forall y.\varphi$: $\bigwedge_{i=1}^{n} \varphi_i \vee \psi_i \equiv \mathsf{OneBehm}(\wedge, x, \varphi)$;
        return $\bigwedge_{i=1}^{n} \varphi_i \vee \forall y.\psi_i$;
      otherwise **if** $\mathsf{VAR}(\Phi) = \{x\}$ **then return** $\Phi \vee 0$
        else return $0 \vee \Phi$ **end**;
  end
end

Fig. 6.11. Computing general Behmann's normal form

The proof of the above lemma is straightforward and follows an easy induction on the structure of Φ along the implementation of the algorithm given in Figure 6.11. Note that we must make a simultaneous induction on both normal forms to have an induction hypothesis that is strong enough to handle the case of negations.

We have now explained all normal forms that we will need for the translation of $\mathsf{MFO}_<$ to LTL_p. As already mentioned, we assume that the given $\mathsf{MFO}_<$ formula has exactly one free first order variable t_0 that determines the present point of time. The translation is given in Figure 6.12, where $\mathsf{MFO2LTL}(t_0, \varphi)$ is the desired LTL_p formula. The translation proceeds in a top-down manner, so that whenever an atom of the form $p^{(t_i)}$ is seen, it fol-

function $\mathsf{mkunary}(t_0, \Phi)$
case Φ **of**
$t_i \doteq t_j$: **if** $t_i \equiv t_j$ **then return** 1
else if $t_i \equiv t_0$ **then return** $n_{t_0}(t_j)$
else if $t_j \equiv t_0$ **then return** $n_{t_0}(t_i)$;
else return $t_i \doteq t_j$ **end**;
$t_i < t_j$: **if** $t_i \equiv t_0$ **then return** $f_{t_0}(t_j)$
else if $t_j \equiv t_0$ **then return** $p_{t_0}(t_i)$;
else return $t_i \leq t_j$ **end**;
$q^{(t_i)}$: **return** $q^{(t_i)}$;
$\neg\varphi$: **return** $\neg\mathsf{mkunary}(t_0, \varphi)$;
$\varphi \wedge \psi$: **return** $\mathsf{mkunary}(t_0, \varphi) \wedge \mathsf{mkunary}(t_0, \psi)$;
$\varphi \vee \psi$: **return** $\mathsf{mkunary}(t_0, \varphi) \vee \mathsf{mkunary}(t_0, \psi)$;
$\exists t_1.\varphi$: **return** $\exists t_1.\mathsf{mkunary}(t_0, \varphi)$;
$\forall t_1.\varphi$: **return** $\forall t_1.\mathsf{mkunary}(t_0, \varphi)$;
end

function $\mathsf{MFO2LTL}(t_0, \Phi)$
case Φ **of**
$p^{(t_0)}$: **return** p;
$\neg\varphi$: **return** $\neg\mathsf{MFO2LTL}(t_0, \varphi)$;
$\varphi \wedge \psi$: **return** $\mathsf{MFO2LTL}(t_0, \varphi) \wedge \mathsf{MFO2LTL}(t_0, \psi)$;
$\varphi \vee \psi$: **return** $\mathsf{MFO2LTL}(t_0, \varphi) \vee \mathsf{MFO2LTL}(t_0, \psi)$;
$\exists t_1.\varphi$: $\Phi_1 := \mathsf{mkunary}(t_0, \varphi)$;
$\bigvee_{i=1}^{n} \varphi_i \wedge \psi_i \equiv \mathsf{OneBehm}(\vee, t_0, \Phi_1)$;
for $i = 1$ **to** n
$\varphi_i' := \mathsf{MFO2LTL}(t_0, \varphi_i)$;
$\psi_i' := \mathsf{MFO2LTL}(t_1, \psi_i)$;
$\bigvee_{j=1}^{m} \psi_j^{<} \wedge \psi_j^{=} \wedge \psi_j^{>} = \mathsf{Separate}(\overleftarrow{\mathsf{F}}\psi_i' \vee \mathsf{F}\psi_i')$;
$\psi_i'' := \bigvee_{j=1}^{m} \left[\psi_j^{<}\right]^{1,0,0}_{p_{t_0}, n_{t_0}, f_{t_0}} \wedge \left[\psi_j^{=}\right]^{0,1,0}_{p_{t_0}, n_{t_0}, f_{t_0}} \wedge \left[\psi_j^{>}\right]^{0,0,1}_{p_{t_0}, n_{t_0}, f_{t_0}}$;
end;
return $\bigvee_{i=1}^{n} \varphi_i' \wedge \psi_i''$;
$\forall t_1.\varphi$: **return** $\neg\mathsf{MFO2LTL}(t_0, \exists t_1.\neg\varphi)$;
end
end

Fig. 6.12. Translating $\mathsf{MFO}_<$ to LTL_p

lows that $t_i \equiv t_0$ must hold. Clearly, $p^{(t_0)}$ is translated to the temporal logic formula p, since we assume that t_0 is our present point of time. Boolean connectives are translated as they are, the correctness follows immediately from the induction step of our recursive implementation.

The crucial case is $\exists t_1.\varphi$. We would like to apply the procedure recursively to φ, but this is not possible, since the application of our procedure requires that φ should have only one free first order variable. It may, however, be the case that the first order variables t_0 and t_1 both occur in φ. Therefore, we want so separate the occurrences of t_0 and t_1 by the previously explained variant of Behmann's normal form. However, the assumption may not hold, i.e., there may be atoms in φ that contain both t_0 and t_1. Note that all atoms where t_0 and t_1 can both occur are of either one of the forms $t_0 < t_i$, $t_0 \doteq t_i$, or $t_i > t_0$. To establish the desired assumption, we fix t_0, i.e., we can view $t_i < t_0$, $t_0 \doteq t_i$, and $t_0 < t_i$ as unary predicates p_{t_0}, n_{t_0}, and f_{t_0} for the past, the present, and the future of t_0. Hence, $p_{t_0}(t_i)$, $n_{t_0}(t_i)$, and $f_{t_0}(t_i)$ mean that t_i is in the past of t_0, equal to t_0, and in the future of t_0, respectively.

The function mkunary implements this translation. As a result, the formula $\Phi_1 := \mathsf{mkunary}(t_0, \varphi)$ in the case $\exists t_1.\varphi$ of $\mathsf{MFO2LTL}(t_0, \Phi)$ has only monadic occurrences of t_0, so that we can apply function OneBehm to separate the atoms containing t_0 from those containing t_1. Keeping in mind that $\forall t.p_{t_0}(t) \leftrightarrow t < t_0$, $\forall t.n_{t_0}(t) \leftrightarrow t \doteq t_0$, $\forall t.f_{t_0}(t) \leftrightarrow t_0 < t$ holds, our given formula $\exists t_1.\varphi$ is therefore equivalent to the $\mathsf{MFO}_<$ formula $\bigvee_{i=1}^{n} \varphi_i \wedge \exists t_1.\psi_i$.

In the resulting formula $\bigvee_{i=1}^{n} \varphi_i \wedge \exists t_1.\psi_i$, the subformulas φ_i are Boolean combinations of atoms $p^{(t_0)}$, and ψ_i is a formula without occurrences of t_0 (note, however, that ψ_i will, in general, contain the predicates p_{t_0}, n_{t_0}, and f_{t_0}). Therefore, we can translate φ_i to LTL_p by simply replacing atoms $p^{(t_0)}$ by p, which is done by another invocation of $\mathsf{MFO2LTL}(t_0, \varphi_i)$. As t_0 no longer occurs in ψ_i, and as ψ_i furthermore contains only one free first order variable, namely t_1, we can apply our procedure recursively as $\mathsf{MFO2LTL}(t_1, \psi_i)$, thus yielding the LTL_p formula ψ_i', where t_1 is seen as the present point of time. Note that ψ_i' will, in general, contain variables p_{t_0}, n_{t_0}, and f_{t_0} that stem from our introduced predicates. As we do not know if t_1 is in the past, the present, or the future of t_0, we obtain the LTL_p formula $\overleftarrow{\mathsf{F}}\,\psi_i' \vee \mathsf{F}\psi_i'$ as an intermediate result.

To complete the translation, we have to eliminate the variables p_{t_0}, n_{t_0}, and f_{t_0} in $\overleftarrow{\mathsf{F}}\,\psi_i' \vee \mathsf{F}\psi_i'$. According to their semantics, p_{t_0} is true only in the past, n_{t_0} only at the present point of time, and f_{t_0} only in the future. For this reason, we separate $\overleftarrow{\mathsf{F}}\,\psi_i' \vee \mathsf{F}\psi_i'$ into past, present, and future parts by the function Separate that should implement the transformation given in Theorem 6.28. If the result is $\bigvee_{j=1}^{m} \psi_j^{<} \wedge \psi_j^{=} \wedge \psi_j^{>}$, then it is not hard to see that p_{t_0}, n_{t_0}, and f_{t_0} are to be interpreted in $\psi_j^{<}$, $\psi_j^{=}$, and $\psi_j^{>}$ as 1 or 0. This is done by the final substitution that eliminates the variables p_{t_0}, n_{t_0}, and f_{t_0}. The case $\forall t_1.\varphi$ is reduced to $\exists t_1.\varphi$. Therefore, we have proved the following theorem, that is due to Kamp [274], Gabbay, Pnueli, Shelah, and Stavi [203]:

Theorem 6.30 (LTL_p and $\mathsf{MFO}_<$). *Given any formula $\Phi \in \mathsf{MFO}_<$ where t_0 is the only first order variable that occurs free in Φ. Then, there is a LTL_p formula $\mathsf{MFO2LTL}(t_0, \Phi)$ such that the following holds for any structure $\mathcal{K}$, any path π of $\mathcal{K}$, and any position $n \in \mathbb{N}$:*

$$(\mathcal{K}, \pi, n) \models \mathsf{MFO2LTL}(t_0, \Phi) \quad \textit{iff} \quad \left[\!\left[[\Phi]_{t_0}^{n} \right]\!\right]_{\xi_\pi} = 1$$

The size of $\mathsf{MFO2LTL}(t_0, \Phi)$ is however nonelementary [221]. We have already seen that we can translate every LTL_p formula to an equivalent $\mathsf{MFO}^3_<$ formula. Hence, it follows that for every $\mathsf{MFO}_<$ formula, there is an equivalent $\mathsf{MFO}^3_<$ formula. However, $\mathsf{MFO}^2_<$ is strictly less expressive, since it does not allow us to express binary temporal operators: Etessami, Vardi, and Wilke have shown the following result [186, 187]:

Theorem 6.31 (Unary LTL_p and $\mathsf{MFO}^2_<$). *Let $\Phi \in \mathsf{MFO}^2_<(\mathsf{succ})$ be the set of $\mathsf{MFO}_<$ formulas with only two first order variables, but where additionally the relation $\mathsf{succ}(x, y) :\Leftrightarrow y \doteq \mathsf{SUC}(x)$ is available.*

Given any formula $\Phi \in \mathsf{MFO}^2_<(\mathsf{succ})$ where t_0 is the only first order variable that occurs free in Φ, there is a LTL_p formula Ψ of size $O(2^{|\Phi|})$ with only unary temporal operators such that the following holds for any structure $\mathcal{K}$, any path π of $\mathcal{K}$, and any position $n \in \mathbb{N}$:

$$(\mathcal{K}, \pi, n) \models \mathsf{MFO2LTL}(t_0, \Phi) \;\; \mathit{iff} \;\; [\![[\Phi]^n_{t_0}]\!]_{\xi_\pi} = 1$$

By Lemma 5.2 on page 287, it follows that $\mathsf{MFO}^2_<(\mathsf{succ})$ is strictly less expressive as $\mathsf{MFO}_<$.

In principle, it is only a matter of taste, whether we want to use the successor function SUC or the successor relation $\mathsf{succ}(x, y) :\Leftrightarrow y \doteq \mathsf{SUC}(x)$. We already know that SUC, and hence, also succ can be defined via $<$, e.g., as follows:

$$\mathsf{succ}(x, y) :\Leftrightarrow x < y \land \forall z.x < z \to y \le z$$

However, we need three variables for that definition, so that we have to explicitly state that we use succ as a basic symbol in $\mathsf{MFO}^2_<(\mathsf{succ})$.

The translation from unary LTL_p to $\mathsf{MFO}^2_<(\mathsf{succ})$ can then be made with the following changes to the algorithm of Figure 6.10:

- $\mathsf{LTL2MFO}(t_0, \mathsf{X}\varphi) := \exists t_1.\mathsf{succ}(t_0, t_1) \land \mathsf{LTL2MFO}(t_1, \varphi)$
- $\mathsf{LTL2MFO}(t_0, \overleftarrow{\underline{\mathsf{X}}}\varphi) := \exists t_1.\mathsf{succ}(t_1, t_0) \land \mathsf{LTL2MFO}(t_1, \varphi)$
- $\mathsf{LTL2MFO}(t_0, \overleftarrow{\mathsf{X}}\varphi) := \forall t_1.\mathsf{succ}(t_1, t_0) \to \mathsf{LTL2MFO}(t_1, \varphi)$

As can be seen, with the help of succ, we only need two variables. The same holds for the translation of $\mathsf{G}\varphi$, $\mathsf{F}\varphi$, $\overleftarrow{\mathsf{G}}\varphi$, and $\overleftarrow{\mathsf{F}}\varphi$ as given in Figure 6.10.

For the translation from $\mathsf{MFO}^2_<(\mathsf{succ})$ to unary LTL_p, we have to face again the problem that Behmann's normal form can not be easily applied, since we have binary relation symbols. In addition to $<$ and $\doteq$, we moreover have the successor relation succ.

The crucial case is again $\exists t_1.\varphi$. In this case, it follows that φ may contain free occurrences of the variables t_0 and t_1, but of not other variable. We have to eliminate one of these variables to apply the procedure recursively. To this end, we first replace $\exists t_1.\varphi$ with the following equivalent formula:

$$\left(\begin{array}{l}\exists t_1.\ t_1 < t_0 \wedge \neg\mathsf{succ}(t_1,t_0) \wedge \varphi \vee \\ \exists t_1.\ \mathsf{succ}(t_1,t_0) \wedge \varphi \vee \\ \exists t_1.\ t_1 \doteq t_0 \wedge \varphi \vee \\ \exists t_1.\ \mathsf{succ}(t_0,t_1) \wedge \varphi \vee \\ \exists t_1.\ t_0 < t_1 \wedge \neg\mathsf{succ}(t_0,t_1) \wedge \varphi \end{array}\right)$$

In every case, we can replace the binary relations of the variables t_0 and t_1 with either 1 or 0, and therefore the binary relations between t_0 and t_1 are eliminated in φ. We therefore obtain the five formulas $\varphi_1, \ldots, \varphi_5$ as shown in Figure 6.13. For each of the five formulas φ_i, we can now separate the subformulas where only t_0 occurs from those where t_1 occurs. We therefore obtain from φ_i a formula of the form $\bigvee_{j=1}^{n_i} \varphi_{i,j} \wedge \psi_{i,j}$, such that t_1 does not occur free in $\varphi_{i,j}$ and t_0 does not occur free in $\psi_{i,j}$. For this reason, we can now recursively apply the procedure to the subformulas $\varphi_{i,j}$ and $\psi_{i,j}$ with the only free variable. It only remains to relate t_1 to t_0 which depends on the different case.

function $\mathsf{MFO}^2_<\mathsf{LTL}(t_0, \Phi)$
  case Φ **of**
    $\neg\varphi$: **return** $\neg\mathsf{MFO}^2_<\mathsf{LTL}(t_0,\varphi)$;
    $\varphi \wedge \psi$: **return** $\mathsf{MFO}^2_<\mathsf{LTL}(t_0,\varphi) \wedge \mathsf{MFO}^2_<\mathsf{LTL}(t_0,\psi)$;
    $\varphi \vee \psi$: **return** $\mathsf{MFO}^2_<\mathsf{LTL}(t_0,\varphi) \vee \mathsf{MFO}^2_<\mathsf{LTL}(t_0,\psi)$;
    $\exists t_1.\varphi$:
      $\varphi_1 := [\varphi]^{1,0,0,0,0}_{t_1<t_0,\mathsf{succ}(t_1,t_0),t_1\doteq t_0,\mathsf{succ}(t_0,t_1),t_0<t_1}$;
      $\varphi_2 := [\varphi]^{0,1,0,0,0}_{t_1<t_0,\mathsf{succ}(t_1,t_0),t_1\doteq t_0,\mathsf{succ}(t_0,t_1),t_0<t_1}$;
      $\varphi_3 := [\varphi]^{0,0,1,0,0}_{t_1<t_0,\mathsf{succ}(t_1,t_0),t_1\doteq t_0,\mathsf{succ}(t_0,t_1),t_0<t_1}$;
      $\varphi_4 := [\varphi]^{0,0,0,1,0}_{t_1<t_0,\mathsf{succ}(t_1,t_0),t_1\doteq t_0,\mathsf{succ}(t_0,t_1),t_0<t_1}$;
      $\varphi_5 := [\varphi]^{0,0,0,0,1}_{t_1<t_0,\mathsf{succ}(t_1,t_0),t_1\doteq t_0,\mathsf{succ}(t_0,t_1),t_0<t_1}$;
      for $i := 1$ **to** 5 **do**
        $\bigvee_{j=1}^{n_i} \varphi_{i,j} \wedge \psi_{i,j} := \mathsf{Separate}(t_0, t_1, \varphi_i)$
      end;
      $\psi_1 := \bigvee_{j=1}^{n_1} \mathsf{MFO}^2_<\mathsf{LTL}(t_0,\varphi_{1,j}) \wedge \overleftarrow{\underline{\mathsf{X}}}\,\overleftarrow{\mathsf{F}}\,(\mathsf{MFO}^2_<\mathsf{LTL}(t_1,\psi_{1,j}))$;
      $\psi_2 := \bigvee_{j=1}^{n_2} \mathsf{MFO}^2_<\mathsf{LTL}(t_0,\varphi_{2,j}) \wedge \overleftarrow{\underline{\mathsf{X}}}\,(\mathsf{MFO}^2_<\mathsf{LTL}(t_1,\psi_{2,j}))$;
      $\psi_3 := \bigvee_{j=1}^{n_3} \mathsf{MFO}^2_<\mathsf{LTL}(t_0,\varphi_{3,j}) \wedge \mathsf{MFO}^2_<\mathsf{LTL}(t_1,\psi_{3,j})$;
      $\psi_4 := \bigvee_{j=1}^{n_4} \mathsf{MFO}^2_<\mathsf{LTL}(t_0,\varphi_{4,j}) \wedge \mathsf{X}\,(\mathsf{MFO}^2_<\mathsf{LTL}(t_1,\psi_{4,j}))$;
      $\psi_5 := \bigvee_{j=1}^{n_5} \mathsf{MFO}^2_<\mathsf{LTL}(t_0,\varphi_{5,j}) \wedge \mathsf{XF}\,(\mathsf{MFO}^2_<\mathsf{LTL}(t_1,\psi_{5,j}))$;
      return $\psi_1 \vee \psi_2 \vee \psi_3 \vee \psi_4 \vee \psi_5$;
    $\forall t_1.\varphi$: **return** $\neg\mathsf{MFO}^2_<\mathsf{LTL}(t_0, \exists t_1.\neg\varphi)$;
    $p^{(t_0)}$: **return** p;
  end
end

Fig. 6.13. Translating $\mathsf{MFO}^2_<(\mathsf{succ})$ to unary LTL_p

The optimality is shown as follows: The following $\mathsf{MFO}^2_<(\mathsf{succ})$ formula states that any two positions t_1 and t_2 that agree on the predicates $p_1, \ldots, p_n$, must also agree on the predicate p_0:

$$\forall t_1.\forall t_2.\ \left(\bigwedge_{i=1}^{n} p_i^{(t_1)} \leftrightarrow p_i^{(t_2)}\right) \rightarrow \left(p_0^{(t_1)} \leftrightarrow p_0^{(t_2)}\right)$$

We show that all LTL_p formulas that are equivalent to the above formula have a size $O(2^n)$. To this end, it is sufficient to prove that every ω-automaton that is equivalent to the above formula must have $\Omega(2^{2^n})$ states. A LTL_p formula with polynomial size $p(n)$ in n, would allow us to translate this LTL_p formula to an automaton with $O(2^{p(n)})$ states, thus contradicting the fact that all equivalent automata must have $\Omega(2^{2^n})$ states.

The desired automaton is best viewed as an attempt to learn a Boolean function $f : \mathbb{B}^n \to \mathbb{B}$, since the value of p_0 is determined by the values of $p_1, \ldots, p_n$. Once the automaton receives an input $(p_1, \ldots, p_n, p_0) \in \mathbb{B}^{n+1}$, it knows the value p_0 of f for the input $(p_1, \ldots, p_n)$. The automaton has to memorize all function values it has seen so far. Hence, the states can be identified as possibly incomplete function tables. As there are three possibilities (1, 0, and 'unknown') for the function value $f(p_1, \ldots, p_n)$, the automaton must have at least 3^{2^n} states.

6.5 Non-Monadic Characterizations

In Section 6.3, we have seen that $\mathsf{MSO}_<$ and its variant S1S are equivalent to ω-automata. In Section 6.4, we have seen that the first order variant of $\mathsf{MSO}_<$, i.e., $\mathsf{MFO}_<$, is equivalent to linear time temporal logic LTL_p. For this reason, we have found characterizations in predicate logic of these logics. It is remarkable that only monadic logics have been used for these characterizations. For this reason, the question has been raised, whether there are also non-monadic fragments of second order logic $\mathsf{SO}_<$ that are equivalent to $\mathsf{MSO}_<$ and ω-automata. *In this section, we briefly mention new results that have been found for the case of finite strings.* It is not clear, if these results do also hold for infinite strings.

Due to Fagin's theorem [189], it is known that every problem in the complexity class NP can be specified by a formula of $\mathsf{ESO}_<$, i.e., a $\mathsf{SO}_<$ formula of the form $\exists p_1. \ldots \exists p_n.\varphi$, where φ is a first order formula and the p_i's are predicates. For this reason, $\mathsf{ESO}_<$ is more powerful than necessary, since problems that can be checked by a finite state automaton require only linear time and no additional space requirements. Hence, it is reasonable to consider fragments of $\mathsf{ESO}_<$ to search for non-monadic logics that are equivalent to $\mathsf{MSO}_<$. In fact, $\mathsf{MSO}_<$ is equivalent to its existential fragment (since we can flatten nested automaton formulas by several determinization steps), and therefore,

$\mathsf{MSO}_<$ can be reduced to its existential fragment, which is also contained in $\mathsf{ESO}_<$.

Clearly, we can reduce the first order part φ to equivalent first order formulas in certain normal forms. Given any fragment $\mathfrak{L} \subseteq \mathsf{FO}$, we denote the corresponding fragment of $\mathsf{ESO}_<$, where the first order part φ belongs to $\mathfrak{L}$ as $\mathsf{ESO}_<(\mathfrak{L})$. In particular, we can transform φ in prenex normal form, and even very restricted quantifier prefixes are sufficient. It is well-known that the quantifier prefix $\forall^*\exists^*$ is sufficient (by skolemization), and Leivant [320] has moreover shown that even the prefix $\forall^*$ is sufficient for the first order part.

Similar to the decidable fragments of FO that we have considered in Section 6.2.3, there are two main directions for searching non-monadic regular fragments: first, restrictions to certain (first order) quantifier prefix classes $\mathsf{FO}(\alpha)$, and secondly, restrictions of the number of variables FO^k.

Eiter, Gottlob and Gurevich considered restrictions of the first order quantifiers for the $\mathsf{ESO}_<$ formulas: For every regular expression α over $\{\forall, \exists\}$, the logic $\mathsf{ESO}_<(\mathsf{FO}(\alpha))$, contains those $\mathsf{ESO}_<$ formulas in prenex normal form, whose first order quantifiers belong to α. In 1998, Eiter, Gottlob and Gurevich in 1998 [153, 154] found the following interesting result for *finite strings*:

Theorem 6.32 (Dichotomy Theorem for Prefix Classes $\mathsf{ESO}_<(\mathsf{FO}(\alpha))$). *The fragments $\mathsf{ESO}_<(\mathsf{FO}(\alpha))$ of existential second order logic over finite strings, where the first order quantifiers are restricted to α, fall into two classes:*

- *If $\alpha \subseteq \exists^*\forall\exists^* \cup \exists^*\forall^2$ holds, then every formula $\varphi \in \mathsf{ESO}_<(\mathsf{FO}(\alpha))$ describes a regular language. Hence, every formula $\varphi \in \mathsf{ESO}_<(\exists^*\forall\exists^* \cup \exists^*\forall^2)$ can be translated to an equivalent finite state automaton.*
- *For every $\alpha \not\subseteq \exists^*\forall\exists^* \cup \exists^*\forall^2$, there is a formula $\varphi \in \mathsf{ESO}_<(\mathsf{FO}(\alpha))$ that defines an irregular language. Moreover, there is a formula $\psi \in \mathsf{ESO}_<(\mathsf{FO}(\alpha))$ that defines an NP-complete language.*

Note that $\alpha \not\subseteq \exists^*\forall\exists^* \cup \exists^*\forall^2$ means that α contains at least one of the prefixes $\forall^3$, $\forall^2\exists$, or $\forall\exists\forall$. Moreover, a class $\mathsf{ESO}_<(\mathsf{FO}(\alpha))$ is closed under complement iff either $\forall\forall$ or $\forall\exists$ occurs belongs to α.

The proof of the first point is quite difficult and can be found in detail in [154]. The proof of the second point can be simply made by describing the irregular language $\{a^n b^n \mid n \in \mathbb{N}\}$ with three formulas $\varphi_1 \in \mathsf{ESO}_<(\forall^3)$, $\varphi_2 \in \mathsf{ESO}_<(\forall^2\exists)$, and $\varphi_3 \in \mathsf{ESO}_<(\forall\exists\forall)$. An example for φ_2 is shown on page 427, formulas φ_1 and φ_3 are similar and can be found in [154].

The above result is quite surprising; it means that the prefix classes $\mathsf{ESO}_<(\mathsf{FO}(\alpha))$ fall into two distinct categories: those that specify only regular languages, and those that allow us to specify a NP-complete language. This means that model checking $\mathsf{ESO}_<(\mathsf{FO}(\alpha))$ is either NP-complete, or very simple, since it can be reduced to checking acceptance of a finite word by a finite state automaton.

In general, we have to distinguish between *structure and expression complexity*. The runtime of a model checking procedure can be measured in terms of the size of the Kripke structure, and the size of the given formula. Fixing a particular formula yields the structure complexity, and fixing a structure yields the expression complexity. Refering to structure complexity, we can therefore state that model checking $\mathsf{ESO}_<(\mathsf{FO}(\alpha))$ with $\alpha \not\subseteq \exists^*\forall\exists^* \cup \exists^*\forall^2$ is NP-complete.

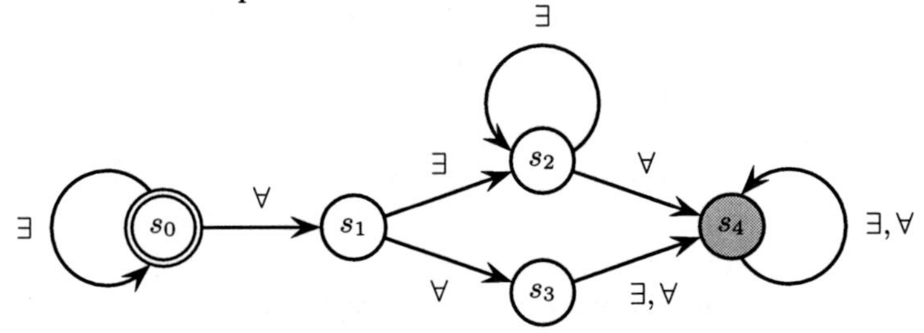

Fig. 6.14. Irregular and regular prefix classes of $\mathsf{ESO}_<(\mathsf{FO}(\alpha))$

Grädel and Rosen [220] considered the restriction to two first order variables, i.e., the logic $\mathsf{ESO}(\mathsf{FO}^2)$, and also found an astonishing result:

Theorem 6.33 (Characterizing Regular Languages by $\mathsf{ESO}_<(\mathsf{FO}^2)$). *Every formula of $\mathsf{ESO}_<(\mathsf{FO}^2)$, the existential second-order logic over finite strings, with only two first-order variables, but arbitrary first order quantification, can be translated to an equivalent ω-automaton.*

The proof given in [220] is based on a translation from $\mathsf{ESO}_<(\mathsf{FO}^2)$ to the logic $\mathsf{ESO}_<(\mathsf{FO}(\exists^*\forall\forall))$, which can be translated by Theorem 6.32 to automata.

We close this section by a remark on the notation often used in the literature: The quantifier hierarchy of a predicate logic is often determined by classes Σ_i and Π_i as follows: In general, $\Sigma_0 = \Pi_0$ is the class of quantifier-free formulas. For every i, Σ_{i+1} is then obtained by closure of Π_i under $\exists$, and Π_{i+1} is obtained by closure of Σ_i under $\forall$. Hence, $\forall x.\exists y.\forall z.\varphi$ with quantifier-free φ belongs to Π_3. Hence, Π_i and Σ_i are negations of each other. For predicate logic, one furthermore adds superscripts to describe the order: Σ_k^i is the Σ_k fragment of $(i+1)$-order logic. Hence, ESO is the class Σ_1^1.

With this notation, it follows for $\mathsf{MSO}_<$, that the quantifier hierarchy collapses: since every $\mathsf{MSO}_<$ formula can be translated to an existential ω-automaton, it follows that $\mathsf{MSO}_<$, and hence, every class Σ_i and Π_i can be translated to Σ_1. The quantifier hierarchy of $\mathsf{MFO}_<$ has been considered by Thomas in [484]. It turned out that the hierarchy of star-free sets obtained by counting the number of alternations between concatenation and Boolean operations (the concatenation hierarchy [79]) coincides with the quantifier hierarchy of $\mathsf{MFO}_<$, when the appropriate translation is made. The quantifier hierarchy of SO over strings and graphs has been only recently considered. See [155] for a recent survey on the obtained results.

7

Conclusions

We have considered the four most important formalisms that are used for specifying and verifying finite state reactive systems, namely, the propositional μ-calculus, ω-automata, temporal logics, and predicate logics. We have considered hierarchies of these formalisms, in particular, the alternation depth hierarchy of the μ-calculus, the (Borel) hierarchy of ω-automata, the (Borel) hierarchy of temporal logics, and the quantifier hierarchy of monadic second order predicate logic. These hierarchies have been established to partition the logics into subsets of increasing complexity and expressiveness. In general, it is often the case that the more expressive a logic is, the more complex will be its verification procedures. Hence, the essential idea followed in this book is to exploit these hierarchies such that the least expressive logic is chosen with the most efficient verification procedure. In this final section, we will briefly summarize the content of the book, and give remarks on topics that are not covered by the book.

In Chapter 3, we studied the model checking problem of the μ-calculus, including its more succinct vectorized form. We have seen that the alternation depth governs the runtime of the verification of μ-calculus formulas: The runtime of all currently known algorithms to solve μ-calculus problems depend exponentially on the alternation depth of the formulas. Therefore, we were particularly interested in alternation-free formulas. The use of vectorized μ-calculus formulas enabled us to translate ω-automata to equivalent μ-calculus formulas whose size depends only linearly on the number of states and transitions of the automaton. Further translations have been given for certain temporal logics, and via ω-automata, also for all temporal logics and the predicate logics considered in Chapter 6. Therefore, the vectorized μ-calculus can be used as a basic verification machinery, which has early been advocated by Emerson [169, 174].

ω-automata were the topic of Chapter 4. We presented the main classes of acceptance conditions, considered their expressiveness and various constructions like Boolean closure and determinization. The relationship between ω-languages and metric spaces allowed us to classify ω-automata by the Borel hierarchy into six classes that moreover have deterministic representatives: $\mathsf{Det}_{\mathsf{G}}$, $\mathsf{Det}_{\mathsf{F}}$, $\mathsf{Det}_{\mathsf{Prefix}}$, $\mathsf{Det}_{\mathsf{FG}}$, $\mathsf{Det}_{\mathsf{GF}}$, and $\mathsf{Det}_{\mathsf{Streett}}$. The first four of these classes can be translated to the alternation-free μ-calculus, while the latter two require alternation depth two. Besides the topological characterization of the automaton hierarchy, we also sketched algebraic automata theory, i.e., the relationship to finite monoids, to establish the connection to first order predicate logic and temporal logics.

In Chapter 5, we considered various subsets of the temporal logic CTL*. We considered direct translations to the μ-calculus and others to ω-automata (for linear time temporal logics). To this end, we reconsidered the automata hierarchy and defined temporal logics TL_{G}, TL_{F}, $\mathsf{TL}_{\mathsf{Prefix}}$, $\mathsf{TL}_{\mathsf{FG}}$, $\mathsf{TL}_{\mathsf{GF}}$, and $\mathsf{TL}_{\mathsf{Streett}}$ in analogy to the automaton classes. We showed that every basic class TL_κ can be translated in linear time to a symbolic description of a NDet_κ automaton, and moreover, that the converse is also true, at least for non-counting automata. The relationship to the alternation depth hierarchy of the μ-calculus is also clear due to the characterization by the ω-automata hierarchy. As a consequence, we have found the logics LeftCTL* and AFCTL* as strict subsets of CTL* that can be translated to the alternation-free μ-calculus.

Predicate logic, as discussed in Chapter 6, introduced another hierarchy namely the quantifier-hierarchy of formulas in prenex normal form. For monadic second order logic, Büchi's result shows that this hierarchy collapses, since all formulas can be reduced to the existential fragment, that is essentially the set of existential automaton formulas.

Therefore, the book investigates hierarchies of the μ-calculus, ω-automata, temporal logics, and predicate logics to identify fragments of certain expressivenesses and complexities. The following table summarizes some complexity results (see page 394 and page 427 for explanations on these classes):

	model checking	satisfiability
ML	P-complete [103, 116, 443]	PSPACE-complete [308]
CTL	P-complete [103, 116, 443]	EXPTIME-complete [192]
CTL$^+$	Δ_2^p-complete [103, 314, 443]	2EXPTIME-complete [266]
LeftCTL*	Δ_2^p-complete	2EXPTIME-complete
AFCTL*	PSPACE-complete	2EXPTIME-complete
LTL	PSPACE-complete [456]	PSPACE-complete [456]
LTL_ω	PSPACE-complete [456, 458]	PSPACE-complete [456, 458]
CTL*	PSPACE-complete [103, 172, 176]	2EXPTIME-complete [168, 177, 498]
$\mathcal{L}_\omega$	non-elementary	non-elementary
$\mathsf{MFO}_<$	non-elementary [221, 473]	non-elementary [221, 473]
$\mathsf{MSO}_<$	non-elementary [221, 473]	non-elementary [221, 473]
$\mathcal{L}_\mu$	UP ∩ coUP [40, 169, 270]	EXPTIME-complete [29, 165, 168]

ML denotes thereby *modal logic*, i.e., the fixpoint-free fragment of the μ-calculus, LTL_ω is LTL_p extended by automaton formulas, but still without path quantifiers. $\mathcal{L}_\omega$ is the branching time extension of LTL_ω where path quantifier are allowed (see Definition 4.6 on page 191). The flat fragment of $\mathcal{L}_\omega$ (Section 4.8.1) probably behaves like CTL*.

There are a lot of other hierarchies that have not been considered in the book due to lack of space. Some of them are refinements of the so-far mentioned hierarchies, others follow different ideas. The Rabin index hierarchy [506] refines the automata hierarchy in that the class $\mathsf{Det}_{\mathsf{Rabin}} / \mathsf{Det}_{\mathsf{Streett}}$ is further structured into the number of necessary acceptance pairs, which is called the Rabin index of the corresponding language. Wagner [506] has shown that this hierarchy is strict, and that the Rabin index can be effectively computed. In Appendix B, we show that μ-calculus formulas can be translated to equivalent Rabin tree automata. It can be shown [22] that the Rabin index on Rabin tree automata matches with the alternation depth hierarchy of the corresponding μ-calculus formulas.

These refinements can also be applied to $\mathsf{TL}_{\mathsf{Streett}}$ and $\mathsf{TL}_{\mathsf{Prefix}}$, and therefore, we can also add more structure to the logics LeftCTL* and AFCTL*. Further hierarchies have been considered by Etessami and Wilke [188], Wilke [511, 512], and Dams [136]. In their work they have established the *until-hierarchy of temporal logic* that is obtained by counting the number of nestings of temporal operators, in particular, the until operators. It can be proved that this hierarchy is strict, i.e., there are formulas of until-depth $n + 1$ that can not be expressed by any other formula of until-depth less or equal to n.

The *quantifier hierarchy* is classically considered for predicate logics [487], and resembles to the alternation depth hierarchy of the μ-calculus, in that alternating nestings of $\forall$- and $\exists$-quantifiers of a formula are counted. This hierarchy is very important for complexity theory. Regular expressions are also structured by the so-called star-height which counts the number of nested Kleene star operations. We have considered star-free regular expressions, as these are expressively equivalent to temporal logic, but we have not considered other star-heights. The minimal star-height of regular language is defined to be the minimal star-height of a regular expression that describes this language. The star-height of regular language is computable [402, 403], but it is still unknown whether there are regular expressions with a star-height of more than one. A further classification of regular expressions is given by the *dot-depth (concatenation hierarchy)* of regular languages Brzozowski and Knast [79], which is the number of concatenation operations of the expression. Thomas has shown that the dot-depth of a regular expression is related with the quantifier-depth of the first order formulas that correspond with that expression. Further comparisons can be found in [403, 405, 487, 489].

Besides other hierarchies, there are further formalisms and fragments that are not covered by this book. Among them are *tree automata* that have only been sketched in Appendix B. In particular, *alternating tree automata* [165, 167, 168, 221, 376, 383, 390] turned out to be an important machinery for explaining many results on expressivenesses and complexities. Another related field is the theory of *infinite games* that turned out to be a third alternative to the μ-calculus (in particular, parity games). The interested reader is referred to [221, 224, 270, 271, 514] for further details. Moreover, monadic second order logic in its more general form over trees and graphs can be used to embed various logics. A recent result of Janin and Walukiewicz [263, 264] is that on infinite computation trees, monadic second-order logic is as expressive as the μ-calculus. On Kripke structures, monadic second-order logic is however more expressive and the subset that corresponds to the μ-calculus is characterized by bisimulation relations. Many other formalisms and logics are still invented, e.g., Müller-Olm's [384] fixpoint logic with chop FLC, that is an extension of the μ-calculus with a sequential composition operator. Müller-Olm proved that FLC does not have the finite model property, and that the sat-problem of FLC is not decidable. Nevertheless, model checking FLC formulas on finite Kripke structure is decidable. Lange and Stirling [313] proved that FLC has the *tree model property*. Moreover, it turns out that FLC is exponentially more succinct than the μ-calculus, and more expressible than the μ-calculus [313]. Lange and Stirling [313] also presented a tableau-based local model checking procedure.

Reconsidering the above table, it turns out the the complexity of the model checking problem of the μ-calculus is still not precisely determined. In particular, it is not clear if the problem can be solved in polynomial time by a deterministic machine, although there are some new results [49, 503]. As the alternation hierarchy of the μ-calculus is however strict, it is likely that a polynomial algorithm, if it should exist, will not focus on the alternation of the operators. There are fragments that are not solely defined via the alternation depth, e.g., those given in [46, 169].

In addition to other logics and hierarchies, there are some important fields in the verification of reactive systems that were not contained in this book. *Compositional reasoning* [244, 332, 339, 361] is a key to integrate fully automated procedures with interactive ones. This can be especially useful to exploit design ideas in order to simplify the proof goals. This has to be incorporated in the translation of system description's given as programs to symbolic representations of Kripke structures [436, 438]. Moreover, such translations have to use sophisticated techniques like data abstraction, quotient constructions, symmetry reduction, and partial order reduction [8, 210, 493, 516] to reduce the size of the problem.

Verification methods for systems with *infinite state spaces* are becoming more and more mature [66, 83, 357, 488]. Finite state automata can be used to represent infinite state sets, when states are encoded as finite words of arbitrary length. It is interesting to note that the symbolic representation by BDDs is only a special case of this representation, which gives a simple explanation of the canonical normal form of BDDs (since minimal automata are unique up to isomorphism).

Finally, we only considered qualitative temporal logic, where it is assumed that every transition of the Kripke structure requires the same amount of time. There are approaches to consider *quantitative temporal aspects* both for discrete time [10, 11, 95, 238, 243, 316, 329, 330, 427] and others that even consider continuous time [9, 30, 90, 91].

A

Binary Decision Diagrams

A.1 Basic Definitions

We have already mentioned in Section 2.1 (see Figure 2.2 on page 52) that the transition relation of a Kripke structure can be encoded by a propositional formula. This form of representing sets is often called an *implicit set representation*, since the elements of the set are not enumerated explicitly. It is possible to implement most algorithms presented in this book with implicit set representations. In the past two decades, this has led to very efficient model checking algorithms [44, 88] that are mostly based on *binary decision diagrams (BDDs)* [74, 77]. In this section, we show the basic algorithms of BDDs and discuss their usage for verification. For further details, we refer to textbooks on BDDs, e.g., [147, 227, 365, 373] or other compendiums, e.g., [467].

The overall idea of implicit set representation is as follows: Assume that our algorithms work on subsets of a finite set set $G = \{e_1, \ldots, e_\ell\}$. The elements of G are identified with variable assignments of a set of propositional variables $V_\Sigma = \{x_1,\ldots,x_n\}$, where $\ell \leq 2^n$ holds. Typically, we choose the smallest number n with that property, but this is only due to efficiency reasons. Identifying variable assignments $\vartheta \subseteq V_\Sigma$ with elements e_i means that there exists a subset $\mathcal{V}_G \subset 2^{V_\Sigma}$ with a bijective function $\Theta : \mathcal{V}_G \to G$. Our algorithms will usually not need that function, since they will exclusively work with the implicit representation.

Having this encoding, it is sufficient to consider the subsets of the propositional variables $V_\Sigma = \{x_1,\ldots,x_n\}$. Recall that a propositional formula with n variables may encode a set with up to 2^n elements. The key observation is that propositional formulas may serve as an efficient representation to store arbitrary subsets of a finite set G. Hence, algorithms and data structures for efficiently manipulating propositional formulas are necessary for the implementation of algorithms that work with these *implicit set representations* like the popular *symbolic model checking procedures* [44, 88]. 'Symbolic representation' is a synonym for 'implicit representation', and 'symbolic model checking' means model checking based on 'implicit set representations'.

In the past two decades, various forms of *decision diagrams* have been developed as normal forms for propositional formulas. Initial work of Lee [318] and Akers [7] on binary decision diagrams has been refined by Bryant [74, 75, 78] to establish *canonical normal forms* that are nowadays simply called BDDs. In the following, we will list the definition and the basic algorithms of BDDs that are necessary to implement the model checking procedures presented in this book in a symbolic manner.

The basic idea of binary decision diagrams is due to Shannon [453] and has already been used as a special case in Lemma 3.12 on page 100. The more general form of this lemma is as follows:

Lemma A.1 (Shannon Expansion of Propositional Formulas). *Given a propositional formula Φ over the variables V_Σ. The following holds for every variable $x \in V_\Sigma$:*

- $\Phi = x \wedge [\Phi]_x^1 \vee \neg x \wedge [\Phi]_x^0$
- $\Phi = (\neg x \vee [\Phi]_x^1) \wedge (x \vee [\Phi]_x^0)$
- $\Phi = \left(x \Rightarrow [\Phi]_x^1 \middle| [\Phi]_x^0\right)$

The lemma lists three equivalent formulas for the same fact: The proposition Φ is factorized into two propositions $[\Phi]_x^1$ and $[\Phi]_x^0$ such that the latter formulas no longer contain occurrences of the variable x. The reduction is thereby done by a case distinction on x. In the following, we will often use the latter form, where $(\alpha \Rightarrow \beta|\, \gamma)$ is to be read as 'if α then β else γ' (see Definition 2.36 on page 74). The following equivalences show that this operator together with the constants $\mathsf{0}$ and 1 is powerful enough to express all propositional formulas:

- $\varphi \wedge \psi = (\varphi \Rightarrow \psi|\, \mathsf{0})$
- $\varphi \vee \psi = (\varphi \Rightarrow 1|\, \psi)$
- $\neg\varphi = (\varphi \Rightarrow \mathsf{0}|\, 1)$

The reduction to the 'if-then-else' operator does not provide us with a canonical normal form. For this reason, we have to further restrict the normal form. Our first additional restriction is that case distinctions are only made on variables. This can be achieved by rewriting with the following equations:

- $((\alpha \Rightarrow \beta|\, \gamma) \Rightarrow \varphi|\, \psi) = (\alpha \Rightarrow (\beta \Rightarrow \varphi|\, \psi)|\, (\gamma \Rightarrow \varphi|\, \psi))$
- $(\mathsf{0} \Rightarrow \varphi|\, \psi) = \psi$
- $(1 \Rightarrow \varphi|\, \psi) = \varphi$

Having rewritten the expressions with the above equations results in 'if-then-else' normal forms where the case distinction is a variable. However, this is still not restrictive enough to result in normal forms that are unique for all equivalent formulas, i.e., in *canonical normal forms*. The next restriction is obtained by eliminating redundant case distinctions, i.e., by rewriting with the following equations:

- $(\alpha \Rightarrow \varphi|\, \varphi) = \varphi$
- $(\alpha \Rightarrow (\alpha \Rightarrow \beta|\, \gamma)|\, \varphi) = (\alpha \Rightarrow \beta|\, \varphi)$
- $(\alpha \Rightarrow \varphi|\, (\alpha \Rightarrow \beta|\, \gamma)) = (\alpha \Rightarrow \varphi|\, \gamma)$
- $(\alpha \Rightarrow \alpha|\, \varphi) = (\alpha \Rightarrow 1|\, \varphi)$
- $(\alpha \Rightarrow \varphi|\, \alpha) = (\alpha \Rightarrow \varphi|\, 0)$

Bryant [74] showed that a canonical normal form is finally obtained when the case distinctions are additionally made in the same order. Hence, we assume that the variables $V_\Sigma = \{x_1,\ldots,x_n\}$ are endowed with a total order $\preceq$. The ordering can be established by rewriting once more with the following equations that have to be formulated for all pairs of variables $x_i,x_j \in V_\Sigma$ with $x_i \preceq x_j$.

- $(x_j \Rightarrow (x_i \Rightarrow \varphi|\, \psi)|\, \alpha) = (x_i \Rightarrow (x_j \Rightarrow \varphi|\, \alpha)|\, (x_j \Rightarrow \psi|\, \alpha))$
- $(x_j \Rightarrow \alpha|\, (x_i \Rightarrow \varphi|\, \psi)) = (x_i \Rightarrow (x_j \Rightarrow \alpha|\, \varphi)|\, (x_j \Rightarrow \alpha|\, \psi))$
- $(x_j \Rightarrow (x_i \Rightarrow \alpha|\, \beta)|\, (x_i \Rightarrow \varphi|\, \psi)) = (x_i \Rightarrow (x_j \Rightarrow \alpha|\, \varphi)|\, (x_j \Rightarrow \beta|\, \psi))$

Rewriting with the above equations will convert every propositional formula into an equivalent one that is a canonical normal form. This means that all propositional formulas that are equivalent to that formula will be converted syntactically to the same formula. In particular, every valid formula will be converted to 1, so that validity and satisfiability can be easily checked once the normal form is obtained.

As an example, consider the formula $x \wedge (\neg x \vee y)$ over the variables $V_\Sigma = \{x, y\}$ with $x \preceq y$. We first replace $\neg$, $\wedge$ and $\vee$ with the if-then-else operator and obtain

$$(x \Rightarrow ((x \Rightarrow 0|\, 1) \Rightarrow 1|\, y)|\, 0)$$

Next, we eliminate case distinctions on expressions that are not variables and obtain:

$$(x \Rightarrow (x \Rightarrow y|\, 1)|\, 0)$$

Finally, eliminating redundant case distinctions results in the following formula:

$$(x \Rightarrow y|\, 0)$$

It can be easily seen that reducing the formula $x \wedge y$ results in the same expression. Hence, the formulas $x \wedge (\neg x \vee y)$ and $x \wedge y$ are equivalent, since they share the same canonical normal form.

In particular, every valid formula results in the canonical normal form 1, and every unsatisfiable formula in the canonical normal form 0. Hence, a formula is satisfiable iff its reduced and ordered if-then-else normal form is different from 0.

The reduced and ordered 'if-then-else' normal form is, in principle, a binary decision diagram. However, the computation as given above is not very efficient. Modern software packages like CUDD [465] make use of efficient data structures and algorithms to directly manipulate the decision diagrams.

In the following, we will briefly list the basics of these data structures and algorithms behind such a BDD package. We start with the following definition of our main data structure with its invariants:

Definition A.2 (Binary Decision Diagram (BDD)). *Given the propositional variables V_Σ together with an injective function $\pi : V_\Sigma \to \{2, \ldots, |V_\Sigma| + 1\}$. A binary decision diagram (BDD) for the variables V_Σ w.r.t. to π is a set of tuples of the form $v = (i, x, j, k, c)$ where $i \in \mathbb{N} \setminus \{0, 1\}$ is the address of v, $x \in V_\Sigma$ is the label of v, j, $k \in \mathbb{N}$ are the children of v, and $c \in \mathbb{N}$ is the reference counter. To access the components of a tuple $v = (i, x, j, k)$, we, furthermore, define*

- $\mathsf{address}(v) = i$
- $\mathsf{label}(v) = x$
- $\mathsf{low}(v) = j$
- $\mathsf{high}(v) = k$
- $\mathsf{refcount}(v) = c$

To access the vertex with address i in a BDD $\mathcal{B}$, we define the partial function $\mathsf{vertex}_\mathcal{B}$ such that $\mathsf{vertex}_\mathcal{B}(i)$ is that tuple $v \in \mathcal{B}$ where $\mathsf{address}(v) = i$ holds. Moreover, we define the partial function $\mathsf{degree}_\mathcal{B}$ on addresses of $\mathcal{B}$ as follows:

$$\mathsf{degree}_\mathcal{B}(i) := \begin{cases} \pi(\mathsf{label}(\mathsf{vertex}_\mathcal{B}(i))) & : \text{for } i > 1 \\ i & : \text{for } i \in \{0, 1\} \end{cases}$$

Then, the following conditions have to hold for $\mathcal{B}$:

- *For every $v \in \mathcal{B}$, either $\mathsf{high}(v) \in \{0, 1\}$ or there must be a vertex $v_1 \in \mathcal{B}$ with $\mathsf{address}(v_1) = \mathsf{high}(v)$.*
- *For every $v \in \mathcal{B}$, either $\mathsf{low}(v) \in \{0, 1\}$ or there must be a vertex $v_0 \in \mathcal{B}$ with $\mathsf{address}(v_0) = \mathsf{low}(v)$.*
- *Uniqueness: For all $x \in V_\Sigma$, $j, k \in \mathbb{N}$, there is at most one vertex $v \in \mathcal{B}$ with $\mathsf{label}(v) = x$, $\mathsf{low}(v) = j$, and $\mathsf{high}(v) = k$.*
- *Reduction: For all $(i, x, j, k, c) \in \mathcal{B}$, we have $j \neq k$.*
- *Ordering: For all $(i, x, j, k, c) \in \mathcal{B}$, we have $\mathsf{degree}_\mathcal{B}(j) < \mathsf{degree}_\mathcal{B}(i)$ and $\mathsf{degree}_\mathcal{B}(k) < \mathsf{degree}_\mathcal{B}(i)$.*

Due to the above uniqueness requirement, we moreover define the partial function $\mathsf{unique}_\mathcal{B}(x, j, k)$ such that it returns the vertex $v \in \mathcal{B}$ with corresponding entries (x, j, k), provided that there is such a $v \in \mathcal{B}$, otherwise it returns $\perp$.

A binary decision diagram as defined above is therefore a graph, where every vertex $v \in \mathcal{B}$ has exactly two successors, namely $\mathsf{low}(v)$ and $\mathsf{high}(v)$. If a successor vertex is different from the leaf vertices 0, 1, then we require that $\mathcal{B}$ must have an entry for that vertex (hence, that vertex is not a leaf). Moreover, the graph must be acyclic due to the ordering restriction. Note that this restriction also forbids that a variable x may appear in the children of a vertex (i, x, j, k, c).

The above definition of $\mathcal{B}$ is in some BDD packages called a *BDD manager*, since $\mathcal{B}$ contains many BDDs. In particular, every vertex $v \in \mathcal{B}$ is the root of a BDD contained in $\mathcal{B}$. It is very important that inside a BDD manager $\mathcal{B}$, all BDDs are uniquely represented. Moreover, due to our requirements, the BDDs are reduced and ordered w.r.t. π. In contrast, some authors distinguish between BDDs and ROBDDs (reduced ordered BDDs).

In a real implementation, the address of a vertex would really be the address of the vertex in the main memory of the computer. Therefore, the access function $\mathsf{vertex}_{\mathcal{B}}(i)$ as required above is just the access to a portion of main memory at a certain address i. The access functions label, low, high, and refcount are trivial. However, the implementation of the function $\mathsf{unique}_{\mathcal{B}}$ is not so simple. In practice, it is implemented by a hash table so that the vertex $\mathsf{unique}_{\mathcal{B}}(x, j, k)$ can be found in time $O(1)$. To this end, a hash function is required that maps the triple (x, j, k) to a number $\hbar(x, j, k)$ that serves as hash key[1].

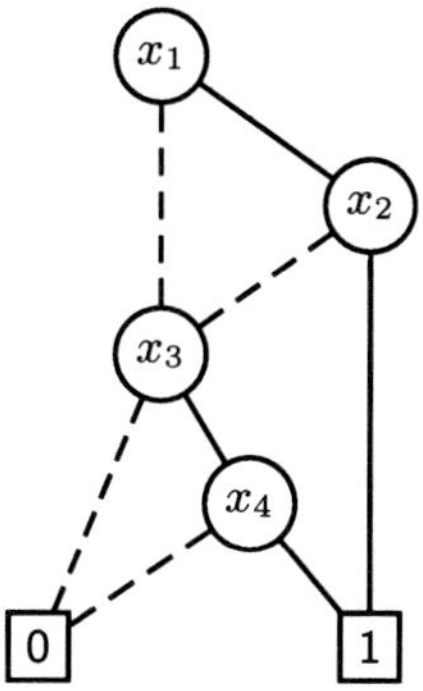

Fig. A.1. A reduced ordered binary decision diagram

Like every graph, a BDD can be drawn as shown in Figure A.1, where low-edges are dashed. The BDD given in Figure A.1 is encoded by the tuples $(2, x_1, 4, 3, 1)$, $(3, x_2, 4, 1, 1)$, $(4, x_3, 0, 5, 2)$, and $(5, x_4, 0, 1, 1)$. We moreover used the function $\pi(x_i) := 6 - i$ for defining the order on the variables.

Note that the reference counter is at least the number of incoming edges of the BDD, but can be larger, since we may have additionally external 'pointers' to a vertex. Vertices $v \in \mathcal{B}$ with reference counter $\mathsf{refcount}(v) = 0$ can be deleted, which in turn will decrease the reference counters of their children.

[1] We give some more details on the construction of such a hash function: The function $\mathsf{pair}(j, k) := \frac{1}{2}(j + k)(j + k + 1) + j$ is a bijection between $\mathbb{N} \times \mathbb{N}$ and $\mathbb{N}$. Hence, we can construct bijections between $\mathbb{N}^n$ and $\mathbb{N}$ by defining $\mathsf{pair}_{n+1}(i_1, \ldots, i_{n+1}) := \mathsf{pair}(\mathsf{pair}_n(i_1, \ldots, i_n), i_{n+1})$. Finally, encoding variables x as numbers, we can use $\hbar(x, j, k) := \mathsf{pair}_3(x, j, k) \bmod p$ with a large prime number p as hash function.

```
function Create_B(x, j, k)
  if j = k then return j end;
  v := unique_B(x, j, k);
  if v ≠ ⊥ then
    i := new_address_B;
    B := B ∪ (i, x, j, k, 1);
    return i
  else
    IncreaseRefcount(v);
    return address(v)
  end
end
```

Fig. A.2. Creating new vertices in a BDD manager

This process, called *garbage collection*, should be applied from time to time to save memory.

The algorithms that we will discuss in the following often have to add a vertex with entries (x, j, k) to a given BDD manager $\mathcal{B}$. Due to the uniqueness requirement, we have to assure that new vertices are only added if there is not already a vertex with the same components (x, j, k) in $\mathcal{B}$. This can be checked with our function $\mathsf{unique}_{\mathcal{B}}$ that returns the address $\mathsf{unique}_{\mathcal{B}}(x, j, k)$ of the vertex with components (x, j, k). As a side effect, we have to increase the reference counter of that vertex, since now there is another pointer to it. If $\mathsf{unique}_{\mathcal{B}}$ returns $\perp$, we know that a new entry has to be added to $\mathcal{B}$. The function $\mathsf{Create}_{\mathcal{B}}$ given in Figure A.2 implements these steps.

As BDDs represent normal forms of propositional formulas, we have to explain the relationship between a BDD and the propositional formula that it represents. Figure A.3 shows a function $\mathsf{FormulaBDD}_{\mathcal{B}}$ that computes for an address i and a BDD $\mathcal{B}$ the associated propositional formula $\mathsf{FormulaBDD}_{\mathcal{B}}(i)$.

```
function FormulaBDD_B(i)
  case i of
    0    : return 0;
    1    : return 1;
    else : v := vertex_B(i);
           φ := FormulaBDD_B(high(v));
           ψ := FormulaBDD_B(low(v));
           x := label(v);
           return (x ⇒ φ| ψ)
  end case
end
```

Fig. A.3. Formula represented by a BDD

Definition A.3 (Associated Formula of a BDD). *Given a BDD $\mathcal{B}$ over the variables V_Σ and a vertex $v \in \mathcal{B}$, the function* $\mathsf{FormulaBDD}_\mathcal{B}$ *given in Figure A.3 computes the associated propositional formula* $\mathsf{FormulaBDD}_\mathcal{B}(\mathsf{address}(v))$.

Hence, it is seen that every vertex $v = (i, x, j, k, c)$ corresponds to a 'case distinction' on the variable x. Due to the requirements given in Definition A.2, it follows that there are no redundant case distinctions with identical cofactors that would correspond with formulas of the form $(x \Rightarrow \varphi | \varphi)$. Furthermore, all common subformulas are shared, and the variable ordering is respected.

Theorem A.4 (BDDs as Canonical Normal Forms). *Given a set of variables V_Σ that are ordered by the function π as required in Definition A.2. Every propositional formula has a BDD that is uniquely determined up to isomorphism. Moreover, all equivalent propositional formulas are represented by the same BDD up to isomorphism. Due to the unique representation in a BDD manager, equivalence of BDDs can be simply checked by comparing their addresses.*

```
function Operands_B(i, m)
  if m = degree_B(i) then
    v := vertex_B(i);
    return (low(v), high(v))
  else return (i, i)
  end
end

function Apply_B(⊙, j, k)
  if j ∈ {0, 1} ∧ k ∈ {0, 1} then
    return ⊙(j, k) (* is either 1 or 0 *)
  end;
  d_j := degree_B(j);
  d_k := degree_B(k);
  m := max{d_j, d_k};
  (j_0, j_1) := Operands(j, m);
  (k_0, k_1) := Operands(k, m);
  i_0 := Apply_B(⊙, j_0, k_0);
  i_1 := Apply_B(⊙, j_1, k_1);
  if m = d_j then x := label(vertex_B(j))
  else x := label(vertex_B(k)) end;
  return Create_B(x, i_0, i_1)
end
```

Fig. A.4. Boolean operations on BDDs

A.2 Basic Algorithms on BDDs

We have already mentioned that Boolean operations can be efficiently implemented on BDDs. For Boolean operations with two arguments like conjunction, disjunction, implication, equivalence, etc., we can use the function apply given in Figure A.4.

Theorem A.5 (Correctness of $\mathsf{Apply}_{\mathcal{B}}$). *Given a BDD manager $\mathcal{B}$ over the variables V_Σ, two vertices $v_j, v_k \in \mathcal{B}$ and a Boolean operation $\odot : \{0,1\} \times \{0,1\} \to \{0,1\}$. The function $\mathsf{Apply}_{\mathcal{B}}$ given in Figure A.4 called with arguments $\odot$, $j := \mathsf{address}(v_j)$, and $k := \mathsf{address}(v_k)$ then adds vertices to $\mathcal{B}$ and returns an address i so that $\mathsf{FormulaBDD}_{\mathcal{B}}(\mathsf{vertex}_{\mathcal{B}}(i))$ corresponds with the Boolean operation $\odot$ applied to $\mathsf{FormulaBDD}_{\mathcal{B}}(v_j)$ and $\mathsf{FormulaBDD}_{\mathcal{B}}(v_k)$.*

Proof. The correctness is seen as follows: The first case, where $j, k \in \{0,1\}$ holds, is clear; we obtain as the result a Boolean constant that is determined by the truth table of the operation $\odot$. In the remaining case, one of the addresses j or k points to a vertex that is labeled with a variable. The correctness then follows from the following equations, where we assume that $f = (x_f \Rightarrow f_1 | f_0)$ and $g = (x_g \Rightarrow g_1 | g_0)$ holds:

- $f \odot g = \begin{cases} (x_f \Rightarrow f_1 \odot g | f_0 \odot g) & : \text{if } \pi(x_f) > \pi(x_g) \\ (x_f \Rightarrow f_1 \odot g_1 | f_0 \odot g_0) & : \text{if } \pi(x_f) = \pi(x_g) \\ (x_g \Rightarrow f \odot g_1 | f \odot g_0) & : \text{if } \pi(x_f) < \pi(x_g) \end{cases}$
- $f \odot 1 = (x_f \Rightarrow f_1 \odot 1 | f_0 \odot 1)$
- $f \odot 0 = (x_f \Rightarrow f_1 \odot 0 | f_0 \odot 0)$
- $1 \odot g = (x_g \Rightarrow 1 \odot g_1 | 1 \odot g_0)$
- $0 \odot g = (x_g \Rightarrow 0 \odot g_1 | 0 \odot g_0)$

The correctness follows by induction, where in the induction steps one of the above equations is used for the proof. Note that the function $\mathsf{Operands}_{\mathcal{B}}(i, m)$ returns $(\mathsf{low}(v), \mathsf{high}(v))$ if $m \leq \mathsf{degree}_{\mathcal{B}}(i)$ holds, and otherwise (i, i). Hence, the recursive call is made with the cofactors of the vertex with the larger degree. When both vertices have the same degree, the recursive call is made with all corresponding cofactors. □

The function $\mathsf{Apply}_{\mathcal{B}}$ can be used to implement Boolean operations with two arguments. This is sufficient to construct for a given propositional formula with the Boolean operators $\neg$, $\wedge$, and $\vee$ a corresponding BDD. The principle can be generalized to implement Boolean operations with more than two arguments. As an example, the function $\mathsf{ITE}_{\mathcal{B}}$ shown in Figure A.5 computes the 'if-then-else' operation for given BDDs [62]. One may also implement conjunction or disjunction with more than two arguments in the same manner.

In addition to Boolean operations, we consider in the following further operations that are important for the implementation of model checking procedures. The next one is the composition of BDDs, which means the replace-

```
function ITE_B(i, j, k)
  if i = 0 then return j
  elseif i = 1 then return k
  elseif j = k then return k
  else
    d_i := degree_B(i);
    d_j := degree_B(j);
    d_k := degree_B(k);
    m = max{d_i, d_j, d_k};
    (i_0, i_1) := Operands(i, m);
    (j_0, j_1) := Operands(j, m);
    (k_0, k_1) := Operands(k, m);
    a := ITE(i_0, j_0, k_0);
    b := ITE(i_1, j_1, k_1);
    if m = d_i then x := label(vertex_B(i))
    elseif m = d_j then x := label(vertex_B(j))
    else x := label(vertex_B(k)) end;
    return Create_B(x, a, b)
  end
end
```

Fig. A.5. If-then-else operation on BDDs

ment of a variable with another BDD. At the syntactical level, this corresponds to the substitution $[\varphi]_x^\alpha$, where x is a variable whose occurrences are replaced with the formula α. Assume that we have already computed BDDs for φ and α, then the algorithm for computing a BDD for $[\varphi]_x^\alpha$ is given in Figure A.6.

Theorem A.6 (Correctness of $\mathsf{Compose}_\mathcal{B}$**).** *Given a BDD manager $\mathcal{B}$ over the variables V_Σ, two vertices $v_\varphi, v_\alpha \in \mathcal{B}$ and a variable $x \in V_\Sigma$. We abbreviate $i_\varphi := \mathsf{address}(v_\varphi)$, $i_\alpha := \mathsf{address}(v_\alpha)$, $\varphi := \mathsf{FormulaBDD}_\mathcal{B}(v_\varphi)$, and $\alpha := \mathsf{FormulaBDD}_\mathcal{B}(v_\alpha)$. The function $\mathsf{Compose}_\mathcal{B}$ given in Figure A.6 called with arguments x, i_φ, and i_α then adds vertices to $\mathcal{B}$ and returns an address i so that $\mathsf{FormulaBDD}_\mathcal{B}(\mathsf{vertex}_\mathcal{B}(i))$ is the canonical representation of $[\varphi]_x^\alpha$.*

Proof. If $i_\varphi \in \{0,1\}$ holds, then the desired result is certainly i_φ itself. Otherwise, i_φ is the address of a vertex $v_\varphi \in \mathcal{B}$. If v_φ is labeled with x, then the associated formula of v_φ is of the form $(x \Rightarrow \varphi_1 | \varphi_0)$, where neither φ_1 nor φ_0 can contain occurrences of x. Hence, the result of the substitution $[\varphi]_x^\alpha$ is $(\alpha \Rightarrow \varphi_1 | \varphi_0)$, which is computed by a call to ITE.

In the remaining case, v_φ is a vertex labeled with a variable different from x. Hence, let $(y \Rightarrow \varphi_1 | \varphi_0)$ and $(z \Rightarrow \alpha_1 | \alpha_0)$ be the formulas associated with v_φ and v_α, respectively, where $x \neq y$. Then, we have the following:

```
function Compose_B(x, i_φ, i_α)
  if i_φ ∈ {0,1} then return i_φ
  else
    v_φ := vertex_B(i_φ);
    if label(v_φ) = x then
      return ITE(i_α, low(v_φ), high(v_φ))
    else
      d_φ := degree_B(i_φ);
      d_α := degree_B(i_α);
      m = max{d_φ, d_α};
      (α0, α1) := Operands(α, m);
      (φ0, φ1) := Operands(φ, m);
      l := Compose_B(x, φ0, α0);
      h := Compose_B(x, φ1, α1);
      if m = d_φ then y := label(v_φ)
      else y := label(vertex_B(i_α)) end;
      return Create_B(y, l, h)
    endif
  endif
end
```

Fig. A.6. Composition of BDDs

$$\begin{aligned}
[(y \Rightarrow \varphi_1 | \varphi_0)]_x^\alpha &= (y \Rightarrow [\varphi_1]_x^\alpha | [\varphi_0]_x^\alpha) \\
&= \left(y \Rightarrow [\varphi_1]_x^{(z \Rightarrow \alpha_1 | \alpha_0)} \middle| [\varphi_0]_x^{(z \Rightarrow \alpha_1 | \alpha_0)} \right) \\
&= \begin{cases} (y \Rightarrow [\varphi_1]_x^\alpha | [\varphi_0]_x^\alpha) & : \text{if } \pi(y) > \pi(z) \\ (y \Rightarrow [\varphi_1]_x^{\alpha_1} | [\varphi_0]_x^{\alpha_0}) & : \text{if } \pi(y) = \pi(z) \\ (z \Rightarrow [\varphi]_x^{\alpha_1} | [\varphi]_x^{\alpha_0}) & : \text{if } \pi(y) < \pi(z) \end{cases}
\end{aligned}$$

□

If a BDD is used to represent a set, it is natural to ask how many elements that set contains. Clearly, this corresponds to the number of paths leading from the root vertex to the 1-leaf, i.e., the number of propositional assignments that satisfy the associated formula. This number can be computed with the function given in Figure A.7.

Theorem A.7 (Correctness of SatCount$_\mathcal{B}$). *Given a BDD manager $\mathcal{B}$ over the variables V_Σ and the address i of a vertex $v \in \mathcal{B}$. The algorithm given in Figure A.7 computes the number* SatCount$_\mathcal{B}(i, |V_\Sigma| + 1)$ *of satisfying assignments of* FormulaBDD$_\mathcal{B}(v)$.

Proof. The correctness is straightforward: if i corresponds to the 1-leaf, then the satisfying assignments are those that assign arbitrary values to the variables with degree in $\{2, \ldots, \hat{d}\}$. The number of these assignments is $2^{|\{2,\ldots,\hat{d}\}|}$, i.e., $2^{\hat{d}-1}$.

```
function SatCount_B(i, d̂)
  if i = 0 then return 0
  else if i = 1 then return 2^(d̂-1)
  else
    d_i := degree_B(i);
    v := vertex_B(i);
    j := low(v);
    k := high(v);
    n_0 := SatCount_B(j, d_i - 1);
    n_1 := SatCount_B(k, d_i - 1);
    return n_0 + n_1
  endif
end
```

Fig. A.7. Counting the satisfying assignments of a BDD

In the case where i is the address of a vertex labeled with x_i having degree d_i, there are two kinds of satisfying assignments: those that assign $x_i := 0$ and those that assign $x_i := 1$. The numbers of these assignments are computed with the corresponding calls to the cofactors. The variables that must thereby be considered are those with degree less than d_i. □

Of course, it is also possible to compute the satisfying assignments in an explicit manner. However, this requires exponential runtime in the worst case, while SatCount$_{\mathcal{B}}$ can be implemented such that it runs in time linear to the number of vertices in the BDD (however, the implementation in Figure A.7 does not have this complexity, since it recomputes the result each time it visits a shared subgraph).

Finally, we consider quantification over propositional variables, i.e., the following functions:

- $\exists x.\varphi := [\varphi]_x^1 \vee [\varphi]_x^0$
- $\forall x.\varphi := [\varphi]_x^1 \wedge [\varphi]_x^0$

We may even quantify over a set of variables at once. The set of variables $\{x_1, \ldots, x_k\}$ is thereby encoded by the formula $x_1 \wedge \ldots \wedge x_k$ that is in turn given as a BDD E. Note that the BDD of this formula is a chain of k vertices that are connected via their high-edges in the order given by the variable ordering. All low-edges directly connect to the 0-leaf. Then, the algorithm is given in Figure A.8.

Theorem A.8 (Correctness of Exists$_{\mathcal{B}}$). *Given a BDD manager $\mathcal{B}$ over the variables V_Σ and the addresses i_e and i_φ of vertices $v_e, v_\varphi \in \mathcal{B}$. Suppose that the associated Formula of i_e is equivalent to $\bigwedge_{i=1}^{k} x_i$, and that φ is the formula associated with i_φ. The algorithm given in Figure A.8 adds vertices to $\mathcal{B}$ and finally returns the address i of the vertex that is associated to $\exists x_1 \ldots . \exists x_k.\varphi$.*

```
function Exists_B(i_e, i_φ)
  if i_e ∈ {0,1} ∨ i_φ ∈ {0,1} then return i_φ end;
  v_e := vertex_B(i_e);
  v_φ := vertex_B(i_φ);
  x_e := label(v_e);
  x_φ := label(v_φ);
  if degree_B(i_e) > degree_B(i_φ) then
  (* x_e does not occur in FormulaBDD_B(i_φ) *)
    return Exists_B(high(v_e), i_φ)
  elseif degree_B(i_e) = degree_B(i_φ) then
    i_0 := exists(high(v_e), low(v_φ));
    i_1 := exists(high(v_e), high(v_φ));
    return Apply_B(∨, i_0, i_1)
  else (* degree_B(i_e) < degree_B(i_φ) *)
    i_0 := exists(i_e, low(v_φ));
    i_1 := exists(i_e, high(v_φ));
    return Create_B(x_φ, i_0, i_1)
  endif
end
```

Fig. A.8. Existential quantification on BDDs

Proof. The correctness is again seen by several case distinctions. If $i_e \in \{0, 1\}$ holds, then the set of variables to quantify over is empty. Hence, the result is φ. If $i_\varphi \in \{0, 1\}$ holds, then no variable occurs in φ, and therefore the result is again φ. This explains the basic cases where either $i_e \in \{0, 1\}$ or $i_\varphi \in \{0, 1\}$ holds.

In the remaining case, i_e and i_φ are addresses of vertices $v_e, v_\varphi \in \mathcal{B}$. Suppose that these vertices are labeled with variables $x_e, x_\varphi \in V_\Sigma$. We then consider the three cases of the algorithm:

$\mathsf{degree}_\mathcal{B}(i_e) > \mathsf{degree}_\mathcal{B}(i_\varphi)$: In this case, we conclude that x_e does not occur in $\mathsf{FormulaBDD}_\mathcal{B}(i_\varphi)$. Hence, the quantification over x_e is irrelevant and the result is simply the quantification over the remaining variables on i_φ.

$\mathsf{degree}_\mathcal{B}(i_e) = \mathsf{degree}_\mathcal{B}(i_\varphi)$: In this case, we have $x_e = x_\varphi$, and therefore, the associated formula $\mathsf{FormulaBDD}_\mathcal{B}(i_\varphi)$ is of the form $(x_e \Rightarrow \varphi_1 | \varphi_0)$. Hence, the existential quantification is the disjunction of the remaining quantification on φ_1 and φ_0.

$\mathsf{degree}_\mathcal{B}(i_e) < \mathsf{degree}_\mathcal{B}(i_\varphi)$: In this case, the formula $\mathsf{FormulaBDD}_\mathcal{B}(i_\varphi)$ is of the form $(x_\varphi \Rightarrow \varphi_1 | \varphi_0)$, where the degree of x_φ is higher than those of the variables that we want to quantify over. The correctness is therefore seen as follows:

$$
\begin{aligned}
\exists x_e.\,(x_\varphi \Rightarrow \varphi_1|\,\varphi_0) &= [(x_\varphi \Rightarrow \varphi_1|\,\varphi_0)]^0_{x_e} \vee [(x_\varphi \Rightarrow \varphi_1|\,\varphi_0)]^1_{x_e}\\
&= \left(x_\varphi \Rightarrow [\varphi_1]^0_x\Big|\,[\varphi_0]^0_x\right) \vee \left(x_\varphi \Rightarrow [\varphi_1]^1_x\Big|\,[\varphi_0]^1_x\right)\\
&= \left(x_\varphi \Rightarrow [\varphi_1]^0_x \vee [\varphi_1]^1_x\Big|\,[\varphi_0]^0_x \vee [\varphi_0]^1_x\right)\\
&= (x_\varphi \Rightarrow (\exists x_e.\varphi_1)|\,(\exists x_e.\varphi_0))
\end{aligned}
$$

□

A.3 Minimization of BDDs Using Care Sets

BDDs are canonical normal forms of formulas w.r.t. a variable ordering. However, if the formula is incompletely specified, we can choose different BDDs that represent formulas that are equivalent on the domain of interest, but may differ otherwise. It is reasonable to describe the domain of interest, also called the *care set*, by another formula d, such that given formulas φ and d, we seek a formula ψ that is equivalent to φ whenever d holds, and that has a BDD as small as possible. Such formulas ψ are called generalized cofactors, and can also be explained in a different manner:

Definition A.9 (Orthonormal Formulas and Generalized Cofactors). *Propositional formulas $\beta_1, \ldots, \beta_n$ over the variables V_Σ form an orthonormal set if the following conditions hold:*

- $\beta_i \wedge \beta_j = 0$ *for* $i \neq j$
- $\left(\bigvee_{i=1}^{n} \beta_i\right) = 1$

If a formula Φ is defined via coefficient formulas φ_i as $\Phi = \bigvee_{i=1}^n \varphi_i \wedge \beta_i$, then the formulas φ_i are called generalized cofactors of Φ w.r.t. β_i.

At the moment it is not clear if generalized cofactors exist for every formula and every set of orthonormal formulas. This is stated in the following lemma, which moreover gives a characterization of the generalized cofactors.

Lemma A.10 (Orthonormal Decomposition and Generalized Cofactors). *Given orthonormal formulas $\beta_1, \ldots, \beta_n$ over the variables V_Σ. For every formula Φ, there are generalized cofactors φ_i such that $\Phi = \bigvee_{i=1}^n \varphi_i \wedge \beta_i$ holds. Moreover, the following are equivalent:*

- $\Phi = \bigvee_{i=1}^{n} \varphi_i \wedge \beta_i$
- $\Phi \wedge \beta_i = \varphi_i \wedge \beta_i$ *for all* i

Proof. Note first that $\beta_j \wedge \beta_j = \beta_j$ holds since

$$\beta_j = \beta_j \wedge 1 = \beta_j \wedge \bigvee_{i=1}^{n} \beta_i = \bigvee_{i=1}^{n} \beta_j \wedge \beta_i = \beta_j \wedge \beta_j$$

Given that Φ is equivalent to $\bigvee_{i=1}^{n} \varphi_i \wedge \beta_i$, it follows that $\Phi \wedge \beta_j$ is equivalent to $\bigvee_{i=1}^{n} \varphi_i \wedge \beta_j \wedge \beta_i$, and therefore, equivalent to $\varphi_j \wedge \beta_j$. Conversely, if $\Phi \wedge \beta_i = \varphi_i \wedge \beta_i$ holds for all i, then we have

$$\bigvee_{i=1}^{n} \varphi_i \wedge \beta_i = \bigvee_{i=1}^{n} \Phi \wedge \beta_i = \Phi \wedge \bigvee_{i=1}^{n} \beta_i = \Phi \wedge 1 = \Phi$$

To prove the existence of the coefficients φ_i, simply define $\varphi_i :\equiv \Phi \wedge \beta_i$. □

The Shannon decomposition is a special form of an orthonormal decomposition, since for every variable x the formulas $\beta_1 :\equiv x$ and $\beta_2 :\equiv \neg x$ are orthonormal. In fact, this can be generalized to arbitrary formulas β: the set $\{\beta, \neg\beta\}$ is orthonormal. Another example of an orthonormal decomposition is the disjunctive normal form, where the base functions β_i are the $2^{|V_\Sigma|}$ minterms.

The above lemma does not state that the coefficient formulas φ_i are uniquely determined for given Φ and β_i. In fact, the characterization $\Phi \wedge \beta_i = \varphi_i \wedge \beta_i$ means that φ_i *only has to agree with Φ whenever β_i holds, and may be arbitrarily defined for the assignments where β_i is false*[2]. It can be shown that the set of cofactors is partially ordered (take the implication as partial order), and that $\Phi \wedge \beta_i$ is the smallest and $\Phi \vee \neg\beta_i$ is the largest cofactor w.r.t. β_i ($\Phi \wedge \beta_i$ is false for all assignments of the 'don't care' set $\neg\beta$, and $\Phi \vee \neg\beta_i$ is true for all of these assignments).

For this reason, there is some freedom for the choice of generalized cofactors. Whenever we have the chance to replace a BDD with one of its cofactors, we clearly want to select the cofactor that has the smallest BDD. However, searching the cofactor that has the minimal BDD is NP-complete [391, 431], and therefore this is not recommended. Instead, good heuristics are used in practice. We will discuss two popular examples, namely the algorithms $\mathsf{Constrain}_{\mathcal{B}}$ [126] and $\mathsf{Restrict}_{\mathcal{B}}$ [128] and refer to [97, 250, 454, 490] for further algorithms.

The function $\mathsf{Constrain}_{\mathcal{B}}$ given in Figure A.9 computes a generalized cofactor of $\mathsf{FormulaBDD}_{\mathcal{B}}(i_\varphi)$ w.r.t. $\mathsf{FormulaBDD}_{\mathcal{B}}(i_d)$ [126, 127]. To understand the implementation of $\mathsf{Constrain}_{\mathcal{B}}$, consider the following equations that can be derived from the implementation given in Figure A.9.

- $\mathsf{Constrain}_{\mathcal{B}}(i_\varphi, \mathsf{0}) = \mathsf{0}$
- $\mathsf{Constrain}_{\mathcal{B}}(i_\varphi, 1) = i_\varphi$
- $\mathsf{Constrain}_{\mathcal{B}}(\mathsf{0}, i_d) = \mathsf{0}$
- $\mathsf{Constrain}_{\mathcal{B}}(1, i_d) = 1$
- $\mathsf{Constrain}_{\mathcal{B}}((x \Rightarrow \varphi_1 | \varphi_0), (y \Rightarrow \mathsf{0} | d_0)) = \mathsf{Constrain}_{\mathcal{B}}(\varphi_0, d_0)$, if $\pi(x) \leq \pi(y)$
- $\mathsf{Constrain}_{\mathcal{B}}((x \Rightarrow \varphi_1 | \varphi_0), (y \Rightarrow d_1 | \mathsf{0})) = \mathsf{Constrain}_{\mathcal{B}}(\varphi_1, d_1)$, if $\pi(x) \leq \pi(y)$

[2] Note that the equivalence $\Phi \wedge \beta_i = \varphi_i \wedge \beta_i$ holds iff $\beta_i \rightarrow (\Phi \leftrightarrow \varphi_i)$ is valid.

```
function Constrain_B(i_φ, i_d)
  if i_d = 0 then return 0
  elseif i_φ ∈ {0, 1} ∨ (i_d = 1) then return i_φ
  else
    d_d := degree_B(i_d);
    d_φ := degree_B(i_φ);
    m = max{d_d, d_φ};
    (φ_0, φ_1) := Operands(i_φ, m);
    (d_0, d_1) := Operands(i_d, m);
    if d_0 = 0 then return Constrain_B(φ_1, d_1)
    elseif d_1 = 0 then return Constrain_B(φ_0, d_0)
    else
      l := Constrain_B(φ_0, d_0);
      h := Constrain_B(φ_1, d_1);
      if m = d_φ then x := label(vertex_B(i_φ))
      else x := label(vertex_B(i_d) end;
      return Create_B(x, l, h);
    endif
  endif
end
```

Fig. A.9. Minimizing BDDs w.r.t. a given domain

- $\mathsf{Constrain}_{\mathcal{B}}((x \Rightarrow \varphi_1|\,\varphi_0)\,,(y \Rightarrow d_1|\,d_0))$
$$= \begin{cases} (x \Rightarrow \mathsf{Constrain}_{\mathcal{B}}(\varphi_1, i_d)|\,\mathsf{Constrain}_{\mathcal{B}}(\varphi_0, i_d)) & \text{: if } \pi(x) > \pi(y) \\ (x \Rightarrow \mathsf{Constrain}_{\mathcal{B}}(\varphi_1, d_1)|\,\mathsf{Constrain}_{\mathcal{B}}(\varphi_0, d_0)) & \text{: if } \pi(x) = \pi(y) \\ (y \Rightarrow \mathsf{Constrain}_{\mathcal{B}}(i_\varphi, d_1)|\,\mathsf{Constrain}_{\mathcal{B}}(i_\varphi, d_0)) & \text{: if } \pi(x) < \pi(y) \end{cases}$$

The last equation states that $\mathsf{Constrain}_{\mathcal{B}}$ simultaneously traverses its argument BDDs until one of the cases given in the first six equations applies. The cases where one argument is a constant are also simple. The interesting cases are therefore handled by the fifth and the sixth equations. Consider first the case where $\pi(x) = \pi(y)$ holds, which means that x and y are the same variable. Then, the BDD of φ is of the form $(x \Rightarrow \varphi_1|\,\varphi_0)$ and the domain formula d is of the form $(x \Rightarrow d_1|\,d_0)$. If $d_0 = 0$ holds, then d is equivalent to $x \wedge d_1$. As we are allowed to change the value of φ if d is false, it follows that *we can replace the low branch φ_0 with an arbitrary formula*. A first idea would be to replace it with a leaf, but we can do even better: If φ_1' is the result of the call $\mathsf{Constrain}_{\mathcal{B}}(\varphi_1, d_1)$, we choose φ_1' also for the low-branch and therefore would obtain $(x \Rightarrow \varphi_1'|\,\varphi_1')$. However, as this case distinction is redundant, it is eliminated so that the resulting BDD is only φ_1'. The case where $d_1 = 0$ holds is completely analogous.

Finally, consider the case where φ is of the form $(x \Rightarrow \varphi_1|\,\varphi_0)$, d is of the form $(y \Rightarrow d_1|\,d_0)$, and $\pi(y) > \pi(x)$. Hence, φ does not depend on y. If $d_0 = 0$ holds, then d is equivalent to $y \wedge d_1$, and therefore we can change φ in all cases where either $\neg y$ or $\neg d_1$ holds. Hence, we can replace φ with a formula of the form $(y \Rightarrow \psi | \varphi')$, where $\varphi' := \mathsf{Constrain}_\mathcal{B}(\varphi, d_1)$ holds, and ψ is completely arbitrary. Again, the best choice for ψ is φ', since then the final result is also φ'. The case where $d_1 = 0$ holds is again completely analogous.

Note that neither $d_0 = 0$ nor $d_1 = 0$ can hold in the algorithm after having computed the pairs (d_0, d_1) and (φ_0, φ_1), if additionally $\pi(x) > \pi(y)$ holds. If this were the case, then we conclude $m = d_\varphi$, and hence $(d_0, d_1) = (d, d)$. Hence, we have $d = 0$, which has, however, been checked before entering these steps of the algorithm. Hence, it is sufficient to check whether $d_0 = 0$ or $d_1 = 0$ holds for the above reductions.

Usually, $\mathsf{Constrain}_\mathcal{B}(i_\varphi, i_d)$ is smaller than the BDD for i_φ. However, this is not always the case: In the case where φ is of the form $(x \Rightarrow \varphi_1 | \varphi_0)$, d is of the form $(y \Rightarrow d_1 | d_0)$ with $\pi(x) < \pi(y)$, but neither $d_0 = 0$ nor $d_1 = 0$ holds, the result is $(y \Rightarrow \mathsf{Constrain}_\mathcal{B}(i_\varphi, d_1) | \mathsf{Constrain}_\mathcal{B}(i_\varphi, d_0))$, which may contain a vertex for y that was not present in φ before. Hence, this case can introduce new vertices in the BDD of φ.

It is possible to refine the function $\mathsf{Constrain}_\mathcal{B}$, so that this case is eliminated. To this end, note that $\Phi \wedge \alpha = \varphi \wedge \alpha$ implies $\Phi \wedge \beta = \varphi \wedge \beta$, provided that $\beta \to \alpha$ holds. Hence, we may weaken β, thus enlarging the domain of interest, for computing a cofactor w.r.t. β.

To eliminate the situation mentioned in the discussion of $\mathsf{Constrain}_\mathcal{B}$, we could therefore existentially quantify over all variables in β that do not occur in φ, hence, computing a cofactor w.r.t. $\alpha := \exists y.\beta$: Note that $\exists y.\beta$ is equivalent to $[\beta]_y^0 \vee [\beta]_y^1$, which is implied by β.

However, this 'weakening' technique reduces the freedom for selecting cofactors, and in the extreme case where β is weakened to 1, the only cofactor is the formula itself. Hence, we only use the 'weakening' technique in the case where φ is of the form $(x \Rightarrow \varphi_1 | \varphi_0)$, d is of the form $(y \Rightarrow d_1 | d_0)$ with $\pi(x) < \pi(y)$, but neither $d_0 = 0$ nor $d_1 = 0$ holds. The result is the function $\mathsf{Restrict}_\mathcal{B}$ given in Figure A.10 [128].

Theorem A.11 (Correctness of $\mathsf{Constrain}_\mathcal{B}$ and $\mathsf{Restrict}_\mathcal{B}$). *Given a BDD manager $\mathcal{B}$ with addresses i_φ and i_d that correspond with formulas φ and d, respectively. The functions $\mathsf{Constrain}_\mathcal{B}$ and $\mathsf{Restrict}_\mathcal{B}$ given in Figures A.9 and A.10 compute generalized cofactors of φ w.r.t. d.*

The computation of $\mathsf{Constrain}_\mathcal{B}$ can be done in time linear to the sizes of i_φ and i_d, which is, however, not the case for $\mathsf{Restrict}_\mathcal{B}$. A further difference between $\mathsf{Constrain}_\mathcal{B}$ and $\mathsf{Restrict}_\mathcal{B}$ is that $\mathsf{Restrict}_\mathcal{B}$ does not enlarge the set of variables that occur in the BDD i_φ, while $\mathsf{Constrain}_\mathcal{B}$ may add additional variables that occur in i_d. $\mathsf{Constrain}_\mathcal{B}$ has, furthermore, the following nice properties:

Lemma A.12 (Properties of $\mathsf{Constrain}_\mathcal{B}$). *The following properties hold for all BDDs, where $\mathsf{Negate}_\mathcal{B}$ negates a BDD (replace the leaf vertices):*

- $\mathsf{Constrain}_\mathcal{B}(\mathsf{Negate}_\mathcal{B}(i_\varphi), i_d) = \mathsf{Negate}_\mathcal{B}(\mathsf{Constrain}_\mathcal{B}(i_\varphi, i_d))$

```
function Restrict_B(i_φ, i_d)
  if i_d = 0 then return 0
  elseif i_φ ∈ {0, 1} ∨ (i_d = 1) then return i_φ
  else
    d_d := degree_B(i_d);
    d_φ := degree_B(i_φ);
    m = max{d_d, d_φ};
    (φ_0, φ_1) := Operands(i_φ, m);
    (d_0, d_1) := Operands(i_d, m);
    if d_0 = 0 then return Restrict_B(φ_1, d_1)
    elseif d_1 = 0 then return Restrict_B(φ_0, d_0)
    elseif m = d_φ then
      x := label(vertex_B(i_φ));
      l := Restrict_B(φ_0, d_0);
      h := Restrict_B(φ_1, d_1);
      return Create_B(x, l, h);
    else
      i_D := Apply_B(∨, d_0, d_1);
      return Restrict_B(φ, i_D)
    endif
  endif
end
```

Fig. A.10. Minimizing BDDs w.r.t. a given domain

- *for every Boolean operation* $\odot$, *we have* $\mathsf{Constrain}_{\mathcal{B}}(\mathsf{Apply}_{\mathcal{B}}(\odot, i_\varphi, i_\psi), i_d) = \mathsf{Apply}_{\mathcal{B}}(\odot, \mathsf{Constrain}_{\mathcal{B}}(i_\varphi, i_d), \mathsf{Constrain}_{\mathcal{B}}(i_\psi, i_d))$
- $\mathsf{Constrain}_{\mathcal{B}}(\mathsf{Compose}_{\mathcal{B}}(x, i_\varphi, i_\alpha), i_d) = \mathsf{Compose}_{\mathcal{B}}(x, i_\varphi, \mathsf{Constrain}_{\mathcal{B}}(i_\alpha, i_d))$ *for* $i_d \neq 0$

As an example, consider the formulas $\varphi_1 :\equiv (x \leftrightarrow y) \wedge (y \leftrightarrow z)$ and $d_1 :\equiv y \vee (x \oplus z)$. The following table shows that there are four generalized cofactors of φ_1 w.r.t. d_1 that are obtained by replacing the entries '?' with 0 or 1:

$x\ y\ z$	φ_1	d_1	ψ_1	φ_2	d_2	ψ_2
0 0 0	1	0	?	0	1	0
0 0 1	0	1	0	1	0	?
0 1 0	0	1	0	1	0	?
0 1 1	0	1	0	0	0	?
1 0 0	0	1	0	0	1	0
1 0 1	0	0	?	1	0	?
1 1 0	0	1	0	0	1	0
1 1 1	1	1	1	1	1	1

The BDDs for φ_1, d_1, $\mathsf{Constrain}_{\mathcal{B}}(i_{\varphi_1}, i_{d_1})$, and $\mathsf{Restrict}_{\mathcal{B}}(i_{\varphi_1}, i_{d_1})$ for the ordering $z \prec y \prec x$ are shown in Figure A.11. As can be seen, the BDDs obtained

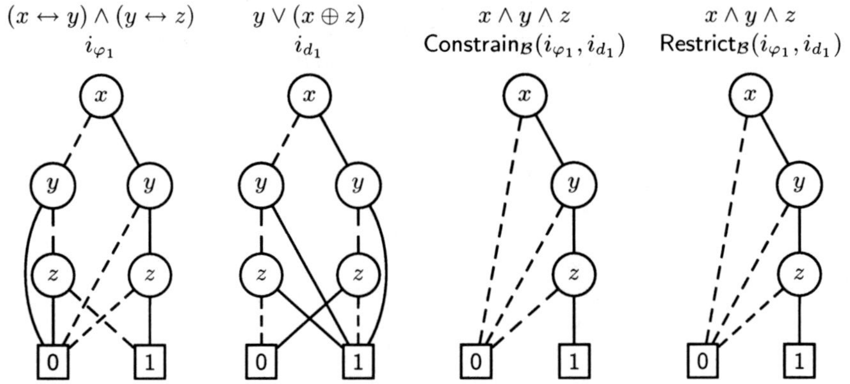

Fig. A.11. First example for computing general cofactors

by $\mathsf{Constrain}_{\mathcal{B}}$ and $\mathsf{Restrict}_{\mathcal{B}}$ are the same in this example, and are not optimal: The cofactor $x \wedge z$ has a smaller BDD (see Figure A.12).

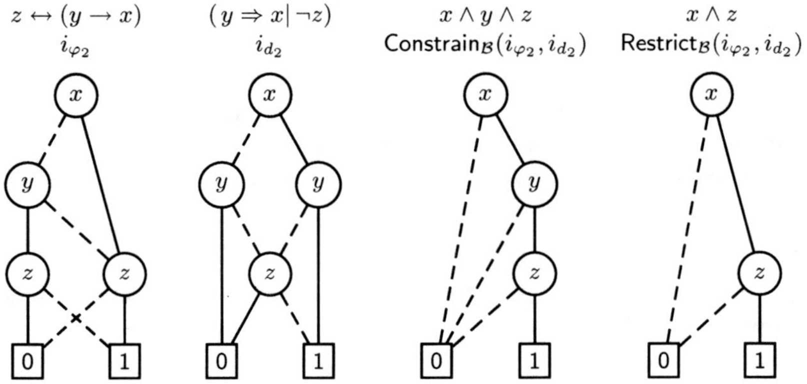

Fig. A.12. Second example for computing general cofactors

The situation is different for the formulas $\varphi_2 :\equiv z \leftrightarrow (y \rightarrow x)$, $d_2 :\equiv (y \Rightarrow x | \neg z)$. Their truth values are also seen in the previous table. The BDDs of φ_2, d_2, $\mathsf{Constrain}_{\mathcal{B}}(i_{\varphi_2}, i_{d_2})$, and $\mathsf{Restrict}_{\mathcal{B}}(i_{\varphi_2}, i_{d_2})$ are shown in Figure A.12. This time $\mathsf{Restrict}_{\mathcal{B}}$ gives us a better result than $\mathsf{Constrain}_{\mathcal{B}}$. Nevertheless, the result is not optimal: the cofactor z has a BDD with only one vertex.

As already mentioned, neither $\mathsf{Constrain}_{\mathcal{B}}$ nor $\mathsf{Restrict}_{\mathcal{B}}$ can guarantee to produce a smaller BDD (see [250] for an example, where a larger BDD is obtained). These functions are therefore called unsafe in [250], and a safe minimization is presented there. However, the compaction algorithm of [250] usually requires more runtime than Constrain$_\mathcal{B}$ or Restrict$_\mathcal{B}$.

Given formulas $\check{\varphi}$, $\hat{\varphi}$ such that $\check{\varphi} \rightarrow \hat{\varphi}$ is valid, we can use generalized cofactors to compute a formula φ such that $\check{\varphi} \rightarrow \varphi$ and $\varphi \rightarrow \hat{\varphi}$ are valid. To this end, define the domain of interest $d :\equiv \check{\varphi} \vee \neg\hat{\varphi}$ and compute a generalized cofactor of $\check{\varphi}$ w.r.t. d. Using Constrain$_\mathcal{B}$ or Restrict$_\mathcal{B}$ to compute the cofactor additionally minimize the BDD.

Another typical example for the application of generalized cofactors is the reduction of a transition relation. Normally, implicit representations of Kripke structures have unreachable states (since the cardinality of the state set must be a power of two). Every propositional formula $\Phi_\mathcal{R}$ for the transition relation is then only of interest for the reachable states. Hence, if we have a formula Φ_{reach} that represents the reachable states or at least a superset of them, we can replace $\Phi_\mathcal{R}$ by any generalized cofactor of $\Phi_\mathcal{R}$ w.r.t. Φ_{reach}.

Moreover, generalized cofactors can be used for the computation of successors and predecessors, which we will explain in the next section.

A.4 Computing Successors and Predecessors

The existential quantification is of essential importance for model checking procedures. Recall that the implicit representation of a Kripke structure is done by encoding the states with propositional variables V_Σ, so that the transition relation is encoded by a propositional formula over $V_\Sigma \cup \{\mathsf{X}x \mid x \in V_\Sigma\}$ (see Figure 2.2 on page 52). Figure A.13 shows again the Kripke structure of Figure 2.2.

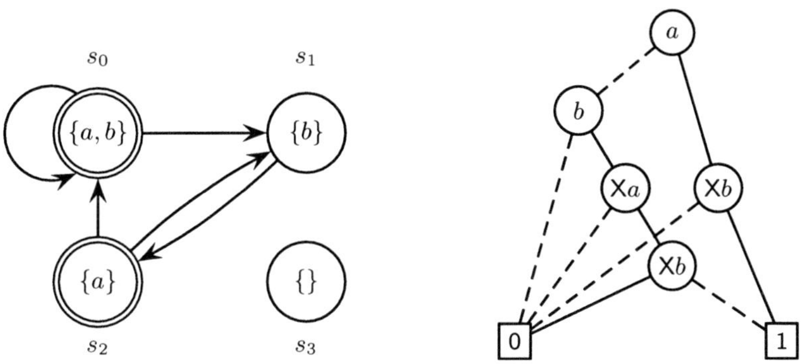

Fig. A.13. Symbolic representation of Kripke structures by BDDs

For example, the set $\{s_0, s_1\}$ is encoded by the formula b, whereas the set $\{s_0, s_1, s_2\}$ is encoded by the formula $a \vee b$. The transition relation is encoded by the propositional formula $\Phi_{\mathcal{R}} :\equiv a \wedge \mathsf{X}b \vee \neg a \wedge b \wedge \mathsf{X}a \wedge \neg \mathsf{X}b$. Using the ordering that is given by the function $\pi(\mathsf{X}b) := 2$, $\pi(\mathsf{X}a) := 3$, $\pi(b) := 4$, and $\pi(a) := 5$, we obtain the BDD shown in Figure A.13 for $\Phi_{\mathcal{R}}$.

Given that Φ_P and Φ_Q are propositional formulas over V_Σ, then these formulas represent certain sets of states P and Q. It is easily seen that $P \setminus Q$, $P \cap Q$, and $P \cup Q$ are then represented by the formulas $\Phi_P \wedge \neg\Phi_Q$, $\Phi_P \wedge \Phi_Q$, and $\Phi_P \vee \Phi_Q$, respectively. This is sufficient to compute sets of states of a Kripke structure where a propositional formula holds. To implement model checking algorithms for the μ-calculus, we additionally need to compute the predecessor and successor sets of a state set.

```
function old2new_B(i_φ)                    function new2old_B(i_φ)
  v_φ := vertex_B(i_φ);                      v_φ := vertex_B(i_φ);
  x_φ := label(v_φ);                         Xx_φ := label(v_φ);
  j_φ := low(v_φ);                           j_φ := low(v_φ);
  k_φ := high(v_φ);                          k_φ := high(v_φ);
  j' := old2new_B(j_φ);                      j' := old2new_B(j_φ);
  k' := old2new_B(k_φ);                      k' := old2new_B(k_φ);
  return Create_B(Xx_φ, j', k')              return Create_B(x_φ, j', k')
end                                        end

function exsuc_B(i_V, i_R, i_P)            function expre_B(i_XV, i_R, i_Q)
  i_R_P := Apply_B(∧, i_R, i_P);             i_XQ := old2new_B(i_Q);
  i_XQ := Exists_B(i_V, i_R_P);              i_R_XQ := Apply_B(∧, i_R, i_XQ);
  return new2old_B(i_XQ)                     return Exists_B(i_XV, i_R_XQ)
end                                        end
```

Fig. A.14. Symbolic computation of predecessor and successors

To this end, we have to replace the variables $x \in V_\Sigma$ with their next-state variant $\mathsf{X}x$ and vice versa. Figure A.14 shows functions old2new$_{\mathcal{B}}$ and new2old$_{\mathcal{B}}$ for that purpose. Additionally, we need conjunction and existential quantification over the variables in V_Σ or the variables in $\{\mathsf{X}x \mid x \in V_\Sigma\}$. We assume in the following, that our BDD manager $\mathcal{B}$ contains vertices i_V and $i_{\mathsf{X}V}$ that represent the formulas $\bigwedge_{x\in V_\Sigma} x$ and $\bigwedge_{x\in V_\Sigma} \mathsf{X}x$, respectively.

Consider first the computation of the BDD representation of the successor set Q of a set of states P. Assume P is represented by Φ_P, and the transition relation $\mathcal{R}$ is represented by $\Phi_{\mathcal{R}}$. Note that Φ_P does not contain next-state variables $\mathsf{X}x$, since it represents a set of states. The formula $\Phi_{\mathcal{R}_P} :\equiv \Phi_{\mathcal{R}} \wedge \Phi_P$ represents the subset of transitions that start in the states of P, i.e., $\mathcal{R}_P := \{(s, s') \in \mathcal{R} \mid s \in P\}$. We are interested in the target states of these transitions, i.e., the set $\{s' \in \mathcal{S} \mid \exists s \in \mathcal{S}.(s, s') \in \mathcal{R}_P\}$. To this end, we hide the target states by an existential quantification over the variables V_Σ, represented by i_V. What we obtain is a BDD that only contains next-state variables $\{\mathsf{X}x \mid x \in V_\Sigma\}$. We obtain the desired representation by replacing all next-state variables $\mathsf{X}x$ by their corresponding current-state variables x. This is done by function $\mathsf{new2old}_{\mathcal{B}}$.

The implementation of the predecessors is very similar. Given a set Q that is represented by the propositional formula Φ_Q, which in turn is represented by a BDD with root vertex i_Q, we first replace the current-state variables x by the corresponding next-state variables $\mathsf{X}x$. This is done by function $\mathsf{old2new}_{\mathcal{B}}$, and the result is the address of a vertex $i_{\mathsf{X}Q}$ that represents the resulting formula $\Phi_{\mathsf{X}Q}$. The result $i_{\mathcal{R}_{\mathsf{X}Q}}$ of the function call $\mathsf{Apply}_{\mathcal{B}}$ therefore represents the set of transitions that end in Q, i.e., the set $\mathcal{R}_{\mathsf{X}Q} := \{(s, s') \in \mathcal{R} \mid s' \in Q\}$. The set $\{s \in \mathcal{S} \mid \exists s' \in \mathcal{S}.(s, s') \in \mathcal{R}_{\mathsf{X}Q}\}$ is then obtained by an existential quantification over the next-state variables $\{\mathsf{X}x \mid x \in V_\Sigma\}$. Recall that these variables are represented by the BDD rooted in $i_{\mathsf{X}V}$ that represents the formula $\bigwedge_{x \in V_\Sigma} \mathsf{X}x$.

Theorem A.13 (Correctness of $\mathsf{exsuc}_{\mathcal{B}}$ and $\mathsf{expre}_{\mathcal{B}}$). *Given a BDD manager $\mathcal{B}$ over the variables $V_\Sigma \cup \{\mathsf{X}x \mid x \in V_\Sigma\}$ that contains vertices v_V and $v_{\mathsf{X}V}$ that represent the formulas $\bigwedge_{x \in V_\Sigma} x$ and $\bigwedge_{x \in V_\Sigma} \mathsf{X}x$, respectively. Let i_V and $i_{\mathsf{X}V}$ be the addresses of v_V and $v_{\mathsf{X}V}$, respectively.*

Let, moreover, $i_{\mathcal{R}}$ be the address of a vertex that represents a transition relation $\mathcal{R}$, and i_Q be the address of a vertex that represents a set of states Q. Then, $\mathsf{exsuc}_{\mathcal{B}}(i_V, i_{\mathcal{R}}, i_Q)$ and $\mathsf{expre}_{\mathcal{B}}(i_V, i_{\mathcal{R}}, i_Q)$ add vertices to $\mathcal{B}$ and return the addresses of vertices that represent the sets $\mathsf{suc}_{\exists}^{\mathcal{R}}(Q)$ and $\mathsf{pre}_{\exists}^{\mathcal{R}}(Q)$, respectively.

As an example, consider again Figure A.13 with $\Phi_{\mathcal{R}} :\equiv a \wedge \mathsf{X}b \vee \neg a \wedge b \wedge \mathsf{X}a \wedge \neg \mathsf{X}b$. The set $P = \{s_0, s_1\}$ is encoded by the formula $\Phi_P :\equiv b$. The computation of the successor representations is, at the propositional level, as follows:

- $\Phi_{\mathcal{R}_P} :\equiv a \wedge b \wedge \mathsf{X}b \vee \neg a \wedge b \wedge \mathsf{X}a \wedge \neg \mathsf{X}b$
- $\Phi_{\mathsf{X}Q} :\equiv \mathsf{X}b \vee \mathsf{X}a \wedge \neg \mathsf{X}b$
- $\Phi_Q :\equiv b \vee a \wedge \neg b$, which is equivalent to $a \vee b$

The predecessors of the set $Q = \{s_0\}$, which is encoded by the formula $\Phi_Q :\equiv a \wedge b$, are computed as follows:

- $\Phi_{\mathsf{X}Q} :\equiv \mathsf{X}a \wedge \mathsf{X}b$
- $\Phi_{\mathcal{R}_{\mathsf{X}Q}} :\equiv a \wedge \mathsf{X}a \wedge \mathsf{X}b$
- $\Phi_P :\equiv a$

Hence, all operations that are necessary for μ-calculus model checking can be efficiently implemented with implicit set representations by BDDs. However, the predecessor and successor computation as given in Figure A.14 is not very efficient. Frequently, there is a bottleneck observed in the computation of $i_{\mathcal{R}_P}$ and $i_{\mathcal{R}_{\mathsf{X}Q}}$ which may introduce many vertices to $\mathcal{B}$ that become irrelevant after existential abstraction. For this reason, many optimizations for the computation of predecessors and successors have been proposed. The most important ones are the following:

1. combination of $\mathsf{Apply}_{\mathcal{B}}$ and $\mathsf{Exists}_{\mathcal{B}}$ in a single function $\mathsf{AndExists}_{\mathcal{B}}$
2. partitioning of the transition relation $\mathcal{R}$ [86, 362]
3. using generalized cofactors of the transition relation $\mathcal{R}$

```
function member(x, i_e)
  if i_e = 1 then return 0
  else
    v_e := vertex_B(i_e);
    if x = label(v_e) then return 1
    else return member(x, high(v_e))
    endif
  endif
end

function ExistsAnd_B(i_e, i_R, i_Q)
  if (i_R = 0) ∨ (i_Q = 0) then return 0
  elseif i_R = 1 then return Exists_B(i_e, i_Q)
  elseif i_Q = 1 then return Exists_B(i_e, i_R)
  else
    d_R := degree_B(i_R);
    d_Q := degree_B(i_Q);
    m = max{d_R, d_Q};
    (r_0, r_1) := Operands(i_R, m);
    (q_0, q_1) := Operands(i_Q, m);
    l := ExistsAnd_B(i_e, r_0, q_0);
    h := ExistsAnd_B(i_e, r_1, q_1);
    if m = d_R then i_m := i_R else i_m := i_Q end;
    x := label(vertex_B(i_m));
    if member(x, i_e) then return Apply_B(∨, l, h)
    else return Create_B(x, l, h)
    endif
  endif
end
```

Fig. A.15. Combination of existential quantification and conjunction

We will briefly discuss these improvements in the following. The function $\mathsf{ExistsAnd}_{\mathcal{B}}$ given in Figure A.15 is easily seen to satisfy the following equation:

$$\mathsf{ExistsAnd}_{\mathcal{B}}(i_e, i_{\mathcal{R}}, i_Q) = \mathsf{Exists}_{\mathcal{B}}(i_e, \mathsf{Apply}_{\mathcal{B}}(\wedge, i_{\mathcal{R}}, i_Q))$$

The correctness is seen by induction on the sum of the numbers of vertices of $i_{\mathcal{R}}$ and i_Q. Hence, $\mathsf{ExistsAnd}_{\mathcal{B}}$ computes a conjunction and existential quantification at once. The successor and predecessor functions can now be implemented more efficiently[3] as follows:

function $\mathsf{exsuc}_{\mathcal{B}}(i_V, i_{\mathcal{R}}, i_P)$
  $i_{\mathsf{X}Q} := \mathsf{ExistsAnd}_{\mathcal{B}}(i_V, i_{\mathcal{R}}, i_P)$;
  return $\mathsf{new2old}_{\mathcal{B}}(i_{\mathsf{X}Q})$
end

function $\mathsf{expre}_{\mathcal{B}}(i_{\mathsf{X}V}, i_{\mathcal{R}}, i_Q)$
  $i_{\mathsf{X}Q} := \mathsf{old2new}_{\mathcal{B}}(i_Q)$;
  return $\mathsf{ExistsAnd}_{\mathcal{B}}(i_{\mathsf{X}V}, i_{\mathcal{R}}, i_{\mathsf{X}Q})$
end

The additional operations $\mathsf{new2old}_{\mathcal{B}}$ and $\mathsf{old2new}_{\mathcal{B}}$ can also be eliminated in that we implement additional functions $\mathsf{ExistsAndX}_{\mathcal{B}}$ and $\mathsf{XExistsAnd}_{\mathcal{B}}$ that work just like $\mathsf{ExistsAnd}_{\mathcal{B}}$, but replace x with $\mathsf{X}x$ or vice versa at the appropriate steps.

The idea of disjunctive partitioning of the transition relation is very simple. Assume that $\Phi_{\mathcal{R}}$ is a disjunction $\Phi_{\mathcal{R}} = \bigvee_{j=1}^{n} \Phi_j$, where the formulas $\Phi_{\mathcal{R}}$, $\Phi_1, \ldots, \Phi_n$ are associated with BDD vertices at the addresses $i_{\mathcal{R}}, i_1, \ldots, i_n$, respectively. Then, the following holds:

$$\begin{aligned}&\mathsf{ExistsAnd}_{\mathcal{B}}(i_V, i_{\mathcal{R}}, i_Q)\\ &\quad = \mathsf{MultiWayApply}(\vee, \mathsf{ExistsAnd}_{\mathcal{B}}(i_V, i_1, i_Q), \ldots, \mathsf{ExistsAnd}_{\mathcal{B}}(i_V, i_n, i_Q))\end{aligned}$$

Hence, the call to $\mathsf{ExistsAnd}_{\mathcal{B}}$ with arguments $(i_V, i_{\mathcal{R}}, i_Q)$ can be replaced by a disjunction of BDDs that are the results of $\mathsf{ExistsAnd}_{\mathcal{B}}(i_V, i_k, i_Q)$. Hence, the calls to $\mathsf{ExistsAnd}_{\mathcal{B}}$ are now made with (hopefully) smaller transition relations so that bottlenecks that may arise due to a call with a large transition relation $i_{\mathcal{R}}$ can be circumvented.

A similar approach can be followed when the transition relation is a conjunction $\Phi_{\mathcal{R}} = \bigwedge_{j=1}^{n} \Phi_{\mathcal{R}_j}$, so that the conjuncts $\Phi_{\mathcal{R}_j}$ do not contain all variables. Computing $\mathsf{degree}_{\mathcal{B}}(i_1), \ldots, \mathsf{degree}_{\mathcal{B}}(i_n)$ shows us which of the BDDs rooted in $i_1, \ldots, i_n$ contain a variable. We can then reorder the conjunction and drive the quantification inwards. For example, assume that $\Phi_{\mathcal{R}_j}$ contains no occurrence of the variables $\{\mathsf{X}x_{j+1}, \ldots, \mathsf{X}x_n\}$. Then, we can proceed as follows for computing predecessors:

$$\begin{aligned}&\exists \mathsf{X}x_1.\Phi_{\mathcal{R}_1}(x_1, \ldots, x_n, \mathsf{X}x_1)\wedge\\ &\quad \exists \mathsf{X}x_2.\Phi_{\mathcal{R}_2}(x_1, \ldots, x_n, \mathsf{X}x_1, \mathsf{X}x_2)\wedge\\ &\quad \vdots\\ &\qquad \exists \mathsf{X}x_{n-1}.\Phi_{\mathcal{R}_{n-1}}(x_1, \ldots, x_n, \mathsf{X}x_1, \ldots, \mathsf{X}x_{n-1})\wedge\\ &\qquad\quad \exists \mathsf{X}x_n.\Phi_{\mathcal{R}_n}(x_1, \ldots, x_n, \mathsf{X}x_1, \ldots, \mathsf{X}x_n) \wedge [\Phi_Q]_{x_1, \ldots, x_n}^{\mathsf{X}x_1, \ldots, \mathsf{X}x_n}\end{aligned}$$

A particular form of conjunctive partitioning is obtained for deterministic systems: Consider a deterministic finite automaton with inputs $i_1, \ldots, i_m$ and state variables $q_1, \ldots, q_n$. The transition relation can be given in the

[3] Efficiency is not meant here as worst-case complexity given by an asymptotic upper bound. Instead, it is seen by most experimental results.

form $\mathcal{R} := \bigwedge_{j=1}^{n} (\mathsf{X}q_j \leftrightarrow \varphi_{\mathcal{R}_j})$, where $\varphi_{\mathcal{R}_j}$ contains only occurrences of the current variables (i.e., no occurrences of variables $\mathsf{X}q_k$ and $\mathsf{X}i_k$). Hence, defining $\Phi_{\mathcal{R}_j} :\equiv \mathsf{X}q_j \leftrightarrow \varphi_{\mathcal{R}_j}$ gives us a conjunctive partitioning of the transition relation as required above, since $\mathsf{X}q_j$ is the only next variable that occurs in this $\Phi_{\mathcal{R}_j}$. For this reason, the predecessors can be computed as follows:

$$
\begin{aligned}
&\exists \mathsf{X}i_1 \ldots \mathsf{X}i_m. \exists \mathsf{X}q_1. (\mathsf{X}q_1 \leftrightarrow \Phi_{\mathcal{R}_1}) \wedge \\
&\quad \exists \mathsf{X}q_2. (\mathsf{X}q_2 \leftrightarrow \Phi_{\mathcal{R}_2}) \wedge \\
&\quad \vdots \\
&\qquad \exists \mathsf{X}q_{n-1}. (\mathsf{X}q_{n-1} \leftrightarrow \Phi_{\mathcal{R}_{n-1}}) \wedge \\
&\qquad\quad \exists \mathsf{X}q_n. (\mathsf{X}q_n \leftrightarrow \Phi_{\mathcal{R}_n}) \wedge [\Phi_Q]_{i_1,\ldots,i_m,q_1,\ldots,q_n}^{\mathsf{X}i_1,\ldots,\mathsf{X}i_m,\mathsf{X}q_1,\ldots,\mathsf{X}q_n}
\end{aligned}
$$

Moreover, an expression of the form $\exists \mathsf{X}q_j. (\mathsf{X}q_j \leftrightarrow \Phi_{\mathcal{R}_j}) \wedge \Psi$ is equivalent to $[\Psi]_{\mathsf{X}q_j}^{\Phi_{\mathcal{R}_j}}$, and can therefore be alternatively computed by $\mathsf{Compose}_{\mathcal{B}}$.

A further variant for computing predecessors and successors more efficiently is obtained by computing generalized cofactors of $\Phi_{\mathcal{R}}$ w.r.t Φ_Q. If we have a generalized cofactor Φ_G of $\Phi_{\mathcal{R}}$ w.r.t. Φ_Q, and the corresponding BDDs rooted at i_G, $i_{\mathcal{R}}$, and i_Q, respectively, then we may replace the computation $\mathsf{Exists}_{\mathcal{B}}(i_e, \mathsf{Apply}_{\mathcal{B}}(\wedge, i_{\mathcal{R}}, i_Q))$ by $\mathsf{Exists}_{\mathcal{B}}(i_e, \mathsf{Apply}_{\mathcal{B}}(\wedge, i_G, i_Q))$, which may already be more efficient. However, for certain cofactors, we can do even better:

Theorem A.14 (Implementing $\mathsf{ExistsAnd}_{\mathcal{B}}$ by Generalized Cofactors). *Given BDDs i_e, $i_{\mathcal{R}}$, i_Q for the computation of $\mathsf{ExistsAnd}_{\mathcal{B}}(i_e, i_{\mathcal{R}}, i_Q)$. Let i_G be a generalized cofactor of $i_{\mathcal{R}}$ w.r.t. i_Q, such that the following holds:*

$$\mathsf{Exists}_{\mathcal{B}}(i_e, i_G) \text{ implies } \mathsf{Exists}_{\mathcal{B}}(i_e, \mathsf{Apply}_{\mathcal{B}}(\wedge, i_{\mathcal{R}}, i_Q))$$

Then, it follows that even the following holds:

$$\mathsf{Exists}_{\mathcal{B}}(i_e, \mathsf{Apply}_{\mathcal{B}}(\wedge, i_{\mathcal{R}}, i_Q)) = \mathsf{Exists}_{\mathcal{B}}(i_e, i_G)$$

In particular, we have:

- $\mathsf{Exists}_{\mathcal{B}}(i_e, \mathsf{Apply}_{\mathcal{B}}(\wedge, i_{\mathcal{R}}, i_Q)) = \mathsf{Exists}_{\mathcal{B}}(i_e, \mathsf{Constrain}_{\mathcal{B}}(i_{\mathcal{R}}, i_Q))$
- $\mathsf{Exists}_{\mathcal{B}}(i_e, \mathsf{Apply}_{\mathcal{B}}(\wedge, i_{\mathcal{R}}, i_Q)) = \mathsf{Exists}_{\mathcal{B}}(i_e, \mathsf{Restrict}_{\mathcal{B}}(i_{\mathcal{R}}, i_Q))$

Let Φ_G, $\Phi_{\mathcal{R}}$, and Φ_Q be the formulas associated with the BDDs i_G, $i_{\mathcal{R}}$, and i_Q, respectively. As Φ_G is a cofactor, we have $\Phi_G \wedge \Phi_Q = \Phi_{\mathcal{R}} \wedge \Phi_Q$. In particular, it follows that $\Phi_{\mathcal{R}} \wedge \Phi_Q$ implies Φ_G. As $\mathsf{Exists}_{\mathcal{B}}$ is monotonic, it follows that $\mathsf{Exists}_{\mathcal{B}}(i_e, \mathsf{Apply}_{\mathcal{B}}(\wedge, i_{\mathcal{R}}, i_Q))$ implies $\mathsf{Exists}_{\mathcal{B}}(i_e, i_G)$. Using the assumption of the theorem, we can therefore conclude the result.

It remains to prove that the cofactors obtained by $\mathsf{Constrain}_{\mathcal{B}}$ and $\mathsf{Restrict}_{\mathcal{B}}$ satisfy the assumption of the above theorem. We do not give proofs of these facts, and refer to [126–128, 490].

A.5 Variable Reordering

BDDs are a canonical normal form for every fixed variable ordering (Theorem A.4). To establish the canonicity, it does not matter which variable ordering we choose, since all of them lead to the desired canonicity. However, different BDDs are obtained for the same formula under different variable orderings, and therefore the size of the BDD of a formula may be influenced by the variable ordering. For example, we have the following result (see also [183]):

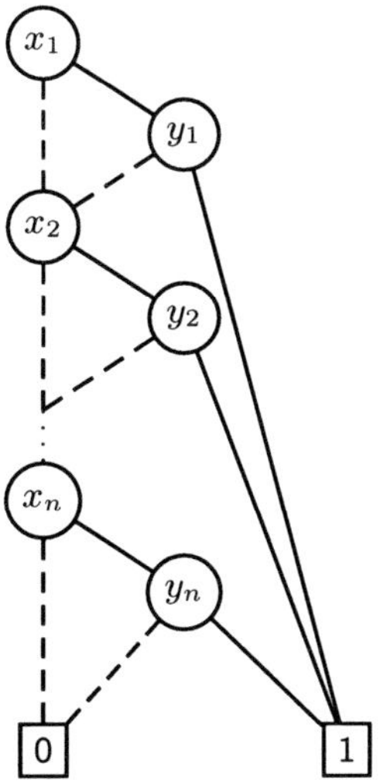

Fig. A.16. BDD mentioned in Lemma A.15

Lemma A.15 (Influence of the Variable Ordering). *The BDD for* $\bigvee_{i=1}^{n}(x_i \wedge y_i)$ *with* $\pi(x_i) = 2n + 3 - 2i$ *and* $\pi(y_i) = 2n + 2 - 2i$ *has exactly* $2n$ *vertices (see Figure A.16). However, the size is exponential for every ordering with* $\pi(x_i) > \max\{\pi(y_j) \mid j \in \{1, \ldots, n\}\}$.

Therefore, the choice of a good variable ordering is essential for the complexity of BDD-based algorithms. The BDD size may depend heavily on the variable ordering, but may also be more or less independent of it: There are formulas where all variable orderings generate polynomial-sized BDDs, while other formulas have BDDs of polynomial and exponential size for different variable orderings, and moreover, there are formulas that only have exponential-sized BDDs [76].

For example, symmetric formulas have polynomial-sized BDDs for every variable ordering. Φ is thereby symmetric, if for all variables $x, y \in V_\Sigma$, Φ

is equivalent to $[\Phi]_{x,y}^{y,x}$. Examples of symmetric formulas are the 'parity function' $x_1 \oplus \ldots \oplus x_n$ or 'threshold functions' that hold when at least k of the n variables are true. In general, the truth value of a symmetric formula only depends on the number of variables that are assigned to 1, and therefore there are only 2^{n+1} different symmetric formulas with n variables (compare this with the number 2^{2^n} of different formulas with n variables). One can prove that symmetric formulas with n variables have BDDs with $O(n^2)$ vertices.

A prominent example for a formula that has only exponentially sized BDDs is the multiplication function. Propositional formulas can be used to encode numerical relations or functions. In the case of the multiplication function, we are interested in formulas Π_i over the variables $x_0, \ldots, x_n$, and $y_0, \ldots, y_n$ such that the following holds (recall Definition 2.9 on page 51 for the definition of $[\![\Phi]\!]_{\vartheta,\{\}}$):

$$\left(\sum_{i=0}^{n} [\![x_i]\!]_{\vartheta,\{\}} \times 2^i\right) \times \left(\sum_{i=0}^{n} [\![y_i]\!]_{\vartheta,\{\}} \times 2^i\right) = \left(\sum_{i=0}^{2n-1} [\![\Pi_i]\!]_{\vartheta,\{\}} \times 2^i\right)$$

Hence, the Π_i can be viewed as the outputs of a multiplier circuit. Bryant [76] has proved the following disappointing fact:

Theorem A.16 (BDD Complexity of Multiplication Function). *For every ordering π, there is a $i \in \{0, \ldots, 2n-1\}$ such that the BDD for Π_i has at least $2^{\frac{n}{8}}$ vertices.*

BDDs can be identified with Boolean functions of type $\mathbb{B}^n \to \mathbb{B}$. Let $G(n)$ be the number of Boolean functions on n Boolean variables that have a BDD with less than $\frac{2^n}{2n}$ vertices. Then, we have $\lim_{n\to\infty} \frac{G(n)}{2^{2^n}} = 0$ (note that 2^{2^n} is the number of Boolean functions of type $\mathbb{B}^n \to \mathbb{B}$). Even more general, this is not only a problem of BDDs, it is just a fact that there are so many Boolean functions that for every normal form the number of polynomially sized normal forms must be negligibly small. Fortunately, many propositional formulas that occur in practice can be represented by BDDs. For example, the representation of the addition function has polynomially sized BDDs (but also BDDs of exponential size). Nevertheless, it is important to compute good variable orderings that keep the BDDs as small as possible.

However, the computation of the optimal variable ordering for a given formula Φ is NP-complete [55]. It is, however, not necessary to test all $n!$ variable orderings in sequence: The best known exact algorithm due to Friedman and Supowit [200] runs in time $O(3^n n^2)$. However, it is unlikely that a polynomial time algorithm exists, and therefore, heuristics are to be used in practice. In general, one distinguishes between static and dynamic approaches to variable ordering: *static approaches* guess a variable ordering in advance and then use this ordering for all BDD operations. In contrast, *dynamic approaches* may change the variable ordering at certain stages.

The basic operation to change the variable ordering is thereby the $\mathsf{Swap}_{\mathcal{B}}$ operation that changes the ordering of adjacent variables. The effect on the

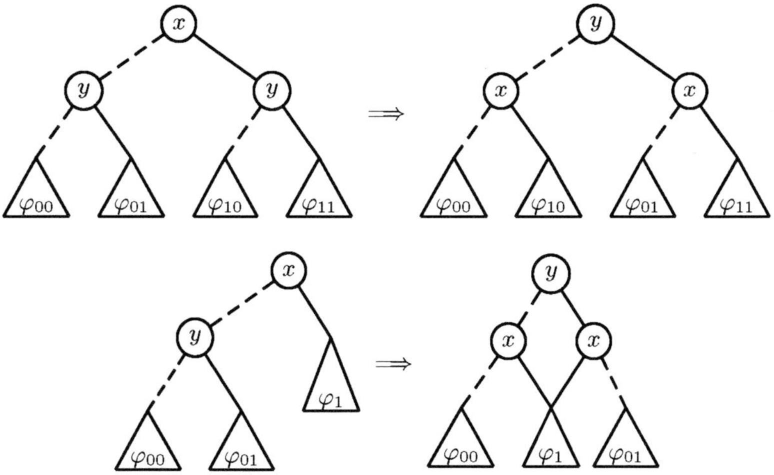

Fig. A.17. $\mathsf{Swap}_{\mathcal{B}}$ operation for reordering BDDs

BDD structure of this operation is shown in Figure A.17, and the correctness is simply seen by the validity of the following formulas, where y must not occur in φ_1 and φ_0:

- $(x \Rightarrow (y \Rightarrow \varphi_{11} | \varphi_{10}) | (y \Rightarrow \varphi_{01} | \varphi_{00}))$
  $= (y \Rightarrow (x \Rightarrow \varphi_{11} | \varphi_{01}) | (x \Rightarrow \varphi_{10} | \varphi_{00}))$
- $(x \Rightarrow \varphi_1 | (y \Rightarrow \varphi_{01} | \varphi_{00})) = (y \Rightarrow (x \Rightarrow \varphi_1 | \varphi_{01}) | (x \Rightarrow \varphi_1 | \varphi_{00}))$
- $(x \Rightarrow (y \Rightarrow \varphi_{11} | \varphi_{10}) | \varphi_0) = (y \Rightarrow (x \Rightarrow \varphi_{11} | \varphi_0) | (x \Rightarrow \varphi_{10} | \varphi_0))$

It is possible to change every possible variable ordering to any other one by means of $\frac{1}{2}n(n-1)$ successive $\mathsf{Swap}_{\mathcal{B}}$ operations, where n is the number of variables. Based on this successive transformation of one variable ordering to another, several heuristics for optimizing the variable ordering have been developed.

For example, the *sifting algorithm* [426] works as follows: for every variable the best position w.r.t. the actual ordering is determined by shifting it upwards and downwards the order. After this, the determined minimal ordering is established. Figure A.18 illustrates this for variable x_4. This procedure is applied to every variable, thus the algorithm requires $O(n^2)$ swap operations.

Many further heuristics for optimizing the variable ordering of BDDs have been proposed and are available in state-of-the-art BDD packages [465]. It is not possible to give a complete overview of these methods here.

search best position for x_4:

$$\begin{array}{ll}
\pi_1 : x_1 \prec x_2 \prec x_3 \prec \boxed{x_4} \prec x_5 \prec x_6 \prec x_7 & \text{initial} \\
\pi_2 : x_1 \prec x_2 \prec x_3 \prec x_5 \prec \boxed{x_4} \prec x_6 \prec x_7 & \mathsf{Swap}_{\mathcal{B}}(x_4, x_5) \\
\pi_3 : x_1 \prec x_2 \prec x_3 \prec x_5 \prec x_6 \prec \boxed{x_4} \prec x_7 & \mathsf{Swap}_{\mathcal{B}}(x_4, x_6) \\
\pi_4 : x_1 \prec x_2 \prec x_3 \prec x_5 \prec x_6 \prec x_7 \prec \boxed{x_4} & \mathsf{Swap}_{\mathcal{B}}(x_4, x_7) \\
\pi_5 : x_1 \prec x_2 \prec x_3 \prec x_5 \prec x_6 \prec \boxed{x_4} \prec x_7 & \mathsf{Swap}_{\mathcal{B}}(x_7, x_4) \\
\pi_6 : x_1 \prec x_2 \prec x_3 \prec x_5 \prec \boxed{x_4} \prec x_6 \prec x_7 & \mathsf{Swap}_{\mathcal{B}}(x_6, x_4) \\
\pi_7 : x_1 \prec x_2 \prec x_3 \prec \boxed{x_4} \prec x_5 \prec x_6 \prec x_7 & \mathsf{Swap}_{\mathcal{B}}(x_5, x_4) \\
\pi_8 : x_1 \prec x_2 \prec \boxed{x_4} \prec x_3 \prec x_5 \prec x_6 \prec x_7 & \mathsf{Swap}_{\mathcal{B}}(x_3, x_4) \\
\pi_9 : x_1 \prec \boxed{x_4} \prec x_2 \prec x_3 \prec x_5 \prec x_6 \prec x_7 & \mathsf{Swap}_{\mathcal{B}}(x_2, x_4) \\
\pi_{10} : \boxed{x_4} \prec x_1 \prec x_2 \prec x_3 \prec x_5 \prec x_6 \prec x_7 & \mathsf{Swap}_{\mathcal{B}}(x_1, x_4)
\end{array}$$

establish the best position of x_4, say π_4:

$$\begin{array}{ll}
\pi_9 : x_1 \prec \boxed{x_4} \prec x_2 \prec x_3 \prec x_5 \prec x_6 \prec x_7 & \mathsf{Swap}_{\mathcal{B}}(x_4, x_1) \\
\pi_8 : x_1 \prec x_2 \prec \boxed{x_4} \prec x_3 \prec x_5 \prec x_6 \prec x_7 & \mathsf{Swap}_{\mathcal{B}}(x_4, x_2) \\
\pi_7 : x_1 \prec x_2 \prec x_3 \prec \boxed{x_4} \prec x_5 \prec x_6 \prec x_7 & \mathsf{Swap}_{\mathcal{B}}(x_4, x_3) \\
\pi_6 : x_1 \prec x_2 \prec x_3 \prec x_5 \prec \boxed{x_4} \prec x_6 \prec x_7 & \mathsf{Swap}_{\mathcal{B}}(x_4, x_5) \\
\pi_5 : x_1 \prec x_2 \prec x_3 \prec x_5 \prec x_6 \prec \boxed{x_4} \prec x_7 & \mathsf{Swap}_{\mathcal{B}}(x_4, x_6) \\
\pi_4 : x_1 \prec x_2 \prec x_3 \prec x_5 \prec x_6 \prec x_7 \prec \boxed{x_4} & \mathsf{Swap}_{\mathcal{B}}(x_4, x_7)
\end{array}$$

Fig. A.18. Example for the sifting algorithm

A.6 Final Remarks

The algorithms that we have presented in this Appendix are not optimal. BDD packages have to implement these algorithms more carefully to avoid repeated computations of the same BDDs. Due to the uniqueness requirement, this would not generate copies of the BDDs, but it would dramatically increase the runtime.

For example, the $\mathsf{SatCount}_{\mathcal{B}}$ algorithm as given in Figure A.7 would have an exponential runtime, since it would traverse a subgraph rooted in a vertex v more than once when different vertices point to v. To avoid this, BDD packages maintain a computed table, where already computed results are stored. If such a computation is required once again, the look-up in the computed table will return the result in time $O(1)$. Using such sophisticated data structures, the following complexities can be obtained:

$$\begin{array}{ll}
\mathsf{Apply}_{\mathcal{B}}(\odot, \varphi, \psi) & O(|\varphi|\,|\psi|) \\
\mathsf{ITE}_{\mathcal{B}}(\alpha, \varphi, \psi) & O(|\alpha|\,|\varphi|\,|\psi|) \\
\mathsf{Compose}_{\mathcal{B}}(x, \varphi, \alpha) & O(|\varphi|^2\,|\alpha|) \\
\mathsf{SatCount}_{\mathcal{B}}(\varphi, \hat{d}) & O(|\varphi|) \\
\mathsf{Constrain}_{\mathcal{B}}(\varphi, d) & O(|\varphi|\,|d|)
\end{array}$$

Moreover, other decomposition types are possible that lead to different forms of decision diagrams [32, 371, 372].

B

Local Model Checking and Satisfiability Checking for the μ-Calculus

In Chapter 3, we discussed several algorithms for checking μ-calculus formulas on a given Kripke structure. The discussed algorithms computed thereby for a given μ-calculus formula Φ and a structure $\mathcal{K}$ the set of states $[\![\Phi]\!]_{\mathcal{K}}$ where Φ holds. These approaches to solve the model checking problem are called *global model checking* procedures, since they compute all states that satisfy Φ. This is more than necessary when one is only interested in the question whether Φ holds in a particular state. Hence, there are also *local model checking* procedures, that try to directly address the problem $(\mathcal{K}, s) \models \Phi$ without necessarily computing all states $[\![\Phi]\!]_{\mathcal{K}}$. Furthermore, it is possible to construct the Kripke structure *on-the-fly*, so that the set of transitions that are required in the local model checking procedure can be computed by need.

Moreover, one is often interested in the *theorem proving problem* or the equivalent *satisfiability problem*: Given a μ-calculus formula Φ, we ask *whether there is a structure $\mathcal{K}$ such that Φ holds in all initial states*. This can be rephrased so that we only ask if there is a structure $\mathcal{K}$ such that Φ holds in a state of this structure (thus making this state the only initial state). This question is also important to determine the equivalence of μ-calculus formulas, since we defined that two formulas are equivalent iff they behave in every state of every structure in the same manner. Hence, φ is equivalent to ψ iff the formula $\neg(\varphi \leftrightarrow \psi)$ is unsatisfiable.

As we have seen in the preceding chapters that many other specification logics can be reduced to the μ-calculus, the approaches considered in this section can also be used to solve the satisfiability problem for other logics and to construct local model checking procedures for them. However, we will not give full details of all proofs, and therefore refer to the original literature for further details, i.e., in particular, Streett and Emerson [168, 171, 478], Stirling and Walker [471, 472], Bradfield and Stirling [63, 67, 68], and Cleaveland [115], Walukiewicz's work [507–510], and Sattler and Vardi's paper [430] for further reading.

For the remainder, it is convenient to assume that the considered formulas fulfill the following syntactic requirements, that can be achieved without loss of generality:

- We only consider formulas in *guarded normal form* (see page 102), so that every bound variable occurs in the scope of a modal operator. Moreover, we assume negation normal form, so that negation symbols only occur before variables (that are not bound).
- We assume that every bound variable is bound only once and has no free occurrences, so that we can define for a formula Φ an associated function that maps a bound variable x to the unique subformula $\mathfrak{D}_\Phi(x)$ of Φ where x is bound. Moreover, we define a partial order $\preceq_\Phi$ on the bound variables such that $x \preceq_\Phi y$ holds if $\mathfrak{D}_\Phi(x)$ is a subformula of $\mathfrak{D}_\Phi(y)$.

B.1 A Partial Local Model Checking Procedure

To start the discussion, we consider the local model checking procedure SimpleLocalCheck of Figure B.1. The procedure is only a partial decision procedure that either computes a result or reports that it can not decide the model checking problem. In particular, given a formula Φ and a state s of a structure $\mathcal{K}$, the call $\mathsf{SimpleLocalCheck}_{\Phi,\mathcal{K}}(s,\Phi)$ will either return 0, 1, or $\perp$. If the result is 1, we know that $(\mathcal{K},s) \models \Phi$ holds. If the result is 0, we know that $(\mathcal{K},s) \models \Phi$ does not hold. In the remaining case, where the result is $\perp$, the procedure is not able to make a decision, i.e., it may be the case that $(\mathcal{K},s) \models \Phi$ holds or not. This is the interesting case that has to be worked out in the following section to obtain a complete decision procedure.

Before extending the procedure to a complete decision procedure, consider how SimpleLocalCheck works: the procedure recursively traverses the syntax tree of Φ (maintaining the context formula Φ to access the definitions $\mathfrak{D}_\Phi(x)$ of bound variables). Additionally, it will exchange the state s in recursive calls when modal operators are evaluated. Furthermore, the recursive calls that have not yet been completed are maintained in a global set *CallStack* to avoid nonterminating runs: As we have only a finite number of states and only finitely many subformulas of Φ, there are only finitely many pairs of arguments (s,φ) for the recursive calls. If a call is found in the *CallStack*, we know that the procedure is caught in an infinite recursion, and therefore, we stop the evaluation and return $\perp$.

There are two kinds of branchings in the recursion steps, namely *conjunctive and disjunctive* ones. Conjunctive branchings are made for the operators $\wedge$, $\Box$, and $\overleftarrow{\Box}$, and disjunctive branchings for the dual operators $\vee$, $\Diamond$, and $\overleftarrow{\Diamond}$. If a call proceeds with a set of conjunctively connected recursions, it will return 1 if all subsequent branches return 1, and it will return 0 if one subsequent branch returns 0. Otherwise, it will return $\perp$. Analogously, if a call

```
function Disj3(Branches)
  f := 0;
  for (s, φ) ∈ Branches do
    b := SimpleLocalCheck_{Φ,K}(s, φ);
    if b = 1 then return 1 end;
    if b = ⊥ then f := 1 end
  end;
  if f then return ⊥
  else return 0 end
end
```

```
function Conj3(Branches)
  f := 0;
  for (s, φ) ∈ Branches do
    b := SimpleLocalCheck_{Φ,K}(s, φ);
    if b = 0 then return 0 end;
    if b = ⊥ then f := 1 end
  end;
  if f then return ⊥
  else return 1 end
end
```

```
function SimpleLocalCheck_{Φ,K}(s, Ψ)
  case Ψ of
    ¬φ: return φ ∉ L(s) ;
    φ ∧ ψ: return Conj3({(s, φ), (s, ψ)}) ;
    φ ∨ ψ: return Disj3({(s, φ), (s, ψ)}) ;
    σx.φ:
      CallStack := {(s, Ψ)} ∪ CallStack;
      b := SimpleLocalCheck_{Φ,K}(s, φ);
      CallStack := CallStack \ {(s, Ψ)};
      return b
    ◇φ: return Disj3({(s', φ) | s' ∈ suc_∃^R({s})}) ;
    □φ: return Conj3({(s', φ) | s' ∈ suc_∃^R({s})}) ;
    ←◇φ: return Disj3({(s', φ) | s' ∈ pre_∃^R({s})}) ;
    ←□φ: return Conj3({(s', φ) | s' ∈ pre_∃^R({s})}) ;
    else (* Ψ is a variable *)
      if BoundVar(Ψ, Φ) then
        if (s, D_Φ(x)) ∈ CallStack then return ⊥
        else return SimpleLocalCheck_{Φ,K}(s, D_Φ(x))
      else
        return Ψ ∈ L(s)
      end
  end
end
```

Fig. B.1. A partial local model checking procedure

generates a set of disjunctively connected recursions, it will return 1 if at least one branch returns 1, and it will return 0 if all branches return 0. We have already implemented some sort of *lazy evaluation* in the procedures Disj3 and Conj3, in that these procedures return as soon as they definitely know the correct function value.

The procedure is certainly correct, i.e., if it returns 1 for (s, Ψ), then $s \in [\![\Psi]\!]_{\mathcal{K}}$ holds, and if it returns 0 for (s, Ψ), then $s \notin [\![\Psi]\!]_{\mathcal{K}}$ holds. However, it may be the case that the procedure returns $\perp$, so that we know nothing. This can only happen when the given formula contains a fixpoint formula, but it may not happen in all of these cases (see Figures B.2 and B.3).

There are different kinds of pairs (s, Ψ), where the procedure returns a value without further recursive calls:

- The formula Ψ to be checked is a variable that is not bound in Φ. In this case, we have $(\mathcal{K}, s) \models \Psi$ iff $\Psi \in \mathcal{L}(s)$ and therefore return the latter.
- The formula Ψ to be checked is a negation $\neg\varphi$: as Φ is in negation normal form, it follows that φ is a variable that is furthermore not bound in Φ (since all occurrences of bound variables must be positive). As $(\mathcal{K}, s) \models \neg\varphi$ iff $\varphi \notin \mathcal{L}(s)$ holds, we return the latter.
- The formula Ψ to be checked is a modal future formula $\Diamond\varphi$ or $\Box\varphi$ and the state s has no successor states. In this case, we have $(\mathcal{K}, s) \not\models \Diamond\varphi$ and $(\mathcal{K}, s) \models \Box\varphi$, no matter what φ is. Note that this implicitly happens, since the procedures Disj3 or Conj3 are then called with the empty set.
- The formula Ψ to be checked is a modal past formula $\overleftarrow{\Diamond}\varphi$ or $\overleftarrow{\Box}\varphi$ and the state s has no predecessor states. This case is analogously handled as the previous one.
- The final case that leads to termination of our procedure is that a call with arguments (s, x) is processed and there is already a call to $(s, \mathfrak{D}_\Phi(x))$ in the *CallStack*.

In all cases, except for the last one, we can decide if $(\mathcal{K}, s) \models \Psi$ holds. The last case mentioned above is the source that generates the return value $\perp$. It may be the case that a previous recursive call will overwrite $\perp$ to 1 or 0, if it is a disjunctive/conjunctive branching when another branch returns 1 or 0, respectively. If this happens, we still obtain a decision, otherwise $\perp$ may propagate further to the top.

For example, consider the formula $\Phi :\equiv \mu x.a \vee \Box x$ and the structure given in the upper part of Figure B.2. Note that Φ holds in a state if and only if all (possibly finite) paths starting in s reach a state where a holds. Hence, Φ holds in the states $\{s_0, s_1, s_3\}$, that can be obtained by the Tarski-Knaster iteration: $Q_0 := \{\}$, $Q_1 := \{s_1, s_3\}$, and finally $Q_2 := \{s_0, s_1, s_3\} = Q_3$.

The lower part of Figure B.2 shows all possible recursive calls of our local model checking procedure (we have thereby neglected a lazy evaluation in the functions Disj3 and Conj3). The labeling $i : (s, \varphi) \vdash b$ of the vertices is thereby to be read as follows: the vertex represents the i-th call that is made with the arguments (s, φ) and returns the result b.

As can be seen, the entire structure is traversed, so that we do not benefit from locality in this example. Instead, all states are considered for the evaluation of Φ, in particular, the states s_0, s_1, s_2, s_3, and s_4, are evaluated in the vertices 0, 5, 10, 15, and 20, respectively.

The situation changes if we use lazy evaluation as implemented in Figure B.1. However, the implementation given in Figure B.1 is nondeterministic,

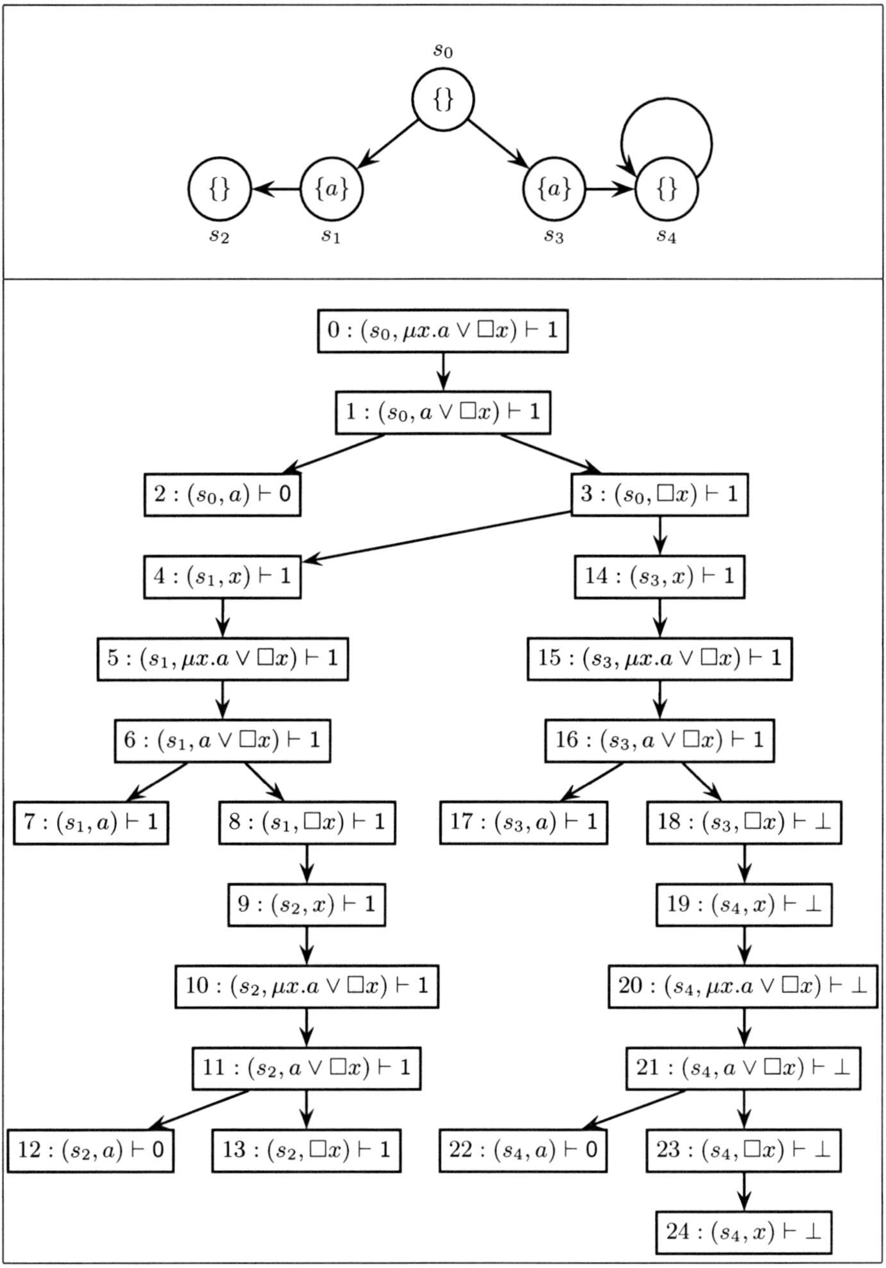

Fig. B.2. Example for local model checking

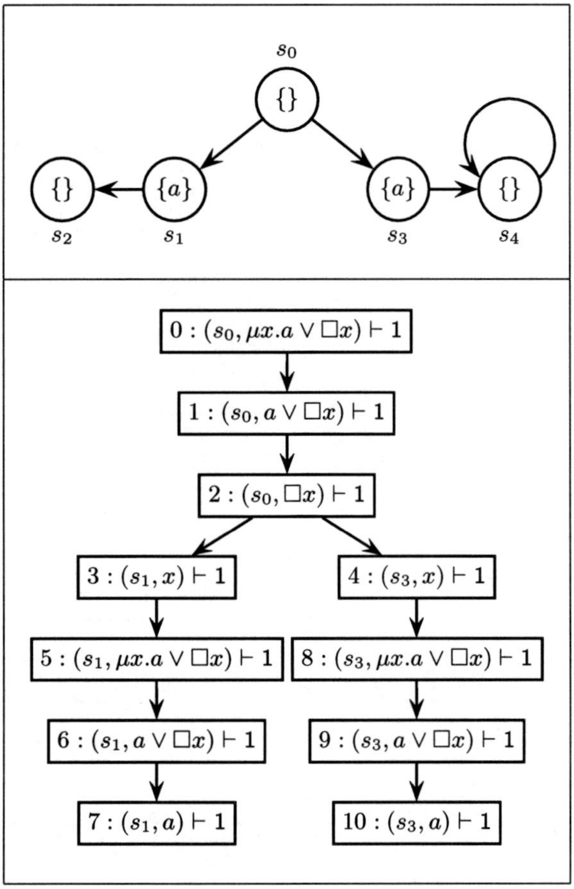

Fig. B.3. Example for local model checking with lazy evaluation

since in the functions Disj3 and Conj3, we iterate through a set that is not ordered. The ordering of these loops may, however, influence the runtime and the number of recursive steps. For example, we have listed in Figure B.3 only the recursive calls that are necessary in our lazy evaluation approach. This requires, however, to choose between the disjunctive branches in a clever way. In conjunctive branches, we do not have the choice, since all branches must evaluate to 1 to propagate this value to the root.

A short form of our procedure can be described by the rules given in Figure B.4. These rules are used in function SimpleLocalCheck to determine the recursive calls together with the combination type (conjunctive or disjunctive). Note that the regeneration rule (9) is only applied if the pair (s, x) is currently not in the open branch *CallStack*. The rules given in Figure B.4 do not, however, make use of lazy evaluation and will therefore construct proof

$$(1)\,\frac{s \vdash_\Phi \varphi \wedge \psi}{s \vdash_\Phi \varphi \quad s \vdash_\Phi \psi}\wedge \qquad (2)\,\frac{s \vdash_\Phi \varphi \vee \psi}{s \vdash_\Phi \varphi \quad s \vdash_\Phi \psi}\vee$$

$$(3)\,\frac{s \vdash_\Phi \Box\varphi}{s_1 \vdash_\Phi \varphi \;\ldots\; s_n \vdash_\Phi \varphi}\wedge \qquad (4)\,\frac{s \vdash_\Phi \Diamond\varphi}{s_1 \vdash_\Phi \varphi \;\ldots\; s_n \vdash_\Phi \varphi}\vee$$

$$(5)\,\frac{s \vdash_\Phi \overleftarrow{\Box}\varphi}{s_1' \vdash_\Phi \varphi \;\ldots\; s_n' \vdash_\Phi \varphi}\wedge \qquad (6)\,\frac{s \vdash_\Phi \overleftarrow{\Diamond}\varphi}{s_1' \vdash_\Phi \varphi \;\ldots\; s_n' \vdash_\Phi \varphi}\vee$$

$$(7)\,\frac{s \vdash_\Phi \mu x.\varphi}{s \vdash_\Phi \varphi} \qquad (8)\,\frac{s \vdash_\Phi \nu x.\varphi}{s \vdash_\Phi \varphi}$$

$$(9)\,\frac{s \vdash_\Phi x}{s \vdash_\Phi \mathfrak{D}_\Phi(x)}$$

In rules (3)-(6), it is assumed that $\{s_1, \ldots, s_n\} = \mathsf{suc}_\exists^{\mathcal{R}}(\{s\})$ and $\{s_1', \ldots, s_n'\} = \mathsf{pre}_\exists^{\mathcal{R}}(\{s\})$ holds.

Fig. B.4. Proof rules for local model checking of the μ-calculus used in Figure B.1

trees that are larger than necessary. We will refine these rules in the next section so that the related local model checking procedure benefits from lazy evaluation, when a clever search strategy is available.

The purpose of our procedure is only for illustrating certain effects. We will refine it in the next section to a complete local model checking procedure, and will thereby derive a *fundamental characterization of least and greatest fixpoint operators: roughly speaking, least fixpoints correspond to finite recursion, while greatest fixpoints are related to nonterminating recursion.* Having established that relationship, we will see how to derive a truth value in the case where a recursive call (s, Ψ) is repeated.

B.2 A Complete Local Model Checking Procedure

In this section, we will improve the model checking procedure of the previous section in two ways: first, we will define criteria to make the procedure complete, so that $\perp$ will never be returned. These criteria will give us a further fundamental insight into the semantics of the μ-calculus: In particular, we will see that *least fixpoints are related to finite recursion, while greatest fixpoints are related with infinite recursion.* Secondly, we will only choose one of the disjunctive branches that return 1 of a call, since that is enough to state that the return value of the root call is also 1. Actually, the procedures of Figure B.1 already worked in this manner. There are two reasons for this: first, the runtime of the model checking procedure is reduced, and secondly, our proofs of its soundness and completeness are simplified. The reason for the latter is that in the obtained proof trees, all branchings are of conjunctive type. Hence, we no longer have to consider complex Boolean combinations of the leaf vertices; instead, the *root vertex is now true if and only if all leaf vertices are true*.

Clearly, in a real implementation, the choice of a branch in a disjunctive branching should be made more carefully by a good strategy. However, we ignore such optimizations here, since we are only interested in a sound and complete model checking procedure. If we were to select in a disjunctive branching a branch that returns 0, no harm is done, since the procedure will then look for another one, until there are no more choices left. In this case, we have to return 0. Hence, bad choices will only increase the runtime, and will neither affect the correctness nor completeness of the procedure.

Recall that the call trees that we have listed in Figures B.2 and B.3 may alternatively be interpreted as proof trees: We have already mentioned that the implementation of our model checking procedure can be based on the proof rules given in Figure B.4. For this reason, complete call trees as given in Figure B.2 may be viewed as proof trees that are constructed by application of the rules of Figure B.4. Hence, the model checking procedure may also be viewed as a procedure that constructs a derivation with the mentioned proof rules.

As we now want to choose between disjunctive branches, the procedure that we will consider in this section has to use modified proof rules. If $(\mathcal{K}, s) \models \varphi$ holds, and the top-level operator of φ leads to a disjunctive branching, at least one of the disjunctive branches must be true. Hence, our proof system will remain complete if we only choose one of the disjunctive branches. The proof rules that we use in this section are therefore given in Figure B.5.

$$(1)\frac{s \vdash_\Phi \varphi \wedge \psi}{s \vdash_\Phi \varphi \quad s \vdash_\Phi \psi} \qquad (2)\frac{s \vdash_\Phi \varphi \vee \psi}{\mathsf{choose}(\{s \vdash_\Phi \varphi, s \vdash_\Phi \psi\})}$$

$$(3)\frac{s \vdash_\Phi \Box\varphi}{s_1 \vdash_\Phi \varphi \ \dots\ s_n \vdash_\Phi \varphi} \qquad (4)\frac{s \vdash_\Phi \Diamond\varphi}{\mathsf{choose}(\{s_1 \vdash_\Phi \varphi, \dots, s_n \vdash_\Phi \varphi\})}$$

$$(5)\frac{s \vdash_\Phi \overleftarrow{\Box}\varphi}{s_1' \vdash_\Phi \varphi \ \dots\ s_n' \vdash_\Phi \varphi} \qquad (6)\frac{s \vdash_\Phi \overleftarrow{\Diamond}\varphi}{\mathsf{choose}(\{s_1' \vdash_\Phi \varphi, \dots, s_n' \vdash_\Phi \varphi\})}$$

$$(7)\frac{s \vdash_\Phi \mu x.\varphi}{s \vdash_\Phi \varphi} \qquad (8)\frac{s \vdash_\Phi \nu x.\varphi}{s \vdash_\Phi \varphi}$$

$$(9)\frac{s \vdash_\Phi x}{s \vdash_\Phi \mathfrak{D}_\Phi(x)}$$

In rules (3)-(6), it is assumed that $\{s_1, \dots, s_n\} = \mathsf{suc}_\exists^{\mathcal{R}}(\{s\})$ and $\{s_1', \dots, s_n'\} = \mathsf{pre}_\exists^{\mathcal{R}}(\{s\})$ holds.

Fig. B.5. Proof rules for local model checking of the μ-calculus with a choice function

```
function Disj2(Branches)
  for (s, φ) ∈ Branches do
    b := LocalCheck_{Φ,K}(s, φ);
    if b = 1 then return 1 end
  end;
  return 0
end
```

```
function Conj2(Branches)
  for (s, φ) ∈ Branches do
    b := LocalCheck_{Φ,K}(s, φ);
    if b = 0 then return 0 end
  end;
  return 1
end
```

```
function LocalCheck_{Φ,K}(s, Ψ)
  case Ψ of
    ¬φ: return φ ∉ L(s) ;
    φ ∧ ψ: return Conj2({(s, φ), (s, ψ)}) ;
    φ ∨ ψ: return Disj2({(s, φ), (s, ψ)}) ;
    σx.φ:
      CallStack := {(s, Ψ)} ∪ CallStack;
      b := LocalCheck_{Φ,K}(s, φ);
      CallStack := CallStack \ {(s, Ψ)};
      return b
    ◇φ: return Disj2({(s', φ) | s' ∈ suc_∃^R({s})}) ;
    □φ: return Conj2({(s', φ) | s' ∈ suc_∃^R({s})}) ;
    ←◇ φ: return Disj2({(s', φ) | s' ∈ pre_∃^R({s})}) ;
    ←□ φ: return Conj2({(s', φ) | s' ∈ pre_∃^R({s})}) ;
    else (* Ψ is a variable *)
      if BoundVar(Ψ, Φ) then
        if (s, D_Φ(x)) ∈ CallStack then
          case D_Φ(x) of
            μx.φ : return 0
            νx.φ : return 1
          end
        else return LocalCheck_{Φ,K}(s, D_Φ(x))
      else
        return Ψ ∈ L(s)
      end
  end
end
```

Fig. B.6. A complete local model checking procedure

Figure B.6 shows the complete local model checking procedure that is obtained from these rules. Apart from the choice between disjunctive branches, there is another, more fundamental change: To make the procedure of Figure B.6 total, a change is made in the case where a call (s, x) is processed and $(s, \mathfrak{D}_\Phi(x))$ already appears in *CallStack*. In the procedure of the previous section, this was the source where $\perp$ has been returned. In the procedure of

Figure B.6, we check whether the fixpoint formula that leads to an infinite recursion is a least or greatest one. If it is a greatest fixpoint formula, we return 1, otherwise the procedure returns 0. Note that the procedure will therefore either return 1 or 0, so that the procedures Disj3 and Conj3 can also be simplified to Disj2 and Conj2, respectively.

Hence, the model checking procedure now implements the view that least fixpoints are related to finite recursion, while greatest fixpoints are related to infinite recursion. In the remainder of this section, we will prove why this view correctly implements the semantics of the μ-calculus.

As all branches in the proof trees are now conjunctive, it follows that a call $\mathsf{LocalCheck}_{\Phi,\mathcal{K}}(s,\varphi)$ returns 1 if and only if all leaf vertices of the generated proof tree are true. When the call returns 0, there is no choice left between disjunctive branches on the path that leads from the root vertex to the false leaf vertex. Moreover, every call to LocalCheck generates a proof tree with leaf vertices that are labeled as follows:

1. $i : (s, x)$ with $x \in V_\Sigma$ (not bound in Φ) generating return value $x \in \mathcal{L}(s)$
2. $i : (s, \neg x)$ with $x \in V_\Sigma$ generating return value $x \notin \mathcal{L}(s)$
3. $i : (s, \Box\varphi)$ where $\mathsf{suc}_\exists^{\mathcal{R}}(\{s\}) = \{\}$ generating return value 1
4. $i : (s, \overleftarrow{\Box}\varphi)$ where $\mathsf{pre}_\exists^{\mathcal{R}}(\{s\}) = \{\}$ generating return value 1
5. $i : (s, \Diamond\varphi)$ where $\mathsf{suc}_\exists^{\mathcal{R}}(\{s\}) = \{\}$ generating return value 0
6. $i : (s, \overleftarrow{\Diamond}\varphi)$ where $\mathsf{pre}_\exists^{\mathcal{R}}(\{s\}) = \{\}$ generating return value 0
7. $i : (s, x)$ with $\mathfrak{D}_\Phi(x) = \sigma x.\varphi$ and $(s, \mathfrak{D}_\Phi(x)) \in$ *CallStack* generating return value $\sigma = \nu$

It is obviously seen that the return values are correct in the first six cases. In the following, we call these cases trivial leaf vertices, and therefore concentrate on leaf vertices of the last kind. To prove the correctness in the latter case, we start with the following definition:

Definition B.1 (Fixpoint Approximation). *Given a fixpoint formula $\sigma x.\varphi$, we define its n-th approximation $\mathsf{apx}_n(\Phi)$ recursively as follows:*

$$\mathsf{apx}_0(\mu x.\varphi) := 0 \qquad\qquad \mathsf{apx}_0(\nu x.\varphi) := 1$$
$$\mathsf{apx}_{n+1}(\mu x.\varphi) := [\varphi]_x^{\mathsf{apx}_n(\mu x.\varphi)} \qquad\qquad \mathsf{apx}_{n+1}(\nu x.\varphi) := [\varphi]_x^{\mathsf{apx}_n(\nu x.\varphi)}$$

The intuition behind $\mathsf{apx}_i(\sigma x.\varphi)$ is that the set $[\![\mathsf{apx}_i(\sigma x.\varphi)]\!]_\mathcal{K}$ is obtained in the Tarski-Knaster iteration for computing $[\![\sigma x.\varphi]\!]_\mathcal{K}$ at step i. We already know that the fixpoint iteration is either monotonically increasing or decreasing. For this reason, $m < n$ implies $[\![\mathsf{apx}_m(\mu x.\varphi)]\!]_\mathcal{K} \subseteq [\![\mathsf{apx}_n(\mu x.\varphi)]\!]_\mathcal{K}$ and $[\![\mathsf{apx}_n(\nu x.\varphi)]\!]_\mathcal{K} \subseteq [\![\mathsf{apx}_m(\nu x.\varphi)]\!]_\mathcal{K}$. Moreover, we have the following result:

Lemma B.2 (Fixpoint Approximation). *For every state s of every Kripke structure $\mathcal{K}$ and all fixpoint formulas $\mu x.\varphi$ and $\nu x.\varphi$, the following holds:*

- *If $(\mathcal{K}, s) \models \mu x.\varphi$ holds, then there is a smallest $n \in \mathbb{N}$ with $s \in [\![\mathsf{apx}_n(\mu x.\varphi)]\!]_\mathcal{K}$.*
- *If $(\mathcal{K}, s) \not\models \nu x.\varphi$ holds, then there is a smallest $n \in \mathbb{N}$ with $s \notin [\![\mathsf{apx}_n(\nu x.\varphi)]\!]_\mathcal{K}$.*

The proof is obvious, since the sequence of states $[\![\mathsf{apx}_n(\sigma x.\varphi)]\!]_{\mathcal{K}}$ for $n \in \mathbb{N}$ is the Tarski-Knaster iteration. The next definition is related to the above one and will be used to define for every fixpoint formula a well-founded partial order on the states of a Kripke structure:

Definition B.3 (Rank of a State w.r.t. a Fixpoint Formula). *Given a Kripke structure $\mathcal{K}$, and a fixpoint formula $\sigma x.\varphi$, we define for every state s a number* $\mathsf{rank}(s, \sigma x.\varphi)$ *as follows:*

$$\mathsf{rank}(s, \mu x.\varphi) := \begin{cases} 0 : \textit{if } s \notin [\![\mu x.\varphi]\!]_{\mathcal{K}} \\ n : \textit{if } n \textit{ is the smallest number with } s \in [\![\mathsf{apx}_n(\mu x.\varphi)]\!]_{\mathcal{K}} \end{cases}$$
$$\mathsf{rank}(s, \nu x.\varphi) := \begin{cases} 0 : \textit{if } s \in [\![\nu x.\varphi]\!]_{\mathcal{K}} \\ n : \textit{if } n \textit{ is the smallest number with } s \notin [\![\mathsf{apx}_n(\nu x.\varphi)]\!]_{\mathcal{K}} \end{cases}$$

The above lemma is the essential key to prove the fact that least and greatest fixpoints correspond to finite and infinite recursions, respectively. To see that least fixpoints are related to finite recursion, note that for all states with $\mathsf{rank}(s, \mu x.\varphi) = 1$, the call $\mathsf{LocalCheck}_{\Phi,\mathcal{K}}(s, \mu x.\varphi)$ returns 1, since the call to $(s, \mu x.\varphi)$ immediately reduces to a call to (s, φ), and when finally a leaf (s, x) should be reached, then 0 is returned. The corresponding proof tree is therefore obviously isomorphic to the proof tree of $\mathsf{apx}_1(\mu x.\varphi)$, i.e., of $[\varphi]_x^{0}$. Hence, we come to the following result:

Lemma B.4 (Completeness of Procedure $\mathsf{LocalCheck}_{\Phi,\mathcal{K}}$). *Given a Kripke structure $\mathcal{K}$ and an arbitrary state s. Then, the following holds:*

- $\mathsf{LocalCheck}_{\Phi,\mathcal{K}}(s, \varphi) = 1$ *iff* $(\mathcal{K}, s) \models \varphi$ *for all formulas φ without fixpoints.*
- *For all formulas φ without fixpoints and all states s with $(\mathcal{K}, s) \models \mu x.\varphi$, we have* $\mathsf{LocalCheck}_{\Phi,\mathcal{K}}(s, \mu x.\varphi) = 1$.

Proof. The first proposition is easily proved by induction on the size of φ. Consider now a particular fixpoint formula $\mu x.\varphi$, where φ contains no further fixpoint operators. We must show that $\mathsf{LocalCheck}_{\Phi,\mathcal{K}}(s, \mu x.\varphi) = 1$ holds for all states s with $\mathsf{rank}(s, \mu x.\varphi) = r > 1$, i.e., the states that satisfy $\mu x.\varphi$. This is not very complicated: As s has rank r, it satisfies by definition the approximation $\mathsf{apx}_r(\mu x.\varphi)$. As this approximation contains no fixpoint operators, the first proposition of the lemma applies. Hence, $\mathsf{LocalCheck}_{\Phi,\mathcal{K}}(s, \mathsf{apx}_r(\mu x.\varphi))$ returns 1. It is now straightforward to convert the proof tree that is obtained from the call $(s, \mathsf{apx}_r(\mu x.\varphi))$ to a corresponding one for the call to $(s, \mu x.\varphi)$.

We recursively construct proof trees for these states along their rank, starting with states of $\mathsf{rank}(s, \mu x.\varphi) = 1$. By definition of the rank, these states are those that satisfy $\mathsf{apx}_1(\mu x.\varphi)$, i.e., $[\varphi]_x^{0}$. It is easily seen that the proof trees for $(s, [\varphi]_x^{0})$ and $(s, \mu x.\varphi)$ are isomorphic (apart from the additional root vertex in the latter call). In fact, all vertices are the same, except that in the former call there may be calls to $(s, 0)$[1], while in the latter the same call is

[1] We assume that 0 is an abbreviation of $a \wedge \neg a$ for some variable a that is not bound. To make the isomorphism between the proof trees more direct, we should rather add cases for Boolean constants 1 and 0 in the procedure LocalCheck.

made for (s, x). As $(s, \mathfrak{D}_\Phi(x))$ already appears in *CallStack* in the latter call, $\mathsf{LocalCheck}_{\Phi,\mathcal{K}}$ will return 0 in both cases. As $\mathsf{apx}_1(\mu x.\varphi)$ contains no fixpoint operators, the call to $(s, \mathsf{apx}_1(\mu x.\varphi))$ returns 1 by the first proposition above, and therefore, also the call to $(s, \mu x.\varphi)$ returns 1. For this reason, the potential calls to $(s, 0)$ or (s, x) will not be leaf vertices, and are instead replaced with other choices of a disjunctive branching.

Consider now a state s with $\mathsf{rank}(s, \mu x.\varphi) = r > 1$. Clearly, s satisfies $\mathsf{apx}_r(\mu x.\varphi)$, which is the formula $[\varphi]_x^{\mathsf{apx}_{r-1}(\mu x.\varphi)}$. Again, this formula contains no fixpoint operators, and therefore $\mathsf{LocalCheck}_{\Phi,\mathcal{K}}(s, [\varphi]_x^{\mathsf{apx}_{r-1}(\mu x.\varphi)})$ returns 1. We now convert this proof tree into a proof tree for $\mathsf{LocalCheck}_{\Phi,\mathcal{K}}(s, \mu x.\varphi)$: The proof tree generated by $\mathsf{LocalCheck}_{\Phi,\mathcal{K}}(s, [\varphi]_x^{\mathsf{apx}_{r-1}(\mu x.\varphi)})$ consists of an upper part that is a proof tree for $\mathsf{LocalCheck}_{\Phi,\mathcal{K}}(s, \varphi)$. There are leaf vertices of this upper part that are labeled with a recursive call of the form (s', x). Clearly, in these cases, we have $\mathsf{rank}(s', \mu x.\varphi) < r$, so that we are already able to construct a proof tree for the calls $(s', \mu x.\varphi)$. Combining these trees, we obtain a successful proof tree for $(s, \mu x.\varphi)$. □

Hence, we see that a successful call $\mathsf{LocalCheck}_{\Phi,\mathcal{K}}(s, \mu x.\varphi)$ *may only generate recursive calls* $(s', \mu x.\varphi)$ *with states* s' *that have a smaller rank than* s*. This is why it must be possible to explain the validity of least fixpoint formulas in finitely many steps (since there is a minimal rank). The proof trees are therefore really trees, i.e., there are no leaf vertices of the form* (s, x) *where* $(s, \mathfrak{D}_\Phi(x))$ *already belongs to the* CallStack. A counterpart to the above lemma is the following theorem:

Theorem B.5 (Correctness of Procedure $\mathsf{LocalCheck}_{\Phi,\mathcal{K}}$**).** *Given a* μ*-calculus formula* Φ *in guarded negation normal form, a structure* $\mathcal{K}$*, and a state* s *of* $\mathcal{K}$*. If the procedure call* $\mathsf{LocalCheck}_{\Phi,\mathcal{K}}(s, \Phi)$ *of the procedure* $\mathsf{LocalCheck}_{\Phi,\mathcal{K}}$ *given in Figure B.6 returns* 1*, then* $(\mathcal{K}, s) \models \Phi$ *holds.*

Proof. As all branches in the proof trees are conjunctive, it follows that a call $\mathsf{LocalCheck}_{\Phi,\mathcal{K}}(s, \varphi)$ returns 1 if and only if all leaf vertices of the generated proof tree are true. Moreover, every leaf vertex is then of one of the forms below:

1. $i : (s, x)$ with $x \in V_\Sigma$ (not bound in Φ) with $x \in \mathcal{L}(s)$
2. $i : (s, \neg x)$ with $x \in V_\Sigma$ with $x \notin \mathcal{L}(s)$
3. $i : (s, \Box\varphi)$ with $\mathsf{suc}_\exists^{\mathcal{R}}(\{s\}) = \{\}$
4. $i : (s, \overleftarrow{\Box}\varphi)$ with $\mathsf{pre}_\exists^{\mathcal{R}}(\{s\}) = \{\}$
5. $i : (s, x)$ with $\mathfrak{D}_\Phi(x) = \nu x.\varphi$ and $(s, \mathfrak{D}_\Phi(x)) \in$ *CallStack*

We have to prove that these leaf vertices are true. If we succeed with that proof, it follows that also the root vertex of our proof tree is true.

The only interesting case is the last one. Hence, consider a leaf vertex v_1 labeled with $i : (s, x)$ with $\mathfrak{D}_\Phi(x) = \nu x.\varphi$ and $(s, \mathfrak{D}_\Phi(x)) \in$ *CallStack*. Hence, there is another vertex v_0 labeled with $j : (s, \nu x.\varphi)$ on the branch that leads to v_1.

It follows that s belongs to a fixpoint of the state transformer $f(Q) := [\![\varphi]\!]_{\mathcal{K}_x^Q}$. In particular, it belongs to the greatest fixpoint and therefore to the set $[\![\nu x.\varphi]\!]_{\mathcal{K}}$. But then, the leaf vertex is true, and so is the root vertex for which the call is made.

A more detailed proof could be obtained by showing that s belongs to all approximations $\mathsf{apx}_n(\nu x.\varphi)$, and hence, it belongs to $[\![\nu x.\varphi]\!]_{\mathcal{K}}$. This can be proved by the observation that the proof trees for $\mathsf{apx}_n(\nu x.\varphi)$ are obtained by appending the proof tree rooted in v_0 to v_1 and so on. □

The above theorem shows that greatest fixpoints allow us to loop infinitely often, in the evaluation made by $\mathsf{LocalCheck}_{\Phi,\mathcal{K}}$. This is forbidden for least fixpoint formulas. We now combine the two previous results to obtain the following final result:

Theorem B.6 (Correctness of Procedure $\mathsf{LocalCheck}_{\Phi,\mathcal{K}}$). *Given a μ-calculus formula Φ in guarded negation normal form, a structure $\mathcal{K}$, and a state s of $\mathcal{K}$. The procedure call $\mathsf{LocalCheck}_{\Phi,\mathcal{K}}(s,\Phi)$ of the procedure $\mathsf{LocalCheck}_{\Phi,\mathcal{K}}$ given in Figure B.6 returns 1 if and only if $(\mathcal{K},s)\models\Phi$ holds (and returns 0 if and only if $(\mathcal{K},s)\not\models\Phi$ holds).*

Proof. One implication has already been proved by the previous theorem. The remaining implication is proved by the help of Lemma B.4. To this end, we first remark that due to the previous theorem, Lemma B.4 can be strengthened as follows:

- For all formulas φ without fixpoints and all states s, we have $(\mathcal{K},s)\models \mu x.\varphi$ if and only if $\mathsf{LocalCheck}_{\Phi,\mathcal{K}}(s,\mu x.\varphi)=1$.
- For all formulas φ without fixpoints and all states s, we have $(\mathcal{K},s)\models \nu x.\varphi$ if and only if $\mathsf{LocalCheck}_{\Phi,\mathcal{K}}(s,\nu x.\varphi)=1$.

The remaining implication is proved by induction on the nesting depth of the fixpoint formulas. The induction base, where formulas without fixpoint operators are considered directly follows from Lemma B.4. The only interesting cases in the induction steps are the fixpoint formulas. These cases can again be reduced to the above statements, when we replace successful calls $(s',\sigma y.\psi)$ with (s',y), and unsuccessful calls $(s',\sigma y.\psi)$ with $(s',\neg y)$ (thus labeling the Kripke structure with variables y representing the validity of subsequent fixpoint formulas). □

Hence, we see that procedure $\mathsf{LocalCheck}$ is correct, and therefore that the evaluation of a least fixpoint formula $\mu x.\varphi$ in a state s must not refer to itself. Instead, it may only recursively call evaluations of $\mu x.\varphi$ in states with a smaller rank, so that the evaluation terminates after finitely many steps. In contrast, the evaluation of a greatest fixpoint formula $\nu x.\varphi$ in a state s may refer to itself. Hence, greatest fixpoints implement infinite recursion.

B.3 Satisfiability of μ-Calculus Formulas

In the previous section, we have seen how a local model checking procedure is obtained by following proof rules that reflect the semantics of the logical operators. We have, furthermore, discussed that this model checking procedure may also be viewed as the construction of a derivation for the proof goal $(\mathcal{K}, s) \models \Phi$ in the calculus that is given by the rules of Figure B.4 and B.5. Hence, it is natural to ask whether we could use the same rules to prove the validity of μ-calculus formulas, i.e., the satisfaction in all structures. In this section, we therefore consider solutions to the validity and the equivalent satisfiability problem: *Given a μ-calculus formula Φ, we ask whether there is a Kripke structure $\mathcal{K}$ and a state s such that $(\mathcal{K}, s) \models \Phi$ holds.* To reduce the validity problem to the satisfiability problem, simply observe that $\neg\Phi$ is unsatisfiable iff Φ is valid.

The rules that we considered so far reduced proof goals $s \vdash_\Phi \varphi$, which mean that $(\mathcal{K}, s) \models \varphi$ is to be proved, to other proof goals of this form. For checking the satisfiability of μ-calculus formulas, there is no longer a Kripke structure available, so that we can not apply the rules in the same manner. Nevertheless, we could start with the construction of a proof tree with an imaginary state s_0, and try to construct a Kripke structure while constructing a proof tree. Our aim is to construct the Kripke structure in such a manner that the proof tree is successful.

Hence, if we reach a vertex labeled with $s \vdash_\Phi x$ where the variable x is not bound in Φ, then we have found the restriction $x \in \mathcal{L}(s)$ for our potential model. If we obtain a vertex labeled with $s \vdash_\Phi \neg x$ with a variable x, then we have found the restriction $x \notin \mathcal{L}(s)$. Clearly, we can not satisfy both restrictions for the same state s. So, if both should appear, we must select another branch in a disjunctive branching vertex that leads to one of these two contradictory leaf vertices. If this is not possible, then the formula is unsatisfiable, otherwise we can try another disjunctive choice.

Proof goals of the form $s \vdash_\Phi x$ and $s \vdash_\Phi \neg x$ assure only the propositional consistency in a state by imposing restrictions on the label $\mathcal{L}(s)$. Additionally, we must construct the transition relation of the Kripke structure by satisfying the subgoals that are generated by the modal rules. In the local model checking procedure, we removed the modal operator and set up new proof goals for the predecessor or successor states. In our satisfiability procedure, we can immediately stop the construction when formulas of type $\Box\varphi$ or $\overleftarrow{\Box}\varphi$ are encountered. The restriction for the transition relation is then that the considered state has no successors and predecessors, respectively. However, if we already constructed predecessor or successor vertices of s_0, we must set up the new proof goals for these states. The same must be done for the existential modal operators $\Diamond\varphi$ and $\overleftarrow{\Diamond}\varphi$. The entire procedure may declare a branch as closed if it ends in a vertex labeled with proof goals of one of the types $s \vdash_\Phi x$ (regardless of whether x is bound or not), $s \vdash_\Phi \neg x$, $s \vdash_\Phi \Box\varphi$, or

$s \vdash_\Phi \overleftarrow{\Box}\varphi$. At the end, we have to check if we can choose between the disjunctive branches such that we can construct a Kripke structure satisfying all the imposed constraints of these branches.

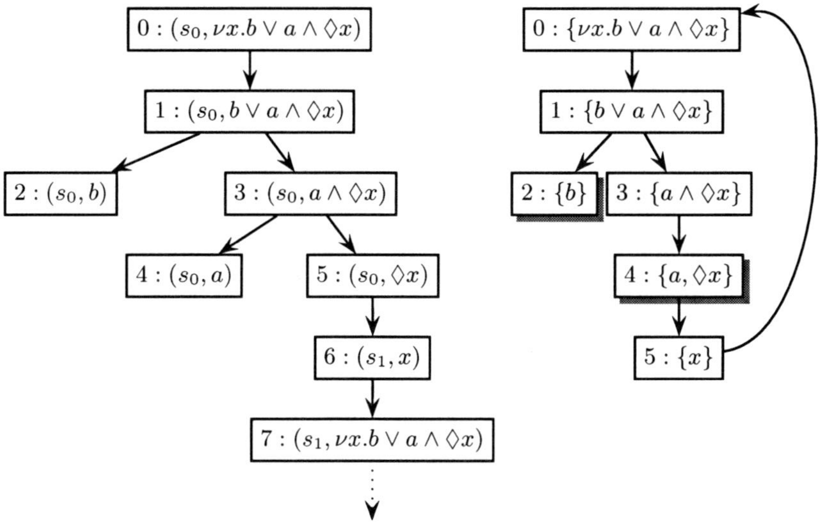

Fig. B.7. From local model checking to satisfiability checking

For example, we show how to construct a model for the formula $\nu x.b \vee a \wedge \Diamond x$. The left-hand side of Figure B.7 shows the initial part of a proof tree for this formula and an imaginary Kripke structure by applying the proof rules of Figure B.4 (without lazy evaluation). Hence, we have branchings of conjunctive and disjunctive types. We prefer these rules for the discussion of satisfiability, since it is easier to argue about different choices between the disjunctive branches when all of them are visible.

As the branching in vertex 1 is a disjunctive one, it is sufficient that only one of the outgoing branches is true. Hence, it is sufficient to impose the restriction that $b \in \mathcal{L}(s_0)$ holds. The simplest model is therefore the structure that has only state s_0, no transitions, and a labeling such that s_0 is labeled with $\{b\}$ (note that there is no restriction for the variable a, so we can determine this arbitrarily).

We now modify the example by setting $b = 0$. In this case, it is no longer possible to satisfy vertex 2, so that we have to proceed to the next disjunctive branch starting in vertex 3. Vertex 4 generates the restriction that s_0 must be labeled with a, and vertex 5 adds the restriction that s_0 must have a successor state that satisfies x. Vertex 6 introduces such a successor state s_1, and vertex 7 unwinds x according to its definition $\mathfrak{D}_\Phi(x)$. Recall that in vertex 6, the local model checking procedure would check whether there is already a vertex labeled with $(s_1, \mathfrak{D}_\Phi(x))$ on the current branch. As we are free to choose the successor state s_1, we identify s_1 with s_0 to find $(s_1, \mathfrak{D}_\Phi(x))$ on the current branch. Hence, the branch is successfully closed, and we have constructed the following Kripke structure: it has only state s_0 that is labeled with $\{a\}$ (again, we can arbitrarily choose the label for b), and the transition relation has the only transition (s_0, s_0).

Consider now the least fixpoint formula $\mu x.b \vee a \wedge \Diamond x$. The proof tree construction is essentially the same as for the greatest fixpoint, hence, we can consider again the left-hand side of Figure B.7. As in the previous example, we find a model by choosing the left branch to vertex 2 in vertex 1, and obtain the same model as above. The situation changes in the special case where $b = \mathtt{0}$ holds. Again, we have to proceed to the other branch of vertex 1 that starts in vertex 3. However, as we now have a least fixpoint formula, we can not simply stop the construction by identifying $s_1 = s_0$ as this would not make the branch successful. Therefore, there is no way to stop the proof tree construction, and hence, there is no successful (finite) proof tree for this formula. We conclude that the formula is not satisfiable. Indeed, we can easily prove by the Tarski-Knaster fixpoint iteration that $[\![\mu x.a \wedge \Diamond x]\!]_{\mathcal{K}} = \{\}$ holds, which means that no state of any structure satisfies this formula.

For this reason, we conclude that the rules we used for local model checking are also useful for reasoning about the satisfiability of μ-calculus formulas. However, an implementation of the satisfiability checking procedure as described informally above would be quite difficult. The problem is that restrictions on the label function and the successors of a state are set up in different branches and may be extended or reduced during the further construction when another disjunctive branch is chosen. Hence, the procedure must work with data structures that allow it to backtrack to previous stages. Moreover, it is difficult to make the procedure complete. The previous example already showed that it is not easily seen when the procedure can terminate. We will therefore not work out this procedure in the following, and follow other approaches that are better to implement.

In general, all known decision procedures for the μ-calculus work in two steps for deciding the satisfiability of a μ-calculus formula Φ [167, 263, 430, 478, 496, 509, 515]: First, they compute the set of so-called *premodels* of Φ, which are Kripke structures with a relaxed notion of the semantics of Φ (explained below). The second step will then check if there is a premodel that is really a model by using the correct semantics of Φ. The modification of the semantics of Φ in a premodel is thereby that the extremality of the fixpoint subformulas is ignored. Hence, a subformula $\sigma x.\varphi$ is viewed as an arbitrary fixpoint, not necessarily the least or greatest one. The second step must therefore check if the extremalities of the fixpoint subformulas can be respected.

The construction of the premodels of Φ is not very difficult, however, it requires exponential time. A traditional approach to construct the models of a formula is to compute its *semantic tableau* [194, 410, 424, 464]: A tableau is thereby a graph that is obtained by application of rules that reflect the semantics of the formula. These rules are applied by traversing the syntax tree of the formula in a top-down manner. In particular, the tableau rules for μ-calculus formulas are obtained by answering the question: *What must hold in a state s to satisfy a formula Φ?* It turns out that ignoring the extremality of fixpoint operators allows us to give quite simple answers to that question.

The tableau rules that we will develop now aim at collecting all restrictions for a state s that must be imposed to satisfy a formula Φ. This starting point is very similar to the proof rules of the local model checking procedure. The difference is that we no longer want to spread the restrictions for a state along different branches, and therefore eliminate the conjunctive branchings for a state.

$$(1)\frac{s \vdash_\Phi \{\varphi \wedge \psi\} \cup \Gamma}{s \vdash_\Phi \{\varphi, \psi\} \cup \Gamma} \qquad (2)\frac{s \vdash_\Phi \{\varphi \vee \psi\} \cup \Gamma}{s \vdash_\Phi \{\varphi\} \cup \Gamma \quad s \vdash_\Phi \{\psi\} \cup \Gamma}$$

$$(3)\frac{s \vdash_\Phi \{\mu x.\varphi\} \cup \Gamma}{s \vdash_\Phi \{\varphi\} \cup \Gamma} \qquad (4)\frac{s \vdash_\Phi \{\nu x.\varphi\} \cup \Gamma}{s \vdash_\Phi \{\varphi\} \cup \Gamma}$$

$$(5)\frac{s \vdash_\Phi \{x\} \cup \Gamma}{s \vdash_\Phi \{\mathfrak{D}_\Phi(x)\} \cup \Gamma}$$

Fig. B.8. Local model checking rules with only disjunctive branching

For this reason, we change the proof goals as follows: the new proof goals consider a set of formulas, and are therefore of the form $s \vdash_\Phi \Gamma$, where Γ is a finite set of formulas. Such a proof goal has the meaning that the conjunction of the formulas in Γ has to be satisfied in state s (as usual, empty conjunction and disjunction are defined as 1 and 0). It is easy to prove that the rules of Figure B.4 can now be rephrased as shown in Figure B.8, where only disjunctions lead to a branching.

Unfortunately, it is not straightforward to formulate modal rules in the style of Figure B.8. We therefore restrict the following considerations to the future fragment to simplify our constructions. In fact, the full μ-calculus with backward modalities adds a further difficulty for satisfiability checking: In contrast to the future fragment, the full μ-calculus does not have the finite model property [476, 496].

In this book, we use *finite Kripke structures* as models for the semantics of the μ-calculus. Hence, the question whether a μ-calculus formula has an infinite model is not well-posed. However, if we consider Kripke structures with infinitely many states, it is reasonable to ask whether this is necessary for satisfiability checking. It turns out that for the full μ-calculus, there are formulas that can only be satisfied in Kripke structures with infinitely many states, but for the fragment without past modalities $\overleftarrow{\Diamond}$ and $\overleftarrow{\Box}$, this is not true:

satisfiable formulas of this fragment always have a finite model, which is called the finite model property.

As an example, Streett's formula [476] $(\nu x.\Diamond x) \wedge \nu y.(\mu z.\overleftarrow{\Box} z) \wedge \Box y$ can only be satisfied in infinite models (see Section 3.8.3): recall that $\nu x.\Diamond x$ holds in a state iff it has at least one infinite path, hence, its negation $\mu z.\Box z$ holds in a state iff it has only finite paths, and therefore $\mu z.\overleftarrow{\Box} z$ holds in a state iff one can go only finitely often backwards from this state. Moreover, $\nu y.\varphi \wedge \Box y$ holds in a state iff all states that can be reached on infinite paths from this state satisfy φ. Hence, $\nu y.(\mu z.\overleftarrow{\Box} z) \wedge \Box y$ holds in a state iff all states that are reachable from this state allow one to go only finitely often backwards. This is only possible if all states on the path are pairwise different, since otherwise the path must have a cycle, which would allow us to go infinitely often backwards. Hence, $\nu y.(\mu z.\overleftarrow{\Box} z) \wedge \Box y$ can only be satisfied on states where all outgoing paths consist of pairwise different states. If we additionally specify that there is an infinite path $\nu x.\Diamond x$, then the only possibility to satisfy this is to use an infinite path without cycles, which must therefore consist of infinitely many different states.

Theorem B.7 (Finite Model Property). *The full μ-calculus (with past modalities) does not have the finite model property, i.e., there are formulas that can only be satisfied in Kripke structures with infinitely many states. However, the fragment without past modalities has the finite model property: every satisfiable formula of this fragment has a finite model.*

By the above example, we have already shown that the full μ-calculus does not have the finite model property. Nevertheless, it has the *tree model property* [496], which means that every model can be represented as an infinite tree where every vertex has only finitely many children (at most $O(|\Phi|)$). The finite model property for the future fragment follows from the remaining theorems of this section. We will even see that this fragment has the *small model property*, that additionally asserts that the size of the finite model can be bounded in terms of the size of the considered formula. The complexity and decidability of the full μ-calculus has been shown by Vardi in [430, 496] using two-way automata, as already used by Streett [476] in the proof of the satisfiability of PDL with looping and converse operators.

We now turn back to the construction of modal rules to complete the set of rules given in Figure B.8. However, even with the restriction to the future fragment, there are some problems to construct modal rules: if we switch from a state to one of its successor states, we have to modify *all* formulas in Γ. For this reason, we have to defer these rules to a point where Γ contains only modal formulas, variables, or negated variables. Hence, consider a proof goal of the form $s \vdash_\Phi \{\Diamond\varphi_1, \ldots, \Diamond\varphi_m, \Box\psi_1, \ldots, \Box\psi_n, \ell_1, \ldots, \ell_k\})$ where the ℓ_is are either variables or negated variables. In the first case, assume that $m > 0$, i.e., there is at least one $\Diamond$-formula. Then, s must have successors, and we have to fulfill the following requirements:

- every successor state $s' \in \mathsf{suc}_\exists^{\mathcal{R}}(\{s\})$ satisfies $\bigwedge_{j=1}^{n} \psi_j$
- for every φ_i there is at least one state $s_i \in \mathsf{suc}_\exists^{\mathcal{R}}(\{s\})$ that satisfies φ_i
- s must satisfy $\bigwedge_{i=1}^{k} \ell_i$

The second case, where $m = 0$ holds, is simpler: This goal can be satisfied if s has no successors at all and is labeled such that $\bigwedge_{i=1}^{k} \ell_i$ holds. However, if s has successors then these states must all satisfy $\bigwedge_{j=1}^{n} \psi_j$.

Hence, we end up with some sort of combined conjunctive and disjunctive branching, and we must, moreover, relate the successor states with subformulas φ_i in the modal rule. As this results in a quite complex combinatorial problem, we still prefer the rules of the previous section for local model checking. For satisfiability checking, we can simplify the above requirements, since we have some freedom for the construction of successor states: First, we may or may not give a state successor states to satisfy a formula, and secondly, we can limit the number of successor states to the number of relevant subgoals that must be satisfied. For this reason, we use the rules given in Figure B.9 to construct semantic tableaux.

$$(1)\ \frac{\{\varphi \wedge \psi\} \cup \Gamma}{\{\varphi, \psi\} \cup \Gamma} \qquad (2)\ \frac{\{\varphi \vee \psi\} \cup \Gamma}{\{\varphi\} \cup \Gamma \quad \{\psi\} \cup \Gamma}$$

$$(3)\ \frac{\{\mu x.\varphi\} \cup \Gamma}{\{\varphi\} \cup \Gamma} \qquad (4)\ \frac{\{\nu x.\varphi\} \cup \Gamma}{\{\varphi\} \cup \Gamma}$$

$$(5)\ \frac{\{x\} \cup \Gamma}{\{\mathfrak{D}_\Phi(x)\} \cup \Gamma}$$

$$(6)\ \frac{\{\Diamond\varphi_1, \ldots, \Diamond\varphi_m, \Box\psi_1, \ldots, \Box\psi_n, \ell_1, \ldots, \ell_k\}}{\{\varphi_1, \psi_1, \ldots, \psi_n\} \ldots \{\varphi_m, \psi_1, \ldots, \psi_n\}}\ m > 0$$

$$(6')\ \frac{\{\Box\psi_1, \ldots, \Box\psi_n, \ell_1, \ldots, \ell_k\}}{\{\}}$$

Fig. B.9. Rules for tableau construction

In these rules, we no longer mention the considered state. Instead, we identify the states with the set of formulas that must be satisfied on them. We will see that this is sufficient, and this insight essentially proves the small model property. The modal rules (6) and (6′) are responsible for the consistency with the successor states. These rules have been simplified for satisfiability checking. Note, however, that these simplifications are not valid for (local) model checking. In model checking, we must consider the successor states of a state when modal rules are applied. However, for satisfiability checking, we *construct* the successor states by need. To be more precise, the reader might have expected the following rules instead of the modal rules of Figure B.9, where the branching in rule (6′) is disjunctive and the branching in rule (6) is still conjunctive:

$$(6)\frac{\{\Diamond\varphi_1,\ldots,\Diamond\varphi_m,\Box\psi_1,\ldots,\Box\psi_n,\ell_1,\ldots,\ell_k\}}{\{\varphi_1,\psi_1,\ldots,\psi_n\}\ldots\{\varphi_m,\psi_1,\ldots,\psi_n\}\ \ \{\psi_1,\ldots,\psi_n\}}\, m>0$$

$$(6')\frac{\{\Box\psi_1,\ldots,\Box\psi_n,\ell_1,\ldots,\ell_k\}}{\{\}\ \ \{\psi_1,\ldots,\psi_n\}}$$

It can be easily seen that we can do without the additional subgoal $\{\psi_1, \ldots,\psi_n\}$ in both rules for satisfiability checking. This subgoal only asserts that all successor states must satisfy the formulas ψ_i, but only introducing successor states for the subgoals $\{\varphi_i,\psi_1,\ldots,\psi_n\}$ makes this a trivial property. Furthermore, we can prune every Kripke structure by deleting some successor states, and only retaining enough successor states to satisfy the subgoals that are generated by the modal rules (see also [159]).

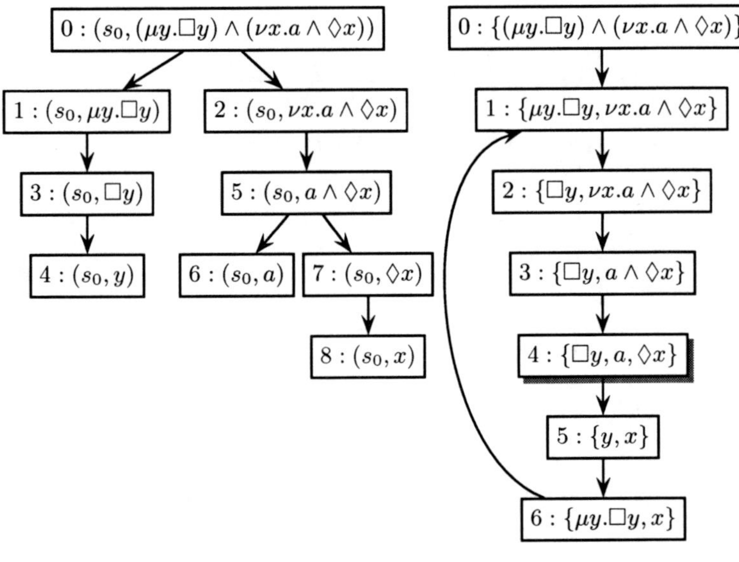

Fig. B.10. From local model checking to satisfiability checking

The tableau rules given in Figure B.9 can be used to construct tableaux, which are graphs whose vertices are labeled with sets of formulas. As examples, the right-hand sides of Figures B.7 and B.10 show the corresponding tableaux that we obtain by the rules of Figure B.9. Figure B.10 shows that conjunctive branches are collected in one branch of the tableau. Figure B.7 shows that disjunctive branchings are retained.

We have to explain how these tableaux are to be read and how we can use them to decide the satisfiability of a μ-calculus formula. We will see that *tableaux encode all premodels* of the considered formula. To this end, we have to formalize the notion of premodels, which first requires the definition of the so-called *Fischer-Ladner closure* $\mathsf{FL}(\Phi)$ of a formula Φ [192].

```
function FL_F(Φ)
  if Φ ∈ F then return F;
  F1 := F ∪ {Φ};
  case Φ of
    is_var(Φ) : return F1;
    ¬φ        : return F1;
    φ ∧ ψ     : F2 := FL_F1(φ); return FL_F2(ψ);
    φ ∨ ψ     : F2 := FL_F1(φ); return FL_F2(ψ);
    ◇φ        : return FL_F1(φ);
    □φ        : return FL_F1(φ);
    μx.φ      : return FL_F1([φ]_x^{μx.φ});
    νx.φ      : return FL_F1([φ]_x^{νx.φ});
  end
end

function FL(Φ)
  return FL_{}(NNF(Φ));
end
```

Fig. B.11. Algorithm for computing the Fischer-Ladner closure

Intuitively, $\mathsf{FL}(\Phi)$ is the set of all subformulas of Φ, where fixpoint formulas $\sigma x.\varphi$ are additionally unwound once. Assigning successively truth values to all formulas of $\mathsf{FL}(\Phi)$ will finally allow us to derive the truth value of Φ in a premodel. The formal definition of $\mathsf{FL}(\Phi)$ is given by the algorithm of Figure B.11. The algorithm terminates since it enriches the function calls $\mathsf{FL}_F(\Phi)$ with the so-far computed set of subformulas F. If $\Phi \in F$ holds, then the algorithm terminates by returning F as the result. It is easily seen that the cardinality of $\mathsf{FL}(\Phi)$ is of order $O(|\Phi|)$, and hence $\mathsf{FL}(\Phi)$ can be efficiently computed. Some authors also include the negations of the subformulas, which would double the size, but would still keep it linear in $|\Phi|$. For the following, it would be no problem to include the negations, but this is simply not necessary.

The next definition introduces the notion of *premodels*. We have explained by the semantics of the μ-calculus, when a state of Kripke structure satisfies a μ-calculus formula. The tableau construction follows the semantics, but does not respect the extremality of the fixpoints. Instead, the rules used for fixpoint formulas just guarantee that the states that satisfy these formulas belong to fixpoints of the related state transformer. This leads to a modified notion of truth that is captured by premodels:

Definition B.8 (Premodel). *Given a μ-calculus formula Φ and a Kripke structure $\mathcal{K} = (\mathcal{I}, \mathcal{S}, \mathcal{R}, \mathcal{L})$ over the variables V_Σ. $\mathcal{K}_\lambda = (\mathcal{I}, \mathcal{S}, \mathcal{R}, \mathcal{L}, \lambda)$ is a premodel of Φ in a state $s_0 \in \mathcal{S}$ iff the mapping $\lambda : \mathcal{S} \to 2^{\mathsf{FL}(\Phi)}$ fulfills the following constraints for all $s \in \mathcal{S}$:*

- $\Phi \in \lambda(s_0)$
- $\varphi \in \lambda(s)$ *implies* $\neg\varphi \notin \lambda(s)$
- $x \in \lambda(s)$ *implies* $x \in \mathcal{L}(s)$ *for every* $x \in V_\Sigma$ *(not bound in Φ)*
- $\neg x \in \lambda(s)$ *implies* $x \notin \mathcal{L}(s)$ *for every* $x \in V_\Sigma$
- $\varphi \wedge \psi \in \lambda(s)$ *implies* $\{\varphi, \psi\} \subseteq \lambda(s)$
- $\varphi \vee \psi \in \lambda(s)$ *implies* $\varphi \in \lambda(s)$ *or* $\psi \in \lambda(s)$
- $\Diamond\varphi \in \lambda(s)$ *implies that there is a successor* $s' \in \mathsf{suc}_\exists^{\mathcal{R}}(\{s\})$ *such that* $\varphi \in \lambda(s')$
- $\Box\varphi \in \lambda(s)$ *implies that for all successors* $s' \in \mathsf{suc}_\exists^{\mathcal{R}}(\{s\})$, *we have* $\varphi \in \lambda(s')$
- $\mu x.\varphi \in \lambda(s)$ *implies that* $\varphi \in \lambda(s)$
- $\nu x.\varphi \in \lambda(s)$ *implies that* $\varphi \in \lambda(s)$

Starting with the condition $\Phi \in \lambda(s)$, the above closure requirements on $\lambda(s)$ determine a labeling of the Kripke structure by following the syntax tree of Φ in a top-down manner. Similar to the tableau rules, these rules follow the semantics of the μ-calculus with the exception that the extremality of the fixpoints is ignored. Starting with a formula $\Phi \in \lambda(s)$, we are forced to add subformulas of Φ, which must be proved in this state. There are only two cases that give us a choice for $\lambda(s)$: first, we can select either φ or ψ when we have $\varphi \vee \psi \in \lambda(s)$, and secondly, we can choose a successor state s' to prove that $\Diamond\varphi \in \lambda(s)$ is satisfied.

It is easily seen that every Kripke structure $\mathcal{K}$ with a state s that satisfies Φ determines a premodel of Φ in state s: We simply define $\lambda(s) := \{\varphi \in \mathsf{FL}(\Phi) \mid s \in [\![\varphi]\!]_{\mathcal{K}}\}$.

Intuitively, the labeling λ may be understood as a plan to prove that $(\mathcal{K}, s) \models \Phi$ holds, in that it is first proved that all formulas in $\lambda(s)$ hold on s.

As we have already seen in the previous section on local model checking, it may not be necessary to consider the entire structure for proving that it satisfies Φ. In this case, we may label the states that are not required for the proof with the empty set, and we may even prune the structure to the states with nonempty labels $\lambda(s)$. The structure will still be a (pre)model, and in the following, we are only interested in the relevant parts of the premodels. This consideration already proves the following:

Lemma B.9. *If a μ-calculus formula Φ has a (pre)model, then there is a (pre)model where all states have at most $|\Phi|$ successors.*

The reason is simply that rule (6) will generate at most $|\Phi|$ subgoals, and therefore, we only need $|\Phi|$ of the successors to prove the satisfiability. The others can be removed without destroying the truth of the formula.

```
function ConjDNF(𝒟_φ, 𝒟_ψ)
  𝒟 := {};
  for 𝒞_φ ∈ 𝒟_φ do
    for 𝒞_ψ ∈ 𝒟_ψ do
      if {¬φ | φ ∈ 𝒞_φ} ∩ 𝒞_ψ = {} then 𝒟 := {𝒞_φ ∪ 𝒞_ψ} ∪ 𝒟 end
    end
  end;
  return 𝒟
end;

function DWC(η)
  case η of
    ¬φ : return {{η}};
    φ ∧ ψ : return ConjDNF(DownwardClose(φ), DownwardClose(ψ));
    φ ∨ ψ : return DownwardClose(φ) ∪ DownwardClose(ψ);
    μx.φ : return DownwardClose(φ);
    νx.φ : return DownwardClose(φ);
    IsBoundVar(η) : return DownwardClose(𝔇_Φ(η));
  else return {{η}};
  end
end

function DownwardClose(η)
  𝒟 := DWC(η);
  return {{η} ∪ 𝒞 | 𝒞 ∈ 𝒟}
end

function ModalVertices(Γ)
  𝒟 := {};
  for φ ∈ Γ do
    𝒟_φ := DownwardClose(φ);
    𝒟 := ConjDNF(𝒟_φ, 𝒟)
  end;
  return 𝒟;
end

function ChoiceVertices(Γ)
  Γ_◇ := {φ | ◇φ ∈ Γ};
  Γ_□ := {φ | □φ ∈ Γ};
  return {{φ} ∪ Γ_□ | φ ∈ Γ_◇};
end
```

Fig. B.12. Computing the AndOrGraph of a formula (I)

```
function AndOrGraph(φ)
  C := {{φ}};
  M := {};
  R_cm := R_mc := {};
  C_new := C;
  M_new := {};
  repeat
    for α ∈ C_new do
      M_α := ModalVertices(α);
      M_new := M_new ∪ M_α;
      R_cm := R_cm ∪ {(α, β) | β ∈ M_α};
    end;
    M_new := M_new \ M;
    M := M ∪ M_new;
    C_new := {};
    for α ∈ M_new do
      C_α := ChoiceVertices(α);
      C_new := C_new ∪ C_α;
      R_mc := R_mc ∪ {(α, β) | β ∈ C_α};
    end;
    C_new := C_new \ C;
    C := C ∪ C_new;
    M_new := {};
  until C_new = {}
  return ({φ}, C, M, R_cm, R_mc)
end
```

Fig. B.13. Computing the AndOrGraph of a formula (II)

As every model defines a premodel, we can first consider the computation of all premodels of a formula, which is a simpler problem. If the formula has no premodels, it is not satisfiable. If it has some premodels, we have to additionally check if one of these premodels is a model. For the computation of all premodels, we can, moreover, reduce the consideration to the relevant premodels: Due to the above explanations, we may prune the (pre)models to the relevant parts that are required to show the satisfiability of the formula. As the essential information of the pruned premodels is then contained in their labels $\lambda(s)$, and we never need different states with the identical labels, we may identify states s with their labels $\lambda(s)$.

Given a μ-calculus formula Φ, we now claim that all these relevant premodels of Φ are encoded in tableaux for Φ, i.e., in all tableaux that start with a root vertex labeled with $\{\Phi\}$. To explain this, we have to distinguish between two kinds of vertices in the tableaux: first, leafs and vertices where one of the modal rules has been applied are called *modal vertices*, and secondly, the root vertex and the children of modal vertices are called *choice vertices*. The tableau of the formula $\Diamond\Diamond x$ shows that there could be vertices that are both modal and choice vertices.

Figures B.12 and B.13 list functions that compute for a μ-calculus formula Φ a bipartite graph AndOrGraph(Φ) with choice vertices $\mathcal{C}$, modal vertices $\mathcal{M}$, and transitions $\mathcal{R}_{cm} \subseteq \mathcal{C} \times \mathcal{M}$ and $\mathcal{R}_{mc} \subseteq \mathcal{M} \times \mathcal{C}$. The graph has a single root vertex c_0, which is a choice vertex. All vertices are subsets of $\mathsf{FL}(\Phi)$, and the root vertex is simply the set $\{\Phi\}$. This bounds the size of $\mathcal{M}$ and $\mathcal{C}$ to $2^{|\mathsf{FL}(\Phi)|}$, i.e., to $2^{|\Phi|}$. As the computation of this graph essentially applies the tableau rules of Figure B.9, we conclude that this graph is essentially a condensed tableau. We will give different interpretations of this graph below, but consider first its construction.

The functions of Figure B.12 make use of disjunctive normal forms of Φ (see page 87), where fixpoint formulas $\sigma x.\varphi$ are replaced with their bodies φ, and bound variables x are replaced with their defining fixpoint formula $\mathfrak{D}_\Phi(x)$. Note that this does not lead to an infinite loop, since (1) the formulas that we consider are in guarded normal form (see Lemma 3.14 on page 102), and (2) since modal formulas are treated like variables in the computation of the disjunctive normal form. Such a disjunctive normal form is represented as a set of sets $\mathcal{D} = \{\mathcal{C}_1, \ldots, \mathcal{C}_n\}$, where $\mathcal{C}_i$ only contains modal formulas, negated variables, and variables that are not bound in Φ. The meaning of $\mathcal{D}$ is clearly the formula $\bigvee_{i=1}^{n} \bigwedge_{\varphi \in \mathcal{C}_i} \varphi$.

Given two such sets $\mathcal{D}_\varphi$ and $\mathcal{D}_\psi$, the function ConjDNF computes the set $\mathcal{D}$ that represents the conjunction of $\mathcal{D}_\varphi$ and $\mathcal{D}_\psi$. $\mathcal{D}$ is obtained by combining all pairs $(\mathcal{C}_\varphi, \mathcal{C}_\psi)$ with $\mathcal{C}_\varphi \in \mathcal{D}_\varphi$ and $\mathcal{C}_\psi \in \mathcal{D}_\psi$ that are consistent, i.e., whose union does not contain a variable with its negation. This is one of two steps in the computation, where two sets $\mathcal{C}_\varphi$ and $\mathcal{C}_\psi$ may be merged that lead to a *locally inconsistent* set, i.e., one that contains both a variable and its negation. These sets are eliminated in function ConjDNF, since they are obviously unsatisfiable.

The other place where a locally inconsistent set may be generated is in function ChoiceVertices, e.g., when $\Gamma_\Diamond$ contains the negation of a formula in $\Gamma_\Box$. Function ChoiceVertices clearly implements the modal rules (6) and (6′), in that it computes for a set of formulas the required subgoals. We could also eliminate the locally inconsistent sets in that function, but doing so would not solve the problem. The reason for this is that the vertices that are generated by function ChoiceVertices are conjunctively connected, and hence, the inconsistency of one of them implies the inconsistency of the modal vertex it stems from. For this reason, we have to remove not only the locally inconsistent vertex, but also the modal vertex it stems from, and all other choice vertices that are children of this modal vertex. For this reason, we retain locally inconsistent sets in function ChoiceVertices. This gives us the possibility to prune the graph afterwards. Alternatively, we may retain the inconsistent vertices, since the remaining steps of our decision procedure will detect such inconsistencies anyway.

The function DownwardClose(η) computes all possible smallest sets that can be used for labeling a state in a premodel that should satisfy η. By construction, these sets obey the rules given in Definition B.8 for conjunctions, disjunctions, fixpoint operators, and negations. The function ModalVertices extends this to a set of formulas Γ. Hence, the result of ModalVertices(Γ) is a set of sets $\mathcal{D} = \{\mathcal{C}_1, \ldots, \mathcal{C}_n\}$, where $\mathcal{C}_i$ only contains modal formulas, negated variables, and variables that are not bound in Φ, and where $\bigvee_{i=1}^{n} \bigwedge_{\varphi \in \mathcal{C}_i} \varphi$ is equivalent to $\bigwedge_{\varphi \in \Gamma} \varphi$.

For this reason, ModalVertices($\{\varphi\}$) contains all possibilities for the label $\lambda(s)$ in a premodel of φ in state s. We can freely choose between one of these labels. Function ChoiceVertices computes then the requirements for successor states of a modal vertex. We must satisfy all of them. This alternating closure under ModalVertices and ChoiceVertices is implemented in function AndOrGraph of Figure B.13.

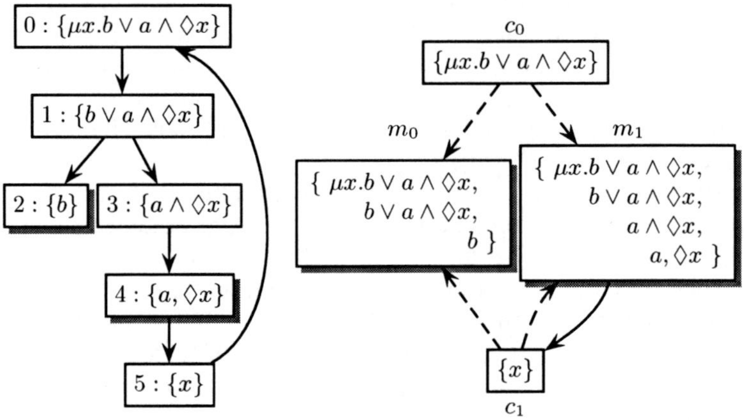

Fig. B.14. Example tableau and AndOrGraph for defining the premodels

For example, Figure B.14 shows on the left-hand side the tableau for $\mu x.b \vee a \wedge \Diamond x$ (similar to the one of Figure B.7), and on the right-hand side the AndOrGraph. The AndOrGraph has the choice vertices c_0 and c_1, and the modal vertices m_0 and m_1 that are connected as shown in Figure B.14. Transitions of $\mathcal{R}_{cm}$ are thereby drawn with dashed lines.

The AndOrGraph of a μ-calculus formula φ can be interpreted in different ways: first, we may interpret it as a board where two players A and B play a game by alternately choosing transitions of the AndOrGraph. Both players consider thereby an additional Kripke structure $\mathcal{K}$ and a state s of $\mathcal{K}$. Player A wins if $\mathcal{K}$ can be converted to a premodel of φ in state s, otherwise player B wins. To this end, player A may choose a transition $(c, m) \in \mathcal{R}_{cm}$ by guessing a label $\lambda(s)$ for state s. After this, player B may choose a transition $(m, c') \in$

$\mathcal{R}_{mc}$. Clearly, player A has a winning strategy if there is a label function λ that makes $\mathcal{K}$ a premodel of φ in s.

There is also a relationship to local model checking: The AndOrGraph contains a path for every choice on disjunctive branches of the local model checking procedure of the previous section. A path in the AndOrGraph therefore combines the conjunctive branches of the proof tree generated by the local model checking procedure under certain choices of disjunctive branches. We therefore distinguish between paths in the AndOrGraph and paths of the proof tree of the local model checking procedure which we will now call traces. Note here that conjunctions are responsible for generating new traces. It is natural to view this as a multithreaded implementation of the local model checking procedure. We will outline this relationship in more detail in Definition B.13 below.

Finally, AndOrGraph(φ) may be interpreted as a deterministic amorphous tree automaton [40, 299]. In general, the transition function of a deterministic tree automaton of branching degree k is a function $\delta : Q \times \Sigma \to Q^k$. The automaton reads a tree where every vertex has exactly k children and is labeled with an input letter. If the automaton is in state q and reads a subtree whose root is labeled with the letter σ, and we have $\delta(q, \sigma) = (q_1, \ldots, q_k)$, then it generates k copies of itself that try to read the subtrees of the input tree from states $q_1, \ldots, q_k$. An amorphous tree automaton is a tree automaton where the branching degree is not fixed, but limited to a maximal branching degree. Hence, the transition function of an amorphous tree automaton is of the form $\delta : Q \times \Sigma \to \bigcup_{i=0}^{n} Q^i$.

It should be clear how AndOrGraph(φ) is interpreted as a tree automaton $\mathfrak{A}_\varphi$: The automaton has states $\mathcal{C}$ and reads downward closed subsets of $\mathsf{FL}(\varphi)$ as inputs. The successor states of a state c and input m are the choice vertices of the set $\{c' \in \mathcal{C} \mid (c, m) \in \mathcal{R}_{cm} \wedge (m, c') \in \mathcal{R}_{mc}\}$.

Consider now an arbitrary premodel $\mathcal{K}$ of φ in state s with label function λ, that is pruned to the necessary states. The automaton $\mathfrak{A}_\varphi$ reads the label $\lambda(s)$ in the initial state. By construction, our automaton is able to read $\lambda(s)$, since its inputs are *all* downward closed sets that contain φ. It may then branch to several successor states, where the labels $\lambda(s')$ of the successor states s' of s have to be read. For this reason, the automaton reads the computation tree of $\mathcal{K}$ that is rooted in state s, and we obtain the following lemma:

Lemma B.10 (Premodels of a Formula). *Given a μ-calculus formula φ and the deterministic amorphous tree automaton $\mathfrak{A}_\varphi$ that is obtained from* AndOrGraph(φ)*. Then, $\mathfrak{A}_\varphi$ has a run for a tree $\mathfrak{T}$ iff $\mathfrak{T}$ is the computation tree of a premodel of φ (pruned to the necessary states). Hence, $\mathfrak{A}_\varphi$ essentially encodes all premodels of φ. Moreover, $\mathfrak{A}_\varphi$ has at most $O(2^{|\Phi|})$ states and for every input letter $m \in \mathsf{FL}(\varphi)$ and every state c, there are at most $O(|\Phi|)$ successor states.*

Hence, the first step of the decision procedure for the μ-calculus has been completed: we are already able to compute the premodels of a formula φ. The next step is to check if one of the obtained premodels is a model.

In Figure B.14, we see that there are two possibilities $m_0, m_1 \in \mathsf{FL}(\Phi)$ for the labeling $\lambda(s_0)$ of the initial state s_0 of a premodel. Choosing m_0 does not require to consider further states of the premodel. Choosing m_1, however, leads to the choice vertex c_1, where we can again choose between m_0 and m_1. Hence, we must add a state s_1 labeled with either $\lambda(s_1) = m_0$ or $\lambda(s_1) = m_1$. It is easily seen that the set of premodels consists therefore of two kinds: first, finite sequences of states where the end state is labeled with m_0, and the others are labeled with m_1, and secondly a single state labeled with m_1 with a self-loop. Clearly, the latter is not a model, but it is a premodel.

One should not be disturbed about the fact that premodels do not always fix a particular subset $\mathcal{L}(s) \subseteq V_\Sigma$ like a Kripke structure. Premodels only determine the information that is necessary to prove the considered formula. It is easy to convert a premodel into a Kripke structure by choosing labels $\mathcal{L}(s)$ that are consistent with $\lambda(s)$. In [430, 496] such complete labelings are called *atoms*. However, we do not need these atoms here, since the tableau rules generate downward closed subsets of $\mathsf{FL}(\Phi)$ as labels.

For a more interesting example, consider Figure B.15. The idea of this example is to show that the conjunction of the CTL formulas $\mathsf{EF}a$ and $\mathsf{EG}\neg a$ is satisfiable. Note, however, that we replaced $\mathsf{EF}a$ with $\mu x.a \vee \Diamond x$ to simplify the tableau construction (as explained on page 300, the correct fixpoint expression is $\mu x.a \wedge (\nu z.\Diamond z) \vee \Diamond x$), therefore the example shows that the conjunction of the CTL formulas $\mathsf{EF}^{fin}a$ and $\mathsf{EG}\neg a$ is satisfiable.

The upper part of Figure B.15 shows a tableau for the conjunction of $\mu x.a \vee \Diamond x$ and $\nu y.\neg a \wedge \Diamond y$. The disjunctive branch that leads to vertex v_4 can be removed since the label of vertex v_4 is locally inconsistent (it contains a and $\neg a$). The lower part contains the AndOrGraph, or if interpreted correctly, the tree automaton that accepts the premodels. It can be seen that it is really a condensed form of the tableau.

The premodels that are encoded in the tree automaton are this time really trees, since we have a conjunctive branching in vertex v_5. In vertex v_{10}, we have a disjunctive branching, so we can choose between the outgoing branches. Two different premodels that are accepted are therefore shown in Figure B.16. As usual, the initial state is drawn with double lines.

We will see that the premodel on the left-hand side is not a model, but the premodel on the right-hand side is a model. How can we determine this? Simply consider what will happen when we apply the local model checking procedure of the previous section to the premodel on the left-hand side. Of course, we should only apply the local model checking procedure to a Kripke structure, but premodels will also work well.

To start with, consider the model checking of $\mu x.a \vee \Diamond x$ in the initial state. As a does not belong to the label, we must proceed to a successor state to evaluate the same formula there. Taking the upper state to evaluate $\mu x.a \vee \Diamond x$ may first check if a holds there, we will then see that a is also not a member of its label, and is therefore forced to check the formula on one of the successor states. As the only successor is the state itself, the procedure detects

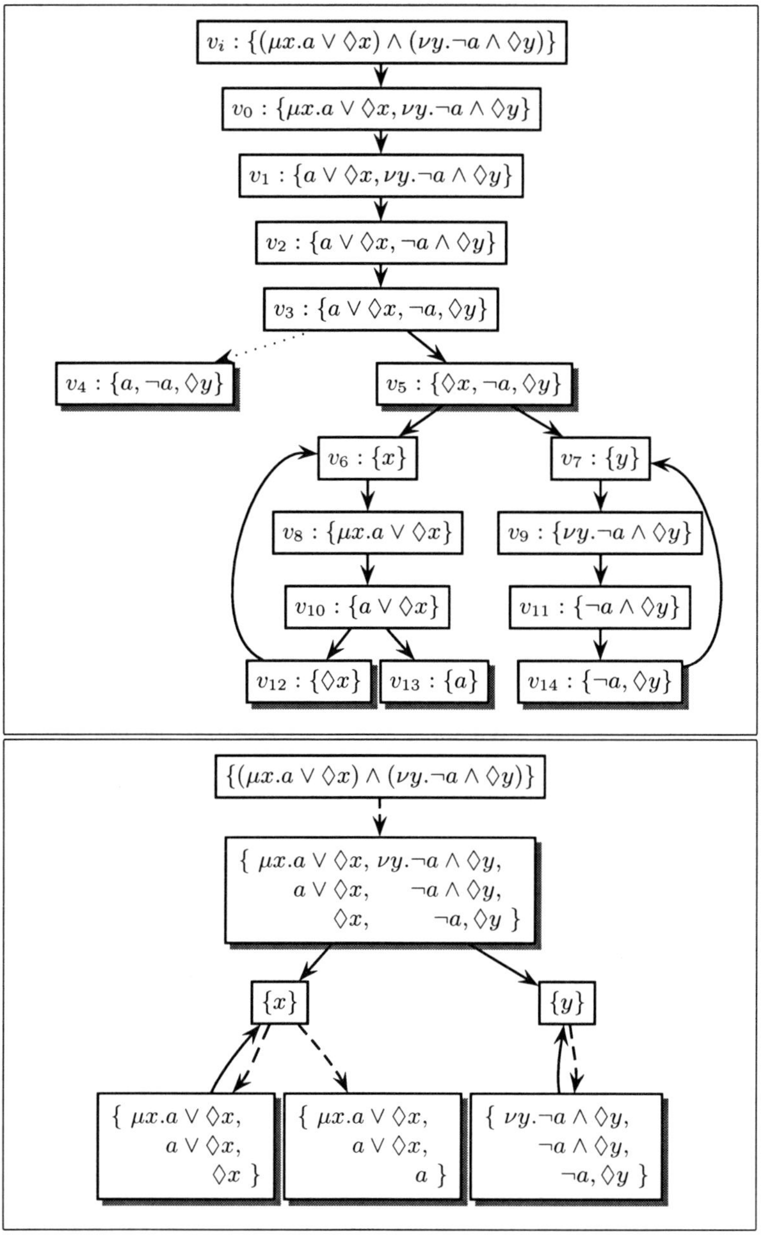

Fig. B.15. An example tableau with its associated deterministic tree automaton

an infinite loop, which is not allowed for least fixpoints. It remains to check the formula in the lower state. However, a is also not included in its label, and therefore the procedure must check $\mu x.a \vee \Diamond x$ on one of the successor

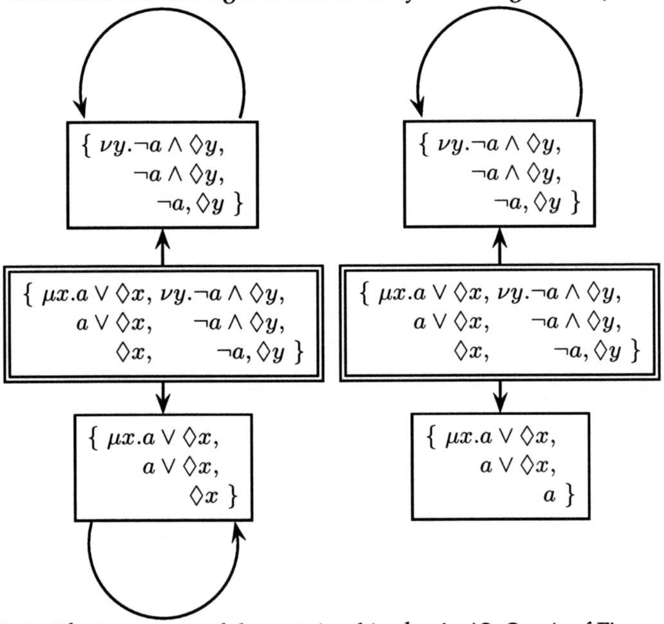

Fig. B.16. The two premodels contained in the AndOrGraph of Figure B.15

states. Again, the procedure detects an infinite recursion of this formula, and therefore the model checking fails. Therefore, the premodel is not a model. The other premodel given on the right hand side is however a model, which can also be checked by our local model checking procedure.

Hence, we see that we can use a local model checking procedure like that of the previous section to check if a premodel is a model. As for every choice vertex, it is sufficient to select one of its successors, the number of different premodels that can be obtained in this way is also finite. We can therefore reduce the satisfiability problem to a finite number of model checking problems, by fixing particular choices of the choice vertices. We therefore define the set of premodels contained in an AndOrGraph as follows:

Definition B.11 (Premodels Contained in AndOrGraph**).** *Given an arbitrary μ-calculus formula φ and $\mathcal{G}_\varphi :=$ AndOrGraph$(\varphi) = (c_0, \mathcal{C}, \mathcal{M}, \mathcal{R}_{cm}, \mathcal{R}_{mc})$. For every total function $\xi : \mathcal{C} \to \mathcal{M}$ with $(c, \xi(c)) \in \mathcal{R}_{cm}$ for every $c \in \mathcal{C}$, we define the following premodel $\mathcal{K}_\xi = (\mathcal{I}, \mathcal{S}, \mathcal{R}_\xi, \mathcal{L}, \lambda)$ contained in $\mathcal{G}_\varphi$:*

- $\mathcal{I} := \{m \in \mathcal{M} \mid \varphi \in m\}$
- $\mathcal{S} := \mathcal{M}$
- $(m, m') \in \mathcal{R}_\xi :\Leftrightarrow \exists c \in \mathcal{C}.(m, c) \in \mathcal{R}_{mc} \wedge m' = \xi(c)$
- $\lambda(m) := m$
- *$\mathcal{L}$ is arbitrary, but consistent with λ*

A premodel is contained in $\mathcal{G}_\varphi$ iff it is obtained by a function $\xi : \mathcal{C} \to \mathcal{M}$ as shown above. The set of premodels contained in $\mathcal{G}_\varphi$ is denoted as premodels$(\mathcal{G}_\varphi)$.

Hence, we have an isomorphism between functions $\xi : \mathcal{C} \to \mathcal{M}$ with the property $(c, \xi(c)) \in \mathcal{R}_{cm}$ (for every $c \in \mathcal{C}$) and premodels contained in $\mathcal{G}_\varphi$, so that there is only a finite number of premodels contained in $\mathcal{G}_\varphi$. Although the set of premodels contained in $\mathsf{AndOrGraph}(\varphi)$ is not the entire set of all premodels of the formula, the formula is satisfiable if and only if one of the contained premodels is a model. To see this, assume that there is a Kripke structure that satisfies a formula φ. Choice vertices stem from disjunctions in φ. As either $(\mathcal{K}, s) \models \varphi$ or $(\mathcal{K}, s) \models \psi$ holds when $(\mathcal{K}, s) \models \varphi \vee \psi$ holds, it must be possible to reduce the further search to one of these two cases. This situation does not change when the proof search comes back to this state in a later step. Hence, it is possible to statically fix the choices as it is done by contained premodels. Hence, we can reduce the satisfiability problem of the μ-calculus to several model checking problems, so that our first decision procedure is now complete.

Theorem B.12 (Satisfiability of μ-Calculus). *A μ-calculus formula φ is satisfiable iff at least one of the premodels in* $\mathsf{premodel}(\mathsf{AndOrGraph}(\varphi))$ *is a model of φ. This can be checked by a (local) model checking procedure.*

It is remarkable that we can restrict the search of models for φ to the finite set $\mathsf{premodels}(\mathcal{G}_\varphi)$, while there are infinitely many different premodels that are accepted by $\mathcal{G}_\varphi$ (when $\mathcal{G}_\varphi$ is interpreted as tree automaton). A proof can be found in [168], where (pre)models *contained* in a tree automaton and (pre)models that are *generated* by a tree automaton are distinguished. This is related with the existence of memoryless winning strategies [167, 221]. Note, however, that the restriction to contained premodels is not legal for model checking.

To roughly determine the runtime of this approach, recall that $|\mathcal{C}| \leq 2^{|\varphi|}$, $|\mathcal{M}| \leq 2^{|\varphi|}$, hence, every choice vertex has at most $2^{|\varphi|}$ successors, while modal vertices have at most $|\varphi|$ successors. For every contained premodel, we therefore have $|\mathcal{S}| = |\mathcal{M}| \leq 2^{|\varphi|}$ and $|\mathcal{R}| \leq |\varphi|\, 2^{|\varphi|}$. Model checking φ in a contained premodel can therefore be done in time $O(|\varphi|\,(|\varphi|\,2^{|\varphi|})^{\mathsf{ad}(\varphi)+1})$. However, there could be $2^{2^{|\varphi|}}$ many contained premodels, thus making the overall procedure doubly exponential.

However, we can do better: As we already know that the invariants of the μ-calculus formula are already respected, the only discrepancy between a premodel and a model is that least and greatest fixpoints are interchanged. Based on the results of the previous section, we therefore only need to check for infinite recursion of least fixpoint formulas (that are not triggered by surrounding greatest fixpoints). However, this has to be done with more care: Note that states of the premodel whose labels contain a least fixpoint formula $\mu x.\varphi$ make a recursive call to that formula. If this state contains occurrences of x in one of its modal formulas, then the call is not immediately satisfied and carries over to the successors. We therefore follow the paths and check if a least fixpoint formula $\mu x.\varphi$ will be regenerated infinitely often along this path. However, this is not so simple: first, a path in the premodel corresponds to several traces of the proof tree of the local model checking procedure, and secondly, a surrounding greatest fixpoint operator may trigger infinitely often a call to an inner least fixpoint. In the latter case, the infinitely many calls are admissible, if they are all satisfied after finitely many steps. The following definition of choice functions and well-founded premodels will provide us with the means to formalize this correctly.

Definition B.13 (Choice Functions, Traces, and Well-Founded Premodels). *Given a premodel $\mathcal{K} = (\mathcal{I}, \mathcal{S}, \mathcal{R}, \mathcal{L}, \lambda)$ of Φ in state s. A choice function χ for $\mathcal{K}$ is a partial function $\chi : \mathcal{S} \times \mathsf{FL}(\Phi) \to \mathcal{S} \times \mathsf{FL}(\Phi)$ such that the following holds:*

- $\varphi \vee \psi \in \lambda(s)$ *implies either* $\chi(s, \varphi \vee \psi) = (s, \varphi)$ *or* $\chi(s, \varphi \vee \psi) = (s, \psi)$
- $\Diamond\varphi \in \lambda(s)$ *implies* $\chi(s, \Diamond\varphi) = (s', \varphi)$ *for some* $s' \in \mathsf{suc}_{\exists}^{\mathcal{R}}(\{s\})$

A choice function $\chi : \mathcal{S} \times \mathsf{FL}(\Phi) \to \mathcal{S} \times \mathsf{FL}(\Phi)$ determines a derivation relation $(s, \varphi) \leadsto_\chi (s', \varphi')$ on $(\mathcal{S} \times \mathsf{FL}(\Phi)) \times (\mathcal{S} \times \mathsf{FL}(\Phi))$ as the smallest relation with the following properties:

- *if* $\varphi \wedge \psi \in \lambda(s)$ *then* $(s, \varphi \wedge \psi) \leadsto_\chi (s, \varphi)$ *and* $(s, \varphi \wedge \psi) \leadsto_\chi (s, \psi)$
- *if* $\varphi \vee \psi \in \lambda(s)$ *then* $(s, \varphi \vee \psi) \leadsto_\chi \chi(s, \varphi \vee \psi)$
- *if* $\Diamond\varphi \in \lambda(s)$ *then* $(s, \Diamond\varphi) \leadsto_\chi \chi(s, \Diamond\varphi)$
- *if* $\Box\varphi \in \lambda(s)$ *then* $(s, \Box\varphi) \leadsto_\chi (s', \varphi)$ *for all* $s' \in \mathsf{suc}_{\exists}^{\mathcal{R}}(\{s\})$
- *if* $\sigma x.\varphi \in \lambda(s)$ *then* $(s, \sigma x.\varphi) \leadsto_\chi (s, \varphi)$
- *if* $x \in \lambda(s)$ *then* $(s, x) \leadsto_\chi (s, \mathfrak{D}_\Phi(x))$

A fixpoint formula $\sigma x.\varphi$ is regenerated from state s_1 to state s_n in the premodel $\mathcal{K}$ if there is a derivation $(s_1, \sigma x.\varphi) \leadsto_\chi \ldots \leadsto_\chi (s_n, \sigma x.\varphi)$ such that x occurs in all formulas of this derivation.

A premodel is well-founded if there is a choice function χ such that for every infinite derivation sequence the outermost fixpoint formula $\sigma x.\varphi \in \mathsf{FL}(\Phi)$ that is regenerated infinitely often is a greatest fixpoint formula.

The above definition establishes the relationship to the local model checking procedure of the previous section. The choice function is thereby an oracle that tells us which of the disjunctive branches in the local model checking we should take. The requirements for the derivation relation simply reformulate the rules of Figure B.4 on page 493. Hence, the derivation sequences are exactly the branches of the proof trees that are constructed by the local model checking procedure under the disjunctive choices made by χ. Note further that the cycles that were found in the local model checking procedure when a leaf vertex is marked with $(s, x) \vdash \ldots$ corresponds to a derivation sequence where $\mathfrak{D}_\Phi(x)$ is regenerated infinitely often. The above definition is therefore consistent with our local model checking procedure.

A path in a premodel may carry several derivations, even one where a least and a greatest fixpoint formula is regenerated infinitely often (see Figure B.17). Furthermore, whenever the rule for conjunction is applied, it generates a new derivation of the same path. It is therefore natural to interpret

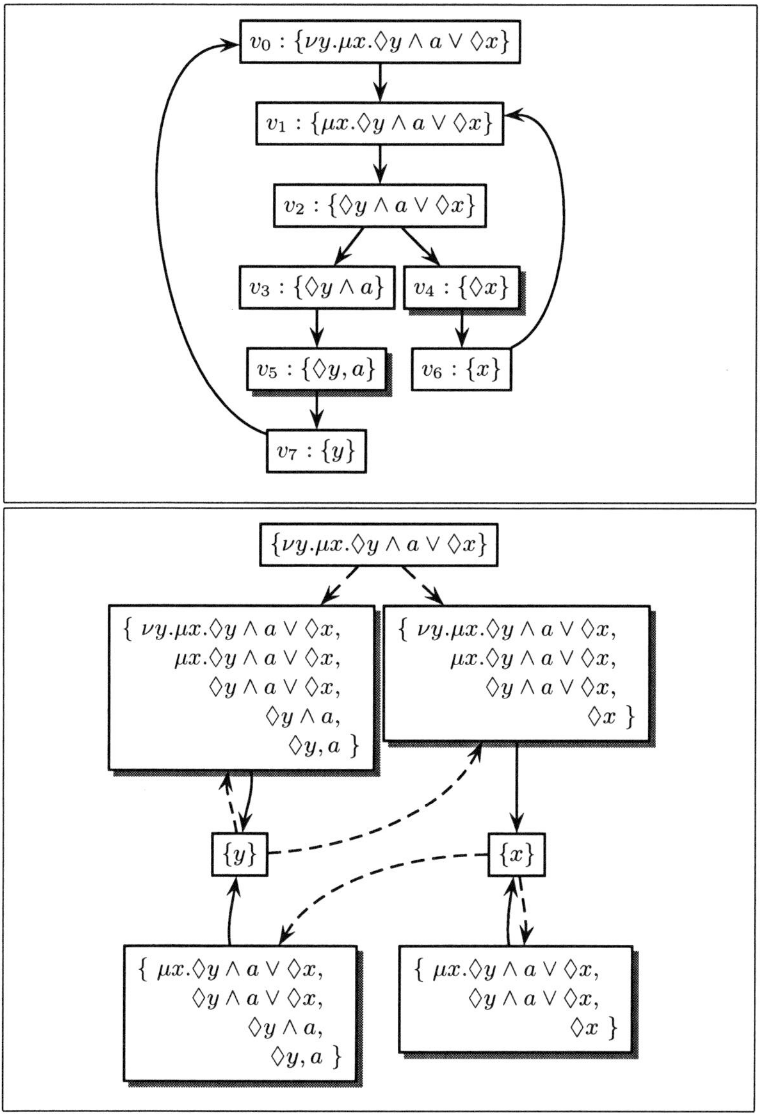

Fig. B.17. An example tableau with its associated deterministic tree automaton

the derivations as threads in a multithreaded implementation of the local model checking procedure.

Note that on every infinite derivation sequence, there must be at least one fixpoint formula $\sigma x.\varphi \in \mathsf{FL}(\Phi)$ that is regenerated infinitely often, since all other rules decrease the size of the formula. Moreover, one of those fixpoint formulas that are regenerated infinitely often, say $\sigma x.\varphi$, is a largest one that contains the others as subformulas. If $\sigma = \nu$ holds, then it follows that between a regeneration of $\sigma x.\varphi$, all other fixpoint formulas disappeared in the derivation, and therefore, every 'call' to them only has finitely many recursion steps between a regeneration of $\sigma x.\varphi$. Hence, the semantics of least fixpoints is determined correctly, which makes the premodel a model. Hence, taking the results of the local model checking procedure, we obtain the fundamental result of Streett and Emerson [477, 478]:

Theorem B.14. *A premodel is a model if and only if it is well-founded.*

Hence, the final step after computing the AndOrGraph is to check if it contains a well-founded premodel. For a given formula Φ, we have to check if AndOrGraph(Φ) contains a premodel $\mathcal{K}_\xi$ with initial state s such that for some choice function χ, on every derivation sequence of $\mathcal{K}_\xi$ and χ starting in (s, Φ), the outermost fixpoint formula $\sigma x.\varphi$ that is regenerated infinitely often is a greatest fixpoint formula.

To this end, it is possible to employ ω-automata that read infinite trees and accept or reject them according to their acceptance condition. In general, the same acceptance conditions are used as for ω-automata on words. However, the expressiveness results are different. For example, Büchi tree automata are less expressive as Rabin tree automata and the reasons for this are quite clear [301]. The most natural acceptance condition to check for well-founded premodels is thereby the parity condition [167, 169, 376], where the alternation depth is used to color the states in a derivation sequence (s, φ) as follows: $\Omega(s, \mu x.\varphi)$ is the smallest odd number greater or equal to $\mathsf{ad}(\mu x.\varphi) - 1$, $\Omega(s, \nu x.\varphi)$ is the smallest even number greater or equal to $\mathsf{ad}(\nu x.\varphi) - 1$, and 0 otherwise (see [167, 169, 221] for more details). Alternatively, we could set up a condition of the form $\mathsf{GF} r_x \rightarrow \mathsf{GF} \bigvee_{y \in \mathsf{Outer}(x)} r_y$ for every least fixpoint variable x where r_x means x is regenerated, and $\mathsf{Outer}(x)$ is the set of variables y whose definitions $\mathfrak{D}_\Phi(y)$ are greatest fixpoint formulas and contain $\mathfrak{D}_\Phi(x)$ as a subformula.

To obtain an ω-tree automaton from AndOrGraph(φ), a 'global' automaton is used in [477, 478] that checks whether an infinite μ-recursion is possible in a path of the tree automaton (that is called the local automaton there). This global automaton is a *universal ω-automaton on infinite words* with $O(|\varphi|)$ states. In particular, the μ-calculus formula itself, i.e., its syntax tree (where leafs with bound variables are redirected back to the root of $\mathfrak{D}_\varphi(x)$) is this automaton.

In [478], it is then estimated that its complement will have at most $O(2^{2^{|\varphi|}})$ states (based on the out-dated complementation procedure of McNaughton), and therefore the product with the tree automaton that checks for premodels will also have $O(2^{2^{|\varphi|}})$ states (note that this product is necessary to obtain the derivation sequences that we want to check). Using the (also outdated) algorithm of Hossley and Rackoff [253] that checks the emptiness of the language that is accepted by an infinite tree automaton in time $O(2^{2^{|C|}})$ results in a quadruply exponential time decision procedure. It has already been remarked in [478] that this can be reduced to triply exponential time.

In the meantime this has been improved to a single exponential time decision procedure by two major improvements: First, algorithms have been found for checking the nonemptiness of Rabin tree automata in single exponential time [165, 168, 304, 409]. Given a Rabin tree automaton with $|\mathcal{C}|$ states and f acceptance pairs, the algorithms of Emerson and Jutla [165, 168] and Pnueli and Rosner [409] check the nonemptiness in time $O((|\mathcal{C}|\, f)^{3f})$. Kupferman and Vardi [304] presented an improved algorithm that runs in time $O(|\mathcal{C}|^{2f+1}\, f!)$ [304]. Secondly, the other necessary improvement was the determinization of ω-automata on words (for the global automaton) in exponential time using Safra's construction [428] (page 228). Both improvements were necessary to finally obtain an exponential time decision procedure for the μ-calculus. Vardi [430, 496] has shown that the satisfiability of the full μ-calculus (including past modalities) can also be decided in exponential time. Therefore, we have the following result [168, 192, 496]:

Theorem B.15 (Complexity of the μ-Calculus Satisfiability). *Satisfiability of the full μ-calculus is decidable in exponential time. The problem is, moreover,* EXPTIME-*complete.*

The algorithm given in [168] for checking nonemptiness of a Rabin tree automaton with states $\mathcal{C}$ and inputs $\mathcal{M}$ is given in Figure B.18. It essentially is based on a pseudo model checking procedure. In principle, we could also define $[\![\Phi]\!]_{\mathcal{G}_\varphi} := \{m \in \mathcal{M} \mid \exists \mathcal{K} \in \mathsf{premodels}(\mathcal{G}_\varphi).m \in [\![\Phi]\!]_{\mathcal{K}}\}$ to apply the local model checking procedure directly on $\mathcal{G}_\varphi = \mathsf{AndOrGraph}(\varphi)$. However, the recursive computation is difficult: It is easily seen that $[\![\varphi \vee \psi]\!]_{\mathcal{G}} = [\![\varphi]\!]_{\mathcal{G}} \cup [\![\psi]\!]_{\mathcal{G}}$ holds, but the same is not the case for conjunctions. Similar problems appear in the algorithms of Figure B.18 (note however that these functions compute subsets of $\mathcal{C}$, i.e., states of the tree automaton). The function TreeRabin given in Figure B.18 computes $\left[\!\!\left[\mathsf{A}\left(\mathsf{F}\alpha \vee \bigvee_{i=1}^{f} \mathsf{GF}\varphi_i \wedge \mathsf{FG}\psi_i\right)\right]\!\!\right]_{\mathfrak{T}}$ in a recursive manner. The base case is finally solved by the function TreeAF, and the recursion step is reduced with function TreeAU. These functions compute the sets $[\![\mathsf{AF}\psi]\!]_{\mathfrak{T}}$ and $[\![\mathsf{A}[\varphi\ \mathsf{U}\ \psi]]\!]_{\mathfrak{T}}$, respectively. Note that the latter requires a special treatment, namely the reduction of the transition relations during the fixpoint iteration, to correctly compute the result. See [168] for the correctness of these algorithms, the version given in [165] is however different.

We do not list further details. The interested reader is invited to consider the original references [165, 167, 168, 477, 478]. Instead, we conclude with some further remarks. The first is that we obtain the small model property as a corollary from Lemma B.10 and Theorem B.12:

Theorem B.16 (Small Model Property). *If a μ-calculus formula Φ without past modalities is satisfiable, it is even satisfiable in a finite model with at most $O(2^{|\Phi|})$ states.*

```
function TreeAX(𝔗, ψ)
  (𝒞, ℳ, ℛ_cm, ℛ_mc) ≡ 𝔗;
  M_1 := pre_∃^{ℛ_mc}(1);
  M_2 := pre_∀^{ℛ_mc}(ψ);
  return pre_∃^{ℛ_cm}(M_1 ∩ M_2);
end

function TreeRabin(𝔗, Γ, α)
  if Γ = {} then return TreeAF(𝔗, α) end;
  {(φ_1, ψ_1), ..., (φ_f, ψ_f)} ≡ Γ;
  Y_0 := {};
  repeat
    Y_1 := Y_0;
    Y_0 := α;
    for i := 1 to f do
      Γ_i := Γ \ {(φ_i, ψ_i)};
      C_1 := TreeRabin(𝔗, Γ_i, α ∨ φ_i);
      C_2 := C_1 ∩ (ψ_i ∪ Y_0) ∩ pre_∃^{ℛ_cm}(1);
      C_3 := TreeAU(𝔗, C_2, α);
      Y_0 := Y_0 ∪ TreeAX(𝔗, C_3);
    end
  until Y_1 = Y_0
end
```

```
function TreeAF(𝔗, ψ)
  (𝒞, ℳ, ℛ_cm, ℛ_mc) ≡ 𝔗;
  C_0 := {};
  repeat
    C_1 := C_0;
    C_0 := ψ ∪ TreeAX(𝔗, C_1);
  until C_1 = C_0;
  return C_0
end
```

```
function TreeAU(𝔗, φ, ψ)
  (𝒞, ℳ, ℛ_cm, ℛ_mc) ≡ 𝔗;
  𝔗' := 𝔗;
  C_0 := 𝒞;
  repeat
    C_1 := C_0;
    C_0 := ψ ∪ φ ∩ TreeAX(𝔗', C_1);
    ℛ_cm := {(c, m) ∈ ℛ_cm | c ∈ C_0};
    ℛ_mc := {(m, c) ∈ ℛ_mc | c ∈ C_0};
    𝔗' := (C_0, ℳ, ℛ_cm, ℛ_mc);
  until C_1 = C_0;
  return C_0
end
```

Fig. B.18. Emerson-Jutla algorithm for checking emptiness of Rabin tree automata

For practical implementation, we note that the tableau construction can often be reduced by logic minimization [358], since the tableau rules transform the μ-calculus formula implicitly in a disjunctive normal form. It is well-known that in such a disjunctive normal form not all minterms are required, since some of them are covered by the remaining ones. We may therefore minimize the formula by choosing a cover of the minterms (thus computing a minimal disjunctive normal form).

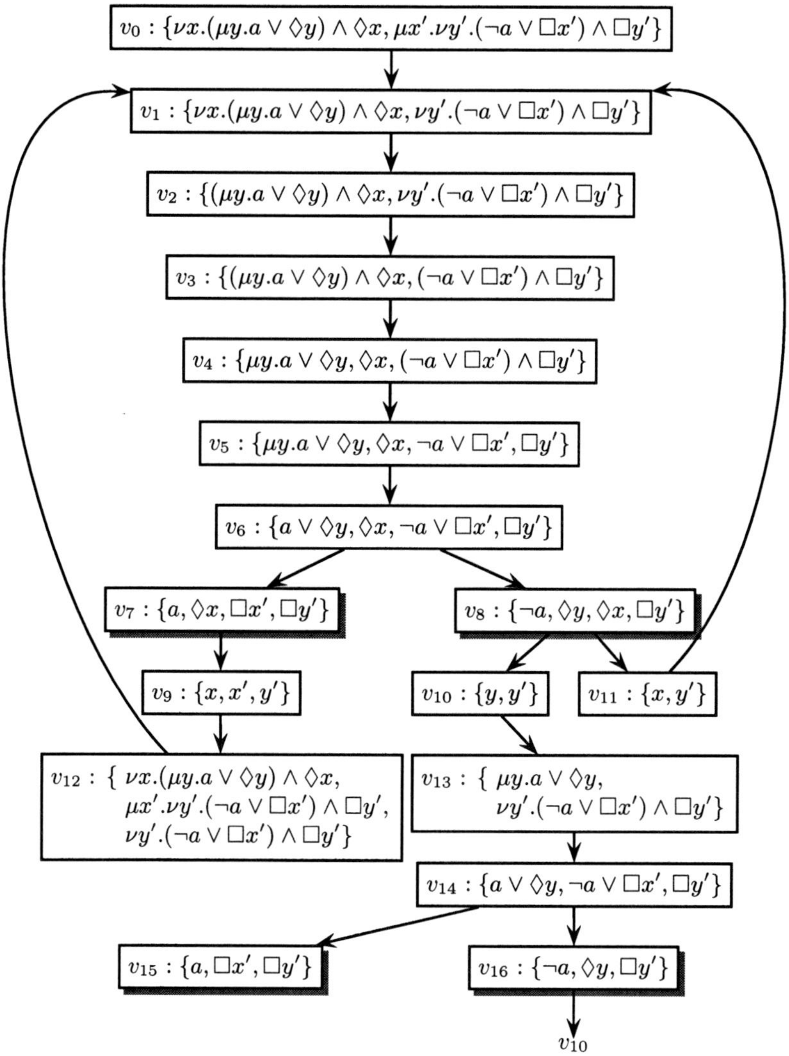

Fig. B.19. Tableau for $\mathsf{EGEF}^{fin} a \wedge \neg\mathsf{EGF} a$

As an example, consider vertex v_6 of Figure B.19. Using the tableau rules as presented, we would obtain the following successors:

- $v_{6,1} : \{a, \Diamond x, \neg a, \Box y'\}$
- $v_{6,2} : \{a, \Diamond x, \Box x', \Box y'\}$
- $v_{6,3} : \{\Diamond y, \Diamond x, \neg a, \Box y'\}$
- $v_{6,4} : \{\Diamond y, \Diamond x, \Box x', \Box y'\}$

Clearly, $v_{6,1}$ is locally inconsistent, since it contains a and $\neg a$. Moreover, $v_{6,4}$ is covered by $v_{6,2}$ and $v_{6,4}$, and can therefore also be deleted without loosing equivalence. This can also be obtained by first removing all fixpoint operators, thus obtaining the following formula: $((a \vee \Diamond y) \wedge \Diamond x) \wedge ((\neg a \vee \Box x') \wedge \Box y')$. Converting this formula into a (minimal) disjunctive normal form results in, e.g., $a \wedge \Diamond x \wedge \Box x' \wedge \Box y' \vee \neg a \wedge \Diamond x \wedge \Diamond y \wedge \Box y'$.

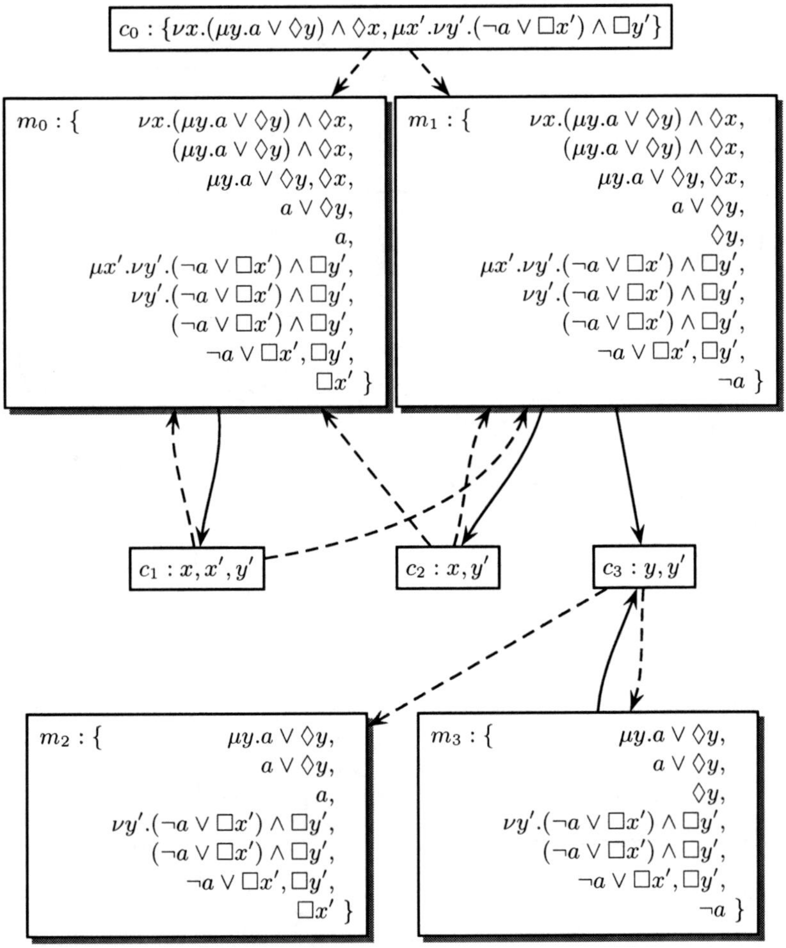

Fig. B.20. AndOrGraph($\mathsf{EGEF}^{fin} a \wedge \neg \mathsf{EGF} a$)

Figure B.20 shows the tree automaton that we obtain from the tableau of Figure B.19. We obtain four choice vertices and four modal vertices, and in each choice vertex, we have the choice between two successors. Therefore, the AndOrGraph contains 2^4 premodels that can be checked for satisfying the considered formula. It turns out that one of them satisfies the formula, and therefore $\nu x.(\mu y.a \vee \Diamond y) \wedge \Diamond x$ does not imply $\nu x'.\mu y'.(a \wedge \Diamond x') \vee \Diamond y'$, or more readable, that $\mathsf{EGEF}^{fin} a$ does not imply $\mathsf{EGF}a$).

The relationship between tableaux and disjunctive normal forms has motivated Walukiewicz to define a 'disjunctive normal form' for μ-calculus formulas. He proved that the satisfiability problem for formulas in this normal form can be decided in linear time (which is possible due to the exponential blow-up in computing the normal form). For the construction [263, 509], the following interesting modal operator was used:

Definition B.17 (Walukiewicz's Modal Operator). *Given a set of μ-calculus formulas $\{\varphi_1,\ldots,\varphi_n\}$, we define (as usual, the empty conjunction is 1, and the empty disjunction is 0; hence, we have $\langle\{\}\rangle = \Box 0$):*

$$\langle\{\varphi_1,\ldots,\varphi_n\}\rangle :\equiv \left(\bigwedge_{i=1}^{n} \Diamond\varphi_i\right) \wedge \left(\Box \bigvee_{i=1}^{n} \varphi_i\right)$$

For $\Gamma \neq \{\}$, it is easily seen that a state s satisfies the formula $\langle\Gamma\rangle$ iff the following two conditions are satisfied:

- every $\varphi \in \Gamma$ is satisfied by at least one successor state $s' \in \mathsf{suc}_\exists^{\mathcal{R}}(\{s\})$
- every successor state $s' \in \mathsf{suc}_\exists^{\mathcal{R}}(\{s\})$ satisfies at least one $\varphi \in \Gamma$

These two conditions are expressed more formally as follows, so that we see that a proof goal of the form $s \vdash_\Phi \langle\Gamma\rangle$ would generate a conjunctive branching with the following branches:

- for every $\varphi \in \Gamma$, we have $[\![\varphi]\!]_{\mathcal{K}} \cap \mathsf{suc}_\exists^{\mathcal{R}}(\{s\}) \neq \{\}$
- $\mathsf{suc}_\exists^{\mathcal{R}}(\{s\}) \subseteq \left[\!\!\left[\bigvee_{\varphi\in\Gamma} \varphi\right]\!\!\right]_{\mathcal{K}}$

In particular, s must have successor states (unless $\Gamma = \{\}$), and the successor states of s can be grouped into nonempty subsets S_φ satisfying the formulas $\varphi \in \Gamma$. Note further that $\langle\{\varphi\}\rangle$ holds in a state s iff $\{\} \neq \mathsf{suc}_\exists^{\mathcal{R}}(\{s\}) \subseteq [\![\varphi]\!]_{\mathcal{K}}$. Finally, the modal operators $\Diamond$ and $\Box$ can be expressed by the above operator:

- $\Diamond\varphi = \langle\{\varphi, 1\}\rangle$
- $\Box\varphi = \langle\{\varphi\}\rangle \vee \langle\{\}\rangle$

The following lemma shows how to combine conjunctions of this operator:

Lemma B.18 (Conjunctions of Modal Operators). *Given sets of μ-calculus formulas $\Phi \neq \{\}$ and $\Psi \neq \{\}$, the following equations are valid:*

- $\langle\{\}\rangle \wedge \langle\Psi\rangle = 0$
- $\langle\Phi\rangle \wedge \langle\Psi\rangle = \langle\{\varphi \wedge \bigvee_{\psi\in\Psi} \psi \mid \varphi \in \Phi\} \cup \{\psi \wedge \bigvee_{\varphi\in\Phi} \varphi \mid \psi \in \Psi\}\rangle$

Proof. The proof of the first equation is simple: $\langle\{\}\rangle$ only holds on those states that have no successor, but $\langle\Psi\rangle$ requires that at least one successor exists. We abbreviate $\chi_\Phi := \bigvee_{\varphi\in\Phi}\varphi$ and $\chi_\Psi := \bigvee_{\psi\in\Psi}\psi$, and $\chi_{\Phi,\Psi} := \left(\bigvee_{\varphi\in\Phi}(\varphi\wedge\chi_\Psi)\right)\vee\left(\bigvee_{\psi\in\Psi}(\psi\wedge\chi_\Phi)\right)$. We first prove that $\chi_{\Phi,\Psi} = \chi_\Phi\wedge\chi_\Psi$ holds:

- $\bigvee_{\varphi\in\Phi}(\varphi\wedge\chi_\Psi) = \left(\bigvee_{\varphi\in\Phi}\varphi\right)\wedge\chi_\Psi = \chi_\Phi\wedge\chi_\Psi$
- $\bigvee_{\psi\in\Psi}(\psi\wedge\chi_\Phi) = \left(\bigvee_{\psi\in\Psi}\psi\right)\wedge\chi_\Phi = \chi_\Psi\wedge\chi_\Phi$

Using this, the remaining proof is simple. □

By induction, we also obtain for $\chi_i := \bigvee_{\varphi\in\Phi_i}\varphi$:

$$\bigwedge_{i=1}^{n}\langle\Phi_i\rangle = \langle\bigcup_{i=1}^{n}\{\varphi\wedge\bigwedge_{j=1,j\neq i}^{n}\chi_j \mid \varphi\in\Phi_i\}\rangle$$

and therefore, we obtain the following tableau rules:

$$\frac{\{\langle\{\varphi_1,\ldots,\varphi_n\}\rangle,\ell_1,\ldots,\ell_k\}}{\{\varphi_1\}\ldots\{\varphi_n\}}\, n>0$$

$$\frac{\{\langle\Phi\rangle,\langle\Psi\rangle\}\cup\Gamma}{\{\langle\{\varphi\wedge\bigvee_{\psi\in\Psi}\psi \mid \varphi\in\Phi\}\cup\{\psi\wedge\bigvee_{\varphi\in\Phi}\varphi \mid \psi\in\Psi\}\rangle,\}\cup\Gamma}$$

As a final remark, we note the close relationship between μ-calculus formulas and alternating tree automata. In fact, Emerson already stated in [167] that μ-calculus formulas can be simply read as alternating tree automata (see also [221]). In principle, the syntax tree of the μ-calculus formula can be used, where leafs marked with bound variables are redirected to their definitions. In [169, 221] it is then described how this automaton reads a Kripke structure from a state s. It turns out that the runs of this automaton are exactly the proof trees of our local model checking procedure, so that we may view the local model checking procedure alternatively as a procedure to determine the word problem of an alternating tree automaton.

The relationship between alternating tree automata and the μ-calculus is even more visible for the vectorized form of the μ-calculus: Alternating automata on words can be written as equation systems [525] of the form $q_i \leftrightarrow \Phi_i$, where q_i is a state variable (with a one-hot encoding) and Φ_i contains only occurrences of $\mathsf{X}q_j$ and the input variables. Hence, alternating automata are backwards deterministic (reconsider here also the ω-automata that are generated from the algorithm of Figure 5.11 on page 342 to see how 'alternating automata' are computed for temporal logic). Looking at the equation systems of the vectorized μ-calculus, we see that they have the same form, except that modal operators are used for the next state. Hence, they are really symbolic descriptions of alternating tree automata, just like the automaton formulas are symbolic descriptions for word automata.

C

Reduction of Structures

In this Appendix, we consider methods to reduce the complexity of model checking problems in that the Kripke structure is reduced without changing the result of the model checking problem. We start in the next section with a formal framework for abstraction, namely Galois connections, and show its equivalence to simulation relations [37, 108, 109, 331]. We then show in Section C.2 how abstract Kripke structures can be computed by Galois connections (or equivalent simulation relations) such that either existential or universal properties are preserved. In Section C.3, we then discuss the optimality of abstractions [137]. We will then, furthermore, briefly consider specialized approaches like symmetry reduction and partial order reductions. Finally, we show in Sections C.4 and C.5 how special abstractions are obtained by data abstraction and the exploitation of symmetries in the Kripke structure. The contents of this section are essentially based on [331], where the use of Galois connections for the abstraction of reactive systems is considered. The definition of the data abstraction as presented here is similar to that defined in [109, 110].

C.1 Galois Connections and Simulations

In this section, we define *Galois connections*, which serve as a basic formalism to formally reason about abstractions. In particular, program analysis is often simplified by *abstract interpretation*, which directly induces a Galois connection [129, 130, 429]. A Galois connection is a pair of functions (α, γ) such that $\alpha : \mathcal{C} \to \mathcal{A}$ maps elements of a concrete set $\mathcal{C}$ to elements of the abstract set $\mathcal{A}$. γ can be viewed in some way as an 'inverse' to γ, since $\gamma : \mathcal{A} \to \mathcal{C}$ maps abstract elements to concrete ones. However, it is not desirable that $\gamma(\alpha(c)) = c$ holds, because this implies that α is a bijection between the sets $\mathcal{C}$ and $\{\alpha(c) \mid c \in \mathcal{C}\}$, and therefore there would be no real abstraction. For this reason, some other properties must be found so that γ can be seen as some sort of inverse of α. Intuitively, these properties assure that $\alpha(c)$ is the least abstraction of c, where 'least' means that $\alpha(c)$ retains as much information from c in $\alpha(c)$ as possible. Conversely, $\gamma(a)$ is the most general concretization of an abstract element c. For this reason, we must assume that the sets $\mathcal{A}$ and $\mathcal{C}$ are ordered in terms of 'information content'.

C.1.1 Basic Properties of Galois Connections

Definition C.1 (Galois Connection). *Given two partially ordered sets $(\mathcal{C}, \preceq_c)$ and $(\mathcal{A}, \preceq_a)$. A pair of functions (α, γ) with $\alpha : \mathcal{C} \rightarrow \mathcal{A}$, $\gamma : \mathcal{A} \rightarrow \mathcal{C}$ is a Galois connection from $(\mathcal{C}, \preceq_c)$ to $(\mathcal{A}, \preceq_a)$ iff the following holds:*

GC1: α is monotonic, i.e., $\forall c_1, c_2 \in \mathcal{C}.\ c_1 \preceq_c c_2 \Rightarrow \alpha(c_1) \preceq_a \alpha(c_2)$
GC2: γ is monotonic, i.e., $\forall a_1, a_2 \in \mathcal{A}.\ a_1 \preceq_a a_2 \Rightarrow \gamma(a_1) \preceq_c \gamma(a_2)$
GC3: $\forall c \in \mathcal{C}.\ c \preceq_c \gamma(\alpha(c))$
GC4: $\forall a \in \mathcal{A}.\ \alpha(\gamma(a)) \preceq_a a$

If, additionally, $a_1 \preceq_a a_2 \Leftrightarrow \gamma(a_1) \preceq_c \gamma(a_2)$ holds, then (α, γ) is a Galois insertion.

We say that $a \in \mathcal{A}$ is an *abstraction of* $c \in \mathcal{C}$ if $\alpha(c) \preceq_a a$ holds. Hence, $\alpha(c)$ is the least abstraction of c. Conversely, we say that $c \in \mathcal{C}$ is a *concretization of* $a \in \mathcal{A}$ if $c \preceq_c \gamma(a)$ holds. Clearly, $\gamma(a)$ is the most general concretization of a.

The essential idea of a Galois connection (α, γ) is as follows: α computes the least abstractions and γ computes the most general concretizations. Galois connections have a couple of useful properties when the partially ordered sets $(\mathcal{C}, \preceq_c)$ and $(\mathcal{A}, \preceq_a)$ are lattices (Section 3.1). We then have the following important properties of Galois connections:

Lemma C.2 (Properties of Galois Connections). *Given a Galois connection (α, γ) from $(\mathcal{C}, \preceq_c)$ to $(\mathcal{A}, \preceq_a)$, the following holds for all $c, c_1, c_2 \in \mathcal{C}$ and all $a, a_1, a_2 \in \mathcal{A}$:*

1. $\alpha(c) = \alpha(\gamma(\alpha(c)))$ *and* $\gamma(\alpha(\gamma(a))) = \gamma(a)$
2. $\alpha(c) \preceq_a a \Leftrightarrow c \preceq_c \gamma(a)$
3. *For all monotonic functions $f_c : \mathcal{C} \rightarrow \mathcal{C}$ and $f_a : \mathcal{A} \rightarrow \mathcal{A}$, we have*

$$[\forall a.\alpha(f_c(\gamma(a))) \preceq_a f_a(a)] \Leftrightarrow [\forall c.f_c(c) \preceq_c \gamma(f_a(\alpha(c)))] \,.$$

If $(\mathcal{C}, \preceq_c)$ and $(\mathcal{A}, \preceq_a)$ are complete lattices with least elements $\bot_c \in \mathcal{C}$ and $\bot_a \in \mathcal{A}$, we, moreover, have the following:

4. $\alpha(\bot_c) = \bot_a$
5. $\alpha(\mathsf{sup}(Q)) = \mathsf{sup}(\{\alpha(c) \mid c \in Q\})$ *and* $\gamma(\mathsf{inf}(Q)) = \mathsf{inf}(\{\gamma(a) \mid a \in Q\})$
6. $\gamma(a) = \mathsf{sup}(\{c \in \mathcal{C} \mid \alpha(c) \preceq_a a\})$ *and* $\alpha(c) = \mathsf{inf}(\{a \in \mathcal{A} \mid c \preceq_c \gamma(a)\})$

Note that the last point states that γ and α uniquely determine each other. Item 2 allows us to lift an inequation $c \preceq_c c_2$ to the abstract level when $c_2 = \gamma(a)$ for some $a \in \mathcal{A}$, and conversely to switch from the abstract level to the concrete level in the same manner. The remaining properties are obvious.

Proof. We prove the above facts in the listed order:

1. By GC3 and GC1 it follows that $\alpha(c) \preceq_a \alpha(\gamma(\alpha(c)))$. Instantiating GC4 with $a := \alpha(c)$ implies $\alpha(\gamma(\alpha(c))) \preceq_a \alpha(c)$ holds. Hence, we have that $\alpha(\gamma(\alpha(c))) = \alpha(c)$. $\gamma(\alpha(\gamma(a))) = \gamma(a)$ is proved analogously.
2. Assume $\alpha(c) \preceq_a a$ holds. By GC2, it follows that $\gamma(\alpha(c)) \preceq_c \gamma(a)$ holds and by GC3, we see that this implies $c \preceq_c \gamma(a)$. To prove the other direction, assume that $c \preceq_c \gamma(a)$ holds. Then, we see by GC1 that $\alpha(c) \preceq_a \alpha(\gamma(a))$ holds and by GC4 that this implies $\alpha(c) \preceq_a a$.
3. Suppose we have for all $a \in \mathcal{A}$ the inequation $\alpha(f_c(\gamma(a))) \preceq_a f_a(a)$. We use GC2 to derive $\gamma(\alpha(f_c(\gamma(a)))) \preceq_c \gamma(f_a(a))$ and by GC3 $f_c(\gamma(a)) \preceq_c \gamma(f_a(a))$. Now, we instantiate $a := \alpha(c)$ for an arbitrary $c \in \mathcal{C}$ and obtain $f_c(\gamma(\alpha(c))) \preceq_c \gamma(f_a(\alpha(c)))$. As f_c is monotonic, we find by GC3 that $f_c(c) \preceq_c f_c(\gamma(\alpha(c)))$, and hence that $f_c(c) \preceq_c \gamma(f_a(\alpha(c)))$. To prove the converse, assume for all $c \in \mathcal{C}$, we have $f_c(c) \preceq_c \gamma(f_a(\alpha(c)))$. Using GC1 and GC4, we obtain $\alpha(f_c(c)) \preceq_a f_a(\alpha(c))$. Instantiating $c := \gamma(a)$ for an arbitrary $a \in \mathcal{A}$, we obtain $\alpha(f_c(\gamma(a))) \preceq_a f_a(\alpha(\gamma(a)))$. By monotony of f_a and GC4, we obtain $f_a(\alpha(\gamma(a))) \preceq_a f_a(a)$, and hence $\alpha(f_c(\gamma(a))) \preceq_a f_a(a)$.
4. As $\bot_c$ is a minimal element, we have $\bot_c \preceq_c \gamma(\bot_a)$. By GC1, we derive from this that $\alpha(\bot_c) \preceq_a \alpha(\gamma(\bot_a))$ and by GC4, we find that $\alpha(\gamma(\bot_a)) \preceq_a \bot_a$. By transitivity of $\preceq_a$, it therefore follows that $\alpha(\bot_c) \preceq_a \bot_a$ holds, and as $\bot_a$ is the minimal element, we must have that $\alpha(\bot_c) = \bot_a$ holds.
5. We prove $\alpha(\mathsf{sup}(Q_c)) = \mathsf{sup}(\{\alpha(c) \mid c \in Q_c\})$ in two steps:
   - For any $c \in Q_c$, it follows from $c \preceq_c \mathsf{sup}(Q_c)$ and the monotony of α that $\alpha(c) \preceq_a \alpha(\mathsf{sup}(Q_c))$ holds. Hence, $\alpha(\mathsf{sup}(Q_c))$ is an upper bound of the set $\{\alpha(c) \mid c \in Q_c\}$. By definition of the supremum, it follows that $\mathsf{sup}(\{\alpha(c) \mid c \in Q_c\}) \preceq_a \alpha(\mathsf{sup}(Q_c))$ must hold.
   - As in the previous item, we derive for any set $Q_a \subseteq \mathcal{A}$ the relation $\mathsf{sup}(\{\gamma(a) \mid a \in Q_a\}) \preceq_c \gamma(\mathsf{sup}(Q_a))$. We now take the set $Q_a := \{\alpha(c) \mid c \in Q_c\}$ and see that $\mathsf{sup}(\{\gamma(\alpha(c)) \mid c \in Q_c\}) \preceq_c \gamma(\mathsf{sup}(\{\alpha(c) \mid c \in Q_c\}))$ holds. By GC3, we have $c \preceq_c \gamma(\alpha(c))$ for any $c \in Q_c$, and therefore $\mathsf{sup}(Q_c) \preceq_c \mathsf{sup}(\{\gamma(\alpha(c)) \mid c \in Q_c\})$. By transitivity of $\preceq_c$, it follows that $\mathsf{sup}(Q_c) \preceq_c \gamma(\mathsf{sup}(\{\alpha(c) \mid c \in Q_c\}))$ holds. Now, we obtain $\alpha(\mathsf{sup}(Q_c)) \preceq_a \alpha(\gamma(\mathsf{sup}(\{\alpha(c) \mid c \in Q_c\})))$ from GC1, the rest follows from GC4.

   The equation $\gamma(\mathsf{inf}(Q_a)) = \mathsf{inf}(\{\gamma(a) \mid a \in Q_a\})$ is proved analogously.
6. To prove the last item, choose an arbitrary $a \in \mathcal{A}$. Using item 2, we see that $\mathsf{sup}(\{c \in \mathcal{C} \mid \alpha(c) \preceq_a a\}) = \mathsf{sup}(\{c \in \mathcal{C} \mid c \preceq_c \gamma(a)\})$. As in particular $\gamma(a) \preceq_c \gamma(a)$ holds, we clearly have $\gamma(a) \preceq_c \mathsf{sup}(\{c \in \mathcal{C} \mid c \preceq_c \gamma(a)\})$. To prove the converse direction, i.e., that $\mathsf{sup}(\{c \in \mathcal{C} \mid c \preceq_c \gamma(a)\}) \preceq_c \gamma(a)$ holds, simply note that $\mathsf{sup}(\{c \in \mathcal{C} \mid c \preceq_c \gamma(a)\})$ denotes the least upper bound of all $c \in \mathcal{C}$ that are smaller or equal than $\gamma(a)$. Hence, it clearly follows that $\mathsf{sup}(\{c \in \mathcal{C} \mid c \preceq_c \gamma(a)\}) \preceq_c \gamma(a)$ holds. The other equation is proved analogously. □

In many cases, the sets $\mathcal{A}$ and $\mathcal{C}$ are sets of sets and the partial orders are in both cases the set inclusion. Then, we have $\mathsf{sup}(X) = \bigcup_{x \in X} x$ and $\mathsf{inf}(X) = \bigcup_{x \in X} x$. The last two items of the previous lemma are then written as follows:

5. $\alpha\left(\bigcup_{c \in X_c} c\right) = \bigcup_{c \in X_c} \alpha(c)$ and $\gamma\left(\bigcap_{a \in X_a} a\right) = \bigcap_{a \in X_a} \gamma(a)$
6. $\gamma(a) = \bigcup_{\alpha(c) \subseteq a} c$ and $\alpha(c) = \bigcap_{c \subseteq \gamma(a)} a$

Hence, α distributes over union and γ over intersection. Hence, the functions are continuous. Moreover, we can prove the following lemma:

Lemma C.3 (Inverse Galois Connection). *Given a Galois connection* (α, γ) *from* $(2^{\mathcal{C}}, \subseteq)$ *to* $(2^{\mathcal{A}}, \subseteq)$*, the pair* $(\alpha^{-1}, \gamma^{-1})$ *is a Galois connection from* $(2^{\mathcal{A}}, \subseteq)$ *to* $(2^{\mathcal{C}}, \subseteq)$*, where* α^{-1} *and* γ^{-1} *are defined as* $\alpha^{-1}(a) := \mathcal{C} \setminus \gamma(\mathcal{A} \setminus a)$ *and* $\gamma^{-1}(c) := \mathcal{A} \setminus \alpha(\mathcal{C} \setminus c)$.

Next, we establish the relationship between binary relations $\sigma \subseteq \mathcal{S}_c \times \mathcal{S}_a$ and Galois connections from from $(2^{\mathcal{S}_c}, \subseteq)$ to $(2^{\mathcal{S}_a}, \subseteq)$. This will be the basis for the alternative definition of simulation by Galois connections.

Lemma C.4 (Galois Connections Induced by Binary Relations). *Given two sets* $\mathcal{S}_c$ *and* $\mathcal{S}_a$ *and a relation* $\sigma \subseteq \mathcal{S}_c \times \mathcal{S}_a$ *on these sets. Then,* $(\alpha_\sigma, \gamma_\sigma)$ *as defined below is a Galois connection from* $(2^{\mathcal{S}_c}, \subseteq)$ *to* $(2^{\mathcal{S}_a}, \subseteq)$*:*

- $\alpha_\sigma(Q_c) := \mathsf{suc}_\exists^\sigma(Q_c) := \{s_a \in \mathcal{S}_a \mid \exists s_c \in \mathcal{S}_c.(s_c, s_a) \in \sigma \land s_c \in Q_c\}$
- $\gamma_\sigma(Q_a) := \mathsf{pre}_\forall^\sigma(Q_a) := \{s_c \in \mathcal{S}_c \mid \forall s_a \in \mathcal{S}_a.(s_c, s_a) \in \sigma \rightarrow s_a \in Q_a\}$

GC1, GC2, GC3, and GC4 follow directly from Lemma 2.6 and Lemma 2.7. The above lemma shows that we can define for any binary relation $\sigma \subseteq \mathcal{S}_c \times \mathcal{S}_a$ a corresponding Galois connection $(\alpha_\sigma, \gamma_\sigma)$. It is remarkable that the converse of the above lemma also holds, i.e., for each Galois connection (α, γ) from $(2^{\mathcal{S}_c}, \subseteq)$ to $(2^{\mathcal{S}_a}, \subseteq)$, we can find a corresponding binary relation $\sigma \subseteq \mathcal{S}_c \times \mathcal{S}_a$. Moreover, this relation σ is uniquely determined.

Lemma C.5 (Binary Relations Induced by Galois Connections). *Given sets* $\mathcal{S}_c$ *and* $\mathcal{S}_a$ *and a Galois connection* (α, γ) *from* $(2^{\mathcal{S}_c}, \subseteq)$ *to* $(2^{\mathcal{S}_a}, \subseteq)$*. Then, there is a unique relation* $\sigma \subseteq \mathcal{S}_c \times \mathcal{S}_a$ *such that the following holds:*

- $\alpha(Q_c) := \mathsf{suc}_\exists^\sigma(Q_c) := \{s_a \in \mathcal{S}_a \mid \exists s_c \in \mathcal{S}_c.(s_c, s_a) \in \sigma \land s_c \in Q_c\}$
- $\gamma(Q_a) := \mathsf{pre}_\forall^\sigma(Q_a) := \{s_c \in \mathcal{S}_c \mid \forall s_a \in \mathcal{S}_a.(s_c, s_a) \in \sigma \rightarrow s_a \in Q_a\}$

Proof. No matter how we define σ, we only need to prove one of the above equations, since α and γ uniquely determine each other and since the previous lemma states that for any relation σ, the right-hand sides of the above equations form a Galois connection. Therefore, we only prove the equation for α for a suitable relation σ.

We define $\sigma := \{(s_c, s_a) \in \mathcal{S}_c \times \mathcal{S}_a \mid s_a \in \alpha(\{s_c\})\}$. Hence, we have to prove that $s_a \in \alpha(Q_c) \Leftrightarrow \exists s_c \in Q_c.s_a \in \alpha(\{s_c\})$, which easily follows from $\bigcup_{s_c \in Q_c} \alpha(\{s_c\}) = \alpha(\bigcup_{s_c \in Q_c} \{s_c\}) = \alpha(Q_c)$ (according to Lemma C.2).

The uniqueness of σ is shown as follows: assume there were two relations σ_1 and σ_2 that fulfill the above requirements. As in particular $s_a \in \alpha(\{s_c\}) \Leftrightarrow (s_c, s_a) \in \sigma$ holds for any σ that fulfills the above relationship for α, we conclude that α uniquely determines the relation σ. □

C.1.2 Galois Simulation

In the previous section, we saw the equivalence between Galois connections and binary relations. *It is therefore only a matter of taste whether we formulate properties by Galois connections or by binary relations.* In particular, simulation relations are binary relations, and therefore we can consider their Galois connections and rephrase properties SIM1, SIM2, and SIM3 for the corresponding Galois connection. This equivalent approach to the simulation preorder is called *Galois-style simulations* in contrast to the *Milner-style simulation* that we gave in Definition 2.10 on page 53.

Definition C.6 (Galois Simulation of Structures). *Given two Kripke structures $\mathcal{K}_c = (\mathcal{I}_c, \mathcal{S}_c, \mathcal{R}_c, \mathcal{L}_c)$ and $\mathcal{K}_a = (\mathcal{I}_a, \mathcal{S}_a, \mathcal{R}_a, \mathcal{L}_a)$ over the variables V_{Σ_c} and V_{Σ_a}, respectively, with $V_{\Sigma_c} \subseteq V_{\Sigma_a}$. Let, moreover, (α, γ) be a Galois connection from $(2^{\mathcal{S}_c}, \subseteq)$ to $(2^{\mathcal{S}_a}, \subseteq)$. We define $\mathcal{K}_c \preccurlyeq^g_{(\alpha,\gamma)} \mathcal{K}_a$ iff the following items are fulfilled:*

- **GSIM1:** $\forall x.\ [\![x]\!]_{\mathcal{K}_a} = \alpha([\![x]\!]_{\mathcal{K}_c}) \wedge \forall x.\alpha([\![x]\!]_{\mathcal{K}_c}) \cap \alpha([\![\neg x]\!]_{\mathcal{K}_c}) = \{\}$
- **GSIM2:** $\forall Q_a \subseteq \mathcal{S}_a.\ \alpha(\mathsf{pre}_{\exists}^{\mathcal{R}_c}(\gamma(Q_a))) \subseteq \mathsf{pre}_{\exists}^{\mathcal{R}_a}(Q_a)$
- **GSIM3:** $\forall s_c \in \mathcal{I}_c.\mathcal{I}_a \cap \alpha(\{s_c\}) \neq \{\}$

We write $\mathcal{K}_c \preccurlyeq^g \mathcal{K}_a$ iff there exists a Galois connection (α, γ) from $(2^{\mathcal{S}_c}, \subseteq)$ to $(2^{\mathcal{S}_a}, \subseteq)$ such that $\mathcal{K}_c \preccurlyeq^g_{(\alpha,\gamma)} \mathcal{K}_a$ holds.

We now compare Galois-style and Milner-style simulations. Clearly, if σ is the corresponding relation to (α, γ), then GSIM3 is equivalent to SIM3. To see this note first that GSIM3 is equivalent to $\forall s_c \in \mathcal{I}_c.\exists s_a \in \mathcal{I}_a.s_a \in \alpha(\{s_c\})$, i.e., to $\forall s_c \in \mathcal{I}_c.\exists s_a \in \mathcal{I}_a.(s_c, s_a) \in \sigma$. The equivalences between SIM1 and GSIM1 and between SIM2 and GSIM2 is not so simple.

Lemma C.7 (Equivalence of GSIM1 and SIM1). *Given two Kripke structures $\mathcal{K}_c = (\mathcal{I}_c, \mathcal{S}_c, \mathcal{R}_c, \mathcal{L}_c)$ and $\mathcal{K}_a = (\mathcal{I}_a, \mathcal{S}_a, \mathcal{R}_a, \mathcal{L}_a)$ over the variables V_{Σ_c} and V_{Σ_a}, respectively with $V_{\Sigma_c} \subseteq V_{\Sigma_a}$. For every Galois connection (α, γ) from $(2^{\mathcal{S}_c}, \subseteq)$ to $(2^{\mathcal{S}_a}, \subseteq)$, the following holds:*

- $\forall x \in V_{\Sigma_c}.\alpha([\![x]\!]_{\mathcal{K}_c}) \cap \alpha([\![\neg x]\!]_{\mathcal{K}_c}) = \{\}$ *is equivalent to* $\forall s_c, s_c' \in \mathcal{S}_c.\forall s_a \in \mathcal{S}_a.s_a \in \alpha(\{s_c\}) \cap \alpha(\{s_c'\}) \rightarrow \mathcal{L}_c(s_c) = \mathcal{L}_c(s_c')$
- *If* $\forall x \in V_{\Sigma_c}.\ [\![x]\!]_{\mathcal{K}_a} = \alpha([\![x]\!]_{\mathcal{K}_c})$ *holds, then* $\forall x \in V_{\Sigma_c}.\alpha([\![x]\!]_{\mathcal{K}_c}) \cap \alpha([\![\neg x]\!]_{\mathcal{K}_c}) = \{\}$ *is equivalent to* $\forall s_c \in \mathcal{S}_c.\forall s_a \in \mathcal{S}_a.s_a \in \alpha(\{s_c\}) \rightarrow \mathcal{L}_c(s_c) = \mathcal{L}_a(s_a)$
- *If* $\forall s_a \in \mathcal{S}_a.\exists s_c \in \mathcal{S}_c.s_a \in \alpha(\{s_c\})$, *i.e.,* $\mathcal{S}_a = \alpha(\mathcal{S}_c)$ *holds, then the following is equivalent:*
  SIM1: $\forall s_c \in \mathcal{S}_c.\forall s_a \in \mathcal{S}_a.s_a \in \alpha(\{s_c\}) \rightarrow \mathcal{L}_c(s_c) = \mathcal{L}_a(s_a)$
  GSIM1: $\forall x.\ [\![x]\!]_{\mathcal{K}_a} = \alpha([\![x]\!]_{\mathcal{K}_c}) \wedge \forall x.\alpha([\![x]\!]_{\mathcal{K}_c}) \cap \alpha([\![\neg x]\!]_{\mathcal{K}_c}) = \{\}$

If α fulfills the property $\forall x \in V_{\Sigma_c}.\alpha([\![x]\!]_{\mathcal{K}_c}) \cap \alpha([\![\neg x]\!]_{\mathcal{K}_c}) = \{\}$, then α is said to be *consistent*. According to the above lemma, this means that states of $\mathcal{S}_c$ that are mapped to the same abstract state are labeled with the same variables.

So, the above lemma shows that under the condition that for every abstract state $s_a \in \mathcal{S}_a$ there is a corresponding concrete state $s_c \in \mathcal{S}_c$, the conditions SIM1 and GSIM1 are equivalent. Clearly, this assumption can be easily established by removing states $s_a \in \mathcal{S}_a$ from $\mathcal{S}_a$ that are not abstractions of a state $s_c \in \mathcal{S}_c$, i.e., use $\mathcal{S}_a' := \alpha(\mathcal{S}_c)$ instead of $\mathcal{S}_a$.

It remains to prove the equivalence of GSIM2 and SIM2. GSIM2 formalizes the following (consider Figure C.1): given a set $Q_a \subseteq \mathcal{S}_a$ of abstract states, we compute the corresponding concrete states $\gamma(Q_a)$, take the predecessor set via $\mathcal{R}_c$ and then compute the abstract states of the predecessors via α. The result must be a subset of the predecessor set that is obtained from Q_a by computing the predecessor set via $\mathcal{R}_a$.

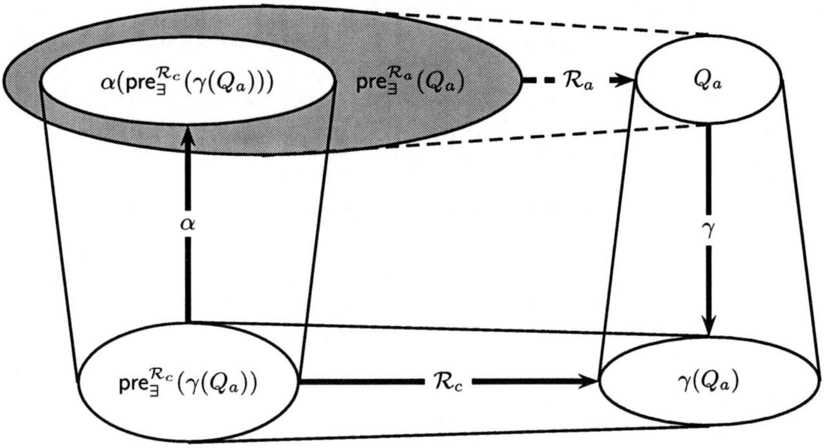

Fig. C.1. Illustration of the $\preccurlyeq^g_{(\alpha,\gamma)}$ preorder (GSIM2).

Hence, GSIM2 states that the predecessor function at the abstract level is an abstraction of the predecessor function at the concrete level. According to Lemma C.2 (item 3), this can be equivalently expressed as $\forall Q_c \subseteq \mathcal{S}_c.\ \mathsf{pre}_\exists^{\mathcal{R}_c}(Q_c) \subseteq \gamma(\mathsf{pre}_\exists^{\mathcal{R}_a}(\alpha(Q_c)))$ (the reader may draw a diagram similar to Figure C.1 for this characterization). As the existential successor and predecessor functions can be distributed over unions and as all successor and predecessor functions are monotonic, we can reduce the last property also to singleton sets Q_c. The next lemma lists further characterizations of GSIM2.

Lemma C.8 (Equivalence of GSIM2 and SIM2). *Given two Kripke structures $\mathcal{K}_c = (\mathcal{I}_c, \mathcal{S}_c, \mathcal{R}_c, \mathcal{L}_c)$ and $\mathcal{K}_a = (\mathcal{I}_a, \mathcal{S}_a, \mathcal{R}_a, \mathcal{L}_a)$ over the variables V_{Σ_c} and V_{Σ_a}, respectively, with $V_{\Sigma_c} \subseteq V_{\Sigma_a}$. Let, moreover, (α, γ) be a Galois connection from $(2^{\mathcal{S}_c}, \subseteq)$ to $(2^{\mathcal{S}_a}, \subseteq)$. Then, the following facts are equivalent to each other:*

1. $\forall Q_a \subseteq \mathcal{S}_a.\ \alpha(\mathsf{pre}_\exists^{\mathcal{R}_c}(\gamma(Q_a))) \subseteq \mathsf{pre}_\exists^{\mathcal{R}_a}(Q_a)$
2. $\forall Q'_c \subseteq \mathcal{S}_c.\ \mathsf{pre}_\exists^{\mathcal{R}_c}(Q'_c) \subseteq \gamma(\mathsf{pre}_\exists^{\mathcal{R}_a}(\alpha(Q'_c)))$
3. $\forall s'_c \in \mathcal{S}_c.\ \mathsf{pre}_\exists^{\mathcal{R}_c}(\{s'_c\}) \subseteq \gamma(\mathsf{pre}_\exists^{\mathcal{R}_a}(\alpha(\{s'_c\})))$
4. $\left(\begin{array}{l}\forall s_c, s'_c \in \mathcal{S}_c. \forall s_a \in \mathcal{S}_a. \\ \qquad (s_c, s'_c) \in \mathcal{R}_c \wedge s_a \in \alpha(\{s_c\}) \rightarrow \exists s'_a \in \alpha(\{s'_c\}).\ (s_a, s'_a) \in \mathcal{R}_a\end{array}\right)$

Moreover, the above properties imply the following ones (which are in each case equivalent to each other):

5. $\forall s'_a \in \mathcal{S}_a.\ \alpha(\mathsf{pre}_\exists^{\mathcal{R}_c}(\gamma(\{s'_a\}))) \subseteq \mathsf{pre}_\exists^{\mathcal{R}_a}(\{s'_a\})$
6. $\left(\begin{array}{l}\forall s_c, s'_c \in \mathcal{S}_c. \forall s_a, s'_a \in \mathcal{S}_a. \\ \qquad (s_c, s'_c) \in \mathcal{R}_c \wedge s'_c \in \gamma(\{s'_a\}) \wedge s_a \in \alpha(\{s_c\}) \rightarrow (s_a, s'_a) \in \mathcal{R}_a\end{array}\right)$

Finally, if the binary relation σ that is induced by (α, γ) is a total function, then the properties 5 and 6 are equivalent to 1-4.

As the first item is exactly the definition of GSIM2 and item 4 is the definition of SIM2, the above lemma states, in particular, that GSIM2 and SIM2 are equivalent. As Lemma C.7 and Lemma C.8 imply that GSIM1, GSIM2, GSIM3 are equivalent to SIM1, SIM2, SIM3, respectively, it now follows that Galois-style simulation and Milner-style simulation are the same:

Theorem C.9 (Correspondence between Galois and Milner Simulation). *Given two Kripke structures $\mathcal{K}_c = (\mathcal{I}_c, \mathcal{S}_c, \mathcal{R}_c, \mathcal{L}_c)$ and $\mathcal{K}_a = (\mathcal{I}_a, \mathcal{S}_a, \mathcal{R}_a, \mathcal{L}_a)$ over the variables V_{Σ_c} and V_{Σ_a}, respectively, with $V_{\Sigma_c} \subseteq V_{\Sigma_a}$. Then, for every simulation relation $\sigma \subseteq \mathcal{S}_c \times \mathcal{S}_a$, there is a Galois connection $(\alpha_\sigma, \gamma_\sigma)$ from $(2^{\mathcal{S}_c}, \subseteq)$ to $(2^{\mathcal{S}_a}, \subseteq)$ such that the following holds:*

$$\mathcal{K}_c \preccurlyeq^g_{(\alpha_\sigma, \gamma_\sigma)} \mathcal{K}_a \Leftrightarrow \mathcal{K}_c \preccurlyeq_\sigma \mathcal{K}_a$$

Conversely, for every Galois connection (α, γ) from $(2^{\mathcal{S}_c}, \subseteq)$ to $(2^{\mathcal{S}_a}, \subseteq)$, there is a simulation relation $\sigma \subseteq \mathcal{S}_c \times \mathcal{S}_a$ such that the following holds:

$$\mathcal{K}_c \preccurlyeq_\sigma \mathcal{K}_a \Leftrightarrow \mathcal{K}_c \preccurlyeq^g_{(\alpha, \gamma)} \mathcal{K}_a$$

Therefore, it follows that $\mathcal{K}_c \preccurlyeq^g \mathcal{K}_a$ holds iff $\mathcal{K}_c \preccurlyeq \mathcal{K}_a$ holds.

The above theorem essentially says that the way that has been taken by process algebras to define the refinement and abstraction of reactive systems with simulation relations [369] coincides with the approach that has been taken by program analysis (abstract interpretation [129, 130]) based on Galois connections.

C.2 Abstract Structures and Preservation Results

In this section, we consider the *construction* of abstract structures: Given a concrete structure $\mathcal{K}_c$, a set of abstract states $\mathcal{S}_a$, and a binary relation $\sigma \subseteq \mathcal{S}_c \times \mathcal{S}_a$, we will construct abstract structures $\mathcal{K}_\sigma^\exists$ and $\mathcal{K}_\sigma^\forall$ such that $\mathcal{K}_\sigma^\exists$ preserves all existential properties and $\mathcal{K}_\sigma^\forall$ preserves all universal properties. Existential properties are all formulas where all subformulas starting with a existential path quantifier E or existential modal operators $\Diamond$, $\overleftarrow{\Diamond}$ occur under an even number of negation symbols, and all subformulas starting with a universal path quantifier A or universal modal operators $\Box$, $\overleftarrow{\Box}$ occur under an odd number of negation symbols. Universal properties are the negations of existential properties.

As we will see, every structure $\mathcal{K}_a$ with $\mathcal{K}_c \preccurlyeq \mathcal{K}_a$ preserves existential properties, i.e., $\mathcal{K}_c \models \Phi_\exists$ implies $\mathcal{K}_a \models \Phi_\exists$ for every existential property $\Phi_\exists$. Analogously, every structure $\mathcal{K}_a$ with $\mathcal{K}_a \preccurlyeq \mathcal{K}_c$ preserves universal properties, i.e., $\mathcal{K}_c \models \Phi_\forall$ implies $\mathcal{K}_a \models \Phi_\forall$ for every universal property $\Phi_\forall$.

Definition C.10 (Abstract Structures Induced by Binary Relations). *Given a Kripke structure $\mathcal{K}_c = (\mathcal{I}_c, \mathcal{S}_c, \mathcal{R}_c, \mathcal{L}_c)$ over the variables V_Σ, a set of abstract states $\mathcal{S}_a$, and a relation $\sigma \subseteq \mathcal{S}_c \times \mathcal{S}_a$. Then, we define the following:*

- $\mathcal{S}_\sigma := \{s_a \mid \exists s_c \in \mathcal{S}_c.(s_c, s_a) \in \sigma\}$
- $\mathcal{I}_\sigma := \{s_a \mid \exists s_c \in \mathcal{I}_c.(s_c, s_a) \in \sigma\}$
- $\mathcal{R}_\sigma^\exists := \{(s_a, s_a') \mid s_a \in \mathsf{suc}_\exists^\sigma(\mathsf{pre}_\exists^{\mathcal{R}_c}(\mathsf{pre}_\exists^\sigma(\{s_a'\})))$
- $\mathcal{R}_\sigma^\forall := \{(s_a, s_a') \mid s_a \in \mathsf{suc}_\forall^\sigma(\mathsf{pre}_\exists^{\mathcal{R}_c}(\mathsf{pre}_\exists^\sigma(\{s_a'\})))$
- $\mathcal{L}_\sigma(s_a) := \bigcup_{(s_c, s_a) \in \sigma} \mathcal{L}_c(s_c)$

The existential abstract structure $\mathcal{K}_\sigma^\exists$ is then defined as $\mathcal{K}_\sigma^\exists := (\mathcal{I}_\sigma, \mathcal{S}_\sigma, \mathcal{R}_\sigma^\exists, \mathcal{L}_\sigma)$, and the universal abstract structure $\mathcal{K}_\sigma^\forall$ is defined as $\mathcal{K}_\sigma^\forall := (\mathcal{I}_\sigma, \mathcal{S}_\sigma, \mathcal{R}_\sigma^\forall, \mathcal{L}_\sigma)$.

As binary relations correspond to Galois connections, we can alternatively formulate the construction of $\mathcal{K}_\sigma^\exists$ and $\mathcal{K}_\sigma^\forall$ in terms of Galois connections.

Definition C.11 (Abstract Structures Induced by Galois Connections). *For every Kripke structure $\mathcal{K}_c = (\mathcal{I}_c, \mathcal{S}_c, \mathcal{R}_c, \mathcal{L}_c)$ over the variables V_Σ, every set of abstract states $\mathcal{S}_a$, and every Galois connection (α, γ) from $(2^{\mathcal{S}_c}, \subseteq)$ to $(2^{\mathcal{S}_a}, \subseteq)$, we define the following:*

- $\mathcal{S}_{(\alpha,\gamma)} := \alpha(\mathcal{S}_c)$
- $\mathcal{I}_{(\alpha,\gamma)} := \alpha(\mathcal{I}_c)$
- $\mathcal{R}_{(\alpha,\gamma)}^\exists := \{(s_a, s_a') \mid s_a \in \mathsf{suc}_\exists^\sigma(\mathsf{pre}_\exists^{\mathcal{R}_c}(\mathsf{pre}_\exists^\sigma(\{s_a'\})))\}$
- $\mathcal{R}_{(\alpha,\gamma)}^\forall := \{(s_a, s_a') \mid s_a \in \mathsf{suc}_\forall^\sigma(\mathsf{pre}_\exists^{\mathcal{R}_c}(\mathsf{pre}_\exists^\sigma(\{s_a'\})))\}$
- $\mathcal{L}_{(\alpha,\gamma)}$ *is defined such that* $\forall x \in V_\Sigma.\, [\![x]\!]_{\mathcal{K}_{(\alpha,\gamma)}^\exists} := \alpha([\![x]\!]_{\mathcal{K}_c})$ *holds.*

The existential abstract structure $\mathcal{K}_{(\alpha,\gamma)}^\exists$ and the universal abstract structure $\mathcal{K}_{(\alpha,\gamma)}^\forall$ are then defined as $\mathcal{K}_{(\alpha,\gamma)}^\exists := (\mathcal{I}_{(\alpha,\gamma)}, \mathcal{S}_{(\alpha,\gamma)}, \mathcal{R}_{(\alpha,\gamma)}^\exists, \mathcal{L}_{(\alpha,\gamma)})$, and $\mathcal{K}_{(\alpha,\gamma)}^\forall := (\mathcal{I}_{(\alpha,\gamma)}, \mathcal{S}_{(\alpha,\gamma)}, \mathcal{R}_{(\alpha,\gamma)}^\forall, \mathcal{L}_{(\alpha,\gamma)})$, respectively.

It is easy to see that if σ is the corresponding relation for the Galois connection (α, γ) then we have $\mathcal{K}_{\sigma}^{\exists} = \mathcal{K}_{(\alpha,\gamma)}^{\exists}$ and $\mathcal{K}_{\sigma}^{\forall} = \mathcal{K}_{(\alpha,\gamma)}^{\forall}$: Note that then $(s_c, s_a) \in \sigma \Leftrightarrow s_a \in \alpha(\{s_c\})$ holds. Hence, it is only a matter of taste whether we prefer the construction of the abstract structure by a Galois connection or by a binary relation between concrete and abstract states.

As can be seen, both structures only differ in their transition relations. We will now prove that $\mathcal{K}_{\sigma}^{\forall} \preccurlyeq_{\sigma^{-1}} \mathcal{K}_c$ and $\mathcal{K}_c \preccurlyeq_{\sigma} \mathcal{K}_{\sigma}^{\exists}$ hold. For this reason, consider first the existential structures $\mathcal{K}_{\sigma}^{\exists}$.

It is easily seen that for arbitrary relations σ the relation $\mathcal{K}_c \preccurlyeq_{\sigma} \mathcal{K}_{\sigma}^{\exists}$ need not hold. The reason for this is simply that σ can only be a simulation relation if σ is total on the set of states that are reachable from the initial states $\mathcal{I}_c$. Restricting $\mathcal{K}_c$ to the reachable states is clearly no severe restriction, and therefore we can demand that σ must be total on $\mathcal{S}_c$. Note that when σ is total on $\mathcal{S}_c$, it follows by Lemma 2.7 that $\forall Q_a \subseteq \mathcal{S}_a.\mathsf{pre}_{\forall}^{\sigma}(Q_a) \subseteq \mathsf{pre}_{\exists}^{\sigma}(Q_a)$ holds. As predecessor and successor functions are monotonic, it hence follows that $\mathsf{suc}_{\exists}^{\sigma}(\mathsf{pre}_{\exists}^{\mathcal{R}_c}(\mathsf{pre}_{\forall}^{\sigma}(\{s'_a\}))) \subseteq \mathsf{suc}_{\exists}^{\sigma}(\mathsf{pre}_{\exists}^{\mathcal{R}_c}(\mathsf{pre}_{\exists}^{\sigma}(\{s'_a\}))) = \mathsf{pre}_{\exists}^{\mathcal{R}_{\sigma}^{\exists}}(\{s'_a\})$ holds. However, to satisfy GSIM2, we need this property for arbitrary sets Q_a and not only for singleton ones. It is proved in the next lemma that GSIM2 also holds.

Lemma C.12 (Existential Abstract Structure Induced by a Binary Relation). *Given a Kripke structure $\mathcal{K}_c = (\mathcal{I}_c, \mathcal{S}_c, \mathcal{R}_c, \mathcal{L}_c)$ over the variables V_{Σ}, a set of abstract states $\mathcal{S}_a$, and a relation $\sigma \subseteq \mathcal{S}_c \times \mathcal{S}_a$ such that the following holds:*

- *σ is total on $\mathcal{S}_c$, i.e., $\forall s_c \in \mathcal{S}_c.\exists s_a \in \mathcal{S}_a.(s_c, s_a) \in \sigma$*
- *σ is consistent, i.e., for all $s_c, s'_c \in \mathcal{S}_c$ and for all $s_a \in \mathcal{S}_a$ with $(s_c, s_a) \in \sigma$ and $(s'_c, s_a) \in \sigma$ it follows that $\mathcal{L}_c(s_c) = \mathcal{L}_c(s'_c)$.*

Then it follows that $\mathcal{K}_c \preccurlyeq_{\sigma} \mathcal{K}_{\sigma}^{\exists}$. Conversely, if $\mathcal{K}_c \preccurlyeq_{\sigma} \mathcal{K}_{\sigma}^{\exists}$ holds, then σ is total on $\mathcal{S}_c$ and consistent.

Now, consider the universal structure $\mathcal{K}_{\sigma}^{\forall}$. Our intention for the construction of the universal abstract structure $\mathcal{K}_{\sigma}^{\forall}$ was that $\mathcal{K}_{\sigma}^{\forall} \preccurlyeq \mathcal{K}_c$ should hold.

Lemma C.13 (Universal Abstract Structure Induced by a Binary Relation). *Given a Kripke structure $\mathcal{K}_c = (\mathcal{I}_c, \mathcal{S}_c, \mathcal{R}_c, \mathcal{L}_c)$ over the variables V_{Σ}, a set of abstract states $\mathcal{S}_a$, and a relation $\sigma \subseteq \mathcal{S}_c \times \mathcal{S}_a$ such that the following hold:*

- *σ is total on $\mathcal{S}_a$, i.e., $\forall s_a \in \mathcal{S}_a.\exists s_c \in \mathcal{S}_c.(s_c, s_a) \in \sigma$*
- *σ is consistent, i.e., for all $s_c, s'_c \in \mathcal{S}_c$ and for all $s_a \in \mathcal{S}_a$ with $(s_c, s_a) \in \sigma$ and $(s'_c, s_a) \in \sigma$ it follows that $\mathcal{L}_c(s_c) = \mathcal{L}_c(s'_c)$.*

Then it follows that $\mathcal{K}_{\sigma}^{\forall} \preccurlyeq_{\sigma^{-1}} \mathcal{K}_c$, where $\sigma^{-1} := \{(s_a, s_c) \mid (s_c, s_a) \in \sigma\}$. Conversely, if $\mathcal{K}_{\sigma}^{\forall} \preccurlyeq_{\sigma^{-1}} \mathcal{K}_c$ holds, then σ is total on $\mathcal{S}_a$ and consistent.

So, we have also achieved our second goal, namely to construct a structure $\mathcal{K}_{\sigma}^{\forall}$ such that $\mathcal{K}_{\sigma}^{\forall} \preccurlyeq_{\sigma^{-1}} \mathcal{K}_c$ holds.

Consider now the preservation of formulas, i.e., we want to know which formulas that hold on $\mathcal{K}_c$ still hold in an abstract structure $\mathcal{K}_a$ when $\mathcal{K}_c \preccurlyeq \mathcal{K}_a$ holds. For this reason, we first give the following definition to formalize what it means that a formula is preserved by a Galois connection (α, γ).

Definition C.14 (Preservation of Formulas). *Given Kripke structures $\mathcal{K}_c = (\mathcal{I}_c, \mathcal{S}_c, \mathcal{R}_c, \mathcal{L}_c)$ and $\mathcal{K}_a = (\mathcal{I}_a, \mathcal{S}_a, \mathcal{R}_a, \mathcal{L}_a)$ over the variables V_Σ, together with a Galois connection (α, γ) from $(2^{\mathcal{S}_c}, \subseteq)$ to $(2^{\mathcal{S}_a}, \subseteq)$. For every formula Φ, we define:*

- *α preserves Φ iff $\forall s_c \in [\![\Phi]\!]_{\mathcal{K}_c}.\alpha(\{s_c\}) \subseteq [\![\Phi]\!]_{\mathcal{K}_a}$*
- *α strongly preserves Φ iff $\forall s_c.s_c \in [\![\Phi]\!]_{\mathcal{K}_c} = \alpha(\{s_c\}) \subseteq [\![\Phi]\!]_{\mathcal{K}_a}$*

We can alternatively formulate the preservation of formulas in terms of a binary relation between $\mathcal{K}_c$ and $\mathcal{K}_a$:

- α preserves Φ iff for all $s_c \in \mathcal{S}_c$

$$(\mathcal{K}_c, s_c) \models \Phi \Rightarrow \forall s_a \in \mathcal{S}_a.(s_c, s_a) \in \sigma \rightarrow (\mathcal{K}_a, s_a) \models \Phi$$

- α strongly preserves Φ iff for all $s_c \in \mathcal{S}_c$

$$(\mathcal{K}_c, s_c) \models \Phi \Leftrightarrow \forall s_a \in \mathcal{S}_a.(s_c, s_a) \in \sigma \rightarrow (\mathcal{K}_a, s_a) \models \Phi$$

Lemma C.15 (Preservation of Formulas). *Given Kripke structures $\mathcal{K}_c = (\mathcal{I}_c, \mathcal{S}_c, \mathcal{R}_c, \mathcal{L}_c)$ and $\mathcal{K}_a = (\mathcal{I}_a, \mathcal{S}_a, \mathcal{R}_a, \mathcal{L}_a)$ over the variables V_Σ, and a Galois connection (α, γ) from $(2^{\mathcal{S}_c}, \subseteq)$ to $(2^{\mathcal{S}_a}, \subseteq)$. Then, α preserves Φ iff $\alpha([\![\Phi]\!]_{\mathcal{K}_c}) \subseteq [\![\Phi]\!]_{\mathcal{K}_a}$. Moreover, α strongly preserves Φ iff $[\![\Phi]\!]_{\mathcal{K}_c} = \gamma([\![\Phi]\!]_{\mathcal{K}_a})$.*

Proof. The first proposition is easily proved:

$$\begin{aligned}
\alpha \text{ preserves } \Phi &\Leftrightarrow \forall s_c \in [\![\Phi]\!]_{\mathcal{K}_c}.\alpha(\{s_c\}) \subseteq [\![\Phi]\!]_{\mathcal{K}_a} \\
&\Leftrightarrow \textstyle\bigcup_{s_c \in [\![\Phi]\!]_{\mathcal{K}_c}} \alpha(\{s_c\}) \subseteq [\![\Phi]\!]_{\mathcal{K}_a} \\
&\Leftrightarrow \alpha(\textstyle\bigcup_{s_c \in [\![\Phi]\!]_{\mathcal{K}_c}} \{s_c\}) \subseteq [\![\Phi]\!]_{\mathcal{K}_a} \\
&\Leftrightarrow \alpha([\![\Phi]\!]_{\mathcal{K}_c}) \subseteq [\![\Phi]\!]_{\mathcal{K}_a}
\end{aligned}$$

To prove the second proposition, note first that if α strongly preserves Φ, then α also (weakly) preserves Φ. Hence, by the above it follows that $\alpha([\![\Phi]\!]_{\mathcal{K}_c}) \subseteq [\![\Phi]\!]_{\mathcal{K}_a}$ holds, which is by Lemma C.2 equivalent to $[\![\Phi]\!]_{\mathcal{K}_c} \subseteq \gamma([\![\Phi]\!]_{\mathcal{K}_a})$.

If α strongly preserves Φ, then it follows $\forall s_c.\alpha(\{s_c\}) \subseteq [\![\Phi]\!]_{\mathcal{K}_a} \rightarrow s_c \in [\![\Phi]\!]_{\mathcal{K}_c}$. Hence, it follows that $\forall s_c.\{s_c\} \subseteq \gamma([\![\Phi]\!]_{\mathcal{K}_a}) \rightarrow s_c \in [\![\Phi]\!]_{\mathcal{K}_c}$, which is equivalent to $\gamma([\![\Phi]\!]_{\mathcal{K}_a}) \subseteq [\![\Phi]\!]_{\mathcal{K}_c}$. Therefore, we have proved that if α strongly preserves Φ, then it follows that $[\![\Phi]\!]_{\mathcal{K}_c} = \gamma([\![\Phi]\!]_{\mathcal{K}_a})$.

To prove the converse (i.e., that $[\![\Phi]\!]_{\mathcal{K}_c} = \gamma([\![\Phi]\!]_{\mathcal{K}_a})$ implies that α strongly preserves Φ), note that $\alpha(\{s_c\}) \subseteq [\![\Phi]\!]_{\mathcal{K}_a}$ is equivalent to $\{s_c\} \subseteq \gamma([\![\Phi]\!]_{\mathcal{K}_a}) = [\![\Phi]\!]_{\mathcal{K}_c}$, and this in turn is equivalent to $s_c \in [\![\Phi]\!]_{\mathcal{K}_c}$. □

Theorem C.16 (Preservation of Existential Properties). *Given structures $\mathcal{K}_c = (\mathcal{I}_c, \mathcal{S}_c, \mathcal{R}_c, \mathcal{L}_c)$ and $\mathcal{K}_a = (\mathcal{I}_a, \mathcal{S}_a, \mathcal{R}_a, \mathcal{L}_a)$ over the variables V_Σ, together with a Galois connection (α, γ) from $(2^{\mathcal{S}_c}, \subseteq)$ to $(2^{\mathcal{S}_a}, \subseteq)$. Given that $\mathcal{K}_c \preccurlyeq^g_{(\alpha,\gamma)} \mathcal{K}_a$ holds, then α preserves all existential properties.*

Therefore, all existential properties are preserved via α to $\mathcal{K}^\exists_\sigma$ and all universal properties are preserved via α^{-1} to $\mathcal{K}^\forall_\sigma$. The construction of the structures $\mathcal{K}^\exists_\sigma$ and $\mathcal{K}^\forall_\sigma$ allows us therefore to check either existential or universal properties in abstract structures instead of given concrete ones.

C.3 Optimal and Faithful Abstractions

We already know that $\mathcal{K}_c \preccurlyeq_\sigma \mathcal{K}^\exists_\sigma$ and $\mathcal{K}^\forall_\sigma \preccurlyeq_{\sigma^{-1}} \mathcal{K}_c$ holds under the conditions that σ is total and σ is consistent. However, we have not yet considered the optimality of the abstractions. To make an effective use of the preservation of formulas, we should find abstract structures that satisfy *as many existential/universal formulas as possible*. Universal properties are satisfied in a state if they hold on every path starting in that state. For this reason, the general strategy is to construct the transition relation such that there are as few paths as possible. For this reason, we should keep $\mathcal{R}^\exists_\sigma$ as small as possible, but of course, condition GSIM2 must be fulfilled. Analogously, we should define $\mathcal{R}^\forall_\sigma$ as large as possible such that GSIM2 is still fulfilled. Hence, for reasons of optimality, we should define

$$\begin{aligned}
\mathcal{R}^\exists_\sigma &:= \min\{\mathcal{R}_a \subseteq \mathcal{S}_a \times \mathcal{S}_a \mid \forall Q_a \subseteq \mathcal{S}_a.\ \alpha(\mathsf{pre}^{\mathcal{R}_c}_\exists(\gamma(Q_a))) \subseteq \mathsf{pre}^{\mathcal{R}_a}_\exists(Q_a)\} \\
\mathcal{R}^\forall_\sigma &:= \max\{\mathcal{R}_a \subseteq \mathcal{S}_a \times \mathcal{S}_a \mid \forall Q_c \subseteq \mathcal{S}_c.\ \alpha^{-1}(\mathsf{pre}^{\mathcal{R}_a}_\exists(\gamma^{-1}(Q_c))) \subseteq \mathsf{pre}^{\mathcal{R}_c}_\exists(Q_c)\}
\end{aligned}$$

It is easily seen that the conditions $\forall Q_c \subseteq \mathcal{S}_c.\ \alpha^{-1}(\mathsf{pre}^{\mathcal{R}_a}_\exists(\gamma^{-1}(Q_c))) \subseteq \mathsf{pre}^{\mathcal{R}_c}_\exists(Q_c)$ and $\forall s'_a \in \mathcal{S}_a.\ \mathsf{pre}^{\mathcal{R}^\forall_\sigma}_\exists(\{s'_a\}) \subseteq \mathsf{suc}^\sigma_\forall(\mathsf{pre}^{\mathcal{R}_c}_\exists(\mathsf{pre}^\sigma_\exists(\{s'_a\})))$ are equivalent. Therefore, the best choice for $\mathcal{R}^\forall_\sigma$ is the maximal relation that still fulfills $\forall s_a, s'_a \in \mathcal{S}_a.\ (s_a, s'_a) \in \mathcal{R}^\forall_\sigma \rightarrow s_a \in \mathsf{suc}^\sigma_\forall(\mathsf{pre}^{\mathcal{R}_c}_\exists(\mathsf{pre}^\sigma_\exists(\{s'_a\})))$. Therefore the definition of $\mathcal{R}^\forall_\sigma$ as we made it in Definitions C.10 and C.11 is in fact the best choice to preserve as many universal properties as possible.

Also, for the definition of $\mathcal{K}^\forall_\sigma$, we should make the set of initial states as large as possible such that GSIM3 for $\mathcal{K}^\forall_\sigma \preccurlyeq_{\sigma^{-1}} \mathcal{K}_c$ is still satisfied. This means we look for the largest set $\mathcal{I}_\sigma$ such that $\forall s_a \in \mathcal{I}_\sigma.\exists s_c \in \mathcal{I}_c.(s_c, s_a) \in \sigma$ holds. Note that the latter is equivalent to $\forall s_a \in \mathcal{I}_\sigma.s_a \in \mathsf{suc}^\sigma_\exists(\mathcal{I}_c)$ and hence to $\mathcal{I}_\sigma \subseteq \mathsf{suc}^\sigma_\exists(\mathcal{I}_c)$. So, we look for the largest subset of $\mathsf{suc}^\sigma_\exists(\mathcal{I}_c)$, and this is obviously $\mathsf{suc}^\sigma_\exists(\mathcal{I}_c) = \alpha(\mathcal{I}_c)$ itself.

Therefore, the definition of $\mathcal{K}^\forall_\sigma$ is optimal: any other structure $\mathcal{K}_a$ with $\mathcal{K}_a \preccurlyeq_{\sigma^{-1}} \mathcal{K}_c$ must have a smaller transition relation or a smaller set of initial states, and therefore it follows that $\mathcal{K}_a \preccurlyeq \mathcal{K}^\forall_\sigma$ holds. *In other words, with respect to the simulation preorder, $\mathcal{K}^\forall_\sigma$ is the largest structure such that $\mathcal{K}_a \preccurlyeq_{\sigma^{-1}} \mathcal{K}_c$ holds, i.e., the maximal structure of the set of all structures that are simulated by $\mathcal{K}_c$.*

Conversely, for the definition of $\mathcal{K}_\sigma^\exists$, we should make the set of initial states as small as possible such that GSIM3 for $\mathcal{K}_c \preccurlyeq_\sigma \mathcal{K}_\sigma^\exists$ is still satisfied. This means we look for the least set $\mathcal{I}_\sigma$ such that $\forall s_c \in \mathcal{I}_c.\exists s_a \in \mathcal{I}_\sigma.(s_c, s_a) \in \sigma$ holds. Note that the latter is equivalent to $\forall s_c \in \mathcal{I}_c.s_c \in \mathsf{pre}_\exists^\sigma(\mathcal{I}_\sigma)$ and hence to $\mathcal{I}_c \subseteq \mathsf{pre}_\exists^\sigma(\mathcal{I}_\sigma)$. Given that σ is a total function, then it follows by Lemma 2.7 that $\mathsf{pre}_\exists^\sigma(Q) = \mathsf{pre}_\forall^\sigma(Q)$ holds. In this case, we look for the least set $\mathcal{I}_\sigma$ such that $\mathcal{I}_c \subseteq \mathsf{pre}_\forall^\sigma(Q) = \gamma(Q)$ holds. Clearly, it follows by Lemma C.2 that the latter condition is equivalent to $\alpha(\mathcal{I}_c) \subseteq \mathcal{I}_\sigma$ so that the minimal solution for $\mathcal{I}_\sigma$ is the set $\alpha(\mathcal{I}_c)$. This is what we have used in the definition of $\mathcal{K}_\sigma^\exists$.

The situation for the transition relation of $\mathcal{K}_\sigma^\exists$ is similar: If σ is a total function, it follows by Lemma 2.7 that $\forall Q_\sigma \subseteq \mathcal{S}_\sigma.\mathsf{pre}_\forall^\sigma(Q_\sigma) = \mathsf{pre}_\exists^\sigma(Q_\sigma)$ holds. As the predecessor and successor functions are continuous, i.e., they distribute over unions, it hence follows that

$$\forall Q_\sigma \subseteq \mathcal{S}_\sigma.\mathsf{suc}_\exists^\sigma(\mathsf{pre}_\exists^{\mathcal{R}_c}(\mathsf{pre}_\forall^\sigma(Q_\sigma))) = \mathsf{suc}_\exists^\sigma(\mathsf{pre}_\exists^{\mathcal{R}_c}(\mathsf{pre}_\exists^\sigma(Q_\sigma))) = \mathsf{pre}_\exists^{\mathcal{R}_\sigma^\exists}(Q_\sigma)$$

Now, if $\mathcal{K}_a = (\mathcal{I}_\sigma, \mathcal{S}_\sigma, \mathcal{R}_a, \mathcal{L}_\sigma)$ is a structure such that $\mathcal{K}_c \preccurlyeq_\sigma \mathcal{K}_a$ holds, it follows by SIM2 and Lemma C.8 that $\forall Q_\sigma \subseteq \mathcal{S}_\sigma.\mathsf{suc}_\exists^\sigma(\mathsf{pre}_\exists^{\mathcal{R}_c}(\mathsf{pre}_\forall^\sigma(Q_\sigma))) \subseteq \mathsf{pre}_\exists^{\mathcal{R}_a}(Q_\sigma)$ holds. Therefore, we conclude by the above equation that $\forall Q_\sigma \subseteq \mathcal{S}_\sigma.\mathsf{pre}_\exists^{\mathcal{R}_\sigma^\exists}(Q_\sigma) \subseteq \mathsf{pre}_\exists^{\mathcal{R}_a}(Q_\sigma)$ which means that $\mathcal{R}_\sigma^\exists \subseteq \mathcal{R}_a$ (simply instantiate Q_σ with a singleton set to see this). Therefore, we have proved the following theorem.

Theorem C.17 (Optimality of Abstract Structures). *Given a Kripke structure $\mathcal{K}_c = (\mathcal{I}_c, \mathcal{S}_c, \mathcal{R}_c, \mathcal{L}_c)$ over the variables V_Σ, a set of abstract states $\mathcal{S}_a$, and a binary relation $\sigma \subseteq \mathcal{S}_c \times \mathcal{S}_a$ with the following properties:*

- *σ is total on $\mathcal{S}_c$, i.e., $\forall s_c \in \mathcal{S}_c.\exists s_a \in \mathcal{S}_a.(s_c, s_a) \in \sigma$*
- *σ is total on $\mathcal{S}_a$, i.e., $\forall s_a \in \mathcal{S}_a.\exists s_c \in \mathcal{S}_c.(s_c, s_a) \in \sigma$*
- *σ is consistent, i.e., for all $s_c, s_c' \in \mathcal{S}_c$ and for all $s_a \in \mathcal{S}_a$ with $(s_c, s_a) \in \sigma$ and $(s_c', s_a) \in \sigma$ it follows that $\mathcal{L}_c(s_c) = \mathcal{L}_c(s_c')$.*

Under these conditions, we have $\mathcal{K}_\sigma^\forall \preccurlyeq_{\sigma^{-1}} \mathcal{K}_c$ and $\mathcal{K}_c \preccurlyeq_\sigma \mathcal{K}_\sigma^\exists$. Moreover, if $\mathcal{K}_a = (\mathcal{I}_a, \mathcal{S}_\sigma, \mathcal{R}_a, \mathcal{L}_a)$ is a structure with $\mathcal{K}_a \preccurlyeq_{\sigma^{-1}} \mathcal{K}_c$, then it follows that $\mathcal{R}_a \subseteq \mathcal{R}_\sigma^\forall$ and $\mathcal{I}_a \subseteq \mathcal{I}_\sigma$ holds, i.e., that $\mathcal{K}_a \preccurlyeq \mathcal{K}_\sigma^\forall$. Finally, if σ is a function, then it follows for any structure $\mathcal{K}_a = (\mathcal{I}_a, \mathcal{S}_\sigma, \mathcal{R}_a, \mathcal{L}_a)$ with $\mathcal{K}_c \preccurlyeq_\sigma \mathcal{K}_a$ that $\mathcal{R}_\sigma^\exists \subseteq \mathcal{R}_a$ and $\mathcal{I}_\sigma \subseteq \mathcal{I}_a$, i.e., that $\mathcal{K}_\sigma^\exists \preccurlyeq \mathcal{K}_a$.

Hence, the structure $\mathcal{K}_\sigma^\forall$ has been defined in an optimal manner. If σ is a total function, then there is also a minimal abstract structure that simulates $\mathcal{K}_c$ via σ, and this minimal structure is $\mathcal{K}_\sigma^\exists$. This means that our definition of the abstract structure is in this case optimal.

One might wonder what happens if σ is not a function. Clearly, we still have $\mathcal{K}_c \preccurlyeq_\sigma \mathcal{K}_\sigma^\exists$ provided that σ is total on $\mathcal{S}_c$ and consistent. However, note that condition (1) we gave before for the minimality of $\mathcal{R}_\sigma^\exists$ need not always have a unique solution. For this reason, we need an alternative notion of optimality in case σ is not a function. This leads to the following definition:

Definition C.18 (Faithful Abstraction). *Given two Kripke structures* $\mathcal{K}_c = (\mathcal{I}_c, \mathcal{S}_c, \mathcal{R}_c, \mathcal{L}_c)$ *and* $\mathcal{K}_a = (\mathcal{I}_a, \mathcal{S}_a, \mathcal{R}_a, \mathcal{L}_a)$, *and a relation* $\sigma \subseteq \mathcal{S}_a \times \mathcal{S}_c$. $\mathcal{K}_a$ *is a faithful abstraction of* $\mathcal{K}_c$ *w.r.t.* σ *iff the following holds:*

- $\mathcal{K}_c \preccurlyeq_\sigma \mathcal{K}_a$
- *For any structure* $\mathcal{K}'_a = (\mathcal{I}'_a, \mathcal{S}'_a, \mathcal{R}'_a, \mathcal{L}'_a)$ *with* $\mathcal{K}_c \preccurlyeq_\sigma \mathcal{K}'_a$ *and* $\mathcal{R}'_a \subseteq \mathcal{R}_a$, *it follows that* $\mathcal{K}_a$ *and* $\mathcal{K}'_a$ *are bisimilar.*

Hence, if $\mathcal{K}_a$ is a faithful abstraction of $\mathcal{K}_c$ via σ, then $\mathcal{K}_a$ is optimal in the following sense: Any structure $\mathcal{K}'_a$ with a smaller transition relation than $\mathcal{K}_a$ that simulates $\mathcal{K}_c$ as well, must be bisimilar to $\mathcal{K}_a$. Therefore, $\mathcal{K}_a$ and $\mathcal{K}'_a$ satisfy the same set of formulas and it is therefore useless to remove further transitions from $\mathcal{R}_a$ (note that the reason for keeping the transition relation as small as possible was to achieve that as many universal properties as possible should be satisfied). *Note that by the above definition, all structures that are faithful abstractions of another structure are bisimilar to each other.*

We now prove the following theorem that provides us with a condition to efficiently check the faithfulness of an abstract structure [331]. Apart from totality, and the properties SIM1 and SIM3, the important condition is that all states $s_c, s'_c \in \mathcal{S}_c$ that have a common abstract state must have the same abstract states (see property A1 in the theorem below).

Theorem C.19 (Faithfulness). *Given a Kripke structure* $\mathcal{K}_c = (\mathcal{I}_c, \mathcal{S}_c, \mathcal{R}_c, \mathcal{L}_c)$, *and a relation* $\sigma \subseteq \mathcal{S}_a \times \mathcal{S}_c$ *that satisfies the following properties:*

A1: for all $s_c, s'_c \in \mathcal{S}_c$ *and all* $s_a, s'_a \in \mathcal{S}_a$, *the following holds*

$$(s_c, s'_a) \in \sigma \wedge (s'_c, s'_a) \in \sigma \wedge (s'_c, s_a) \in \sigma \rightarrow (s_c, s_a) \in \sigma$$

A2: σ *is total on* $\mathcal{S}_c$, *i.e.,* $\forall s_c \in \mathcal{S}_c . \exists s_a \in \mathcal{S}_a . (s_c, s_a) \in \sigma$
A3: σ *satisfies SIM1, i.e.,* σ *preserves labels:*
$\forall s_c \in \mathcal{S}_c . \forall s_a \in \mathcal{S}_a . (s_c, s_a) \in \sigma \rightarrow \mathcal{L}_c(s_c) = \mathcal{L}_a(s_a)$
A4: σ *satisfies SIM3, i.e.,* $\forall s_c \in \mathcal{I}_c . \exists s_a \in \mathcal{I}_a . (s_c, s_a) \in \sigma$

Under these conditions, the structure $\mathcal{K}_\sigma^\exists$ *as given in Definition C.10 is a faithful abstraction of* $\mathcal{K}_c$ *w.r.t.* σ.

Proof. Using the given assumptions, we prove that $\mathcal{K}_\sigma^\exists$ is bisimilar to $\mathcal{K}_a$. For this reason, we define $(s_a, s'_a) \in \varrho :\Leftrightarrow \exists s_c \in \mathcal{S}_c . (s_c, s_a) \in \sigma \wedge (s_c, s'_a) \in \sigma$ and prove that ϱ is a bisimulation relation between $\mathcal{K}_\sigma^\exists$ and $\mathcal{K}_a$. We first abbreviate some further conditions:

A1′: $\forall s_c, s'_c \in \mathcal{S}_c . \forall s_a, s'_a \in \mathcal{S}_a . (s_c, s'_a) \in \sigma \wedge (s'_a, s_a) \in \varrho \rightarrow (s_c, s_a) \in \sigma$
A5: $(s_a, s'_a) \in \mathcal{R}_\sigma^\exists \Leftrightarrow \exists s_c, s'_c \in \mathcal{S} . (s_c, s_a) \in \sigma \wedge (s_c, s'_c) \in \mathcal{R}_c \wedge (s'_c, s'_a) \in \sigma$
A6: $\mathcal{K}_c \preccurlyeq_\sigma \mathcal{K}_a$
A7: $\mathcal{R}_a \subseteq \mathcal{R}_\sigma^\exists$

A1′ is obtained from A1 by definition of ϱ, A5 is the definition of $\mathcal{R}_\sigma^\exists$ according to Definition C.10, and A6 and A7 stem from our proof goal to establish the faithfulness. The bisimilarity is now seen as follows:

BISIM1: Given $(s_a, s'_a) \in \varrho$, it follows that there is an $s_c \in \mathcal{S}_c$ such that $(s_c, s_a) \in \sigma \wedge (s_c, s'_a) \in \sigma$ holds. As σ preserves labels, it follows that $\mathcal{L}_c(s_c) = \mathcal{L}_a(s_a)$ and $\mathcal{L}_c(s_c) = \mathcal{L}_a(s'_a)$, and hence that $\mathcal{L}_a(s_a) = \mathcal{L}_a(s'_a)$.

BISIM2a: Given $(s_a, s'_a) \in \mathcal{R}_\sigma^\exists$ and $(s_a, s''_a) \in \varrho$. We prove that there is an $s'''_a \in \mathcal{S}_a$ with $(s''_a, s'''_a) \in \mathcal{R}_a$ and $(s'_a, s'''_a) \in \varrho$. Consider the following diagram:

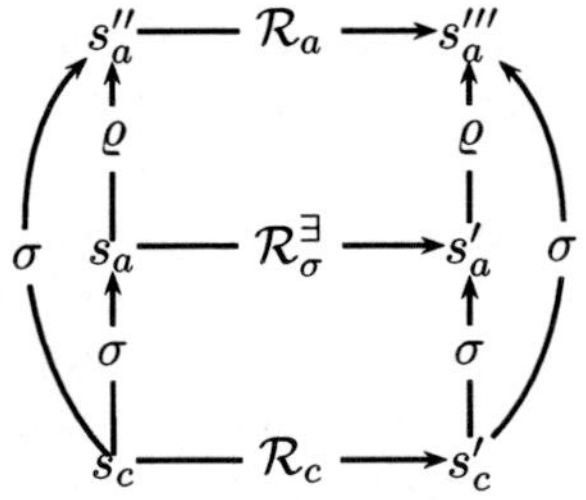

By definition of $\mathcal{R}_\sigma^\exists$ (A5), there are $s_c, s'_c \in \mathcal{S}$ with $(s_c, s_a) \in \sigma \wedge (s_c, s'_c) \in \mathcal{R}_c \wedge (s'_c, s'_a) \in \sigma$. Due to A1′, it follows again that also $(s_c, s''_a) \in \sigma$ holds. By A6, it moreover follows that $\mathcal{K}_c \preccurlyeq_\sigma \mathcal{K}_a$, and therefore by condition SIM2 that there must be a s'''_a such that $(s''_a, s'''_a) \in \mathcal{R}_a$ and $(s'_c, s'''_a) \in \sigma$. From the definition of ϱ, it follows now that $(s'_a, s'''_a) \in \varrho$ holds.

BISIM2b: Given $(s_a, s'_a) \in \mathcal{R}_a$ and $(s_a, s''_a) \in \varrho$. We prove that there is an $s'''_a \in \mathcal{S}_a$ with $(s''_a, s'''_a) \in \mathcal{R}_\sigma^\exists$ and $(s'_a, s'''_a) \in \varrho$. Consider the following diagram:

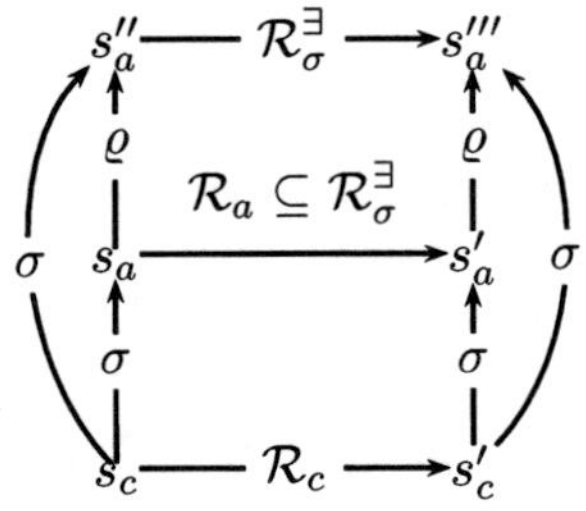

First, if follows from A7, that also $(s_a, s'_a) \in \mathcal{R}_\sigma^\exists$ holds. Hence, there are $s_c, s'_c \in \mathcal{S}$ with $(s_c, s_a) \in \sigma \wedge (s_c, s'_c) \in \mathcal{R}_c \wedge (s'_c, s'_a) \in \sigma$. Due to A1′, it follows now that also $(s_c, s''_a) \in \sigma$ holds.

By A2, it moreover follows that $\mathcal{K}_c \preccurlyeq_\sigma \mathcal{K}_\sigma^\exists$, and therefore by condition SIM2 that there must be a s'''_a such that $(s''_a, s'''_a) \in \mathcal{R}_\sigma^\exists$ and $(s'_c, s'''_a) \in \sigma$. From the definition of ϱ, it follows now that $(s'_a, s'''_a) \in \varrho$ holds.

BISIM3a: Given $s_a \in \mathcal{I}_\sigma$, we have to show that there is an $s'_a \in \mathcal{I}_a$ with $(s_a, s'_a) \in \varrho$. We simply take $s'_a := s_a$ since for any state s_a we have by the definition of ϱ and A2, that $(s_a, s_a) \in \varrho$.

BISIM3b: This is proved in the same manner as BSIM3a.

□

Hence, even if σ is not a total function, we can nevertheless establish with the notion of faithfulness some criteria for the optimality of abstractions. The above theorem then gives criteria for σ that guarantees the faithfulness of the abstract structure $\mathcal{K}_\sigma^\exists$ as given in Definition C.10.

Consider condition A1 of the above theorem: it says that if two concrete states $s_c, s_c' \in \mathcal{S}_c$ share a common abstract state, then they must have the same abstract states. Therefore, σ induces an equivalence relation $\approx_a$ on the set of abstract states and an equivalence relation $\approx_c$ on the set of concrete states, such that either no states of two classes $\widetilde{s_c}$ and $\widetilde{s_a}$ are σ related with each other or all states of $\widetilde{s_c}$ are related with all states of $\widetilde{s_a}$. For this reason, we can define quotients of the structures $\mathcal{S}_c$ and $\mathcal{S}_a$ and a corresponding relation $\widetilde{\sigma}$ that relates classes iff all states of $\widetilde{s_c}$ are related with all states of $\widetilde{s_a}$. It is then easy to see that $\widetilde{\sigma}$ is a total function. This relates the above result to our previous results on optimality.

To conclude this section, we reconsider the collapsing operation of Definition 2.16. Recall that this operation is our basic means to find structures that are larger in terms of the simulation preorder (Lemma 2.17). Therefore, a simulation relation between $\mathcal{K}$ and $\mathsf{collapse}(\mathcal{K})$ exists, and we have already given one in Lemma 2.17. We will now show that this simulation relation looks like in terms of Galois connections.

Definition C.20 (Galois Connection for Collapsing). *Given a Kripke structure $\mathcal{K} = (\mathcal{I}, \mathcal{S}, \mathcal{R}, \mathcal{L})$ over V_Σ, we define for any set of states $Q \subseteq \mathcal{S}$ and for any set of sets of variables $Q_\Sigma \subseteq 2^{V_\Sigma}$ the following functions $\alpha_\Sigma : 2^{\mathcal{S}} \to 2^{2^{V_\Sigma}}$ and $\gamma_\Sigma : 2^{2^{V_\Sigma}} \to 2^{\mathcal{S}}$:*

$$\alpha_\Sigma(Q) := \{\mathcal{L}(s) \mid s \in Q\} \qquad\qquad \gamma_\Sigma(Q_\Sigma) := \{s \in \mathcal{S} \mid \mathcal{L}(s) \in Q_\Sigma\}$$

Lemma C.21 (Galois Connection for Collapsing). *Given a Kripke structure $\mathcal{K} = (\mathcal{I}, \mathcal{S}, \mathcal{R}, \mathcal{L})$ over V_Σ, and the functions α_Σ, γ_Σ as given in Definition C.20. Then, $(\alpha_\Sigma, \gamma_\Sigma)$ is a Galois connection from $(2^{\mathcal{S}}, \subseteq)$ to $(2^{2^{V_\Sigma}}, \subseteq)$. Moreover, the corresponding binary relation is $\sigma_\Sigma := \{(s, \vartheta) \mid \vartheta = \mathcal{L}(s)\}$.*

Proof. We prove that $(\alpha_\Sigma, \gamma_\Sigma)$ is a Galois connection by proving that it is induced by the relation σ_Σ as defined above. To see that it holds, simply note that $(s, \vartheta) \in \sigma_\Sigma \Leftrightarrow \vartheta \in \alpha_\Sigma(\{s\})$ holds, i.e., it follows that $\forall Q.\alpha_\Sigma(Q) = \mathsf{suc}_\exists^{\sigma_\Sigma}(Q)$ (since the existential successor function distributes over unions). To prove $\forall Q_\Sigma.\gamma_\Sigma(Q_\Sigma) = \mathsf{pre}_\forall^{\sigma_\Sigma}(Q_\Sigma)$, consider the following:

$$\begin{aligned} s \in \mathsf{pre}_\forall^{\sigma_\Sigma}(Q_\Sigma) &\Leftrightarrow \forall \vartheta \subseteq V_\Sigma.(s, \vartheta) \in \sigma_\Sigma \to \vartheta \in Q_\Sigma \\ &\Leftrightarrow \forall \vartheta \subseteq V_\Sigma.\vartheta = \mathcal{L}(s) \to \vartheta \in Q_\Sigma \\ &\Leftrightarrow \mathcal{L}(s) \in Q_\Sigma \\ &\Leftrightarrow s \in \gamma_\Sigma(Q_\Sigma) \end{aligned}$$

Hence, $(\alpha_\Sigma, \gamma_\Sigma)$ and σ_Σ correspond, and therefore $(\alpha_\Sigma, \gamma_\Sigma)$ is by Lemma C.5 a Galois connection. □

Now, consider the abstract structure $\mathcal{K}^{\exists}_{\sigma_\Sigma}$ that is constructed for σ_{σ_Σ} according to Definition C.10. Abstract states are sets of variables of V_Σ, and according to the definition, the structure is computed as follows:

- $\mathcal{S}_{\sigma_\Sigma} := \{\mathcal{L}(s) \mid s \in \mathcal{S}\}$
- $\mathcal{I}_{\sigma_\Sigma} := \{\mathcal{L}(s) \mid s \in \mathcal{I}\}$
- $\mathcal{R}_{\sigma_\Sigma} := \{(\mathcal{L}(s), \mathcal{L}(s')) \mid (s, s') \in \mathcal{R}\}$
- $\mathcal{L}_{\sigma_\Sigma}(\vartheta) := \vartheta$

It is interesting to see that there are some alternative ways how this structure can be obtained: It is easy to see that the collapsed structure can be constructed as abstraction via the above Galois connection or alternatively via the collapsing operation. Also, we can construct it as quotient by an appropriate equivalence relation. These alternatives are given in the following theorem.

Theorem C.22. *Given a Kripke structure $\mathcal{K} = (\mathcal{I}, \mathcal{S}, \mathcal{R}, \mathcal{L})$ over V_Σ. Then, the following structures are isomorphic to each other:*

- collapse($\mathcal{K}$) *as given in Definition 2.16*
- $\mathcal{K}^{\exists}_{(\alpha_{\sigma_\Sigma}, \gamma_{\sigma_\Sigma})}$ *as given in Definition C.11 for the Galois connection $(\alpha_{\sigma_\Sigma}, \gamma_{\sigma_\Sigma})$ given in Definition C.20*
- $\mathcal{K}^{\exists}_{\sigma_{\sigma_\Sigma}}$ *as given in Definition C.10 for the relation σ_{σ_Σ} given in Definition C.20*
- *The quotient structure $\mathcal{K}_{/\approx_\sigma}$ as given in Definition 2.24 for the equivalence relation $\approx_\sigma$ that is defined as follows: $s \approx_{\sigma_\Sigma} s' :\Leftrightarrow \mathcal{L}(s) = \mathcal{L}(s')$.*

The proof of the above facts is immediately seen by the definition of the structures. Let us finally note that the relation σ_{σ_Σ} given in Definition C.20 is a total function on $\mathcal{S}_c$. Moreover, σ_{σ_Σ} preserves labels, hence satisfies SIM1 and also satisfies SIM3. Therefore, we see again that $\mathcal{K} \preccurlyeq$ collapse($\mathcal{K}$) holds, and know now by Theorem C.17 that the structure collapse($\mathcal{K}$) has been constructed in an optimal manner for the relation σ_{σ_Σ}.

C.4 Data Abstraction

We have already seen that instead of checking existential and universal properties in a structure $\mathcal{K}$, we can alternatively check these properties in other structures $\mathcal{K}^{\exists}$ and $\mathcal{K}^{\forall}$ with $\mathcal{K}^{\exists} \preccurlyeq \mathcal{K}$ and $\mathcal{K} \preccurlyeq \mathcal{K}^{\forall}$. Choosing a small abstract structure $\mathcal{K}_a$ may yield significant improvements on the runtimes of the verification. The remaining problem is, however, to easily determine abstract structures without computing the most general (bi)simulation relations. Moreover, the problem is that the abstraction can be too coarse so that we do not have $\mathcal{K}_a \models \Phi$, although $\mathcal{K}_c \models \Phi$ holds.

Another problem is that once we have chosen a structure $\mathcal{K}_a$, we have to prove that $\mathcal{K}_c \preccurlyeq \mathcal{K}_a$ holds. In general, this problem is as complex as the verification of $\mathcal{K}_c \models \Phi$ itself, so that we would gain nothing if we could not find better tests for $\mathcal{K}_c \preccurlyeq \mathcal{K}_a$. Note that checking whether a Kripke structure simulates another one is polynomial, since we only have to evaluate an alternation-free fixpoint [27, 369, 370]. Nevertheless, this is as complex as checking alternation-free μ-calculus formulas.

In the previous sections, we have seen how we can define for a given concrete structure $\mathcal{K}_c = (\mathcal{I}_c, \mathcal{S}_c, \mathcal{R}_c, \mathcal{L}_c)$ over the variables V_{Σ_c} and a given set of abstract states $\mathcal{S}_a$, an abstract structure $\mathcal{K}_\sigma$ for *any relation* $\sigma \subseteq \mathcal{S}_c \times \mathcal{S}_a$. Alternatively, we can construct the same structure in terms of a Galois connection (α, γ) from $(2^{\mathcal{S}_c}, \subseteq)$ to $(2^{\mathcal{S}_a}, \subseteq)$. We have also seen that under the reasonable condition that σ is total, σ will be a simulation relation between $\mathcal{K}_c$ and $\mathcal{K}_a$. Therefore, having constructed the abstract structure $\mathcal{K}_\sigma$ according to Definition C.10 or C.11, we can replace the test $\mathcal{K}_c \preccurlyeq \mathcal{K}_\sigma$ by checking the assumptions of Theorem C.17. Moreover, if σ is a total function, then Theorem C.17 tells us that the construction of $\mathcal{K}_\sigma$ (and $\mathcal{K}_{(\alpha,\gamma)}$) is optimal, i.e. we have constructed a structure such that σ is even the *greatest simulation relation* between $\mathcal{K}_c$ and $\mathcal{K}_\sigma$. Therefore, if we do not have $\mathcal{K}_a \models \Phi$, then it makes no sense to look for other abstract structures $\mathcal{K}'_a$ such that $\mathcal{K}_c \preccurlyeq_\sigma \mathcal{K}_a$ holds for reducing the model checking problem. In this case, we must choose another relation σ that is more detailed. In the previous section, we have also seen that the condition that σ must be a function can be weakened to the condition that σ fulfills the 'zigzag' property (A1 in Theorem C.19) so that a faithful abstraction is obtained.

Note that in the previous sections, we did not change the set of variables. However, it is often the case that we know that the property that is to be verified does not depend on all program variables. Instead, it may only be of interest whether a numeric variable equals zero or not, or if a queue is empty or not. In these cases, it is reasonable to replace the numeric data type by an abstract one that only contains two values: One that represents the number zero, and another that represents all other numeric values. For this reason, we consider in this section how we can construct Galois connections for such *data type abstractions*.

We have not introduced data types other than Boolean variables on the states of the Kripke structures. Higher data types that are finite, can be encoded with bitvectors in our Kripke structures. For this reason, we assume that the set of variables V_Σ is partitioned into disjoint subsets, i.e., $V_\Sigma = \bigcup_{i=0}^{n} \mathcal{V}_i$ with $\mathcal{V}_i \cap \mathcal{V}_j = \{\}$. Thus, we can *interpret* each subset $\mathcal{V}_i$ as a 'bitvector' that represents some higher-order data type χ by means of an interpretation function $\Phi_\chi : 2^{\mathcal{V}_i} \to \chi$. For example, if $\{b_n, \ldots, b_0\} = \mathcal{V}_b$ is a class of the partition of V_Σ, we can interpret each subset $\vartheta \subseteq \mathcal{V}_b$ as a natural (i.e., unsigned) number as follows: $\Phi_u(\vartheta) := \sum_{i=0}^{n} f_\vartheta(b_i)2^i$, where $f_\vartheta(b_i) := 1$ iff $b_i \in \vartheta$ and $f_\vartheta(b_i) := 0$ iff $b_i \notin \vartheta$. Alternatively, we could interpret ϑ as an integer (i.e., signed) number using the two-complement as follows: $\Phi_s(\vartheta) := -f_\vartheta(b_n)2^n + \sum_{i=0}^{n-1} f_\vartheta(b_i)2^i$.

As we do not have higher data types, we must therefore perform the abstraction in terms of our bitvectors. An abstraction from such 'data types' can therefore be given via *abstraction functions* of the form $\hbar : 2^{V_\Sigma} \to 2^{V_\Omega}$ that map a bitvector $\vartheta \in 2^{V_\Sigma}$ to another bitvector $\zeta \in 2^{V_\Omega}$. Given such an abstraction function, we can define a corresponding Galois connection from the set of structures over V_Σ to the set of structures over V_Ω (both sets are thereby ordered with the simulation preorder, where we identify bisimilar structures). This is shown in the following section. Using this Galois connection, we obtain for any structure over V_Σ another structure over V_Ω, which means that we have replaced some higher data type modeled by bitvectors of V_Σ to some other higher data type modeled by bitvectors of V_Ω. Clearly, we must also adapt the given specification. This is shown in Section C.4.2.

C.4.1 Abstract Interpretation of Structures

Given sets of variables V_Σ and V_Ω, each function $\hbar : 2^{V_\Sigma} \to 2^{V_\Omega}$ is an abstraction function. We already mentioned that with suitable interpretation functions $\Phi_\tau : V_\Sigma \to \tau$ and $\Phi_\pi : V_\Omega \to \pi$ to higher data types τ and π, respectively, such an abstraction function $\hbar : 2^{V_\Sigma} \to 2^{V_\Omega}$ can be viewed as an abstraction from the data type τ to the type π. We use such abstraction functions $\hbar : 2^{V_\Sigma} \to 2^{V_\Omega}$ to define a corresponding Galois connection.

Definition C.23 (Abstract Interpretation of Structures). *Given a Kripke structure $\mathcal{K}_c = (\mathcal{I}_c, \mathcal{S}_c, \mathcal{R}_c, \mathcal{L}_c)$ over V_Σ and an abstraction function $\hbar : 2^{V_\Sigma} \to 2^{V_\Omega}$. The abstract structure $\mathsf{abs}_\hbar(\mathcal{K}_c)$ w.r.t. $\hbar$ is defined as $\mathsf{abs}_\hbar(\mathcal{K}_c) := (\mathcal{I}_c, \mathcal{S}_c, \mathcal{R}_c, \hbar \circ \mathcal{L}_c)$. Also, for any structure $\mathcal{K}_a = (\mathcal{I}_a, \mathcal{S}_a, \mathcal{R}_a, \mathcal{L}_a)$ over V_Ω, the concretization $\mathsf{rep}_\hbar(\mathcal{K}_a)$ w.r.t. $\hbar$ is defined as $\mathsf{rep}_\hbar(\mathcal{K}_a) := (\mathcal{I}_c', \mathcal{S}_c', \mathcal{R}_c', \mathcal{L}_c')$, where*

- $\mathcal{S}_c' := \{(s_a, \vartheta) \mid s_a \in \mathcal{S}_a \land \vartheta \subseteq V_\Sigma \land \hbar(\vartheta) = \mathcal{L}_a(s_a)\} \subseteq \mathcal{S}_a \times 2^{V_\Sigma}$
- $\mathcal{I}_c' := \{(s_a, \vartheta) \mid s_a \in \mathcal{I}_a \land \vartheta \subseteq V_\Sigma \land \hbar(\vartheta) = \mathcal{L}_a(s_a)\}$
- $((s_1, \vartheta_1), (s_2, \vartheta_2)) \in \mathcal{R}_c' :\Leftrightarrow (s_1, s_2) \in \mathcal{R}_a$
- $\mathcal{L}_c'((s_a, \vartheta)) := \vartheta$

Note that the structures $\mathcal{K}$ and $\mathsf{abs}_\hbar(\mathcal{K})$ are almost the same: They only differ in their labels in that $\mathcal{L}(s)$ is replaced with $\hbar(\mathcal{L}(s))$. Therefore, the structure $\mathsf{abs}_\hbar(\mathcal{K})$ is a structure over the variables $\bigcup_{s \in \mathcal{S}_c} \hbar(\mathcal{L}_c(s)) \subseteq V_\Omega$.

Conversely, the concretization $\mathsf{rep}_\hbar(\mathcal{K}_a)$ of the abstract structure $\mathcal{K}_a$ is a structure over V_Σ. Note also that the structure $\mathsf{rep}_\hbar(\mathcal{K}_a)$ is significantly larger than the structure $\mathcal{K}_a$ since each abstract state of $\mathcal{S}_a$ may be multiplied by any set $\vartheta \subseteq V_\Sigma$ such that the set of reachable states may be multiplied by $2^{|V_\Sigma|}$. Hence, we will often work with $\mathsf{collapse}(\mathsf{rep}_\hbar(\mathcal{K}_a))$ instead of $\mathsf{rep}_\hbar(\mathcal{K}_a)$ (this structure has at most $2^{|V_\Sigma|}$ states).

In Definition C.23, we explained the construction of functions $\mathsf{abs}_\hbar$ and $\mathsf{rep}_\hbar$) for an abstraction function $\hbar : 2^{V_\Sigma} \to 2^{V_\Omega}$. We now prove that the pair $(\mathsf{abs}_\hbar, \mathsf{rep}_\hbar)$ is a Galois connection from the set of structures over V_Σ to the set of structures over V_Ω.

Theorem C.24 (Abstract Interpretation of Structures). *Given an abstraction function* $\hbar : 2^{V_\Sigma} \to 2^{V_\Omega}$*, and the functions* $\mathsf{abs}_\hbar$ *and* $\mathsf{rep}_\hbar$ *as given in Definition C.23. Then,* $(\mathsf{abs}_\hbar, \mathsf{rep}_\hbar)$ *is a Galois connection from the set of structures over* V_Σ *to the set of structures over* V_Ω*, both ordered with the simulation order (where we identify bisimilar structures to obtain a partial order from the simulation preorder).*

Proof. The proof is not too difficult, but quite involved with technical details. We just mention some major steps.

- Consider any structure $\mathcal{K}_c = (\mathcal{I}_c, \mathcal{S}_c, \mathcal{R}_c, \mathcal{L}_c)$ over V_Σ. The structure $\mathsf{rep}_\hbar(\mathsf{abs}_\hbar(\mathcal{K}_c)) = (\mathcal{I}'_c, \mathcal{S}'_c, \mathcal{R}'_c, \mathcal{L}'_c)$ is then defined as follows:
  - $\mathcal{S}'_c := \{(s_c, \vartheta) \mid s_c \in \mathcal{S}_c \land \vartheta \subseteq V_\Sigma \land \hbar(\vartheta) = \hbar(\mathcal{L}_c(s_c))\} \subseteq \mathcal{S}_c \times 2^{V_\Sigma}$
  - $\mathcal{I}'_c := \{(s_c, \vartheta) \mid s_c \in \mathcal{I}_c \land \vartheta \subseteq V_\Sigma \land \hbar(\vartheta) = \hbar(\mathcal{L}_c(s_c))\}$
  - $((s_1, \vartheta_1), (s_2, \vartheta_2)) \in \mathcal{R}'_c :\Leftrightarrow (s_1, s_2) \in \mathcal{R}_c$
  - $\mathcal{L}'_c((s_c, \vartheta)) := \vartheta$

  Hence, it is easy to see that $\preceq_c :\Leftrightarrow \{(s_c, (s_c, \mathcal{L}_c(s_c))) \mid s_c \in \mathcal{S}_c\}$ is a simulation relation between $\mathcal{K}_c$ and $\mathsf{rep}_\hbar(\mathsf{abs}_\hbar(\mathcal{K}_c))$.
- Consider any structure $\mathcal{K}_a = (\mathcal{I}_a, \mathcal{S}_a, \mathcal{R}_a, \mathcal{L}_a)$ over V_Ω. The structure $\mathsf{abs}_\hbar(\mathsf{rep}_\hbar(\mathcal{K}_a)) = (\mathcal{I}'_a, \mathcal{S}'_a, \mathcal{R}'_a, \mathcal{L}'_a)$ is then defined as follows:
  - $\mathcal{S}'_a := \{(s_a, \vartheta) \mid s_a \in \mathcal{S}_a \land \vartheta \subseteq V_\Sigma \land \hbar(\vartheta) = \mathcal{L}_a(s_a)\}$
  - $\mathcal{I}'_a := \{(s_a, \vartheta) \mid s_a \in \mathcal{I}_a \land \vartheta \subseteq V_\Sigma \land \hbar(\vartheta) = \mathcal{L}_a(s_a)\}$
  - $((s_1, \vartheta_1), (s_2, \vartheta_2)) \in \mathcal{R}'_a :\Leftrightarrow (s_1, s_2) \in \mathcal{R}_a$
  - $\mathcal{L}'_a((s_a, \vartheta)) := \hbar(\vartheta) = \mathcal{L}_a(s_a)$

  Hence, $\preceq_a := \{((s_a, \vartheta), s_a) \mid s_a \in \mathcal{S}_a \land (s_a, \vartheta) \in \mathcal{S}'_a\}$ is a simulation relation between $\mathsf{abs}_\hbar(\mathsf{rep}_\hbar(\mathcal{K}_a))$ and $\mathcal{K}_a$.

□

Hence, we have obtained a Galois connection between structures from our data abstraction function $\hbar$. The operations we are now interested in are operations on structures over V_Σ that we want to lift to operations on structures over V_Ω. In particular, we are interested in the preservation of the simulation preorder. By Lemma C.2, it holds for any structure $\mathcal{K}_c$ over V_Σ and any structure $\mathcal{K}_a$ over V_Ω that $\mathsf{abs}_\hbar(\mathcal{K}_c) \preccurlyeq \mathcal{K}_a$ holds iff $\mathcal{K}_c \preccurlyeq \mathsf{rep}_\hbar(\mathcal{K}_a)$. In particular, this means that $(\mathsf{abs}_\hbar, \mathsf{rep}_\hbar)$ is a so-called *conservative connection*.

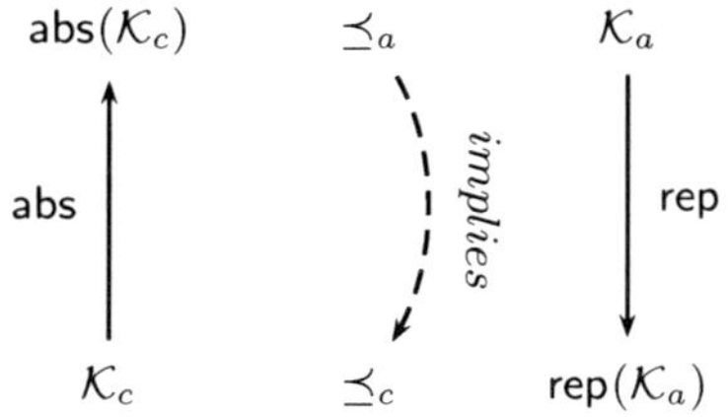

Fig. C.2. A conservative connection (abs, rep)

Definition C.25 (Conservative Connection). *Given functions* $\alpha : \mathcal{C} \to \mathcal{A}, \gamma : \mathcal{A} \to \mathcal{C}$ *between partially ordered sets* $(\mathcal{C}, \preceq_c)$ *and* $(\mathcal{A}, \preceq_a)$*, the pair* (α, γ) *is a conservative connection from* $(\mathcal{C}, \preceq_c)$ *to* $(\mathcal{A}, \preceq_a)$ *iff* $\forall c \in \mathcal{C}.\forall a \in \mathcal{A}.\alpha(c) \preceq_a a \to c \preceq_c \gamma(a)$ *holds.*

Clearly, every Galois connection from $(\mathcal{C}, \preceq_c)$ to $(\mathcal{A}, \preceq_a)$ is also a conservative connection from $(\mathcal{C}, \preceq_c)$ to $(\mathcal{A}, \preceq_a)$. For Kripke structures, the situation is depicted in Figure C.2. Before explaining how conservative connections are used for the efficient verification of universal properties, let us consider some example conservative connections.

Lemma C.26 (Examples of Conservative Connections). *In general, the following are conservative connections:*

- *Every Galois connection is a conservative connection. In particular, for any abstraction function* $\hbar : 2^{V_\Sigma} \to 2^{V_\Omega}$*, the pair* $(\mathsf{abs}_\hbar, \mathsf{rep}_\hbar)$ *is a conservative connection.*
- *For* $V_\Omega \subseteq V_\Sigma$*, we define* $\mathsf{abs}(\mathcal{K}_c) := \mathcal{K}_{c \downarrow V_\Omega}$ *and* $\mathsf{rep}(\mathcal{K}_a) := \mathcal{K}_a \times \mathcal{K}_{id}$*, where* $\mathcal{K}_{id}$ *is over* $V_\Sigma \setminus V_\Omega$ *as given in Lemma 2.33 on page 68.*
- *Given that* $(\mathsf{abs}_1, \mathsf{rep}_1)$ *and* $(\mathsf{abs}_2, \mathsf{rep}_2)$ *are conservative connections, then* $(\mathsf{abs}_1 \circ \mathsf{abs}_2, \mathsf{rep}_2 \circ \mathsf{rep}_1)$ *is a conservative connection.*
- *Define* $\mathsf{abs}(\mathcal{K}) := \mathsf{collapse}(\mathcal{K})$ *and* $\mathsf{rep}(\mathcal{K}) := \mathsf{collapse}(\mathcal{K})$*, then* $(\mathsf{abs}, \mathsf{rep})$ *is a conservative connection.*
- *Given that* $(\mathsf{abs}_1, \mathsf{rep}_1)$ *is a conservative connection, so is* $(\mathsf{abs}_2, \mathsf{rep}_2)$*, provided that for any structure* $\mathcal{K}$ *we have* $\mathsf{abs}_2(\mathcal{K}) \preceq_1 \mathsf{abs}_1(\mathcal{K})$ *and* $\mathsf{rep}_1(\mathcal{K}) \preceq_2 \mathsf{rep}_2(\mathcal{K})$*.*

The proofs of the above facts are all quite simple, so we omit them. The basic idea to use conservative connections for the efficient verification of universal properties is the following: *The basic problem that we want to solve is to check for a given universal formula* Φ *whether* $\mathcal{K}_c \models \Phi$ *holds in a given structure* $\mathcal{K}_c$*. Given that we have a conservative connection* $(\mathsf{abs}, \mathsf{rep})$ *and another structure* $\mathcal{K}_a$ *such that we already know that* $\mathsf{abs}(\mathcal{K}_c) \preceq_a \mathcal{K}_a$ *holds (or that we can test this efficiently), then we can immediately conclude that* $\mathcal{K}_c \preceq_c \mathsf{rep}(\mathcal{K}_a)$ *holds.* Hence, using conservative connections, we can reduce $\mathcal{K}_c \models \Phi$ to $\mathsf{abs}(\mathcal{K}_c) \preceq_a \mathcal{K}_a$ and $\mathsf{rep}(\mathcal{K}_a) \models \Phi$ for an appropriate structure $\mathcal{K}_a$. Hence, we have the following reduction rule:

$$\frac{\mathcal{K}_c \models \Phi}{\mathsf{abs}(\mathcal{K}_c) \preccurlyeq \mathcal{K}_a \qquad \mathsf{rep}(\mathcal{K}_a) \models \Phi}$$

For example, define $\mathcal{K}_a := \mathsf{abs}(\mathcal{K}_c)$. Hence, it immediately follows that $\mathsf{abs}(\mathcal{K}_c) \preceq_a \mathcal{K}_a$ holds, and it only remains to check $\mathsf{rep}(\mathsf{abs}(\mathcal{K}_c)) \models \Phi$. As another example, define $\mathcal{K}_a := \mathsf{collapse}(\mathsf{abs}(\mathcal{K}_c))$. Again, it follows that $\mathsf{abs}(\mathcal{K}_c) \preceq_a \mathcal{K}_a$ holds and therefore, we can replace for every universal property Φ the test $\mathcal{K}_c \models \Phi$ by $\mathsf{rep}(\mathsf{collapse}(\mathsf{abs}(\mathcal{K}_c))) \models \Phi$. In particular, using the Galois connection $(\mathsf{abs}_\hbar, \mathsf{rep}_\hbar$ obtained from a function $\hbar : 2^{V_\Sigma} \to 2^{V_\Omega}$ allows us to reduce $\mathcal{K}_c \models \Phi$ to the simpler problem $\mathsf{rep}_\hbar(\mathsf{collapse}(\mathsf{abs}_\hbar(\mathcal{K}_c))) \models \Phi$. Hence, we can have the following reduction rule:

$$\frac{\mathcal{K}_c \models \Phi}{\mathsf{rep}_{\hbar}(\mathsf{collapse}(\mathsf{abs}_{\hbar}(\mathcal{K}_c))) \models \Phi}$$

Note that $\mathsf{abs}_{\hbar}(\mathcal{K}_c)$ only changes the labels of $\mathcal{K}_c$, the collapse operation combines all states with the same labels, and finally the result is converted back to the original set of variables.

In general, we also have the following reduction rules for any universal properties:

$$\frac{\mathcal{K}_c \models \Phi}{\mathcal{K}_c \preccurlyeq \mathcal{K}_c' \quad \mathcal{K}_c' \models \Phi} \qquad \frac{\mathcal{K}_c \models \Phi}{\mathsf{collapse}(\mathcal{K}_c) \models \Phi}$$

We can combine these to obtain the following reduction rule:

$$\frac{\mathcal{K}_c \models \Phi}{\mathsf{collapse}(\mathsf{rep}_{\hbar}(\mathsf{collapse}(\mathsf{abs}_{\hbar}(\mathcal{K}_c)))) \models \Phi}$$

The remaining problem $\mathsf{collapse}(\mathsf{rep}_{\hbar}(\mathsf{abs}_{\hbar}(\mathcal{K}_c))) \models \Phi$ can be significantly simpler[1] than $\mathcal{K}_c \models \Phi$.

Moreover, it should be mentioned that these rules can be applied in a *compositional manner*. Assume we have to check $\mathcal{K}_1 \times \mathcal{K}_2 \models \Phi$ for a universal property Φ. Then, we can refine the above rules as follows:

$$\frac{\mathcal{K}_1 \times \mathcal{K}_2 \models \Phi}{\mathcal{K}_1 \preccurlyeq \mathcal{K}_1' \quad \mathcal{K}_2 \preccurlyeq \mathcal{K}_2' \quad \mathcal{K}_1' \times \mathcal{K}_2' \models \Phi} \qquad \frac{\mathcal{K}_1 \times \mathcal{K}_2 \models \Phi}{\mathsf{collapse}(\mathcal{K}_1) \times \mathsf{collapse}(\mathcal{K}_2) \models \Phi}$$

$$\frac{\mathcal{K}_1 \times \mathcal{K}_2 \models \Phi}{\mathsf{rep}_{\hbar}(\mathsf{collapse}(\mathsf{abs}_{\hbar}(\mathcal{K}_1))) \times \mathsf{rep}_{\hbar}(\mathsf{collapse}(\mathsf{abs}_{\hbar}(\mathcal{K}_2))) \models \Phi}$$

Hence, we can apply the operations all in a compositional manner. This avoids having to perform these operations on large product structures. The correctness of the above rules is seen by the following theorem:

Theorem C.27. *Given an abstraction function* $\hbar : 2^{V_\Sigma} \to 2^{V_\Omega}$*, and the functions* $\mathsf{abs}_{\hbar}$ *and* $\mathsf{rep}_{\hbar}$ *described in Definition C.23. Then, the following holds:*

- $\mathsf{abs}_{\hbar}(\mathcal{K}_1 \times \mathcal{K}_2) = \mathsf{abs}_{\hbar}(\mathcal{K}_1) \times \mathsf{abs}_{\hbar}(\mathcal{K}_2)$
- $\mathsf{rep}_{\hbar}(\mathcal{K}_1 \times \mathcal{K}_2) = \mathsf{rep}_{\hbar}(\mathcal{K}_1) \times \mathsf{rep}_{\hbar}(\mathcal{K}_2)$

As an example, consider a counter modulo 6. The counter has three propositional variables b_2, b_1, and b_0 to represent the current value of the counter, i.e., the numbers $0, \ldots, 5$ as natural numbers. Additionally, there is an enable input e that instructs the counter to increment its value. If e is false, the counter stores its current value.

[1] The number of transitions is usually increased, but in general we can hope that the representation of the transition relations as logical formulas or as OBDDs will be much smaller.

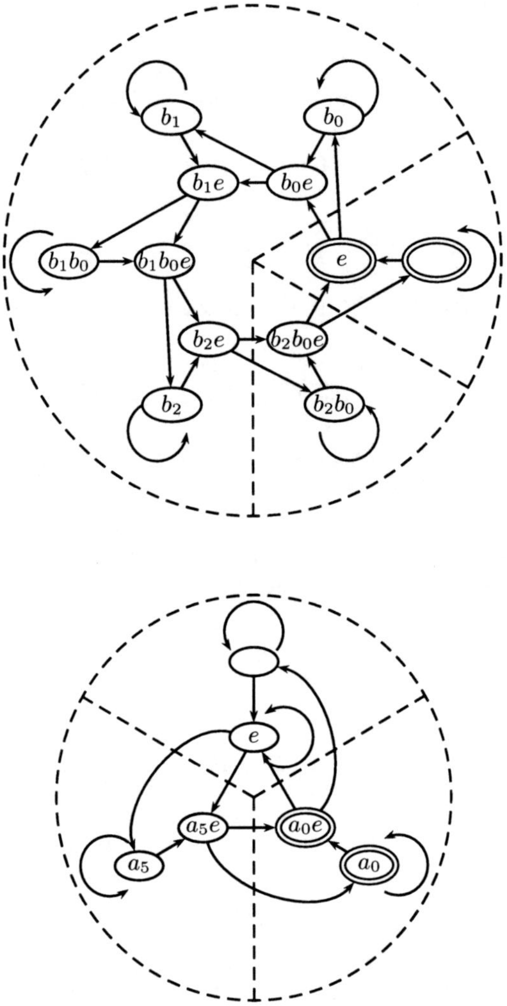

Fig. C.3. Abstraction of a 3-bit modulo 6 counter

A Kripke structure $\mathcal{K}_c$ that models such a counter is given in the upper half of Figure C.3. Clearly, it is a structure over the variables $V_\Sigma := \{b_2, b_1, b_0, e\}$. In this Kripke structure, we use the following standard encoding of natural numbers for the counter's value: A subset $\vartheta \subseteq \{b_n, \ldots, b_0\}$ is mapped to the natural number $\Phi_u(\vartheta) := \sum_{i=0}^{n} f_\vartheta(b_i)2^i$, where $f_\vartheta(b_i) := 1$ iff $b_i \in \vartheta$ and $f_\vartheta(b_i) := 0$ iff $b_i \notin \vartheta$.

We want to prove that whenever we are in a state where the counter has the value 5 and increment, then an overflow occurs that means that the next value of the counter is 0. Hence, we want to prove the following specification

$\Phi := \mathsf{AG}([b_2 \wedge \neg b_2 \wedge b_0 \wedge e] \rightarrow \mathsf{X}[\neg b_2 \wedge \neg b_2 \wedge \neg b_0])$, which is clearly a ACTL^* formula. To verify this property with our abstraction technique, we use the following abstraction function $\hbar_b : 2^{\{b_2,b_1,b_0\}} \rightarrow 2^{\{a_5,a_0\}}$:

$$\hbar_b(\vartheta) := \begin{cases} \{a_0\} : \text{if } \vartheta = \{\}, \text{ i.e., } \Phi_s(\vartheta) = 0 \\ \{a_5\} : \text{if } \vartheta = \{b_2, b_0\}, \text{ i.e., } \Phi_s(\vartheta) = 5 \\ \{\} \quad : \text{otherwise} \end{cases}$$

We extend $\hbar_b$ to an abstraction function $\hbar : 2^{\{b_2,b_1,b_0,e\}} \rightarrow 2^{\{a_5,a_0,e\}}$ as follows: $\hbar(\vartheta) := \hbar_b(\vartheta \setminus \{e\}) \cup (\vartheta \setminus \{b_2, b_1, b_0\})$. Finally, we collapse the structure: the lower part of Figure C.3 shows the resulting structure $\mathsf{collapse}(\mathsf{abs}_\hbar(\mathcal{K}_c))$. To finally verify our specification Φ that is given over variables $\{b_2, b_1, b_0, e\}$, we must compute a representation of the structure, i.e., $\mathsf{rep}_\hbar(\mathsf{collapse}(\mathsf{abs}_\hbar(\mathcal{K}_c)))$.

C.4.2 Abstract Specifications

The considerations of the previous section lead to the following reduction rule:

$$\frac{\mathcal{K}_c \models \Phi}{\mathsf{abs}(\mathcal{K}_c) \preccurlyeq \mathcal{K}_a \qquad \mathsf{rep}(\mathcal{K}_a) \models \Phi}$$

Hence, we can reduce the problem $\mathcal{K}_c \models \Phi$ to $\mathsf{rep}(\mathcal{K}_a) \models \Phi$. While the remaining model checking problem can become significantly simpler, it is still given at the concrete level. We therefore consider in this section conditions to lift specifications to the abstract level. Therefore, we want to use the following alternative reduction rule:

$$\frac{\mathcal{K}_c \models \Phi}{\mathsf{abs}(\mathcal{K}_c) \preccurlyeq \mathcal{K}_a \qquad \mathcal{K}_a \models \mathsf{abs}(\Phi)}$$

Of course, we first have to define an abstraction $\mathsf{abs}(\Phi)$ of the specification Φ. To this end, we use the following function for specifications given in CTL^*:

Definition C.28 (Lifting Specifications at the Abstract Level). *Given an abstraction function $\hbar : 2^{V_\Sigma} \rightarrow 2^{V_\Omega}$ and a CTL^* formula Φ, we define $\mathsf{abs}_\hbar(\Phi)$ as follows:*

- *if Φ is propositional then define* $\mathsf{abs}_\hbar(\Phi) := \bigvee_{\vartheta \in \mathsf{models}_{V_\Sigma}(\Phi)} \mathsf{minterm}_{V_\Omega}(\hbar(\vartheta))$
- $\mathsf{abs}_\hbar(\neg\varphi) := \neg \mathsf{abs}_\hbar(\varphi)$
- $\mathsf{abs}_\hbar(\varphi \wedge \psi) := \mathsf{abs}_\hbar(\varphi) \wedge \mathsf{abs}_\hbar(\psi)$ *and* $\mathsf{abs}_\hbar(\varphi \vee \psi) := \mathsf{abs}_\hbar(\varphi) \vee \mathsf{abs}_\hbar(\psi)$
- $\mathsf{abs}_\hbar(\mathsf{X}\varphi) := \mathsf{X}\ \mathsf{abs}_\hbar(\varphi)$
- $\mathsf{abs}_\hbar([\varphi\ \underline{\mathsf{U}}\ \psi]) := [\mathsf{abs}_\hbar(\varphi)\ \underline{\mathsf{U}}\ \mathsf{abs}_\hbar(\psi)]$
- $\mathsf{abs}_\hbar([\varphi\ \mathsf{B}\ \psi]) := [\mathsf{abs}_\hbar(\varphi)\ \mathsf{B}\ \mathsf{abs}_\hbar(\psi)]$
- $\mathsf{abs}_\hbar(\mathsf{E}\varphi) := \mathsf{E}\ \mathsf{abs}_\hbar(\varphi)$ *and* $\mathsf{abs}_\hbar(\mathsf{A}\varphi) := \mathsf{A}\ \mathsf{abs}_\hbar(\varphi)$

Lifting specifications at the abstract level enables us to check $\mathsf{abs}_{\hbar}(\mathcal{K}_c) \models \mathsf{abs}_{\hbar}(\Phi)$ instead of $\mathcal{K}_c \models \Phi$. As $\mathsf{abs}_{\hbar}(\mathcal{K}_c)$ can be significantly smaller than the low-level structure $\mathcal{K}_c$, we can gain large improvements on the complexity of the verification. For example, reconsider the example of Figure C.3, where our goal was to check $\Phi := \mathsf{AG}([b_2 \wedge \neg b_2 \wedge b_0 \wedge e] \rightarrow \mathsf{X}[\neg b_2 \wedge \neg b_2 \wedge \neg b_0])$. Using the abstraction function $\hbar : 2^{\{b_2,b_1,b_0,e\}} \rightarrow 2^{\{a_5,a_0,e\}}$, we compute the abstract specification: $\mathsf{abs}_{\hbar}(\Phi) = \mathsf{AG}([a_5 \wedge \neg a_0 \wedge e] \rightarrow \mathsf{X}[\neg a_5 \wedge a_0])$. Clearly, we now prefer to check $\mathsf{abs}_{\hbar}(\Phi)$ in $\mathsf{abs}_{\hbar}(\mathcal{K}_c)$. In general, it is however not possible to lift specification at the abstract level. Therefore, we must impose some criteria for specifications:

Definition C.29 ($\hbar$-Invariant Specifications). *Given a Kripke structure $\mathcal{K} = (\mathcal{I}, \mathcal{S}, \mathcal{R}, \mathcal{L})$ over some set of variables V_Σ, an abstraction function $\hbar : 2^{V_\Sigma} \rightarrow 2^{V_\Omega}$, and a* CTL* *formula Φ. Φ is $\hbar$-invariant w.r.t. $\mathcal{K}$ iff the following holds:*

$$\forall s \in \mathcal{S}.\ \mathcal{L}(s) \in \mathsf{models}_{V_\Sigma}(\Phi) \Leftrightarrow \hbar(\mathcal{L}(s)) \in \mathsf{models}_{V_\Omega}(\mathsf{abs}_{\hbar}(\Phi))$$

To prove the correctness of our reduction rule, we have to show the implication of $(\mathsf{abs}_{\hbar}(\mathcal{K}_c), s) \models \mathsf{abs}_{\hbar}(\Phi)$ and $(\mathcal{K}_c, s) \models \Phi$. Assume first that Φ is propositional. Then, it is easy to see that $(\mathcal{K}_c, s) \models \Phi$ is equivalent to $\mathcal{L}_c(s) \in \mathsf{models}_{V_\Sigma}(\Phi)$, and analogously that $(\mathsf{abs}_{\hbar}(\mathcal{K}_c), s) \models \mathsf{abs}_{\hbar}(\Phi)$ is equivalent to $\hbar(\mathcal{L}_c(s)) \in \mathsf{models}_{V_\Omega}(\mathsf{abs}_{\hbar}(\Phi))$. Hence, we must prove that $\hbar(\mathcal{L}_c(s)) \in \mathsf{models}_{V_\Omega}(\mathsf{abs}_{\hbar}(\Phi))$ implies $\mathcal{L}_c(s) \in \mathsf{models}_{V_\Sigma}(\Phi)$. For $\hbar$-invariant specifications Φ this is trivial, since $\mathcal{L}(s) \in \mathsf{models}_{V_\Sigma}(\Phi)$ is equivalent to $\hbar(\mathcal{L}(s)) \in \mathsf{models}_{V_\Omega}(\mathsf{abs}_{\hbar}(\Phi))$.

However, this implication does not hold for specifications that are not $\hbar$-invariant. For example, consider the specification $\Psi := b_2 \wedge \neg b_1 \wedge \neg b_0$, which says that the counter's value is 4. The abstract form of Ψ is $\mathsf{abs}_{\hbar}(\Psi) := \neg a_5 \wedge \neg a_0$. Let s be the state of the concrete Kripke structure given in the upper part of Figure C.3 that has the label $\overline{b_2} b_1 b_0 e$, i.e., the counter's value is 3. Clearly, we have $(\mathcal{K}_c, s) \not\models \Psi$, but $(\mathsf{abs}_{\hbar}(\mathcal{K}_c), s) \models \mathsf{abs}_{\hbar}(\Psi)$. Note that Ψ says that the counter's value is 4, while $\mathsf{abs}_{\hbar}(\Psi)$ only says that the counter's value is neither 0 nor 5. Ψ is not $\hbar$-invariant, since in the concrete model, there are two labels $\vartheta_1, \vartheta_2 \subseteq V_\Sigma$ such that $\hbar(\vartheta_1) = \hbar(\vartheta_2)$ and $[\![\mathsf{abs}_{\hbar}(\Psi)]\!]_{\hbar(\vartheta_1)} = \mathsf{true}$, while we have $[\![\Psi]\!]_{\vartheta_1} = \mathsf{false}$ and $[\![\Psi]\!]_{\vartheta_2} = \mathsf{true}$.

Theorem C.30 (Abstract Verification). *Given a Kripke structure $\mathcal{K}$ over the variables V_Σ, an abstraction function $\hbar : 2^{V_\Sigma} \rightarrow 2^{V_\Omega}$, and a* CTL* *formula Φ that is $\hbar$-invariant w.r.t. $\mathcal{K}$. Then the following holds:*

$$(\mathsf{abs}_{\hbar}(\mathcal{K}), s) \models \mathsf{abs}_{\hbar}(\Phi) \textit{ if and only if } (\mathcal{K}, s) \models \Phi$$

Therefore, if follows for any ACTL* *formula Φ, that*

$$(\mathsf{collapse}(\mathsf{abs}_{\hbar}(\mathcal{K})), \mathsf{collapse}(s)) \models \mathsf{abs}_{\hbar}(\Phi) \textit{ implies } (\mathcal{K}, s) \models \Phi$$

The proof is done by induction on Φ, where we assume that Φ is in negation normal form. We only give an idea for the propositional case, the other steps are trivial. If Φ is propositional, then also $\mathsf{abs}_\hbar(\Phi)$ is propositional and the proof is as follows:

$$
\begin{aligned}
&(\mathsf{abs}_\hbar(\mathcal{K}), s) \models \mathsf{abs}_\hbar(\Phi) \\
&\quad \Leftrightarrow \hbar(\mathcal{L}(s)) \in \mathsf{models}_{V_\Omega}(\mathsf{abs}_\hbar(\Phi)) \\
&\quad \Leftrightarrow \hbar(\mathcal{L}(s)) \in \mathsf{models}_{V_\Omega}(\textstyle\bigvee_{\vartheta \in \mathsf{models}_{V_\Sigma}(\Phi)} \mathsf{minterm}_{V_\Omega}(\hbar(\vartheta))) \\
&\quad \Leftrightarrow \hbar(\mathcal{L}(s)) \in \textstyle\bigcup_{\vartheta \in \mathsf{models}_{V_\Sigma}(\Phi)} \mathsf{models}_{V_\Omega}(\mathsf{minterm}_{V_\Omega}(\hbar(\vartheta))) \\
&\quad \Leftrightarrow \hbar(\mathcal{L}(s)) \in \textstyle\bigcup_{\vartheta \in \mathsf{models}_{V_\Sigma}(\Phi)} \{\hbar(\vartheta)\} \\
&\quad \Leftrightarrow \hbar(\mathcal{L}(s)) \in \{\hbar(\vartheta) \mid \vartheta \in \mathsf{models}_{V_\Sigma}(\Phi)\}
\end{aligned}
$$

Moreover, $(\mathcal{K}, s) \models \Phi$ is equivalent to $\mathcal{L}(s) \in \mathsf{models}_{V_\Sigma}(\Phi)$. Now, note that Φ is $\hbar$-invariant. Hence, $\mathcal{L}(s) \in \mathsf{models}_{V_\Sigma}(\Phi)$ is equivalent to $\hbar(\mathcal{L}(s)) \in \mathsf{models}_{V_\Omega}(\mathsf{abs}_\hbar(\Phi))$, and therefore, we can see that $(\mathcal{K}, s) \models \Phi$ is the same as $(\mathsf{abs}_\hbar(\mathcal{K}), s) \models \mathsf{abs}_\hbar(\Phi)$.

Intuitively, $\hbar$ invariance means that we can not distinguish states that are mapped to the same label with our concrete specification. This means[2] that whenever we have $\hbar(\mathcal{L}(s_1)) = \hbar(\mathcal{L}(s_2))$, then it follows that for any $\hbar$-invariant formula, we have $(\mathcal{K}, s_1) \models \Phi$ iff $(\mathcal{K}, s_2) \models \Phi$.

C.5 Symmetry and Model Checking

In this section, we consider the exploitation of symmetries for reducing model checking problems. The reduced model $\mathcal{K}_G$ is thereby obtained from the original structure $\mathcal{K}$ by a quotient construction similar to Definition 2.24. Recall that Definition 2.24 requires an equivalence relation that preserves labels. For symmetry reduction, we no longer enforce the preservation of labels and use instead another relation to declare different labels to be 'equivalent'. Hence, we can then also combine states with different labels, when the labels are equivalent to each other.

The investigation of symmetries that can be exploited in verification procedures is based on the consideration of *automorphisms*. In a general sense, a morphism is a function that maps some mathematical structure to another structure such that some basic mathematical relations of the structure are preserved. If the morphism maps the structure to a substructure of itself, then it is called an *endomorphism*. If, furthermore, the endomorphism is a bijective function, i.e., the structure is mapped onto itself, the morphism is called an automorphism.

---

[2] The proof is as follows: $(\mathcal{K}, s_1) \models \Phi$ holds iff $\mathcal{L}(s_1) \in \mathsf{models}_{V_\Sigma}(\Phi)$ which is equivalent to $\hbar(\mathcal{L}(s_1)) \in \mathsf{models}_{V_\Omega}(\mathsf{abs}_\hbar(\Phi))$. As $\hbar(\mathcal{L}(s_1)) = \hbar(\mathcal{L}(s_2))$ holds, we also have $\hbar(\mathcal{L}(s_2)) \in \mathsf{models}_{V_\Omega}(\mathsf{abs}_\hbar(\Phi))$ and by $\hbar$-invariance, it follows then that $\mathcal{L}(s_2) \in \mathsf{models}_{V_\Sigma}(\Phi)$ and therefore $(\mathcal{K}, s_2) \models \Phi$ must hold.

For instance, consider linear functions $f : \mathbb{R}^n \rightarrow \mathbb{R}^m$ that are defined by a $m \times n$ matrix $\mathfrak{A}$ as follows: $f(\mathbf{x}) := \mathfrak{A}\mathbf{x}$ (matrix multiplication). f is a morphism as it preserves the vector addition and the scalar multiplication by real numbers. If $n = m$, then f is an endomorphism and if the matrix $\mathfrak{A}$ is not singular then f is an automorphism.

Automorphisms are always related with some form of symmetry of the structure, since the resulting mathematical structure is isomorphic to the given one. Whenever a property holds for all symmetric structures, it is sufficient to consider only one of its symmetric images. This is the key to the reductions considered in this section.

The first papers on symmetry reductions are [113, 180, 260] and the more detailed journal versions [104, 178, 261]. Ip and Dill [260] considered only reductions of the structures that can be used for checking safety properties. The authors of [113, 180] considered symmetry reductions with respect to CTL* formulas. [113] restricted the symmetries that can be used for symmetry reductions in the way that variables occurring on the formula to be checked are not allowed to be permuted. In this sense, [180] is an extension thereof, since there, symmetries were defined both on formulas and models and the combination of both is then used for reduction. This work has been extended in [179, 181] by various forms of fairness constraints. An interesting combination of symmetry and partial order reduction has been presented in [164] and a combination of symmetry reduction and on-the-fly model checking has been given in [226]. The following section follows mainly [178], however, it is based on the Kripke structures introduced in this book. Hence, the proofs and definitions have been adapted. More recent work [182, 457] is concerned with reductions of systems that are 'almost symmetric'.

C.5.1 Symmetries of Structures

In the following, both automorphisms of the models and the specifications are defined. We start with the definition of the automorphisms of the models. To simplify the notation, we often write $f(M)$ instead of $\{f(x) \mid x \in M\}$ in the following.

Definition C.31 (Symmetry Automorphisms of Structures). *Given a Kripke structure $\mathcal{K} = (\mathcal{I}, \mathcal{S}, \mathcal{R}, \mathcal{L})$ for a set of variables V_Σ. Each function $f : \mathcal{S} \cup V_\Sigma \rightarrow \mathcal{S} \cup V_\Sigma$ that satisfies the following properties is an automorphism of $\mathcal{K}$:*

- *$f(s) \in \mathcal{S}$ and $f(x) \in V_\Sigma$ for each $s \in \mathcal{S}$ and each $x \in V_\Sigma$*
- *$f_{|\mathcal{S}} : \mathcal{S} \rightarrow \mathcal{S}$ and $f_{|V_\Sigma} : V_\Sigma \rightarrow V_\Sigma$ are bijective functions*
- *f preserves labels up to permutation, i.e., $f(\mathcal{L}(s)) = \mathcal{L}(f(s))$ for each $s \in \mathcal{S}$*
- *f preserves transitions, i.e., $(s,t) \in \mathcal{R}$ implies $(f(s), f(t)) \in \mathcal{R}$*
- *f preserves initial states, i.e., $s \in \mathcal{I}$ iff $f(s) \in \mathcal{I}$*

The set of automorphisms of $\mathcal{K}$ is denoted with $\mathsf{Auto}(\mathcal{K})$.

An automorphism f preserves the main properties of the structure, i.e., the labels, the transitions, and the initial states. Hence, f is a morphism, i.e., a mapping that preserves the habit of its domain. As $f_{|\mathcal{S}}$ and $f_{|V_\Sigma}$ are bijective, f is an isomorphism.

In principle, the functions used in the above definition are pairs of two functions, namely $f_{|\mathcal{S}} : \mathcal{S} \to \mathcal{S}$ and $f_{|V_\Sigma} : V_\Sigma \to V_\Sigma$. It is required that these functions are bijective. It should be noted here that bijective functions on finite sets are permutations, and hence the relationship with permutation groups [327] becomes clear. The set of automorphisms together with the function composition $\circ$ forms a commutative group (see Section 4.7.1), i.e., it is a set with an operation $\circ$ that fulfills the following properties:

Lemma C.32 (Automorphism Group of a Structure). *For any Kripke structure $\mathcal{K}$ over a set of variables V_Σ, the set of automorphisms $\mathsf{Auto}(\mathcal{K})$ is a commutative group w.r.t. function composition $\circ$, i.e., the following holds:*

Closure: $\forall f, g \in \mathsf{Auto}(\mathcal{K}). f \circ g \in \mathsf{Auto}(\mathcal{K})$
Associativity: $\forall f, g, h \in \mathsf{Auto}(\mathcal{K}). f \circ (g \circ h) = (f \circ g) \circ h$
Neutral Element: $\forall g \in \mathsf{Auto}(\mathcal{K}). f_{id} \circ g = g$ *and* $f_{id} \in \mathsf{Auto}(\mathcal{K})$ *for* $f_{id}(i) := i$
Inverse Elements: $\forall f \in \mathsf{Auto}(\mathcal{K}). \exists g \in \mathsf{Auto}(\mathcal{K}). f \circ g = f_{id}$
Commutativity: $\forall f, g \in \mathsf{Auto}(\mathcal{K}). f \circ g = g \circ f$

A subgroup of a group is a subset of that group that also fulfills the above properties, i.e., it is a group w.r.t. the same operation, but the operation only works on a subset of the considered group. In general, it can be shown that a subset G of a group is a subgroup iff for each $e_1, e_2 \in G$ implies that $e_1 \circ e_2^{-1} \in G$ (where e_2^{-1} denotes the inverse of e_2). This property can be used to efficiently check whether a subset is a subgroup or not (provided that e_2^{-1} and $\circ$ can be efficiently computed).

As an example, consider the Kripke structure given in the left-hand side of Figure C.4. It is easily seen that the following function f_1 is an automorphism: $f_1(s_1) := s_3$, $f_1(s_4) := s_7$, $f_1(s_5) := s_6$, $f_1(s_3) := s_1$, $f_1(s_7) := s_4$, $f_1(s_6) := s_5$, and $f_1(s) = s$ for $s \in \{s_0, s_2, s_8\}$. The variables are mapped as follows $f_1(a_1) := a_2$ and $f_1(a_2) := a_1$. Clearly, applying f_1 to the structure again results in the same structure, i.e., an isomorphic structure so that f_1 is indeed an automorphism. Hence, the inverse f_1^{-1} is also an automorphism and as $f_1 \circ f_1 = f_{id}$ holds, it follows that $\{f_{id}, f_1, f_1^{-1}\}$ is a subgroup of $\mathsf{Auto}(\mathcal{K})$. The group $\{f_{id}, f_1, f_1^{-1}\}$ describes some part of the symmetry of the structure that can be used to reduce it.

We now show how smaller structures are defined that can be used for model checking when a subgroup G of $\mathsf{Auto}(\mathcal{K})$ is chosen. The key to the construction is that we can define for a given subgroup an equivalence relation on the states (and vice versa) such that a quotient structure according to Definition 2.24 can be constructed. We also define an equivalence relation on the set of labels s.t. we can consider $\widetilde{\mathcal{L}}(\widetilde{s})$ for each class of states $\widetilde{s}$ as a set of variables instead of a set of sets of variables.

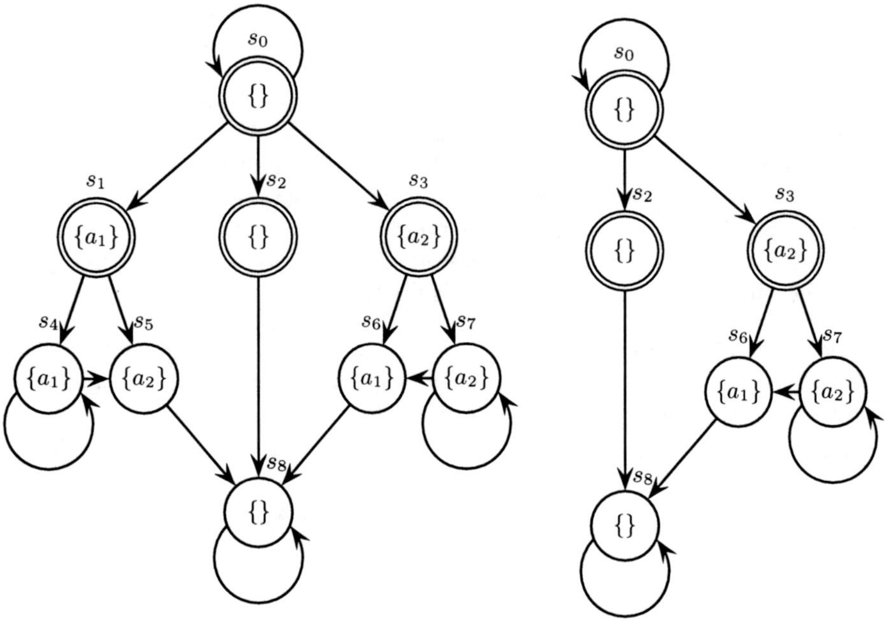

Fig. C.4. Example for a symmetry reduction

Definition C.33 (Induced Equivalence by Automorphism Subgroups). *Let $\mathcal{K} = (\mathcal{I}, \mathcal{S}, \mathcal{R}, \mathcal{L})$ be a Kripke structure over the variables V_Σ and let G be a subgroup of $\mathsf{Auto}(\mathcal{K})$. Then, we define the relations $\approx_G^{\mathcal{S}}$ and $\approx_G^{\Sigma}$ on $\mathcal{S} \times \mathcal{S}$ and $2^{V_\Sigma} \times 2^{V_\Sigma}$, respectively, as follows:*

$$s_1 \approx_G^{\mathcal{S}} s_2 :\Leftrightarrow \exists f \in G. s_2 = f(s_1)$$
$$\vartheta_1 \approx_G^{\Sigma} \vartheta_2 :\Leftrightarrow \exists f \in G. \vartheta_2 = \{f(x) \mid x \in \vartheta_1\}$$

If G is a subgroup, then both $\approx_G^{\mathcal{S}}$ and $\approx_G^{\Sigma}$ are equivalence relations. As quotients can only be constructed for equivalence relations on states, it is therefore necessary that we restrict the following investigations to subgroups of $\mathsf{Auto}(\mathcal{K})$.

Before formally proving that the induced relation $\approx_G^{\mathcal{S}}$ is indeed an equivalence relation (provided that G is a subgroup of $\mathsf{Auto}(\mathcal{K})$), let us consider an example. The structure on the right-hand side of Figure C.4 has been obtained by a quotient construction using the equivalence $\approx_G^{\mathcal{S}}$ for the group $G := \{f_{id}, f_1, f_1^{-1}\}$. The following equivalence classes form the states of the quotient structure: $\{s_0\}$, $\{s_1, s_3\}$, $\{s_2\}$, $\{s_4, s_7\}$, $\{s_5, s_6\}$, $\{s_8\}$. To obtain the structure given on the right-hand side of Figure C.4, we used the canonical selection function ζ with $\zeta(s_0) = s_0$, $\zeta(s_1) = \zeta(s_3 = s_3$, $\zeta(s_2) := s_2$, $\zeta(s_4) = \zeta(s_7) = s_7$, $\zeta(s_5) = \zeta(s_6) = s_6$, and $\zeta(s_8) = s_8$.

Lemma C.34 (Induced Equivalence by Automorphism Subgroups). *Let $\mathcal{K} = (\mathcal{I}, \mathcal{S}, \mathcal{R}, \mathcal{L})$ be a Kripke structure over the variables V_Σ and let G be a subset of* $\mathsf{Auto}(\mathcal{K})$*. If G is a subgroup of* $\mathsf{Auto}(\mathcal{K})$*, then both $\approx_G^{\mathcal{S}}$ and $\approx_G^{\Sigma}$ are equivalence relations. Moreover, $s_1 \approx_G^{\mathcal{S}} s_2$ implies $\mathcal{L}(s_1) \approx_G^{\Sigma} \mathcal{L}(s_2)$.*

Proof. Reflexivity, symmetry, and transitivity of both relations can be reduced to the existence of the neutral element in G, the existence of inverse functions in G and the closure of G, respectively. As associativity and commutativity trivially hold for G, this proves the above lemma.

Reflexivity: We have to show that $s \approx_G^{\mathcal{S}} s$ holds for each $s \in \mathcal{S}$ and $\vartheta \approx_G^{\Sigma} \vartheta$ holds for each $\vartheta \subseteq V_\Sigma$. By definition of $\approx_G^{\mathcal{S}}$ and $\approx_G^{\Sigma}$, this is the same as $\exists f_1 \in G.s = f_1(s)$ and $\exists f_2 \in G.\vartheta = \{f_2(x) \mid x \in \vartheta\}$. As $f_{id} \in G$, i.e., the identity function (the neutral element w.r.t. $\circ$), we can use $f_1 = f_2 = f_{id}$ to see that both properties hold.

Symmetry: We have to show that $s_1 \approx_G^{\mathcal{S}} s_2$ implies $s_2 \approx_G^{\mathcal{S}} s_1$ and that $\vartheta_1 \approx_G^{\Sigma} \vartheta_2$ implies $\vartheta_2 \approx_G^{\Sigma} \vartheta_1$. By definition of $\approx_G^{\mathcal{S}}$ and $\approx_G^{\Sigma}$, this means that we have to show that for all $s_1, s_2 \in \mathcal{S}$ $\exists f_1 \in G.s_2 = f_1(s_1)$ implies $\exists g_1 \in G.s_1 = g_1(s_2)$ and for all $\vartheta_1, \vartheta_2 \subseteq V_\Sigma$, $\exists f_2 \in G.\vartheta_2 = f_2(s_1)$ implies $\exists g_2 \in G.\vartheta_1 = g_2(\vartheta_2)$. As for each $f_1, f_2 \in G$ the inverse functions are also in G, we can define $g_1 := f_1^{-1}$ and $g_2 := f_2^{-1}$.

Transitivity: We have to show that $s_1 \approx_G^{\mathcal{S}} s_2$ and $s_2 \approx_G^{\mathcal{S}} s_3$ implies $s_1 \approx_G^{\mathcal{S}} s_3$ and analogously for $\approx_G^{\Sigma}$. By definition of $\approx_G^{\mathcal{S}}$, it is equivalent to show that for arbitrary $f, g \in G$ with $s_2 = f(s_1)$ and $s_3 = g(s_2)$, there is a $h \in G$ such that $s_3 = h(s_1)$. Due to the closure of G, h exists since we define $h := g \circ f$. This is proved analogously for $\approx_G^{\Sigma}$.

Finally, let $s_1, s_2 \in \mathcal{S}$ with $s_1 \approx_G^{\mathcal{S}} s_2$ be given. Hence, we have $\exists f \in G.s_2 = f(s_1)$ which implies that $\exists f \in G.\mathcal{L}(s_2) = \mathcal{L}(f(s_1)) = f(\mathcal{L}(s_1))$. This means that $\mathcal{L}(s_1) \approx_G^{\Sigma} \mathcal{L}(s_2)$. □

If G is a subgroup of $\mathsf{Auto}(\mathcal{K})$, and consequently $\approx_G^{\mathcal{S}}$ is an equivalence relation, we can construct quotient structures according to Definition 2.24 on page 61. The key idea of symmetry reductions is to use $\approx_G^{\mathcal{S}}$ for an arbitrary subgroup G the quotient construction and to switch from the structure $\mathcal{K}$ to the quotient of $\mathcal{K}$ with $\approx_G^{\mathcal{S}}$. We have already seen that the truth of CTL* formulas is not affected by the quotient construction provided that the quotient is computed for a bisimulation relation. In particular, such a bisimulation relation preserves labels, which is, however, not the case for the relation $\approx_G^{\mathcal{S}}$: In general, $\widetilde{\mathcal{L}}(\widetilde{s})$ is a set of sets of variables.

However, we know that all labels $\vartheta \in \widetilde{\mathcal{L}}(\widetilde{s})$ belong to the same equivalence class w.r.t. $\approx_G^{\Sigma}$. Hence, these sets are permutations of each other, i.e., $\forall \vartheta_1, \vartheta_2 \in \widetilde{\mathcal{L}}(\widetilde{s})$, there is a $f \in G$ such that $\vartheta_2 = f(\vartheta_1)$. If we weaken the notion of bisimilarity to bisimilarity up to permutation, then we have the following lemma.

Lemma C.35 (Bisimulation up to G-Permutations). *Let $\mathcal{K} = (\mathcal{I}, \mathcal{S}, \mathcal{R}, \mathcal{L})$ be a Kripke structure over the variables V_Σ, G be a subgroup of $\mathsf{Auto}(\mathcal{K})$, and $\zeta : \mathcal{S} \to \mathcal{S}$ a canonical selection function for $\approx_G^{\mathcal{S}}$. Then, the following holds for the canonical quotient structure $\mathcal{K}_\zeta$:*

Canonical Selection: for $s_1 \in \mathcal{S}$, $s_2 \in \mathcal{S}_\zeta$ with $s_1 \approx_G^{\mathcal{S}} s_2$, it follows that $s_2 = \zeta(s_1)$
PBISIM1: for all $s_1 \in \mathcal{S}$, $s_2 \in \mathcal{S}_\zeta$ with $s_1 \approx_G^{\mathcal{S}} s_2$, there is a $f \in G$ such that $\mathcal{L}(s_2) = f(\mathcal{L}(s_1))$
PBISIM2a: for all $(s_1, s_1') \in \mathcal{R}$, $s_2 \in \mathcal{S}_\zeta$ with $s_1 \approx_G^{\mathcal{S}} s_2$, there is a $s_2' \in \mathcal{S}_\zeta$ such that $(s_2, s_2') \in \mathcal{R}_\zeta$
PBISIM2b: for all $(s_2, s_2') \in \mathcal{R}_\zeta$, $s_1 \in \mathcal{S}$ with $s_1 \approx_G^{\mathcal{S}} s_2$, there is a $s_1' \in \mathcal{S}$ such that $(s_1, s_1') \in \mathcal{R}$
PBISIM3a: $\forall s_1 \in \mathcal{I}.\exists s_2 \in \mathcal{I}_\zeta.s_1 \approx_G^{\mathcal{S}} s_2$
PBISIM3b: $\forall s_2 \in \mathcal{I}_\zeta.\exists s_1 \in \mathcal{I}.s_1 \approx_G^{\mathcal{S}} s_2$

This means that $\mathcal{K}$ and $\mathcal{K}_\zeta$ are bisimilar up to permutations of G and $\approx_G^{\mathcal{S}}$ restricted to $\mathcal{S} \times \mathcal{S}_\zeta$ is a bisimulation relation.

Proof. Assume there are states that satisfy $s_1 \approx_G^{\mathcal{S}} s_2$. According to Lemma 2.28, we have $\zeta(s_1) = \zeta(s_2)$, and hence $\zeta(s_1) = s_2$ (since s_2 is a fixpoint of ζ by Lemma 2.27). This proves the first item and we are free to replace s_2 in the above propositions with $\zeta(s_1)$.

Hence, PBISIM1 follows almost directly from Lemma C.34, since $s \approx_G^{\mathcal{S}} \zeta(s)$ implies $\mathcal{L}(s) \approx_G^{\Sigma} \mathcal{L}(\zeta(s))$, which means that there is a $f \in G$ such that $\mathcal{L}(\zeta(s)) = f(\mathcal{L}(s))$. The proof of PBISIM2a is also simple: Just define $s_2' := \zeta(s_1')$ and observe that due to definition of $\mathcal{R}_\zeta$, we derive from $(s_1, s_1') \in \mathcal{R}$ that $(s_2, s_2') \in \mathcal{R}_\zeta$ holds.

The proof of PBISIM2b is slightly more difficult: As $(s_2, s_2') \in \mathcal{R}_\zeta$ holds, there must be $(q_1, q_1') \in \mathcal{R}$ with $\zeta(q_1) = s_2$ and $\zeta(q_1') = s_2'$. As also $\zeta(s_1) = s_2$ holds, it follows that $\zeta(s_1) = \zeta(q_1)$, i.e., $q_1 \approx_G^{\mathcal{S}} s_1$. By definition of $\approx_G^{\mathcal{S}}$, this means that there is a $f \in G$ such that $s_1 = f(q_1)$. We choose such an f and define $s_1' := f(q_2)$. As f preserves transitions, it follows from $(q_1, q_1') \in \mathcal{R}$ that also $(f(q_1), f(q_1')) \in \mathcal{R}$, i.e., $(s_1, s_1') \in \mathcal{R}$ must hold. Moreover, by construction of s_1', we have $s_1' \approx_G^{\mathcal{S}} q_1'$, which means that $\zeta(s_1') = \zeta(q_2)$ and hence, $\zeta(s_1') = s_2'$ holds.

PBISIM3a and PBISIM3b are trivial, simply recall that $s_1 \approx_G^{\mathcal{S}} s_2$ with $s_2 \in \mathcal{S}_\zeta$ implies $s_2 = \zeta(s_1)$. Hence, use $s_2 = \zeta(s_1)$ in the proof of PBISIM3a and $s_1 := s_2$ in the proof of PBISIM3b. □

According to the above lemma, the quotient obtained by a symmetry reduction is bisimilar to the original structure up to permutation of labels. Clearly, this is not sufficient to preserve truth values for *arbitrary* CTL^* formulas. However, whenever the truth value of a formula is robust w.r.t. to the permutations in G, it can alternatively be checked in $\mathcal{K}_zeta$ since $\mathcal{K}$ and $\mathcal{K}_zeta$ do not distinguish between these formulas.

C.5.2 Symmetries in the Specification

In the last section, we defined automorphism subgroups that reflect the symmetries of structures to compute quotient structures. In this section, we define the automorphisms of formulas that reflect the symmetries that are inherent in the specification. The main result of this section is that if an automorphism subgroup G is chosen that matches with the symmetries of the specification, then the truth of the specification is preserved by the quotient construction.

The main property that is to be preserved by the automorphism subgroup of a formula is its truth value. Hence, the automorphisms of a formula Φ should be all functions that map $\mathsf{VAR}(\Phi)$ bijectively to $\mathsf{VAR}(\Phi)$ such that the truth value of Φ is retained in any structure. As this property is hard to check, we impose a stronger one, hence ignoring some symmetries. For every function $f : \mathsf{VAR}(\Phi) \to \mathsf{VAR}(\Phi)$, we define $f(\Phi)$ as the formula that is obtained by replacing all occurrences of variables x in Φ with $f(x)$.

Definition C.36 (Automorphisms of CTL^* Formulas). *Given a CTL^* formula Φ over the variables V_Σ. The automorphisms $\mathsf{Auto}(\Phi)$ of Φ is the set of bijective functions $f : \mathsf{VAR}(\Phi) \to \mathsf{VAR}(\Phi)$ that is computed by the algorithm of Figure C.5. It is assumed that the function* new_var *introduces a new variable that does not belong to V_Σ (hence, extending V_Σ to $V_{\Sigma'}$).*

For example, let Φ be the CTL^* formula $a_2 \wedge a_1 \wedge \mathsf{G}(\neg a_1 \vee \neg a_2) \vee \mathsf{F}(a_2 \wedge a_1 \wedge a_3) \wedge (a_2 \vee a_1)$. We have $\mathsf{VAR}(\Phi) = \{a_1, a_2, a_3\}$, hence, all permutations on $\mathsf{VAR}(\Phi)$ are $\mathsf{Perm}(\{a_1, a_2, a_3\}) = \{f_{123}, f_{132}, f_{213}, f_{231}, f_{312}, f_{321}\}$, where f_{ijk} denotes the function that is defined as $f_{ijk}(a_1) = a_i$, $f_{ijk}(a_2) = a_j$ and $f_{ijk}(a_3) = a_k$. According to the algorithm in Figure C.5, we first compute $\mathsf{topprop}(\Phi) = (\{\vartheta_1 = \mathsf{G}(\neg a_1 \vee \neg a_2), \vartheta_2 = \mathsf{F}(a_2 \wedge a_1 \wedge a_3)\}, a_2 \wedge a_1 \wedge \vartheta_1 \vee \vartheta_2 \wedge (a_2 \vee a_1))$. Next, we compute $\mathsf{Auto}(\mathsf{G}(\neg a_1 \vee \neg a_2)) = \mathsf{Auto}(\neg a_1 \vee \neg a_2) = \{f_{123}, f_{213}\}$ and $\mathsf{Auto}(\mathsf{F}(a_2 \wedge a_1 \wedge a_3)) = \mathsf{Auto}(a_2 \wedge a_1 \wedge a_3) = \mathsf{Perm}(\{a_1, a_2, a_3\})$. Moreover, $\mathsf{Auto}(a_2 \wedge a_1 \wedge \vartheta_1 \vee \vartheta_2 \wedge (a_2 \vee a_1))) = \{f_{123}, f_{213}\}$, hence, $\mathsf{Auto}(\Phi) = \{f_{123}, f_{213}\}$.

Note again that, in general, $\mathsf{Auto}(\Phi)$ as computed in Figure C.5 is only a subset of the automorphisms to avoid theorem proving for CTL^* (for reasons of complexity). For example, we obtain $\mathsf{Auto}(\neg \mathsf{AG}(a_1 \wedge a_3) \vee \mathsf{EF}(a_1 \vee a_2)) = \{f_{123}\}$. However, as the formula is valid, we could also use $\mathsf{Perm}(\{a_1, a_2, a_3\})$ as $\mathsf{Auto}(\Phi)$, instead. Nevertheless, a high degree of symmetry can be found, such that the set $\mathsf{Auto}(\Phi)$ is often a large[3] subset of $\mathsf{Perm}(\mathsf{VAR}(\Phi))$.

Symmetries often occur in parameterized specifications, i.e., specifications that are to be proved for structures that are generated with a certain regular pattern. For example, consider a specification of the following form: whenever some property a holds *exactly one of the outputs* o_1,

[3] For the representation of large permutation subgroups, note that each such group is generated by a set of basic permutations. A basic permutation is a permutation that exchanges exactly two elements. Hence, for n elements there are only n basic permutations.

```
function topprop(Φ)
    case Φ of
      is_prop(Φ)        : return ({}, φ);
      ¬φ                : (E, φ') ≡ topprop(φ); return (E, ¬φ');
      φ1 ∧ φ2           : (E1, φ1') ≡ topprop(φ1); (E2, φ2') ≡ topprop(φ2);
                          return (E1 ∪ E2, φ1' ∧ φ2');
      φ1 ∨ φ2           : (E1, φ1') ≡ topprop(φ1); (E2, φ2') ≡ topprop(φ2);
                          return (E1 ∪ E2, φ1' ∨ φ2');
      otherwise         : ϑ = new_var; return ({}, ϑ);
    end
end

function Auto(Φ)
    case Φ of
      is_prop(Φ)            : return {f ∈ Perm(VAR(Φ)) | Φ = f(Φ) is valid};
      ¬φ, φ ∧ ψ, φ ∨ ψ:       ({ϑ1 = φ1, ..., ϑm = φm}, Ψ) ≡ topprop(Φ);
                              return Auto(Ψ) ∩ ⋂_{i=1}^{n} Auto(φi);
      Xφ, Gφ, Fφ            : return Auto(φ);
      [φ U ψ], [φ U̲ ψ]      : return Auto(φ) ∩ Auto(ψ);
      [φ B ψ], [φ B̲ ψ]      : return Auto(φ) ∩ Auto(ψ);
      Eφ, Aφ                : return Auto(φ);
    end
end
```

Fig. C.5. Computing automorphisms of a CTL* formula Φ

..., o_n *holds*. This is given by the following propositional formula $a \rightarrow (\bigvee_{i=1}^{n} o_i) \wedge \bigwedge_{i=1}^{n}\left(o_i \rightarrow \bigwedge_{j=1,j\neq i}^{n} \neg o_j\right)$. It can be easily seen that $\mathsf{Auto}(\Phi) = \mathsf{Perm}(\{o_1,\ldots,o_n\})$ and hence consists of $n!$ different automorphisms.

The next theorem now gives a criterion for the preservation of CTL* formulas.

Theorem C.37 (Symmetry Reduction for CTL*). *Let $\mathcal{K} = (\mathcal{I},\mathcal{S},\mathcal{R},\mathcal{L})$ be a Kripke structure over the variables V_Σ and let Φ be a CTL* path formula over V_Σ. Let be G a subgroup of $\mathsf{Auto}(\mathcal{K})$ such that $\{f_{|\mathsf{VAR}(\Phi)} \mid f \in G\} \subseteq \mathsf{Auto}(\Phi)$ holds. Then, for all paths π in $\mathcal{K}$ and all canonical selection functions $\zeta : \mathcal{S} \to \mathcal{S}$ for $\approx_G^{\mathcal{S}}$, the following holds:*

$$(\mathcal{K},\pi) \models \Phi \ \ \textit{iff} \ \ (\mathcal{K}_\zeta,\pi_\zeta) \models \Phi \ \ \textit{where}\ \pi_\zeta := \lambda t.\zeta(\pi^{(t)})$$

Note that the theorem implies that truth values of Φ in different structures $\mathcal{K}_{\zeta_1}$, $\mathcal{K}_{\zeta_2}$ obtained by different canonical selection functions ζ_1 and ζ_2 must be the same. Hence, the truth value of Φ does not depend on the choice of ζ, in particular, it does not depend on the choice of a label of $\widetilde{\mathcal{L}}(\widetilde{s})$.

The proof of the above theorem requires some technical preparations. In particular, the proof will be done by induction on some subformulas of the given CTL^* formula Φ that are called significant subformulas. These are defined as follows:

Definition C.38 (Significant Subformulas). *Given a* CTL^* *formula* Φ *over the variables* V_Σ. *Then, the set* $\mathsf{sig}(\Phi) := \mathsf{sig}_1(\Phi) \cup \{\Phi\}$, *where* $\mathsf{sig}_1(\Phi)$ *is defined below, is called the set of significant subformulas of* Φ.

function $\mathsf{sig}_1(\Phi)$
  case Φ **of**
    $\mathsf{is\_prop}(\Phi)$: **return** $\{\}$;
    $\neg\varphi$: **return** $\mathsf{sig}_1(\varphi)$;
    $\varphi \wedge \psi$, $\varphi \vee \psi$: **return** $\mathsf{sig}_1(\varphi) \cup \mathsf{sig}_1(\psi)$;
    $\mathsf{X}\varphi$, $\mathsf{G}\varphi$, $\mathsf{F}\varphi$: **return** $\mathsf{sig}_1\varphi \cup \{\Phi\}$;
    $[\varphi\ \mathsf{U}\ \psi]$, $[\varphi\ \underline{\mathsf{U}}\ \psi]$: **return** $\mathsf{sig}_1(\varphi) \cup \mathsf{sig}_1(\psi) \cup \{\Phi\}$;
    $[\varphi\ \mathsf{B}\ \psi]$, $[\varphi\ \underline{\mathsf{B}}\ \psi]$: **return** $\mathsf{sig}_1(\varphi) \cup \mathsf{sig}_1(\psi) \cup \{\Phi\}$;
    $\mathsf{E}\varphi$, $\mathsf{A}\varphi$: **return** $\mathsf{sig}_1(\varphi) \cup \{\Phi\}$;
  end
end

The key property of significant subformulas of Φ is that their automorphism group includes the automorphism group of Φ (see the lemma below). This property will be useful in the proof of Theorem C.37. Intuitively, the lemma holds because each $\varphi \in \mathsf{sig}(\Phi)$ contributes to the computation of $\mathsf{Auto}(\Phi)$ by an intersection with $\mathsf{Auto}(\varphi)$, hence, the result must be a subset of $\mathsf{Auto}(\varphi)$.

Lemma C.39. *Given a* CTL^* *formula* Φ *over the variables* V_Σ, *then for each* $\varphi \in \mathsf{sig}(\Phi)$, *we have* $\mathsf{Auto}(\Phi) \subseteq \mathsf{Auto}(\varphi)$. *Hence,* $\mathsf{Auto}(\Phi) \subseteq \bigcap_{\varphi \in \mathsf{sig}(\Phi)} \mathsf{Auto}(\varphi)$.

With the help of the above lemma, we are now able to prove Theorem C.37. Let $c(\Psi)$ for any CTL^* formula Ψ be the number of temporal operators and path quantifiers occurring in Ψ. We can define a partial order $\preceq$ on the set of significant subformulas by $\varphi_1 \preceq \varphi_2 :\Leftrightarrow c(\varphi_1) \leq c(\varphi_2)$. Hence, we can apply induction along the significant subformulas of Φ. We omit the details of the proof.

References

[1] ABADI, M., AND MANNA, Z. Nonclausal deduction in first-order temporal logic. *Journal of the ACM 37*, 2 (1990), 279–317.

[2] ACCELLERA. Property specification language reference manual. http://www.haifa.il.ibm.com/projects/verification/sugar, January 2003.

[3] ACKERMANN, W. Über die Erfüllbarkeit gewisser Zählausdrücke. *Mathematische Annalen 100* (1928), 638–649.

[4] ADLER, M., AND IMMERMAN, N. An $n!$ lower bound on formula size. In *Symposium on Logic in Computer Science (LICS)* (2001), IEEE Computer Society, pp. 197–208.

[5] AGRAWAL, M., KAYAL, N., AND SAXENA, N. PRIMES is in P, 2002.

[6] AHO, A. V., HOPCROFT, J. E., AND ULLMAN, J. D. *The Design and Analysis of Computer Algorithms*. Addison Wesley, 1974.

[7] AKERS, S. Binary decision diagrams. *IEEE Transactions on Computers C-27*, 6 (June 1978), 509–516.

[8] ALUR, R., BRAYTON, R., HENZINGER, T., QADEER, S., AND RAJAMANI, S. Partial-order reduction in symbolic state space exploration. In *Conference on Computer Aided Verification (CAV)* (1997), vol. 1254 of *LNCS*, Springer, pp. 340–351.

[9] ALUR, R., FEDER, T., AND HENZINGER, T. The benefits of relaxing punctuality. In *Symposium on Principles of Distributed Computing* (1991), ACM, pp. 139–152.

[10] ALUR, R., AND HENZINGER, T. A really temporal logic. In *Symposium on Foundations of Computer Science (FOCS)* (New York, 1989), IEEE Computer Society, pp. 164–169.

[11] ALUR, R., AND HENZINGER, T. Real-time logics: Complexity and expressiveness. In *Symposium on Logic in Computer Science (LICS)* (Washington, D.C., June 1990), IEEE Computer Society, pp. 390–401.

[12] ALUR, R., AND HENZINGER, T. Logics and models of real-time: A survey. In *Real-Time: Theory in Practice* (1991), vol. 600 of *LNCS*, Springer, pp. 74–106.

[13] AMIR, A. Separation in nonlinear time models. *Information and Control 66* (1985), 177–203.

[14] AMLA, N., EMERSON, E., KURSHAN, R., AND NAMJOSHI, K. Model checking synchronous timing diagrams. In *Conference on Formal Methods in Computer*

Aided Design (FMCAD) (Austin, Texas, USA, 2000), vol. 1954 of *LNCS*, Springer, pp. 283–298.

[15] ANDRÉKA, H., NÉMETI, I., AND VAN BENTHEM, J. Modal logic and bounded fragments of predicate logic. *Journal of Philosophical Logic 27*, 3 (1998), 217–274.

[16] ANDREWS, P. Theorem proving via general matings. *Journal of the Association for Computing Machinery 28*, 2 (April 1981), 193–214.

[17] ANDREWS, P. *An Introduction to Mathematical Logic and Type Theory: To Truth through Proof.* Computer Science and Applied Mathematics Series. Academic, New York, 1986.

[18] ANDREWS, P., ISSAR, S., NESMITH, D., AND PFENNIG, F. The TPS theorem proving system. In *Conference on Automated Deduction (CADE)* (1990), M. Stickel, Ed., Springer, pp. 641–642.

[19] APT, K. Ten years of Hoare's logic: A survey – part I. *ACM Transactions on Programming Languages and Systems (TOPLAS) 3*, 4 (1981), 431–483.

[20] ARMONI, R., BUSTAN, D., KUPFERMAN, O., AND VARDI, M. Resets vs. aborts in linear temporal logic. In *Conference on Tools and Algorithms for the Construction and Analysis of Systems (TACAS)* (Warsaw, Poland, 2003), H. Garavel and J. Hatcliff, Eds., vol. 2619 of *LNCS*, Springer, pp. 65–80.

[21] ARMONI, R., FIX, L., FLAISHER, A., GERTH, R., GINSBURG, B., KANZA, T., LANDVER, A., MADOR-HAIM, S., SINGERMAN, E., TIEMEYER, A., VARDI, M., AND ZBAR, Y. The ForSpec temporal logic: A new temporal property-specification language. In *Conference on Tools and Algorithms for the Construction and Analysis of Systems (TACAS)* (Grenoble, France, 2002), vol. 2280 of *LNCS*, Springer, pp. 296–311.

[22] ARNOLD, A. The μ-calulcus alternation hierarchy is strict on binary trees. *Theoretical Informatics and Applications 33*, 4-5 (1999), 329–340.

[23] ARNOLD, A., AND CRUBILLE, P. A linear algorithm to solve fixed-point equations on transition systems. *Information Processing Letters 29*, 2 (1988), 57–66.

[24] ARNOLD, A., AND NIWIŃSKI, D. Fixed point characterization of Büchi automata on infinite trees. *Information Processing and Cybernetics 26* (1990), 451–459.

[25] AUBIN, R. Mechanizing structural induction. *Theoretical Computer Science 9* (1979), 329–362.

[26] AZIZ, A., SINGHAL, V., BALARIN, F., BRAYTON, R., AND SANGIOVANNI-VINCENTELLI, A. Equivalences for fair Kripke structures. In *Colloquium on Automata, Languages and Programming (ICALP)* (Jerusalem, Israel, July 1994).

[27] BALCAZAR, J., GABARRO, J., AND SANTHA, M. Deciding bisimilarity is P-complete. *Formal Aspects of Computing 4*, 6 (1992), 638–648.

[28] BANIEQBAL, B., AND BARRINGER, H. A study of an extended temporal logic and a temporal fixed point calculus. Technical Report UMCS-86-10-2, University of Manchester, 1986.

[29] BANIEQBAL, B., AND BARRINGER, H. Temporal logic with fixed points. In *Temporal Logic in Specification* (1987), pp. 62–74.

[30] BARRINGER, H., KUIPER, R., AND PNUELI, A. A really abstract current model and its temporal logic. In *Symposium on Principles of Programming Languages (POPL)* (1986), pp. 173–183.

[31] BASIN, D. A., AND KLARLUND, N. Hardware verification using monadic second-order logic. In *Conference on Computer Aided Verification (CAV)* (Liege, Belgium, July 1995), P. Wolper, Ed., vol. 939 of *LNCS*, Springer, pp. 31–41.

[32] BECKER, B., AND DRECHSLER, R. How many decomposition types do we need? In *European Design and Test Conference (EDTC)* (Paris, March 1995), IEEE Computer Society, pp. 438–443.

[33] BEER, I., BEN-DAVID, S., EISNER, C., FISMAN, D., GRINGAUZE, A., AND RODEH, Y. The temporal logic Sugar. In *Conference on Computer Aided Verification (CAV)* (Paris, France, 2001), vol. 2102 of *LNCS*, Springer, pp. 363–367.

[34] BEHMANN, H. Beiträge zur Algebra der Logik, insbesondere zum Entscheidungsproblem. *Mathematische Annalen 86* (1922), 163–229.

[35] BEKIČ, H. Definable operations in general algebras, and the theory of automata and flow charts. In *Programming Languages and Their Definition - Hans Bekič (1936-1982).* (1984), C. Jones, Ed., vol. 177 of *LNCS*, Springer, pp. 30–55.

[36] BEN-ARI, M., MANNA, Z., AND PNUELI, A. The temporal logic of branching time. In *Symposium on Principles of Programming Languages (POPL)* (1981), pp. 164–176.

[37] BENSALEM, S., BOUAJJANI, A., LOISEAUX, C., AND SIFAKIS, J. Property preserving simulations. In *Workshop on Computer Aided Verification (CAV)* (July 1992), G. Bochmann and D. Probst, Eds.

[38] BERARD, B., BIDOIT, M., FINKEL, A., LAROUSSINIE, F., PETIT, A., PETRUCCI, L., SCHNOEBELEN, P., BERARD, B., BIDOIT, M., FINKEL, A., LAROUSSINIE, F., PETIT, A., PETRUCCI, L., AND SCHNOEBELEN, P. *Systems and Software Verification. Model-Checking Techniques and Tools.* Springer, 2001.

[39] BERNAYS, P., AND SCHÖNFINKEL, M. Zum Entscheidungsproblem der mathematischen Logik. *Mathematische Annalen 99* (1928), 342–372.

[40] BERNHOLTZ, O., VARDI, M. Y., AND WOLPER, P. An automata-theoretic approach to branching-time model checking. In *Conference on Computer Aided Verification (CAV)* (Stanford, California, USA, June 1994), D. L. Dill, Ed., vol. 818 of *LNCS*, Springer, pp. 142–155.

[41] BERRY, G. The constructive semantics of pure Esterel. http://www-sop.inria.fr/meije/esterel/, July 1996.

[42] BERRY, G. The foundations of Esterel. In *Proof, Language and Interaction: Essays in Honour of Robin Milner*, G. Plotkin, C. Stirling, and M. Tofte, Eds. MIT, 1998.

[43] BERRY, G., AND GONTHIER, G. The Esterel synchronous programming language: Design, semantics, implementation. *Science of Computer Programming 19*, 2 (1992), 87–152.

[44] BERTHET, C., COUDERT, O., AND MADRE, J. C. New ideas on symbolic manipulations of finite state machines. In *Conference on Computer Aided Design (ICCAD)* (1990).

[45] BEVIER, W., HUNT, W., MOORE, J., AND YOUNG, W. An approach to system verification. *Journal of Automated Reasoning 5*, 4 (1989), 411–428.

[46] BHAT, G., AND CLEAVELAND, R. Efficient local model checking for fragments of the modal μ-calculus. In *Conference on Tools and Algorithms for the Construction and Analysis of Systems (TACAS)* (Passau, Germany, March 1996), T. Margaria and B. Steffen, Eds., vol. 1055 of *LNCS*, Springer, pp. 107–126.

[47] BIBEL, W. *Automated Theorem Proving*. Vieweg, 1987.

[48] BIBEL, W., EDER, E., AND FRONHÖFER, B. Towards an advanced implementation of the connection method. In *International Joint Conference on Artificial Intelligence (IJCAI)* (August 1983), pp. 920–922.

[49] BJÖRKLUND, H., SANDBERG, S., AND VOROBYOV, S. A discrete subexponential algorithm for parity games. In *Symposium on Theoretical Aspects of Computer*

Science (STACS) (Berlin, Germany, 2003), vol. 2607 of *LNCS*, Springer, pp. 663–674.

[50] BLÄSIUS, K., AND BÜRCKERT, H.-J. *Deduktionssysteme*. Oldenbourg, 1987.

[51] BLEDSOE, W., AND LOVELAND, D. *Automated Theorem Proving: after 25 years*, vol. 29 of *Contemporary Mathematics*. American Mathematical Society (AMS), 1984.

[52] BLOEM, R., RAVI, K., AND SOMENZI, F. Efficient decision procedures for model checking of linear time logic properties. In *Conference on Computer Aided Verification (CAV)* (Trento, Italy, 1999), N. Halbwachs and D. Peled, Eds., vol. 1633 of *LNCS*, Springer.

[53] BOCHMANN, G. Hardware specification with temporal logic: An example. *IEEE Transactions on Computers C-31*, 3 (March 1982), 223–231.

[54] BOIGELOT, B., RASSART, S., AND WOLPER, P. On the expressiveness of real and integer arithmetic automata. In *Colloquium on Automata, Languages and Programming (ICALP)* (July 1998), vol. 1443 of *LNCS*, Springer, pp. 152–163.

[55] BOLLIG, B., AND WEGENER, I. Improving the variable ordering of OBDDs is NP-complete. *IEEE Transactions on Computer Aided Design 45*, 9 (1996), 993–1002.

[56] BÖRGER, E., GRÄDEL, E., AND GUREVICH, Y. *The classical decision problem*. Springer, 1997.

[57] BOSE, B., ESEN TUNA, M., AND CHOPPELLA, V. A tutorial on digital design derivation using DRS. In *Conference on Formal Methods in Computer Aided Design (FMCAD)* (Palo Alto, CA, USA, November 1996), M. Srivas and A. Camilleri, Eds., vol. 1166 of *LNCS*, Springer, pp. 270–274.

[58] BOSE, B., AND JOHNSON, S. DDD-FM9001: Derivation of a verified microprocessor. In *Conference on Correct Hardware Design and Verification Methods (CHARME)* (Arles, France, May 1993), Springer, pp. 191–202.

[59] BOUHOULA, A., AND RUSINOWITCH, M. Automatic case analysis in proof by induction. In *International Joint Conference on Artificial Intelligence (IJCAI)* (Chambery, France, 1993).

[60] BOYER, R., AND MOORE, J. *A Computational Logic Handbook*. Academic, New York, 1979.

[61] BOYER, R., AND MOORE, J. *A Computational Logic Handbook*. Academic, New York, 1988.

[62] BRACE, K., RUDELL, R., AND BRYANT, R. Efficient implementation of a BDD package. In *Design Automation Conference (DAC)* (Orlando, Florida, June 1990), ACM Press, pp. 40–45.

[63] BRADFIELD, J. *Verifying Temporal Properties of Systems*. Progress in Theoretical Computer Science. Birkhäuser, Boston, Basel, Berlin, 1992.

[64] BRADFIELD, J. The modal μ-calculus alternation hierarchy is strict. In *Conference on Concurrency Theory (CONCUR)* (1996), U. Montanari and V. Sassone, Eds., vol. 1119 of *LNCS*, Springer, pp. 233–246.

[65] BRADFIELD, J. Simplifying the modal μ-calculus alternation hierarchy. In *Symposium on Theoretical Aspects of Computer Science (STACS)* (1998), M. Morvan, C. Meinel, and D. Krob, Eds., vol. 1376 of *LNCS*, Springer, pp. 39–49.

[66] BRADFIELD, J., AND STIRLING, C. Local model checking for infinite state spaces. In *Workshop on Computer Aided Verification (CAV)* (July 1991), K. Larsen and A. Skou, Eds.

[67] BRADFIELD, J., AND STIRLING, C. Verifying temporal properties of processes. *Theoretical Computer Science 96*, 1 (1992), 157–174.

[68] BRADFIELD, J., AND STIRLING, C. Modal logics and μ-calculi: An introduction. In *Handbook of Process Algebra*, J. Bergstra, A. Ponse, and S. Smolka, Eds. Elsevier Science, 2001, pp. 293–330.

[69] BRAYTON, R. K., HACHTEL, G. D., SANGIOVANNI-VINCENTELLI, A., SOMENZI, F., AZIZ, A., CHENG, S. T., EDWARDS, S., KHATRI, S., KUKIMOTO, Y., PARDO, A., QADEER, S., RANJAN, R. K., SARWARY, S., SHIPLE, T. R., SWAMY, G., AND VILLA, T. VIS: a system for verification and synthesis. In *Conference on Computer Aided Verification (CAV)* (New Brunswick, NJ, USA, July / August 1996), R. Alur and T. A. Henzinger, Eds., vol. 1102 of *LNCS*, Springer, pp. 428–432.

[70] BROWN, S., AND ROSE, J. FPGA and CPLD architectures: A tutorial. *IEEE Design and Test of Computers 13*, 2 (2003), 42–57.

[71] BROWNE, M., CLARKE, E., DILL, D., AND MISHRA, B. Automatic verification of sequential circuits using temporal logic. *IEEE Transactions on Computers C-35*, 12 (December 1986), 1034–1044.

[72] BROWNE, M., CLARKE, E., AND GRUMBERG, O. Characterizing finite Kripke structures in propositional temporal logic. *Theoretical Computer Science 59* (July 1988), 115–131.

[73] BRUYERE, V., HANSEL, G., MICHAUX, C., AND VILLEMAIRE, R. Logic and p-recognizable sets of integers. *Bulletin of the Societe Mathematique Belgique 1* (1994), 191–238.

[74] BRYANT, R. Graph-based algorithms for Boolean function manipulation. *IEEE Transactions on Computers C-35*, 8 (August 1986), 677–691.

[75] BRYANT, R. Graph-based algorithms for Boolean function manipulation. In *Design Automation Conference (DAC)* (1990), ACM Press.

[76] BRYANT, R. On the complexity of VLSI implementations and graph representations of Boolean functions with application to integer multiplication. *IEEE Transactions on Computers 40*, 2 (February 1991), 205–213.

[77] BRYANT, R. Symbolic Boolean manipulation with ordered binary decision diagrams. Tech. Rep. CMU-CS-92-160, School of Computer Science, Carnegie Mellon University, Pittsburgh, PA 15213, July 1992.

[78] BRYANT, R. Symbolic Boolean manipulation with ordered binary-decision diagrams. *ACM Computing Surveys 24*, 3 (September 1992), 293–318.

[79] BRZOZOWSKI, J., AND KNAST, R. The dot-depth hierarchy of star-free languages is infinite. *Journal of Computer and System Sciences 16* (1978), 37–55.

[80] BÜCHI, J. On a decision method in restricted second order arithmetic. In *International Congress on Logic, Methodology and Philosophy of Science* (Stanford, CA, 1960), E. Nagel, Ed., Stanford University Press, pp. 1–12.

[81] BÜCHI, J. Weak second order arithmetic and finite automata. *Z. Math. Logik Grundlagen Math. 6* (1960), 66–92.

[82] BÜCHI, J., AND LANDWEBER, L. Solving sequential conditions finite-state strategies. *ACM Transactions 138* (1969), 295–311.

[83] BULTAN, T., GERBER, R., AND PUGH, W. Symbolic model checking of infinite state systems using Presburger arithmetic. In *Conference on Computer Aided Verification (CAV)* (June 1997), O. Grumberg, Ed., vol. 1254 of *LNCS*, Springer, pp. 400–411.

[84] BULTAN, T., GERBER, R., AND PUGH, W. Model-checking concurrent systems with unbounded integer variables. *ACM Transactions on Programming Languages and Systems (TOPLAS) 21*, 4 (1999), 747–789.

[85] BUNDY, A. A survey of automated deduction. Informatics research report edi-inf-rr-0001, Division of Informatics, University of Edinburgh, 1999.

[86] BURCH, J., CLARKE, E., AND LONG, D. Symbolic model checking with partitioned transition relations. In *Conference on Very Large Scale Integration (VLSI)* (Edinburgh, Scotland, August 1991), A. Halaas and P. Denyer, Eds., North Holland, pp. 49–58.

[87] BURCH, J., CLARKE, E., MCMILLAN, K., AND DILL, D. Sequential circuit verification using symbolic model checking. In *Design Automation Conference (DAC)* (Los Alamitos, CA, June 1990), ACM Press, pp. 46–51.

[88] BURCH, J., CLARKE, E., MCMILLAN, K., DILL, D., AND HWANG, L. Symbolic model checking: 10^{20} states and beyond. In *Symposium on Logic in Computer Science (LICS)* (Washington, D.C., June 1990), IEEE Computer Society, pp. 1–33.

[89] BURCH, J., CLARKE, E., MCMILLAN, K., DILL, D., AND HWANG, L. Symbolic model checking: 10^{20} states and beyond. *Information and Computation 98*, 2 (June 1992), 142–170.

[90] BURGESS, J. Axioms for tense logics II: time periods. *Notre Dame Journal of Formal Logic 23*, 4 (1982), 375–383.

[91] BURGESS, J., AND GUREVICH, Y. The decision problem for linear temporal logic. *Notre Dame Journal of Formal Logic 26*, 2 (1985), 115–128.

[92] BURSTALL, R. Proving properties of programs by structural induction. *The Computer Journal 12* (1969), 41–48.

[93] BUTLER, M., AND LANGBACKA, T. Program derivation using the refinement calculator. In *Higher Order Logic Theorem Proving and its Applications* (Turku, Finland, August 1996), J. V. Wright, J. Grundy, and J. Harrison, Eds., vol. 1125 of *LNCS*, Springer, pp. 93–108.

[94] CAMILLERI, A., GORDON, M., AND MELHAM, T. Hardware verification using higher order logic. In *Working Conference From HDL Descriptions to Guaranteed Correct Circuit Designs* (Amsterdam, September 1986), D. Borrione, Ed., North Holland, pp. 41–66.

[95] CAMPOS, S., AND CLARKE, E. Real-time symbolic model checking for discrete time models. In *Theories and Experiences for Real-Time System Development* (May 1994), T. Rus and C. Rattray, Eds., AMAST Series in Computing, World Scientific.

[96] CHANDRA, A., KOZEN, D., AND STOCKMEYER, L. Alternation. *Journal of the ACM 28*, 1 (1981), 114–133.

[97] CHANG, S., CHENG, D., AND MAREK-SADOWSKA, M. Minimizing ROBDD size of incompletely specified multiple output functions. In *European Design and Test Conference (EDTC)* (Paris, February 1994), IEEE Computer Society, pp. 620–624.

[98] CHELLAS, B. *Modal Logic: An Introduction*. Cambridge University Press, 1980.

[99] CHURCH, A. A note on the Entscheidungsproblem. *Journal of Symbolic Logic 1* (1936), 101–102.

[100] CHURCH, A. A formulation of the simple theory of types. *Journal of Symbolic Logic 5* (1940), 56–68.

[101] CLARKE, E., AND DRAGHICESCU, I. Expressibility results for linear-time and branching-time logics. In *Linear Time, Branching Time and Partial Order in Logics and Models for Concurrency* (Noordwigherhout, Netherland, May/June 1988), vol. 354 of *LNCS*, Springer, pp. 428–437.

[102] CLARKE, E., AND EMERSON, E. Synthesis of synchronization skeletons for branching time temporal logic. In *Workshop on Logics of Programs* (Yorktown Heights, New York, May 1981), vol. 131 of *LNCS*, Springer.

[103] CLARKE, E., EMERSON, E., AND SISTLA, A. Automatic verification of finite-state concurrent systems using temporal logic specifications. *ACM Transactions on Programming Languages and Systems (TOPLAS) 8*, 2 (April 1986), 244–263.

[104] CLARKE, E., ENDERS, R., FILKORN, T., AND JHA, S. Exploiting symmetry in temporal logic model checking. *Formal Methods in System Design 9*, 1-2 (1996), 77–104.

[105] CLARKE, E., GRUMBERG, O., AND HAMAGUCHI, K. Another look at LTL model checking. In *Conference on Computer Aided Verification (CAV)* (Stanford, California, USA, June 1994), D. L. Dill, Ed., vol. 818 of *LNCS*, Springer, pp. 415–427.

[106] CLARKE, E., GRUMBERG, O., HIRAISHI, H., JHA, S., LONG, D., MCMILLAN, K., AND NESS, L. Verification of the Futurebus+ cache coherence protocol. In *Conference on Computer Hardware Description Languages and Their Applications (CHDL)* (Ottawa, Canada, April 1993), D. Agnew, L. Claesen, and R. Camposano, Eds., Elsevier Science, pp. 5–20.

[107] CLARKE, E., GRUMBERG, O., AND KURSHAN, R. A synthesis of two approaches for verifying finite state concurrent systems. In *Symposium on Logical Foundations of Computer Science: Logic at Botik '89* (New York, July 1989), vol. 363 of *LNCS*, Springer.

[108] CLARKE, E., GRUMBERG, O., AND LONG, D. Model checking and abstraction. In *Symposium on Principles of Programming Languages (POPL)* (Albuquerque, New Mexico, January 1992), ACM, pp. 342–354.

[109] CLARKE, E., GRUMBERG, O., AND LONG, D. Model checking and abstraction. *ACM Transactions on Programming Languages and Systems (TOPLAS) 16*, 5 (September 1994), 1512–1542.

[110] CLARKE, E., GRUMBERG, O., AND LONG, D. Model checking. In *Deductive Program Design* (Marktoberdorf, Germany, 1996), vol. 152 of *Nato ASI Series F*, Springer.

[111] CLARKE, E., GRUMBERG, O., AND PELED, D. *Model Checking*. MIT, London, England, 1999.

[112] CLARKE, E., GRUMBERG, O., AND PELED, D. *Model Checking*. MIT, 2000.

[113] CLARKE, E. M., FILKORN, T., AND JHA, S. Exploiting symmetry in temporal logic model checking. In *Workshop on Computer Aided Verification (CAV)* (June/July 1993), Courcoubetis, Ed., pp. 450–462.

[114] CLARKE, E. M., AND WING, J. M. Formal methods: State of the art and future directions. Tech. Rep. CMU-CS-96-178, Carnegie Mellon University, September 1996. ftp://reports.adm.cs.cmu.edu/usr/anon/1996/CMU-CS-96-178.ps.

[115] CLEAVELAND, R. Tableaux-based model checking in the propositional μ-calculus. *Acta Informatica 27*, 8 (1989), 725–747.

[116] CLEAVELAND, R., KLEIN, M., AND STEFFEN, B. Faster model checking for the μ-calculus. In *Conference on Computer Aided Verification (CAV)* (Montreal, June/July 1992), G. Bochmann and D. Probst, Eds., vol. 663 of *LNCS*, Springer, pp. 410–422.

[117] CLEAVELAND, R., AND STEFFEN, B. Computing behavioral relations, logically. In *Colloquium on Automata, Languages and Programming (ICALP)* (Madrid, Spain,

July 1991), J. L. Albert, B. Monien, and M. R. Artalejo, Eds., vol. 510 of *LNCS*, Springer, pp. 127–138.

[118] CLEAVELAND, R., AND STEFFEN, B. A linear-time model checking algorithm for the alternation-free μ-calculus. In *Conference on Computer Aided Verification (CAV)* (Aalborg, Denmark, July 1991), K. Larsen and A. Skou, Eds., vol. 575 of *LNCS*, Springer, pp. 48–58.

[119] CLEAVELAND, R., AND STEFFEN, B. A linear-time model checking algorithm for the alternation-free μ-calculus. *Formal Methods in System Design 2*, 2 (April 1993), 121–147.

[120] COHEN, J., PERRIN, D., AND PIN, J.-E. On the expressive power of temporal logic. *Computer and System Sciences 46*, 3 (1993), 271–294.

[121] COHN, A. A proof of correctness of the VIPER microprocessor: The first level. In *VLSI Specification, Verification and Synthesis* (Boston, 1987), G. Birtwistle and P. Subrahmanyam, Eds., Kluwer, pp. 27–71.

[122] COMPTON, K., AND HAUCK, S. Reconfigurable computing: A survey of systems and software. *ACM Computing Surveys 34*, 2 (June 2002), 171–210.

[123] CONSTABLE, R. *Implementing Mathematics with the Nuprl Proof Development System*. Prentice Hall, 1986.

[124] COOK, S. The complexity of theorem proving procedures. In *Symposium on Theory of Computing* (1971), pp. 151–158.

[125] CORNES, C., COURANT, J., FILLIATRE, J., HUET, G., MANOURY, P., PAULIN-MOHRING, C., MUNOZ, C., MURTHY, C., PARENT, C., SAÏBI, A., AND WERNER, B. The Coq proof assistant reference manual version 5.10. Technical Report 177, INRIA, http://pauillac.inria.fr/coq/, 1995.

[126] COUDERT, O., BERTHET, C., AND MADRE, J. Verification of sequential machines using Boolean functional vectors. In *Workshop on Applied Formal Methods for Correct VLSI Design* (Leuven, Belgium, November 1989), L. Claesen, Ed., North Holland, pp. 111–128.

[127] COUDERT, O., BERTHET, C., AND MADRE, J. Verification of synchronous sequential machines using symbolic execution. In *Workshop on Automatic Verification Methods for Finite State Systems* (Grenoble, France, June 1989), vol. 407 of *LNCS*, Springer, pp. 365–373.

[128] COUDERT, O., AND MADRE, J. A unified framework for the formal verification of sequential circuits. In *Conference on Computer Aided Design (ICCAD)* (November 1990), IEEE Computer Society.

[129] COUSOT, P., AND COUSOT, R. Abstract interpretation: A unified lattice model for static analysis of programs by construction or approximation of fixpoints. In *Symposium on Principles of Programming Languages (POPL)* (1977), pp. 238–252.

[130] COUSOT, P., AND COUSOT, R. Abstract interpretation and application to logic programs. *Logic Programming 13*, 2-3 (1992), 103–179.

[131] COUVREUR, J.-M. On-the-fly verification of linear temporal logic. In *Symposium of Formal Methods Europe (FME)* (Toulouse, France, 1999), vol. 1708 of *LNCS*, Springer, pp. 233–252.

[132] CRAIGEN, D., GERHART, S., AND RALSTON, T. Formal methods reality check: Industrial usage. *IEEE Transactions on Software Engineering 21*, 2 (February 1995), 90–98.

[133] CULLYER, W. Implementing safety critical systems: The VIPER microprocessor. In *VLSI Specification, Verification, and Synthesis* (Boston, 1988), G. Birtwistle and P. Subrahmanyam, Eds., Kluwer, pp. 1–26.

[134] D'AGOSTINO, M. Are tableaux an improvement of truth-tables? Cut-free proofs and bivalence. *Logic, Language, and Information 1*, 3 (1992), 127–139.

[135] DAM, M. CTL* and ECTL* as fragments of the modal μ-calculus. *Theoretical Computer Science 126*, 1 (1994), 77–96.

[136] DAMS, D. Flat fragments of CTL and CTL*: Separating the expressive and distinguishing powers. *Logic Journal of the IPGL 7*, 1 (1999), 55–78.

[137] DAMS, D., GERTH, R., AND GRUMBERG, O. Abstract interpretation of reactive systems. *ACM Transactions on Programming Languages and Systems (TOPLAS) 19*, 2 (1997), 253–291.

[138] DANIELE, M., GIUNCHIGLIA, F., AND VARDI, M. Improved automata generation for linear temporal logic. In *Conference on Computer Aided Verification (CAV)* (Trento, Italy, 1999), vol. 1633 of *LNCS*, Springer.

[139] DAVEAU, J.-M., FERNANDES MARCHIORO, G., AND JERRAYA, A. VHDL generation from SDL specification. In *Conference on Computer Hardware Description Languages and Their Applications (CHDL)* (Toledo, Spain, April 1997), C. Delgado Kloos and E. Cerny, Eds., Chapman and Hall.

[140] DAVIS, M. The prehistory and early history of automated deduction. In *Automation of Reasoning: Classical Papers on Computational Logic 1957-1966*, J. Siekmann and G. Wrightson, Eds. Springer, Berlin, 1983.

[141] DAVIS, M., LOGEMANN, G., AND LOVELAND, D. A machine program for theorem proving. *Communications of the ACM (CACM) 5*, 7 (1962), 394–397.

[142] DE BAKKER, J., AND DE ROEVER, W. A calculus for recursive program schemes. In *Colloquium on Automata, Languages and Programming (ICALP)* (1973), pp. 167–196.

[143] DEMRIE, S., AND SCHNOEBELEN, P. The complexity of propositional linear temporal logics in simple cases. In *Symposium on Theoretical Aspects of Computer Science (STACS)* (1998), M. Morvan, C. Meinel, and D. Krob, Eds., no. 1373 in LNCS, Springer, pp. 61–72.

[144] DERSHOWITZ, N., OKADA, M., AND SIVAKUMAR, G. Canonical conditional rewrite systems. In *Conference on Automated Deduction (CADE)* (Argonne, Illinois, USA, 1988), Springer.

[145] DIJKSTRA, E. *A Discipline of Programming*. Prentice Hall, 1976.

[146] DREBEN, B., AND GOLDFARB, W. *The decision problem: Solvable classes of quantificational formulas*. Addison-Wesley, 1979.

[147] DRECHSLER, R., AND BECKER, B. *Binary Decision Diagrams: Theory and Implementation*. Kluwer, 1998.

[148] EBBINGHAUS, H., AND FLUM, J. *Finite Model Theory*. Springer, 1995.

[149] EBBINGHAUS, H., FLUM, J., AND THOMAS, W. *Einführung in die mathematische Logik*. Wissenschaftliche Buchgesellschaft Darmstadt, 1978.

[150] EDER, E. *On the Relative Complexities of First Order Calculi*. Vieweg, 1991.

[151] EILENBERG, S. *Automata, Languages, and Machines*, vol. B. Academic, New York, 1976.

[152] EITER, T., GOTTLOB, G., AND GUREVICH, Y. Normal forms for second-order logic over finite structures, and classification of NP optimization problems. *Annals of Pure and Applied Logic 78*, 1 (1996), 111–125.

[153] EITER, T., GOTTLOB, G., AND GUREVICH, Y. Existential second-order logic over strings. In *Symposium on Logic in Computer Science (LICS)* (1998), IEEE Computer Society, pp. 16–27.

[154] EITER, T., GOTTLOB, G., AND GUREVICH, Y. Existential second-order logic over strings. *Journal of the ACM 47*, 1 (2000), 77–131.

[155] EITER, T., GOTTLOB, G., AND SCHWENTICK, T. Second-order logic over strings: Regular and non-regular fragments. In *Developments in Language Theory* (Vienna, Austria, 2002), W. Kuich, G. Rozenberg, and A. Salomaa, Eds., vol. 2295 of *LNCS*, Springer, pp. 37–56.

[156] ELGOT, C. Decision problems of finite automata design and related arithmetics. *ACM Transactions 98* (1961), 21–52.

[157] ELGOT, C., AND RABIN, M. Decidability and undecidability of extensions of second (first) order theories of (generalized) successor. *Symbolic Logic 31* (1966), 169–181.

[158] EMERSON, E. *Temporal and Modal Logic*, vol. B. Elsevier Science, 1990, ch. Temporal and Modal Logics, pp. 996–1072.

[159] EMERSON, E. Automated temporal reasoning about reactive systems. In *Logics for Concurrency: Structure versus Automata* (1996), F. Moller and G. Birtwistle, Eds., vol. 1043 of *LNCS*, Springer, pp. 41–101.

[160] EMERSON, E., AND CLARKE, E. Characterizing correctness properties of parallel programs as fixpoints. In *Colloquium on Automata, Languages and Programming (ICALP)* (Berlin, 1980), vol. 85 of *LNCS*, Springer, pp. 169–181.

[161] EMERSON, E., AND CLARKE, E. Using branching-time temporal logic to synthesize synchronization skeletons. *Science of Computer Programming 2*, 3 (1982), 241–266.

[162] EMERSON, E., AND HALPERN, J. Decision procedures and expressiveness in the temporal logic of branching time. *Computer and System Sciences 30*, 1 (1985), 1–24.

[163] EMERSON, E., AND HALPERN, J. "sometimes" and "not never" revisited: On branching versus linear time temporal logic. *Journal of the ACM 33*, 1 (January 1986), 151–178.

[164] EMERSON, E., JHA, S., AND PELED, D. Combining partial order and symmetry reductions. In *Conference on Tools and Algorithms for the Construction and Analysis of Systems (TACAS)* (Enschede, The Netherlands, 1997), E. Brinksma, Ed., vol. 1217 of *LNCS*, Springer, pp. 19–34.

[165] EMERSON, E., AND JUTLA, C. The complexity of tree automata and logics of programs. In *Symposium on Foundations of Computer Science (FOCS)* (White Plains, New York, 1988), pp. 328–337.

[166] EMERSON, E., AND JUTLA, C. On simultaneously determinizing and complementing ω-automata. In *Symposium on Logic in Computer Science (LICS)* (1989), pp. 333–342.

[167] EMERSON, E., AND JUTLA, C. Tree automata, μ-calculus and determinacy. In *Symposium on Foundations of Computer Science (FOCS)* (San Juan, Puerto Rico, 1991), pp. 368–377.

[168] EMERSON, E., AND JUTLA, C. The complexity of tree automata and logics of programs. *SIAM Journal on Computing 29*, 1 (1999), 132–158.

[169] EMERSON, E., JUTLA, C., AND SISTLA, A. On model checking for fragments of μ-calculus. In *Conference on Computer Aided Verification (CAV)* (Stanford, California, USA, June/July 1993), C. Courcoubetis, Ed., vol. 697 of *LNCS*, Springer, pp. 385–396.

[170] EMERSON, E., JUTLA, C., AND SISTLA, A. On model checking for μ-calculus and its fragments, 1999.

[171] EMERSON, E., JUTLA, C., AND SISTLA, A. On model checking for the μ-calculus and its fragments. *Theoretical Computer Science 258*, 1-2 (2001), 491–522.

[172] EMERSON, E., AND LEI, C.-L. Modalities for model checking: Branching time strikes back. In *Symposium on Principles of Programming Languages (POPL)* (New York, January 1985), ACM, pp. 84–96.

[173] EMERSON, E., AND LEI, C.-L. Temporal model checking under generalized fairness constraints. In *Hawaii International Conference on System Sciences* (North-Holland, CA, 1985), vol. 1, Western Periodicals, pp. 277–288.

[174] EMERSON, E., AND LEI, C.-L. Efficient model checking in fragments of the propositional μ-calculus. In *Symposium on Logic in Computer Science (LICS)* (Washington, D.C., 1986), IEEE Computer Society, pp. 267–278.

[175] EMERSON, E., AND LEI, C.-L. Temporal reasoning under generalized fairness constraints. In *Symposium on Theoretical Aspects of Computer Science (STACS)* (Orsay, France, January 1986), B.Monien and G.Vidal-Naquet, Eds., Springer, pp. 21–36.

[176] EMERSON, E., AND LEI, C.-L. Modalities for model checking: Branching time strikes back. *Science of Computer Programming 8* (1987), 275–306.

[177] EMERSON, E., AND SISTLA, A. Deciding branching time logic. In *Symposium on Theory of Computing* (1984), pp. 14–24.

[178] EMERSON, E., AND SISTLA, A. Symmetry and model checking. *Formal Methods in System Design 9* (1996), 105–131.

[179] EMERSON, E., AND SISTLA, A. Utilizing symmetry when model-checking under fairness assumptions: An automata-theoretic approach. *ACM Transactions on Programming Languages and Systems (TOPLAS) 19*, 4 (1997), 617–638.

[180] EMERSON, E., AND SISTLA, A. P. Symmetry and model checking. In *Workshop on Computer Aided Verification (CAV)* (June/July 1993), C. Courcoubetis, Ed., pp. 463–478.

[181] EMERSON, E., AND SISTLA, A. P. Utilizing symmetry when model checking under fairness assumptions: an automata-theoretic approach. In *Conference on Computer Aided Verification (CAV)* (Liege, Belgium, July 1995), P. Wolper, Ed., vol. 939 of *LNCS*, Springer, pp. 309–324.

[182] EMERSON, E., AND TREFLER, R. From asymmetry to full symmetry. In *Conference on Correct Hardware Design and Verification Methods (CHARME)* (Bad Herrenalb, Germany, September 1999), L. Pierre and T. Kropf, Eds., vol. 1703 of *LNCS*, Springer, pp. 142–156.

[183] ENDERS, R., FILKORN, T., AND TAUBNER, D. Generating BDDs for symbolic model checking in CCS. In *Workshop on Computer Aided Verification (CAV)* (Aalborg, Denmark, July 1991), K. Larsen and A. Skou, Eds., vol. 575 of *LNCS*, Springer, pp. 203–213.

[184] ENDERTON, H. B. *A Mathematical Introduction to Logic*. Academic, New York, New York, 1972.

[185] ETESSAMI, K., AND HOLZMANN, G. Optimizing Büchi automata. In *Conference on Concurrency Theory (CONCUR)* (University Park, USA, 2000), vol. 1877 of *LNCS*, Springer, pp. 153–168.

[186] ETESSAMI, K., VARDI, M., AND WILKE, T. First-order logic with two variables and unary temporal logic. In *Symposium on Logic in Computer Science (LICS)* (Warsaw, Poland, 1996), IEEE Computer Society, pp. 108–117.

[187] ETESSAMI, K., VARDI, M., AND WILKE, T. First-order logic with two variables and unary temporal logic. *Information and Computation 179*, 2 (2002), 279–295.

[188] ETESSAMI, K., AND WILKE, T. An Until-hierarchy for temporal logic. In *Symposium on Logic in Computer Science (LICS)* (New Brunswick, New Jersey, 1996), pp. 108–117.

[189] FAGIN, R. Generalized first-order spectra and polynomial-time recognizable sets. *SIAM AMS Proceedings 7* (1974), 43–73.

[190] FAGIN, R. Finite model theory - a personal perspective. *Theoretical Computer Science 116*, 1-2 (1993), 3–31.

[191] FISCHER, M., AND RABIN, M. Super-exponential complexity of Presburger arithmetic. In *Complexity of Computation* (Providence, RI, 1974), R. Karp, Ed., vol. 7, American Mathematical Society, pp. 27–41.

[192] FISHER, M., AND LADNER, R. Propositional dynamic logic of regular programs. *Computer and System Sciences 18*, 2 (1979), 194–211.

[193] FISLER, K. Extending formal reasoning with support for hardware diagrams. In *Conference on Theorem Provers in Circuit Design (TPCD)* (Bad Herrenalb, Germany, September 1994), T. Kropf and R. Kumar, Eds., vol. 901 of *LNCS*, Springer, pp. 298–303. published 1995.

[194] FITTING, M. First-order modal tableaux. *Journal of Automated Reasoning 4* (1988), 191–213.

[195] FITTING, M. *First-Order Logic and Automated Theorem Proving*. Texts and Monographs in Computer Science. Springer, 1990.

[196] FLOYD, R. Assigning meaning to programs. In *Symposia in Applied Mathematics: Mathematical Aspects of Computer Science* (1967), vol. 19, pp. 19–31.

[197] FRANCEZ, N. *Fairness*. Springer, New York, 1987.

[198] FREGE, G. *Begriffsschrift, eine der arithmetischen nachgebildete Formelsprache des reinen Denkens*. Louis Nebert, Halle, 1879.

[199] FRIBOURG, L. A strong restriction of the inductive completion procedure. In *Colloquium on Automata, Languages and Programming (ICALP)* (1986), pp. 105–115.

[200] FRIEDMAN, S., AND SUPOWIT, K. Finding the optimal variable ordering for binary decision diagrams. *IEEE Transactions on Computers 39* (1990), 710–713.

[201] FÜRER, M. Alternation and the Ackermann case of the decision problem. *L'Enseignment Mathematique* 27 (1981), 137–162.

[202] GABBAY, D., HODKINSON, I., AND REYNOLDS, M. *Temporal Logic: Mathematical Foundations and Computational Aspects*, vol. 1. Oxford Science Publications, 1994. ISBN 0 19 853769 7.

[203] GABBAY, D., PNUELI, A., SHELAH, S., AND STAVI, J. On the temporal analysis of fairness. In *Symposium on Principles of Programming Languages (POPL)* (New York, 1980), ACM, pp. 163–173.

[204] GAREY, M., AND JOHNSON, D. *Computers and Intractability: A Guide to the Theory of NP-Completeness*. Studienreihe Informatik. Freeman, San Francisco, 1979.

[205] GARLAND, S., AND V. GUTTAG, J. Inductive methods for reasoning about abstract data types. In *Symposium on Principles of Programming Languages (POPL)* (San Diego, California, 1988), pp. 219–228.

[206] GARLAND, S., AND V. GUTTAG, J. An overview of LP, the larch prover. In *Conference on Rewriting Techniques and Applications (RTA)* (Chapel Hill, North Carolina, USA, 1989), N. Dershowitz, Ed., Springer, pp. 137–151.

[207] GASTIN, P., AND ODDOUX, D. Fast LTL to Büchi automata translation. In *Conference on Computer Aided Verification (CAV)* (Paris, France, 2001), vol. 2102 of *LNCS*, Springer, pp. 53–65.

[208] GERTH, R., PELED, D., VARDI, M., AND WOLPER, P. Simple on-the-fly automatic verification of linear temporal logic. In *Protocol Specification, Testing, and Verification (PSTV)* (Warsaw, June 1995), North Holland.

[209] GINZBURG, A. *Algebraic Theory of Automata.* Academic, New York, 1969.

[210] GODEFROID, P. *Partial-Order Methods for the Verification of Concurrent Systems - An Approach to the State Explosion Problem.* PhD thesis, Université de Liege, Institut Montefiore, 1995.

[211] GÖDEL, K. Die Vollständigkeit der Axiome des logischen Funktionenkalküls. *Monatshefte für Mathematik und Physik 37* (1930), 349–360.

[212] GÖDEL, K. Über formal unentscheidbare Sätze der Principia Mathematica und verwandter Systeme. *Monatshefte für Mathematik und Physik 38* (1931), 173–198.

[213] GÖDEL, K. Ein Spezialfall des Entscheidungsproblems der theoretischen Logik. *Ergebnisse der mathematischen Kolloquien* 2 (1932), 27–28.

[214] GOLDFARB, W. The unsolvability of the Gödel class with identity. *Journal of Symbolic Logic 49* (1984), 1237–1252.

[215] GORDON, M. Why higher-order logic is a good formalism for specifying and verifying hardware. In *Formal Aspects of VLSI Design*, G. Milne and P. Subrahmanyam, Eds. North Holland, Computer Laboratory, University of Cambridge, 1986, pp. 153–177.

[216] GORDON, M., AND MELHAM, T. *Introduction to HOL: A Theorem Proving Environment for Higher Order Logic.* Cambridge University Press, 1993.

[217] GRÄDEL, E. Decision procedures for guarded logics. In *Conference on Automated Deduction (CADE)* (1999), vol. 1632 of *LNAI*, Springer, pp. 31–51.

[218] GRÄDEL, E., KOLAITIS, P., AND VARDI, M. On the decision problem for two-variable first-order logic. *The Bulletin of Symbolic Logic 3*, 1 (1997), 53–69.

[219] GRÄDEL, E., AND OTTO, M. On logics with two variables. *Theoretical Computer Science 224*, 1-2 (1999), 73–113.

[220] GRÄDEL, E., AND ROSEN, E. Two-variable descriptions of regularity. In *Symposium on Logic in Computer Science (LICS)* (1999), IEEE Computer Society.

[221] GRÄDEL, E., THOMAS, W., AND WILKE, T. *Automata, Logics, and Infinite Games*, vol. 2500 of *LNCS*. Springer, 2002.

[222] GRAF, S., AND LOISEAUX, C. A tool for symbolic program verification and abstraction. In *GI/ITG Workshop Formale Methoden zum Entwurf korrekter Systeme* (Bad Herrenalb, March 1993), T. Kropf, R. Kumar, and D. Schmid, Eds., GI/ITG, Universität Karlsruhe, Interner Bericht Nr. 10/93, pp. 122–138.

[223] GUPTA, A. Formal hardware verification methods: A survey. *Formal Methods in System Design 1*, 2-3 (1992), 151–238.

[224] GUREVICH, Y., AND HARRINGTON, L. Trees, automata, and games. In *Symposium on Theory of Computing* (San Francisco, USA, 1982), pp. 60–65.

[225] GURUMURTHY, S., KUPFERMAN, O., SOMENZI, F., AND VARDI, M. On complementing nondeterministic büchi automata. In *Conference on Correct Hardware Design and Verification Methods (CHARME)* (2003), LNCS, Springer.

[226] GYURIS, V., AND SISTLA, A. On-the-fly model checking under fairness that exploits symmetry. In *Conference on Computer Aided Verification (CAV)* (Haifa, Israel, 1997), O. Grumberg, Ed., vol. 1254 of *LNCS*, Springer, pp. 232–243.

[227] HACHTEL, G., AND SOMENZI, F. *Logic Synthesis and Verification Algorithms.* Kluwer, 1996.

[228] HAILPERN, B. T. *Verifying Concurrent Processes Using Temporal Logic*, vol. 129 of *LNCS*. Springer, Berlin, 1982.

[229] HAILPERN, J. Y., AND OWICKI, S. S. Verifying network protocols using temporal logic. In *Trends and Applications 1980: Computer Network Protocols* (1980), pp. 18–28.

[230] HALBWACHS, N. *Synchronous programming of reactive systems*. Kluwer, 1993.

[231] HALL, A. Seven myths of formal methods. *IEEE Software 7*, 5 (September 1990), 11–19.

[232] HALPERN, J., MANNA, Z., AND MOSZKOWSKI, B. A hardware semantics based on temporal intervals. In *Colloquium on Automata, Languages and Programming (ICALP)* (New York, 1983), vol. 154 of *LNCS*, Springer, pp. 278–291.

[233] HANNA, F., AND DAECHE, N. Specification and verification of digital systems using higher-order predicate logic. *IEEE Proceedings 133 Part E*, 5 (September 1986), 242–254.

[234] HARDIN, R., KURSHAN, R., SHUKLA, S., AND VARDI, M. A new heuristic for bad cycle detection using BDDs. In *Conference on Computer Aided Verification (CAV)* (June 1997), O. Grumberg, Ed., vol. 1254 of *LNCS*, Springer.

[235] HAREL, D. *First-Order Dynamic Logic*, vol. 68 of *LNCS*. Springer, 1979.

[236] HAREL, D. Statecharts: A visual formulation for complex systems. *Science of Computer Programming 8*, 3 (1987), 231–274.

[237] HAREL, D., KOZEN, D., AND TIURYN, J. *Dynamic Logic*. MIT, Cambridge, Massachusetts, 2000.

[238] HAREL, E., LICHTENSTEIN, O., AND PNUELI, A. Explicit clock temporal logic. In *Symposium on Logic in Computer Science (LICS)* (Washington, D.C., June 1990), IEEE Computer Society, pp. 402–413.

[239] HENNESSY, M., AND MILNER, R. Algebraic laws for non-determinism and concurrency. *Journal of the ACM 32*, 1 (1985), 137–161.

[240] HENRIKSEN, J., JENSEN, J., JORGENSEN, M., KLARLUND, N., PAIGE, R., RAUHE, T., AND SANDHOLM, A. Mona: Monadic second-order logic in practice. In *Conference on Tools and Algorithms for the Construction and Analysis of Systems (TACAS)* (1995), E. Brinksma, R. Cleaveland, K. Larsen, T. Margaria, and B. Steffen, Eds., vol. 1019 of *LNCS*, Springer, pp. 89–110.

[241] HENZINGER, T., KUPFERMAN, O., AND QADEER, S. From pre-historic to postmodern symbolic model checking. In *Conference on Computer Aided Verification (CAV)* (1998), vol. 1427 of *LNCS*, Springer, pp. 195–206.

[242] HENZINGER, T., KUPFERMAN, O., AND RAJAMANI, S. Fair simulation. In *Conference on Concurrency Theory (CONCUR)* (July 1997), vol. 1243 of *LNCS*, Springer.

[243] HENZINGER, T., MANNA, Z., AND PNUELI, A. Timed transition systems. In *Real-Time: Theory in Practice* (Mook, June 1991), Springer, pp. 226–251.

[244] HENZINGER, T., QADEER, S., AND RAJAMANI, S. You assume, we guarantee: Methodology and case studies. In *Conference on Computer Aided Verification (CAV)* (Vancouver, BC, Canada, 1998), vol. 1427 of *LNCS*, Springer, pp. 440–451.

[245] HERBERT, J. Temporal abstraction of digital designs. In *Fusion of Hardware Design and Verification* (Glasgow, Scotland, July 1988), G. Milne, Ed., North Holland, pp. 1–26.

[246] HILBERT, D., AND ACKERMANN, W. *Grundzüge der theoretischen Logik*. Springer, 1972.

[247] HITCHCOCK, P., AND PARK, D. Induction rules and termination proofs. In *Colloquium on Automata, Languages and Programming (ICALP)* (1973), pp. 225–251.

[248] HOARE, C. An axiomatic basis for computer programming. *Communications of the ACM 12* (1969), 576–580.

[249] HOJATI, R., TOUATI, H., KURSHAN, R., AND BRAYTON, R. Efficient ω-regular language containment. In *Conference on Computer Aided Verification (CAV)* (Montreal, Canada, 1992), vol. 663 of *LNCS*, Springer.

[250] HONG, Y., BEEREL, P., BURCH, J., AND MCMILLAN, K. Safe BDD minimization using don't cares. In *Design Automation Conference (DAC)* (San Diego, CA, 1997), ACM Press, pp. 208–213.

[251] HOPCROFT, J., AND ULLMAN, J. *Introduction to Automata Theory, Languages and Computation*. Addison Wesley, 1979.

[252] HOSSLEY, R. *Finite Tree Automata and ω-Automata*. PhD thesis, MIT, Cambridge, Massachusetts, 1970.

[253] HOSSLEY, R., AND RACKOFF, C. The emptiness problem for automata on infinite trees. In *Symposium on Switching and Automata Theory* (1972), pp. 121–124.

[254] HUET, G., AND HULLOT, J.-M. Proofs by induction in equational theories with constructors. *Computer and System Sciences 25*, 2 (1982), 239–266.

[255] HUGHES, G., AND CRESSWELL, M. *An Introduction to Modal Logics*. Methuen, London, 1968.

[256] HUNT, W. *FM8501: A Verified Microprocessor*. PhD thesis, University of Texas, Austin, 1985.

[257] HUNT, W. Microprocessor design verification. *Journal of Automated Reasoning 5*, 4 (1989), 429–460.

[258] IMMERMAN, N. Languages that capture complexity classes. *SIAM Journal on Computing 16*, 4 (1987), 760–778.

[259] IMMERMAN, N., AND VARDI, M. Model checking and transitive-closure logic. In *Conference on Computer Aided Verification (CAV)* (June 1997), O. Grumberg, Ed., vol. 1254 of *LNCS*, Springer.

[260] IP, C., AND DILL, D. Better verification through symmetry. In *Conference on Computer Hardware Description Languages and Their Applications (CHDL)* (Ottawa, Canada, April 1993), D. Agnew, L. Claesen, and R. Camposano, Eds., Elsevier Science, pp. 87–100.

[261] IP, C., AND DILL, D. Better verification through symmetry. *Formal Methods in System Design 9*, 1-2 (1996), 41–75.

[262] ISLI, A. Mapping an LPTL formula into a Büchi alternating automaton accepting its models. In *International Conference on Temporal Logic (ICTL)* (Bonn, Germany, 1994), pp. 85–90.

[263] JANIN, D., AND WALUKIEWICZ, I. Automata for the μ-calculus and related results. In *Symposium on Mathematical Foundations of Computer Science (MFCS)* (Prague, Czech Republic, 1995), J. Wiedermann and P. Hájek, Eds., vol. 969 of *LNCS*, Springer, pp. 552–562.

[264] JANIN, D., AND WALUKIEWICZ, I. On the expressive completeness of the propositional μ-calculus with respect to the monadic second order logic. In *Conference on Concurrency Theory (CONCUR)* (Pisa, Italy, August 1996), V. Sassone and U. Montanari, Eds., vol. 1119 of *LNCS*, Springer, pp. 1–17.

[265] JENSEN, J., JORGENSEN, M., AND KLARLUND, N. Monadic second order logic for parameterized verification. BRICS Report RS-94-10, Department of Computer Science, University of Aarhus, 1994.

[266] JOHANNSEN, J., AND LANGE, M. CTL$^+$ is complete for double exponential time. In *Colloquium on Automata, Languages and Programming (ICALP)* (2003), LNCS, Springer.

[267] JOUANNAUD, J.-P., AND KOUNALIS, E. Automatic proofs by induction in equational theories without constructors. In *Symposium on Logic in Computer Science (LICS)* (Cambrigde, Massachusetts, USA, 1986), pp. 358–366.

[268] JOUANNAUD, J.-P., AND KOUNALIS, E. Automatic proofs by induction in theories without constructors. *Information and Computation 82*, 1 (1989), 1–33.

[269] JOYCE, J. Hardware verification of VLSI regular structures. Technical Report 109, University of Cambridge Computer Laboratory, July 1987.

[270] JURDZIŃSKI, M. Deciding the winner in parity games is in UP ∩ co-UP. *Information Processing Letters 68*, 3 (1998), 119–124.

[271] JURDZIŃSKI, M. Small progress measures for solving parity games. In *Symposium on Theoretical Aspects of Computer Science (STACS)* (Lille, France, 2000), vol. 1770 of *LNCS*, Springer, pp. 290–301.

[272] KAHR, A., WANG, H., AND MOORE, E. Entscheidungsproblem reduced to the AEA case. *Proceedings of the National Academy of Sciences, USA 48* (1962), 365–377.

[273] KALMÁR, L. Über die Erfüllbarkeit derjenigen Zählausdrücke, welche in der Normalform zwei benachbarte Allzeichen enthalten. *Mathematische Annalen 108* (1933), 466–484.

[274] KAMP, H. *Tense Logic and the Theory of Linear Order*. PhD thesis, University of California, Los Angeles, 1968.

[275] KAPLAN, S., AND REMY, J.-L. *Resolution of Equations in Algebraic Structures*, vol. 2. Academic, New York, 1989, ch. Completion algorithms for conditional reasoning.

[276] KAPUR, D., AND MUSSER, D. Proof by consistency. *Artificial Intelligence 31*, 2 (1987), 125–157.

[277] KAUFMANN, M., AND MOORE, J. Design goals for ACL2. Technical Report 101, Computational Logic, Inc., 1994.

[278] KELB, P., MARGARIA, T., MENDLER, M., AND GSOTTBERGER, C. MOSEL: A flexible toolset for monadic second-order logic. In *Conference on Tools and Algorithms for the Construction and Analysis of Systems (TACAS)* (Enschede, The Netherlands, 1997), E. Brinksma, Ed., vol. 1217 of *LNCS*, Springer, pp. 183–202.

[279] KERBER, M. How to prove higher order theorems in first order logic. SEKI Report SR-90-19, University of Kaiserslautern, 1990.

[280] KERBER, M. How to prove higher order theorems in first order logic. In *International Joint Conference on Artificial Intelligence (IJCAI)* (1991), pp. 137–142.

[281] KESTEN, Y., PNUELI, A., AND RAVIV, L. Algorithmic verification of linear temporal logic specifications. In *Colloquium on Automata, Languages and Programming (ICALP)* (Aalborg, Denmark, 1998), vol. 1443 of *LNCS*, Springer, pp. 1–16.

[282] KEUTZER, K. The need for formal verification in hardware design and what formal verification has NOT done for me lately. In *Higher Order Logic Theorem Proving and its Applications* (Davis, California, August 1991), M. Archer, J. Joyce, K. Levitt, and P. Windley, Eds., IEEE Computer Society, pp. 77–86.

[283] KFOURY, A., AND PARK, D. On termination of program schemes. *Information and Control 29* (1975), 243–251.

[284] KLARLUND, N. Progress measures for complementation of ω-automata with application to temporal logic. In *Symposium on Foundations of Computer Science (FOCS)* (1991), IEEE Computer Society, pp. 358–367.

[285] KLEENE, S. Representation of events in nerve nets and finite automata. In *Automata Studies*, C. Shannon and J. McCarthy, Eds. Princeton University Press, Princeton, NJ, 1956, pp. 3–41.

[286] KOUNALIS, E., AND RUSINOWITCH, M. Mechanizing inductive reasoning. In *Conference on Artificial Intelligence* (Boston, Massachusetts, 1990), pp. 240–245.

[287] KOWALSKI, R. A proof procedure using connection graphs. *Journal of the ACM 22*, 4 (1975), 572–595.

[288] KOZEN, D. Results on the propositional μ-calculus. In *Colloquium on Automata, Languages and Programming (ICALP)* (1982), pp. 348–359.

[289] KOZEN, D. Results on the propositional μ-calculus. *Theoretical Computer Science 27* (December 1983), 333–354.

[290] KOZEN, D., AND PARIKH, R. A decision procedure for the propositional μ-calculus. In *Second Workshop on Logics of Programs* (1983).

[291] KOZEN, D., AND TIURYN, J. Logics of programs. In *Handbook of Theoretical Computer Science*, J. V. Leeuwen, Ed., vol. B. Elsevier Science, North-Holland, Amsterdam, 1990, pp. 789–840.

[292] KRIPKE, S. Semantical considerations on modal logic. In *Colloquium on Modal and Many Valued Logics* (August 1963), vol. 16 of *Acta Philosophica Fennica*, pp. 83–94.

[293] KRISHNAN, S., PURI, A., AND BRAYTON, R. Deterministic ω-automata vis-a-vis deterministic Büchi automata. In *Symposium on Algorithms and Computation (ISAAC)* (Beijing, China, 1994), vol. 834 of *LNCS*, Springer.

[294] KRÖGER, F. *Temporal Logic of Programs*, vol. 8 of *EATCS Monographs on Theoretical Computer Science*. Springer, 1987.

[295] KROPF, T. *Formal Hardware Verification - Methods and Systems in Comparison*, state of the art report ed., vol. 1287 of *LNCS*. Springer, August 1997.

[296] KUKULA, J., SHIPLE, T., AND AZIZ, A. Techniques for implicit state enumeration of EFSMs. In *Conference on Formal Methods in Computer Aided Design (FMCAD)* (Palo Alto, CA, USA, November 1998), vol. 1522 of *LNCS*, Springer.

[297] KUMAR, R., BLUMENRÖHR, C., EISENBIEGLER, D., AND SCHMID, D. Formal synthesis in circuit design - a classification and survey. In *Conference on Formal Methods in Computer Aided Design (FMCAD)* (Palo Alto, CA, USA, November 1996), M. Srivas and A. Camilleri, Eds., vol. 1166 of *LNCS*, Springer, pp. 294–309.

[298] KUMAR, R., SCHNEIDER, K., AND KROPF, T. Structuring and automating hardware proofs in a higher-order theorem-proving environment. *Formal Methods in System Design 2*, 2 (1993), 165–230.

[299] KUPFERMAN, O., AND GRUMBERG, O. Branching time temporal logic and amorphous tree automata. In *Conference on Concurrency Theory (CONCUR)* (Hildesheim, Germany, 1993), vol. 715 of *LNCS*, Springer, pp. 262–277.

[300] KUPFERMAN, O., AND GRUMBERG, O. Buy one, get one free!!! *Logic and Computation 6*, 4 (August 1996), 523–539.

[301] KUPFERMAN, O., SAFRA, S., AND VARDI, M. Y. Relating word and tree automata. In *Symposium on Logic in Computer Science (LICS)* (Liege, Belgium, 1996).

[302] KUPFERMAN, O., AND VARDI, M. Weak alternating automata are not that weak. In *Israeli Symposium on Theory of Computing and Systems* (1997), IEEE Computer Society, pp. 147–158.

[303] KUPFERMAN, O., AND VARDI, M. Freedom, weakness, and determinism: From linear-time to branching-time. In *Symposium on Logic in Computer Science (LICS)* (1998), pp. 81–92.

[304] KUPFERMAN, O., AND VARDI, M. Weak alternating automata and tree automata emptiness. In *Symposium on Theory of Computing* (Dallas, 1998).

[305] KUPFERMAN, O., AND VARDI, M. On bounded specifications. In *Logic for Programming, Artificial Intelligence, and Reasoning (LPAR)* (Havanna, Cuba, 2001), vol. 2250 of *LNAI*, Springer, pp. 24–38.

[306] KUPFERMAN, O., AND VARDI, M. $\Pi_2 \cap \Sigma_2 \equiv$ AFMC. In *Colloquium on Automata, Languages and Programming (ICALP)* (2003), LNCS, Springer.

[307] KÜSTERS, R., AND WILKE, T. Deciding the first level of the μ-calculus alternation hierarchy. In *Conference on the Foundations of Software Technology and Theoretical Computer Science (FSTTCS)* (Kanpur, India, 2002), M. Agrawal and A. Seth, Eds., vol. 2556 of *LNCS*, Springer, pp. 241–252.

[308] LADNER, R. The computational complexity of provability in systems of propositional modal logic. *SIAM Journal of Computing 6*, 3 (1977), 467–480.

[309] LALLEMENT, G. *Semigroups and Combinatorial Applications*. Wiley, 1979.

[310] LAMPORT, L. "sometime" is sometimes "not never"-on the temporal logic of programs. In *Symposium on Principles of Programming Languages (POPL)* (New York, 1980), ACM, pp. 174–185.

[311] LAMPORT, L. What good is temporal logic? In *Congress on Information Processing* (Amsterdam, 1983), R. Mason, Ed., North Holland, pp. 657–667.

[312] LANDWEBER, L. Decision problems for ω-automata. *Mathematical Systems Theory 3*, 4 (1969), 376–384.

[313] LANGE, M., AND STIRLING, C. Model checking fixed point logic with chop. In *Conference on Foundations of Software Science and Computation Structures (FOSSACS)* (April 2002), M. Nielsen and U. Engberg, Eds., vol. 2303 of *LNCS*, Springer, pp. 250–263.

[314] LAROUSSINIE, F., MARKEY, N., AND SCHNOEBELEN, P. Model checking ctl$^+$ and fctl is hard. In *Conference on Foundations of Software Science and Computation Structures (FOSSACS)* (2001), vol. 2030 of *LNCS*, Springer, pp. 318–331.

[315] LAROUSSINIE, F., AND SCHNOEBELEN, P. Specification in CTL+past for verification in CTL. *Information and Computation 156*, 1-2 (1999), 236–263.

[316] LAROUSSINIE, F., SCHNOEBELEN, P., AND TURUANI, M. On the expressivity and complexity of quantitative branching-time temporal logics. *Theoretical Computer Science 297*, 1-3 (2003), 297–315.

[317] LASSEZ, J.-L., NGUYEN, V., AND SONENBERG, E. Fixed point theorems and semantics. A folk tale. *Information Processing Letters 14*, 3 (1982), 112–116.

[318] LEE, C. Representation of switching circuits by binary decision diagrams. *Bell Systems Technical Journal 38* (1959), 985–999.

[319] LEESER, M. *Reasoning about the Function and Timing of Integrated Circuits with PROLOG and Temporal Logic*. PhD thesis, University of Cambridge Computer Laboratory, February 1988.

[320] LEIVANT, D. Descriptive characterizations of computational complexity. *Journal of Computer and System Sciences 39* (1989), 51–83.

[321] LENZI, G. A hierarchy theorem for the μ-calculus. In *Colloquium on Automata, Languages and Programming (ICALP)* (Paderborn, Germany, 1996), vol. 1099 of *LNCS*, Springer, pp. 87–97.

[322] LESCANNE, P. Computer experiments with the REVE term rewriting system generator. In *Symposium on Principles of Programming Languages (POPL)* (Austin, Texas, January 1983), pp. 99–108.

[323] LEWIS, H. *Unsolvable classes of quantificational formulas*. Addison-Wesley, 1979.

[324] LICHTENSTEIN, O., AND PNUELI, A. Checking that finite state concurrent programs satisfy their linear specification. In *Symposium on Principles of Programming Languages (POPL)* (New York, January 1985), ACM, pp. 97–107.

[325] LICHTENSTEIN, O., PNUELI, A., AND ZUCK, L. Checking that finite-state concurrent programs satisfy their specification. In *Symposium on Principles of Programming Languages (POPL)* (1985), pp. 97–107.

[326] LICHTENSTEIN, O., PNUELI, A., AND ZUCK, L. The glory of the past. In *Conference on Logics of Programs* (New York, 1985), vol. 193 of *LNCS*, Springer, pp. 196–218.

[327] LIPSON, J., Ed. *Elements of Algebra and Algebraic Computing*. Benjamin Cummings, 1981.

[328] LOGOTHETIS, G., AND SCHNEIDER, K. Abstraction from counters: An application on real-time systems. In *Design, Automation and Test in Europe (DATE)* (Paris,France, March 2000), IEEE Computer Society, pp. 486–493.

[329] LOGOTHETIS, G., AND SCHNEIDER, K. A new approach to the specification and verification of real-time systems. In *Euromicro Conference on Real Time Systems* (Delft, The Netherlands, June 2001), IEEE Computer Society, pp. 171–180.

[330] LOGOTHETIS, G., AND SCHNEIDER, K. Symbolic model checking of real-time systems. In *Symposium on Temporal Representation and Reasoning* (Cividale del Friuli, Italy, June 2001), IEEE Computer Society, pp. 214–223.

[331] LOISEAUX, C., GRAF, S., SIFAKIS, J., BOUAJJANI, A., AND BENSALEM, S. Property preserving abstractions for the verification of concurrent systems. *Formal Methods in System Design 6* (February 1995), 11–44.

[332] LONG, D. *Model Checking, Abstraction, and Compositional Verification*. PhD thesis, Carnegie Mellon University, 1993.

[333] LONG, D., BROWNE, A., CLARKE, E., JHA, S., AND MARRERO, W. An improved algorithm for the evaluation of fixpoint expressions. In *Conference on Computer Aided Verification (CAV)* (Stanford, California, USA, June 1994), D. L. Dill, Ed., vol. 818 of *LNCS*, Springer, pp. 338–350.

[334] LOVELAND, D. *Automated Theorem Proving*. North Holland, 1978.

[335] LÖWENHEIM, L. Über Möglichkeiten im Relativkalkül. *Mathematische Annalen 76* (1915), 447–470.

[336] MACHTEY, M., AND YOUNG, P. *An Introduction to the General Theory of Algorithms*. North Holland, 1978.

[337] MADER, A. *Verification of Modal Properties Using Boolean Equation Systems*. PhD thesis, Technical University of Munich, Germany, 2000.

[338] MAIDL, M. The common fragment of CTL and LTL. In *Symposium on Foundations of Computer Science (FOCS)* (2000), pp. 643–652.

[339] MAIER, P. Compositional circular assume-guarantee rules cannot be sound and complete. In *Conference on Foundations of Software Science and Computation Structures (FOSSACS)* (April 2003), A. Gordon, Ed., vol. 2620 of *LNCS*, Springer, pp. 343–357.

[340] MALACHI, Y., AND OWICKI, S. Temporal specifications of self-timed systems. In *VLSI Systems and Computations* (Rockville, MD, 1981), H. Kung, B. Spoull, and G. Steele, Eds., IEEE Computer Society, pp. 203–212.

[341] MALER, O. *Finite Automata: Infinite Behaviour, Learnability and Decomposition*. PhD thesis, The Weizmann Institute of Science, Rehovot, Israel, 1990.

[342] MALER, O., AND PNUELI, A. Tight bounds on the complexity of cascaded decomposition of automata. In *Symposium on Foundations of Computer Science (FOCS)* (St. Louis, Miss., 1990), IEEE Computer Science, pp. 672–682.

[343] MANNA, Z., AND PNUELI, A. The modal logic of programs. In *Colloquium on Automata, Languages and Programming (ICALP)* (1979), vol. 71 of *LNCS*, Springer, pp. 385–409.

[344] MANNA, Z., AND PNUELI, A. Verification of concurrent programs: Temporal proof principles. In *Workshop on Logics of Programs* (New York, 1981), vol. 131 of *LNCS*, Springer, pp. 200–252.

[345] MANNA, Z., AND PNUELI, A. Verification of concurrent programs: A temporal proof system. In *School on Advanced Programming* (1982), pp. 163–255.

[346] MANNA, Z., AND PNUELI, A. Verification of concurrent programs: The temporal framework. In *Correctness Problems in Computer Science* (London, 1982), R. Boyer and J. Moore, Eds., Academic, New York, pp. 215–273.

[347] MANNA, Z., AND PNUELI, A. How to cook a temporal proof system for your pet language. In *Symposium on Principles of Programming Languages (POPL)* (New York, 1983), ACM, pp. 141–154.

[348] MANNA, Z., AND PNUELI, A. On the relation of programs and computations to models of temporal logic. In *Temporal Logic in Specification* (Altrincham,UK, 1987), B. Banieqbal, H. Barringer, and A. Pnueli, Eds., Springer, pp. 124–164.

[349] MANNA, Z., AND PNUELI, A. Specification and verification of concurrent programs by ∀ automata. In *Symposium on Principles of Programming Languages (POPL)* (1987), pp. 1–12.

[350] MANNA, Z., AND PNUELI, A. The anchored version of the temporal framework. In *Linear Time, Branching Time and Partial Order in Logics and Models for Concurrency* (Noordwigherhout, Netherland, May/June 1988), vol. 354 of *LNCS*, Springer, pp. 428–437.

[351] MANNA, Z., AND PNUELI, A. A hierarchy of temporal properties. In *Symposium on Principles of Distributed Computing* (1990), pp. 377–408.

[352] MANNA, Z., AND PNUELI, A. *The temporal Logic of Reactive and Concurrent Systems*. Springer, 1992.

[353] MANNA, Z., AND WOLPER, P. Synthesis of communicating processes form temporal logic specifications. *ACM Transactions on Programming Languages and Systems (TOPLAS) 6*, 1 (1984), 68–93.

[354] MARGARIA, T., AND MENDLER, M. Modeling sequential circuits in second-order monadic logic. In *GI/ITG/GME Workshop: Methoden des Entwurfs und der Verifikation digitaler Systeme* (Kreischa, March 1996), B. straube and J. Schoenherr, Eds., Berichte aus der Informatik, Shaker, pp. 21–30.

[355] MARKEY, N. Temporal logic with past is exponentially more succinct. *Bulletin of the European Association for Theoretical Computer Science 79* (2003), 122–128.

[356] MARTIN, D. Borel determinacy. *Ann. Math. 102* (1975), 363–371.

[357] MAYR, R. *Decidability and Complexity of Model Checking Problems for Infinite-State Systems*. PhD thesis, Technische Universität München, 1998.

[358] MCCLUSKEY, E. *Logic Design Principles*. Prentice Hall, 1986.

[359] McCulloch, W., and Pitts, W. A logical calculus of ideas immanent in nervous activity. *Bulletin of Mathematical Biophysics 5* (1943), 115–133.
[360] McMillan, K. *Symbolic Model Checking*. Kluwer, Norwell Massachusetts, 1993.
[361] McMillan, K. Circular compositional reasoning about liveness. Technical report, Cadence Berkeley Labs, 1999.
[362] McMillan, K. L. A conjunctively decomposed Boolean representation for symbolic model checking. In *Conference on Computer Aided Verification (CAV)* (New Brunswick, NJ, USA, July/August 1996), R. Alur and T. A. Henzinger, Eds., vol. 1102 of *LNCS*, Springer, pp. 13–25.
[363] McNaughton, R. Testing and generating infinite sequences by a finite automaton. *Information and Control 9*, 5 (1966), 521–530.
[364] McNaughton, R., and Papert, S. *Counter-free Automata*. MIT, 1971.
[365] Meinel, C., and Theobald, T. *Algorithms and Data Structures in VLSI Design: OBDD – Foundations and Applications*. Springer, 1998.
[366] Meyer, A. Weak monadic second order theory of successor is not elementary recursive. In *Logic Colloquium* (1975), Springer, pp. 132–154.
[367] Michel, M. Complementation is more difficult with automata on infinite words. Manuscript, CNET, Paris, 1988.
[368] Miller, S., and Srivas, M. Formal verification of the AAMP5 microprocessor: A case study in the industrial use of formal methods. In *Workshop on Industrial-Strength Formal Specification Techniques (WIFT)* (Boca Raton, FL, 1995), IEEE Computer Society, pp. 2–16.
[369] Milner, R. An algebraic definition of simulation between programs. In *International Joint Conference on Artificial Intelligence (IJCAI)* (September 1971), pp. 481–489.
[370] Milner, R. *A Calculus of Communicating Systems*, vol. 92 of *LNCS*. Springer, New York, 1980.
[371] Minato, S. Zero-suppressed BDDs for set manipulation in combinatorial problems. In *Design Automation Conference (DAC)* (Dallas, TX, June 1993), ACM Press, pp. 272–277.
[372] Minato, S. Implicit manipulation of polynomials using zero suppressed BDD. In *European Design and Test Conference (EDTC)* (Paris, March 1995), IEEE Computer Society, pp. 449–457.
[373] Minato, S. *Binary Decision Diagrams and Applications for VLSI CAD*. Kluwer, 1996.
[374] Miyano, S., and Hayashi, T. Alternating automata on ω-words. *Theoretical Computer Science 32* (1984), 321–330.
[375] Mortimer, M. On languages with two variables. *Zeitschrift für Mathematische Logik und Grundlagen der Mathematik 21* (1975), 135–140.
[376] Mostowski, A. Regular expressions for infinite trees and a standard form of automata. In *Computation Theory* (1984), A. Skowron, Ed., vol. 208 of *LNCS*, Springer, pp. 157–168.
[377] Moszkowski, B. *Reasoning about Digital Circuits*. PhD thesis, Stanford University, Stanford, CA, 1983.
[378] Moszkowski, B. Executing temporal logic programs. Tech. Rep. 71, University of Cambridge Computer Laboratory, August 1985.
[379] Moszkowski, B. A temporal logic for multilevel reasoning about hardware. *IEEE Computer* (February 1985), 10–19.

[380] MULLER, D. Infinite sequences and finite machines. In *Symposium on Switching Circuit Theory and Logical Design* (New York, 1963), pp. 3–16.

[381] MULLER, D., SAOUDI, A., AND SCHUPP, P. Alternating automata, the weak monadic theory of the tree, and its complexity. In *Colloquium on Automata, Languages and Programming (ICALP)* (1986), L. Kott, Ed., Springer, pp. 275–283.

[382] MULLER, D., SAOUDI, A., AND SCHUPP, P. Weak alternating automata give a simple explanation of why most temporal and dynamic logics are decidable in exponential time. In *Symposium on Logic in Computer Science (LICS)* (1988), pp. 422–427.

[383] MULLER, D., AND SCHUPP, P. Alternating automata on infinite trees. *Theoretical Computer Science 54* (1987), 267–276.

[384] MÜLLER-OLM, M. A modal fixpoint logic with chop. In *Symposium on Theoretical Aspects of Computer Science (STACS)* (1999), vol. 1563 of *LNCS*, Springer, pp. 510–520.

[385] MUSSER, D. On proving inductive properties of abstract data types. In *Symposium on Principles of Programming Languages (POPL)* (1980), pp. 154–162.

[386] M.Y.VARDI, AND WOLPER, P. Reasoning about infinite computations. *Information and Computation 115*, 1 (1994), 1–37.

[387] NIWIŃSKI, D. The propositional μ-calculus is more expressive than the propositional dynamic logic of looping, 1984. Unpublished manuscript.

[388] NIWIŃSKI, D. On fixed point clones. In *Colloquium on Automata, Languages and Programming (ICALP)* (1986), L. Kott, Ed., vol. 226 of *LNCS*, Springer, pp. 464–473.

[389] NIWIŃSKI, D. Fixed points vs. infinite generation. In *Symposium on Logic in Computer Science (LICS)* (Washington, D.C., July 1988), IEEE Computer Society, pp. 402–409.

[390] NIWIŃSKI, D. Fixed point characterization of infinite behaviour of finite-state systems. *Theoretical Computer Science 189*, 1-2 (1997), 1–69.

[391] OLIVEIRA, A., CARLONI, L., VILLA, T., AND SANGIOVANNI-VINCENTELLI, A. Exact minimization of Boolean decision diagrams using implicit techniques. Technical Report UCB ERL M96/16, University of California, 1996.

[392] OSTROFF, J. Real-time computer control of discrete event systems modeled by extended state machines: A temporal logic approach. Tech. Rep. 8618, University of Toronto, September 1989.

[393] OTTO, M. Eliminating recursion in the μ-calculus. In *Symposium on Theoretical Aspects of Computer Science (STACS)* (Trier, Germany, 1999), vol. 1563 of *LNCS*, Springer, pp. 531–540.

[394] OWICKI, S., AND GRIES, D. An axiomatic proof technique for parallel programs. *Acta Informatica 6*, 4 (1976), 319–340.

[395] OWICKI, S., AND GRIES, D. Verifying properties of parallel programs: An axiomatic approach. *Communications of the ACM 19*, 5 (1976), 279–284.

[396] OWRE, S., RUSHBY, J., SHANKAR, N., AND SRIVAS, M. A tutorial on using PVS for hardware verification. In *Conference on Theorem Provers in Circuit Design (TPCD)* (Bad Herrenalb, Germany, September 1994), T. Kropf and R. Kumar, Eds., vol. 901 of *LNCS*, Springer, pp. 258–279. published 1995.

[397] PARK, D. Finiteness is μ-ineffable. *Theoretical Computer Science 3* (1976), 173–181.

[398] PAULSON, L. *Isabelle: A Generic Theorem Prover*, vol. 828 of *LNCS*. Springer, 1994.

[399] PÉCUCHET, J. On the complementation of Büchi automata. *Theoretical Computer Science 47*, 3 (1986), 95–98.

[400] PELED, D., PRATT, V., AND HOLZMAN, G., Eds. *Partial Order Methods in Verification* (1996), vol. 29 of *DIMACS*, American Mathematical Society (AMS).

[401] PERRIN, D. *Mathematical Foundation of Computer Science*, vol. 176 of *LNCS*. Springer, 1984, ch. Recent results on automata and infinite words, pp. 134–148.

[402] PERRIN, D. *Handbook of Theoretical Computer Science*, vol. B. North Holland, 1990, ch. Finite automata.

[403] PERRIN, D., AND PIN, J. First order logic and star free sets. *Computer and System Sciences 32*, 3 (1986), 393–406.

[404] PERRIN, D., AND SCHUPP, P. Automata on the integers, recurrence distinguishability, and the equivalence and decidability of monadic theories. In *Symposium on Logic in Computer Science (LICS)* (1986), pp. 301–304.

[405] PIN, J. Logic, semigroups and automata on words. *Annals of Mathematics and Artificial Intelligence 16* (1996), 343–384.

[406] PINTER, S., AND WOLPER, P. L. A temporal logic for reasoning about partially ordered computations. In *Symposium on Principles of Distributed Computing* (1984), pp. 28–37.

[407] PNUELI, A. The temporal logic of programs. In *Symposium on Foundations of Computer Science (FOCS)* (New York, 1977), vol. 18, IEEE Computer Society, pp. 46–57.

[408] PNUELI, A. The temporal semantics of concurrent programs. *Theoretical Computer Science 13* (1981), 45–60.

[409] PNUELI, A., AND ROSNER, R. On the synthesis of a reactive module. In *Symposium on Principles of Programming Languages (POPL)* (Austin, Texas, 1989), ACM, pp. 179–190.

[410] PNUELI, A., AND SHERMAN, R. Semantic tableau for temporal logic. Technical Report Cs81-82, The Weizmann Institute, 1981.

[411] PRATT, V. Semantical considerations of Floyd-Hoare logic. In *Symposium on Foundations of Computer Science (FOCS)* (1976), pp. 109–121.

[412] PRATT, V. Models of program logics. In *Symposium on Foundations of Computer Science (FOCS)* (1979), pp. 115–122.

[413] PRATT, V. A decidable μ-calculus: Preliminary report. In *Symposium on Foundations of Computer Science (FOCS)* (1982), pp. 421–427.

[414] PRAWITZ, D. An improved proof procedure. *Theoria 26* (1960).

[415] PRESBURGER, M. Über die Vollständigkeit eines gewissen Systems der Arithmetik ganzer Zahlen, in welchem die Addition als einzige Operation hervortritt. In *Sprawozdanie z I Kongresu Matematyków Krajów Słowiańskich* (Warszawa, Skład Głowny, 1929), F. Leja, Ed., pp. 92–101.

[416] PRIOR, A. *Time and Modality*. Clarendon, Oxford, 1957.

[417] PRIOR, A. *Past, Present and Future*. Clarendon, Oxford, 1967.

[418] RABIN, M. Decidability of second-order theories and automata on infinite trees. *Transaction of the American Mathematical Society 141* (1969), 1–35.

[419] RABIN, M. Weakly definable relations and special automata. In *Symposium on Mathematical Logic and Foundations of Set Theory* (1970), North Holland, pp. 1–23.

[420] RABIN, M. Automata on infinite objects and Church's problem. In *Regional Conference Series in Mathematics* (1972), vol. 13, American Mathematical Society.

[421] RABIN, M., AND SCOTT, D. Finite automata and their decision problems. *IBM Journal of Research and Development 3* (1959), 115–125.

[422] RAMSEY, F. On a problem in formal logic. *Proceedings of the London Mathematical Society 30* (1928), 264–268.

[423] RAVI, K., BLOEM, R., AND SOMENZI, F. A comparative study of symbolic algorithms for the computation of fair cycles. In *Conference on Formal Methods in Computer Aided Design (FMCAD)* (2000), vol. 1954 of *LNCS*, Springer.

[424] REEVES, S. Semantic tableau as a framework for automated theorem proving. Tech. rep., Department of Computer Science, Queen Mary College,, University of London, Mile End Road, London E1 4NS, 1987.

[425] ROBINSON, J. A machine oriented logic based on the resolution principle. *Journal of Automated Reasoning 12*, 1 (1965), 23–41.

[426] RUDELL, R. Dynamic variable ordering for ordered binary decision diagrams. In *Conference on Computer Aided Design (ICCAD)* (Santa Clara, California, November 1993), IEEE Computer Society, pp. 42–47.

[427] RUF, J., AND KROPF, T. Using MTBDDs for discrete timed symbolic model checking. *Multiple-Valued Logic - An International Journal* (1998). Special Issue on Decision Diagrams.

[428] SAFRA, S. On the complexity of ω-automata. In *Symposium on Foundations of Computer Science (FOCS)* (1988), pp. 319–327.

[429] SANCHIS, L. Data types as lattices: Retractions, closures and projections. *Informatique Théorique et Applications 11*, 4 (1977), 329–344.

[430] SATTLER, U., AND VARDI, M. The hybrid μ-calculus. In *International Joint Conference on Automated Reasoning (IJCAR)* (Siena, Italy, June 2001), vol. 2083 of *LNAI*, Springer, pp. 76–91.

[431] SAUERHOFF, M., AND WEGENER, I. On the complexity of minimizing the OBDD size for incompletely specified functions. *IEEE Transactions on Computer Aided Design 15*, 11 (1996), 1435–1437.

[432] SCHLÖR, R., AND DAMM, W. Specification and verification of system-level hardware design using timing diagrams. In *European Design and Test Conference (EDTC)* (Paris, France, February 1993), G. Goossens and B. Lin, Eds., IEEE Computer Society, pp. 518–524.

[433] SCHNEIDER, K. *Ein einheitlicher Ansatz zur Unterstützung von Abstraktionsmechanismen der Hardwareverifikation*, vol. 116 of *DISKI (Dissertationen zur Künstlichen Intelligenz)*. Infix, Sankt Augustin, 1996. ISBN 3-89601-116-2.

[434] SCHNEIDER, K. CTL and equivalent sublanguages of CTL*. In *Conference on Computer Hardware Description Languages and Their Applications (CHDL)* (Toledo,Spain, April 1997), C. Delgado Kloos, Ed., IFIP, Chapman and Hall, pp. 40–59.

[435] SCHNEIDER, K. A verified hardware synthesis for Esterel. In *Workshop on Distributed and Parallel Embedded Systems (DIPES)* (Schloß Ehringerfeld, Germany, 2000), F. Rammig, Ed., Kluwer, pp. 205–214.

[436] SCHNEIDER, K. Embedding imperative synchronous languages in interactive theorem provers. In *Conference on Application of Concurrency to System Design (ICACSD)* (Newcastle upon Tyne, UK, June 2001), IEEE Computer Society, pp. 143–156.

[437] SCHNEIDER, K. Improving automata generation for linear temporal logic by considering the automaton hierarchy. In *Logic for Programming, Artificial Intelligence, and Reasoning (LPAR)* (Havanna, Cuba, 2001), vol. 2250 of *LNAI*, Springer, pp. 39–54.

[438] SCHNEIDER, K. Proving the equivalence of microstep and macrostep semantics. In *Conference on Theorem Proving in Higher Order Logic* (Hampton, Virginia, USA, 2002), vol. 2410 of *LNCS*, Springer, pp. 314–331.

[439] SCHNEIDER, K., AND HOFFMANN, D. A HOL conversion for translating linear time temporal logic to ω-automata. In *Higher Order Logic Theorem Proving and its Applications* (Nice, France, September 1999), Y. Bertot, G. Dowek, C. Paulin-Mohring, and L. Théry, Eds., vol. 1690 of *LNCS*, Springer, pp. 255–272.

[440] SCHNEIDER, K., KUMAR, R., AND KROPF, T. Automating most parts of hardware proofs in HOL. In *Workshop on Computer Aided Verification (CAV)* (Aalborg, July 1991), K. Larsen and A. Skou, Eds., vol. 575 of *LNCS*, Springer, pp. 365–375.

[441] SCHNEIDER, K., KUMAR, R., AND KROPF, T. Structuring hardware proofs: First steps towards automation in a higher-order environment. In *Conference on Very Large Scale Integration (VLSI)* (Edinburgh, Scotland, August 1991), A. Halaas and P. Denyer, Eds., IFIP Transactions, North Holland, pp. 81–90.

[442] SCHNEIDER, K., AND WEINDEL, H. An efficient decision procedure for S1S. In *GI/ITG/GMM Workshop: Methoden des Entwurfs und der Verifikation digitaler Systeme* (1997), M.Pfaff and R. Hagelauer, Eds., pp. 129–138.

[443] SCHNOEBELEN, P. The complexity of temporal logic model checking. In *Advances in Modal Logic (AiML)* (Toulouse, France, 2003), World Scientific.

[444] SCHÜTZENBERGER, M. Certain elementary families of automata. In *Symposium of Mathematical Theory of Automata* (Polytechnic Institute of Brooklyn, 1962), pp. 139–152.

[445] SCHÜTZENBERGER, M. On finite monoids having only trivial subgroups. *Information and Control* (1965), 190–194.

[446] SCHUELE, T., AND SCHNEIDER, K. Symbolic model checking by automata based set representation. In *GI/ITG/GMM Workshop: Methoden und Beschreibungssprachen zur Modellierung und Verifikation von Schaltungen und Systemen* (Tübingen, Germany, February 2002), pp. 229–238.

[447] SCHÜLE, T., AND SCHNEIDER, K. Exact runtime analysis using automata-based symbolic simulation. In *Formal Methods and Models for Codesign (MEMOCODE)* (Mont Saint-Michel, France, 2003), IEEE Computer Society.

[448] SCHÜTTE, K. Untersuchungen zum Entscheidungsproblem der mathematischen Logik. *Mathematische Annalen 109* (1934), 572–603.

[449] SCHUTTEN, R., AND FITZPATRICK, T. Design for verification, 2003.

[450] SCHWARTZ, R., MELLIAR-SMITH, P., AND VOGT, F. An interval logic for higher-level temporal reasoning. In *Symposium on Principles of Distributed Computing* (1983), pp. 173–186.

[451] SCOTT, D. A decision method for validity of sentences in two variables. *Journal of Symbolic Logic 27* (1962), 377.

[452] SEIDL, H. Fast and simple nested fixpoints. *Information Processing Letters 59*, 6 (1996), 303–308.

[453] SHANNON, C. A symbolic analysis of relay and switching circuits. *Transactions American Institute of Electrical Engineers 57* (1938), 713–723.

[454] SHIPLE, T., HOJATI, R., SANGIOVANNI-VINCENTELLI, A., AND BRAYTON, R. Heuristic minimization of BDDs using don't cares. In *Design Automation Conference (DAC)* (San Diego, CA, June 1994), ACM Press.

[455] SIEFKES, D. *Decidable Theories I: Büchi's Monadic Second Order Successor Arithmetic*. Lecture Notes in Mathematics. Springer, 1970.

[456] SISTLA, A., AND CLARKE, E. The complexity of propositional linear temporal logics. *Journal of the ACM 32*, 3 (July 1985), 733–749.

[457] SISTLA, A., AND GODEFROID, P. Symmetry and reduced symmetry in model checking. In *Conference on Computer Aided Verification (CAV)* (Paris, France, 2001), vol. 2102 of *LNCS*, Springer, pp. 91–103.

[458] SISTLA, A., VARDI, M., AND WOLPER, P. The complementation problem for Büchi automata with applications to temporal logic. In *Colloquium on Automata, Languages and Programming (ICALP)* (New York, 1985), vol. 194 of *LNCS*, Springer, pp. 465–474.

[459] SISTLA, A., VARDI, M., AND WOLPER, P. The complementation problem for Büchi automata with applications to temporal logic. *Theoretical Computer Science 49* (1987), 217–237.

[460] SISTLA, A. P. *Theoretical Issues in the Design of Distributed and Concurrent Systems*. PhD thesis, Harvard University, Cambridge, MA, 1983.

[461] SKOLEM, T. Logisch-kombinatorische Untersuchungen über die Erfüllbarkeit oder Beweisbarkeit mathematischer Sätze nebst einem Theoreme über dichte Mengen. *Videnskapsselskapets skrifter, I. Mathematisk-naturvidenskabelig klasse 4* (1920).

[462] SKOLEM, T. Über die mathematische Logik. *Norsk mathemtisk tidsskrift 10* (1928), 125–142.

[463] SKOLEM, T. Über gewisse Satzfunktionen in der Arithmetik. *Skr. Norske Videnskaps-Akademie i Oslo 7* (1930).

[464] SMULLYAN, R. *First Order Logic*. Springer, 1968.

[465] SOMENZI, F. CUDD: CU decision diagram package, release 2.3.0, 1998. ftp://vlsi.colorado.edu/pub/ and http://vlsi.Colorado.EDU/.

[466] SOMENZI, F. Binary decision diagrams, 1999.

[467] SOMENZI, F. Efficient manipulation of decision diagrams. *Software Tools for Technology Transfer (STTT) 3*, 2 (2001), 171–181.

[468] SOMENZI, F., AND BLOEM, R. Efficient Büchi automata from LTL formulae. In *Conference on Computer Aided Verification (CAV)* (Trento, Italy, 2000), vol. 1633 of *LNCS*, Springer, pp. 247–263.

[469] STAIGER, L., AND WAGNER, K. Automatentheoretische Charakterisierungen topologischer Klassen regulärer Folgenmengen. *Elektron. Informationsverarb. Kybernet. 10* (1974), 379–392.

[470] STICKEL, M. Automated deduction by theory resolution. *Journal of Automated Reasoning 1*, 4 (1985), 333–355.

[471] STIRLING, C., AND WALKER, D. Local model checking in the modal μ-calculus. *Theoretical Computer Science 89*, 1 (1991), 161–177.

[472] STIRLING, C., AND WALKER, D. J. Local model checking in the modal μ-calculus. In *Theory and Practice of Software Development (TAPSOFT)* (March 1989), J. Diaz and F. Orejas, Eds., vol. 351 of *LNCS*, Springer, pp. 369–383.

[473] STOCKMEYER, L. *The complexity of decision problems in automata theory and logic*. PhD thesis, Department of Electrical Engineering, MIT, Boston, 1974.

[474] STOCKMEYER, L. The polynomial time hierarchy. *Theoretical Computer Science 3* (1977), 1–22.

[475] STRAUBING, H. *Finite automata, formal logic, and circuit complexity*. Birkhäuser, 1994.

[476] STREETT, R. Propositional dynamic logic of looping and converse is elementarily decidable. *Information and Control 54*, 1-2 (1982), 121–141.

[477] STREETT, R., AND EMERSON, E. The propositional μ-calculus is elementary. In *Colloquium on Automata, Languages and Programming (ICALP)* (Antwerp, Belgium, 1984), vol. 172 of *LNCS*, Springer, pp. 465–472.

[478] STREETT, R., AND EMERSON, E. An automata theoretic decision procedure for the propositional μ-calculus. *Information and Computation 81*, 3 (1989), 249–264.

[479] SURÁNYI, J. *Reduktionstheorie des Entscheidungsproblems im Pädikatenkalkül der ersten Stufe.* Verlag der Ungarischen Akademie der Wissenschaften, 1959.

[480] TAHAR, S. *Eine Methode zur formalen Verifikation von RISC-Prozessoren.* PhD thesis, Universität Karlsruhe, Institut für Rechnerentwurf und Fehlertoleranz, December 1994.

[481] TAKAHASHI, M., AND YAMASAKI, H. A note on ω-regular languages. *Theoretical Computer Science 23* (1983), 217–225.

[482] TARSKI, A. A lattice-theoretical fixpoint theorem and its applications. *Pacific J. Math 5* (1955), 285–309.

[483] THOMAS, W. Star free regular sets of ω-sequences. *Information and Control 42* (1979), 148–156.

[484] THOMAS, W. Classifying regular events in symbolic logic. *Computer and System Sciences 25* (1982), 360–376.

[485] THOMAS, W. Computation tree logic and regular ω-languages. In *Linear Time, Branching Time and Partial Order in Logics and Models for Concurrency* (Noordwigherhout, Netherland, May/June 1988), vol. 354 of *LNCS*, Springer, pp. 690–713.

[486] THOMAS, W. Automata on infinite objects. In *Handbook of Theoretical Computer Science* (Amsterdam, 1990), J. van Leeuwen, Ed., vol. B, Elsevier Science, pp. 133–191.

[487] THOMAS, W. Languages, automata, and logic. Technical Report 9607, Christian-Albrechts-Universität Kiel, Institut für Informatik und Praktische Mathematik, May 1996.

[488] THOMAS, W. A short introduction to infinite automata. In *Conference on Developments on Language Theory* (2001), vol. 2295 of *LNCS*, Springer.

[489] THOMAS, W., AND LESCOW, H. Logical specifications of infinite computations. In *A Decade of Concurrency, Reflections and Perspectives, REX School/Symposium* (Noordwijkerhout, The Netherlands, 1994), vol. 803 of *LNCS*, Springer, pp. 583–621.

[490] TOUATI, H., SAVOJ, H., LIN, B., BRAYTON, R., AND SANGIOVANNI-VINCENTELLI, A. Implicit state enumeration of finite state machines using BDD's. In *Conference on Computer Aided Design (ICCAD)* (1990), pp. 130–132.

[491] TRACHTENBROT, B., AND BARSDIN, J. Finite automata, behaviour and synthesis. *Mir, Moscow (in russian)* (1970).

[492] TURING, A. On computable numbers, with an application to the Entscheidungsproblem. *Proceedings of the London Mathematical Society 42* (1937), 230–265.

[493] VALMARI, A. A stubborn attack on the state explosion problem. In *Workshop on Computer Aided Verification (CAV)* (June 1990), R. P. Kurshan and E. Clarkes, Eds.

[494] VARDI, M. An automata-theoretic approach to linear temporal logic. In *Logics for Concurrency - Structure versus Automata* (1996), vol. 1043 of *LNCS*, Springer, pp. 238–266.

[495] VARDI, M. Why is modal logic so robustly decidable? In *Descriptive Complexity and Finite Models* (1996), no. 31 in DIMACS Workshop, American Mathematical Society, pp. 149–184.

[496] VARDI, M. Reasoning about the past with two-way automata. In *Colloquium on Automata, Languages and Programming (ICALP)* (Aalborg, Denmark, 1998), vol. 1443 of *LNCS*, Springer, pp. 628–641.

[497] VARDI, M. Branching vs. linear time: Final showdown. In *Conference on Tools and Algorithms for the Construction and Analysis of Systems (TACAS)* (Genova, Italy, 2001), vol. 2031 of *LNCS*, Springer, pp. 1–22.

[498] VARDI, M., AND STOCKMEYER, L. Improved upper and lower bounds for modal logics of programs. In *Symposium on Theory of Computing* (1985), pp. 240–251.

[499] VARDI, M., AND WOLPER, P. Automata theoretic techniques for modal logics of programs. In *Symposium on Theory of Computing* (1984).

[500] VARDI, M., AND WOLPER, P. Yet another process logic. In *Workshop on Logics of Programs* (Berlin, 1984), vol. 164, Springer, pp. 501–512.

[501] VARDI, M., AND WOLPER, P. An automata-theoretic approach to automatic program verification. In *Symposium on Logic in Computer Science (LICS)* (June 1986), IEEE Computer Society, pp. 332–344.

[502] ČERNÁ, I., AND PELÁNEK, R. Relating hierarchy of linear temporal properties to model checking. Technical report, Faculty of Informatics, Masaryk University, 2003. http://www.fi.muni.cz/informatics/reports.

[503] VÖGE, J., AND JURDZINSKI, M. A discrete strategy improvement algorithm for solving parity games. In *Conference on Computer Aided Verification (CAV)* (Chicago, IL, USA, 2000), vol. 1855 of *LNCS*, Springer, pp. 202–215.

[504] WAGNER, K. Eine Axiomatisierung der Theorie der regulären Folgenmengen. *Journ. of Inform. Cybernetics 12* (1976), 337–354.

[505] WAGNER, K. *Zur Theorie der regulären Folgenmengen*. PhD thesis, Friedrich Schiller Universität, Jena, 1976.

[506] WAGNER, K. On ω-regular sets. *Information and Control 43* (1979), 123–177.

[507] WALUKIEWICZ, I. *A Complete Deductive System for the μ-Calculus*. PhD thesis, Warsaw University, 1993.

[508] WALUKIEWICZ, I. A complete deductive system for the μ-calculus. In *Symposium on Logic in Computer Science (LICS)* (1993), IEEE Computer Society, pp. 136–147.

[509] WALUKIEWICZ, I. Notes on the propositional μ-calculus: Completeness and related results. BRICS Notes Series NS-95-1, Basic Research in Computer Science (BRICS), February 1995.

[510] WALUKIEWICZ, I. Completeness of Kozen's axiomatisation of the propositional μ-calculus. *Information and Computation 157*, 1-2 (2000), 142–182.

[511] WILKE, T. *Classifying discrete temporal properties*. PhD thesis, Christian-Albrechts Universität Kiel, 1998.

[512] WILKE, T. Classifying discrete temporal properties. In *Symposium on Theoretical Aspects of Computer Science (STACS)* (Trier, Germany, 1999), C. Meinel and S. Tison, Eds., vol. 1563 of *LNCS*, Springer, pp. 32–46.

[513] WILKE, T. CTL^+ is exponentially more succinct than CTL. Aachener Informatik-Berichte 99-7, Fachgruppe Informatik der RWTH Aachen, 52056 Aachen, Germany, 1999.

[514] WILKE, T. Alternating tree automata, parity games, and modal μ-calculus. http://www.ti.informatik.uni-kiel.de/ALS, 2000. (unpublished manuscript).

[515] WILKE, T. Alternating tree automata, parity games, and modal μ-calculus. *Bulletin of the Societe Mathematique Belgique 8*, 2 (2001).

[516] WILLEMS, B., AND WOLPER, P. Partial-order methods for model checking: From linear time to branching time. In *Symposium on Logic in Computer Science (LICS)* (New Brunswick, July 1996), pp. 294–303.

[517] WINDLEY, P. Microprocessor verification. In *Higher Order Logic Theorem Proving and its Applications* (1991), IEEE Computer Society, pp. 32–37.

[518] WOLPER, P. Temporal logic can be more expressive. In *Symposium on Foundations of Computer Science (FOCS)* (New York, 1981), IEEE Computer Society, pp. 340–348.

[519] WOLPER, P. Temporal logic can be more expressive. *Information and Control 56*, 1-2 (1983), 72–99.

[520] WOLPER, P. Constructing automata from temporal logic formulas: A tutorial. In *Summer School on Formal Methods in Performance Analysis* (2001), vol. 2090 of *LNCS*, Springer, pp. 261–277.

[521] WOLPER, P., AND BOIGELOT, B. An automata-theoretic approach to Presburger arithmetic constraints. In *Static Analysis Symposium (SAS)* (Glasgow, September 1995), vol. 983 of *LNCS*, Springer, pp. 21–32.

[522] WOLPER, P., AND BOIGELOT, B. On the construction of automata from linear arithmetic constraints. In *Conference on Tools and Algorithms for the Construction and Analysis of Systems (TACAS)* (Berlin, March 2000), vol. 1785 of *LNCS*, Springer, pp. 1–19.

[523] WOLPER, P., VARDI, M., AND SISTLA, A. Reasoning about infinite computations paths. In *Symposium on Foundations of Computer Science (FOCS)* (New York, 1983), IEEE Computer Society, pp. 185–194.

[524] X.1, C. V. X. F. *Functional Specification and Description Language (SDL) Criteria for Using Formal Description Techniques (FDT's)*, vol. IXth Plenary Assembly. CCITT, Melbourne, November 1988.

[525] YU, S. *Regular Languages*. Springer, 1997, ch. 2, pp. 41–110.

[526] ZILLER, R. Finding bad states during symbolic supervisor synthesis. In *GI/ITG/GMM Workshop: Methoden und Beschreibungssprachen zur Modellierung und Verifikation von Schaltungen und Systemen* (Tübingen, Germany, 25-27 February 2002), pp. 209–218.

[527] ZUCK, L. *Past Temporal Logic*. PhD thesis, Weizmann Institute, Rehovot, Israel, 1986.

Index

Monographs in Theoretical Computer Science · An EATCS Series

K. Jensen
Coloured Petri Nets
Basic Concepts, **Analysis Methods**
and Practical Use, Vol. 1
2nd ed.

K. Jensen
Coloured Petri Nets
Basic Concepts, ***Analysis Methods***
and Practical Use, Vol. 2

K. Jensen
Coloured Petri Nets
Basic Concepts, Analysis Methods
and ***Practical Use,*** **Vol. 3**

A. Nait Abdallah
The Logic of Partial Information

Z. Fülöp, H. Vogler
Syntax-Directed Semantics
Formal Models Based on Tree Transducers

A. de Luca, S. Varricchio
Finiteness and Regularity
in Semigroups and Formal Languages

E. Best, R. Devillers, M. Koutny
Petri Net Algebra

S.P. Demri, E. S. Orłowska
Incomplete Information:
Structure, Inference, Complexity

J.C.M. Baeten, C.A. Middelburg
Process Algebra with Timing

L. A. Hemaspaandra, L.Torenvliet
Theory of Semi-Feasible Algorithms

Texts in Theoretical Computer Science · An EATCS Series

J. L. Balcázar, J. Díaz, J. Gabarró
Structural Complexity I
2nd ed. (see also overleaf, Vol. 22)

M. Garzon
Models of Massive Parallelism
Analysis of Cellular Automata
and Neural Networks

J. Hromkovič
Communication Complexity
and Parallel Computing

A. Leitsch
The Resolution Calculus

G. Păun, G. Rozenberg, A. Salomaa
DNA Computing
New Computing Paradigms

A. Salomaa
Public-Key Cryptography
2nd ed.

K. Sikkel
Parsing Schemata
A Framework for Specification
and Analysis of Parsing Algorithms

H. Vollmer
Introduction to Circuit Complexity
A Uniform Approach

W. Fokkink
Introduction to Process Algebra

K. Weihrauch
Computable Analysis
An Introduction

J. Hromkovič
Algorithmics for Hard Problems
Introduction to Combinatorial Optimization,
Randomization, Approximation, and Heuristics
2nd ed.

S. Jukna
Extremal Combinatorics
With Applications in Computer Science

P. Clote, E. Kranakis
Boolean Functions and Computation
Models

L. A. Hemaspaandra, M. Ogihara
The Complexity Theory Companion

C.S. Calude
Information and Randomness.
An Algorithmic Perspective
2nd ed.

J. Hromkovič
Theoretical Computer Science
Introduction to Automata, Computability,
Complexity, Algorithmics, Randomization,
Communication and Cryptography

A. Schneider
Verification of Reactive Systems
Formal Methods and Algorithms

Former volumes appeared as EATCS Monographs on Theoretical Computer Science

Vol. 5: W. Kuich, A. Salomaa
Semirings, Automata, Languages

Vol. 6: H. Ehrig, B. Mahr
Fundamentals of Algebraic Specification 1
Equations and Initial Semantics

Vol. 7: F. Gécseg
Products of Automata

Vol. 8: F. Kröger
Temporal Logic of Programs

Vol. 9: K. Weihrauch
Computability

Vol. 10: H. Edelsbrunner
Algorithms in Combinatorial Geometry

Vol. 12: J. Berstel, C. Reutenauer
Rational Series and Their Languages

Vol. 13: E. Best, C. Fernández C.
Nonsequential Processes
A Petri Net View

Vol. 14: M. Jantzen
Confluent String Rewriting

Vol. 15: S. Sippu, E. Soisalon-Soininen
Parsing Theory
Volume I: Languages and Parsing

Vol. 16: P. Padawitz
Computing in Horn Clause Theories

Vol. 17: J. Paredaens, P. DeBra, M. Gyssens, D. Van Gucht
The Structure of the Relational Database Model

Vol. 18: J. Dassow, G. Páun
Regulated Rewriting in Formal Language Theory

Vol. 19: M. Tofte
Compiler Generators
What they can do, what they might do, and what they will probably never do

Vol. 20: S. Sippu, E. Soisalon-Soininen
Parsing Theory
Volume II: LR(k) and LL(k) Parsing

Vol. 21: H. Ehrig, B. Mahr
Fundamentals of Algebraic Specification 2
Module Specifications and Constraints

Vol. 22: J. L. Balcázar, J. Díaz, J. Gabarró
Structural Complexity II

Vol. 24: T. Gergely, L. Úry
First-Order Programming Theories

R. Janicki, P. E. Lauer
Specification and Analysis of Concurrent Systems
The COSY Approach

O. Watanabe (Ed.)
Kolmogorov Complexity and Computational Complexity

G. Schmidt, Th. Ströhlein
Relations and Graphs
Discrete Mathematics for Computer Scientists

S. L. Bloom, Z. Ésik
Iteration Theories
The Equational Logic of Iterative Processes

CPSIA information can be obtained at www.ICGtesting.com
Printed in the USA
LVOW102135260213

321855LV00001B/13/P